THE GOSPEL
ACCORDING TO LUKE X–XXIV

VOLUME 28A

THE ANCHOR BIBLE is a fresh approach to the world's greatest classic. Its object is to make the Bible accessible to the modern reader; its method is to arrive at the meaning of biblical literature through exact translation and extended exposition, and to reconstruct the ancient setting of the biblical story, as well as the circumstances of its transcription and the characteristics of its transcribers.

THE ANCHOR BIBLE is a project of international and interfaith scope: Protestant, Catholic, and Jewish scholars from many countries contribute individual volumes. The project is not sponsored by any ecclesiastical organization and is not intended to reflect any particular theological doctrine. Prepared under our joint supervision, THE ANCHOR BIBLE is an effort to make available all the significant historical and linguistic knowledge which bears on the interpretation of the biblical record.

THE ANCHOR BIBLE is aimed at the general reader with no special formal training in biblical studies; yet, it is written with most exacting standards of scholarship, reflecting the highest technical accomplishment.

This project marks the beginning of a new era of cooperation among scholars in biblical research, thus forming a common body of knowledge to be shared by all.

William Foxwell Albright
David Noel Freedman
GENERAL EDITORS

THE ANCHOR BIBLE

The Gospel According to
LUKE
(X–XXIV)

Introduction, Translation, and Notes

by

JOSEPH A. FITZMYER, S.J.

DOUBLEDAY & COMPANY, INC.
GARDEN CITY, NEW YORK
1985

NIHIL OBSTAT
Joseph N. Tylenda, S.J., *Censor Deputatus*

IMPRIMI POTEST
V. Rev. Joseph P. Whelan, S.J., *Provincial*
Maryland Province, Society of Jesus

IMPRIMATUR
Rev. Msgr. John F. Donoghue, *Vicar General*
Archdiocese of Washington
16 February 1983

The *nihil obstat* and *imprimatur* are official declarations that a book or pamphlet is free of doctrinal or moral error. No implication is contained therein that those who have granted the *nihil obstat* and *imprimatur* agree with the content, opinions, or statements expressed.

Library of Congress Cataloging in Publication Data
(Revised for volume 2)
Bible. N.T. Luke. English. Anchor Bible.
The Gospel according to Luke.

(The Anchor Bible; v. 28–28A)
Includes bibliographies and index.
1. Bible. N.T. Luke—Commentaries. I. Fitzmyer,
Joseph A. II. Title. III. Series: Bible. English.
Anchor Bible. 1964; v. 28–28A.
BS192.2.A1 1964.G3   vol. 28A   [BS2593]   220.7'7s   [226'.4077]
ISBN 0-385-00515-6 (v. 1)
ISBN 0-385-15542-5 (v. 2)
Library of Congress Catalog Card Number 80–702

PREFACE

In the course of my study of the Lucan Gospel this commentary has grown beyond all that I had originally envisaged. I have sought to write a new, modern commentary on the Gospel according to Luke in the "classic" mode. In it I have tried to restore the esteem that Luke once enjoyed in the past among the evangelists. In recent decades a very pejorative view of this writer had emerged (see pp. 4-5), and it has been my aim to show that there is another way of reading "the Rev. Mr. Luke," one which still has something to say to a twentieth-century Christian. I only hope that these two volumes measure up to that goal in some way.

The reader of the second volume will in time note some differences from the first volume. Some of them are owing to the publication of more recent works that influenced my study of the Gospel. For instance, my translation of the Gospel was initially based on the 25th ed. of Nestle-Aland, but once the 26th ed. of that critical text appeared, I began to make more and more use of it, even though I never followed its text slavishly. Similarly, I have consulted the newer commentaries (e.g. that of I. H. Marshall, which only came into my hands as I was completing the manuscript of vol. 28, and that of E. Schweizer) and the study of Lucan language by J. Jeremias. Had I had such excellent studies from the beginning, my work would have been greatly reduced.

Secondary literature on the Lucan Gospel is enormous. I have tried to cull from it the best that I could—or at least the best that would fit into the way I should prefer a twentieth-century Christian to read this Gospel. I have not been able to incorporate every view that differs from mine. I have been trying to write my own commentary on the Lucan Gospel in dialogue, to be sure, with other commentators; but sometimes views, based on quite different approaches, have had to be left without comment.

In referring to the secondary literature, I have often used an author's name and a short title. If the reader is interested in pursuing a topic further, he/she should refer first to the bibliography which follows the passage under discussion. In those sectional bibliographies one will usually find books and articles that bear on the passage as a whole. If the book or article indicated by a short title is not found in such sectional bibliographies, then one should consult the list of General Works Frequently Quoted with Short Titles (pp. xxx-xxxvi). Often enough, the names of commentators are merely listed, especially when various interpretations are being set forth; in these cases short titles are not used, and the reader is expected to consult the list of commentaries and monographs in vol. 28, pp. 271-283. Secondary literature dealing with specific verses is usually cited in full in the notes on the verses concerned. In the sectional bibliographies divisions are sometimes found; in such cases the more generic bibliographical material precedes the specific.

The reader will best use this commentary not only with a good modern English translation of the Bible, but also with a synopsis of the first three canonical Gospels. *Gospel Parallels: A Synopsis of the First Three Gospels* (ed. B. H. Throckmorton, Jr.; 4th ed.; London/Toronto/Camden, NJ: Nelson, 1979) is readily available. For those who read Greek, there is K. Aland, ed., *Synopsis of the Four Gospels: Greek-English Edition of the Synopsis Quattuor Evangeliorum with the Text of the Revised Standard Version* (3d ed.; New York: United Bible Societies, 1979) or, better still, K. Aland, ed., *Synopsis quattuor evangeliorum: Locis parallelis evangeliorum apocryphorum et patrum adhibitis* (10th ed.; Stuttgart: Deutsche Bibelstiftung, 1978). Also useful is the more recent Greek synopsis with German and English titles, A. Huck and H. Greeven, *Synopse der drei ersten Evangelien mit Beigabe der johanneischen Parallelstellen* (13th ed.; Tübingen: Mohr [Siebeck], 1981). In using the last mentioned, the reader should be aware that the Greek text differs at times from N-A²⁶ and UBSGNT³, which I have in great part followed (at least in the latter part of this commentary).

A recently published commentary on the Lucan Gospel by C. H. Talbert *(Reading Luke: A Literary and Theological Commentary on the Third Gospel* [New York: Crossroad, 1982]) sets out with the premise that a "widespread loss of confidence in the two-source theory . . . has occurred during the past fifteen years" (p. 1). Anyone who uses this commentary of mine will realize that I do not share that alleged "loss of confidence." It is characteristic of a small group of students of the Synoptic relationships, mostly American, a few British, and still fewer Continental scholars. I have preferred to line myself up with what is still the majority opinion in this matter, espoused by many German, Belgian, French, Scandinavian, and American scholars, both Protestant and Roman Catholic. Fortunately, there is much good in Talbert's commentary, which saves it from the fate that it might otherwise encounter. Moreover, two recent successful books about controversial NT topics, published in this country, made profitable use of the modified form of the Two-Source Theory, *Peter in the New Testament* (eds. R. E. Brown et al.) and *Mary in the New Testament* (eds. R. E. Brown et al.). In the initial session of discussions on each of these topics the question of Synoptic relationships was broached; surprisingly, all present voted unanimously for the modified form of the Two-Source Theory.

On pp. 82-85 of vol. 28 I spoke of the problem one has in trying to decide whether a given passage that has not been derived from "Mk" or "Q" comes from "L" or has been freely composed by the evangelist. When I composed the list of "L" passages that appears on pp. 83-84, I did so on the basis of studies made of the Gospel up to that time of writing. Having pursued my research and analysis still further, I see today that that list needs some adjustment. The vast majority of the passages assigned to "L" at first still remains in that category, but there are some slight corrections to be made. They will be found on p. 1600, along with other corrigenda in vol. 28. At the end of this volume the reader will also find additional bibliography for some parts of vol. 28.

The reader should recall the two important points incorporated into the preface of vol. 28 (pp. viii-ix) about the stages of the gospel tradition and the mode of referring to the OT, especially to the Psalter.

It is again my pleasant task to express my thanks to various persons who helped me in many ways to finish this commentary on the Lucan Gospel. Once again I must thank Henry J. Bertels, S.J. and William J. Sheehan, C.S.B. of the Woodstock Theological Center Library, for much assistance; Raymond E. Brown, S.S., who has read and corrected part of my manuscript on the passion narrative; David Noel Freedman, the general editor of the Anchor Bible series, for many critical comments and suggestions which have improved the text of the commentary; Estelle Laurence, the copy editor; and Eve F. Roshevsky and her staff at Doubleday & Company, who have seen this volume to the end of its publication.

When Jerome was writing his commentary on Matthew's Gospel, he included the remark, "In the words of the Gospels the Spirit has been joined to the letter; and whatever at first sight seems to be cold, if you touch it, grows hot."* So Jerome wrote about Matthew. But that can also be said about the Gospel of Luke and its portrait of Jesus of Nazareth. At least with such a conviction have I composed this commentary. May hearts of readers still be set on fire by reading about the risen Christ in the Gospel of Luke who begs them to touch the text of his words.

JOSEPH A. FITZMYER, S.J.
Department of Biblical Studies
School of Religious Studies
The Catholic University of America
Washington, DC 20064

---

* In evangelicis sermonibus semper litterae iunctus est spiritus; et quidquid primo frigere videtur aspectu, si tegigeris, calet (In Matth. 2.14,14 [CCLat 77. 121]).

CONTENTS

PRINCIPAL ABBREVIATIONS

AAGA[3]	M. Black, *An Aramaic Approach to the Gospels and Acts* (3d ed.; Oxford: Clarendon, 1967)
AAS	*Acta apostolicae sedis*
AASOR	Annual of the American Schools of Oriental Research
AbhKPAW	*Abhandlungen der königlichen preussischen Akademie der Wissenschaften*
AbhTANT	Abhandlungen zur Theologie des Alten und Neuen Testaments
ABR	*Australian Biblical Review*
AD	G. R. Driver, *Aramaic Documents of the Fifth Century B.C.* (Oxford: Clarendon, 1957)
AER	*American Ecclesiastical Review*
AGSU	Arbeiten zur Geschichte des Spätjudentums und Urchristentums
AJP	*American Journal of Philology*
AJT	*American Journal of Theology*
ALBO	Analecta lovaniensia biblica et orientalia
AnBib	Analecta biblica
ANEP	J. B. Pritchard, *The Ancient Near East in Pictures* (Princeton: Princeton University, 1954)
ANET	J. B. Pritchard, *Ancient Near Eastern Texts* (Princeton: Princeton University, 1950) and *Supplement* (1968)
Ang	*Angelicum*
AnGreg	Analecta gregoriana
ANT	M. R. James, *The Apocryphal New Testament* (Oxford: Clarendon, 1924)
AOS	American Oriental Society
AP	A. Cowley, *Aramaic Papyri of the Fifth Century B.C.* (Oxford: Clarendon, 1923).
APOT	*Apocrypha and Pseudepigrapha of the Old Testament* (ed. R. H. Charles; 2 vols.; Oxford: Clarendon, 1913)
app. crit.	*apparatus criticus*
ASAE	*Annales du service des antiquités de l'Egypte*
ASNU	Acta seminarii neotestamentici upsaliensis
ASOR	American Schools of Oriental Research
AsSeign	*Assemblées du Seigneur*
ASTI	*Annual of the Swedish Theological Institute*
ATLA	American Theological Library Association
ATR	*Anglican Theological Review*
A.U.C.	AB URBE CONDITA (from the foundation of Rome, in Roman dates)
AUSS	*Andrews University Seminary Studies*

AzNTT   Arbeiten zur neutestamentlichen Textforschung

BA   *Biblical Archaeologist*
BAC   Biblioteca de autores cristianos
BAGD   Bauer-Arndt-Gingrich-Danker, *Greek-English Lexicon of the New Testament* (2d ed.; Chicago: University of Chicago, 1979)
BASOR   *Bulletin of the American Schools of Oriental Research*
BBB   Bonner biblische Beiträge
BDB   Brown-Driver-Briggs, *Hebrew and English Lexicon of the Old Testament* (Oxford: Clarendon, 1952)
BDF   Blass-Debrunner-Funk, *Greek Grammar of the New Testament* (Chicago: University of Chicago, 1961)
BDR   Blass-Debrunner-Rehkopf, *Grammatik des neutestamentlichen Griechisch* (Göttingen: Vandenhoeck & Ruprecht, 1976)
Beginnings   F. J. Foakes Jackson and K. Lake, eds., *The Beginnings of Christianity: The Acts of the Apostles* (5 vols.; London: Macmillan, 1920-1933; repr., Grand Rapids: Baker, 1979)
BeO   *Bibbia e oriente*
BETL   Bibliotheca ephemeridum theologicarum lovaniensium
BEvT   Beiträge zur evangelischen Theologie
BFCT   Beiträge zur Förderung christlicher Theologie
BGBE   Beiträge zur Geschichte der biblischen Exegese
BGU   *Ägyptische Urkunden aus den Museen zu Berlin: Griechische Urkunden I-VIII* (Berlin: Weidmann, 1892-1933)
BHT   Beiträge zur historischen Theologie
Bib   *Biblica*
BibLeb   *Bibel und Leben*
BibOr   Biblica et orientalia
BibS(N)   Biblische Studien (Neukirchen: Erziehungsverein, 1951-)
(bis)   two occurrences
BJ   *La Bible de Jérusalem*
BJRL   *Bulletin of the John Rylands* (University) *Library* (of Manchester)
BK   *Bibel und Kirche*
BKAT   Biblischer Kommentar: Altes Testament
BLit   *Bibel und Liturgie*
BMAP   E. G. Kraeling, *The Brooklyn Museum Aramaic Papyri* (New Haven: Yale University, 1953)
BN   *Biblische Notizen*
BNTC   Black's New Testament Commentaries
Boh   Bohairic (an ancient Coptic version of the NT)
BR   *Biblical Research*
BSac   *Bibliotheca sacra*
BT   *The Bible Translator*
BTB   *Biblical Theology Bulletin*
BTS   *Bible et terre sainte*
BVC   *Bible et vie chrétienne*

BW	*Biblical World*
BWANT	Beiträge zur Wissenschaft vom Alten und Neuen Testaments
BZ	*Biblische Zeitschrift*
BZNW	Beihefte zur *ZNW*
CB	*Cultura bíblica*
CBQ	*Catholic Biblical Quarterly*
CCD	*Confraternity of Christian Doctrine* (version of the Bible)
CCER	*Cahiers du cercle Ernest Renan*
CCLat	Corpus christianorum, series latina
CHR	*Church History Review*
CIG	*Corpus inscriptionum graecarum*
CII	*Corpus inscriptionum iudaicarum* (2 vols.; ed. J.-B. Frey; Vatican City: Institute of Christian Archaeology, 1936, 1952)
CIS	*Corpus inscriptionum semiticarum*
CivCatt	*Civiltà cattolica*
CJRT	*Canadian Journal of Religious Thought*
CNT	Commentaire du Nouveau Testament
Comm. in	Commentary on
ConB	Coniectanea biblica
ConNT	*Coniectanea neotestamentica*
CQR	*Church Quarterly Review*
CRev	*Classical Review*
CSCO	Corpus scriptorum christianorum orientalium
CSEL	Corpus scriptorum ecclesiasticorum latinorum
CSS	Cursus sacrae Scripturae
CTJ	*Calvin Theological Journal*
CTM	*Concordia Theological Monthly*
CurrTM	*Currents in Theology and Mission*
DBS	*Dictionnaire de la Bible, Supplément*
DJD	Discoveries in the Judaean Desert (of Jordan) (Oxford: Clarendon)
DS	Denzinger-Schönmetzer, *Enchiridion symbolorum*
DunRev	*Dunwoodie Review*
E	English version (bracketed, immediately following chapter and verse)
EBib	Études bibliques
EKK	Evangelisch-katholischer Kommentar
ELS	D. Baldi, *Enchiridion locorum sanctorum* (Jerusalem: Franciscan, 1955)
Ep.	*Epistula,* Epistle
ESBNT	J. A. Fitzmyer, *Essays on the Semitic Background of the New Testament* (London: Chapman, 1971; repr., Missoula, MT: Scholars, 1974)

EstBíb	*Estudios bíblicos*
EstEcl	*Estudios eclesiásticos*
ETL	*Ephemerides theologicae lovanienses*
ETR	*Études théologiques et religieuses*
EvQ	*Evangelical Quarterly*
EvT	*Evangelische Theologie*
EWNT	*Exegetisches Wörterbuch zum Neuen Testament* (eds. H. Balz and G. Schneider; 3 vols.; Stuttgart: Kohlhammer, 1978-1983)
Expos	*Expositor*
ExpTim	*Expository Times*
FBBS	Facet Books, Biblical Series
FC	Fathers of the Church
FGT	V. Taylor, *Formation of the Gospel Tradition* (London: Macmillan, 1949)
frg.	fragment
FRLANT	Forschungen zur Religion und Literatur des Alten und Neuen Testaments
FTG	M. Dibelius, *From Tradition to Gospel* (New York: Scribner's, 1935)
GCS	Griechische christliche Schriftsteller
GKC	Gesenius-Kautzsch-Cowley, *Hebrew Grammar* (Oxford: Clarendon, 1946)
Gos.	Gospel
GR	*Greece and Rome*
Greg	*Gregorianum*
HALAT	W. Baumgartner, *Hebräisches und aramäisches Lexikon zum Alten Testament* (Leiden: Brill, 1967, 1974, 1983, 198?)
HeB	*Homiletica en Biblica*
Hennecke-Schnee-melcher, *NTApocrypha*	E. Hennecke and W. Schneemelcher, *New Testament Apocrypha* (2 vols.; London: Lutterworth, 1963, 1965)
HeyJ	*Heythrop Journal*
HibJ	*Hibbert Journal*
HJPAJC	E. Schürer, *The History of the Jewish People in the Age of Jesus Christ (175 B.C.-A.D. 135)* (2 vols. [so far]; rev. ed. G. Vermes et al.; Edinburgh: Clark, 1973, 1979)
HNT	Handbuch zum Neuen Testament
HSCP	*Harvard Studies in Classical Philology*
HSM	Harvard Semitic Monographs
HST	R. Bultmann, *History of the Synoptic Tradition* (Oxford: Blackwell, 1968)
HTKNT	Herders theologischer Kommentar zum Neuen Testament
HTR	*Harvard Theological Review*

HTS	Harvard Theological Studies
HUCA	*Hebrew Union College Annual*
IB	*Interpreter's Bible* (Nashville: Abingdon, 1952)
ICC	International Critical Commentary
IDB	*Interpreter's Dictionary of the Bible* (4 vols.; Nashville: Abingdon, 1962)
IDBSup	*Interpreter's Dictionary of the Bible, Supplementary Volume* (1976)
IEJ	*Israel Exploration Journal*
ILS	H. Dessau, ed., *Inscriptiones latinae selectae*
Int	*Interpretation*
IPLCG	B. M. Metzger, *Index to Periodical Literature on Christ and the Gospels* (NTTS 6; Leiden: Brill, 1966)
ITQ	*Irish Theological Quarterly*
JAAR	*Journal of the American Academy of Religion*
JAC	*Jahrbuch für Antike und Christentum*
JANESCU	*Journal of the Ancient Near Eastern Society of Columbia University*
JAOS	*Journal of the American Oriental Society*
JB	*Jerusalem Bible*
JBC	*The Jerome Biblical Commentary* (eds. R. E. Brown et al.; Englewood Cliffs, NJ: Prentice-Hall, 1968)
JBL	*Journal of Biblical Literature*
JBR	*Journal of Bible and Religion*
JETS	*Journal of the Evangelical Theological Society*
JJS	*Journal of Jewish Studies*
JNES	*Journal of Near Eastern Studies*
Josephus *Ag.Ap.*	*Against Apion*
Ant.	*Antiquities*
J.W.	*The Jewish War*
JPOS	*Journal of the Palestine Oriental Society*
JQR	*Jewish Quarterly Review*
JR	*Journal of Religion*
JRS	*Journal of Roman Studies*
JSJ	*Journal for the Study of Judaism in the Persian, Hellenistic and Roman Period*
JSNT	*Journal for the Study of the New Testament*
JSOT	*Journal for the Study of the Old Testament*
JTS	*Journal of Theological Studies*
KD	*Kerygma und Dogma*
"L"	The Lucan private source
LAE	A. Deissmann, *Light from the Ancient East* (2d ed.; London: Hodder & Stoughton, 1927)

LCL	Loeb Classical Library
LD	Lectio divina
LQ	*Lutheran Quarterly*
LSJ	Liddell-Scott-Jones, *Greek-English Lexicon* (Oxford: Clarendon, 1940)
LTK	*Lexikon für Theologie und Kirche* (11 vols.; 2d ed.; eds. J. Höfer and K. Rahner; Freiburg im B.: Herder, 1957-1967)
LumVie	*Lumière et vie*
LumVieSup	Supplement to *LumVie*
LXX	Septuagint
"M"	The Matthean private source
m.	Mishna
MeyerK	H. A. W. Meyer, Kritisch-exegetischer Kommentar über das Neue Testament
"Mk"	The Marcan source
MM	J. H. Moulton and G. Milligan, *The Vocabulary of the Greek Testament* (London: Hodder & Stoughton, 1930)
MNT	R. E. Brown et al., eds., *Mary in the New Testament* (Philadelphia: Fortress; New York: Paulist, 1978)
MNTC	Moffatt New Testament Commentaries
MPAT	J. A. Fitzmyer and D. J. Harrington, *A Manual of Palestinian Aramaic Texts* (BibOr 34; Rome: Biblical Institute, 1979)
MScRel	*Mélanges de science religieuse*
MT	Masoretic Text
MTS	Münchener theologische Studien
MTZ	*Münchener theologische Zeitschrift*
N-A²⁶	Eb. and E. Nestle, K. Aland, et al., *Novum Testamentum graece* (26th ed.; Stuttgart: Deutsche Bibelstiftung, 1979)
NAB	*New American Bible* (successor to *CCD)*
NCCHS	R. C. Fuller et al., eds., *A New Catholic Commentary on Holy Scripture* (London: Nelson, 1969)
NEB	*New English Bible*
NedTT	*Nederlands theologisch Tijdschrift*
NHS	Nag Hammadi Studies
NICNT	New International Commentary on the New Testament
NIDNTT	C. Brown, ed., *New International Dictionary of New Testament Theology* (3 vols.; Grand Rapids: Zondervan, 1975-1978)
NIV	*New International Version* (of the Bible)
NJV	*New Jewish Version* (of the Bible)
NKZ	*Neue kirchliche Zeitschrift*
NorTT	*Norsk teologisk Tidsskrift*
NovT	*Novum Testamentum*
NovTSup	Supplement to *NovT*
NRT	*La nouvelle revue théologique*

ns	new series (in any language)
NT	New Testament
NTA	*New Testament Abstracts*
NTAbh	Neutestamentliche Abhandlungen
NTB	C. K. Barrett, *The New Testament Background: Selected Documents* (London: SPCK, 1956)
NTD	Das Neue Testament deutsch
NTS	*New Testament Studies*
NTTS	New Testament Tools and Studies
OGIS	W. Dittenberger, *Orientis graeci inscriptiones selectae* (Leipzig: Hirzel, 1903-1905)
OL	Old Latin (Vetus latina)
OS	Old Syriac (Vetus syra)
os	old series (in any language)
OT	Old Testament
OxyP	Oxyrhynchus Papyri
PCB	M. Black and H. H. Rowley, eds., *Peake's Commentary on the Bible* (London: Nelson, 1963)
PEQ	*Palestine Exploration Quarterly*
PG	J. Migne, ed., Patrologia graeca
PJ	*Palästina-Jahrbuch*
PL	J. Migne, ed., Patrologia latina
ProcCTSA	*Proceedings of the Catholic Theological Society of America*
Prot. Jas.	*Protevangelium of James*
PSBA	*Proceedings of the Society of Biblical Archaeology*
PW	*Paulys Real-Encyclopädie der classischen Altertumswissenschaft* (ed. G. Wissowa; Stuttgart: Metzler, 1893-)
"Q"	Quelle (source of the Double Tradition in Luke and Matthew)
QD	Quaestiones disputatae
QDAP	*Quarterly of the Department of Antiquities in Palestine*
RAC	*Reallexikon für Antike und Christentum* (ed. T. Klausner; Stuttgart: Hiersmann, 1950-)
RB	*Revue biblique*
RBén	*Revue bénédictine*
RCB	*Revista de cultura bíblica*
RechBib	Recherches bibliques
REG	*Revue des études grecques*
REJ	*Revue des études juives*
RevArch	*Revue archéologique*
RevExp	*Review and Expositor*
RevistB	*Revista bíblica*
RevQ	*Revue de Qumrân*

RevScRel	Revue des sciences religieuses
RevThom	Revue thomiste
RGG	Die Religion in Geschichte und Gegenwart (7 vols.; 3d ed.; ed. K. Galling; Tübingen: Mohr [Siebeck], 1957-1965)
RHE	Revue d'histoire ecclésiastique
RHPR	Revue d'histoire et de philosophie religieuses
RHR	Revue de l'histoire des religions
RIDA	Revue internationale du droit de l'antiquité
RivB	Rivista biblica
RivBSup	Supplement to RivB
RNT	Regensburger Neues Testament
RSPT	Revue des sciences philosophiques et théologiques
RSR	Recherches de science religieuse
RSV	Revised Standard Version
RTL	Revue théologique de Louvain
RTP	Revue de théologie et de philosophie
RTR	Reformed Theological Review
RUO	Revue de l'université d'Ottawa
Sah	Sahidic (an ancient Coptic version of the NT)
SANT	Studien zum Alten und Neuen Testaments
SB	Sources bibliques
SBA	Studies in Biblical Archaeology
SBB	Stuttgarter biblische Beiträge
SBFLA	Studii biblici franciscani liber annuus
SBL	Society of Biblical Literature
SBLDS	SBL Dissertation Series
SBLMS	SBL Monograph Series
SBLSBS	SBL Sources for Biblical Study
SBLSP	SBL Seminar Papers (Chico, CA: Scholars)
SBS	Stuttgarter Bibelstudien
SBT	Studies in Biblical Theology
SC	Sources chrétiennes
ScCatt	Scuola cattolica
ScEccl	Sciences ecclésiastiques
ScEsp	Science et esprit
Scr	Scripture
SE I, II, III, etc.	Studia evangelica I (TU 73; ed. F. L. Cross; Berlin: Akademie, 1959): II (TU 87, 1964); III (TU 88, 1964); IV (TU 102, 1968); V (TU 103, 1968); VI (TU 112; ed. E. A. Livingstone, 1973)
SEA	Svensk exegetisk årsbok
SHT	Studies in Historical Theology
SJLA	Studies in Judaism in Late Antiquity
SJT	Scottish Journal of Theology
SNT	Studien zum Neuen Testament
SNTSMS	Studiorum Novi Testamenti Societas, Monograph Series

SPAW	*Sitzungsberichte der preussischen Akademie der Wissenschaften*
SPB	Studia postbiblica
SQE	K. Aland, *Synopsis quattuor evangeliorum* (10th ed.; Stuttgart: Deutsche Bibelstiftung, 1978)
ST	*Studia theologica*
Str-B	[H. Strack und] P. Billerbeck, *Kommentar zum Neuen Testament* (6 vols.; Munich: Beck, 1922-1961)
StudNeot	Studia Neotestamentica, Studia
SUNT	Studien zur Umwelt des Neuen Testaments
SVTP	Studia in Veteris Testamenti pseudepigrapha
SymBU	Symbolae biblicae upsalienses
SymOs	*Symbolae osloenses*
Syr[h]	Syriac version of the NT, Harclean
T.	*Testament*
TAG	J. A. Fitzmyer, *To Advance the Gospel: New Testament Studies* (New York: Crossroad, 1981)
TBl	*Theologische Blätter*
TBT	*The Bible Today*
TCGNT	B. M. Metzger, *A Textual Commentary on the Greek New Testament* (London/New York: United Bible Societies, 1971)
TD	*Theology Digest*
TDNT	G. Kittel and G. Friedrich, eds., *Theological Dictionary of the New Testament* (10 vols.; Grand Rapids: Eerdmans, 1964-1976; Engl. version of *TWNT)*
TDOT	G. J. Botterweck and H. Ringgren, eds., *Theological Dictionary of the Old Testament* (Grand Rapids: Eerdmans, 1974-)
TF	*Theologische Forschung*
Tg.	Targum
TGl	*Theologie und Glaube*
THKNT	Theologischer Handkommentar zum Neuen Testament
TLZ	*Theologische Literaturzeitung*
TPAPA	*Transactions and Proceedings of the American Philosophical Association*
TPQ	*Theologisch-praktische Quartalschrift*
TQ	*Theologische Quartalschrift*
TRu	*Theologische Rundschau*
TS	*Theological Studies*
TSK	*Theologische Studien und Kritiken*
TTod	*Theology Today*
TTZ	*Trierer theologische Zeitschrift*
TU	Texte und Untersuchungen
TvT	*Tijdschrift voor Theologie*
TWNT	G. Kittel and G. Friedrich, eds., *Theologisches Wörterbuch zum Neuen Testament* (10 vols.; Stuttgart: Kohlhammer, 1933-1979)
TynNTC	Tyndale New Testament Commentary

TZ   *Theologische Zeitschrift*

UBS   United Bible Societies
UBSGNT³   *UBS Greek New Testament* (3d ed.; New York: UBS, 1975)
USQR   *Union Seminary Quarterly Review* (New York, NY)
USR   *Union Seminary Review* (Richmond, VA)
UT   C. H. Gordon, *Ugaritic Textbook* (Analecta orientalia 38; Rome: Biblical Institute, 1965)

VC   *Vigiliae christianae*
VCaro   *Verbum Caro*
VD   *Verbum domini*
VF   *Verkündigung und Forschung*
Vg   Vulgate (Vulgata latina)
VKGNT   K. Aland, ed., *Vollständige Konkordanz zum griechischen Neuen Testament* (2 vols.; Berlin/New York: de Gruyter, 1975-1983)
VoxT   *Vox theologica*
VS   Verbum salutis
VSpir   *Vie spirituelle*
VT   *Vetus Testamentum*

WA   J. A. Fitzmyer, *A Wandering Aramean: Collected Aramaic Essays* (SBLMS 25; Missoula, MT: Scholars, 1979)
WJT   *Westminster Journal of Theology*
WMANT   Wissenschaftliche Monographien zum Alten und Neuen Testament
WUNT   Wissenschaftliche Untersuchungen zum Neuen Testament

ZA   *Zeitschrift für Assyriologie*
ZBG   M. Zerwick, *Biblical Greek* (Rome: Biblical Institute, 1963)
ZKT   *Zeitschrift für katholische Theologie*
ZNW   *Zeitschrift für die neutestamentliche Wissenschaft*
ZRGG   *Zeitschrift für Religions- und Geistesgeschichte*
ZSSR   *Zeitschrift der Savigny Stiftung für Rechtsgeschichte, romantistische Abteilung*
ZST   *Zeitschrift für systematische Theologie*
ZTK   *Zeitschrift für Theologie und Kirche*
>   becomes
<   derived from

GRAMMATICAL ABBREVIATIONS

absol.	absolute	adv.	adverb
acc.	accusative	aor.	aorist
act.	active	art.	article
adj.	adjective	cl.	clause

conj.	conjunction	n.	noun
cp.	compare	neut.	neuter
dat.	dative	nom.	nominative
def.	definite	obj.	object
dem.	demonstrative	opt.	optative
dir.	direct	pass.	passive
fem.	feminine	pers.	person
fut.	future	pf.	perfect
gen.	genitive	pl.	plural
impers.	impersonal	prep.	preposition
impf.	imperfect	pres.	present
impv.	imperative	pron.	pronoun
indef.	indefinite	ptc.	participle
indic.	indicative	rel.	relative
indir.	indirect	sg.	singular
infin.	infinitive	subj.	subject
interj.	interjection	subjunc.	subjunctive
intrans.	intransitive	trans.	transitive
lit.	literally	vb.	verb
masc.	masculine	voc.	vocative

Dead Sea Scrolls and Related Texts

CD	Cairo (Genizah text of the) Damascus (Document)
Ḥev	Naḥal Ḥever texts
Mas	Masada texts
Mird	Khirbet Mird texts
Mur	Wadi Murabbaʻat texts
p	Pesher (commentary)
Q	Qumran
1Q, 2Q, etc.	Numbered caves of Qumran, yielding written material; followed by abbreviation of biblical or apocryphal book
1QapGen	*Genesis Apocryphon* of Qumran Cave 1
1QH	*Hôdāyôt (Thanksgiving Psalms)* from Cave 1
1QIsa[a,b]	First or second copy of Isaiah from Cave 1
1QpHab	*Pesher on Habakkuk* from Cave 1
1QM	*Milḥāmāh* (War Scroll)
1QS	*Serek hayyaḥad (Rule of the Community, Manual of Discipline)*
1QSa	Appendix A *(Rule of the Congregation)* of 1QS
1QSb	Appendix B *(Collection of Benedictions)* of 1QS
4QDibHam	*Dibrê hammĕʼôrôt (Sayings of the Luminaries)* from Cave 4
4QEn	Enoch texts from Cave 4
4QFlor	*Florilegium* from Cave 4
4QMess ar	Aramaic "Messianic" text from Cave 4
4QPBless	*Patriarchal Blessings* from Cave 4
4QPrNab	*Prayer of Nabonidus* from Cave 4
4QpsDan[a]	Copy a of Pseudo-Daniel texts from Cave 4

4QTLevi   *Testament of Levi* from Cave 4
6QD   Damascus Document from Cave 6
11QMelch   *Melchizedek* text from Cave 11
11QPsᵃ   First copy of Psalms from Cave 11
11QTemple *Temple Scroll* from Cave 11
11QtgJob   *Targum of Job* from Cave 11

Targumic Material

Tg. Neb.   *Targum of the Prophets (= Tg. Jonathan)*
Tg. Neof. 1 *Targum Neofiti 1* (of the Pentateuch)
Tg. Onq.   *Targum Onqelos* (of the Pentateuch)
Tg. Yer. I *Targum Yerušalmi I (= Tg. Pseudo-Jonathan,* of the Pentateuch)

Orders and Tractates in Mishnaic and Related Literature

To distinguish the same-named tractates in the Mishna, Tosepta, Babylonian Talmud, and Jerusalem Talmud, an italicized m., t., b., or y. is used before the title of the tractate. Thus *m. Para, t. Para, b. Para, y. Para.*

GENERAL WORKS FREQUENTLY QUOTED WITH SHORT TITLES
(for commentaries quoted with short titles, see pp. 271-279 of vol. 28)

Alon, A. *The Natural History of the Land of the Bible* (Garden City, NY: Doubleday, 1978).

Bailey, J. A. *The Traditions Common to the Gospels of Luke and John* (NovTSup 7; Leiden: Brill, 1963).

Bammel, E., ed. *The Trial of Jesus: Cambridge Studies in Honour of C. F. D. Moule* (SBT 2/13; London, SCM; Naperville, IL: Allenson, 1970).

Benoit, P. *Exégèse et théologie* (3 vols.; Paris: Cerf, 1961, 1961, 1968).

——— *The Passion and Resurrection of Jesus* (New York: Herder and Herder, 1969).

Betz, O., et al., eds. *Abraham unser Vater: Juden und Christen im Gespräch über die Bibel: Festschrift für Otto Michel zum 60. Geburtstag* (AGSU 5; Leiden: Brill, 1963).

Blinzler, J., et al., eds. *Neutestamentliche Aufsätze für Prof. Josef Schmid zum 70. Geburtstag* (Regensburg: Pustet, 1963).

Böcher, O., and K. Haacker, eds. *Verborum veritas: Festschrift für Gustav Stählin zum 70. Geburtstag* (Wuppertal: Brockhaus, 1970).

Bousset, W. *Kyrios Christos* (Nashville: Abingdon, 1970).

Bovon, F. *Luc le théologien: Vingt-cinq ans de recherches (1950-1975)* (Neuchâtel/Paris: Delachaux et Niestlé, 1978).

Braumann, G., ed. *Das Lukas-Evangelium: Die redaktions- und kompositionsgeschichtliche Forschung* (Wege der Forschung 280; Darmstadt: Wissenschaftliche Buchgesellschaft, 1974).

Braun, H. *Qumran und das Neue Testament* (2 vols.; Tübingen: Mohr [Siebeck], 1966).

Brown, R. E. *The Birth of the Messiah: A Commentary on the Infancy Narratives in Matthew and Luke* (Garden City, NY: Doubleday, 1977).

—— *The Gospel according to John (i-xii): Introduction, Translation, and Notes; The Gospel according to John (xiii-xxi): Introduction, Translation, and Notes* (AB 29, 29A; Garden City, NY: Doubleday, 1966, 1970).

—— *New Testament Essays* (Milwaukee: Bruce, 1965).

—— et al., eds. *Peter in the New Testament: A Collaborative Assessment by Protestant and Roman Catholic Scholars* (Minneapolis, MN: Augsburg; New York: Paulist, 1973).

Brown, S. *Apostasy and Perseverance in the Theology of Luke* (AnBib 36; Rome: Biblical Institute, 1969).

Bultmann, R. *Glauben und Verstehen: Gesammelte Aufsätze* (Tübingen: Mohr [Siebeck], 1933).

—— *Marburger Predigten* (Tübingen: Mohr [Siebeck], 1956).

—— *Theology of the New Testament* (2 vols.; London: SCM, 1955-1956).

Bundy, W. E. *Jesus and the First Three Gospels: An Introduction to the Synoptic Tradition* (Cambridge, MA: Harvard University, 1955).

Burger, C. *Jesus als Davidssohn: Eine traditionsgeschichtliche Untersuchung* (FRLANT 98; Göttingen: Vandenhoeck & Ruprecht, 1970).

Cadbury, H. J. *The Style and Literary Method of Luke* (HTS 6; Cambridge, MA: Harvard University, 1920).

Carlston, C. E. *The Parables of the Triple Tradition* (Philadelphia: Fortress, 1975).

Casetti, P., et al., eds. *Mélanges Dominique Barthélemy: Etudes offertes à l'occasion de son 60ᵉ anniversaire* (Orbis biblicus et orientalis 38; Fribourg: Editions universitaires; Göttingen: Vandenhoeck & Ruprecht, 1981).

Cerfaux, L. *Recueil Lucien Cerfaux: Etudes d'exégèse et d'histoire religieuse* (3 vols.; Gembloux: Duculot, 1954, 1954, 1962).

Conzelmann, H. *An Outline of the Theology of the New Testament* (New York/Evanston: Harper & Row, 1968).

—— et al., eds. *Zur Bedeutung des Todes Jesu: Exegetische Beiträge* (Gütersloh: Mohn, 1967).

Cranfield, C. E. B. *The Gospel according to Saint Mark* (Cambridge Greek Testament Commentary; Cambridge: University Press, 1959).

Cullmann, O. *The Christology of the New Testament* (Philadelphia: Westminster, 1959).

Dalman, G. *The Words of Jesus* (Edinburgh: Clark, 1909).

—— *Die Worte Jesu* (2d ed.; Leipzig: Hinrichs, 1930; repr., Darmstadt: Wissenschaftliche Buchgesellschaft, 1965).

Delorme, J., ed. *The Eucharist in the New Testament: A Symposium* (Baltimore: Helicon; London: Chapman, 1964).

Derrett, J. D. M. *Law in the New Testament* (London: Darton, Longman & Todd, 1970).

Descamps, A., and A. de Halleux, eds. *Mélanges bibliques en hommage au R. P. Béda Rigaux* (Gembloux: Duculot, 1970).

Dhanis, E., ed. *Resurrexit: Actes du symposium international sur la résurrection de Jésus (Rome 1970)* (Rome: Editrice vaticana, 1974).

Dibelius, M. *Botschaft und Geschichte* (2 vols.; Tübingen: Mohr [Siebeck], 1953, 1956).

Dietrich, W. *Das Petrusbild der lukanischen Schriften* (BWANT 94; Stuttgart: Kohlhammer, 1972).

Dillon, R. J. *From Eye-Witnesses to Ministers of the Word: Tradition and Composition in Luke 24* (AnBib 82; Rome: Biblical Institute, 1978).

Dodd, C. H. *The Parables of the Kingdom* (New York: Scribner's, 1961).

Dupont, J. *Les béatitudes* (3 vols.; EBib; Paris: Gabalda, 1958, 1960, 1973).

——— ed. *Jésus aux origines de la christologie* (BETL 40; Gembloux: Duculot; Leuven: Leuven University, 1975).

Eichholz, G. *Gleichnisse der Evangelien: Form, Überlieferung, Auslegung* (3d ed.; Neukirchen-Vluyn: Neukirchener-V., 1979).

Ellis, E. E., and E. Grässer, eds. *Jesus und Paulus: Festschrift für Werner Georg Kümmel zum 70. Geburtstag* (Göttingen: Vandenhoeck & Ruprecht, 1975).

Eltester, W., ed. *Judentum—Urchristentum—Kirche: Festschrift für Joachim Jeremias* (BZNW 26; Berlin: Töpelmann, 1960).

——— *Neutestamentliche Studien für Rudolf Bultmann zu seinem siebzigsten Geburtstag am 20. August* (BZNW 21; Berlin: Töpelmann, 1954).

Epp, E. J., and G. D. Fee, eds. *New Testament Textual Criticism: Its Significance for Exegesis: Essays in Honour of Bruce M. Metzger* (Oxford: Clarendon, 1981).

Feld, H., and J. Nolte, eds. *Wort Gottes in der Zeit: Festschrift Karl Hermann Schelkle zum 65. Geburtstag dargebracht . . .* (Düsseldorf: Patmos, 1973).

Field, F. *Notes on the Translation of the New Testament* (Cambridge: University Press, 1899).

Finegan, J. *The Archeology of the New Testament* (Princeton: Princeton University, 1969).

——— *Die Überlieferung der Leidens- und Auferstehungsgeschichte Jesu* (BZNW 15; Giessen: Töpelmann, 1934).

Flender, H. *St Luke: Theologian of Redemptive History* (Philadelphia: Fortress, 1967).

Foerster, W. *Herr ist Jesus: Herkunft und Bedeutung des urchristlichen Kyrios-Bekenntnisses* (Neutestamentliche Forschungen 2/1; Gütersloh: Bertelsmann, 1924).

France, R. T., and D. Wenham, eds. *Gospel Perspectives: Studies of History and Tradition in the Four Gospels* (2 vols.; Sheffield: JSOT, 1980-1981).

Gnilka, J., ed. *Neues Testament und Kirche: Für Rudolf Schnackenburg* (Freiburg im B.: Herder, 1974).

Grässer, E. *Das Problem der Parusieverzögerung in den synoptischen Evangelien und in der Apostelgeschichte* (BZNW 22; Berlin: Töpelmann, 1957; 2d ed., 1966).

Guillaume, J.-M. *Luc interprète des anciennes traditions sur la résurrection de Jésus* (EBib; Paris: Gabalda, 1979).

Haenchen, E. *The Acts of the Apostles: A Commentary* (Philadelphia: Westminster, 1971).

——— *Der Weg Jesu: Eine Erklärung des Markus-Evangeliums und der kanonischen Parallelen* (Sammlung Töpelmann 2/6; 2d ed.; Berlin: de Gruyter, 1968).

Hahn, F. *Mission in the New Testament* (SBT 47; Naperville, IL: Allenson, 1965).

———— *The Titles of Jesus in Christology: Their History in Early Christianity* (London: Lutterworth, 1969).

Haubeck, W., and M. Bachmann, eds. *Wort in der Zeit: Neutestamentliche Studien: Festgabe für Karl Heinz Rengstorf zum 75. Geburtstag* (Leiden: Brill, 1980).

Hobart, W. K. *The Medical Language of St. Luke* (Dublin: Hodges, Figgis; London: Longmans, Green, 1882).

Hoffmann, P., et al., eds. *Orientierung an Jesus: Zur Theologie der Synoptiker: Für Josef Schmid* (Freiburg im B.: Herder, 1973).

Huck, A., and H. Greeven. *Synopse der drei ersten Evangelien mit Beigabe der johanneischen Parallelstellen: Synopsis of the First Three Gospels with the Addition of the Johannine Parallels* (13th ed.; Tübingen: Mohr [Siebeck], 1981).

Iersel, B. M. F. van. *"Der Sohn" in den synoptischen Jesusworten: Christusbezeichnung Jesu?* (NovTSup 3; 2d ed.; Leiden: Brill, 1964).

Jeremias, G., et al., eds. *Tradition und Glaube: Das frühe Christentum in seiner Umwelt: Festgabe für Karl Georg Kuhn zum 65. Geburtstag* (Göttingen: Vandenhoeck & Ruprecht, 1971).

Jeremias, J. *Abba: Studien zur neutestamentlichen Theologie und Zeitgeschichte* (Göttingen: Vandenhoeck & Ruprecht, 1966).

———— *The Eucharistic Words of Jesus* (Philadelphia: Fortress, 1977).

———— *Jerusalem in the Time of Jesus* (Philadelphia: Fortress, 1969).

———— *New Testament Theology: The Proclamation of Jesus* (New York: Scribner's, 1971).

———— *The Parables of Jesus* (rev. ed.; New York: Scribner's, 1963).

———— *The Prayers of Jesus* (SBT 2/6; Naperville, IL: Allenson, 1967).

———— *Die Sprache des Lukasevangeliums* (MeyerK; Göttingen: Vandenhoeck & Ruprecht, 1980).

Jülicher, A. *Die Gleichnisreden Jesu* (2 vols.; Tübingen: Mohr [Siebeck], 1910; repr., Darmstadt: Wissenschaftliche Buchgesellschaft, 1963).

Kaestli, J.-D. *L'Eschatologie dans l'oeuvre de Luc* (Geneva: Labor et Fides, 1969).

Käsemann, E. *New Testament Questions of Today* (Philadelphia: Fortress, 1969).

———— *Essays on New Testament Themes* (SBT 41; London: SCM, 1964).

Kissinger, W. S. *The Parables of Jesus: A History of Interpretation and Bibliography* (ATLA Bibliography Series 4; Metuchen, NJ: Scarecrow, 1979).

Kümmel, W. G. *Promise and Fulfilment: The Eschatological Message of Jesus* (SBT 23; Naperville, IL: Allenson, 1957).

———— *The Theology of the New Testament according to Its Major Witnesses, Jesus—Paul—John* (Nashville, TN: Abingdon, 1973).

Kuss, O. *Auslegung und Verkündigung: Aufsätze zur Exegese des Neuen Testamentes* (Regensburg: Pustet, 1963).

Lambrecht, J. *Once More Astonished: The Parables of Jesus* (New York: Crossroad, 1981).

Lehmann, M. *Synoptische Quellenanalyse und die Frage nach dem historischen Jesus* (BZNW 38; Berlin: de Gruyter, 1970).

Linnemann, E. *Jesus of the Parables: Introduction and Exposition* (New York: Harper & Row, 1966).

———— *Studien zur Passionsgeschichte* (FRLANT 102; Göttingen: Vandenhoeck & Ruprecht, 1970).

Lohfink, G. *Die Sammlung Israels: Eine Untersuchung zur lukanischen Ekklesiologie* (SANT 39; Munich: Kösel, 1975).

Lohse, E. *History of the Suffering and Death of Jesus Christ* (Philadelphia: Fortress, 1967).

———— et al., eds. *Der Ruf Jesu und die Antwort der Gemeinde: Exegetische Untersuchungen Joachim Jeremias zum 70. Geburtstag gewidmet von seinen Schülern* (Göttingen: Vandenhoeck & Ruprecht, 1970).

Lövestam, E. *Spiritual Wakefulness in the New Testament* (Lunds Universitets Årsskrift 1/55.3; Lund: Gleerup, 1963).

Lührmann, D. *Die Redaktion der Logienquelle* (WMANT 3; Neukirchen-Vluyn: Neukirchener-V., 1969).

Manson, T. W. *The Sayings of Jesus as Recorded in the Gospels according to St. Matthew and St. Luke Arranged with Introduction and Commentary* (London: SCM, 1971).

Marshall, I. H. *The Gospel of Luke: A Commentary on the Greek Text* (New International Greek Testament Commentary; Grand Rapids, MI: Eerdmans, 1978).

———— *Luke: Historian and Theologian* (Grand Rapids, MI: Zondervan, 1970).

Ménard, J.-E. *L'Evangile selon Thomas* (NHS 5; Leiden: Brill, 1975).

Merklein, H., and J. Lange, eds. *Biblische Randbemerkungen: Schüler-Festschrift für Rudolf Schnackenburg zum 60. Geburtstag* (Würzburg: Echter-V., 1974).

Miyoshi, M. *Der Anfang des Reiseberichts Lk 9,51-10,24: Eine Redaktionsgeschichtliche Untersuchung* (AnBib 60; Rome: Biblical Institute, 1974).

Montefiore, H., and H. E. W. Turner. *Thomas and the Evangelists* (SBT 35; Naperville, IL: Allenson, 1962).

Moule, C. F. D. *An Idiom Book of New Testament Greek* (Cambridge: University Press, 1953).

Mussner, F. *Praesentia salutis: Gesammelte Studien zu Fragen und Themen des Neuen Testamentes* (Düsseldorf: Patmos, 1967).

Neirynck, F., ed. *L'Evangile de Luc: Problèmes littéraires et théologiques: Mémorial Lucien Cerfaux* (BETL 32; Gembloux: Duculot; Leuven: Leuven University, 1973).

Ott, W. *Gebet und Heil: Die Bedeutung der Gebetsparänese in der lukanischen Theologie* (SANT 12; Munich: Kösel, 1965).

Perkins, P. *Hearing the Parables* (New York: Paulist, 1981).

Perrin, N. *Rediscovering the Teaching of Jesus* (New York: Harper & Row, 1967).

Pesch, R., and R. Schnackenburg, eds. *Jesus und der Menschensohn: Für Anton Vögtle* (Freiburg im B.: Herder, 1975).

Potterie, I. de la, ed. *De Jésus aux évangiles: Tradition et rédaction dans les évangiles synoptiques: Donum natalicium Iosepho Coppens . . .* (BETL 25; 2 vols.; Gembloux: Duculot, 1967).

Rehkopf, F. *Die lukanische Sonderquelle: Ihr Umfang und Sprachgebrauch* (WUNT 5; Tübingen: Mohr [Siebeck], 1959).

Rese, M. *Alttestamentliche Motive in der Christologie des Lukas* (SNT 1; Gütersloh: Mohn, 1969).

Robinson, J. A. T. *Twelve New Testament Studies* (SBT 34; Naperville, IL: Allenson, 1962).

Robinson, J. M. *The Problem of History in Mark and Other Marcan Studies* (Philadelphia: Fortress, 1982).

Roloff, J. *Das Kerygma und der irdische Jesus: Historische Motive in den Jesus-Erzählungen der Evangelien* (Göttingen: Vandenhoeck & Ruprecht, 1970).

Sabbe, M., ed. *L'Evangile selon Marc: Tradition et rédaction* (BETL 34; Gembloux: Duculot, 1974).

Schenke, L. *Studien zur Passionsgeschichte des Markus: Tradition und Redaktion in Markus 14,1-42* (Forschung zur Bibel 4; Würzburg: Echter-V., 1971).

Schmid, J. *Matthäus und Lukas: Eine Untersuchung des Verhältnisses ihrer Evangelien* (Biblische Studien 23/2-4; Freiburg im B.: Herder, 1930).

——— *The Regensburg New Testament: The Gospel according to Mark* (Staten Island, NY: Alba House, n.d.).

Schnackenburg, R., et al., eds. *Die Kirche des Anfangs: Festschrift für Heinz Schürmann zum 65. Geburtstag* (Leipzig: St. Benno, 1977).

Schneider, G. *Parusiegleichnisse im Lukas-Evangelium* (SBS 74; Stuttgart: Katholisches Bibelwerk, 1975).

——— *Verleugnung, Verspottung und Verhör Jesu nach Lukas, 22,54-71: Studien zur lukanischen Darstellung der Passion* (SANT 22; Munich: Kösel, 1969).

Schrage, W. *Das Verhältnis des Thomasevangeliums zur synoptischen Tradition und zu den koptischen Evangelienübersetzungen: Zugleich ein Beitrag zur gnostischen Synoptikerdeutung* (BZNW 29; Berlin: de Gruyter, 1964).

Schramm, T. *Der Markus-Stoff bei Lukas: Eine literarkritische und redaktionsgeschichtliche Untersuchung* (SNTSMS 14; Cambridge: University Press, 1971).

Schulz, S. *Q: Die Spruchquelle der Evangelisten* (Zürich: Theologischer-V., 1972).

Schürmann, H. *Quellenkritische Untersuchung des lukanischen Abendmahlsberichtes Lk 22, 7-38. I. Teil: Der Paschamahlbericht Lk 22, (7-14.)15-18; II. Teil: Der Einsetzungsbericht Lk 22, 19-20; III. Teil: Jesu Abschiedsrede Lk 22, 21-38* (NTAbh 19/5, 20/4-5; Münster in W.: Aschendorff, 1953, 1955, 1957).

——— *Traditionsgeschichtliche Untersuchungen zu den synoptischen Evangelien: Beiträge* (Düsseldorf: Patmos, 1968).

——— *Ursprung und Gestalt: Erörterungen und Besinnungen zum Neuen Testament* (Düsseldorf: Patmos, 1970).

Schweizer, E. *Das Evangelium nach Lukas übersetzt und erklärt* (NTD 3; 18th ed.; Vandenhoeck & Ruprecht, 1982).

——— *The Good News according to Mark: A Commentary on the Gospel* (London: SPCK, 1971).

Streeter, B. H. *The Four Gospels: A Study of Origins, Treating of the Manuscript Tradition, Sources, Authority, & Dates* (London: Macmillan, 1924).

Taylor, V. *Behind the Third Gospel: A Study of the Proto-Luke Hypothesis* (Oxford: Clarendon, 1926).

——— *The Gospel according to St. Mark: The Greek Text with Introduction, Notes, and Indexes* (London: Macmillan, 1953).

——— *The Passion Narrative of St Luke: A Critical and Historical Investigation* (SNTSMS 19; ed. O. E. Evans; Cambridge: University Press, 1972).

Thrall, M. E. *Greek Particles in the New Testament* (NTTS 3; Leiden: Brill, 1962).
Tödt, M. E. *The Son of Man in the Synoptic Tradition* (New Testament Library; Philadelphia: Westminster, 1965).
Torrey, C. C. *Our Translated Gospels: Some of the Evidence* (New York: Harper & Bros., 1936).
Trilling, W. *Christusverkündigung in den synoptischen Evangelien: Beispiele gattungsgemässer Auslegung* (Biblische Handbibliothek 4; Munich: Kösel, 1969).
Unnik, W. C. van, ed. *Neotestamentica et patristica: Eine Freundesgabe, Herrn Professor Dr. Oscar Cullmann zu seinem 60. Geburtstag überreicht* (NovTSup 6; Leiden: Brill, 1962).
Vögtle, A. *Das Evangelium und die Evangelien: Beiträge zur Evangelienforschung* (Düsseldorf: Patmos, 1971).
Voss, G. *Die Christologie der lukanischen Schriften in Grundzügen* (Studia neotestamentica, Studia II; Paris/Bruges: Desclée de Brouwer, 1965).
Weiser, A. *Die Knechtsgleichnisse der synoptischen Evangelien* (SANT 29; Munich: Kösel, 1971).

TRANSLATION
AND COMMENTARY

IV. THE JOURNEY TO JERUSALEM
(CONTINUED)

60. THE MISSION OF THE SEVENTY(-TWO)
(10:1-12)

10 ¹ Later on the Lord appointed seventy(-two) others and sent them on in twos ahead of him to every town and place that he himself intended to visit. ² He said to them, "The harvest is abundant, but laborers are few; so beg the owner of the harvest to send out laborers enough for his harvest. ³ Now go; and look, I am sending you out like lambs among wolves. ⁴ Do not carry a purse or a knapsack or sandals; and do not exchange greetings with anyone on the way. ⁵ Whenever you enter a house, say first of all, 'Peace be to this house!' ⁶ And if a peaceful person dwells there, your peace will rest upon him. But if not, it will come back to you. ⁷ Stay at that one house, eating and drinking what they have; for the laborer deserves his pay. Do not move from house to house. ⁸ Whenever you enter a town and people welcome you, eat what is put before you. ⁹ Cure the sick in that town and say to them, 'The kingdom of God has drawn near to you.' ¹⁰ But if you enter a town and the people do not welcome you, go out into its streets and say, ¹¹ 'The very dust from your town which has clung to our feet we wipe off in protest against you.' Rather, be sure of this, the kingdom of God has drawn near. ¹² I tell you, it shall be more tolerable on that day for Sodom than for that town."

COMMENT

As part of his recently begun travel account (9:51) Luke now introduces Jesus sending out further disciples to prepare the way for him (10:1-12). Earlier he had dispatched the Twelve on a mission to preach and heal (9:1-6). Now seventy(-two) disciples are sent off. Though Luke depicts Jesus himself en route to Jerusalem, he never indicates whence these disciples are dispatched or whither they return—save from Jesus and to Jesus.

These twelve verses form a mission-charge to the disciples, but they are part of a longer discourse, which ends with Jesus' woes uttered against towns in Galilee and his remarks about the disciples as representatives of himself and of the One who sent him (10:13-15,16). The exact relation of these added sayings will be discussed below; but one should note the joining of such disparate material, which is characteristic of the travel account, in which the evangelist is hardly concerned about (historical) transitions. The concatenation of sayings-material in this account reveals what Luke meant in his prologue when he protested that he was writing "systematically" *(kathexēs,* lit. "in order," 1:3). Luke is concerned more about the literary concatenation of sayings than about their historical or plausible transitions.

The mission-charge (10:1-12) is a "doublet" of the rules for missionary activity already set forth for the Twelve in 9:1-6 (see p. 81). The sayings used in this episode come from "Q," being paralleled (in a different order) in Matt 9:37-38, 10:7-16 (and 11:24). These verses were undoubtedly a unit already collected in "Q"; they are preserved here in their more original shape. Matthew's one account of a mission (of the Twelve) uses material from both "Mk" and "Q," conflating the sayings into one sermon (chap. 10). F. Hahn *(Mission,* 33) thinks that vv. 2-12 represent the original form of "Q" and come from a tradition earlier than Mark 6:6b-13. That may be, but one has to allow for some Lucan redaction of these verses. Verse 1 is clearly of Lucan composition (the evangelist's introduction to the separate mission of "seventy[-two] others"). P. Hoffmann ("Lukas 10,5-11," 39-42) has made a strong case for the Lucan redaction of vv. 10-11, where direct discourse has been introduced. But his attempt to show that v. 8 is modified by Lucan redaction is less convincing; the similar beginnings of vv. 5,8,10 are almost certainly to be attributed to the "Q" source; Matthew has the same in 10:11. Verse 7 undoubtedly manifests Lucan redaction; it is repetitious in that part *c* says what part *a* has already said, whereas part *b* was probably already in "Q," since it is paralleled in Matt 10:10b. Moreover, v. 12 has been redactionally modified by Luke, even if it is parallel to Matt 10:15 (see also Matt 11:24 and COMMENT on 10:13-15; cf. J. Jeremias, *Die Sprache,* 182-186).

Two of the sayings in this mission-charge have parallels in the Coptic *Gospel of Thomas.* The first is a parallel to v. 2 in § 73: "Jesus said, 'The harvest is great, but laborers are scarce; so beg the Lord to send laborers to the harvest.' " The only real differences from Luke 10:2 are the use of "the Lord" instead of "the owner of the harvest" and the omission of "his." Since the Synoptic form of this saying is passed on identically by both Matthew and Luke, one might wonder whether the Coptic form depends on an extracanonical tradition; that is, however, hardly likely (cf. W. Schrage, *Das Verhältnis,* 153). The other saying, parallel to 10:8, is found in § 14b: "When you go into a land and walk about in its districts, if they welcome you, eat what they put before you and heal the sick among them." This Coptic form of the saying is joined to another which is parallel to Mark 7:15 and omitted by Luke. The Coptic form of the saying in v. 8 is almost certainly dependent on the Lucan form (see W. Schrage, ibid. 52-55). In both instances the Coptic sayings offer parallels only to isolated sayings and have no real parallel to the episode as a whole (as is true with so many of the sayings preserved in that apocryphal Gospel).

Since none of the other Gospels knows of a separate sending-out of "other" disciples than the Twelve and since what is addressed here to the "others" is already found in part in the charge to the Twelve in Matthew, Luke has clearly created this literary "doublet" from the "Q" material that is parallel to Mark 6:6b-13. Information that was preserved in the "Mk" and "Q" sources about *a* sending-out of disciples by Jesus has been used by Luke to fashion two separate mission-charges, one to the Twelve and one to the "seventy(-two) others." Further support for this conclusion is found in Luke 22:35 (see COMMENT there), where Jesus, addressing the Twelve at the Last Supper, asks them, "When I sent you out without a purse, knapsack, or *sandals,* was there anything that you lacked?" That question, including "sandals," refers not to 9:3, addressed to the Twelve, but to 10:4, addressed to the "others." In other words, the double sending-out of disciples during Jesus' earthly ministry is a Lucan creation.

Since sayings of Jesus in both chaps. 9 and 10 sound like community regulations for missionary work, especially with an air of expectancy about the approach of the kingdom, it has often seemed that they reflect the early activity of the Christian community rather than a historical sending-out of disciples during Jesus' Galilean ministry. R. Bultmann *(HST* 145) thought that, since these regulations were no longer applicable to missionary endeavors in Mark's day, he made them into a charge to disciples during Jesus' own ministry. Though no one contests that early Christians were convinced that their missionary activity was rooted in a commission of Jesus, or at least of the risen Lord, the issue is rather whether these regulations, related in the Synoptics to a mission during the Galilean ministry of Jesus himself, reflect actually a historical sending-out by Jesus during that ministry. Other sayings from early church practice have at times been retrojected into that ministry and put on the lips of Jesus. But, as J. M. Creed has recognized *(The Gospel,* 125), there is no conclusive reason to say that Jesus did not associate to himself disciples and prepare them for preaching the advent of the kingdom by sending them on this temporary mission. F. Hahn *(Mission,* 46) is also willing to trace the radical demands of the regulations back to Jesus himself. The only real problem with the rooting of these instructions in a mission-charge of Jesus' ministry is that such a preparation would suggest a greater degree of allegiance to him than the disciples' eventual defection would seem to tolerate. Hence the hesitation about such a sending-out during the Galilean ministry. That Luke should make two out of the tradition that he inherited is not surprising, since in the Lucan Gospel the disciples are never said to have deserted Jesus.

The details in this mission-charge are more specific than in 9:1-6. The two important notes that emerge are urgency and hostility. *Impedimenta* cannot be tolerated in the preaching of the kingdom, and the curing of the sick must be handled with the speed expected of workers at harvest time. But the disciples must realize that they are not being sent to carry out ordinary social obligations and amenities, for what they are to preach and do will set them apart. There will be no time for ordinary greetings, scruples over what sort of food one eats, or searching for better quarters. Their message is to be, "The kingdom of God has drawn near to you!" Their concern for God's kingdom must be that of reapers confronted with a harvest that is to be gathered in before it spoils.

They are, however, being sent out like lambs among wolves, i.e. defenseless, weak creatures, whose status will always be precarious when strong confrontation and attack are imminent.

Verses 5-7 deal with the conduct of disciples in houses, and vv. 8-9 with that in towns.

Seventy(-two) other disciples are now sent out in the Lucan Gospel in addition to the Twelve in 9:1-6 because of the abundance of the harvest. Luke's reason for this "doublet" seems to be that the "mission" will not be restricted to the Twelve; "others" will share in the testimony to be borne to Jesus and to his own word or message. The significance of this "doublet" is realized when one recalls how in Acts the role of the Twelve eventually becomes insignificant (see p. 255).

In this mission-charge disciples are being instructed not only to go forth to preach and to cure, but to beg God for laborers enough to cope with the abundance of the evangelical harvest. The success of the harvest will depend not only on the disciples' cooperation, but also on their prayer. The owner of the harvest is God, whose kingdom is to be preached. In 8:11 his word was compared to seed sown in the ground. Now the preaching of the kingdom is indirectly compared with a harvest; though the figure differs somewhat, it is clearly related. Jesus' saying stresses the need of disciples as collaborators; he who was sent to preach (4:18) now sends out "others," and in numbers (10:1); they will be his representatives (10:16).

The mission-charge proper ends with a minatory statement that compares towns like Jesus' hometown, Nazareth, that may reject his message, or the Samaritan villages, on which the disciples wanted to call down consuming fire (9:53-54), with a famous OT town, Sodom, destroyed by fire and brimstone (Gen 19:24). When judgment comes, Sodom with all its wickedness will be thought to have fared better than such towns with their rejection of God's special envoys. The minatory statement becomes the springboard for further woes in the immediately following section, part of this Lucan discourse.

This episode is important for Lucan eschatology (see pp. 231-235). It hints at the coming visit of "the Lord" (v. 1), alludes to the harvest to be reaped from evangelical preaching (v. 2), and suggests that no matter how bad it will be for Sodom, it will be even worse for such a town (v. 12).

In chaps. 9 and 10, with their mission-charges, Luke is also speaking to the Christian community of his day, relating details of its missionary endeavors to the ministry of Jesus himself. Thus the teaching of the Christian community in the Period of the Church is rooted in his teaching and in a command of Jesus himself.

NOTES

10 1. *Later on.* Lit. "after these things." This is a stereotyped Lucan transitional phrase. See 5:27; 12:4; 17:8; 18:4; Acts 7:7; 13:20; 15:16; 18:1. Cf. p. 111. It is not to be pressed in a temporal sense.

the Lord. See NOTE on 7:13.

appointed. Only in 10:9 does the reader learn that the seventy(-two) were intended to preach the kingdom and cure the sick. Nothing is said, as in 9:1, about Jesus giving them a share in his "power" and "authority." That would seem to be presupposed in the appointment.

seventy(-two) others. I.e. other than the Twelve, but possibly also other than the messengers in 9:52. Does it imply that the Twelve remained with Jesus during this mission? H. Conzelmann *(Theology,* 67 n. 1) thinks that this is likely. It is impossible to think that the number was part of "Q," since this verse is from Luke's own pen.

Instead of simply *heterous,* "others," read in mss. P⁷⁵, B, L, etc., many important mss. (ℵ, A, C, D, K, W, X, etc.) read *kai heterous,* which would mean "even seventy/seventy-two others." It is difficult to say which is to be preferred.

Should one read "seventy" or "seventy-two"? The former is attested in such mss. as ℵ, A, C, K, L, W, X, etc., whereas the latter has the support of P⁷⁵, B, D, 0181, and the OL and OS traditions. The UBS Committee, in assessing the external evidence, thought it almost equally balanced, and considered the attempts to answer which was preferable by invoking the internal symbolism intended as inconclusive. Whose symbolism is it (Jesus'? the pre-Synoptic tradition's? the evangelist's?)? K. Aland *(TCGNT* 151) argues strongly for "seventy-two" (without any brackets) because of the varied external evidence and because, whereas seventy is a frequently used OT number, seventy-two is not (being found only in Num 31:38). Hence a change from seventy-two to seventy in copying would be more likely than vice versa. For pre-P⁷⁵ discussions, see B. M. Metzger, "Seventy or Seventy-Two Disciples?" 299-306; S. Jellicoe, "St Luke and the 'Seventy(-two),' " 319-321. See also Luke 10:17.

If the number were seventy, would it reflect such OT usage as the seventy elders chosen by Moses to assist him (Exod 24:1; Num 11:16,24)? Or possibly the seventy offspring of Jacob (Exod 1:5; Deut 10:22)? It is hardly likely that the seventy years of

Zech 7:5 would be involved. It has often been thought to reflect the nations of the world in the table of Gen 10:2-31 and would symbolize the coming evangelization of the Gentiles and diaspora Jews by the disciples, whereas the Twelve would have been sent to Israel itself. See further *1 Enoch* 89:59; cf. Deut 32:8. But in the MT of Genesis the descendants of Japheth, Ham, and Shem number seventy, whereas in the LXX they are seventy-two. The number seventy is surely an approximation or "round number" for a more original seventy-two.

The trouble with this interpretation is that the "seventy(-two) others" are sent in this verse "to every town and place that Jesus himself intended to visit," and Luke 24:47 destines the Twelve for "all nations." Because of such problems, some commentators (e.g. J. Schmid, *Evangelium nach Lukas,* 184) simply take the seventy/seventy-two as a round number.

in twos. Luke's composition borrows a detail from Mark 6:7, which he omitted in 9:1; he writes *ana dyo* instead of the Marcan *dyo dyo,* "two by two." See *ana pentēkonta* in NOTE on 9:14. Thus Jesus is made to send out thirty-five/thirty-six pairs of disciples, but Luke never calls them *mathētai* in this whole section. The custom of traveling in pairs is said to be Jewish, but it is not found in the OT. It turns up here and elsewhere in the NT and becomes famous in the later rabbinical tradition. See J. Jeremias, "Paarweise Sendung." The pair could be meant for mutual support on the journey, but it is more probably to be explained by the notion of the testimony of two witnesses in judicial cases. See Deut 19:15; Num 35:30. A juridical note is suggested at the end of this episode (vv. 10-11), and a "warning" (lit. "testimony") was mentioned explicitly in the parallel in 9:5. NT pairs can be found in Paul and Barnabas (Acts 13:1 [but cf. 13:13]); Paul and Silas (Acts 15:40); Peter and John (Acts 8:14); Barnabas and Mark (Acts 15:40); Judas and Silas (Acts 15:32); and possibly Andronicus and Junia(s) (Rom 16:7).

ahead of him. Lit. "before his face," a Septuagintism. See p. 115.

that he himself intended to visit. I.e. they were to go on ahead as heralds—heralds not only of his coming ministry, but perhaps even of his eschatological visit.

2. *The harvest is abundant.* See Matt 9:37-38. In the Lucan Gospel this harvest becomes a figure for the season when the mature preaching of the kingdom takes place. Recall 8:15,16-17. The time has come for its widespread announcement and the great numbers that will accept the message. In the OT the harvest was a figure of God's eschatological judgment of the nations. See Joel 4:1-13; Isa 27:11-12. In John 4:36-38 missionary results are described, as here, in terms of it: disciples will have the joy of reaping what they have not sown. But the image also carries a warning as well as a promise, as the sequel of this episode makes clear.

but laborers are few. Lucan style makes use of the contrasting particles *men . . . de* in this and the preceding cl.; see p. 108.

beg the owner. I.e. God, who is the *kyrios.* The disciples being commissioned are instructed to pray that God will provide adequately for the task of the harvest. See p. 245. The vb. *deēthēte* is often used of prayer of petition. See 22:32; Acts 8:22,24; 10:2; Ps 30:8 (LXX). Cf. H. Greeven, *TDNT* 2. 40-42. This instruction implies that the work of Jesus and the mission of the disciples are under the providence of God himself, who is creating a new phase of salvific preaching and will be the judge of it on a given "day" (v. 12).

3. *Now go.* Thus the mission-charge is given. Luke uses *hypagete.*

and look, I am sending you. Lit. "Behold, I send you." See NOTE on 9:2. This is one of the I-sayings of Jesus in the Synoptic tradition. See *HST* 158. The sender is Jesus, as the "Lord," expressing his fundamental commission.

like lambs among wolves. The image shifts from reapers at a harvest to animals that do not associate. Luke has nothing about "prudence" and "simplicity," which are Matthean additions (10:16). The contrast of lambs and wolves suggests the perils, opposition, and hostility which will mark the mission of the seventy(-two), as that of Jesus himself. H. Lignée ("La mission," 65) thinks that the figure signifies that the disciples are being sent into the pagan world; but that is not immediately obvious. *1 Enoch* 89:14,18-20 uses the opposition of sheep and wolves in a very similar way, and the peril expressed in the opposition known to any Palestinian shepherd could be applied to any mission of Christian disciples, who are considered as defenseless as young sheep. A later rabbinical tradition knows of a saying of Hadrian to R. Yehoshua' about what he considered great in sheep (= Israel) that can continue to live among seventy wolves (= the nations); the rabbi replied, "Great is the shepherd who delivers it and watches over it and destroys them [the wolves] before them [Israel]." See J. Jeremias, *TDNT* 1. 340.

4. *a purse or a knapsack or sandals.* See Luke 9:3, where only *pēra,* "knapsack," occurs. The same threesome *(ballantion, pēra, hypodēmata)* occur again in 22:35. Mark 6:9 mentioned "sandals" (with a different word, *sandalia,* which Luke avoided in his parallel). Matt 10:9-10, which is somewhat parallel to this Lucan verse, has been influenced by Mark 6:8-9.

do not exchange greetings with anyone on the way. This strange injunction has been variously interpreted. Prima facie, it seems to mean that the disciples are not to waste time on the mission talking to people because the harvest is ripe and has to be brought in before it spoils. Their greetings should rather be directed to "houses" and "towns" as the following verses suggest. In this sense it recalls the injunction given by Elisha to Gehazi in 2 Kgs 4:29. However, it has also been interpreted not so much of haste as of dedication; the disciples are to concentrate on preaching and curing, not on worldly matters. The relationship demanded by kingdom-preaching is not measured by ordinary social courtesy, gear, or greetings. But the injunction may couch a warning about the hostility that the disciples are to expect as Jesus' heralds—a hostility that is expressed in terms of reapers and no greetings to passersby in Ps 129:8; and in the aloofness of the Essenes to all non-community-members (1QS 5:10-11,15). See further A. O'Hagan, " 'Greet No One.' " To interpret this injunction as a prohibition to visit or receive hospitality from relatives on a missionary journey is eisegetical, *pace* B. Lang ("Grussverbot"). For "on the way," see COMMENT on 9:51-56.

5. *Peace be to this house!* Or "household, family." The Lucan form of this greeting, in direct discourse, is more Semitic than its Matthean parallel (10:12, "salute it"). The greeting is an extension of the OT greeting, "peace be with you," found in Luke 24:36. Cf. Judg 6:23; 19:20. In contrast to banal greetings used on the road, the commissioned disciple is to announce the peace that the salvation of Jesus brings. Luke constantly links peace with God's salvation. See p. 225. This characteristic of the Period of Jesus is to be extended to all who accept the kingdom of God. It should, however, be noted that Luke does not associate peace with the Spirit (as does Paul),

but with Jesus himself, *pace* H. Lignée, "La mission," 69. The greeting used is related to another, reflected in Gal 6:16; for the antiquity of the latter, see Pss 125:5; 128:6; cf. A. Hurvitz, *Leshonenu* 27-28 (1964) 297-302.

6. *a peaceful person.* Lit. "a son of peace," i.e. a person open to and receptive of the prime quality of Christian salvation brought by Jesus. Peace is not to be understood in this context as merely the opposite of war, but in the OT sense of *šālôm,* the root of which is *šlm,* "completeness, wholeness." It expresses rather the comprehensive bounty of God's salvific presence and activity. For the figurative use of *huios,* "son," cf. 5:34; 16:8b; 20:34,36; Acts 4:36; a Septuagintism. See p. 115. Matt 10:11 eliminates the Semitism and speaks instead of a "worthy" person. Cf. F. W. Danker, "The *huios* Phrases in the New Testament," *NTS* 7 (1960-1961) 94; W. Klassen, " 'A Child of Peace' (Luke 10. 6) in First Century Context," *NTS* 27 (1980-1981) 488-506.

your peace. I.e. the peace that you bring as my envoy.

will rest. The greeting will be effective in that its saving power will affect people.

But if not. Another instance of the favorite Lucan particles *ei de mē ge.* See NOTE on 5:36; cf. 13:9; 14:31-32. See M. E. Thrall, *Greek Particles,* 9-10.

it will come back to you. I.e. it will not be lost, for such peace requires an apt reception. The consequences differ for a person of a house from those stated for a town in v. 12.

7. *Stay at that one house.* Luke uses *en autē tē oikia.* M. Black (*AAGA*[3] 98) thinks that the phrase is a "misrendering of an Aramaic demonstrative" and that Luke would be "reproducing unedited a translation Greek version of the saying of Jesus from his source." This seems unlikely; the phrase is a simple extension of one often used in the LXX. See p. 117. For a similar regulation given to the Twelve, see 9:4. The reason for the regulation is stated at the end of this verse. Note that Matt 10:13 speaks of a "worthy" house, a Matthean modification.

eating and drinking what they have. On the Greek expression Luke uses, see E. Delebecque, "Sur un hellénisme," 590-593.

for the laborer deserves his pay. The "Q" parallel in Matt 10:10b has *trophē,* "sustenance," instead of *misthos,* "pay." That is again a Matthean modification of the "Q" source. For the idea expressed here, see 1 Cor 9:14; 1 Tim 5:18. Cf. *Did.* 13.1: "Every true prophet who wishes to settle among you is worthy of his sustenance."

8. *enter a town.* The whole town is to be confronted with the preaching and healing; the disciples are to perform a public, official act.

eat what is put before you. I.e. accept the hospitality of the townspeople, such as it is.

9. *Cure the sick.* Cf. Luke 9:2. The Matthean parallel (10:8) expands the activity in which the disciples are to engage: "raise the dead, cleanse lepers, expel demons—you freely received, give freely."

The kingdom of God has drawn near to you. I.e. in the very preaching of it by the disciples sent out by Jesus. See v. 11c. The statement is the same as Mark 1:15, which Luke omitted in his parallel to that passage. C. H. Dodd *(Parables,* 28-30) tried to argue that *ēngiken* means "has come," but W. G. Kümmel *(Promise and Fulfilment,* 24) has more rightly insisted (along with others, e.g. J. M. Robinson, *The Problem of History,* 72 n. 1) that it has to be understood as "has approached, has drawn near." Cf. M. Black, "The Kingdom of God Has Come," 289-290; W. R. Hutton, "The Kingdom of God Has Come," *ExpTim* 64 (1952-1953) 89-91. The implication is that the day of the kingdom's full arrival is still in the future. Even if "we meet something which is rare" here in Luke (H. Conzelmann, *Theology,* 107), he thus preserves some of the primitive futurist eschatology of the early community. Perhaps he also implies that the kingdom has drawn near because Jesus himself is soon to stand at the gates of the towns. See v. 1; cf. NOTE on 4:43 and pp. 231-235. See further Luke 11:20.

10. *do not welcome you.* See Luke 9:5.

11. *The very dust.* See NOTE on 9:5. The disciples are charged not merely to knock the dust from their feet but to proclaim the meaning of the action to the unreceptive town. The proximity of the kingdom does not prevent its being rejected.

Rather. The strong adversative conj. *plēn,* "but, rather," is used, as in 6:24,35; cf. 10:14,20; 11:41; 12:31; 13:33; 17:1; 18:8; 19:27; 22:21,22,42; 23:28.

the kingdom of God has drawn near. See NOTE on v. 9. The repetition of the proclamation is significant.

12. *more tolerable on that day for Sodom.* I.e. the day of the arrival of God's complete dominion in human history and its consequent judgment will be more catastrophic for a town that rejects the Christian message than the fate of Sodom, the notorious town of sinners in Jewish history. The Lucan Jesus alludes to the destruction of Sodom in Gen 19:24-28. It is spoken of as if its fate were to be reenacted in the eschaton, when the unreceptive town will suffer a fate worse than that of Sodom. Cf. Luke 10:14. The adj. *anektos* describes what can be endured, tolerated, and it connotes condemnation and punishment. For "on that day," see Luke 6:23; 21:34; cf. 2 Thess 1:10. The "day" is that of judgment, as Luke 10:14 suggests. It echoes Zech 12:3-4; Isa 10:20; Jer 30:8 (LXX 37:8).

BIBLIOGRAPHY (10:1-12)

(in addition to the titles given in 9:1-6)

Black, M. "The Kingdom of God Has Come," *ExpTim* 63 (1951-1952) 289-290.

Delebecque, E. "Sur un hellénisme de Saint Luc," *RB* 87 (1980) 590-593 (on v. 7).

Gamba, G. G. *La portata universalistica dell'invio dei settanta(due) discepoli, Lc 10:1 e ss.* (Turin: Scuola grafica salesiana, 1963).

Harvey, A. E. " 'The Workman Is Worthy of His Hire': Fortunes of a Proverb in the Early Church," *NovT* 24 (1982) 209-221.

Hoffmann, P. "Lukas 10,5-11 in der Instruktionsrede der Logienquelle," *EKK Vorarbeiten* 3 (1971) 37-53.

Jellicoe, S. "St Luke and the 'Seventy(-two),' " *NTS* 6 (1959-1960) 319-321.

Jeremias, J. "Paarweise Sendung im Neuen Testament," *New Testament Essays: Studies in Memory of Thomas Walter Manson 1893-1958* (ed. A. J. B. Higgins; Manchester: Manchester University, 1959) 136-143; reprinted, *Abba* 132-139.

Lang, B. "Grussverbot oder Besuchsverbot? Eine sozialgeschichtliche Deutung von Lukas 10,4b," *BZ* 26 (1982) 75-79.

Lignée, H. "La mission des soixante-douze: Lc, 1-12.17-20," *AsSeign* 45 (1974) 64-74.

Metzger, B. M. "Seventy or Seventy-Two Disciples?" *NTS* 5 (1958-1959) 299-306.

Miyoshi, M. *Der Anfang, 59-94.*

O'Hagan, A. " 'Greet No One on the Way' (Lk 10,4b)," *SBFLA* 16 (1965-1966) 69-84.

Schulz, S. " 'Die Gottesherrschaft ist nahe herbeigekommen' (Mt 10,7/Lk 10,9): Der kerygmatische Entwurf der Q-Gemeinde Syriens," *Das Wort und die Wörter: Festschrift Gerhard Friedrich* (eds. H. Balz and S. Schulz; Stuttgart: Kohlhammer, 1973) 57-67.

Venetz, H.-J. "Bittet den Herrn der Ernte: Überlegungen zu Lk 10,2/Mt 9,37," *Diakonia* 11 (1980) 148-161.

61. WOES UTTERED AGAINST THE TOWNS OF GALILEE
(10:13-15)

10   [13] "Woe to you, Chorazin! Woe to you, Bethsaida! Had the miracles performed in your midst been done in Tyre and Sidon, the people there would have sat in sackcloth and ashes and reformed their lives long ago! [14] Rather, it shall be more tolerable at the judgment for Tyre and Sidon than for you. [15] As for you, Capernaum, you don't expect to be exalted to the skies, do you? No, *you shall go down to death's abode!*"[a]

[a] Isa 14:15

COMMENT

The next few verses in the Lucan Gospel create something of a problem. As they stand, vv. 13-15 and 16 form part of Jesus' instructions to the seventy(-two) disciples. Whereas v. 16 would seem to be a logical conclusion to the mission-charge in vv. 2-12, it is separated from them by vv. 13-15, which utter woes on Galilean towns, Chorazin (otherwise unmentioned in the account of the Galilean ministry just completed), Bethsaida (evangelized in 9:10-17 and the scene of the feeding of the five thousand), and Capernaum (a town which already had witnessed his ministry and cures, 4:23; 7:1). Moreover, v. 16 has a Matthean counterpart at the end of the mission-charge given to the Twelve (10:40); but see COMMENT on v. 16 for further discussion of its Synoptic relationship. Verses 13-15 are more like an aside or a soliloquy than an integral part of the instructions to the disciples, since the Galilean villages named scarcely seem to be examples of the towns and places "which he himself intended to visit" on his way to Jerusalem. Again, the woes are hardly pertinent to the work expected of the disciples in the mission-charge. Indeed, if it were not for v. 16, the aside that Jesus utters here might even appear as a sort of filler-episode, words uttered while the seventy(-two) were off on their mission, from which they are said to return in v. 17.

Verses 13-15, the woes against Chorazin, Bethsaida, and Capernaum, were derived by Luke from "Q" (see p. 76). Their Matthean counterpart is found, not with the instructions given to the Twelve, but as a sequel to Jesus' testimony to John the Baptist (11:7-19), and occurs just before Jesus' utterance of thanks to his Father (11:25-27). Matt 11:20 is a generic rubric, composed by Matthew (see *HST* 333; F. Mussner, *Die Wunder Jesu*, 25) to introduce the woes in vv. 21-24. Their Matthean form is longer and undoubtedly reflects the original "Q" version of these sayings. Luke 10:13-15 parallels only Matt 11:21-23a. It is strange that one saying, the comparison (of Capernaum) with Sodom, appeared substantially in two different places in "Q" and is retained by Matthew in 10:15 and 11:24. Luke has eliminated the parallel to the latter, the comparison with Sodom, because it duplicates 10:12, the comparison of an inhospitable town with Sodom, redacted by Luke to suit the saying about the kingdom in v. 11.

As the woes originally stood in "Q," they consisted of a *pronouncement* (an accusation against Chorazin and Bethsaida [Matt 11:21a]; and against Capernaum [11:23a]), an *explanation* (that mighty deeds would have led to repentance in Tyre and Sidon [11:21b]; and in Sodom [11:23b]), and a *comparison* (the greater tolerance for Tyre and Sidon at the judgment [11:22]; and for Sodom [11:24]). In curtailing the sayings, Luke eliminated the second explanation and the comparison of Capernaum with Sodom. Although the woe-form exemplified in the "Q" version is not found explicitly in the OT, the woes against these Galilean cities can profitably be compared with such OT passages as Amos 6:4-7; Mic 2:1; Hab 2:6-7; and Zeph 2:5. (See further J. A. Comber, "The Composition," 498-499.)

Forty-five words of Matt 11:21-23a are found to be identical in Luke 10:13-15. Matthew probably changed the more original vb. *egenēthēsan*, "had been done" (Luke 10:13; cf. Matt 11:23) to a stylistic variant, *egenonto;* he probably also introduced *legō hymin* to produce *plēn legō hymin*, "rather, I say to you," which he uses again in 11:24 and 26:64 and which Luke never uses. But Luke has probably retained the more original "Q" expression *en tē krisei,* "at the judgment," whereas Matthew has modified it to *en hēmera kriseōs,* "on the day of judgment" (11:22,24; cf. 10:15; 12:36). (Cp. Luke 11:31-32; Matt 12:41-42; cf. J. Jeremias, *Die Sprache,* 186.)

Luke has added the woes to the mission-charge because of a catchword bond: *anektoteron estai,* "it shall be more tolerable," occurs in v. 12 and in v. 14. In doing this, he has simply taken over the woes from a different part of "Q," without any inverting of material (e.g. putting vv. 13-15 before v. 16, as has been suggested by T. W. Manson, *Sayings,* 76-77). The Matthean counterpart of v. 16 (10:40) suggests that it (or some saying like it) was actually part of the mission-charge in "Q," and so is unrelated to the woes.

Judged form-critically, Jesus' aside is a minatory saying *(HST* 111-112), a prophetic proclamation invoking eschatological judgment on unrepentant Galilean towns. Bultmann (ibid.) regarded the sayings as "a community for-mulation," which looked back on Jesus' activity in Capernaum as already finished and as a failure. A similar evaluation of the sayings can be found in J. M. Creed, *The Gospel,* 146, quoting A. Loisy, "the pronouncement of a Christian prophet casting a retrospective glance at the work of Jesus in Gali-lee." There may be a grain of truth in that view (e.g. in the sharpening of the threat), but the success of Jesus' activity in Capernaum recorded in 4:23, already dependent on an earlier tradition (see COMMENT and NOTE on 4:23), has to be considered. It could well have been the basis of an admonition of the historical Jesus to a smug Galilean town that his former activity in it was not sufficient for an expectation of exaltation. If one detects in these sayings a prophetic proclamation, it does not follow that they stem only from some early Christian prophetic tradition, *pace* E. Käsemann, *New Testament Ques-tions,* 94-95. The "Q" saying, mentioning Chorazin, which does not otherwise figure in the early Jesus-tradition, may be a good sign for attributing these woes to Jesus himself. (See further F. Mussner, *Die Wunder,* 27; W. Grundmann, *Evangelium nach Lukas,* 211.)

In this aside, Jesus appears as God's mouthpiece and does not hesitate to utter a prophetic proclamation, a foreboding directed against Galilean towns that had witnessed his preaching and miracles. He pointedly compares those towns, which have been favored with his "miracles" or "mighty deeds" *(dynameis,* v. 13), with the (in)famous pagan Phoenician towns of Tyre and Sidon against which prophets of old once inveighed. Though Jesus' words (v. 15) allude to the oracle against the king of Babylon in Isa 14:4b-21, who would have exalted himself to the heavens like the Canaanite astral deities, *Hêlēl* (Day Star) and *Šaḥar* (Dawn), the reader of the Lucan Gospel will think of Chorazin and Bethsaida, neighboring Galilean towns, now compared with Tyre and its neighbor Sidon, as objects of similar prophetic oracles and taunts. In Ezekiel 28 the oracle of divine judgment against Tyre (vv. 2-19) is followed by that against its neighbor Sidon (vv. 20-23), both being singled out for their pagan decadence. Those two cities are often linked in prophetic writings (Jer 25:22; 47:4; Zech 9:2). Such pagan cities were punished by God, even though they had not had the opportunity of hearing reform-preachers. The inhabitants of these cities would long since have cast themselves in the role of mourners and penitents and sought to reform themselves had such a preacher accosted them (recall the reaction of pagan Nineveh to the preach-ing of Jonah, Jonah 3:5-9). The inhabitants of Chorazin, Bethsaida, and Ca-pernaum, favored with the prophetic preaching and "mighty deeds" of Jesus, smugly went their own ways, however, and refused belief. What could have contributed to Capernaum's glory at the judgment would lead only to its disgrace.

Luke retained these minatory sayings, uttered against towns that the historical Jesus once evangelized, because he felt that they had a pertinence for Christian readers of his own day and for generations to follow. The Jesus who appears in this aside as an accuser and judge now so accosts the Christian reader. His words stress the responsibility incumbent on persons confronted with his word. Not to accept his challenge is to reject the message that comes through him as God's spokesman. What could lead to exaltation thus might lead only to disgrace and humiliation.

By making the woes part of the mission-charge of the "seventy(-two) others," and thus depicting Jesus comparing Galilean towns of his own ministry with pagan towns, Luke undoubtedly has in mind the implications of Jesus' words of instruction for the Gentile mission. The passage thus contributes to the universalism of the Christian mission and evangelization.

NOTES

10   13. *Woe to you.* See NOTE on 6:24.

Chorazin! Because of its occurrence with Bethsaida and Capernaum, it is to be understood as a town in Galilee. Its site is not known with certainty. It has often been identified with modern Kh. Kerazeh, ruins about two and a half miles northwest of Tell Ḥum. See NOTE on Capernaum, 4:23. The remains of a third–fourth century synagogue have been found there, together with an Aramaic inscription honoring Judan, son of Yishmael, who constructed its colonnade and staircase. See *MPAT* § A16; cf. J. Naveh, *'l psyps w'bn: On Stone and Mosaic, The Aramaic and Hebrew Inscriptions from Ancient Synagogues* (Jerusalem: Israel Exploration Society, 1978) 36-38 (§ 17*). A passage in the Babylonian Talmud *(b. Menaḥ.* 85a) mentions a place, *Krzyym (Karzayîm),* from which came good wheat, as not being near Jerusalem. Eusebius *(Onom.* 303, 174) knows of Chorazin as "a village in Galilee against which Christ uttered a woe after he had preached to it; now it is a desert, two miles from Capernaum." But Jerome *(Comm. in Is.* 3; PL 24. 127) located it with Capernaum, Tiberias, and Bethsaida on the shore of Lake Gennesaret. Hence the hesitation about its identification. See further C. Kopp, *The Holy Places of the Gospels* (New York: Herder and Herder, 1963) 187-189; J. Finegan, *Archeology,* 57-58; *ELS* 305-308.

Bethsaida! See NOTE on 9:10. It is actually a town where a miracle took place.

the miracles performed in your midst. Lit. "the mighty deeds (which) occurred in you." Luke uses *dynameis,* the pl. of *dynamis,* "power," as in 19:37, to refer to the wondrous acts of Jesus wrought in these towns. See COMMENT on 4:31-37; NOTES on 4:14; 5:17; 6:19; 8:46. The specific form of the effects of his power is not further described. Nor is it said that these deeds were performed by Jesus alone; in 9:1 he shared his "power and authority" with the Twelve.

in Tyre and Sidon. I.e. in the well-known Phoenician trade cities of the pagan world —outside of Galilee, to which the Lucan Jesus has otherwise restricted his evangelization up to this point. On Tyre and Sidon, see NOTE on 6:17. There Luke speaks of them as towns from which people flocked to hear Jesus, as well as from Judea and Jerusalem; they formed part of the audience to which his sermon on the plain was directed. This detail adds poignancy to his remark here.

would have sat in sackcloth and ashes. I.e. would have adopted an ancient form of penitential conduct or mourning. The phrase is an abridgement of an OT expression, "to cover oneself with sackcloth and sit in ashes" (Jonah 3:6 LXX; cf. Job 2:8). The combination of sackcloth and ashes occurs also in Isa 58:5; Esth 4:2-3 (LXX); Dan 9:3 (LXX), in slightly variant expressions. Josephus also knows of the use of sackcloth and ashes *(spodos* and *tephra).* See *J.W.* 2.12,5 § 237; *Ant.* 5.1,12 § 37; 19.8,2 § 349; 20.6,1 § 123. They are often mentioned in a context of weeping, lamentation, and fasting—but without implying mourning for death. Here they connote sorrowful repentance for sin and disbelief, finding expression in a participial phrase subordinated to the vb. *metenoēsan,* "would have repented."

The n. *sakkos* is a grecized form of Hebrew *śāq* or Aramaic *śaqqā',* the name for a cloth made of rough goat's hair and used as a loin covering for the naked body as a sign of mourning or penitence. Its use is often mentioned in the OT. E.g. Gen 37:34; 2 Sam 3:31; 1 Kgs 21:27; Ps 69:11; Isa 20:2; 32:11. It was black in color (Rev 6:12; *1 Clem.* 8:3; cf. Isa 50:3). The word was borrowed in the Greek world to designate a "coarse cloth of hair," used for bags or sacks (Herodotus, *Hist.* 9.80; Aristophanes, *Acharn.* 745 [cf. Josh 9:4]). Plutarch *(Superst.* 7, 168D) also knows of the penitential use of sackcloth for sins (using the diminutive *sakkion).*

Spodos, "wood-ashes, embers," has been known in Greek since the time of Homer *(Od.* 9.375). It was also used in the Greek world as a sign of mourning (Euripides, *Suppl.* 827, 1160). In the LXX it often translates Hebrew *'ēper,* which usually means merely "dust." But the meaning "ashes" is found in Num 19:9-10.

reformed their lives. Lit. "repented." See NOTE on 3:3; cf. p. 237.

long ago! The adv. *palai* stands emphatically at the head of the apodosis of this contrary-to-fact condition. In my translation it has been put at the end for emphasis.

14. *Rather.* Luke again uses the adversative conj. *plēn.* See NOTE on 10:11.

more tolerable. See NOTE on 10:12.

at the judgment. P⁴⁵ and ms. D omit this phrase, but it is to be retained, being found in the best mss. The parallel in Matt 11:22-24 reads "in the day of judgment," a phrase found in Prov 6:34 (LXX); Jdt 16:17. The Lucan phrase is probably that of the "Q" source. The reference is to the day of divine retribution. See Mal 3:5-21 (3:5-4:5E); cf. Jude 6; 4QEnᵇ 1 iv 11; 4QEnᵈ 1 xi 1; 4QEnᵉ 1 xxii 2-3; 1QM 1:5 for similar references to that eschatological event.

15. *Capernaum.* See NOTE on 4:23, where it was first mentioned as a town that had witnessed Jesus' healings and other (mighty) deeds. Cf. 7:1-10.

to be exalted to the skies, do you? I.e. because I have performed cures in the midst of your people. The question is introduced by *mē,* expecting a negative answer. These words may allude to Isa 14:13, but apart from the gen. *ouranou,* "sky, heaven," there is not another verbal echo. See, however, the following NOTE.

There is, however, a textual problem. I have read *mē heōs ouranou hypsōthēsē,* which is found in P⁴⁵, P⁷⁵, ℵ, B*, D, OL, etc., but mss. A, B², C, R, W, Θ, and the Koine text-tradition read instead *hē heōs ouranou hypsōtheisa,* "(As for you, Capernaum), the (city) exalted to the skies," which gives the Galilean town a slightly different status. The preferred reading is sometimes considered suspect, because it agrees with the form in Matt 11:23 (and could have been harmonized by copyists). Moreover, it is difficult to say whether *mē* has been produced by a dittography of *m* (with which *Kapharnaoum* ends) or whether *hē* (written in uncial mss. without breathings) was produced by haplography of the same letter. See further *TCGNT* 30-31.

you shall go down to death's abode! Lit. "to Hades." Some Greek mss. (P⁴⁵, א, A, C, L, R, W, Θ, and the Koine text-tradition) read *katabibasthēsē*, "you will be driven down," certainly a more forceful threat. However, *katabēsē* is the reading of mss. P⁷⁵, B, D, and of the Syriac tradition; it is preferred because it represents a wide geographical spread of texts. The latter reading, then, is a clear echo of Isa 14:15 (LXX), *eis hadou katabēsē*, "you shall go down into Hades" (and into the depths of the earth)—part of the taunt addressed to the king of Babylon (14:4). Capernaum will thus join earlier tyrants in Sheol. Cf. Isa 14:11; Ezek 26:20; 31:16-17; *Ps. Sol.* 1:5 for similar threats. "Going down to Hades" means at least Capernaum's disgrace; whether it also connotes its punishment is difficult to say. The contrast of *ouranos* and *hadēs* and the allusion to Isaiah 14 would suggest the latter.

The Greek name *hadēs* was properly that of the god of the netherworld as the place of the dead (so Homer, *Il.* 15.188). A remnant of this meaning is still seen in the use of the gen. case with preps. that would otherwise govern other cases (e.g. *eis* in the LXX of Isa 14:15, quoted above, "into [the house of] Hades"). In time it came to be the name for the grave (Pindar, *Pyth. Od.* 5.96) or for a region or abode of the dead (Euripides, *Alcest.* 13), having gates (Vettius Valens, 179.13; cf. Homer, *Il.* 5.646; Isa 38:10; Wis 16:13; Matt 16:18). In the LXX, *hadēs*, with rare exceptions, translates Hebrew *šĕ'ôl*, "Sheol" (e.g. Isa 14:9,11,15; Qoh 9:10), which originally meant the realm to which all human beings go at death (Ps 89:49), a place of shadowy existence (Isa 14:9) below the waters of the ocean (Job 26:5-6; see NOTE on 8:31), and of inactivity (Ps 6:6). Sometimes it carries the connotation of a region opposed to heaven (see Amos 9:2; Ps 139:8), which would be the sense in Luke 10. In postexilic Judaism *šĕ'ôl* underwent a development with the emergence of the ideas of resurrection (see Dan 12:2) and of retribution for the conduct of earthly life. It became a place divided into separate locales, one for the upright, and three for sinners. This distinction is clearly found in *1 Enoch* 22:3-13. Cf. 4QEnᵉ 1 xxii 1-8; 4QEnᵈ 1 xi 1-3 (known in the Greek version as *hoi topoi hoi koiloi*, "the hollow places"); also *1 Enoch* 63:10; 99:11; cf. *2 Esdr.* 7:36; Josephus, *Ant.* 18.1,3 § 14 (but see *J.W.* 2.8,14 § 163). This is partly reflected in Luke 16:22-26. J. Jeremias *(TDNT* 1. 148) would distinguish Hades from *gehenna* (on which see NOTE on 12:5), but this is far from certain. See O. Böcher *(EWNT* 1. 73), who equates them.

BIBLIOGRAPHY (10:13-15)

Comber, J. A. "The Composition and Literary Characteristics of Matt 11:20-24,"
    CBQ 39 (1977) 497-504.
Lührmann, D. *Redaktion,* 60-64.
Mussner, F. *Die Wunder Jesu: Eine Hinführung* (Munich: Kösel, 1967) 24-28.
Schulz, S. *Q: Die Spruchquelle,* 360-366.

62. THE DISCIPLES AS REPRESENTATIVES
(10:16)

10   ¹⁶ Whoever listens to you listens to me; whoever rejects you rejects me; and whoever rejects me rejects him who sent me.

COMMENT

This verse forms the conclusion to the mission-charge given to the
"seventy(-two) others" (10:2-12) and has a counterpart at the end of the
instruction given to the Twelve in the Matthean Gospel. It formulates the
principle on which both the Twelve and the "others" have been sent out.
They have not only been given a share in Jesus' "power and authority" (9:1)
and been sent on ahead of him (10:1), but they have been commissioned to
speak in his name and in the name of the one who sent Jesus himself (cf.
4:43). The saying comments on the different ways that the message carried by
the disciple-representatives will be received by people who hear them.

The three-part saying has been most likely derived by Luke from "Q" (see
p. 77). Its Matthean counterpart (10:40) would suggest that the mission-
charge in "Q" ended with such a saying. The Matthean form, however, creates a slight problem, and it is likely that Matthew has substituted for the
three-part saying, preserved in Luke, a fuller form, derived from "M," which
is similar in its formulation of the basic principle, but different enough in
expression (reception of a prophet and of a righteous one) to suggest that it
comes from an independent tradition (so too *HST* 143). For the Matthean
form actually consists of two verses (10:40-41), joined by *dechesthai,* "receive," as the catchword bond; and to which v. 42 (about the reception of a
child) has been added by still another catchword bond, *misthos,* "wages."
Hence, though Matt 10:40 superficially sounds like Luke 10:16, it probably

represents another tradition, with a fuller formulation, which Matthew has preferred to substitute for the ending of the instruction. That saying has its counterpart in the "Mk" tradition (see p. 81); and so we have a Matthean "doublet" (see Mark 9:37; Matt 18:5; Luke 9:48 [see COMMENT there]; cf. Mark 9:41). The Johannine tradition (see NOTE) has also preserved diverse forms of these sayings, which probably do not all go back to a single utterance of the historical Jesus, *pace* T. W. Manson, *Sayings,* 78. The diverse formulations, however, reveal that concerns in the subsequent Christian community were in part responsible for the shape that they have taken.

Form-critically speaking, we have to class the saying with the "I-sayings" of Jesus (so *HST* 153; derived from a "Jewish tradition" [ibid. 147]). But this does not mean that it is wholly a fabrication of even a Palestinian Christian community. At issue, once again, is the question whether the historical Jesus had disciples during his ministry and made use of them to help in that ministry.

The Lucan form of the saying, both positive and negative in its expression, probably preserves the "Q" formulation of the mission-charge. In effect, it puts more stress on the negative side by using the vb. *athetein,* "reject," four times over (see M. Miyoshi, *Der Anfang,* 91; cf. J. Jeremias, *Die Sprache,* 187).

On the one hand, the saying lends authority to the preaching of the disciples. The principle implied in it is that of representation, akin to the institution of *šālîaḥ* of contemporary Judaism: The one sent is to be regarded as the sender himself. The disciples, therefore, speak and act in the name of Jesus, just as he speaks and acts in the name of the one who sent him. This aspect of the saying is not to be neglected in the Lucan use of it, for it enhances the Lucan notion of *asphaleia* (1:4; see pp. 300-301). It inculcates the notion that what the church of Luke's day is teaching is rooted in the teaching of Jesus himself.

But, on the other hand, the saying concentrates on the reaction of hearers: some listen, some reject, implying a process of discernment. It does not deal with passive listening; and those who fail to listen in the proper sense are actively nullifying the message being brought to them. Implicit in the saying is a judgment about the response to the word preached by the disciples, and so the saying is related to the eschatological judgment of v. 14. The persons who accept or reject the teaching of such representatives accept or reject the message of Jesus and of God himself. In this way, this saying too has its own minatory aspect. It is, therefore, not without some connection to the woes that immediately precede it. (See further W. Thüsing, "Dienstfunktion," 79.)

NOTES

10 16. *Whoever listens to you.* I.e. hears the word or message that you preach. The vb. *akouein* means not only to hear physically, but to accept with faith the message announced by the disciples. See 6:47.

listens to me. For the disciple is, in effect, preaching only what Jesus himself was sent to preach (4:43). The "word" is one, and the third part of the verse makes it clear that it is the word of God himself.

whoever rejects you. I.e. refuses to accept the message you announce as coming from me and ultimately from God himself. The vb. *athetein* etymologically means to "nullify, set at nought," and has already been used in 7:30 of the thwarting of God's design. See NOTE there. The overtones of that thwarting are undoubtedly to be heard here in the rejection of the disciples' message.

whoever rejects me rejects him who sent me. Thus Jesus insists that he has not come to preach on his own authority. Recall 4:14,42-43; 5:17. So the Lucan Jesus affirms what the Johannine Jesus utters in very similar language on several occasions. Cf. John 5:23; 7:28; 12:44-45,48; 13:20.

BIBLIOGRAPHY (10:16)

Esteban, J. "Un texto de S. Lucas sobre la obediencia," *Manresa* 34 (1962) 29-34.
Miyoshi, M. *Der Anfang,* 69-73, 91-94.
Thüsing, W. "Dienstfunktion und Vollmacht kirchlicher Ämter nach dem Neuen Testament," *BibLeb* 14 (1973) 77-88, esp. 78-80.

63. THE RETURN OF THE SEVENTY(-TWO)
(10:17-20)

10 ¹⁷ The seventy(-two) returned full of joy and reported, "Lord, with the use of your name even the demons submit to us!" ¹⁸ Jesus said to them, "I was watching Satan fall, like lightning, from heaven. ¹⁹ See, I have given you authority to tread upon serpents and scorpions, and over all the power of the Enemy; and nothing shall harm you at all. ²⁰ So do not rejoice at this that spirits submit to you; rather, rejoice that your names stand written in heaven!"

COMMENT

Luke appends to his story of Jesus' sending out "seventy(-two) others" an account of their return, their elation at the success of their mission, and Jesus' threefold comment on their report (10:17-20). It is a more expressive note than that recorded on the return of "the apostles" in 9:10. This notice is exclusive to Luke, as was the mission-charge to the "seventy(-two) others." Whereas Luke 9:10 reflected Mark 6:30, there is nothing in the Synoptic tradition of this notice.

Jesus' coming praise of the Father (10:21-24) has a counterpart in the Matthean Gospel, in 11:25-27, where it follows immediately on the woes uttered against the Galilean towns. The Matthean order probably reflects the part of "Q," which both evangelists have used. But Luke has inserted between the end of the mission-charge, of which he had made the woes a part, and the praise of the Father this episode about the return of the disciples. It gives to the passage about the praise of the Father a better psychological background, following not immediately on the instruction to the disciples, but on the report of their success. This passage then builds up to the authority of the Son.

If the sayings in this episode were a unit inherited by Luke, then it would have to be attributed to "L." R. Bultmann *(HST* 158 n. 1) rightly ascribes v. 17 to Luke's pen; it is composed by Luke in view of what is to be said in v. 20. Bultmann regards v. 18 (the falling of Satan) as inherited by Luke "from tradition," but he questions whether vv. 18 and 19 were originally uttered together, and similarly vv. 19 and 20. True, there is no intrinsic connection among the three sayings. It is perhaps best to regard the pericope itself as a unit created by Luke; the three isolated sayings may have been inherited by him from "L," but v. 20 may also be of Lucan composition. It is, however, another matter to think that vv. 19 and 20 reflect only Christian tradition, "when the Church was in danger of overrating miracle" (ibid. 158). If we admit that the original sense of v. 18 is irretrievably lost, the strangeness of the saying may be the best reason for ascribing it to Jesus himself (cf. J. Jeremias, *Die Sprache,* 187-189).

Form-critically considered, the episode might at first appear like a pronouncement story, with v. 20 as the pronouncement. Though it has a narrative introduction, which almost certainly comes from Luke's pen, the saying of the disciples (with "Lord") is only an introductory foil for the use of the inherited isolated sayings. It is difficult, indeed, to say which of the three is really the most important. As Luke has fashioned the episode, the third saying corresponds to his introduction and therefore gets pride of place. The first two sayings are to be classed as "I-sayings"; the last is hortatory.

Jesus' threefold answer to the report of the seventy(-two) puts their elated reaction to their own mission in its proper perspective. Coming on the heels of Jesus' saying about representation (v. 16), his threefold reaction to their report spells out the effects of that representation and relates it to heaven's perspective. One cannot miss the contrast between Satan's fall from heaven and the disciples' names being written in heaven, on the one hand, and that between what was accomplished in his "name" and the implication of their work, on the other, that their "names" are really recorded in heaven.

Initially, Jesus' first remark (v. 18) seems to be cast in terms of a vision. But, as the NOTE makes clear, this is not to be understood either as an ecstatic vision that Jesus had during their mission or as a preexistent vision of Satan's fall aeons earlier or as a proleptic vision of Satan's coming fate. Rather, Jesus' "watching" is a symbolic way of summing up the effects of the disciples' mission; his contemplation revealed how their activity expressed victory over Satan's power or influence. The evil that Satan symbolizes has met with ignominious defeat, and he has been dethroned from his prosecutor's role in the heavenly court. For H. Conzelmann (Theology, 28) the Period of Jesus is one "free from Satan"; yet here we see that it is precisely the period in which Satan's fall is contemplated, even though we are not sure in what sense his power to cause evil is at an end (as 22:3,31-32 will make clear, even before the Period of Jesus comes to an end). (See further pp. 186-187; cf. S. Brown, Apostasy and Perseverance, 6-7.) Jesus summarizes the effects of the mission of the seventy(-two) in terms of the fall of Satan.

His second remark (v. 19) supplies a further explanation of the defeat of evil brought about by the disciples' mission. Satan has fallen from heaven, the height of his influence, and evil in all its manifestations (physical, symbolic, and personal—see NOTE) is now subjected to that "authority" that comes from Jesus himself. The disciples as representatives of Jesus (10:16) and as ones sent on ahead of him (10:1) have been able to confront evil in its varied manifestations.

Jesus' last remark (v. 20) puts the mission of the disciples in its proper heavenly perspective. It is not just that Satanic evil has been eclipsed—this is not the reason for their joy—rather, the real reason for it is that God himself has inscribed the names of these representatives of Jesus in the book of life, in the heavenly registry of his own favored people (see NOTE on v. 20 for the ancient image used here). Jesus directs the attention of the disciples away from thoughts about sensational success to a consideration of their heavenly status. Their names have been recorded in God's book of life, just as those of his chosen people of old. This should be the real basis for their "joy." Possessing power over demons or spirits is no guarantee of life; but being registered in the book of life is another matter.

Luke has indulged in a bit of apocalyptic writing here in preserving the first comment of Jesus about Satan's fall from heaven; but it is used in a hortatory context and differs considerably from the apocalyptic mode of Rev 12:9-12. If there is a hortatory aspect to the episode, it is scarcely a warning against pride (as it has sometimes been naïvely interpreted—because it has been wrongly related to Isa 14:15 [see NOTE on v. 18]).

NOTES

10   17. *The seventy(-two).* The same textual variant occurs here as in v. 1. See NOTE there.

returned. Or "came back." Luke notes the return of the seventy(-two) with the same vb. that he used for the Twelve in 9:10, there called "the apostles." We are not told when or how the thirty-five or thirty-six pairs came back—on the same day, several days later?

full of joy. Lit. "with joy" *(meta charas).* This detail has already colored the Lucan account. See 1:14; 2:10; 8:13; cf. 24:41,52. It is expressive here of the disciples' reaction to the success of their mission. They have not only announced the kingdom and cured the sick (v. 9), but have had unexpected effects.

Lord. See NOTE on 5:8, and pp. 202-203.

with the use of your name. Lit. "in/with your name," i.e. at the invocation of your name. The use of the name of Jesus becomes a frequent theme in Luke's second volume. See Acts 3:6; 4:10,17-18,30; 5:40; 9:27. The connotation is that the power associated with the person of Jesus becomes effective through the invocation of his name. Cf. Mark 16:17b. Recall Acts 19:13-14 where even itinerant Jewish exorcists are depicted using his name.

even the demons. I.e. spirits or beings regarded in protological thinking as the causes of evil. See NOTE on 4:33. This was more than the disciples, who were instructed to cure the sick (v. 9), might have expected; their report associates their work with that of the Twelve (9:1).

submit to us! I.e. in an exorcistic sense; the demons were obedient to the commands and rebukes of the disciples, as they were to Jesus' (4:39). By contrast, recall the failure of the disciples in 9:40. The vb. *hypotassein* used here by Luke is also used of demons and spirits in Greek magical papyri. See *LAE* 258. In v. 20 "spirits" will be used instead of "demons."

18. *I was watching Satan fall, like lightning, from heaven.* The best Greek word order here is *etheōroun ton satanan hōs astrapēn ek tou ouranou pesonta;* but ms. B and Origen read *etheōroun ton satanan ek tou ouranou hōs astrapēn pesonta,* whereas P[75] and Epiphanius read *etheōroun ton satanan hōs astrapēn pesonta ek tou ouranou.* Since in early mss. there was no punctuation, the best reading above (the first) could be understood in two ways and consequently gave rise to the variants. It could be taken as I have translated it, and this would be closer to the word order of P[75], whereas one could also translate the verse, "I was watching Satan fall like lightning-from-heaven" (closer to ms. B). The latter translation understands the prepositional phrase *ek tou ouranou* as a descriptive modifier of lightning and takes *ouranos* (= sky) as the place from which swift-flashing lightning seems to descend to earth in popular descriptions. This sense is preferred by P. Joüon, "Notes philologiques," 353 (c.-à-d., "comme un

éclair qui vient [ou: sort] du ciel"; cf. Luke 11:16); F. W. Lewis, " 'I Beheld,' " 233. The other (preferred) translation alludes to the OT description of Satan as "the adversary," a functionary of the heavenly court of Yahweh prosecuting humanity; it would refer to his being deposed from his role. His fall would be the end of his accusation of humanity before God. Just when this fall takes place is not stated. Cf. Luke 22:3,31-32.

Luke, though he had spoken of "the devil" *(diabolos,* "accuser") in 4:2-13; 8:12, now uses for the first time the name *Satanas,* a grecized form of Hebrew *śāṭān* or Aramaic *śāṭānāʾ* (as a common n., *śāṭān* occurs in 4QTLevi ar[a] 1:17 [*MPAT* § 21], "adversary"), a specific name for the arch-devil, "Satan." His heavenly role is best seen in Job 1:6-12; 2:1-7, where God is depicted allowing him to test the blamelessness, uprightness, and fidelity of his servant Job. In Zech 3:1-2 he also appears in a vision at the right of "the angel of the Lord" as an accuser. Cp. 1 Chr 21:1; there he is said to have incited David to sin in taking up Israel's numerical census, whereas the parallel in 2 Sam 24:1 ascribes the same sin to "the anger of the Lord." In the parallel of 1 Chronicles postexilic theology has been at work, removing God from any causality of human sin and ascribing its origin to a personification of evil. Another form of the mythical origin of sin is found in a more primitive expression in 1 Kgs 21:19-23 ("a lying spirit"). The name Satan occurs in intertestamental writings also as *Maś-ṭēmāh,* a fem. *maqtal* n. type, with the *nun* of the root assimilated to the initial *m.* It is an abstraction, "Opposition, Prosecution." See 1QM 13:4,11; CD 16:5; 1QS 3:23; *Jub.* 10:8. See NOTE on 4:2. "Satan" will appear again in Luke 11:18; 13:16; 22:3,31; Acts 5:3; 26:18.

The vb. *etheōroun* is in the impf. tense and is taken by many commentators as expressive of continuous action, "I was watching," or "I watched repeatedly." E.g. J. M. Creed, *The Gospel,* 147. I have preferred it myself, though I recognize that this Greek vb. is used only in the pres. and impf. and that *theasthai* is used for other forms. See BDF § 101. Creed would interpret the vb. as referring to some "ecstatic vision" (ibid.; similarly E. E. Ellis, *Gospel of Luke,* 157; *HST* 161). Certainly to be excluded is the meaning of it as a vision of the preexistent Jesus, since his preexistence is not something that Luke reckons with in his Gospel; so too W. Foerster, *TDNT* 7. 157. Likewise to be excluded is that of a proleptic vision of something to take place at the last judgment; the Lucan Jesus is not an apocalyptist of the sort responsible for Rev 12:9-12.

The ptc. *pesonta* is aor., expressing punctiliar action. See ZBG § 269 for a good discussion of the relation of this ptc. to the main vb. The fall has nothing to do with Gen 6:1-4, even though later rabbinic tradition often thought of the fall of Satan as connected with that passage, probably in an effort to explain the strange *Nĕphîlîm,* "fallen ones" (?), which appear there. See Str-B 2. 167-168. Because there is a reference to Isa 14:15 in v. 15 (see NOTE), some commentators think that Jesus alludes to Isa 14:12 ("How you are fallen from heaven, O Day Star, son of dawn"). E.g. see I. H. Marshall, *Luke,* 428-429. However, in that taunt addressed to the king of Babylon he has exalted himself to the sky like astral deities; there is no mention of Satan in that text—a later tradition prone to identify Satan and Lucifer notwithstanding.

19. *See.* Lit. "behold"; Luke uses *idou,* which introduces something new (see BAGD 371), revealing the original independence or isolation of this verse.

I have given. The preferred reading here is the pf. indic. *dedōka,* found in mss. P⁷⁵, ℵ, B, C*, L, W, etc. But some mss. (P⁴⁵, A, C³, D, Θ, and the Koine text-tradition) have the pres. *didōmi,* "I am giving." This pres. tense would rather refer to a promise being made by Jesus to Christian missionaries of the future. It is better, however, to understand it of the "power and authority" implied in the mission-charge already given to the "seventy(-two) others."

authority. This is probably an allusion to the authority mentioned in 9:1 (addressed to the Twelve; cf. Mark 6:7); it is now stated as implied in the mission-charge to the others (vv. 2-12). The n. *exousian* governs two unequal objs., an infinitival cl. and a prepositional phrase.

to tread upon serpents and scorpions. Though many commentators think that the first three words of this saying *(patein epanō opheōn)* are modeled on or allude to Ps 91:13 ("you will trample upon the lion and the dragon" [MT: *tirmōs kĕpîr wĕtannîm;* LXX: *katapatēseis leonta kai drakonta]),* it is a farfetched allusion, *pace* P. Grelot, "Étude critique de Luc 10,19," 90. Greek *ophis,* "serpent, snake," never renders Hebrew *tannîm,* "dragon," in the LXX. The animals mentioned here were neither "half demonic" nor symbols of demons (so E. E. Ellis, *Gospel of Luke,* 157), as G. Foerster rightly notes *(TDNT* 5. 579). The serpent and the scorpion were not only well-known sources of physical evil in Palestinian life, but were OT symbols of all kinds of evil. The seductive serpent of Gen 3:1-14, used to explain the "origin" of evil in human life, appears in the LXX as *ho ophis.* See further Num 21:6-9; Sir 21:2, cf. Pss 58:4; 140:3. For the scorpion as a means of divine chastisement, see 1 Kgs 12:11,14; 2 Chr 10:11,14; Sir 39:30. The combination of serpents and scorpions is already found in Deut 8:15. Cf. Luke 11:11-12. For the juxtaposition of them and Satan in the later targumic tradition, see P. Grelot, "Étude critique," 92-96. Cf. A. Alon, *Natural History,* 182-187, 203-209.

over all the power of the Enemy. A different phrase, introduced by *epi,* expresses the same idea in parallelism; it too depends on *exousia.* See NOTE on "authority" above. "The Enemy" *(ho echthros)* is a synonym for "Satan," the prosecuting adversary. Cf. Rev 9:10-11. For the expected subjection, see NOTE on 4:34.

nothing shall harm you at all. Or possibly, "he (i.e. the Enemy) shall harm you in nothing," understanding the negative *ouden,* placed emphatically at the head of the cl., as an adv. acc. In the preferred translation *ouden* acts as the subj. of the cl. Either translation is possible, and both suit the context.

20. *So.* The verse is introduced by the conj. *plēn* (see NOTE on 10:11), and this is indicative of the verse's original independent status. I have used "rather" at the beginning of the second cl. of this verse, which it logically introduces.

spirits. See NOTE on "even the demons" (v. 17).

your names stand written in heaven! Lit. "your names have been written (and remain so [pf.]) in the heavens." Cf. 1QS 7:2. Jesus' words allude to the OT idea of the heavenly book of the living or of life, the registry of those who belong to God's upright people. The image is drawn from the ancient records of cities or kingdoms, which listed the citizens who belonged to them. For the OT background, see Exod 32:32-33; Pss 69:28; 56:9; 87:6; Isa 4:3; 34:16; Dan 12:1; Mal 3:16-17. The idea is further reflected in several NT passages: Phil 4:3; Heb 12:23; Rev 3:5; 13:8. Cf. the use of it in intertestamental literature: *Jub.* 30:19-23; *1 Enoch* 47:3; 104:1,7; 108:3,7; 1QM 12:2;

4Q*180* 1:3 (see the photo: *whw' ḥrwt 'l lhwt[ ]*; cf. J. Strugnell, "Notes en marge du volume V des 'Discoveries in the Judaean Desert of Jordan,' " *RevQ* 7 [1969-1971] 163-276, esp. 253); 4QDibHam 6:14 (see M. Baillet, "Un recueil liturgique de Qumrân, Grotte 4: 'Les paroles des luminaires,' " *RB* 68 [1961] 195-250, esp. 232). The idea itself is rooted in ancient Sumerian and Akkadian literature. See S. M. Paul, "Heavenly Tablets," 345-353.

BIBLIOGRAPHY (10:17-20)

Foerster, W. *TDNT* 7. 151-163, esp. 158-160.
Grelot, P. "Étude critique de Luc 10,19," *RSR* 69 (1981) 87-100.
Joüon, P. "Notes philologiques sur les évangiles," *RSR* 18 (1928) 345-359, esp. 353.
Kruse, H. " 'Dialektische Negation' als semitisches Idiom," *VT* 4 (1954) 385-400, esp. 389.
Kümmel, W. G. *Promise and Fulfilment,* 113-114.
Lewis, F. W. " 'I Beheld Satan Fall as Lightning from Heaven' (Luke x. 18)," *ExpTim* 25 (1913-1914) 232-233.
Lowther Clarke, W. K. "Studies in Texts," *Theology* 7 (1923) 101-104.
Miyoshi, M. *Der Anfang,* 95-119.
Müller, U. B. "Vision und Botschaft: Erwägungen zur prophetischen Struktur der Verkündigung Jesu," *ZTK* 74 (1977) 416-448.
Paul, S. M. "Heavenly Tablets and the Book of Life," *JANESCU* 5 (1973) 345-353.
Puig Tàrrech, A. "Lc 10,18: La visió de la caiguda de Satanàs," *Revista catalana de teologia* 3 (1978) 217-243.
Spitta, F. "Der Satan als Blitz," *ZNW* 9 (1908) 160-163.
Webster, C. A. "St. Luke x. 18," *ExpTim* 57 (1945-1946) 52-53.
Zerwick, M. " 'Vidi satanam sicut fulgur de caelo cadentem' (Lc 10,17-20)," *VD* 26 (1958) 110-114.

64. JESUS' PRAISE OF THE FATHER; THE BLESSEDNESS OF THE DISCIPLES
(10:21-24)

10 ²¹ At that moment Jesus found delight in the holy Spirit and said, "I praise you, Father, Lord of heaven and earth, because you have hidden these things from the wise and the intelligent, yet have revealed them to small children. Indeed, Father, this has been your good pleasure. ²² All things have been entrusted to me by my Father. No one knows who the Son is but the Father, or who the Father is but the Son or the one to whom the Son chooses to reveal him." ²³ Turning to the

disciples, Jesus said to them privately, "Blessed are the eyes that see what you see! [24] I tell you, many prophets and kings have wanted to see what you now see and have not seen it, to hear what you hear and have not heard it."

COMMENT

Luke now appends to Jesus' comments on the success of the disciples' mission a double-episode, in which he records Jesus' praise of God as his Father (10:21-22) and his declaration of the favored status of his disciples as eyewitnesses of his ministry and teaching (10:23-24). The double-episode acts as further commentary on the disciples' relationship to him. They have not only been his representatives (v. 16), with their names inscribed in heaven (v. 20), but they are "children" favored with a revelation about him and his heavenly Father; in this status their real beatitude is found (vv. 21-24).

Luke has derived these sayings from two different parts of "Q" and joined them as a fitting further comment of Jesus on the status of the disciples, to whom he had shortly before addressed his instructions. The Matthean counterparts of these sayings are found in different contexts (11:25-27 and 13:16-17). Jesus' praise of the Father is a sequel in Matthew to the woes on the Galilean cities, which, as does the connection in Luke 10:13-15 and 21-22, shows that the woes and the praise of the Father were once closely related in "Q." Luke separated the woes to make them part of the mission-charge; now he picks up their sequel and appends it to Jesus' comments on the mission-success of the seventy(-two), adding it to a beatitude about their eyewitness-status. The latter saying forms part of the parable-discourse in Matthew 13, where it is inserted into a Marcan setting. Luke *may* have preserved the original order of these sayings in "Q," and possibly Matthew has moved the beatitude to another context, but it is really impossible to say. I prefer to think that they were not originally joined in "Q."

This Lucan double-episode has a threefold grouping of sayings of Jesus: his praise of the Father, a revelatory utterance, and a beatitude pronounced over the disciples. In this it has a certain similarity to Matt 11:25-30 (see also p. 76), where a slightly different threefold group of sayings is found: Jesus' praise of the Father, a revelatory utterance, and a consolation for the heavily burdened. E. Norden (*Agnostos theos,* 279-280, 301) regarded Matt 11:25-30 as a unit derived from "Q." He has been followed at times by others (e.g. K. Stendahl, "Matthew," *PCB* 784; T. Arvedsen, *Das Mysterium Christi,* 5-9). The third saying in vv. 28-30, however, is found exclusively in that Gospel and has been derived from "M" (a possibility that Norden did not deny). Bultmann *(HST* 159) was certainly right in recognizing its independence from vv. 25-27; and he has been followed by many others (e.g. H. D. Betz, "The Logion of the Easy Yoke and of Rest (Matt 11:28-30)," *JBL* 86 [1967] 17-18; M. J. Suggs, *Wisdom,* 79-81; cf. W. Bousset, *Kyrios Christos,* 84). It has no counterpart in the Lucan Gospel. Though this may seem like an argument from silence, Luke would hardly have suppressed such a part of "Q," since it would have suited so well the immediate context about the success of the disciples and their return had it been there. Moreover, a form of Matt 11:28-30 is found in *Gos. of Thom.* § 90: "Jesus said, 'Come to me, for convenient is my yoke, and my lordship is gentle, and you will find repose for yourselves.' "

Were the sayings in vv. 21-22 originally a unit? That to which *tauta,* "these things" (v. 21), originally referred is not only obscure, but it is not certain that *panta,* "all things" (v. 22), refers to the same. Jesus' praise of the Father in v. 21b speaks of the Father's revelation and says nothing about himself, whereas v. 22 is concerned with the Son's revelation. For this reason some commentators have suggested that vv. 21-22 were not initially a unit. So R. Bultmann *(HST* 159-160), who characterized v. 21b-c as a "Hellenistic revelation saying," but v. 22 as a saying derived from a lost Jewish (Aramaic) writing, which Jesus may have used. Yet even though there are differences in vv. 21-22, the contrast of the Father and the Son, made explicit in v. 22, is already implicit in v. 21b; this seems to provide enough indication that the two revelatory sayings, one from the Father, and one from the Son, were a unit.

This unit (vv. 21-22) is the only saying in the Synoptic Gospels in which Jesus is made to speak as he often does in the Johannine Gospel. It has been called "a meteorite fallen from the Johannine sky" (K. A. von Hase, *Geschichte Jesu* [2d ed.; Leipzig: Breitkopf und Härtel, 1891] 422). Here alone the Synoptic Jesus speaks of a mutual knowledge in a way akin to what has been called Hellenistic mysticism, and in addition he designates himself absolutely "the Son" (three times in one verse; recall, however, Mark 13:32, which is omitted by Luke). It thus raises the question whether the Synoptic tradition here meets the Johannine in some way. Two passages of the Fourth Gospel, in particular, are often compared with these verses: "As the Father knows me, so I too know the Father" (10:15); and ". . . as you have granted him [your Son, the Son of v. 1] authority over all mankind [lit. flesh], that he might give eternal life to all those whom you have given him" (17:2). Similar echoes, not as closely parallel, could be found in John 3:35; 6:65; 7:29; 13:3; 14:7,9-11; 17:25. One explanation of the resemblances might be that the Johannine tradition has borrowed from the Synoptic; but I am reluctant to adopt such an explanation. It seems more likely that the Synoptic tradition has preserved a form of saying which was more at home in the developing Johannine tradition which has affected it, even though we cannot be more specific about the manner of the contact.

Lucan composition in this episode is evident in the introductory temporal phrase ("at that moment") and in the mention of Jesus' delight in the holy Spirit. In vv. 23-24 he has fashioned the introductory participial cl., making the beatitude refer expressly to the disciples (Matt 13:16 is less clear). He has also redactionally modified v. 21 in the use of the compound vb. *apekrypsas,* "you have hidden," to make it parallel *apekalypsas* (whereas Matthew has retained the simple vb. *ekrypsas* from "Q"). Moreover, Luke has sharpened the form of the revelatory utterance and of the beatitude. In the former, the "Q"-form (retained by Matthew) expressed merely the fact of the revealed knowledge of the Father and the Son, but Luke's reformulation centers the reader's attention on the nature of the Father and the Son by the use of the indirect questions, "Who the Son is" and "Who the Father is." The reformulation serves not merely to make known God as Father, but to manifest the relationship of Jesus to him precisely as Son. Similarly, in the beatitude, in emphasizing "what you see," he lauds the disciples not just for the fact of seeing, but for *what* they have seen and heard. However, Luke has probably retained the original formulation of "Q" in the phrase "prophets and kings," whereas Matthew has changed it to "prophets and righteous ones" (13:17; cf. Matt 10:41 ["M"]; 23:29). (Cf. J. Jeremias, *Die Sprache,* 189.)

Ever since E. Norden's discussion of Matt 11:25-30, parallels to Jesus' revelatory utterance (esp. v. 22) have been sought in Hellenistic and other ancient literature. Norden set forth the six Matthean verses in cola and strophes, stressed the threefold form (address of praise to the Father, content of the revelation [couched in the third sg.], and appeal for acceptance of it by worthy listeners), and sought for parallels to it in Hellenistic or Hellenistic Jewish literature *(Agnostos theos,* 280). He appealed to Sir 51:1-30 (dividing it into three parts: 1-12, 13-22, 23-30) and to the Hermetic tractate I *(Poimandres* 32). For the latter, see A. D. Nock and A.-J. Festugière, *Corpus hermeticum* (4 vols.; Collection Budé; Paris: "Les belles-Lettres," 1945-1954), 1. 19; W. Scott, *Hermetica* (4 vols.; Oxford: Clarendon, 1924-1936), 1. 132-133 (neither edition gives the full text that Norden cites on p. 293; nor does he himself on p. 110, to which he refers!). Norden found further traces of the same revelatory tradition in form or content in Sir 24:1-2,5-6,18-19 (part of this text is now found in Hebrew in 11QPsª 21:11-17; for its pertinence to the discussion of Matthew, see M. J. Suggs, *Wisdom,* 80-81); *Odes Sol.* 33:6-11; and various Pauline passages. Norden has at times trimmed the evidence to suit his needs and wrenched some Pauline material from its contexts; he also insinuated all too early dates for the tradition that he was using, calling it "a very ancient motif of oriental, and also Jewish, literature which certainly goes back to Egypt" *(Agnostos theos,* 290). Whereas his sole "Egyptian" source was the Greek Hermetic tractate, which is not to be dated without further ado earlier than A.D. 125 (see C. H. Dodd, *The Fourth Gospel* [Cambridge: University Press, 1953] 11-12; cf. E. Haenchen, *ZTK* 53 [1956] 191), his oldest material was really the Greek text of Sirach (dated ca. 132 B.C.); the *Odes of Solomon* are certainly not older than the Hermetic literature, whatever their provenience may be.

R. Bultmann *(HST* 160) added to the discussion a more ancient Egyptian text, drawn from Akhenaton's *Hymn to the Aton* (ad fin.): ". . . and there is no other that knows thee/Save thy Son Nefer-kheperu-Re Wa-en-Re [= Akhenaton],/For thou hast made him well-versed in thy plans and in thy strength" (J. A. Wilson, *ANET* 371).

In more recent discussions much has been made of the OT and Jewish background of these sayings. M. J. Suggs *(Wisdom,* 89-95), while rightly stressing with H. Koester the Hellenization of Palestinian Judaism in the late pre-Christian centuries, invokes "the most illuminating parallels" for these sayings in Wis 2:17-18; 4:10,13-15, with an emphasis on election, eschatological knowledge, the intimate relation of Father and Son, and the failure of people to recognize the Son or the Father. W. D. Davies also sought to show the pertinence of some Qumran literature to the understanding of such sayings of Jesus (" 'Knowledge' in the Dead Sea Scrolls," 133-139), appealing to such texts as 1QS 4:2-5,18-25; 11:2-4,6; 1QpHab 2:7-10 (are all of them cogent?). J. M. Robinson ("Die Hodajot-Formel in Gebet und Hymnus des Frühchristentums," *Apophoreta: Festschrift für Ernst Haenchen . . .* [BZNW 30; Berlin: Töpelmann, 1964] 194-235) further compared the introductory formula (10:21b) with that in the Qumran *Thanksgiving Psalms,* as well as the thanksgiving tradition in early Christianity.

All of these parallels provide a background for Jesus' praise of his Father and his revelatory utterance; they shed light not only on the genre of the sayings, but also raise a question about their authenticity (to which I shall return below).

Form-critically considered, vv. 21-24 are to be classed as sayings of Jesus; those in vv. 21-22 have been classed as "I"-Sayings by R. Bultmann *(HST* 159-160); but they could also be understood as wisdom-sayings, even though the word *sophia* does not occur in them. They have been so regarded by a number of modern writers (e.g. M. J. Suggs, A. Feuillet, F. Christ). Verses 23-24 are rather to be classed as prophetic sayings, with v. 23b more specifically as a beatitude. In both parts of the unit of sayings, one should note the heavy OT influence, both in form and in content. (See NOTES for details.)

In this Lucan double-episode, Jesus is depicted as one who finds delight in his relation to the Spirit of God and to God himself, whom he acknowledges as Father. His Spirit-inspired prayer recognizes this Father as the Lord or Sovereign of heaven and earth, of that realm from which Satan has been seen falling and in which his disciples' names have been inscribed. But God is also Lord of the realm in which Jesus' own ministry and teaching have been manifested. He extols this Lord and Father, who has seen fit to reveal eschatological secrets, not to the wise and intelligent of this world, but to his chosen disciples, the "small children" or the *in-fantes*, so characterized because they stand in the tradition of the genuine recipients of Israel's wisdom of old. What they have seen and heard has been a revelation from the Father himself. It has come to the disciples because it is a manifestation of the Father's bounteous providence for his people, a manifestation of his "good pleasure" (recall NOTE on 2:14). Verse 22 explains that what has been revealed to the disciples is not only the relation of Jesus to his heavenly Father, but also of them to him. He alone it is who reveals all "these things" (v. 21) as the Son; he is the revealer of the Father and of all that pertains to him. The Lord of heaven and earth has entrusted "all things" to Jesus precisely as "the Son." If the sense of "these things" in its original setting escapes us, in this Lucan context it refers to the hidden meaning of what the disciples have seen and heard in the ministry and teaching of Jesus and to their relation to him. Again, if the sense of "all things" is obscure in its original setting, in the Lucan context it refers primarily to the knowledge of the Son about the Father and the knowledge that only he can transmit to his followers. "Who the Son is" and "who the Father is" are the important content of the Son's revelation—and their relation is not to be understood in an ontological sense, but in their joint concern for people with receptive ears. In the long run, this is the reason for the association of the beatitude uttered over the disciples in v. 23b. If Jesus' words in v. 21b have, in effect, contrasted the disciples with their contemporaries, "the wise and the intelligent," for whom "these things" lie still hidden, his words in vv. 23b-24 further contrast them with people who lived long before them. They have been eyewitnesses of the Son's unique revelation: his preaching, his activity, his personal impact on human beings, and now of his relation to the Father. Of old, prophets and kings longed to see the inbreaking of God's salvific work in human history through a promised messianic agent; now the "small children" of this age have witnessed it. In its own way the final saying of Jesus fits in with the Lucan fulfillment theme (see pp. 292-293).

Verse 22c expresses the sheer gratuity of the definitive revelation that has now been made to human beings: "to whom the Son chooses to reveal him" (i.e. the Father). That revelation is made to "small children," to the disciples of Jesus, the Christian community, and not to the wise and the intelligent of this world.

Jesus as the Son and the revealer of the Father thus appears in the Synoptic tradition playing a role so familiar to the Johannine Jesus. The eschatological secrets revealed to the "small children" eventually become a secret even about the godhead itself (v. 22). Without using the title "Son of God" or making that the obj. of a revelation explicitly, these sayings assert a *unique* relation of Jesus to the Father, precisely as "the Son," who alone through this mutual relationship (of fatherhood and sonship) is able to reveal. The later Christian tradition of the first century eventually gave Jesus the title "God" *(theos,* in John 1:1; 20:28; Heb 1:8), a confessional title indeed. But Paul, in writing to the Corinthians ca. A.D. 57, could already speak of him as "the Son" (1 Cor 15:28), in the same absolute way as this title appears here in the Synoptic tradition. (See also M. Hengel, *The Son of God: The Origin of Christology and the History of Jewish-Hellenistic Religion* [Philadelphia: Fortress, 1976] 9). Thus the title used here brings a corrective to the later confessional title *(theos),* in that Jesus is seen as *ho huios,* "the Son"; he is not *ho patēr,* he is not *'abbā'.*

This title, "the Son," now appears in a saying found in Stage III of the gospel tradition. To what extent can the sayings, especially those in vv. 21-22, be traced back to Stage I, i.e. to the historical Jesus himself? There is probably no more disputed saying in the Synoptic tradition than this one, when the question of its authenticity is raised. Norden was reluctant to consider any of the six verses in the Matthean parallel as Jesus' *autophōnia (Agnostos Theos,* 303-308). A. von Harnack was skeptical in the extreme *(The Sayings of Jesus: The Second Source of St. Matthew and St. Luke* [New York: Putnam; London: Williams & Norgate, 1908] 272-301). This approach has not gone without an assessment (see J. Chapman, "Dr Harnack on Luke X 22: No Man Knoweth the Son," *JTS* 10 [1908-1909] 552-566). R. Bultmann, following M. Dibelius, considered vv. 21-22 as a "Hellenistic revelation saying" similar to Matt 28:18, and hence as a transmitted saying of the risen Lord. For him vv. 23-24 came from "a possible Christian origin" *(HST* 128, 160). In more recent times, commentators have been less sure about such negative assessments (see A. M. Hunter, "Crux criticorum," 241-242, 245; M. J. Suggs, *Wisdom,* 72-77). When one considers the parallels to the sayings in other ancient literature, the relation of the sayings to the Johannine tradition, the redaction of the evangelists, and the specific content of the utterances, one realizes the problem. Yet even when one takes these factors into account, there is no firm basis for denying all connection of these Stage-III sayings with the historical Jesus. He must have said or insinuated something similar to what is recorded here to give rise to the rapid conclusion, which emerged not long after his death, that he was indeed the Son of God (albeit not yet understood in the sense of Nicaea). Although I am inclined to regard the substance of these sayings as authentic, that substance should more likely be traced to an implicit christology expressed in Jesus' words and deeds in his earthly ministry.

Lastly, let it be recalled that, as Jesus prays to God here, addressing him simply as Father, so he will soon teach his disciples to pray (11:2-4).

NOTES

10 21. *At that moment.* Lit. "in/at that hour," an alleged Aramaism. See p. 117. This is the Lucan introductory formula (see 2:38); the Matthean (11:25) is *en ekeinō tō kairō,* "at that time." Whereas Matthew's phrase relates these sayings of Jesus to his moving about in Galilee with disciples (e.g. when the Baptist sent messengers to him, 11:2,7), Luke's formula relates the sayings to the return of the seventy(-two) and Jesus' comment on the report about their mission (10:17-21).

Jesus. The best Greek mss. of the Lucan Gospel (P⁴⁵, P⁷⁵, ℵ, B, D, Ξ, etc.) and ancient versions omit this name; it is found, however, in mss. A, C, W, Ψ. It is used in my translation not because it is the preferred Greek reading, but because the English version calls for a name-subject, as the Koine text-tradition also recognized.

found delight. The vb. *agalliasthai* plays upon a Lucan motif, the first chords of which were struck in the infancy narrative (1:47; cf. 1:14,44; Acts 2:46). It gives expression to Jesus' joy in the presence of the Spirit to his own ministry. The connection of it with *chairete,* "rejoice" (v. 20), is purely coincidental.

in. Whether one reads the prep. *en* with mss. ℵ, D, L, Ξ, 33 or omits it with mss. P⁷⁵, A, B, C, K, W, Θ, the sense is little affected. The English translation demands it in either case. The omission may be affected by the following phrase. In the LXX *agalliasthai* is used both with the simple dat. and with preps. *(en* or *epi).*

the holy Spirit. The def. art. *tō* and the adj. *hagiō* have been omitted in a number of mss. (P⁴⁵, A, W, Δ, Ψ) and various ancient versions; at times the prep. *en* is involved in this omission. See preceding NOTE. To omit it might seem to mean that Jesus found delight in (his own) spirit, i.e. internally. The omission would be supported by the fact that nowhere else in the Bible does one read of someone (even Jesus) finding delight or exulting in the holy Spirit. Yet that is also a reason for preferring "the holy Spirit" as the more difficult textual reading—which is actually better attested. See further *TCGNT* 152. Cf. 2:25,27; 4:1.

The holy Spirit is to be understood as the source and inspiration of Jesus' joy and praise of the Father. See pp. 227-231.

I praise you. I.e. I acknowledge you for what you are and extol you. Another possible translation is, "I thank you." With the acc., the vb. *exomologeisthai* means "admit, confess, acknowledge" (someone or something); but with the dat., as here, the sense is "praise, extol" (as in 2 Sam 22:50; Pss 6:5; 9:1; 35:18; 45:17; 86:12; 118:28). In all these instances from the LXX, however, it translates the Hebrew *hôdāh* (hiphil of *ydy),* which often carries the further nuance of "thank." Many of the Qumran *Thanksgiving Psalms* begin thus, *'wdkh 'dwny ky(')* . . . "I praise/thank you, Lord, because . . ." (1QH 2:20,31; 3:19,37; 4:5; 7:26, etc.), using an OT formula. See Pss 18:50; 30:13; 35:18; 71:22—even with the conj. *hoti* (= Hebrew *ky),* Pss 52:11; 57:10; 86:12; 108:5; 118:21. This sort of laudatory formula, used of God, was well established in Palestinian Jewish tradition, from which it was borrowed by early Christians. See J. M. Robinson, "Die Hodajot-Formel." Cf. 1 Cor 1:4-7, for an earlier Christian use of it. Whether the formula was "cultic" (T. Arvedsen), "baptismal" (M. Rist, "Is Matt. 11:25-30 a Primitive Baptismal Hymn," *JR* 15 [1935] 63-77), or "eucharistic" (J. M.

Robinson) need not detain us. The most striking Qumran parallel to the present text is found in 1QH 7:26-27: "I [give you thanks, O Lord], because you have given me insight into your truth and made known to me your marvellous mysteries and (given knowledge of) your kindnesses to a man [of wickedness, and of] the multitude of your mercies to one perverse in heart." Not only the wisdom-content of the saying but the form itself, coming from a pre-Christian Palestinian Jewish tradition, is revealing. Jesus' praise so expressed is a form of his prayer to God. See p. 245.

Father. God has already been referred to as *ho patēr* in sayings of Jesus: 6:36 (the disciples' Father) and 9:26 (Jesus probably referring to himself as the Son of Man, but not further explaining his relation to "the Father"). In this first saying, Jesus now addresses God as Father, using the voc. *páter,* as in 11:2. See NOTE there. At the beginning of the next sentence, the def. art. with the nom. case *ho patēr* is substituted for the Greek voc. *páter.* The substitution is a literary variant, since the use of the def. art. with the nom. case for the voc. is known elsewhere in Greek. See BDF § 147.3; cf. Luke 8:54; 11:39; 18:11,13; John 13:13; Eph 5:14; Rev 6:10 within the NT.

In addressing God as Father, Jesus moves with this formula beyond the Qumran acclamation of similar thrust, in which the title *'dwny,* "Lord," is normally used. See preceding NOTE. Though the sense of "Father" is not further explained, the mutuality of relationship implied in the terms "son" and "father" becomes clear in v. 22. On God as "Father," see COMMENT on 11:1-4.

Lord of heaven and earth. Though *kai tēs gēs,* "and of earth," was omitted in ms. P⁴⁵ and in Marcion's version, it is to be retained, being found in the best Greek mss. and being a venerable Jewish formula. See also Acts 17:24. In Aramaic, it is found in 1QapGen 22:16,21, *mārêh šĕmayyā' wĕ'ar'ā',* where it translates the Hebrew of Gen 14:19,22, *qōnēh šāmayim wā'āreṣ,* "creator/maker of heaven and earth." Cf. Jdt 9:12 *(despota tōn ouranōn kai tēs gēs);* Tob 7:17 *(ho kyrios tou ouranou kai tēs gēs* [mss. B, A; ms. S reads simply *ho kyrios tou ouranou*—unfortunately the verse is not preserved in the Tobit frgs. of Qumran Cave 4; see J. T. Milik, "La patrie de Tobie," *RB* 73 (1966) 522]). In later rabbinic writings it is found in further *developed* forms. See Str-B 2. 176.

these things. To what *tauta* referred in the original saying is impossible to say. See W. Bousset, *Kyrios Christos,* 84-85 for a discussion of the matter. To leave it simply as "the knowledge of God's will" (J. M. Creed, *The Gospel,* 148) is too vague; similarly for "the presence of the Kingdom" (A. M. Hunter, "Crux," 243). Because of the relation of this saying to the woes against the Galilean towns (10:13-15) in "Q" (see COMMENT), Arvedsen maintained that "these things" were to be understood as part of an initiation formula of inclusion and exclusion in a mystery-liturgy which used ancient cultic blessings and curses such as one finds in Deut 27-28 or 11:13-21 *(Das Mysterium,* 77-104); but that explanation is too farfetched. The same context of a relation to the woes more rightly made W. D. Davies think that "these things" in Luke should be related to "events of eschatological significance" (the fate of the Galilean towns, the fall of Satan, and the inscribing of the disciples' names in heaven); see " 'Knowledge' in the Dead Sea Scrolls," 137-138. This also finds support in the beatitude of vv. 23-24. That *tauta* should have an eschatological connotation is not impossible here, but its eschatological significance must also include something about the relationship of the disciples to Jesus and of his relationship to God. This is the burden of the immediately preceding context in the Lucan Gospel (e.g. 10:16), and it receives further clarification in the next verse, as well as in the beatitude of vv. 23-24.

you have hidden . . . from the wise and intelligent. I.e. the learned ones of this world. Jesus' praise of the Father acknowledges that he has actually hidden "these things" from the wise. It ascribes to God an activity similar to the hardening of Pharaoh's heart (Exod 7:3). The vb. *apekrypsas* is the aor. indic. and cannot be interpreted as if it were a concessive ptc., "although you have hidden," *pace* I. H. Marshall, *Luke,* 434. Further, it goes too far to equate the "wise and the intelligent" with "the arrogant" (so A. Oepke, *TDNT* 3. 973); that is too strong a nuance and is scarcely called for in the context. The last phrase in this lemma makes one think of Paul's strictures in 1 Cor 1:19-25 against the "wise man" and the "scribe" and of his appeal to Isa (29:14 [LXX]), where the adjs. *sophos* and *synetos,* used in Luke, are found in parallelism. The pair is often found in the OT wisdom-literature (Job 34:34; Prov 16:21; Qoh 9:11; Sir 3:29; 9:14-15; Hos 14:10). As used in this verse, it suggests that the wise and the intelligent, with all their learning, cannot fathom God's salvific activity, even when it is directed at them. For another attempt to explain this phrase, see G. Schwarz, *"Hoti ekrypsas tauta apo . . . syneton,"* BN 9 (1979) 22-25.

revealed them to small children. I.e. to infants *(nēpioi,* persons incapable of proper human speech), the opposite of the wise and the intelligent in human society. Paul uses *nēpioi* of immature Christians (1 Cor 3:1), but that is hardly the meaning in Luke. The word is rather to be understood in the LXX sense, where *nēpios* sometimes translates Hebrew *petî,* "simple" (Pss 19:8; 116:6; 119:130), the childlike persons to whom the law would give understanding and enable them to open themselves to God. The same sense of *petî/pĕtā'îm* is found in Qumran literature. See 1QH 2:9; frg. 15:4; 11QPsᵃ 18:2,4. See further J. Dupont, "Les 'simples' *(petâyim)* dans la Bible et à Qumrân: À propos des *nēpioi* de Mt. 11,25; Lc. 10,21," *Studi sull'oriente e la Bibbia offerti al P. Giovanni Rinaldi . . .* (Genoa: Studio e vita, 1967) 329-336. In the Lucan context the "small children" are the disciples, contrasted with the scribes and others of Jesus' ministry who do not listen to him (5:30; 15:2; 19:47).

Though the idea of gods "revealing" things to human beings is not foreign to Greek religion, it is noteworthy that the vb. *apokalyptein* used in this verse and elsewhere (e.g. 12:2; 17:30) is not normally found in Greek literature for such activity; instead vbs. like *epideiknynai, hypodeiknynai,* or *sēmainein* are employed. See further A. Oepke, *TDNT* 3. 566. Jesus' words about the revelation of the Father stand in the OT tradition, in which the LXX uses *apokalyptein* to translate Hebrew *gālāh,* "reveal." E.g. 1 Sam 3:7,21; Dan 2:19; 10:1 (Theodotion).

Indeed. On the good Greek particle *nai,* see NOTE on 11:28.

this has been your good pleasure. Lit. "in this way good pleasure has taken shape *(or* has come into being) before you," a reverential way of speaking about God—what happens takes place in his presence. See BAGD 257. The cl. describes God's gracious and condescending action in regard to the elect in the matter of revelation. It has not been his good pleasure to reveal these things to everyone. The prepositional phrase *emprosthen sou,* "before you" (in a spatial sense), has its counterpart in the LXX, where it is used frequently with vbs. of motion (to place, lead, send, go [in, out], etc.), translating either Hebrew *lipnê* and its compounds or Aramaic *qŏdām* and its compounds. It occurs also in the LXX with *ginesthai,* "to be, become," which is used here, but rather in a temporal sense. See 1 Kgs 3:12; 22:54; 2 Kgs 18:5. The closest one comes to the Lucan phraseology is 2 Chr 13:13, but there the sense of *ginesthai* in the LXX is different. Cf. 2 Chr 15:8. Luke uses the prep. *emprosthen* in 5:19; 7:27; 12:8; 14:2; 19:4,27,28; 21:36; Acts 10:4; 18:17.

22. *All things have been entrusted to me by my Father.* I.e. in my ministry and for the good of human beings. Again, to what *panta* referred in the original saying is difficult to say. It might be thought to refer to the totality of cosmic power and sovereignty implied in the title "Lord of heaven and earth," with which Jesus has just hailed the Father, but it more likely refers to the knowledge of the mutual relation of himself and God, the content of the revelation gratuitously to be given. If this cognitive sense of *panta* is preferred, it is not to be forthwith understood of the eternal relations of the Trinity, such as would emerge in later Christian theology. The Lucan formulation, "who the Son is" and "who the Father is" already represents a later development beyond the Matthean form of the saying. Jesus is depicted as one who has received from the Father, and what he has received he passes on; and since only he does, this implies that his sonship is unique.

The vb. is *paradidonai,* often used of passing on a traditional teaching. See 1 Cor 11:23; 15:3; cf. B. Gerhardsson, *Memory and Manuscript* (ASNU 22; Lund: Gleerup, 1961) 288-302.

At the beginning of this verse in some mss. (A, C, K, W, X, Δ, Θ, Ψ, etc.) one finds the phrase "and turning to the disciples, he said." But it is omitted by better mss. (P[45], P[75], ℵ, B, D, L, Ξ, etc.). It is almost certainly derived secondarily from the beginning of v. 23.

An echo of Jesus' words is found in *Gos. of Thom.* § 61b: "To me were given some of the things of my Father." See p. 86.

No one knows who the Son is but the Father. The intimate relationship of Father and Son is known only to those involved—and to those to whom it is eventually revealed by one who is involved in that relationship. This relationship stresses the uniqueness of the sonship enjoyed by Jesus. Even if the NT elsewhere refers to Christians as "sons of God" (Gal 3:26; Rom 8:19), what is stated here about Jesus' own sonship implies a difference. Note that in this one verse Jesus refers to himself three times absolutely as "the Son." See p. 205. Cf. Mark 13:32; Matt 24:36; 28:19; John 3:35,36; 5:19-26; 6:40; 8:36; 14:13; 17:1.

For the negative expression, "no one . . . but" (= "any"), see 4:26-27; 18:19. Cf. ZBG § 469-470.

who the Father is but the Son. Antithetic parallelism exists between this cl. and the preceding. The uniqueness of the knowledge of the relationship implies the uniqueness of the relationship itself.

or the one to whom the Son chooses to reveal him. The pronominal obj. of the vb. is lacking in the Greek text; it has to be supplied and is to be understood as referring to the Father, not to "himself," *pace* P. Winter, "Mt XI 27," 131. If the vb. were middle, the revelation of Jesus himself might be possible, but it is act.

23. *Turning to the disciples.* Luke uses the aor. pass. ptc. *strapheis* (in an intrans. sense) with *pros* and the acc., as in 7:44; 23:28.

privately. See NOTE on 9:10.

Blessed are the eyes that see what you see! For a beatitude pronounced over a part of the body, see NOTE on 6:20. The beatitude expresses the privileged role of the disciples as eyewitnesses; they are the ones who will be called upon to be witnesses to him after his ascension. See R. J. Dillon, *Eye-witnesses,* 270, 291. See p. 243.

24. *I tell you.* Most Greek mss. read *legō gar hymin,* "for I tell you," but the conj. *gar* is omitted by ms. P[75] and a few others. Its force is not causal or inferential, but merely transitional. In the Matthean counterpart (13:17) the original reading of "Q" is retained, *amēn gar legō hymin*—one of the instances in which Luke has omitted *amēn*.

many prophets and kings have wanted to see what you now see. The eschatological secrets that the disciples as "little children" now see and hear were perceived neither by earthly kings nor even by the prophets of old who longed to see them. The Lucan Jesus thus plays on the theme of fulfillment; it will appear again in 24:25,44. Cf. 1 Pet 1:10-12. The Johannine Jesus speaks in a different vein of Abraham (8:56) and of Isaiah (12:41).

to hear what you hear. I.e. that the age of God's new mode of salvation has been proclaimed. This is why the disciples' ears are "blessed." Cf. J. Horst, *TDNT* 6. 553.

BIBLIOGRAPHY (10:21-24)

Arvedsen, T. *Das Mysterium Christi: Eine Studie zu Mt 11.25-30* (Arbeiten und Mitteilungen aus dem neutestamentlichen Seminar zu Uppsala 7; Uppsala: Lundqvist, 1937).

Biencek, J. *Sohn Gottes als Christusbezeichnung der Synoptiker* (AbhTANT 21; Zürich: Zwingli, 1951).

Cerfaux, L. "L'Évangile de Jean et 'le logion johannique' des Synoptiques," *L'Evangile de Jean: Etudes et problèmes* (ed. F.-M. Braun; RechBib 3; Bruges: Desclée de Brouwer, 1958) 147-159.

———— "Les sources scripturaires de *Mt.,* XI, 25-30," *ETL* 30 (1954) 740-746; 31 (1955) 331-342; reprinted, *Recueil Lucien Cerfaux* 3. 139-159.

Charlier, C. "L'Action de grâces de Jésus (Luc 10,17-24 et Matth. 11,25-30)," *BVC* 17 (1957) 87-99.

Christ, F. *Jesus Sophia: Die Sophia-Christologie bei den Synoptikern* (AbhTANT 57; Zürich: Zwingli, 1970) 81-99.

Cullmann, O. *Christology,* 280-288.

Davies, W. D. " 'Knowledge' in the Dead Sea Scrolls and Matthew 11:25-30," *HTR* 46 (1953) 113-139.

Feuillet, A. "Jésus et la sagesse divine d'après les évangiles synoptiques," *RB* 62 (1955) 161-196.

Grimm, W. "Der Dank für die empfangene Offenbarung bei Jesus und Josephus," *BZ* 17 (1973) 249-256.

———— "Selige Augenzeugen, Luk. 10,23f: Alttestamentlicher Hintergrund und ursprünglicher Sinn," *TZ* 26 (1970) 172-183.

Hahn, F. *Titles,* 307-333.

Hoffmann, P. "Die Offenbarung des Sohnes: Die apokalyptischen Voraussetzungen und ihre Verarbeitung im Q-Logion Mt 11,27 par Lk 10,22," *Kairos* 12 (1970) 270-288.

Hunter, A. M. "Crux criticorum—Matt. xi.25-30—A Re-appraisal," *NTS* 8 (1961-1962) 241-249.

Iersel, B. M. F. van, *"Der Sohn,"* 146-161.

Irenée de Lyon, S. "En quel sense nul ne connaît le Père, sinon le Fils, et par combien de manières adaptées aux temps le Fils révèle le Père," *BVC* 11 (1955) 53-56. [French translation of *Adv. haer.* 4.6.]

Jeremias, J. *New Testament Theology,* 56-61.

Klijn, A. F. J. "Matthew 11:25//Luke 10:21," *New Testament Textual Criticism* (eds. E. J. Epp and G. D. Fee) 1-14.

Kloppenborg, J. S. "Wisdom Christology in Q," *Laval théologique et philosophique* 34 (1978) 129-147.

Kümmel, W. G. *Promise and Fulfilment,* 111-113.

Légasse, S. "La révélation aux *nēpioi,"* *RB* 67 (1960) 321-348.

Luck, W. "Weisheit und Christologie in Mt 11,25-30," *Wort und Dienst* 13 (1975) 35-51.

Lührmann, D. *Redaktion,* 64-68.

Miyoshi, M. *Der Anfang,* 120-152.

Norden, E. *Agnostos Theos* (Stuttgart: Teubner, 1913; reprinted, Darmstadt: Wissenschaftliche Buchgesellschaft, 1956) 277-308.

Suggs, M. J. *Wisdom, Christology, and Law in Matthew's Gospel* (Cambridge, MA: Harvard University, 1970) 71-97.

Winter, P. "Mt XI 27 and Lk X 22 from the First to the Fifth Century: Reflections on the Development of the Text," *NovT* 1 (1956) 112-148.

Zerwick, M. "El júbilo del Señor (Lc 10,21-24)," *RevistB* 20 (1958) 23-28.

65. THE COMMANDMENT FOR ETERNAL LIFE
(10:25-28)

10 [25] Once a lawyer stood up, trying to test Jesus with a question, "Teacher, what am I to do to inherit eternal life?" [26] Jesus said to him, "What is written in the Law? How do you read it?" [27] He said in reply, *"You must love the Lord your God with all your heart, with all your soul, with all your might,*[a] and with all your mind; and you must love *your neighbor as yourself."*[b] [28] Jesus then said to him, "You have answered correctly; do this and you shall live."

[a] Deut 6:5   [b] Lev 19:18

COMMENT

Jesus has just contrasted the disciples as "small children" with "the wise and intelligent" (10:21). Now Luke's continuing narrative (10:25-28) in the travel account introduces one of the latter to question Jesus and test his teaching. The beatitude pronounced over the disciples who have seen and heard is now followed with a parenetic counsel about eternal life, a counsel about the practical love of God and of one's neighbor.

At first, the episode (vv. 25-28) seems to resemble Mark 12:28-31 (= Matt 22:34-40) in that in both Mark/Matthew and Luke someone questions Jesus and two verses from the OT (Deut 6:5 and Lev 19:18) are joined in an answer. Moreover, Luke has omitted the counterpart of Mark 12:28-34 at 20:40 (avoiding a doublet? [see p. 81]). In the Marcan episode a Scribe asks Jesus which commandment is the first of all; the Matthean setting is similar, but the scene is more elaborate and the questioner is a "lawyer." In both Mark and Matthew Jesus answers, making Deut 6:5 the first and Lev 19:18 the second commandment. In Mark the Scribe further comments on Jesus' answer. Luke, however, depicts a "lawyer" asking Jesus about eternal life and Jesus countering with a question which draws forth from the lawyer the double quotation of Deut 6:5 and Lev 19:18, to which Jesus answers with a confirmation. A further question (v. 29) from the lawyer closely connects this episode with the following (vv. 30-37). Moreover, the lawyer's initial question is found echoed in Luke 18:18, posed by a "magistrate," which introduces a different story about commandments of the Decalogue. Thus the initial, seeming similarity of the Marcan and Lucan episodes soon gives way to the impression that one may be dealing with different traditions or perhaps different incidents in the life of Jesus.

Some commentators think that Luke may have reworked the Marcan episode to make it the introduction to his story about the good Samaritan (so G. Schneider, *Evangelium nach Lukas,* 247; J. Schmid, *Evangelium nach Lukas,* 190-191; E. Klostermann, *Lukasevangelium,* 118). Others, because of a number of small agreements in the Lucan story with those of Matthew (e.g. "lawyer," "teacher," "in the law," the omission of Deut 6:4 [see T. Schramm, *Markus-Stoff,* 47 n. 4]), think that Luke has substituted here a form of the episode that existed in "Q," and which Matthew used in his reworking of the Marcan form (so *HST* 22-23; F. W. Beare, *The Earliest Records of Jesus* [Oxford: Blackwell, 1962] 159).

But the whole form of this episode in the Lucan Gospel is so different from the Marcan story that it should rather be ascribed to "L." The use of "lawyer" instead of "one of the Scribes" and the omission of the first part of the Shema' (Deut 6:4; cf. Mark 12:29b) could easily be explained by Luke's redactional concern for the predominantly Gentile audience for whom he was writing, if these elements were really part of his inherited story. Luke may, however, be influenced by "Mk" (see T. Schramm, *Markus-Stoff,* 49).

Whether the Marcan and the Lucan forms of the story go back to the same incident in the ministry of Jesus is hard to say. There is no need to appeal to Jesus' "repeating" of the same teaching in various ways, *pace* T. W. Manson *Sayings,* 260; cf. I. H. Marshall, *Luke,* 441. It is more likely that the different forms of the one questioning of Jesus about important commandments of the Law which exist in the gospel tradition emerged in the post-Easter transmission of what he did and said (cf. J. Jeremias, *Die Sprache,* 190).

As the episode stands in the Lucan Gospel, it is to be form-critically regarded as a pronouncement-story. R. Bultmann *(HST* 51) notes that whereas the Marcan story (12:28-34) takes the form of a school debate, in which the answerer is praised at the end, the Lucan story has become a controversy dialogue, in which Jesus' first answer is really a counter-question and his final comment merely confirms the lawyer's response. Jesus' final comment, "Do this and you shall live," is actually a weak pronouncement, and the cutting edge in the episode is rather the lawyer's answer. That, of course, becomes Jesus' pronouncement too, by virtue of his confirmation.

Jesus' counter-question elicits from the lawyer two commands from the Mosaic Law, the first taken from the expanded Shema' (Deut 6:4-9), which the faithful Jew was to recite twice a day (see Deut 6:7; cf. *m. Ber.* 1:1-4), and the second from Lev 19:18. The first command insisted on the absolute love of Yahweh in a total personal response; the three (or four) faculties (heart, soul, might, [and mind]) were meant to sum up the totality of undivided dedication to him. The second command, which is quite distinct in the OT, being derived from the so-called Holiness Code of Leviticus (chaps. 17-26), enjoins the Israelite to love his "neighbor," i.e. his fellow Israelite. In effect, it demands of the Israelite the same attitude toward one's neighbor as toward Yahweh himself. The love of Yahweh was commended particularly in the deuteronomic writings (see Deut 11:13,22; 19:9; 30:16; cf. Josh 22:5; 23:11; W. L. Moran,"The Ancient Near Eastern Background of the Love of God in Deuteronomy," *CBQ* 25 [1963] 77-87; G. Wallis, *TDOT* 1. 101-118).

Jesus' confirmation of the lawyer's double response makes the double commandment of love into a norm for the conduct of the Christian disciple. No love of God is complete without that of one's neighbor. Jesus' parenetic counsel is given, then, in OT terminology, and the following episode will attempt to define who the "neighbor" is. But it must be recalled that the Lucan Jesus, in his sermon on the plain, has already insisted on the love of one's enemies (6:27-35).

Elsewhere in the NT, Christians are enjoined to love their neighbors by writers who also appeal to Lev 19:18 (see Gal 5:14; Rom 13:9; Jas 2:8—where the love of the neighbor is regarded as the summation of the Mosaic Law). In this Lucan episode, however, it is joined to the counsel of the total personal love of God himself, as it is also in the Marcan and Matthean episodes.

Because the joining of the two commands is found on Jesus' lips in the Marcan and Matthean stories and on a lawyer's lips in this Lucan episode, the question has been raised about the occurrence of the joint command in pre-Christian Judaism. Was the double commandment a teaching of the rabbis already in Jesus' day? A form of the double command is found in the *Testaments of the Twelve Patriarchs:* In the *T. Issachar* 5:2, "Love the Lord and the neighbor"; in *T. Dan* 5:3, "Love the Lord with all your life and each other with a true heart"; cf. *T. Issachar* 7:6. Though it is now known that some parts of this writing, preserved in its entirety only in Greek, did exist in Semitic form in pre-Christian Palestinian Judaism (e.g. 4QTLevi, 4QTNaph, 4QTBenj [as yet in great part unpublished]), nothing is known about the *T. Dan* or *T. Issachar* in this period. Moreover, the Greek form of the *Testaments* has usually been suspected of Christian interpolations. Hence appeal cannot be made to such writings without further ado. However, a form of it may be couched by Philo of Alexandria in terms of Greek virtues in the following comment: "Among the great number of particular propositions and principles [studied in Sabbath schools], two, as it were, stand as preeminent topics: one of duty toward God in piety and holiness *(eusebeia kai hosiotēs),* one of duty toward human beings in generosity and justice *(philanthropia kai dikaiosynē)" (De spec. leg.* 2.15 § 63). But whether this is a reflection of the uniting of Deut 6:5 and Lev 19:18 is another matter. The double form is, however, attested later in Christian writings, which is not surprising (see *Did.* 1:2; *Barn.* 19:2,5; Justin, *Dial.* 93:2-3; *Mart. Pol.* 3:3). (See further G. Bornkamm, "Das Doppelgebot"; C. Burchard, "Das doppelte Liebesgebot.")

Whether one can establish the preexistence of the double command in prior Jewish tradition or not, it stands here so formulated, and what is significant is that it is presented as a "reading" of the "Law." In effect, the Lucan Jesus finds the basic counsel of Christian life in the words of Scripture itself, "Do this and you shall live," or in this you shall find life eternal. The different forms which the love-command takes in the gospel tradition suggest finally that Jesus himself was the catalyst for the development of the double command in the Christian tradition.

NOTES

10   25. *Once.* Luke uses *kai idou,* "and behold" as a simple introductory formula. See p. 121. No other indication of time or place is provided. Though the following episode might argue for a Jerusalem locale (so E. E. Ellis, *Gospel of Luke,* 159), that is not to be claimed for this questioning of Jesus.

a lawyer. See NOTE on 7:30. Matt 22:35 also makes the interrogator a "lawyer," but the form of the phrase is quite different *(heis ex autōn nomikos);* it does not argue for a common source behind these episodes.

trying to test. The same vb. *ekpeirazein* was used in 4:12. Note the different, simple form of the vb. in Matt 22:35. Cf. P. Thomson, " 'Tempted Him' (Luke x.25)," *Exp-Tim* 37 (1925-1926) 526. The phrase reveals a hostile attitude. Contrast Mark 12:28.

Teacher. The address and the question echo that put to John the Baptist in 3:10,12. See NOTES there.

to inherit eternal life? The question appears again in Luke 18:18. See NOTE there. It is sparked in a Jewish mind by Dan 12:2: "Many of those who sleep in the dust of the earth will awake, some to life eternal, some to shame and eternal disgrace." Both the LXX and Theodotion's Greek read *zōēn aiōnion.* Cf. 4 Macc 15:3. The question put to Jesus makes its own contribution to the Lucan treatment of an important effect of the Christ-event in his writings. See p. 222. In Mark 12:28 the concern is with the Mosaic Law; here in Luke the question is phrased more generally to suit readers not concerned with the Law. Cf. Acts 16:30.

26. *Jesus.* The name is supplied in my translation; the Greek text has simply, "and he said."

What is written in the Law? See Luke 2:23. "Law" is a reference to the *Tōrāh* of Moses; the lawyer's answer draws two passages from the Pentateuch.

How do you read it? See 4:16; 6:3; Acts 8:28,30,32; 13:27; 15:21 for the Lucan use of *anaginōskein* for "reading" of the Scriptures (or Moses).

27. *He said in reply.* Luke uses the Septuagintal formula *apokritheis eipen.* See p. 114.

You must love the Lord your God . . . The lawyer at first quotes Deut 6:5; the Lucan text of which agrees with the LXX, save for the addition of "and with all your mind" (in the fourth place), the substitution of *ischys* for *dynamis* (in the third prepositional phrase), and the substitution of the prep. *en* (+ dat.) for *ex* (+ gen.) in the last three phrases. The LXX actually has the prep. *ex* in all phrases. Some mss. of Luke (A, C, W, Θ, Ψ, and the Koine text-tradition) have *ex* in all instances; but that is probably the result of a copyist's harmonization with the LXX. The original Hebrew of Deut 6:5 has only three phrases (heart, soul, might). A corrector of ms. B of the LXX has introduced *dianoia,* "mind," for *kardia,* "heart." Mark 12:30 also has four phrases, but in a different order (= Lucan 1, 2, 4, 3); Matt 22:37 has only three (= Lucan 1, 2, 4). Where the fourth phrase comes from is not clear. See further K. J. Thomas, "Liturgical Citations."

The aspects of the human person so expressed have to be understood in the OT sense: *kardia,* "heart," as denoting the more responsive and emotional reactions of a human being; *psychē,* "soul," the vitality and consciousness of a person; *ischys,* "might," the powerful and instinctive drive; and *dianoia,* "mind," the intelligent and planning qualities. As a group, they sum up the totality of personal life.

In the OT quotation *kyrios* refers here to Yahweh. See p. 201.

your neighbor as yourself. The lawyer's second response joins Lev 19:18b to the first, but as a unit. It is quoted verbatim according to the LXX, which agrees with the Hebrew (my translation has repeated the vb., "you must love," which is not in the Lucan Greek text). One is to have the same esteem and care for a neighbor that one would have for oneself. In Leviticus "neighbor" stands in parallelism with "the children of your own people," i.e. fellow Israelites. The love is eventually extended in Lev 19:34 to the "sojourner" *(gēr)* in the land (cf. Deut 10:19), but not to others, e.g. *gôyîm*. See Str-B 1. 353-354. The Essenes of Qumran were "to love all the sons of light . . . and hate all the sons of darkness"; 1QS 1:9-10; also 2:24; 5:25; 1QM 1:1. Cf. Josephus, *J. W.* 2.8,7 § 139. The "sons of light" were members of their own community.

28. *You have answered correctly.* See Luke 7:43. Jesus can only agree with the Law and the lawyer's quoting of it.

do this and you shall live. I.e. find eternal life. See v. 25. Only the person who *puts* the command of love *into practice* will find life. The vb. *zēsē* may allude to Lev 18:5, which promises life to the person who obeys Yahweh's statutes and ordinances. Cf. Gal 3:12. Jesus' words thus add a counsel of practice to the theoretic recognition of the love-commands in the Torah. Addressed to the Christian reader, they form part of Lucan parenesis.

BIBLIOGRAPHY (10:25-28)

Bornkamm, G. "Das Doppelgebot der Liebe," *Neutestamentliche Studien* (ed. W. Eltester) 85-93.

Bultmann, R. "Aimer son prochain, commandement de Dieu," *RHPR* 10 (1930) 222-241; reprinted (in German), *Glauben und Verstehen,* 229-244.

Burchard, C. "Das doppelte Liebesgebot in der frühen christlichen Überlieferung," *Der Ruf Jesu* (eds. E. Lohse et al.) 39-62.

Crossan, J. D. "Parable and Example in the Teaching of Jesus," *NTS* 18 (1971-1972) 285-307.

Denaux, A., and P. Kevers. "De historisch-kritische Methode," *Collationes* 26 (1980) 387-404.

Diezinger, W. "Zum Liebesgebot Mk xii,28-34 und Parr.," *NovT* 20 (1978) 81-83.

Ernst, J. "Die Einheit von Gottes- und Nächstenliebe in der Verkündigung Jesu," *TGl* 60 (1970) 3-14.

Furnish, V. P. *The Love Command in the New Testament* (Nashville: Abingdon, 1972) 34-45.

Heutger, N. "Die lukanischen Samaritanererzählungen in religionspädagogischer Sicht," *Wort in der Zeit* (eds. W. Haubeck and M. Bachmann) 275-287.

Jones, P. R. "The Love Command in Parable: Luke 10:25-37," *Perspectives in Religious Studies* 6 (1979) 224-242.

Lohfink, N. "Das Hauptgebot," *Das Siegeslied am Schilfmeer: Christliche Auseinandersetzungen mit dem Alten Testament* (Frankfurt am M.: Knecht, 1965) 129-150.

Nissen, A. *Gott und der Nächste im antiken Judentum: Untersuchungen zum Doppelgebot der Liebe* (WUNT 15; Tübingen: Mohr [Siebeck], 1974).

Piper, J. "Is Self-Love Biblical?" *Christianity Today* 21 (1976-1977) 1150-1153.

Stern, J. B. "Jesus' Citation of Dt 6,5 and Lv 19,18 in the Light of Jewish Tradition," *CBQ* 28 (1966) 312-316.

Thomas, K. J. "Liturgical Citations in the Synoptics," *NTS* 22 (1975-1976) 205-214.

Venetz, H. "Theologische Grundstrukturen in der Verkündigung Jesu? Ein Vergleich von Mk 10,17-22; Lk 10,25-37 und Mt 5,21-48," *Mélanges Dominique Barthélemy* (eds. P. Casetti et al.) 613-650.

Zerwick, M. " 'Diliges Deum tuum ex toto corde tuo' (Lc 10,25-29)," *VD* 26 (1948) 365-369.

66. THE PARABLE OF THE GOOD SAMARITAN
(10:29-37)

10   [29] But the lawyer was anxious to justify himself; so he said to Jesus, "But who is my neighbor?" [30] Jesus took him up and said to him, "A certain man was traveling down from Jerusalem to Jericho, when he fell in with robbers. They stripped him, beat him, and went off leaving him half-dead. [31] Now by coincidence a priest was going down that same road; when he saw the man, he passed by on the other side. [32] Similarly, a levite also came upon that place, saw him, and passed by on the other side. [33] But a Samaritan who was on a journey came upon him. When he saw him, he was moved to pity. [34] He went up and bandaged his wounds, pouring olive oil and wine over them. He set him on his own mount, led him to a public inn, and made provision for him there. [35] The next day he took out two pieces of silver, gave them to the innkeeper, and said, 'Provide for him, and on my way back I shall reimburse you for whatever you spend over and above this.' [36] Which of these three seems to you to have been neighbor to the man who fell into the hands of the robbers?" [37] He answered, "The one who showed him kindness." So Jesus said to him, "Go and do the same yourself."

COMMENT

This episode in the Lucan travel account (10:29-37) is intimately connected with the preceding one by the introductory question put by the lawyer to Jesus, "But who is my neighbor?" Jesus' answer to it is provided in the story of the good Samaritan.

The story is recorded only in the Lucan Gospel and, apart from the introductory verse, which is most likely of Lucan composition and fashioned by him to join this story to the preceding episode, it comes to the evangelist from his private source "L." Only secondarily has it been joined to the preceding, since it does not really answer the lawyer's second question. It is one of the parables of mercy (see p. 258) which give this Gospel a distinctive tone and help to create a distinctive Lucan picture of Jesus. The concluding remark of Jesus in v. 37 may be a Lucan redactional addition. (Cf. J. Jeremias, *Die Sprache*, 190-193.)

From a form-critical point of view, it has often been called a parable. But the text lacks this customary appellation (contrast 12:16; 18:9) and would be so understood only in a generic sense of *parabolē* (see NOTE on 5:36). The concluding words of Jesus (v. 37) use *homoiōs*, "likewise, in the same way," and suggest a comparison of the lawyer and the Samaritan; they thus make of this story indirectly a parable or an extended simile. The point of the story, however, is made without the concluding remark of Jesus. Like a few other distinctive Lucan stories (12:16-21; 16:19-31; 18:9-14), it is better understood as an "example" (in rhetoric, *exemplum*). It supplies a practical model for Christian conduct with radical demands and the approval/rejection of certain modes of action. The point of the story is not conveyed by some analogy to a spiritual truth, but by the narrative thrust of the "example" itself.

The storytelling devices are to be noted in the episode: the threesome in the dramatis personae (the priest, the levite, and the Samaritan [like the Englishman, the Irishman, the Scotsman]); the Palestinian details (olive oil, wine, animal, and inn); the answer of the Jewish lawyer, which studiously avoids saying "the Samaritan" and uses only "the one who showed him kindness"; and a certain in-built improbability (would a Jew normally regard a Samaritan as a model of kindness, picture him traveling in Judea, or think that a Judean innkeeper would trust him?—to query in this way, however, is to miss the point of the *story*). To argue that "the narrative is not fiction, but history," because Jesus would not speak against priests or levites (so A. Plummer, *The Gospel*, 285-286) is to miss the thrust of the narrative.

Crucial to the understanding of the story which Jesus tells (vv. 30-35) are certain noteworthy details: (1) The privileged status of the priest and the levite in Palestinian Jewish society—their levitical and/or Aaronic heritage, which associated them intimately with the Temple cult and the heart of Jewish life as worship of Yahweh. New light has been shed on this in the Temple Scroll from Qumran Cave 11 (see NOTE on 10:32). (2) The defilement considered to be derived from contact with a dead (or apparently dead) body (see NOTE on 10:31); this affected those of the priestly and levitical status more seriously than other Jews. (3) The attitude shared by Palestinian Jews concerning the Samaritans, summed up so well in the Johannine comment, "Jews, remember, use nothing in common with Samaritans" (John 4:9; see COMMENT and NOTES on 9:52-53). Their history made them schismatics in the eyes of the Jews, and relations with them have been exemplified in the lack of welcome accorded Jesus and his disciples in 9:52-54 as they tried to pass through Samaritan territory. These details underlie the story's basic contrast: the pity and kindness shown by a schismatic Samaritan to an unfortunate, mistreated human victim stands out vividly against the heartless, perhaps Law-inspired insouciance of two representatives of the official Jewish cult, who otherwise would have been expected by their roles and heritage to deal with the "purification" of physically afflicted persons (see the role of the "priest" in Leviticus 12, 13, 15).

The point of the story is summed up in the lawyer's reaction, that a "neighbor" is anyone in need with whom one comes into contact and to whom one can show pity and kindness, even beyond the bounds of one's own ethnic or religious group. The regulations on defilement from contact with a dead body were also to be found in the *Samaritan* Pentateuch, but they did not hinder the Samaritan of the story from being motivated by his own pity and kindness, which enabled him to transcend such restrictions. The sense that is given to "neighbor" by Jesus' "example" changes considerably the sense of the word as it was used in the lawyer's question. As J. M. Creed puts it *(The Gospel,* 151), "The scribe *[sic]* asks for a definition of what is meant by 'neighbour,' when it is said that a man must love his neighbour as himself. In the quotation from the law and in the scribe's question, the neighbour is mentioned as the proper *object* of benevolent action. The parable, it is true, gives by implication an answer to the question, viz. your neighbour is anyone in need with whom you are thrown into contact, but the word neighbour is now used in a quite different sense, viz. to denote the person who himself shews benevolence or 'neighbourliness' to others." In effect, the question that Jesus asks at the end of the story and the response that the lawyer begrudgingly makes to it casts the question into a larger perspective and unmasks the lawyer's effort to justify himself. It is no longer whether the victim of the highway robbery could be considered legally a "neighbor" to either the priest, the levite, or the Samaritan, but rather which one of them acted as a "neighbor" to the unfortunate victim. As T. W. Manson *(Sayings,* 263) once put it, "The principle underlying the question is that while mere neighbourhood does not create love, love does create neighbourliness." No definition of "neighbor" emerges from the "example," because such a casuistic question is really out of place. Love does not define its object.

In the Lucan context the "kindness" *(eleos)* shown by the Samaritan to the half-dead victim becomes a concrete example of the love of one's neighbor advocated in v. 28; it is an essential part of the way to "eternal life." The incorporation of this episode into this Gospel emphasizes that part of the sermon on the plain that deals with human love (6:27-35). It also contributes to the larger picture of Lucan "universalism," which includes a Samaritan and makes of him a paradigm for Christian conduct; it suggests that even a Samaritan has found the way to eternal life. The priest and the levite were not lacking in their love of God—the dedication of their status attests to that; but their love of neighbor was put to the test and was found wanting, whereas the Samaritan's shone true.

This episode has often been understood quite differently from the interpretation of it presented here. Over the centuries the history of its exegesis has witnessed many modes of exposition, most of them allegorical and extrinsic. From Marcion and Irenaeus, through the Middle Ages and the Reformation period, until the nineteenth century, it has often been given a christological explanation (Christ is the good Samaritan), an ecclesiological explanation (the inn is the church), a sacramental explanation, or an extrinsic soteriological explanation. Interpretations of this sort have not been wanting in modern times (see the writings of H. Binder, J. Daniélou, and B. Gerhardsson in the BIBLIOGRAPHY on pages 888-889). In one form or other, modern commentators usually prefer the mode of interpretation which began with A. Jülicher, viz. which seeks to cope with the thrust of the narrative or description itself. (See further W. Monselewski, *Der barmherzige Samariter;* H. G. Klemm, *Das Gleichnis.*) Similarly allegorical or extrinsic in the long run are attempts, such as that of J. D. M. Derrett ("Law in the New Testament," 22-37), to regard the "parable" as a midrash on Hos 6:6, "I am interested in merciful kindness, not sacrifice." Equally farfetched is the explanation which analyzes the name "Samaritan" by the Hebrew *šomrônî* (cf. 2 Kgs 17:29) and relates it by popular etymology to the vb. *šmr,* "watch, guard," seeing a connection with Jesus as the Good Shepherd in John 10:11. Luke would be the first to stress the love of Jesus for the afflicted and distressed of humanity, but that is not the point of this so-called parable.

Is this Lucan parable anti-Semitic? It can, of course, be read that way, as if Luke were suggesting a Samaritan as a paradigm for Christian conduct in contrast to the two Jews. S. Sandmel *(Anti-Semitism in the New Testament* [Philadelphia: Fortress, 1978] 77) thinks that this parable is not in itself anti-Jewish, but "in the total context of Luke it does lend itself to a possible alignment with other anti-Jewish passages," among which he lists 14:15-24; 17:11-19, and various places in the passion narrative. (See further R. Reuther, *Faith and Fratricide* [New York: Seabury, 1974] 84.) To read the parable in this way, however, is just another subtle way of allegorizing it. The emphasis in this Lucan passage lies in the last injunction, "Go and do the same yourself," and if it has an interest in the Samaritan, it is simply the Lucan stress on universalism which makes him seek out those in Palestinian society who were not the most important. Even H. Conzelmann *(Theology,* 146) refused to see in "the extreme sharpness of polemic" that Luke manifests at times between Christians and Jews any espousal of "Christian anti-Semitism," a "development" that he ascribes to early Catholicism. In the long run, to read the Lucan Gospel in this way is to import into it anachronistic issues that were not really Luke's concern.

NOTES

10   29. *anxious to justify himself.* Lit. "desiring to vindicate himself," i.e. to show that he was right in posing the question that he had originally proposed to Jesus, even though it found such a simple answer. One may debate whether in the Lucan context this implies that the lawyer has not put into practice the second part of the love-command; recall the polemical attitude of v. 25. For the Greek phrase, see Greek *Enoch* 102:10; also J. Jeremias, "Beobachtungen zu neutestamentlichen Stellen an Hand des neugefundenen griechischen Henoch-Textes," *ZNW* 38 (1939) 115-124, esp. 117-118. Cf. Luke 16:15; 18:14.

who is my neighbor? The implication in the question is, Where does one draw the line? Jesus' "example" will extend the answer beyond that given in Lev 19:16,33-34.

30. *took him up.* By replying to what he asked. See the LXX of Job 2:4; 40:1; Dan 3:28.

A certain man. Luke uses for the first time the indef. *anthrōpos tis;* he will use it again in 12:16; 14:2,16; 15:11; 16:1,19; 19:12; 20:9; Acts 9:33. It occurs only in the Lucan writings of the NT. Almost as frequently he uses *anēr tis* (Luke 8:27; Acts 5:1; 8:9; 10:1; 13:6; 16:9; 17:5; 25:14) or *tis anēr* (Acts 3:2; 14:8; 17:34). J. Jeremias *(Die Sprache,* 191) has tried to ascribe *anthrōpos tis* to one of Luke's sources, and *anēr tis* to Luke's own pen. This, however, is far from certain, since the use of *anthrōpos/anēr* with indef. *tis* is exclusive to Luke among the evangelists; both should be reckoned as part of his own style. See further *tis* + a noun (p. 111).

was traveling down from Jerusalem to Jericho. According to Josephus, *J.W.* 4.8,3 § 474, this was a distance of 150 *stadioi* (about eighteen miles) through "desert and rocky" country. Reference would be to the Roman road through passes and the Wadi Qelt; one would descend from over 2500 feet above sea level (Jerusalem) to 770 feet below it (Jericho). See J. Finegan, *Archeology,* 86-87. Josephus also mentions it as the way taken by the Legio X Fretensis en route from Jericho for the siege of Jerusalem *(J.W.* 5.2,3 § 69-70). See R. Beauvery, "La route romaine de Jérusalem à Jéricho," *RB* 64 (1957) 72-101.

Jerusalem. See NOTE on 2:22. See further I. de la Potterie, "Les deux noms de Jérusalem dans l'évangile de Luc," 69 (1981) 57-70; J. Jeremias, "IEROUSALĒM/ IEROSOLYMA," *ZNW* 65 (1974) 273-276.

Jericho. This "town of palm trees" (2 Chr 28:15) will be mentioned again at 18:35; 19:1. It is not the Jericho of OT times (= Tell es-Sulṭan), but the town founded by Herod the Great about a mile and a half to the south on the western edge of the Jordan plain, where the Wadi Qelt opens on to it (= Tulul Abu el-'Alayiq). See Josephus, *J.W.* 4.8,2 § 452-453; J. Finegan, *Archeology,* 83-85.

fell in with robbers. Josephus tells of Essenes who carried on their journeys only arms, precisely as protection against highway robbers—using of the latter the very word *lēstai* that Luke employs here *(J.W.* 2.8,4 § 125; cf. 2.12,2 § 228). From the time of Jerome at least, the site of "the Ascent of Adummim" (Josh 18:17) has been singled out as the place where this traveler met violence, since *'Adummîm* is related to the word for "blood." See D. Baldi, *ELS* 544-570; cf. J. Finegan, *Archeology,* 87-88.

stripped him. Lit., "who also having stripped him," i.e. of his clothes, and left him unconscious; this explains why he looked like a corpse.

beat him. Lit., "having laid blows (on him)."

31. *by coincidence.* This phrase is emphatically placed at the head of the sentence. *Synkyria,* "coincidence," occurs only here in the NT; the ms. P^{75c} reads instead *syntychian,* which has the same meaning.

a priest. One who probably had been serving in the Jerusalem Temple and was making his way home after the end of his course. See NOTE on 1:5. Later rabbinic tradition knows of Jericho as a place where some priests lived. See Str-B 2. 182.

passed by on the other side. Luke uses a rare doubly compounded vb., *anti-par-erchesthai,* another sense of which is found in Wis 16:10. The implication of his passing by is to avoid contamination by contact with or proximity to a dead body. See Num 5:2c; 19:2-13. A priest was to defile himself only to bury persons of his immediate family (Ezek 44:25-27); but cp. Lev 5:3; 21:1-3; Num 6:6-8; and the later tradition in *m. Nazir* 7:1.

32. *a levite.* The name originally designated a member of the tribe of Levi, a descendant of Jacob's third son (Gen 29:34). In the OT "levite" was commonly used for those descendants who were not Aaronids, but who were entrusted with minor services related to the Temple cult and rites. Their status varied in the course of OT times, especially as priestly clans became more numerous. Relatively few of them returned from the Babylonian Captivity (see Ezra 2:36-43), but these soon acquired a status entitling them to receive tithes for priestly service (Neh 10:37-38). Cf. 11QTemple 21:2-5; 22:8-11. See J. Milgrom, "Studies in the Temple Scroll," *JBL* 97 (1978) 501-523.

Verse 32 is omitted in ms. ℵ by haplography. See the end of v. 31.

came upon that place. The transmitted Greek text is not clear here. In addition to the ptc. *elthōn,* "coming," some mss. read *genomenos* at the beginning of the cl. (P^{45}, A, C, D, E, etc.). Some mss. omit *elthōn* (P^{45}, D, Π, 63, 68, etc.). The expression *genomenos kata* is used by Luke in Acts 27:7, meaning "being (present) at . . ." The critical text of N-A^{26} and *UBSGNT*^{3} reads both ptcs., putting, however, *genomenos* in square brackets. I have omitted it in my translation as redundant.

33. *Samaritan.* See NOTE on 9:52; Str-B 1. 538-560. He is the foil to the two respected members of the Palestinian Jewish community mentioned in vv. 31-32, who would have regarded him almost as a pagan.

The attempt of J. Halévy *(REJ* 4 [1882] 249-255) to regard *Samaritēs* as a Lucan substitution for *Israelitēs* (to be understood as "layman") in the so-called original story is farfetched. It would introduce a nuance of contrast between the lay and the clerical; it stems only from nineteenth-century anticlericalism.

who was on a journey. Lit. "making (his) way, being a traveler," since he is depicted outside of Samaria and traveling the same road in Judea.

came upon him. For *erchesthai kata,* see Acts 16:7.

was moved to pity. Or "he had pity (on him)"; no prepositional phrase is used here, as it is in 7:13. See COMMENT on 7:11-17. See H. Köster *(TDNT* 7. 553), for whom the vb. *splanchnizesthai* is used here of one human being toward another in "the basic and decisive attitude in human and hence in Christian acts."

34. *pouring olive oil and wine over them.* They were the provender that the Samari-

tan had with him on his journey. A mixture of them for medicinal purposes is known from Theophrastus, *Hist. plant.* 9.11,1 and from the later rabbinic tradition *(m. Šabb.* 19:2). In the OT olive oil is said to be a softener of wounds (Isa 1:6); elsewhere in the NT it is used to anoint the sick (Mark 6:13; Jas 5:14). The acidic nature of wine would serve as an antiseptic. In 2 Sam 16:2 it is used as a drink for someone who faints, but here as a medical application. Cf. Str-B 1. 428. The two items are mentioned as staples of the land in Rev 6:6; 18:13. Cf. Exod 23:11.

set him on his own mount. Lit. "having made him mount his own animal" or "(acquired) beast." Only Luke uses *epibibazein* in the NT. See 19:35; Acts 23:24; cf. LXX 2 Kgs 9:28; 23:30.

led him to a public inn. Luke uses *agein,* "lead," properly here. See my article, "The Use of *Agein* and *Pherein* in the Synoptic Gospels," *Festschrift to Honor F. Wilbur Gingrich* (eds. E. H. Barth and R. E. Cocroft; Leiden: Brill, 1972) 147-160. On *pandocheion,* "public inn," see NOTE on 2:7. Cf. J. R. Royse, "A Philonic Use of *pandocheion* (Luke x 34)," *NovT* 23 (1981) 193-194. Since the time of the Crusaders it has been localized at the Ascent of Adummim. See NOTE on 10:30.

35. *two pieces of silver.* Lit. "two denarii." See NOTE on 7:41; cf. Matt 20:2. The Samaritan is depicted making use of his material possessions (oil, wine, mount, silver money) to aid an unfortunate human victim. See p. 249.

on my way back. Lit. "on my returning"; the dat. of the articular infin. is used. See p. 119. The vb. *epanerchesthai* turns up again in 19:15.

I shall reimburse you. Lit. "I shall pay you back." Luke uses the vb. *apodidonai* in two senses: (a) neutrally: "give over/back, hand over" (see 4:20; 9:42; 16:2; Acts 4:33; 5:8; 7:9; 19:40); (b) with the connotation of debt: "pay back what is owed, reimburse" (7:42; 10:35; 12:59; 19:8; this may also be the connotation in 20:25 [see NOTE there]). Cf. A. Sand, *EWNT* 1. 306-309.

36. *Which of these three seems to you to have been neighbor to the man.* The counter-question put by Jesus to the lawyer changes the original question. See COMMENT.

37. *The one who showed him kindness.* Lit. "the one doing mercy with him." See NOTE on Luke 1:72; for the Septuagintism involved, see p. 115. Recall Mic 6:8.

Go and do the same yourself. Lit. "go and you (too) do likewise"; the sg. pron. *sy* is added for emphasis before the impv. Ms. P[45] even adds an additional *kai* before the impv., also for emphasis. The sg. impv. *poreuou* is found only once in Matthew and three times in John; but Luke uses it 12 times (5:24; 7:50; 8:48; 10:37; 13:31; 17:19; Acts 8:26; 9:15; 10:20; 22:10,21; 24:25). For "do the same," see Luke 3:11; 6:31. These Lucanisms suggest that this final remark of Jesus may be a redactional addition to the original story. Cf. 1 Kgs 2:31 LXX.

BIBLIOGRAPHY (10:29-37)

Binder, H. "Das Gleichnis vom barmherzigen Samariter," *TZ* 15 (1959) 176-194.

Biser, E. "Wer ist mein Nächster?" *Geist und Leben* 48 (1975) 406-414.

Bishop, E. F. F. "People on the Road to Jericho: The Good Samaritan—and the Others," *EvQ* 42 (1970) 2-6.

Bowman, J. "The Parable of the Good Samaritan," *ExpTim* 59 (1947-1948) 151-153, 248-249.

Castellino, G. "Il sacerdote e il levita nella parabola del buon samaritano," *Divinitas* 9 (1965) 134-140.

Cerfaux, L. "Trois réhabilitations dans l'Evangile," *Bulletin des facultés catholiques de Lyon* 72 (1950) 5-13; reprinted, *Recueil Lucien Cerfaux*, 2. 51-59.

Cranfield, C. E. B. "The Good Samaritan (Luke 10:25-37)," *TTod* 11 (1954) 368-372.

Crespy, G. "La parabole dite 'Le bon Samaritain'! Recherches structurales," *ETR* 48 (1973) 61-79 (translated into English in the following).

Crossan, J. D., ed. "The Good Samaritan," *Semeia* 2 (1974) [whole issue].

Daniel, C. "Les Esséniens et l'arrière-fond historique de la parabole du Bon Samaritain," *NovT* 11 (1969) 71-104.

Daniélou, J. "Le bon Samaritain," *Mélanges bibliques rédigés en l'honneur de André Robert* (Paris: Bloud et Gay, 1957) 457-465.

Derrett, J. D. M. "Law in the New Testament: Fresh Light on the Parable of the Good Samaritan," *NTS* 11 (1964-1965) 22-37.

Diego, J. R. de. "¿Quién es mi prójimo?" *EstEcl* 41 (1966) 93-109.

Downey, G. "Who Is My Neighbor? The Greek and Roman Answer," *ATR* 47 (1965) 3-15.

Eichholz, G. *Gleichnisse der Evangelien*, 148-178.

Eulenstein, R. " 'Und wer ist mein Nächster?': Lk. 10,25-37 in der Sicht eines klassischen Philologen," *TGl* 67 (1977) 127-145.

Eynde, P. van den. "Le bon samaritain," *BVC* 70 (1966) 22-35.

Funk, R. W. " 'How Do You Read?' A Sermon on Luke 10:25-37," *Int* 18 (1964) 56-61.

——— "The Old Testament in Parable: A Study of Luke 10:25-37," *Encounter* 26 (1965) 251-267.

Furness, J. M. "Fresh Light on Luke 10[25-37]," *ExpTim* 80 (1968-1969) 182.

Gerhardsson, B. "The Good Samaritan—The Good Shepherd?" *ConNT* 16 (1958) 1-31.

Gewalt, D. "Der 'barmherzige Samariter': Zu Lukas 10,25-37," *EvT* 38 (1978) 403-417.

Giavini, G. "Il 'prossimo' nella parabola di buon samaritano," *RivB* 12 (1964) 419-421.

Gordon, J. C. "The Parable of the Good Samaritan (St. Luke x. 25-37): A Suggested Re-orientation," *ExpTim* 56 (1944-1945) 302-304.

Hermann, I. "Wem ich der Nächste bin: Auslegung von Lk 10,25-37," *BibLeb* 2 (1961) 17-24.

Kieffer, R. "Analyse sémiotique et commentaire: Quelques réflexions à propos d'études de Luc 10. 25-37," *NTS* 25 (1978-1979) 454-468.

Klemm, H. G. *Das Gleichnis vom barmherzigen Samariter: Grundzüge der Auslegung im 16./17. Jahrhundert* (BWANT 6/3 [103]; Stuttgart: Kohlhammer, 1973).

Lambrecht, J. *Once More*, 93-130.

Leenhardt, F.-J. "La parabole du Samaritain (Schéma d'une exégèse existentialiste)," *Aux sources de la tradition chrétienne: Mélanges offerts à M. Maurice Goguel à l'occasion de son soixante-dixième anniversaire* (Neuchâtel/Paris: Delachaux et Niestlé, 1950) 132-138.

Linnemann, E. *Jesus of the Parables,* 51-58.

Masson, W. J. "The Parable of the Good Samaritan," *ExpTim* 48 (1936-1937) 179-181.

Mattill, A. J., Jr. "The Good Samaritan and the Purpose of Luke-Acts: Halévy Reconsidered," *Encounter* 33 (1972) 359-376.

Monselewski, W. *Der barmherzige Samariter: Eine auslegungsgeschichtliche Untersuchung zu Lukas 10,25-37* (BGBE 5; Tübingen: Mohr [Siebeck], 1967).

Ramaroson, L. "Comme 'le bon Samaritain,' ne chercher qu'à aimer (Lc 10,29-37)," *Bib* 56 (1975) 533-536.

Reicke, B. "Der barmherzige Samariter," *Verborum veritas* (eds. O. Böcher and K. Haacker) 103-109.

Scholz, G. "Ästhetische Beobachtungen am Gleichnis vom reichen Mann und armen Lazarus und an drei anderen Gleichnissen (Lk 16, 19-25 [26-31]; 10, 34; 13, 9; 15, 11-32)," *Linguistica biblica* 43 (1978) 67-74.

Sellin, G. "Lukas als Gleichniserzähler: Die Erzählung vom barmherzigen Samariter (Lk 10:25-27)," *ZNW* 65 (1974) 166-189; 66 (1975) 19-60.

Silva, R. "La parábola del buen samaritano," *CB* 23 (1966) 234-240.

Spicq, C. "The Charity of the Good Samaritan—Luke 10:25-37," *Contemporary New Testament Studies* (ed. M. R. Ryan; Collegeville, MN: Liturgical, 1965) 218-224.

Trudinger, L. P. "Once Again, Now 'Who Is My Neighbour?' " *EvQ* 48 (1976) 160-163.

Wickham, E. S. G. "Studies in Texts: Luke x. 29," *Theology* 60 (1957) 417-418.

Wilkinson, F. H. "Oded: Proto-Type of the Good Samaritan," *ExpTim* 69 (1957-1958) 94.

Wink, W. "The Parable of the Compassionate Samaritan: A Communal Exegesis Approach," *RevExp* 76 (1979) 199-217.

Young, N. H. "Once Again, Now 'Who Is My Neighbour': A Comment," *EvQ* 49 (1977) 178-179.

Zerwick, M. " 'Homo quidam descendebat ab Jerusalem in Jericho' (Lc 10,30-37)," *VD* 27 (1949) 55-59.

——— "The Good Samaritan," *Furrow* 6 (1955) 291-295.

Zimmermann, H. "Das Gleichnis vom barmherzigen Samariter: Lk 10,25-37," *Die Zeit Jesu: Festschrift für Heinrich Schlier* (eds. G. Bornkamm and K. Rahner; Freiburg im B.: Herder, 1970) 58-69.

67. MARTHA AND MARY
(10:38-42)

10 [38] As they moved on, Jesus entered a village where a woman named Martha welcomed him into her home. [39] She had a sister named Mary, who sat down at the Lord's feet and listened to what he was saying. [40] But Martha was preoccupied with the details of serving. She came to Jesus and said, "Sir, are you not concerned that my sister has left me alone to do all the serving? Tell her, please, to come and lend me a hand." [41] But the Lord said to her in reply, "Martha, Martha, you are fretting and disturbed about many details; [42] there is need of only one thing. For Mary has chosen the best part; it shall not be taken away from her."

COMMENT

After the story of the good Samaritan, the Lucan travel account calls the reader's attention to Jesus' progress on his journey toward Jerusalem by relating a visit in a certain village to Martha and Mary (10:38-42). It is an episode unrelated to the preceding passages, unless one wants to see in it another way of inheriting eternal life (v. 25), as does A. Plummer (The Gospel, 290).

The story of the visit to Martha and Mary comes to Luke from his special source "L," being recounted nowhere else in the Synoptic gospel tradition. A contact with the developing Johannine tradition is not impossible (see p. 88); but there is no way of being certain. If the village were named in "L," the name has been suppressed by Luke in the interest of his geographical perspective (see pp. 164-171). Here Jesus is still en route to Jerusalem; he has not yet reached it or its environs. (Cf. J. Jeremias, Die Sprache, 193-194.)

From a form-critical consideration, the episode is to be regarded as a pronouncement-story. Bultmann (HST 33) classed it as a biographical apophthegm, despite its text-critical problems, considering it an "ideal construction," inherited from a Hellenistic tradition. V. Taylor, however, preferred to regard it as a story about Jesus (FGT 75), and M. Dibelius (FTG 119) as a legend (with its basis in historical reality, p. 293). Taylor thought that the interest in the story lay in the incidents rather than in the words of Jesus or in Jesus' "fellowship with His friends" (FGT 156). Yet even if one were to admit that this episode has interest because of Jesus' dealings with women, its most memorable part is precisely the pronouncement about Mary's portion. Taylor has paid too much attention to Dibelius' analysis.

In the preceding episode there was a contrast between the Samaritan and the Jewish priest and levite; in this one the contrast is seen between the reactions of Martha, the perfect hostess, and of Mary, the perfect disciple. Perhaps this note of contrast is responsible for the collocation of the episodes. But that is a superficial consideration at most, even if Martha's distraction is gently reproved, whereas Mary's attention is clearly approved. According to W. Grundmann *(Evangelium nach Lukas,* 225), this episode is linked to the preceding chiastically; the latter gave a concrete illustration of the love of one's neighbor (the second command), whereas this one illustrates the love of God (the first command). This stretches a point. The love of God might be a motivation for listening to Jesus' instruction, but there is no reference to such motivation in it to link this passage with vv. 25-28. (See further G. Schneider, *Evangelium nach Lukas,* 252.)

This passage is somewhat subtle, since Jesus' answer to Martha's fretting request seems at first to reassure her, telling her that she need prepare only *one* dish. But when his pronouncement is complete, one realizes that the "one thing" means more than "one dish" and has taken on another nuance. It has become the "best part," and he who has been part of it guarantees that it will not be taken away from Mary to send her to help distracted Martha.

The episode makes listening to the "word" the "one thing" needed. In a way it repeats the Lucan message of 8:15,21. Priority is given to the hearing of the word coming from God's messenger over preoccupation with all other concerns. Martha wanted to honor Jesus with an elaborate meal, but Jesus reminds her that it is more important to listen to what he has to say. The proper "service" of Jesus is attention to his instruction, not an elaborate provision for his physical needs ("pursuit of life," 8:14; cf. 21:34). Recall Ps 55:23 (LXX).

Moreover, Luke in this scene does not hesitate to depict a woman as a disciple sitting at Jesus' feet; this goes beyond 8:2-3. *Pace* E. Laland, the episode is scarcely introduced to instruct women about the proper entertainment of traveling preachers. Jesus rather encourages a woman to learn from him; contrast the attitude of the sages in later rabbinic tradition (see A. Oepke, *TDNT* 1. 781-782). Jesus' own attitude here may rather reflect Prov 31:26.

On the heels of the good Samaritan episode, this one emphasizes the listening to the word of Jesus, something that goes beyond love of one's neighbor. Martha's service is not repudiated by him, but he stresses that its elaborate thrust may be misplaced. A *diakonia* that bypasses the word is one that will never have lasting character; whereas listening to Jesus' word is the lasting "good" that will not be taken away from the listener.

To read this episode as a commendation of contemplative life over against active life is to allegorize it beyond recognition and to introduce a distinction that was born only of later preoccupations. The episode is addressed to the Christian who is expected to be *contemplativus(a) in actione.*

NOTES

10   38. *As they moved on.* Lit. "in their moving on," another example of *en* + dat. of the articular infin. See p. 119. Some mss. (A, C, D, W, etc.) read *egeneto de en . . . autous kai autos eisēlthen,* "As they moved on, he happened to enter . . ." The vb. *poreuesthai* calls attention to the journey motif. See COMMENT on 9:51-56.

a village. Lit. "a certain village," which remains nameless in the Lucan tradition. See 9:56. It is closer to Galilee than to Jerusalem. From John 11:1; 12:1-3 one learns that Martha and Mary, the sisters of Lazarus, lived in Bethany, a village near Jerusalem, to be named in 19:29.

Martha. Though the name means "lady, mistress," it is not being used as a symbolic name suiting her role in this episode. It is the fem. form *(Mār[ĕ]tā')* of the Aramaic n. *mārê',* "lord," not of *mār, pace* I. H. Marshall, *Luke,* 451; Str-B 2. 184. Cf. *WA,* 89. It is attested on a first-century ossuary from Giv'at ha-Mivtar (in northeast Jerusalem). See *MPAT* § 87. It is also found in Greek papyri from Egypt (BGU 1153:1,3; 1155:4) and in Plutarch, *Marius* 17.2.

welcomed him. I.e. as a guest. Recall 7:36; cf. 19:6; Acts 17:7. Contrast Luke 9:53.

into her home. This phrase is omitted in mss. P[45], P[75], B, and the Sahidic version; both N-A[26] and *UBSGNT[3]* omit it. Some form of the phrase, however, is found in important mss.: *auton eis tēn oikian* (P[3], א*, C*, L, Ξ [with *autēs* added in some]); *auton eis ton oikon autēs* (A, D, K, P, W, Δ). Both N-A[25] and Merk read it. It is not easy to decide whether the omission is better. See *TCGNT* 153.

39. *Mary.* She is also called Martha's sister in John 11:1. She is not to be identified with Mary Magdalene of 8:2. See NOTE there. On the name, see NOTE on 1:27. The best reading here gives the Greek form as *Mariam* (P[75], א, B[2], C*, L, P), whereas some mss. (P[45], A, B*, C[3], D) have *Maria.*

sat down. The preferred reading is the aor. pass. ptc. *parakathestheisa* (P[3], P[75], א, A, B, C*, L), used in the reflexive sense, "having seated herself beside." Other mss. (P[45], C[3], D, W) read *parakathisasa,* which hardly differs in meaning; *pace* E. E. Ellis, *Gospel of Luke,* 162, there is no reason to think that Jesus was already reclining at the table; the meal is only being prepared.

at the Lord's feet. Her position is that of a listening disciple (see NOTE on 8:35; cf. Acts 22:3); it reveals her "zealous readiness to learn" (K. Weiss, *TDNT* 6. 630). For this use of "Lord," see the NOTE on 7:13. "Lord" is read in mss. P[3], א, B[2], D, L, Ξ, etc.; but mss. P[45], P[75], A, B*, C[2], W, etc. have instead *Iēsou,* "of Jesus." Possibly "Lord" is read because of v. 41.

listened. Or "kept listening," since the vb. *ēkouen* is impf. in the best mss.; a few (P[45], L, Ξ) have the aor. *ēkousen.*

what he was saying. Lit. "his word," i.e. his instruction. See NOTE on 1:4.

40. *was preoccupied with the details of serving.* Lit. "was being distracted about much serving." The implication is that Martha too would gladly have listened to his

instruction, but allowed herself to be drawn away (in different directions) by her elaborate plans of providing for Jesus' meal. The description of her stands in contrast to Mary's "sitting." She serves as did the women in 8:2-3.

came. Lit. "having taken a position by/at." See NOTE on 2:9.

Sir. See NOTE on 5:12.

come and lend me a hand. Or, "Speak to her, please, that she may help me," since *hina* may be introducing a purpose cl. However, in Hellenistic usage, with the subjunc. it can often replace an infin. See ZBG § 407.

41. *the Lord.* See NOTE on 7:13. On Westcott and Hort's suspicion of vv. 41-42a, see p. 130.

said to her in reply. Lit. "answering, he said," a Septuagintism. See p. 114.

Martha, Martha. The repeated name gently chides. See further 6:46; 22:31; Acts 9:4; 22:7; 26:14.

you are fretting and disturbed about many details. The text-critical situation for this and the following cl. is complicated by many variants; only the most important are listed here. The best reading is *merimnas kai thorybazē peri polla* (translated above); see mss. P³, P⁴⁵, P⁷⁵, ℵ, B, C, D, L, W, etc. But *thorybazesthai* is a rare Greek vb. and has been replaced in some mss. (A, K, P, Δ, Π, Ψ) by *tyrbazein,* "trouble." On *merimnas,* cf. 1 Cor 7:34.

Jesus' comment to Martha casts light on what he will say in 12:37; 22:37; he has not come to be served (Mark 10:45 [omitted, however, by Luke]).

42. *there is need of only one thing.* The best reading is now *henos de estin chreia,* "but of one (thing) there is need" (mss. P⁴⁵, P⁷⁵, A, C*, K, P, Δ, Π, Ψ, etc.). One ms. (38) reads *oligōn* instead of *henos,* "but of a few (things) there is need"—i.e. a few dishes. However, a number of mss. (P³, ℵᶜ, B, C², L, 33, etc.) have combined the two readings: *oligōn de estin chreia ē henos,* "but of a few things there is need, or of (only) one." Because the latter seemed unintelligible and the transmission was so uncertain, some ancient versions (OL, OS) omitted this and the preceding cl.

However, the recent discovery of P⁷⁵, the oldest text of Luke, more or less decides the issue in favor of the reading in the lemma. Moreover, the contrast of the "one" and the "many" almost calls intrinsically for this reading, as M. Dibelius *(FTG* 119) well saw. See Luke 18:22. Cf. G. D. Fee, " 'One Thing Is Needful?' Luke 10:42," *New Testament Textual Criticism* (eds. E. J. Epp and G. D. Fee) 61-76.

For Mary. The proper name is omitted in mss. ℵ, A, C, D, L, W, etc., but read in P³, P⁷⁵, B, etc. The conj. *gar* is found in the latter as well as in ℵ, L, Ψ; but *de* is read in mss. A, C, W, etc.

the best part. Lit. "the good part." The positive degree of the adj. is often used in Hellenistic Greek for either the superlative or comparative, both of which were on the wane. See BDF § 245; ZBG § 146. See p. 124. By this phrase stress is put on the exclusive listening to the word of Jesus. The word *meris,* "part," is used in the LXX for a portion of food (Gen 43:34; Deut 18:8; 1 Sam 1:4), but also for "portion" in a higher sense (Pss 16:5; 119:57).

it. Lit. "which"; the rel. pron. *hētis* would carry the nuance of "which for that reason." See ZBG § 218.

from. Some mss. add the prep. *ap'* to the compound vb. (P[75], $\aleph$[2], A, C, W, etc.), but it does not affect the sense.

This last statement of Jesus gathers further meaning in the light of Luke 8:18; 12:19-21,33.

BIBLIOGRAPHY (10:38-42)

Augsten, M. "Lukanische Miszelle," *NTS* 14 (1967-1968) 581-583.

Baker, A. "One Thing Necessary," *CBQ* 27 (1965) 127-137.

Bonnardière, A.-M. de la. "Marthe et Marie, figures de l'église d'après S. Augustin," *VSpir* 86 (1952) 404-427.

Bover, J. M. "Porro unum est necessarium (Lc 10,42)," *Valoración sobrenatural del "Cosmos": La inspiración bíblica: Otros estudios* (XIV semana bíblica española, 21-26 Sept. 1953; Madrid: Consejo superior de investigaciones científicas, 1954) 383-389.

Fee, G. D. " 'One Thing Is Needful?' Luke 10:42," *New Testament Textual Criticism* (eds. E. J. Epp and G. D. Fee) 61-75.

George, A. "L'Accueil du Seigneur: Lc 10,38-42," *AsSeign* ns 47 (1970) 75-85.

Gillieson, T. "A Plea for Proportion: St. Luke x. 38-42," *ExpTim* 59 (1947-1948) 111-112.

Kemmer, A. "Maria und Martha: Zur Deutungsgeschichte von Lk 10,38ff. im alten Mönchtum," *Erbe und Auftrag* 40 (1964) 355-367.

Knockaert, A. "Structural Analysis of the Biblical Text," *Lumen vitae* 33 (1978) 471-481.

Laland, E. "Die Martha-Maria-Perikope Lukas 10,38-42," *ST* 13 (1959) 70-85.

——— "Marthe et Marie: Quel message l'église primitive lisait-elle dans ce récit? Luc 10,38-42," *BVC* 76 (1967) 29-43.

Matanic, A. "La pericopa di Lc. 10,38-42, spiegata da Ugo di St-Cher, primo esegeta degli Ordini Mendicanti (+1263)," *Divinitas* 13 (1969) 715-724.

Nicolas, J.-H. "La meilleure part: Marthe et Marie," *VSpir* 75 (1946) 226-238.

Nolle, L. "Bethany," *Scr* 4 (1949-1951) 262-264.

O'Rahilly, A. "The Two Sisters," *Scr* 4 (1949-1951) 68-76.

Puzo, F. "Marta y María: Nota exegética a Lc 10,38-42 y 1 Cor 7,29-35," *Miscelanea bíblica Andres Fernandez (= EstEcl* 34 [1960]) 851-857.

Stevenson, M. "Martha and Mary," *ExpTim* 28 (1916-1917) 478.

Sudbrack, J. " 'Nur eines ist notwendig' (Lk 10,42)," *Geist und Leben* 37 (1964) 161-164.

Vitti, A. M. "Maria optimam partem elegit (Lc. 10, 38-42)," *VD* 10 (1930) 225-230.

Zerwick, M. " 'Optima pars' (Lc 10,38-42)," *VD* 27 (1949) 294-298.

68. THE "OUR FATHER"
(11:1-4)

11 ¹ Once when he happened to be praying in a certain place and after he had finished, one of his disciples said to him, "Lord, teach us to pray, just as John taught his disciples." ² He said to them, "Whenever you pray, say:

" 'Father!

May your name be sanctified!

May your kingdom come!

³ Give us each day our bread for subsistence.

⁴ Forgive us our sins,

    for we too forgive everyone who does wrong to us.

And bring us not into temptation.' "

COMMENT

Luke now incorporates into his travel account an episode in which Jesus, at the request of his disciples, teaches them to pray (11:1-4). Though the Lucan form of the prayer does not use the title "Our Father," I shall speak of it as the Lucan form of the "Our Father," because this title, derived from Matt 6:9, has become traditional and is commonly used.

The Lucan form of the prayer fits well into this context of the Gospel, coming shortly after Jesus' own prayer to the Father (10:21-22), his "example" of neighborly love (10:29-37), and his emphasis on the hearing of the word as the "one thing" necessary (10:38-42). This complex of episodes thus reveals in its own way what the ideal attitude of the Christian disciple toward God should be and the sentiments that that attitude should evoke. The passage, moreover, is the first of three Lucan episodes dealing with prayer (see *HST* 324), being followed by the parable of the persistent friend (11:5-8) and sayings on the efficacy of prayer (11:9-13), the climax of which tells of the gift of the Spirit to be given to those who call on the heavenly Father in prayer.

Three forms of the "Our Father" are known from antiquity. The shortest is the Lucan, with five impvs.; Matt 6:9-13 is longer, with seven impvs.; and a still longer form, with seven impvs. and a doxology, is found in *Did.* 8:2. Apart from the doxology, which is also found in various forms in some mss.

of Matt 6:13, probably based on 1 Chr 29:11-13, and appears to be an early liturgical adaptation of the prayer itself, the *Didache*-form is almost certainly dependent on the Matthean. Matthew and Luke have both derived their prayer from "Q." In the Matthean Gospel the "Our Father" forms part of the sermon on the mount and is presented as an example of prayer contrasted with the display of hypocrites (6:5-6) and the prattling of Gentiles (6:7-8). The collocation there is topical, as it is here, but in a different way.

In the number of impvs., the Lucan form is undoubtedly closer to that of "Q" and to the wording of Jesus himself. This is maintained because of Matthew's penchant for adding phrases to the words of Jesus (see p. 631), even though one can never exclude the possibility that he inherited the prayer in a longer form from an earlier liturgical tradition, which had already added the extra elements. Instead, Matthew has appended phrases: to the end of the opening address *(pace* J. Jeremias, *The Prayers of Jesus,* 32), to the end of the second-person wishes expressed to God, and to the end of the first-pl. petitions asked of God. Thus, "our" and "Who (are) in heaven" *(ho en tois ouranois,* a favorite Matthean attributive [see 5:16,45; 6:1; 7:11,21; 10:32-33; 12:50; 16:17; 18:10,14,19—perhaps derived from Mark 11:25-26; it is never used by Luke, who may have known it, as 11:13 may disclose]); "your will be done on earth as in heaven"; and "deliver us from evil *(or* the evil One)." These elements, which suit indeed the spirit of the prayer, have scarcely been excised by Luke, even though Augustine *(Enchiridion* 116 [CCLat 46.111]) once thought so; similarly M. D. Goulder ("The Composition"). (See further J. Jeremias, *The Lord's Prayer,* 11-12.)

Whereas the Matthean formulation and additions give the prayer a more Jewish cast than the Lucan, Luke has slightly redacted the wording of the prayer. He has changed the aor. impv. *dos* (of "Q") to the pres. *didou* and altered the adv. *sēmeron,* "today," to the distributive phrase *to kath' hēmeran,* "each day." He has disturbed the parallelism in *opheilēmata,* "debts," and *opheiletais,* "debtors" (which Matthew has [from "Q"]; cf. *Did.* 8:2, the sg. *opheilēn,* "debt"), changing the first to *hamartias,* "sins." Luke thus eliminates the Semitic religious connotation of "debt," which may not have been comprehensible to his Gentile Christian readers. He has further altered the perf. *aphēkamen,* "we have forgiven," to a more general pres. *aphiomen,* "we forgive," and made "debtors" more universal, "everyone who does wrong to us" (see NOTE on 11:4; cf. J. Jeremias, *Die Sprache,* 195-196).

The Lucan form of the prayer is introduced by a narrative statement providing a twofold setting for the teaching of it, Jesus himself at prayer and a disciple's request. This has often been thought to represent the "original context" in which Jesus uttered the prayer (e.g. E. E. Ellis, *Gospel of Luke,* 164; I. H. Marshall, *Luke,* 456). That, however, is far from certain. Given the typically Lucan opening, *kai egeneto,* and his emphasis on Jesus at prayer and on counsels to pray (see p. 244), the introduction seems rather to have been

fashioned by Luke's redactional pen. This secondary narrative setting gives to
the Lucan episode the character of a pronouncement-story; but in reality the
prayer must be considered form-critically as another example of sayings of
Jesus. The Lucan setting for the teaching of this prayer provides a solemnity
of occasion, as Jesus instructs his followers in an important feature in their
lives as his disciples and in their relation to God.

The Lucan form of the prayer consists of an address ("Father"), two wishes
uttered before God (in the second sg.), and three petitions asked of him (in
the first pl.). (The Matthean form has an expanded address, three wishes, and
four petitions.)

In this mode of prayer Jesus instructs and authorizes his disciples to address God as "Father," using the very title that he himself employed in his
prayer of praise (10:21 [twice]) and will employ again (22:42). Gal 4:6 and
Rom 8:15, which preserve an early tradition about Spirit-inspired prayer, not
only include the Aramaic counterpart of the address, 'abbā', but reflect a
recollection about how Jesus himself addressed God—in a way exclusive to
himself and otherwise unknown in pre-Christian Palestinian Jewish tradition.
The nuance of intimacy that it carries is thus extended to use by the Christian
community. "Father" is no longer meant in the corporate or collective, national, or covenantal sense of old (see NOTE on 11:2), but suggests an intimate
relationship between the disciples and God that is akin to that of Jesus himself; God is not merely the transcendent lord of the heavens, but is near as a
father to his children. Neither Matthew nor Luke explain the fatherhood of
God further, but the connotation of the Aramaic 'abbā', correctly translated
by Luke (páter), reveals its proper nuance.

The use of the first pl. in the latter part of the prayer reveals further that it
is a prayer addressed to God in their *communal* existence as disciples of
Jesus. (See further N. Perrin, *Rediscovering,* 41; J. Jeremias, *Abba,* 15-67; *The
Prayers of Jesus,* 94-107.)

The two wishes express a form of praise of God which the Christian community utters in its capacity as children of the Father. Neither of them expresses something that human beings can or are expected to bring about. The
parallelism in them formulates a double wish that God may eschatologically
see to the hallowing of his name and the advent of his kingship among human
beings. The first wish concerns the "name" of God and reflects the OT way of
referring to God found in such passages as 2 Sam 6:2; Jer 7:11; Amos 9:12.
But even more specifically, it reflects the OT idea that God would see that his
name would be "sanctified," i.e. vindicated, recognized as holy, and so extolled. This wish probably echoes the prophecy of Ezek 36:22-28. The
prophet was told to instruct the house of Israel that Yahweh was about to
"vindicate the holiness" of his great name, which had been "profaned among
the nations." In restoring Israel and in giving it "a new heart" and "a new
spirit," Yahweh would be removing it from all pagan uncleanness and mani-

festing it as *holy,* i.e. set apart and dedicated to the service of his "holy name." Beneath this conviction runs the current of Israel's basic dedication: "So you shall be holy, because I am holy" (Lev 11:45; see further Isa 5:16; Ezek 20:41; 38:23). As a wish to be expressed by the Christian community, the vindication of the holiness of God's name includes a mode of his activity to be carried out primarily through Jesus, but also through his disciples. The Christian community thus acknowledges this quality and this mode of God's action in human history.

In the second wish the community prays that God's kingly dominion over human life and existence be eschatologically achieved and established, be brought to full realization. For the sense of "kingdom" in the Lucan Gospel, see pp. 154-156; for the various modes of its "coming," see 10:9,11; 17:20; 22:16,18. Again, this is a wish that primarily refers to God's own activity (now in and through Jesus); but in its post-Easter existence the community prays that it will be somehow identified with the working out of such activity. There is scarcely a hint in either of these wishes of an awareness of the delay of the parousia. The double wish expresses the Christian community's praise of God, a manifestation of its faith-relationship to him as Father. On this basis it builds its petitions.

The second part of the Lucan "Our Father" adds to the praise a triple petition. The Christian community is to request the "Father" to sustain it in its daily need of food, to entreat his forgiveness for sin, and to beg of him that it be not confronted with temptation to apostasy. The second petition has an explicative cl.: the disciples state their own attitude of forgiveness toward all who wrong them (cf. Matt 18:23-35). All three petitions thus express a humble confidence and reliance, but also a conviction that they will be heard. Two of them reflect an OT attitude: Just as Israel of old was supplied its daily sustenance in the desert, "bread from heaven . . . a day's portion every day . . . that I may test them, whether they will walk in my law or not" (Exod 16:4; cf. Ps 78:24), so now the Christian community is to pray for its sustenance and to ask that it be not brought to the test. The second petition recognizes that even as children of the "Father" Christian disciples are involved in sin, that they sin and are sinned against. This part of their prayer also echoes OT pleas (see Pss 25:11; 51:5-6; 130:8). The explanation added to it is not to be understood as a *do ut des* attitude or as a "condition," *pace* I. H. Marshall, *Luke,* 460; rather, it springs from the realization that God's forgiveness cannot be expected if human forgiveness is withheld. This petition thus reveals a new sense in which God's fatherhood implies an awareness of human brotherhood.

Are all the wishes and petitions to be understood eschatologically? The stress on the futuristic, eschatological significance of them is more readily admitted for the Matthean "Our Father" than for the Lucan. The redactional changes in the latter have modified this stress. In the Lucan form the wishes are undoubtedly still to be understood as eschatological. But the petitions, especially that for daily sustenance and for preservation from apostasy, are more properly to be understood of the Christian disciples' present condition. The same is probably true of the second petition (for forgiveness) too.

For what kind of bread is the Christian community to pray? The NOTE on v. 3 sets forth the historical and modern attempts to explain the adj. *epiousios*. After long consideration, I have reverted to the explanation given by Origen, "our bread for subsistence," i.e. our essential bread. Though he eventually allegorized it as "the bread of heaven" and started a tradition of understanding it as "supersubstantial" (Jerome's word), referring it to the Eucharist, many patristic writers frankly understood it as the bread "that sustains this life," "what is suited to the essence, life, and constitution of our body." (So Cyril of Alexandria, Cyril of Jerusalem, Basil, Chrysostom, Euthymius Zigabenus [for the vagaries of patristic and medieval interpretation, see J. Hennig, "Our Daily Bread," and J. Carmignac, *Recherches].)* The OT background of God feeding his people with manna would support this natural, material understanding of *ton arton hēmōn ton epiousion.* This seems to be the best explanation of the bread for which Christians are to pray, as far as Stage I of the gospel tradition would be concerned.

But just as the manna was eventually allegorized in the pre-Christian Jewish tradition itself as "the bread of angels" (Ps 78:25 LXX; the MT there calls it *leḥem 'abbîrîm,* "the bread of the mighty" *[NAB];* Wis 16:20), so it is difficult to restrict "our bread for subsistence" to the natural sense in Stage III of the gospel tradition, especially in a NT writer like Luke for whom "the breaking of the bread" (24:35; Acts 2:42,46; 20:7,11) has Eucharistic overtones. In this context the Christian community would be thus praying for the "bread of subsistence" in the kingdom.

In many respects the "Our Father" is a thoroughly Jewish prayer, for almost every word of it could be uttered by a devout Jew—with the exception perhaps of the adj. *epiousios* (depending on how that is understood) and of the initial address (the Matthean form would be more customary than the Lucan). Parallels to the address (in the Matthean form), to the wishes, and to the petitions have been found in Jewish prayer-forms. For "Our Father," see Isa 63:16; 64:7; 1 Chr 29:10; Tob 13:4; Sir 51:10 (Hebrew); for "who (are) in heaven," see *Mekilta* of Exod 20:25, "their Father in heaven, the Holy One." (On the Lucan "Father," see NOTE.) For the first wish, cf. "May his great name be extolled and hallowed in the world which he has created according to his will" *(Qaddiš;* see *Encyclopedia judaica* [Jerusalem: Keter, 1971] 10. 660). For the second, cf. "May he cause his kingdom to rule in your lifetime and in your days, and in the lifetime of all the House of Israel" *(Qaddiš;* ibid.). For the first petition, see Prov 30:8, "Provide me only with the food I need" *(NIV;* MT *leḥem ḥuqqî,* rendered in the targum as *laḥmā' <dĕ>mistî).* For the second petition, cf. "Forgive us, Our Father, for we have sinned; pardon us, Our King, for we have transgressed" *(Amidah* 6; see L. Finkelstein, *JQR* 16 [1925-1926] 146-147). For the last petition, cf. "Bring me not into the power of sin, or into the power of guilt, or into the power of temptation" *(b. Berak.* 60b). Even though many of the Jewish prayers that are often used for such comparisons (see further J. J. Petuchowski and M. Brocke, *The Lord's Prayer and Jewish Liturgy)* date from centuries well after the NT (e.g. the *Qaddiš* is first referred to in the sixth century A.D.; the Babylonian talmudic tractate *Berakot* is Amoraic [fourth-fifth centuries A.D.]) and may have been themselves influenced by the NT forms, the parallels reveal the basically Jewish form and content of the prayer.

To the extent that one can reconstruct the original Aramaic form of the prayer, one may dare to say:

'Abbā',	Father!
yitqaddaš šĕmāk,	May your name be sanctified!
tē'têh malkûtāk,	May your kingdom come!
laḥmánā' dî mistĕyā' hab lánāh yômā' dĕnāh,	Give us this day our bread for subsistence.
ûšĕbuq lánāh ḥôbaynā' kĕdî šĕbáqnā' lĕḥayyābaynā',	Forgive us our debts, as we have forgiven our debtors.
wĕ'al ta'ĕlinnánā' lĕnisyôn.	And bring us not into temptation.

If one were to prefer "bread for the future," it would be *laḥmánā' dî limḥar.* The Matthean additions would run thus: *'Ăbûnā' dî bišmayyā',* "Our Father, who (are) in heaven"; *tihwêh rĕ'ûtāk hêk dî bišmayyā' 'ap 'al 'ar'ā',* "May your will be (done), as in heaven, also on earth"; and *bĕram 'aṣṣélnā' min bĕ'îšā',* "but rescue us from evil *(or* the evil One).''

That the prayer might have been uttered by Jesus in Hebrew, rather than in Aramaic, is a possibility that no one can exclude; but that raises the whole question of whether Jesus would naturally have been using Hebrew rather than the commonly spoken Aramaic in his teaching (see further *WA* 38-46). I prefer the Aramaic explanation. The reconstruction of the original Aramaic form of the "Our Father" will always remain problematic, conditioned above all by our knowledge of the Palestinian Aramaic of Jesus' days.

Significantly, the Lucan form of the prayer contains elements that can be illustrated from numerous passages in the Third Gospel which depict Jesus himself at prayer, so that it becomes a succinct summary of his teaching. (See further P. Edmonds, "The Lucan Our Father.")

NOTES

11 1. *when he happened to be praying.* Lit. "and it happened, in his praying, . . . (that) one of his disciples said . . ." Luke again uses *kai egeneto* without the conj. *kai,* but with a finite vb. *(eipen,* see p. 119). In 9:18 the disciples were also present when Jesus was at prayer.

after he had finished. Lit. "when he finished." This cl. is subordinate to the articular infin. *en tō einai.*

one of his disciples. See NOTES on 5:30; 6:13,17; 8:9; 9:10,40. The disciple remains unnamed.

Lord. See NOTE on *kyrie* (voc.) in 5:8.

teach us to pray. The disciples, struck by Jesus' constant example in this Gospel, desire to commune with God as their master does. But they add another reason.

just as John taught his disciples. See NOTE on 5:33, where reference is also made to the prayer of the disciples of the Baptist. Nowhere do we learn what or how they were taught to pray. It is insinuated that reference is being made to some prayer-form used by John that is different from the ordinary. For Essene forms of prayer in contemporary Judaism, see 1QS 10:1-11:22 and the whole of the *Hôdāyôt (Thanksgiving Psalms).* See further J. A. T. Robinson, "The Baptism of John and the Qumran Community," *HTR* 50 (1957) 177; H. Braun, *Qumran* 1. 88.

2. *Whenever you pray.* The preferred reading is the pres. subjunc. *proseuchēsthe* (of mss. ℵ, B, D, L, Ξ, Ψ, and the Koine text-tradition); some mss. (P75, A, C, P, W, etc.) have, however, the pres. indic. *proseuchesthe.* The subjunc. is preferred with the conj. *hotan,* expressing a present general temporal idea, "whenever." See ZBG § 325. The Lucan formulation has a slightly different nuance from Matt 6:9, "So *(houtōs)* you are to pray." Neither stresses the duty to pray; but the Lucan formulation presents the "Our Father" as the *mode* of *all* Christian prayer, whereas the Matthean gives it merely as *an* example. This Lucan introduction has tended to make the "Our Father" a very common Christian prayer; but it was apparently understood otherwise in the early church, where its use was reserved for the baptized and its utterance surrounded with a certain awe (as witnessed in the ancient Roman liturgy, *Audemus dicere,* "we make bold to say"). See further T. W. Manson, "The Lord's Prayer," *BJRL* 38 (1955-1956) 99-113, 436-448.

Father! Luke uses the simple Greek voc. *páter,* as in 10:21 (see NOTE there), equaling Aramaic *'abbā',* the original address used by Jesus. Moreover, the fact that *'abbā'* is preserved in Mark 14:36; Gal 4:6; Rom 8:15 argues for this Lucan form of address as more original than Matthew's "Our Father who (are) in heaven." Some Lucan mss. (A, C, D, W, and the Koine text-tradition) add, however, "Our" and "who (are) in heaven" at this point, but these additions are the result of a copyist's harmonization with the Matthean formula.

In the OT God is referred to as Father. The people of Israel are his children, his firstborn, and their king is his son (Deut 14:1; Hos 11:1-3; 2 Sam 7:14). The title is used of God explicitly when he is considered as creator (Deut 32:6; Mal 2:10), as lord of his chosen people (Jer 3:19; 31:9; Isa 63:16; Tob 13:4), as one sinned against by

Israel (Jer 3:4-5; Mal 1:6), and as the one from whom mercy and forgiveness come (Ps 103:13; Isa 64:7-8 [64:8-9E]). God is acknowledged by Israel as "our Father," and David is to address him as "my Father" (Ps 89:27). In all these passages God is Father in a corporate, national, or covenantal sense. The use of the title by an individual in prayer is rare in pre-Christian Palestinian Judaism; it may occur in Sir 23:1,4; 51:10, but these passages are problematic and uncertain. See J. Jeremias, *Prayers,* 23 n. 51, 28.

Against this pre-Christian Jewish background, the use of *'abbā'* or *páter* is regarded as "striking and unusual" and even "quite extraordinary" (W. G. Kümmel, *Theology of the New Testament,* 40). Even if one takes into consideration all the rabbinical references to God as Father from "ancient Palestinian Judaism" collected by J. Jeremias *(Prayers,* 16-29), one is struck by his conclusion: *"There is as yet no evidence in the literature of ancient Palestinian Judaism that 'my Father' is used as a personal address to God" (Prayers,* 29 [his italics]). A fortiori, no evidence for the simple *'abbā'.* See my forthcoming article, "Abba and Jesus' Relation to God," *Mélanges Jacques Dupont* (Paris: Cerf, 198?).

Aramaic *'abbā'* in its origin may be a child's word, expressive of family intimacy. The form is in the emphatic state in Aramaic, and that is why it turns up literally translated as *ho patēr* in Mark 14:36, etc., whereas Lucan *páter* is the better Greek translation of it. Cp. *malkā',* "O King," Dan 2:4 with the voc. *basileu* in the LXX.

The simplicity of the address, "Father," stands in contrast with the elaborate modes of addressing God used in many Jewish prayers. R. Bultmann *(Theology,* 1.23-24) compared

> the ornate, emotional, often liturgically beautiful, but often overloaded forms of address in Jewish prayers with the stark simplicity of "Father"! The "Prayer of Eighteen Petitions," for instance, which the devout Jew is expected to say three times daily, begins, "Lord God of Abraham, God of Isaac, God of Jacob! God Most High, Creator of heaven and earth! Our Shield and the Shield of our fathers!" The "Lord's Prayer" stands out above Jewish prayers not only in its simple address but in its direct simplicity throughout . . . God is near; He hears and understands the requests which come thronging to Him, as a father understands the requests of his own child. . . .

Jesus teaches his disciples to address God as he himself addressed him (10:21). But it is important to note, as has G. Bornkamm *(Jesus of Nazareth* [New York: Harper & Row, 1975] 128), "there is nowhere a passage where he himself joins with his disciples in an 'Our Father.'" From Jesus' own use of *'abbā'* some commentators have sought to conclude to Jesus' awareness of his own "unique sonship," an implication already discussed in the prayer of 10:21. See further G. Dalman, *Words of Jesus,* 190; cf. J. D. G. Dunn, *Jesus and the Spirit* (London: SCM, 1975) 21-37.

May your name be sanctified! Luke preserves the aor. pass. impv. (third sg.) *hagiasthētō* of "Q," as does Matt 6:9 and *Did.* 8:2. It expresses a punctiliar mode of action suited for the eschatological nuance of this wish. Cf. John 12:28 for a Johannine way of expressing this praise. For the sense of the wish, see COMMENT.

May your kingdom come! Codex Bezae adds at the beginning of this wish, "upon us" *(eph' hēmas).* Some minor mss. (162, 700), Marcion, and some patristic writers

(Gregory of Nyssa, Maximus the Confessor) have a different form of this petition: "May your holy Spirit come upon us and purify us" (a modification probably derived from the use of the prayer in a baptismal liturgy; it is hardly [pace R. Leaney, "The Lucan Text of the Lord's Prayer," 103-111] an original part of the prayer or even of the Lucan form of it). Cf. B. M. Metzger, *Manuscripts of the Greek Bible* (New York: Oxford University, 1981) 122. The best Lucan mss. read *elthetō* (second aor. impv. third sg.), again expressing punctiliar action suited to the eschatological nuance of the wish. The "coming" of God's kingdom is not an OT notion.

Some mss. (A, C, D, W, Δ, Θ, and the Koine text-tradition) add, "May your will be done on earth as in heaven." This is again, however, the result of a copyist's harmonization with the Matthean form of the prayer.

3. *Give us each day.* For the adv. *sēmeron,* "today," of "Q" (see Matt 6:11), Luke has substituted the phrase *to kath' hēmeran,* "each day, daily" (see Luke 9:23; 16:19; 19:47; 22:53; Acts 2:46,47; 3:2; 16:11; 17:11). The phrase is also used in a distributive sense in Aristophanes, *Knights* 1126. Cf. the LXX of Lev 23:37, where *eis hēmeran* is added. The distributive sense suits the pres. impv. *didou,* expressive of continuous action ("keep on giving"), which Luke has also substituted. It divests the "Q" form of the petition of its eschatological thrust (aor. impv. *dos).* See BDF § 335, 336.3; ZBG § 242.

our bread for subsistence. The phrase *ton arton hēmōn ton epiousion* also occurs in Matt 6:11 and *Did.* 8:2. The sense of the adj. *epiousios* has been obscure since the beginning. Origen *(De oratione* 27.7; GCS, 2.366-367) maintained that it was unknown both in Greek literature and in ordinary Greek parlance and that it had been invented by the evangelists. The word is not found with certainty in any extrabiblical text; it is often said to occur in a fifth-century A.D. papyrus (see F. Preisigke, *Sammelbuch griechischen Urkunden aus Ägypten* [Strassburg: Trübner, 1915-1958], 1.5224:20 *epiousi[ ],* supposedly = Latin *diaria,* "daily ration"), but the papyrus is no longer accessible for checking and the original publisher (A. Sayce) was notorious for his inaccuracy in reading and transcribing. See B. M. Metzger, "How Many Times," 52-54.

Ancient versions and writers rendered *epiousios* in various ways: (a) Old Syriac (followed by the Armenian): *'myn',* "continual"; (b) Old Latin *(Vetus Itala): quotidianus,* "daily"; (c) Peshitta: *děsunqānan,* "of our need"; (d) Origen: *eis tēn ousian symballomenon arton,* "bread being of service for (our) being" *(De oratione* 27.7; GCS, 2.367); (e) John Chrysostom: *ton ephēmeron,* "daily" *(Hom. in Matt.* 19.5; PG 57.280); (f) Jerome: *quotidianus,* "daily" (in the Vg of Luke), but *supersubstantialis,* "supersubstantial" (in the Vg of Matthew and in some other writings: *Comm. in Ps.* 135.25; CCLat 78.295; *Comm. in Matt.* 6.11; CCLat 77.37); *substantivum (sive superventurum),* "substantive *(or* about to come)" *(Comm. in Ezek.* 6.18,5-9; CCLat 75.239); *praecipuum, egregium, peculiarem,* "principal, choice, peculiar" (because he understood *epiousios* as = to *periousios* of e.g. LXX Deut 7:6; *Comm. in Tit.* 2.14; PL 26.622-623). But Jerome also said that he had found "in evangelio quod appellatur secundum Hebraeos [which we usually call today *The Gospel of the Nazaraeans* (see Hennecke-Schneemelcher, *NTApocrypha,* 1. 147)] *maar* [= Hebrew *māḥār,* "tomorrow"], quod dicitur crastinum . . . *Panem nostrum crastinum,* id est futurum, *da nobis hodie" (Comm. in Matt.* 6.11; CCLat 77.37; cf. *Comm. in Ps.* 135.25; CCLat 78.295), "Our bread of the morrow (that is, future bread) give us today."

Modern commentators are likewise divided in explaining the meaning of the adj. The most commonly used explanations are the following (for a list of those who use each one, see J. Carmignac, *Recherches,* 118-221). Etymologically, *epiousios* is explained as derived from:

(a) *epi + ousia* ("substance, being, essence"): "bread for subsistence, necessary for existence, essential." This explanation follows Origen's analysis. See above. The prep. *epi* is explained as expressing purpose or goal (see BAGD 289a) or as an empty prefix (H. Bourgoin, *"Epiousios* expliqué par la notion de préfixe vide," 91-96). Some who use this explanation restrict it to a material sense of "bread" or "food" required for daily survival. Cf. Prov 30:8. Others follow Origen in giving it an added (allegorical) nuance, "the living bread which came down from heaven" (cf. John 6:41,51,58), food of "the tree of life," or "the bread of angels." Cf. Ps 78:25 LXX. Even though one encounters difficulty in saying what the underlying Aramaic might have been for this meaning of the adj., it is still the best explanation of the Greek word in the existing prayer (in all three extant forms). Most likely it would have been understood originally in the material sense. See COMMENT, p. 900. Cf. Acts 14:17; 17:25c.

(b) *epi + ousa* (pres. ptc. of *eimí,* "be," with which *hēmera,* "day," has to be understood): "bread for the current day, for today, daily." This explanation follows John Chrysostom's analysis (see above); he understood it in a material sense and insisted on it because of Jesus' words about no anxiety for the morrow (Matt 6:34). It seems to gain support because it may reflect the manna to be gathered *děbar yôm běyômô,* "a day's portion for its day" (Exod 16:4; LXX: *to tēs hēmeras eis hēmeran).* This explanation has been insisted on recently by J. Starcky, arguing for a Hebrew *Vorlage* of the prayer ("La quatrième demande du Pater," 401-409); and by P. Grelot, arguing instead for an Aramaic *Vorlage* ("La quatrième demande du 'Pater,' " 299-314), basing his explanation on *sěkôm yôm běyômeh* of *Tg. Neof. 1* on Exod 16:4. However, if "daily" were meant, there are all sorts of words in the Greek language that could have expressed that unambiguously: *ephēmerios, kathēmerios, hēmerinos, kathēmerinos,* etc. Moreover, the adj. is actually tautological in such an explanation, the phrase of Exod 16:4 notwithstanding. Finally, aside from the late date of *Tg. Neof. 1,* the word *sěkôm* is simply unattested in the Aramaic of the Middle phase (in the period between 200 B.C. and A.D. 200). Was it in use then?

(c) *epi + iousa* (pres. ptc. of *eîmí,* "come," with which *hēmera* is again understood): "bread for the coming (day)" or "for the future." The phrase is attested in Greek literature: *hē epiousa hēmera* (Aristophanes, *Eccles.* 105; Polybius, *Hist.* 2.25,11; Acts 7:26); even abbreviated, *hē epiousa* (Acts 16:11; 20:15; 21:18; 23:11—but cf. Plato, *Crito* 44a, where it seems to mean "today"). To this explanation could be related the meaning that Jerome said he found in *The Gospel of the Nazaraeans* (see above), "of the morrow" *(crastinum).* This explanation would suit well the eschatological interpretation of the "Our Father." If it were understood in the material sense, it would be difficult to reconcile with the saying of Jesus about no anxiety for the morrow (Matt 6:34—it would be less of a difficulty in the Lucan Gospel, where that saying is omitted; cf. *Mekilta,* "Wayyassa'," 3.27). But, like the foregoing explanation, it presupposes that *hēmera* is to be understood in *epiousios*—which is far from certain. For this

reason, B. Orchard ("The Meaning of *ton epiousion"*) has recently insisted on a different sense of *epeimi,* not a temporal sense, but simply "come upon" (LSJ 614b): "the
bread that we come upon." Though this solves one problem, it makes the bread that
Christians are to pray for a strange sort of bread; the petition is scarcely that we learn
to be satisfied with "the bread that is made present."

For other less likely explanations, see BAGD 297. The problematic *Greek* adj.—and
one has to insist that it is a problem on the Greek level of the tradition—is probably
best explained by Origen, but without his allegorical interpretation of it.

4. *Forgive us our sins.* Luke has changed *opheilēmata,* "debts," to *hamartias,* "sins,"
probably to make the petition more intelligible for Gentile Christian readers, since,
though *opheilēma* is found in classical and Hellenistic Greek in the sense of a "debt,"
the religious sense of it is unattested there. See MM 468; BAGD 598. In an Aramaic
text, however, from Qumran Cave 4 (4QMess ar 2:17) "sin and debt" (or "guilt") are
found in juxtaposition *(ḥṭ'h wḥwbt',* see *MPAT* § 28). The "forgiveness" of "sins"
would be just as intelligible in Palestinian Judaism as that of "debts." See 11QtgJob
38:2-3 *(wšbq lhwn ḥṭ'yhwn bdylh,* "and he [God] forgave them [Job's friends] their sins
because of him [Job]"; see *MPAT* § 5:38,2-3). The change from "debts" to "sins" also
adapts the "Our Father" to an important Lucan way of expressing an effect of the
Christ-event. See pp. 223-224.

The ms. D and the OL version read "debts," again harmonizing the Lucan text with
the Matthean.

for we too forgive everyone who does wrong to us. Luke uses the pres. *aphiomen*
instead of the perf. *aphēkamen* of "Q" (see Matt 6:12), "we have forgiven"; *Did.* 8:2
has the regular form of the pres. *aphiemen,* which also appears in some Lucan mss.
(‎‭ℵ*, L, Θ). Luke has used the vb. *opheilein,* meaning "owe," "be indebted [to]," but in
the sense of "do wrong to." See BAGD 599; F. Hauck, *TDNT* 5. 560; cf. W. Dittenberger, *Sylloge inscriptionum graecarum* (4 vols.; Hildesheim: Olms, 1960) §
1042:15. For Luke that forgiveness becomes universal *(panti,* "everyone") and is related to God's present forgiveness (and not just in the eschaton).

bring us not into temptation. The Lucan Jesus will formulate an echo of this petition
in a cautionary word to his disciples in 22:40,46, "Pray that you enter not into temptation." Here the prayer is phrased differently, and more boldly; they are to pray that
God will not bring them to temptation/test. In the OT God is often said to bring his
people Israel to a/the test. See Exod 16:4; 20:20; Deut 8:2,16; 13:4; 33:8; Judg 2:22.
Echoing such a mode of thinking Jesus now instructs his disciples to pray that God
will not bring them to *the* test (of apostasy). As in the OT, there is involved here a
protological way of thinking that human beings may end up in a status of apostasy
and that God is somehow the cause of it. It is labeled protological because it is an
attempt to explain the condition of apostasy, but it is not a fully logical attempt. All
the good and the evil that come to human beings (in this way of thinking) are ascribed
to God, the cause of everything. There had not yet emerged in the history of ideas the
distinction between God's absolute and permissive will; so everything was ascribed to
him. When that distinction emerged (in the debates about predestination), God was
then said to permit people to fall into temptation or apostasy, but he did not will it
absolutely. This distinction was not known in OT times and was not operative in the
thinking of Jesus as he formulated this petition of the "Our Father." This kind of

thinking is found elsewhere in the NT, e.g. in Rom 9:18b, where Paul says that God "hardens the heart of whomever he wills" (in a context of the hardening of the heart of the Pharaoh [see Exod 9:12]). A reaction to the way of protological thinking present in this petition of the "Our Father" begins to appear in the NT, in Jas 1:13-15, "Let no one say when he is tempted, 'I am tempted by God'; for . . . he himself tempts no one." Later Marcion objected to that mode of thinking too. See J. Carmignac, *Recherches*, 236-304. Attempts to get around this way of translating the petition are well known in modern Romance languages ("et ne nous laissez pas succomber à la tentation" [contrast the Traduction oecuménique and the *BJ:* "et ne nous soumets pas à la tentation"]; "y no nos dejes caer en la tentación"). The positive value of *peirasmos*, "test, temptation," is expressed elsewhere in the NT (see Jas 1:12; Rev 2:10; 1 Pet 4:12-13); but this view is not shared by Luke. See S. Brown, *Apostasy*, 15-16. For Luke this "temptation" is not restricted to an eschatological trial, but is extended to the constant danger of apostasy; cf. 8:14-15; Acts 20:19. See J. M. Creed, *The Gospel*, 157.

Some Lucan mss. ($\aleph^1$, A, C, D, R, W, and the Koine text-tradition) add "But deliver us from evil," again the result of a copyist's harmonization with the Matthean form. The doxology is completely lacking in Lucan mss. at this point (on its different forms in Matthew and the *Didache,* see *TCGNT* 16-17). It was probably added to reduce the impact of the Matthean form of the prayer ending with the temptation petition.

BIBLIOGRAPHY (11:1-4)

Ashton, J. "Our Father," *The Way* 18 (1978) 83-91.

Bandstra, A. J. "The Original Form of the Lord's Prayer," *Calvin Theological Journal* 16 (1981) 15-37.

Brown, R. E. "The Pater Noster as an Eschatological Prayer," *TS* 22 (1961) 175-208; reprinted, *New Testament Essays* (Milwaukee, WI: Bruce, 1965) 217-253.

Bussche, H. van den. *Understanding the Lord's Prayer* (New York: Sheed and Ward, 1963).

Carmignac, J. "Hebrew Translations of the Lord's Prayer: An Historical Survey," *Biblical and Near Eastern Studies: Essays in Honor of William Sanford LaSor* (ed. G. A. Tuttle; Grand Rapids, MI: Eerdmans, 1978) 18-79.

——— *Recherches sur le "Notre Père"* (Paris: Letouzey et Ané, 1969; abundant older bibliography can be found in this work; see review of it by R. E. Brown, *CBQ* 32 [1970] 264-266).

Dalman, G. *Die Worte Jesu,* 283-365 (Anhang A: Das Vaterunser).

Dewailly, L.-M. " 'Donne-nous notre pain': Quel pain? Notes sur la quatrième demande du Pater," *RSPT* 64 (1980) 561-588.

Edmonds, P. "The Lucan Our Father: A Summary of Luke's Teaching on Prayer?" *ExpTim* 91 (1979-1980) 140-143.

Elliott, J. K. "Did the Lord's Prayer Originate with John the Baptist?" *TZ* 29 (1973) 215.

Fiebig, P. *Das Vaterunser: Ursprung, Sinn und Bedeutung des christlichen Hauptgebetes* (Gütersloh: Bertelsmann, 1927).

Freudenberger, R. "Zum Text der zweiten Vaterunserbitte," *NTS* 15 (1968-1969) 419-432.

Goulder, M. D. "The Composition of the Lord's Prayer," *JTS* 14 (1963) 32-45.

Jeremias, J. *Abba,* 15-67.

——— "Abba," *The Central Message of the New Testament* (London: SCM, 1965) 9-30.

——— *The Lord's Prayer* (Facet Books, Biblical Series 8; Philadelphia: Fortress, 1973).

——— *The Prayers of Jesus* (Philadelphia: Fortress, 1978).

Kruse, H. " 'Pater Noster' et passio Christi," *VD* 46 (1968) 3-29.

Kuhn, K.-G. *Achtzehngebet und Vaterunser und der Reim* (WUNT 1; Tübingen: Mohr [Siebeck], 1950).

Kuss, O. "Das Vaterunser," *Auslegung und Verkündigung,* 2. 277-333.

Leaney, R. "The Lucan Text of the Lord's Prayer (Lk xi 2-4)," *NovT* 1 (1956) 103-111.

Lohmeyer, E. *Das Vater-unser* (2d ed.; Göttingen: Vandenhoeck & Ruprecht, 1947).

Marchel, W. *Abba Père! La prière du Christ et des chrétiens* (AnBib 19; Rome: Biblical Institute, 1963) 191-202.

Ott, W. *Gebet und Heil,* 112-123.

Petuchowski, J. J., and M. Brocke. *The Lord's Prayer and Jewish Liturgy* (New York: Seabury, 1978).

Schürmann, H. *Praying with Christ: The "Our Father" for Today* (New York: Herder and Herder, 1964); *Das Gebet des Herrn als Schlüssel zum Verstehen Jesu* (4th ed.; Freiburg im B.: Herder, 1981).

Tilborg, S. van. "A Form-Criticism of the Lord's Prayer," *NovT* 14 (1972) 94-105.

Van Bruggen, J. "The Lord's Prayer and Textual Criticism," *Calvin Theological Journal* 17 (1982) 78-87 (with a reply by J. A. Bandstra, pp. 88-97).

Vögtle, A. "Der 'eschatologische' Bezug der Wir-Bitten des Vaterunser," *Jesus und Paulus: Festschrift für Werner Georg Kümmel zum 70. Geburtstag* (Göttingen: Vandenhoeck & Ruprecht, 1975) 344-362.

Willis, G. G. "Lead Us Not into Temptation," *Downside Review* 93 (1975) 281-288.

The Meaning of epiousios

Baker, A. "What Sort of Bread Did Jesus Want Us to Pray for?" *New Blackfriars* 54 (1973) 125-129.

Black, M. "The Aramaic of *ton arton hēmōn ton epiousion* (Matt vi. 11 = Luke xi. 3)," *JTS* 42 (1941) 186-189.

Bourgoin, H. "*Epiousios* expliqué par la notion de préfixe vide," *Bib* 60 (1979) 91-96.

Braun, F.-M. "Le pain dont nous avons besoin: *Mt* 6, 11; *Lc* 11, 3," *NRT* 100 (1978) 559-568.

Carmignac, J. *Recherches,* 118-221 (with older bibliography).

Debrunner, A. "*Epiousios,*" *Glotta* 4 (1913) 249-253.

Dewailly, L.-M. "Vilket bröd avses i Fader vår?" *SEA* 45 (1980) 77-89.

Dornseiff, F. *"Epiousios* im Vaterunser," *Glotta* 35 (1956) 145-149.

Falcone, S. A. "The Kind of Bread We Pray for in the Lord's Prayer," *Essays in Honor of Joseph P. Brennan* (ed. R. F. McNamara; Rochester, NY: St. Bernard's Seminary, 1976) 36-59.

Foerster, W. *"Epiousios,"* *TDNT* 2. 590-599.

Foucault, J.-A. de. "Notre pain quotidien," *REG* 83 (1970) 56-62.

Grelot, P. "La quatrième demande du 'Pater' et son arrière-plan sémitique," *NTS* 25 (1978-1979) 299-314.

Hauck, F. *"Artos epiousios,"* *ZNW* 33 (1934) 199-202.

Hemmerdinger, B. "Un élément pythagoricien dans le Pater," *ZNW* 63 (1972) 121.

Hennig, J. "Our Daily Bread," *TS* 4 (1943) 445-454.

Metzger, B. M. "How Many Times Does 'Epiousios' Occur outside the Lord's Prayer?" *ExpTim* 69 (1957-1958) 52-54; "Num bis relata sit, extra orationem dominicam, vox *epiousios?*" *VD* 34 (1956) 349-350.

Müller, C. *"Epiousios,"* *EWNT* 2. 79-81.

Orchard, B. "The Meaning of *ton epiousion* (Mt 6:11 = Lk 11:3)," *BTB* 3 (1973) 274-282.

Schmid, W. *"Epiousios,"* *Glotta* 6 (1915) 28-29.

Shearman, T. G. "Our Daily Bread," *JBL* 53 (1934) 110-117.

Starcky, J. "La quatrième demande du Pater," *HTR* 64 (1971) 401-409.

Wimmerer, R. "Noch einmal *epiousios,"* *Glotta* 12 (1923) 68-82.

69. THE PARABLE OF THE PERSISTENT FRIEND
(11:5-8)

11 ⁵ Then he said to them, "Suppose one of you has a friend, and he comes at midnight and says, 'My friend, lend me three loaves of bread, ⁶ since a friend of mine on a journey has just arrived and I have nothing to put before him.' ⁷ And suppose the man inside replies, 'Do not bother me! The door is already bolted, and my children and I are in bed. I cannot get up and give you anything now.' ⁸ I tell you, even if he will not get up and give it to him because he is his friend, because of his persistence he will rouse himself and give him as much as he needs."

COMMENT

Following on the Lucan form of the "Our Father" at this point in the travel account is a parable drawn from Palestinian folk-traditions about a person who is surprised at midnight by the arrival of an unexpected friend and who finds that he does not have the wherewithal to show him hospitality (11:5-8). It forms the second of three passages topically arranged, dealing with a favorite Lucan theme, viz. prayer (see pp. 244-247).

This parable is found only in the Lucan Gospel and is derived from "L." In form, it is devoid of any introductory comparison and begins instead with a rhetorical question. Moreover, it also lacks an explicit conclusion or application. Cf. J. Jeremias, *Die Sprache,* 196-198.

Coming on the heels of the "Our Father," it acts as a further "exhortation to prayer" *(HST* 199), even though one may wonder whether it were originally proposed apropos of some specific petition now lost in the gospel tradition. In the Lucan context, it points up the mode of prayer of petition exemplified in the "Our Father" itself. In the Matthean Gospel, by contrast, the "Our Father" is followed by a caution about God's forgiveness being conditional on human willingness to forgive others. Here in the Lucan context it serves to stress persistence in human prayer to God, as a later exclusively Lucan parable will also do (18:1-8). The stress is peculiarly Lucan and stands in contrast to the advice given in Matt 6:8 about God's knowing well in advance what humans need. It emphasizes the certainty that the prayer will be heard; the "friend" who has the unexpected guest on his hands will not take no for an answer; implied is the neighbor's realization that he and his family will only get sleep if he yields to the persistent request of the "friend." The neighbor who yields to persistence becomes the foil for the heavenly Father. But, as G. B. Caird notes *(Gospel of St Luke,* 152), "God does not have to be waked or cajoled into giving us what we need—many gifts he bestows on the ungodly and ungrateful; but his choicest blessings are reserved for those who will value them and who show their appreciation by asking until they receive." Indeed, Luke's Greek word for "persistence" actually means "shamelessness."

It may, however, be a mistake to press the parable too much and to ask what sort of picture of God it conveys. To avoid such an implication, some commentators have even proposed that it is not a parable about a persistent friend, but rather about a friend roused at midnight by a request for help (see J. Jeremias, *Parables,* 157-158; G. Schneider, *Evangelium nach Lukas,* 260; J. Schmid, *Evangelium nach Lukas,* 198-199). Jeremias would distinguish the Lucan context and conclusion (v. 8), which makes it "an exhortation to unwearied prayer" (especially because of vv. 9-13), from the real parable: vv.

5-7 should be regarded as one continuous rhetorical question—Can you imagine such a thing happening? Unthinkable! "Under no circumstances would he [the neighbor] leave his friend's request unanswered," if one understands the custom of oriental hospitality. The central figure is not the petitioning friend, but the one roused from sleep. Thus God becomes the one who hearkens to the cry of the needy and comes to their help. While this *may* have been the meaning of the parable in Stage I—much depends on whether the Greek text of v. 7 can be forced to be read as the continuation of the question begun in v. 5—the parable has certainly been used by Luke for another purpose, already stated above.

NOTES

11   5. *he said to them.* Luke uses again the prep. *pros* + acc. See p. 116.

Suppose one of you has a friend. Lit. "Who of you will have a friend and he will come to him at midnight and will say to him?" The sentence has an awkward change of subj.; the peculiar use of personal prons. makes it impossible to translate it exactly into English. The parable begins with a rhetorical question introduced by *tís ex hymōn,* "Who of you?" or "Which one of you?" Cf. 11:11; 12:25; 14:28; 15:4; 17:7; cf. 14:5; Hag 2:3; Isa 42:23; 50:10 for OT parallels. In the OT the phrase does not introduce a parable. There is little certainty that it is a sign of *ipsissima verba* of Jesus, *pace* J. Jeremias, *Parables,* 103. The question actually presents a situation challenging the hearer to a judgment about it.

The situation is one drawn from Palestinian folk-customs: A traveler, moving by night to avoid the heat of the day, arrives at the house of a friend; his late arrival is unexpected and his friend discovers that his cupboard is bare. Yet it is imperative that he grant hospitality to his unexpected guest; what is his host to do? There are no shops; bread would not be baked until morning.

The third vb. *(eipē,* "will say") is actually a subjunc. in the best mss.; but some others (A, D, K, R, W, etc.) read *erei,* a fut. indic., parallel to the first two. This is probably owing to scribal harmonization.

My friend. The repetitive use of forms of *philos,* "friend," builds up the background of ancient Near Eastern hospitality, which the protasis in v. 8 eventually exploits. "Friend" is used in two senses; the neighbors are friends, and so are the host and guest. The apostrophe that is used is significantly absent in v. 7. As the parable now stands in the Lucan context, its absence there is probably to be understood as a mark of annoyance.

three loaves of bread. Lit. "three breads," maybe something like three rolls. According to J. Jeremias *(Parables,* 157), it is the equivalent of a meal for one person, and it would be expected that the friend return them once the housewife had baked hers. But A. Plummer *(The Gospel,* 299) is probably right in thinking that there is no need to seek any meaning in the number three.

6. *since.* See NOTE on 1:34.

has just arrived. The best mss. read the second aor. *paregeneto;* but ms. D reads the historical pres. *parestin ap' agrou,* "has arrived from (the) country."

7. *replies.* Lit. "will say in reply" *(apokritheis eipē* [see p. 114]). Whether this is to be taken as a real reply or as a continuation of the supposition of vv. 5-6, see COMMENT on pp. 910-911.

already bolted. I.e. for some time now. Cf. 14:17.

in bed. Eis + acc. is used without a vb. of motion as a substitute for the prep. *en.* See BDF § 205. One has to envisage a single-room house with members of the family asleep on mats; to get up and draw the bolt would be to disturb everyone.

get up. See NOTE on 1:39 *(anastas).*

8. *I tell you.* Jesus introduces the final point of his parable, by addressing the listeners directly—the "them" of v. 5. Similar endings of parables can be found in 14:24 (see NOTE there); 15:7,10; 16:9; 18:8,14; 19:26. The Greek formulation in such a cl. varies at times.

his friend. The best reading is *philon autou,* "his friend." But variants occur in some mss. (D: *auton philon autou,* "he is his friend"; A, R, 565, 1424: *auton philon,* "he is a friend").

because of his persistence. Lit. "because of his shamelessness indeed," i.e. his importunity in begging and begging at this late hour of the night. It forces the one asked to be gift-ready. In this interpretation the *anaideia* is a quality of the petitioner. Some commentators have attempted to make it rather a quality of the neighbor roused from sleep: "he will fulfil the request because of *his* own shamelessness, namely, that which will be brought to light through his refusal" (A. Fridrichsen, "Exegetisches," 40-43). But that interpretation fails because the *autou,* "his," that modifies *anaideia* has to be understood in the same sense as the *autou* with the preceding *philon,* "his friend," a reference to the begging neighbor. See further K. E. Bailey, *Poet and Peasant* (Grand Rapids: Eerdmans, 1976) 119-133.

rouse himself. See NOTE on 7:14.

as much as he needs. I.e. not just what was asked for.

BIBLIOGRAPHY (11:5-8)

Berger, K. "Materialien zu Form und Überlieferungsgeschichte neutestamentlicher Gleichnisse," *NovT* 15 (1973) 1-37, esp. 33-36.

Bornkamm, G. " 'Bittet, suchet, klopfet an': Predigt über Luk. 11, 5-13," *EvT* 13 (1953) 1-5.

Derrett, J. D. M. "The Friend at Midnight: Asian Ideas in the Gospel of St. Luke," *Donum gentilicium: New Testament Studies in Honour of David Daube* (ed. E. Bammel et al.; Oxford: Clarendon, 1978) 78-87.

Fridrichsen, A. "Exegetisches zum Neuen Testament," *SymOs* 13 (1934) 38-46, esp. 40-43.

Jeremias, J. *Parables,* 157-160.

Jülicher, A. *Gleichnisreden,* 2. 268-276.

Martin, A. D. "The Parable concerning Hospitality," *ExpTim* 37 (1925-1926) 411-414.

Ott, W. *Gebet und Heil,* 23-31, 99-102.

Rickards, R. R. "The Translation of Luke 11.5-13," *BT* 28 (1977) 239-243.

Zerwick, M. "Vivere ex verbo Dei: 11) Perseveranter orare (Lc 11,5-13)," *VD* 28 (1950) 243-247.

70. THE EFFICACY OF PRAYER
(11:9-13)

11 ⁹ "So I tell you, 'Ask, and it will be given to you; search, and you will find; knock, and the door will be opened for you. ¹⁰ For everyone who asks, obtains; he who searches, finds; and the door will be opened for him who knocks. ¹¹ Suppose one of you is a father and your son asks you for a fish, will you hand him a serpent instead? ¹² Or suppose he asks for an egg, will you hand him a scorpion? ¹³ If you then, evil as you are, know how to give your children good gifts, how much more surely will the heavenly Father give the holy Spirit to those who ask him?' "

COMMENT

The third episode dealing with prayer at this point in the travel account (11:9-13) is closely related to the two preceding. In fact, the first saying of Jesus in it drives home the need for persistence in prayer again. But it now goes further.

The episode has its counterpart in the Matthean sermon on the mount (7:7-11) and has been derived by both evangelists from "Q." Save for the introductory cl. (v. 9a), which probably was part of "Q" itself (and dropped by Matthew), the wording of the three pairs in vv. 9b,c,d, and 10 is identical with that in Matt 7:7-8 (see p. 76). In the saying in the latter part of the episode both evangelists have another threesome, but the three pairs are not identical. Luke has fish/serpent, egg/scorpion, good gifts/holy Spirit (vv. 11-13), whereas Matthew has bread/stone, fish/serpent, good gifts/good things (7:9-11). Which is the more original? Luke has certainly redacted the end of the saying by the addition of "holy Spirit" in accord with his emphasis on the Spirit (see pp. 227-231; cf. *HST* 327). Given the collocation of "serpents and scorpions" in the "L" passage of 10:19, the probability is that Luke has omitted the bread/stone contrast in favor of his second pair (unless one wants to insist that he has merely added it redactionally to a form of the saying in which he also had bread/stone as the first pair—a form attested in many mss. [see NOTE on 11:11]). Sayings reminiscent of vv. 9-10 are found in *Gos. of Thom.* § 2,92,94; but in each case they are either overlaid with other material or modified so that they scarcely represent a tradition independent of the Synoptics (see pp. 86-87). None of them has preserved the pairs found in vv. 11-13. Luke has most likely substituted a favorite word, *hyparchontes* (v. 13; see p. 111), for the simple *ontes* of "Q," and added *patera,* "father," for *anthrōpos,* "man," in v. 11 (see Matt 7:9; cf. J. Jeremias, *Die Sprache,* 198).

Though T. W. Manson *(Sayings,* 81) and some other commentators call vv. 11-13 a "parable" (since it has the rhetorical-question construction found in vv. 5-7), the comparison is again at most implicit. It is better to regard all the utterances in this passage as Logia or wisdom-sayings of Jesus (see *HST* 80), expressing not secular wisdom, but a piety reckoning with the hearing of prayer by God (ibid. 104). Whether all the sayings in this episode belong together as a unit or represent the joining of utterances used on different occasions is hard to say. Verse 10 is repetitious of v. 9; some commentators even think that it is a poetic form of v. 9. It is, however, clear that a catchword bonding has been operative *(aiteite,* v. 9; *aitōn,* v. 10; *aitēsei,* v. 11; and *aitēsei,* v. 12).

At first, vv. 9-10 may sound like simple worldly wisdom; but the three pairs, twice repeated, emphasize, especially in this Lucan context, persistence in unwearying prayer. Three human modes of petition are mentioned (asking, searching, knocking at a door), and each is promised a reward (gift, discovery, welcome). They are not to be allegorized as human endeavor resulting in progress, but express rather the kinds of simple petition the Christian disciple is to present to the heavenly Father. Verse 10 is so formulated that it sounds like a universal law "that each of these three actions on the part of man meets with a corresponding response from God" (J. M. Creed, *The Gospel,* 158).

Verses 11-13 implicitly compare the heavenly Father with an earthly parent. The discussion in vv. 5-8 concerned friends, now it involves the father-son relationship. The argument moves from the absurd to the reasonable, from the lesser to the greater. An earthly father will not give a son who begs of him something for sustenance (a fish or an egg) something similar-looking, but which is a possible source of evil to him. The good that the son seeks will surely be given, without any deception or equivocation. God too will give only good to his children who seek it from him. Indeed, he will give them the supreme gift, the holy Spirit. His bounty thus transcends that of earthly parents because he is essentially good and not evil, as they are known to be. Human bounty is still only a trifle in comparison with that of the heavenly Father. What is given is not only "as much as he needs" (v. 8), but the supreme gift of the Spirit.

NOTES

11 9. *So I tell you.* This introductory cl. has the prepositive indir. obj. *(hymin legō)* found elsewhere in Luke only in "L" or "Q" passages. See 6:27; 7:14; 16:9; 23:43; cf. the use in Matt 16:18; 21:24. It formulates a prophetic admonition about prayer.

Ask, and it will be given to you. I.e. by God (the so-called theological pass. is again used; see ZBG § 236 or NOTE on 5:20).

search, and you will find. I.e. with the help of God (as the parallelism suggests). Forms of this saying are known in many literatures. Cf. Str-B 1. 458.

will be opened. I.e. by God. The best reading here is *anoigēsetai,* but some mss. (D, E, W) have another form of the fut. pass., *anoichthēsetai.* See NOTE on v. 10.

10. *will be opened.* Or possibly, "is opened." N-A²⁶ reads *anoig[ēs]etai,* because the textual evidence is about equally mixed between the fut. and the pres. Mss. P⁷⁵, B, D read the pres. *anoigetai,* but A, E, W have a form of the fut. pass. *anoichthēsetai,* whereas P⁷⁵, C, and the Freer and Lake families of minuscules have *anoigēsetai.* The fut. looks like a scribal assimilation to that form in v. 9, but the pres. is judged as an assimilation to the pres. of the other vbs. in v. 10. In any case, the meaning is little affected.

11. *Suppose one of you is a father.* Lit. "Which one of you (as) a father will a son ask for a fish and will he hand him a serpent instead of a fish?" Another rhetorical question is used. As in v. 5, the mixture of subjs. and personal prons. complicates the sentence structure, making it difficult to render exactly in good English.

Kai, "and," is read by mss. P⁴⁵, P⁷⁵, B before "instead of a fish"; it is the *lectio difficilior,* to be retained in preference to the interrogative negative *mē* of mss. ℵ, A, D, W, Θ, and the Koine text-tradition. See *TCGNT* 157.

for a fish, will you hand him a serpent instead? Similarity of appearance between a fish and a serpent is intended. The implication is that a parent would not deceive his/ her child. At times water snakes *(topidonotus tesselatus)* have been caught by fishermen in the Lake of Gennesaret; they feed on small fish, used as bait. See B. Hjerl-Hansen, "Le rapprochement."

Many mss. insert before "a fish" the words, *arton, mē lithon epidōsei autō ē kai,* "bread, you will not hand him a stone, will you; or even . . ." (so the Hesychian and Koine text-traditions, A, D, R, W, the Lake and Freer families of minuscules, etc.). But this added pair is suspect of scribal harmonization with Matt 7:9-10; the shorter reading (found only in P⁴⁵, P⁷⁵, B, 1241) is to be preferred.

12. *an egg . . . a scorpion?* A scorpion with claws and tail rolled up is said to resemble an egg. See H. Pegg, " 'A Scorpion for an Egg' (Luke xi. 12)."

13. *evil as you are.* No proof is offered for this; it is an implied appeal to experience.

the heavenly Father. The textual reading is not certain. It could be "the Father from heaven" *(ho patēr ho ex ouranou,* P⁷⁵, ℵ, L, 33) or "the Father will give from heaven" *(ho patēr ex ouranou dōsei),* or "your heavenly Father" *(hymōn ho ouranios,* P⁴⁵, 1242). The last could be influenced by the parallel in Matt 7:11. On the first possibility, see E. Delebecque, "Sur un hellénisme," 590-593.

the holy Spirit. Actually the Greek text lacks the def. art. This is the Lucan redactional modification for the more original *agatha,* "good things," preserved in Matt 7:11. *Pneuma agathon,* "a good Spirit," is read in mss. P⁴⁵, L, etc. Codex Bezae has *agathon doma,* "a good gift." Cf. Luke 10:21.

Here Luke makes Jesus speak of the gift to be given in the Period of the Church (24:49; Acts 1:4,7-8). He has introduced into a Saying of Jesus the vocabulary of the early church. See pp. 227-230.

BIBLIOGRAPHY (11:9-13)
(in addition to the titles given in 11:5-8)

Brox, N. "Suchen und finden: Zur Nachgeschichte von Mt 7,7b/Lk 11,9b," *Orientierung an Jesus* (eds. P. Hoffmann et al.) 17-36.

Delebecque, E. "Sur un hellénisme," *RB* 87 (1980) 590-593 (on v. 13).

Hjerl-Hansen, B. "Le rapprochement poisson-serpent dans la prédication de Jésus (Mt. VII, 10 et Luc. XI, 11)," *RB* 55 (1948) 195-198.

Kraeling, C. H. "Seek and You Will Find," *Early Christian Origins: Studies in Honor of Harold R. Willoughby* (ed. A. Wikgren; Chicago: Quadrangle Books, 1961) 24-34.

Leonardi, G. " 'Cercate e troverete . . . lo Spirito Santo' nell'unità letteraria di Luca 11,1-13," *Quaerere Deum* (Settimana biblica 25; eds. A. Bonora et al.; Brescia: Paideia, 1980).

Pegg, H. " 'A Scorpion for an Egg' (Luke xi. 12)," *ExpTim* 38 (1926-1927) 468-469.

71. THE BEELZEBUL CONTROVERSY
(11:14-23)

11 14 Now Jesus was casting out a demon which was mute; and when the demon had come forth, the mute person began to speak to the surprise of all the crowd. 15 But some of them said, "By Beelzebul, the prince of demons, he casts them out." 16 And others, to put him to a test, kept demanding of him a sign from heaven. 17 But Jesus realized what they were thinking and said to them, "Every kingdom divided against itself ends in ruins, and one house falls upon another. 18 Now if even Satan is divided against himself, how will his kingdom stand? You say it is by Beelzebul that I cast out demons. 19 If indeed I cast them out by Beelzebul, by whom do your own people cast them out? For this very reason they will sit in judgment over you. 20 But if it is by

*the finger of God*ᵃ that I cast out demons, then surely the kingdom of God has already reached you.

²¹ When a powerful man fully armed stands guard over his court-yard, his belongings are safe and sound. ²² But when a more powerful man attacks and overpowers him, he carries away all the weapons on which he had relied and divides up his booty.

²³ The one who is not with me is against me; and the one who does not gather with me scatters."

ᵃ Exod 8:15 (8:19E)

COMMENT

The travel account continues with a story about some people in the crowd around Jesus commenting on his expelling a demon and asserting that he is in league with Beelzebul or Satan. Coming immediately after the three episodes that contain his instruction on prayer (11:1-4,5-8,9-13), which give no indication of the presence of a crowd, this episode is a good example of the problem created by the concatenation of inherited passages in the travel account. In 10:38 Jesus enters a village and is welcomed by Martha into her house. After that we read immediately about his being at prayer "in a certain place" (11:1), when one of his disciples asks him to teach them to pray. This is the setting for the triple instruction on prayer—which apparently takes place in the absence of a crowd. Now all of a sudden Jesus is in the midst of a crowd, expelling a demon (11:14-23). It becomes the occasion of a debate about where he gets this power. It is a form of the Beelzebul controversy known elsewhere in the gospel tradition, which Luke now makes part of his travel account. (Codex Bezae had its way of solving the problem mentioned above, by introducing v. 14 as follows: "When he had said these things, a mute demoniac was brought to him [historic pres.]; and when he cast it out, they were surprised.")

This is the first of three episodes that Luke uses from the source "Q," dealing with either demons or signs (from heaven): 11:14-23,24-26,29-32 (with an insert from "L" in vv. 27-28). The Matthean counterparts to these episodes occur in a slightly different order in 12:22-30,43-45,38-42. Mark has a variant of this Beelzebul tradition in 3:22-27, which Luke chose to omit when he returned to the use of Marcan material after his Little Interpolation (6:20-8:3; see pp. 67, 699). Matthew makes some use of the Marcan tradition in his form of "Q," but Luke is scarcely affected by it. Matthew may also have a further variant of the tradition in 9:32-34. It is possible that Luke 9:50 is a variant of the last verse of this episode, despite its different wording (see

NOTE on 9:50). The variant that is found in *Gos. of Thom.* § 35 is clearly dependent on Matt 12:29 and has little to do with the Lucan form.

It is generally thought that in this episode Luke has by and large preserved the wording of "Q." See B. S. Easton. The "Q" material is actually restricted to vv. 15b,17,18a-b,19-20,23 and probably includes parts of vv. 14,21-22. Luke himself has added v. 16, as a foreshadowing of 11:29 (using, indeed, a phrase from Mark 8:11 [omitted as part of his Big Omission, see pp. 770-771]). He has also repeated part of v. 15b in v. 18c. How much of vv. 14,21-22 is Lucan composition or redaction is not easy to say. A few expressions resemble terms in the Matthean counterparts: "mute" (v. 14a; cf. Matt 12:22); "the crowds" (pl., v. 14c; cf. Matt 12:23); "a powerful man" (v. 21; cf. Matt 12:29). But for the most part these verses have been independently redacted by both evangelists. Though it is sometimes contested (see C. S. Rodd, "Spirit or Finger," *ExpTim* 72 [1960-1961] 157-158; J. E. Yates, *SE II* 295-299), Luke has undoubtedly preserved "the finger of God" in v. 20 from "Q," even though he has not always otherwise preserved the mention of the Spirit when it was present in his sources (see p. 228). Matt 12:28 has changed it to "the Spirit of God." (Cf. N. Perrin, *Rediscovering*, 63; J. Jeremias, *Die Sprache*, 199-202.)

Form-critically considered, the episode is an expanded pronouncement-story, a form of a controversy dialogue *(HST* 13; *FGT* 120). It has been preserved here as a more unified story than that in Mark 3:22-27 (or 30). It echoes a Palestinian debate between Jesus and his Jewish peers, even though one has the suspicion that v. 19 may stem from an early church-controversy, rather than the ministry of Jesus itself. The pronouncement is couched now in vv. 19-20. This story has been further expanded by two sayings, one parabolic (vv. 21-22), the other minatory (v. 23).

The story presents Jesus defending himself against accusations of his contemporaries, rejecting their slanderous claims that he was in league with Beelzebul or Satan and that thereby he could help people to become free of demons. The episode opens with an expression of surprise that Jesus has expelled a demon and an accusation that he has done this as an agent of Beelzebul. In his reaction to this accusation, Jesus uses two images, the divided kingdom and the falling house (or household). The images evoke civil war. Jesus' reaction to the slander: He is in no way in league with the forces of evil. Implicitly he challenges his critics to think about what they are saying. Can society in any form tolerate division and dissension in such essential matters? Verse 19 even pushes his argument further, becoming an *argumentum ad hominem,* as Jesus implies that the Palestinian exorcists too must then be in league with Beelzebul. The third step in his argument is reached when he draws just the opposite conclusion from his activity and the power of God that is implied in it: the OT anthropomorphism, "the finger of God," serves to relate his activity to Yahweh's agents of old; if he too is such an agent, then his critics might well recognize that the kingdom of God preached of old has perhaps arrived among them in a new form. Jesus thus resolutely rejects any association with evil in his activity. The kingdom, for which he taught his disciples to pray (11:2), is already manifesting its presence among the people of Palestine, even if some of them are too blind to recognize it. Indeed, it may even be thought to have come earlier than expected *(ephthasen,* v. 20). Not only has the kingdom taken on this form among his Palestinian peers (cf. 17:21), but even those among them who also cast out demons may turn out to be the ones to sit in judgment on those who accuse him of sharing evil's power. In sum, God is with Jesus, evil is not. (The Lucan addition in v. 16, about some people demanding a sign from heaven, really distracts from the thrust of the rest of the episode. Why Luke added it here, apart from a concern to foreshadow 11:29, is hard to say. Its addition, however, does heighten the criticism leveled against Jesus.)

In the added saying of vv. 21-22 Jesus speaks of "a more powerful man," echoing the saying of John the Baptist in 3:16 and recalling the vanquishing of Satan in the temptation-scenes (4:1-13; see COMMENT, pp. 512-513). Beelzebul may be depicted as "a powerful man," armed and guarding his courtyard, but now "a more powerful man" has come to defeat and despoil him, kit and caboodle.

The minatory saying in v. 23 has its counterpart in Matt 12:30, which shows that it too formed part of the "Q" unit. In its present context, it states that human beings cannot be neutral in their reaction to Jesus' struggle against the evil represented by demonic forces. To be on his side one must gather in with him, as a shepherd his sheep into the fold (cf. 12:32; Mark 14:27) or as a harvester his wheat into the granary (see 3:17; cf. 12:17); one cannot be a divisive element scattering the flock (John 10:12; Mark 14:27).

The whole story has an eschatological nuance, especially the pronouncement in vv. 19-20, as it now stands: Judgment *will* come for those who slander Jesus because in his conduct the kingdom is already being met.

NOTES

11 14. *Now Jesus was casting out a demon.* Lit. "and he was casting out" (the periphrasis of the impf. *ēn* + pres. ptc. *ekballōn* introduces the episode, as in 1:21). See p. 122.

demon. See NOTE on 4:33. In this episode the *daimonion* is clearly distinguished from both Beelzebul (v. 15) and Satan (v. 18); it is considered to be the cause of the dumbness.

which was mute. Lit. "and it was mute," or simply, "a mute (demon)," depending on the reading preferred: *kai auto ēn,* omitted in mss. P⁴⁵, P⁷⁵, ℵ, A*, B, L, etc., but retained in mss. Aᶜ, C, R, W, Θ, Ψ, and the Koine text-tradition. N-A²⁶ brackets the three words; it is hard to decide. In Matt 12:22 the person is said to be "blind and mute"; in Mark 3:22 no mention is made of an exorcism as the occasion for the criticism of Jesus. On the meaning of *kōphos*, see NOTE on 1:22.

when the demon had come forth. Lit. "and it happened, when the demon came forth, (that) the mute (person) began to speak." Luke uses *egeneto de* + finite vb. (without a conj.) and also a gen. absol. as a temporal cl. See p. 119. The vb. *elalēsen* is understood as an ingressive aor. See BDF § 331.

to the surprise of all the crowd. Lit. "and the crowds (pl.) were surprised" *(ethaumasan).* On "crowd(s)," see NOTE on 3:7. The unexpected had happened. Cf. 1:63; 2:18; 8:25; 9:43. The reality of the expulsion is taken for granted; no one contests that aspect of Jesus' activity.

15. *some of them said.* In Matt 12:24 the critics become "the Pharisees," who are distinguished from "the crowds" (Matt 12:23). Ms. P⁴⁵ reads: "Some of them spoke (as) strong ones *(ochyroi),* saying . . ."

By. The prep. *en* is used to express agency. See NOTE on 4:1.

Beelzebul. This name occurs only here and in vv. 18-19 in the Lucan writings. Cf. Mark 3:22; Matt 10:25; 12:24,27. Mss. ℵ, B of the Lucan Gospel read *Beezeboul;* the Latin and Syriac versions reflect rather the form *Beelzebub.* In any case, Luke has preserved a Jewish Greek name. See p. 113.

The forms *Beelzeboul* and *Beezeboul* (the latter representing an assimilation of *l* to the following *z* and a simplification) preserve the name of an old Canaanite god, meaning "Baal, the Prince," or "Baal of the Exalted Abode." Elements of the name have been found in the Ugaritic title of Baal Puissant, *zbl b'l arṣ (UT* 49.I:14-15; 49.III:3,9,21, etc.), "Exalted One/Prince, Lord of Earth." See W. F. Albright, "Zabûl Yam and Thâpit Nahar in the Combat between Baal and the Sea," *JPOS* 16 (1936) 17-18; H. L. Ginsberg, *ANET* 140. In the OT (1 Kgs 8:13; 2 Chr 6:2; Ps 49:15; Isa 63:15; Hab 3:11) *zēbûl* refers to God's "exalted abode" (whether heaven or, by extension, the Temple). See further 1QS 10:3; 1QM 12:1,2; 1QH 3:34. The form *zbl* (Ugaritic) or *zēbûl* (Hebrew) is the pass. ptc. of *zbl,* "carry, lift up." This ancient name for the Canaanite *Bĕ'el šĕmayin,* "Lord of the Heavens," the rival of Yahweh, "Lord of the Heavens" *(mārê' šĕmayyā',* Dan 5:23), in Hellenistic times, is applied to Satan because of Ps 96:5, "All the gods of the nations are idols," which becomes in the LXX, ". . . are demons" *(daimonia).*

"Beelzebub" of the Latin and Syriac traditions and of the literature that depends on them (e.g. Milton's *Paradise Lost)* is derived from the name of a (Philistine?) god of the town Ekron preserved in 2 Kgs 1:2-3,6,16, *Ba'al-zĕbûb.* This seems to have been a deliberate caconymic, a (polemical) distortion of the foregoing name to depreciate the pagan god, making it "Lord of the Flies." See the LXX: *Baal muian theon,* "Baal, the Fly-God"; the same interpretation is in Josephus, *Ant.* 9.2,1 § 19. Cf. *HALAT,* 250.

Other explanations which have been attempted are less than convincing: (a) Beelzebul/Beelzebub is a corruption/distortion of Aramaic *bĕ'el-dĕbāb,* "adversary" (lit. "master of a complaint"), i.e. prosecutor (in a lawsuit); intriguing, but fraught with problems; (b) *Beelzeboul* represents Aramaic *bĕ'el zibbûl,* "Lord of Dung"; a comprehensible name for Satan, but where is *zibbûl* attested meaning "dung" in any contemporary Aramaic? (c) *Beelzeboul* is a distortion of *Ba'al-zĕbûb,* which really means "Baal, the Flame" (F. C. Fensham). See further L. Gaston, "Beelzebul," *TZ* 18 (1962) 247-255; E. C. B. MacLaurin, "Beelzeboul," *NovT* 20 (1978) 156-160.

the prince of demons. This epithet of Beelzebul plays on the meaning of his name, but only in part (see above). Some commentators (O. Böcher, *EWNT* 1.508; W. Foerster, *TDNT* 1. 606) think that this phrase means that Beelzebul is only a potentate in Satan's kingdom and not identical with Satan himself. This view, however, ignores the def. art. preceding *archōn*, "prince." Even though Satan is usually kept distinct in earlier Jewish literature from demons and spirits (see NOTES on 4:2; 10:18), that is no guarantee against the identification in the tradition preserved here: the use of Beelzebul in v. 15 and Satan in v. 18 suggests that the former has already become merely an alternate name for Satan, as had "Belial" (1QS 1:18,24; 2:5,19, etc.; cf. 2 Cor 6:15), "Maṣṭemah" (1QS 3:23; 1QM 13:4,11; CD 16:5; *Jub.* 10:8), or "Asmodaeus" (Tob 3:8,17). Cf. O. Merk, *EWNT* 1.403; L. Gaston, *TZ* 18 (1962) 247-255; R. Schnackenburg, LTK[2] 2. 97. Cp. the conflation in Rev 12:9.

In casting out demons "by Beelzebul," Jesus would be depicted by his critics as an agent of Beelzebul. In Mark 3:22 he is said rather either "to have Beelzebul" or that "Beelzebul has [him]."

16. *others, to put him to a test.* This testing has really nothing to do with the criticism leveled against Jesus in this story. On "testing," see NOTE on 4:2. Luke's redaction is manifest here in his use of a favorite word, *heteroi,* "others." See p. 110.

a sign from heaven. See COMMENT; also NOTE on v. 29.

17. *realized what they were thinking.* Lit. "but he himself, knowing their thoughts." On the literary use of *autos de,* see p. 120. Jesus' comment makes use of two parable-like utterances.

divided against itself. Luke uses *eph' heautēn,* which may be derived from Mark 3:24. A kingdom divided against itself and houses falling on one another are a graphic description of civil war. Such an upheaval would be occurring in Beelzebul's kingdom, if Jesus were really driving out demons by Beelzebul's power. It would be counterproductive.

one house falls upon another. Or "against" another, since the prep. *epi* has the same meaning as in the preceding and following phrases. See BAGD 560. Here *oikos* could even mean "family," as it can also in 10:5; 19:9; Acts 16:15. Then its meaning would be more pregnant in the image of a civil war.

18. *even Satan.* This again seems to imply that, for Luke, Beelzebul is Satan (on this name see NOTES on 4:2; 10:18). The introduction of Satan must affect one's thinking about the Period of Jesus as Satan-free. See p. 187.

his kingdom. Recall 4:5-6.

19. *by whom do your own people cast them out?* Lit. "your sons," *huios* being used to denote membership in a guild or class (see NOTE on 5:34; cf. BAGD 834), i.e. your exorcists. Those who are leveling accusations against Jesus have forgotten the exorcisms carried out by his Jewish contemporaries. See Mark 9:38; Acts 19:13-14. Josephus *(Ant.* 8.2,5 § 46) writes of a certain Eleazar, his fellow-tribesman, who in the presence of Vespasian and his attendants "freed people seized by demons" *(hypo tōn daimoniōn lambanomenous apolyonta);* he passed a ring with roots prescribed by Solomon under its seal before the nose of the afflicted to draw out the demons through their nostrils. The *Genesis Apocryphon* also depicts Abram driving out an evil spirit that had afflicted Pharaoh and his household (1QapGen 20:29). For later stories of exorcisms in rabbinical writings, see Str-B 4/1. 533-535; cf. L. J. McGinley, *Form-*

Criticism of the Synoptic Healing Narratives (Woodstock, MD: Woodstock College, 1944) 101-103. Cf. Josephus, *J.W.* 7.6,3 § 185; 1 Sam 16:14-23.

they will sit in judgment over you. Lit. "they will be your judges," when the eschaton comes. Jesus' use of an *argumentum ad hominem* summons his critics to an existential judgment about themselves.

20. *by the finger of God.* I.e. without the aid of rings, charms, and incantations as used by other exorcists. Jesus' words allude to the story of the third plague in Exod 8:15 (8:19E). Cf. Exod 31:18; Deut 9:10; Ps 8:4. The OT image recalls God's intervention on behalf of his people at the time of the hardening of Pharaoh's heart against them. In Jesus, God's power now intervenes again to release humans from evil, this time from psychic evil. See p. 223. The OT anthropomorphism obviously expresses the ease with which Jesus has expelled the demon. The expression, "finger of God," has also been found in a Greek ostracon (an adjuration, in fact) from Ashmunen in Egypt (see *LAE* 306); but it dates from the late imperial period and mentions a woman Maria, and so could be influenced by such a NT passage as this. For a possible Egyptian background to the anthropomorphism, see B. Couroyer in the BIBLIOGRAPHY.

the kingdom of God. See NOTE on 4:43; cf. pp. 154-156.

has already reached you. Luke uses *ephthasen,* the aor. of *phthanein,* "come before, precede," which can also mean "have just arrived" or simply "arrive" (BAGD 856; MM 667). Attempts have been made to interpret the vb. as a timeless aor. (with a fut. meaning), "the kingdom will be upon you immediately." See J. Y. Campbell, "The Kingdom of God Has Come," *ExpTim* 48 (1936-1937) 91-94; cf. K. W. Clark, "Realized Eschatology," *JBL* 59 (1940) 367-383. But without necessarily subscribing to C. H. Dodd's "realized eschatology" (see his *Parables,* 44), one can accept his insistence on the interpretation of this vb. in a genuine aor. meaning. See *ExpTim* 48 (1936-1937) 138-142. There is a sense in which one has to admit that even for Luke the kingdom has arrived in Jesus' preaching (and activity). See W. G. Kümmel, *Promise and Fulfilment,* 105-109: *phthanein* does not merely equal *engizein,* "draw near." As I. H. Marshall *(Luke,* 476) notes, Jesus' words refer to the arrival of the kingdom *eph' hymas,* "unto you"; "the kingly and saving power of God has drawn near to the hearers and is there for them to grasp; and the proof that it is near to them is that its power has been evidenced in the lives of other people. . . ." See further NOTE on 10:9. It is baffling why this activity of Jesus "excludes any idea of the immanence of the Kingdom" (H. Conzelmann, *Theology,* 107 n. 2).

21. *a powerful man.* The image is not that of a householder (as in Matthew), but of a lord of a castle. See J. Schmid, *Evangelium nach Lukas,* 204; also S. Légasse, "L'"homme fort' de Luc xi 21-22," *NovT* 5.5-9. It is applied to Satan.

his courtyard. Luke, following "Q," differs from the Matthean parallel, which is influenced by Mark 3:27, and speaks of a "house" *(oikian).* On *aulē,* "courtyard," see NOTE on 2:8.

belongings. Luke uses the ptc. *ta hyparchonta,* as in 8:3; 12:15,33,44; 14:33; 16:1; 19:8; Acts 4:32. See p. 111.

are safe and sound. Lit. "in peace," i.e. in a situation without war. See p. 225.

22. *a more powerful man.* Lit. "one more powerful than he." The image could refer either to God himself or, more probably, to Jesus, armed with the word of God,

vanquishing Satan (recall p. 513), and now disarming and despoiling him. Is there an allusion here to Isa 53:12c? Possibly. Cf. *T. Levi* 18:12.

attacks. Lit. "having come upon (him)." See NOTE on 1:35. Instead of *epelthōn,* which expresses a coming or an advance in a hostile sense, P⁴⁵ reads *epanelthōn,* "having come against," and P⁷⁵ uses the simple vb., *elthōn,* in the same sense. See BAGD 310.

23. *who is not with me is against me.* The image is at first military: fighting with or against someone. This supplies the connection of this verse with the foregoing saying of vv. 21-22. One has to take sides with Jesus or with Satan. Whoever tries to stand aloof from Jesus' cause abets that of the evil one.

gather . . . scatters. The pair occurs elsewhere (Matt 25:24-26; John 11:52).

BIBLIOGRAPHY (11:14-23)

Barnett, P. W. "The Jewish Sign-Prophets—A.D. 40-70: Their Intentions and Origin," *NTS* 27 (1980-1981) 679-697.

Beauvery, R. "Jésus et Béelzéboul (Lc 11,14-28)," *AsSeign* 30 (1963) 26-36.

Böcher, O. *Das Neue Testament und die dämonischen Mächte* (SBS 58; Stuttgart: Katholisches Bibelwerk, 1972) 9-11.

Bryant, H. E. "Note on Luke xi. 17," *ExpTim* 50 (1938-1939) 525-526.

Couroyer, B. "Le 'doigt de Dieu' (Exode, VIII, 15)," *RB* 63 (1956) 481-495.

Easton, B. S. "The Beelzebul Sections," *JBL* 32 (1913) 57-73.

George, A. "Note sur quelques traits lucaniens de l'expression 'Par le doigt de Dieu' (Luc XI,20)," *ScEccl* 18 (1966) 461-466; reprinted in his *Études sur l'oeuvre de Luc* (SB; Paris: Gabalda, 1978) 128-132.

Grässer, E. "Zum Verständnis des Gottesherrschaft," *ZNW* 65 (1974) 3-26.

Hamerton-Kelly, R. G. "A Note on Matthew XII. 28 Par. Luke XI. 20," *NTS* 11 (1964-1965) 167-169.

Hermann, I. " '. . . dann ist das Gottesreich zu euch gekommen': Eine Homilie zu Luk 11,14-20," *BibLeb* 1 (1960) 198-204.

Käsemann, E. "Lukas 11,14-28," *Exegetische Versuche und Besinnungen* (2d ed.; Göttingen: Vandenhoeck & Ruprecht, 1960), 1. 242-248.

Kruse, H. "Das Reich Satans," *Bib* 58 (1977) 29-61.

Kümmel, W. G. *Promise and Fulfilment,* 24, 105-109.

Légasse, S. "L''homme fort' de Luc xi 21-22," *NovT* 5 (1962) 5-9.

Linton, O. "The Demand for a Sign from Heaven (Mk 8, 11-12 and Parallels)," *ST* 19 (1965) 112-129.

Lorenzmeier, T. "Zum Logion Mt 12,28; Lk 11,20," *Neues Testament und christliche Existenz: Festschrift für Herbert Braun* (eds. H. D. Betz and L. Schottroff; Tübingen: Mohr [Siebeck], 1973) 289-304.

Perrin, N. *Rediscovering,* 63-67, 77.

Zerwick, M. "In Beelzebub principe daemoniorum (Lc. 11,14-28)," *VD* 29 (1951) 44-48.

72. THE RETURN OF THE EVIL SPIRIT
(11:24-26)

11 ²⁴ "When an unclean spirit comes out of a person, it roams through areas without water in search of a resting-place. Failing to find one, it then says, 'I shall return to the house that I left.' ²⁵ When it goes back, it finds it swept out and set in order. ²⁶ Then it goes off and brings along seven other spirits more evil than itself; they enter in and dwell there. And the last state of that person is worse than it was before."

COMMENT

To the last minatory saying of Jesus in the preceding episode (v. 23), Luke now adds another, about the return of an evil spirit to a demoniac (11:24-26), cautioning Christian disciples about too great assurance over manifestations of the defeat of physical or psychic evil.

Luke has derived this episode from "Q" (see p. 78). Its parallel is found in Matt 12:43-45; apart from a few Lucan omissions, it is almost word-for-word identical (see p. 76). Luke has omitted that the house is found "vacant" (v. 25; cf. Matt 12:44 [but see NOTE on 11:25]); and "with him" (v. 26; cf. Matt 12:45). He may also have omitted the conclusion, "So it will be for this wicked generation too" (Matt 12:45d). But that may rather be a Matthean modification, added because "wicked generation" precedes in 12:39. The addition makes the Matthean form more parable-like (see *HST* 164; he thinks that Matthew has preserved the original ending of "Q"). Part of the problem is the answer to the question, Who inverted the order of "Q," Matthew or Luke? (Recall COMMENT on 11:14-23.) It is hard to say. Many commentators think that Luke has preserved the original order of "Q" (so J. M. Creed, T. W. Manson, G. Schneider, et al.). But if the Matthean conclusion is not original, then it is easier to understand the Lucan inversion and insertion of vv. 27-28. (Cf. J. Jeremias, *Die Sprache,* 202.)

Form-critically considered, the episode preserves a minatory saying of Jesus. It warns against a smugness about the defeat of evil. Once driven out, how can one be certain that it will not reinvade human existence? In the Lucan context, the episode seems to mean that it is not sufficient that a demon be driven out; the person represented by the house swept clean and set in order must be on Jesus' side (see v. 23) and also listen to the word of God and observe it (v. 28); so E. Klostermann, *Lukasevangelium*, 127. The episode deals with the reinvasion of an exorcised person; it says nothing about a relapse into sin (recidivism), as it has often been interpreted. The teaching in the episode is couched in the typical protological thinking of ancient Palestinian demonological beliefs (that spirits, especially evil ones, must dwell somewhere and are not satisfied with nomadic roaming through arid, desert wastelands). We are not told in the episode by what power the unclean spirit has been expelled: whether by "the finger of God," by Jesus' "power" (see 5:17), or by that of Jewish exorcists (see v. 19). If the last group were meant, then Jesus' words would have added force; but they may envision even exorcisms performed by him (so G. Schneider). In any case, the episode adds a caution to that expressed in v. 23. The house must not remain merely in a state of readiness for reception; it must be filled with the word of God.

NOTES

11   24. *an unclean spirit.* See NOTE on 4:33. In the immediate context, it could refer to that mentioned in v. 14.

it roams through areas without water. Desert places were often considered the abode of demons. Recall "the wilderness" and Azazel of Lev 16:10; cf. Isa 34:13-14; Bar 4:35; Luke 8:29; Rev 18:2. For the continuation of this belief in later rabbinical literature, see Str-B 4/1. 516.

in search of a resting-place. Homeless, the demon is considered to be like a nomad. The Greek word *anapausis*, used here, is the same that is found in Isa 34:14 LXX, the "resting-place," sought by the "night hag" *(RSV* for Hebrew *Lîlît).*

it then says. The adv. *tote* is read by mss. P⁷⁵, ℵ², B, L, Θ, etc., but omitted by P⁴⁵, ℵ*, A, C, D, W, etc., the evidence being almost equal. N-A²⁶ brackets it; it is suspect because it may be a scribal harmonization with Matt 12:44.

I shall return. I.e. to a settled life. Cf. Josephus, *Ant.* 8.2,5 § 47.

25. *swept out and set in order.* I.e. ready to attract a passerby, or prepared for the reception of a guest. The best mss. have only two pf. ptcs., but mss. ℵ², B, C, L, R, Ξ, Ψ, etc., read before them the pres. ptc. *scholazonta*, "being vacant." It is again suspect as a scribal or copyist's harmonization with Matt 12:44. The first return of the demon is to inspect the abode.

26. *brings along seven other spirits.* The "seven spirits" probably symbolize the totality of evil or uncleanness. See NOTE on 8:2. They are scarcely brought along "out of sheer benevolence" (T. W. Manson, *Sayings,* 87). Rather, eight may be better able to resist another expulsion than one. However, the seven spirits may be considered as the counterparts of the seven angels of the presence (Tob 12:15). The vb. *paralambanein* was already used in 9:10,28.

the last state of that person. Lit. "the last things of that human being become worse than the first," a saying preserved also in 2 Pet 2:20. Cf. John 5:14.

926

LUKE X–XXIV

§ IVA

926   L U K E   X – X X I V   § IVA

BIBLIOGRAPHY (11:24-26)

Böcher, O. *Das Neue Testament und die dämonischen Mächte* (SBS 58; Stuttgart: Katholisches Bibelwerk, 1972) 9-11.
Jeremias, J. *Parables,* 197-198.
Nyberg, H. S. "Zum grammatischen Verständnis von Matth. 12, 44-45," *ConNT* 2 (1936) 22-35; reprinted 13 (1949) 1-11.
Plummer, A. "The Parable of the Demon's Return," *ExpTim* 3 (1891-1892) 349-351.

73. THOSE WHO ARE REALLY BLESSED
(11:27-28)

11   27 While he was saying this, a woman in the crowd happened to raise her voice and say to him, "Blessed is the womb that bore you and the breasts that you fed on." 28 But he replied, "Blessed rather are those who listen to the word of God and observe it."

COMMENT

Luke interrupts his use of "Q" material in the travel account to insert a saying of Jesus about the real blessedness of those who are associated with him (11:27-28). Coming immediately after vv. 23 and 24-26, it provides a further commentary on the cautions he has just uttered there; but otherwise it is hard to say why Luke has put this episode here.

The episode is peculiar to Luke, being derived from "L." Some commentators wonder whether it might be "a variant of the saying on the true kinship of Jesus" recorded in 8:19-21 (so J. M. Creed, *The Gospel,* 162; cf. W. E. Bundy, *Jesus,* 349; E. Klostermann, *Lukasevangelium,* 127). This, however, seems unlikely, given the difference of setting (an outdoor crowd), comment (from a woman), and wording (a beatitude). Further, as R. Bultmann *(HST* 30-31) has noted, there is in the earlier scene a "transmutation of the idea of kinship," which is lacking here. Still others wonder whether the story may have been in "Q" and omitted by Matthew, who made the Marcan equivalent (3:31-35) of what Luke has in 8:19-21 follow upon his use of the return of the evil spirit (Matt 12:43-45,46-50). (See H. Schürmann, "Das Thomasevangelium" [see p. 104], 231.) G. B. Caird *(Gospel of St Luke,* 156) ascribes it to "the compiler of Q," without further ado. But there is not the slightest hint that Matthew ever knew of this story. It is hardly a Lucan composition; and so it should be ascribed to "L." (Cf. J. Jeremias, *Die Sprache,* 203.)

Bultmann has rightly classified the episode as a biographical apophthegm, i.e. a pronouncement-story (see *FGT* 72; M. Dibelius *[FTG* 162] calls it a chria).

The woman calling out from the crowd extols Jesus in a typically maternal way, being charmed by his eloquence; it is reminiscent of Prov 23:24-25. The immediately preceding episode may not adequately explain why she is charmed; it is hardly likely that she is a mother with the experience of a lapsed penitent in her own family, *pace* A. Plummer, *The Gospel,* 305. The collocation of the episodes is Lucan, and the woman's comment is to be understood as made on Jesus' preaching in general. Her reaction to him stands in contrast to that in vv. 15-16.

Her comment about how wonderful a mother so eloquent a preacher-son must have had serves as a foil for Jesus' remark about who is truly blessed. As in 8:19-21, he again shifts all the attention to those who listen to God's word and observe it. Indeed, at first his words sound more negative toward his mother than those in 8:21. This impression is created in part by the contrast of the two beatitudes and in part by the force of the particle *menoun,* "rather." The first beatitude extols indeed the mother who has produced such a son; it echoes in a way the words of Mary's canticle in 1:48, "From now on all generations will count me blessed," offering an explanation of them. The second one seems to say that one should not judge God's blessings by charming words or exorcisms (11:24-26) but rather by obedient observance of his word. Put this way, it contrasts mother and son more than is intended. In Luke 1:45 Elizabeth made it clear that Mary was "blessed" or an object of praise, not just because she was to be Jesus' mother, but because she had believed: what had been told to her was to be fulfilled by the Lord. Similarly here; the second beatitude is phrased generically, praising "those who hear and observe," and states a reason for their happiness. The second does not negate the first, but formulates rather what Jesus considers of prime importance and merely corrects the inadequacy of the first. The particle *menoun* does not mean "nay, rather . . ." but "yes, rather . . ." for v. 28 admits that Jesus' mother is worthy of praise, not just because she has given birth to him, but because she too—in the Lucan story—is among those who have listened to the word of God, believed it (1:45), and acted on it (8:21; cf. Acts 1:14). Thus the minatory statements in vv. 23 and 24-26 find a commentary in this further remark of Jesus about who is truly blessed.

A form of this saying, combining it with Luke 23:29 and changing "God" to "the Father," is found in *Gos. of Thom.* § 79: "A woman from the crowd said to him, 'Blessed are the womb that bore you and the breasts that nourished you.' He said to her, 'Blessed are those who have heard the word of the Father (and) have truly kept it. For days will come when you will say,

"Blessed is the womb that has not conceived and the breasts that have not given milk." ' " Compare the Mishnaic praise of one of the five disciples of R. Yohanan b. Zakkai, i.e. R. Joshua b. Hananiah: "Joshua b. Hananiah—happy is she that bare him" *(m. Abot* 2:8).

NOTES

11 27. *While he was saying this . . .* Lit. "and it happened, in his saying these things, (that) a woman from the crowd, lifting up her voice, said to him." Luke again uses *egeneto de* + a finite vb. *(eipen),* without a conj., but with an articular infin. and a circumstantial ptc. *(eparasa).* See p. 119.

in the crowd. In this context the phrase refers to 11:14. See NOTE on 3:7. The word order in the Greek text is strange (see C. F. D. Moule, *Idiom Book,* 168), and some mss. have tried to ameliorate it (A, C, R, W, Θ, Ξ, etc.).

raise her voice. This classical Greek expression is used only by Luke in the NT. See Acts 2:14; 14:11; 22:22; cf. Luke 17:13—p. 110.

Blessed. See NOTE on 6:20.

the womb that bore you and the breasts that you fed on. Lit. "that you sucked." This Jewish circumlocution, mentioning the maternal organs by synecdoche, is normally found in expressions of praise for a mother. It is undoubtedly inspired by Gen 49:25e, "blessings of breast and womb," in Jacob's blessing of Joseph. Expressions similar to Jesus' words here are found in *Syr. Bar.* 54:10; *m. Abot* 2:8; and in later rabbinical writings; see Str-B 2. 187-188. The fifth-century midrash *Genesis Rabbah* (98:20) interpreted the words of Gen 49:25e as a blessing on Rachel. And a very close parallel to Jesus' words turns up in the late targums of Gen 49:25e (Ps.-Jonathan, Neofiti, and the Fragmentary Targum [with slight variants])—are they influenced by this NT passage? Cf. M. McNamara, but use with caution.

Failure to recognize the traditional Jewish synecdoche being used here has led a modern would-be interpreter of Jesus in the NT to write, ". . . her [the woman in the crowd] image of a woman was sexually reductionist in the extreme: female genitals and breasts. 'Blessed is . . . sucked!' Jesus clearly felt it necessary to reject this 'baby-machine' image and insist again on personhood being primary for all. . . ." (L. Swidler, "Jesus Was a Feminist," *New York Times,* December 18, 1971, 29). Alas, poor Luke! How distorted can the NT "message" get?

28. *rather.* The compound Greek particle *menoun* (used only four times in the NT and, against classical usage, at the head of a sentence) can have three different senses: (a) adversative, "nay, rather," "on the contrary": so commonly in classical Greek (Sophocles, *Ajax* 1363; Aristophanes, *Eccl.* 1102) and in the NT (Rom 9:20; 10:18); this would mean that Jesus was rejecting the woman's blessing of his mother (it seems to be the sense advocated by T. W. Manson, I. H. Marshall, M. P. Scott, et al.). (b) affirmative, "indeed," expressive of agreement with what was said. See Phil 3:8. (c) corrective, "yes, but rather," meaning that what was said is true as far as it goes (Plato, *Rep.* 489D). M. E. Thrall *(Greek Particles in the New Testament,* 34-35) points out that for Luke the first two uses are to be eliminated since, when he wants to express contradiction, he uses *ouchi, legō hymin* (12:51; 13:3,5); and for affirmation he

employs *nai* (7:26; 10:21; 11:51; 12:5). Hence, the last corrective sense is to be preferred. Cf. C. F. D. Moule, *Idiom Book,* 163-164.

who listen to the word of God and observe it. Jesus' words in 8:21 are echoed here. See NOTE there; cf. 6:47; 8:15. Whereas Luke used *poiountes* ("doing it") in 8:21, here he uses *phylassontes* ("guarding it"). For the sense of it, see 18:21; Acts 7:53; cf. Jas 1:22. Recall the OT use of *'śh* (= *poiein* in LXX) and *šmr* (= *phylassein* in the LXX) in such passages as Deut 4:6; 28:13,15.

In effect, Jesus' beatitude echoes that of Elizabeth in 1:42.

BIBLIOGRAPHY (11:27-28)

Black, M. "The Aramaic Liturgical Poetry of the Jews," *JTS* os 50 (1949) 179-182.

Brown, R. E., et al. *Mary in the New Testament* (Philadelphia: Fortress; New York: Paulist, 1978) 170-172.

Dewailly, L.-M. *Jésus-Christ, Parole de Dieu* (2d ed.; Paris: Cerf, 1969) 141-145.

Jacquemin, P.-E. "L'Accueil de la parole de Dieu Lc 11,27-28," *AsSeign* 66 (1973) 10-19.

McNamara, M. *The New Testament and the Palestinian Targum to the Pentateuch* (AnBib 27; Rome: Biblical Institute, 1966) 131-133.

Mussner, F. "Lk 1,48f; 11,27f und die Anfänge der Marienverehrung in der Urkirche," *Catholica* 21 (1967) 287-294.

Riedl, J. "Selig, die das Wort Gottes hören und befolgen (Lc 11,28): Theologisch-biblische Adventsbesinnung," *BibLeb* 4 (1963) 252-260.

Scott, M. P. "A Note on the Meaning and Translation of Luke 11,28," *ITQ* 41 (1974) 235-250.

Zimmermann, H. " 'Selig, die das Wort Gottes hören und es bewahren': Eine exegetische Studie zu Lk 11,27f," *Catholica* 29 (1975) 114-119.

74. THE SIGN OF JONAH
(11:29-32)

11 ^{29} With the crowds pressing closely about him, Jesus started to say, "This generation is an evil generation; it demands a sign, but no sign will be given to it except the sign of Jonah. ^{30} For just as Jonah was a sign to the Ninevites, so will the Son of Man be to this generation. ^{31} At the judgment the Queen of the South will arise together with the men of this generation and will condemn them. She came from the ends of the earth to listen to the wisdom of Solomon; but now here is something greater than Solomon! ^{32} At the judgment Ninevites

will stand up together with this generation and will condemn it. For they reformed their lives at the preaching of Jonah; but now here is something greater than Jonah!"

COMMENT

Luke now adds to his collection of Jesus' sayings at this point in the travel account several utterances for which he has already prepared in v. 16, when he added to the Beelzebul controversy a note that some people were trying to put Jesus to the test, demanding of him "a sign from heaven." Nothing was made of that detail there; now Luke depicts Jesus replying to such a demand with his saying about "the sign of Jonah" (11:29-32). We have noted earlier that this episode is related to those in vv. 14-23 and 24-26 (see p. 917). In fact, from v. 14 to v. 54 Jesus is in some form of debate with Palestinian questioners.

Luke has derived this episode from "Q," and its parallel is found in Matt 12:38-42 (see p. 78). The "Q" material also has a counterpart in Mark 8:11-12, which, however, lacks a specific reference to Jonah and the added saying about Solomon and the Queen of the South. These two forms of a response by Jesus to sign-seekers create a complicated problem. In an attempt to unravel the strands, one should realize that four forms of the response are found in the gospel tradition: (1) In Mark 8:11-12 Pharisees seek from Jesus "a sign from heaven"; Jesus sighs and says, "I tell you truly, no sign will be given this generation." (2) The parallel to this Marcan passage in Matt 16:1,4 depicts Pharisees and Sadducees similarly asking for "a sign from heaven"; here Jesus says, "No sign will be given to it except the sign of Jonah." (This Matthean passage is regarded as the parallel to Mark 8:11-12, because from 14:1 on Matthew has been following closely the Marcan order [from 6:14 on]; see *SQE* 560). In effect, the Matthean Jesus here promises no more of a sign than in Mark, since no explanation is given of "the sign of Jonah." No explanation is given in Matthew 16, because it has already been explained in Matthew 12; the reader is simply expected to know what it is—a modern writer would use a footnote cross-reference. (3) Luke 11:29-32 depicts Jesus saying to the crowds that no sign will be given to this generation "except the sign of Jonah," to which is added an explanation (v. 30) and then a double comparison (about the Queen of the South and Jonah, vv. 31-32). (4) To this Lucan form of the saying Matt 12:38-42 corresponds, except that Pharisees request a sign from Jesus; again Jesus says that no sign will be given "except the sign of Jonah the prophet." The latter is now explained in v. 40 by reference to Jonah's stay in the belly of the fish "for three days and three nights," and then in vv. 41-42 with a further reference to Jonah and then to the Queen of the South. Thus, unlike the other two Synoptic Gospels, Matthew has a doublet: one episode from "Mk" (16:1,4), and one from "Q" (12:38-42).

These four forms of the saying about sign-seeking raise various questions. *First,* are the Marcan and "Q" forms provided by the tradition variants of one saying of Jesus; or do they represent two different answers that Jesus gave on different occasions? In the first case, the Marcan form would represent a pared-down version or recollection. The second case is not impossible, but there is no way to be sure about it; reputable commentators (e.g. M.-J. Lagrange) have espoused it. (We may be faced here with the same sort of situation as with the traditions in "Mk" and "Q" about the temptations of Jesus, except that there Matthew and Luke have combined things in one episode.) *Second,* in the "Q" form of the episode, the formulation in Luke 11:31-32 is almost word-for-word identical with its parallel in Matthew; the correspondence in Luke 11:29-30 with Matt 12:38-39 is less close but sufficiently so to maintain the origin in "Q." The problem is caused, however, by Matt 12:40. Did "Q" contain the reference to Jonah's stay in the fish's belly? It is unlikely that Luke would have omitted it, if it had been there. It is rather Matthew who has added it, allegorizing, as it were, a detail in the OT story about Jonah in hindsight-reflection on Jesus' resurrection. The "sign of Jonah" as a reference to Jesus' resurrection is scarcely to be attributed to Jesus himself; it is simply another instance of Matthean additions to the words of Jesus (see pp. 631, 897). This addition makes "the sign of Jonah" in Matthew double, the resurrection and that of "Q" (see below). *Third,* since the saying about the Queen of the South is found in both Matthew and Luke, it must have been in "Q." But it is intrusive in the story about the sign of Jonah. Could it have been uttered independently by Jesus on another occasion and added later by topical arrangement when "Q" was being formed? It could have been joined to the sign-of-Jonah saying for three reasons: (a) the common reference to "this generation"; (b) the common description of Jesus as "something greater than" Solomon or Jonah; and (c) the coming of an OT figure from afar (Jonah to preach, the queen to listen). But maybe the topical arrangement stems from Jesus himself. This, however, gives rise to another question, about the order of the added sayings, since they differ in Matthew and Luke. *Fourth,* which is the more original order of the added sayings in "Q"? Most commentators think that Luke has preserved it: the Queen of the South rising in judgment, then the Ninevites (11:31-32). This order is also seen to be chronological. It has been suggested that Matthew has inverted this sequence in order to put the example of Jonah and the Ninevites closer to his addition in v. 40. This is plausible enough. But the Matthean order (without v. 40) would more easily explain the topical arrangement mentioned above (the "sign of Jonah" of v. 39, followed by some form of Luke 11:30, which has been omitted by Matthew in favor of his v. 40, and then by v. 41; this would provide a place to which to attach v. 42, see D. Correns, "Jona und Salomo.") Then Luke's change of order would be in the interest of investing the preaching of Jonah with wisdom-overtones (recall Luke 7:35). In the long run, we cannot say for certain who inverted the order of "Q" in these sayings.

In the Lucan form v. 29a is from the evangelist's pen; it may even have been composed as a replacement for what he used in 11:16. Luke has probably preserved the original wording of vv. 29b,c,30. Verses 31-32 are almost identical with Matt 12:41-42 (save for the order); fifty-three out of fifty-five words are the same (reference to them could have been added on p. 76). Cf. J. Jeremias, *Die Sprache*, 203-204.

In terms of form-critical assessment, the episode basically preserves minatory sayings of Jesus (see *HST* 112, 117-118). They thus join those of 11:23,24-26. But the introduction of the saying about the Queen of the South has also added a bit of a wisdom-saying, giving this nuance to both statements about "something greater."

Before trying to understand the meaning of the passage and the sense of "the sign of Jonah" in the Lucan version, it would be wise to recall the elements of the story of Jonah in the OT. The four chapters of the Book of Jonah are marked by parallelism: chaps. 3 and 4 correspond to chaps. 1 and 2 (in diptych-like fashion). In part one the word of Yahweh comes to Jonah of Gathhepher in Galilee and tells him to go and cry out against Nineveh, the great city of the Assyrians, that it might repent of its wickedness. Jonah is reluctant, flees from Joppa on a ship headed in the opposite direction (to Tarshish in the west), and is punished for trying to flee from Yahweh himself. Thrown overboard by sailors in a storm, he is swallowed up by a great fish appointed by Yahweh. He spends three days and three nights in its belly (from which he even utters a psalm of thanksgiving). He is eventually spewed forth upon dry land. In part two the word of Yahweh comes to Jonah again, sending him a second time to Nineveh. He goes and preaches there until all Nineveh sits in sackcloth, fasts, and repents of its wickedness—from the king to toddlers to animals. At which Yahweh repents. Seeing Yahweh's graciousness but being distressed at this rescue of an evil pagan city, the Galilean prophet retires east of it to see what may become of Nineveh. To shield himself from the sun and the heat, Jonah builds himself a booth, and Yahweh supplies added shade by making a plant sprout, which makes Jonah happy. The next day the plant withers, and Jonah loses his added shield against the sun and heat; again he is distressed—distressed enough to want to die. But Yahweh's word takes him up short: Did you, Jonah, make the plant grow? Do you now show pity for it? Should I not show pity for Nineveh, with its 120,000 inhabitants who repented at your preaching? Thus runs the classic OT account of Yahweh's universal salvific concern. In it should be noted the contrast between the recalcitrant, angry Jewish prophet and the obedience and/or repentance of all others in the story (sailors, Ninevites, animals, fish, plants). Jonah's stay in the fish's belly was a punishment of the prophet, who is eventually saved by God for his own designs. That stay is not a "sign" to Jonah's contemporaries; nothing in the story suggests that he referred to it in preaching to the Ninevites. They know nothing about the "miraculous salvation" of Jonah, *pace* G. Schneider, *Evangelium nach Lukas,* 271.

The Lucan Jesus alludes to this story as he reacts to the request that came from the crowds that he show them "a sign from heaven"; the request was made in 11:16 by those who would put him to a test. They sought from him more than what he had been trying to show them in his miracles; they wanted a flamboyant manifestation, in a way reminiscent of the third temptation in 4:9-11 (see COMMENT on pp. 511-512), as a sign of his credibility. Jesus' answer: "No sign will be given to it except the sign of Jonah" (v. 29c). This is explained in v. 30: as Jonah was a sign to the Ninevites, so will Jesus as the Son of Man be a sign to this generation.

In what sense was Jonah a sign to the Ninevites? To many commentators the sign is the person of Jonah, and by this is sometimes implied "Jonah as saved from the fish"—yet that would be to read a nuance of Matt 12:40 into the "Q" form and into Luke's use of it. Not even Luke 16:31, with its reference to someone raised from the dead, makes it necessary to think that Luke's reference to Jesus as the Son of Man demands this here. As v. 30 stood in "Q," independently of vv. 31-32, it would have to refer to the person of Jonah as manifested to the Ninevites in the Book of Jonah, part two. When joined to the sayings in vv. 31-32, however, it would have carried a further nuance: the person of Jonah and *his preaching,* as a result of which the Ninevites reformed their lives. In the total Lucan context, this is clearly the sense of "the sign of Jonah." (Matthew has this sense too [see v. 41], but he has added a second sense in his reference to the resurrection by the allusion to the stay in the fish's belly in v. 40.)

Hence in this Lucan passage one must note: Just as Jonah was a prophet sent from afar to preach repentance to the Ninevites, so too does Jesus appear to this generation. The title given to him, "Son of Man," is a reference neither to his resurrection nor to his parousia *(pace HST* 117-118), but to his earthly ministry. He comes from afar in the sense of a heaven-sent prophet like Jonah; but he is something greater than Jonah. His preaching is the only sign that will be given to this generation; indeed, the note of irony is unmistakable, since this sign is already being given. The reaction to him has been recorded in 7:31-34. That reaction evokes his present warning: The Ninevites, who heeded the preaching of Jonah, reformed their lives; they will then rise and point an accuser's finger at this "evil generation" in the day of judgment.

By putting the saying about the Queen of the South before that about the Ninevites, Luke enhances the warning with a wisdom-motif. In not heeding Jesus' preaching, the men of his generation have failed to recognize the heaven-sent wisdom which he has come to preach. For this reason the Queen of the South, who came from the ends of the earth to listen to Solomon's wisdom, will rise too at the judgment to point an accusing finger at those who challenge Jesus, for "something greater than Solomon" is here.

Coming immediately after Jesus' saying about those who are really blessed ("who listen to the word of God and observe it," v. 28), this episode suggests an identification of Jesus' preaching and wisdom with that "word of God." Moreover, the two OT figures, Solomon and Jonah, who address their message to pagans (the queen and the Ninevites), succeed in their tasks. These pagans who listened to the authorities of old are precisely the ones who will rise to express condemnation of "this generation." The implications of this episode for Lucan universalism in salvation are not to be missed.

In what sense would Jesus be understood as "something greater" than Solomon and Jonah? These two OT foils to his activity were a king and a prophet; both of these titles are given to Jesus in the Lucan story (see pp. 213-215). But he has already been identified as one who sits on David's throne (1:32), indeed, even as "the Son of God" (1:35; cf. 3:22; 8:28; 9:35; 22:70). The reader of the Lucan Gospel, who recalls these titles, realizes how much greater is this "Son of Man" who now preaches to this generation as a heaven-sent prophet coming from afar.

Again, the eschatological reference to "the judgment" is not to be overlooked. The Lucan use of the "Q" references to it has in no way attentuated the force of the warning that they try to convey. Whether that judgment is imminent is not said.

The story carries its own message to Christians of every generation who are distracted from the main message of this preacher from afar and want him rather to give them "a sign from heaven" to reassure them. The credence put in private revelations of one sort or another over the centuries is but an example of how the attitude of "the men of this generation" persists in human existence, even Christian experience.

NOTES

11 29. *the crowds.* I.e. those mentioned in 11:14. See NOTE on 3:7. In the Matthean parallel (12:38) the setting is more specific: questions from Scribes and Pharisees.

pressing closely about. Or possibly, "were gathering even more."

started to say. See 3:8. E. Klostermann *(Lukasevangelium,* 128) may be right in thinking that v. 16 was the real introduction to this episode; having used it there, Luke now fashions this introduction anew.

This generation. See NOTES on 7:31; 9:41. Cf. Mark 8:12; Matt 12:39; 16:4; both of these evangelists speak of an "evil and adulterous generation." See further 11:30,31,32,50,51; 17:25; 21:32.

an evil generation. The predicate finds a Hebrew equivalent in 1QSb 3:7: *dôr*

'awlā[h], "a generation of wickedness." It is probably called "evil" because it is seeking a sign of credibility.

it demands a sign. Recall 11:16. Though *sēmeion* is the usual word in the Johannine
Gospel for Jesus' miracles, it is never so used in the Synoptics (although Luke combines it with *dynameis* and *terata* in Acts 2:22). *Sēmeion* refers here to a flamboyant
portent to be perceived by the senses which would express or vindicate Jesus' authority or credibility. His contemporaries, who do not accept his preaching and perversely
relate his exorcisms to Beelzebul (11:14-23), seek instead from him a "sign from
heaven." In Acts 5:36 Luke refers to Theudas, who gave himself out to be somebody;
Josephus tells how he sought to establish his credibility *(Ant.* 20.5,1 § 97): He led a
group of followers with all their possessions, claiming to be a prophet, and that "at his
command the river would be parted and give them easy passage." The demand made
of Jesus must be understood against the background of such claims. There is, however,
an OT background to signs from heaven. See Isa 7:11; Judg 6:17. See further the
development of the sense of "sign" in the OT, especially in the postexilic writings and
in the LXX (K. H. Rengstorf, *TDNT* 7. 208-225). Recall the Pauline comment in 1
Cor 1:22.

no sign will be given to it. Here the answer agrees in sense, if not in wording, with
the formula in Mark 8:12. The Marcan formula, introduced by *amēn legō hymin,*
contains a Hebraism *(ei dothēsetai),* an oath-formula (Greek *ei* = Hebrew *'im).* Sense:
No flamboyant portent will be supplied. A similar answer will be given again in Luke
16:31.

except the sign of Jonah. I.e. a sign drawn from ancient history. Reference is made
to Jonah, son of Amittai, usually identified with the prophet from Gathhepher in
Galilee in the days of Jeroboam II (2 Kgs 14:25), who became the hero of the Book of
Jonah. Some mss. (A, C, W, Θ, and the Koine text-tradition) add, "the prophet," but
this is missing in mss. P[45], P[75], ℵ, B, D, L, etc., and is suspect because of scribal
harmonization with Matt 12:39. For the sense of "the sign of Jonah," see COMMENT.

The history of the interpretation of this passage has even included an attempt to
identify "Jonah" with John the Baptist. See C. R. Bowen, J. H. Michael. At work in
such thinking is the parallelism of "Simon Bar-Jona" of Matt 16:17 and "Simon the
son of John" of John 1:42. The alleged equation of Hebrew *Yōnāh* with a shortened
form of *Yĕhôḥānān* is unknown in any contemporary Hebrew or Aramaic sources.
The confusion is found in some mss. of the LXX of 2 Kgs 25:23; 1 Chr 26:3; 1 Esdr
9:1,23 (see J. Jeremias, *TDNT* 3. 407); but these are Christian copies of the LXX and
the NT parallelism mentioned above may be responsible for the variants in mss. A and
B of the LXX.

According to J. Jeremias, "the sign of Jonah must refer to the miracle of the
deliverance of Jonah from the belly of the great fish (Jon. 2). For the contemporaries
of Jonah this event was the outstanding miracle in the life of Jonah. The term 'sign' is
in fact used of this miracle" (ibid. 409). How any of the sources that Jeremias cites can
be considered "contemporaries of Jonah" is puzzling (3 Macc 6:8; Josephus, *Ant.*
9.10,2 § 213; or the sources mentioned in Str-B 1. 645-649). He cites *Pirqe de-Rabbi
Eliezer* 10 as a Jewish text which uses indeed "signs" *('wtwt)* of Jonah's deliverance;
but he does not tell his readers that this writing comes from the eighth century A.D.
and is written in artificial Hebrew reminiscent of the Geonic period. The chances are

936   LUKE X-XXIV   § IVA

that this late haggadah is influenced by Christian discussions of "the sign of Jonah." Strikingly, the résumé of the Book of Jonah given by Josephus *(Ant.* 9.10,2 § 208-214) does not call Jonah's deliverance a "sign," much less a miracle of any sort; and the editor of the English translation notes that the summary "omits the chief message of the story, the need of repentance" (R. Marcus, LCL 6. 113).

30. *the Ninevites.* Luke uses simply *Nineuitais* (which lacks a counterpart in Matt 12:40 because of that evangelist's modification); but in v. 32 the "Q" phrase *andres Nineuitai* occurs (also in Matt 12:41). The latter form corresponds to classical Greek usage, which Luke often employs in Acts (1:11; 2:14,22; 3:12; 5:35; 13:16; 21:28).

the Son of Man. I.e. Jesus (see NOTE on 5:24 and pp. 208-210), understood in his role as a heaven-sent messenger who confronts his generation with his preaching and wisdom (7:34-35).

At the end of this Lucan verse ms. D and some OL mss. insert a form of the Matthean addition (12:40).

will be. I.e. in the rest of Jesus' preaching to them; irony is at work. Bultmann *(HST* 118) understands it thus: "Just as Jonah came to the Ninevites from a distant country, so will the Son of Man come to this generation from heaven; i.e. the sign asked for the preaching of Jesus is the Son of Man himself, when he comes to judgement." This interpretation presupposes that vv. 31-32 were always part of the original saying; there is, however, no guarantee that the future tense of the vb. has to be understood of Jesus' parousia.

31. *At the judgment.* I.e. the day of divine retribution. See NOTE on 10:14. This phrase does not imply a reference to Jesus' resurrection, as some interpreters have supposed.

the Queen of the South. I.e. the Queen of Sheba, known from 1 Kgs 10:1-29; 2 Chr 9:1-12. Sheba (Hebrew *Šĕbā')* was a kingdom of Semitic people in southwest Arabia, not far from Teima. See Gen 10:28; Job 6:19. In the Greek of the LXX the name became *Saba,* and when Josephus speaks of it, he identifies it as "the royal city (i.e. capital) of Ethiopia" *(Ant.* 2.10,2 § 249; cf. 8.6,5 § 165). This linking seems to be based on Isa 43:3, where Ethiopia and Sheba *(Kûš ûSĕbā')* are mentioned together. Later rabbinic tradition made of Sheba a land of sorcerers. See L. Ginzberg, *Legends of the Jews* (7 vols.; Philadelphia: Jewish Publication Society, 1904-1938) 6. 292.

will arise together with. This may simply mean "will rise from the dead" along with; but it may also reflect the Hebrew/Aramaic legal expression *qwm 'm,* "stand up with," i.e. to take the position of an accuser, if the expression attested in rabbinic writings be also contemporary. See J. Jeremias, *TDNT* 3. 408 n. 15; *AAGA*[3] 134. Cf. *m. Sanh.* 10:3.

the men of this generation. Luke uses *tōn andrōn tēs geneas tautēs,* not *anthrōpōn,* but that expression is dependent on the phrase *andres Nineuitai* in v. 32, the form which was in "Q." See Matt 12:41. The queen is not thought of as rising up against only the males of Nineveh; that would counter the thrust of the Jonah story in the OT, where humans and beasts, herds and flocks sat in sackcloth and fasted (Hebrew: *hā'ādām wĕhabbĕhēmāh habbāqār wĕhaṣṣō'n,* Jonah 3:7). For a different view of the matter, see N. M. Flanagan, "Mary in the Theology of John's Gospel," *Marianum* 40 (1978) 288-304, esp. 290. This is a good example of a NT instance in which *anēr* has to be understood in a generic sense, not specifically as "man, male." See NOTE on v. 30.

She came from the ends of the earth. The expression *ta perata tēs gēs* imitates a LXX phrase (Pss 2:8; 22:28; 46:10; 59:14; 65:6). This description of the queen reflects also on that of Jonah, who was ordered by God to go to distant Nineveh in the east, but who fled first to Tarshish in the west.

to listen to the wisdom of Solomon. In the OT the Queen of Sheba "heard of Solomon's fame" and "came to test him with hard questions," all of which Solomon answered (1 Kgs 10:1-3); then she "saw all the wisdom of Solomon" (v. 4) and told him, "Your wisdom and prosperity surpass the report that I had heard" (v. 7c). Cf. 1 Kgs 3:5-14; 10:23-24; Josephus, *Ant.* 8.6,5-6 § 165-175, esp. § 171 *(tēn sophian kai tēn phronēsin).*

but now. Lit. "and behold" (introductory *kai idou,* a Septuagintism; cf. p. 121). Verse 32c begins in the same way.

something greater than Solomon! The phraseology recalls that of 7:35. God's wisdom is vindicated by the judgment that will be passed, not on Jesus by his generation, but on it by those who accept him and so prove to be "her [wisdom's] children." A sapiential theme of the OT is now linked to a prophetic theme: the Son of Man, who preaches God's word, is greater than wise Solomon (and the mouthpiece-prophet, Jonah [v. 32]).

32. *At the judgment.* See NOTE on v. 31.

they reformed their lives at the preaching of Jonah. I.e. they recognized the sign given to them, the prophet's call to repentance *(metanoia,* see p. 237). On *kērygma,* "preaching," see p. 147. Cf. H. Braun, "Umkehr in spätjüdisch-häretischer und in frühchristlicher Sicht," *Gesammelte Studien zum Neuen Testament und seiner Umwelt* (Tübingen: Mohr [Siebeck], 1962) 70-72.

BIBLIOGRAPHY (11:29-32)

Bacon, B. W. "What Was the Sign of Jonah?" *Biblical World* 20 (1902) 99-112.

Bonsirven, J. "Hora talmudica: À propos du logion sur le signe de Jonas," *RSR* 24 (1934) 450-455.

Bowen, C. R. "Was John the Baptist the Sign of Jonah?" *AJT* 20 (1916) 414-421.

Correns, D. "Jona und Salomo," *Wort in der Zeit* (eds. W. Haubeck and M. Bachmann), 86-94.

Edwards, R. A. *The Sign of Jonah in the Theology of the Evangelists and Q* (SBT 2/18; Naperville, IL: Allenson, 1971).

Hoffmann, P. *Studien zur Theologie der Logienquelle* (NTAbh 2/8; 2d ed.; Münster in W.: Aschendorff, 1975) 181.

Howton, J. "The Sign of Jonah," *SJT* 15 (1962) 288-304.

Lührmann, D. *Redaktion,* 34-43, 43-48.

Merrill, E. H. "The Sign of Jonah," *JETS* 23 (1980) 23-30.

Michael, J. H. "The Sign of John," *JTS* 21 (1919-1920) 146-159.

Mussner, F. "Wege zum Selbstbewusstsein Jesu: Ein Versuch," *BZ* 12 (1968) 161-172, esp. 169-171.

Schmitt, G. "Das Zeichen des Jona," *ZNW* 69 (1978) 123-129.

Schulz, S. *Q: Die Spruchquelle,* 250-257.

Seidelin, P. "Das Jonaszeichen," *ST* 5 (1951) 119-131.

Thibaut, R. "Le signe de Jonas," *NRT* 60 (1933) 532-536.

Tödt, H. E. *The Son of Man in the Synoptic Tradition* (London: SCM, 1965) 52-54, 211-214, 271-274.

Vögtle, A. "Der Spruch von Jonaszeichen," *Synoptische Studien Alfred Wikenhauser zum siebzigsten Geburtstag . . . dargebracht* (eds. J. Schmid and A. Vögtle; Munich: Zink, 1953) 230-277; reprinted in *Das Evangelium,* 103-136.

75. SAYINGS ABOUT LIGHT
(11:33-36)

11 ^{33} "No one lights a lamp and then puts it away in a crevice or under a bushel, but rather on the stand so that those who come in can see its radiance. ^{34} Now your eye is the lamp of the body. If your eye is clear-sighted, then your whole body has light; but if it is bad, then your body is in darkness. ^{35} See to it, then, that the light which enters you is not darkness. ^{36} If your whole body has light, with no part of it in darkness, it will all have as much light as when a lamp shines on you with its rays."

COMMENT

Luke now joins further sayings of Jesus to the warnings of vv. 14-32. In themselves, they are unrelated to what immediately precedes, being drawn from independent contexts. But they are grouped about the idea of light and its effect or influence (11:33-36); catchword bonding (light, lamp) makes them into a unit.

Verses 33-35 are clearly derived from "Q"; their parallels, however, are found in different parts of the Matthean sermon on the mount (5:15; 6:22-23; see p. 78). The first saying (v. 33 = Matt 5:15) is, moreover, a doublet of Luke 8:16 (= Mark 4:21; see p. 81). Another form of it is found in *Gos. of Thom.* § 33b (discussed on p. 717). Verses 34-35 are very close in their wording to Matt 6:22-23. By inserting the introductory "See to it" *(skopei),* Luke has made the more original exclamation (preserved in Matt 6:23) into a warning, which builds on the saying of v. 34. A form of v. 34 is also preserved in *Gos. of Thom.* § 24c: "There is light within a man of light, and it *(or* he) lights up the whole world; if it *(or* he) does not shine, there is darkness." This transforms the saying in the sense of v. 33; it is scarcely a more primitive form of it, being somewhat influenced by John 1:9; 5:35. Verse 36 is problematic. Did it belong to "Q" or not? F. Hahn, R. A. Edwards et al. think so. Matthew would then have eliminated the verse because of its tautological nature. But it may also have been a Lucan addition (so S. Schulz), a platitudinous attempt to explain further vv. 34 and/or 35. (See further COMMENT on 8:16-18. Cf. J. Jeremias, *Die Sprache,* 204-205.)

Form-critically, this material is to be classed with dominical sayings, specifically wisdom-sayings (see *HST* 92, 96). T. W. Manson *(Sayings,* 93) prefers to regard vv. 34-35 as a distinct parable in poetic form.

As a unit in this part of the travel account, these sayings explain further the nature of the "something greater" than Solomon or Jonah that is here: In Jesus a light has been given, which needs no further sign from heaven to authenticate it. The infancy narrative has already presented him as a "light" (2:32); now that motif is exploited. The light is not hidden away; if it does not illumine, it is not because of its being concealed or snuffed out, but because people of this generation are not clear-sighted, and darkness is part of them.

The first saying (v. 33) presents the person and preaching of Jesus as the light. The doublet in 8:16 concentrated more on the disciples' hearing of the word, whereas now it bears on Jesus himself. Though the Matthean parallel (5:15) depicts the lamp shining on all who are in the house, the Lucan form, which has been assimilated to the wording of 8:16c, illumines "those who come in" (to the house), i.e. possible converts from among those still outside. The sapiential character of the saying implies a counsel to disciples who also must display a radiance to others, to those who come under their influence in missionary endeavors.

The second saying (v. 34) is a further sapiential utterance which comments on the condition of those who listen—those who see the light, or should be able to see it. There is a certain obscurity to it, as R. Bultmann *(HST* 92) recognized. It is a primitive way of expressing consciousness of light and darkness: A person with good sight, who sees light, is considered to be illumined within; a person with bad sight, who does not see light, is filled with darkness within. On the surface, the saying deals with the physical condition of a person's eyes, clear-sighted or bad. But in the context, in which "bad" is expressed by the adj. *ponēros,* the same word used for the "evil" generation of v. 29, the sapiential saying takes on another nuance. The clear-sightedness becomes a dedication to the word of God preached (the "light"); and the badness results in a "darkened" existence. The disciple is thus cautioned (v. 35) to make sure that light illumines his/her existence and that darkness does not influence it. If the body is truly receptive of light, "with no part of it in darkness," it will accept illumination from the true light when it shines—the word of God preached by Jesus.

These sayings about light, depicting Jesus as such and stressing the need of a clear eye for illumined existence, are addressed in the Lucan context to people of Jesus' own generation and their sign-seeking. Of old, Israel had been destined to be a "light to the nations" in the Servant Song of Isa 49:6. Jesus now shines in that capacity, as a light not hidden away from his generation. But is the eye of this generation clear-sighted and not bad? Can it say with the psalmist of old, "Yes, Lord, you light my lamp; my God illumines my darkness" (Ps 18:29)? That is a question that Christians of every generation may ask themselves: Does the God-given light illumine them, with no part of them in darkness?

NOTES

11 33. *puts it away in a crevice.* Or possibly "a cellar." The best mss. read *kryptēn*, "crevice, cellar." But P⁴⁵, Ψ, etc., have *krypton*, "hiding place." Some interpreters (C. H. Dodd, J. Jeremias, G. Schneider et al.) think that "cellar" is more appropriate here, a reference to a non-Palestinian house in the Hellenistic world. That would be possible, if it could be shown that that is the only meaning of *kryptē.*

or under a bushel. Lit. "or under a bushel-measure." See NOTE on 8:16. This phrase is omitted in important mss. here (P⁴⁵, P⁷⁵, L, Ξ, 0214, etc.), but read by others (ℵ, B, C, D, W, Θ, and the Koine text-tradition). N-A²⁶ has set it in square brackets, being unable to decide. See *TCGNT* 159.

those who come in can see its radiance. Matt 5:15 reads rather "shines on all in the house," probably the original wording of "Q," which Luke has changed to make the end of this verse agree with the addition he made to the Marcan form in 8:16c (save for the use of *phengos*, "radiance," instead of *phōs*, "light" there).

34. *your eye is the lamp of the body.* I.e. that whereby the person is illumined— because the eye is the organ whereby light is perceived. The function of "lamp" has changed here. That Greek *sōma* means "person" can be seen from Rom 12:1; Phil 1:20; Eph 5:28; Plutarch, *Moral.* 142E; Aeschines, *Orat.* 2.58; MM 621. There is no reason to appeal to questionable Aramaic expressions (especially of late date), as does T. W. Manson, *Sayings,* 93.

clear-sighted. The Greek adj. *haplous* basically means "simple" (i.e. single, not double or triple); it is so used in Greek papyri (MM 58). A moral sense of it is also known, "sincere" *(Barn.* 19:2) or (because of its relation to the n. *haplotēs,* "simplicity, generosity, liberality") "generous." The moral sense might seem preferable because of the contrast with *ponēros* later in the verse.

light . . . darkness. These natural phenomena are often used in Greek literature (e.g. Euripides, *Iphig. Taur.* 1026; Plutarch, *Moral.* 82B) and in the OT (e.g. Ps 112:4; Isa 42:6-7; 45:7; 59:9-10; Job 29:3; Prov 4:18-19; Mic 7:8) as symbols of good and evil. Here the pair is similarly used, but in a specific sense: acceptance of the person and preaching of Jesus or not. See further NOTE on 16:8b.

bad. The adj. *ponēros* designates primarily physical badness, "in poor condition, sick" (BAGD 690). Cf. Plato, *Hippias Min.* 374D *(ponēria ophthalmōn).* Though it also occurs in the NT in the sense of "evil eye" (Matt 20:15; Mark 7:22), this meaning is not suitable here. However, a nuance of moral evil is suggested by the relation of this expression to the "evil generation" of v. 29.

35. *the light which enters you.* Lit. "which is in you." The oxymoron is heightened by the introduction of Luke's initial caution, "See to it."

36. *it will all have as much light.* The sense of this verse is quite contested. First of all, C. C. Torrey *(The Four Gospels: A New Translation* [London/New York: Harper, 1933] 145, 309-310), invoking a mistranslation of Aramaic *nāhîr lehweh kollā',* in which the last word—actually the subj.—has been translated as adjectival *holon* ("it . . . all"), would render it: "If, however, your whole body is lighted up, with no part dark, then all about you will be light; just as the lamp lights you with its brightness." This is not impossible, if the theory of mistranslation is admissible. Second, it could simply mean, "If the heart is truly receptive of light, it will receive light from the true light when it shines, that is from Christ" (so J. M. Creed, *The Gospel,* 164, following E. Klostermann, *Lukasevangelium,* 129. For a third sense, see I. H. Marshall, *Luke,* 490 (§ 2).

BIBLIOGRAPHY (11:33-36)

Benoit, P. "L'Oeil, lampe du corps," *RB* 60 (1953) 603-605.

Brandt, W. "Der Spruch vom lumen internum," *ZNW* 14 (1913) 97-116, 177-201.

Edlund, C. *Das Auge der Einfalt: Eine Untersuchung zu Matth. 6,22-23 und Luk. 11,34-35* (ASNU 19; Copenhagen: Munksgaard; Lund: Gleerup, 1952).

Hahn, F. "Die Worte vom Licht 11,33-36," eds. P. Hoffmann et al., *Orientierung an Jesus* 107-138.

Schulz, S. *Q: Die Spruchquelle,* 468-470, 474-476.

Sjöberg, E. "Das Licht in dir: Zur Deutung von Matth. 6,22f Par.," *ST* 5 (1951) 89-105.

76. SAYINGS AGAINST THE PHARISEES AND THE LAWYERS (11:37-54)

11 37 When he had said this, a Pharisee invited him to dine with him. So he entered his home and reclined at table. 38 When the Pharisee saw this, he was surprised that Jesus did not first wash before the meal. 39 But the Lord said to him, "You Pharisees usually clean the outside of the cup and the platter; but the inside of you is full of greed and wickedness. 40 Foolish people! Did not the one who made the outside also make the inside? 41 Give away rather its contents as alms, and all will be clean for you.

42 Woe to you Pharisees! You tithe mint and rue and every edible herb, but disregard justice and the love of God. These were rather the things one should practice, without neglecting the others. 43 Woe to you Pharisees! You love the front seat in synagogues and greetings of respect in the marketplaces. 44 Woe to you, because you are like unmarked graves over which people walk without realizing it."

45 One of the lawyers said to him in reply, "Teacher, in saying these things, you are also insulting us." 46 And he said, "Woe to you lawyers too! You weigh down people with burdens they can scarcely carry and you will not lift a single finger to the burdens. 47 Woe to you, because you build the tombs of the prophets whom your fathers murdered. 48 Thereby you give testimony that you approve of the deeds of your fathers; they murdered the prophets, and you build their tombs! 49 For this reason God's wisdom has said, 'I shall send to them prophets and emissaries; and some of these they will kill and persecute.' 50 Consequently, the blood of all the prophets which has been shed since the foundation of the world shall be required of this generation—51 from the blood of Abel to the blood of Zechariah, who perished between the altar and the sanctuary. Yes, and I tell you, it shall be required of this generation! 52 Woe to you lawyers! You have carried off the key of knowledge; you did not enter yourselves and have hindered those who would enter."

53 When Jesus had gone out of there, the Scribes and the Pharisees began to react violently against him and to check his utterances closely in many things, 54 plotting to catch him in something that he might say.

COMMENT

Luke continues his travel account with sayings of Jesus against Pharisees and Lawyers (or Scribes). They include six woes, three uttered against each group (11:37-54), in a parallelism reminiscent of the beatitudes and woes of 6:20-26.

The source of this material in Luke and of its counterpart in Matthew 23 is not easily determined. One senses a great similarity between these two passages in content and generic topics and wording, but specific phrasing and the order of the topics vary considerably. The material is used by Matthew in one of his five great sermons, and a number of commentators think that at least some of the material used by him has come from "M" as well as from

"Q" (see B. H. Streeter, *The Four Gospels*, 253-254; T. W. Manson, *Sayings*, 95-96). Matthew has also made use of Mark 12:38-39.

As for the Lucan form of these sayings, certain features are to be noted: (1) Luke has himself fashioned the introductory vv. 37-38 and 45. Verses 37-38 introduce not only the whole set of sayings but also the first one about the cup and the platter (vv. 39-40) as well as the woes against the Pharisees (vv. 42-44). Verse 37, composed by Luke, was modeled on 6:37 (see *HST* 334); v. 38, with the detail about Jesus failing to wash, is a takeoff on Mark 7:2, a passage omitted from "Mk" as a result of the Big Omission (see p. 67). Luke's style has further left its traces in v. 39 in the use of "the Lord" and "said to him" (see NOTES). Moreover, the first saying (about cleansing the cup) is only loosely connected with Jesus' own failure to wash. (2) Whereas the sayings in Matthew 23 are directed consistently against the Scribes and the Pharisees (vv. 2,13,15,23,25,27,29—seven woes in all), Luke has made of the inherited material two sets of three woes: vv. 42-44 against the Pharisees; vv. 46-52 against their lawyers. This 2 × 3 parallel is a Lucan creation; it may result also in the dropping of "woe" from before the first saying (vv. 39-40). (3) Luke has added v. 41, which has no parallel in Matthew; it stems from his own composition, stressing almsgiving and using his favorite adversative conj. *plēn*, "except, but, rather" (p. 111) and another favorite, "all." (4) He has further added the narrative of vv. 53-54, which together with vv. 37-38 form a secondary framework for the sayings themselves. G. B. Caird *(Gospel of St Luke*, 158) would ascribe vv. 42-52 to "Q" and vv. 37-41,53-54 to "L."

It is indeed unlikely that vv. 39-40,42-44,46-52 have been derived from "L." It is too difficult to ascribe the similarity of content and generic topics and wording to the block of material in Matthew 23 to such a coincidence as would be demanded by the independent derivation of these sayings from "M" and "L." No, for these Lucan verses one must postulate "Q," and thus agree (in general) with many older commentators (A. von Harnack, W. Bussmann, R. Bultmann, et al.). If one allows for the use of "M" along with "Q" in Matthew 23, one should recognize nevertheless two other Lucan features in this section: (a) a comparative shortening of the sayings (cf. 11:43 with Matt 23:6; 11:44 with Matt 23:27; 11:47-48 with Matt 23:29-31; 11:51 with Matt 23:35-36); and (b) the elimination of material that would not readily be appreciated or understood by the Gentile Christian readers of this Gospel (e.g. Luke's change to the generic "every edible herb," v. 42; his dropping of "the weightier matters of the law," Matt 23:23; of "being called Rabbi," 23:8; of "whitewashed graves," 23:27; of synagogue-beatings, 23:34; of "son of Barachiah," 23:35; of the locking of the "kingdom of heaven," 23:13). (Cf. J. Jeremias, *Die Sprache*, 205-210.)

Furthermore, Luke has probably introduced "God's wisdom" (v. 49, where the Matthean parallel puts the words on Jesus' own lips), a motif close to the sapiential cast of 11:31 (cf. 7:35); and the "key of knowledge" (v. 52), being the only Synoptic evangelist to speak of *gnōsis* (see 1:77). Who changed the order of the woes? It is hard to say; Matthew has the following order (in the Lucan numbering): 43,46,52,42,(39),44,47. Verses 49-51 were already joined to vv. 46-48 in "Q," even if we prefer to attribute "God's wisdom" to Luke's pen. The conclusions in vv. 53-54 are to be compared with similar conclusions in 6:11; 19:47; 20:19; 22:2, all of which have counterparts in Mark. This one alone stems from Lucan composition, but it helps to trace the growing hostility to Jesus' ministry that punctuates the Lucan account.

Verse 43 has a doublet in 20:46, which is derived from Mark 12:38-39 (see p. 81). Moreover, a form of vv. 39-40 is found in *Gos. of Thom.* § 89: "Jesus said, 'Why do you wash the outside of the cup? Do you not realize that the one who made the inside is also the one who made the outside?' " This simpler form may seem to be more primitive; but it is probably a later simplification of the saying in an effort to emphasize divine unity (see J.-E. Ménard, *L'Evangile selon Thomas,* 191); cf. § 22 (and p. 87). Again, a form of v. 52 is preserved in *Gos. of Thom.* § 39a: "Jesus said, 'The Pharisees and the Scribes have taken the keys of knowledge; they have hidden them and have not entered, and those who wished to enter they have not permitted.' " To it is joined a form of Matt 10:16b. The opening of this form is Matthean; but the reference to the "keys of knowledge" is Lucan, apart from the pl.; the hiding is probably a development of the Matthean "locking up." These are a development beyond the canonical forms. (Cf. OxyP 655:39-50; *ESBNT* 413-414.)

Form-critically considered, the passage is made up of a narrative framework, composed by Luke (vv. 37-38, 53-54), a secondary narrative introduction (v. 45), and sayings of Jesus. R. Bultmann *(HST* 131-132) classed vv. 39-41,42 as legal sayings, and vv. 43-44,46-48,49-51 as minatory sayings (ibid. 113-114). The six woes, however, are found in vv. 42-44,46,47,52, which should mean that v. 42 belongs with the minatory sayings. Verse 49 might also be regarded in the Lucan context as a wisdom-saying.

In this section of the travel account Luke depicts Jesus in controversy with specific Palestinian religious figures. It seems unlikely that Jesus himself uttered a harangue such as this against these leaders—especially on the occasion of an invitation to dinner. The differences in the Lucan and Matthean contexts reveal the secondary grouping of sayings in the units preserved. The Lucan introduction sets the stage for them in any case: Jesus has accepted an invitation to dine with a Pharisee but pays no attention to the custom of washing (probably his hands) before the meal—something that his host would consider of prime importance.

The shock of his host elicits from Jesus the first remark about cleansing— not oneself or one's hands—but (strangely) about the ritual cleansing of utensils. Outward cleansing is insufficient, being superficial; one must clean the inside of the cup or the platter as well. The "inside" of such utensils, however, becomes the symbol of the inside of human beings—full of greed and wickedness. Jesus recommends that one consider the maker of the vessel: He made the inside as well as the outside. The reference to the maker gives a dimension to the saying that does not escape the reader—God himself, whom Luke elsewhere (Acts 1:24; 15:8; see NOTE on 16:15) calls "the knower of hearts." He would see the greed and the wickedness within. To this the Lucan Jesus adds his own counsel: Give away the contents of the cup or platter as alms to the poor, and thus cleanliness will be achieved in every way; greed and wickedness will not only be washed out of one's life, but even that status before God that ritual cleanness was to achieve will be gained—"all will be clean for you." Thus concern for outward, superficial regulations will give way to real concern for inner cleanliness.

Three woes are now addressed to Pharisees, those contemporaries of Jesus whose lives were strictly regulated by the interpretation of the Mosaic Law as proposed by their Scribes. The first one (v. 42) contrasts their concern for minutiae and for the building of fences around the Law (see *Pirqe 'Abot* 1:1) with their neglect of what is really important: They tithe tiny herbs and forget about justice and the love of God. Jesus does not do away with tithing, but says rather, "First things first." His counsel about justice and the love of God may be an echo of Mic 6:8: "Do justice, love kindness, and walk humbly with your God." The second woe (v. 43) castigates the Pharisees for self-aggrandizement. In the Lucan context, coming after the concern criticized in the first woe, this may imply that the concern to carry out minutiae in legal regulations leads to self-satisfaction and the seeking of recognition in public. The third woe (v. 44) criticizes the Pharisees for not realizing that they are not what they seem to be; people do not realize what evil is really within the Pharisees and so risk contamination from them. They are like unmarked graves with bones of the dead within; they seem to be holy, but they deceive others. As T. W. Manson *(Sayings,* 99) remarks, there is in these woes "no polemic against Pharisaism as a system." One has to read them as they are presented, keeping out of mind the overtones of the Matthean counterparts. They are a condemnation of bad Pharisees such as could be made, and was made, by Pharisees themselves. To these the woes really apply.

There follow three woes addressed to the lawyers among the Pharisees, dealing with the Law, the prophets, and wisdom. After a query from a lawyer, Jesus addresses the first woe against the lawyers (v. 46). It echoes the first woe against the Pharisees, castigating the lawyers for minute legalistic interpretations of the Mosaic Law and the "traditions of the elders" (Mark 7:5; cf. Gal 1:14). Their interpretations created a mass of regulations incumbent on all the people. Jesus' words do not mean that they impose burdens on others but do not keep them themselves; they do keep them themselves, but their preoccupation with minutiae and their failure to concentrate on justice and the love of God renders the service of God burdensome. The lawyer's job is not finished when he points out to the weak in his following that they have sinned and must repent; he must raise his finger to lighten the load, bringing his followers to a lightsome comprehension of God's law as an expression of God's love for his people. This the lawyers have not done. The second woe (vv. 47-48, with its appended sayings, vv. 49-51) would seem to be more appropriately addressed to the Pharisees than to the lawyers, but it criticizes them for building monumental tombs to the honor and memory of prophets killed by their forebears, which means their approval of what was done to these mouthpieces of God. They honor only prophets who are dead, because they do not want to hear such mouthpieces adding things to the Torah. Their collaboration in the crimes of their forebears reflects a reaction to Jesus himself, the latest of the "prophets and emissaries," to whom they refuse to listen and whom they refuse to acknowledge. Also implied is that this latest of the prophets may share a like fate with those that are already done away with. But God's wisdom will not be thwarted, and Jesus' words take on a critical edge: Unless this generation breaks with the past, it will answer for all the injustice done to God's chosen ones from Abel to Zechariah—from the first to the last person murdered in the first and last books of the Hebrew canon of the OT. The third woe against the lawyers (v. 52) reveals the sad plight of these learned men. The key of knowledge was given to them, the key to unlock the knowledge of God and his will in the Torah and its traditions; it was the key to the house that wisdom built (Prov 9:1). They have not entered that house themselves and have prevented others from entering it. Their neglect is thus castigated.

So runs Jesus' criticism of recognized spiritual leaders of his own day.

In the narrative verses at the end (53-54), the lawyers become "Scribes," and mention is made of the opposition to Jesus that his sayings have created among them and the Pharisees.

These minatory sayings against the religious leaders of the Jews become in time warnings against the city of Jerusalem and its inhabitants (see 13:1-9; 13:34-35; 19:41-44; 21:20-24; 23:28-31).

NOTES

11 37. *When he had said this.* Luke uses the articular infin., *en tō lalēsai,* of the past, as in 2:27; 3:21. See pp. 119-120, 148. The ms. D and some OS versions read: "But a certain Pharisee begged him to dine with him."

a Pharisee. See NOTE on 5:17. In this passage the Pharisees will appear especially as the meticulous practitioners of their ancient religious customs. Some mss. (A, C, W, Θ, and the Koine text-tradition) add *tis,* "a certain," probably under the influence of 7:36, which is so similar to this verse. Cf. also 14:1.

invited. Lit. "asks," a historic pres. See p. 107; cf. 7:36.

to dine. The Greek vb. *aristan* can refer to breakfast, but in this instance it probably means the noonday meal. See John 21:12,15.

38. *saw this, he was surprised that.* I.e. shocked. Ms. D and the OL, OS versions read: "passing judgment in his own mind, he began to ask why . . ." It is implied that Jesus has read his thoughts.

first wash before the meal. I.e. perform the ceremonial washing of the hands (at least). See Mark 7:1-5; cf. Gen 18:4; Judg 19:21; Josephus, *J.W.* 2.8,5 § 129. Recall Jesus' contact with "crowds" and the expulsion of a demon in the foregoing Lucan context.

39. *the Lord.* For this absolute use, see NOTE on 7:13 and pp. 202-203.

said to him. Luke uses here *pros* + acc. See p. 116.

You Pharisees. Ms. D adds, "hypocrites," borrowed from Matthew. Though Luke speaks of their "hypocrisy" (12:1), he never uses the adj. of the Pharisees. The nom. case *(hoi Pharisaioi)* is used as a voc. See NOTE on 10:21.

platter. Whereas Matt 23:25 has *paropsis,* "(food) dish," Luke uses *pinax,* "platter."

greed and wickedness. Matt 23:25 has "greed and intemperance" *(akrasia;* but cf. the *app. crit.).* Luke's formulation has improved the contrast over that in Matthew. He says nothing about the source of the greed. Cf. Mark 12:40.

40. *Foolish people!* This may be a Lucan substitution for "blind Pharisee!" of "Q" (Matt 23:26; cf. Luke 12:20 ["L"]). Only Luke among the Synoptics uses *aphrōn,* "foolish." For its OT background, see T. Donald, "The Semantic Field of 'Folly' in Proverbs, Job, Psalms, and Ecclesiastes," *VT* 13 (1963) 285-292.

the one who made the outside. I.e. the cupmaker who fashioned the vessel. Prima facie, this refers to the human artisan; but in the context of the address to "foolish people," the further sense of God as the "Maker" is connoted. For another sense of the ptc. *poiēsas,* "set aright," see J. M. Creed, *The Gospel,* 166. Despite the difference in wording in Matt 23:26, the contrast of the "outside" and the "inside" is present and evidence of "Q."

41. *its contents.* Lit. "the things being inside." For ancient attempts to understand the ptc. *ta enonta* differently, see A. Plummer, *The Gospel,* 311.

give as alms. I.e. to the poor. See pp. 247-251; cf. G. Brans, "Christus' leer over de hoeveelheid der aalmoes," *ETL* 6 (1929) 463-469.

An attempt was made years ago by J. Wellhausen *(Einleitung in die drei ersten Evangelien* [Berlin: G. Reimer, 1905] 36-37) to explain *dote eleēmosynēn,* "give as alms," as a mistranslation of *zakkau,* "cleanse," instead of *dakkau,* which Matthew would have more correctly translated as *katharison,* "cleanse." This was queried by G. Dalman *(Die Worte Jesu,* 50, 71), who regarded the confusion as unrealistic. However, M. Black *(AAGA³* 2) not only called Wellhausen's conjecture "brilliant," but considered it as a "deliberate interpretation of the Aramaic" underlying the Greek sayings. All of this needs further scrutiny. Attempts to uncover the Aramaic of Jesus' sayings have to be built on more than individual words. In this case, no little part of the hesitation about the correctness of the suggestion is whether v. 41 is really parallel to Matt 23:26. If I am right, it is not. Luke has used v. 40 as the equivalent of Matt 23:26 and then freely added the further recommendation about the contents to be given away as alms. See C. F. D. Moule, *Idiom Book,* 186. But the Wellhausenian suggestion is widely followed. See G. B. Caird, *Gospel of St Luke,* 158; *FGT* 110-111.

For an entirely different mode of explanation, see J. Neusner, "First Cleanse the Inside." Cf. H. Maccoby, "The Washing of Cups," *JSNT* 14 (1982) 3-15.

and all will be clean. This part of the verse is introduced by *kai idou,* omitted in translation. See p. 121.

42. *Woe.* See NOTE on 6:24.

You tithe. My translation has omitted the conj. *hoti,* "because." It is often said to be a mistranslation of Aramaic *dî,* which should have been translated rather "who"; cf. 6:24-27. "Tithing" refers to the practice of giving a tenth of produce or booty for the support of a king, the Temple, or its ministers. The custom varied in OT times. The regulations which would govern Jesus' allusion here are found in Deut 14:22-27 (cf. Deut 12:6-9) and Deut 14:28-29 (cf. Deut 26:12-15); these are not absolutely clear. Still others (from the Priestly Code) are found in Lev 27:30-33; Num 18:12; Neh 10:37-38; 12:44; 13:5,12; 2 Chr 31:5-12. Cf. Mal 3:8,10. Herbs are not mentioned in these passages, which in time developed into the rabbinic tractates on the subject, *m. Ma'aśerôt, Ma'aśer šeni,* etc. Though these tractates were compiled at the beginning of the third century A.D., they illustrate the kind of mentality to which Jesus refers here. The first of these begins thus: "They have laid down a general rule about tithes: Whatever is used for food, is kept watch over, and grown from the soil is subject to tithes." See further *NIDNTT* 3. 851-855.

mint and rue and every edible herb. Greek *hēdyosmon* (lit. "sweet smelling") was a popular name for *minthē,* "green mint" (= mentha viridis); see Theophrastus, *Hist. plant.* 7.7,1. It may be the same as Hebrew *dandānāh,* mentioned in *m. Šeb.* 7:1, though that has also been translated as "miltwaste" or "ceterach." Str-B 1. 933 claims that there is no explicit mention of the tithing of mint in rabbinic literature. Greek *pēganon,* "rue" (= ruta graveolens), is discussed in Theophrastus, *Hist. plant.* 1.3,4; it was the equivalent of Hebrew *pêgām,* mentioned in *m. Šeb.* 9:1 among herbs *exempt* from tithing! See D. Correns, "Die Verzehntung der Raute," *NovT* 6 (1963-1964) 110-112. Greek *lachanon* was a generic name for "garden, pot herb," used in the LXX for Hebrew *yereq,* "green(s)" (Gen 9:3).

Instead of the last two herbs Matt 23:23 has "dill and cummin" *(anēthon* and *kyminon).* Greek *anēthon* (= anethum graveolens) is known from Theophrastus, *Hist. plant.* 1.11,2 and was the equivalent of Hebrew *šebet;* according to *m. Ma'aś.* 4:5, it was to be tithed. Greek *kyminon* (= cuminum cyminum) is also known from the same place in Theophrastus; it was the equivalent of Hebrew *kammôn* and was to be tithed, according to *m. Dem.* 2:1.

Of the three mentioned by Luke only one herb ("mint") had possibly to be tithed; the generic third expression is probably Lucan and reflects his lack of accurate knowledge of things Palestinian, since *m. Šeb.* 9:1 mentions at least six herbs which were not to be tithed. Cf. Luke 18:12.

justice. Greek *krisis* usually means "judgment"; but it has here rather the sense of "right, sense of justice," as in Acts 8:33 (= Isa 53:8); Matt 12:18 (= Isa 42:1); John 7:24 (?); *1 Clem.* 8:4. This and the next phrase reformulate Luke 10:27.

the love of God. Only here and in Matt 12:42 does the n. *agapē* occur in the Synoptic tradition. Cf. John 5:42. Matt 23:23 reads rather "mercy and faith" *(to eleos kai tēn pistin).*

These were rather the things. Luke uses the contrary-to-fact sense of impf. *edei.* See

BDF § 360.1. In this case, it has nothing to do with an expression of God's will. See pp. 179-180, *pace* H. Conzelmann, *Theology,* 153 n. 1. It expresses what should have been, but was not, the obj. of emphasis for those who criticize Jesus. Beginning with this phrase, all is omitted in ms. D, probably owing to the influence of Marcion, who would certainly not have agreed with the last part. See *TCGNT* 149. Note that concern for trifles is not condemned. This whole part of the verse was certainly part of "Q," as R. Bultmann *(HST* 131) recognized. Cf. T. W. Manson, *Sayings,* 98.

43. *the front seat in synagogues.* I.e. places of honor, distinct from "the chair of Moses" (Matt 23:2), in an ancient synagogue. See NOTE on 4:15. Cf. 20:46c.

greetings of respect in the marketplaces. For the later tradition about the need to greet first one who is an expert in the Torah, see Str-B 1. 382 (f). Cf. Luke 20:46b; Hermas, *Vis.* 3.9,7.

44. *Woe to you.* Mss. A, D, W, Θ, and the Koine text-tradition add, "Scribes and Pharisees, hypocrites," a scribal harmonization with Matt 23:27.

unmarked graves. I.e. graves dug in the ground and filled with the bones of the dead, which could be the source of ritual defilement for Jews. See Num 19:11-22; Lev 21:1-4,11. Because they are unmarked, people do not recognize them for what they are, and so unwittingly come into contact with them. Matt 23:27 refers to the yearly custom of whitewashing graves before Passover. See Str-B 1. 936-937 for the later legislation about it. Greek *adēla* is not a mistranslation, *pace* G. Schwarz, " 'Unkenntliche Gräber'?" *NTS* 23 (1976-1977) 345-346; it is a deliberate change of "Q" by Luke, to avoid having to explain the whitewashing.

45. *One of the lawyers.* Luke uses again *nomikoi* instead of "Scribes." See NOTE on 7:30. They are understood here as the legal specialists among the Pharisees.

said to him in reply. Lit. "having answered, he says." Again, the ptc. *apokritheis* with a vb. of saying is used (see p. 114), this time with the historic pres. *legei.* See p. 107.

Teacher. See NOTES on 3:12; 7:40.

you are also insulting us. I.e. the best instructed among the Pharisees. He understands Jesus' words as critical of his professional group, which was responsible for the details of Pharisaic piety.

46. *burdens they can scarcely carry.* I.e. duties deduced by legal interpretation that augment the obligations beyond the written law itself; e.g. the thirty-nine classes of work that one could not do on the Sabbath lest the third commandment be violated. See *m. Šabb.* 7:2. It was because of the lawyers that the Torah, which should have been a source of joyful service to God, became a burden. Cf. Acts 15:10. Contrast the invitation of the Matthean Jesus (11:30), which has no parallel in Luke, surprisingly enough.

you will not lift a single finger to the burdens. I.e. to be of help to people. Unstressed *kai autoi* begins this cl. See p. 120. *Pace* W. Grundmann *(Evangelium nach Lukas,* 249), the text does not imply that the lawyers give easier interpretations of the Law for themselves. Cf. Str-B 1. 913-914.

47. *build the tombs of the prophets.* I.e. to honor and perpetuate the memory of them —so on the surface of things. Cf. J. Jeremias, *Heiligengräber in Jesu Umwelt.* In the context, the nuance may also be present: "the heavy tombs they build are designed to

ensure that they shall never return to trouble the living" (G. B. Caird, *The Language and Imagery of the Bible* [Philadelphia: Westminster, 1980] 208).

whom your fathers murdered. Lit. "and your fathers murdered them." See Acts 7:52. *Pateres* is used in the sense of "forebears," as in Luke 1:55; 6:23,26.

48. *you give testimony that you approve of the deeds of your fathers.* Lit. "you are witnesses and you approve." Cf. Acts 8:1. Some mss. (P[75], A, C, D, W, Θ, and the Koine text-tradition) read the vb. *martyreite*, "you testify"; but *martyres este kai syneudokeite* (preferred here) is read in ℵ, B, L, 700*, etc. By building the tombs, association in the guilt of their forebears is manifested.

they murdered the prophets, and you build their tombs! The literary use of *men . . . de* marks the balanced contrast here. See p. 108. Luke reads *oikodomeite,* whereas Matt 23:31 has *huioi este . . .* "you are sons of those who murder the prophets." M. Black *(AAGA*[3] 12) has tried to explain this difference by an appeal to Aramaic, *'twn bnyn 'twn,* which could be rendered either as "you are building" or "you are sons." If one judges just on the basis of these few words, it is possible; but the real question is whether Luke has any parallel to Matt 23:31.

49. *God's wisdom has said.* So Luke introduces the saying that follows; Matt 23:34 puts the saying directly on the lips of Jesus himself. It may sound like a quotation from the OT or from an intertestamental Jewish writing. But its source has never been found. In what sense is "wisdom of God" to be understood? Does it refer to God himself or to Jesus? Other NT passages could be invoked in favor of Jesus as God's wisdom (1 Cor 1:24,30; 2:7; Col 2:3). Is Luke alluding to the implications of 7:35; 11:31? Later patristic commentators understood it clearly of Jesus. See Hippolytus, *Frg. in Prov* (PG 10.628); Cyprian, *Testim.* 2.2 (CSEL 3. 64). H. Conzelmann *(Theology,* 110 n. 1) is convinced that for Luke there is no identification of Jesus and Sophia; here "Sophia is pre-existent, but not Jesus."

I shall send to them prophets and emissaries. Or possibly "prophets and apostles" *(apostolous).* Matt 23:34 has rather "prophets, wise men, and Scribes." The meaning "apostles" may well be intended by Luke in this Stage III of the gospel tradition, especially since he is aware that some of the Christian *apostoloi* had already been done away with. See Acts 12:2-5; cf. p. 254. The words of this saying suggest indirectly that Jesus himself is such a "prophet and emissary" (see NOTE on 4:24) and even a spokesman of God's wisdom. For the killing of prophets and emissaries already sent, see 13:33,34 (and NOTES there).

50. *the blood of all the prophets which has been shed.* Cf. Jer 7:25, "from the day your fathers came out of the land of Egypt until today, I have persistently sent all my servants the prophets to them. . . ." Cf. Rev 18:24.

since the foundation of the world. This phrase *(apo katabolēs kosmou,* always anarthrous, yet not found in the LXX) occurs elsewhere in the NT (Matt 13:35; 25:34; John 17:24; Eph 1:4; Heb 4:3; 9:26; 1 Pet 1:20; Rev 13:8; 17:8), and *ek katabolēs* is found in Hellenistic Greek writers (Polybius, *Hist.* 1.36,8; 24.8,9; Diodorus Siculus, *Bibl. hist.* 12.32,2).

required. An OT expression is used (see Gen 9:5; 42:22; 2 Sam 4:11; Ps 9:13; Ezek 3:18,20) to formulate the debt that will be demanded of "this generation" so that the deaths of the prophets of old will be avenged.

of this generation. An echo of vv. 29,30,31; cf. 11:51. See V. Burch, "The Petitioning

Blood of the Prophets (Luke xi.49-51)," *ExpTim* 30 (1918-1919) 329-330. A. Plummer *(The Gospel,* 314) thinks that this is a reference to the destruction of Jerusalem. Cf. 21:32.

51. *from the blood of Abel.* Allusion is made to his murder by Cain in Gen 4:8-10. Cf. *1 Enoch* 22:7. Luke has omitted the adj. *dikaiou,* "innocent," which Matt 23:35 has retained. Though Abel was not a prophet, the use of this saying by Luke fits his general view of the OT in which most of it is regarded as some sort of prophecy.

to the blood of Zechariah. This is usually understood as a reference to Zechariah the priest, the son of Jehoiada, who was stoned by the people whom he addressed as God's mouthpiece "in the court of the house of the Lord," during the reign of King Joash (2 Chr 24:20-22). He was not usually regarded as a prophet—no more than Abel was. Since a span of time is implied "from Abel to Zechariah," it has often been suggested that two figures are singled out, one from the first book of the Hebrew OT canon and one from the last, both of whom were murdered. Hence the preference for this Zechariah. But was the so-called Hebrew OT canon closed or formed at the time that this saying of Jesus was fashioned (or recorded in "Q")? What guarantee is there that the order of books was the same then as it is today in the MT? Indeed, one might argue from this reference that it was. But that really has to be established independently of this reference in order to make certain the identity of Zechariah here. Indeed, in codex L of the Hebrew OT, Chronicles stands at the head of the "Writings"; see O. Eissfeldt, *The Old Testament: An Introduction* (New York: Harper & Row, 1965) 443.

If this phrase, "to the blood of Zechariah," stood in "Q," then Matthew must have added to it, "the son of Barachiah" (23:35). This addition would make of him a prophet (see Zech 1:1); but nothing is known of the violent death of this prophet, much less of its occurrence "between the altar and the sanctuary." If, however, the phrase stood in "Q" along with the addition which Matthew has, then Luke would have excised the latter in the interest of less confusion—which seems more probable. For the treatment of this Zechariah and the consideration of him as a prophet in later rabbinic tradition, see Str-B 1. 940-942.

For later attempts to identify this Zechariah with the father of John the Baptist (see *Prot. Jas.* 23-24; Origen *Comm. in Matth.* 25 [GCS 38.42-44]) or with Zechariah son of Baris (see Josephus, *J.W.* 4.5,4 § 335-343), see T. W. Manson, *Sayings,* 104-105. Cf. J. Chapman, "Zacharias, Slain between the Temple and the Altar," *JTS* 13 (1911-1912) 398-410.

Yes, and I tell you. See NOTE on 7:28; cf. 12:5.

52. *the key of knowledge.* This is not an appositional gen., but a key which gives access to knowledge. Whereas the Matthean form of this saying (23:13) speaks of the Scribes and Pharisees locking up the "kingdom of heaven" (which may well have been the "Q" form), Luke's saying is devoid of any reference to the kingdom, although it is often so interpreted. Because Luke's form also speaks of people wanting to "enter," it seems that his form of the saying is alluding to Wisdom's house (Prov 9:1). This would mean wisdom in a broad sense, referring to God's salvific plan. See p. 179.

53. *When Jesus had gone out of there.* I.e. the house of the Pharisee entered in v. 37c. This is a rare reference to Jesus' movement in this part of the travel account. See p. 825. The implication is that he was followed out by others.

For vv. 53-54 ms. D and some others read, "While he was saying these things to them, the Pharisees and the lawyers began to react violently and to fight with him in the presence of all the people about many things, seeking some pretext to catch him in order that they might be able to accuse him."

began to react violently against him. Lit. "began to have it in for him terribly." Luke uses here *deinōs enechein,* which J. M. Creed *(The Gospel,* 169) considers an abbreviation for the classical Greek *enechein cholon tini,* "harbor a grudge against." See Herodotus, *Hist.* 1.118; 6.119; 8.27; cf. MM 214. In any case, it is an expression of extreme hostility toward Jesus.

check his utterances closely. Lit. "to question him closely." The vb. *apostomatizein* really means "to mouth (something) from memory," but it ill suits the verse; in earlier instances it has been found to mean "to teach by dictation" (LSJ 1. 226) or "to make repeated answers" (MM 70).

54. *plotting to catch him in something he might say.* Lit. "lying in wait to trap (him) in something from his mouth." See Acts 23:21. Some mss. (A, C, D, W, Θ, Ψ, and the Koine text-tradition) add: "in order that they might accuse him."

BIBLIOGRAPHY (11:37-54)

Christ, F. *Jesus Sophia: Die Sophia-Christologie bei den Synoptikern* (Zürich: Zwingli, 1970) 120-135.

Derrett, J. D. M. "You Build the Tombs of the Prophets (Lk. 11,47-51, Mt. 23,29-31)," *SE IV* (TU 102) 187-193.

Ellis, E. E. "Lk xi.49-51: An Oracle of a Christian Prophet?" *ExpTim* 74 (1962-1963) 157-158.

Frizzi, G. "Carattere originali e rivelanza degli 'apostoli inviati' in Q/*Lc.* 11,49-51; 13,34-35/*Mt.* 23,34-36.37-39," *RivB* 21 (1973) 401-412.

Jeremias, J. *Heiligengräber in Jesu Umwelt (Mt. 23,29; Lk. 11,47): Eine Untersuchung zur Volksreligion der Zeit Jesu* (Göttingen: Vandenhoeck & Ruprecht, 1958).

——— "Drei weitere spätjüdische Heiligengräber," *ZNW* 52 (1961) 95-101.

Klein, G. "Die Verfolgung der Apostel, Luk 11,49," *Neues Testament und Geschichte . . . Oskar Cullmann zum 70. Geburtstag* (eds. H. Baltensweiler and B. Reicke; Zürich: Theologischer-V.; Tübingen: Mohr, 1972) 113-124.

Neusner, J. " 'First Cleanse the Inside:' The 'Halakhic' Background of a Controversy-Saying," *NTS* 22 (1975-1976) 486-495.

Pernot, H. "Matthieu, XXIII,29-36; Luc, XI,47-51," *RHPR* 13 (1933) 263-267.

Pesch, W. *Der Lohngedanke in der Lehre Jesu verglichen mit der religiösen Lohnlehre des Spätjudentums* (MTS I/7; Munich: Zink, 1955) 40-50.

Sand, A. *Das Gesetz und die Propheten: Untersuchungen zur Theologie des Evangeliums nach Matthäus* (Biblische Untersuchungen 11; Regensburg: Pustet, 1974) 84-95.

Schulz, S. *Q: Die Spruchquelle,* 94-114, 336-345.

Seitz, O. J. F. "The Commission of Prophets and 'Apostles': A Re-examination of Matthew 23,34 with Luke 11,49," *SE IV* (TU 102) 236-340.

Steck, O. H. *Israel und das gewaltsame Geschick der Propheten* (WMANT 23; Neukirchen-Vluyn: Neukirchener-V., 1967) 26-33, 50-53, 282-283.

Vincent, H. "Le tombeau des prophètes," *RB* 10 (1901) 72-88.

77. THE LEAVEN OF THE PHARISEES
(12:1)

12 ¹ Meanwhile thousands of people had gathered closely in a crowd so that they were actually trampling on one another. At first Jesus began to speak to his disciples: "Beware of the leaven of the Pharisees, that is, their hypocrisy."

COMMENT

Luke continues his travel account with further sayings of Jesus, addressed at first to the disciples, even though a huge crowd is present. The first one is an isolated comment on the leaven of the Pharisees (12:1), which serves as a transition from the subject matter at the end of chap. 11. Topical arrangement calls for its addition to the woes uttered against the Pharisees (11:42-44) and their lawyers (11:46-52). What follows in the rest of chap. 12 has been called a "parade example of Lucan redaction" (E. Klostermann, *Lukasevangelium,* 132).

The first saying is often ascribed to "Q" (so G. Schneider, *Evangelium nach Lukas,* 277; I. H. Marshall, *Luke,* 510), but it is more likely derived by Luke from "L" (so T. W. Manson, S. Schulz), even though a form of the saying is preserved in Mark 8:15 (used also by Matt 16:6,12), since only five words *(apo tēs zymēs tōn Pharisaiōn,* "from the leaven of the Pharisees") are common to Mark and Luke. Both the Marcan and Lucan traditions undoubtedly go back to some saying of Jesus himself about "the leaven of the Pharisees," but they are differently preserved. Only Luke has identified it with "hypocrisy"—strangely enough, since the Lucan Jesus elsewhere never calls the Pharisees "hypocrites," as does the Matthean. In Mark the leaven is not identified; in Matt 16:12 it is rather said to be "the teaching" of the Pharisees and Sadducees. Being a Greek term with no real equivalent in Hebrew or Aramaic, "hypocrisy" is almost certainly an explanation added by the evangelist to explain the leaven in Stage III of the gospel tradition.

The introductory phrases of v. 1 are of Lucan composition (see *HST* 335; J. Jeremias, *Die Sprache,* 211).

Form-critically considered, the saying belongs to the minatory class of Jesus' logia. Caution is expressed, but no threat of punishment.

Jesus warns his disciples about that characteristic of the lives of some of his contemporaries that he finds objectionable, their hypocrisy. He compares it to leaven, to that element in the making of bread, which is good in itself, but which works only by corruption and affects the whole loaf. This latter is the main point of his comparison. For the Lucan Jesus "hypocrisy" is a dissembling attitude in one's piety. This explains why Jesus could call some Pharisees "unmarked graves" (11:44); they do not come across on the surface as that which they really are. It is not their "typical hybris," *pace* W. Popke *(EWNT* 2. 261), but their dissemblance in conduct. In any case, disciples are not to let themselves be so contaminated; they should rather cultivate sincerity and openness.

NOTES

12 1. *Meanwhile.* Lit. "at which (things)," i.e. in the situation created by what precedes, in the context of the plotting against him; on *en hois,* see Acts 24:18 (variant); 26:12. Cf. BAGD 585.

thousands of people had gathered closely in a crowd. Lit. "myriads (tens of thousands) of the crowd having been brought together"; a gen. absol. (see p. 108 § 2) describes by hyperbole the large number of listeners. The numerical note makes one think of the numerical summaries which punctuate the narrative of Acts (2:41; 4:4; 5:14; 6:1,7; 9:31; 11:21,24; 12:24; 14:1). It is a Lucan device to stress Jesus' popularity with the crowds. See 11:29; cf. NOTE on 3:7. Thus Luke contrasts the reaction of crowds to that of prominent Jews.

Instead of "crowds," ms. P[45] and a few others read "people." Ms. D, however, begins thus: "As many crowds were surrounding him so that they were choking each other," i.e. cutting off breath for each other.

At first. The position of the adv. *prōton* may favor this sense (of Jesus first speaking to the disciples); but it could also be taken with the following impv., as E. Klostermann *(Lukasevangelium,* 133) prefers, "above all, beware."

began to speak. See 3:8; 4:21; 7:15,24,49; 11:29; 13:26; 14:18, etc.

to his disciples. Luke again uses *pros* + acc. See p. 116.

Beware of the leaven. Lit. "look to yourselves *(or* be on your guard) against . . ." with *prosechein.* See p. 113. For this Lucan usage, cf. 17:3; 20:46; 21:34; Acts 5:35; 20:28. It is also a Septuagintism; see Gen 24:6; Exod 10:28; 34:12; Deut 4:9. Let not this kind of leaven affect your lives.

"Leaven" *(zymē),* though often called "yeast," was actually old, sour dough which had been stored away (see Luke 13:21) and subjected to fermenting juices until it was to be used in new dough as a rising agent (to make the new bread light); see C. L. Mitton, "Leaven," 339. The fermenting involved some corruption. Its all-pervasive effect was figuratively used in a good (see 1 Cor 5:6-8) as well as a bad sense (as here). Plutarch *(Quaest. rom.* 109) recounts that in Roman religion the priest of Jupiter, the *Flamen dialis,* was forbidden to touch *zymē,* because it comes from corruption and corrupts, because it makes dough slack and feeble. Cf. Aulus Gellius, *Noct. Att.* 10.15,19; H. Windisch, *TDNT* 2. 905; Ignatius, *Magn.* 10.

Pharisees. See NOTE on 5:17. In Mark 8:15 the leaven is that of "the Pharisees and Herod," and in Matt 16:6,12 of the "Pharisees and Sadducees."

hypocrisy. The abstract n. occurs only here in Luke. See NOTE on 6:42; cf. 12:56; 13:15. *Hypokrisis* occurs only once in the LXX: 2 Macc 6:25. Aquila and Theodotion, however, use it in Isa 32:6 to translate Hebrew *ḥōnep,* "ungodliness." Cf. U. Wilckens, *TDNT* 8. 559-571. On the word order in some mss., see *TCGNT* 159.

For manifestations of Essene opposition to the Pharisees, their conduct, and interpretation of the Law, see the deriding term *dôrĕšê haḥălāqôt,* "seekers after smooth things" in 1QH 2:15,32; 4QpIsaᶜ 23 ii 10; 4QpNah 3-4 ii 2,4; 3-4 iii 6-7; CD 1:18; or *dôrĕšê rĕmiyyāh,* "seekers of deceit," in 1QH 2:34; cf. *mlysy rmyh,* 1QH 4:10. These are probably figurative ways of referring to "false expositions" of the Torah. See further R. Meyer, *TDNT* 9. 30. Thus the reaction of the Lucan Jesus recorded in this verse may well fit into a larger Palestinian background.

BIBLIOGRAPHY (12:1)

Bertrand, D. "Hypocrites selon Luc 12,1-59," *Christus* 21 (1974) 323-333.
Iwand, H. J. *Die Gegenwart des Kommenden: Eine Auslegung von Lk 12* (BibS[N] 50; Neukirchen-Vluyn: Neukirchener-V., 1966).
Mitton, C. L. "Leaven," *ExpTim* 84 (1972-1973) 339-343.
Negoiță, A., and C. Daniel. "L'Enigme du levain: Ad Mc. viii 15; Mt. xvi 6; et Lc. xii 1," *NovT* 9 (1967) 306-314.

78. EXHORTATION TO FEARLESS CONFESSION
(12:2-9)

12 ²"There is nothing so covered up that it will not be uncovered, nothing so secret that it will not become known. ³Accordingly, what you have said in the dark will be heard in broad daylight; what you have whispered behind closed doors will be proclaimed on the housetops.

⁴To you my friends I say, Do not fear those who kill the body and afterward can do no more. ⁵I shall show you whom you should fear: Fear him who after the killing has authority to hurl you into gehenna. Yes, and I tell you, he is the one to fear. ⁶Do not five sparrows sell for

two pennies? Yet not one of them is forgotten in God's sight. ⁷ Indeed, even the hairs on your head have all been numbered. You must not be afraid; you are worth far more than many sparrows.

⁸ But this I say to you, If anyone acknowledges me before men, the Son of Man will acknowledge him before God's angels. ⁹ And everyone who disowns me in the sight of men will be disowned in the sight of God's angels."

COMMENT

Further sayings of Jesus are now recorded (12:2-9). These words of encouragement or warning stem from diverse contexts in the ministry of Jesus and scarcely represent a unit derived from it; they are hardly an ideal unit even in their present contexts. Some commentators consider vv. 2-3 as the real end of Jesus' harangue against the Pharisees, following on 11:52 (so G. Friedrich, *TDNT* 3. 705; T. W. Manson, *Sayings*, 105). But Luke has created the context, as will appear below (see D. Lührmann, *Redaktion*, 49 n. 2).

Luke has derived these sayings from "Q" (see p. 78); the parallels are found similarly ordered in Matt 10:26-33, where they form part of the mission-charge addressed to the "twelve disciples." Here Luke has given them a different setting. The first saying (12:2) is a doublet of 8:17, which has been derived from Mark 4:22 (see p. 717—also for the forms of the saying in *Gos. of Thom.* § 5b,6d). Matthew has added to it an introductory caution (10:26a), relating the sayings to his context. The second saying (12:3) is preserved in a more primitive form (with the fut. pass. vbs.) in Luke than in Matthew; but Luke has added "behind closed doors," which disturbs the parallelism between ears and housetops and which is absent in Matt 10:27. Though vv. 2-3 were related in "Q," they were not so originally, *pace* J. Schmid, *Evangelium nach Lukas*, 215. (See J. Ernst, *Evangelium nach Lukas*, 393.) In 12:4a Luke has added an introductory phrase, as he has also in v. 5a,c (in the last instance with *nai, legō hymin* [cf. 7:26; 11:51]). The rest of these verses is preserved in more original form in Matthew. It is, however, difficult to say whether Matt 10:29 ("two sparrows for a penny") or Luke 12:6a ("five sparrows sell for two pennies") is more original; possibly the Lucan form is influenced by 9:13. In any case, the sense is not affected. Luke's fondness for the prep. *enōpion*, "before, in the sight of" (see pp. 110, 114), and for the periphrastic vb. "to be" + ptc. (see p. 122) reveals his redactional hand in v. 6b. By contrast, 12:7 is more primitive than Matthew's form (10:30). One may wonder whether Luke 21:18 is a doublet of v. 7 (see p. 81). In 12:8 Luke has substituted the title, "Son of Man," for the more original "I" of Matt 10:32 (see p. 210). In both vv. 8-9 "God's angels" is probably more primitive (despite its introductory *enōpion)* than Matthew's reference to "the Father" in 10:32-33 (cf. Matt 10:29); similarly for the fut. pass. vbs. (cf. 12:2-3). Verse 9 is also a doublet of 9:26, which has been derived from Mark 8:38; there both forms of the saying have "the Son of Man," which has influenced the Lucan redaction of v. 8 (see p. 784; and NOTE on 9:26).

Verses 2-3 preserve wisdom-sayings of Jesus (see *HST* 83), marked by a characteristic parallelism; that they were nothing more than "secular meshallim" made into "dominical sayings," i.e. a warning against entrusting secrets (ibid. 102) may be too negative a judgment about them. In the Lucan context, these wisdom-sayings assume a minatory character too. Verses 4-5 are to be classed as prophetic minatory sayings, whereas vv. 6-7 are hortatory. Verses 8-9 are also minatory (ibid. 112), both promising salvation and threatening damnation.

The meaning of Jesus' proverb-like words in vv. 2-3 can be summed up thus: "Truth will out" *(FGT* 111). More specifically, they denote that the real core of a person cannot be covered up or kept hidden forever; a time comes when it is ruthlessly exposed. Even the secret utterances of a person will be heard. In 8:17 the doublet saying had to do with a manifestation of the word of God (see p. 718)—the bold proclamation of what the disciples had heard in private (as it is also in Matt 10:26-27). But here it refers much more to a person's inner makeup. What is said or done in secret is not hidden from God, and in the end all will come to light. These words might seem like a commentary on 11:44, the warning to the Pharisees as "unmarked graves." But in the Lucan context, they serve much more as a commentary on "hypocrisy" (12:1); it too will be exposed for what it is (see J. Schmid, *Evangelium nach Lukas,* 215).

In vv. 4-7 Jesus counsels his disciples, now addressed as "friends," to fearless conduct and confession in the face of persecution. Encouragement and warning are combined again. Fearlessness is recommended in persecution, and even in martyrdom. Loss of the life known to "the body" may cause fear; but it is nothing compared with that which one should have for him who has authority to hurl one into gehenna, i.e. God himself. Disciples are not to fear loss of physical life at the hands of other human beings; they should rather fear the consequences of apostasy. The death of the loyal martyr is rewarded by God, who recognizes what the person stood for. In its kernel (apart from Lucan redaction) it is to be regarded as an authentic saying of Jesus. It also contains an aspect of Lucan individual eschatology (see J. Dupont, "L'Après-mort").

Verses 6-7 seek to combine with the foregoing encouragement a reflection about God's care of Jesus' disciples. Real fear is pitted against sham fear. They are not spared from persecution or martyrdom, but in these circumstances the disciples are not to fear at all. The reason given makes use of an argument *a minori ad maius:* If God in his care forgets not even sparrows, five of which can be bought as food in the marketplace for two pennies, and if he in his knowledge has even numbered the hairs of a person's head, how much more care and concern will he in his wisdom manifest for the disciples and friends of Jesus? If God's unrestricted providence extends to such minutiae, will it not be concerned also with the disciples of the heaven-sent mouthpiece of God? The sayings stress how little reason there is to be afraid of other human beings in the setting of persecution and martyrdom. For the disciples' names already stand written in heaven (10:20).

Verses 8-9 add a double Son-of-Man saying, stressing that the loyal acknowledgment of Jesus before the rest of humanity is required of his followers. The one who acknowledges his allegiance to Jesus, not only as the Son of Man but as all that he is (Messiah, bearer of the Spirit, etc.), is promised an eschatological reward in the acknowledgment that Jesus as the Son of Man will exercise at the judgment in the heavenly court (see Luke 9:26, which specifies the moment; cf. 22:69; Acts 17:31). For those disciples who disown him, however, he will be there to react in kind. Promise and warning are again combined. The present is thus given an eschatological dimension.

The kernel of the saying must be regarded as authentic, *pace* P. Vielhauer, E. Käsemann, D. Lührmann, et al. (See K. Berger, "Zu den sogenannten Sätzen heiligen Rechtes," *NTS* 17 [1970-1971] 10-40; C. Colpe, *TDNT* 8.400-477, esp. 438; J. M. McDermott, "Luke, xii, 8-9: Stone of Scandal," 532-533.) There is little reason to regard it as an early Christian formulation, a sentence of holy law (to use Käsemann's terminology *[New Testament Questions,* 77]). This is maintained, even though we regard "Son of Man" as a secondary Lucan addition.

This passage in particular has played a large role in the discussion of whether Jesus ever referred to someone other than himself as an expected apocalyptic figure. The question dates back to R. Bultmann, *Theology,* 1. 29. (See further F. Hahn, A. J. B. Higgins, H. E. Tödt, I. H. Marshall, J. M. McDermott, G. Haufe, et al.) It is too vast a problem to be discussed here, but I am reluctant to admit the distinction in Stage I of the gospel tradition (see pp. 208-211).

NOTES

12 2. *will not be uncovered.* Probably intended as a theological pass. (see NOTE on 5:20), as with the other pass. vbs. in these verses.

3. *Accordingly.* Or possibly "because"; *anth' hōn,* lit. "in return for which." See 1:20; 19:44; Acts 12:23; cf. Jdt 9:3; BDF § 208.1. This phrase is not found in Matt 10:27. The expression occurs frequently in the LXX. See Jer 5:14,19; 7:13; 16:11, especially with retributive force.

in the dark. A figure for secrecy, found in Sophocles, *Antig.* 692.

whispered. Lit. "said to the ear." This stands in parallelism to "in the dark."

behind closed doors. Lit. "in the inner/hidden rooms," to which outsiders have no ready access. This phrase is absent in Matt 10:27. Cf. Judg 16:9; 1 Kgs 22:25.

4. *To you my friends.* This is the only place in the Synoptic tradition where Jesus so addresses his disciples. Cf. John 15:13-15.

Do not fear. The Lucan text has the aor. pass. here and three times in v. 5, whereas Matt 10:28,31 has the pres. Contrast Luke 12:7, where the pres. also occurs. This seems to indicate that the pres. was the more original form in "Q."

those who kill the body. I.e. put an end to physical human life. Matt 10:28b adds, "but cannot kill the soul," which Luke has apparently omitted as unclear. Cf. 4 Macc 13:14-15.

afterward. Luke has added his favorite *meta tauta.* See NOTE on 10:1.

can do no more. Here the classical Greek use of *echein* (lit. "have") occurs with an infin. in the sense of "to be able." See NOTE on 7:40; cf. 14:14; Acts 4:14; 23:17-19; 25:26.

5. *I shall show you.* A Lucan redactional addition. See 6:47.

Fear him who . . . has authority to hurl you . . . Matt 10:28 reads, "but fear rather him who can destroy both soul and body in gehenna." This does not refer to the Son of Man in judgment, or to the devil or Satan (as K. Stendahl and G. W. H. Lampe would have it, *PCB*, 783, 834), or to the power of evil, Apollyon (Rev 9:11—W. D. Niven), but to God (so O. Böcher, *EWNT* 1. 575; I. H. Marshall, *Luke*, 513; J. M. Creed, *The Gospel*, 171, et al.). Reference is made to what the Book of Revelation calls "the second death" (2:11; 20:6,14; 21:8). In the NT one is otherwise counseled to resist Satan, not fear him (Jas 4:7; 1 Pet 5:9). The fear of God, however, is not beneath a follower of Jesus (cf. Acts 9:31); nor is it merely an element of Lucan bourgeois piety (cf. Rom 11:20; 2 Cor 7:1; Phil 2:12; 1 Pet 1:17; 2:17). One meets here the typical protological way of thinking, found elsewhere in the NT, when an action such as the hurling of people into gehenna is ascribed to God. Modern systematic theology would explain the presence of persons in gehenna in other ways. It is Luke's way of repeating an OT teaching: "Fear of the Lord is the beginning of knowledge" (Prov 1:7).

after the killing. I.e. by human beings.

gehenna. Luke retains Jewish Greek vocabulary. See p. 113. It could also be translated "hell," as long as one does not overload that word with all the connotations of later theology. The Greek name *geenna,* retained from "Q," is not found in the LXX or in the writings of Philo or Josephus. It is a form derived from Hebrew *gê(')* *Hinnōm,* "valley of (the son[s] of) Hinnom," which is diversely translated in the LXX: *pharanx Onom* (Josh 15:8b); *napē Onnam* (Josh 18:16a); *Gaibenenom* (Jer 7:32; 2 Kgs 23:10); or *Gaienna* (Josh 18:16b [in ms. B, copied by Christian scribes and possibly influenced by the NT spelling]). It refers to the valley or Wadi er-Rababi, which runs first north-south west of Jerusalem, then east-west south of it, to empty into the Kidron Valley. In earlier OT times there was in it a high place called Topheth, where sons and daughters of Judah were offered in burnt-sacrifice to Baal-Molech. See Jer 7:32; 19:4-6; 32:34-35; 2 Kgs 16:3; 21:6; 23:10; cf. 2 Chr 28:3; 33:6. In later times it was the area for continually burning potters' kilns and rubbish dumps. Cf. Jer 18:1-4; 19:2,10-13; Neh 2:13. Because fire had been earlier associated with Sheol (Deut 32:22) and was regarded as a punitive element (Isa 32:10), in the last pre-Christian centuries there emerged in Judaism a belief in a lake or abyss of fire wherein wicked, unrighteous, and apostate Jews would be punished in the afterlife. Traces of this belief can be found in Jdt 16:17; *1 Enoch* 10:13; 18:11-16; 27:1-3; 90:26; *Jub.* 9:15; *2 Esdr.* 7:36; and possibly in 1QH 3:29-36. Cf. Rev 9:1-2,11; 19:20; 20:1-3,10,14-15; 21:8; now Satan, the wicked, the beasts of the land and the sea, and death itself are thrown into it. The name "gehenna," however, appears in 2 Esdr 2:29; 7:36 (often dated ca. A.D. 100; but this writing is extant only in later Latin, Syriac, Coptic, and Ethiopic versions, i.e. Christian translations possibly dependent on the NT itself). In the time of Jesus gehenna had become the place for torment of all sinners after judgment, or at least after death (J. Dupont, "L'Après-mort," 12). Whether it is associated with what some call the "intermediate state" (e.g. J. M. Creed, *The Gospel*, 171) cannot be ascertained. For later Jewish developments in rabbinic literature, see Str-B 4/2. 1022-1118. For further bibliography, see *NIDNTT* 2. 210.

6. *five sparrows . . . for two pennies?* The sparrows, though a threat to crops, were regarded as good to eat, well worth their cheap price, and sought after as food by the poor. See MM 594; *LAE*, 272-275. See O. Bauernfeind, *TDNT* 7. 732; cf. Str-B 1. 583 for similar comparisons using sparrows.

pennies. The Greek *assarion,* which is a Latin loanword, was used in "Q." *Assarius,* the Roman "as," was a copper coin = one sixteenth of a denarius. See NOTE on 7:41.

is forgotten in God's sight. Rather they are present to God's mind. See Isa 49:15 for a similar comparison; cf. Acts 10:31. Cf. Matt 10:29.

7. *the hairs on your head have all been numbered.* I.e. by divine knowledge; none of them will be lost without God's foresight—a curious hyperbole for a common affliction of humanity, baldness. See Luke 21:18; Acts 27:34, and the OT way of putting it (1 Sam 14:45; 2 Sam 14:11; 1 Kgs 1:52).

you are worth far more than many sparrows. Lit. "you are superior to many sparrows." The difference is not quantitative, but qualitative.

8. *men . . . Son of Man . . . angels.* There is an obvious play on the words here, necessitating the use of "men" for *anthrōpōn.* On "Son of Man," see NOTE on 5:24; cf. pp. 208-211.

acknowledges me. Luke preserves the vb. *homologēsē* with the prep. *en* from "Q." This is usually considered a Semitic construction, equaling Hebrew *hôdāh lě-,* which is not found in the LXX. See O. Michel, *TDNT* 5. 208 n. 27; BDF § 220.2. It is scarcely derived from the Syriac, *pace* A. Plummer, *The Gospel,* 320; it is just the other way round.

God's angels. I.e. the members of the heavenly court at the final judgment. See 2:13; 15:10; Acts 10:3; John 1:51; Gal 4:14; Heb 1:6 (dependent on the LXX of Ps 97:6?). The frequency of these references elsewhere argues for the antiquity of the phrase in "Q," which Matthew rather has changed. However, G. Dalman *(Words of Jesus,* 197) thinks that Luke has used "angels of God" in order "to avoid the expression 'in the presence of God.' " But Luke does not avoid this expression elsewhere (either with *emprosthen* [Acts 10:4] or with *enōpion* [Luke 1:19; 12:6; 16:15]).

9. *disowns.* Lit. "denies." See NOTE on 9:23. As with "acknowledges" (v. 8), this vb. does not necessarily demand a judicial context or court-setting, even though the Son of Man's reaction to it might be so understood. It would refer to any mode of the

disciple's acknowledgment or disowning. Cf. Luke 22:34,57,61; Acts 3:12-15; 7:35; also H. Riesenfeld, "The Meaning of the Verb *arneisthai*," *ConNT* 11 (1947) 207-219, esp. 215.

BIBLIOGRAPHY (12:2-9)

Bornkamm, G. "Das Wort Jesu vom Bekennen," *Monatsschrift für Pastoraltheologie* 34 (1938) 108-118; reprinted, *Geschichte und Glaube: Erster Teil: Gesammelte Aufsätze Band III* (Munich: Kaiser, 1968) 25-36.
Catchpole, D. R. "The Angelic Son of Man in Luke 12:8," *NovT* 24 (1982) 255-265.
Dupont, J. "L'Après-mort dans l'oeuvre de Luc," *RTL* 3 (1972) 3-21.
Hahn, F. *Titles*, 28-34.
Haufe, G. "Das Menschensohn-Problem in der gegenwärtigen wissenschaftlichen Diskussion," *EvT* 26 (1966) 130-141.
Higgins, A. J. B. " 'Menschensohn' oder 'ich' in Q: Lk 12,8-9/Mt 10,32-33?" *Jesus und der Menschensohn* (eds. R. Pesch and R. Schnackenburg) 117-123.
Kümmel, W. G. "Das Verhalten Jesus gegenüber und das Verhalten des Menschensohns: Markus 8,38 par und Lukas 12,3f par Matthäus 10,32f," *Jesus und der Menschensohn* (eds. R. Pesch and R. Schnackenburg) 210-224.
Lindars, B. "Jesus as Advocate: A Contribution to the Christology Debate," *BJRL* 62 (1980) 476-497.
McDermott, J. M. "Luke, xii, 8-9: Stone of Scandal," *RB* 84 (1977) 523-537.
——— "Luc, xii, 8-9: Pierre angulaire," *RB* 85 (1978) 381-401.
Marshall, I. H. "Uncomfortable Words, VI: 'Fear Him Who Can Destroy both Soul and Body in Hell' (Mt 10:28 R.S.V.)," *ExpTim* 81 (1969-1970) 276-280.
Niven, W. D. "Luke xii.4," *ExpTim* 26 (1914-1915) 44-45.
Pesch, R. "Jésus, homme libre," *Concilium* 93 (1974) 47-58.
——— "Über die Autorität Jesu: Eine Rückfrage anhand des Bekenner- und Verleugnerspruchs Lk 12,8f par.," *Die Kirche des Anfangs* (eds. R. Schnackenburg et al.) 25-55.
Tödt, H. E. *The Son of Man*, 55-60, 339-347.

79. THE HOLY SPIRIT
(12:10-12)

12 ¹⁰ "As for anyone who will speak out against the Son of Man, he will be forgiven; but anyone who reviles the holy Spirit will not be forgiven. ¹¹ When they hale you into synagogues and before magistrates and authorities, do not worry about the defense you will make or what you will say. ¹² For the holy Spirit will teach you at that very moment what you must say."

COMMENT

Catchword bonding results in the addition of another Son-of-Man saying to those in vv. 8-9 at this point in the travel account. Luke introduces sayings of Jesus which move from the Son of Man to the holy Spirit (12:10-12). Whereas the saying in v. 8 spoke of Jesus as the Son of Man in glory or judgment, this verse now speaks of him in his mortal condition. There is a certain parallelism between v. 10a and v. 8, and between v. 10b and v. 9 (see E. Lövestam, *Spiritus blasphemia,* 70). But the collocation of these sayings is certainly Lucan; they were not so joined in "Q"; the different position of them in Matthew reveals this. The collocation is probably owing not only to the catchword bonding, but also to the common topic of a position which one assumes with regard to Jesus.

The saying in v. 10 has its counterpart in Matt 12:32, where that evangelist has added this "Q" saying to the form of the blasphemy-saying which he has derived from Mark 3:28 (in place of 3:29), thus making it part of the Beelzebul controversy (the context which he has inherited from "Mk"). Common to the "Q" saying in both Luke and Matthew is the mention of "the Son of Man," whereas the saying in Mark 3:28 speaks of "sins and blasphemies" which will be forgiven "the sons of men"; and this becomes in Matthew merely "men" *(tois anthrōpois).* It is not easy to say whether the "Mk" or "Q" form of the saying is the more original (see E. Lövestam, *Spiritus blasphemia,* 71-73). But some form of it is almost certainly to be attributed to Jesus himself in Stage I (so O. Hofius, *EWNT* 1. 532.)

Luke is responsible for the introductory *pas hos,* "As for anyone," and for the abbreviation of the saying, i.e. his elimination of the reference to the Jewish ages, "either in this world or in the next" (in his concern for his predominantly Gentile readers). Luke is also influenced in his redaction by the form of the saying preserved in Mark 3:28-29, which makes use of the vb. *blasphēmein,* "revile, blaspheme." In the Marcan context it is part of the Beelzebul controversy and was omitted by Luke as he resumed his own narrative in 8:4 after his Little Interpolation (see pp. 67, 699). Yet another form of this saying is found in *Gos. of Thom.* § 44: "Whoever reviles the Father will be forgiven, and whoever reviles the Son will be forgiven; but whoever reviles the holy Spirit will not be forgiven, either on earth or in heaven." This form is clearly of later vintage, being dependent on the emerging belief in the Trinity and transforming the Jewish expression "this world and the world to come" to a form dependent on Matt 28:18 (cf. Luke 12:56; Col 1:20). The Lucan form of this saying further lacks the explanation of the "unforgivable sin," which is found in Mark 3:29, also omitted by Matthew in favor of the added "Q" saying.

The second saying (vv. 11-12) about the support of Christian disciples to be expected from the holy Spirit has its counterpart in Matt 10:19-20, where it forms an earlier part of his mission-charge to the "twelve disciples." Luke has redacted the "Q" saying by introducing reference to synagogues, magistrates, and authorities; this is absent from Matthew. This redactional modification specifies that the persecution referred to in vv. 4-7,8-9 will come from either Jewish or Gentile sources (see Luke 21:12). On the other hand, "the holy Spirit" is probably the more original expression of "Q," which Matt 10:20 has made into "the Spirit of your Father," adapting the saying to references to the Father in 10:29,32,33. "Holy Spirit" is also found in another form of this saying preserved in Mark 13:11, from which Luke will derive his doublet in 21:14-15 (see p. 81). There the Spirit has been eliminated by Luke, and Jesus himself becomes the support of the disciples who will have to speak in defense of themselves and their ministry.

The logion of v. 10 has been classed by R. Bultmann *(HST* 130-131) among legal sayings of Jesus, i.e. those concerned with "the law of Jewish piety." He considers the "Mk" form to be more original, but recognizes that others (e.g. A. Fridrichsen, "Le péché") consider "Q" to be more original. But because of the collocation which Luke has made of this saying (v. 10) in the context of exhortation of disciples in apostolic activity, it adds a hortatory connotation about their fearless testimony in the face of persecution. It is more than a mere legal saying. Verses 11-12 are, moreover, consolatory, not minatory; they come out of a context that is not parenesis, but paraclesis (see J. Schmid, *Evangelium nach Lukas,* 217; G. Schneider, *Evangelium nach Lukas,* 260).

The sense of v. 10 is not easy to determine. At first, v. 10a seems to contradict v. 9. This impression undoubtedly comes from the original isolated character of the sayings, which are now joined in this Lucan context. Indeed, E. Klostermann *(Lukasevangelium,* 134) even thinks that v. 10 would have better followed vv. 11-12. Whereas vv. 8-9 were clearly addressed to disciples

(Christian followers of Jesus), the "anyone" of v. 10 seems to include at least a larger audience, if not a different one. Moreover, the contrast of the speaking against the Son of Man and the holy Spirit compares a lesser figure with a greater. What is said or done against Jesus as the Son of Man has reference to his ministry (see p. 210); he is rejected in his mortal condition by people. (In the Marcan context it takes the form of ascribing his driving out of demons to Beelzebul; that is the blasphemy [3:22]; similarly in the Matthean context [12:32; cf. 12:27-29].) No matter how one explains the blasphemy against the Son of Man, the real problem is the nature of the unforgivable sin against the holy Spirit.

What is the unforgivable sin? Various explanations have been given of it. (a) It is explained in Mark 3:29-30 as the accusation that Jesus himself "has an unclean spirit"—he drives out demons, not because he is influenced by the holy Spirit, but because he has an unclean spirit; and so it is "an everlasting sin." (This explanation is dropped in Matt 12:32, *pace* E. E. Ellis *[Gospel of Luke,* 176], where that evangelist uses the "Q" saying instead.) (b) Patristic interpreters understood the speaking against the Son of Man as forgivable because it came from non-believers, whereas the blaspheming against the holy Spirit was the unforgivable apostasy of Christian disciples (see Theognostus of Alexandria, *Hypotyposes* 3 [PG 10. 240-241]; Origen, *Comm. in Ioan.* 2.10 [GCS 4. 65]). (c) A slightly different form of the preceding explanation explains the sin against the Son of Man as the rejection of him by his contemporaries in Palestine during his ministry, who will be given the opportunity after his resurrection, the outpouring of the Spirit, and the preaching of disciples to "repent and be baptized . . . in the name of Jesus Christ" (Acts 2:38), but who will then commit the unforgivable sin, if they still refuse. (See Acts 13:45; 18:6; 26:11; J. Ernst, *Evangelium nach Lukas,* 395; R. J. Karris, *Invitation to Luke,* 153; O. Hofius, *EWNT* 1. 532.) (d) Another explanation relates v. 10 closely to vv. 11-12 and understands it as the non-acceptance of the testimony which the holy Spirit will put into the mouths of the disciples (see J. M. Creed, *The Gospel,* 172; E. Klostermann, *Evangelium nach Lukas,* 134). (e) The unforgivable sin is not to be understood merely as the rejection of Christian preaching or the gospel, but the persistence in consummate and obdurate opposition to the influence of the Spirit which animates that preaching; it involves a mentality which obstinately sets the mind against the Spirit of God, and as long as that obstinate mindset perdures, God's forgiveness cannot be accorded to such a person. It is the extreme, unaltered form of opposition to God himself. So, with varying nuances, A. Plummer, *The Gospel,* 321; T. W. Manson, *Sayings,* 110; E. Lövestam, *Spiritus blasphemia,* 51-57. This last explanation is to be preferred.

In a Gospel such as this, with so much emphasis on the forgiveness of sins (see pp. 223-224), it is strange that the evangelist would have incorporated this saying of Jesus. But Luke has his reasons for it, as later passages in his writings will make clear: the denial of Peter (22:34,57,61); Acts 3:12-15; 7:35,51-52. One must also recall Heb 6:4-6; 1 John 5:16. Moreover, it is important not to read into the gospel tradition about this saying the obvious queries of later Christians: Well, could they not repent and seek forgiveness? That is to miss the point of the saying, the implication of which is that the person is obstinate in the blasphemy, i.e. obstinate in opposition to God himself (O. E. Evans).

Finally, in vv. 11-12, where the catchword bonding ("the holy Spirit") has related the second saying to the preceding, Jesus promises the Spirit as support for persecuted disciples haled before worldly authorities, either Jewish or Gentile, in their missionary activity. Jesus is not yet empowered to give the Spirit in his ministry (see H. Conzelmann, *Theology*, 179), but he promises that the Spirit of God, which has been depicted thus far in the Lucan story as the source of Jesus' own power (3:22; 4:1,14,18; 10:21), will also be the source of strength and eloquence in the disciples when they are called upon to defend themselves and their mission. He who is the bearer of the Spirit (11:13; cf. Acts 2:33) will give it in a specific sense. In Acts 4:8 Peter will explicitly be "filled with the holy Spirit," as he replies to "rulers, elders, and Scribes" gathered in Jerusalem with "Annas, Caiaphas, John, and Alexander" (chief priests). Cf. also 4:25-31; 5:29-32; 6:9-10; 7:51-56. Human helplessness and inarticulateness will give way to the strength and eloquence that comes from God's Spirit.

The complex of v. 10 and vv. 11-12 makes clear how great a calling and responsibility the Christian disciple-missionary has—to carry forth as witness Jesus' own word and to cope with such opposition that may even involve resistance to the holy Spirit. See W. Grundmann, *Evangelium nach Lukas*, 255.

NOTES

12 10. *anyone.* Luke writes *pas hos*, lit. "everyone who," combining his favorite "all" (see NOTES on 3:16; 4:15) with the rel. pron. See further 2:20; 3:19; 12:8,48; 19:37; 24:25; Acts 2:21; 13:39; 26:2.

will speak out against the Son of Man. Lit. "will utter a word against" *(erei logon eis)*, whereas Matt 12:32 uses *eipē logon kata* + gen. (which has the same meaning). For the OT background of this latter expression, see E. Lövestam, *Spiritus blasphemia*, 21. For such opposition to Jesus as the earthly Son of Man, see Luke 22:65; 23:39. On "Son of Man," see NOTE on 5:24; cf. pp. 208-211. The title was already in "Q," but was it part of the original saying? V. Taylor *(FGT* 112) may be right in querying it.

he will be forgiven. Lit. "it will be forgiven him," i.e. by God (the theological pass. is used; see NOTE on 5:20). The fut. pass. of the vb. *aphethēsetai autō* may represent Aramaic *šbq l.* See 11QtgJob 38:2-3 *(MPAT* 5:38.2-3). But the pass. of *aphienai* is used with the dat. in the LXX to translate other (Hebrew) vbs., *kpr* or *slḥ*. See Isa 22:14; 33:24. On the forgiveness of sins in Lucan writings, see pp. 223-224.

who reviles the holy Spirit. Lit. "to the one blaspheming against the holy Spirit." Luke uses the prep. *eis* with *blasphēmein*, as does Mark 3:29. These are the only places in the NT where this construction occurs; cf. Dan 3:96 (LXX); Bel 8 (Theodotion); elsewhere the vb. governs the acc. as dir. obj. Luke is thus influenced here by the Marcan passage which he has omitted earlier. See COMMENT. "Reviling" or "blaspheming" the holy Spirit is not limited to the use of injurious language, but includes other activity in opposition. The "holy Spirit" is being used somewhat like "the finger of God" in 11:20, as a way of expressing God's salvific intervention in human activity; if this is rejected or abused, so is God himself. For the OT background of the saying, involving successors of Moses who share in his participation in God's Spirit, which is eventually grieved by the Israelites in the desert, see Num 11:17; 27:18; Deut 34:9; Isa 63:7-14; Ps 106:32-33. On "blasphemy," see Lev 24:11-23; Num 15:30-31. Cf. E. Lövestam, *Spiritus blasphemia*, 35-43.

the holy Spirit. See NOTE on 1:15; cf. pp. 227-231.

will not be forgiven. Lit. "it will not be forgiven," i.e. by God, as above. Salvation in the form of forgiveness of sins will never be available for such blasphemers.

11. *into synagogues.* See NOTE on 4:15; cf. 21:12; Acts 22:19; 26:11; 2 Cor 11:24 (alluding to Deut 25:2-3; see also *m. Mak.* 3:10). Cf. Str-B 3. 527-530.

before magistrates and authorities. Undoubtedly Gentile authorities are meant in contrast to those in synagogues (see 21:12, "kings and prefects"), although *archai kai exousiai* could also be Jewish. See Titus 3:1. For a different sense of this phrase, referring to angels, see Col 1:16; 2:15; Eph 3:10. The latter, however, is scarcely intended here.

do not worry about the defense you will make. Lit. "do not be anxious (about) how or what you will say in defense," a difficult Greek phrase in this context, in which "what" again follows closely. Ms. D, ancient versions, and patristic citations write simply "how" *(pōs)*, eliminating the first *tí*, probably because one follows in the next phrase. But *pōs ē tí* is also found in Matt 10:19. Cf. *TCGNT* 159-160.

12. *will teach you.* The vb. *didaskein*, "teach," is used of the Spirit only here in the Lucan writings. Cf. John 14:26; 1 Cor 2:13.

at that very moment. A Lucan Septuagintism. See pp. 117-118. For a curious parallel to this instruction, see Philo's paraphrase of the comments of the angel who appears to Balaam in Num 22:32-35 *(De vita Mos.* 1.49 § 274): "Pursue your journey. Your hurrying will avail you not. I shall prompt the words you need without your mind's consent, and direct the organs of your speech as justice and convenience may require. I shall guide the reins of your speech, and, though you understand it not, use your tongue for each prophetic utterance."

BIBLIOGRAPHY (12:10-12)

Boring, M. E. "The Unforgivable Sin Logion Mark III 28-29/Matt XII 31-32/Luke XII 10: Formal Analysis and History of the Tradition," *NovT* 18 (1976) 258-279.

Colpe, C. "Der Spruch von der Lästerung des Geistes," *Der Ruf Jesu* (eds. E. Lohse et al.) 63-79.

Denney, J. "Speaking against the Son of Man and Blaspheming the Spirit," *Expos* 7/4 (1907) 521-532.

Evans, O. E. "The Unforgivable Sin," *ExpTim* 68 (1956-1957) 240-244.

Fitzer, G. "Die Sünde wider den Heiligen Geist," *TZ* 13 (1957) 161-182.

Fridrichsen, A. "Le péché contre le Saint-Esprit," *RHPR* 3 (1923) 367-372.

Giblet, J. "Les promesses de l'Esprit et la mission des apôtres dans les évangiles," *Irénikon* 30 (1957) 5-43, esp. 17-19.

Holst, R. "Reexamining Mk 3:28f. and Its Parallels," *ZNW* 63 (1972) 122-124.

Lövestam, E. *Spiritus blasphemia: Eine Studie zu Mk 3,28f par Mt 12,31f, Lk 12,10* (Scripta minora regiae societatis humaniorum litterarum lundensis 1966-1967:1; Lund: Gleerup, 1968).

Marshall, I. H. "Hard Sayings—VII," *Theology* 67 (1964) 65-67.

Roulin, P. "Le péché contre l'Esprit Saint," *BVC* 29 (1959) 38-45.

Schippers, R. "The Son of Man in Matt. xii. 32 = Lk. xii. 10, Compared with Mk. iii. 28," *SE IV* (TU 102) 231-235.

Williams, J. G. "A Note on the 'Unforgivable Sin' Logion," *NTS* 12 (1965-1966) 75-77.

80. WARNING AGAINST GREED
(12:13-15)

12   [13] Then someone in the crowd said to him, "Teacher, tell my brother to share the family inheritance with me." [14] But Jesus said to him, "Sir, who set me over you as judge or arbiter?" [15] Then he said to the people, "Take care! Be on guard against every form of greed, because one's life does not depend upon one's belongings, even when they are more than sufficient."

COMMENT

The sayings of Jesus addressed to his disciples in the presence of a great crowd (12:1-12,22-34) are interrupted by a request from an individual in the crowd who asks Jesus to intervene in a dispute between him and his brother over inheritance (12:13-15). This, in turn, provides a setting for the coming parable of the rich fool (vv. 16-21). The topic thus moves from sayings about allegiance to himself to attitudes about worldly possessions (12:13-34). Earlier a warning about hypocrisy led to sayings on fearless confession, etc.; now a refusal to be concerned about material inheritance leads to a warning about greed and the folly of the rich.

This passage and the following parable are derived by Luke from "L," being found only in this Gospel (see p. 83). This is at least true of vv. 13-14; Lucan composition may be responsible for v. 15, as R. Bultmann (HST 193, 335) thinks. The introductory cl. makes use of a favorite Lucan expression (eipen de pros autous), and the sentiment is otherwise quite characteristic of the Lucan Jesus' attitude toward wealth, despite the strange wording (not without textual difficulties). This makes it unlikely that vv. 13-21 were originally a unit, pace T. W. Manson, Sayings, 270. Moreover, despite the claims of I. H. Marshall, H. Schürmann, J. Ernst, there is simply no "evidence" that these verses ever stood in "Q." That Matthew has omitted them, or that he has echoed them in 6:19-20,25 is simply farfetched. Cf. J. Schmid, Evangelium nach Lukas, 218.

Form-critically considered, vv. 13-14 are a pronouncement-story; the pronouncement in v. 14 is occasioned by the request of a friendly bystander. It has been called a "scholastic dialogue" by R. Bultmann (HST 54-55), who doubts that it can be traced back to Jesus himself. But there is no reason to ascribe such an attitude to the early Christian community, even despite 1 Cor 6:4-8. To the pronouncement has been added, however, a minatory saying about greed (v. 15). Though some commentators (e.g. FGT 23-24) would regard vv. 14-15 as the pronouncement, I prefer to consider v. 15 as an appended saying, which may reflect an early Christian attitude, rather than an authentic logion of Jesus.

A form of vv. 13-14 is found in Gos. of Thom. § 72: "[A man said to him], 'Tell my brothers that they should divide my father's possessions with me.' He said to him, 'Sir, who made me a divider?' He turned to his disciples (and) said to them, 'Am I a divider?' " This (secondary) form of the saying has nothing corresponding to v. 15 and is another reason for not regarding vv. 13-15 as an original unit. Cf. J.-E. Ménard, L'Evangile selon Thomas, 173.

The saying uttered by Jesus in response to the request makes clear that he has not come to settle such legal questions as were otherwise submitted to religious teachers (Palestinian rabbis) of the time. He rejects the role of judge or arbiter in family disputes about inheritance (as well as other material concerns). Given the attitude to be expressed in 12:51-53, one can understand Jesus' refusal to get involved here. He has, moreover, identified his own family with those who listen to the word of God and act on it; he will not get involved in the material disputes of another. He is, furthermore, disturbed that two brothers dispute over such material possessions (land, money, goods). Needed is not a casuistic settlement by a "teacher," but a realization that covetousness is at the root of such family disputes.

The saying in v. 15 adds commentary to the foregoing pronouncement, providing it with another basic attitude. It exposes the underlying covetousness of the request for arbitration. Jesus warns against every kind of greed. He refuses to identify authentic Christian existence with the possession of material wealth, even inherited—especially when abundant. It is much more important to *be* than to *have*—to be one who listens to God's word and acts on it than to live in an unnecessary abundance of wealth. His words remind us of Lev 19:18 and prepare (esp. v. 15c) for the coming parable.

NOTES

12   13. *someone in the crowd said to him.* See 13:23; 9:57. This is probably a Lucan composition, introducing the "L" material. The setting is scarcely historical.

Teacher. See NOTES on 3:12; 7:40. Since the question of inheritance is treated in the Pentateuch (e.g. Deut 21:15-17; Num 27:1-11; 36:7-9), a religious teacher or Scribe would be the usual one to whom such a problem would be brought.

The regulations for inheritance in later rabbinic interpretation of Num 27:1-11; Deut 21:15-17 are found in *m. B. Bat.* 8:1-9:10. The problem has nothing to do with Josephus, *J.W.* 2.8,3 § 122 (common ownership among Essenes), *pace* I. H. Marshall, *Luke,* 522. Cf. Str-B 3. 545-549.

my brother. We are not told just what was in dispute. Did the older brother refuse to allow this one to take "that portion of the property that was coming" to him (15:12)? Did he prefer to hold it jointly? Given Jesus' reply, the details of the dispute are unimportant, and the problem goes against what is counseled in Ps 133:1.

inheritance. Luke uses the usual secular Greek word *klēronomia,* as in 20:14. The same sense is found in the LXX (Num 26:54,56; 27:7-11); Josephus *(J.W.* 2,12,8 § 249), and Greek papyrus texts (MM 346-347). Cf. *EWNT* 2. 736.

14. *Sir.* Lit. "man" (voc. of *anthrōpos).* See NOTE on 5:20; cf. 22:58,60. It is a rebuking term, implying aloofness.

judge or arbiter? Marcion and ms. D read only "judge." "Arbiter" *(meristēs,* lit. "portioner") is replaced in some mss. by *dikastēs,* "arbitrator," probably under the influence of Acts 7:27,35. Cf. Exod 2:14 for the opposite role.

15. *he said to the people.* Lit. "said to them" *(pros +* acc. *autous;* see p. 116); reference is made to the crowd.

Take care! Be on guard against. Lit. "look and guard yourselves from."

every form of greed. Greek *pleonexia* is frequently found in parenetic passages of the NT (Rom 1:29; 2 Cor 9:5; Col 3:5; Eph 4:19; 5:3; 2 Pet 2:3,14). From the following parable it will appear that greed is the height of folly. "Greed" is the lust to have more, more than is needed, the boundless grasping after more. Cf. 1 Tim 6:10 (love of money as the root of all evil).

one's life does not depend upon one's belongings. Fullness of life consists not in what one has or in what one has labored and sweated for. See 9:25, where what is said there about life is to be understood spiritually, but is now extended to physical life itself. Patristic allusions to this verse often recast it: "Possessions are not life." The substantive ptc. of *hyparchein* with a dat. is used only by Luke in the NT (8:3 [see NOTE there]; Acts 4:32). Cf. J. Jeremias, *Die Sprache,* 215.

even when they are more than sufficient. See Luke 21:4; cf. Qoh 2:3-11; Job 31:24-28. The greedy person acts as if the important thing in life is only secured when he/she has amassed the superfluous. Cf. E. Klostermann, *Lukasevangelium,* 135. For a possible mingling of two disparate phrases in this peculiar ending of the verse, see C. F. D. Moule, "H. W. Moule on Acts iv. 25," *ExpTim* 65 (1953-1954) 220-221. Luke uses here his favorite articular infin. with the prep. *en.* See p. 119.

BIBLIOGRAPHY (12:13-15)

Baarda, T. "Luke 12, 13-14: Text und Transmission from Marcion to Augustine," *Christianity, Judaism, and Other Greco-Roman Cults: Studies for Morton Smith at Sixty* (SJLA 12; ed. J. Neusner; Leiden: Brill, 1975) 1. 107-162.

———— "Over exegese gesproken," *VoxT* 39 (1969) 146-154.

Daube, D. "Inheritance in Two Lukan Pericopes," *ZSSR* 72 (1955) 326-334.

Degenhardt, H.-J. *Lukas, Evangelist der Armen,* 68-76.

Neuhäusler, E. "Allem Besitz entsagen," *Anspruch und Antwort Gottes: Zur Lehre von den Weisungen innerhalb der synoptischen Jesusverkündigung* (Düsseldorf: Patmos, 1962) 170-185.

Tarelli, C. C. "A Note on Luke xii. 15," *JTS* 41 (1940) 260-262.

81. THE PARABLE OF THE RICH FOOL
(12:16-21)

12 16 He proposed to them a parable: "There was once a rich man with a farm that produced abundant crops, 17 and he thought to himself, 'What should I do? I do not have space enough to store my produce.' 18 'This is what I will do,' he said; 'I will tear down my barns and build bigger ones; I will gather into them all my grain and other goods. 19 Then I will say to myself, "Friend, you have many good

things stored up for years to come; so take it easy; eat, drink, and be merry.' " [20] But God said to him, 'You fool, this very night is your life demanded of you. Now who will get all that you have prepared?' "

[21] So it will be with anyone who piles up treasure for himself but is not rich with God.

COMMENT

Luke continues to add from his special source ("L," see p. 83) the so-called parable of the rich fool (12:16-21). It is meant as a commentary on Jesus' saying about greed (12:15), which manifests itself not only in disputes about inheritance, but in lustful ambition to provide for oneself more than is necessary. In particular, it offers a commentary on v. 15c. (See *HST* 61.)

The introduction to the parable is typically Lucan (see NOTE on 12:16). Verse 21 is a secondary addition (of Lucan composition) to the parable, being introduced by "so"; the sense of the parable is complete without it, *pace* P. Joüon, "La parabole du riche insensé"; and the verse is missing in some manuscripts. Moreover, a form of the parable, with nothing corresponding to v. 21, is found in *Gos. of Thom.* § 63: "Jesus said, 'There was a rich man who had much money. He said, "I will make use of my money to sow and reap, to plant and fill my barns with produce so that I shall lack nothing." These were the thoughts of his heart, but that very night he died. Let the one who has ears take heed' " (see further J. N. Birdsall). In this form of the story, however, the rich man is not treated as a fool, and it has lost the cutting edge of the Lucan parable, viz. God's verdict.

As for the form of the episode, though it is called a "parable" by Luke (v. 16), it is really another "example" (see COMMENT on 10:29-37) according to our modern categories of figures, supplying a practical model for Christian conduct with an implicit demand for radical action.

The message of the episode is simple, casting 9:25 in narrative form. The amassing of a superabundance of material possessions for the sake of *la dolce vita* becomes the height of folly in the light of the responsibility of life itself and the assessment of it which will take place once it is over. *Pace* J. Jeremias (*Parables*, 165), Jesus' words do not merely refer to "the approaching eschatological catastrophe, and the coming Judgement," but to the death of the individual person and his/her individual fate. The point of his story is brought home in the realization that the rich man was on the point of achieving an ambition in this present life, without ever reflecting on what would be the aftermath of that ambition, either in his own existence or for the stores so amassed. Jesus' words thus bring a consideration of death into human existence: A human being shall one day answer for the conduct of life beyond all the foresight exerted to enhance one's physical well-being with abundance. In the story the "rich man" is a farmer; but he stands for humans seduced by "every form of greed" (12:15), whether peasant or statesman, craftsman or lawyer, nurse or doctor, secretary or professor. All can become fools in God's sight. (See further J. Dupont, "L'Après-mort dans l'oeuvre de Luc," *RTL* 3 [1972] 3-21; "Die individuelle Eschatologie," 38.)

Running through the story is the God-fool contrast; recall Ps 14:1, "The fool (LXX: *aphrōn)* says in his heart, 'There is no God.' " One lives without reckoning with God; and, Luke's story adds, without acknowledging the obligation to use one's wealth for others and realizing that death's call may come at the height of the ambitious pursuit. The fool's godlessness manifests itself in his lust for more, whereas the fear of the Lord which is the beginning of wisdom (Prov 1:7; 9:10) never crosses his mind.

The application in v. 21 adds a further warning for the person "not rich with God." It makes even clearer that the goal of life is not the piling up of treasure "for himself." As part of Lucan teaching on the use of material possessions (see pp. 247-251), it implies the use of wealth on behalf of others as the way to become "rich with God."

It may seem that God is unjust to demand the rich man's life precisely at the moment when he is achieving a life's ambition, for in itself the amassing of wealth is indifferent. The reason why it is hard for the rich to get through the eye of the needle (18:25) is not because of amassing in itself, but because of the iniquitous seduction that invariably comes with it (see NOTE on 16:11), distracting that person from the consideration of what life is all about. Again, this may sound like bourgeois piety; but it is part of the message of the Lucan Jesus.

For a Roman philosopher's way of putting the lesson of this episode, see Seneca, *Ep. mor.* 17.5. Compare also the attitude expressed about the amassing of wealth in a foolish way which is found in *1 Enoch* 97:8-10: "Woe to you who acquire silver and gold, but not in righteousness, and say, 'We have become very rich and have possessions and have acquired everything that we desired. Now let us do what we have planned, for we have gathered silver and filled our storehouses, and as many as water are the husbandmen of our houses.' Like water your life will flow away, for riches will not stay with you; they will quickly go up from you, for you acquired everything in wickedness, and you will be given over to a great curse." See S. Aalen, "St Luke's Gospel and the Last Chapters of I Enoch," *NTS* 13 (1966-1967) 1-13; G. W. E. Nickelsburg, "Riches, the Rich, and God's Judgment in 1 Enoch 92-105 and the Gospel according to Luke," *NTS* 25 (1978-1979) 324-344, esp. 329-330, 334-337.

NOTES

12 16. *proposed to them a parable.* See NOTE on 5:36; cf. p. 116 *(eipen pros* + acc.). See also 6:39.

There was once a rich man. Lit. "of a certain rich man yielded well the farm/ property"; for the word order, see BDF § 473.1. The details of the story would well be at home in a Palestinian setting.

produced abundant crops. The vb. *euphorein,* "yield well," occurs only here in the Greek Bible; it is used by Josephus, *J.W.* 2.21,2 § 592.

17. *thought to himself.* Luke again uses *dialogizesthai,* as in 5:22. See NOTE there. The Septuagintism *legōn,* ptc. "saying," has been omitted in the translation. See p. 115.

What should I do? Cp. the soliloquy in 12:45; 15:17a; 16:3-4; 18:4-5; 20:13; also Sir 11:19. The rich man wonders about the future of his store.

18. *build bigger ones.* Ms. D and some OL versions read, "I shall make them bigger." In either case, it expresses the final decision at the supreme moment of ambition. The "barns" are to be understood as warehouses for storage.

all my grain and other goods. This is the reading of mss. P75, א2, B, L, 070, etc.; mss. D, א*, and the OL read, "all my produce" *(panta ta genēmata mou),* whereas mss. A, Q, W, Θ, Ψ, and the Koine text-tradition have "all my produce and my goods," an obvious scribal conflation of the two preceding readings. "Other goods" refers to more than farm produce; it makes the story applicable to others than just farmers.

19. *to myself, "Friend . . ."* Lit. "to my soul, 'Soul . . .' " Here Greek *psychē* is used in two senses: (1) as a vivid Semitic substitute for the reflexive pron. "myself." See v. 22; cp. Luke's use of *en heautō* in v. 17; (2) in an underlying synecdoche, as the fool addresses his whole self, using only a part of him. See NOTES on 6:9; 9:24. For the voc. use of *psychē,* see Chariton, *Aphrod.* 3.2. Cf. Greek *Enoch* 97:8.

stored up for years to come; so take it easy; eat, drink. These words are omitted in ms. D and OL versions; Westcott-Hort bracketed them, but N-A26 and *UBSGNT*3 admit them without comment. See p. 130.

stored up. See NOTE on 2:34. Cf. Greek *Enoch* 97:8.

take it easy. Lit. "take your rest," as after eating well. Cf. Sir 11:18-19 (especially in the Hebrew) for the same sentiment expressed here.

eat, drink, and be merry. These are acts symbolic of carefree, luxurious, even dissipated living; cf. 1 Cor 15:32 (= Isa 22:13); Qoh 8:15 (nothing better under the sun than "to eat and drink and enjoy oneself" [the LXX uses the same three Greek vbs. as Luke]); Tob 7:10; *1 Enoch* 97:8-9; Euripides, *Alcest.* 788-789; Menander, *Frg.* 301; *Gilgamesh* X.iii *(ANET* 90). See further *HST* 204. Note also the frequency of the egoistic assertions in vv. 17b-c,18,19, which mark the superficial self-confidence of the speaker.

20. *God said to him.* I.e. in a dream of the night; the direct address is part of the story's development. He is addressed by the lord of life, without whom he has schemed.

You fool. Lit. "Fool!" On *aphrōn,* see NOTE on 11:40; cf. D. Zeller, *EWNT* 1. 444-446. The "summons" comes when it is least expected.

this very night. The ambitious scheme will never be realized; at the height of the planning the God-fool contrast enters human existence, and death exposes the basic poverty of the fool.

is your life demanded of you. Lit. "they exact your soul from you," with a poignant pres. tense. The mss. **ℵ**, A, W, Θ, Ψ, and the Koine text-tradition read the compound *apaitousin,* whereas others (P[75], B, L, Q, 070, 33) have the simple vb. *aitousin;* see *TCGNT* 160. The sense is not affected. For the expression, see Wis 15:8. The indef. (impers.) third pl. is a substitute for the pass. (see 6:38; 16:9; 23:31); in this case, for the theological pass. (see BDF § 130.2; ZBG § 236). The same use of the third pl. is found in Hebrew: Prov 9:11b; Job 4:19c; 6:2b. Cf. Str-B 2. 221.

It is hardly likely that the pl. is to be understood of "angels" of death (cf. Job 33:23 LXX; Heb 2:14), *pace* W. Grundmann, *Evangelium nach Lukas,* 258; I. H. Marshall, *Luke,* 524; much less of "robbers" as in 10:30.

who will get all that you have prepared? Lit. "what you have made ready, to whom will it be/go?" Herein lies the height of the folly. The rhetorical question is poignant. The vb. *hetoimazein* has already been used in other contexts (1:17,76; 2:31; 3:4; 9:52).

21. *who piles up treasure for himself.* The whole verse is omitted in ms. D and some OL versions (a,b). See p. 130. But it is found in P[45], P[75], etc; see *TCGNT* 160.

for himself. I.e. not for others, like the poor, widows, orphans, sojourners in the land. See Deut 24:17-22; cf. 2 Cor 6:10b. Verse 33 will provide further comment on this verse.

is not rich with God. I.e. by storing up what really counts in the sight of God (among which would be the proper use of material possessions for others). Divine scrutiny of the life given will not be concerned with barns bursting at their seams.

Some mss. (U, the Freer family of minuscules) add to this verse, "Saying this, he called out, 'Let the one who has ears to hear take heed.' " Cf. 8:8; it has also been added elsewhere in some mss. (8:15; 13:9; 21:4). Even though the form of this parable in *Gos. of Thom.* § 63 includes it, it is scarcely an original ending, being derived mainly from lectionary use. See further J. N. Birdsall, "Lk xii. 16ff."; and the discussion of this hortatory utterance by J. M. Robinson, *The Problem of History,* 43-44.

BIBLIOGRAPHY (12:16-21)

Birdsall, J. N. "Lk xii. 16ff. and the Gospel of Thomas," *JTS* 13 (1962) 332-336.
Derrett, J. D. M. "The Rich Fool: A Parable of Jesus Concerning Inheritance," *HeyJ* 18 (1977) 131-151.
Dupont, J. *Les béatitudes* 3. 113-118.
——— "Die individuelle Eschatologie im Lukasevangelium und in der Apostelgeschichte," *Orientierung an Jesus* (eds. P. Hoffmann et al.) 37-47, esp. 38-41.
Eichholz, G. "Vom reichen Kornbauern (Luk. 12, 13-21)," *Gleichnisse der Evangelien,* 179-191.
Gaide, G. "Le riche insensé Lc 12, 13-21," *AsSeign* ns 49 (1971) 82-89.
Jeremias, J. *Parables,* 164-165.

Joüon, P. "Notes philologiques sur les Évangiles—Luc 12,21," *RSR* 18 (1928) 353-354.

——— "La parabole du riche insensé *(Luc,* 12,13-21)," *RSR* 29 (1939) 486-489.

Lambrecht, J. *Once More,* 7, 59, 80.

Linnemann, E. *Jesus of the Parables,* 4-5, 15-16, 22, 45.

Reid, J. "The Poor Rich Fool: Luke xii. 21," *ExpTim* 13 (1901-1902) 567-568.

Seng, E. W. "Der reiche Tor: Eine Untersuchung von Lk. xii 16-21 unter besonderer Berücksichtigung form- und motivgeschichtlicher Aspekte," *NovT* 20 (1978) 136-155.

82. WORRY ABOUT EARTHLY THINGS
(12:22-32)

12 [22] He said to his disciples, "For this reason I say to you, Do not worry about your life—what you will eat; nor about your body—what you will put on. [23] For life means more than food, and the body more than clothing. [24] Look at the ravens! They neither sow nor reap; they have neither a storeroom nor a barn. Yet God feeds them. How much more you are worth than birds! [25] Which one of you by worrying can add a moment of time to his span of life? [26] If you cannot achieve even a tiny little thing, then why worry about the rest? [27] Look at the lilies —how they grow! They neither toil nor spin; yet I tell you, not even Solomon in all his splendor was robed as one of these. [28] If God so lavishly clothes the grass which grows in the field today and is tossed into the furnace tomorrow, how much more so will he clothe you, O people of little faith! [29] Do not seek continually for what you are to eat and drink; do not be anxious about these things. [30] For they are all the things the pagans of this world run after! But your Father is well aware that you need them. [31] Seek rather for his kingdom, and these things will be given to you in addition. [32] Do not be afraid, little flock, for it has pleased your Father to entrust to you his kingdom."

COMMENT

At this point in the travel account Jesus again addresses his disciples in the crowd. The subject of these sayings is worry about earthly matters (12:22-32); they are the beginning of a variety of counsels that fill the rest of this chapter.

This immediate collection (vv. 22-32) acts as a commentary on the parable of the rich fool.

Verse 22a is transitional, being composed by Luke; in "Q," from which he has derived the sayings of vv. 22b-31 (see p. 78), they were not specifically addressed to the "disciples," but they already formed a unit there, even though it is hard to say that they were all uttered on one occasion by Jesus. The parallel to these sayings is found in Matt 6:25-33, again in a part of the sermon on the mount. Catchword bonding ("worry," vv. 22c,25,26) is responsible for the unit, and it probably governs Luke's use of the sayings here too (see vv. 11-12). In "Q" an intrusive verse was already present (Matt 6:27 = Luke 12:25). It represents an "independent logion" (*HST* 88), but has been attached to the unit because of the ptc. *merimnōn,* "worrying," even though it deals with neither food nor clothing. Luke has further modified his form of v. 26, which differs considerably from (the repetitious) Matt 6:28a. Luke has made some further minor redactional changes, the chief of which are: the dropping of "your" *(hymōn)* twice in v. 22; the substitution of his favorite vb. *katanoein,* "look at," in vv. 24,27; his better Greek sg. vbs. with neut. pl. subjs. in v. 27; his use of *meteōrizesthai,* "be anxious," in v. 29. Finally, he has added v. 32, a saying regarded by R. Bultmann *(HST* 111) as a "secondary community formulation," uttered by the risen Christ and promising salvation. But it is almost certainly of pre-Lucan origin (so J. Jeremias, *Die Sprache,* 218), even if it is difficult to agree with W. Pesch that it is to be traced to Jesus himself.

A form of v. 22 is also found in the Coptic *Gos. of Thom.* § 36: "Jesus said, 'Fret not from morning to evening and from evening to morning about what you are going to put on." An earlier form of this is found in the older Greek text of the same Gospel (OxyP 655:1-17): "[Jesus says, 'Be not solicitous f]rom morning un[til evening, or] from eve[ning until mo]rning either [for y]our [sustenance], what [you will] eat, [or] for [your] clo[thing], what you [will] put on. [You] are worth [far] more than [the lili]es whi[ch g]row but do not s[pi]n, and have n[o] clo[thi]ng. And you, what do [you lack]? Who of you can add to his stature/span of life? *He* will [gi]ve you your clothing." The Coptic form is much shorter than the Greek; the latter represents a condensation of Luke 12:22-27a or Matt 6:25-28, and the Coptic is a further (modified) reduction of 12:22 alone. (See further J.-E. Ménard, *L'Evangile selon Thomas,* 134-136.)

Form-critically considered, these sayings are hortatory logia, prophetic counsels against worry about food and drink or clothes. Some of them are marked by (poetic?) parallelism (12:22c,d,23; see *FGT* 109); others are marked by the use of impvs. (vv. 22,24,27,29,31,32), followed often by subsidiary comments or explanations.

As a group, these sayings in vv. 22b-31 exhort Jesus' disciples to a correct and fundamental view of concern for everyday, earthly life—details of food and clothing. Coming immediately after his warning against "every form of greed" (v. 15) and the example of the rich fool (vv. 16-21), they furnish yet another perspective on material possessions: Cast off worry about food and clothing; realize that life itself is a greater concern than these needs of material existence. Jesus draws from the Palestinian countryside vivid details to press his point: Be as free from worry as the ravens, the lilies, even the grass in the field. They all thrive without worry, because God himself cares for them. Ravens have no barns or warehouses; lilies neither toil nor spin, and grass grows lavishly. Further comparison is made with reference to a king of Israel and to pagans: The lilies are more resplendent than Solomon of old in all his renowned raiment; food and drink are the things that pagans run after. Yet what are you in comparison with all these? So concludes the argument from smaller to greater. The Christian disciple is far more important. (See p. 248.)

The crucial point of the exhortation occurs in vv. 30b-31: "Your Father is well aware that you need these things; seek rather his kingdom, and these things will be given to you in addition." Priority of values is proposed again. In 11:2 the disciples were instructed to pray, "May your kingdom come," now they learn that they too are to have a specific share in it.

Verses 25-26 press the point still further: Worry cannot add an extra moment to one's life; so if this "tiny little thing" cannot be achieved by human concern, why worry about the rest? Direction in life should come from a preoccupation with God and his kingdom; concern for earthly details may prove to be only an obstacle to the single-minded pursuit of and service to the kingdom.

Verse 32 adds a further counsel, as the "disciples" of v. 22 are now addressed as "little flock." It betrays the self-conscious awareness of the early Christian community in its struggle for recognition, unity, and cohesion. Reassurance is given to it, which should transcend all fear, despite the small size of the group. Here one should recall the idyllic summaries of Acts 2:42-47; 4:32-35; and the divisive episode of Ananias and Sapphira (Acts 5:1-10). Jesus' words could envisage the scattering of the group after his death; their reward is promised as a share in the kingdom itself (see W. Pesch, *Die kleine Herde*). Whether one can be sure that the words in this verse go back to Jesus himself or not, they are used by Luke to exhort his own community to steadfastness in the pursuit of all that the preceding collection of sayings of Jesus still has to say to it.

NOTES

12   22. *said to his disciples.* The Lucan composing hand is seen in *eipen pros* + acc. See p. 116. "His" is omitted in some important mss. (P[75], B, 1241) and OL versions (c, e); N-A[26] has bracketed the possessive. Cf. *TCGNT* 161. Note the double introduction, v. 22a (Lucan), v. 22b ("Q").

For this reason. In the Lucan context a conclusion is drawn from the rich man's conduct and fate.

Do not worry about your life. Lit. "about the soul" *(psychē),* considered as involved in eating. It stands in contrast to *sōma,* "body," which wears the clothes. God who gives "life" will see that human beings obtain what is needed for mere existence, because "life" has a larger dimension than mere existence. Food and clothing are meant to serve "life." The vb. *merimnan* means to "take anxious thought," but it also connotes exertion and the putting forth of effort (see J. Jeremias, *Parables,* 214-215); yet the basic idea of worry cannot be glossed over. Cf. R. Bultmann, *TDNT* 4. 591.

23. *life.* Again, lit. "the soul." See NOTES on 1:46; 9:24.

24. *Look at.* Luke has substituted *katanoein,* "consider, think about," a vb. he has used in 6:41; 12:27; 20:23; Acts 7:31,32; 11:6; 27:39. Matthew uses it only in 7:3 (= Luke 6:41). See p. 110; cf. J. Jeremias, *Die Sprache,* 217. Matt 6:26 reads rather *emblepsate,* which expresses the same idea more literally, "look at." The argument proceeds here *a minori ad maius,* as it does in v. 28. Birds are mentioned because of their continual pecking for food; below lilies will be joined with raiment.

the ravens! These birds are mentioned only here in the NT; Matt 6:26 has changed the specific to the more generic, "birds of the sky," a phrase that Luke also uses elsewhere (8:5; 9:58; 13:19). The ravens are mentioned because they cry for food in Ps 147:9; Job 38:41; they are cared for by God himself, even if they are unclean birds (forbidden as food to Israelites, Lev 11:15; Deut 14:14). They were known in antiquity as careless creatures that even fail to return to their nests. See Servius' comments on Virgil, *Georg.* 1.414 (ed. G. Thilo 3. 268), which quote Pliny the Elder, *Nat. Hist.* 35.7,23?. See further E. Fuchs, "Die Verkündigung Jesu"; S. Schulz, *Q: Die Spruchquelle,* 149-150.

neither sow nor reap. Lit. "they do not sow, nor do they reap," the negative advs. are not uniformly transmitted in various mss. See the *app. crit.* Such refined activity and storage in barns are mentioned to contrast the constant pecking of worthless birds with God's abundant providence.

you are worth. See 12:7.

25. *Which one of you.* See NOTE on 11:5.

can add a moment of time to his span of life? Or "a cubit to his stature." On *hēlikia,* see NOTE on 2:52. The n. *pēchys* occurs in Greek literature from Homer on in the sense of "forearm" *(Il.* 5.314), and as a measure of length (from the point of the elbow to the tip of the middle finger), "cubit" (46.2 centimeters or about 18 inches), in Herodotus, *Hist.* 1.178. As a measure of length, it occurs in the LXX (e.g. Gen 6:15-16; 7:20; Exod 25:9,16,22 [10,17,23E]) and in the NT (John 21:8; Rev 21:17). But it seems to occur in a temporal sense in Diogenes Laertius, *Plato* 3.11; and a related form *pēchuion*, "small amount," is similarly used in Mimnermus, *Anth. lyr. gr.* 2.3. Hence the hesitation of commentators. Most prefer the temporal sense in Luke because it avoids the grotesque idea that the addition of 18 inches to one's height would be a "tiny little thing" *(elachiston)*. However, the *NEB*, Manson, Danker, et al. prefer "stature." As one might expect, the *JB* mixes the two images. Cf. MM 279; J. Schneider, *TDNT* 2. 941-943. In any case, the implication is that only God can prolong human life or add such stature; consumption of food alone will not achieve it. The vb. *prostithenai*, "add," is a Lucan favorite. See p. 111. For the form of the saying, cp. Prov 6:27-28. For a measure of length used to measure time, see Ps 39:5. For a farfetched attempt to retrovert this phrase into Aramaic, see G. Schwarz, *"Prostheinai epi tēn hēlikian autou pēchyn hena,"* *ZNW* 71 (1980) 244-247.

27. *the lilies.* Matt 6:28 adds "of the field." Greek *krinon* is specifically the "white lily" *(lilium candidum)*. See Theophrastus, *Hist. plant.* 6.6,8; Theocritus, *Cycl.* 11.56. It was, however, also used generically for many lilylike flowers. Since the "white lily" is usually a woodland plant, it is hard to think of it in a Palestinian setting ("a field"). Hence *krina* is often understood generically of other colorful, beautiful flowers that dot the Palestinian countryside in the spring; e.g. the scarlet anemone, the Easter daisy, the autumn crocus, ranunculi, even poppies—all of which have been suggested at times as meant by *krina.* See G. Dalman, "Die Lilie der Bibel," *PJ* 21 (1925) 98-100; G. B. King, " 'Consider the Lilies,' " *Crozer Quarterly* 10 (1933) 28-36; E. Ha-Reubeni, "Les lis des champs," *RB* 54 (1947) 362-364; A. Alon, *Natural History,* 155-174. Even if the flower cannot be specifically identified, the import of Jesus' words is clear: The "lilies" do nothing to achieve their own beauty.

how they grow! . . . *spin.* Ms. D, OS versions, and Marcion read, "neither spin nor weave," which critical editions of the Greek NT once preferred. E.g. Nestle-Aland[25]; cf. E. Klostermann, *Lukasevangelium,* 137; T. C. Skeat, "The Lilies of the Field," *ZNW* 37 (1938) 211-214. Though the reading preferred here has been suspected of being a copyist's harmonization with Matt 6:28, it is found in good mss. (P[45], P[75], B, ℵ, A, and the Koine text-tradition). Cf. *TCGNT* 161. Underlying "toil" and "spin" may be a play on the Aramaic vbs. *'ămal* and *'ăzal,* as suggested by T. W. Manson, *Sayings,* 112.

Solomon in all his splendor. Allusion is made to his proverbial wealth and raiment (1 Kgs 10:4-5,21,23; 2 Chr 9:4,20,22).

one of these. See p. 122.

28. *the grass.* Jesus' words now reduce the colorful lily to mere "grass" for the sake of the argument, again *a minori ad maius.* Recall the OT descriptions of the transitory and passing nature of grass (Isa 37:27; 40:6-8; Job 8:12; Pss 37:2; 90:5-6; 102:12; 103:15). His words, however, now give a new turn to the image, in stressing God's providence even for grass.

O people of little faith! A Greek compound adj. *oligopistos,* added to the tradition already in "Q," lacks any real equivalent in the Semitic languages, and hence is scarcely traceable to Jesus himself. It is found elsewhere in Christian writers, dependent on the NT. Luke uses it only here; but cf. Matt 6:30; 8:26; 14:31; 16:8. The apostrophe stresses the attitude of one who does not trust God to provide what is needed for mere material existence.

29. *Do not seek.* Matt 6:31 has rather, "Do not therefore worry."

do not be anxious. Luke uses a rare Greek vb. *meteōrizesthe,* which is found with this meaning in Polybius, *Hist.* 5.70,10; OxyP 1679:16; Josephus, *Ant.* 16.4,6 § 135. Its more usual meaning, however, is "to be raised on high, be elated, overweening." This has been preferred in the past (cf. Vg "nolite in sublime tolli"; Luther, Tyndale), but it ill suits the Lucan context. Matt 6:31 has nothing corresponding to it; did he omit what was in "Q"? See further K. H. Rengstorf, *Evangelium nach Lukas,* 162; K. Deissner, *TDNT* 4. 630-631; J. Molitor, *BZ* 10 (1966) 107-108.

30. *the pagans of this world.* Lit. "the nations of the world," who know not God (1 Thess 4:5). Their hectic "running after" food and drink creates the anxiety of their lives and the lack of inner peace.

your Father. I.e. God as the heavenly provider. See 2:49; 6:36; 9:26; 11:2,13; 22:29; 24:49. Alas, he can be forgotten. See Hos 9:1-4.

31. *his kingdom.* Matt 6:33 adds "and his righteousness." See Matt 5:6. Jesus exhorts his disciples to allow God's kingship to dominate their lives so that they will even seek to spread its influence. See pp. 154-157 and NOTE on 4:43. Earlier he had instructed them to pray that it might "come" (11:2). Now he insists on a hierarchy of values: Whoever seeks this kingdom will receive from God what is needed for the sustenance of material life. See p. 68.

32. *Do not be afraid.* The stock OT reassurance is repeated. See NOTE on 1:13; cf. 2:10; 5:10; 8:50; Acts 18:9; 27:24. The reassurance is given to the flock despite its small size. Cf. 10:3 (it is like lambs among wolves); Acts 20:29.

little flock. This may be an allusion to Isa 41:14 LXX, "Jacob, smallest of Israel, I shall help you" (contrast the MT). In this saying the *small* community of Jesus' followers is promised God's *greatest* gift.

to entrust to you his kingdom. I.e. to make you part of it. The giving of the kingdom echoes that of Dan 7:13-14, where it is promised to one like a Son of Man (= "the saints" of Israel in the Danielic context); now it becomes the heritage of Jesus' disciples. See 22:29-30, where Jesus himself confers *his own* kingship on his apostles.

BIBLIOGRAPHY (12:22-32)

Avanzo, M. "Jésus y la conducción de la comunidad," *RevistB* 37 (1975) 16-22.

Degenhardt, H.-J. *Lukas, Evangelist der Armen,* 80-85.

Fuchs, E. "Die Verkündigung Jesu: Der Spruch von den Raben," *Der historische Jesus und der kerygmatische Christus* (eds. H. Ristow and K. Matthiae; 3d ed.; Berlin: Evangelische Verlagsanstalt, 1964) 385-388.

Meyer, B. F. "Jesus and the Remnant of Israel," *JBL* 84 (1965) 123-130.

Montgomery, J. A. "Some Correspondence between the Elephantine Papyri and the Gospels," *ExpTim* 24 (1912-1913) 428-429.

Nötscher, F. "Das Reich (Gottes) und seine Gerechtigkeit (Mt 6,33 vgl. Lc 12,31)," *Bib* 31 (1950) 237-241.

Pesch, R. *Die kleine Herde: Zur Theologie der Gemeinde* (Reihe 10; Graz: Styria, 1973).

Pesch, W. "Zur Formgeschichte und Exegese von Lk 12,32," *Bib* 41 (1960) 25-40.

Riesenfeld, H. "Vom Schätzesammeln und Sorgen—Ein Thema urchristlicher Paränese: Zu Mt VI 19-34," *Neotestamentica et patristica* (see p. xxxvi) 47-58.

83. TREASURE IN HEAVEN
(12:33-34)

12 [33] "Sell your belongings and give them away as alms. Provide yourselves with purses that will not wear out, a treasure in heaven that will not fail, where no thief gets near to it, no moth destroys it. [34] For where your treasure is, there your heart will also be."

COMMENT

The exhortation addressed to the disciples continues with a radical counsel about disposing of earthly possessions in favor of a treasure in heaven (12:33-34).

The first piece of advice in v. 33a undoubtedly stems from Luke's pen (it echoes 11:41; cf. S. Schulz, *Q: Die Spruchquelle,* 142). The rest of this verse and v. 34 are derived from "Q." The Matthean parallel is found in 6:19-21, in a different part of the sermon on the mount (or possibly in 6:20-21 [so G. Schneider, *Evangelium nach Lukas,* 286]). Once again, we are confronted with a generic similarity of the sayings in the two Gospels, but also with enough specific diversity to create problems in deciding whether another source ("M" or "L") was used in conjunction with "Q." T. W. Manson *(Sayings,* 114), following W. Bussmann, thinks that Luke is following "Q," whereas Matthew has made use of "M" instead. W. Grundmann *(Evangelium nach Lukas,* 262), however, considers the two verses to be the foil to the parable of the rich fool and believes that they originally followed on the heels of it in "L." It is impossible to be sure. If Luke had before him a form of the sayings, as they are preserved in Matthew, then they have been considerably abridged by him. Because v. 34 is almost identical in both Matthew and Luke, this abridgement seems to be the more likely. In v. 33b,c,d Luke has eliminated the picturesque but repetitious details about thieves burrowing through walls in order to steal, probably because he thinks of a different type of house known to his community. Moreover, J. Jeremias *(Die Sprache,* 218) attributes to Lucan redaction the vbs. "gets near" *(engizei)* and "destroys" *(diaphtheirei)*. In v. 34 Luke has made "your" pl. to conform with the second pl. in v. 33; Matt 6:21 has the sg., but it is otherwise identical.

Another form of the saying is found at the end of *Gos. of Thom.* § 76 (added to the parable of the hidden pearl): "You too must seek for the treasure which does not fail (but) which remains, there where no moth gets near to eat and no worm destroys." That is scarcely more original than the canonical forms.

These sayings are again hortatory logia *(HST* 77); v. 34 is, moreover, a maxim which could be at home in secular literature (ibid. 82, 84). It is devoid of an eschatological connotation, such as is present in v. 33b,c,d.

In these verses the Lucan Jesus speaks radically about material possessions, presenting the proper stance that disciples are to adopt vis-à-vis such matters. They are to "sell them" and give the proceeds away "as alms." In this way they will fashion for themselves "purses" which will not wear out and store up rather in heaven an impregnable treasure. Jesus will return to this theme again in 16:13, putting it even more starkly there. In Acts Luke depicts the early Christian community, living out such counsel in idyllic fashion (2:42-47; 4:32-35), until it is disturbed by the deception of Ananias and Sapphira (5:1-10).

In a way v. 34 sums it all up. The heart as the seat of human yearning must have its proper attraction: a heavenly treasure. The maxim does not tell the reader what that treasure is or even why it lasts; it suggests rather why the seeking for the kingdom can find an obstacle in the seeking for food, drink, and clothing—attractions that seduce. Even though the maxim in itself is devoid of an eschatological dimension, yet in the context it assumes one; however, that background is not the eschatological crisis, but the fate of the individual after death (so W. Pesch, "Zur Exegese," 374). In such a context one must guard that the heart is not seduced by earthly possessions.

With these two verses Jesus' counsels about greed come to an end. The next sayings will move to a new topic.

NOTES

12   33. *Sell your belongings.* See also Luke 18:22; cf. Matt 19:21. The motivation for this has been expressed in 12:21, in order to become "rich with God." See pp. 249-250 and NOTE on 8:3.

give them away as alms. Cf. Luke 11:41. Recall the less radical advice of Tobit to his son, 4:7-11. Cf. Sir 35:2.

Provide yourselves with purses . . . Lit. "make yourselves purses that do not grow old," and do not allow the money to be lost. This instruction has no counterpart in Matt 6:19.

a treasure in heaven that will not fail. Cf. 16:9c; 18:22e. Luke has added the descriptive adj. to the treasure of "Q"; it is to be understood as a treasure not to be lost through death. Cp. 12:16-21. Cf. Sir 29:11-12; Col 3:2.

where no thief gets near to it. I.e. to steal it.

no moth destroys. I.e. as in a clothes closet, where expensive garments (a form of ancient wealth) would be stored.

34. *where your treasure is, there your heart will also be.* The maxim has parallels in secular Greek literature, but none of them is so succinctly put as here. See Sextus Empiricus, *Hypotyp.* 1.136; Epictetus, *Diatr.* 2.22,19. The sense: If you put your treasure in heaven, then your heart will be set on heavenly things.

BIBLIOGRAPHY (12:33-34)

Degenhardt, H.-J. *Lukas Evangelist der Armen,* 85-93.

Mees, M. "Das Sprichwort Mt. 6,21/Lk. 12,34 und seine ausserkanonischen Parallelen," *Augustinianum* 14 (1974) 67-89.

Pesch, W. "Zur Exegese von Mt 6,19-21 und Lk 12,33-34," *Bib* 41 (1960) 356-378.

84. SAYINGS ABOUT VIGILANCE AND FAITHFULNESS
(12:35-46)

12 ³⁵ "Keep your aprons on and your lamps burning! ³⁶ Be like those who await their master at whatever hour he returns from the wedding party, prepared to open for him as soon as he arrives and knocks. ³⁷ Blessed are those servants whom the master finds on the alert when he arrives! Believe me, he will put on an apron, make them recline at table, and will come and serve them. ³⁸ Should he come about midnight or shortly before dawn and so find them, blessed are those people!

³⁹ But consider this too: If the master of the house were to know at what time the burglar was coming, he would not let his house be broken into. ⁴⁰ So you too must be ready, because the Son of Man arrives at a time when you least expect him."

⁴¹ Then Peter said to him, "Lord, do you tell this parable for us or for all the people?" ⁴² The Lord answered, "Well, who is the faithful and prudent manager whom the master puts over his staff to distribute to them a food allowance at the proper time? ⁴³ Blessed is that servant whom the master finds at his job when he arrives! ⁴⁴ I can tell you

truly, he will put that person in charge of all he possesses. [45] But suppose that servant says to himself, 'My master is taking his time in arriving,' and begins to mistreat servants and maids, to eat and drink and get drunk; [46] then that servant's master will arrive at a time when he does not expect him, at an hour he does not suspect. He will dismember him and assign him a fate fit for the faithless."

COMMENT

At this point in the travel account the Lucan Jesus changes his topic. From concern about earthly possessions he moves on to advice about watchfulness and fidelity (12:35-46). He continues to address the disciples (cf. v. 54), and in this change of topic, which is unique to Luke (since the sayings are found in another context in Matthew), Jesus implies a relationship between the topics. Watchfulness and faithfulness are not unrelated to the treasure in heaven and the meaning of life itself. Freedom from care, like that of the ravens and the lilies, receives another dimension or perspective, when it is related to vigilance and fidelity in human life. Though the Lucan joining is prima facie literary, it is not without some rooting in human life itself, for detachment from material things of earthly existence (the treasures that are attacked by thieves and moths) is related to the expectation of human life (a treasure not yet within reach, a blessedness to be pronounced by the master of life).

The sayings recorded here do not represent a unified group; they are only loosely joined. Verses 35-38 are undoubtedly derived from "L," being unique to the Lucan Gospel (so W. Grundmann, *Evangelium nach Lukas,* 264; cf. D. Lührmann, *Redaktion,* 69; C. H. Dodd, *Parables,* 127-132). R. Bultmann *(HST* 118) toyed with the idea that these verses were originally part of "Q" and that Matthew, instead of using them, substituted the parable of the ten virgins (from "M"); he has been followed by many others (J. M. Creed, *The Gospel,* 176; T. W. Manson, *Sayings,* 115; I. H. Marshall, *Luke,* 533; G. Schneider, *Evangelium nach Lukas,* 288). Apart from the common theme of watchfulness, however, the question of detail shifts the emphasis. Hence it is better to regard vv. 35-38 as derived from "L," since vv. 35-38 are not common to Matthew and Luke. However, vv. 39-40 do have a parallel in Matt 24:43-44 and have been derived from "Q" (see p. 78); Luke has probably abbreviated the wording, although G. Schneider (ibid. 289) ascribes the modification to Matthew. Another (independent?) form of this saying is recorded in Mark 13:35-36, at the end of the Marcan eschatological discourse. Having made use of the "Q" form of the saying here, Luke does not pick up a doublet from "Mk" in chap. 21 (see p. 82). The form in "Mk" is probably the reason

why Matthew has introduced the corresponding "Q" material into his eschatological discourse.

Luke has freely composed the transitional vv. 41-42a (so rightly *HST* 335);
it is highly doubtful that they were ever part of "Q," *pace* I. H. Marshall,
Luke, 533. Likewise derived from "Q," however, are vv. 42b-46, which have
their parallels in Matt 24:45-51, being again part of the eschatological discourse. The wording in vv. 42b-46 is especially close to that of Matthew (see
p. 76). The latter, however, has changed "faithless" of "Q" to "hypocrites"
and has added the "weeping and gnashing of teeth" in 24:51 (as also in 8:12;
13:42,50; 22:13; 25:30).

A form of v. 39 is also preserved in *Gos. of Thom.* § 21, as part of the
answer that Jesus gives to Mary (Magdalene) about the disciples: "So I say, If
the master of the house knows that the burglar is coming, he will be on guard
before he comes (and) will not let him break into the house of his domain to
carry off his vessels. But you must be on guard against the world. . . ." (See
also § 103.) This form is more influenced by Matthew than by Luke. See also
Mark 3:27. Cf. J.-E. Ménard, *L'Evangile selon Thomas,* 112; W. Schrage, *Das
Verhältnis,* 67-69. It may be a reason, however, to suspect that "Son of Man"
has been secondarily introduced into the original saying (see p. 210).

Form-critically considered, vv. 35-38 preserve a hortatory admonition to
watchfulness during the absence of the master. Bultmann *(HST* 118) regards
vv. 37-38 as an allegorical development of the comparison made in v. 36, but
he refuses to call it a parable. Others (e.g. G. Schneider, *Evangelium nach
Lukas,* 289) plainly refer to vv. 35-38 as the parable of the "waiting servants."
Part of the problem is that the transitional verse (41-42a) uses the word
"parable" of the preceding sayings—but in what sense? And are vv. 35-38
included? Verses 39-40 are at least the remnant of a parable, even though they
lack an introductory comparative phrase; the application is included in v. 40.
And "parable" in v. 41 must refer at least to it. In reply to Peter's question,
Jesus' words eventually take the form of another parable or similitude (vv.
42b-46), even though they lack an explicit comparison and application; they
begin with a question (see *HST* 171). In all, these verses present a series of
eschatological counsels. But to what term do they refer? Before we try to
answer that question, it is well to consider the content of the sayings themselves.

The sayings fall into three sections: the first deals with the watchful servants of an absent master; the second with a watchful master; and the third
with the manager of an absent master. As a group they present parable-like
sayings about servants and masters and the relation between them.

As they stand today in the Lucan Gospel, the first set of sayings (vv. 35-38)
urges disciples to eschatological vigilance and readiness, for in their present
condition they are like servants who are expected to carry out their duties in
the absence of their master, whose return can occur at any time. If he on his

return finds them on the alert, he will reward them. He will even go to the extent of serving them himself in a reversal of roles. This means giving them a share in his banquet (implied: the eschatological banquet [see NOTE on 13:29]). The theme of reward is secondary (even when the beatitude is reiterated in v. 38), whereas that of readiness and watchfulness predominates.

The remnant of the parable in vv. 39-40 stresses the theme of watchfulness, depicting a householder on guard over his house to prevent it from being burglarized; the time element is crucial, but it has nothing to do with a delay *(pace* H. Conzelmann, *Theology,* 108; that first appears in v. 45). It is simply that the time of the burglary is not known; it is impossible to make provision against it (E. Linnemann, *Jesus of the Parables,* 135). *Pace* G. Schneider *(Evangelium nach Lukas,* 289), it is wrong to call this "the parable of the burglar." It is rather the parable of the householder faced with word of a prowling burglar. In the application, the attention of the disciples is drawn to the coming of the Son of Man. Here again the title is being used to depict him in his role as judge of human life (see 9:26; 17:22,24,26,30; 18:8; 21:27,36), before whose scrutiny the disciples will have to stand. In the Lucan Gospel Jesus is clearly this Son of Man, but again in what sense?

Peter's question sharpens the application: Do you mean us (the disciples) or all the people? Jesus' answer is not perfectly formulated. It begins with a rhetorical counter-question, which quickly takes on parable-like properties. The first part of the details says the same thing as the comparison in vv. 36-38, even though the subject of the comment is now a "faithful and prudent manager," not just a group of ordinary servants. He is expected to be ready and watchful, administering faithfully. Not only are readiness and watchfulness expected, but fidelity and prudent conduct. This becomes more apparent when the second part is added about the manager. He may have normally been faithful and prudent, but reveals another side of himself in arrogance and abuse of power, as he realizes that his absent master is tarrying. Again, the theme of reward which reappears is secondary. The primary emphasis is on whether the manager will be found *faithful* and *prudent when* his absent master arrives to scrutinize how well he has carried out his task, how well he has cared for his master's servants. The timing and the fidelity are crucial. One should not fail to notice, however, how the punishment of the manager, if he abuses his authority, corresponds to the double life that he would be leading: He will be dismembered, or "cut in two." We may be dealing with a parable-like saying that has more than one point to make; it is difficult to say how much allegory is involved in this saying.

The big problem in these sayings (or parables) is the term to which the watchfulness refers. Most modern commentators recognize that we are dealing with the Lucan formulation of a tradition about Jesus' sayings on watchfulness and fidelity, and their place in Christian conduct. In Stage III of the gospel tradition it is clear that Jesus is the Son of Man and that his parousia or second coming is meant; this is clear in the Lucan story, especially in view of Acts 1:11c; 7:56; 17:30-31. (See further pp. 232-233.)

One may further ask whether, in view of 12:20 and its reference to death, the term might not be considered here to be also the death of the individual. Though this question cannot be wholly excluded, the main emphasis seems to be on the parousia, in light of the reference to the coming Son of Man in v. 40.

Problematic is whether such sayings about readiness and watchfulness are traceable to Jesus himself, or whether they reflect community exhortations born of their expectation of his parousia. To my way of thinking, it is an oversimplification of the NT data to ascribe the sayings about watchfulness in vv. 39-40, 42b-46 solely to early church creation "like all other parousia parables and traditions in Q" (S. Schulz, *Q: Die Spruchquelle,* 269; cf. D. Lührmann, *Redaktion,* 70). Although the thief metaphor is rare in pre-Christian Jewish literature, watchfulness connected with the eschatological day of Yahweh is abundant in OT prophets (Isa 13:6; Ezek 30:3; Joel 1:15; 2:1; Amos 5:18; Obad 15; Zeph 1:14-18). Even though that has to be understood at times in terms of specific events in the history of Israel, it became a theme which transcended them, calling for watchfulness in conduct (see Mal 3:23-24 [4:5-6E]); cf. E. Lövestam, *Spiritual Wakefulness,* 8-20. Recall the vigil kept by the Essenes of Qumran: "Let the Many watch *(yšqwdw)* in common for a third of all the nights of the year, to read the Book and study the Law" (1QS 6:7). Jesus' words about vigilance could well have been uttered in such a context; they could have fitted into his preaching about the "coming" of the kingdom and the implication of judgment associated with it (see 9:26 [cf. pp. 155-156]). That they were secondarily associated with Son of Man sayings, however, is not impossible; just as they may have been secondarily allegorized. Matthew has related such sayings to his eschatological discourse; that relationship may well be as secondary as the Lucan relation of them to the travel account. But it is impossible to eliminate all futurist eschatological nuances from all his sayings about watchfulness (see further W. G. Kümmel, *Promise and Fulfilment,* 55; W. Foerster, *Herr ist Jesus,* 231-232; 268-270).

NOTES

12 35. *Keep your aprons on.* Lit. "let your loins be girded" (pf. ptc., expressing condition), i.e. let the long, ankle-length robe be adjusted by a waist-belt to ensure readiness for action or departure. This instruction may be an allusion to that given to the Israelites at the first celebration of Passover: to be in readiness for a hasty exodus from Egypt and the arrival of the destroying angel (Exod 12:11,22-23). But the expression became in the OT a common instruction for readiness or service. See 1 Kgs 18:46; 2 Kgs 4:29; 9:1; Job 38:3; 40:7; cf. 11QtgJob 30:1; 34:2-3 *(MPAT* 36, 42); 1QM 15:14;

16:11; Eph 6:14; 1 Pet 1:13. Philo *(Sacr. Abel.* 63) explains it as "ready for service." Cf. Luke 17:8.

your lamps burning! Cf. Luke 8:16; 11:33. The lighted lamps connote watchfulness. Cf. Exod 27:20; Lev 24:2. A. Plummer *(The Gospel,* 330) goes so far as to see in this detail "the parable of the Ten Virgins condensed (Mt. xxv. 1)." But this is farfetched, since Luke speaks of *lychnoi,* whereas that parable uses *lampades;* here the servants with the lamps are within, there the virgins are without, and the foolish among them knock (not the master). It is one thing to say that Matthew substituted the parable for this passage (allegedly from "Q"), and another to say that this is a condensed form of that parable. See further I. H. Marshall, *Luke,* 535.

36. *who await their master.* The disciples are compared to "servants" *(douloi)* of the "master" *(kyrios).* This verse thus adds a warning to the counsel of v. 35, in the form of a comparison; they must be ready to serve, not just to open the door. The use of *kyrios* may connote the parousiac arrival of the Lord, the Son of Man (v. 40), at least in this stage of the gospel tradition (III).

at whatever hour he returns from the wedding party. Lit. "whenever he breaks loose from the wedding celebrations." The vb. *analyein* can also mean simply "return," as in Wis 2:1; Tob 2:9 [mss. B, A]; 2 Macc 8:25; Josephus, *Ant.* 11.3,2 § 34 (from a feast); MM 36. No stress should be put on "wedding celebrations," since *gamoi* (pl.) often means no more than "celebration" (in general). See Luke 14:8; Esth 2:18; 9:22.

knocks. At Stage III this detail takes on the connotation of Christ knocking at the door. See Rev 3:20. It is part of the way that Jesus' words have been divested of their parabolic setting in later parts of the NT (R. Bauckham). Cf. *Did.* 16.1.

37. *Blessed.* See NOTE on 6:20. The beatitude is uttered over those just compared to faithful, alert servants. See the Pauline way of putting it in 1 Cor 16:13: "Be watchful, stand firm in your faith, be courageous . . ." Cf. Rev 16:15.

finds on the alert. Lit. "watching." Cf. J. M. Nützel, *EWNT* 1. 638-639.

when he arrives! In Stage III of the tradition, this would refer to the parousia, or possibly to the moment of death (in this Lucan context; see 12:20).

Believe me. Lit. "Amen, I tell you." See NOTE on 4:24.

he will put on an apron. Lit. "will gird himself," in order to serve. Since servants were not usually so treated (see Luke 17:7), the reversal of roles is significant. He will give them a share in his banquet (as at the parousia). See Luke 13:29; 22:27-30; cf. Rev 19:9. Cf. Horace, *Serm.* 2.6,107-109.

38. *about midnight or shortly before dawn.* Lit. "in the second or third watch" (of the night). Cf. 2:8. Reference may be made to the Roman custom of dividing the night (from 6 P.M. to 6 A.M.) into four equal periods (6-9, 9-12, 12-3, 3-6) or "watches" *(phylakai),* when sentinels were posted (see Vegetius, *De re mil.* 3.8); or possibly to the Hellenistic and Jewish custom of three watches (6-10, 10-2, 2-6). See Judg 7:19. Josephus *(Ant.* 18.9,6 § 356) speaks of the "fourth watch," but alludes to a three-watch night in *J. W.* 5.12,2 § 510. Cf. Mark 13:35-36. Luke seems to reckon elsewhere with four watches. See Acts 12:4. Cf. E. Haenchen, *Acts,* 382.

Ms. D and some ancient versions read: "Should he come during the evening watch and find them, he will do so, and even if it is in the second or third watch." Still other mss. have combinations of these texts. See the *app. crit.* In any case, the sense of the expression is: No matter when the master arrives, be ready.

blessed are those people! The mss. P⁷⁵, א¹, B, D, L, etc., read simply the dem. pron. *ekeinoi,* "those (people)," but many others (e.g. A, Q, W, Θ, Ψ, 070) add *douloi,* "servants," probably under the influence of v. 37.

39. *at what time.* Lit. "at what hour"; Matt 24:43-44 reads "at what watch" (of the night). Luke is the one who has changed "watch" to "hour" because of *phylakē* (v. 38) and to agree with "hour" of v. 46 below. It is also a more traditional Christian term. Cf. 1 John 2:18. It does not limit the thievery to the night. For the motif of the unexpected burglar, see 1 Thess 5:2-4; 2 Pet 3:10; Rev 3:3; 16:15.

he would not let . . . This is the reading in mss. P⁷⁵, א*, D, and in some ancient versions (OL and OS); but many mss. (A, B, L, Q, W, Θ, Ψ, 070) read "he would stay awake and not let . . ." But this is suspect, because it looks like a copyist's harmonization with Matt 24:43.

be broken into. Lit. "be dug through," i.e. probably a reference to the mud-brick walls of houses in Palestine.

40. *the Son of Man.* See NOTE on 5:24; pp. 208-211.

Some mss. (part of the Freer family of minuscules) omit this entire verse.

41. *Peter.* See NOTES on 4:38; 8:45. The question stems not from "Peter's impulsiveness," *pace* A. Plummer, *The Gospel,* 331; nor does Peter speak up as a "representative disciple" (E. E. Ellis, *Gospel of Luke,* 181). Peter's appearance here is one of the ways in which Luke highlights the role of Peter as spokesman, a role already found in "Mk." See R. E. Brown et al., eds., *Peter,* 113-114; cf. W. Dietrich, *Das Petrusbild der lukanischen Schriften* (BWANT 94; Stuttgart: Kohlhammer, 1972) 48-49 n. 74. Peter's question stands in contrast to the last interlocutor in the Lucan story who interrupted Jesus, the lawyer of 11:45. See further COMMENT on 5:1-11.

Lord. Or possibly "Sir." See NOTES on 5:8,12.

this parable. See NOTE on 5:36. On *legein* with *pros* + acc., see p. 116.

for us or for all the people? Who are meant by the contrast? Since the last time that we read of "the apostles" was in 9:10, it is scarcely likely that Peter's words refer to them as "us." In the immediate Lucan context a distinction has been made between "the crowd(s)" (12:1,13,54) and the "disciples" (12:1,22). Hence, Peter's "us" must refer to the disciples, and *pantas,* "all," to the crowd(s). So Peter's question would have to be understood on the level of Stage I; but it must be remembered that this question is a Lucan creation, stemming from Stage III. This may reflect the thinking of community officials of Luke's time. It has nothing to do with "the Twelve," who are not mentioned, and who by Luke's time are no more than a distant memory.

42. *The Lord.* See NOTE on 7:13.

the faithful and prudent manager. Such an authority figure will appear again in 16:1,8,10-12. Some ancient versions (OL, OS) and ms. D add: "and good." Luke has substituted "manager" *(oikonomos)* for the "servant" *(doulos)* of "Q," retained by Matt 24:45. Cf. 1 Cor 4:1-5. See J. Jeremias, *Parables,* 56 n. 25.

puts over his staff. The implication is that the "manager" represents someone placed in authority over others, not just over material possessions, but over those who are under the *kyrios.* The evangelist could be referring to community officials.

to distribute to them a food allowance. An infin. of purpose is introduced by a gen. of the def. art. *(tou).* See BDF § 390.4; 400.5.

Luke has substituted for *trophē,* "food," of "Q" (see Matt 24:45) the rare word *sitometrion,* "measure of grain," which is known in no Greek literary texts, but is found in some of the Greek papyri from Egypt. See MM 576.

at the proper time? The phrase *en kairō* (even without the def. art.) is used in a generic sense. See NOTE on 4:13. Cf. 20:10 (without the prep. *en).*

43. *Blessed.* See NOTE on 6:20 and on v. 37.

that servant. Here *doulos* is used, as in Matt 24:46, retained from "Q."

44. *I can tell you truly.* See NOTE on 9:27. Luke has eliminated the *amēn* of "Q" (see Matt 24:47), substituting for it *alēthōs.* Contrast v. 37b.

in charge of all he possesses. I.e. he will give him a share in all of his own power and wealth. On *tois hyparchousin,* see NOTE on 8:3.

45. *that servant.* Luke has retained the designation of "Q," whereas Matt 24:48 immediately characterizes him as "that evil servant," which is a bit strange, since it is not yet clear why he is "evil."

says to himself. See NOTE on 12:17.

taking his time in arriving. Delay in arrival is now introduced in the parable. A Greek expression is used, which is derived from the LXX *(chronizein* + an infin.; see Deut 23:22). Implied is the servant's realization of an opportunity to exploit his power and authority.

to eat and drink and get drunk. Matt 24:49 reads, "eats and drinks with drunken revelers." The combination of the three vbs. is found in the LXX of Cant 5:1; it echoes a stereotyped mode of conduct.

46. *at a time.* Lit. "on a day," a phrase reminiscent of the OT "day of Yahweh" motif. E.g. Joel 2:31.

He will dismember him. Lit. "he will cut him in two," which some commentators say must be understood literally. E.g. J. M. Creed, *The Gospel,* 177; A. Plummer, *The Gospel,* 332. It is rather to be understood figuratively of severe punishment. Possibly the punishment is meant as characteristic of the double standards of that allegedly "faithful and prudent manager." See further O. Betz, "Dichotomized Servant," 44-47; J. Jeremias, *Parables,* 57 nn. 30-31; P. Ellingworth, "Luke 12.46—Is There an Anticlimax here?" *BT* 31 (1980) 242-243.

a fate fit for the faithless. Lit. "and his portion will be with the unbelievers," or (better) with those who lack fidelity. The negative adj. *apistōn* plays upon *pistos,* "faithful," of v. 42. Matthew has changed it to "hypocrites" (24:51), *pace* O. Betz *(RevQ* 5 [1964-1966] 45). Recall the frequency of "hypocrites" in the Matthean Gospel (6:2,5,16; 7:5; 15:7; 22:18; 23:13,14,15; 24:51). Cf. NOTE on 12:1.

BIBLIOGRAPHY (12:35-46)

Bauckham, R. "Synoptic Parousia Parables and the Apocalypse," *NTS* 23 (1976-1977) 162-176.

Betz, O. "The Dichotomized Servant and the End of Judas Iscariot (Light on the Dark Passages: Matthew 24,51 and parallel; Acts 1,18)," *RevQ* 5 (1964-1966) 43-58.

Clarke, A. K., and N. E. W. Collie. "A Comment on Luke xii 41-58," *JTS* 17 (1915-1916) 299-301.

Deterding, P. E. "Eschatological and Eucharistic Motifs in Luke 12:35-40," *Concordia Journal* 5 (1979) 85-94.

George, A. "L'Attente du maître qui vient: Lc 12,32-48," *AsSeign* 50 (1974) 66-76.

Gollinger, H. " 'Ihr wisst nicht, an welchem Tag euer Herr kommt': Auslegung vom Mt 24,37-51," *BibLeb* 11 (1970) 238-247.

Jeremias, J. *Parables,* 48-66, 90-96, 101-102.

Joüon, P. "La parabole du portier qui doit veiller (Mc 13, 33-37) et la parabole des serviteurs qui doivent veiller (Lc 12, 35-40)," *RSR* 30 (1940) 365-368.

Lövestam, E. *Spiritual Wakefulness,* 92-107.

Schneider, G. *Parusiegleichnisse im Lukas-Evangelium* (SBS 74; Stuttgart: Katholisches Bibelwerk, 1975) 20-37.

Smitmans, A. "Das Gleichnis vom Dieb," *Wort Gottes in der Zeit,* 43-68.

Tödt, H. E. *The Son of Man,* 88-94.

Weiser, A. *Die Knechtsgleichnisse,* 161-225.

85. THE SERVANT'S REWARD
(12:47-48)

12 ⁴⁷ "Now that servant who knows the master's wishes and does not anticipate them or acts against them will have to stand many blows. ⁴⁸ But the one who does not know them yet does what deserves punishment will stand but few blows. Much will be required of everyone to whom much has been given! And even more will be demanded of the one to whom more has been entrusted!"

COMMENT

Jesus' sayings about the obligation of service continue with comments on diverse punishment to be meted out to incompetent servants. They stress the responsibility of the servant for his/her failure to carry what is expected. The preceding parable centered on trust and fidelity; now Jesus' words turn to the just deserts of incompetence.

Verses 47-48 have been derived by Luke from "L," being unique to his Gospel (see p. 84). They are added by catchword bonding (see "that servant" in vv. 45,47 [although the Greek word order is changed]). Moreover, the dem. adj. "that" is explained by what follows. (Cf. J. Jeremias, *Die Sprache,* 222.)

Form-critically considered, the sayings are admonitions (*HST* 117, 168). The words in v. 48b,c are really an added proverb, once independent and not really organically connected with the preceding. Together with it, they produce a parable-like saying. A synonymous parallelism marks the group of the last two sayings. Verse 48a should probably be regarded as a parenthesis; it formulates antithetically a parallelism with v. 47. Verse 48b states the principle that underlies the warning expressed in v. 47. Verse 48c drives home the message of the principle.

In these sayings Jesus turns his attention to the servant who does not carry out what he/she is supposed to; hence he/she is responsible for the reward (punishment) received. The punishment is meted out according to the knowledge and culpability involved. A more severe beating is given to the willful disobedience of the lazy loafer who knows what is expected than to the dimwit who does not. The proverb explains why: Much will be required (by God) of the gifted servant, and even more of the really talented one. The words could have been directed by Jesus in Stage I of the tradition against leaders of the Palestinian community (see J. Schmid, *Evangelium nach Lukas,* 224); but as they now stand in the Lucan context they envisage those entrusted with service to the Christian community.

As a group these sayings provide a further commentary on the answer Jesus gave to Peter's question in vv. 42-46. That answer spoke first of the faithful and prudent manager, but turned to the shyster who would exploit his/her position. The latter provides a transition to this stern comment on the incompetent disciple who would flout his/her master's wishes, and even on the one who would try to carry them out without discernment or understanding. The presupposition in the sayings is that servants entrusted with tasks have also been given the wherewithal to carry them out.

NOTES

12   47. *who knows the master's wishes.* Lit. "knowing the will of his master." Cf. Acts 22:14; Rom 2:18. The contrast here and in the first part of v. 48 is between the disobedient servant who knows and the one who is unwitting. Behind this contrast lies the OT teaching on deliberate sins (committed with a high hand) and those done in ignorance. See Num 15:27-30; 1QS 5:12; 4QpPs^a 3-10 iv 15; CD 8:8; 10:3. Cf. *m. Šabb.* 7:1.

   and does not anticipate them or acts against them. Lit. "and not preparing (for it) or doing (something) against his will." The ms. P^{45} omits the negative *(mē)* before the first ptc., which would imply conspiracy even against the master's will. Cf. Jas 4:17.

   will have to stand many blows. In classical Greek the vb. *derein* meant "to flay," but in the NT it always has the meaning "to beat, whip," as it also has in Aristophanes, *Frogs* 618; Epictetus, *Diatr.* 3.19,5. Cf. Luke 20:10-11; 22:63; Acts 5:40; 16:37; 22:19. With the fem. acc. pl. adjs. *pollas* ("many"), *oligas* ("few"), one has to understand the n. *plēgas,* "blows." See BDF § 154, 241.6.

   48. *Much will be required . . . given!* Lit. "as for everyone to whom much has been

given, much will be required of him." For the *casus pendens,* here a dat., see pp. 124-125. On the relative *pas hos,* see NOTE on 12:10. It may be an anacoluthon, but it is not particularly Semitic, *pace* J. Jeremias *(Die Sprache,* 222). Cf. BDF § 295, 466.3. This part of the verse enunciates the principle that underlies Jesus' comment in v. 47.

The pass. is again theological, i.e. required, given by God. See NOTE on 5:20. For the OT notions reflected here, see Amos 3:2; Wis 6:6.

will be demanded . . . entrusted! Lit. "(from the one) to whom they entrust much, they will demand more of him." Luke again uses the third pl. indefinitely (impersonally) as a substitute for the pass. See NOTE on 12:20.

BIBLIOGRAPHY (12:47-48)

Iwand, H. J. *Die Gegenwart des Kommenden: Eine Auslegung von Lk 12* (BibS[N] 50; Neukirchen-Vluyn: Neukirchener-V., 1966) 42-44.
Weiser, A. *Die Knechtsgleichnisse,* 178-225.

86. THE ENIGMA OF JESUS' MISSION
(12:49-53)

12 ⁴⁹ "I have come to cast fire upon the earth, and how I wish it were already ablaze! ⁵⁰ I have a baptism in which to be baptized, and how hard pressed I am until it is accomplished! ⁵¹ Do you think that I have come to put peace on earth? No, I tell you, rather discord! ⁵² For from now on five members of one family will be divided, three against two and two against three; ⁵³ father will be divided against son and *son against father,* mother against daughter and *daughter against mother,* mother-in-law against bride and *bride against mother-in-law."* [a]

[a] Mic 7:6

COMMENT

The sayings about servants and masters have come to an end at this point in the travel account, and Jesus moves on to other topics. The first of these is a series of comments on his own ministry (12:49-53). In the foregoing vv. 36-40,43,45-46 reference has been made to the "coming" of a master *(kyrios),* a burglar, and the Son of Man. This has probably suggested the addition of these comments about Jesus' own coming (vv. 49,51).

The first comment (v. 49) is derived from "L," being unique to this Gospel (see p. 84). The second comment (v. 50) is parallel to this, *pace* H. Conzelmann *(Theology,* 109), not in contrast to the first. The second one has a relation to Mark 10:38 (in an episode about the sons of Zebedee, which Luke will omit in chap. 18): "Can you drink the cup that I am to drink or be baptized with the baptism that I shall undergo?" Since the comment is clearly pre-Lucan, v. 50 could be considered as derived from "L," but it has been so heavily modified by Luke that it borders on Lucan composition. Verses 51 and 53, however, the third comment, come from "Q," having a parallel in Matt 10:34-36, where it forms part of the mission-charge to the "twelve disciples" (see p. 78). Luke has redactionally added v. 52 and modified the beginning of v. 53. Its Matthean counterpart preserves the "Q" form better, even though neither Matthew nor Luke quotes Mic 7:6 exactly. In both it is no more than an allusion.

Forms of some of these sayings of Jesus are preserved in the Coptic *Gospel of Thomas.* In § 10 we have a saying corresponding to v. 49: "Jesus said, 'I have cast fire upon the world, and look, I am guarding it until it blazes.' " In § 16 there is a saying corresponding to vv. 51-53: "Jesus said, 'Perhaps people think that I have come to cast peace upon the world; they do not realize that it is divisions that I have come to cast upon the earth, fire, sword, and war. For five will be in a house: three will be against two, and two against three; the father against the son, and the son against the father; and they will stand as solitaries *(or* monks?)." Logion 10 is almost certainly a derivative of the Lucan v. 49, whereas logion 16 is a hybrid of the Lucan and Matthean forms of the sayings; moreover, the last reference to *'mmonachos,* "solitaries," clearly betrays its later formulation. (See further J.-E. Ménard, *L'Evangile selon Thomas,* 94-95, 103-105; W. Schrage, *Das Verhältnis,* 49-51, 57-61.)

From the form-critical perspective, vv. 49-51 enshrine "I-sayings" of Jesus, reminiscent of the Johannine tradition. R. Bultmann *(HST* 153-154) considers vv. 49-50 to be *vaticinia ex eventu* and v. 50 as a secondary parallel to v. 49, even though they do not match perfectly. But as W. G. Kümmel *(Promise and Fulfilment,* 69-70) and others have pointed out, it is difficult to deny that this is a real prediction by Jesus. Part of the difficulty is how specifically one wants to understand the figurative reference to baptism in Stage I of the gospel tradition. To my way of thinking, it is quite possible that Jesus realized during the course of his ministry that his continued preaching of the kingdom and of God's word was meeting with staunch and growing opposition from opponents who might one day adopt extreme measures against him. There is no need to load that realization with all the specifics of the trial and crucifixion as we know them from Stage III of that tradition.

Jesus is depicted commenting on parallel aspects of his earthly ministry. First, he longs to see the earth ablaze and consumed by the fire which his coming was meant to enkindle. He states clearly the aims of his ministry under the figure of a discriminating fire, the fire of *krisis*. Second, he views his ministry as a "baptism," not only of water, but again of "fire" (recall 3:16). But it is not one that he merely administers to others, but that he must undergo; he who baptizes with fire must himself face the testing and *krisis* that that figure connotes. He longs that this be accomplished, because it is related to the aim of the ministry set forth in v. 49. At this point we are not told what that figurative baptism is; in time the reader of the Lucan Gospel will learn what is meant. Bultmann *(HST* 153) speaks of it as Jesus' "martyr-dom"; others (e.g. O. Cullmann, *Christology,* 67; H. Koester, *TDNT* 7. 884-885) speak even more bluntly of his death. That is to read by hindsight into the statement of even the Lucan Jesus more than may be really meant. See p. 778. Third, he defines the effect of his ministry as discord. The consequences of the fire and the baptism, therefore, may seem to contradict an important way in which Luke depicts Jesus, as bringing "peace on earth" (see 2:14; 19:38; cf. p. 225). Though peace is an important effect of the Christ-event in the Lucan view, the evangelist has here retained from "Q" an interpretation of Jesus' ministry in terms of its opposite. Yet even that effect of his ministry has been foreshadowed in the infancy narrative: Jesus was a child set "for the fall and rise of many in Israel" (2:34). He now spells out a mode which that discord may take: division within families, even alluding to the lament of the prophet Micah (7:1-7) about the disappearance of the godly from the earth and the consequent state of human society in which not only neighbors, but even members of families suffer. The Lucan Jesus has come during the era of Augustan peace, as a sign of peace among human beings; he has not come as the fiery reformer that John once expected (see pp. 663-665). Yet his ministry is now described by him as a source of discord among the very people he came to serve and save. Even in his own family the Lucan Jesus' career brought a "sword" to pierce his mother's "own soul" (2:35 [see NOTE there]) —and this despite the Lucan esteem for Mary as the first believer (see p. 430).

It is not easy to relate the Lucan form of these sayings to that in Mark 10:38 or to say to what extent they can be used to gauge the consciousness of the historical Jesus. Like those in 10:21-24, we are dealing with sayings having the formulation of Stage III of the gospel tradition. That that formulation has been colored by the events of the trial, passion, and crucifixion is quite likely. But the ascription of *all* such testimony in the tradition to community formulation is unwarranted. W. Grundmann *(Evangelium nach Lukas,* 269), followed by I. H. Marshall *(Luke,* 546), appeals to the self-testimony of the Qumran Teacher of Righteousness in the *Hôdāyôt* or *Thanksgiving Psalms* for parallels; but neither of them documents this testimony specifically. In this connection, it might be profitable to consider the following lines: "And I became a mocking-song for the ungodly, and against me streamed the assem-bly of the wicked" (1QH 2:11-12); ". . . I became a man of dispute for those who mouth error, and [a man of pe]ace for all who look upon what is right"

(1QH 2:14-15); "You (O Lord) have redeemed the life of the poor one whom they have plotted to destroy by shedding his blood because of service rendered to you, but they knew nothing about my steps proceeding from you" (1QH 2:32-33). (See further G. Jeremias, *Der Lehrer der Gerechtigkeit* [SUNT 2; Göttingen: Vandenhoeck & Ruprecht, 1963]).

NOTES

12   49. *I have come.* Luke uses the aor. indic. *ēlthon,* not the pf., as in 5:32. Cf. the unclean spirit's cry in 4:34; also the Son-of-Man sayings in 7:34; 9:58. For the Johannine usage, see John 3:2; 5:43; 7:28; 12:27,47; 16:28; 18:37. For the expression of intention by the use of this vb. with a following infin., see J. Jeremias, *New Testament Theology,* 293 n. 6.

to cast fire upon the earth. H. Conzelmann *(Theology,* 109) interprets this immediately as "the eschatological conflagration." Granted that there is not an exact parallel between v. 49 (expressive of Jesus' goal) and v. 50 (an ominous reference to his end), the mention of fire is rather figurative. In the OT it is sometimes used as a means of purification (Lev 13:52; Num 31:23), of discernment or discrimination (Jer 23:29; Isa 33:14), and of judgment (Gen 19:24; Exod 9:24; Ps 66:12 [joined with water]; Isa 43:2). Cf. *1 Enoch* 91:9; 100:1-2,9; Luke 3:9; 9:54. Whichever of these nuances one prefers, the "fire" has also to be related to that of Luke 3:16, the effect of which is now seen to touch even "the earth."

how I wish it were already ablaze! Lit. "what do I wish if it were already ablaze." These words are not easy to interpret. For some commentators, Jesus utters a wish that is unfulfilled, with a contrary-to-fact protasis as the obj. of *thelō,* "I wish." See BDF § 299.4, 359-360. The whole is introduced by interrogative *tí,* which may echo a Hebrew/Aramaic *māh;* and the conj. *ei,* "if," may equal Hebrew *'im* or Aramaic *hēn.* See *AAGA*[3] 123. These would facilitate the translation in the lemma above. But it is complicated by the fact that *thelein* (or its synonym *boulesthai*) is found elsewhere in Greek followed by *ei.* See Herodotus, *Hist.* 6.52; 9.14; also in Sir 23:14, which may be a Semitism (the Hebrew text is missing). This may be an extension of the of *ei* to introduce the obj. cl. after vbs. of surprise, emotion, etc. See LSJ 481 (V). See further F. H. Seper, *"Kai tí thelō ei ēdē anēphthē* (Lc 12,49b)," *VD* 36, 147-153; A. Plummer, *The Gospel,* 334; C. F. D. Moule, *Idiom Book,* 137, 187. Cf. H. Braun, *Qumran,* 1. 89.

50. *I have a baptism in which to be baptized.* Lit. "I have to be baptized [in/with] a baptism." For the use of *echein,* "have," with an infin., see NOTE on 7:40. Cf. J. Jeremias, *Die Sprache,* 169. A cognate acc. is used with the pass. vb. The word "baptize/baptism" is often regarded as a Christian word, and for this reason many think that Jesus' formulation of the ordeal that faces him in terms of that is therefore derived from the Christian community. This, however, is far from certain. For Josephus knew of John and spoke of him as the *baptistēs;* he refers to his *baptismos* or *baptisis (Ant.* 18.5,2 § 116-117). These ns. are unknown in the LXX, but the cognate vbs. *baptein* and *baptizein* do occur, usually as the translation of Hebrew *ṭābal,* "dip." Though ritual washings are mentioned in Qumran literature, this Hebrew word is not used. The problem is to understand why Jesus would express an ordeal to be faced as a

"baptism." Having already been baptized in John's sense (3:21), he cannot refer merely to that. See p. 482. But, as mentioned above, because of the association of baptism with "fire" (3:16), with the connotations of the latter suggested in the preceding notes, it is possible that Jesus would have used such an expression. See further H. Schürmann, *Traditionsgeschichtliche Untersuchungen,* 53. J. A. T. Robinson *(Twelve . . . Studies,* 21) thinks that Jesus is hinting at "his redemptive suffering." Yet it is no more than a hint. See Mark 10:38-39.

how hard pressed I am. Or, less likely, "how great is my distress" (see BAGD 789); the latter is preferred by those who relate this expression to the Gethsemane scene. The vb. *synechein,* however, has many uses in the Lucan writings (4:38; 8:37,45; 19:43; 22:63; Acts 7:57; 18:5; 28:8—a Lucan favorite; see p. 111). Basically, it means "hold together, grip, press close," but the absolute use of it, as here, is found elsewhere only in 2 Esdr 16:10 (= Neh 6:10). H. Koester *(TDNT* 7. 884-885) is right in preferring not to interpret it as the fear of death; that would be too specific. He suggests, "How I am totally governed by this." See further p. 180.

until it is accomplished! Or "fulfilled," i.e. brought to fulfillment.

51. *to put peace on earth?* The best mss. read *dounai,* "give," but ms. D and some ancient versions have *poiēsai,* "make"; still others, *balein,* "cast" (1424, OL [b, l, g, r¹]). The latter is probably the result of a copyist's harmonization with v. 49 or with Matt 10:34. The vb. *dounai* may be used in the Semitic sense of "set, put." See Mic 3:5 LXX. Recall 2:14.

rather discord! Or "division," since the n. *diamerismos* is echoed in the following vbs. (vv. 52-53). Matt 10:34 makes use of the figurative "sword."

52. *from now on.* A sign of Lucan redaction. See NOTES on 1:48; 5:10. Conzelmann *(Theology,* 109) rightly understands this temporal designation, not of "the End," but of the epoch of conflict now beginning in the Lucan story.

will be divided. Luke again uses the future of the vb. "to be" + pf. ptc. *(diamemeris-menoi).* See pp. 122-123. This stands in contrast to the fut. pass. in v. 53. The periphrasis stems from Luke's pen.

53. *son against father.* This and the other expressions in the verse (italicized in the translation) may allude to Mic 7:6, which reads, "A son treats his father with contempt, a daughter rises up against her mother, a daughter-in-law against her mother-in-law; a man's enemies are those of his own household." Thus the Greek of Luke (as well as of Matthew) differs considerably from that of the LXX. Cf. Zech 13:3.

BIBLIOGRAPHY (12:49-53)

Black, M. "Uncomfortable Words: III. The Violent Word," *ExpTim* 81 (1969-1970) 115-118.

Braumann, G. "Leidenskelch und Todestaufe (Mc 10,38f.)," *ZNW* 56 (1965) 178-183.

Bruston, C. "Une parole de Jésus mal comprise," *RHPR* 5 (1925) 70-71.

Delling, G. *"Baptisma baptisthēnai,"* NovT 2 (1957-1958) 92-115; reprinted, *Studien zum Neuen Testament und zum hellenistischen Judentum: Gesammelte Aufsätze 1950-1968* (Göttingen: Vandenhoeck & Ruprecht, 1970) 236-256.

Feuillet, A. "La coupe et le baptême de la passion *(Mc,* X, 35-40; cf. *Mt,* XX, 20-23; *Lc,* XII, 50)," *RB* 74 (1967) 356-391.

George, A. "La venue de Jésus, cause de division entre les hommes Lc 12,49-53," *AsSeign* ns 51 (1972) 62-71.

Graystone, G. " 'I Have Come to Cast Fire on the Earth . . . ,' " *Scr* 4 (1949-1951) 135-141.

Kaestli, J.-D. "Luc 12:49-59: Diverses paroles eschatologiques," *L'Eschatologie,* 19-23.

Kuss, O. "Zur Frage einer vorpaulinischen Todestaufe," *MTZ* 4 (1953) 1-17; reprinted, *Auslegung und Verkündigung,* 1. 162-186.

Roberts, T. A. "Some Comments on Matthew x. 34-36 and Luke xii. 51-53," *ExpTim* 69 (1957-1958) 304-306.

Schürmann, H. "Wie hat Jesus seinen Tod bestanden und verstanden?" *Orientierung an Jesus* (eds. P. Hoffmann et al.) 325-363.

Seper, F. H. *"Kai tí thelō ei ēdē anēphthē* (Lc 12,49b)," *VD* 36 (1958) 147-153.

Vögtle, A. "Todesankündigungen und Todesverständnis Jesu," *Der Tod Jesu: Deutungen im Neuen Testament* (ed. K. Kertelge; Freiburg: Herder, 1976) 51-113, esp. 80-88.

Ward, R. A. "St Luke xii. 49: *kai tí thelō ei ēdē anēphthē,"* *ExpTim* 63 (1951-1952) 92-93.

87. THE SIGNS OF THE TIMES
(12:54-56)

12 ⁵⁴ Then Jesus said to the crowds, "When you see a cloud forming in the west, you immediately say, 'It is going to rain'; and so it does. ⁵⁵ When you notice wind blowing from the south, you say, 'It is going to be very hot'; and so it is. ⁵⁶ Hypocrites! You have learned to interpret the look of the earth and the sky. How is it you have not learned to interpret the season that is here?"

COMMENT

Having addressed the disciples in various sayings and parables (12:22-53), Jesus now turns his attention again to the crowds following him. This is still part of the travel account. Jesus utters his surprise at his contemporaries' inability to understand what is going on in their midst, in their very own day (12:54-56). It becomes an echo of his words of judgment in 7:31-35.

The sayings recorded here have a remote parallel in Matt 16:2-3. But the text of those verses is critically uncertain; they may have been interpolated at a later date and have been bracketed in N-A[26] (see *TCGNT* 41). Apart from the text-critical problem, however, only six Greek words out of forty-seven/ forty-eight in the Lucan text of this passage agree with the Matthean vocabulary. Whereas the introductory clause (v. 54a) is of Lucan composition, the rest of the sayings are not marked by his style (except possibly the adv. *eutheōs,* "immediately" [see J. Jeremias, *Die Sprache,* 224]). But the remote similarity of the passage with Matt 16:2-3 may suggest that it is pre-Lucan. It is scarcely derived from "Q" *(pace* R. A. Edwards, G. Schneider, *Evangelium nach Lukas,* 293-294), and should be regarded as "L" (see p. 80 and W. Grundmann, *Evangelium nach Lukas,* 272). The Lucan form of the sayings lacks the vivid colors of the Matthean.

A form of v. 56 is found (in part) in *Gos. of Thom.* § 91: "You assess the look of the sky and the earth, but you have not recognized what *(or* him who) is before you; you do not know how to assess this season." In this case the saying is more dependent on Luke than on Matthew, although the remark in the second part (possibly referring to Jesus himself) is a development beyond either of them. See further J.-E. Ménard, *L'Evangile selon Thomas,* 192-193; W. Schrage, *Das Verhältnis,* 175-177.

Form-critically, the sayings are minatory (see *HST* 116; but he also refers to them as a "similitude," without a comparison [p. 172]). Many others label the verses simply as a "parable" (e.g. T. W. Manson, *Sayings,* 121). They end with a rhetorical question, and thus have a form of application.

Jesus turns to the crowds and continues his remarks with ominous words. As weatherwise Palestinian farmers, they have learned to read the face of nature, with its clouds and winds. They should, then, be able to assess the critical moment in which they exist. He thus contrasts the people's "meteorological sensitiveness" with their "religious sensitiveness" (T. W. Manson, *Sayings,* 121). Without referring directly to himself or his message (as he may do in the *Gospel of Thomas* form), Jesus upbraids his audience for their lack of comprehension. Coming on the heels of sayings concerned with judgment, this aspect of judgment underlies the present set of sayings too. What the audience fails to notice is the critical import of his appearance and message about God and his kingdom (see 7:22-23; 11:20). There is no hint in this passage about a delay; rather "the season that is here" is precisely the time for repentance and conversion (see Acts 3:19-20; 17:30-31 for the consequences).

NOTES

12 54. *to the crowds.* See 12:1,13; cf. NOTE on 3:7. The implication is that the disciples have understood the significance of Jesus' appearance, in contrast to the crowds.

a cloud forming in the west. I.e. over the Mediterranean Sea, whence come the rain clouds that condense on the hills of central Palestine. Cf. 1 Kgs 18:44. See D. Baly, *The Geography of the Bible* (rev. ed.; New York: Harper & Row, 1974) 43-53. The "west" is expressed by *dysmai,* lit. "the settings" (of the sun). See 13:29.

55. *wind blowing from the south.* Lit. "the south-wind blowing." I.e. the wind that comes from the Arabian steppes in the southeast. Cf. Jer 4:11.

It is going to be very hot. Lit. "it will be a scorcher," i.e. the burning heat of the sun. The Greek *kausōn* is used in the LXX (e.g. Job 27:21; Hos 12:2 [12:1E]; 13:15; Jonah 4:8; Isa 49:10; Jer 18:17) of a wind coming from the east (= Hebrew *qādîm),* resembling the sirocco or (Arabic) *ḥamsīn.* Some mss. (P45, ℵ*, W) read *erchetai,* "is coming," instead of *estai,* "will be." Cf. Jas 1:11; J. Schneider, *TDNT* 3. 644.

56. *Hypocrites! Pace* G. Klein *(ZTK* 61 [1964] 380 n. 45), this epithet has not been added by Luke, who rarely uses it otherwise. See NOTES on 6:42; 12:1; cf. U. Wilckens, *TDNT* 8. 567 n. 41. It is used in this verse of the crowds. The use implies that Jesus is unmasking their attitude; their problem is much more an unwillingness to interpret than an inability.

the look of the earth and the sky. This is the best order of the words; in various mss. other word orders are found. The sense, however, is not changed.

you have not learned to interpret. This is the reading of mss. P75, ℵ, B, L, Θ, 33, etc.; but ms. D and the OL and OS versions have simply, "do you not interpret?"

the season that is here? Lit. "this (critical) time" *(kairon,* used as in 1:20 [see NOTE there]). Contrast the use in 4:13; 8:13; 12:42; 13:1. It refers to the significant era, which in Lucan salvation-history is the Period of Jesus. See pp. 181-187. In Matt 16:3 the phrase is "the signs of the times," whence the common name for this episode in the gospel tradition. H. Conzelmann *(Theology,* 109): "The message is that one must not be led astray by the delay." But where in the passage is there mention of or allusion to a "delay"?

BIBLIOGRAPHY (12:54-56)

George, A. " 'Interpréter ce temps' Luc 12,54-56," *BVC* 64 (1965) 18-23.
Klein, G. "Die Prüfung der Zeit (Lukas 12,54-56)," *ZTK* 61 (1964) 373-390.
Kümmel, W. G. *Promise and Fulfilment,* 22.
Wood, H. G. "Interpreting This Time," *NTS* 2 (1955-1956) 262-266.

88. AGREEMENT WITH ONE'S OPPONENT
(12:57-59)

12 ⁵⁷ "But why can you not judge for yourselves what is right? ⁵⁸ As you go with your opponent to a magistrate, make an effort to settle with him on the way; otherwise he may drag you off to the judge, and the judge may hand you over to the jailer, who may put you in prison. ⁵⁹ I tell you, you will not get out of there until you have paid the last cent."

COMMENT

Jesus' sayings continue now on what may be a completely unrelated topic, for they concern reconciliation with an opponent (12:57-59). A superficial reason for the inclusion of them here in the travel account may be the reference to "on the way" (v. 58).

The saying in v. 57 is clearly transitional, being a rhetorical question composed by Luke to join vv. 58-59 to the preceding saying about the assessment of the critical season (see S. Schulz, *Q: Die Spruchquelle*, 421). The transitional nature can be seen in use of the second pl. "you" in v. 57 in contrast to the second sg. "you" in the inherited material of vv. 58-59. The latter are derived from "Q," and their parallel is found in Matt 5:25-26, again a part of the sermon on the mount (see p. 78). The Matthean setting is really more apt for them. Luke's redaction can be seen in v. 58 ("make an effort," "to settle," "drag," "jailer") and in v. 59 (the omission of "amen" and the use of "cent"). (See further J. Jeremias, *Die Sprache*, 225.) The Lucan redaction has actually made use of more technical Roman judicial terms in contrast to the Matthean form (see E. Klostermann, *Lukasevangelium*, 141).

From a form-critical viewpoint, the sayings are again minatory. But many commentators speak of them as a parable or similitude that has lost its comparison and application. (So *HST* 172; T. W. Manson, *Sayings*, 122; I. H. Marshall, *Luke*, 550.) However, this is problematic and depends on how the passage as a whole is to be understood.

Prescinding from any possible nuances that may come from the Matthean use of the sayings and also—for the moment—from the greater Lucan context, we read of Jesus challenging his audience to timely and prudent reconciliation with one's opponent. Prima facie, he warns his listeners to think about the consequences of being haled into court; he implies, moreover, that those who would follow him should learn to work out compromises in life in order to avoid such conflicts. This is what it means to "judge what is right."

If this is the intent of Jesus' words here, one realizes that they are wholly unrelated to the foregoing context in the Lucan travel account. But they are not radically different from the advice that Paul sends to his Corinthian converts in 1 Cor 6:1-8, especially v. 7. Is such advice so out of place on the lips of Jesus, even of the Lucan Jesus?

This question has to be asked because the tendency of modern commentators to allegorize the would-be parable (see the form-critical remarks above) and interpret Jesus' words in terms of a greater Lucan context. So R. Bultmann *(HST* 172): "As in your civil life at times you place the greatest emphasis on not having to appear before the judge, so you should take care that you need fear no accuser before the heavenly judge." E. Klostermann *(Lukasevangelium,* 141) goes even further in identifying the "opponent" with "der Satan." G. Schneider *(Evangelium nach Lukas,* 295) thinks that this piece of tradition is neither a prudential regulation *(Klugheitsregel)* nor a pure parable; he prefers to call it (with H. Schürmann) a "minatory parable," or a prophetic threat of judgment. But the problem is whether Luke intended the sayings to be so understood (at Stage III of the gospel tradition); what meaning they may have carried in Stage I is hopelessly lost to us. Are we to think in terms of the contrast of civil and religious life, of which Bultmann spoke, and whether the Lucan collocation of the sayings imposes that interpretation? This becomes more pertinent when one considers the following context, the sayings of Jesus about a historical incident in Palestine of Jesus' time. To my way of thinking, it is far from clear that this Lucan episode is to be so understood. It is a piece of prudential advice, stemming from Jesus, which has lost its specific reference, and is best interpreted even here as no more than that.

NOTES

12 57. *judge for yourselves.* I.e. without help from me or others. See 21:30.

what is right? Lit. "what is the just *(or* proper) thing (to do)." Cf. Acts 4:19.

58. *make an effort.* Lit. "give activity *(or* pains)." Apart from Eph 4:19, the n. *ergasia* is found only in Lucan writings (Acts 16:16,19; 19:24,25). Cf. Josephus, *Ant.* 3.1,7 § 35. The expression used by Luke may be a Latinism (= *da operam* [see BDF § 5.3]). It stresses that the opportunity should be exploited.

to settle with him. Lit. "to be reconciled of him," reading the prep. *apo* with the best Greek mss., but which is omitted in mss. B, 892, 1241. The parallel in Matt 5:25 reads, "Come to an understanding with your opponent quickly while you go with him on the way."

drag you off. Luke uses the compound vb. *katasyrein,* the simple form of which *(syrein)* occurs also in Acts 8:3; 14:19; 17:6; the latter is found elsewhere in the NT only in John 21:8; Rev 12:4.

the jailer. Whereas Matt 5:25 has simply "the guard" *(hypēretēs),* Luke uses the proper term for the constable of a debtors' jail, *praktōr.*

59. *the last cent.* Lit. "the last *lepton,*" a small copper coin, two of which = a *kodrantēs* (see Mark 12:42), the name used in Matt 5:26 for the last coin. (Matthew's word *kodrantēs* is a loanword = Latin *quadrans,* "a quarter" of the Roman "as" [see NOTES on 12:6; 7:41].) Luke's change has exaggerated the extent of the judge's punishment in order to show that after his verdict is given it is too late for a compromise. The small copper coin will appear again in 21:2. In first-century Palestine the *lepton* was the smallest coin in use.

BIBLIOGRAPHY (12:57-59)

Caird, G. B. "Expounding the Parables: I. The Defendant (Matthew 5:25f.; Luke 12:58f.)," *ExpTim* 77 (1965-1966) 36-39.

Jeremias, J. *Parables,* 43-44, 96, 180.

Schürmann, H. "Eschatologie und Liebesdienst in der Verkündigung Jesu," *Kaufet die Zeit aus: Beiträge zur christlichen Eschatologie: Festgabe für Professor Dr. Theodorich Kampmann* (ed. H. Kirchhoff; Paderborn: Schöningh, 1959) 39-71; reprinted, *Ursprung und Gestalt,* 279-298.

89. TIMELY REFORM: THE PARABLE OF THE BARREN FIG TREE
(13:1-9)

13 ¹ At that time some people who were present told Jesus about the Galileans whose blood Pilate had mingled with their sacrifices. ² He replied to them, "Do you suppose that these Galileans were greater sinners than all the others in Galilee, because they suffered this fate? ³ No, I tell you; unless you reform your lives, you shall all perish in a similar way. ⁴ Or those eighteen who were killed when the tower in Siloam fell upon them—do you suppose that they were more guilty than all the other people living in Jerusalem? ⁵ No, I tell you; unless you reform your lives, you shall all perish in the same way."

⁶ Then he proposed this parable: "A certain man had a fig tree planted in his vineyard; he came up to it, looking for fruit, but found none. ⁷ So he said to the gardener, 'Look here, for three years now I

have come looking for fruit on this fig tree, and I find none. Cut it down! Why should it even use up the soil?' [8] But he replied, 'Leave it, sir, for this year yet, until I loosen the soil around it and put in some fertilizer. [9] Perhaps it will bear fruit later on; but if not, then you can cut it down.' "

COMMENT

As the crowd listens to Jesus at this stage in the travel account, people arrive to tell him about what has happened to some Galileans whom Pilate has put to death; this comes immediately after his remarks on reconciliation with one's opponent, and the episode has a certain poignancy. It occasions Jesus' remarks about the guilt of the Galileans—and other Jerusalemites, whom he himself introduces—and an appeal for repentance. To it he adds a parable about a barren fig tree, exhorting his audience to timely reform (13:1-9).

The story about the murdered Galileans, the eighteen killed at Siloam, and the parable of the barren fig tree are found only in the Lucan Gospel and have been inherited by the evangelist from "L" (see p. 84). One may wonder whether the story and the parable were originally joined as they are here; there is certainly no intrinsic connection between them. R. Bultmann *(HST* 23) considers vv. 1-5 a "unitary composition" which serves Luke as an introduction to the parable. There Bultmann seems to consider these verses as a controversy-dialogue occasioned by a question from people present, but later on *(HST* 54-55) he treats them as a scholastic dialogue formulated by the early church "in the spirit of Jesus" and in dependence on Josephus *(Ant.* 18.4,1 § 86-87). This is far from clear. In any case, vv. 1-5 are a pronounce-ment-story *(FGT* 69), with Jesus' questions and the punch line repeated (vv. 3,5). To it has been added the parable (vv. 6-9), which lacks an explicit application (it is implied in the preceding vv. 3,5). It may be viewed as a parable of mercy (see p. 258), or perhaps even as a parable of crisis, contain-ing a call for repentance before it is too late. Some commentators think that the parable has "a parallel" in Mark 11:12-14 (the cursing of the fig tree; cf. Matt 21:18-19), which Luke omits in chap. 19 (e.g. G. Schneider, *Evangelium nach Lukas,* 296). This, however, seems most unlikely, since the Marcan passage, though parabolic in its thrust, is not a parable, and only the most obvious words are common to the two episodes ("fig tree," "fruit," "he came," "found none"). Otherwise there is nothing common. (See further T. W. Manson, *Sayings,* 274; cf. C.-H. Hunzinger, *TDNT* 7. 755-757.)

Jesus, having learned about the fate of the Galileans killed by Pilate, draws a moral from it. Though a Galilean himself, he does not launch into a chau-vinistic criticism of the Roman prefect; instead he uses the incident to call for repentance. He insists that those Galileans did not suffer that fate because they were greater sinners than others in Galilee; but their sudden death challenges those still alive to repentance, to a reformation of life (= an acceptance in faith of the saving word of God that he has come to announce). The existence of others can also be suddenly terminated in a similar way.

Jesus plays at one-upmanship, matching the story of the deliberate, gruesome death of the Galileans with that of the accidental death of eighteen Jerusalemites killed by the sudden collapse of a tower in the old wall of the city near the pool of Siloam. They may have been no more guilty than the first (the Galileans) or than others in Jerusalem, yet they too met a sudden death. Death may face anyone as rapidly as it faced the Galileans and the eighteen Jerusalemites, for at any moment, even that very night, "life" may be "demanded" of one for scrutiny and assessment (see 12:20).

The parable drives home the critical nature of human existence: "As a final period of grace is given to this fig tree, so Jesus' summons to repentance goes forth in the short period of grace before God's judgment; it is the last hour" (ibid.). This is the basic intent of the parable. Hunzinger counsels against allegorizing the details of the parable; but G. Schneider *(Evangelium nach Lukas,* 298) has rightly seen that the parable in the Lucan context may have a further allegorical thrust. Here one must distinguish the stages of the gospel tradition again. In Stage I the parable undoubtedly had the intent stated above and was probably aimed by Jesus at his Palestinian contemporaries. But one does not have to go to the extent of some commentators, seeing the vineyard as Israel, the fig tree as Jerusalem (or an individual Jew), the gardener as Jesus, and the three years as his ministry. It is sufficient to see the general thrust of the parable as envisaging his contemporaries. But in Stage III of the gospel tradition the horizon of application is enlarged; the stories and the parable hardly have in view solely Jesus' contemporaries, but also the Christian individual faced with the prospect of a sudden end of life. In this context the barren fig tree takes on a different meaning, the symbol of the human being whose life is marked by unproductivity. Why should such a person, having been given life and existence, continue to use up natural resources so unproductively. If one bears no fruit and continues one's unproductivity and procrastination, then that person should be ready to face the fate of the barren fig tree. As a sequel to the preceding comments of Jesus about reform of life, the parable takes on a significantly ominous thrust. The Galileans may have died by the malice of some human being; the eighteen Jerusalemites by chance (they happened to be in the wrong place at the wrong time). But the fig tree will die expressly because of inactivity and unproductiveness. In the long run this becomes "the greater sin." The guilt that comes from one's own procrastination or lack of decision is greater than that implied by death at someone else's hands or unexpected calamity. Jesus' parable thus stresses that the last period of grace has been granted to reform such procrastination. See p. 189.

On the implication in the parable of a delay or postponement of the end-time, see pp. 232-233.

NOTES

13 1. *At that time.* In Luke's phrase *en autō tō kairō* the critical sense of *kairos* is not necessary. See NOTE on 12:56. For the construction used here, see p. 118. It introduces a transition composed by Luke to join this episode to the foregoing. The transition creates the impression of a report about something that has recently happened. J. Blinzler ("Die Niedermetzelung," 32) tries to pinpoint this "time" to 14 Nisan 29 B.C., a year before Jesus' death at Passover. But there is no certainty to such speculation.

some people . . . were present. Or possibly, "some had just arrived," since the vb. *pareinai* can mean not only "be present, be alongside of," but also "have just come, arrive." See BAGD 624; BDF § 322. Cf. Acts 10:21; 17:6. There is an almost word-for-word parallel to this phrase in Diodorus Siculus, *Bibl. hist.* 17.8,2 ("some people arrived announcing that many of the Greeks were in revolt").

the Galileans. I.e. inhabitants of Galilee in the north of Palestine, a designation which will be given to Peter (22:59) and to Jesus himself (23:6). Cf. Acts 5:37. How many Galileans? The thrust of the story suggests fewer than eighteen.

whose blood Pilate had mingled with their sacrifices. I.e. people whom Pilate, through his soldiers, had cut down while they were slaughtering sacrificial animals, possibly Passover lambs. Since "sacrifices" *(thysiai)* were to be offered (even by lay people) only in Jerusalem, the forecourt of the priests in the Jerusalem Temple must be envisaged here, even though it is not named. There even the Passover lambs were to be killed. See J. Blinzler, "Eine Bemerkung zum Geschichtsrahmen des Johannesevangeliums," *Bib* 36 (1955) 27-31. The Galileans would then be understood as pilgrims who had come to Jerusalem for a feast. It is hardly likely, *pace* O. Cullmann *(The State in the New Testament* [New York: Scribner's, 1956] 14), that "sacrifices" should be understood of people (either Romans or their underlings) whom anarchic Galilean zealots might have killed or that Pilate would have exploited such an occasion to kill Galileans.

On Pilate, see NOTE on 3:1; cf. pp. 176-177.

The incident to which Luke refers is not mentioned elsewhere either in the gospel tradition or in other ancient writers. On a possible source that Luke may have had, see p. 89. Given Josephus' knowledge of Pilate's other overt attacks on Jews in Palestine, it is difficult to think that this incident would have escaped his attention, even if fewer than eighteen Galileans were done away with. Attempts have been made to explain the Lucan story by referring to other incidents of Pilate's attacks on the Jewish people over whom he ruled in various accounts of Josephus: (1) Pilate's sending of cavalry and infantrymen into a village (Tirathana) near Mt. Gerizim to prevent a group of Samaritans, led by one of their demagogues, from climbing their sacred mountain; the soldiers killed some and put the rest to flight *(Ant.* 18.4,1 § 86-87). So R. Bultmann

(HST 23) and many others (J. Wellhausen, E. Meyer, E. Hirsch, E. Mireaux, K. Rengstorf, etc.). This would make Luke guilty of anachronistic confusion (since the episode happened in A.D. 35, and it became the occasion for L. Vitellius, the legate of Syria, to send Pilate back to Rome to answer to the emperor for the slaughter). But the passage in Josephus speaks of "Samaritans," not Galileans, makes no mention of "sacrifices," and locates the incident at a village near the base of Mt. Gerizim, not on it, where Samaritan sacrifices would have taken place. (2) Pilate's introduction into Jerusalem of effigies of Roman emperors on military standards, which caused rebellious Jerusalemites to march to Caesarea Maritima in protest against the move *(J.W.* 2.9,2 § 169-174; *Ant.* 18.3,1 § 55-59). So C. H. Kraeling, *HTR* 35 (1942) 286-288. (3) Pilate's use of Temple treasury funds to build an aqueduct to bring water into Jerusalem *(J.W.* 2.9,4 § 175-177; *Ant.* 18.3,2 § 60-62). So A. T. Olmstead, *Jesus in the Light of History* (New York: Scribner's, 1942) 147-149. Here Josephus speaks of "the Jews" *(Ioudaioi),* not of "Galileans." (4) Archelaus' slaughter of three thousand in Jerusalem about the time of Passover *(J.W.* 2.1,3 § 8-13; *Ant.* 17.9,3 § 213-218). So S. E. Johnson ("A Note") and some others. (5) The murder of six thousand "Jews" by Alexander Janneus (103-76 B.C.) because he had been pelted by them with lemons during the celebration of Succoth or Tabernacles *(J.W.* 13.13,5 § 372). So T. Zahn *(Evangelium des Lucas,* 521 n. 68). What either of the last two have to do with the Lucan story about "Pilate" and his slaughter of "Galileans" is hard to understand; but it is indicative of the straits to which commentators have been reduced.

There is no way of telling whether this episode is historical or the result of a Lucan confusion of it with some other incident in first-century Palestinian history. For a fuller discussion of the problem, see J. Blinzler, "Die Niedermetzelung." Luke's picture of Pilate in this episode is not contradicted by the brutal person depicted in Josephus' writings. However, it is hardly likely that the unexplained reference to the death of Galileans is a fabrication out of whole cloth. Cf. G. Schwarz, "Lukas XIII, 1-5."

In any case, this reference to Palestinian history—along with the succeeding story provided by Jesus himself—gives him a springboard for his pronouncement, no matter how reliable the history may be.

2. *replied to them.* Luke uses again *apokritheis eipen,* a Septuagintism. See p. 114; cf. J. Jeremias, *Die Sprache,* 226.

were greater sinners than all the others. Lit. "sinned beyond all the Galileans." In using the prep. *para* + acc., Luke preserves a Semitic expression, a circumlocution for comparison (for or instead of Aramaic or Hebrew *min,* "from"). See J. Jeremias, *Parables,* 141. For an Aramaic parallel, see 1QapGen 20:6-7, lit. "Above *['al]* all women is she beautiful indeed," i.e. she is more beautiful than all women. This use of *para* (in a comparative sense) is found again in 13:4; 18:14. See p. 124.

because they suffered this fate? Calamity in life was often believed to be the result of past sin. See Job 4:7; 8:4,20; 22:5; Exod 20:5c; 1QapGen 20:16-29 (the affliction sent to Pharaoh and his household because of the carrying off of Sarai); John 9:2-3. Jesus' words do not query that belief, but make instead a plea for repentance.

3. *No, I tell you.* A strong contrary statement is thus introduced. See 1:60; 13:5; 16:30.

unless you reform your lives. Cf. 13:5. A call for *metanoia.* See NOTE on 3:3; cf. pp.

237-239. For the OT background of this plea, see Ps 7:13 (LXX); Jer 12:17 (LXX). Only repentance can ensure one against the certain annihilation of the wicked, with which all are threatened unless they turn from sin.

you shall all perish in a similar way. Prima facie, this refers to a form of natural death, which will come unexpectedly; but in the context of judgment, which has been running through this part of the Lucan travel account, a broader sense of perishing must be envisaged.

4. *Or those eighteen . . . them.* Jesus mentions the calamity which afflicted a greater number of people, in this case by accidental death. On the *casus pendens,* see pp. 124-125.

the tower in Siloam. This undoubtedly refers to a tower that formed part of the old (first) wall of ancient Jerusalem, which according to Josephus *(J. W.* 5.4,2 § 145) turned from the east southward "above the fountain of Siloam." Nothing more is known about a tower there; nor does Josephus mention such a calamity as this. See J. Finegan, *Archeology,* 114. Cf. John 9:7,11.

more guilty. Lit. "were debtors beyond all who . . ." The Greek *opheiletai* probably reflects the Aramaic sense of *ḥayyāb,* "debtor," used in a religious sense. See 11QtgJob 21:5; 34:4. See p. 117.

living in Jerusalem? The best mss. (P⁴⁵, P⁷⁵, B, D, L, etc.) read simply *tous katoikountas Ierousalēm,* lit. "dwellers of Jerusalem"; others (ℵ, A, W, Θ, Ψ, and the Koine text-tradition) read a prep. *(en)* before the name. On *Ierousalēm,* see NOTES on 2:22, 10:30, and p. 824.

The reference to two ostensibly historical incidents does not necessarily mean that Jesus indirectly anticipates the annihilation of his contemporaries in the destruction of Jerusalem, *pace* J. M. Creed, *The Gospel,* 181. He has not yet formulated here what he will in 21:24.

6. *he proposed this parable.* See NOTE on 5:36.

a fig tree planted in his vineyard. For the planting of fig trees in a vineyard, see Mic 4:4; Pliny, *Nat. Hist.* 17.35,200; however, Theophrastus, *De caus. plant.* 3.10,6 counsels against it. It should be recalled that a fig tree often stood in the OT as a symbol of Judah or Israel (Hos 9:10; Mic 7:1; Jer 8:13; 24:1-10). See further C.-H. Hunzinger, *TDNT* 7. 751-757.

found none. This marks his disappointment and frustration. Cf. Luke 3:9.

7. *said to the gardener.* Lit. "to the vinedresser." See MM 27. Luke uses again *eipen pros* + acc. See p. 116.

for three years now. Lit. "behold three years from the (time) when I continue coming." See A. Plummer, *The Gospel,* 340. A parenthetical nom. is used after *idou,* "behold." See BDF § 144. On the pres. tense, see BDF § 322. The construction with *aph' hou* is found in Thucydides, *Hist.* 1.18,1. The "three years" cannot be understood allegorically of Jesus' ministry; Luke knows nothing of a three-year ministry.

Why should it even use up the soil? Lit. "why should it waste even the earth?"

8. *he replied.* The gardener acts as the advocate, pleading the cause of the unproductive tree. Luke uses *apokritheis* with the historic pres. *legei.* See p. 107.

for this year yet. The salutary period of grace before the critical showdown is thus limited.

9. *but if not.* Luke uses the balancing *men . . . de* of literary Greek. See p. 108. At

the end of this verse there is added in some mss. (Γ and others), "As he said this, he called out, 'Let the one who has ears to hear take heed.' " See NOTES on 8:8 and 12:21.

BIBLIOGRAPHY (13:1-9)

Bartsch, H.-W. "Die 'Verfluchung' des Feigenbaums," *ZNW* 53 (1962) 256-260.

Blinzler, J. "Die letzte Gnadenfrist: Lk 13,6-9," *BLit* 37 (1963-1964) 155-169.

—— "Die Niedermetzelung von Galiläern durch Pilatus," *NovT* 2 (1957-1958) 24-49.

Denney, J. "Three Motives to Repentance, Luke XIII. 1-9," *Expos* 4/7 (1893) 232-237.

Dodd, C. H. *Parables,* 47.

Dupont, J. "Les paraboles du sénevé et du levain," *NRT* 89 (1967) 897-913.

Faccio, H. M. "De ficu sterili (Lc 13,6-9)," *VD* 29 (1951) 233-238.

Jeremias, J. *Parables,* 169-171.

Johnson, S. E. "A Note on Luke 13:1-5," *ATR* 17 (1935) 91-95.

Kahn, J. G. "La parabole du figuier stérile et les arbres récalcitrants de la Genèse," *NovT* 13 (1971) 38-45.

Kuss, O. "Zum Sinngehalt des Doppelgleichnisses vom Senfkorn und Sauerteig," *Bib* 40 (1959) 641-653; reprinted, *Auslegung und Verkündigung,* 1. 85-97.

Schürer, E. *HJPAJC* 1. 357-398.

Schwarz, G. "Lukas XIII, 1-5: Eine Emendation," *NovT* 11 (1969) 121-126.

Ternant, P. "Le dernier délai de la conversion Lc 13," *AsSeign* 16 (1971) 59-72.

Zeitlin, S. "Who Were the Galileans? New Light on Josephus' Activities in Galilee," *JQR* 64 (1973-1974) 189-203.

90. THE CURE OF THE CRIPPLED WOMAN ON THE SABBATH
(13:10-17)

13 [10] Jesus was teaching on the Sabbath in one of the synagogues, [11] when a woman was present, infirm and afflicted by a spirit for eighteen years, bent over and unable to straighten up in any way. [12] When Jesus saw her, he addressed her and said, "Woman, you are rid of your infirmity!" [13] And he laid his hands on her. Instantly she straightened up and continued to glorify God. [14] The leader of the synagogue, however, annoyed that Jesus had cured her on the Sabbath, remarked to the crowd, "There are six days when one has to work; come on one of

these to be cured, and not on the day of Sabbath." [15] But the Lord said to him in reply, "Hypocrites! Does not each of you release his ox or ass from the manger on the Sabbath to lead it off to water? [16] This woman is a daughter of Abraham, and Satan has kept her tied up for eighteen long years. Did she not have to be released from that bond, even on the day of Sabbath?" [17] As he said this, all his opponents were struck with shame, while the whole crowd rejoiced at all the wonderful things he was doing.

COMMENT

Luke now depicts Jesus, though still on his journey to Jerusalem, visiting a synagogue in an unnamed village on a Sabbath, and while there curing a crippled woman, which results in a debate about the Sabbath (13:10-17). Coming on the heels of the parable of the barren fig tree, the episode has given rise to considerable discussion as to its place and meaning. Whereas M.-J. Lagrange (*Luc*, 381) believes that Luke would have followed a "chronological order," A. Loisy (*L'Evangile selon Luc*, 364) preferred the patristic view that the cured woman symbolizes the church and is contrasted with the barren fig tree, the symbol of the synagogue, a contrast which he considers to dominate the arrangement. As far as the first explanation is concerned, how one could establish such a chronological order is baffling; as for the second explanation, there is not the slightest suggestion in the text that such allegory is at work (see J. M. Creed, *The Gospel*, 182). E. Klostermann (*Lukasevangelium*, 144) certainly comes closer to the truth, when he suggests that Luke is simply following the order of his own source ("L"). The mention of "a daughter of Abraham" (v. 16) as a literary preparation for v. 28 is scarcely cogent; and it is probably sheer chance that the number eighteen appears in this and the foregoing episode (cf. vv. 4,11,16), though one cannot deny that it may have served as a catchword-bond for the episodes.

The cure of the crippled woman is recounted only by Luke, derived by him from "L" (see p. 84). It has often been thought to be a secondary variant of the cure of the man with dropsy (14:1-6); but that suggestion raises more problems than it solves (apart from the mention of an "ox" and "the day of Sabbath" there is scarcely any connection). Bultmann (*HST* 12) wanted to explain the genesis of this episode as something composed by Luke on the basis of the saying in v. 15, which Bultmann would consider the pronouncement in the story. But, as many others have argued, v. 15 alone is scarcely the pronouncement; v. 16 would have to be included. This raises the further question about the form-critical nature of the episode. For V. Taylor (*FGT* 155) this is one of the alleged pronouncement-stories which is more dominated by the narrative elements (as in some other Lucan instances); he is thus inclined to classify this episode with stories about Jesus. Part of the difficulty is that the controversy arises only once the miracle has been recounted, and this has been seen as a reason for regarding the episode as a whole as a more recent formation (so E. Lohse, "Jesu Worte"). But all the elements of the typical miracle-story, save the request for a miracle, are present. The reaction in v. 17b may be the typical ending, whereas v. 17c is part of Lucan redaction (see NOTE). In any case, this episode is on the border between a miracle-story and a pronouncement-story; and M. Dibelius *(FTG* 97) rightly recognized its "hybrid form." The story itself probably reflects one of the real-life situations of Jesus' own ministry: a cure and debate over the Sabbath in Stage I of the gospel tradition.

The episode depicts Jesus once again making use of his "power" (recall 4:14,36; 5:17) to heal an unfortunate human being afflicted with physical evil. This rare miracle-story in the travel account tells of his conquest of evil on his journey up to Jerusalem, the city of destiny, where he will meet evil in another form in his own life. He uses that power to heal not only in a synagogue, but even on a Sabbath. The temporal and spatial setting for the cure thus enhances the effect wrought on "a daughter of Abraham" for whom in God's providence Jesus was sent, because she had "to be released." The impersonal vb. *dei,* lit. "it is necessary" (v. 16), alludes to the necessary realization of God's plan of salvation-history, working itself out in Jesus' ministry (see pp. 179-180). The irony in the episode is seen in that the opposition to Jesus' curing act comes from a "leader of the synagogue," who himself uses the same impersonal vb. *dei* (v. 14) to express the human obligation of work (on six other days!).

The episode is but another one in the Lucan Gospel in which Jesus is portrayed stressing that the welfare of a human being takes precedence over even such religious obligations as the observance of the Sabbath. Recall 6:1-11, where Jesus "the Son of Man" (in Stage III) is presented as "lord of the Sabbath" (v. 5) and as one who has authority over it. The reader of this Lucan episode is expected to recall that earlier episode and its meaning.

Coming on the heels of the preceding episode in the travel account, which dealt with the need of repentance and timely reform, this episode implicitly singles out the "leader of the synagogue" (v. 14) and "all his (= Jesus') opponents" (v. 17) as prime examples of those who stand in need of such reform. "Hypocrites" (in the pl.) is addressed in the story to "the crowd" (v. 14), but the epithet is evoked by the subterfuge of the leader (sg.) who addresses his remarks, not to Jesus, but to the crowd. Jesus' accusation is not meant for them solely, apart from the leader. It characterizes the attitude of those who stand in need of timely reform.

Jesus' argument is an example of reasoning *a minori ad maius*—what the later rabbinical tradition called *qal wāḥômer* ("light and heavy," i.e. from the light instance to the more grave). If it is permitted to care for household animals on the Sabbath, it is also permitted to care for human infirmity; if one can loose the tether of animals to lead them from the feeding-trough to water, one can loose the bonds of an afflicted human being and bring her to health.

It is characteristic of Luke that in this episode he makes a woman the object of Jesus' compassion on the Sabbath; it contributes to the universalism of Jesus' message in this Gospel (see p. 191). He will do the same for a man in 14:1-6.

Finally, the reader of this episode cannot fail to note the way it says something about how the Lucan Jesus perceives himself. Having cured this unfortunate "daughter of Abraham" on a Sabbath in a synagogue, it implicitly depicts him acting with authority toward the Sabbath and the traditions of old and upbraiding the hypocrisy of reactions which would criticize him for so acting.

NOTES

13   10. *was teaching.* Jesus' cure of the woman takes place in the context of his teaching, on which the major emphasis in the travel account falls. On the Lucan use of *didaskein,* "teach," see p. 148. The periphrastic conjugation is again used, *ēn* + pres. ptc. *didaskōn.* See p. 122.

on the Sabbath. Luke uses the pl. *en tois sabbasin,* but in vv. 14-16 the sg. *sabbaton* will occur. See NOTE on 4:31.

in one of the synagogues. This locale echoes that of 4:15. See NOTE there. It is the last time that the Lucan Jesus will appear in such a setting. For the Septuagintism employed, see pp. 121-122.

11. *when a woman was present, infirm and afflicted by a spirit for eighteen years.* Lit. "and behold a woman, having a spirit of infirmity for eighteen years." The physical illness is described in the following cl., and according to the best Greek mss. it is caused by the spirit. This cl. is simply introduced by the interjection *kai idou* (see p. 121) and lacks a vb. Ms. D sought to remedy the lack of it, reading *en astheneia ēn pneumatos.* This would mean that she "was in/with an infirmity of spirit," which clearly carries another meaning. But the best reading attributes her infirmity to a "spirit." See NOTE on 4:33. The expression "a spirit of infirmity or sickness" is undoubtedly an Aramaism; cp. *rûaḥ šiḥlānāyāʾ,* "spirit of purulence/pestilence" (1QapGen 20:26,16). See p. 117. Cf. v. 16b.

bent over and unable to straighten up. Lit. "being bent double and not able to lift up (the head)"—or possibly "to straighten" (her back). The description of the woman's infirmity in this verse was one of the main arguments used by W. K. Hobart *(The Medical Language of St. Luke,* 20-22) to try to show that the writer of this Gospel was a medical man. See pp. 51-53, 60. For a more modern study of the phenomenon, see J. Wilkinson ("The Case"), who identifies the affliction as *spondylitis ankylopoietica,* which produces a fusion of spinal joints.

12. *he addressed her.* Or "he called out to her." Jesus acts spontaneously; no request is made of him to intervene on her behalf.

you are rid of. Lit. "you have been released from," and are free of; the pf. tense in the theological pass. (see NOTE on 5:20; cf. 7:48) expresses the condition resulting from the past action.

13. *laid his hands on her.* See NOTE on 4:40; cf. 5:13.

Instantly. A favorite reaction to a miraculous act of Jesus in the Lucan Gospel. See NOTE on 1:64. The instantaneous cure on the Sabbath stands in contrast to the eighteen years of infirmity.

straightened up. Lit. "was straightened up," the aor. pass., again used in a theological sense, i.e. by God.

continued to glorify God. Or "and was (continually) glorifying God," with the impf. tense expressing durative action. Cf. 2:20. God's salvific bounty, manifested to her through Jesus' words and deed, elicits from her the praise of him who is the source of her benefaction. On the Septuagintism used here, see p. 114.

14. *leader of the synagogue.* See 8:49.

the crowd. Luke's favorite word for people attending Jesus' teaching or cures (see NOTE on 3:7) now designates the synagogue-congregation. The leader's warning is addressed to the people, not merely as a criticism of Jesus' action on the Sabbath, but as a warning to them about him. From this indirect insinuation arises the charge of hypocrisy that follows.

six days. An allusion to the prohibition of work in Exod 20:9 or Deut 5:13.

15. *the Lord.* See NOTE on 7:13; cf. pp. 202-203.

Hypocrites! This epithet is again addressed to the crowd, being pl., as in 12:56; see NOTES on 6:42; 12:1.

release. Note the play on the use of *lyein,* "loose," here and in v. 16.

his ox or ass. The OT pair of household animals is so mentioned in Deut 5:14; 22:4; Isa 32:20. Cf. Gen 32:5; 34:28. The first of them will appear again in Luke 14:5. For later rabbinical regulations about the care of such animals on the Sabbath, see Str-B 2. 199; I. H. Marshall, *Luke,* 558.

the manger. I.e. the feeding-trough. See Luke 2:7,12,16.

16. *a daughter of Abraham.* I.e. one of God's chosen people. Cf. 4 Macc 15:28. In 19:9 the toll-collector Zacchaeus will be recognized as a "son of Abraham." See p. 192.

Satan. See NOTES on 4:2; 10:18. This is the closest that Luke comes to associating an evil "spirit" (v. 11) with Satan. It should not be understood as a simple identification. Jesus' words stress that God's activity is now present to counteract the worst of evil afflicting human beings. This mention of Satan in the Period of Jesus creates a problem for the alleged "Satan-free" character of this period. See p. 187.

has kept her tied up. I.e. like an animal tethered to a trough, but even worse. The figurative expression characterizes her crippling infirmity (cf. 8:29; Mark 7:35); the evil which afflicts her is worse than bonds tethering animals to troughs.

eighteen long years. Lit. "behold, ten and eight years."

Did she not have to be released from that bond. Again the impersonal *edei* (impf.), "it was necessary," expresses the relation of this merciful act of Jesus to salvation-history. See pp. 179-180; cf. v. 14. G. Schwarz *("Lythēnai apo tou desmou toutou," BN*

15 [1981] 47) maintains that "this figurative use of *deō* and *desmos* is un-Greek"; and he seeks to retroject the Lucan text into Aramaic. This is, however, highly questionable. Not only is his translation into Aramaic doubtful, but this figurative use of the vb. *dein* ("bind") and *desmos* ("bond") is well attested in Greek, both classical and Hellenistic. See Theognis, *Eleg.* 178; *Anthol. pal.* 11.138; *Tab. defix.* 96.108; W. Dittengerger, *Sylloge* 809:14; 1175:14; MM 142, 144; *LAE* 306.

17. *As he said this.* The first cl. of v. 17 is omitted in ms. D.

all his opponents. They are unnamed and stand in contrast to "the whole crowd." The wording of this phrase and the reference to "shame" are undoubtedly an allusion to Isa 45:16 (LXX), which also uses *hoi antikeimenoi autō,* "those opposing him," and speaks of shame. Luke has redacted the allusion by adding his favorite "all" *(pantes,* see NOTES on 3:16; 4:15; 9:1—but this adj. is omitted in some mss. [P⁴⁵, D] and in the OL). Note also *pas ho ochlos,* lit. "all the crowd." See 6:19; Acts 21:27.

the wonderful things. I.e. the cure of the crippled woman among other things. This is a rare instance in the Synoptics where such an adj. *(endoxos,* "wondrous, splendid") is used of one of Jesus' miracles, which are not usually regarded as causing wonder. Cf. the LXX of Exod 34:10, for the OT background of this usage, translated as "marvels" in the *RSV.*

BIBLIOGRAPHY (13:10-17)

Lohse, E. "Jesu Worte über den Sabbat," *Judentum—Urchristentum—Kirche* (ed. W. Eltester) 79-89.

Neirynck, F. "Jesus and the Sabbath: Some Observations on Mark II, 27," *Jésus aux origines* (ed. J. Dupont) 227-270.

Roloff, J. *Das Kerygma,* 66-69.

Wilkinson, J. "The Case of the Bent Woman in Luke 13:10-17," *EvQ* 49 (1977) 195-205.

91. THE PARABLE OF THE MUSTARD SEED
(13:18-19)

13 ¹⁸ So he said, "What is the kingdom of God like, and to what should I compare it? ¹⁹ It is like a mustard seed which a man took and sowed in his garden; it grew to be a tree, and *the birds of the sky built their nests in its branches.* "ᵃ

ᵃ Ps 104:12; Dan 4:9,18

COMMENT

Luke finishes off the first part of his travel account with two parables of Jesus, the first about a mustard seed (13:18-19), the second about leaven (13:20-21). Form-critically considered, both of them are parables of the kingdom and they relate his foregoing call for timely reform and a proper understanding of himself and of his ministry to afflicted human beings to a broader dimension of his preaching. Recall 4:43.

The parables are paired: one about a man, the other about a woman; and both of them have the same formulation, "which a man took and . . ." "which a woman took and . . ." The paired parables precede the second mention of Jerusalem in the course of the Lucan travel account.

The Synoptic relationship of the parable of the mustard seed is complicated. A form of it is found in Matt 13:31-32, the wording of much of which is similar to Luke; there it is also followed by the parable of the leaven (13:33). This reveals that the paired parables were already found in "Q." Even though Matthew presents them as parables of "the kingdom of heaven," characteristically using the phrase that Luke avoids, he also has the wording, "like a mustard seed which a man took and . . . his . . . and became [Matthew, however, has the historical pres.] a tree"; "built their nests in its branches." Another form of the parable is found in Mark 4:30-32, being part of the Marcan sermon in parables. The similarity of the Lucan parables, however, to the Marcan is minimal; it has in common only the words *elegen,* "said," *basileia tou theou,* "kingdom of God," *kokkō sinapeōs,* "a mustard seed," and *ta peteina tou ouranou,* "the birds of the sky." The Marcan form is otherwise longer and fuller. Matthew makes use of the parable in his own sermon in parables, thus showing that he has followed Mark and altered the form of the parable inherited from him with the wording of "Q," which is most likely preserved almost as is in the Lucan form (with the possibility that Luke may have changed the more primitive "kingdom of heaven" to "kingdom of God"). Thus the source of the Lucan parable is "Q." Even though Luke must have known the Marcan form of it, with its description of the mustard seed as the "smallest of all seeds on the earth," he has not made use of it. (See pp. 71-72, 80-87.)

Still another form of the parable is found in *Gos. of Thom.* § 20: "The disciples said to Jesus, 'Tell us what the kingdom of heaven is like.' He said to them, 'It is like a mustard seed, smaller than all seeds. But when it falls on ground which is cultivated, it sends forth a great branch (and) becomes a shelter for birds of the sky.' " In this later, developed form, the parable has acquired an introductory question and is more dependent on the Marcan/ Matthean form than on the Lucan. It further makes mention of the ground "which is cultivated," thus slightly allegorizing the parable itself. (See J.-E. Ménard, *L'Evangile selon Thomas,* 109 ["le texte de Thomas ne présente pas de signes convaincants d'antériorité"]; cf. W. Schrage, *Das Verhältnis,* 61-66.)

In the parable of the mustard seed Jesus shows how from a small beginning the kingdom of God grows inevitably into a great phenomenon in human history. His own preaching of the kingdom will have an inevitable result in its fully realized form. In the Lucan formulation, which makes no mention of the size of the seed—for what reason this is not picked up one can only speculate —the parable is not per se one of contrast, but of growth. The growth and development *(ēuxēsen kai egeneto,* lit. "it grew and became") of the mustard seed are implied as taking place through the mysterious operation of divine power in the plant; that power is already operative. The parable implies the same divine operation of which Ezek 17:22-24 spoke explicitly, in connection, however, with a cedar (cf. Ezek 31:2-9). The inevitability of the growth of the mustard seed into a "tree" which provides nesting-shelter for the birds of the sky is a characteristic of the kingdom which the Lucan Jesus preaches. The lesson of the parable stresses the organic unity between Jesus' present mission in Israel and a future form of the kingdom of God (see N. A. Dahl, "The Parables of Growth").

The parable of the mustard seed draws its illustration of the kingdom from a plant known to inhabitants of Palestine. Its growth from a small seed into a "tree" in which birds can find shelter illustrates Jesus' preaching of the kingdom. God's divine operation is active in it just as it is in the growth of the plant. Are human beings ready to build their "nests" in it? That is the challenge that the Lucan Jesus offers at this point in the travel account.

NOTES

13 18. *So he said.* The Lucan setting for this comment of Jesus is still that of the synagogue of v. 10.

the kingdom of God. See NOTE on 4:43 and pp. 154-156.

like. This introductory comparative formula *(homoios* + dat.) is also found in 6:47,48,49; 7:31,32; 12:36; 13:21 (and in the Matthean parallels), but it is not found in "Mk." See NOTE on 7:31.

to what should I compare it? See NOTE on 7:31. The rhetorical question is double here; cf. v. 20 below.

19. *a mustard seed.* Lit. "a seed *(or* grain) of mustard." Luke does not add the Marcan description of the seed's size. See NOTE on 17:6. The mustard plant was grown in Palestine, but it is not mentioned in the OT; it appears later in rabbinic literature. See *m. Kil.* 2:9; 3:2; *m. Nid.* 5:2; cf. C.-H. Hunzinger, *"Sinapi," TDNT* 7. 287-291. Luke uses the Greek name *sinapi,* as do the other evangelists; its classical Greek name was *napy.* Theophrastus *(Hist. plant.* 7.1,2-3) classes mustard among the *lachana,* "edible garden herbs" (see NOTE on 11:42), and knows that it grows into

dendron, "tree," even though it is usually regarded as a bush. See K. W. Clark, "The Mustard Plant."

a man. Luke retains from "Q" the word *anthrōpos*, the generic term for "man, human being," but because it stands in parallelism with "woman" in v. 21, it has to be translated here specifically as "a man." See further 22:57,58,60.

sowed. Lit. "tossed into his garden"; the Lucan phrase sounds as if the man's action were less deliberate than the Matthean description of it, "sowed in his field." According to *m. Kil.* 2:9, mustard was not to be grown in a "field," but in 3:2 in a "garden bed." Who has preserved the original of "Q," Luke or Matthew? In either case, it differs from the Marcan phrase, "sown in the ground/earth."

grew to be a tree. Lit. "grew and became into a tree," with the prep. *eis* expressing the goal or end condition. See BDF § 229a-b. For the Septuagintism, *ginesthai eis*, see Gen 20:12, etc. Later on, rabbinic literature knows of the mustard plant growing to the height of a fig tree. See *y. Pe'a* 7.4.

birds of the sky . . . A composite allusion is made to Ps 104:12 (LXX) and Dan 4:9,18. Cf. Greek of the LXX and Theodotion 4:12,22. See NOTE on 8:5. Whether birds could "make nests" in a mustard plant is debated; the OT stereotyped expression is being applied in a literary manner to the mustard plant. The birds are to be understood merely as human beings (in general) who would seek shelter in the kingdom. Despite the allusion to Daniel, where they seem to symbolize the nations of the world, one should beware of allegorizing this OT detail, already present in the tradition prior to both "Q" and "Mk," as meaning the Gentiles. So G. Schneider, *Evangelium nach Lukas*, 302, among others. It is hardly likely that the Lucan Jesus is already thinking of the mission of the disciples to the end of the earth (Acts 1:7-8). Note, moreover, that Luke has not added his favorite adj., "all" (cf. Acts 10:12); it is found in the LXX of Dan 4:21. See A. Alon, *Natural History*, 211-232.

BIBLIOGRAPHY (13:18-19)

Bartsch, H.-W. "Eine bisher übersehene Zitierung der LXX in Mark. 4,30," *TZ* 15 (1959) 126-128.

Bowen, C. R. "The Kingdom and the Mustard Seed," *AJT* 22 (1918) 562-569.

Clark, K. W. "The Mustard Plant," *Classical Weekly* 37 (1943-1944) 81-83.

Crossan, J. D. "The Seed Parables of Jesus," *JBL* 92 (1973) 244-266, esp. 253-259.

Dahl, N. A. "The Parables of Growth," *ST* 5 (1951) 132-166; reprinted in *Jesus in the Memory of the Early Church* (Minneapolis: Augsburg, 1976) 141-166.

Dupont, J. "Les paraboles du sénevé et du levain," *NRT* 89 (1967) 897-913.

Haenchen, E. *Der Weg Jesu*, 180-186.

Hunter, A. M. "The Interpretation of the Parables," *ExpTim* 69 (1957-1958) 100-104.

Jeremias, J. *Parables*, 146-149.

Kuss, O. "Zum Sinngehalt des Doppelgleichnisses vom Senfkorn und Sauerteig," *Bib* 40 (1959) 641-653; reprinted, *Auslegung und Verkündigung*, 1. 85-97.

———— "Zur Senfkornparabel," *TGl* 41 (1951) 40-49; reprinted, *Auslegung und Verkündigung*, 1. 78-84.

McArthur, H. K. "The Parable of the Mustard Seed," *CBQ* 33 (1971) 198-210.

Mussner, F. "1Q Hodajoth und das Gleichnis von Senfkorn (Mk 4,30-32 Par.)," *BZ* 4 (1960) 128-130.

Schultze, B. "Die ekklesiologische Bedeutung des Gleichnis vom Senfkorn (Matth. 13,31-32; Mk. 4,30-32; Lk. 13,18-19)," *Orientalia christiana periodica* 27 (1961) 362-386.

Wenham, D. "The Synoptic Problem Revisited: Some New Suggestions about the Composition of Mark 4:1-34," *Tyndale Bulletin* 23 (1972) 3-38.

Zinng, P. *Das Wachsen der Kirche: Beiträge zur Frage der lukanischen Redaktion und Theologie* (Orbis biblicus et orientalis 3; Göttingen: Vandenhoeck & Ruprecht; Fribourg: Universitätsverlag, 1974) 100-115.

92. THE PARABLE OF THE YEAST
(13:20-21)

13 [20] Again he said, "To what should I compare the kingdom of God? [21] It is like leaven, which a woman took and mixed with three measures of flour until the whole was fermented."

COMMENT

Still another aspect of the kingdom is brought out by Jesus' parable of the yeast, which should more properly be called that of the leaven (13:20-21).

This parable too comes from "Q" and its order is dictated by this source; it has nothing to do with the order of Mark (which lacks this parable completely; see pp. 68-69,81). Apart from the introductory formulas, the wording of the parable in Matthew and Luke is almost identical.

Another form of the parable is found in *Gos. of Thom.* § 96, where it has been recorded quite independently of the parable of the mustard seed; this may, indeed, reflect that the parable once existed apart from the pair used by Luke. "The kingdom of the Father is like a woman; she took a bit of leaven, hid it in dough, (and) made it into big loaves. Whoever has ears take heed." Later development of the tradition is clearly seen in "the kingdom of the Father." Moreover, the point of the parable has changed: the bit of leaven becomes big loaves, and the kingdom itself is likened to a woman. The three measures of flour have disappeared. Is it possibly influenced by 1 Cor 5:6 (see O. Cullmann, "Das Thomasevangelium und die Frage nach dem Alter der in ihm enthaltenen Tradition," *TLZ* 85 [1960] 321-334, esp. 332)? Hardly, since the sense of the Pauline assertion, "a little leaven leavens the whole mass of dough," reflects more the "Q" form of thinking. (See further J.-E. Ménard, *L'Evangile selon Thomas*, 196-197; W. Schrage, *Das Verhältnis*, 183-185.)

The Lucan parable compares the kingdom of God with leaven and alludes to its power to affect the whole lump of dough into which it is mixed (or "hidden"). The kingdom, once present in human history—even in a hidden way, cannot help but leaven the whole of it because of its characteristic active ingredients. Flour is important for bread, but without leaven there is no real bread! Its power is needed above all.

The two parables, stressing the inevitable growth of the kingdom and its active power, thus terminate part *a* of the Lucan travel account (9:51-13:21). There follows the second mention of Jerusalem, which is often used to divide this part of the Lucan Gospel (see p. 825).

NOTES

13   20. *To what should I compare.* See NOTE on 7:31. The rhetorical question here is single; contrast v. 18.

21. *leaven.* See NOTE on 12:1.

mixed. Lit. "hid" or "hid (away) in," depending on whether one reads *ekrypsen* (with mss. B, K, L, N, etc.) or *enekrypsen* (with mss. P⁷⁵, ℵ, A, D, W, Θ, Ψ, etc.). The latter reading, though supported by many of the best mss., is sometimes thought to be influenced by the Matthean parallel, which has *enekrypsen* (13:33).

three measures of flour. Luke retains from "Q" the word *saton* for "measure," a grecized form of Aramaic *sā'tā'*, the equivalent of Hebrew *sĕ'āh*, a common grain measure. See Josephus, *Ant.* 9.4,5 § 85, where he says that a *saton* was the equivalent of one and a half Italian *modii* (cf. *Ant.* 9.4,4 § 71), i.e. about a peck and a half. The woman was using a sizable amount of flour; this enhances the power of the leaven. But "three measures" may be a stereotyped expression; see Gen 18:6.

fermented. Or "leavened."

BIBLIOGRAPHY (13:20-21)

Allis, O. T. "The Parable of the Leaven," *EvQ* 19 (1947) 254-273.

Funk, R. W. "Beyond Criticism in Quest of Literacy: The Parable of the Leaven," *Int* 25 (1971) 149-170.

Schulz, S. *Q: Die Spruchquelle*, 307-309.

Waller, E. "The Parable of the Leaven: A Sectarian Teaching and the Inclusion of Women," *USQR* 35 (1979-1980) 99-109.

b. From the Second to the Third Mention of Jerusalem
as Destination (13:22-17:10)

93. RECEPTION AND REJECTION IN
THE KINGDOM
(13:22-30)

13 ²² Jesus continued on his journey through towns and villages, teaching and making his way toward Jerusalem. ²³ Once someone asked him, "Sir, is it true that only a few are to be saved?" He said to him, ²⁴ "Strive to enter through the narrow door, for many, I tell you, will seek to get in, but will not be able—²⁵ especially once the master of the house gets up and locks the door. Then you may stand outside, knock at the door, and cry, 'Open up for us, Sir!' But he will only answer, 'I do not know you or where you are from.' ²⁶ Then you will start saying, 'We ate and drank with you, and you taught us in our streets.' ²⁷ Yet he will only say to you, 'I do not know you or where you are from. *Depart from me, all doers of evil.'* [a] ²⁸ Then there will be weeping and grinding of teeth there, when you will see Abraham, Isaac, and Jacob, and all the prophets in the kingdom of God, and yourselves thrown out. ²⁹ Then people will come *from the east and the west, from the north* [b] and the south and will recline at table in the kingdom of God. ³⁰ Yes, some of those who are now last will be first, and some of those first will be last."

[a] Ps 6:9   [b] Ps 107:3

COMMENT

Luke begins the second part of his travel account (part *b* in the outline on p. 139) with a group of Jesus' utterances about salvation and reception or non-reception into the kingdom (13:22-30). In effect, these utterances set a tone for the entire second part; they are also closely connected with the two final parables which ended the first part, in that they too deal with the kingdom.

R. Bultmann *(HST* 130) calls these utterances a Lucan "eschatological discourse." Whether that is the right way to label them or not—I should prefer a "kingdom discourse"—Bultmann is certainly right in viewing vv. 22-30 as composed "from all sorts of pieces of information" in the tradition; it is scarcely a "homogeneous discourse," *pace* M.-J. Lagrange, *Luc,* 387.

As a unit, the episode has been fashioned by Luke. But out of what? It is introduced by two verses which appear only in this Gospel. At first sight, one might think that they have been derived from "L," but the introductory v. 22 is almost certainly of Lucan composition (see *HST* 334). It is a summary statement of the evangelist, using his characteristic language (see NOTES and p. 80).

Verse 23 is more problematic. T. W. Manson regarded it as part of "Q" *(Sayings,* 124); and others as pre-Lucan (see I. H. Marshall, *Luke,* 563; M.-J. Lagrange, *Luc,* 388). But it too is best explained as a question ascribed to an unnamed listener fashioned by Luke himself to introduce the traditional material which follows (so *FTG* 162; S. Schulz, *Q: Die Spruchquelle,* 310).

The material in vv. 24-29 has some parallels in Matthean passages; but the relationship differs with each verse. Verse 24 has a counterpart in the Matthean sermon on the mount (7:13-14), where Jesus speaks of two gates and two ways which lead to life or destruction. The Lucan form speaks only of a "narrow door," and it is linked to vv. 25-27a by catchword bonding; both have to do with a "door." Luke may have modified his source to create this bond. The "narrow door" of v. 24, however, becomes in vv. 25-27a a locked door. As Bultmann put it, "the door in v. 25 is quite different from that in v. 24 where the *polloi* ["many"] certainly do not seek this door [i.e. the one locked in v. 25]" *(HST* 130).

Verses 25-27 resemble part of the parable of the ten virgins in Matt 25:10-12 (actually only the cry, "Open up for us, Sir!") and part of the sermon on the mount again in Matt 7:23 (actually the use of Ps 6:9). Otherwise v. 25 is peculiar to Luke; it may have come from his source. Matthew has none of this, because of the parable of the ten virgins (see I. H. Marshall, *Luke,* 563). These Lucan verses, moreover, have a bond in the answer which comes from the house-master within, "I do not know you or where you are from." Some commentators (e.g. J. Jeremias; F. Mussner; A. Denaux; G. Schneider, *Evangelium nach Lukas,* 306) even regard these verses as parable-like; but that judgment is too much influenced by the Matthean parallel.

The closest parallel with Matthean material is found in vv. 28-29 (= Matt 8:11-12). These Lucan verses are joined to the preceding utterance only in a loose way, and Luke has probably inverted the order of the sayings to associate the weeping and grinding of teeth with the evil-doers of v. 27.

Though I ascribe vv. 24-29 to "Q" (see p. 78), along with a number of others (G. Schneider, E. Hirsch, R. A. Edwards), I have to admit that the parallel Matthean material is at times quite diverse. How much of the difference is to be ascribed to Matthean redaction, or to Lucan redaction—or, in the extreme, to the use rather of "L"—who can say? T. W. Manson went so far as to attribute the Matthean counterparts of vv. 24-27 to "M" *(Sayings,* 124); and others have suggested that Matthew combined "Q" with "M." There is no certainty that vv. 24-29 formed a unit in "Q."

Finally, v. 30 contains an attached isolated saying, which is now given a contextual sense that it probably did not have in its original setting (in Stage I of the gospel tradition). It has been derived by Luke from "L" (see p. 82 for a discussion of the passage in relation to his avoidance of doublets).

Form-critically considered, most of the utterances recorded in this passage are to be explained as minatory sayings of Jesus. Bultmann *(HST* 93) was inclined to regard v. 24 as a wisdom-saying (but I should hesitate to include v. 23 with it, as he seems to). It serves, nevertheless, to introduce the minatory sayings that follow. Verse 30 is problematic; Bultmann *(HST* 117) could not decide whether it was a wisdom- or minatory saying. As it appears in the Lucan context, it is minatory.

In the course of his teaching, while en route to Jerusalem, Jesus is asked how many will share in the salvation promised in the kingdom: Are only a few to be saved? The question comes out of a background belief among Palestinian Jews that "all Israelites have a share in the world to come" *(m. Sanh.* 10:1). What, then, would be the relation of human beings to the kingdom that Jesus was preaching? Jesus does not answer the question directly. He gives rather a practical warning that people should strive or struggle to enter the kingdom by its "narrow door." This is Jesus' concern; he leaves to God himself the answer about how many will find salvation. He puts emphasis instead on the effort that human beings will have to exert to get in. Verse 24b adds another consideration: Many will not succeed in entering, and the explanation comes from the following verses; they will try to get in only when it is already too late for them. Jesus hints at the traffic-jam situation before the narrow door, but continues that the door may also be found to be closed before such persons realize.

The connection between vv. 24 and 25 is not clear (see NOTES); but in any case v. 25 makes it plain that entry into the kingdom will also depend on the master of the house (i.e. the master of the kingdom, as emerges in v. 28). What was a narrow door has become a door which the master within can close and lock in order to keep out those whom he does not know. It is a door not only to the kingdom of salvation, but to the joys of its festive banquet. The master is indirectly identified as Jesus himself (not God, as Matt 25:12 might suggest), for those outside appeal to him as contemporaries who shared food with him and listened to his teaching. Still the answer comes, "I do not know you or where you are from" (v. 27b). Jesus' teaching in these utterances plays upon the OT idea of people being known by God (see Jer 1:5; Amos 3:2; Hos 5:3; 13:5), i.e. those who are his chosen ones (cf. Ps 138:6). In this case the master not only denies that he knows them, but positively excludes them: "Depart from me, all doers of evil," quoting Ps 6:9.

In vv. 28-29 the notion of the door, narrow or closed, has completely disappeared; the theme has become the joyous banquet of the kingdom at which those admitted recline with the master, the patriarchs of Israel of old, and all the prophets. Those admitted will be people who come not only from among Jesus' contemporaries who have striven to walk through the narrow door while it was still open, but also people from east and west, north and south (in an allusion to Ps 107:3). The joy of those admitted to the banquet of the kingdom is contrasted with the weeping and grinding of teeth of those locked out. Verse 28 expresses in terms of exclusion what v. 29 does in terms of inclusion.

Verse 28c speaks of "yourselves thrown out." Who are they? The Matthean counterpart of vv. 28-29 (Matt 8:11-12) envisages evil Christian disciples. But the Lucan form of the sayings envisages some of Jesus' Palestinian contemporaries. In order to enter the door of the kingdom, the Lucan Jesus warns, one needs more than the superficial acquaintance of a contemporary (v. 26b); one has to reckon with the narrowness of the door and the contest-like struggle (= effort) to get through it. Understood against the background of Jesus' earlier call for timely reform (13:3,5), this warning about how many will get into the kingdom before the master has closed the door puts that call in a new light. See p. 150.

The people coming from the four winds will be admitted into the banquet of the kingdom with the patriarchs and prophets of old and will thus join reconstituted Israel (see further p. 58). These new people are Gentiles in the Lucan view; but Jesus' utterances do not mean that none of his Palestinian Jewish contemporaries succeeded in entering by the narrow door. They say only that "many" would "not be able" to do so. Those who did succeed belong to reconstituted Israel, now to be joined by the Gentiles from the four winds.

Does the formulation of these vv. 28-29 go back to Jesus himself (in Stage I)? This is difficult to say. We have already noted the difference of order of the sayings in Luke and Matthew. Moreover, the relation of Gentiles and Jews in the kingdom may reflect much more of the early community's preoccupation with it than Jesus' own. But does the warning about the Gentiles and the kingdom have "no reference to the Person of Jesus"? So R. Bultmann (HST 116) puts it. That may well be somewhat exaggerated.

Lastly, v. 30 shows that the kingdom brings into human relations a reversal, for it turns upside down all human calculations. "Some of those who are now last will be first, and some of those first will be last." This reversal echoes in its own way what was said by Simeon about the child Jesus, destined for the fall and rise of many in Israel (see pp. 422-423).

NOTES

13 22. *continued on his journey.* Lit. "was making his way through." Luke employs the impf. of continuous action, *dieporeueto* (cf. 6:1; 18:36), a compound of *poreuesthai,* "go, move along, proceed on one's way," the vb. often used to express Jesus' journey. See pp. 167, 169, and NOTE on 9:56. The verse alludes to 9:51; it has nothing to do with John 10:22-23 and gives no firm chronological or geographical data.

through towns and villages. Luke uses the pl. of the phrase employed in 8:1. See NOTE there. The distributive sense of the prep. *kata* is almost exclusively Lucan in the NT, though it does occur in Titus 1:5. This phrase is a vague introduction, characteristic of other Lucan summaries. It is not even clear whether it is to be taken with the preceding vb. or the following ptc.

teaching. See NOTES on 4:15,31; cf. p. 148.

making his way toward Jerusalem. Luke repeats the idea expressed in the main vb., but uses the abstract *poreia,* "journey," with the middle voice ptc. of *poiein* as a classical literary substitute for mere *poreuomenos.* See ZBG § 227; BDF § 310.1; cf. NOTE on 5:33. See further A. J. C. M., *"Poieisthai: poiein*—Sur les critères déterminant le choix entre l'actif *poiein* et le moyen *poieisthai,"* *Mnemosyne* 34 (1981) 1-62.

Jerusalem. The form of the name is *Hierosolyma* (see NOTES on 2:22; 10:30; and p. 824) in the best mss. (P[75], ℵ, B, L, 892); some others (A, D, W, and the Koine text-tradition) read *Ierousalēm.*

23. *Sir.* See NOTE on 5:12; cf. p. 203. Jesus is addressed by an unnamed interrogator, asking about his "teaching." Cf. 9:57; 11:1,27,45; 12:13.

is it true that only a few are to be saved? Jesus' interrogator puts a theoretical question to him. The phraseology makes one think of 1 Cor 1:18, reflecting an early Christian discussion, but the question may well have come out of a Palestinian Jewish background. In the COMMENT I have quoted a Jewish belief recorded in the Mishnah *(Sanh.* 10:1). That could be compared with *4 Ezra* 8:1, "This age the Most High has made for many, but the age to come for few" *(APOT* 2. 592). Cf. *4 Ezra* 7:47; 9:15 ("There are more who perish than shall be saved, even as the flood is greater than a drop"); Isa 60:21. The question has to be understood in the Lucan context as prepared for by Jesus' call for timely reform (13:3,5).

The direct question is introduced by *ei,* which usually means "if," but which can introduce an indirect question, "whether." Its use in a direct question is not known in classical Greek, but is a Septuagintism (Gen 17:17; 44:19; Amos 3:3-6; 6:12; cf. BDF § 440.3; ZBG § 401). Further Lucan examples are found in 14:3 (as a variant reading); 22:49; Acts 1:6; 7:1; 19:2.

He said to him. The typically Lucan expression *eipen pros* + acc. is used again. See p. 116.

24. *Strive to enter through the narrow door.* I.e. through the only door to the kingdom there is. Jesus' warning makes use of the language of a contest *(agōn)* or struggle in order to stress the need of effort to walk into the kingdom through the narrow door. The path to salvation is not through a wide, open entrance. The call for timely reform (13:3,5) is now cast in terms of a narrowness of entrance through which only a few can

pass at any one time. It is not yet said whether the striving will succeed in opening the door; nor are we yet told who opens it.

Some mss. (A, W, Ψ, and the Koine text-tradition) read *pylēs*, "gate," but this is a copyist's harmonization with Matt 7:13.

many . . . will not be able. So Jesus answers indirectly the question put to him. Many may crowd before the narrow door, but not all of them will succeed in passing through it.

I tell you. The simple *legō hymin* is used here, as in 7:9,28; 10:12,24; 11:8,9; 12:4,8; 13:35.

25. *especially once the master of the house gets up and locks the door.* Now it becomes apparent that the door is also controlled by the master within. To the narrowness of the door is added a warning not to wait until the last minute, for salvation in the kingdom is gained through a door that the master opens for those whom he knows. Jesus' words add a temporal dimension. All human striving may be too late, if it comes only at the last minute. At the moment it is not clear who the master is, God or Jesus; v. 26 will clarify that. For *egerthē*, "gets up," see NOTE on 7:14.

The transition from v. 24 to v. 25 is problematic. Verse 25 begins with a temporal prepositional phrase *aph' hou an . . .* lit. "from (the time) when/at which . . ." See BAGD 87a. Does it introduce a subordinate cl. following upon v. 24 (which should end with a comma), or does it introduce a subordinate cl., the apodosis of which is *kai apokritheis erei,* "But he will only answer"? The problem is compounded by the possibility that vv. 25-27 come originally from an entirely separate context and are here only loosely joined to the preceding saying. I have joined these vv. 25-27 loosely to the foregoing with a dash. See further M.-J. Lagrange, *Luc,* 388-389; E. Klostermann, *Lukasevangelium,* 146.

Then you may stand outside . . . Lit. "and you will begin to stand outside and knock at the door, saying." This cl. is actually coordinate to the preceding, both being introduced by *aph' hou.* The additional description creates a dramatic scenario.

Open up for us, Sir! The cry resembles that of the five foolish virgins in Matt 25:10c, "Sir, Sir, open up for us." Some Lucan mss. (A, D, W, Θ, Ψ, and the Koine text-tradition) add a second *kyrie,* undoubtedly the result of a copyist's harmonization with Matthew.

I do not know you or where you are from. Lit. "I do not know you, whence you are." The same remark is repeated in v. 27. The master of the house rejects those whom he does not know. In the present Lucan context it adds another reason why the "many" will not be able to enter: the door is not only narrow, but it is controlled by the master within.

26. *Then you will start saying.* The best reading is *arxesthe,* "you will start" (fut. indic. middle); but many mss. (א, A, D, K, L, N, W, etc.) read *arxēsthe* (aor. subjunc. middle), which is the same as the vb. in v. 25b. In an independent sentence the latter is strange; but it does not affect the sense.

We ate and drank with you. I.e. we are your acquaintances and contemporaries, seen by you at table and taught by you in the streets. What do you mean, You do not know us! The master's answer stresses that more than superficial acquaintance is needed.

27. *Depart from me, all doers of evil.* Luke writes *apostēte ap' emou pantes ergatai adikias,* whereas a slightly different form is found in the LXX of Ps 6:9, *apostēte ap'*

emou, pantes hoi ergazomenoi tēn anomian, "Depart from me, all (you) practicing lawlessness." The suffering psalmist, whose prayer has been heard by Yahweh, charges his adversaries to leave him. The psalmist's words are now used in a minatory dismissal. Matt 7:23 reads instead: *apochōreite ap' emou hoi ergazomenoi tēn anomian,* which is closer to the LXX (except for the vb. and the absence of "all"). Which was the form in "Q"? P. Hoffmann thinks the Matthean was and that Luke has restored *pantes,* changed *anomia* to *adikia* (cf. Luke 16:8 bis; 18:6; Acts 1:18; 8:23—never used by Matthew) and the ptc. to *ergatai.* Cf. Luke 10:2,7; 13:27; Acts 19:25 (also used by Matthew!). Cf. 1 Macc 3:6.

28. *weeping and grinding of teeth.* This phrase occurs also in the Matthean parallel (8:12b). Matthew, however, has added it elsewhere (13:42,50; 22:13; 24:51; 25:30).

you will see Abraham, Isaac, and Jacob. The three patriarchs of Israel occur again in Acts 3:13; 7:32. Cf. Matt 8:11. The threesome occurs frequently in the OT (Deut 1:8; 6:10; 9:5,27; 1 Kgs 18:36; 2 Kgs 13:23).

all the prophets. Matt 8:11 does not include these OT figures; and they were most likely not part of "Q." The phrase is never used in Mark or John, and it appears only once in Matthew (11:13). However, it occurs several times in Lucan writings (11:50; 24:27; Acts 3:18,24; 10:43). So Luke has added it redactionally to his source. See also E. Klostermann, *Lukasevangelium,* 147.

in the kingdom of God. The phrase is understood in a spatial sense. See p. 156. Thus Luke (and his source) have related the forebears of Israel to the main theme of Jesus' preaching. Inside the house of the kingdom all is joy, quite different from the weeping and grinding of teeth, the condition of those "outside" and "there" *(ekei,* v. 28). See pp. 153-156, 190.

and yourselves thrown out. In Matt 8:12 those excluded are the "children of the kingdom," i.e. those destined to inherit it. In the Lucan context they are those who boast of being contemporaries of the master of the house (or kingdom). Cf. Rev 11:2.

29. *people will come.* Matt 8:11 says that "many" will come from the east and the west. Luke, however, because he has used the saying with "many" failing to get into the kingdom in v. 24, now deletes the *polloi* here.

from the east and the west, from the north. This much of the geographical origins of the newcomers is derived from Ps 107:3. It is likely that one should also add "and the south" to that allusion. The difficulty is that the Hebrew text of Ps 107:3 ends with "and from the sea," *ûmiyyam* (lit. translated in the LXX as *kai thalassēs).* The Hebrew text seems to be corrupt in its transmission, since "from the sea" would mean "from the west" (an area already mentioned in the Hebrew text). The same reading is found in 4QPsᶠ (as yet unpublished; information courtesy of E. C. Ulrich). *Ûmiyyām* should probably be read as *ûmiyyāmîn* (two letters having been lost in copying), "from the south." Hence "and the south" is scarcely a Lucan redactional addition, *pace* E. Klostermann, *Lukasevangelium,* 147. For similar OT phrases, see Isa 49:12; 43:5-6. Could some sea to the "south" be meant in these OT passages?

will recline at table in the kingdom. I.e. and share in the eschatological banquet to be provided by God for his chosen ones. See the OT motif and its development in Isa 25:6-8; 55:1-2; 65:13-14; *1 Enoch* 62:14; *2 Bar.* 29:4; *Pirqe 'Aboth* 3:20. Luke alludes to it again in 14:15; 22:16,29-30; cf. Rev 3:20; 19:9.

30. *Yes.* Lit. "and behold" (introductory *kai idou,* see p. 121).

some of those who are now last will be first. The expression lacks any definite articles; hence not all those who are last. This saying is similar to that preserved in Mark 10:31, "But many who are first will be last, and the last first" (= Matt 19:30). The Lucan form is, however, closer to Matt 20:16, but it inverts the order of last/first. Luke's form stresses that some of the newcomers (the last) will be considered more important than old-timers.

On a possible echo of v. 30 in *Gos. of Thom.* § 4, see p. 86.

BIBLIOGRAPHY (13:22-30)

Dupont, J. " 'Beaucoup viendront du levant et du couchant . . .' (Matthieu 8,11-12; Luc 13,28-29)," *ScEccl* 19 (1967) 153-167.

Grässer, E. *Parusieverzögerung,* 192-193.

Grimm, W. "Zum Hintergrund von Mt 8, 11f/Lk 13, 28f," *BZ* 16 (1972) 255-256.

Hoffmann, P. *"Pantes ergatai adikias:* Redaktion und Tradition in Lc 13,22-30," *ZNW* 58 (1967) 188-214.

Mees, M. "Ausserkanonische Parallelstellen zu den Gerichtsworten *Mt.* 7,21-23; *Lk.* 6,46; 13,26-28 und ihre Bedeutung für die Formung der Jesusworte," *Vetera christianorum* 10 (1973) 79-102.

Mussner, F. "Das 'Gleichnis' vom gestrengen Mahlherrn (Lk 13,22-30): Ein Beitrag zum Redaktionsverfahren und zur Theologie des Lukas," *TTZ* 65 (1956) 129-143; reprinted, *Praesentia salutis,* 113-124.

Packett, E. B. "Luke 13:25," *ExpTim* 67 (1955-1956) 178.

Rosaz, M. "Passer sur l'autre rive," *Christus* 26 (1979) 323-332.

Schulz, S. *Q: Die Spruchquelle,* 309-312, 323-336.

Schwarz, G. "Matthäus VII 13a: Ein Alarmruf angesichts höchster Gefahr," *NovT* 12 (1970) 229-232.

Seynaeve, J. "La parabole de la porte étroite: L'Acceptation 'pratique' du Christ, Lc 13,22-30," *AsSeign* 52 (1974) 68-77.

Zeller, D. "Das Logion Mt 8,11f/Lk 13,28f und das Motiv der 'Völkerwallfahrt,' " *BZ* 15 (1971) 222-237; 16 (1972) 84-93.

94. HEROD'S DESIRE TO KILL JESUS; HIS DEPARTURE FROM GALILEE
(13:31-33)

13 ³¹ At that very time some Pharisees came and said to Jesus, "Leave here and move on, because Herod would like to kill you." ³² He said to them, "Go tell that fox, 'Look, I shall be casting out demons and healing people today and tomorrow; and on the third day

I shall reach my goal.' [33] But today, tomorrow, and the next day, I must keep on my way, because it is impossible that a prophet will perish outside of Jerusalem."

COMMENT

Next in Luke's travel account comes a report about Herod's seeking to kill Jesus and the latter's significant reaction to it and its place in his own destiny (13:31-33). The passage is exclusive to the Third Gospel.

There seems to be a consensus among commentators that the report of the Pharisees to Jesus about Herod's attitude toward him is a piece of authentic tradition rooted in Stage I of the gospel material. V. Taylor *(FGT* 158) speaks of the episode's "freshness of originality," and even A. Denaux, who espouses the theory of Lucan redaction for the bulk of the episode, admits an authentic kernel in it ("L'Hypocrisie"). Cf. J. B. Tyson, "Jesus and Herod Antipas." But Denaux's evidence for his theory of Lucan redaction is not that cogent. It is better to regard this episode as derived by the evangelist from his source "L," which he has embedded in material from "Q" both preceding and following (13:24-29 and 13:34-35). Denaux rightly thinks that, though this episode and the following one are closely linked in the present Lucan Gospel, they did not exist together in a pre-Lucan stage. What Luke has derived from "L" he introduces with a temporal phrase of his own (v. 31a). (See further M. Rese ["Einige"].)

Form-critically considered, this episode is to be regarded as a pronouncement-story. Bultmann *(HST* 35) classed it among his biographical apophthegms. Actually, in its present form it is a narrative with two pronouncements, one in v. 32 and the other in v. 33. In analyzing the episode Bultmann suggests two possibilities: Either the real pronouncement is in v. 32, and v. 33 is an added "unattached saying" (added because of the catchword bonding, "today, tomorrow . . ."), or v. 32b ("Look . . .") is a later secondary addition to vv. 31,32a,33. The former alternative seems the more likely. However, V. Taylor *(FGT* 75, 153) preferred to classify this episode as a story about Jesus, because, he thought, the interest lay rather in the narrative incident than in the pronouncement(s). Given the collocation of this episode immediately after the second reference to Jesus' journey to Jerusalem in this account (13:22), Luke's interest in it clearly lies in the goal (v. 32) or in the keeping of Jesus on the way to the city of destiny (v. 33). Hence, the episode in its present form is best regarded as a pronouncement-story with a double pronouncement. One could, however, further debate whether v. 33 was really part of "L" or stems from Lucan composition, as a sort of commentary on v. 32, which it parallels (in part at least).

H. Conzelmann *(Theology,* 68) recognizes the importance of this episode for the geographical perspective of the Lucan Gospel. The tradition enshrined in it not only presupposes a stay of Jesus in Galilee and a connection with Herod (recall 9:9; cf. 23:6-12), but it may even reflect the reason for Jesus' departure from Galilee and the journey to Jerusalem in the first place. Conzelmann is right, however, in insisting that the notice given here is not merely the report of a stage of the journey, but that it expresses the theological necessity of the journey, and one of fairly long duration. Its purpose is not merely to note a change of locale, but to stress the inevitability of Jesus' reaching a place of suffering (and of death). This is part of his destiny, and someone like Herod is not to stand in the way of it. The note of necessity leads to the lament of Jesus over Jerusalem in the next episode because "Jesus will not only be killed *in* Jerusalem, but *through* Jerusalem" (G. Schneider, *Evangelium nach Lukas,* 309). This gives to the present episode its real significance in the Lucan travel account.

Precisely at the time when Jesus had warned his contemporaries that they would not be guaranteed access to the kingdom merely because of superficial acquaintance with him (13:26-28), he is warned about a contemporary's desire to do away with him. Herod had already imprisoned and beheaded John the Baptist (3:19-20; 9:9a), and Jesus was aware of this. Herod's own curiosity about Jesus (9:9c) was not explained earlier; now it is unmasked. Later on, it will be explained (23:8), but Herod will make no attempt to preserve Jesus from the "chief priests and the Scribes" (23:10), will treat Jesus with contempt, and will send him back to Pilate (23:11). The Pharisees who report this desire of Herod to Jesus now urge him to move on. Jesus' uncompromising reply makes use of an unflattering term about the tetrarch of Galilee, the holder of political power, summing up his estimate of Herod's character and expressing his defiance of Herod's pretensions. Though Jesus does not trust Herod, he uses the warning to make a fundamental declaration about his own ministry and journey. He will go on teaching and freeing human beings from evil until he reaches his "goal" or destiny (v. 32). His ministry has no political connotations (recall 4:43), and he will continue, not out of fear of Herod, a political authority, but because he *must*—because he is subject to another authority.

No hint is given in v. 32 about the nature of that goal, but the added pronouncement in v. 33 hints at a possible end of his journey and ministry: he may share a prophet's end in the city toward which he has been moving with resolute determination (9:51). Jesus' role as a prophet moving along his way to Jerusalem thus emerges very clearly in this episode (see pp. 213-215).

We raised above the possibility that v. 33 might be redacted at least by Luke. When one reads that verse, coming on the heels of v. 32 (with its own suggestions about Jesus' "end"), one cannot help but wonder how much of all this can be traced back to Jesus of Nazareth himself in Stage I of the gospel tradition. This is difficult to say. In Stage III Luke has clearly depicted Jesus moving resolutely toward Jerusalem (9:51) and now referring to it as a place to which he *must* proceed before his end/goal is reached and as a place outside of which a prophet will not perish. There is a clear intimation of Jesus' end as a prophet's death. This is the picture of the Lucan Jesus, sketched with hindsight by the evangelist. How much of it can be traced back to Jesus himself? See p. 778.

NOTES

13 31. *At that very time.* A Lucanism, allegedly an Aramaism. See pp. 117-118. So Luke joins this episode with the preceding, and with this stage of the travel account. If the story, taken in isolation, implies that Jesus is still in Herod's territory, it may reflect why he originally left Galilee. In the Lucan context, however, it serves another purpose.

some Pharisees. Otherwise unnamed. Whence do they come? Are they to be understood as coming from Jerusalem, the city to which Jesus is headed? This is not likely. In 5:17 (see NOTE there) there were Pharisees among those who came to listen to him from every village of Galilee and Judea and from Jerusalem. Cf. 6:17. If there is anything authentic in their report to Jesus about Herod's desire, one would expect that they would be coming from his territory (3:1; 23:7). A. Denaux ("L'Hypocrisie," 261-263) has painted too black a picture of Luke's pejorative attitude toward the Pharisees. Their report is not simply a mark of their "hypocrisy." That is as bad an interpretation of this phrase as that suggested by older commentators that the Pharisees told Jesus about Herod's desire in order to lure him to Jerusalem so that he might fall more easily into their hands there than in Galilee. One must recall that for Luke Christianity in the long run is a logical sequel to Pharisaic Judaism (see the end of Acts); this does not prevent him from listing Pharisees at times among the adversaries of Jesus. But here he says *tines Pharisaioi,* "some Pharisees," and they are depicted giving Jesus sage advice; these at least are well disposed toward him. Jesus' own remark in the episode is directed not against them, but against Herod. Though the Lucan Jesus does speak of hypocrisy as the leaven of the Pharisees (12:1), he never directs the term "hypocrites" at them. See 12:56; 13:15; and NOTES there. Moreover, there is no reason to think that these Pharisees are emissaries of Herod himself; such a connection is not apparent in the text. Indeed, J. B. Tyson ("Jesus and Herod Antipas," 245) plausibly argues for the historicity of this incident from the fact that Pharisees appear here not as antagonists of Jesus but as friends.

Herod. Herod Antipas, tetrarch of Galilee. See NOTES on 3:1; 9:7. In the Lucan story Jesus has already left his territory, but problems with Palestinian geography will occur again (see 17:11); Luke's knowledge of it is not to be pressed. Herod himself does not appear here; he may be presumed to be enjoying his "love of tranquillity" (see Josephus, *Ant.* 18.7,2 § 245) in his own territory. See p. 89.

would like to kill you. Lit. "wishes to kill you." By sheer coincidence these words echo those said about Herod apropos of John the Baptist (Mark 6:19). For a different view of this matter, see A. Denaux, "L'Hypocrisie," 265-268.

32. *Go tell that fox.* This is not a command that Jesus gives to the Pharisees whom he would send back, but rather his rhetorical comment on their warning and the situation that faces him. He sees through Herod's character.

In both classical and Hellenistic Greek *alōpex,* "fox," was an epithet for a crafty or sly person. See Pindar, *Pyth. Od.* 2.77-78; Plato, *Resp.* 2.8 § 365c; Plutarch, *Solon* 30.2; Epictetus, *Diatr.* 1.3,7-8). In the OT *šû'āl* is used of foolish prophets (Ezek 13:4); but in rabbinic literature it later carries the Greek connotation. See Str-B 2. 200-201. M. Dibelius *(FTG* 162-163) thinks that Jesus would hardly have used the epithet and that it betrays Luke's interest in the great ones of the earth. Possible, but far from certain! It is, moreover, farfetched to think that "fox" is used with further connotations of a contrast with "lion"—or of Saul with David, *pace* W. Grimm. For *poreutheis* + finite vb., see p. 115.

casting out demons and healing people. So Jesus sums up his ministry in contrast to the threat on his life; he will not stop the ministry to others out of fear of Herod. The pres. tense is used here with a fut. nuance. See C. F. D. Moule, *Idiom Book,* 7; cf. BDF § 323. On "demons," see NOTE on 4:33.

today and tomorrow. I.e. for a time yet, day by day. Cf. LXX of Exod 19:10 *(sēmeron kai aurion,* followed in v. 11 by *tē gar hēmera tē tritē).*

on the third day. See NOTE on 9:22.

I shall reach my goal. Lit. ". . . I am brought to an end," i.e. by God (the theological pass., see NOTE on 5:20). For the fut. sense of the pres. tense, see above.

In what sense is this "end" to be understood? Luke had used *teleioun* in 2:43 in a temporal sense, of completing a period time; in Acts 20:24 he uses it in a spatial sense: Paul "finishes" his course *(dromon,* "race"). The spatial sense could be meant here: on the third day Jesus will be brought to the end/goal of his journey; he will reach the city of destiny. Is it possible that the Lucan Jesus means more: "being brought to the end/goal of my life"? Given the opening verse of the travel account, with its reference to his being "taken up" (9:51), and the allusion to his "departure" *(exodos)* in the transfiguration scene (9:31), it is not impossible that he is hinting at this sense of end/goal here. For a non-telic interpretation of this saying, see J. Wellhausen, *Das Evangelium Lucae,* 75-76. In any case, one should not import into the meaning of *teleioun* the sense of "perfecting" found in Heb 5:9; 7:28; 9:9; 10:1.

33. *But.* Luke again uses the strong adversative *plēn.* See p. 111.

today, tomorrow. This phrase repeats that of v. 32. There is no justification in any of the mss. for W. Grundmann's suggestion that the phrase be dropped here and that the following phrase be understood as "on the fourth day" *(Evangelium nach Lukas,* 289). Cf. J. M. Creed, *The Gospel,* 187. This phrase acquires further meaning as a commentary on that of v. 32.

and the next day. Lit. "on the immediately following [day, *hēmera* being understood]." Luke uses the pres. ptc. middle of *echein,* "have," in the sense of "clinging" in a stereotyped phrase (see Acts 20:15; 2 Macc 12:39), also known in extrabiblical Greek (Josephus, *Ant.* 6.11,9 § 235; 7.1,3 § 18). Cf. MM 270.

I must keep on my way. Lit. "it is necessary for me to move along." See pp. 179-180 for the nuance of necessity expressed in impers. *dei;* the terminology is heavily Lucan. See pp. 112, 168-169, 824; NOTES on 4:30; 9:31.

it is impossible. The vb. *endechesthai* occurs only here in the NT; it is used impersonally, "it is possible," as in 2 Macc 11:18; Josephus, *Ant.* 9.10 § 210; and in Greek papyri. See MM 212. For an attempt to give this vb. the meaning, "it is not appropriate," see T. W. Manson, *Sayings,* 277. The "impossibility" will be echoed in another way in 22:22.

that a prophet will perish outside of Jerusalem. I.e. it is not destined that Herod will kill me, but that Jerusalem will. Behind this statement lies a traditional belief about the fate of various prophetic figures in the city of Jerusalem. Possibly envisaged is the killing of the prophet Uriah in Jerusalem by King Jehoiakim (Jer 26:20-23); or the attempt on Jeremiah's life in Jerusalem (Jer 38:4-6)—or even on Amos' life (Amos 7:10-17), though that took place in Bethel, not in Jerusalem. There is also the story of the Jerusalem-slaying of Zechariah (2 Chr 24:20-22; see NOTE on 11:51), who later becomes a prophet (son of Berechiah, see Zech 1:1; cf. Matt 23:35 and still later traditions). There is also the embellishment of an OT story about King Manasseh. He shed much innocent blood "till he had filled Jerusalem from one end to another" (2 Kgs 21:16; cf. 24:4). This account becomes in later tradition a story of his polluting the Temple and the city and of his killing all the righteous people among the Hebrews: "He spared not even the prophets, some of whom he slaughtered daily, so that Jerusalem ran with blood" (Josephus, *Ant.* 10.3,1 § 38). In still later legends there is the story of the killing of the prophet Isaiah. See *Mart. Isa.* 5:1-14 *(APOT* 2. 162); Justin Martyr, *Dial. cum Tryph.* 120. 14-15. All of this has to be recalled against the background of the more generic murder of prophets, not necessarily in Jerusalem. See 1 Kgs 18:4,13; 19:10,14 (interpreted by A. Denaux as applicable here in terms of Jesus as Elijah, but that is farfetched). Cf. Str-B 1. 943.

Whatever the allusion may be, the Lucan Jesus refers to himself in these words as *a* prophet, as one who is to perish in Jerusalem. Herod will not interfere, for Jerusalem, Jesus' goal, has the first claim on him as a heaven-sent mouthpiece of God. See further pp. 219-220; and NOTE on 4:24.

Jerusalem. The form of the Greek name is *Ierousalēm,* as it will again appear in v. 34. See p. 824 and NOTES on 2:22; 10:30.

BIBLIOGRAPHY (13:31-33)

Blinzler, J. *Herodes Antipas und Jesus Christus* (Stuttgart: Katholisches Bibelwerk, 1947) 16-20.

Bunn, L. H. "Herod Antipas and 'That Fox,' " *ExpTim* 43 (1931-1932) 380-381.

Denaux, A. "L'Hypocrisie des Pharisiens et le dessein de Dieu: Analyse de Lc., XIII, 31-33," *L'Evangile de Luc* (ed. F. Neirynck) 245-285.

Farley, F. A. "A Text (Luke xiii. 33)," *ExpTim* 34 (1922-1923) 429-430.

Ferraro, G. " 'Oggi e domani e il terzo giorno' (osservazioni su *Luca* 13,32,33)," *RivB* 16 (1968) 397-407.

Gilbert, A. H. *"Sēmeron kai aurion, kai tē tritē* (Luke 13:32)," *JBL* 35 (1916) 315-318.

Grimm, W. "Eschatologischer Saul wider eschatologischen David: Eine Deutung von Lc. xiii 31 ff," *NovT* 15 (1973) 114-133.

Hoehner, H. W. *Herod Antipas* (Grand Rapids, MI: Zondervan, 1980) 191, 202, 214-218.

Jeremias, J. "Die Drei-Tage-Worte der Evangelien," *Tradition und Glaube* (ed. G. Jeremias) 221-229.

Lehmann, M. *Synoptische Quellenanalyse und die Frage nach dem historischen Jesus: Kriterien der Jesusforschung untersucht in Auseinandersetzung mit Emmanuel Hirschs Frühgeschichte des Evangeliums* (BZNW 38; Berlin: de Gruyter, 1970) 146-148.

Rese, M. "Einige Überlegungen zu Lukas XIII, 31-33," *Jésus aux origines* (ed. J. Dupont) 201-225.

Schnider, F. *Jesus der Prophet* (Göttingen: Vandenhoeck & Ruprecht; Fribourg: Universitätsverlag, 1974) 167-172.

Steck, O. H. *Israel und das gewaltsame Geschick der Propheten: Untersuchungen zur Überlieferung des deuteronomistischen Geschichtsbildes im Alten Testament, Spätjudentum und Urchristentum* (WMANT 23; Neukirchen-Vluyn: Neukirchener-V., 1967) 40-58.

Tyson, J. B. "Jesus and Herod Antipas," *JBL* 79 (1960) 239-246.

Verrall, A. W. "Christ before Herod (Luke xxiii 1-16)," *JTS* 10 (1908-1909) 321-353, esp. 352-353.

95. THE LAMENT OVER JERUSALEM
(13:34-35)

13 [34] "O Jerusalem, Jerusalem, city that murders prophets and stones those who are sent to you! How often did I want to gather your children together just as a hen gathers her brood under her wings, but you would not have it! [35] Now look, your *house* is *abandoned!*[a] I tell you, you will not see me until the time comes when you say, '*Blest is the one who comes in the name of the Lord.*' "[b]

[a] Jer 22:5   [b] Ps 118:26

COMMENT

The preceding episode in the travel account ended with Jesus answering Herod's threat and implicitly recognizing that he himself might face a prophet's fate in Jerusalem, the city to which he was headed. The last word of that episode, significantly, was "Jerusalem," and it occurs again at the very beginning of this one. Now Jesus addresses an apostrophe to "Jerusalem, Jerusalem," using a double voc. in OT fashion (see Gen 22:11; Exod 3:4) and uttering a lament over its sad condition (13:34-35).

Luke has derived this short passage from "Q" (see p. 78). Its Matthean counterpart is found in 23:37-39, which follows on the lengthy list of invectives and woes addressed to the Scribes and Pharisees in chap. 23 of that Gospel. Many commentators agree with R. Bultmann that Matthew has undoubtedly preserved the more original order of passages in "Q." There Jesus laments over Jerusalem within the city itself; here in Luke the lament is put on the lips of Jesus while he is still en route to the city. In this Lucan setting the lament takes on a different function. This passage is another one of those "Q" texts in which the Lucan and Matthean wording is very close (see pp. 75-76). Luke has apparently altered the text slightly to improve its Greek language.

From a form-critical viewpoint, we must understand the passage as a minatory saying, a threat of eventual judgment uttered by a prophetic figure and teacher of wisdom who approaches the city of Jerusalem. Bultmann *(HST* 114-115) would have us believe that it was "originally a Jewish prophecy" (whether Jesus himself quoted it or the early community ascribed it to him), uttered by some supra-historical entity like Wisdom. He further queries whether v. 35b-d was originally part of this prophecy or rather "a Christian addition foretelling the death and parousia of Jesus," or whether the words, "I tell you, you will not see me," are the Christian expansion. Part of the reason for this query is the problem that the sayings raise, about the number of times Jesus would have been in Jerusalem ("How often did I want . . ."), when in the Synoptic tradition only one visit to Jerusalem is presented. This, however, is to allow the tail to wag the dog. The first decision which must be made is whether *posakis,* "how often," is to be understood of literal, historical visits to Jerusalem itself. Refuge is sometimes taken by commentators in the view that, though Jesus is presented in the Synoptics visiting Jerusalem only once, he must have done so more often. But the rhetoric of the saying is not being coped with in such a view. Even if Jesus visited Jerusalem only once, he could still have wanted many times over to gather Jerusalem's children to himself. It can, however, be admitted that Jesus does speak like "God's wisdom" in this passage (recall 11:49—a passage related to the tradition preserved here). There is no need to invoke "a saying of divine wisdom" *(pace* G. Schneider, *Evangelium nach Lukas,* 310), which is made into a saying of Jesus. Minatory sayings could easily be uttered by prophetic wisdom-teachers. Cf. the saying on wisdom taking up its abode in Jerusalem in Sir 24:7-12, which provides a plausible (deuterocanonical) OT background to this episode.

As the episode is used in the Lucan context, it fits naturally in with the preceding pronouncement-story; both episodes are related to his *exodos* (9:31;

see p. 793). In Stage III of the gospel tradition, the episode clearly portrays Jesus referring to himself as a heaven-sent messenger and herald of God's wisdom commenting on the sad condition of Jerusalem, the metropolis of God's people. The form which the saying might have had in Stage I of that tradition is another question; it might have been uttered by Jesus in view of a vague premonition of what might face him in that city, once he arrived there. (See further p. 778.)

The lament which the Lucan Jesus utters here echoes OT lamentations pronounced over Jerusalem of old; compare the lament over the death of Josiah, traditionally ascribed to Jeremiah (2 Chr 35:25). The irony in Jesus' plaintive cry is evident. What a glorious destiny this city of David might have had and might still have; but how it is turning out instead. The metropolis of the people of God, which should be most receptive to Jesus and his preaching, will turn out to be the city which refuses him—in spite of an initial, enthusiastic welcome, really superficial—and will one day rue his coming to it in another capacity.

In the Lucan story recounted thus far people have come to Jesus from Jerusalem to listen to him (5:17; 6:17). Among them have been some who would not readily accept his preaching of the kingdom. These have been, in part at least, the "children" of Jerusalem whom Jesus would gladly have gathered to himself. Reactions to him coming from Jerusalemites have been recorded in 5:21,30; 6:2,7; 7:30; 11:45; reactions are still to be recounted from others in 19:39,47; 20:19; 22:2.

In comparing himself to a mother-bird, Jesus uses a readily understood figure for his own love and concern for his contemporaries, manifesting thereby in a new way the salvific interest of God himself, which he was sent to proclaim (4:43). But Jerusalem will not seek its security in the protective wings of heaven-sent wisdom. So it will be left like a helpless fledgling, its "house" will be left abandoned. Whether "house" is understood as the Jerusalem Temple or in a broader sense of God's people resident there (see NOTE on 13:35), the message of judgment is ominously the same.

In either case, Jerusalem will not look on this heaven-sent bearer of God's wisdom (11:49) until it sees him coming in another role. The saying preserved in "Q" and even as used in Matthew undoubtedly referred to Jesus' parousiac coming, his coming as judge. But in the Lucan Gospel it takes on another, more immediate connotation, *pace* E. E. Ellis, *Gospel of Luke,* 191: It refers, first of all, to Jesus' coming to Jerusalem as king "in the name of the Lord" (see 19:38), i.e. as the regal herald of God's kingdom; but then also as the rejected king proceeding to his crucifixion and mourned by the "daughters of Jerusalem" (23:28,38). Beyond these immediate references, which are an intrinsic part of the Lucan story line, there may also be reference to his judicial, parousiac coming, at the time of the eschaton (see Acts 1:11): The time will come when even Jerusalem will be ready to sing out, "Blest is the one who comes in the name of the Lord," but then it will be too late (see T. W. Manson, *Sayings,* 128).

This blessing, then, sums up the irony of minatory sayings uttered by Jesus in his apostrophe over Jerusalem.

NOTES

13   34. *O Jerusalem, Jerusalem.* See 13:33, which occasions the addition of this apostrophe to the City of David. See NOTE on 9:31.

that murders prophets and stones those who are sent to you! Lit. "to it." The Greek text shifts to the third sg. after the initial address, only to return to the second sg. in the next sentence. English style demands the uniform address used in my translation. The participles are in the pres. tense, expressive of Jerusalem's ever-present attitude toward heaven-sent messengers. On Jerusalem as murderer of prophets, see NOTE on 13:33; recall also the wisdom-saying of 11:49-51. On stoning, see 1 Sam 30:6; 1 Kgs 12:18; 21:13. When Josephus recounts the complaint of the Israelites in the desert against Moses (Exod 14:10-12), the complaint becomes a desire to stone him *(Ant.* 2.15,4 § 327). Recall also elements of the story of Stephen (Acts 6:10-14; 7:35-37,48,52,58).

How often did I want. Jesus' rhetorical exclamation makes use of the same vb. for his desire *(thelein)* that will be used at the end of the verse for the refusal of the Jerusalemites.

to gather your children together. This is to be understood, not of numerous visits of Jesus to the city of Jerusalem, but of his untold desires, expressive of his abiding concern to spread the message of God's kingdom in Jerusalem and see its inhabitants respond to this heaven-sent message.

Matt 23:37 has the more usual second aor. infin. *episynagagein,* which Luke has probably changed to the first aor. infin. *episynaxai;* there is no difference in meaning in this stylistic change.

as a hen gathers her brood under her wings. I.e. in a gesture of care and protection. A similar figure is found in Deut 32:11, "Like an eagle that stirs up its nest, that flutters over its young, spreading out its wings. . . ." There the Hebrew *qēn,* "nest," is rendered in the LXX by *nossia,* "brood," the word used by Luke here. Some commentators try to give *qēn* that meaning in Deut 32:11, "nestlings" (BDB 890); but is that a meaning based on the Greek translation? Cf. Pss 17:8; 36:8; Ruth 2:12. With this figure Jesus expresses his concern to bring his contemporaries of Jerusalem into the care which he was sent to manifest as the new herald of God's salvific kingdom.

but you would not have it! Lit. "and you did not want [it]," i.e. you rejected such care. Cf. the description of wisdom in *1 Enoch* 42:1-3. The main purpose of Jesus as the kingdom-preacher has thus been thwarted. Recall the Lucan Jesus' wry comment in 5:39 ("No one who has sipped an old wine prefers a new wine"). See p. 423.

35. *your house is abandoned!* Some mss. (D, N, Θ, Ψ, etc.) add the adj. *erēmos,* "deserted," possibly in dependence on Jer 22:5; the best mss. (P⁷⁵, ℵ, A, D, K, L, R, W, etc.), however, omit it.

The words are possibly an allusion to Jer 22:5 *(eis erēmōsin estai ho oikos houtos,* "this house will become a waste"). Cf. similar expressions in Jer 12:7; Ps 69:26; 1 Kgs 9:7-8; Tob 14:4 (mss. B, A). The abandonment of the house is also part of the commentary in the Qumran text, 4QFlor 1:5-6.

What is the sense of *oikos,* "house"? Many commentators take it as a reference to the Temple of Jerusalem, relating the saying to Jesus' announcement of its destruction. See Mark 13:2, etc. So S. Schulz, W. Grundmann, et al. But it is possible to understand *oikos* in the broader sense of "household." Cf. 4QFlor 1:10, where *bêt,* "house," is explained by *zarʿăkā,* "your seed/offspring." Cf. pp. 54, 56. See F. D. Weinert, "Luke, the Temple, and Jesus' Saying about Jerusalem's Abandoned House (Luke 13:34-35)," *CBQ* 44 (1982) 68-76.

I tell you. The Greek text may simply have *legō hymin,* as in 13:24 (see NOTE there; so in mss. P⁴⁵, ℵ*, L, etc.); but many other mss. (P⁷⁵, ℵ², A, B, D, R, W, etc.) include the conj. *de,* "but." The latter is the better text-tradition, even though the conj. is not needed in the English translation. At the end of these words, some mss. (A, W, Ψ, and the Koine text-tradition) add *hoti* to introduce the direct quotation; it is omitted, however, in the best mss. (P⁴⁵, P⁷⁵, ℵ, B, D, L, R, etc.).

until the time comes when you say. The Greek text is not uniformly transmitted. Some mss. read *heōs hēxei hote eipēte,* lit. "until it will come when you will say" [aor. subjunc.]. The Matthean parallel omits the words *hēxei hote,* joining *heōs* (followed by *an)* to *eipēte* (the normal construction [the conj. *hote* is not normally used with the subjunc.; see BDF § 382.2]). In some mss. of Luke (P⁴⁵, ℵ, N, etc.), the particle *an* is also added; but that would not affect the sense. The reading *(an) hēxei hote* is attested only in mss. A, D, W, Ψ, *f*¹, 28, and in the OL version; it is considered the *lectio difficilior* and is retained for that reason. See also *TCGNT* 163.

Matt 23:39 has a further phrase, *ap' arti,* "from now on." This phrase, however, is almost certainly secondary, being used elsewhere in the Matthean Gospel (26:29,64).

Blest is the one who comes in the name of the Lord. An allusion to Ps 118:26 (LXX, which is an accurate rendering of the Hebrew, *bārûk habbā' bĕšem Yahweh); see* NOTE on 7:19. The quotation will be used again in Luke 19:38, modified with an addition and probably with another connotation. The use of the words here refers to the coming quotation of them, at the time of Jesus' royal entry into Jerusalem. They are derived from the last of the so-called Egyptian Hallel psalms (113-118), which were used in the liturgies of great Jewish feast days. Though Psalm 118 is actually a hymn of thanks addressed to God for deliverance from battle, its v. 26 was chanted by people of Jerusalem as a greeting to pilgrims coming to the city for the celebration of feast days, especially Passover. See Str-B 1. 850.

BIBLIOGRAPHY (13:34-35)

Christ, F. *Jesus Sophia: Die Sophia-Christologie bei den Synoptikern* (ATANT 57; Zürich: Zwingli, 1970) 136-152.

Conzelmann, H. *Theology,* 109-110, 133, 139, 199.

Grässer, E. *Die Naherwartung Jesu* (SBS 61; Stuttgart: Katholisches Bibelwerk, 1973) 109-112.

Hoffmann, P. *Studien zur Theologie der Logienquelle* (NTAbh ns 8; Münster: Aschendorff, 1972) 171-180.

Kümmel, W. G. *Promise and Fulfilment,* 79-81, 100.

Schulz, S. *Q: Die Spruchquelle,* 346-360.

Suggs, M. J. *Wisdom, Christology, and Law in Matthew's Gospel* (Cambridge, MA: Harvard University, 1970) 63-71.

96. THE CURE OF THE MAN WITH DROPSY
(14:1-6)

14   [1] Once when Jesus went into the house of a prominent Pharisee to take a meal with him on a Sabbath and people were watching him closely, [2] there happened to be a man in front of him afflicted with dropsy. [3] Jesus addressed the lawyers and the Pharisees, saying, "Is it lawful to cure people on the Sabbath or not?" [4] But they kept silent. So he took hold of the man, healed him, and sent him away. [5] Then he said to them, "Suppose a child or an ox of anyone of you falls into a well—would you not immediately pull it up, even on the Sabbath?" [6] And to this they could find no answer.

COMMENT

Having finished his lament over Jerusalem, the Lucan Jesus moves on; it will be only at v. 25 that we are told that he is once again en route. He is now depicted entering the house of a leader of the Pharisees to share a festive meal with him on a Sabbath. While there, he cures a man of dropsy and queries those present about the legitimacy of such a cure on the Sabbath (14:1-6).

This episode is found only in this Gospel. What is traditional or pre-Lucan in it is probably derived from "L" (see p. 84). It is clearly used as a means to introduce the following episodes of Jesus' dinner-table discourses (vv. 7-14,15-24), a "literary device to provide a setting for the sayings" (J. M. Creed, *The Gospel,* 188). On the literary composition of vv. 1-14 as a *symposion,* "banquet-discourse," see X. de Meeûs, "Composition." A. Plummer has tried to consider this episode as the beginning of a new section in the Lucan travel account; but that is questionable.

In this case, however, the story of the cure of the man with dropsy is so heavily couched in Lucan phraseology that one realizes that the "L" material is at a minimum and that Lucan composition is responsible for a large part of the episode. F. Neirynck ("Jesus and the Sabbath," 230) regards it as "almost completely due to Lukan redaction." See NOTES for detailed comments on favorite Lucan expressions. It is not clear, however, how such expressions would argue for the episode as a community-formation *(Gemeindebildung)*, as several commentators (E. Lohse, J. Roloff) would have it.

Some interpreters (e.g. G. Schneider, *Evangelium nach Lukas,* 312) toy with the idea that v. 5 may be derived from "Q," since a similar saying is found embedded in otherwise Marcan material in Matt 12:11. But that is far from clear; the wording is so different that v. 5 is better ascribed to "L." Schneider even raises the question whether vv. 1-6 might not be "Q" material which Matthew has omitted.

This raises a further problem, for Jesus' query in v. 3b, which silences the lawyers and Pharisees, is similar to that in 6:9, in the cure on the Sabbath of a man with a stunted right hand. Is it a doublet? In dealing with the doublets (pp. 81-82), I hesitated to list this one, because the wording is so different. Who can tell whether we are dealing here with material which goes back to the same incident in Stage I of the gospel tradition? Though in both episodes Jesus is being watched by Pharisees and Scribes/lawyers and poses a question about the legitimacy of healing on a Sabbath, the combination of the question in v. 3b with the further one in v. 5 creates a serious difference. It argues, indeed, for a different incident. (See further *FTG* 55.)

It is, moreover, not easy to classify this episode form-critically. R. Bultmann *(HST* 12), who regards this episode as a mere variant of Mark 3:1-6, classes it as a pronouncement-story, specifically as a controversy dialogue. Verse 5 would be for him an added "isolated saying," which Matthew has introduced into his Marcan material in 12:11-12. So for Bultmann the pronouncement would be v. 3b; yet he admits that the Lucan episode, apart from the introductory v. 1, is "compact in structure." M. Dibelius *(FTG* 55), however, more rightly sees that Jesus' saying in v. 5 carries the real weight of the story (a paradigm, as he calls it). V. Taylor *(FGT* 155) related this episode to that of the crippled woman cured by Jesus on a Sabbath (13:10-17), preferring to regard both of them as stories about Jesus. In this case, however, the emphasis is not on the narrative (the miracle that Jesus performs, not by word, but by touch), but on the implicit pronouncement in the two questions with which he reduces to silence those who were watching him closely. Hence the episode should be understood as a pronouncement-story, as Bultmann recognized, even if one cannot be certain that the question in v. 5 was originally an isolated saying.

Jesus' action in curing the man and his words about his doing so rightly on a Sabbath cast him once again in the role of a heaven-sent messenger or teacher acting with authority. He uses his power to cope with evil afflicting an unfortunate human being, and that even on the Sabbath. Again, the episode reminds the reader of the way the evangelist has presented Jesus in 6:5 as the

"Lord of the Sabbath." Implicitly, Jesus also criticizes his contemporaries for their lack of concern for a fellow human being.

Jesus' second question to the lawyers and the Pharisees about rescuing a child or an ox from a well on the Sabbath calls to mind the restriction in the rule book of a nearly contemporary Palestinian Jewish community, which forbade such activity on the Sabbath: "Let no one assist a beast in giving birth on the Sabbath day. Even if it drops (its newborn) into a cistern or into a pit, one is not to raise it up on the Sabbath" (CD 11:13-14). Here Jesus is depicted attributing to his contemporaries a more humane view, perhaps closer to that in later rabbinic literature: "They may not deliver the young of cattle on a feast-day, but they may give help (to the dam)" *(m. Šabb.* 18:3; cf. *b. Šabb.* 128b). The attitude presupposed by Jesus in that second question reflects Deut 22:4, the Mosaic injunction to help a brother whose ox or ass falls by the way.

So ends the third and last Sabbath-healing and controversy in the Lucan Gospel (see 6:6-11; 13:10-17).

NOTES

14 1. *Once when Jesus went.* Lit. "and it happened, when he went . . . and behold there was . . ." Luke uses his favorite introduction, *kai egeneto* and a finite vb. with the conj. *kai* (see p. 119); joined with it is the prep. *en* with the articular infin. (also p. 119). Though at first sight the apodosis of this construction might seem to be *kai autoi ēsan* . . . (v. 1b), it is rather that introduced by another favorite expression, *kai idou* . . . (v. 2). See E. Klostermann *(Lukasevangelium,* 149). Cf. 5:1,17. Note that all the details about the setting remain vague; they are typical of literary introductions. Time and place are not determined. There is no reason to think (with A. Plummer, *The Gospel,* 353) that the style reflects an Aramaic source.

into the house of a prominent Pharisee. Lit. "into the house of a certain one of the leaders of the Pharisees." On Pharisees, see NOTE on 5:17. The Lucan Jesus seems to be unaware of what was recorded in 11:53-54. His going to the house of a Pharisee reminds the reader of 7:36; 11:37; he has probably been invited again. The Pharisee will implicitly reappear as the host in vv. 8,9,10,12. Just what Luke might have meant specifically by a "leader" *(archōn)* of the Pharisees is not clear. *Hoi archontes* will appear again in 23:13,35; 24:20; Acts 3:17; 4:5,8; 13:27; 14:5.

There is not a shred of evidence to suggest that because Jesus' host is a "ruler" the setting for the meal is in Jerusalem or that the "rulers" represent "churchmen," displaying thoroughly false standards of values, *pace* E. E. Ellis, *Gospel of Luke,* 192; cf. A. Plummer, *The Gospel,* 353.

to take a meal with him on a Sabbath. Lit. "on a Sabbath to eat bread." Cf. 14:15. Guests were often invited to a Sabbath meal at the end of the Sabbath synagogue service, which according to Josephus *(Life* 54 § 279), usually took place at midday (at the sixth hour). The meal would have been prepared on the day before (on the Parasceve, Day of Preparation). See *m. Šabb.* 4:1-2 for regulations about keeping things hot. Cf. Str-B 2. 202-203.

This is but another of Luke's dinner episodes. See 5:29; 7:36; 9:13-17; 10:39; 11:37; 22:14; 24:30.

people were watching him closely. Lit. "and they were watching him closely," i.e. in order to see whether he would observe the Sabbath carefully. Recall the watching of Jesus in 11:53-54; it will be recorded again in 20:20. The expressions are characteristically Lucan: the unstressed *kai autoi* (see p. 120) and the vb. "to be" with the pres. ptc. See p. 122.

2. *there happened to be a man in front of him.* Lit. "and behold there was a certain man . . ." We are not told how such a person was among those invited; his presence is not explained. Is he an unfortunate intruder (so E. E. Ellis, *Gospel of Luke,* 192) or was he planted? If he were an invited guest, why does Jesus eventually send him off? On *anthrōpos tis,* see NOTE on 10:30.

afflicted with dropsy. I.e. suffering from edema, an abnormal accumulation of serous fluids in connective tissues or cavities of the body accompanied by swelling, distention, or defective circulation. It is usually symptomatic of more serious problems.

3. *Jesus addressed the lawyers.* Lit. "having replied, Jesus said to the lawyers." Luke again uses *apokritheis* with *eipen pros* + acc., characteristic expressions. See pp. 114, 116. Nothing has been said to Jesus so far, at least in this account; hence *apokritheis* is to be understood as a stereotyped introductory formula. Cf. 13:14. The alternative would be to regard his words as a comment on the ptc. *paratēroumenoi,* "watching" (him), or on their "unspoken suspicions" (J. M. Creed, *The Gospel,* 189). In other words, he is answering their thoughts. On "lawyers," see NOTE on 7:30.

Is it lawful. Or "is it possible" (according to the Law)? Cf. 6:9. Some mss. (P45, A, W, *f*1,13, and the Koine text-tradition) introduce the question with the conj. *ei,* "whether" (see 13:23 and NOTE there); the best mss. (P75, ℵ, B, D, L, Θ, Ψ, etc.), however, omit it. Those that do read *ei* omit *ē ou,* "or not," at the end of the sentence.

to cure people on the Sabbath or not? Thus the dilemma is put to the leaders of the Pharisees, not to Jesus himself.

4. *they kept silent.* I.e. they would not commit themselves. But to be silent is to agree (especially when legal matters are the issue).

took hold . . . healed . . . sent him away. Jesus cures the man with a gesture, without an authoritative word; he allows him to go on his way. If he were among the invited guests, the departure may suggest his desire to make the most of his gained freedom. The vb. *apelysen* does not mean simply "he let go of him," but rather "he let him go (away, home)." This does not suggest that some of the Pharisaic leaders might have contested what he had done. On "healed," see NOTES on 4:40; 6:18; 9:42.

5. *he said to them.* Again, Luke uses *eipen pros* + acc., as in v. 3a.

Suppose a child or an ox . . . falls into a well. Lit. "a son or an ox of which one of you will fall . . . and you will not immediately . . ." The parataxis in Luke's Greek text is not easily put into English in this instance. Though some commentators (e.g. J. M. Creed, *The Gospel,* 189) think that Jesus is arguing *a fortiori,* it is rather an argument *a pari,* because a human being (a child) is already part of the comparison. The pair used in the illustration may seem to be incongruous, "a child or an ox," since a child would be more important than an animal. This has led to attempts to improve the text on the part of some copyists. Instead of *huios,* "son," some mss. (‭א‬, K, L, Ψ, etc.) read *onos,* "ass"; a few mss. (Θ, 2174), the Vg, and the Curetonian Syriac version read both words, *onos, huios,* "an ass, a son . . ." Codex Bezae even has *probaton,* "a lamb," but the best texts (P⁴⁵, P⁷⁵, [A], B, and the Koine text-tradition) as well as the OL and OS versions read "a child or an ox." Actually, P⁷⁵ has the abbreviation *ȳs ē bous,* which one might have been tempted to read as "a pig or an ox" (with all its obvious problems). See further V. Martin and R. Kasser, *Papyrus Bodmer XIV: Evangile de Luc chap. 3-24* (Cologny-Geneva Bibliothèque Bodmer, 1961) 18-19. The reading "ass" is probably derived from 13:15, and the "lamb" from Matt 12:11. What we have retained is also the *lectio difficilior.* Cf. J. R. Harris, "A Speculation in Textual Criticism," *Expos* 7/3 (1907) 444-454; Str-B 1. 629.

Pace M. Black *(AAGA³* 168-169), it is highly unlikely that any play on underlying Aramaic words is involved in this pair and its use in this verse. Where is such a confusion between *bĕ'îrā'* and *bĕrā'* otherwise attested in antiquity? The problem is one of transmission of the Greek text, and to try to solve it on the basis of a mistranslation of Aramaic is misleading. See further M. Black, *JTS* ns 1 (1950) 60-62; H. Connolly "The Appeal to Aramaic Sources of Our Gospels," *Downside Review* 66 (1948) 25-37, esp. 31.

would you not immediately pull it up, even on the Sabbath? Though the Greek text has no special emphasis, the thrust of the contrast in the question puts it on "you"— any one of *you.*

6. *to this they could find no answer.* Lit. "and they were not able to reply to these things." The reaction is thus stronger than in v. 4a. It is assumed that Jesus' words have reduced his observers to silence. In effect, they agree that they would do exactly what he intimated they would—at least for a child or ox of their own. But then what about a human being not related to them? Cf. 20:26; Acts 11:18; 12:17; 15:12; 22:2, for similar Lucan endings that record the silence of bystanders or others. For the sense of *pros* + acc. used here, see 18:1 (and NOTE there); 20:19; Acts 24:16.

BIBLIOGRAPHY (14:1-6)

Black, M. "The Aramaic Spoken by Christ and Luke 14.5," *JTS* ns 1 (1950) 60-62.

Ernst, J. "Gastmahlgespräche: Lk 14,1-24," *Die Kirche des Anfangs* (eds. R. Schnackenburg et al.) 57-78.

Liese, H. "Dominus ad cenam invitatus die Sabbati: Luc. 14, 1-12," *VD* 11 (1931) 257-261.

Lohse, E. "Jesu Worte über den Sabbat," *Judentum—Urchristentum—Kirche* (ed. W. Eltester) 79-89.

Meeûs, X. de. "Composition de Lc., XIV et genre symposiaque," *ETL* 37 (1961) 847-870.

Neirynck, F. "Jesus and the Sabbath: Some Observations on Mark II,27," *Jésus aux origines* (ed. J. Dupont) 227-270.

Roloff, J. "Die Sabbatszenen des lukanischen Sondergutes (Lk.13,10-17; 14,1-6)," *Das Kerygma,* 66-69.

Simson, P. "L'Evangile (Lc 14,1-11): Le code de bienséance de l'assemblée chrétienne," *AsSeign* os 70 (1975) 31-41.

97. SAYINGS ON CONDUCT AT DINNERS
(14:7-14)

14   [7] Then Jesus proposed a parable to those who had been invited, as he noticed how they were seeking out the first places. [8] He said to them, "When you are invited by someone to a banquet, do not recline at the first place. It may be that someone more distinguished than you has been invited by your host [9] and he who has invited you and him may come to you and say, 'Give this man your place.' Then in your embarrassment you would proceed to take the last place. [10] Rather, when you are invited, go settle down in the last place, so that when your host comes in he can say to you, 'Move up to a higher place, my friend.' Then you will enjoy honor before all who are at table with you. [11] For everyone who *exalts* himself will *be humbled,* and the one who *humbles* himself will *be exalted.*"[a]

[12] And Jesus said to his host, "When you are going to give a luncheon or a dinner, do not call your friends, or even your brothers, your relatives, your rich neighbors, lest they only invite you in turn and so you are repaid. [13] Rather, when you are going to give a dinner party, invite the poor, the crippled, the lame, and the blind. [14] Then you will be blessed, for they do not have the wherewithal to repay you; you will be repaid instead at the resurrection of the upright."

[a] Ezek 21:31

COMMENT

The setting for this episode is still that of the preceding: Jesus is at dinner on a Sabbath in the house of one of the leaders of the Pharisees; his words are directed to the Pharisees and lawyers of v. 3. He uses the occasion to offer sage advice about conduct at dinners as he observes his contemporaries at this festive meal. He comments on the attitude of both fellow guests and host (14:7-14). The episode is thus divided into two parts (vv. 7-11 and vv. 12-14).

These dinner-table sayings of Jesus are recorded only here in the Lucan Gospel, being for the most part derived from "L" (see p. 84). They are, moreover, only loosely joined to the preceding and following episodes; there is no reason to think of these three episodes from "L" as having formed a pre-Lucan unit. Verse 11, however, is different. The Greek text of it is almost word-for-word identical (save for *kai* instead of *de)* with 18:14, where it forms the ending of another "L" passage (the parable of the Pharisee and the toll-collector, 18:9-14). It is, furthermore, very close in wording to Matt 23:12, and less so to Matt 18:4 (in the first of these parallels the Matthean introductory *hostis,* "whoever," is probably the original form, which Luke has changed to his more usual *pas hos,* "everyone who"). This makes it likely that v. 11 has been introduced into the "L" material from "Q" (see p. 81).

The introductory verse is, in part, transitional, being fashioned by Luke's redactional pen. He introduces the sayings which follow by portraying Jesus proposing a parable to the invited guests and their host. The expression "parable" refers only to vv. 7-11, yet they do not turn out to be a parable in the usual sense. R. Bultmann *(HST* 179) recognized that the stylistic relationship of the passage to similitudes or parables is only "faint," and that in reality it resembles more "warnings" (see *HST* 103-104, where he calls vv. 8-10 a secular rule of prudence). Verse 11 is rightly regarded by Bultmann as a wisdom-saying of Jesus added to the rest *(HST* 103). Has the exhortation to take the lowest seat at the banquet developed out of an original parable intended to ward off self-righteous claims before God (so *FTG* 248)? Is this the reason why the sayings, now hortatory in character, are introduced as a "parable"? This is hardly an accurate assessment, for it would mean that an eschatologically oriented parable has been secularized in the transmission of the pre-Lucan tradition—which is hardly likely; it would most likely be just the other way round. J. M. Creed *(The Gospel,* 198-199) suggests that, because the saying is introduced as a "parable," this word "gives the correct clue to its interpretation: i.e. it is not a direct injunction as to proper behaviour at a dinner (though this certainly seems to be suggested by the words *epechōn . . . exelegonto* ["as he noticed how they were seeking out the first places"]), but the proper behaviour at a feast affords an analogy to the attitude demanded by the Kingdom of God." But, in this suggestion, Creed has gone to the opposite extreme, since the connection between Jesus' saying in vv. 8-10—even the appended saying of v. 11—and the kingdom is scarcely evident. Moreover, Creed's words within the parentheses are telling; they hit the sense precisely. Jesus' saying is a bit of secular, prudential wisdom, just as his words in 12:57-59 about agreement with one's opponent were. Hence, despite the Lucan introductory expression, "parable," Jesus' sayings recorded here are to be regarded form-critically as hortatory counsels, to which a wisdom-saying (v. 11) has been appended. The same characterization can be used for the saying in vv. 12-14, which is in no way parabolic. (Recall also the diverse meanings of *parabolē* listed in the NOTE on 5:36.)

The joining of the two sayings (vv. 8-10 and 12-14) is in part explained by their similar structure. Both have a similar beginning ("When you are invited . . ."; "When you are going to give a luncheon . . ."), a similar negative imperative ("do not recline . . ."; "do not call . . ."), and a similar negative purpose/result cl. ("lest someone more distinguished . . ." [modified in my translation]; "lest they only invite you in turn . . ."). The parallelism is thus probably responsible for the pair of sayings.

In these sayings, loosely connected to the topic of festive dining of the preceding episode (vv. 1-6), the Lucan Jesus offers indirect counsel to his disciples about modes of conduct toward other human beings. He does this by commenting, first of all, on the maneuvering of his fellow guests, which he has observed, as they sought out for themselves the best places. He castigates them for seeking out positions of prestige. Specifically, they are places of honor at a banquet. He lets it be known that real honor will come not from one's self-seeking choices, but from what is bestowed on one by another. Honor before one's peers comes not from what one does on one's own behalf, but depends on the estimate others have of one. Jesus' main point is expressed at the end of v. 10, "Then you will enjoy honor before all who are at table with you." The added wisdom-saying introduces a further dimension: Its theological pass. expresses God's judgment as the source of the honor *(doxa)*. God will humble the one who exalts himself and exalt the one who humbles himself. Hence the attitude of Christian disciples should be humility, not status-seeking. (Maybe the addition of the wisdom-saying in v. 11 is the reason why this otherwise prudential saying appears to Luke as a "parable.")

In the second saying Jesus moves from self-seeking ambition to selfish recompense and tries to counteract this as well. He counsels this time, not his fellow guests, but his host. He suggests that the kind of people one should invite to dinners is not one's friends, brothers, relatives, or rich neighbors, but the poor, the crippled, the lame, and the blind. Four affluent types of human beings, able to recompense, are contrasted with four unfortunate types, unable to do so. Real love never reckons with recompense; and because this is so, generosity will find its reward at the resurrection. The reciprocity expected must give way to a return in another, unexpected form—a return, not from the unfortunates who have not the wherewithal to reciprocate the host's kindness and graciousness, but from God himself. The host who invites such unfortunates will find himself among the "upright" at the resurrection.

The sayings of the Lucan Jesus in vv. 12-14 fit into the general Lucan theme of the use of material possessions and of the concern for the poor and unfortunate of this world (see pp. 192, 247-251).

Lastly, one should mention that another form of vv. 8-10 is recorded after

LUKE X–XXIV

§ IVA

Matt 20:28 in some Greek mss. (D, Φ) and ancient versions (OL, Vg, Curetonian Syriac): "Seek to grow from a small (status), and from a greater (one) to be less. When you enter (a house) and are asked to dine, do not recline in the prominent places lest someone more renowned than you come in and the host should come to you and say, 'Move further down'; then you will be embarrassed. But if you settle down in a lower place and someone less important than you comes in, the host will say to you, 'Come up further'; this will be (more [ms. Φ]) to your advantage." Whether this is a development of the Lucan episode or an independent tradition is hard to say.

NOTES

14 *7. proposed a parable to those who had been invited. Luke fashions his introductory verse again with *elegen pros* + acc. See p. 116. On "parable," see NOTE on 5:36; cf. 13:6; 18:1. Here it introduces a bit of sage advice, prudential in itself, but with an added dimension because of v. 11. Whether that addition is enough to give the saying parabolic character may be debated.

as he noticed. Lit. "fixing" (his attention on [some object like *ton noun,* "his mind" is probably to be understood]). The vb. *epechein* is thus often used by itself of paying heed to something. See Acts 3:5; 1 Tim 4:16; Sir 34:2; 2 Macc 9:25; cf. MM 232. Jesus sees the lawyers and Pharisees (mentioned in v. 3) maneuvering for position.

the first places. See 20:46; cf. 11:43. Seeking out such places was also known in the Greek world. See Theophrastus, *Charact.* 21.2. Josephus *(Ant.* 15.2,4 § 21) knows of the prestige associated with such places.

8. *to a banquet.* Lit. "to wedding celebrations," but *gamos,* especially in the pl. (as here), can also be used in a generic sense. See NOTE on 12:36. The phrase is omitted in ms. P⁷⁵ and in some mss. of the OL. The formal order of places would not have been restricted to wedding celebrations.

do not recline. In the NT only Luke uses *kataklinein* for "recline." See NOTE on 7:36; cf. 9:14-15; 24:30.

It may be that someone more distinguished than you has been invited. Lit. "lest someone . . ." The conj. *mēpote* would normally introduce a negative purpose cl., but the sense is in this instance clearly one of result. On the tendency to confuse these two types of cl. in Hellenistic Greek, see ZBG § 351-353. Some would prefer to understand *mēpote* as expressive of apprehension. See BDF § 370.2. In any case the motivation for not taking a higher place is not moral, but practical and prudential.

9. *Give this man your place.* I.e. make room for him. See Epictetus, *Dissert.* 4.1,105; Josephus, *Ant.* 12.4,9 § 210 (the same Greek word, *topos,* is used of a "place" at a king's feast).

Then . . . you would proceed to take the last place. Lit. "and then you will begin with shame to occupy the last place." Jesus' words thus drive home the reversal of human values which so much of his preaching demands—a reversal of status, condition, or role.

10. *go settle down.* Lit. "going, fall/lean back . . ." Similar advice is later attrib-

uted in the rabbinical tradition to R. Simeon b. Azzai: "Stay two or three seats below your place and sit until they say to you, 'Go (farther) up.' Do not begin by going up because (then) they may say to you, 'Go down.' It is better that they should say to you 'Go up, go up,' than that they should say to you, 'Go down, go down' " *(Leviticus Rabb.* 1 [fifth century A.D.]). A similar saying is recorded in *Abot de Rabbi Nathan* 25. See Str-B 1. 916. Are these rabbinical traditions possibly influenced by the early Christian tradition?

Move up to a higher place. Jesus' words echo those of Prov 25:6-7, but adapt them to a banquet setting. The saying in Proverbs runs: "Do not put yourself forward in the presence of a king or stand in the place of the great; for it is better to be told, 'Come up here,' than to be put lower in the presence of the prince." Cf. Sir 3:17-20.

Then you will enjoy honor before all. Lit. "you will have glory before all." Two of Luke's favorite words are used here *(enōpion,* "before," see p. 110; and *pas,* "all").

11. *everyone who exalts himself.* See 18:14. These words of wisdom allude to Ezek 21:31 (LXX: "You abased what is lofty and exalted what is lowly"; cf. 21:26E). See also Ezek 17:24. The allusion thus puts Jesus' previous saying (end of v. 10) into a larger perspective: Self-assertion will not suffice when God's judgment is to intervene.

will be humbled. I.e. by God (see NOTE on 5:20); the theological pass. is used.

12. *to his host.* Lit. "to the one who had invited/called him"; from v. 1 he is known as one of the prominent Pharisees.

a luncheon or a dinner. As in 11:37-38 *ariston* refers to a noonday meal, the Roman *prandium,* whereas *deipnon* refers to a main meal, taken toward evening. Cf. Str-B 2. 204-206.

your brothers, your relatives. M.-J. Lagrange *(Luc,* 402) thinks that *adelphous* has the sense of close relatives, "because one does not always have 'brothers.' " But it is hard to give *adelphous* such a meaning here, when it is followed by *syngeneis,* "relatives."

rich neighbors. This is the reading in the best Greek mss., but some mss. (D, etc.) and ancient versions (OL, Vg) separate these words, "neither the neighbors nor the rich." This, however, creates a fivesome, to which the foursome below would not be parallel.

lest they only invite you in turn. Lit. "lest even they invite you," *kai autoi* is intensive here. See p. 120. I.e. lest the social convention of *do ut des* be further promoted. Cf. Xenophon, *Symp.* 1.15.

and so you are repaid. Lit. "and (lest that) be your recompense." The n. *antapodoma* normally carries the sense of "recompense" in the LXX. See also Rom 11:9; cf. P. Joüon, "Notes philologiques sur les évangiles," *RSR* 18 (1928) 354.

13. *the poor, the crippled, the lame, and the blind.* This foursome will appear again in v. 21 below. The first mentioned would not have the money to reciprocate (see NOTE on 4:18), the other three would not have the power or capability. Three of the four ("the lame, the blind, the crippled") are mentioned (along with "one who has a permanent blemish in his flesh") as those to be excluded from the eschatological war of the "sons of light against the sons of darkness" in the Qumran *War Scroll* (1QM 7:4) and also excluded from the community meal in 1QSa 2:5-6. Cf. 2 Sam 5:8 (LXX); Lev 21:17-23; 4QDᵇ. See *ESBNT* 198-199, 202. By contrast, the invitation of such persons by the Christian disciple will reveal his concern to relieve the need of fellow

human beings. Cf. Deut 14:28-29; 16:11-14; 26:11-13; Tob 2:2 for the OT background to Jesus' counsel.

See the similar principle attributed in later rabbinical literature to R. Jose b. Yohanan: "Let your house be opened wide and let the needy be members of your household" *(m. Abot* 1:5).

the crippled. The best reading is *anapeirous* (mss. P[75], ℵ, A, B, D); the more common, classical Greek form is *anapērous,* which is also found in some mss. See Plato, *Crito,* 53A, where it is coupled with the "lame" and the "blind," as here.

14. *blessed.* I.e. *makarios,* the obj. of a beatitude (see NOTES on 6:20; 7:23).

the wherewithal to repay you. I.e. they will not be able to return the hospitality, because they either have nothing or are incapable of supplying a similar repast. For the vb. *echein* with an infin., see NOTE on 7:40.

you will be repaid. I.e. by God. For the theological pass., see NOTE on 5:20.

at the resurrection of the upright. Or "of the righteous ones." Mention is made of eschatological retribution at the time of the resurrection; recall 13:27. Compare also the other references to the "resurrection" in Lucan writings (20:35; Acts 17:32; 23:6; 24:15). Here the words of Jesus are addressed to Pharisees and lawyers, who presumably believed in the resurrection. The background of the phrase used may well be Dan 12:2-3. Note the Greek form in Theodotion.

BIBLIOGRAPHY (14:7-14)

Degenhardt, H.-J. "Gastmahlgespräche und Eintrittsbedingungen für die Jünger-schaft Jesu: Lk 14,7-35," *Lukas Evangelist der Armen,* 97-113.
Jeremias, J. *Parables,* 191-193.
Jülicher, A. *Gleichnisreden,* 246-254.
Navone, J. "The Parable of the Banquet," *TBT* 14 (1964) 923-929.
Shillito, E. "The Gospel according to St. Luke xiv. 7-33," *ExpTim* 52 (1940-1941) 432-434.
Stöger, A. "Sentences sur les repas: Lc 14,1. 7-14," *AsSeign* ns 53 (1970) 78-88.

98. THE PARABLE OF THE GREAT DINNER
(14:15-24)

14 [15] One of those with him at table who heard all this remarked, "Blessed, then, is the one who will share the meal in the kingdom of God." [16] So Jesus said, "A man was once giving a great dinner, to which he had invited many guests. [17] At the time for the dinner he sent his servant to inform those invited, 'Please come now, for things are at last prepared.' [18] But they all at once began to decline. The first one

said to him, 'I have bought a field, and I have to go out and inspect it. Please convey my regrets.' [19] Another said, 'I have bought five yoke of oxen, and I am on my way to try them out. Please convey my regrets.' [20] Yet another said, 'I have just been married, and for this reason I cannot come.' [21] When the servant came back, he reported all this to his master. The master of the house became angry and said to his servant, 'Go out quickly into the streets and lanes of the town and bring in here the poor, the crippled, the blind, and the lame.' [22] Again the servant said, 'Sir, what you ordered has been done, and there is still room.' [23] Then the master said to the servant, 'Go out then into the highways and the hedgerows and make people come in so that my house will be filled! [24] For I tell you, not one of those men who were originally invited shall taste of my dinner.' "

COMMENT

At this point in the Lucan travel account Jesus' dinner-table talk moves on from topics of guest places at dinner and the proper guests to invite to that of the acceptance of invitations to a festive meal. The setting for this new topic is still the same: Jesus is reclining at table on a Sabbath in the house of the prominent Pharisee of v. 1. One of the guests who has been listening to his counsels about not maneuvering for the best positions and about inviting the poor, the crippled, the lame, and the blind shows some comprehension of what Jesus has been saying as he remarks on the good fortune of the person who will be able to partake of the kingdom-meal (v. 15). He must be presumed to have heard what Jesus had said in 13:28-29 about those who will come from the east and the west, from the north and the south to recline in God's kingdom with Abraham, Isaac, and Jacob and all the prophets. The eschatological dimension of dining (in the kingdom) is suggested to him by Jesus' most recent reference to the host's proper recompense at "the resurrection of the upright" (v. 14). He understands that recompense to be a share in the eschatological banquet of the kingdom.

The fellow guest's remark becomes the cue for Jesus to add a parable to his preceding topics of table-talk (14:16-24). Thus the climax of this group of topically arranged sayings of Jesus, having to do with dining, is now reached, in this parable of the great dinner. From a form-critical point of view, this episode creates no problem, since the bulk of it is a kingdom-parable, presented in a "thorough-going narrative form" (R. Bultmann, *HST* 175).

Its Synoptic relationship and its place in the gospel tradition are, however, other matters. It is clearly Luke who has joined this episode to the preceding two; this parable has a counterpart in the Matthean Gospel, where it appears in an entirely different context (being the third of three parables, along with that of the two sons and the wicked vineyard tenants, in chaps. 21-22, uttered when Jesus is already in Jerusalem).

The parable of the great dinner in Luke's Gospel is certainly related to that of the royal wedding celebration in Matthew's, but how closely? Older commentators (e.g. A. Plummer, *The Gospel,* 359-360) and some more recent ones (e.g. E. E. Ellis, *Gospel of Luke,* 194) prefer to think of it either as a distinct story or an "independent parable with the same theme." H. Schürmann *(Das Lukasevangelium,* 236) and J. Ernst *(Evangelium nach Lukas,* 442) prefer to ascribe the Lucan form of the parable to "L." Though such solutions are not absolutely impossible, they give the impression of being pat and easy. No little part of the problem is how one assesses the form of the parable which is found in *Gos. of Thom.* § 64. This is one of the longest units in that Coptic non-canonical Gospel. The text of it runs as follows:

> Jesus said, "A man (once) had guests. When he had prepared the dinner, he sent his servant to summon the guests. He went to the first one (and) said to him, 'My master summons you.' (But) he said, 'I have financial claims on some merchants; they are coming to me this evening. I must go and give them orders. I ask to be excused from the dinner.' He went to another one (and) said to him, 'My master summons you.' (But) he said to him, 'I have just bought a house, and people require me for a day. I shall have no time.' He came to another one (and) said to him, 'My master summons you.' (But) he said to him, 'My friend is getting married, and I am the one to arrange (the) dinner.' He went to (still) another one (and) said to him, 'My master summons you.' (But) he said, 'I have just bought a village, and I am on my way to collect the rent. I shall not be able to come. I ask to be excused.' The servant came (back) and told his master, 'Those whom you summoned to the dinner have asked to be excused.' The master (then) said to the servant, 'Go out into the streets and bring in those whom you will find that they may eat my dinner. But buyers and sellers shall not come into the places of my Father.' " (See p. 87.)

As a number of commentators have pointed out (e.g. H. Montefiore, "A Comparison of the Parables of the Gospel according to Thomas and of the Synoptic Gospels," in H. Montefiore and H. E. W. Turner, *Thomas and the Evangelists,* 61), the form of the parable in the *Gospel of Thomas* does not include "details which are evidently intended by the synoptic evangelists to be understood allegorically." However, W. Schrage *(Das Verhältnis,* 133-137) thinks that form in the *Gospel of Thomas* depends on Matthew and Luke, and more so on the latter than on the former, even though he cannot fully establish its dependence. Similarly, J.-E. Ménard *(L'Evangile selon Thomas,* 165) seems to hint at the dependence of the *Gospel of Thomas* on Luke, when he points out that the excuses in the former come from proprietors and a bridegroom's friend, not from simple peasants, such as the Lucan story depicts. But none of this is conclusive. If the form in the *Gospel of Thomas* depended on Matthew or Luke, would not some of the allegorical aspect have rubbed off on it?

When one looks more carefully at the form of the parable in the *Gospel of Thomas*, one sees that the point of it is clear: Those who were invited to the dinner and have refused to respond to the servant's summons will find no place at the Father's banquet; their places will be taken by others brought in from outside, and they will be excluded only because they have excluded themselves. In the context of the *Gospel of Thomas*, which normally strings together sayings and parables of Jesus that are quite unrelated, this form of the parable follows on a form of that of the rich fool (cf. Luke 12:16-21; see p. 971). In effect, the two parables caution the rich.

The parable in the *Gospel of Thomas* is closer to the Lucan form than to the Matthean. It contains no introductory formula of comparison (cf. Matt 22:2). The already-invited guests are summoned to the festive dinner (not a marriage celebration for a son) by a man (not a king) who sends out once (not twice) one servant (not several) to them. Though the guests now summoned in the *Gospel of Thomas* number four (whereas Luke has only three), they ask to be excused with individually formulated reasons (unlike the Matthean summary statements: "they would not come," or "they made light of it and went off, one to his farm, another to his business, while the others seized his servants, treated them shamefully, and killed them"). Even the concluding sentence of the parable in the *Gospel of Thomas* resembles (remotely) Luke 14:24 in its comment on those originally invited; the Matthean form has none of this.

However, the form in the *Gospel of Thomas* is closer to the Matthean in the ending of the story, since the master simply sends his servant to bring in those he finds in the streets. In the Lucan form, the servant is sent out twice: once into the streets and lanes of the town, and again into the highways and hedgerows (outside the town) to find people to fill his master's house.

In my opinion, one should regard the form of the parable in the *Gospel of Thomas* as more primitive and closer to what might have come from the lips of Jesus himself in Stage I of the gospel tradition. In this, I agree with J. Jeremias *(Parables,* 176), E. Haenchen ("Das Gleichnis"), G. Schneider *(Evangelium nach Lukas,* 317), N. Perrin *(Rediscovering,* 113). H. Koester ("Apocryphal and Canonical Gospels," *HTR* 73 [1980] 105-130), who is at pains to argue for primitive and authentic material in the so-called apocryphal Gospels, surprisingly makes no mention of this form of the parable in the *Gospel of Thomas* (see his pp. 112-119).

It is, however, possible that the formulation of the excuses in the *Gospel of Thomas* may be somewhat expanded; perhaps even the adding of the fourth guest is part of the expansion beyond the primitive form of Stage I. Otherwise, one can easily explain the peculiarly Matthean or Lucan variants of the story as the redaction of each evangelist (or, in a less likely hypothesis, in the early Christian form that came to them). Why Matthew has varied the form of the parable as he has does not concern us here; the Lucan variants, however, are easily explained.

Because of the relation of the parable forms in the *Gospel of Thomas* and in Luke, I prefer to think that both the Matthean and Lucan forms are derived in the main from "Q" (see p. 78). The bulk of the Lucan form (vv. 16-21) corresponds sufficiently to Matt 22:2-10 to warrant this, as many other commentators have noted (R. A. Edwards, S. Schulz, D. Lührmann, *Redaktion,* 87, et al.).

In using the material from "Q," Luke has prefixed to it his own transitional verse, the remark of a fellow guest about the eschatological dinner in the kingdom (14:15). Though R. Bultmann *(HST* 109) considers this beatitude as a prophetic or apocalyptic saying of Jesus, borrowed from the tradition and accidentally put on the lips of a fellow guest, there is no reason why this saying should not be regarded simply as a Lucan composition—a macarism similar to 11:27, which calls forth a comment from Jesus (in this case, a parable). At any rate, Bultmann rightly considers v. 15 as part of Luke's "editorial construction of the story of the supper." Similarly, H. Conzelmann, *Theology,* 111. M. Dibelius *(FTG* 161) understands the remark as a chria-like formulation, i.e. "a short pointed saying of general significance, originating in a definite person and arising out of a definite situation" (ibid. 152).

The present Lucan story in vv. 16-23 is an intelligible unit, even though the parable proper, derived from "Q," is limited to vv. 16-21. Verse 21b, however, with its foursome, "the poor, the crippled, the blind, and the lame," is of Lucan redaction, assimilating the newly introduced diners to the proper guests to invite in v. 13 of the preceding episode. The individual excuses were probably in the "Q"-form of the parable, which Matthew for his own reasons has summarily reduced. The individual excuses have their own form in the *Gospel of Thomas.* Although both Luke and Matthew have a salvation-history allegorization of the parable, that was not part of "Q," for the shape of the allegorization is quite different and hence independently produced. Verses 22-23 are the results, then, of Lucan redaction, if not of Lucan composition, added to the original parable. So I prefer to regard these verses, along with many commentators (e.g. J. Jeremias, *Parables,* 176; A. Vögtle, "Die Einladung," 183-184; *pace* E. Linnemann, *Jesus of the Parables,* 159). Note the Lucan favorite expression in *eipen pros* + acc. (v. 23; see p. 116). Finally, even though v. 24 has a counterpart at the end of the parable in the *Gospel of Thomas,* in its present formulation it should be regarded as the product of Lucan redaction.

The sense of the parable is not difficult to discern. As a whole, it makes the same point as does the form in the *Gospel of Thomas:* Those who say no to the master's summons to come to the dinner now prepared will never taste of it. *Pace* J. Jeremias *(Parables,* 176), the sense of the original is not "It may be too late." It is rather a minatory parable which emphasizes the seriousness of the preaching addressed by Jesus to his compatriots and seeks to elicit from them acceptance, not refusal; they are addressed with an insistent invitation (see 16:16b). Those who are excluded from the banquet have only themselves to thank; God will not drag the unwilling into it against their will. In the Lucan context of the fellow guest's remark about the good fortune of those who will partake of the kingdom's eschatological dinner, Jesus' parable makes it clear that the refusal to accept his preaching now will mean eventual exclusion from the joy of that festive meal, in which Abraham, Isaac, and Jacob and all the prophets will share. In the fuller Lucan context of the Gospel, in which the master of the house has already been depicted closing the door of the kingdom and excluding contemporaries of Jesus as people not known to him (13:25,27), the exclusion of those invited to dine in this parable envisages again those contemporaries, and more specifically the lawyers and the Pharisees, some of whom are dining with him and hearing his parable. In the setting of this parable, they are those who "were originally invited" (14:24).

The Lucan form of the parable goes still further, allegorizing the original in terms of Luke's ideas of salvation-history. In the separate sending of the servant "into the streets and lanes of the town" and then "into the highways and the hedgerows" (outside the town), the implication is clear that first further contemporaries of Jesus' *patris* (recall 4:24; see p. 528) are invited, the outcasts of the town, Jewish people of less noble standing. Then those from outside the *patris* are also brought in, viz. the Gentiles. This allegorization of the original parable (see J. Jeremias, *Parables,* 64) fits into a Lucan motif which finds even more explicit expression elsewhere in his writings, e.g. in Acts 13:46: "It was necessary that the word of God be addressed to you first [i.e. Jews and God-fearers in the synagogue of Antioch in Pisidia]. Since you reject it and consider yourselves not worthy of eternal life, we are now turning to the Gentiles." See further Acts 18:6; 3:26; 28:23-28. Indeed, the servant is told to "make people come in" (i.e. compel them with persuasion to do so) so that the house of the kingdom will eventually be filled.

Thus the Lucan Jesus is seen desperately trying to coax his contemporaries into a proper understanding of his role as kingdom-preacher. He is portrayed foreseeing the places at the kingdom-banquet occupied by none of those originally invited, because they have excluded themselves, but by strangers from the highways and hedgerows.

Lest one think that Luke's form of the parable is too negative against the contemporaries of Jesus, one should not miss the distinction between the "lawyers and the Pharisees" of v. 3 and "the poor, the crippled, the blind, and the lame" brought in from "the streets and lanes of the *town."* Thus, Luke is at pains to show that some of the Palestinian contemporaries of Jesus did accept him. These four groups will enter the banquet hall along with those from the highways and hedgerows to become reconstituted Israel, the refashioned people of God (see pp. 190-191). In all, God's will is not foiled by the rejection of human beings; the places at the kingdom-banquet will be filled. But a mirror is held up before the lawyers and Pharisees in which they can see that they are regarding something else as more important than God's invitation offered in Jesus' preaching (see G. Schneider, *Evangelium nach Lukas,* 319).

As T. W. Manson *(Sayings,* 130) once noted, the Lucan Jesus does not teach "a mechanically operating predestination, which determines from all eternity who shall or who shall not be brought into the Kingdom. Neither does He proclaim that man's entry into the Kingdom is purely his own affair. The two essential points in His teaching are that no man can enter the Kingdom without the invitation of God, and that no man can remain outside it but by his own deliberate choice. Man cannot save himself; but he can damn himself."

Finally, is the parable another expression of Lucan anti-Semitism? See COMMENT on 10:29-37.

NOTES

14   15. *One of those with him at table.* I.e. one of the lawyers and the Pharisees of v. 3, or perhaps another invited guest.

Blessed. See NOTE on 6:20.

who will share the meal in the kingdom of God. An allusion to the kingdom-banquet mentioned in 13:29. See NOTE there; cf. pp. 154-157, 190; in the light of v. 14 it means a share in the eternal reward of the upright, salvation itself. Cf. 22:16,29-30.

This is not a pious remark of a fellow guest striving to save the evening by changing the topic and thereby rescuing the host from Jesus' implied criticism in vv. 12-14. It is Luke's transitional introduction, reminding the reader of still another dimension of dining (already referred to in 13:29). Jesus' answer will say, in effect, to this fellow guest, "You are right; but if invited, will you be among those to decline?"

The beatitude enhances the coming parable with an OT background motif; see NOTE on 13:29.

will share the meal. Lit. "will eat bread." This is an OT expression (e.g. Gen 37:25; 2 Sam 9:7,10; 12:20; 2 Kgs 4:8; Qoh 9:7). *Artos,* "bread," is being used in a more generic sense, as in 14:1. But some mss. (A*, W, f^{13}, and the Koine text-tradition) read *ariston,* "lunch, midday meal." This must be regarded as a simple copyist's corruption of *arton,* for the best mss. (P[75], ℵ[1], A[c], B, D, K, etc.) read the latter.

16. *A man.* On *anthrōpos tis,* see NOTE on 10:30. J. Jeremias *(Parables,* 178) would have us believe that this person is to be understood as a toll-collector (see NOTE on 3:12), because Jesus would have known of a story about a toll-collector, named Bar Ma'yan, who died and was given a great funeral. He was so rewarded because once, when he had prepared a great dinner and invited town councilors who refused to come, he brought in the poor of the town and fed them lest the food be wasted. This

story is preserved in two parts of the Palestinian Talmud *(y. Sanh.* 6.23c; *y. Hag.* 2.77d;* its Aramaic form is readily accessible in G. Dalman, *Aramäische Dialektproben* [2d ed.; Leipzig: Hinrichs, 1927; reprinted, Darmstadt: Wissenschaftliche Buchgesellschaft, 1960] 33 § 2). These stories, however, scarcely antedate the fourth century A.D.; that Jesus would have known them is unlikely.

a great dinner. The *Gospel of Thomas* also speaks of a "dinner" (with the Greek word *deipnon,* preserved in the Coptic text); Matt 22:2 speaks of *gamous tō huiō autou,* "a wedding celebration for his son." Instead of the neut. *deipnon mega* mss. B³, D read *deipnon megan,* making the n. masc. See BDF § 49.1.

had invited many guests. The story presupposes that a preliminary invitation has already been sent out to the "many." This innocuous use of *polloi,* "many," has nothing to do with the Hebrew *ha-rabbîm* of Qumran literature, where "the many" is, indeed, the name for an in-group (the community itself) or the "elect," *pace* J. A. Sanders ("The Ethic," 260). In the Lucan parable the *polloi* turn out not to be the elect!

17. *his servant.* In the Matthean parallel it is "his servants" (22:3). The sg. is not to be allegorized in terms of Jesus; this would be to go beyond the thrust of the Lucan parable, or that in the *Gospel of Thomas,* where it is also sg. (see J. M. Creed, *The Gospel,* 191).

to inform those invited. Many commentators refer to what seems to have been a custom at times in antiquity of sending some servant (called in Latin *vocator)* to summon invited guests as the hour of the dinner approached. This may be reflected in Esth 5:8 and 6:14. Cf. Terence, *Hauton.* 169; Apuleius, *Metam.* 3.12. J. Jeremias *(Parables,* 176) claims it was a "special courtesy practised by upper circles in Jerusalem," but he can only appeal to a fifth-century midrashic text for evidence *(Lam. Rab.* 4:2).

things are at last prepared. Lit. "(things) are now for some time ready." For the sense of the adv. *ēdē,* see NOTE on 11:7. The preferred reading, *hoti ēdē hetoima estin,* is found in ms. B and in the OL version. It is the *lectio difficilior.* Mss. P⁷⁵, ℵ*, L, R, Θ use the third pl. vb. *eisin,* whereas mss. A, D, W, Ψ, and the Koine text-tradition have . . . *estin panta,* "all is at length ready." Cf. Matt 22:4 for the influence on the copyists.

18. *they all at once began to decline.* The prepositional phrase *apo mias,* lit. "from one," is probably an Aramaism, related to later Christian Palestinian Aramaic *min ḥădā'* or Syriac *men ḥădā'.* See p. 117. Compare the contemporary use of similar preps. with the numeral *ḥad* in Palestinian Aramaic: *bḥd',* "together" (1QapGen 12:16); *kḥd',* "together" (11QtgJob 30:5); *lḥd',* "exceedingly, very" (1QapGen 20:33). See *AAGA*³ 113. Another prepositional phrase, *epi mias,* found in Greek *Enoch* 99:9, has been introduced into the discussion of this Lucan phrase (by J. Jeremias, "Beobachtungen zu neutestamentlichen Stellen an Hand des neugefundenen griechischen Henoch-Textes," *ZNW* 38 [1939] 118; S. Aalen, "St Luke's Gospel"), but the relevance of *epi mias* to Lucan *apo mias* is far from clear.

If the Aramaic explanation suggested above is unacceptable, one could think of the phrase as a Greek ellipsis and understand with it either *phōnēs* "with one (voice)," i.e. with one accord (cf. Herodian, *Hist.* 1.4,8; Lucian, *Nigrinus,* 14), or *gnōmēs,* "with one (opinion)," i.e. mutually. Cf. Aristophanes, *Lys.* 1000; Philo, *De spec. leg.* 3.12 73.

The first one. The threesome in the dramatis personae is to be noted: a farmer with a field, a peasant with yokes of oxen, and a newlywed. Recall the priest, the levite, and the Samaritan in 10:29-37. See COMMENT there. The storytelling technique in the parable should not be missed: the threesome, the three sendings of the servant, the three excuses (two regrets and one "I cannot come" [cp. the *Gospel of Thomas]).* This is why one should not scrutinize how real or weak the excuses seem to be; if any of the "invited" guests actually accepted the summons, there would be no story. However, to see Holy War reasons involved in each of the excuses given by the three is eisegetical, *pace* P. H. Ballard ("Reasons") and J. D. M. Derrett ("The Parable").

I have bought a field. I.e. a piece of farmland outside the town, which he feels obliged to inspect. The reader should not ask why he did not inspect it before he bought it; that would be to miss the point of the story. E. Linnemann *(Jesus of the Parables,* 89 n. a) does precisely this when she suggests that the aor. should be translated, "I am in the act of buying."

T. W. Manson *(Sayings,* 130) has caught the point when he writes, "The claims of mammon take precedence."

have to go out and inspect it. Lit. "I have a need to go out . . ." Luke used *echein anankēn* + infin., as in classical and Hellenistic Greek. See 1 Cor 7:37; Heb 7:27; Plutarch, *Cato Min.* 24.6; Josephus, *Ant.* 16.9,3 § 290. The expression is not found in the LXX.

Please convey my regrets. Lit. "I ask you, hold me excused." This may be a Latinism, since a very similar form turns up in Martial, *Epigr.* 2.79, "excusatum habeas me rogo." The Greek vb. *paraiteisthai* normally means "request, ask for," but when used in the context of invitations, it came to carry the nuance of "decline, excuse," even in extrabiblical Greek. See Polybius, *Hist.* 5.27,3; Josephus, *Ant.* 7.8,2 § 175; 12.4,7 § 197; MM 484. A similar, but not identical expression is found in OxyP2.292,6 (A.D. 25): *parakalō se . . . echein auton synestaménon,* "I beg you to have him as (your) protégé."

20. *I have just been married.* Lit. "I married a woman/wife." In this case, the excuse may reflect the status of a newlywed recognized in Deut 24:5. Cf. Deut 20:7. The husband understandably prefers to spend time with his bride. For a similar sentiment in the Greek world, cf. Herodotus, *Hist.* 1.36. The aor. no more reflects a Semitic pf. here, *pace* J. Jeremias, *Parables,* 177, than it does in v. 18.

Most mss. read *gynaika egēma kai dia touto,* "I have married (with the classical Attic aor.) a woman, and for this reason . . ." Ms. D and the Sinaitic and Curetonian Syriac versions have *gynaika elabon dio,* "I have taken a wife; wherefore . . ." The latter is preferred by G. D. Kilpatrick ("The Aorist of *gamein* in the New Testament," *JTS* 18 [1967] 139-140) as the correct text. But are the reasons cogent enough to prefer this weakly attested reading to that of the best Greek mss.?

E. Linnemann *(Jesus of the Parables,* 89) would have us believe that v. 20 was not part of the original parable; her reasons are farfetched and militate against the threefold structure of the parable. See further P. H. Ballard, "Reasons," 342.

21. *the servant came back.* Luke uses the vb. *paraginesthai.* See NOTE on 13:1; also p. 111. It means, he "came to" (his master).

into the streets and lanes of the town. Palestinian poor and unfortunate in the town are to be brought in. For *plateiai* as city "streets," see Luke 10:10; Rev 11:8; 21:21; for the combination of *plateiai* and *rhymai,* see the LXX of Isa 15:3.

the poor . . . the lame. A slightly different word order from the mention of the foursome in v. 13; they constitute the outcasts or subclasses of the town's society. Cf. Matt 22:10, which reads "the bad and the good." Was this the original of "Q," which Luke replaced with his phrase from v. 13? Or is Matthew preparing for the appended parable in his Gospel in vv. 11-14? It is hard to say. Contrast 1QSa 2:5-7, where such persons are excluded from dining. See further H. Braun, *Qumran,* 1. 90.

22. *what you ordered has been done.* This report on the first sending-out of the servant into the streets and lanes stands in contrast to the absence of a report on the further command in v. 23.

23. *into the highways and the hedgerows.* Lit. "into the roads and hedges/fences," i.e. vineyards, gardens, or fields surrounded by hedges or fences, alongside of which ran the "roads" outside the town. In the parable of the persistent friend (11:5-6), he comes *ex hodou,* lit. "from (the) highway," i.e. he was on a journey. See further W. Michaelis, *TDNT* 5. 68.

make people come in. Lit. "force (them) to enter." The language is not to be abused; it means merely that the poor and others will understandably resist in their modesty such an invitation, until they are gently taken and led into the house. See W. Grundmann, *Evangelium nach Lukas,* 300. Recall Gen 19:3. Compare the use of *anankazein* in Mark 6:45; Matt 14:22 (= to urge by convincing speech). Note a milder form of the command in 16:16c.

From Augustine *(Contra Gaud. Don.* 1.25,28 [CSEL 53. 226-227]) on, this phrase has often been understood of physical force which may be used to make converts; thus he became the spiritual father of the Inquisition (J. Schmid, *Evangelium nach Lukas,* 246). See further F. A. Norwood, " 'Compel.' "

my house will be filled! I.e. with those partaking of the bounty of the master's banquet. Here the parable proper ends. We are not told of the execution of this command; it is of little interest in the parable. The full house is taken for granted; this is the parable's main point. See H. Conzelmann, *Theology,* 111.

24. *For I tell you.* Since "you" is pl. *(hymin),* the question arises about who is speaking. It is scarcely being said to the servant (sg.). It is a stereotyped introduction to the conclusion of a parable, such as one finds elsewhere. See NOTE on 11:8. In Stage I of the gospel tradition, it could have had a merely generic meaning; but in Stage III it takes on a further connotation.

not one of those men who were originally invited. Some mss. (D, ℵ) read *anthrōpōn,* "human beings," but the best Greek mss. have *andrōn.*

shall taste of my dinner. I.e. shall have a share in the joy of the festive occasion that I have made ready. The fut. vb. *geusetai* corresponds to the fut. *phagetai* in v. 15. In Stage III of the gospel tradition the saying refers to the eschatological banquet of the kingdom. Jesus then becomes the host. Recall the ending of the parable in *Gos. of Thom.* § 64.

BIBLIOGRAPHY (14:15-24)

Aalen, S. "St Luke's Gospel and the Last Chapters of I Enoch," *NTS* 13 (1966-1967) 1-13.

Baker, J. "Christ's Challenge to Straight Thinking," *ExpTim* 67 (1955-1956) 179-181.

Ballard, P. H. "Reasons for Refusing the Great Supper," *JTS* 23 (1972) 341-350.

Bultmann, R. "Lukas 14, 16-24," *Marburger Predigten* (Tübingen: Mohr [Siebeck], 1956) 126-136.

Derrett, J. D. M. "The Parable of the Great Supper," *Law,* 126-155.

Dormeyer, D. "Literarische und theologische Analyse der Parabel Lukas 14, 15-24," *BibLeb* 15 (1974) 206-219.

Dupont, J. "In parabola magni convivii (Matth. 22, 2-14; Luc. 14, 16-24) historia salutis delineatur," *Acta congressus internationalis de theologia concilii Vaticani II: Romae diebus 26 septembris—1 octobris 1966 celebrati* (Vatican City: Polyglott Press, 1968) 455-459.

Eichholz, G. "Vom grossen Abendmahl (Luk. 14, 16-24) und von der königlichen Hochzeit (Matth. 22, 1-14)," *Gleichnisse der Evangelien,* 126-147.

Galbiati, E. "Gli invitati al convito (Luc 14,16-24)," *BeO* 7 (1965) 129-135.

Glombitza, O. "Das grosse Abendmahl (Luk. xiv 12-24)," *NovT* 5 (1962) 10-16.

Haenchen, E. "Das Gleichnis vom grossen Mahl," *Die Bibel und wir: Gesammelte Aufsätze, zweiter Band* (Tübingen: Mohr [Siebeck], 1968) 135-155.

Hahn, F. "Das Gleichnis von der Einladung zum Festmahl," *Verborum veritas,* 51-82.

Hart, J. H. A. "Possible References to the Foundation of Tiberias in the Teaching of Our Lord," *Expos* 8/1 (1911) 74-84.

Jeremias, J. *Parables,* 176-180.

Jülicher, A. *Gleichnisreden,* 2. 67-79, 202-214.

Liese, H. "Cena magna: Lc. 14,16-24," *VD* 13 (1933) 161-166.

Linnemann, E. *Jesus of the Parables,* 88-97, 158-168.

———— "Überlegungen zur Parabel vom grossen Abendmahl: Lc 14,15-24/Mt 22,1-24," *ZNW* 51 (1960) 246-255.

Mouson, J. "Explicatur parabola de magno convivio (Mt. xxii, 1-14; Lc. xiv, 16-24)," *Collectanea mechliniensia* 28 (1958) 610-613.

Norwood, F. A. " 'Compel Them to Come In': The History of Luke 14:23," *Religion in Life* 23 (1953-1954) 516-527.

Palmer, H. "Just Married, Cannot Come," *NovT* 18 (1976) 241-257.

Perkins, P. *Hearing the Parables,* 94-98.

Perrin, N. *Rediscovering,* 110-114.

Resenhöfft, W. "Jesu Gleichnis von den Talenten, ergänzt durch die Lukas-Fassung," *NTS* 26 (1979-1980) 318-331.

Sanders, J. A. "The Ethic of Election in Luke's Great Banquet Parable," *Essays in Old Testament Ethics (J. Philip Hyatt, In Memoriam)* (eds. J. L. Crenshaw and J. T. Willis; New York: Ktav, 1974) 245-271.

Schlier, H. "The Call of God," *The Relevance of the New Testament* (New York: Herder and Herder, 1968) 249-258.

Schulz, S. *Q: Die Spruchquelle,* 391-403.

Swaeles, R. "L'Evangile (Lc 14, 16-24): La parabole des invités qui se dérobent," *AsSeign* os 55 (1962) 32-50.

Trilling, W. "Zur Überlieferungsgeschichte des Gleichnisses vom Hochzeitsmahl Mt 22,1-14," *BZ* 4 (1960) 251-265.

Via, D. O., Jr. "The Relationship of Form to Content in the Parables: The Wedding Feast," *Int* 25 (1971) 171-184.

Vögtle, A. "Die Einladung zum grossen Gastmahl und zum königlichen Hochzeitsmahl: Ein Paradigma für den Wandel des geschichtlichen Verständnishorizonts," *Das Evangelium und die Evangelien,* 171-218.

Weiser, A. *Die Knechtsgleichnisse,* 58-71.

Zimmermann, H. *Jesus Christus: Geschichte und Verkündigung* (2d ed.; Stuttgart: Katholisches Bibelwerk, 1975) 110-121.

99. CONDITIONS OF DISCIPLESHIP
(14:25-33)

14 ²⁵ Many crowds of people were traveling along with Jesus, and once he turned and said to them, ²⁶ "If anyone comes to me and does not hate his father and his mother, his wife and his children, his brothers and his sisters—yes, even his own life—he cannot be a disciple of mine. ²⁷ Whoever does not carry his own cross and walk behind me cannot be a disciple of mine.

²⁸ For which one of you would plan to build a tower and would not first sit down to reckon whether one has enough to complete it? ²⁹ Otherwise one might lay the foundation and never be able to finish; then all who notice this might begin to ridicule him, ³⁰ 'Here is someone who began to build but could not finish!' ³¹ Or what king would march forth to engage another king in battle and would not first sit down and deliberate whether with ten thousand troops he could meet him who comes against him with twenty thousand? ³² If he could not, he would send a delegation to ask for terms of peace, while the other is still afar off.

³³ Similarly, then, everyone of you who does not say good-bye to all he has cannot be a disciple of mine."

COMMENT

In the Lucan travel account Jesus' dinner-table talk has now come to an end, and the evangelist proceeds to call the reader's attention to Jesus' progress on his journey to Jerusalem and to the crowds accompanying him. He now portrays Jesus speaking about the conditions of real discipleship (14:25-33). The immediately preceding context spoke of an invitation extended far and wide to people on streets and lanes, highways and hedgerows to come into the banquet of the kingdom—so that "my house will be filled" (v. 23). Now Jesus' words add a different consideration: the conditions of discipleship in the kingdom. Their effect in the Lucan Gospel is to parallel the parable of the wedding garment in Matt 22:11-14, which is there added to that of the royal wedding celebration (and which Luke does not have). Entry into the kingdom has its own conditions, and these Lucan verses stand in antithetic parallelism to vv. 15-24. In the larger context of the travel account this passage with its various references to following Jesus (along a way), walking behind him, planning preparations for an undertaking, and distance provides details for the Lucan picture of Christian discipleship (see pp. 241-251). It is, however, farfetched to see these verses as the climax of the last two chapters and to interpret them as directed against "the Jews" who failed to satisfy the conditions necessary to inherit the kingdom, *pace* A. Loisy *(L'Evangile selon Luc,* 388). That is to miss the point of the instructions intended precisely for Christian disciples.

After the introductory v. 25, which by its vagueness reveals that it comes from the evangelist's pen (see J. Jeremias, *Die Sprache,* 241), Luke derives vv. 26-27 from "Q" (see p. 79). Its Matthean parallel is found in 10:37-38, where it forms part of the mission discourse to the "twelve disciples." The two sayings about the hating of parents and relatives and the carrying of one's cross appear in the same order in Matthew and Luke, despite their different wording; they were evidently united in "Q." The *Gospel of Thomas* likewise presents a form of these two sayings joined together in § 55, but it also has a form of the first one alone in § 101. There is still another form of the first saying in Luke 18:29 (a doublet?). That passage is derived from Mark 10:29 (cf. Matt 19:29). From "Mk" Luke seems to have taken the expression "brothers and sisters," which he adds here to v. 26, but which he reduces to merely "brothers" in 18:29 (see NOTE there).

R. Bultmann *(HST* 160) regards the Lucan formulation ("does not hate") as more original than the Matthean ("loves . . . more than me"); "for the former could hardly have developed from the latter." He also considers the Lucan phrase, "be a disciple of mine," as more primitive than Matthew's wording, "worthy of me" (= early Christian terminology). However, the

Matthean form is probably more primitive in its parallelism of father/mother and son/daughter. Luke has changed the second one to wife/children, added a third (brothers/sisters), and also the echo of 9:23 in v. 27—what Bultmann calls "pedantic additions." Verse 27 is a doublet of 9:23b-d,24 (see pp. 81, 784).

In the *Gospel of Thomas* the form of these sayings is as follows: (§ 55) "Jesus said, 'Whoever hates not his father and his mother cannot become my disciple, and (whoever) hates (not) his brothers and his sisters and takes (not) up his cross, as I do, shall not be worthy of me.' " (§ 101) " < Jesus said, > 'Whoever hates [no]t his fath[er] and his mother, as I (do), cannot become my d[iscipl]e; and whoever loves [not] his fa[ther a]nd his mother, as I (do), shall not become my d[isciple]. For my mother [   ], but [my] true [mother] gave me life." The first part of logion § 55 is closer to Matthew in its parallelism, but its ending follows Luke, as does its use of the vb. "hate." The second part of it combines an element from Luke (brothers/sisters) with the substance of Matt 10:38. There is nothing here that shows independence of the canonical forms of these sayings (see further W. Schrage, *Das Verhältnis,* 120). This has to be stressed, *pace* H. Montefiore, "Comparison," in H. Montefiore and H. E. W. Turner, *Thomas and the Evangelists,* 42. The first part of logion § 101 repeats § 55; its second part is a free composition modeled on the first and making use of gnostic ideas. (See further J.-E. Ménard, *L'Evangile selon Thomas,* 157-158, 202.)

Verses 28-32 have been derived by Luke from his source "L" (see p. 84); they contain a few redactional Lucanisms (see NOTES on these verses). Verse 33, however, is a conclusion to this passage, which has been composed by Luke, in order to add a further condition of discipleship, his favorite idea of disposing of material possessions. He makes the verse end with a refrain of vv. 26 and 27.

From a form-critical point of view, Jesus' words in vv. 26-27 may possibly be classed as "I-sayings" (so *HST* 163, which regards them as derived from the primitive Palestinian church), or as hortatory, prophetic words directed at the disciples among the crowds. There is no need to ascribe v. 26 to "Christian prophets" speaking in the name of the ascended Lord, as does Bultmann. N. Perrin *(Rediscovering,* 141) rightly recognizes the authentic character of this saying. The second saying (v. 27), about carrying one's cross, has all the problems noted about its doublet in 9:23 (see p. 784). It is probably a pre-Lucan, early Christian reformulation of something that Jesus may well have said. Verses 28-30 and 31-32 present two parables, even though they lack the explicit formula of comparison. In the first instance the comparison is implied in the rhetorical question, "Which one of you . . . ?" That serves to introduce the pair of parables. Luke, however, makes up for the lack of a comparative formula in his appended v. 33, "Similarly, then, everyone of you . . ."

Jesus' words to the crowds that accompany him form in this part of Luke's travel account a connected discourse, which they did not form originally, and set forth three conditions of discipleship, uncompromising demands made of those who would follow him: the willingness to leave family ties, the willingness to face radical self-denial, and the willingness to give up one's material possessions. In addition, he casts these conditions of discipleship in a demand for serious consideration and no-nonsense, prior deliberation about the costs of such following. The engagement is not to be undertaken lightly.

The first condition (v. 26) calls for a willingness to put parents, family, relatives, even one's own life, in subordination to discipleship. In preserving the vb. "hate" from "Q," Luke presents Jesus' first condition much more radically than does Matthew; there Jesus speaks of loving him more than parents or children (Matt 10:37). Indeed, the Lucan form has heightened the demand by the addition, "yes, even his own life." In effect, it asks the Christian disciple how much he/she esteems this Jesus to whom allegiance is being given. "Only the person who is capable of a radical and painful decision, to set all natural, human relations behind the connection with Jesus (cf. 9:59-62; 8:19-21; 11:27-28) and to give up life itself in martyrdom, can really become a disciple of Jesus" (J. Schmid, *Evangelium nach Lukas*, 247-248). On the following of Jesus, see pp. 241-243.

The second condition (v. 27) calls for the disciple to carry his/her cross and walk behind Jesus; to carry one's cross has already been explained in 9:23 as an image of self-denial (see COMMENT on 9:23-27). The Lucan Jesus here makes it one of the three conditions. In its own way it clarifies Luke's addition to the first condition, the hating of one's "own life," for it may even lead to a destiny similar to that which Jesus will face.

The third condition (v. 33) calls for a radical renunciation of all one's material possessions. It needs no explanation, but one should recall the Lucan theme into which it fits (see pp. 247-251).

The seriousness demanded by the three conditions is now presented in the twin parables (vv. 28-32). Jesus counsels his followers not to decide on discipleship without advance, mature self-probing. One must consider not only the demands to be made but also the consequences of what may only be begun and be left half-done because of a lack of follow-through. Ridicule or surrender to unconditional terms should deter one from rash and unreflective decisions.

In these parables Jesus counsels the disciple to consider seriously what forces and resources the would-be disciple has. But the added condition in v. 33 counsels renunciation of all the material possessions that one has. Note the contrast: What one *has* in the former sense is infinitely more important than what one *has* in the latter—to what one will be expected to say good-bye. In the latter case, the radical condition calls for the renunciation of "all." In the Lucan two-volume story, what Jesus is depicted demanding here provides a background for the idyllic summaries in Acts 2:42-47 and 4:32-37 as well as for the unedifying, yet salutary and instructive, story of Ananias and Sapphira (5:1-11).

NOTES

14 25. *Many crowds.* See the NOTE on 3:7. In this context many people are following Jesus because of the blessings and wonderful things that he has associated with the kingdom. Some Greek mss. (D, Θ) and ancient versions (OL, Curetonian Syriac) omit *polloi,* "many." For the vb. *syneporeuonto,* see 7:11 and NOTE on 4:30. Cf. 24:15.

said to them. The Lucan pen is detected in *eipen pros* + acc. See p. 116.

26. *comes to me.* Jesus clearly distinguishes "discipleship" proper from mere "coming" to him. Many will come to him, but only some will fulfill the conditions required, which are sternly set forth in this passage more so than in any other Gospel.

hate. From 16:13 one learns that *misein,* "hate," is the opposite of *agapan,* "love." *Misein* has already been used in 6:22,27 to describe the attitude of outsiders toward Christian disciples; now it is used by the Lucan Jesus as a figure to express the character of allegiance to himself demanded of the disciple. One is called to such "hatred" to the extent that such persons would be opposed to Jesus; the choice that the disciple has to make is between natural affection for kin and allegiance to Jesus. "In most cases these two are not incompatible; and to hate one's parents *as such* would be monstrous. . . . But Christ's followers must be ready, if necessary, to act towards what is dearest to them as if it were an object of hatred. . . . Jesus, as often, states a principle in a startling way, and leaves His hearers to find out the qualifications" (A. Plummer, *The Gospel,* 364).

For the OT background of such love and hatred, see Gen 29:31-33; Deut 21:15-17. Compare the attitude demanded of members of the pre-Christian Palestinian Jewish community at Qumran; they were to hate all the sons of darkness (1QS 1:10), i.e. all those who were not members of their group; cf. 1QS 9:21; Josephus, *J.W.* 2.8,7 § 139; Ps 139:21-22; K. Stendahl, "Hate, Non-Retaliation, and Love: 1QS x. 17-20 and Rom. 12:10-21," *HTR* 55 (1962) 343-355.

Matthew has softened the demand of Jesus by his redactional wording, "loves . . . more than me" (Matt 10:37).

his father and his mother. This OT expression is pre-Lucan, being found also in Matt 10:37. See also Luke 2:33; 8:51; 18:20 (= Exod 20:12). Hebrew has no single word for "parents," like Greek *goneis* (used by Luke in 2:27,41,43; 18:29; 21:16). Cf. J. Jeremias, *Die Sprache,* 96-97. For the OT background to this part of the saying, see Deut 33:9. Likewise in the OT background is the story of Elisha as a disciple of Elijah in 1 Kgs 19:19-21.

his wife and his children. This is a Lucan redactional alteration of the "Q" formulation, being more comprehensive and changed in view of 14:20. Cf. Acts 21:5. Matthew (10:37) has "son or daughter," which is more traditional. See Exod 20:10; Lev 12:6; 18:10; Deut 16:11,14, etc. The Lucan formulation, however, is not without its OT background. See Num 16:27; Deut 3:19; Jdt 7:14,27.

his brothers and his sisters. This Lucan addition to "Q" is derived from 18:29 (=

Mark 10:29). The phrase has apparently no real counterpart in the LXX, although the singular brother/sister is found in Lev 21:3; Num 6:7. In Joel 2:13 one ms. (A) adds, "and sisters," but the rest of the mss. lack it. The phrase "brothers and sisters" occurs in Mark 3:32; but Luke has made of it merely "your brothers" (8:20, to agree with 8:19 [?]; see NOTE).

yes, even his own life. Lit. "and still even his own soul." This added phrase echoes 9:23; cf. 17:33. Its formulation reminds one of John 12:25b. For *psychē* in the sense of "life," see NOTE on 9:24. Cf. 6:9.

I read here *eti de kai tēn psychēn heautou* (with mss. P⁴⁵, ℵ, A, D, W, Θ, Ψ, *f*¹,¹³, and the Koine text-tradition [see J. Jeremias, *Die Sprache,* 241]). Cf. Luke 9:42; 14:32; 15:20; Acts 2:26. The ms. P⁷⁵ omits *de,* but *eti te kai,* which is also found in Acts 21:28, is only weakly supported by mss. B, L, R, 33, 892. It is therefore a puzzle why it has been preferred by N-A²⁶ and *UBSGNT*³. The change in meaning is in any case insignificant.

A similar saying is preserved in *Poimandres* 4.6: "If you do not hate your body *(sōma)* first *(or* above all), O child, you will not be able to love yourself."

cannot be a disciple of mine. The same cl. appears again at the end of vv. 27,33. Matt 10:37 has redactionally modified the saying, "is not worthy of me."

Jesus' disciples have been mentioned in 5:30; 6:1,13 (the calling of twelve of them),17,20; 8:9,22; 9:14,16,18,40,43b,54; 10:23; 12:1,22. They will be further mentioned in 16:1; 17:1,22; 18:15; 19:29,37,39; 20:45; 22:11,39,45. In Acts the word *mathētai,* "disciples," becomes the usual word for Christians: 6:1,2,7; 9:1,10,19,26,38; 11:26,29; 13:52; 14:20,22,28; 15:10; 16:1; 18:23,27; 19:1,9,30; 20:1,30; 21:4,16*(bis).*

It is strange that the word *mathētēs* does not appear with any certainty in the LXX; it is found as a variant only in some mss. of Jer 13:21; 20:11; 26:9 (= MT 46:9). In later targums and rabbinical writings *talmîd(ā')* is the usual Aramaic word for "disciple." This word is found in the OT only in 1 Chr 25:8 (in parallelism with *mēbîn),* "small and great, teacher and pupil alike" *(RSV);* there it has none of the connotation of the NT or later rabbinic usage. However, Josephus presents Joshua as *mathētēs* of Moses *(Ant.* 6.5,4 § 84), and Elisha as a "disciple" of Elijah *(Ant.* 8.13,7 § 354).

Perhaps K. H. Rengstorf is right in that the relationship of Jesus' followers to him in Stage I of the gospel tradition was not clearly that of *mathētēs* to *didaskalos,* "teacher," or *rabbi.* See *TDNT* 4. 455. But Luke certainly presents it thus here. Moreover, it is not peculiar to Luke, for he has at least inherited this relationship from "Mk," if not also from "Q."

T. W. Manson *(The Teaching of Jesus* [Cambridge: University Press, 1955] 237-240) has argued that the variant forms of this saying in Matthew and Luke are derived from a common Aramaic original, which used the word *šwly' (šĕwilyā'),* "apprentice," which was confused with *šwy,* "equal, corresponding to; worthy." This, however, is scarcely likely. Though the latter word is well attested in contemporary Aramaic, *šwly'* is not. It is much more likely that Matthew has simply changed the saying to suit a contemporary Christian view of discipleship.

27. *does not carry his own cross.* See NOTE on 9:23. Whereas Luke has *bastazein,* "take up, carry, bear" (cf. 7:14; 10:4; 11:27; 22:10 and John 19:17), Matt 10:38 uses *lambanein,* "take hold of, grasp, take upon oneself." Both words are used in the LXX to translate Hebrew *nāśā'* (2 Kgs 18:14; Job 21:3; 1 Chr 15:15; 2 Kgs 7:8). There is,

therefore, no need to suspect an Aramaic vb. *šĕqal* behind this difference. This last vb. does occur in contemporary Aramaic (1QapGen 21:9), in the sense of "lifting up" (one's eyes), but not of "carrying," *pace AAGA*[3] 195-196. Moreover, Aramaic *nĕsā'* is also attested. See 11QtgJob 11:4.

walk behind me. I.e. follow as a disciple. See NOTE on 5:11; 9:23.

The whole verse (27) is omitted in some mss. (M*, R, Γ, 29, etc.) and ancient versions. See *TCGNT* 164. The omission is the result of homoeoteleuton, both vv. 26 and 27 ending with the same cl.

28. *For.* The conj. binds the parables closely to the preceding.

to build a tower. I.e. some sort of fortification to protect a house, land, or vineyard. See Mark 12:1. Some commentators query whether Jesus would be referring to some recent event; if so, there is no way to be sure about it. One could refer to the account of the towers built by Herod in Jerusalem given by Josephus *(J.W.* 5.4,3 § 156-171). M.-J. Lagrange *(Luc,* 410-411) thinks that the builder is not a king (as in the following parable), but some rich person.

sit down. Lit. "having sat down." This ptc. functions like *anastas,* "rising up," when used with a following finite vb. The similar use of *kathisas* is Lucan. See 5:3; 14:31; 16:6; Acts 16:13; 12:21; 25:17.

reckon. Lit. "calculate," i.e. count with pebbles. The vb. *psēphizein/psēphizesthai* was often used in antiquity for tallying in business and for voting. See Polybius, *Hist.* 5.26,13; Herodotus, *Hist.* 9.55; cf. Epictetus, *Disc.* 3.15,8 ("Reckon, sir, first what the task is, then your own nature, what you are able to carry"); Philo, *De Abrahamo* 21 § 105: "Virtue's nature is most peaceable; she is careful to test her own strength before the conflict, so they say, so that if she is able to contend to the end she will take the field; but if she finds her strength too weak, she may shrink from entering the contest at all."

29. *begin to ridicule him.* The pron. *autō,* if masc. and referring to the builder, is awkward because of the preceding gen. absol. See BDF § 423.1; cf. p. 108. Could it refer to the tower *(pyrgos),* i.e. "it"? The pron. is omitted in some mss. (P[45], D).

30. *Here is someone who began . . .* Lit. "that fellow began," with the derogatory use of the dem. *houtos.*

31. *what king.* I.e. a ruler who must consider national policy, not just private finances, as in the preceding parable.

to engage another king in battle. I.e. and win with success. For this military use of the vb. *symballein,* see 1 Macc 4:34; 2 Macc 8:23; 14:17. Contrast Luke 2:19. See NOTE there.

with ten thousand troops. The same phrase is found in 1 Macc 4:29, but this is scarcely an allusion to that passage.

32. *If he could not.* See NOTES on Lucan particles in 5:36; 10:6.

delegation. Lit. "an embassy," an abstraction for "ambassadors." Cf. Luke 19:14; Josephus, *Ant.* 4.8,41 § 296.

to ask for terms of peace. Lit. "to ask for the things pertaining to peace." See 19:42. The implication is that the first king is ready to submit (or even surrender) to the second. For the sense of *eirēnē,* see pp. 224-225.

The best Greek mss. read *ta pros eirēnēn* (ℵ², A, D, L, R, W, Θ, Ψ, and the Koine text-tradition); but some mss. omit *ta,* having simply *pros eirēnēn* (ℵ*, Γ, 1241, etc.).

The meaning is not, however, affected. The expression used here is found in *T. Judah* 9:7 *(aitousin hēmas ta pros eirēnēn,* "they asked of us terms of peace"). Is there an allusion to the submission of King Toi of Hamath to David? H. St. J. Thackeray ("A Study in the Parable") once thought so. He compared the LXX of 2 Sam 8:10; 11:7, *erōtēsai . . . (ta) eis eirēnēn* to Hebrew *šā'al lěšālôm* (cf. Ps 122:6), and concluded that the phrase meant "to ask after his welfare," "inquire about his health," "salute." This would be a roundabout way of expressing submission to a king with superior forces. Possibly, but the allusion is not evident.

33. *Similarly, then . . .* For similar conclusions to Lucan parables, see 12:21; 15:7,10; 17:10; 21:31. One should put no punctuation between "everyone of you" and "who." See 12:21.

does not say good-bye to all he has. Luke uses the same vb. *apotassesthai* as in 9:61. The counsel given here echoes that of 12:33; it will be echoed again in 18:22. See p. 250. On "all," see NOTES on 3:16; 4:15; 9:1. On *hyparchousin,* see NOTE on 8:3.

BIBLIOGRAPHY (14:25-33)

Blinzler, J. "Selbstprüfung als Voraussetzung der Nachfolge," *BLit* 37 (1963-1964) 288-299.

Denney, J. "The Word 'Hate' in Luke xiv, 26," *ExpTim* 21 (1909-1910) 41-42.

Derrett, J. D. M. "Nisi dominus aedificaverit domum: Towers and Wars (Lk xiv 28-32)," *NovT* 19 (1977) 241-261.

Dinkler, E. "Jesu Wort vom Kreuztragen," *Neutestamentliche Studien für Rudolf Bultmann zu seinem siebzigsten Geburtstag am 20. August 1954* (BZNW 21; Berlin: Töpelmann, 1954) 110-129; reprinted, *Signum crucis: Aufsätze zum Neuen Testament und zur christlichen Archäologie* (Tübingen: Mohr [Siebeck], 1967) 77-98.

Eichholz, G. "Vom Bauen und vom Kriegführen (Luk. 14, 28-32)," *Gleichnisse der Evangelien,* 192-199.

Finlayson, T. C. "Christ Demanding Hatred: Luke xiv. 26," *Expos* 1/9 (1879) 420-430.

Fletcher, D. R. "Condemned to Die: The Logion on Cross-Bearing: What Does It Mean?" *Int* 18 (1964) 156-164.

Hunzinger, C.-H. "Unbekannte Gleichnisse Jesu aus dem Thomas-Evangelium," *Judentum—Urchristentum—Kirche* (ed. W. Eltester) 209-220.

Jarvis, P. G. "Expounding the Parables: V. The Tower-builder and the King Going to War (Luke 14:25-33)," *ExpTim* 77 (1965-1966) 196-198.

Jülicher, A. *Gleichnisreden,* 202-214.

Louw, J. "The Parables of the Tower-Builder and the King Going to War," *ExpTim* 48 (1936-1937) 478.

Mechie, S. "The Parables of the Tower-Building and the King Going to War," *ExpTim* 48 (1936-1937) 235-236.

Moore, T. V. "The Tower-Builder and the King: A Suggested Exposition of Luke xiv. 25-35," *Expos* 8/7 (1914) 519-537.

Perrin, N. *Rediscovering,* 126-128.

Schulz, S. *Q: Die Spruchquelle,* 430-433.

Seynaeve, J. "Exigences de la condition chrétienne: Lc 14," *AsSeign* ns 54 (1972) 64-75.

Thackeray, H. St. J. "A Study in the Parable of the Two Kings," *JTS* 14 (1913) 389-399.

100. THE PARABLE OF SALT
(14:34-35)

14 ³⁴ "Salt, then, is good. But if salt becomes tasteless, with what can it be made salty? ³⁵ It would be fit neither for the ground nor for the dung-heap; instead people would just throw it out.

So let the one who has ears to hear take heed."

COMMENT

At this point in the travel account Luke abruptly adds a parable about salt to Jesus' sayings about the conditions of discipleship (14:34-35). It is only loosely connected with the preceding, but is obviously intended as a further comment on those conditions.

The parable is derived by Luke from "Q" (see p. 79). Its Matthean counterpart is found in the sermon on the mount (5:13): "You are the salt of the earth. But if salt becomes tasteless, with what can it be salted? It is no longer good for anything except to be thrown out and trampled under foot by human beings." However, the Lucan form also has some similarity to a form of the saying preserved in Mark 9:50: "Salt is good; but if salt becomes unsalted, with what will you make it salty? Have salt in yourselves, and be at peace with one another." Neither Matthew nor Luke, both of whom have been following the Marcan order (Matt 17:1-18:9 = Mark 9:2-48; Luke 9:28-50 = Mark 9:2-40), have included this Marcan form of the parable in their Gospels. It is found in the block of Marcan material which Luke omits in his Little Omission (Mark 9:41-10:12 [see pp. 67, 823]). In omitting this material, Luke thus avoids a doublet (see pp. 81-82). Nevertheless, Luke uses the Marcan form in part to reword the "Q"-form adopted. He begins the parable as does Mark 9:50 and uses the vb. *artyein,* "make salty." He further changes the second part of the saying about the uselessness of such salt. Finally, he adds the stray logion about hearing (v. 35b), which is found with the parable neither in Matthew nor in Mark (see Luke 8:8).

Form-critically considered, the sayings about salt are an implicit similitude, metaphorical sayings which have become a popular proverb *(HST* 168), devoid of any explicit comparison. They even sound like a proverb of secular wisdom. However, they have an application, not from their own wording, but from the context in which they are used. They are intended here to have a hortatory function (see *FTG* 247); this function is further enhanced by the added saying in v. 35b.

In the Matthean form of the similitude the disciples are portrayed as "the salt of the earth" (parallel to "the light of the world"), and the salt is used to describe the influence of the disciples on other human beings. If they have no influence, they are useless and worth getting rid of. In the Marcan form the saying is also applied to the disciples, but it is understood as expressing their good relations with one another: "Have salt in you and be at peace with one another." Neither of these aspects is true of the Lucan form.

Coming on the heels of the three conditions of discipleship set forth in vv. 25-33, in which the question was entirely about the relation of the disciples to Jesus, the similitude has to be understood of the same relationship. Salt expresses the willingness of the disciple to offer himself/herself in allegiance to Jesus. Just as salt can lose its saltiness, so too can the allegiance deteriorate. If the connection is lost, with what will it be restored? The disciple would be fit for nothing but to be thrown out. Just as the tower-builder and the king could become useless in attaining their first-intended goal, so can the disciple, even once oriented to Jesus. As salt is useful as long as it keeps its seasoning power, so too a disciple, who has decided to follow Jesus, as long as he/she remains ready for the challenge of such allegiance. "The true disciple is as salt; the half-hearted disciple, like tasteless salt, is worse than useless" (J. M. Creed, *The Gospel,* 193).

NOTES

14 34. *Salt, then, is good.* Compare the wording of Mark 9:50. As the saying develops, its goodness is not explained (whether as a seasoning or a preservative or a destroyer [see Judg 9:45]), but the retention of the goodness emerges as important. Salt does not appear in the OT in a figurative sense.

Since sodium chloride is a chemically stable compound, some commentators wonder whether the figure used here refers to ordinary salt as we know it or to "one of the complex salts of Palestine, which can lose savor through physical disintegration or through mixture with gypsum" (E. P. Deatrick, "Salt," 44; cf. O. Cullmann, "Das Gleichnis," 193-194; F. Hauck, *TDNT* 1. 229). Possibly, but then one wonders whether one is not pressing the similitude too far again. It is readily understood in either case. Cf. G. Schwarz, *"Kalon to halas,"* BN 7 (1978) 32-35.

if salt becomes tasteless. Lit. "is made insipid," for the vb. *mōrainein* carries also the connotation of making/being foolish *(mōros).* Thus the vb. has the same meaning as

Hebrew *tāpēl*, which means "tasteless" in Job 6:6 ("Can that which is tasteless be eaten without salt?"), but "insipid" in Lam 2:14 (Jerusalem's prophets seeing visions which are "worthless and insipid"). The LXX paraphrases in both cases.

It is possible that the Marcan form *analon*, lit. "without salt, tasteless," is an attempt to translate *tāpēl* literally, whereas the Lucan form gives it a figurative meaning, "insipid." See J. Jeremias, *Parables*, 168-169; *AAGA*³ 166.

A similar saying is preserved in the Babylonian Talmud (fourth-fifth centuries A.D.) attributed to R. Joshua b. Hananiah (ca. A.D. 120): "There was once a mule which had a foal. On this was hung a chain with the inscription that it should raise 100,000 zuz from its father's family. He was asked, 'Can then a mule bear offspring?' He said, 'These are fables.' He was then asked, 'When salt loses its savor, wherewith shall it be salted?' He answered, 'With the young of a mule.' He was then asked, 'Does then the unfruitful mule have young?' He answered, 'Can salt lose its savor?' " So the rabbinical tradition reacts to the parable of Jesus.

with what can it be made salty? Luke uses the vb. *artyein*, which properly means "fit out, equip, make ready," but which was also used in a culinary sense, "to season, make savory." It is thus a more classical and literary expression than the Matthean (and probably "Q") vb. *halizein*, "to salt." It is also found in the papyri of the Hellenistic period (see MM 80), whereas *halizein* is not. *Pace* E. P. Deatrick ("Salt," 45-46), who has adopted a translation of Tyndale and Luther, the Greek cannot mean, "what can be salted therewith?" The subj. of the vb. is clearly the salt itself (or at least the residue thereof).

35. *fit.* Or "suited," see 9:62, where the same adj., *euthetos,* is found.

neither for the ground nor for the dung-heap. In Matt 5:13 the disciples are said to be "the salt of the earth" *(gē),* but here in Luke *gē* is clearly being used in another sense, "ground, soil," being in parallelism with *kopria,* "dung-heap." Though salt is known to have been a fertilizer for soil in which certain kinds of vegetables were to be planted, the insipid salt would not be able to be used for that purpose; and it would probably even ruin a dung-heap. A. Plummer *(The Gospel,* 366) rightly notes that it is really futile to discuss what is meant by *gē* and *kopria;* "they do not symbolize anything. Many things which have deteriorated or become corrupt are useful as manure, or to mix with manure. Savourless salt is not even of this much use: and disciples without the spirit of self-devotion are like it."

F. Perles ("Zwei Übersetzungsfehler," 96) once suggested that *eis gēn* was a mistranslation of Aramaic *lĕtabbālā',* "for seasoning," because this *tbl* had been confused with Hebrew and Aramaic *tēbēl.* The original would have read, "not for seasoning and not for dunging" *(lā' lĕtabbālā' wĕlā' lĕzabbālā').* M. Black *(AAGA*³, 166-167) further claims (without documentation) that Hebrew *tēbēl,* "used in the Targum [which one?], is occasionally rendered in the LXX by *gē.*" As a matter of fact, in the over twenty-five hundred instances of *gē* in the LXX, it renders *tēbēl* four times (Isa 14:21; 26:9,18; 1 Chr 16:30); in each case when *tēbēl* stands in parallelism to *'ereṣ,* the LXX translates both by *gē.* If one wants to find the Aramaic use of *tbl,* one need only turn to 11QtgJob 24:8, where *tb[l']* is partially preserved; or 29:3 where it clearly occurs ("on the face of the earth"). In the corresponding Hebrew texts (Job 34:13; 37:12) *tēbēl* occurs, but the LXX has a complete paraphrase ("who has made the < earth > under the heaven and all that is in it," 34:13; "upon the earth," 37:12 [here the MT is unclear, almost untranslatable]). What one can make of all this is baffling. As M.-J. Lagrange *(Luc,* 413-414) and J. M. Creed *(The Gospel,* 196) stated before me, I cannot see the relevance of this suggestion to the understanding of the Greek text. Moreover, no one has ever explained how *zabbālā'* would become *kopria,* "dung-heap."

people would just throw it out. Lit. "they would just throw (it) out," the indefinite or impersonal third pl. is used as a substitute for the pass. (see ZBG § 3), an Aramaism most probably.

In the Lucan context this cl. of the parable reflects most on v. 33 of the preceding episode.

let the one who has ears. See NOTE on 8:8, from which Luke derives this comment word for word. From each one of those listening to Jesus in the crowds (v. 25) the comment calls for a positive decision. Cf. p. 700.

BIBLIOGRAPHY (14:34-35)

Bauer, J. B. " 'Quod si sal infatuatum fuerit' (Mt 5,13; Mc 9,50; Lc 14,34)," *VD* 29 (1951) 228-230.

Cullmann, O. "Das Gleichnis vom Salz: Zur frühesten Kommentierung eines Herrenworts durch die Evangelisten," *Vorträge und Aufsätze 1925-1962* (ed. K. Froehlich; Tübingen: Mohr [Siebeck], 1966) 192-201.

———— "Que signifie le sel dans la parabole de Jésus? Les évangélistes, premiers commentateurs du logion," *RHPR* 37 (1957) 36-43; reprinted, *La foi et le culte de l'église primitive* (Neuchâtel: Delachaux et Niestlé, 1963) 211-220.

Deatrick, E. P. "Salt, Soil, Savior," *BA* 25 (1962) 41-48.

Dupont, J. "Renoncer à tous ses biens (Luc 14,33)," *NRT* 93 (1971) 561-582.

Gressmann, H. "Mitteilungen 14. Salzdüngung in den Evangelien," *TLZ* 36 (1911) 156-157.

Hauck, F. *TDNT* 1. 228-229.

Jeremias, J. *Parables,* 168-169.

Nauck, W. "Salt as a Metaphor in Instructions for Discipleship," *ST* 6 (1952) 165-178.

Perles, F. "Zwei Übersetzungsfehler im Text der Evangelien," *ZNW* 19 (1919-1920) 96.

Schulz, S. *Q: Die Spruchquelle,* 470-472.

101. THE PARABLE OF THE LOST SHEEP
(15:1-7)

15 ¹ Now all the toll-collectors and sinners were drawing near to Jesus to listen to him. ² But both the Pharisees and Scribes kept grumbling at him, "This fellow welcomes sinners and eats with them."

³ So Jesus proposed to them this parable, ⁴ "Which one of you that owns a hundred sheep and loses one of them, would not leave the ninety-nine in the desert and go after the lost one until he has found it? ⁵ And when he finds it, would he not gladly lift it to his shoulders, ⁶ return to his dwelling, call together his friends and neighbors, and say, 'Celebrate with me, because I have found my sheep that was lost'? ⁷ Similarly, I tell you, there will be more joy in heaven over one sinner who reforms than over ninety-nine upright persons who need no reform."

COMMENT

Having portrayed Jesus instructing the crowds accompanying him en route to Jerusalem concerning various conditions of discipleship (14:25-35), Luke now presents him addressing with further parables Pharisees and Scribes who grumble at his welcoming toll-collectors and sinners and his dining with them. Among the parables that Luke now appends to that of the salt (14:34-35) are three about joy over the finding of what has been lost (chap. 15); they will be followed by other parables and sayings in the next chapters.

The three parables of chap. 15, that of the lost sheep (vv. 4-7), of the lost coin (vv. 8-10), and of the lost or prodigal son (vv. 11-32), are so distinctive of the Lucan portrait of Jesus that this part of his account has been called "the heart of the Third Gospel" (L. Ramaroson, "Le coeur"). The three were scarcely uttered as a unit in Stage I of the gospel tradition; but coming from different contexts, they have been built into an "artistically constructed unit with a single theme" (I. H. Marshall, *Luke,* 597). They make a major contribution to the Lucan theme of God's love and mercy for sinful human beings and of Jesus' call for repentance and conversion. Indeed, the note of "joy" that is part of the first two parables is explicitly applied to God himself in the concluding verse of each (vv. 7,10).

The parables of chap. 15, however, are part of a still larger unit in the Lucan travel account, which begins here and extends to the end (at least of the specifically Lucan form of that account [18:14], if not to its very end [19:27]). This unit has been called by T. W. Manson "the Gospel of the Outcast" (Sayings, 282), for here Luke's use of his "L" material seems to reveal a deliberate attempt to show God's concern for those human beings whom people tend to despise or condemn. This is evident not only in the parables of chap. 15 (dealing with a shepherd, a poor [perhaps miserly] woman, and a prodigal son), but in other episodes later on (the dishonest manager [16:1-8a], the dishonest judge [18:1-8], the rich man and Lazarus [16:19-31], the ten lepers [17:11-19], the Pharisee and the toll-collector [18:9-14], and even in the story of Zacchaeus [19:1-10]). It thus introduces into the end of the travel account a note of importance for the Lucan portrait of Jesus; it prepares (indirectly) for the ministry in Jerusalem and the passion narrative. (See pp. 257-258.)

Another attempt has been made (by C. J. A. Hickling) to explain chaps. 15 and 16 as a unit, as a Lucan tract on Jesus and the Pharisees. Whereas such a treatment does highlight certain aspects of these chapters—especially Jesus' reproof of the Pharisees in 16:14-15—it unduly strains the interpretation of other incidents in these chapters. After all, chap. 16 is addressed "to the disciples," and it is slightly eisegetical to read the story of the rich man and Lazarus (16:19-31) as directed solely at Pharisees.

It is even more eisegetical to think that Luke has composed the unit of chap. 15 as an echo or reflection of Jer 31:10-20, which portrays God as a shepherd gathering in Israel as his flock, Rachel weeping for her children and refusing to be consoled, and Ephraim, the repentant son of Joseph. This explanation of the unit has been proposed by H. B. Kossen, but it is far-fetched. (See also E. E. Ellis, Gospel of Luke, 196.)

That chap. 15 is an artistic unit in the Lucan Gospel must be admitted. But how did Luke compose it? We can discern in it four main sections: (a) an introduction (vv. 1-3); (b-c) a pair of parallel parables (vv. 4-6,8-9), each fitted with a concluding application (vv. 7,10); (d) a third parable (vv. 11-32), more elaborate, but also centering on joy over the finding of what was lost.

In the introduction, v. 3 is of Lucan composition (see NOTE). Though W. R. Farmer maintains that vv. 1-2 are pre-Lucan, J. Jeremias has more plausibly shown (Die Sprache, 243-244) that they are really of Lucan composition, being mostly a reworking of his own redaction in 5:29-30 (or 32) of Mark 2:15-17. This is a preferable explanation. In a sense, the introductory three verses are not in accord with the rest, since they present Jesus proposing a "parable," when in reality he proposes three of them, and the first seems to imply that there might have been shepherds among the Pharisees and Scribes. In noting this, however, we may be trying to derive from the text more than it says.

The pair of parables (vv. 4-6 and 8-9) has a counterpart in the pair of parables in 13:18-21 (the mustard seed and the yeast) and in the pair of sayings on the conditions of discipleship in 14:28-32 (cf. 12:24-27). As in the pair of parables of chap. 13, this pair again makes use of a man and a woman, a moderately rich shepherd and a poor woman. The pair is clearly marked by the introductory "or" (v. 8), resembling that of 14:31. Was the pair originally joined in Stage I of the gospel tradition? We have no way of being certain in answering this question. The similarity of structure and wording in the two parables might suggest this and has been used by numerous commentators to maintain that Jesus so uttered them as a pair (T. W. Manson, *Sayings,* 283; J. Lambrecht, *Once More,* 28). One should note at least that the applications in vv. 7,10 are secondary. They may well have been in the pre-Lucan tradition (at least v. 7), but they add an aspect which is allegorizing—extending the joy over the finding to God himself. These applications should rather be attributed to Stage II of the gospel tradition.

Did the pair exist in the pre-Lucan tradition? There is a parallel to the parable of the lost sheep in Matt 18:12-13; and it too has an application (v. 14), though of different character. This might seem to suggest that this parable at least was part of "Q," and commentators have reacted differently to this parallel. Some (like T. W. Manson, *Sayings,* 283), stressing the differences between the Lucan and Matthean form and wishing to attribute the pair to Jesus himself, think that Matthew really inherited his form from "M," and Luke the pair from "L." Still others (G. Schneider, *Evangelium nach Lukas,* 324-325; J. Lambrecht, *Once More,* 37-42) think that the pair was actually in "Q" and that Matthew has not only eliminated the parable of the lost coin, but heavily redacted the first parable because of the use he makes of it in his sermon on the community in chap. 18, where it is not addressed to Scribes and Pharisees, but to Christian disciples ("it is not the will of my Father in heaven that one of these little ones should perish," v. 14). (See p. 79.)

But if the pair of parables stood in "Q," then it is difficult to explain why Matthew would have omitted the second, thus disrupting the pair (when he has not only the pairs of the mustard seed and the yeast [13:31-33] and the hidden treasure and the pearl [13:44-46])—to say nothing of the fundamental postulate of "Q" itself, that such passages are found in both Matthew and Luke, not in Mark!

I think that Luke more likely found the first parable (lost sheep) in "Q" and may either have found the other (lost coin) in "L" or have freely composed the parallel. I have already opted for the former (see p. 84); and the study of the Lucan language in these verses by J. Jeremias *(Die Sprache,* 243-248) seems to confirm that. If both parables are to be traced to Stage I of the gospel tradition, they would *not* have been uttered on the same occasion. R. Bultmann *(HST* 171) attributes the second parable to early church tradition,

not to Jesus, because the first of the pair already has an application; similarly
E. Klostermann, *Lukasevangelium*, 155. (But on this, see J. Dupont, *Béati-tudes*, 2. 248.) Bultmann, however, is right in thinking that the Matthean
form of the parable of the lost sheep is more original, for Luke has clearly
redacted his form of it (and of the second parable) to make the theme common in all three parables used in chap. 15: He has substituted the ptcs.
apolesas and *apolōlos*, "lost," for the more original *planēthē* and *planōmenon*,
"wandered off," to suit the theme of the lost and the found. J. Jeremias
(Parables, 40, 42, 69-70, 103, 177) has argued for the Lucan form as the more
primitive; but most of his arguments are not convincing (see W. L. Peterson,
"The Parable," 139-141).

Still another form of the parable of the lost sheep is found in *Gos. of Thom.*
§ 107: "Jesus said, 'The kingdom is like a shepherd who had a hundred sheep.
One among them went astray, the biggest one. He left the ninety-nine (and)
sought for that one (sheep) until he found it. When he had (thus) exerted
himself, he said to (that) sheep, "I love you more than the ninety-nine."' "
This form of the story makes it explicitly a kingdom-parable and adds a note
not found in either the Matthean or Lucan form, the greater love of the
shepherd for the stray. Yet another form is found in the *Gospel of Truth*
(31:35-32:9): "He [the Beloved Son] is the shepherd who left behind the
ninety-nine sheep which had not strayed. He went searching for the one
which had strayed. He rejoiced when he found it. For 99 is a number (reckoned) on the left hand which holds it. But when the one is found, the entire
sum passes over to the right (hand)."

The form of the story in the *Gospel of Truth* is almost certainly under
gnostic influence, with its peculiar numerology (on which see K. Grobel, *The
Gospel of Truth* [Nashville: Abingdon, 1960] 129-131). It has often been said
that the form in the *Gospel of Thomas* has also become a vehicle for expressing gnostic teaching (see N. Perrin, *Rediscovering*, 99; cf. J.-E. Ménard,
L'Evangile selon Thomas, 205; W. Schrage, *Das Verhältnis*, 195-196). Against
this view W. L. Peterson ("The Parable," 127-138) has strongly argued and
apparently with good reason; but when he presses further and tries to establish that the form in the *Gospel of Thomas* is "more primitive than the synoptic versions of the parable" (ibid. 147), I fail to follow him. The greater love of
the shepherd for the stray is colored by the Johannine identification of Jesus
as the good shepherd (10:11-17); and the making of the parable into one
about the kingdom is scarcely more primitive than the Synoptic forms. Fidelity to the eschatological tone of Ezek 34:16 in the *Gospel of Thomas* and the
alleged xenophobic intent scarcely support all the conclusions that are drawn.

When the passage is form-critically considered, it is seen to be a parable (so
C. H. Dodd, *Parables*, 6) or (if one prefers R. Bultmann's view, *HST* 171) a
similitude, introduced by a rhetorical question and fitted with an application
(v. 7).

The setting for the parable proper depicts outcasts of first-century Palestinian society coming to Jesus en route to Jerusalem and Scribes and Pharisees in the same society grumbling at his consorting with toll-collectors and sinners (v. 1; cf. v. 2). The setting recalls 5:29-32. In this case the parable proper is offered as a defense of Jesus' own conduct; this and the following parable make the same basic point. The introduction makes it clear who is meant by the "lost" in the Lucan parables. The point of the parable is not only the shepherd's gracious willingness and initiative to seek out the lost, but also to celebrate its finding with joy. The willingness of the moderately rich shepherd to abandon ninety-nine sheep to search for one stray becomes the basis of the joyful celebration. It symbolizes God's mercy and gracious initiative manifest in the ministry of Jesus to "sinners"—who are the "lost." The parable expresses what the Lucan Jesus will say of himself in 19:10, "the Son of Man has come to seek out and to save what was lost."

The application in v. 7 goes a step further, adding the dimension of heavenly joy not just over the lost sinner who has been found, but over the repentance of that sinner. The joining of the application to the parable proper brings out that that repentance does not take place without the prevenience and initiative of the gracious shepherd. If this application were already in the pre-Lucan gospel tradition, then it still fits well with the Lucan theme of repentance (on which see pp. 237-239); cf. C. H. Dodd, *Parables,* 92.

One should hesitate to reduce this parable, as does N. Perrin *(Rediscovering,* 100), to a mere story "of panic and pleasure, of a sudden crisis that changes all values and of a new situation of joy and gladness." That is to miss the point of the parable, which is not a description of the change in situation of a first-century Palestinian, but rather of the joy (of God) at the finding of a "lost" sinner.

NOTES

15 1. *all the toll-collectors and sinners.* This (pre-Lucan) combination of persons in Palestinian society of the first century has already been met with in 5:30 (see NOTE there; cf. F. Herrenbrück, "Wer waren die 'Zöllner'?" *ZNW* 72 [1981] 178-194) and 7:34. In this Gospel they stand for the outcasts, the irreligious, and the immoral; in this episode they flock to Jesus as they had to John the Baptist in 3:12-13, anxious to hear him—thus they are foils to the grumbling Pharisees and Scribes. For the meaning of *telōnai,* see NOTE on 3:12. For the characteristic Lucan use of hyperbole in "all," see NOTES on 3:16; 4:15; 9:1. Some mss. (W, etc.) and some ancient versions (Latin and Syriac) omit this adj.

were drawing near to Jesus to listen to him. Luke uses the impf. of the vb. *eimi* with a pres. ptc. *engizontes.* See pp. 122-123. According to W. R. Farmer *(NTS* 8 [1961-1962] 303), this usage "at the beginning of an introductory sentence" is not Lucan, but pre-

Lucan. This, however, is strange, because Luke often uses the same construction at the beginning of passages clearly stemming from his pen. See 1:21; 2:33; 3:23; 4:31, etc.

2. *both the Pharisees and Scribes.* See NOTES on 5:17 and 21. The same order of names is found in 5:30, whereas more frequently the order is reversed. See 5:21; 6:7; 11:53; cf. 7:30; 14:3. The conj. *te,* "both," read in mss. P[75], ℵ, B, D, L, Θ, etc., is omitted by others (mss. W, Ψ, *f*[1,13] and the Koine text-tradition).

kept grumbling at him. As they do in 5:30, and as people will again do in 19:7; the impf. tense expresses the continuity of such criticism.

This fellow. The pejorative sense of the demonstrative *houtos,* "that one," is used here. The criticism leveled against him reflects that of 5:29-32. Cf. 7:39. The basis of the criticism may be echoed in the later Tannaitic Midrash, *Mek. Amalek* 3 on Exod 18:1 (65a) that a person should not associate with the godless. See Str-B 2. 208.

eats with them. Cf. Gal 2:12-13.

3. *proposed to them this parable.* Some commentators, realizing that the sg. *parabolēn* actually introduces three parables before the next introductory phrase (16:1), suggest the translation, "a parabolic discourse" (A. Loisy, *L'Evangile selon Luc,* 392; M.-J. Lagrange, *Luc,* 416). It is possible that it is introductory to the parable in vv. 11-32, before which Luke subsequently inserted the pair of parables, in order to create this threesome on the lost and the found. For the Lucan formulation here, see NOTE on 5:36.

4. *Which one of you.* Luke uses *tís anthrōpos ex hymōn,* "what man among you," a variant of the simpler *tís ex hymōn.* See NOTE on 11:5. Note the parallel introductory rhetorical question in v. 8. The man is a "shepherd," even though the name is not used of him. He is understood as a symbol of the loving God (as in the OT; cf. Ps 23:1-3; Ezek 34:11-16).

that owns a hundred sheep. Lit. "having a hundred sheep." The ms. D reads the rel. pron. with the fut., *hos hexei,* "who will have." A hundred sheep contrast well with one stray, and the point of the parable is thus made; the shepherd who is good will leave even ninety-nine to go in search of one. He is not an inordinately rich sheep-owner, but a moderately rich one, and is thus contrasted with the poor woman in the next parable. For the use of the numbers one hundred, ninety-nine, and one in rabbinical sayings of Palestinian origin, see *m. Pe'a* 4:1-2; cf. Str-B 1. 784-785. Cf. Gen 32:14.

loses. Lit. "(having) lost." Instead of the ptc. *apolesas,* mss. B*, D have the subjunc. *apolesē,* "will lose." The loss of the sheep enhances for the shepherd its value, and he willingly foregoes his concern for the ninety-nine in order to retrieve the lost one.

would not leave the ninety-nine in the desert. J. Jeremias *(Parables,* 133) thinks that the shepherd would have counted the sheep as he was putting them into the fold at night. Perhaps; but it is really missing the point of the parable to ask whether a shepherd would actually have left the other sheep in the desert—i.e. would have left such dumb animals alone, unattended. Matt 18:12 reads rather, "on the mountains" *(epi ta orē).* Neither locality in Palestine is unlikely, when one realizes that modern Bedouin shepherds of Jordan or Israel graze their flocks in sparsely grown, predominantly stony areas between Bethlehem and the Dead Sea. Either could well be called "mountains" or "desert," and there is no need to postulate questionable Aramaic phrases like *bĕṭûrā' (pace* J. Jeremias, *Parables,* 39-40, 133) to explain the variants.

The LXX of 1 Sam 17:28 may be the source of the Lucan phrase! Cf. E. E. F. Bishop, *ATR* 44 (1962) 44-57.

The modern goatherd Muhammed edh-Dhib, who went in search of a stray goat in high cliffs above the northwestern shore of the Dead Sea, eventually discovered Qumran Cave 1 in 1947. See R. de Vaux, *Archaeology and the Dead Sea Scrolls* (Schweich Lectures 1959; London: British Academy, 1973) vii n. 1.

and go after the lost one. I.e. as a good shepherd would. Cf. Ezek 34:11-12,16; John 10:11-12. It is taken for granted to be the reaction of such a shepherd. Cf. 19:10.

until he has found it? The cl. expresses the persistence of the searcher. The Lucan form contrasts with the Matthean (18:13), "if he will happen to find it." The best reading is *heōs heurē auto,* but some mss. (‫א‬, A, N, Δ, Ψ, *f*[1,13], etc.) read *heōs hou;* the meaning is not thereby changed.

5. *lift it to his shoulders.* This detail is not found in Matt 18:13. According to Jeremias *(Parables,* 134), this action was necessary, because a stray sheep would lie helpless and would not move on its own, even if prodded. Perhaps, but again this may be missing the point. For the detail expresses the concern of the shepherd. It may, indeed, be a literary touch introduced by Luke, not only from the ancient Near Eastern art forms of the *kriophoros,* the figure known in ancient Assyria and Syria of the tenth-eighth centuries B.C., but in the Greek world as well (Hermes Criophorus, Pausanias, *Boeotia* 9.22,1). See Calpurnius Siculus, *Eclog.* 5.39; cf. A. Parrot, "Le 'bon pasteur': A propos d'une statue de Mari," *Mélanges syriens offerts à M. René Dussaud* (2 vols.; Paris: Geuthner, 1939) 1. 171-182; G. E. Wright, "The Good Shepherd," *BA* 2 (1939) 44-48; V. Muller, "The Prehistory of the 'Good Shepherd,'" *JNES* 3 (1944) 87-90. The famous marble statuette of the Good Shepherd, dating from the third century A.D. and presently in the Lateran Museum, Rome, probably comes from a catacomb and was undoubtedly inspired by this passage (and John 10:11). See O. Marucchi, *Manual of Christian Archeology* (Paterson, NJ: St. Anthony Guild, 1935) 338-340; J. Stevenson, *The Catacombs: Rediscovered Monuments of Early Christianity* (London: Thames and Hudson, 1978) 98-100; J. Finegan, *Light from the Ancient Past* (Princeton: Princeton University, 1951) 383-384 and fig. 167. Cf. Isa 40:11; 49:22.

6. *call together his friends and neighbors.* This detail is lacking in Matt 18:13, but has its parallel in v. 9 of this Gospel. The vb. *synkalein* is a favorite of Luke's. See 9:1; 23:13; Acts 5:21; 10:24; 28:17.

Celebrate with me. I.e. share my joy over the finding of the stray sheep. The same note will be repeated in vv. 9 and 23-24 (in different ways). It strikes the chord of the theme that unites these parables in chap. 15.

7. *Similarly, I tell you.* Again, cf. v. 10.

there will be more joy. The fut. probably refers to the time of judgment. On "more joy," see p. 124.

in heaven. I.e. among God's angels (as in v. 10) or on the part of God himself, if the phrase is meant as a substitute for the divine name. In this application, joy and celebration occur not only on earth, but also in heaven; indeed, they are the result of the initiative of divine love seeking out the lost sinner.

over one sinner who reforms. Both M. Black *(AAGA*[3] 184) and J. Jeremias *(Die Sprache,* 247) maintain that an alliteration, present in underlying Aramaic words *(ḥedwā', "joy,"* and *ḥădā' ḥăṭĕyā', "one sinner"),* points to a pre-Lucan formulation of this application. This is possible. On *metanoein,* see p. 237.

ninety-nine upright persons who need no reform. If by the ninety-nine are meant the Scribes and Pharisees, then the conclusion is ironic—i.e. over ninety-nine allegedly upright persons. But it may only be a typically Lucan way of exaggerating God's joy at a repentant sinner. Cf. Ezek 18:23. Joy over ninety-nine who have no need of repentance cannot be compared with the divine joy over *a* penitent! "The glad tidings of God's love for the penitent sinner proclaimed by Jesus" is Luke's favorite theme, "and into this parable that theme is concentrated" (J. M. Creed, *The Gospel,* 196). See p. 258.

Contrast the Matthean application (18:14), where the stress is put not on joy in heaven, but on the Father's will that not one of these little ones will be lost.

Bibliography on Chapter 15 as a Whole

Adam, A. "Gnostische Züge in der patristischen Exegese von Luk. 15," *SE III* (TU 88) 299-305.

Cantinat, J. "Les paraboles de la miséricorde (Lc, XV, 1-32)," *NRT* 77 (1955) 246-264.

Dupont, J. "Réjouissez-vous avec moi! Lc 15,1-32," *AsSeign* ns 55 (1974) 70-79.

Farmer, W. R. "Notes on a Literary and Form-Critical Analysis of Some of the Synoptic Material Peculiar to Luke," *NTS* 8 (1961-1962) 301-316.

Giblin, C. H. "Structural and Theological Considerations on Luke 15," *CBQ* 24 (1962) 15-31.

Hickling, C. J. A. "A Tract on Jesus and the Pharisees? A Conjecture on the Redaction of Luke 15 and 16," *HeyJ* 16 (1975) 253-265.

Jeremias, J. "Tradition und Redaktion in Lukas 15," *ZNW* 62 (1971) 172-189.

Kossen, H. B. "Quelques remarques sur l'ordre des paraboles dans Luc XV et sur la structure de Matthieu XVIII 8-14," *NovT* 1 (1956) 75-80.

Lambrecht, J. "Parabels over 'het verlorene' (Lc. 15)," *Collationes* 22 (1976) 449-479.

Perrin, N. *Rediscovering,* 90-102.

Ramaroson, L. "Le coeur du troisième évangile: Lc 15," *Bib* 60 (1979) 248-260.

Rasco, E. "Les paraboles de Luc XV: Une invitation à la joie de Dieu dans le Christ," *De Jésus aux évangiles* (ed. I. de la Potterie) 165-183.

Soltau, W. "Die Anordnung der Logia in Lukas 15-18," *ZNW* 10 (1909) 230-238.

Waelkens, R. "L'Analyse structurale des paraboles: Deux essais: Luc 15,1-32 et Matthieu 13,44-46," *RTL* 8 (1977) 160-178.

BIBLIOGRAPHY (15:1-7)

Bishop, E. F. F. "The Parable of the Lost or Wandering Sheep: Matthew 18.10-14; Luke 15.3-7," *ATR* 44 (1962) 44-57.

Bussby, F. "Did a Shepherd Leave Sheep upon the Mountains or in the Desert? A Note on Matthew 18.12 and Luke 15.4," *ATR* 45 (1963) 93-94.

Buzy, D. "La brebis perdue," *RB* 39 (1930) 47-61.

Cantinat, J. "La brebis et la drachme perdues (Lc 15,1-10)," *AsSeign* os 57 (1965) 24-38.

Derrett, J. D. M. "Fresh Light on the Lost Sheep and the Lost Coin," *NTS* 26 (1979-1980) 36-60.

Dupont, J. "Les implications christologiques de la parabole de la brebis perdue," *Jésus aux origines* (ed. J. Dupont) 331-350.

——— "L'opzione pastorale nella parabola della pecora smarrita (Mt 18,12-14)," *Chiesa per il mondo: Miscellanea teologico-pastorale nel LXX del card. Michele Pellegrino . . .* (2 vols.; ed. G. Ghiberti; Bologna: EDB, 1974) 1. 97-104.

——— "La parabole de la brebis perdue (Matthieu 18, 12-14; Luc 15, 4-7)," *Greg* 49 (1968) 265-287.

Faccio, H. "De ove perdita (Lc 15, 3-7)," *VD* 26 (1948) 221-228.

Galbiati, E. "La parabola della pecora e della dramma ritrovate (Luca 15, 1-10)," *BeO* 6 (1964) 129-133.

Jeremias, J. *Parables,* 38-40, 132-136.

Kamphaus, F. " '. . . zu suchen, was verloren war,' Homilie zu Lk 15,1-10," *BibLeb* 8 (1967) 201-204.

Linnemann, E. *Jesus of the Parables,* 65-73.

Monnier, J. "Sur la grâce, à propos de la parabole de la brebis perdue," *RHPR* 16 (1936) 191-195.

Perkins, P. *Hearing the Parables,* 29-33, 38, 47, 52.

Peterson, W. L. "The Parable of the Lost Sheep in the Gospel of Thomas and the Synoptics," *NovT* 23 (1981) 128-147.

Schmidt, W. "Der gute Hirt: Biblische Besinnung über Lukas 15,1-7," *EvT* 24 (1964) 173-177.

Schnider, F. "Das Gleichnis vom verlorenen Schaf und seine Redaktoren: Ein intertextueller Vergleich," *Kairos* 19 (1977) 146-154.

Schulz, S. *Q: Die Spruchquelle,* 387-391.

Topel, J. "On Being 'Parabled,' " *TBT* 87 (1976) 1010-1017.

Trilling, W. "Gottes Erbarmen (Lk 15,1-10)," *Christusverkündigung in den synoptischen Evangelien: Beispiele gattungsgemässer Auslegung* (Biblische Handbibliothek 4; Munich: Kösel, 1969) 108-122.

102. THE PARABLE OF THE LOST COIN
(15:8-10)

15   8 "Or again, what woman who has ten silver coins—if she should lose one of them, would she not light a lamp, sweep out the house, and search carefully until she finds it? 9 And when she finds it, would she not call together her friends and neighbors, and say, 'Celebrate with me, because I have found the silver coin that I lost?' 10 Similarly, I tell you, there is joy before God's angels over one sinner who reforms."

COMMENT

The second of the paired parables at this point in the Lucan travel account tells of a woman who has lost a silver coin and also expends much energy to find it; when she has found it, she too invites friends and neighbors to share her joy over the finding of what was lost (15:8-9). This parable also has an appended application (v. 10).

We have already expressed (in the COMMENT on vv. 1-7) our preference for the derivation of this parable from "L." As in the former case, it could be regarded as a parable or a similitude.

The parable of the lost coin makes almost the same point as that of the lost sheep, but now, instead of a moderately rich shepherd, the main figure is a poor woman who has lost one of her ten drachmas. Luke may intend to depict her as miserly. In any case, she serves to portray divine initiative in seeking out what was lost, again the sinner, as the introduction suggests (v. 2). The appended application allegorizes the sense of the parable in stating that the joy is limited not to earth, but is found even "before God's angels" (v. 10). The paired parables thus insist that, through the preaching of Jesus, God's initiative and grace are extended in boundless fashion; they pass over the defection of the sinner and seek out instead such a one for reform. If a human being will exert such effort to recover her property, how much more will God himself expend? This is the Lucan Jesus' answer to the criticism of the Scribes and Pharisees, the reason why he consorts and dines with such sinful people.

NOTES

15 8. *what woman.* Recall the parallel introductory rhetorical question in v. 4; see p. 191. In this case, the syntax is not perfect, for the *tís gynē* is a nom. absol. (see pp. 124-125). Hence the dash in the translation.

who has ten silver coins. Lit. "having ten drachmas," i.e. ancient silver coins, the value of which is difficult to estimate. The Attic *drachmē* was worth about one quarter of a silver shekel, which was in use in Palestine (Josephus, *Ant.* 3.8,2 § 195). Herod the Great once rewarded soldiers in his army with a hundred and fifty drachmas and their officers with larger sums (Josephus, *J.W.* 1.16,3 § 308); but soldiers of Mark Antony looked on a gift of a hundred drachmas each as a token of his stinginess (Appian, *Bell. civ.* 3.7,43 § 177). There was a time when its purchasing power was considerable, enough to buy a sheep, or the equivalent of a day's wage. In the days of Nero, however, the *denarius* replaced the *drachmē,* which it equaled, but it was then 1/6000 of a talent *(talanton)* or 1/100 of a pound or mina *(mna).* In any case, ten drachmas were not a great sum of money. The *drachmē* is mentioned only here in the NT. See W. Pesch, *EWNT* 1. 855-857; H. Chantraine, "Drachme," *Der kleine Pauly* (5 vols; eds. K. Ziegler and W. Sontheimer; Stuttgart: Druckmüller, 1964-1975) 2. 155-156.

According to J. Jeremias *(Parables,* 133), E. F. F. Bishop, and others, the ten drachmas were part of the woman's dowry (her headdress bedecked with coins [see S. Weir, "A Bridal Headdress from Southern Palestine," *PEQ* 105 (1973) 101-109 and pls. V-XII]), and from this would have stemmed her concern to retrieve the missing one. But, as E. Klostermann *(Lukasevangelium,* 157) pointed out years ago, there is not a hint in the text that so identifies the ten coins.

if she should lose one. The best reading is *ean apolesē drachmēn mian,* "if she will lose one drachma," but ms. D smooths out the problematic syntax mentioned in par. 1 above by reading a paratactic ptc. *kai apolesasa mian,* "and having lost one."

The contrast of ten and one hundred is really not intended in the parallel. Just as having ninety-nine did not deter the shepherd's concern to go to find the stray sheep, so having nine drachmas did not dispense the woman from looking for the one lost.

light a lamp, sweep out the house, and search carefully. Three acts describe her unwearied, unstinted effort to find the lost coin. The darkness of an ancient (probably windowless) house in Palestine is alluded to. Cf. *Midr. Cant.* 1:1 (79b), which has similar details.

until she finds it? Recall the same detail in v. 4.

9. *would she not call together.* See v. 6. The "friends and neighbors" are female in the Greek text. Contrast v. 6.

10. *Similarly, I tell you.* See v. 7.

there is joy. Luke improves the wording here by using *ginetai chara* (so mss. P75, ℵ, B, L, 33, etc.), whereas mss. D, N, *f* 13 harmonize the text with v. 7, *chara estai.*

before God's angels. I.e. by God himself in the presence of angels, or perhaps with them. Luke uses the prep. *enōpion* (see p. 110) and the description of the heavenly court that he has used in 12:8-9. See NOTE there. Again, the point is that the joy is not confined to earth alone.

over one sinner who reforms. The main part of v. 7 is repeated here (without any reference to the others).

BIBLIOGRAPHY (15:8-10)
(in addition to the titles given in 15:1-7)

Güttgemanns, E. "Struktural-generative Analyse des Bildworts 'Die verlorene Drachme' (Lk 15, 8-10)," *Linguistica biblica* 6 (1971) 2-17.
Walls, A. F. " 'In the Presence of the Angels' (Luke xv 10)," *NovT* 3 (1959) 314-316.

103. THE PARABLE OF THE PRODIGAL SON
(15:11-32)

15 [11] Then Jesus said, "There was once a man who had two sons; [12] and the younger of them said to his father, 'Father, give me that portion of the property which is coming to me.' So he divided his estate between them. [13] Not long afterward the younger son gathered together all he had and left home for a distant land, where he squandered his property, living a dissolute life.

[14] When he had spent everything, a severe famine came upon that land, and he began to be in want. [15] So he went and hired himself out to one of the citizens of that land, who sent him off to his farm to feed the pigs. [16] He longed to have his fill even of the carob pods on which the pigs used to feed; but nobody would give him anything. [17] Finally, he came to himself and said, 'How many hired hands working for my father have more than enough to eat, and here am I dying of hunger. [18] I shall get up then and go to my father and say to him, "Father, I have sinned against heaven and before you. [19] I no longer deserve to be called your son; treat me as one of your hired hands." ' [20] So he got up and went back to his father.

While he was still a long way off, his father saw him and had pity on him. He ran to meet him, threw his arms around his neck, and kissed him. [21] The son said to him, 'Father, I have sinned against heaven and before you; I no longer deserve to be called your son.' [22] But his father said to the servants, 'Quick! Bring the best robe and put it on him; give him a ring for his finger and sandals for his feet. [23] Bring out the fatted calf and slaughter it; let us feast and be merry, [24] because this son of mine was dead and has come back to life; he was lost and has been found.' And they began to make merry.

[25] Now the elder son was in the field; as he was coming in and drew near to the house, he heard music and dancing. [26] He called one of the servant boys and asked what it was all about. [27] He told him, 'Your brother has come; and your father has slaughtered the fatted calf, because he has got him back safe and sound.' [28] Then the elder brother became angry and refused to go in. So his father went out and pleaded with him. [29] But he replied to his father, 'Look, I have been serving you so many years, and I have never disregarded a single command of yours; yet you never gave me even a goat that I might make merry with my friends. [30] Now that son of yours has come back, who has devoured your estate with prostitutes, and you have slaughtered for him the fatted calf!' [31] But the father said to him, 'Son, you are always with me. All that I have is yours. [32] But we had to make merry and celebrate! For that brother of yours was dead and has come back to life; he was lost and has been found.' "

COMMENT

To the two preceding parables about the finding of the lost, Luke now adds a third (15:11-32) related to the same theme. It has been traditionally called "the parable of the prodigal son," a marginal title found in English Bibles of the sixteenth century (undoubtedly derived from a similar title in the Latin Vulgate, *De filio prodigo).* The traditional German title, *Der verlorene Sohn,* better expresses the relation of this parable to the preceding.

Regarded as "the greatest of all His [Jesus'] parables" (J. E. Compton), it has, more than any other Gospel passage, entered into varied discussions and presentations of human conduct. From the earliest patristic commentaries on this parable (e.g. of Tertullian, Clement of Alexandria, Gregory Thaumaturgus, Ambrose, Jerome, and Augustine), it has been the subject of elaborate interpretation and recognized as an authentic commentary of Jesus of Nazareth on an all-too-familiar human situation. It has lent itself as a subject for great painters (Dürer, Beham, Rembrandt, L. Bassano, G. van Honthorst), dramatists (Tudor Dramatists; Gascoigne's *Glasse of Government),* choreographers (Balanchine), musicians (Animuccia, Prokofiev, Britten), litterateurs (A. Gide, *L'Enfant prodigue),* and philosophers (Nietzsche). One has only to look at the elaborate bibliography on this story in W. S. Kissinger,

Parables of Jesus, 351-370—scarcely exhaustive—to get an impression of the many ways in which this parable has been reworked. Moreover, parallels to it have been uncovered in Babylonian and Canaanite literature, in the Lotus Sutra, and in Greek papyri. Yet none of the parallels or the retellings can measure up to or compare with the moving force of this story put on the lips of Jesus in this Gospel. See pp. 257-258.

One can agree with G. V. Jones *(The Art,* 174) that the story which this parable unfolds "combines into a succinct pattern such themes as Freedom and Responsibility, Estrangement, the Personalness of Life, Longing and Return, Grace, Anguish, and Reconciliation . . . universal characteristics of life and . . . basic human needs." But emphasis on such themes, while appropriate to a discussion of parables in general, still has to reckon with the fact that this is a parable of the Lucan Jesus, an important element in this part of the Lucan Gospel ("the Gospel of the Outcast"), and a major contribution to the Lucan theme of divine forgiveness of the lost sinner.

The story is preserved only in the Lucan Gospel, and the evangelist has derived it from his source "L" (see p. 84). Luke's redactional pen has left at times some distinctive traces: the introductory *eipen de* (vv. 11,21; see J. Jeremias, *Die Sprache,* 33); the litotes "not long afterward" (v. 13; see NOTE); the ptc. *anastas* (vv. 18,20; see p. 110); *eipen pros* with the acc. (v. 22; see p. 116); "he was lost" (vv. 24,32—the thematic link with vv. 6,9); the optative mood in the indirect question, "what it was all about," along with the vb. *pynthanesthai,* "asked" (v. 26; see p. 112).

From a form-critical point of view, the story is clearly a parable in narrative form, but lacking an explicit application. For years it has been recognized that the traditional English title, "the prodigal son," and the traditional German title, *Der verlorene Sohn,* scarcely sum up more than an aspect of the story. The parable of "the two sons" (T. W. Manson, *Sayings,* 284) is hardly an improvement, but that suggested by J. Jeremias *(Parables,* 128), "the parable of the Father's Love," comes closer to an adequate summary, for the central figure in the story is really the father: "There was once a man who had two sons."

No little part of the problem in properly assessing the message of the story is the relation of its first part (vv. 11-24) to its second (vv. 25-32). Since the time of J. Wellhausen *(Das Evangelium Lucae,* 81-85), attempts have been made in various ways to separate the two parts, suggesting that the second part is a later or secondary expansion of the first. But R. Bultmann *(HST* 196) rightly rejected the view that vv. 25-32 are an "allegorical fabrication" of the first part and insisted that the second part "makes plain by contrast the paradoxical character of divine forgiveness." Bultmann rightly saw, moreover, that this parable was of the sort in which "two types are contrasted with each other" (as in that of the two debtors [7:41-42], the Pharisee and the toll-collector [18:9-14], the two sons [Matt 21:28-31], the wise and foolish virgins

[Matt 25:1-13]). Even though it is a two-peaked parable, the central figure in it is the father.

More recently, J. T. Sanders ("Tradition and Redaction") has queried the existence of two-peaked parables and argued for a concentration of Lucanisms in the second part. The original parable would have dealt only with the younger son and his return, which Luke would have turned into a subtle criticism of the Pharisees and Scribes of v. 2, thus providing a bridge to chap. 16. But his philological arguments, grammatical and stylistic, have been found wanting (see the studies of E. Schweizer, J. Jeremias, C. E. Carlston, and J. J. O'Rourke). Apart from minor redactional changes, such as those we have mentioned above, style is relatively uniform throughout and stems mainly from a pre-Lucan tradition. The same sort of study invalidates the claim of L. Schottroff ("Das Gleichnis") that the parable is wholly a Lucan creation (see further I. H. Marshall, *Luke*, 605-606). Such study does not establish the authenticity of the parable, but commentators such as A. Jülicher, R. Bultmann, J. M. Creed, F. Hauck, and many others see no decisive reasons not to ascribe the parable as a whole to Stage I of the gospel tradition.

There may be a sense in which an important distinction should be made in the discussion of this parable. Perhaps one should distinguish the meaning of it as it was told in Stage I of the gospel tradition from the Lucan context in which it is now found. On the lips of Jesus it may well have stressed the boundless, unconditioned love of the father who not only welcomes back with love his (repentant) son who has wronged him, but will not even allow the attitude of the ever-faithful elder son to deter him from expressing that love and acceptance of the younger son, who "was dead and has come back to life." All of this would still be true of the parable in the Lucan context, but there is more; and it can be seen in two ways. First is the relation this parable has to the two preceding, which stress joy over finding what was lost. Luke may well have added the parallel conclusions of vv. 24,32, "he was lost and has been found." In this parable joy takes the form of feasting, making merry, and dining on the fatted calf, but now it is over finding what was lost. Second, the still fuller Lucan context, including the introductory vv. 1-2, relates the parable to the grumbling Pharisees and Scribes. The attitude of the elder son is now understood in terms of them specifically, and this fuller Lucan context thus allegorizes such notions in the story as the father's "command" *(entolē,* v. 29) or the elder son's service (v. 29).

As it now stands in the Lucan Gospel, the parable presents the loving father as a symbol of God himself. His ready, unconditioned, and unstinted love and mercy are manifested not only toward the repentant sinner (the younger son) but toward the uncomprehending critic of such a human being. The parable portrays the message of Jesus, the kingdom-preacher, especially with the Lucan stress on the divine willingness to accept the repentant sinner into that kingdom. This parable probes the human psyche and touches it deeply in the cry of the young son, "Father, I have sinned against heaven and before you. I no longer deserve to be called your son." In the Lucan Gospel as a whole the story exemplifies the proclamation of the Lord's year of favor, which Jesus was sent to announce to the downtrodden (4:18-19). As the Son of Man who has come to seek out and to save what was lost (19:10), he will not be deterred from such a proclamation by the attitude of those who might prefer their own sense of uprightness to joining in joy and love for those who react with repentance to such a proclamation.

Thus chap. 15 ends with its proclamation of the mercy of a loving father made manifest to the repentant sinner, no matter how gross the sinful conduct has been. It identifies Jesus himself as the incomparable herald of that proclamation. He turns, moreover, to consort and dine with "toll-collectors and sinners" because such persons can find acceptance with God himself. Even though this parable does not stress the seeking out of the lost, as did the two preceding, it does insinuate that Jesus is in the long run the *true* elder brother. The whole chapter thus resounds with joy celebrating the finding of that which was lost (vv. 6,9,24,32).

Along with other commentators, T. W. Manson *(Sayings,* 286) speaks of a "theological problem raised by the parable": There seems to be no place in it for the teaching that God's forgiveness of sinners actually comes through the "sacrificial death of Jesus." Manson rightly rejects such criticism of the Lucan parable because it misses its point, which is not to be a summary of "the Christian doctrine of the Atonement" or a compendium of all of Christian theology. In the Lucan setting its primary purpose is to "justify the attitude of Jesus to sinners by showing that His way is the fulfilment of God's will concerning them, and that the way of the scribes and the Pharisees is the wrong way. . . . Jesus in this parable lays down the fundamental principle of God's relation to sinful men: that God loves the sinner while he is still a sinner, *before* he repents; and that somehow it is this Divine love that makes the sinner's repentance possible." One detects in such criticism the tendency to expect that Luke must teach what Paul teaches (see pp. 27-29).

Scholars with expertise in ancient law have tried to clarify the legal situation of inheritance in Palestine (see the contributions of J. D. M. Derrett, D. Daube, and L. Schottroff). But the sources with which they work (mostly rabbinical) stem from a later date, and there is little unanimity in their presentation of the details. Fortunately, the understanding of the parable does not depend on a minute discussion of them. Derrett would further have us believe that the parable arose originally in a synagogue sermon (of Hanukkah) based on Deut 33:6-26 and Mal 1:6a, elaborated by Deut 21-22. But all of that is farfetched, bordering on eisegesis.

NOTES

15 11. There was once a man who had two sons. He is presumably a Palestinian Jewish farmer or landowner, who is relatively well off. The phrase, "two sons," prepares for the two-part parable, even though the second son does not appear until v. 25. On *anthrōpos tis,* see NOTE on 10:30.

12. *the younger.* Nothing is said about him being married; so he is presumably about twenty years of age.

Father. On the voc. *páter,* see NOTE on 10:21. Here it is used immediately of the boy's human father.

that portion of the property which is coming to me. Lit. "that portion of the property falling to me." The n. *ousia,* "substance, property," is used in the LXX (Tob 14:13 [mss. B, A]; 3 Macc 3:28), Josephus *(Ant.* 7.5,5 § 114; *J.W.* 4.4,3 § 241), and papyri (see MM 467), sometimes even in the sense of "land." The vb. *epiballein* is a stock expression for "falling to, coming to." See Tob 3:17; 1 Macc 10:30; and in extrabiblical Greek (Diodorus Siculus, *Bibl. Hist.* 14.17; OxyP 715:13-15). Cf. BDF § 308; MM 235.

According to Jewish customs in Palestine, a father could dispose of his property either by a will (Greek *diathēkē)* to be executed after his death (Num 36:7-9; 27:8-11) or by a gift to his children during his lifetime (Greek *dōrēma;* Latin *donatio inter vivos).* The counsels of Sir 33:19-23 against the latter reveal that it must have been common enough. In any case, the firstborn son was to inherit or receive a "double portion," i.e. twice the amount that would be given to each of the other sons. See Deut 21:17. In this case, since there were only two sons, the elder would receive two thirds and the younger one third of the property. (J. D. M. Derrett would restrict it to two ninths for a gift to a younger son.) In any case, the son by the gift would acquire title to the property, but the usufruct or interest on the property would continue to come to the father until his death. If the son sold the property, the purchaser would take possession of it only at the death of the father. In doing so, the younger son would have no further claims on the property, either capital or usufruct.

he divided his estate between them. This need not mean that he made over at that time the property to both of them. In allotting to the younger son the third as a gift, he would in effect be dividing the estate *(bios).* In the rest of the parable the father acts as though he were still in possession of the property: He commands the servants (v. 22), orders the slaughter of the fatted calf (v. 23), and speaks of "all that I have" (v. 31).

13. *Not long afterward.* Lit. "after not many days," a litotes. This figure has been used by Luke seventeen times (21:9; Acts 1:5; 12:18; 14:28; 15:2; 17:4,12; 19:11,23,24; 20:12; 21:39; 26:19,26; 27:14,20; 28:2—studied and categorized by F. Rehkopf ("Grammatisches zum Griechischen des Neuen Testaments," *Der Ruf Jesu* [eds. E. Lohse et al.] 213-225). Cf. John 2:12.

gathered together all he had. The vb. *synagein,* "bring together," probably carries the connotation of "converting everything" into cash. It is so used by Plutarch *(Cato Min.* 6.7 § 672c), "converting the inheritance into money." See MM 600. The young son was apparently within his rights to do this.

left home for a distant land. Lit. "went off on a journey to a distant land," i.e. emigrated, probably to some country where diaspora Jews lived. See 19:12.

squandered his property. Lit. "scattered his substance." Instead of *tēn ousian autou,* the reading of the best mss., Codex Bezae has *heautou ton bion,* "his own estate." Cf. Prov 29:3.

living a dissolute life. Lit. "living dissolutely," the adv. *asōtōs* (= *a*-privative + *sōzein*) means "in a way not (bound to be) salutary"; it was used of profligate conduct (LXX Prov 7:11; Demosthenes, *Or.* 40.58; Lucian, *Kataplous* 17). We are not told what this dissolute manner of life was; in v. 30 the elder son describes it as a devouring "your estate with prostitutes."

14. *When he had spent.* Luke uses the gen. absol. See p. 108.

a severe famine. A stock expression used elsewhere in Greek literature: Thucydides, *Pel. Wars* 3.85; Herodotus, *Hist.* 1.94; cf. W. Dittenberger, *Sylloge* 3.495:59.

he began to be in want. Luke uses unstressed *kai autos.* See p. 120.

15. *went and hired himself out.* Lit. "going, he joined himself closely to." The details that follow reveal that the citizen who becomes this Jewish boy's employer is a Gentile. For the same use of the ptc. *poreutheis* ("went and"), see 9:12,13; 13:32; 14:10; 17:14; 22:8.

one of the citizens. On *heis* with the gen., see p. 122. Cf. vv. 19,26.

who sent him off. Lit. "and he sent him off," i.e. the citizen did; for a similar abrupt change of subject, see 7:15.

to feed the pigs. Though from a good Jewish family, he becomes a swineherd. Since pigs, though cloven-footed, do not chew the cud, they are considered "unclean" animals for a Jew. See Lev 11:7; Deut 14:8; cf. 1 Macc 1:47. This detail suggests the degradation to which the young son has been brought. For a kindred, later rabbinic attitude to swineherding, see *b. B. Qam,* 82b, "Cursed be the man who raises pigs, and cursed be the man who teaches his son Greek wisdom." Cf. NOTE on 8:32.

16. *He longed to have his fill.* Lit. "to be sated." See 6:21; 9:17. The best reading is *epethymei chortasthēnai ek* (mss. P⁷⁵, ℵ, B, D, L, R, *f*¹,¹³); but some other mss. (A, Θ, Ψ, and the Koine text-tradition) and ancient versions (OL, Vg, Syriac, Bohairic) read *gemisai tēn koilian autou apo,* "to fill his belly from." Ms. W conflates the two forms. The young son longed to eat what the pigs were eating, but was too disgusted to partake of it. This grotesque image is used to stress his dire need. The impf. *epethymei* (without *an*) expresses an unfulfilled or unattainable wish (see BDF § 359.2); in this case it was psychologically unattainable.

even of the carob pods. Lit. "of the little horns," a n. used specifically of the leguminous fruit of the carob tree, often called St. John's bread. The tree is found all over the Mediterranean area. Its long pods contain a sweet pulp and indigestible seeds and were used for food for animals, sometimes even for humans.

nobody would give him anything. I.e. anything else, anything suitable (see J. Willcock, "Luke xv. 16," *ExpTim* 29 [1917-1918] 43), other than the carob pods. How then did he get his food? We are not told, since it does not matter.

17. *he came to himself.* Lit. "having come to himself," i.e. to his senses. This realization and the remorse are the beginning of his repentance. *Pace* J. Dupont ("Le fils prodigue," 67), his remorse must include a realization of what he has done to his father and a regret for his misconduct. He does not selfishly contrast his status with

that of his father's hired hands. The expression *erchesthai eis heauton* is also found in extrabiblical Greek *(T. Jos.* 3:9; Diodorus Siculus, *Bibl. Hist.* 13.95,2; Epictetus, *Disc.* 3.1,15).

and said. In a soliloquy. See NOTE on 12:17.

How many hired hands. Lit. "how many salaried (ones)," i.e. laborers, not part of the household, who were paid a wage *(misthos)* at the end of the day (Lev 25:50; Job 7:1; Tob 5:14).

18. *I shall get up then and go.* Lit. "rising, I shall set out for." Luke uses the aor. ptc. *anastas* with a finite vb., as in v. 20—a Septuagintism (see p. 114; cf. Gen 22:3,19; 24:10; 43:8; Tob 8:10), not an Aramaism.

I have sinned against heaven and before you. The son's confession, though it uses two different preps. *(eis* and *enōpion),* employs only stylistic variants. "Heaven" is a surrogate for "God," as in Dan 4:26; 1 Macc 3:18, and the young son acknowledges that his conduct has wronged not only his own father but God too. There is no need to understand the first part as meaning, "My sin is so great that it reaches to heaven," or to think that the first part refers to the son's dissolute life and the second to the squandering of his father's property. The expression is simply a paraphrase of an OT confession; see Exod 10:16 (Pharaoh's confession to Moses and Aaron: "against the Lord your God and against you"). In Hebrew the vb. *ḥāṭā'* is usually followed by the simple prep. *lĕ-,* which is variously translated into Greek in the LXX, either by the dat. or by preps. *eis, enanti,* or *enōpion.* See Exod 10:16; 1 Sam 7:6; 24:12; Deut 1:41. See also G. Lohfink, " 'Ich habe gesündigt gegen den Himmel und gegen dich': Eine Exegese von Lk 15, 18-21," *TQ* 155 [1975] 51-52. On *enōpion,* see p. 114.

19. *deserve to be called your son.* After the gift was made, the son has no further legal claim on his father. But the realization of the grossness of his conduct brings him to acknowledge that even psychologically he no longer deserves to be regarded as a son.

as one of your hired hands. I.e. he asks to be allowed to work for his father as a day laborer. Thus the parable does not idealize the sinner.

20. *While he was still a long way off.* The reader is not to ask how the father would have seen him at such a distance as this might suggest; that would be to miss the point of the story. For the gen. absol., see p. 108.

had pity on him. See NOTE on 7:13 and COMMENT there (p. 656).

He ran to meet him. This detail expresses the father's initiative, his basic and prevenient love for the son who left him. As the story develops, this is but the beginning of the manifestations of paternal love and joy. No matter what was done in the past, it is now a time only for love.

threw his arms around his neck. Lit. "fell upon his neck"; the same expression occurs in Acts 20:37, probably imitating the LXX of Gen 33:4; 45:14-15; or 3 Macc 5:49.

and kissed him. Not just in the sense of greeting or welcome, but as a manifestation of forgiveness. See 2 Sam 14:33.

21. *Father . . . son.* The young son repeats his confession, already preformulated in vv. 18-19; but before his real request can be made, the father breaks in. Some mss., however, add at the end, "Treat me as one of your hired hands." So ℵ, B, D, 33, 700,

etc. This addition, however, looks like a copyist's harmonization; it is lacking in mss. P[75], A, L, W, Θ, Ψ, *f* [1,13], and the Koine text-tradition. See *TCGNT* 164.

22. *his father said to the servants.* This would seem to imply that the father was still in some sense the master of the household and owner of the property. On *eipen pros* + acc., see p. 116.

the best robe. Lit. "the first robe," i.e. the one of first quality or value, as the adj. *prōtos* is used in the LXX of Ezek 27:22 *(RSV,* "best"); Amos 6:6; Cant 4:14. Attempts have been made to understand *prōtos* in the sense of *proteros,* "former," i.e. the robe he used to wear. But that obscures the gift-nature of the robe, which along with the ring and sandals marks the father's generosity. Cf. Gen 41:42. In other words, he treats his younger son not as he asks to be treated (as a day laborer), but as an honored guest.

a ring for his finger. See 1 Macc 6:15.

23. *the fatted calf.* See also v. 27. In a culture in which meat was not often eaten, this slaughtering of an animal fattened up for a special occasion also marks the esteem of the father on the return of his young son. The term itself is derived from the LXX of Judg 6:28 (ms. A); Jer 26:21 (= MT 46:21).

let us feast and be merry. A similar phrase appears in 12:19; see NOTE there. Cf. v. 32a below.

24. *was dead and has come back to life.* See v. 32b. A figurative sense of the adj. *nekros* is found in 9:60. Here it is used in still a different figurative sense: either as "thought to be dead" (because he was no longer part of the father's household *[familia]*) or morally "dead" (because of his dissolute life). "Life" would then mean either life in the family or spiritual life (that of a reformed penitent).

was lost and has been found. This is the catchword bond uniting this parable to the two preceding (see vv. 6,9; cf. v. 32c). Since B. Weiss, commentators have at times queried whether Luke has added this to the inherited parable. See E. Klostermann, *Lukasevangelium,* 160. This is highly probable.

25. *in the field.* The elder son, who now appears, was presumably at work for his father—on a "field" still belonging to the father, but destined as a result of the division (v. 12c) to come to this son at the death of the father (as v. 31c implies). Cf. 17:7.

as he was coming in and drew near to the house. Instead of the temporal cl. read by most Greek mss., Codex Bezae has two coordinated ptcs., *elthōn de kai engisas,* "coming (in) and drawing near"; they would modify the main vb. *ēkousen,* "he heard." Cf. 7:12.

music and dancing. Lit. "an orchestra and (choral) dances." The first word *symphonia* is also found in the Greek versions of Dan 3:5, translating Aramaic *sûmpōnyāh* (actually a Greek loanword); since it is there the name of a musical instrument and usually translated "bagpipe," attempts have been made to use that term here. See P. Barry, "On Luke xv. 25, *symphōnia:* Bagpipe," *JBL* 23 (1904) 180-190. But the suggestion is farfetched for many reasons. See G. F. Moore, *"Symphōnia* Not a Bagpipe," *JBL* 24 (1905) 166-175; M.-J. Lagrange, *Luc,* 426-427.

26. *one of the servant boys.* The same sense of *pais* is found in 7:7. On the Lucan use of *heis* ("one") with the gen., see pp. 121-122.

asked what it was all about. Lit. "inquired what this might be," expressed in the optative mood. See BDF § 299.1; § 386.1. Cf. 18:36; Acts 21:33.

27. *because he has got him back safe and sound.* Lit. "because he recovered him healthy." The ptc. *hygiainonta* is used in a figurative sense.

28. *became angry and refused to go in.* The elder brother's scornful reaction is not concealed; presumably it is made known to the father.

went out and pleaded with him. Luke is concerned to bring together the loving father and the resentful elder son, who has otherwise always treated his father with respect.

29. *I have been serving you so many years.* The elder son uses the vb. *douleuein,* which implies that he puts himself not in the category of a hired hand *(misthios),* but of a slave *(doulos):* "serving you faithfully like a slave." Cf. Gen 31:41. In the fuller Lucan context the vb. alludes as well to the loyal service of keeping the commandments on the part of Jesus' critics.

I have never disregarded a single command of yours. Conscious of his fidelity, he stresses it—recognizing that virtue is worse rewarded than vice. Cf. 17:9-10.

you never gave me even a goat. Some mss. (P75, B, etc.) read *eriphion,* "a kid," i.e. a young he-goat; ms. D has *eriphon ex aigōn,* derived probably from the LXX of Gen 38:20. A "goat" would have been of far less value than a fatted calf. His reproach to his father centers on his years-long service, which should have merited for him such a minor form of feasting.

30. *that son of yours.* Thus the elder son expresses the height of his scorn; he cannot bring himself to speak of the younger son as "my brother." The dem. adj. *houtos* is used pejoratively. Cf. 15:2; 18:11; Acts 17:18.

devoured your estate with prostitutes. "We are not told and must not ask how tidings of his younger brother's fortunes had reached him" (J. M. Creed, *The Gospel,* 201). The Latin Vulgate reads *devoravit substantiam suam,* "devoured his own substance, property," which probably reflects a variant in ms. D of v. 13b. The Greek form is more pointed in its formulation.

31. *Son.* Lit. "child," or "(my) child," an affectionate form of address used by the father for the elder son; it is found also in extrabiblical Greek, even for adults. See Herodian, *Hist.* 1.6,4; Achilles Tatius, *Leucip.* 8.4,3. See NOTE on 2:48.

you are always with me. The father expresses no recrimination and does not say that the elder son is wrong; nor does he comment on the uprightness or fidelity of the elder son. All that is taken for granted. Instead, he stresses only their intimate association: "You are always with me" (= you have never died; you have never been lost).

All that I have is yours. I.e. all the property *(ousia,* v. 12), which remains to the father after the "gift" by which one third was given to the younger son; it will all become the property of the elder son, once the father dies—as well as the remains of the usufruct from the gift. See NOTE on v. 12. As the firstborn, the elder son inherits it all.

32. *we had to make merry and celebrate!* Lit. "it was necessary to make merry . . . ." The pron. *hēmas* is supplied as the subj. of the infins. Thus the father vindicates his outward celebration and inner rejoicing. The use of the impf. of *dei,* "it is necessary," echoes the Lucan use of it as an expression of an aspect of salvation-history; that may be hinted at here too.

that brother of yours. The father's response echoes the formulation of the elder brother's comment in v. 30: there *ho huios sou houtos* was used, now *ho adelphos sou houtos.* The father's remark thus becomes gently critical: "It is *your* brother who has returned!"

was dead and has come back to life . . . The telling echo of v. 24. Here in the Greek text the simple vb. *ezēsen* ("lived") is the preferred reading (mss. P⁷⁵, א*, B, L, R, Δ, etc.), whereas several other mss. (א², A, D, W, Θ, Ψ, and the Koine text-tradition) read *anezēsen,* which harmonizes this verse with the preferred reading in v. 24. Thus the second half of the parable ends with the same words of the father, who manifests his love in yet another way even toward the upright elder son; this is why the father remains the central figure in the parable even to the end.

We never learn—and one misses the point to ask—about the subsequent reaction of the elder son (Did he yield to his father's persuasion? Did he go in and greet his younger brother? Did he join in the feasting?). Nor do we learn to what status the younger son was restored. All such questions distract from the Lucan story about *the loving father* "who had two sons."

BIBLIOGRAPHY (15:11-32)

Alonso Díaz, J. "Paralelos entre la narración del libro de Jonás y la parábola del hijo pródigo," *Bib* 40 (1959) 632-640.

Blinzler, J. "Gottes grosse Freude über die Umkehr des Sünders: Lk 15.11-32," *BLit* 37 (1963-1964) 21-28.

Brandenburg, H. *Das Gleichnis vom verlorenen Sohn* (2d ed.; Gladbach: Schriftenmissions-V., 1959).

Braumann, G. "Tot-Lebendig, verloren-gefunden (Lk 15,24 und 32)," *Wort in der Zeit* (eds. W. Haubeck and M. Bachmann) 156-164.

Broer, I. "Das Gleichnis vom verlorenen Sohn und die Theologie des Lukas," *NTS* 20 (1973-1974) 453-462.

Carlston, C. E. "A *Positive* Criterion of Authenticity?" *BR* 7 (1962) 33-44, esp. 36-39.

——— "Reminiscence and Redaction in Luke 15:11-32," *JBL* 94 (1975) 368-390.

Cerfaux, L. "Trois rehabilitations dans l'évangile," *Recueil Lucien Cerfaux,* 2. 51-59.

Compton, J. E. "The Prodigal's Brother," *ExpTim* 42 (1930-1931) 287.

Crossan, J. D., ed. *Polyvalent Narration* (= *Semeia* 9; Missoula, MT: Society of Biblical Literature, 1977).

Daube, D. "Inheritance in Two Lukan Pericopes," *ZSSR* 72 (1955) 326-334.

Derrett, J. D. M. "Law in the New Testament: The Parable of the Prodigal Son," *NTS* 14 (1967-1968) 56-74.

Dumais, M. "Approche historico-critique d'un texte: La parabole du père et de ses deux fils (Luc 15, 11-32)," *ScEsp* 33 (1981) 191-214.

Dupont, J. *Béatitudes,* 2. 237-242.

——— "L'Evangile *(Lc 15,11-32):* L'Enfant prodigue," *AsSeign* os 29 (1966) 52-68.

——— "Le fils prodigue: Lc 15,1-3.11-32," *AsSeign* ns 17 (1969) 64-72.

Eichholz, G. *Gleichnisse der Evangelien,* 200-220.

Fuchs, E. "Das Fest der Verlorenen: Existentiale Interpretation des Gleichnisses vom verlorenen Sohn," *Glaube und Erfahrung: Zum christologischen Problem im Neuen Testament* (Tübingen: Mohr [Siebeck], 1965) 402-415.

Giblet, J. "La parabole de l'accueil messianique (Luc 15, 11-32)," *BVC* 47 (1962) 17-28.

Golenvaux, C. "L'Enfant prodigue," *BVC* 94 (1970) 88-93.

Goppelt, L. *Theologie des Neuen Testaments: Erster Teil: Jesu Wirken in seiner theologischen Bedeutung* (Göttingen: Vandenhoeck & Ruprecht, 1975) 179-188.

Grelot, P. "Le père et ses deux fils: Luc, xv, 11-32: Essai d'analyse structurale," *RB* 84 (1977) 321-348; "De l'analyse structurale à l'herméneutique," ibid. 538-565.

Hirsch, E. *Frühgeschichte des Evangeliums* (2 vols.; Tübingen: Mohr [Siebeck], 1941) 2. 220-223.

Hofius, O. "Alttestamentliche Motive im Gleichnis vom verlorenen Sohn," *NTS* 24 (1977-1978) 240-248.

Jeremias, J. *Parables,* 87, 105, 128-132.

——— "Tradition und Redaktion in Lukas 15," *ZNW* 62 (1971) 172-189.

——— "Zum Gleichnis vom verlorenen Sohn, Luk. 15, 11-32," *TZ* 5 (1949) 228-231.

Jones, G. V. *The Art and Truth of the Parables* (London: SPCK, 1964) 167-205.

Jülicher, A. *Gleichnisreden,* 2. 333-365.

Jüngel, E. *Paulus und Jesus: Eine Untersuchung zur Präzisierung der Frage nach dem Ursprung der Christologie* (2d ed.; Tübingen: Mohr [Siebeck], 1964) 160-164.

Klötzli, E. *Ein Mensch hatte zwei Söhne: Eine Auslegung von Lukas 15,11-32* (Zürich/Frankfurt: Gotthelf, 1966).

Linnemann, E. *Jesus of the Parables,* 73-81.

O'Rourke, J. J. "Some Notes on Luke xv. 11-32," *NTS* 18 (1971-1972) 431-433.

Osborn, R. T. "The Father and His Two Sons: A Parable of Liberation," *Dialog* 19 (1980) 204-209.

Penning de Vries, P. "Der nie verlorene Vater (Lk 15, 11-32)," *Geist und Leben* 44 (1971) 74-75.

Perkins, P. *Hearing the Parables,* 53-62, 134-136, 140-142.

Pesch, R. "Zur Exegese Gottes durch Jesus von Nazaret: Eine Auslegung des Gleichnisses vom Vater und den beiden Söhnen (Lk 15,11-32)," *Jesus: Ort der Erfahrung Gottes: Festschrift für Bernhard Welte* (ed. B. Casper; Freiburg im B.: Herder, 1976) 140-189.

Pöhlmann, W. "Die Absichtung des verlorenen Sohnes (Lk 15:12f.) und die erzählte Welt der Parabel," *ZNW* 70 (1979) 194-213.

Price, J. L. "Luke 15:11-32," *Int* 31 (1977) 64-69.

Rengstorf, K. H. *Die Re-investitur des Verlorenen Sohnes in der Gleichniserzählung Jesu: Luk. 15, 11-32* (Arbeitsgemeinschaft für Forschung des Landes Nordrhein-Westfalen, Geisteswissenschaften, Heft 137; Cologne/Opladen: Westdeutscher-V., 1967).

Robilliard, J.-A. "La parabole du fils aîné: Jésus et l'amour miséricordieux," *VSpir* 106 (1962) 531-544.

Rubsys, A. L. "The Parable of the Forgiving Father," *Readings in Biblical Morality* (ed. C. L. Salm; Englewood Cliffs, NJ: Prentice-Hall, 1967) 103-108.

Sanders, J. T. "Tradition and Redaction in Luke xv. 11-32," *NTS* 15 (1968-1969) 433-438.

Schniewind, J. "Das Gleichnis vom verlorenen Sohn," *Die Freude der Busse: Zur Grundfrage der Bibel* (2d ed.; Göttingen: Vandenhoeck & Ruprecht, 1960) 34-87.

Schottroff, L. "Das Gleichnis vom verlorenen Sohn," *ZTK* 68 (1971) 27-52.

Schweizer, E. "Antwort," *TZ* 5 (1949) 231-233 (answers J. Jeremias, "Zum Gleichnis").

———— "Zur Frage der Lukasquellen, Analyse von Luk. 15,11-32," *TZ* 4 (1948) 469-471.

Scott, B. B. "The Prodigal Son: A Structuralist Interpretation," *Polyvalent Narration* (ed. J. D. Crossan) 45-73.

Silva, R. "La parábola del hijo pródigo," *CB* 23 (1966) 259-263.

Siniscalco, P. "La parabola del figlio prodigo (Lc. 15,11-32) in Ireneo," *Studi in onore di Alberto Pincherle (= Studi e materiali di storia delle religioni* 38 [1967]) 536-553.

Stickler, H. E. "The Prodigal's Brother," *ExpTim* 42 (1930-1931) 45-46.

Tolbert, M. A. "The Prodigal Son: An Essay in Literary Criticism from a Psychoanalytic Perspective," *Polyvalent Narration* (ed. J. D. Crossan) 1-20.

Vazques Mendel, M. A. "El perdón libera del odio: Lectura estructural de Lc 15, 11-32," *Communio* 11 (1978) 271-312.

Via, D. O., Jr. "The Prodigal Son: A Jungian Reading," *Polyvalent Narration* (ed. J. D. Crossan) 21-43.

104. THE PARABLE OF THE DISHONEST MANAGER
(16:1-8a)

16 ¹ Then Jesus said to the disciples. "There was once a rich man who had a manager, and he heard complaints that this man was squandering his property. ² So he called him in and said, 'What is this I hear about you? Draw up for me an account of your management, for you can no longer be manager here.' ³ Then the manager said to himself, 'What am I going to do? My master is taking my job away from me. I cannot dig; to beg, I am ashamed. ⁴ Ah, I know what I shall do so that, when I am removed from management, people will welcome me into their homes.' ⁵ Then he summoned each of his master's debtors. He said to the first, 'How much do you owe my master?' 'One hundred jugs of olive oil,' he answered. ⁶ So he said to the man, 'Here, take your bond, sit down and—hurry—write it for fifty.' ⁷ Then he said to another, 'You, how much do you owe?' He answered, 'A hundred bushels of wheat.' To him he said, 'Here, take your bond and write it for eighty.' ⁸ᵃ And the master praised that dishonest manager because he had acted prudently."

COMMENT

To the parables in chap. 15 Luke now adds further parables and sayings of Jesus, and at this point in the travel account the theme changes somewhat. Whereas the theme in chap. 15 was joy over the finding of what was lost, in this chapter it has to do mainly with the proper attitude toward and use of material possessions. In a way, this new theme was foreshadowed in chap. 15 in the example given by the younger son who squandered his possessions by dissolute living. Now we find two parables, that of the dishonest manager (vv. 1-8a) and that of the rich man and Lazarus (vv. 19-31), which explicitly develop this new theme; there are also sayings appended to the first parable (vv. 8b-13) and others that reprove avaricious Pharisees (vv. 14-15). Only two sayings distract from the theme, that about the law (vv. 16-17) and that about divorce (v. 18). Since most of the material in chap. 16 is exclusive to Luke (vv. 1-12, 14-15, 19-31), one wonders why he inserted here the sayings on the law and divorce, which have counterparts in the Synoptic tradition. It is, consequently, difficult to discern what thread, apart from the theme about the use of material possessions, unites the chapter. (For attempts, see BIBLIOGRA-PHY, page 1102.) In its own way, a good bit of the material in chap. 16 contributes to "the Gospel of the Outcast" (see COMMENT on 15:1-7). I shall discuss the material in the chapter in six sections: vv. 1-8a, 8b-13, 14-15, 16-17, 18, 19-31.

The parable of the dishonest manager has always been puzzling. The lectionaries in Christian liturgy have often compounded the problem of interpreting it by including with the parable proper only some of the appended sayings, thus giving the impression that they too were part of the parable. Older commentators, from patristic times on, failing to fathom the meaning of the parable (or the appended sayings), often contented themselves with homilies about drawing up one's account of management (v. 2), about who the prospective "friends" (v. 9) might be, or about who the "trustworthy/faithful manager" (v. 10) was (St. Paul, the local bishop, etc.). Voices, however, were raised even in antiquity against such multivalent use of elements in the story (see Cyril of Alexandria, Comm. in Luc. 16:1; PG 72.809). Modern commentators have not helped much either, because there has been a great deal of disagreement about where the parable proper ends, even though there is fairly general agreement today that in the unit of vv. 1-13 we have a parable and appended sayings.

Luke has inherited the unit mostly from his source "L" (see p. 84). Only v. 13 has a parallel in Matt 6:24, showing that it has been added from "Q" (see p. 79). This means that most of vv. 1-12 already existed in the pre-Lucan tradition. Lucan redaction in these verses is minimal (see J. Jeremias, *Die*

Sprache, 255-257), apart from the introductory sentence (v. 1a, with its *elegen pros* + acc. [see p. 116]), which Luke composed.

Even though the episode is not explicitly entitled *parabolē,* the first part of the unit is almost unanimously regarded as such (see *HST* 175-176, a "similitude," even though it is for him "entirely narrative in form"; *FTG* 248, a "parabolic narrative"; cf. J. M. Creed, *The Gospel,* 201).

Two main questions confront the interpreter of this story: (a) Where to end the parable proper? (b) What is the meaning of the parable? The main problem concerns v. 8, and it has a bearing on both questions. Moreover, v. 8 has three problems: (1) Does it, in whole or in part, belong to the parable? (2) Who is *ho kyrios* in it? and (3) What is the force of the second *hoti?*

As to the first question, where to end the parable proper, four main views have been current in modern times:

(1) Verses 1-9 make up the parable: the story proper (vv. 1-7) and its application (vv. 8-9). This view was largely the result of the lectionary use of the parable; it sought to relate v. 9 closely to v. 4 in the first part. Invariably, Jesus was regarded as the *kyrios* of v. 8a, and his application of the story was given in vv. 8b-9. With varying nuances, this interpretation was used by D. R. Fletcher, P. Gächter, J. Knabenbauer, M.-J. Lagrange, A. Rücker, et al.; it has been largely abandoned today, but remnants of it can still be found in those who view the parable differently (e.g. T. W. Manson, *Sayings,* 290-293).

(2) Verses 1-7 make up the parable; the rest is secondary addition. In other words, only vv. 1-7 would be traceable to Jesus, the rest is derived either from the evangelist or the tradition before him. So R. Bultmann *(HST* 175, 199-200), who classifies it among the "many similitudes" whose "original meaning . . . has become irrecoverable," although it "obviously meant to say that one can learn even from the slyness of a deceiver; but in what way?" Again, with varying nuances, this view is proposed by W. Grundmann, H. Drexler, A. R. C. Leaney, H. Preisker, W. Michaelis, et al. If one limits the parable to the narrative story in this way, it ends all too abruptly, and one never learns the reaction of the "rich man" or "master" which one is led to await from the beginning.

(3) Verses 1-8 make up the parable. This has the advantage of ending the story with a reaction to the manager's activity, but it raises the question about the *kyrios* of v. 8a. Is he the master of vv. 3,5, the rich man of v. 1? Or is he Jesus? In either case, one wonders about the sense of the approval expressed, to say nothing of the added application in the comment in v. 8b. This represents the majority view in the interpretation of the parable, being used— again, with varying nuances—by J. M. Creed, A. Descamps, E. E. Ellis, E. Klostermann, A. Plummer, K. H. Rengstorf, J. Schmid, et al. T. W. Manson *(Sayings,* 292) sums up the interpretation well: "Whether it is the employer or Jesus that speaks, we must take the purport of the speech to be: 'This is a

fraud; but it is a most ingenious fraud. The steward is a rascal; but he is a wonderfully clever rascal.' "

Common to all three of the foregoing views is the interpretation that the manager, having squandered his master's property, proceeded to falsify the accounts of his master's debtors in order to feather his own nest. The lesson is drawn for Christian disciples from the manager's evil behavior either by contrast or by irony (depending on the commentator). Some commentators who adopt the fourth view about the division of the story will also use this ironic interpretation.

(4) Verses 1-8a make up the parable, and in this case the *kyrios* is the master of vv. 3,5, the rich man of v. 1. This view was adopted by B. Weiss, F. Tillmann, B. T. D. Smith, W. O. E. Oesterley, L. M. Friedel, J. Volckaert, P. Samain, G. Schneider, et al., some of whom, however, would still make Jesus the *kyrios* of v. 8a (and use the interpretation just mentioned). In this case, the question is, In what sense did the master approve of what the manager had done? To answer that question, I have to turn to the second main question mentioned above, What is the meaning of the parable?

To answer this question, one has to isolate four further questions involved in the story:

(1) In what way was the manager dishonest in that he is given the title "the dishonest manager" (v. 8a)? At the outset the manager is reported as one who has been squandering his master's property (v. 1). We are not told how. It could refer to some form of mismanagement: negligence, swindling, incompetent discretion—it does not matter. The manager does not deny the accusation, does not try to defend himself, and makes no attempt to beg off (contrast Matt 18:26). This in itself would be reason enough to call him a "dishonest manager." Did he compound this situation by further falsifying accounts? By further dishonest behavior?

(2) What is the economic situation reflected in this parable? The "rich man" is probably an absentee landlord, the owner of a Galilean *latifundium*, who entrusted the transaction of all usual business in the management of his estate to a "manager" *(oikonomos)*. The latter was not merely a head-servant placed in charge of the household staff (as in 12:42), but a trained, trusted, and duly empowered agent of the master. He was able to act in the name of the master in transactions with third parties (e.g. the renting of plots of ground to tenant-farmers, the making of loans against a harvest, the liquidation of debts, the keeping of accounts of all such transactions). According to accepted practice, such an agent, however, often lent his master's property out to others at a commission or an interest which was added to the principal in promissory notes or bonds. The notes or bonds frequently mentioned only the amount owed, i.e. the principal plus the interest. This custom was widespread in the ancient eastern Mediterranean world, being attested in Greco-Roman Egypt, Palestine, Syria, Assyria, and Babylonia. Indeed, it was appar-

ently still in vogue in the early part of this century (1903) in India, where M. D. Gibson observed it and proposed an interpretation of this parable on the basis of it. Her interpretation was supported by others (see *ESBNT* 174 n. 23) and was eventually bolstered by ancient evidence gathered by J. D. M. Derrett (see BIBLIOGRAPHY). The same custom seems to be known also in later rabbinic texts in which casuistry solved the problem of reconciling this practice with the prohibition of usury or interest in the OT (see Deut 15:7-8; 23:20-21; Exod 22:24; Lev 25:36-37)—a problem that one encounters in Luke 19:23, which seems to reckon with interest. Josephus seems to be aware of a form of the practice since he records that, when Herod Agrippa I, being almost bankrupt (ca. A.D. 33-34), borrowed money through an agent Marsyas from a Near Eastern banker, he had to write a bond for 20,000 Attic drachmas, even though he received 2500 drachmas less *(Ant.* 18.6,3 § 157). (See further the texts of Murabba'at [18 r 4 (DJD 2. 101); 114 (DJD 2.240-241)]; J. D. M. Derrett, *Law,* 56-59.)

(3) Why does the master praise the manager? Though the master may not have known the amount of commission that his manager was acquiring, he must be presumed to have known about the customary practice. There was no "agency for wrongdoing" (i.e. no legal system in which an agent's evil conduct would become the responsibility of the master), and the master would scarcely have approved of the manager's falsification of accounts (or probably even any direct violation of the Torah). The master praises the manager for his prudence, because he realizes that the manager has eliminated his own commission from the original usurious bonds. Such reduction of sums is not attested elsewhere, as far as I know. But it should be noted that the manager does not employ the technical expression for the cancellation of a debt, *ekeleuse to cheirographon chiasthēnai,* "he ordered the receipt crossed out" (i.e. marked with a Greek *chi),* P. Flor. I.61:65 (A.D. 65). Luke's text says only that the debtor is to write a new *cheirographon* (without using that word) for fifty or eighty, eliminating the commission. Such an action of the manager could well bring the praise or approval of his master.

(4) What is the point of the parable? The parable is not a warning against the destructive nature of riches, or an approval of the dishonesty of the manager (vv. 1-2), or an approval of any falsification of accounts. The master's approval bears on the prudence of the manager who realized how best to use what material possessions were his to ensure his future security. The "dishonest manager" thus becomes a model for Christian disciples, not because of his dishonesty (his initial mismanagement and squandering), but because of his prudence. Faced with a crisis, he judged prudently how to cope with it. Christian disciples are also faced with a crisis by the kingdom/judgment preaching of Jesus, and the prudent use of material possessions might be recommended in the light of that crisis. The manager may still be one of the outcasts in the world that Luke knew, but even he has a message for the

Christian disciple. It must be remembered that, if the manager makes use of his wealth to ensure his future, it is a wealth that he has only because of the master's gracious appointment of him as *oikonomos* to begin with. J. D. M. Derrett would rather see the point of the parable in the proper management of God's wealth entrusted to disciples. In a sense, this is comprehensible, but it shifts the emphasis so that the import of the parable is no longer recognizable. It reckons not with the cutting down of the figures and what that would mean to the manager himself.

Is any allegorization of the parable possible, beyond that which Luke suggests by the added sayings? (See *ESBNT* 178.)

What the meaning of this parable is in itself is one thing; what it becomes in the Lucan context, when the following sayings are appended, is another, especially when one reads it as a preparation for the parable of the rich man and Lazarus (16:19-31).

NOTES

16 1. *said to the disciples.* The audience thus changes from the grumbling Pharisees and Scribes of 15:2, the former of whom will reappear in v. 14. They must be presupposed to be listening to all this. On the other hand, what is said to them is also said to disciples. The best reading in mss. P⁷⁵, ℵ, B, D, L, R, etc., is "the disciples," but some others (mss. A, W, Θ, Ψ, *f*¹·¹³, and the Koine text-tradition) add *autou*, "his disciples."

There was once a rich man. I.e. an owner of large estate somewhere in Palestine. Notice that the second parable in this chapter begins the same way (v. 19). On *anthrōpos tis,* see NOTE on 10:30.

who had a manager. The Greek *oikonomos* was often, but not necessarily, a slave born in the household (= Hebrew *ben bayit,* "a son of the house" [Gen 15:3] or *yĕlîd bayit,* "born of the house" [Gen 14:14]), who was especially trained and tested in the supervision of a farm-estate. In the Roman world of the time he was called *vilicus* (or *villicus*). Columella *(De re rustica* 11.1,7) gives instructions about how the manager should have been trained and tested to see whether he really had competence, fidelity, and good will toward his master *(domino fidem ac benevolentiam).* These things are precisely what is lacking in the manager of this story. See further K. Schneider, "Vilicus, vilica," PW 2/8.2 (1958) 2136-2141; K. D. Fabian, "Vilicus," *Der kleine Pauly* 5. 1272-1273; cf. W. Erdman, "Ein römischer procurator omnium bonorum in Judäa z. Z. Christi," *ZSSR* 64 (1944) 370-376.

heard complaints . . . Lit., "and he [the manager] was accused to him [the rich man] as one squandering . . .," i.e. accusations were made to the master. The vb. *diaballein* often carries the connotation of calumny, "to bring charges with hostile intent," i.e. either falsely or slanderously (see 4 Macc 4:1; OxyP 900:13; Josephus, *Ant.* 7.11,3 § 267); but it need not carry such a negative connotation, as is clear from the LXX of Dan 3:8; 2 Macc 3:11; Josephus, *Ant.* 12.4,4 § 176. As the story develops here, the latter sense is meant.

squandering his property. The same vb. *diaskorpizein* has been used in the parable of the prodigal son (15:13) to describe his wasteful use of his property. For this squandering, the agent is called a "dishonest manager" in v. 8a. The "property" is expressed here by *ta hyparchonta.* See NOTE on 8:3.

2. *What is this I hear about you?* Lit. "what this I am hearing about you," a shortened expression similar to what one also finds in the LXX of Gen 12:18; 20:9; 42:28, etc. It should not be translated, "Why do I hear this about you?"

Draw up for me an account of your management. Lit. "render a word of your management." For the expression *apodidonai (ton) logon,* see Matt 12:36; Acts 19:40; Heb 13:17. The sense: Hand over or give me an inventory of my possessions and prepare an account of the transactions you have made, listing the debtors and what they owe. The inventory, account, and list would facilitate the transfer of the manager's task to another. On the Lucan use of the vb. *apodidonai,* see NOTE on 10:35.

you can no longer be manager here. The master has decided to dismiss him from his job; presumably the master has substantiated the charges.

3. *said to himself.* For soliloquy in a parable, see NOTE on 12:17.

My master is taking my job away from me. The wording here may reflect the LXX of Isa 22:19. This comment is introduced by *hoti,* after the rhetorical question.

I cannot dig. Lit. "I am unable to dig," i.e. not physically strong enough to dig, since he has been trained to a white-collar job and is unprepared for hard, physical labor.

to beg, I am ashamed. To the physical inability is added a psychological one. Some mss. (P[75], B) add *kai,* "and," before the second admission.

4. *I know.* Lit. "I have known," or "I have come to know," an example of the "dramatic" aor. See ZBG § 258. It expresses the decision that has been made.

so that . . . people will welcome me into their homes. Lit. "they will receive me," with an indefinite third pl. vb. (a Semitic substitute for the pass. voice). See BDF § 130.2; ZBG § 1. His decision has been taken to ensure his future security.

5. *each of his master's debtors.* I.e. those with whom he had transacted business; in the following, only two are mentioned and they are to be understood as sample cases.

How much do you owe my master? The question is asked to advance the story, since he may be presumed to have a good idea how much was owed; in v. 6 he gives the bond or promissory note to the debtor. He would have had such in his keeping.

One hundred jugs of olive oil. Lit. "a hundred baths of olive oil." The bath (Greek *batos,* from Hebrew *bat* [see p. 113]), a liquid measure which Josephus equates with seventy-two Greek *xestai* or Roman *sextarii (Ant.* 8.2,9 § 57). Each bath was equivalent to about nine gallons. Cf. LXX 2 Esdr 7:22. Hence one hundred baths would be roughly nine hundred gallons of oil. Instead of *batous,* mss. D and 124 read *kadous,* "jars." *Kados* is a Greek variant of *kabos* (= Hebrew *qab),* a liquid measure roughly equivalent to four *xestai;* hence a considerably smaller amount.

6. *take your bond.* Lit. "receive your letters," *grammata,* the sg. of which is used by Josephus *(Ant.* 18.6,3 § 156) of a promissory note or IOU. The "bond," which could also be called *cheirographon* (lit. "[something] written by hand"), must be understood to be of the *atokos* type, i.e. "without interest." This does not mean that interest was not demanded, but only that no interest was explicitly expressed in the bond. In it the debtor as a rule expressed only the total which he owed, without specifying the princi-

pal and the interest. See P. W. Pestman, "Loans Bearing No Interest?" *Journal of Juristic Papyrology* 16-17 (1971) 7-29; J. D. M. Derrett, " 'Take Thy Bond . . . and Write Fifty' (Luke xvi.6): The Nature of the Bond," *JTS* 23 (1972) 438-440.

write it for fifty. This does not mean a cancellation of half the debt or a falsification of accounts, *pace* J. Jeremias, *Parables,* 181. It means that the debtor actually owed the master only fifty jugs of oil, and that the other fifty were the manager's commission. The amount of interest (100%) seems exorbitant; it may be nothing more than the (fantastically) high figures used in parabolic stories (see J. Jeremias, *Parables,* 28, 181), but J. D. M. Derrett *(Law,* 69-72) has tried to show that the interest of 100% is not unknown (in Indian sources!).

Loans of consumer goods (grain, wine, salt, oil, beer, etc.) were made at especially high interest rates. For instance, a loan of wheat is recorded in OxyP 1040, in which four *artabae* were lent and were to be returned *epi diaphorō hēmiolias,* "with an addition of one-half," in all, six *artabae* of wheat. This bond is not of the *atokos* type, but rather of the *syn hēmiolia* ("with a half") type, in which the interest of 50% is explicitly recorded. See N. Lewis, "The Meaning of *syn hēmiolia* and Kindred Expressions in Loan Contracts," *TPAPA* 76 (1945) 126-139.

7. *A hundred bushels of wheat.* Lit. "a hundred kors of grain." The kor (Greek *koros,* from Hebrew *kōr* [see p. 113]) was a dry measure, which Josephus equates with ten Attic *medimnoi (Ant.* 15.9,2 § 314), but elsewhere *(Ant.* 3.15,3 § 321) with 4/7 of a *medimnos.* The *medimnos* was about one and a half bushels. So one hundred kors of grain might actually be considerably more than "a hundred bushels." But it is impossible to reckon this amount with any accuracy.

To him he said. Luke retains the historic pres. *legei* of his source. See p. 107.

write it for eighty. In this case the commission would have been only 25 percent, i.e. on eighty kors (principal). Interest of a quarter or a third for wheat seems to have been common. See J. D. M. Derrett, *Law,* 66-68.

8a. *the master praised.* Lit. "the master approved of the manager of dishonesty." *Ho kyrios* is thus understood of the "rich man" (v. 1) or the "master" (vv. 3,5). The vb. *epēnesen* directly commends the prudent action taken by the manager. It may also indirectly reflect the master's official approval or ratification of his agent's reduction of the amounts; but this is not necessary to the story. In any case, it does not mean that the master approved of the dishonesty recorded in vv. 1c-2.

For a farfetched attempt to translate *epēnesen* as ironic or to understand it *sensu malo* as "condemned," see G. Schwarz, " '. . . lobte den betrügerischen Verwalter'? (Lukas 16,8a)," *BZ* 18 (1974) 94-95.

For attempts to understand *ho kyrios* in v. 8a as Jesus, see J. Jeremias, *Parables,* 45-46; I. H. Marshall, "Luke xvi, 8"; H. Drexler, "Miszellen" (he calls the explanation proposed here [see *ESBNT* 161-184] "pointless," but scarcely gives any reason for such judgment); E. E. Ellis, *Gospel of Luke,* 199.

that dishonest manager. Lit. "the manager of dishonesty." The gen. of quality is found in the LXX (see Ezek 14:4; 44:12); it is often called in NT study a Hebraic gen., because it seems to reflect the use of the Hebrew construct chain, where Indo-European languages would use an adj. See p. 124; cf. BDF § 165; ZBG § 40. Contrast "mammon of dishonesty" (v. 9) with "dishonest mammon" (v. 11). Compare "that dishonest judge" (18:6, see NOTE there).

because he had acted prudently. I.e. he had sized up the urgency of the situation facing him; in this he becomes a model for the Christian disciple faced with the crisis which Jesus' kingdom/judgment preaching brings into his/her life. H. Preisker ("Lukas 16, 1-7") thinks that the adv. *phronimōs* is used differently here from elsewhere in the Synoptics (except Matt 10:16b), for otherwise it describes the person who has grasped the eschatological dimension of the human situation (Matt 7:24; 24:45; 25:2,4,8,9; Luke 12:42). But J. Jeremias *(Parables,* 46) more rightly sees that this dimension is connoted here too.

Bibliography on Chapter 16 as a Whole

Feuillet, A. "Les paraboles de Luc: Chap. 16. Recherches sur la conception chrétienne du droit de propriété et sur les fondements scripturaires de la doctrine sociale de l'église," *Esprit et vie* 89 (1979) 241-250, 257-271.

Hickling, C. J. A. "A Tract on Jesus and the Pharisees? A Conjecture on the Redaction of Luke 15 and 16," *HeyJ* 16 (1975) 253-265.

Rodenbusch, E. "Die Komposition von Lucas 16," *ZNW* 4 (1903) 243-254.

Samain, E. "Approche littéraire de Lc 16," *Foi et vie* 72 (1973) 39-62; with an added note by T. Snoy, 62-68.

For bibliography on vv. 1-13 prior to 1926, see B. M. Metzger, *IPLCG,* 318-321; W. S. Kissinger, *Parables of Jesus,* 398-408.

Bibliography (16:1-8a)

Bailey, K. E. *Poet and Peasant: A Literary-Cultural Approach to the Parables in Luke* (Grand Rapids, MI: Eerdmans, 1976) 86-110.

Baverstock, A. H. "The Parable of the Unjust Steward: An Interpretation," *Theology* 35 (1937) 78-83.

Bigo, P. "La richesse comme intendance, dans l'évangile: A propos de Luc 16:1-9," *NRT* 87 (1965) 267-271.

Blinzler, J. "Kluge Ausnützung der Gegenwart zur Sicherung der Zukunft: Lk 16,1-8," *BLit* 37 (1963-1964) 357-368.

Boyd, W. F. "The Parable of the Unjust Steward (Luke xvi. 1ff.)," *ExpTim* 50 (1938-1939) 46.

Bretscher, P. G. "Brief Studies: The Parable of the Unjust Steward—A New Approach to Luke 16:1-9," *CTM* 22 (1951) 756-762.

Caemmerer, R. R. "Investment for Eternity: A Study of Luke 16:1-13," *CTM* 34 (1963) 69-76.

Camps, G. M. and B. M. Ubach, "Un sentido bíblico de *adikos, adikia* y la interpretación de Lc 16,1-13," *EstBíb* 25 (1966) 75-82.

Clavier, H. "L'Ironie dans l'enseignement de Jésus," *NovT* 1 (1956) 3-20.

Comiskey, J. P. "The Unjust Steward," *TBT* 52 (1971) 229-235.

Coutts, J. "Studies in Texts: The Unjust Steward, Lk. xvi, 1-8a," *Theology* 52 (1949) 54-60.

Davidson, J. A. "A 'Conjecture' about the Parable of the Unjust Steward (Luke xvi,1-9)," *ExpTim* 66 (1954-1955) 31.

Degenhardt, H.-J. *Lukas Evangelist der Armen,* 114-120.

Derrett, J. D. M. "Fresh Light on St Luke xvi: I. The Parable of the Unjust Steward," *NTS* 7 (1960-1961) 198-219; reprinted, *Law,* 48-77.

Drexler, H. "Miszellen: Zu Lukas 16,1-7," *ZNW* 58 (1967) 286-288.

Dupont, J. *Béatitudes,* 1. 107-111; 2. 118-122, 168-172.

——— "L'Exemple de l'intendant débrouillard: Lc 16,1-13," *AsSeign* ns 56 (1974) 67-78.

——— "La parabole de l'intendant avisé (Luc, 16, 1-13)," *LumV suppl. biblique de "Paroisse et liturgie"* 12 (1953) 13-19.

Feuillet, A. "Les riches intendants du Christ (Luc xvi, 1-13)," *RSR* 34 (1947) 30-54.

Firth, C. B. "The Parable of the Unrighteous Steward (Luke xvi. 1-9)," *ExpTim* 63 (1951-1952) 93-95.

Fitzmyer, J. A. "The Story of the Dishonest Manager (Lk 16:1-13)," *TS* 25 (1964) 23-42; reprinted, *ESBNT,* 161-184.

Fletcher, D. R. "The Riddle of the Unjust Steward: Is Irony the Key?" *JBL* 82 (1963) 15-30.

Friedel, L. M. "The Parable of the Unjust Steward," *CBQ* 3 (1941) 337-348.

Fyot, J.-L. "Sur la parabole de l'intendant infidèle," *Christus* 6 (1959) 500-504.

Gächter, P. "Die Parabel vom ungetreuen Verwalter (Lk 16,1-8)," *Orientierung* 27 (1963) 149-150.

Galbiati, E. "Il fattore infedele (Luca 16,1-9)," *BeO* 3 (1961) 92-96.

Gander, G. "Le procédé de l'économe infidèle, décrit Luc 16.5-7, est-il répréhensible ou louable?" *VCaro* 7 (1953) 128-141.

Gibson, M. D. "On the Parable of the Unjust Steward," *ExpTim* 14 (1902-1903) 334.

Hüttermann, F. "Stand das Gleichnis vom ungerechten Verwalter in Q?" *TGl* 27 (1935) 739-742.

Jalland, T. G. "A Note on Luke 16,1-9," *SE I,* 503-505.

Jeremias, J. *Parables,* 19, 23, 42, 45-48, 181-182.

Jülicher, A. *Gleichnisreden,* 2. 495-514.

Kamlah, E. "Die Parabel vom ungerechten Verwalter (Luk. 16, 1ff.) im Rahmen der Knechtsgleichnisse, *Abraham unser Vater* (eds. O. Betz et al.) 276-294.

Kannengiesser, C. "L'Intendant malhonnête," *Christus* 18 (1971) 213-218.

Knox, W. L. *The Sources of the Synoptic Gospels* (2 vols.; Cambridge: University Press, 1957) 2. 93-96.

Kosmala, H. "The Parable of the Unjust Steward in the Light of Qumran," *ASTI* 3 (1964) 114-121.

Krämer, M. "Ad parabolam de villico iniquo: Lc 16,8.9," *VD* 38 (1960) 278-291.

Krüger, G. "Die geistesgeschichtlichen Grundlagen des Gleichnisses vom ungerechten Verwalter Lk 16,1-9," *BZ* 21 (1933) 170-181.

Kümmel, W. G. "Der Begriff des Eigentums im Neuen Testament," *Heilsgeschehen und Geschichte: Gesammelte Aufsätze 1933-1964* (eds. E. Grässer et al.; Marburger theologische Studien 3; Marburg: Elwert, 1965) 271-277, esp. 274.

Liese, H. "Villicus iniquitatis: Lc. 16, 1-9," *VD* 12 (1932) 193-198.

Lindars, B. "Jesus and the Pharisees," *Donum gentilicium: New Testament Studies in Honour of David Daube* (eds. E. Bammel et al.; Oxford: Clarendon, 1978) 51-63, esp. 53-56.

Lunt, R. G. "Expounding the Parables: III. The Parable of the Unjust Steward (Luke 16:1-15)," *ExpTim* 77 (1965-1966) 132-136.

———— "Towards an Interpretation of the Parable of the Unjust Steward (Luke xvi. 1-18," *ExpTim* 66 (1954-1955) 335-337.

Maass, F. "Das Gleichnis vom ungerechten Haushalter, Lukas 16,1-8," *Theologia viatorum* 8 (1961-1962) 173-184.

Marshall, I. H. "Luke xvi, 8—Who Commended the Unjust Steward?" *JTS* 19 (1968) 617-619.

Merkelbach, R. "Über das Gleichnis vom ungerechten Haushalter (Lucas 16, 1-13)," *VC* 33 (1979) 180-181.

Molina, J.-P. "Luc 16/1 à 13: L'Injuste *Mamon,*" *ETR* 53 (1978) 371-376.

Moore, F. J. "The Parable of the Unjust Steward," *ATR* 47 (1965) 103-105.

Perkins, P. *Hearing the Parables,* 165-171, 185.

Preisker, H. "Lukas 16,1-7," *TLZ* 74 (1949) 85-92.

Samain, P. "Le bon usage des richesses, en Luc XVI, 1-12," *Revue diocésaine de Tournai* 2 (1947) 330-335.

Smith, B. T. D. *The Parables of the Synoptic Gospels: A Critical Study* (Cambridge: University Press, 1937) 108-112.

Tillmann, F. "Zum Gleichnis vom ungerechten Verwalter. Lk 16,1-9," *BZ* 9 (1911) 171-184.

Topel, L. J. "On the Injustice of the Unjust Steward: Lk 16:1-13," *CBQ* 37 (1975) 216-227.

Volckaert, J. "The Parable of the Clever Steward," *Clergy Monthly* 17 (1953) 332-341.

Williams, F. E. "Is Almsgiving the Point of the 'Unjust Steward'?" *JBL* 83 (1964) 293-297.

Williams, F. J. "The Parable of the Unjust Steward (Luke xvi. 1-9)," *ExpTim* 66 (1954-1955) 371-372.

Zerwick, M. "De villico iniquo," *VD* 25 (1947) 54-55, 172-176.

Zimmermann, H. "Die Botschaft der Gleichnisse Jesu," *BibLeb* 2 (1961) 92-105, 171-174, 254-261 (esp. 254-261).

105. THREE APPLICATIONS OF THE PARABLE
(16:8b-13)

16 8b "For the children of this world are more prudent in dealing with their own generation than are the children of light. 9 I tell you, use the mammon of dishonesty to make friends so that, when it gives out, you will be welcomed into dwellings that are everlasting."

¹⁰ "The one who is faithful in little things is also faithful with much; the one who is dishonest in little things is also dishonest with much. ¹¹ If, then, you are not faithful when handling dishonest mammon, who will trust you with real wealth? ¹² And if you are not faithful with another's goods, who will give you goods of your own?"

¹³ "No servant can serve two masters; either he will hate the one and love the other, or he will be devoted to the one and despise the other. You cannot serve both God and mammon."

COMMENT

To the parable of the dishonest manager (16:1-8a) the gospel tradition at an early stage appended other sayings of Jesus—possibly because the parable, being repeated in areas where the economic situation was not fully understood, was already lending itself to forms of allegorization. Three further applications have been made of the parable in the Lucan context. C. H. Dodd has called them "notes for three separate sermons on the parable as text" *(Parables,* 17). They reveal how the early Christian community was moralizing the story. The applications are found in vv. 8b-9,10-12,13. They undoubtedly stem from different settings, and at least the first was quickly associated with the parable itself.

The first application (16:8b-9) may not even have been a unit originally, since v. 9 begins with a pre-Lucan expression, *(kai egō) hymin legō,* lit. "and I tell you," which is used elsewhere as introductory (see 5:24; 6:27; 11:9; *pace* A. Descamps, it is not of Lucan redaction; see J. Jeremias, *Die Sprache,* 106). These two verses are of marked Semitic phraseology and betray a Palestinian background (with "children of this world," "the children of light," "the mammon of dishonesty," "dwellings that are everlasting"). Verse 9 seems to have been fashioned in the pre-Lucan tradition in imitation of v. 4; it scarcely owes its existence to Luke himself. The two verses undoubtedly came to Luke from "L" (see p. 84), along with the parable itself, and joined to it because of the catchword bonds in "prudently" (v. 8a) and "more prudent" (v. 8b) and in "manager of dishonesty" (v. 8a, see NOTE there) and "mammon of dishonesty" (v. 9).

The second application (vv. 10-12) is likewise derived from "L" (see p. 84), but whether it too was already appended to the foregoing verses is another question. Each of these three verses is marked by a form of antithetic parallelism; the first is declarative, the second and third shorter and interrogative. J. Jeremias *(Die Sprache,* 61-62) stresses that this is a pre-Lucan formulation. In vv. 10-11 the antithesis plays on *pistos/pisteuein,* "(be) faithful" and *adikos,* "dishonest," whereas in v. 12, which also uses "faithful," the antithesis involves "another's goods" and "your own" (goods). In reality, these verses are more closely related to Jesus' sayings about vigilance and faithfulness in 12:42b-46 (derived from "Q," see p. 985). There Jesus spoke of a "faithful and prudent manager," and vv. 10-12 would be more at home in that context; they may even have belonged to such a part of the gospel tradition. Here they form a unit and have been added to the foregoing verses because of the catchword bond, "mammon of dishonesty" (v. 9) and "dishonest mammon" (v. 11).

Lastly, Luke himself, having derived v. 13 from "Q" (see its counterpart in the Matthean sermon on the mount, 6:24), has appended it here because of the catchword bond "mammon" in vv. 9, 11, and 13d. The only difference between the Matthean and Lucan forms of the saying is the presence of *oiketēs*, "servant," in v. 13 of the latter. Many commentators judge that it is a Lucan addition, as is likely (see A. Jülicher, *Gleichnisreden*, 2. 109; E. Klostermann, *Lukasevangelium*, 164; J. Jeremias, *Die Sprache*, 258). Otherwise, twenty-seven out of twenty-eight Greek words are identical (see p. 76). Yet another form of this saying is preserved in *Gos. of Thom.* § 47: "Jesus said, 'It is impossible for a man to mount two horses (or) to stretch two bows. And it is impossible for a servant to serve two masters—otherwise he will honor the one and contemn the other." The *Gospel of Thomas* form is closer to Luke (with "servant") than to Matthew. The first part of its saying (about two horses and two bows) is probably only an analogical extension of the "Q" saying; though it could conceivably be more primitive than "Q," nothing argues in favor of it, and analogical imitation is a more plausible explanation. (See W. Schrage, *Das Verhältnis*, 109-111; J.-E. Ménard, *L'Evangile selon Thomas*, 147-149 [who even thinks that the form has been gnosticized in its use of *šᵉmše*, "serve."])

From a form-critical point of view, all the appended sayings are wisdom-utterances of Jesus (see *HST* 70, 75-77). Only one of them (v. 9) is an exhortation in imperative form; the rest enshrines declaratory principles.

The first application (vv. 8b-9) equates the children of this world with the manager of v. 8a. Because of their "prudence," both surpass the children of light (Christian disciples) in their dealings with this generation. In other words, Christians can learn something from the prudence of such people. Verse 8b is a generalizing comment on the conclusion of the parable itself, stressing prudence in Christian life. Verse 9 spells out the eschatological implication of the exhortation hidden in the declaration of v. 8b. Christian disciples are to make prudent use of material possessions, now called "the mammon of dishonesty," to make friends who will welcome them into dwellings that are everlasting, when the mammon itself gives out. Thus the prudence of the decision made by the manager of v. 4 is allegorized to become an exhortation to the prudent use of material possessions. As NOTE will make clear, "mammon of dishonesty" is not to be understood as if the saying were recommending the use of dishonest means to attain a good end.

What is the prudent use of "mammon of dishonesty" which is being recommended? In itself, the saying does not go into detail. It could be almsgiving, which would fit into a Lucan theme in the Gospel (see p. 249). But that too would be a further allegorizing of the parable.

The second application (vv. 10-12) is different, drawing a lesson from the parable as a whole and its implication about responsible management. The manager is nowhere in the parable said explicitly to have been unfaithful; yet that is certainly the implication of vv. 1b-2 and the reason why he is removed from his job. Verses 10-12 allegorize this aspect of the parable. The eschatological nuance of v. 9 disappears, and the emphasis is shifted to day-to-day responsibility and fidelity. Three points are made: The contrast of faithfulness in little things of life and in big things (the smallest amount and much), cf. 19:13,16-19; a contrast of handling ordinary possessions and really valuable goods; and a contrast of responsibility in handling what belongs to another and what may become one's own. The three contrasts thus sum up the role of fidelity in Christian life.

Finally, the third application (v. 13), which really has nothing to do with the parable proper, sums up a general attitude toward wealth. Even though Luke has derived it from an earlier Christian tradition, it fits well into his own treatment of the ideal Christian attitude toward material possessions (see pp. 247-251). It also comments on vv. 10-12. The saying puts the attitude toward money very radically: God or mammon! Which is going to govern one's life? For no one can serve both of them! If one allows oneself to get involved in the servile pursuit of wealth and reduces oneself to a slave of it, then one cannot really serve God. Mammon thus becomes the god that one serves. So the saying puts the question to the Christian reader: Which do you want to serve?

When the parable (vv. 1-8a) is separated from the appended applications, which the early Christian tradition soon associated with it, its teaching is consistent in itself. When considered separately, it has its own message. But when the applications are properly viewed, they too become forceful allegorizations which still have something to say to Christians of today. There is no need to invoke irony to save the relation of the applications to the parable itself (see further *ESBNT* 180 and n. 32).

NOTES

16   8b. *For.* This part of v. 8 begins with the conj. *hoti,* which creates an initial problem, coming so closely after another *hoti* which introduces the obj. cl. of the vb. *epēnesen.* Years ago J. Wellhausen *(Das Evangelium Lucae,* 86) wanted to understand

the second *hoti* as equal to Hebrew *lē'mōr* ("saying"), as introducing *dir.* discourse. Jesus' statement would then be, "The children of this world . . ." followed by v. 9, "I tell you . . ." This suggestion, however, is overly subtle and has convinced few people. I. H. Marshall ("Luke xvi. 8—Who Commended the Unjust Steward?" *JTS* 19 [1968] 617-619) thought that v. 8 was merely another example of the Lucan use of indir. discourse, followed by dir. discourse; he thus tried to support Wellhausen and compared Luke 5:14; Acts 1:4; 23:22; 25:4-5 (quoting as well BDF § 470.2 and H. J. Cadbury, "Lexical Notes on Luke-Acts," *JBL* 48 [1929] 412-425). But none of these examples is a valid parallel. Luke 5:14 does indeed have dir. discourse continuing indir. discourse (expressed, however, by an infin.!), but it lacks precisely *hoti* (even in a sense of *recitativum).* In Acts 1:4 the anacoluthon comes after two infin.-objs. of *parēngeilen;* in Acts 23:22 the *hoti* introduces, not dir. discourse, but a second instance of indir. discourse; and Acts 25:4-5 has nothing similar. The upshot is that we are thrust back on the comment of J. M. Creed *(The Gospel,* 203) that the second *hoti* in v. 8 must be translated as "for" or "because." It creates a secondary joining, which introduces a new lesson to be drawn from the parable; it thereby reveals the kind of suture it really is. Cf. 16:15c.

the children of this world. This is probably only a Greek reflection of the Palestinian expression *kl bny tbl,* "all the children of the world" (CD 20:34), a Qumran designation for all humans outside their community, a sense that is akin to that used here. In this case, the Greek expression connotes individuals whose outlook is totally conditioned by this world/age and have no care for the godly aspects of human existence. A slightly different sense of the phrase will be used in 20:34, where "the children of this age" (mortal human beings in earthly existence) stand in contrast to "children of God" who are "like angels."

more prudent in dealing with their own generation. Lit. "more prudent with reference to *(eis)* their own generation." The prep. *eis* expresses relationship (BAGD 866). Just what is meant here by *genea,* "generation," is problematic. It may mean "people of their own clan/kind" (BAGD 154). In any case, the prudence of such people in their dealings with one another is being proposed to Christian disciples eager to become part of the kingdom.

the children of light. Lit. "the sons of light." This is a designation of Christian disciples, as it is in 1 Thess 5:5; Eph 5:8; John 12:36. This expression is found neither in the OT nor in later rabbinic literature; but it is known to be a favorite designation of the (Essene) Qumran community, being used both in Hebrew *(bĕnê 'ôr,* 1QS 1:9; 2:16; 3:13,24,25; 1QM 1:3,9,11,13; 4QFlor 1-2 i 8-9; 4Q*177* 10-11:7; 12-13 i 7,11) and in Aramaic *(bĕnê nĕhôrā',* 4Q'Amram^b 3:1 *[MPAT* § 23.3:1]; 4Q'Amram^e 1:[9-10] *[MPAT* § 26.1:9-10]). The frequent Qumran counterpart, "sons of darkness" *(bĕnê ḥôšek* or *bĕnê ḥăšôkā'),* has no parallel in the NT. Though the expression, "sons of . . ." is thoroughly Semitic (see NOTE on 10:6) and though "light" and "darkness" are found as a symbolic pair for ethical good and evil, weal and woe (see NOTE on 11:34), the division of humanity into two groups by the expressions, "sons of light" and "sons of darkness," is found nowhere else outside Qumran literature—and by implication also in the NT. See further *ESBNT* 208-211; H. Braun, *Qumran,* 1. 90-91.

9. *I tell you.* Jesus is now made to draw a further application. This phrase is undoubtedly the mark of an originally separate saying.

use the mammon of dishonesty to make friends. Lit. "make for yourselves friends out of the mammon of dishonesty." Unfortunately, we are not told who these "friends" are; commentators speculate: God (T. W. Manson, *Sayings,* 293), the poor (W. Manson, *Gospel of Luke,* 183-184), angels (W. Grundmann, *Evangelium nach Lukas,* 321). Nor are we told how to make such friends. By giving alms?

The prep. *ek,* "out of," has been variously interpreted. J. C. Wansey ("The Parable of the Unjust Steward: An Interpretation," *ExpTim* 47 [1935-1936] 39-40), in an attempt to get rid of the obvious meaning, suggested that it was corrupted by scribal haplography from *ektos,* "without": "Make friends without the mammon . . ." E. Delebecque *(Etudes grecques sur l'évangile de Luc* [Paris: "Les belles lettres," 1976] 93) would understand it in a separatist sense, like Hebrew *min,* "apart from." P. Colella ("De mamona iniquitatis," *RivB* 19 [1971] 427; "Zu Lk 16 7," *ZNW* 64 [1973] 124-126) prefers to understand it, again in a Hebrew sense, as an expression of comparison, "rather than": "Make for yourselves friends rather than mammon." But all these are desperate attempts to get around a sense of "mammon of dishonesty," which may be unnecessary. The prep. *ek* denotes the means by which the friends are to be made; this is a natural sense and finds its counterparts not only in Luke (8:3), but also in extrabiblical Greek (Xenophon, *Anab.* 6.4,9; Josephus, *Life* 29 § 142). Indeed, it could also reflect a Semitic *min* (CD 2:12, *wlml' pny tbl mzr'm,* "to fill the face of the universe with [lit. "from"] their seed").

mammon. The n. *mamōnas* is a grecized form of either Hebrew *māmôn* or Aramaic *māmônā'.* See p. 113. Though unknown in OT Hebrew, it is found in Qumran literature both in Hebrew (1QS 6:2; 1Q27 1 ii 5; CD 14:20) and in Aramaic (11QtgJob 11:[8] = Hebrew Job 27:17); it is also found in later targums (e.g. *Neofiti 1* of Gen 14:16,21). Augustine *(De serm. Dom.* 2.14,47; *CCLat* 35.138; *Sermo 113* 2.2; *PL* 38.648) knows of it as a Punic word, even though it is so far unattested in Phoenician or Punic. Many etymological explanations of the word have been suggested (from *matmôn,* "something hidden"; *ma'môn,* "credit in a bank," *mahmôn,* "abundance," *man* + *mā',* Lat. "quidquid"), but they are all improbable, involving alleged assimilations that never occur. The best explanation of the word remains that it is a *maqtāl* noun type of the root *'mn,* "be firm" (the Hebrew causative of which is *he'ĕmîn,* "believe, trust in"; cf. *amēn): ma'mān* > *ma'môn* (accented long *a* > *ô* [so-called Canaanite shift]) > *māmôn* (with the quiescence of the *aleph,* the *a* is lengthened). It would mean "that in which one puts trust," from which a semantic shift to "money, possessions" would not be difficult. In Aramaic it would be an aramaized loanword from Hebrew. See further A. M. Honeyman, "The Etymology of Mammon," *Archivum linguisticum* 4 (1952) 60-65; F. Vattioni, "Mammona iniquitatis," *Augustinianum* 5 (1965) 379-386; H. P. Rüger, *"Mamōnas," ZNW* 64 (1973) 127-131.

mammon of dishonesty. The exact Semitic equivalent of this Greek expression has not yet been discovered elsewhere. However, in Qumran literature one finds a kindred phrase, *hôn ḥāmās,* "wealth of violence" (1QS 10:19), and *hôn hāriš'āh,* "the wealth of evil" (CD 6:15; cf. CD 8:5; 19:17). In none of these instances does the phrase clearly mean "ill-gotten gain" or wealth iniquitously acquired. Even in the two Lucan passages (16:9,11) the phrase seems to mean "mammon that leads to dishonesty," stressing the *tendency* or iniquitous seduction of mammon to enslave those who pursue it and to lead to forms of dishonesty.

It is sometimes said that *māmôn dišqar* occurs in the targums in the meaning of "possessions acquired dishonestly" (so F. Hauck, *TDNT* 4. 390); if so, this is a later nuance. Hauck cites only the fifth-century targum of Prov 15:27, which translates Hebrew *bōṣēă' bāṣa'*, "he who is greedy for gain" (which is not quite the same thing). Cf. Str-B 2. 220; *1 Enoch* 63:10.

when it gives out. I.e. when the mammon gives out and the crisis arrives. The best reading is *eklipē* (third sg. second aor. subjunc.), "it (i.e. the mammon) fails, gives out" (mss. P⁷⁵, B, ℵ*, Ψ, L, D); but patristic quotations (Irenaeus, Clement of Alexandria, Basil, Chrysostom) and some mss. of the Koine text-tradition have *eklipēte*, "(when) you (pl.) give out," i.e. die; this reading becomes in the Latin Vulgate (and the tradition dependent on it) *cum defeceritis*. It is almost certainly derived from an early exegetical tradition.

Hence the sense of the exhortation: Use prudently the wealth you have—the mammon of dishonesty—to ensure your status at the eschaton.

you will be welcomed. Lit. "they will welcome you," the indef. third pl. is again to be understood as a substitute for the pass. (see NOTE on 16:4). There is no need to invoke the theological pass. here.

into dwellings that are everlasting. Lit. "into everlasting tents," an expression found elsewhere only in *2 Esdras* 2:11 (which may come from the third century A.D. and be dependent on this Lucan passage). It clearly has an eschatological connotation.

10. *faithful in little things.* Lit. "faithful in the smallest (thing)." Cf. 19:17; *2 Clem.* 8.5-6.

11. *dishonest mammon.* Instead of the so-called Hebraic gen. of v. 9, one actually has here the Greek adj. "dishonest mammon."

who. To some commentators this means "God." See I. H. Marshall, *Luke,* 623. This is possible, but the sense of the question comes across without necessarily thinking of God.

real wealth. Lit. "the true wealth." The contrast in this verse is between *adikos,* "dishonest," and *alēthinos,* "true." The neut. *to alēthinon* means "what is really good" (BAGD 37).

12. *goods of your own.* This expression is a bit obscure. Some interpreters think that what comes to one by inheritance is meant. That is possible, but there may be a contrast between material possessions (which do not really belong to human beings) and a person's real wealth or worth (which cannot be taken away). The best reading is *hymeteron,* "your own" (in mss. P⁷⁵, ℵ, A, D, R, W, etc.); but a few mss. (B, L, etc.) have *hēmeteron,* "our own," which just compounds the difficulty. Since Greek *ypsilon* and *ēta* were pronounced alike during many centuries, this may be the cause of the confusion; but it is also suspected of having been changed to "our" (= belonging to the Father and the Son) by later theological interpretation. See *TCGNT* 165.

13. *No servant.* The Lucan addition of *oiketēs* is more generic than *oikonomos* used in vv. 1,3,8.

serve two masters. I.e. at the same time and with the same devotion. The two following contrasts explain why. The first uses the OT love/hatred pair of Qoh 3:8; it expresses an emotional reaction, whereas the second puts the problem more in terms of an intellectual reaction. Note the chiastic arrangement.

You cannot serve both God and mammon. The starkness of the summary scarcely needs a comment. The vb. *douleuein* carries a different connotation when used of God and personified money. For the former it connotes an honorable dependence and devotion, but for the latter an enslavement to procure it and all that that entails. The picture of the rich man in 16:19-21 will spell out the enslavement. Cf. *2 Clem.* 6.1.

BIBLIOGRAPHY (16:8b-13)
(in addition to the titles given in 16:1-8a)

Anderson, F. C. "Luke xvi. 10," *ExpTim* 59 (1947-1948) 278-279.

Degenhardt, H.-J. *Lukas Evangelist der Armen,* 120-131.

Descamps, A. "La composition littéraire de Luc XVI 9-13," *NovT* 1 (1956) 47-53.

Hiers, R. H. "Friends by Unrighteous Mammon: The Eschatological Proletariat (Luke 16:9)," *JAAR* 38 (1970) 30-36.

Hof, O. "Luthers Auslegung von Lukas 16,9," *EvT* 8 (1948-1949) 151-166.

Maillot, A. "Notules sur Luc 16 8b-9," *ETR* 44 (1969) 127-130.

Middleton, R. D. "St. Luke xvi. 9," *Theology* 29 (1934) 41.

Paul, G. "The Unjust Steward and the Interpretation of Lk 16. 9," *Theology* 61 (1958) 189-193.

Safrai, S., and D. Flusser. "The Slave of Two Masters," *Immanuel* 6 (1976) 30-33.

Schulz, S. *Q: Die Spruchquelle,* 459-461.

Snoy, T. "Le problème de la finale de la parabole de l'intendant avisé," *Foi et vie* 72 (1973) 66-68.

106. AVARICIOUS PHARISEES ARE REPROVED (16:14-15)

16 ¹⁴ Listening to all this were avaricious Pharisees who sneered at him. ¹⁵ So he said to them, "You are the ones who are always justifying your position in the sight of human beings; but God knows what is in your hearts. For what is of highest human value is an abomination in God's sight."

COMMENT

To the parable of the dishonest manager (16:1-8a) and its appended sayings (vv. 8b-13) Luke now adds three further sayings of Jesus, which he fashions into an editorial unit, before the parable of the rich man and Lazarus (16:19-31). In themselves they are not related topically, are derived from different sources, and are addressed to the Pharisees explicitly. The Pharisees have been listening to the preceding parable, and the last saying about serving God and mammon probably suggested the introduction of them at the beginning of this unit. The first saying of this unit, vv. 14-15, would lead logically to the parable in vv. 19-31; but Luke has inserted other material before that.

As with most of the preceding material (vv. 1-12), the saying in the first part (vv. 14-15) is exclusive to the Lucan Gospel. Apart from the introductory verse, which is in large measure of Lucan composition (especially *ēkouon de*, lit. "and there were listening"; and the ptc. *hyparchontes*, "being"—see J. Jeremias, *Die Sprache*, 258; cf. *HST* 335; J. Schmid, *Evangelium nach Lukas*, 261), the rest is inherited by Luke from "L" (p. 84), but it scarcely followed on the heels of vv. 8b-12 in that source.

Form-critically considered, the saying in v. 15 is partly polemical and minatory and partly a wisdom-utterance (introduced by *hoti*, v. 15d; cf. *HST* 73). The last part is proverbial in character. The whole verse constitutes Jesus' answer to the ridicule of the Pharisees.

Jesus' words are addressed to money-loving or avaricious Pharisees. Coming immediately after Jesus' saying about serving God or mammon in the present Lucan context, they offer a commentary on v. 13, especially the last part of it: Coveting mammon is the real abomination in God's sight. Leading up to that last part, however, is a probing contrast: Vindication of oneself or one's uprightness in the sight of human beings means nothing to God, who knows what is in the human heart. Mammon may enable a person to secure esteem or an image of uprightness in human society, but that is not what really counts. The depths of the human heart and its desires or loves are known to God; and what he knows should constitute the real estimate of a human being. Whether one explains the Pharisaic quest of money as a sign of God's reward for upright conduct and piety (see E. Klostermann, *Lukasevangelium*, 166) or as a means enabling one to give alms to the poor (J. M. Creed, *The Gospel*, 206) matters little. Either could lead to pride and a false estimate of one's worth. God judges otherwise than human beings.

NOTES

16   14. *Listening to all this.* I.e. the words especially about the incompatibility of service of God and mammon. Implied is the Pharisees' wonder why they should not be compatible. The best mss. (P[75], ℵ, B, L, R, Ψ, 1241) and ancient versions read only *tauta panta*, "all these things," but some other mss. (A, W, Θ, *f*[1,13], and the Koine text-tradition) have *tauta panta kai hoi Ph.;* the *kai* would then be adverbial, "the Pharisees too" or "even the Pharisees." This adds an emphasis to the contrast between them and the "disciples" of v. 1.

avaricious Pharisees. Lit. "Pharisees being money-loving." Luke again uses the ptc.

of *hyparchein* (= the vb. "to be") with a predicate adj. See 11:13; 23:50; Acts 2:30; 3:2; 16:20,37; 17:24,29; 22:3; 27:12. Cf. 20:47. The change of audience here does not connote a change of theme, *pace* E. E. Ellis, *Gospel of Luke,* 202; the theme begun in v. 1 is clearly continued, though with a variation.

On "Pharisees," see NOTE on 5:17. T. W. Manson *(Sayings,* 295) thinks that the saying in v. 15 was originally addressed, not to Pharisees, but to Sadducees, who, he claims, would not have cared for "treasure in heaven" (12:33) because of their disbelief in the resurrection (Acts 23:8), and whose very name, related to the root *ṣdq,* "be righteous," would imply their concern for esteem among other human beings. This view, however, is all too speculative; moreover the relation of Pharisaic piety to righteousness is not unknown.

sneered at him. Lit. "turned up the nose at him." The grumbling of 15:2 has now become ridicule or scorn. An OT expression is used here; see Prov 1:30; Jer 20:7; Ps 2:4.

15. *justifying your position in the sight of human beings.* Lit. "the ones vindicating yourselves before men" *(anthrōpōn),* i.e. striving to preserve an image of uprightness before other human beings (see 10:29; 18:9,14; 20:20). Jesus' words imply that the Pharisaic attitude toward money is rooted in something deeper, in a quest for an image of uprightness before others.

God knows what is in your hearts. Lit. "knows your hearts," i.e. your inmost depths; the "heart" is being thought of as the seat of human emotion, desire, and reaction. Recall 1:51; 3:15; 5:22; 10:27. For God as *kardiognōstēs,* "knower of hearts," see Acts 1:24; 15:8; cf. Acts 8:21. This characterization of God is based on such OT passages as 1 Sam 16:7; 1 Kgs 8:39; 1 Chr 28:9; Ps 7:10; Prov 21:2; 24:12. Jesus is thus implying that his critics' piety is but empty show.

For. See NOTE on 16:8b.

what is of highest human value is an abomination in God's sight. Lit. "what is high among human beings is an abomination before God," i.e. in the ordinary run of things, because normally most human beings do not think the things of God. Just what is meant specifically by "the high/lofty" is not said; but in the Lucan context of this chapter it can easily be understood as mammon or the coveting of it. Lucan redaction has undoubtedly introduced the prep. *enōpion.* See p. 110. The proverb makes use of the frequent term of the LXX, *bdelygma,* the translation of Hebrew *šiqqûṣ* or *tôʿēbāh,* "abomination." See e.g. Deut 24:4; 1 Kgs 11:5; Dan 9:27 (alluded to in Mark 13:14); 11:31. Instead of *tou theou,* "God," ms. B reads *kyriou,* "the Lord," a reading which may be influenced by the LXX of Prov 1:7. Addressed to the Pharisees, this proverb echoes Luke 11:42-44. Moreover, the "great chasm" between human and divine perceptions foreshadows that to come in v. 26.

Compare the later rabbinic parallel of the *Mekilta* on Exod 20:18: "One who is proud of heart is designated an abomination, as it is said, 'Everyone that is proud in heart is an abomination of the Lord' (Prov 16:5)." See J. Z. Lauterbach, ed., *Mekilta de-Rabbi Ishmael* (3 vols.; Philadelphia: Jewish Publication Society of America, 1976) 2. 275.

BIBLIOGRAPHY (16:14-15)

Degenhardt, H.-J. *Lukas Evangelist der Armen,* 131-133.
Hanson, R. P. C. "A Note on Luke xvi. 14-31," *ExpTim* 55 (1943-1944) 221-222.

107. TWO SAYINGS ABOUT THE LAW
(16:16-17)

16   16 "Up until John it was the law and the prophets; from that time on the kingdom of God is being preached, and everyone is pressed to enter it. 17 But it is easier for the sky and the earth to pass away than for one stroke of a letter of the law to drop out."

COMMENT

The second set of sayings in this Lucan editorial unit preceding the parable of the rich man and Lazarus has almost nothing to do with material possessions or ambitious esteem before other human beings, topics of Jesus' comments in vv. 1-15. It deals instead with the law and its relation to the kingdom (16:16-17), a far larger concern.

The sayings of Jesus preserved in these verses are not exclusive to the Lucan Gospel, as was much of the material in vv. 1-15; a form of them is found also in the Matthean Gospel, not joined as they are here, but used in different contexts. The Lucan sayings correspond to Matt 11:12-13 (where a form of the first is added to Jesus' testimony to John the Baptist [= Luke 7: 24-30; see p. 671]) and Matt 5:18 (where a form of the second is used as a part of the proposition or thesis of the sermon on the mount, after the introductory beatitudes and other sayings). They have been derived by Luke from "Q" and most likely as a unit (see p. 79). It has been plausibly argued that the three sayings in vv. 16-18 were found in the same order in "Q" as they are here in Luke and that it is Matthew who has redistributed them (see *FGT* 93; cf. I. H. Marshall, *Luke,* 627).

Verse 16 creates the biggest problem. It has three parts; 16a corresponds to Matt 11:13, and 16b-c to Matt 11:12. There is no way of telling which evangelist has preserved either the original order of these sayings (in Stage I of the gospel tradition) or the order in "Q" (of Stage II). Good arguments have been brought forth for both sides; but none brings with them conviction, although the majority of commentators favors the Lucan order. The same has to be said about the formulation of the sayings.

The Matthean form of v. 16 seems to be the more primitive. I ascribe the asyndetic joining of the first saying to the preceding matter to Luke's source (it is non-Lucan; see J. Jeremias, *Die Sprache,* 60-61). But 16b is Lucan (the use of *apo tote,* "from that time on" and "the kingdom of God is being preached"; see p. 182). In v. 17 Luke has simplified the inherited material for the sake of his predominantly Gentile readers. See further H. Schürmann, *Traditionsgeschichtliche Untersuchungen,* 126-136; P. Hoffmann, *Studien,* 53-56; I. H. Marshall, *Luke,* 626-627.

Form-critically considered, both verses contain isolated sayings of Jesus about the law of Moses; their original context is hopelessly lost. Only indirectly can the first part of v. 16 be considered a saying about John the Baptist (but see *HST* 164). They are probably derived from authentic sayings of Jesus uttered at diverse times in his ministry, and have been subsequently joined because of their common topic. It is far from certain that v. 16 is a creation of the early Christian community, *pace* R. Bultmann, *HST* 164: "derives from the early Palestinian Church"; S. Schulz, *Q: Die Spruchquelle,* 263; and others (see N. Perrin, *Rediscovering,* 74-77 for a more convincing defense of the saying as authentic; cf. W. G. Kümmel, *Promise and Fulfilment,* 121-124; E. Käsemann, *Essays,* 42-43).

The first saying (v. 16), even though it is strange in its present Lucan setting in the travel account, is an important element in Lucan theology, and especially in Luke's view of three periods of salvation-history (see pp. 182-187). True, it mentions only two of them; but they have to be considered in the Lucan two-volume work as a whole; at this point there is no need to make mention of the third period, and Acts 1:6b has to be related to this verse in order to understand it properly. Verse 16 now makes not only John the Baptist but also the time of his appearance a transition; it at once ends the Period of Israel and begins or inaugurates the Period of Jesus. In this we have accepted and retained the basic distinction of H. Conzelmann *(Theology,* 12-17), even if we have modified it in our sketch of Lucan theology, by understanding John as a transitional figure who inaugurates the second period and introduces Jesus, who is the kingdom-preacher par excellence in the Lucan writings. In this sense, John is a precursor of Jesus, not as a Christian or a kingdom-preacher himself, but the Jewish reform-preacher who prepares Israel for the preaching of the kingdom. Hence "up until John it was the law and the prophets," i.e. the law of Moses and the preaching of the prophets (and their books) were the way in which God's presence and will toward Israel were made manifest. "From that time on the kingdom of God is being preached," i.e. by Jesus, whose invitation is radical and demanding, pressuring human beings to accept it. Hence, this saying of Jesus (v. 16) means that a new era in salvation-history was initiated at the time of John. As E. Käsemann has put it, "the Old Testament epoch of salvation history concludes with the Baptist, who himself already belongs to the new epoch. . . ." *(Essays,* 42-43). (See further pp. 181-187.)

The second saying (v. 17) is retained by Luke as a further comment on the relation of the kingdom preached by Jesus to the law. It is used by Luke with hyperbole to stress rhetorically the continuity of Jesus' kingdom-preaching with the manifestation of God's will in the law of old. The former is but the logical and legitimate outgrowth of the latter (see p. 9). But Luke does not think in terms of a literal interpretation of the law and the prophets, as his use of "Moses and all the prophets" (24:27) or "in the law of Moses, in the prophets and in the Psalms" (24:44) makes clear. Luke has his own way of reading "the law and the prophets," in which he finds "all that was written" about the Christ; he knows that it must all see fulfillment. In yet another sense the continuing or abiding validity of the law will be stressed in Jesus' words at the end of the coming parable, "If they listen not to Moses and the prophets . . ." So both Pharisees and Christian disciples are in a way under the law, now filled out in the preached gospel, which challenges them all with its pressing demand. For in the demands of the kingdom itself the law is vindicated.

NOTES

16 16. *Up until John.* I.e. up until John inclusive, in that he was a Jewish reform-preacher; but also exclusive, because he was "something greater than a prophet" (7:26), for with his appearance (3:1-17) a new period of salvation-history was inaugurated. Recall also the Lucan notion of *archē,* "beginning." See NOTES on 1:3; 3:23; cf. Acts 1:22. Luke uses the prep. *mechri* in Acts 10:30; 20:7; but it is difficult to derive from either of these passages a nuance which would solve the hesitation about the inclusive/exclusive senses applicable here. Some mss. (A, D, W, Θ, Ψ, and the Koine text-tradition) read the prep. *heōs* instead of *mechri,* but the sense of the phrase is unaffected; *heōs* is probably the result of scribal harmonization with Matt 11:13. The order of the elements in v. 16 is undoubtedly more primitive here in Luke than in the Matthean parallel (11:12-13).

the law and the prophets. This is a summary way of referring to OT preaching. Apart from the prologue to Sirach, it is not found as such in the OT or in rabbinical literature. But the coupling can be found in 1QS 1:3; 8:15-16; CD 5:21-6:1 (= 6QD 3:4); 4QDibHam 3:12 *(RB* 68 [1961] 204). Cf. H. Braun, *Qumran,* 1. 91. In this detail Luke has preserved the more primitive order, the law or "Moses" before the prophets. See 16:29,31; Acts 13:15; 24:14; 28:23; cf. John 1:45; Rom 3:21, and contrast Acts 26:22. Even Matthew has this order in 5:17; 7:12; 22:40, although in the parallel to this passage it is reversed, "the prophets and the law." It is possible that the phrase connotes two parts of the Hebrew Scriptures; reference to a third will be found in 24:44 ("the psalms").

from that time on. I.e. from the appearance of John in 3:1-17, even though John himself is never depicted in the Lucan Gospel as a kingdom-preacher. Compare the formulation in Matt 11:12.

the kingdom of God. See NOTE on 4:43; cf. 8:1; Acts 8:12.

is being preached. I.e. by Jesus (and eventually his disciples). See 9:2; 10:9. Possibly one should translate, "has been preached," i.e. is (still) being preached. On the sense of *euangelizesthai,* see p. 148. Only Luke links this vb. with "the kingdom of God."

everyone is pressed to enter it. Lit. "everyone is forced into it," i.e. with a demanding, urgent invitation (of the kingdom-preacher himself). The translation understands *biazetai* as a pass. parallel to *euangelizetai,* "is preached." This use of the vb. *biazein* is attested in OxyP 2.294:16-17: *egō de biazomai hypo philō[n] genesthai oikiakos tou archistatoros Apollōniou,* "I (Sarapion) am being pressed by friends to become a member of the household of Apollonius, the chief usher" (at the court of the prefect of Egypt). The sentence is found in a letter written from Alexandria by Sarapion to his brother Dorion in the ninth year of Tiberius, ca. A.D. 22. See BAGD 140; MM 109. It is also supported by the middle-voice use (= act. transitive sense) of the vb. meaning "invite" in the LXX of Gen 33:11; Judg 13:15, and of the compound *parabiazesthai* in Luke 24:29; Acts 16:15. In a sense, it bears out the saying in 14:23 ("make people come in") and corresponds to the varied reactions of people to Jesus' preaching in this Gospel: on the one hand, favorable (4:36; 5:26; 7:16-17; 9:43; 18:43), but on the other, negative (4:28; 9:53; 15:2; 16:14; 19:7). Recall the words of Simeon in 2:34. This pass. understanding of *biazetai* has been proposed since the early part of this century, but not many have adopted it; among those who have are F. Godet, P.-H. Menoud, W. G. Kümmel " 'Das Gesetz' " (but cf. *Promise and Fulfilment,* 121-124), J. M. Bover and J. O'Callaghan, C. Spicq (?).

This part of v. 16 has been a *crux interpretum* for two reasons: (a) the sense of *biazetai* itself, and (b) the tendency to make it say something like Matt 11:12. The vb. *biazein* means "to force," but it is most frequently used in the middle voice, "make use of force," either in a positive sense ("try hard" [see Epictetus, *Disc.* 4.7,20-21]) or in a negative, hostile sense ("uses force on/against" [see LXX Esth 7:8; Appian, *Bell. civ.* 5.35 § 139]). The positive sense, with varying nuances, has been preferred by commentators such as H. Conzelmann, J. M. Creed, F. W. Danker, E. Klostermann, N. Perrin, A. Plummer, K. H. Rengstorf, G. Schneider, G. Schrenk; but the problem has always been to explain how that sense would be true of "everyone" *(pas).* Subterfuges are used to explain it: Even toll-collectors and sinners are trying hard to get into the kingdom; or people of violence are the ones who get in. But none of these explanations carries conviction. With varying nuances, the negative sense has been preferred by commentators such as E. Dinkler, A. Loisy, A. R. C. Leaney, M. Black, A. Schlatter: "uses violence against it." But who is meant by "everyone" *(pas)?* In the latter case, one senses the tendency to make the Lucan form of the saying assert what Matt 11:12 does (the second reason given above). Here the discussions of commentators move back and forth between Stages I and III of the gospel tradition (e.g. I. H. Marshall, *Luke,* 629; T. W. Manson, *Sayings,* 134-135) and fail to keep them distinct, as has to be done.

It may very well be that the Matthean form of the saying in 11:12 is closer to the original, and that that is why Matthew has made use of it where he does (appended to the testimony of Jesus about John). It means there something entirely different: the subj. of *biazetai* is "the kingdom of heaven," and force is used against *it:* "From the days of John the Baptist until now the kingdom of heaven suffers violence *(biazetai)* and men of violence *(biastai)* plunder *(harpazousin)* it." In the Matthean context the threefold reference to violence *(biazetai, biastai, harpazousin)* undoubtedly refers to what has happened to John himself, who is a kingdom-preacher in that Gospel. See p. 184. Such a sense ill suits the Lucan context (and Gospel as a whole), and that is undoubtedly why Luke changed the wording of the inherited "Q" saying. See further C. Spicq, *Notes de lexicographie néo-testamentaire* (2 vols.; Fribourg: Editions universitaires; Göttingen: Vandenhoeck & Ruprecht, 1978) 1. 189-194.

17. *easier for the sky and the earth to pass away.* Or "heaven and earth." See Luke 10:21 (and NOTE there); Acts 17:24; cf. Luke 21:33. The phrase expresses the whole created universe, imitating OT passages (Isa 51:6; Job 14:12). See further 12:56; Acts 4:24; 14:15; 17:24. They will pass away because they are the sum of corruptible, material creation.

than for one stroke of a letter of the law to drop out. Lit. "for one serif . . ." e.g. the tittle which distinguishes similar-looking Hebrew letters, one from the other. See Eusebius, *Comm. in Ps. 33.1* (PG 23.292). *Pace* T. W. Manson *(Sayings,* 135) and S. Schulz *(Q: Die Spruchquelle,* 115 n. 155), the *keraia,* "(little) hook," does not refer to the ornamental "crowns" found on letters in manuscripts of the Torah. Str-B 1. 248-249 may offer references to such in late rabbinical and even medieval manuscripts, but where does one find them in first-century Palestinian copies? Again, *pace* G. Schwarz *("Iōta hen ē mia keraia,"* ZNW 66 [1975] 268-269), the *keraia* scarcely refers to the Hebrew letter *waw.*

Whatever the sense of the *keraia,* it is clear that the Lucan Jesus sees his preaching of the kingdom as something more abiding than the universe itself, because it is the real meaning of the continuing validity of the law.

BIBLIOGRAPHY (16:16-17)

Bammel, E. "Is Luke 16,16-18 of Baptist's Provenience?" *HTR* 51 (1958) 101-106.

Banks, R. J. *Jesus and the Law in the Synoptic Tradition* (SNTSMS 28; Cambridge: University Press, 1975) 203-226.

Braumann, G. " 'Dem Himmelreich wird Gewalt angetan,' " *ZNW* 52 (1961) 104-109.

Catchpole, D. R. "On Doing Violence to the Kingdom," *Journal of Theology for Southern Africa* 25 (1978) 50-61.

Danker, F. W. "Luke 16:16—An Opposition Logion," *JBL* 77 (1958) 231-243.

Godet, F. *Commentaire sur l'évangile de Saint Luc,* 2. 259.

Hoffmann, P. *Studien zur Theologie der Logienquelle* (NTAbh ns 8; Münster in W.: Aschendorff, 1972) 50-79.

Kaestli, J.-D. *L'Eschatologie,* 24-27.

Kümmel, W. G. " 'Das Gesetz und die Propheten gehen bis Johannes'—Lukas 16,16 im Zusammenhang der heilsgeschichtlichen Theologie der Lukasschriften," *Verborum veritas* (eds. O. Böcher and K. Haacker) 89-102; see also G. Braumann, ed., *Das Lukas-Evangelium,* 398-415.

Ligier, L. *Péché d'Adam et péché du monde* (2 vols.; Théologie 43, 48; Paris: Aubier, 1960, 1961) 2. 74-116.

Menoud, P.-H. "Le sens du verbe *biazetai* dans Lc 16,16," *Mélanges bibliques . . . Béda Rigaux* (eds. A. Descamps and A. de Halleux) 207-212.

Moore, E. "*Biazō, harpazō* and Cognates in Josephus," *NTS* 21 (1974-1975) 519-543.

Perrin, N. *Rediscovering,* 74-77.

Schnackenburg, R. *God's Rule and Kingdom* (New York: Herder and Herder, 1963) 129-132.

Schulz, S. *Q: Die Spruchquelle,* 114-116, 261-267.

Schürmann, H. " 'Wer daher eines dieser geringsten Gebote auflöst . . .': Wo fand Matthäus das Logion Mt. 5,19," *BZ* 4 (1960) 238-250; reprinted, *Traditionsgeschichtliche Untersuchungen,* 126-136.

Thiering, B. E. "Are the 'Violent Men' False Teachers?" *NovT* 21 (1979) 293-297.

Wink, W. *John the Baptist in the Gospel Tradition* (SNTSMS 7; Cambridge: University Press, 1968) 20-23.

108. ON DIVORCE
(16:18)

16 [18] "Anyone who divorces his wife and marries another woman commits adultery; and anyone who marries a woman divorced from her husband commits adultery."

COMMENT

The third saying in this Lucan editorial unit seems to move to an entirely different topic—even less related to the general theme of chap. 16 than the sayings on the law in the two preceding verses—viz. the prohibition of divorce (16:18). It is scarcely to be understood as an example of the "law," since it goes beyond it in imposing a prohibition not contained in it. Given the Palestinian understanding of the relation of a woman to a man in marriage (see further below), it indirectly belongs to the topic of a man's possessions.

Luke has derived this isolated saying on divorce from "Q" (see p. 79). Its counterpart is found in the sermon on the mount as one of the six antitheses toward the beginning of that sermon (Matt 5:32). It is almost as isolated there as it is here in Luke, being unrelated to the topics of the other five antitheses, although agreeing with them in form. Another wording of the prohibition is preserved in Matt 19:9, which is a Matthean doublet, being derived from Mark 10:11 (which is part of Luke's Little Omission; see p. 67; also pp. 81-82). The "Q"-form of the saying began with a ptc., *ho apolyōn*, "the one divorcing" (to which Luke has added his favorite *pas*, "everyone"), whereas the "Mk"-form uses a rel. cl., *hos an apolysē*, "whoever divorces." The "Mk"-form also supplies a context for the saying, which is thus no longer an isolated saying, but a pronouncement-story with allusions to Gen 1:27; 2:24; this is preserved in Matthew 19. Moreover, in both instances of the Matthean doublet Matthew has secondarily introduced an exceptive phrase ("except for unchastity," *RSV)* to meet a new contingency in the early Christian community for which he composed his Gospel—phrases which were scarcely part of the otherwise authentic saying of Jesus prohibiting divorce, ultimately derived from Stage I of the gospel tradition.

Paul also knew of this tradition and has preserved a form of the saying in 1 Cor 7:10-11: "To the married I give charge—not I, but the Lord—that a wife should not be separated from (her) husband (but if she is separated, let her remain unmarried or else be reconciled with her husband) and that a man should not divorce (his) wife." The Pauline form of the prohibition is the *earliest* attestation of it, found in Paul's First Letter to the Corinthians, written ca. A.D. 57; he has set the saying in indir. discourse to suit the epistolary style of his letter. In v. 13c Paul also says that a woman should not divorce her husband. In doing so, he has adapted Jesus' words to a Hellenistic Christian-community setting, since it reckons with the possibility of the woman divorcing her husband, a practice which was hardly true of the original Palestinian context. In comparing Luke's form with Paul's, we can see that Luke has actually preserved a *more primitive* form of the saying, since it forbids a *man* to divorce his wife and remarry (even though the prepositional phrase *apo andros* in v. 18c, "from (her) husband," may have been secondarily added). The Lucan saying is thus cast completely from the OT or Jewish point of view, commenting on the action of the husband who would divorce his wife and marry again (or who might marry a divorced woman). Underlying it are the Palestinian and OT ideas of the wife as the chattel of the husband (implicit in such passages as Exod 20:17; 21:3,22; Jer 6:12; Num 30:10-14; Esth 1:20-22; and especially Sir 23:22-27) and of the permission to divorce the wife allowed to the husband in Deut 24:1-4. (For further details on the relation of the Lucan saying to the other NT forms of the prohibition, see my extended discussion in *TS* 37 [1976] 197-226; *TAG* 79-111.)

From a form-critical viewpoint, the prohibition of divorce is a dominical saying cast in a declaratory legal form, reminiscent of OT casuistic law. See *HST* 132; B. Schaller, "Die Sprüche," 245; K. Haacker, "Ehescheidung," 30.

As in 1 Cor 7:10-11 and Mark 10:11, the Lucan form of the saying forbids divorce absolutely, i.e. without any exceptions (cp. Matt 5:32; 19:9 mentioned above). Though the Lucan form says nothing about the woman having to remain *agamos,* "unmarried," or being reconciled to her husband, as does 1 Cor 7:11 (possibly a Pauline addition), it not only prohibits divorce to the man but includes a judgment about the husband's marriage after such a separation, relating both to adultery, which is proscribed in the OT. Verse 18c spells out another aspect of it: Anyone who marries a divorced woman also commits adultery. In branding the man's actions as adulterous, Jesus is clearly going beyond the OT teaching on divorce, which permitted the husband to do so (Deut 24:1-4). We are, however, now aware that some Palestinian Jews in the time of Jesus, the Essenes of Qumran, had also developed a prohibition of polygamy and divorce (based on Deut 17:17)—thus setting themselves apart from other Jews of the time. See 11QTemple 57:17-19: "He shall not take in addition to her another wife, for she alone shall be with him all the days of her life; and if she dies, he shall take for himself another (wife) from his father's house, from his clan." Note the "she alone" *(hy'h lbdh).* (Cf. also CD 4:20-5:1.) For detailed discussion of these passages, see my article referred to above, pp. 213-221; also see my article "Divorce among First-Century Palestinian Jews." This Essene teaching may take some of the edge of originality off Jesus' teaching, but it has provided an intelligible Palestinian matrix for it.

Jesus thus proclaims monogamy and speaks out against successive polygamy, which would have been made possible by divorce. In doing so, he was speaking out against a practice which was widespread in Palestinian Judaism of his day. Why did he take such a stance? It is difficult to answer this question. It has been plausibly suggested, however, by A. Isaksson *(Marriage and Ministry,* 147) that Jesus presents marriage as indissoluble as an extension of the OT attitude toward members of priestly families who were to serve in the Jerusalem Temple: "They shall not marry a harlot or a woman defiled; neither shall they marry a woman divorced from her husband, for the priest is holy to his God" (Lev 21:7; cf. Ezek 44:22). Isaksson sees this as the motivation for Jesus' prohibition of divorce: "Jesus taught his disciples they were chosen for and consecrated to the service of God." His suggestion fits in with other considerations of the Christian community as a temple in a new sense (2 Cor 6:14-7:1; 1 Cor 3:16-17; Eph 2:18-22) or of the general priestly character of Christian disciples (Rev 1:6; 1 Pet 2:5,9). This aspect, however, is not particularly Lucan. Though Luke has preserved for us a form of the absolute prohibition of divorce (along with Paul and Mark), it is still puzzling why it has been introduced into this part of his travel account.

NOTES

16 18. *Anyone who divorces.* Lit. "everyone divorcing." In the saying of Jesus on divorce preserved in the Synoptics the vb. *apolyein* is always used (Mark 10:11; Matt 5:32; 19:9). It is also used in Matt 1:19, where Joseph's first decision is to "divorce" Mary because he suspects her of unchastity during the betrothal. Cf. Deut 22:20-21. This sense of *apolyein* is found in Hellenistic writers (Dionysius of Halicarnassus, *Rom. Ant.* 2.25,7; Diodorus Siculus, *Bibl. hist.* 12.18,1-2). However, BAGD (p. 96) says that "this [use] is in accord not w. Jewish . . . , but w. Greco-Rom. custom," even though the authors cite an example of this use from Josephus, *Ant.* 15.7,10 § 259. Indeed, B. K. Diderichsen *(Den markianske skilsmisserperikope: Dens genesis og historiske placering* [Copenhagen: Gyldendal, 1962] 20-47, 347) tried to say that Jesus' original saying meant only "anyone who leaves his wife (in the sense of abandoning her and the children in order to follow Jesus as a disciple; cf. 14:26; 18:29) and marries another . . ." This sense would have been lost later, and the word would have been understood of divorce. Such a meaning of *apolyein,* however, is farfetched and contradicts the sense of *chōrizein* in 1 Cor 7:10 (and elsewhere in Hellenistic writings). Moreover, the meaning "divorce" is clearly found in a Greek document of remarriage from Palestine itself (Mur 115:3-4 [dated A.D. 124]: "Since it happened earlier to the same Elias [son] of Simon to become estranged and divorce Salome . . ."). The two vbs. used in this Murabba'at text, *apallagēnai kai apolyein,* are probably Greek attempts to translate Aramaic terms which are often used in Jewish writs of divorce, *šābeq wamĕtārek,* "divorce and repudiate." See Mur 19:2-4 (dated A.D. 111). Even though MM (66-67) is unable to give any instance of *apolyein* meaning "divorce" in the papyri from Egypt, this Murabba'at evidence is significant. Cf. *1 Esdr* 9:36; G. Schneider, *EWNT* 1.336-337; E. Lövestam, "Apolyein—en gammalpalestinensisk skilsmässoterm," *SEA* 27 (1962) 132-135.

and marries another woman. The Greek vb. *gamein* is used, as in the best reading in 14:20. Cf. the Semitic variant there, *labein,* "to take" (a wife) in ms. D. This cl. is sometimes regarded as an addition made by Luke to the original saying, being derived from Mark 10. See H. Baltensweiler, *Die Ehe,* 60-64; G. Schneider, *Evangelium nach Lukas,* 339. But since it is present in other forms of the prohibition either Pauline or Synoptic (Mark 10:11; 19:9), it is probably to be regarded as part of the original prohibition, even if it is absent in Matt 5:32, *pace* S. Schulz, *Q: Die Spruchquelle,* 117. See F. Neirynck, "De Jezuswoorden," 133.

commits adultery. The vb. *moicheuein* alludes to the prohibition of adultery in the Decalogue (Exod 20:13 [20:14E]; Deut 5:17 [5:18E]) and elsewhere in the OT (Lev 20:10; Deut 22:22). Luke 18:20 and John 7:53-8:11 imply that the prohibition of it was still regarded as in force. Note that in Matt 5:32 it is said that the husband causes the woman to commit adultery (if she remarries). See the commentary on this verse in Hermas, *Mand.* 4.1,4-11.

anyone who marries a woman divorced. Some mss. (ℵ, A, W, Θ, Ψ, *f*1,13, and the Koine text-tradition) add *pas* to the beginning of this phrase, "everyone who . . ."

(probably in imitation of the beginning of the verse). But mss. P75, B, D, L, 1241, etc., omit it. This part of the saying criticizes the second man involved.

from her husband. A few mss. (D, 28, etc.) omit this phrase, but nothing is lost by this omission. On the sense of the prep. *apo,* see NOTE on 1:26.

BIBLIOGRAPHY (16:18)

Baltensweiler, H. *Die Ehe im Neuen Testament: Exegetische Untersuchungen über Ehe, Ehelosigkeit und Ehescheidung* (AbhTANT 52; Zürich: Zwingli, 1967).

Bammel, E. "Markus 10,11f. und das jüdische Eherecht," *ZNW* 61 (1970) 95-101.

Berrouard, M.-F. "L'Indissolubilité du mariage dans le Nouveau Testament," *Lum Vie* 4 (1952) 21-40.

Bonsirven, J. *Le divorce dans le Nouveau Testament* (Paris/Tournai: Desclée, 1948).

Catchpole, D. R. "The Synoptic Divorce Material as a Traditio-Historical Problem," *BJRL* 57 (1974-1975) 92-127.

Derrett, J. D. M. *Law,* 363-388.

Descamps, A.-L. "Les textes évangéliques sur le mariage," *RTL* 9 (1978) 259-286; 11 (1980) 5-50.

Donahue, J. R. "Divorce: New Testament Perspectives," *The Month* 242 (1981) 113-120.

Dupont, J. *Mariage et divorce dans l'évangile: Matthieu 19,3-12 et parallèles* (Bruges: Abbaye de Saint-André; Desclée de Brouwer, 1959) 45-88, 124-153.

Fitzmyer, J. A. "Divorce among First-Century Palestinian Jews," *H. L. Ginsberg Volume* (Eretz-Israel 14; Jerusalem: Israel Exploration Society, 1978) 103*-110*, 193.

———— "The Matthean Divorce Texts and Some New Palestinian Evidence," *TS* 37 (1976) 197-226; reprinted, *TAG,* 79-111.

Greeven, H. "Ehe nach dem Neuen Testament," *NTS* 15 (1968-1969) 365-388.

Haacker, K. "Ehescheidung und Wiederverheiratung im Neuen Testament," *TQ* 151 (1971) 28-38.

Harrington, W. "Jesus' Attitude toward Divorce," *ITQ* 37 (1970) 199-209.

Isaksson, A. *Marriage and Ministry in the New Temple* (ASNU 24; Lund: Gleerup, 1965).

Kornfeld, W., and H. Cazelles. "Mariage," *DBS* 5 (1957) 905-935, esp. cols. 926-935.

Lövestam, E. "De synoptiska Jesus-orden om skilsmässa och omgifte: Referensramar och implikationer," *SEA* 43 (1978) 65-73.

MacRae, G. W. "New Testament Perspectives on Marriage and Divorce," *Divorce and Remarriage in the Catholic Church* (ed. L. G. Wrenn; New York: Newman, 1973) 1-15.

Mueller, J. R. "The Temple Scroll and the Gospel Divorce Texts," *RevQ* 10 (1979-1981) 247-256.

Myre, A. "Dix ans d'exégèse sur le divorce dans le Nouveau Testament," *Le divorce: L'Eglise catholique ne devrait-elle pas modifier son attitude séculaire à l'égard de l'indissolubilité du mariage?* (Montreal: Fides, 1973) 139-162.

Neirynck, F. "Huwelijk en Echtscheiding in het Evangelie," *Collationes brugenses et gandavenses* 6 (1960) 123-130.

———— "De Jezuswoorden over Echtscheiding," *Mislukt Huwelijk en Echtscheiding: Een multidisciplinaire Benadering* (ed. V. Heylen; Sociologische Verkenningen 2; Antwerp: Patmos, 1972) 127-141.

Nembach, U. "Ehescheidung nach alttestamentlichem und jüdischem Recht," *TZ* 26 (1970) 161-171.

Pesch, R. *Freie Treue: Die Christen und die Ehescheidung* (Freiburg im B.: Herder, 1971) 56-60.

———— "Die neutestamentliche Weisung für die Ehe," *BibLeb* 9 (1968) 208-221.

Richards, H. J. "Christ on Divorce," *Scr* 11 (1959) 22-32.

Schaller, B. "Die Sprüche über Ehescheidung und Wiederheirat in der synoptischen Überlieferung," *Der Ruf Jesu* (eds. E. Lohse et al.) 226-246.

Schneider, G. "Jesu Wort über die Ehescheidung in der Überlieferung des Neuen Testaments," *TTZ* 80 (1971) 65-87.

Schubert, K. "Ehescheidung im Judentum zur Zeit Jesu," *TQ* 151 (1971) 23-27.

Schulz, S. *Q: Die Spruchquelle,* 116-120.

Stock, A. "Matthean Divorce Texts," *BTB* 8 (1978) 24-33.

Tosato, A. *Il matrimonio nel giudaismo antico e nel Nuovo Testamento* (Rome: Città Nuova Editrice, 1976).

———— "The Law of Leviticus 18:18: A Reexamination," *CBQ* 46 (1984) 199-214.

Trevijano Etcheverría, R. "Matrimonio y divorcio en Mc 10,2-12 y par.," *Burgense* 18 (1977) 113-151.

Vargas-Machuca, A. "Divorcio e indisolubilidad del matrimonio en la Sagrada Escritura," *EstBíb* 39 (1981) 19-61.

Vawter, B. "The Biblical Theology of Divorce," *ProcCTSA* 22 (1967) 223-243.

———— "Divorce and the New Testament," *CBQ* 39 (1977) 528-542.

Wrege, H.-T. *Die Überlieferungsgeschichte der Bergpredigt* (WUNT 9; Tübingen: Mohr [Siebeck], 1968) 66-70.

109. THE PARABLE OF THE RICH MAN AND LAZARUS
(16:19-31)

16   [19] "There was once a rich man who used to dress in *purple and fine linen*[a] and feast sumptuously every day. [20] At his door squatted a beggar named Lazarus, covered with sores and [21] longing to be fed, if only with the scraps that dropped from the rich man's table. Dogs too used to come to lick at his sores. [22] One day the beggar died and was carried away by the angels to Abraham's bosom. The rich man also

[a] Prov 31:22

died and was buried. [23] But in death's abode the rich man was tormented. Once he looked up and saw Abraham at a distance with Lazarus at his side. [24] 'Father Abraham,' he called out, 'Have mercy on me! Send Lazarus to dip the tip of his finger in water that he might cool my tongue, for I am in great pain in these flames.' [25] Abraham replied, 'Remember, my child, that you received your blessings during your life, while Lazarus had only misfortunes. Now he is comforted here, and you are in great pain. [26] Besides, between us and you a great chasm has been fixed so that those who might want to cross over from this side to you cannot; and none can come over from there to us.' [27] Yet he pleaded, 'Then I beg you, Father, send him at least to my father's house, [28] where I have five brothers, that he might warn them, lest they too come to this place of torment.' [29] Abraham replied, 'They have Moses and the prophets; let them listen to them.' [30] 'No, Father Abraham,' he said, 'but if someone will come back from the dead to them, they will reform their lives.' [31] Abraham said to him, 'If they listen not to Moses and the prophets, they will not be convinced even if someone rises from the dead.' "

COMMENT

At this point in his travel account, Luke adds the parable of the rich man and Lazarus (16:19-31). It is to be understood as addressed to the Pharisees of v. 14 (at 17:1 Jesus will turn his attention to his disciples again). The story is a fitting conclusion to the theme of chap. 16 (see COMMENT on 16:1-8a), even though it is introduced awkwardly after Jesus' saying on divorce (v. 18).

This story is again exclusive to Luke, being derived by him from his source "L" (see p. 84). A few traces of Lucan redaction can be detected in it: "There was once a rich man" *(anthrōpos tis ēn plousios,* v. 19; cf. 16:1; see NOTE on 10:30); "a beggar named Lazarus" (v. 20; cp. 1:5; 10:38; Acts 8:9; 9:33; 10:1; 16:1); "one day the beggar died" (v. 22, lit. "happened to die"; see NOTE); "tormented" (v. 23, lit. "being *[hyparchōn]* in torments"); unstressed *kai autos* (v. 24); *eipen de* (vv. 25,27,31); and certain elements in v. 25 (see J. Dupont, *Béatitudes,* 3. 60-62). The amount of non-Lucan formulation in the story is, however, noteworthy (see J. Jeremias, *Die Sprache,* 260-262), stemming from the pre-Lucan source. (See further *HST* 178; G. Schneider, *Evangelium nach Lukas,* 340.)

Form-critically considered, the story belongs to the parables of Jesus. Indeed, Codex Bezae explicitly introduces it as such, "And he uttered another parable" *(heteran parabolēn),* but this introduction is lacking in the majority of Greek mss. Bultmann *(HST* 178) says of it, "Pure narrative without introduction or application" (cf. Ambrose *[Expos. ev. sec. Luc.* 8.13 (CSEL 32.397)], "narratio magis quam parabola videtur, quando etiam nomen exprimitur"). More specifically, as we already noted apropos of the good Samaritan (see COMMENT on 10:29-37), the story is better understood as an "example" (in rhetoric, *exemplum).* It further shares with the story of the prodigal son a two-peaked character and a contrast of the two (in this case, main) figures (see COMMENT on 15:11-32). M. Dibelius *(FTG* 251 n. 2) notes that the parabolic law of antithesis is exemplified in it.

Bultmann *(HST* 178) has further rightly recognized that the story has two points: (a) Verses 19-26 depict the reversal of fortunes of this life in the hereafter; in the matter of material possessions there is a counterbalancing of the earthly with the afterlife. (b) Verses 27-31 insist that even the return of a messenger from the dead will not bring about reform among the obdurate rich. In the first part, a comparison is made between the rich man and Lazarus; Lazarus does not enter into the discussion, which takes place between the rich man and Abraham. The dialogue continues in the second part, but Lazarus is less involved, whereas the five brothers become the focus of attention.

The two parts of the story, however, have raised a number of questions. The first part is paralleled in other, extrabiblical literature; does it depend on such? What meaning would the second part have prior to Jesus' own death and resurrection—or at least without reference to them? To what extent does either part of the story go back to Jesus himself?

Years ago H. Gressmann ("Vom reichen Mann") drew attention to an Egyptian folktale, copied in Demotic on the back of a Greek document dated in the seventh year of the emperor Claudius (A.D. 47), telling about the retribution in the afterlife for conditions in this: a reincarnated Egyptian Si-Osiris, born miraculously to Satme Khamuas, takes his father on a tour of Am^ente, the realm of the dead, to show him what happened to a rich man who had died, was honorably lamented, shrouded in fine linen, and sumptuously buried, and to a poor man who had also died, but who was carried out unmourned on a straw mat to a common necropolis of Memphis. The rich man was seen in torment with the axle of the hinge of the hall's door fixed in his right eye socket; but in another hall Osiris, ruler of Am^ente, sat enthroned and near him was the poor man, robed in the rich man's fine linen. Si-Osiris' words to his father: "May it be done to you in Am^ente as it is done in Am^ente to this pauper and not as it is done to this rich man in Am^ente." (See further F. L. Griffith, *Stories of the High Priests of Memphis* [Oxford: Clarendon, 1900] 42-43.)

Gressmann then cited Luke 16:19-31 and seven other tales about retribution in the afterlife from rabbinic sources of later date, the earliest of which is found in two forms in the Palestinian Talmud *(y. Sanh.* 6.23c and *y. Hag.* 2.77d—scarcely before A.D. 400). Gressmann thought that Alexandrian Jews had brought the Egyptian folktale to Palestine, where it developed as the story of a poor Torah scholar and a rich toll-collector named Bar Ma'yan (see NOTE on 14:15). J. Jeremias *(Parables,* 183) claims that Jesus was familiar with this Palestinian tale and even alluded to it in the parable of the great dinner (14:15-24). That the story existed in Palestine in the time of Jesus is possible; indeed, K. Grobel ("'. . . Whose Name was Neves'") has exploited the Egyptian tale even more than Gressmann did, pointing out further parallels (not all of which are convincing). But there are distinctive elements in the first part of the story that are present neither in the Egyptian folktale nor in the story of Bar Ma'yan (the dogs, Abraham's bosom, the dialogue between the rich man and Abraham). If the Lucan parable echoes such folktales, it has refashioned them, and there is no reason to think that this refashioning was not done by Jesus himself.

R. Bultmann *(HST* 197) calls attention to still "another Jewish legend" which tells of a rich and godless married couple. The woman dies, and a boy journeys to Hades, sees the woman in fiery torment, and brings back a message for the husband, "Tell my husband to turn over a new leaf, for the power of repentance is great," and the husband repents. Bultmann comments, "In the form in which we find it, this story is relatively old; it is hard to imagine that it derives from the gospel story" (ibid.). It may be "relatively old," and it may be "hard to imagine that it derives from the gospel story," but such a comment is hardly sufficient for Bultmann's "alternative suggestion" that "a Jewish story lies behind Lk. 16[19-31]" (ibid.) or his eventual conclusion that a Synoptic similitude such as this has been taken "from the Jewish tradition by the Church and put into Jesus' mouth" (ibid. 203). Bultmann ascribes to his conclusion "very great probability." The "Jewish legend" is found in M. J. Bin Gorion, *Der Born Judas: Legenden, Märchen und Erzählungen* (6 vols.; Leipzig: Insel-V., 1922-1924) 6. 75ff. From what period does it date?

That Jesus could have borrowed a motif from such a Jewish tradition is certainly admissible; he could even have joined it secondarily to the tale about retribution in the afterlife from the Egyptian tradition. But there is a certain unity to the two parts of the Lucan parable, which transcends such distinct motifs. As we have already seen, the parable as a whole is scarcely a product of Lucan composition. In the long run, there is no solid reason not to ascribe it as a unit to Jesus himself.

In any case, the parable as told by the Lucan Jesus carries its own double message. In the present context its connection with the parable and sayings of vv. 1-13 is not hard to see. It further illustrates the teaching of the Lucan Jesus about the prudent use of material possessions and gives new meaning to the "dwellings that are everlasting" (v. 9). It is a vivid restatement of the beatitude and the woe of 6:20,24, and illustrates the proverb at the end of 16:15, "What is of highest human value is an abomination in God's sight." See further A. Feuillet, "La parabole du mauvais riche."

In the first part of the parable (vv. 19-26) Jesus clearly asserts the reversal of fortunes in the afterlife: a person may expect compensation after death for the use of material possessions at his/her disposal (see 16:12). The luxurious way of life of the rich man and his (implied) lack of concern for the poor Lazarus at his door stand in obvious contrast with their destinies after death: Lazarus in bliss in the bosom of Abraham and the rich man in torment in Hades. The vivid details of the description need little comment. The rich man, having no need to work, is arrayed in royal purple and fine linen and feasts sumptuously; the destitute Lazarus is, on the contrary, ulcerous and famished. After death their fortunes are reversed, and then not even Lazarus can help the tormented rich man. Their fates are sealed. The story *says* nothing about judgment, but inculcates only the reversal of fortunes.

In the second part (vv. 27-31) Jesus' words insist that not even the miraculous return of someone from the dead will bring about reform among the obdurate rich who heed not Moses and the prophets. Coming shortly after vv. 16-17 on the continuing validity of the law and the prophets, this part of the parable adds emphasis to that saying of Jesus. Bultmann *(HST* 203) has related this part of the parable to Deut 30:11-14, where Moses insists that the observance of the law is not difficult and does not need someone to scale the heavens to make its requirements obvious or travel beyond the sea to bring them close to home. He further refers to *1 Enoch* 108 (unfortunately not extant among the Enochic fragments of Qumran, but possibly a genuine part of early Enochic literature; *pace* J. T. Milik, *The Books of Enoch* [Oxford: Clarendon, 1976] 48, 57, 78, 98, 107, it is not certainly a "Christian Apocalypse of Enoch"). That chapter breathes, according to Bultmann, the rancor of Judaism in its comments on the fate of the rich and sinners and of the pious and the poor. Such passages in Deuteronomy and in Enochic literature make it possible that the words of Jesus in the second part had a meaning for Palestinian Jews in Stage I of the gospel tradition—even without any allusion to Jesus' own death and resurrection. Bultmann misses the point when he thinks that Jesus' words say that it is not right "to ask God for a miracle as a confirmation of his will" *(HST* 203). Rather, as J. M. Creed *(The Gospel,* 209) has noted, "The purpose for which the rich man desires Lazarus to be sent is not to authenticate God's word already given, but to move his brethren to repent lest they come to Hell."

On the lips of the Lucan Jesus, however, the words take on a further nuance (in Stage III). They are addressed not only to the rich among the Pharisees of Palestine, but to Christians as well, and an allusion to Jesus' own death and resurrection is unmistakable.

J. Jeremias *(Parables,* 186), T. W. Manson *(Sayings,* 301), and others are right in thinking that the main stress in the parable lies in the second part. Jesus' words are not meant as a "comment on a social problem," but as a warning to people like the brothers of the rich man. They face a crisis in their lives and do not realize it. However, the Lucan Jesus is undoubtedly saying something, especially in the first part, about retribution in the afterlife. As I. H. Marshall puts its *(Luke,* 633), this "does not do justice to the first part of the parable with its lengthy description of the two men." Jesus may be using in that part folkloric material and the details may be derived from such a background; to identify it as such does not eliminate the critical character of the message itself. Indeed, the first part of the parable inculcates that there is a reward-aspect to human conduct and that Christian disciples are called upon to recognize it.

This Lucan parable teaches the same basic idea that Paul develops in Rom 10:5-17. Luke is stressing that salvation involves a reaction of faith (v. 31) to the word of God preached through Moses and the prophets. He does not say explicitly that "faith comes from what is heard" *(hē pistis ex akoēs,* Rom 10:17)—and we should not expect him to do so (see pp. 27-29). Yet in his own way Luke teaches a message similar to that of Rom 10:5-10.

T. W. Manson *(Sayings,* 301) is right in emphasizing the relation of this parable to what he has called "the Gospel of the Outcast" (see COMMENT on 15:1-7) at this point in the Lucan writings, for it calls indirectly for "generous and gracious help for all the victims of poverty, sickness, or any other ill that may come" upon human beings.

Because this parable is the only one in the gospel tradition in which a person is given a name, the relation of it to the story of the raising of Lazarus in John 11:1-44 naturally comes up. In particular, v. 31, with its comment on someone rising from the dead makes one think of Lazarus' resuscitation in the Johannine Gospel. There a man is raised from the dead, does return to terrestrial life, and some people do come to faith (John 11:45). Ever since Origen *(In Ioann.* frg. 77; GCS 10. 543-544) the question has been raised whether the same figure is involved in both stories. J. Weiss once suggested that the name Lazarus might have been inserted into the parable under the influence of John 11 at the time of the formation of the NT canon, or that the story of the raising of Lazarus was already part of the gospel tradition at the time Luke was composing his Gospel and that he added the name and adjusted the ending of the parable to reflect the Johannine tradition. More recently, R. Dunkerley ("Lazarus") has suggested that the second part of the parable may even have been added under the influence of the Johannine tradition. In all of this, we can only speculate. There is no hard evidence to establish a connection between this Lucan parable and the Johannine miracle-story. (See further R. E. Brown, *John, I-XII,* 428-429; R. Schnackenburg, *The Gospel according to St John* [3 vols.; New York: Seabury, 1980, 1980, 1982] 2. 341-342. See p. 88.)

NOTES

16   19. *There was once a rich man.* See 16:1. The story begins with the description of the life-styles of two Palestinian Jews, as vv. 22,24,25,27,30 reveal. In the majority of the Greek mss. the rich man is nameless, but ms. P[75], the oldest Greek text of the Lucan Gospel, adds *onomati Neuēs,* "by the name of Neues." The name itself is unintelligible and is probably a shortened form of *Nineuēs,* which is also found in the ancient Sahidic version, *epefran pe nineuē,* "whose name was Nineveh." It further occurs in Sahidic homilies of later centuries in which he is reproached for not having pitied his "neighbor" or "confrere," Lazarus. See L. T. Lefort, "Le nom du mauvais riche (Lc 16,19) et la tradition copte," *ZNW* 37 (1938) 65-72. "Nineveh" is a peculiar *personal* name, but perhaps it echoes some aspect of the well-known Assyrian city of the same name.

A. von Harnack ("Der Name des reichen Mannes in Luc. 16,19," *TU* 13/1 [1895] 75-78) suggested that *Nineuēs* was a corruption of Phinehas, the name of the rich man preserved in Priscillian, *Tract. IX, Ad populum I* (CSEL 18.91), spelled *Finees;* and in Ps.-Cyprian, *De pascha computus* 17 (CSEL 3/3.265), spelled *Finaeus.* This name is probably derived from Exod 6:25 or Num 25:7, where Phinehas and Eleazar occur together (as father and son).

K. Grobel tried to explain the Coptic name *Nineuē* as two words, *nine,* "nothing," and *oue,* "one, someone," hence "Nobody." See " '. . . Whose Name Was Neves,' " 381. But *nine* is attested only in Fayyumic, not Sahidic. It is a desperate effort to solve the problem of the name.

A marginal note in a thirteenth-century ms. of Peter of Riga's *Aurora* reads: "Amonofis dicitur esse nomen divitis," "Amenofis [i.e. Amenophis] is said to be the name of the rich man." See M. R. James, "Notes," *JTS* 4 (1902-1903) 242-243.

In English we often refer to the rich man as *Dives,* which is a deliberate misunderstanding of the Latin Vg, "Homo quidam erat dives," as "There was a certain man, Dives." See further B. M. Metzger, "Names for the Nameless in the New Testament: A Study in the Growth of Christian Tradition," *Kyriakon: Festschrift Johannes Quasten* (eds. P. Granfield and J. A. Jungmann; Münster in W.: Aschendorff, 1970) 1. 79-99; J. A. Fitzmyer, "Papyrus Bodmer XIV: Some Features of Our Oldest Text of Luke," *CBQ* 24 (1962) 175-177; H. J. Cadbury, "A Proper Name for Dives," *JBL* 81 (1962) 399-402; "The Name for Dives," *JBL* 84 (1965) 73; *TCGNT* 165-166.

Pace T. W. Manson *(Sayings,* 296-297), it is eisegetical to read this parable as addressed to Sadducees (see v. 14) or to make the rich man a Sadducee, a "priestly aristocrat of Jerusalem." What point would the story make on those who deny the resurrection (20:27; Acts 23:8), "the persistence of the soul after death, penalties in the underworld, and rewards" (Josephus, *J. W.* 2.8,14 § 165)?

who used to dress in purple and fine linen. Lit. "and he was usually clothed in purple and byssus." His garments, described in OT terms (Prov 31:22), insinuate that he lived like a king. "Purple and fine linen" were also the gifts given to Sarai, when Pharaoh restored her to her husband in the *Genesis Apocryphon* (1QapGen 20:31). See 1 Macc 8:14 for "purple" as the raiment of royalty; it was probably fine wool dyed with imported Phoenician purple (made from the murex). "Fine linen" would refer to undergarments made of *bûṣ*, "byssus" (a Hebrew word, borrowed from Egyptian, along with the product from Egypt; see T. O. Lambdin, "Egyptian Loanwords in the Old Testament," *JAOS* 73 [1953] 147-148; cf. A. Hurvitz, "The Usage of *šš* and *bwṣ* in the Bible and Its Implication for the Date of P," *HTR* 60 [1967] 117-121). Cf. Ezek 27:7,16; Rev 18:12. Cf. P. Battifol, "Trois notes exégétiques: Sur Luc. xvi, 19," *RB* 9 (1912) 541 (on Philostratus, *Vita Apoll.* 2.20); R. Delbrueck, "Antiquarisches zu den Verspottungen Jesu," *ZNW* 41 (1942) 128-129.

and feast sumptuously every day. Lit. "splendidly making merry daily," the vb. used is *euphrainein,* as in 12:19; 15:23,24,29,32. Cf. Jas 5:5.

20. *squatted.* Lit. "had been thrown." The pass. of *ballein* is often used to describe an afflicted person, bedridden or crippled. See Rev 2:22; Matt 8:6,14; 9:2; Josephus, *J.W.* 1.32,3 § 629; *Ant.* 9.10,2 § 209.

a beggar named Lazarus. Lit. "and a certain poor (man), Lazarus by name." The name *Lazaros* also occurs in Josephus, *J.W.* 5.13,7 § 567; it is a grecized, shortened form of Hebrew or Aramaic *'El'āzār,* known from the OT (e.g. Exod 6:23, son of Aaron); the latter has been found on numerous ossuaries of the Jerusalem area from the first centuries B.C. and A.D. See J. T. Milik, "Le iscrizioni degli ossuari," in B. Bagatti and J. T. Milik, *Gli scavi del 'Dominus Flevit' (Monte Oliveto—Gerusalemme), Parte I: La necropoli del periodo romano* (Pubblicazioni dello studium biblicum franciscanum 13; Jerusalem: Franciscan Press, 1958) 92-93 (with a full list of occurrences). Josephus uses the fuller Greek form *Eleazaros* for over twenty persons. See *Ant.* 18.4,5 § 103. One ossuary from Palestine has the name of the person in both Greek and Hebrew: *Eliezros Eleazarou/'Elî'ēzer ben Lāzār,* "Eliezer (son of) Eleazar/Lazar." See *CII* 2. 1337. On the problem of the shortening of the name in Aramaic, see J. A. Fitzmyer, "Another View of the 'Son of Man' Debate," *JSNT* 4 (1979) 58-68, esp. 62-64.

The name *'El'āzār* means "God has helped," and it is a fitting name for the beggar in this parable, who was not helped by a fellow human being, but in his afterlife is consoled by God.

covered with sores. Lit. "ulcerated," a pf. pass. ptc. *heilkōmenos* related to the n. *helkos,* "abscess, ulcer." T. W. Manson *(Sayings,* 298) would have us believe that Greek *ptōchos,* "poor" = Aramaic *miskēnā',* used as a euphemism for "leper." But where is it so used? See E. Littmann, "Torreys Buch über die vier Evangelien," *ZNW* 34 (1935) 31; "Zur Bedeutung von *miskin,"* ZA 17 (1903) 262-265. Then the problem is to explain what he would be doing begging in public. See I. H. Marshall, *Luke,* 635.

21. *longing to be fed.* This is actually the same Greek expression *(epithymōn chortasthēnai)* as that used of the prodigal son in 15:16.

if only with the scraps that dropped from the rich man's table. Lit. "from the (things) falling from the table of the rich man." Some mss. (א², A, D, W, Θ, Ψ, 063, and the Koine text-tradition) and ancient versions read *tōn psichiōn,* "tiny crumbs"; that phrase is absent in mss. P⁷⁵, א*, B, L, and some ancient versions; it probably reflects Matt 15:27. My translation is not an attempt to follow the *textus receptus;* in either case the sense is not affected. At the end of this sentence some mss. *(f¹³)* and the Sixto-Clementine Vg add "and nobody would give him anything," an obvious scribal harmonization with Luke 15:16.

Dogs too. J. D. M. Derrett ("Fresh Light," *Law, 89)* would have us believe that they belonged to the rich man himself. Nothing in the text indicates that.

to lick at his sores. The best reading is *epeleichon,* as in mss. ℵ, A, B, L, Θ, Ψ, 33; some others (W, *f*¹³, and the Koine text-tradition) have *apeleichon,* "to lick away"; ms. 157 has *perieleichon,* "to lick around." The attention of the dogs has only added to his miseries. The description of the beggar is vivid and detailed to bring out the lack of concern for him on the part of the rich man.

22. *One day the beggar died.* Lit. "and it happened that the poor man died." Luke uses *egeneto de* with infins. See p. 118.

carried away by the angels. I.e. left unburied by human beings, he was carried off by heavenly beings. This seems to reflect the belief found in Shepherd of Hermas, *Vis.* 2.2,7; *Sim.* 927,3; and still later in Diogenes Laertius, *Lives* 8.31 (where Pythagoras attributes the role to Hermes, the "herald of the gods" in Greek mythology). Apart from *T. Asher* 6:4-6, where something similar is found, the carrying off of the dead by angels is not found in Jewish writings before the mid-second century. See Str-B 2.223-225.

to Abraham's bosom. I.e. to a place of honor, rest, and bliss in the afterlife. This designation is unknown elsewhere in pre-Christian Jewish literature, finding its way (from here?) into late midrashim *(Echa rabb.* 1.85; *Pesqita rabb.* 43 § 108b) and the Babylonian Talmud *(b. Qidd.* 72a-b). The sense of the phrase in some of these passages is disputed. See L. Ginzberg, *The Legends of the Jews* [7 vols.; Philadelphia: Jewish Publication Society of America, 1912-1938] 5. 268). It probably represents a development of the OT idea of sleeping with one's fathers or ancestors. See 1 Kgs 1:21; 2:10; 11:21; 4 Macc 13:17, etc.). In using *kolpos,* "bosom," it may suggest either a place of honor for a guest at a banquet at the right of the host (see John 13:23) or an association of intimacy (see John 1:18). See further R. Meyer, *TDNT* 3. 824-826; F. Planas, "En el seno de Abrahan," *CB* 15 (1958) 148-152; Str-B 2. 225-227. For an attempt to interpret the phrase as "Abraham's lap," see P. Haupt, "Abraham's Bosom," *AJP* 42 (1921) 162-167. Note that the sg. *kolpon* of this verse becomes the pl. *kolpois* in v. 23.

was buried. I.e. with due pomp and ceremony. In this case, there was no question of the man being left unburied. See *1 Enoch* 103:5-6.

23. *in death's abode.* Lit. "in Hades," see NOTE on 10:15. In this parable Hades is a locale distinct from "Abraham's bosom," with a great chasm separating them. But it may be that two different locales in Sheol are really meant. See further L. W. Grensted, "The Use of Enoch in St. Luke xvi. 19-31," *ExpTim* 26 (1914-1915) 333-334.

was tormented. Lit. "being *(hyparchōn,* see p. 111) in torments." Cf. 4 Macc 13:15: "For a great struggle of soul and danger in eternal torment await those who transgress God's commandment." The implication in this part of the parable is not simply that having wealth in this life leads necessarily to torment in the hereafter, but the failure to make prudent use of it, as vv. 9,14-15 have already suggested.

he looked up and saw. Lit. "raising his eyes, he sees"—the historic pres. of the pre-Lucan source is preserved. See p. 107. The expression itself is a Septuagintism. See p. 114. For the dead of one locale being able to see those in the other, see 2 Esdr 7:85,93; *2 Bar* 51:5-6.

Lazarus at his side. Lit. "at his bosom" or "in his lap." See NOTE on v. 22. Some mss. (D, Θ) and the OL version add a ptc., *anapauomenon,* "resting."

24. *Father Abraham.* The rich Jew in torment insists on his kinship with Abraham, "the father of all Hebrews," as Josephus called him *(Ant.* 14.10,22 § 255). See 3:8 and NOTE there; also 1:73. See p. 188. The rich man will call Abraham "Father" again in vv. 27,30.

he called out. Lit. "and calling, he said," unstressed *kai autos* is used. See p. 120.

Have mercy on me! See 17:13; 18:38,39. He who showed no mercy to the poor beggar at his door during his earthly life now seeks for mercy from Abraham (and implicitly from God).

Send Lazarus. The rich man recognizes the beggar and mentions him by name. This detail implies that he was known to the rich man in life as the beggar at his door. His request is callous, stemming from his selfish concern.

that he might cool my tongue. I.e. that part of him with which he feasted during life. Hyperbole is used in this verse to express the severity of the torment. For "thirst" as a part of the torment of Hades, see 2 Esdr 8:59. For water in Hades, see *1 Enoch* 22:9.

I am in great pain. See NOTE on 2:48.

in these flames. For flames associated with Hades, see Sir 21:9-10; 1QH 17:13 (damaged text!); *1 Enoch* 10:13; 63:10 (flames of the torment of Sheol). Cf. Isa 66:24.

25. *my child.* Abraham addresses him with *teknon* (cf. 15:31 [see NOTE there], the same term used of the elder brother of the prodigal), acknowledging indeed the rich man's kinship, but not his right to a share in Abraham's merits. See NOTE on 2:48.

you received your blessings during your life. I.e. on earth. The "blessings" and "misfortunes" are literally expressed as "your good things" and Lazarus' "evil things"; the contrast here recalls the beatitude and woe of 6:20,24.

he is comforted. Lit. "he is consoled," i.e. by God (the theological pass., see NOTE on 5:20). The vb. *parakalein* recalls the woe of 6:24. See NOTE there.

here. The best reading is the adv. *hōde,* "here," but mss. *f*¹ and Marcion read the dem. pron. *hode,* "this one," viz. Lazarus, in contrast to *sy,* "you," in the last cl. of the verse.

26. *Besides.* Lit. "in all these things," an expression used in the LXX (Sir 48:15; Job 12:9) to express addition. Not only should the rich man's request not be granted, but it cannot—the situation is irreversible. The phrase does not mean "in spite of all this," *pace* C. F. Evans, "Uncomfortable Words," 229. A. Plummer *(The Gospel,* 396) queried whether the phrase could mean, "In all these regions, from end to end." Similarly, M.-J. Lagrange *(Luc,* 447). That would be to understand some word like *chōriois* with the phrase, which is possible; but it is not necessary. Some mss. (A, D, W, Θ, Ψ, and the Koine text-tradition) read *epi* instead of *en;* this would clearly mean "in addition" (cf. 3:20), but *en* is the reading in mss. P⁷⁵, ℵ, B, L, etc.

a great chasm. Lit. "a great yawning," i.e. an unbridgeable gulf between the locale of bliss and that of torment. The phrase itself is found in the LXX of 2 Sam 18:17, with a different meaning. The separation of locales is implied in *1 Enoch* 18:11-12 (4QEnᶜ 1 viii 27-30). Plato, in the myth of Er, also speaks of a *chasma* of the heavens and earth (but again in a different sense; see *Resp.* 10.614D). See further E. F. F. Bishop, "A Yawning Chasm," *EvQ* 45 (1973) 3-5; D. de Bruyne, "Notes de philologie biblique: I. Chasme (Luc 16, 26)," *RB* 30 (1921) 400-405.

has been fixed. I.e. by God (another instance of the theological pass.; see NOTE on

5:20). The vb. used is *stērizein*. See NOTE on 9:51. The sense is that the fate of the two men is fixed irrevocably, as the answer of the rich man which follows reveals.

27. *Then I beg you, Father*. See NOTE on v. 25.

send him at least to my father's house. I.e. let him appear in a dream or a vision to my family. Note the subtle play on "father" in this verse; the rich man's natural father is contrasted with "Father Abraham." Messengers from the dead are known in Greek literature. See Plato, *Resp.* 10.614D; Lucian, *Demonax* 43. Cf. 1 Sam 28:7-20.

28. *five brothers*. Cp. 14:19.

he might warn them. Or "might testify to them," i.e. might go as an eyewitness and bear testimony under oath (BAGD 186; cf. Acts 18:5), not only that there is a life after death, but that retribution for one's conduct is part of it.

29. *Abraham replied*. Lit. "says," the historic pres. See p. 107. Some mss. (A, D, W, Θ, Ψ, *f*[1.13], and the Koine text-tradition) add the pron. *autō*, "to him," but mss. P[75], ℵ, B, L, 892, etc., omit it.

They have Moses and the prophets. See v. 31 and the NOTE on 16:16. Implied in the patriarch's answer is that the essential message in the Hebrew Scriptures is still a valid guide for the conduct of his offspring. Those who will not submit themselves to God's word will not be convinced by a sign, even the miraculous return of one from the realm of death. "Moses and the prophets" is scarcely a veiled reference to the Sadducees, *pace* T. W. Manson *(Sayings,* 297); the phrase does not occur in the OT, but is found in Essene literature. See NOTE on 16:16.

let them listen to them. Contrast the advice given to the disciples on the mountain of transfiguration (9:35, see NOTE there).

30. *Father Abraham*. See NOTE on v. 24. The rich man persists in his petition.

if someone will come back from the dead. The vb. in many of the best mss. is *poreuthē*, "go forth"; but ms. P[75] reads *egerthē*, "were to be raised," and ms. ℵ has *anastō*, "were to rise." The latter is a copyist's harmonization with v. 31. There is no distinction between *tis apo nekrōn* in this verse and *tis ek nekrōn* in v. 31. See P. Joüon, "Notes philologiques," 354.

they will reform their lives. The rich man uses a fut. more vivid condition. The Lucan theme of repentance and conversion appears again. See pp. 237-238.

31. *they will not be convinced*. Abraham's answer is just as emphatic as the insistent petition of the rich man. Instead of the majority Greek reading *(peisthēsontai,* the subjunc. of emphatic fut., "will [not] be convinced"), ms. D and Latin and Syriac versions have *pisteusousin* (fut. indic.), "they will (not) believe." In this way, the sign-seeking generation (11:29) is answered again.

even if someone rises from the dead. The best reading is *anastē*, "rises," but ms. P[75] again has *egerthē*, "is raised" (see v. 30), and ms. W and the OL version have *apelthē*, "comes (from)." Ms. D conflates *anastē kai apelthē pros autous*, "rises and comes (from the dead) to them." See p. 195 on *anastē* and NOTE on 9:8; cf. p. 195.

Those who reject or care not about God's word in "Moses and the prophets" will not be moved by the testimony of such a messenger even from death's realm. For the Christian reader of the Lucan Gospel, the reference to Jesus' own death and resurrection is obvious. See 9:22; cf. 18:33.

BIBLIOGRAPHY (16:19-31)

Alexandre, M. "L'Interprétation de *Luc* 16,19-31 chez Grégoire de Nysse," *Epektasis: Mélanges patristiques offerts au Cardinal Jean Daniélou* (eds. J. Fontaine and C. Kannengiesser; Paris: Beauchesne, 1972) 425-441.

Barth, K. "Miserable Lazarus (Text: Luke 16:19-31)," *USR* 46 (1934-1935) 259-268.

Bornhäuser, K. *Studien zum Sondergut des Lukas* (Gütersloh: Bertelsmann, 1934) 138-160.

Cantinat, J. "Le mauvais riche et Lazare," *BVC* 48 (1962) 19-26.

Cave, C. H. "Lazarus and the Lukan Deuteronomy," *NTS* 15 (1968-1969) 319-325.

Degenhardt, H.-J. *Lukas Evangelist der Armen,* 133-135.

Derrett, J. D. M. "Fresh Light on St Luke xvi: II. Dives and Lazarus and the Preceding Sayings," *NTS* 7 (1960-1961) 364-380; reprinted, *Law,* 78-99.

Díaz, J. "La discriminación y retribución immediatas después de la muerte (Precisiones neotestamentarias y de la literatura judía contemporánea)," *XVI semana bíblica espanola* (Madrid: Consejo superior de investigaciones científicas, 1956) 85-157.

Dunkerley, R. "Lazarus," *NTS* 5 (1958-1959) 321-327.

Dupont, J. "L'Après-mort dans l'oeuvre de Luc," *RTL* 3 (1972) 3-21.

——— *Béatitudes,* 3. 60-64, 111-112, 162-182.

Eichholz, G. *Gleichnisse der Evangelien,* 221-228.

Evans, C. F. "Uncomfortable Words—V. '. . . Neither Will They Be Convinced,' " *ExpTim* 81 (1969-1970) 228-231.

Feuillet, A. "La parabole du mauvais riche et du pauvre Lazare (Lc 16, 19-31) antithèse de la parabole de l'intendant astucieux (Lc 16, 1-9)," *NRT* 101 (1979) 212-223.

George, A. "La parabole du riche et de Lazare: Lc 16,19-31," *AsSeign* ns 57 (1971) 80-93.

Glombitza, O. "Der reiche Mann und der arme Lazarus: Luk. xvi 19-31, Zur Frage nach der Botschaft des Textes," *NovT* 12 (1970) 166-180.

Gressmann, H. "Vom reichen Mann und armen Lazarus: Eine literargeschichtliche Studie," *AbhKPAW* phil.-hist. Kl. 7, 1918 (Berlin: Königliche Akademie der Wissenschaften, 1918).

Grobel, K. " '. . . Whose Name Was Neves,' " *NTS* 10 (1963-1964) 373-382.

Huie, W. P. "The Poverty of Abundance: From Text to Sermon on Luke 16:19-31," *Int* 22 (1968) 403-420.

Jülicher, A. *Gleichnisreden,* 2. 617-641.

North, B. *The Rich Man and Lazarus: A Practical Exposition of Luke xvi,19-31* (London: Banner of Truth Trust, 1960).

Pax, E. "Der reiche und der arme Lazarus: Eine Milieustudie," *SBFLA* 25 (1975) 254-268.

Perkins, P. *Hearing the Parables,* 53-62, 64-66, 134-138, 140-142, 156, 171.

Renié, J. "Le mauvais riche (Lc., xvi, 19-31)," *Année théologique* 6 (1945) 268-275.

Rimmer, N. "Parable of Dives and Lazarus (Luke xvi. 19-31)," *ExpTim* 66 (1954-1955) 215-216.

Sahlin, H. "Lasarus-gestalten i Lk 16 och Joh 11," *SEA* 37-38 (1972-1973) 167-174.

Schnider, F., and W. Stenger. "Die offene Tür und die unüberschreitbare Kluft: Strukturanalytische Überlegungen zum Gleichnis vom reichen Mann und armen Lazarus (Lk 16, 19-31)," *NTS* 25 (1978-1979) 273-283.

Standen, A. O. "The Parable of Dives and Lazarus and Enoch 22," *ExpTim* 33 (1921-1922) 523.

110. WARNING AGAINST STUMBLING BLOCKS
(17:1-3a)

17 ¹ Then Jesus said to his disciples, "It is impossible that scandals not occur. But woe betide the one through whom they do occur! ² It will be better for such a one to be thrown into the sea with a millstone around his neck than that he should cause one of these little ones to stumble. ³ᵃ So be on your guard!"

COMMENT

Luke now continues his travel account with further sayings of Jesus, which are completely unrelated to the foregoing chapter or parable. Four sets of isolated sayings of Jesus now bring the second part of the travel account to a close: 17:1-3a, on scandals or stumbling blocks; 17:3b-4, on the duty of Christian forgiveness; 17:5-6, on the power of Christian faith; and 17:7-10, on the inadequacy of Christian service. The sayings are, moreover, unrelated to each other. The only link that they seem to have is a bearing on various aspects of discipleship. The first of them concerns scandals or stumbling blocks put before disciples by others that cause them to sin or be disloyal (17:1-3a).

Luke has composed the introductory sentence in which he depicts Jesus again turning his attention to the disciples (v. 1a). Superficially, the saying about stumbling blocks is related to Mark 9:42 and Matt 18:6-7. Whereas Matt 18:6 is dependent on Mark 9:42, the Lucan formulation coincides with the Marcan form only in three phrases, "into the sea," "around his neck," and "one of these little ones." The woe in v. 1c has, however, a similarity with Matt 18:7, which has no Marcan counterpart. The Matthean text of it reads: "Woe to the world because of scandals; for it is necessary that they occur, but woe betide the person through whom the scandal occurs." The similarity of the Lucan and Matthean woes suggests that part of the Lucan statement is derived from "Q," and since the sayings in the next sections (vv. 3b-4,5-6) are derived from that source, it seems likely that a form of vv. 1b-2 also existed in that source (see G. Schneider, *Evangelium nach Lukas,* 345). Luke would be preserving the sayings in the "Q" order. He has, however, also been influenced by Mark 9:42—a passage which would correspond to his Little Omission (see pp. 67, 72, 824). He has undoubtedly redacted what he inherits from both "Q" and "Mk" in this set of sayings (vv. 1b-2). (See further J. Jeremias, *Die Sprache,* 163, 262.) The final warning in v. 3a is of Lucan composition (see S. Schulz, *Q: Die Spruchquelle,* 320; G. Schneider, *Evangelium nach Lukas,* 346).

Form-critically considered, the sayings about scandals belong to the legal category. R. Bultmann *(HST* 144) regards v. 2 as an old proverb taken over by "the Christian Church" and preserved in the Lucan form "without Christian alterations"; he considers the Marcan phrase "these little ones *who believe"* as a christianized form of the proverb, to which Matthew has added "in me." (Bultmann further compares Mark 9:36,41.) That the Lucan form (derived from "Q") is more primitive than the "Mk" may be admitted; that there is nothing more than a Christian adoption of an old proverb is another matter. Bultmann's view is based on sheer surmise. In any case, one should note the litotes and the woe in v. 1b,c.

The Lucan Jesus warns his disciples about the inevitability of scandal in Christian life. He is depicted as enough of a realist to know that human beings will at times affect one another in such a way that even some of his followers will sin by causing others to sin. His warning takes the form of a woe uttered against the person who might be the source of such disedification. The severity of the fate that Jesus envisages, weighted drowning in a sea, could not be more expressive; it needs no elaborate explanation. It is the basis of his final warning, "Be on your guard," lest you become such a person.

The saying envisages the problem of seduction to apostasy, of putting stumbling blocks before disciples otherwise required to be loyal and faithful. The disciple who would cause another to waver in fidelity is not worth continued existence in this life; he heaps guilt only upon himself, and the eschatological connotation of the warning is not hard to perceive.

Christian disciples are designated as "these little ones," a phrase which reminds the reader of the Lucan Gospel about the "small children" of 10:21. The phrase connotes a certain helplessness, a condition which should not be exploited by subversive activity on the part of any Christian disciple.

From the present context we cannot tell who such persons are from whom the "scandals" come. In Acts 20:29-30 Paul in his last discourse to the elders of Ephesus at Miletus is presented warning them against "fierce wolves" who will enter the flock, "men speaking perverse things, to draw away disciples after them." Such persons are undoubtedly among those against whom the Lucan Jesus now utters his woe.

NOTES

17 1. *said to his disciples.* Luke again uses *eipen pros* + acc. See p. 116. In v. 5 the "disciples" will become "the apostles." Despite such specific designations, Jesus' words are being addressed to Luke's Christian readers.

impossible that scandals not occur. The n. *skandalon* is hardly ever found in classical Greek; a related form of it, *skandalēthron,* "a stick of a mousetrap," occurs rarely. E.g. Aristophanes, *Acharn.* 687. In Hellenistic Greek *skandalon* begins to make an appearance, and in the LXX it and the related vb. *skandalizein* usually translate forms of the Hebrew roots *yqš,* "catch in a trap, snare" (see Josh 23:13; Judg 2:3; 8:27), or *kšl,* "stumble" (see Lev 19:14; 1 Sam 25:31; Ps 119:165). In time the two ideas were assimilated so that the n. and the vb. both connote a "cause of ruin" for someone. See further G. Stählin, *TDNT* 7. 339-358. Specifically, in Jesus' saying the "scandal" has to be understood of an enticement to apostasy or abandonment of allegiance (to God or to his word as proclaimed by Jesus). See 7:23 and NOTE there. Since, however, the warning of Jesus is couched in generic terms, it is impossible to exclude a wider connotation, viz. a seduction to sin in general. This connotation is not, however, in the forefront of the present Lucan context. For the Lucan construction of the neut. *anendekton,* lit. "inadmissible" (hence, "impossible") with the gen. of the articular infin., see BDF § 400.4. Cf. Luke 4:42 (J. Jeremias, *Die Sprache,* 28). For an attempt to make *skandalon* out to be a "snare, lure" rather than a "stumbling block," see MM 576.

But woe betide. Luke again uses the strong adversative conj. *plēn* (see NOTE on 10:11), followed by *ouai.* See NOTE on 6:24. This is the best reading, preserved in mss. P⁷⁵, ℵ, B, D, L, Ψ, *f*¹,¹³, etc.; but some mss. (A, W, Θ, the Koine text-tradition) and the Latin and Syriac versions have merely *ouai de.*

2. *It will be better.* Lit. "it is (more) advantageous"; the same vb., *lysitelein,* is found in Tob 3:6; Andocides, *Or.* 1.125 ("it is better to die than to live"). The compound vb. means really *lysei ta telē,* "it pays the taxes, repays the outlay." See A. Plummer, *The Gospel,* 399.

with a millstone around his neck. Lit. "if a millstone be laid about his neck." For a contemporary Palestinian basalt millstone discovered in the excavation of Khirbet Qumran, see R. de Vaux, *Archaeology and the Dead Sea Scrolls* (Schweich Lectures 1959; London: Oxford University, 1973) pl. XXb. Mss. P⁷⁵, ℵ, B, D, L, Θ, and *f*¹,¹³ have *lithos mylikos,* "a stone belonging to a mill," but mss. A, Ψ, and the Koine text-tradition have *mylos onikos,* "a mill turned by an ass," the phrase used in Mark 9:42 and Matt 18:6 and introduced into mss. of the Lucan Gospel by copyists' harmonization. For a later form of this saying, see *1 Clem.* 46.8. For a millstone as an instrument of death or destruction, see Judg 9:53; Rev 18:21.

than that. The Greek *hina* is used in a non-purpose sense. See 1:43; cf. J. Jeremias, *Die Sprache,* 58.

one of these little ones. For the construction, see p. 122. In *1 Clem.* 46.8 they become "one of my elect."

3a. *be on your guard!* See NOTE on 12:1; cf. especially 21:34. This impv. is problematic; as I have taken it, it serves as the conclusion to the preceding sayings; but it could also be meant as the introduction to the following set of sayings—or at least as transitional. See further E. Klostermann, *Lukasevangelium,* 171.

BIBLIOGRAPHY (17:1-3a)

Kafka, G. "Bild und Wort in den Evangelien," *MTZ* 2 (1951) 263-287, esp. 263-265.
Trilling, W. *Hausordnung Gottes: Eine Auslegung von Matthäus 18* (Düsseldorf: Patmos, 1960) 30-35, 57-60.

111. ON FORGIVENESS
(17:3b-4)

17 3b "If your brother sins, rebuke him; if he reforms his conduct, forgive him. 4 Even if he sins against you seven times in a day and seven times turns back to you to say, 'I am sorry,' you are to forgive him."

COMMENT

The second of these four sets of sayings concerns the duty of Christian forgiveness (17:3b-4). It envisages the case of a Christian disciple who has sinned in some way against a fellow-disciple.

The sayings in this set are derived by Luke from the source "Q" (see p. 79) and have their counterparts in Matt 18:15,21-22, where they form part of the ecclesiastical discourse in that Gospel. Lucan redaction accounts for the presence of the vbs. *epitimēson,* "rebuke" (v. 3b), *metanoēsē,* "reforms" (v. 3c), *epistrepsē,* "turns back" (v. 4b), and *metanoō,* "I am sorry" (v. 4b), since none of these vbs. occurs in the Matthean parallels and they are frequently used by Luke elsewhere (see NOTES on vv. 3b-4). Luke has, moreover, probably preserved the order of the sayings of "Q" in vv. 3b-4, whereas Matthew has separated the first from the second by the insertion of 18:16-18 (on fraternal correction). (See further S. Schulz, *Q: Die Spruchquelle,* 320.) The Lucan double saying preserves better the parallelism of the utterances, which probably reflects that of "Q" and is otherwise disturbed in Matthew.

The sayings touch upon a good Lucan theme, forgiveness. Usually, the Lucan Jesus' emphasis is on the forgiveness of human sins by God (see pp. 223-224), but here it takes a new direction, the foregiveness of sins committed by one human being against another, by one Christian disciple against another. What should the latter's attitude be toward it? Jesus sees the need to rebuke or admonish the offender—to tell him/her wherein the wrong lies. Then if the admonition or rebuke is accepted, forgiveness must follow. The goal of the rebuke is repentance, which is to be followed by forgiveness. One should recall the second petition of the Lucan "Our Father" (11:4a,b). The second saying of Jesus preserved here goes even further, instructing the disciples that forgiveness is to be accorded whenever repentance is manifested. "Seven times" is used to denote totality (and is not to be taken literally, as "seven times in a day" makes clear). The willingness to forgive must be boundless. The Lucan theme of repentance and conversion recurs here (see pp. 237-239). (Note that the Petrine question in Matt 18:21 is a secondary formulation, as is also the answer "seventy times seven" [so the *RSV*]; but the Matthean expression *hebdomēkontakis hepta* is derived from Gen 4:24, where it stands as a translation of Hebrew *šib'îm wĕšib'āh*, which in that context must mean "seventy-sevenfold," as the *RSV* renders the Genesis passage. Cf. *T. Benj.* 7:4.)

NOTES

17 3b. *brother.* The n. *adelphos* is probably to be understood as a fellow-disciple, as in Acts 1:15; 6:3; 9:30; 10:23. For the OT background of Jesus' teaching, see Lev 19:17.

sins. The mss. D, Ψ, 063, *f* 13, and the Koine text-tradition add *eis se,* "against you," which is probably derived from v. 4 by copyists' harmonization; the phrase is omitted in mss. ℵ, A, B, L, W, Θ, *f* 1, etc. The omission of it makes the saying more generic.

rebuke him. See NOTE on 4:35. The vb. *epitiman* carries the nuance of a frank, but gentle admonition: politely tell him that he is wrong. Such a rebuke is counseled instead of the harboring of a grudge or detraction to some third party. See *T. Gad* 6:3: "So love one another from the heart; if anyone sins against you, speak to him peaceably, banishing the poison of hatred, and keeping not guile in your soul. If he confesses and repents, forgive him."

reforms his conduct. Lit. "repents." See NOTE on 3:3; cf. p. 237.

forgive him. See NOTE on 5:20; cf. pp. 223-224.

4. *seven times.* See NOTES on 8:2; 11:26. Cf. I. Abrahams, "Numbers, Typical and Important," *Encylopaedia judaica* (New York: Macmillan, 1971) 12. 1254-1261, esp. 1257.

in a day. See Ps 119:164.

and seven times turns back. Some mss. (A, W, Θ, 063, *f* 1,13, and the Koine text-tradition) add *tēs hēmeras,* "in a day," undoubtedly from a copyist's harmonization with the first part of v. 4; mss. ℵ, B, D, L, Ψ, 892, etc., omit the phrase. On the vb. *epistrephein,* see NOTES on 1:16,17; cf. pp. 237-238.

I am sorry. Lit. "I repent, reform."

you are to forgive. Lit. "you shall forgive," the fut. *aphēseis* is emphatic and stands in contrast to the impv. *aphes* at the end of v. 3.

BIBLIOGRAPHY (17:3b-4)

Lührmann, D. *Redaktion,* 111-114.
Schulz, S. *Q: Die Spruchquelle,* 320-322.

112. ON FAITH
(17:5-6)

17 ⁵ Then the apostles said to the Lord, "Increase our faith." ⁶ But the Lord said, "If you had faith the size of a mustard seed, you would say to this mulberry tree, 'Be uprooted and planted in the sea,' and it would obey you."

COMMENT

Yet another aspect of Christian discipleship now emerges in Jesus' saying about the kind and power of faith expected of his followers (17:5-6). The apostles beg Jesus for faith and their request evokes from him a response.

This saying is derived by Luke from "Q" (see p. 79); its parallel is found in Matt 17:20, where it is appended to the Matthean form of the story of the cure of the epileptic boy (cf. Luke 9:37-43a) and made the commentary on the disciples' inability to exorcise the demon that afflicted the boy and on their "little faith" *(oligopistia,* a favorite Matthean theme [see Matt 6:30; 8:26; 14:31; 16:8; and especially 17:20]). In both the Lucan and Matthean forms of Jesus' response to the apostles, he speaks of faith the size of a mustard seed; but in Luke he refers the power of faith to a mulberry tree, whereas in Matthew he refers it to a mountain: "He said to them, 'Because of your little faith. Amen, I tell you, if you have faith the size of a mustard seed, you will say to this mountain, "Move from here over there," and it will be moved; and nothing will be impossible to you' " (Matt 17:20).

The difference of reference is partly owing to a Matthean doublet, since Matt 21:21 has another form of the saying in a comment on the withered fig tree: "Jesus spoke up and said to them, 'Amen, I tell you, if you have faith and waver not, you will not only do what has been done to this fig tree, but even if you say to this mountain, "Be lifted up and thrown into the sea," it will be done.' " The form of this Matthean saying is derived from Mark 11:22-23 (a Marcan passage omitted by Luke—and there is no echo of the cursing of the fig tree in the Lucan formulation of the saying preserved in this chapter [see S. Schulz, *Q: Die Spruchquelle,* 466]). However, Matt 21:21 has affected Matt 17:20 (otherwise derived from "Q," and not from "M," *pace* T. W. Manson, *Sayings,* 140-141). Hence, Luke has here preserved the more original form of "Q," with the mulberry tree, which Matthew has assimilated to the form he derived in 21:21 from "Mk." Bultmann *(HST* 75) regards the Matthean form as the more original; but what would have prompted Luke to change "mountain" to "mulberry tree"? For this reason the other explanation is more plausible (see S. Schulz, *Q: Die Spruchquelle,* 466-467). Luke has most likely composed the transitional v. 5, introducing "the apostles," who address "the Lord," who then responds in v. 6 (see *HST* 334-335; *FTG* 162; W. Grundmann, *Evangelium nach Lukas,* 332).

Form-critically considered, the saying of Jesus about the power of faith belongs to non-proverb-like wisdom-sayings *(HST* 81), which formulate a paradox similar to the saying about the camel and the eye of the needle (Luke 18:25).

The request made of Jesus by the apostles for an increase of faith comes into the Lucan travel account abruptly. Little that precedes immediately prepares for its introduction; in fact, this is the first time that this aspect of Christian life appears in the instruction being given in this part of the Lucan Gospel. Jesus' answer to the request does not really meet it. His words rather put the apostles immediately on the spot: The amount of faith is not important, but the kind of faith is, i.e. genuine faith. If it were no bigger than a grain of mustard, yet genuine, it would have wondrous power. Jesus' words are couched in a mixed condition, which begins with a protasis expressing reality, but ends with an apodosis contrary to fact. It implies that the faith of the apostles is not even the size of a mustard seed.

In 1 Cor 13:2 Paul speaks of a faith that "moves mountains," relating it to speaking in tongues, prophetic powers, and a knowledge of mysteries—in effect, of a charismatic faith, which may be different from the essential Christian faith or reaction to the kerygma or gospel. Luke does not speak of that sort of faith; he is rather envisaging the reaction of human beings to the proclamation of Jesus himself or his disciples. Even though there is an absolute formulation about faith and nothing is said explicitly about a relationship to God or Jesus, that must be implied, *pace* N. Perrin, *Rediscovering,* 138. To divest the Lucan notion of faith of its implied object (God or his word as proclaimed by Jesus) is to water down a key concept. (See further pp. 235-237.) Moreover, the Lucan introduction envisages this reaction to Christian proclamation as something that can be increased. Even if Jesus' reply means that the faith of the apostles was actually smaller than a mustard seed, he does insinuate that the fundamental attitude of a Christian disciple should be precisely, "Grant us more faith." Jesus' words also imply that genuine Christian faith could grow and would have a power that would be limitless (expressed by the grotesque image of an uprooted mulberry tree being *planted* in the sea). (An "increase" in faith may also be the meaning of the Pauline phrase, "through faith for faith," in Rom 1:17.)

This saying of Jesus has also been preserved in the *Gospel of Thomas*, where it is given an entirely different twist. In § 48, Jesus is made to say: "If two make peace, one with the other, in the same house, they will say to the mountain, 'Move away,' and it will move away." And again in § 106: "Jesus said, 'When you make the two one, you will become sons of man; and when you say, "Mountain, move away," it will move away.'" The second form, with two being made one, is clearly gnostic; but both forms in the apocryphal Gospel depend on Matt 17:20. There is no hint of faith in these forms, which are more concerned with a return to unity. See J.-E. Ménard, *L'Evangile selon Thomas*, 149-151, 204.

NOTES

17 5. *the apostles.* For Luke, this means the Twelve. See NOTE on 6:13; cf. pp. 253-254.

the Lord. As again in v. 6. See NOTE on 7:13; cf. pp. 202-203. J. Jeremias *(Die Sprache,* 158) is right in thinking that the absolute use of "the Lord" is pre-Lucan, but when it occurs in statements of the evangelist himself, it is in this Gospel certainly redactional. See also S. Schulz, *Q: Die Spruchquelle,* 466. For a similar intervention of disciples, see Luke 11:1; 12:41.

Increase our faith. Lit. "add faith to us," which could mean, Add more faith to what we already have, or add faith to the other gifts that we have received. Since "apostles" say this, a certain amount of faith must be understood as present; hence the former sense would be preferred, i.e. grant us more faith. In Stage I of the gospel tradition, the request would not be about faith in the full Christian sense; but in Stage III the connotation of it as such could be present (especially in view of the compositional character of this verse). On the Lucan favorite vb. *prostithenai,* see p. 111. On faith, see NOTE on 5:20.

6. *If you had faith the size of a mustard seed.* Lit. "if you have faith like a seed *(or* a grain) of mustard," the protasis uses the pres. *echete,* of a "real" condition. But the apodosis continues in the sense of an "unreal" or contrary-to-fact condition. Mss. D, E, G correct the protasis and read the impf. *eichete.* The implication would then be that the apostles do not have as much as a mustard-seed amount of faith. See BDF § 372.1a. On the size of the mustard seed, see NOTE on 13:19.

to this mulberry tree. The Greek n. *sykaminos* occurs in the LXX (1 Kgs 10:27; 1 Chr 27:28; 2 Chr 1:15; 9:27, etc.) as the translation of Hebrew *šiqmāh,* which is really the "sycamore tree." See Luke 19:4, *sykomorea.* Luke may not have differentiated

them. In any case, it designates a relatively large tree. Such a tree was not to be
planted within twenty-five cubits of a cistern, i.e. about thirty-seven ft., according to
the later tradition of *m. B. Bat.* 2:11. Ms. D reads "to this mountain, 'Move from here
over there,' and it would move, and . . . ," an obvious scribal harmonization with
Matt 17:20. The adj. *tautē*, "this," is omitted in some mss. (P75, א, D, L, etc.). See
further C.-H. Hunzinger, *TDNT* 7. 289-291; A. Alon, *Natural History*, 68-69.

   Be uprooted and planted in the sea. Ms. D reads *metaphyteuthēti eis tēn thalassan*,
"be transplanted into the sea," a minor variant. The person with genuine faith would
be able to effect things in a manner beyond all expectation. Cf. Jer 1:10. Two figures
are obviously mixed here, "being planted" and "in the sea." This is an inconsistency
that does not bother Luke. In the earlier tradition it was probably a mountain that was
thrown into a sea, which would be intelligible. But now a mulberry tree being
"planted" in the sea is strange, to say the least.

BIBLIOGRAPHY (17:5-6)

George, A. "La foi des apôtres: Efficacité et gratuité: Lc 17,5-10," *AsSeign* ns 58
   (1974) 68-77.
Schulz, S. *Q: Die Spruchquelle*, 465-468.

113. WE ARE UNPROFITABLE SERVANTS
(17:7-10)

17 7 "Which one of you who has a servant that plows or tends sheep,
when he returns home from the field, would say to him, 'Come at once
and sit down to eat'? 8 Would he not rather say, 'Prepare my dinner;
put on your apron and wait on me while I eat and drink; afterward
you can eat and drink yourself.' 9 Does he thank that servant for carrying out his orders? 10 So it is with you. When you have carried out all
your orders, learn to say, 'We are unprofitable servants; we have only
done our duty.' "

COMMENT

The last set of sayings of Jesus in this group of four with which the second
part of the travel account closes deals with the inadequacy of service of
Christian disciples. In this concluding set Jesus inculcates the idea that after
all that Christian disciples have done they are still "unprofitable servants"

(17:7-10). In using the saying here in the travel account, Luke is emphasizing the relation of human service to Christian destiny.

Verses 7-10 are exclusive to the Lucan Gospel, having been derived from the source "L" (see p. 84). Apart from a few distinctive Lucan redactional traits (the adv. *eutheōs,* "at once," v. 7; the phrase *meta tauta,* "afterward," v. 8; the adj. *panta,* "all," v. 10; and the vb. *diatassein,* "order," vv. 9,10), the rest is derived from the pre-Lucan source.

The bulk of the material is a parable or similitude. R. Bultmann (*HST* 170) regards vv. 7-10 "as a similitude: *Master and Servant* . . . with no conjunction of comparison," but with a rhetorical question and a concluding application, "So it is with you." Years ago B. S. Easton *(Gospel according to St. Luke,* 258) and more recently P. S. Minear ("A Note," 82-83) have queried whether the application in v. 10 is integrally part of the parable. Easton wrote: "The parable ends with a question [in v. 9] that is its own answer." There is clearly wisdom in recognizing this, since it enables one to distinguish the sense of the parable in Stage I of the gospel tradition from that of the Lucan context in Stage III.

Details in the parable proper (having a servant, a farm with fields to be plowed and sheep to be tended) seem out of place if the parable were originally addressed either to "disciples" (v. 1) or "apostles" (v. 5), the sayings may originally have been directed either to Pharisees (so J. Jeremias, *Parables,* 193) or to the crowds (P. S. Minear, "A Note," 84). It would have been a "demand for renunciation of all Pharisaic self-righteousness" (J. Jeremias) or a "ruling out" of "any expectation of rewards according to merit" (P. S. Minear, who depends on H. Conzelmann, *Theology,* 234). In Stage I of the gospel tradition, this could have been the meaning of the parable proper.

In distinguishing the parable in vv. 7-9 from its application in v. 10, we can see that the former concentrates on the master, whereas the latter explains the attitude of the servant. This distinction, however, raises the question whether the application was framed by Luke himself or already existed in the pre-Lucan source. The latter alternative seems the more likely.

In the Lucan context (Stage III) the application in v. 10 clearly applies the parable to the "disciples" (v. 1) or the "apostles" (v. 5). Minear has shown that *doulos,* "slave, servant" could already have taken on the Christian nuance of the Pauline usage (e.g. Rom 1:1; 1 Cor 7:22; Gal 1:10). Cf. Acts 4:29; 16:17. Moreover, plowing, shepherding, and serving took on in time Christian nuances (1 Cor 9:7,10; Rom 15:25), well before Luke composed his two volumes. The upshot is that Jesus' words about the inadequacy of service could now be understood in a specific Christian sense.

In the present Lucan setting Jesus' words stress that the Christian disciple who is a "servant" or "slave," and has well carried out his task, can only regard himself as an unprofitable servant. Their stress strikes home in two ways: (1) The conduct of such a Christian disciple in fulfilling his/her appointed tasks does not necessarily guarantee his/her salvation; having done all that is expected, the disciple still realizes that the destiny that awaits him/her is a grace. (2) There is no room for human boasting. The Lucan Jesus formulates what Paul teaches in terms of human *kauchēsis:* "It is excluded" (Rom 3:27; cf. 1 Cor 1:29; Eph 2:9).

NOTES

17   7. *Which one of you.* See NOTE on 11:5. Envisaged is a small farmer who has one servant who not only works his farm (plowing and tending sheep) but also prepares his meals. Some mss. (P[75], D, L, 1241) omit the prep. *ex,* but the sense of the introductory phrase is not changed thereby.

when he returns home from the field. The servant or slave has presumably already done a good day's work in the field; nothing in the text reveals that he has been loafing or shirking his duty. Cf. 15:25.

would say to him. The question expects the answer "no." Codex Bezae and some OL versions add *mē,* making more explicit the question expecting the negative answer (complicating the already tortuous syntax of the Greek). The servant is not met with an invitation to dine, because further tasks and chores await him. Contrast 12:37.

at once. The adv. *eutheōs* is Lucan. See 5:13; 12:36,54; 14:5; 21:9; Acts 9:18,20,34; 12:10; 16:10; 17:10,14; 21:30; 22:29.

8. *Would he not rather say.* The sentence is introduced by *all' ouchi,* announcing a question that expects the answer "yes." See BDF § 448.4.

Prepare my dinner. Lit. "prepare what I am to dine on."

put on your apron . . . Lit. "having girt yourself, wait on me." See NOTE on 12:35. For *diakonein* in the sense of "serving tables," see Acts 6:2. For the broader Christian sense, see Rom 15:25; Acts 1:17,25.

afterward. Lit. "after these (things)." See NOTE on 10:1.

9. *Does he thank . . . ?* Lit. "he does not thank, does he . . . ?" The question expects the answer "no," being introduced with *mē.* See BDF § 427.2. It thus concludes the parable proper.

10. *So it is with you.* The application is thus made to the "disciples" of v. 1 or the "apostles" of v. 5, the audience proper for the four groups of sayings at the end of part two of the travel account. For a similar mode of application, see 21:31; contrast 22:26. Before these words some mss. (A, W, Θ, Ψ, 063, and the Koine text-tradition) have added *ou dokō,* which seems to mean "I do not think (so)," an answer to the negative question with which v. 9 ends. B. M. Metzger *(TCGNT* 166) thinks that it was a marginal comment which found its way eventually into the Western text-tradition.

The point of the application is: If a human master can make such demands on his servants, how much more can God expect of Christian servants in his kingdom?

When you have carried out all your orders. Lit. "all that has been ordered," by whom is not said; possibly the pass. ptc. is to be understood as a theological pass. See NOTE on 5:20. "All" is understood of "all our duties" as Christians by J. M. Creed *(The Gospel,* 216), but P. S. Minear would restrict the pron. to the "three duties specifically assigned to apostles: plowing, shepherding, deaconing" ("A Note," 85).

The last suggestion tends to allegorize the parable too much. It would seem to refer in Stage III to all the tasks of Christian disciples called to be instruments of proclaiming God's merciful love to human beings. On Luke's rhetorical predilection for "all," see NOTES on 3:16; 4:15; 9:1.

learn to say . . . The entire saying was omitted in Marcion's text of Luke.

We are unprofitable servants. I.e. we recognize that what we have managed to do in God's service is still inadequate. The sense of the adj. *achreios* is disputed. Literally, it means "useless, worthless" and is used in this sense in the only other place in the NT in which it occurs (Matt 25:30, for the servant who has done nothing). It was often used of slaves (Ps.-Plato, *Alcib.* 1.17 122B; Achilles Tatius, *Erot.* 5.17,8). But that sense of the word seems ill-suited here because the presupposition is that the servant in the parable has done all that he was supposed to do—*a fortiori* for the Christian disciple. The adj. was omitted in the Sinaitic Syriac version, apparently as tautological, and some modern commentators have followed this omission. See BAGD 128. In the LXX of 2 Sam 6:22 it occurs in the sense of "unworthy, miserable," and some commentators would prefer that sense. See J. Jeremias, *Parables,* 193, n. 98; W. Grundmann, *Evangelium nach Lukas,* 334. A. Plummer *(The Gospel,* 402) tries to defend the sense of "unprofitable," because "nothing has been *gained* by them for their master. He has got no more than his due. . . . That God does not need man's service is not the point. Nor are the rewards which he gives in return for man's service here brought into question. The point is that man can make no just *claim* for having done *more* than was due." No matter how much a person does in God's service, there is a sense in which he/she is still "unprofitable."

Still another interpretation has been suggested, exploiting more the etymology than historical usage (see, though, Homer, *Od.* 18.163; Theocritus, *Poem.* 25.72—are they pertinent?), by J. J. Kilgallen ("What Kind of Servants are We? Luke 17,10," *Bib* 63 [1982] 549-551): *achreioi* would mean "those to whom something is not due, owed"; hence, "We are servants to whom no favor is owed." It is not clear how this is to be understood with the last comment.

we have only done our duty. Lit. "we have done what we are bound to do." Compare the later dictum of Antigonus of Socho: "Be not like slaves that serve the master for the sake of receiving a bounty; but be like slaves that serve the master not for the sake of receiving a bounty; and let the fear of heaven be upon you" *(m. Abot* 1:3). Or the advice attributed to R. Yohanan b. Zakkai: "He used to say, 'If you have achieved much in the Law, claim not merit for yourself; for this purpose were you created" *(m. Abot* 2:8).

Finally, in the Lucan context of the last three sayings that preceded this parable, the sense of duty is thus given to the avoidance of scandal (vv. 1-3a), to forgiveness (vv. 3b-4), and to faith (vv. 5-6).

BIBLIOGRAPHY (17:7-10)

Bultmann, R. *Marburger Predigten,* 148-158.

Derrett, J. D. M. "The Parable of the Profitable Servant (Luke xvii.7-10)," *SE VII* (TU 126 [1982]) 165-174.

Greeven, H. " 'Wer unter euch . . . ?' " *Wort und Dienst* 3 (1952) 86-101.

Holstein, H. "Serviteurs inutiles?" *BVC* 48 (1962) 39-45.

Jeremias, J. *Parables*, 193.

Jülicher, A. *Gleichnisreden*, 2. 11-23.

Maasewerd, T. "Unbekanntes Evangelium," *BLit* 28 (1960-1961) 291-296.

Minear, P. "A Note on Luke 17:7-10," *JBL* 93 (1974) 82-87.

Neuhäusler, E. *Anspruch und Antwort Gottes: Zur Lehre von den Weisungen innerhalb der synoptischen Jesusverkündigung* (Düsseldorf: Patmos, 1962) 34-36.

Pesch, W. *Der Lohngedanke in der Lehre Jesu verglichen mit der religiösen Lohnlehre des Spätjudentums* (MTS 7; Munich: Zink, 1955) 20-22.

Schmid, J. "Zwei unbekannte Gleichnisse Jesu," *Geist und Leben* 33 (1960) 428-433, esp. 431-433.

Sudbrack, J. " 'Armselige Knechte sind wir: Unsere Schuldigkeit war es, was wir taten': Meditation über Lk 17,7-10," *Geist und Leben* 41 (1968) 308-312.

Ward, A. M. "Uncomfortable Words: IV. Unprofitable Servants," *ExpTim* 81 (1969-1970) 200-203.

Weiser, A. *Die Knechtsgleichnisse*, 105-120.

c. From the Third Mention of Jerusalem as Destination to the End of the Lucan Travel Account (17:11-18:14)

114. THE CLEANSING OF TEN LEPERS
(17:11-19)

17 ¹¹ While Jesus was making his way toward Jerusalem and was passing between Samaria and Galilee, ¹² ten lepers happened to meet him, as he was entering a certain village; but they kept their distance. ¹³ They raised their voices to call out, "Jesus, Master, have mercy on us!" ¹⁴ He looked at them and said, "Go, *show* yourselves *to the priests.*"[a] And as they went, they happened to be made clean. ¹⁵ One of them, when he saw that he was cured, came back, glorifying God in a loud voice. ¹⁶ He fell at the feet of Jesus and thanked him—and he was a Samaritan. ¹⁷ At that Jesus said, "Were not ten made clean? Where are the other nine? ¹⁸ Can it be that none has been found to come back and give glory to God but this stranger?" ¹⁹ So he said to him, "Get up and be on your way; your faith has brought you salvation."

[a] Lev 13:49

COMMENT

In the episode of Jesus' cleansing of ten lepers (17:11-19), the reader comes to the beginning of the third part of the Lucan travel account (part *c* in the outline on p. 140). The third mention of Jerusalem as Jesus' destination is met in v. 11a. Though the latter part of the verse (11b) creates a classic *crux interpretum*, with its geographical references to Samaria and Galilee (see NOTE on v. 11), it alerts the reader once again to the Lucan geographical perspective (see pp. 164-171), to the evangelist's theological concern to move Jesus to the city of destiny, where salvation is to be definitively achieved for human beings. The third part of the travel account stretches to 18:14, the end of the specifically Lucan account, or to 19:27, its end in the Gospel as a whole, the last part of the account (18:15-19:27) being that wherein Luke incorporates material from "Mk" about the journey.

The story of the cleansing of the ten lepers is recounted solely by Luke. The introductory verse (11) and the final verse (19) are clearly of Lucan composition, both containing several of his favorite constructions. The rest of the episode (vv. 12-18) may be derived from a pre-Lucan source (e.g. "L" [see p. 84]), but the Lucan redaction of the material is very pronounced, almost as heavy in these verses as in vv. 11,19. This has led a commentator like W. Bruners *(Die Reinigung,* 297-306) to argue that "Luke is the author of the whole narrative" (ibid. 298); he cites the characteristically Lucan language and style, the similarity of the episode with other Lucan miracle-stories (esp. 5:12-16), the influence of the LXX of 2 Kgs 5:1-15 (the cure of Naaman the Syrian) and argues strongly for the Lucan composition of 17:11-19 as a literary unit. Many other commentators, however, are not so certain, and prefer to reckon with a pre-Lucan form of the story, which in the earlier tradition may have been affected by the account of the cleansing of a leper (Mark 1:40-45 [cf. Luke 5:12-16]) or even by the OT story of Naaman. R. Bultmann *(HST* 33) went so far as to call the story "secondary," being of Hellenistic origin (whence, for him, come most of the miracle-stories) and nothing more than an "imaginary" transposition of Mark 1:40-45, "in which gratitude and ingratitude are depicted on one and the same dramatic canvas" (ibid.; cf. pp. 57, 60, 220, 239; similarly, J. M. Creed, *The Gospel,* 216). Many others, however, who will not accept Bultmann's origin of the pericope, ascribe it nevertheless to a pre-Lucan source. (So, with varying nuances, H. D. Betz, "The Cleansing," 317-321; cf. *TLZ* 106 [1981] 338-339; G. Schneider, *Evangelium nach Lukas,* 350; J. Ernst, *Evangelium nach Lukas,* 482; R. Pesch, *Jesu ureigene Taten?* 114-123.) At issue here is the line that has to be drawn between Lucan composition and Lucan redaction, and no certainty is possible in this matter. (See NOTES on this passage for further comments.)

The form-critical category of the episode is also problematic. M. Dibelius assigned it a special category, a "legend of Jesus," one of the "religious stories in which Jesus brings to light His purity, wisdom, and virtue, or in which the Divine protection and care of Jesus are revealed" *(FTG* 120). Dibelius refused to classify it with "paradigms" (his label for pronouncement-stories), because it does not conclude with a saying "which can be used by the Church" or with "tales" (his label for miracle-stories), because interest in the miracle does not dominate in the pericope, or with "legends" about a Samaritan, because not the Samaritan, but Jesus "stands in the centre." R. Bultmann, however, saw more clearly when he categorized the episode as a "biographical apophthegm," with its pronouncement couched in vv. 17-18. Though V. Taylor at first considered 17:11-19 as a pronouncement-story—noting that its relation to Mark 1:40-45 "must always remain obscure" *(FGT* 75)—he later queried whether the episode were not really a story about Jesus, a pericope in which the narrative element was predominant (ibid. 153-155).

Though the episode begins as a miracle-story (vv. 12-14), recounting a healing wrought by Jesus, it contains an injunction from him which might at first sight seem to be a pronouncement, "Go, show yourselves to the priests." Yet that injunction really serves as an expression of Jesus' powerful word, such as one would expect in a miracle-story (contrast Mark 1:41,44, where there is both a word of power and the injunction to manifest its effect to "the priest"). Here, the miracle-story itself has been made subservient to something more (vv. 15-18), to a pronouncement which contrasts gratitude with ingratitude, Jews with a Samaritan, and the sight of faith with the miracle itself. The emphasis does not lie on the narrative elements, as Dibelius rightly saw, but on the pronouncement of Jesus about the reaction of the Samaritan, who was a "stranger." Hence, as H. D. Betz ("The Cleansing," 322-323) has rightly noted, we have here an apophthegm or pronouncement-story (one need not insist on its being "biographical," in Bultmann's sense); it is a pronouncement-story, which has not grown from a simple saying (as is sometimes the case [see 17:20-21]). Rather, it is a miracle-story that has become a pronouncement-story either under Luke's pen or—more likely—in the pre-Lucan tradition (depending on how one resolves the earlier problem). (See further E. Klostermann, *Lukasevangelium,* 173.) In adding v. 19, Luke has further related Jesus' pronouncement to faith and salvation—in effect, added a further pronouncement.

W. Bruners *(Die Reinigung,* 118) would have us believe that the form of 17:11-19 is an "imitated prophetic narrative with surpassing character," i.e. a story that invests Jesus with prophetic characteristics, but which makes him greater than Elisha (of the Naaman story in 2 Kings 5). Bruners thus imports into the interpretation of the Lucan Gospel a form-critical category used by W. Richter in OT investigation. But it is far from clear whether this is relevant here; and, as H. D. Betz *(TLZ* 106 [1981] 339), has rightly noted, this Lucan passage has nothing to do with the prophetic or with Elisha.

Betz ("The Cleansing," 321) has tried to detect various layers in the pre-Lucan tradition of this story. The oldest layer would have recounted the healing of ten lepers, of whom only one returns to glorify God and thank Jesus; Jesus' double question asks why the nine others did not return. The second layer would have made the one healed leper who returns a Samaritan, and Jesus' third question (v. 18) would have been added. Such a growth of the tradition is, of course, not impossible. But the whole analysis is quite speculative.

The Lucan story at this point in the travel account depicts Jesus making use of his "power" (recall 4:14,36; 5:17 [see NOTE there]) once again to aid unfortunate human beings afflicted with an evil which ostracized them from normal society; he liberates these outcasts from their evil condition. He is again presented as the beneficent healer who lavishes his bounty on those who need him most. The lepers appear at a distance, outside of an unnamed Palestinian village, as Jesus is about to enter it on his way to Jerusalem. The lepers call out to him in prayer for mercy and pity; he answers with an injunction alluding to the directive of Lev 13:49 and telling them to go present themselves to the priests for examination. There is no indication in the text of the miracle-story proper (vv. 12-14) that Jesus knows of any distinction among them. Bultmann *(HST* 33) completely misses the point, as do others who follow him, when he queries, "What could a Samaritan want with Jewish priests?" Similarly, A. Plummer's comment, "The Samaritan would go to a priest of the temple on Mount Gerizim" *(The Gospel,* 404). That may be, but it scarcely affects the thrust of the story itself. Likewise immaterial would be the comment that Lev 13:49 also stood in the Samaritan Pentateuch (see A. von Gall, *Der hebräische Pentateuch der Samaritaner* [Giessen: Töpelmann, 1914-1918; reprinted, Berlin, 1966] 231). The point in the story is, in the long run, the contrast between ingratitude and gratitude (as Bultmann eventually recognized), but also between Jews and a Samaritan, and above all between the miracle of healing and the eyes of faith. Jesus' pronouncement, in the form of three questions, highlights that contrast, hyperbolically referring to the Samaritan as a "stranger" *(allogenēs,* lit. "one of another race"), i.e. one not of the house of Israel. The contrast stresses the seeing (i.e. the understanding) that came to the Samaritan, which was not shared by the "other nine." That seeing enabled a human being to turn (be converted), to glorify God, and to thank Jesus himself. Jesus' words in v. 19 (the Lucan appendage) relate the Samaritan's "seeing" further to faith and to salvation. His initial cry for "mercy" (v. 13b) thus terminated in his conversion to God and his agent, Jesus.

Though we have retained the traditional title of this episode, "The Cleansing of Ten Lepers," one may ask (with O. Glombitza, "Der dankbare

Samariter") whether it might not be better entitled "The Thankful Samaritan," or even with W. Grundmann *(Evangelium nach Lukas,* 334), "The Healing of the Ten Lepers and the Thankful Samaritan." The thankful Samaritan is viewed against the background of the other nine.

Is there more in the episode? H. D. Betz ("The Cleansing," 325) would have us believe so, for he thinks that the author's intention "is clearly polemical": Though ten lepers experience a miraculous healing, nine of them miss "salvation"; because the "seeing," not the healing, is decisive, the narrator intends a sharp critique of the belief in healing miracles—which cannot be identical with the experience of salvation itself. Such a critique led him to compose the story. Betz goes so far in his mode of interpretation as to say that "a Samaritan, a member of a group to whom the Jews generally deny the external and internal religious presuppositions for attaining salvation, is granted that very salvation through Christian faith" (ibid. 326). This is subtle indeed. Perhaps the word *pistis* in v. 19 carries the connotation of Christian faith in Stage III of the gospel tradition, but would it have it in earlier stages? Finally, it is not at all evident that the healing miracle in the episode "can only be taken as a *parody"* (ibid. 327). What normal reader of the Lucan Gospel would come away from this story with such an impression? (See further I. H. Marshall, *Luke,* 649.)

The question has at times been asked whether this Lucan episode is anti-Semitic in its contrast of Jewish lepers and the Samaritan. The same sort of question surfaced in the discussion of 10:29-37 (see COMMENT there).

NOTES

17   11. *While Jesus was making his way toward Jerusalem.* Lit. "in making his way to J.," *en* + dat. of the articular infin. in a temporal sense. See p. 119. Note the similarity of wording of this introduction with that in 9:51-52. Luke uses here *Ierousalēm* (contrast the form at the beginning of part *b* of the travel account, 13:22). See NOTES on 2:22; 10:30; cf. p. 824. On the vb. *poreuesthai,* see NOTE on 4:30 and pp. 168-169. Some mss. (A, D, W, Θ, Ψ, *f* [1,13], and the Koine text-tradition) add the pron. *auton* before the infin. *poreuesthai,* "in his making his way"; but mss. P[75], ℵ, B, L, etc., omit it.

and was passing. The phrase *kai autos* (unstressed) introduces a second paratactic circumstance, which is related to the *kai egeneto* construction. See p. 121.

between Samaria and Galilee. This phrase enshrines Luke's "geographical ineptitude" (see p. 164), and it is not easy to explain what is meant here. First, the best reading is *dia meson Samareias kai Galilaias,* "through the middle of/between Samaria and Galilee" (in mss. P[75(?)], ℵ, B, L, 1424). Other mss. read either simply adverbial *meson,* "in the midst of" (ms. D), or *ana meson,* "between" (*f* [1,13]), or *dia mesou,* "through the midst of" (A, W, Θ, Ψ, and the Koine text-tradition; cf. 4:30). The variants, however, are undoubtedly grammatical corrections introduced by copyists who sought to remedy the difficult reading *dia meson*, because *dia* + acc. usually means "because of, for the sake of," whereas *dia* + gen. normally has the sense of "through" (with a spatial, temporal, or instrumental nuance). *Dia* + acc. in a spatial sense, "through," is found rarely in classical Greek poetry (Homer, *Il.* 7.247; 11.118; Aeschylus, *Supp.* 14) and in Hellenistic Greek prose (W. H. Waddington, *Inscriptions grecques et latines de la Syrie* [Paris: Didot, 1870] § 1866b). See BDF § 222; BAGD 181. This rare usage may be reflected here. However, J. Blinzler ("Die literarische Eigenart" [see pp. 830-831], 46-52) would excise *meson Samareias kai* as a marginal gloss eventually introduced into the text and would read only *dia Galilaias,* "through Galilee." Seductive though this solution is, it is really a tampering with the text, which can find no support in the tradition. *Dia meson* has to be retained and understood as "between/through the middle of," despite the geographical problem that it creates.

Second, if one presses the prepositional phrase, it would say that Luke depicts Jesus passing through an area between Samaria and Galilee; but what area that would be is baffling. If the sense is simply "between Samaria and Galilee," it would mean that Jesus, in traveling from Galilee to Jerusalem (i.e. from north to south) would now be moving from east to west or—more likely—from west to east. That is equally baffling. M.-J. Lagrange *(Luc,* 457) explains that Jesus had stopped at the border of Samaria; now he comes as close to Samaria as possible to descend to the Jordan Valley and Jericho.

However, H. Conzelmann *(Theology,* 68-73), comparing Acts 9:31 (which speaks of the church throughout Judea, Galilee, and Samaria being at peace), Pliny, *Nat. Hist.* 5.14, 68-69; 5.15,70, and Strabo, *Geogr.* 16.34 § 760, concludes that Luke writes as one "from abroad," with an inaccurate knowledge of Palestinian geography, who thinks of "Galilee as inland, but adjoining Judaea, and of Samaria as being to the north of Judaea" (p. 70). Some explanation like this is to be preferred, since no brief can be held for the accuracy of Luke's Palestinian geography. Its deficiency is manifest in this verse which he himself has composed; but it is not crucial to his story. *Nothing specific* is intended by it; it is not meant to locate the event of the cleansing with geographical precision and should be understood only in a general way (note the vagueness of "a certain village" in v. 12).

Samaria. This area of Palestine is again mentioned by Luke in Acts 1:8; 8:1,5,9,14; 9:31; 15:3. The Greek *Samareia* occurs often in the LXX for Hebrew *Šōmĕrôn* (1 Kgs 13:32; 16:28,29,32, etc.) or Aramaic *Šāmĕráyin* (Ezra 4:17). It was originally the name of a city, but was later transferred to a region or province. In NT times it stretched in the hill country from the Plain of Esdraelon/Jezreel to the northern border of Judea. See Josephus, *Life* 52 § 269; *Ant.* 20.6,1 § 118; see further pp. 828-829.

Galilee. This area of Palestine has been mentioned in 1:26; 2:4,39; 3:1; 4:14 (see NOTE there), 31,44 (see NOTE there); 5:17; 8:26; it will be mentioned again in 23:5,49,55; Acts 9:31; 10:37; 13:31. The Greek name *Galilaia* is found in the LXX as the translation of Hebrew *Gālîl* (Josh 20:7; 21:32; 1 Kgs 9:11; 1 Chr 6:76) or *Gālîlāh* (2 Kgs 15:29), meaning "circle, circuit, district." Cf. Isa 8:23 (9:1E), *gĕlîl haggôyim,* "district of the Gentiles." In postexilic times it was the name of the northern part of Palestine, surrounded by the Jordan River, the plain of Jezreel/Esdraelon, Mt. Carmel, Ptolemais, Tyre, and Syria. It was the tetrarchy of Herod Antipas. See NOTE on 3:1. See Josephus' description of Upper and Lower Galilee (J. W. 3.3,1 § 35-40).

12. *ten lepers.* Lit. "ten leprous men," the number "ten" probably being intended as a round number; "four lepers" are mentioned together in 2 Kgs 7:3. On the Lucan use of *anēr*, "man," see J. Jeremias, *Die Sprache,* 134-135. Does it argue for Lucan redaction or composition? On leprosy, see NOTE on 5:12.

happened to meet him. Luke began v. 11 with *kai egeneto,* which is followed (after a temporal infinitival cl. and a paratactic *kai autos* cl.) by *kai* and a finite vb. See p. 119. This is a mark at least of Lucan redaction. See J. Jeremias, *Die Sprache,* 264. The pron. *autō,* "him," is omitted in mss. P75, B, D, L, but is read by mss. ℵ, A, W, Θ, Ψ, 063, *f* 1,13, and the Koine text-tradition; it is bracketed in N-A26 and *UBSGNT*3.

as he was entering a certain village. A Lucan use of the gen. absol. (see p. 108), but it is not a good example of it, since it is not really "absol." (i.e. absolved from connection with the rest of the sentence). See 9:52,56; 10:38. *Pace* H. D. Betz ("The Cleansing," 317), there is not a hint in the text that Jesus enters the village as a "divine man" *(theios anēr).*

they kept their distance. Lit. "they stood at a distance," which is unspecified, but based on Num 5:2-3; Lev 13:46.

13. *They raised their voices.* This could mean in a shout, but as the story develops it must have the connotation of "in prayer." This is a Lucan formula. See NOTE on 11:27; cf. J. Jeremias, *Die Sprache,* 264.

Jesus. We are not told how they knew his name, but Luke has already supplied an explanation in his statement that "reports of him circulated throughout the neighboring countryside" (4:14, i.e. neighboring on Galilee).

Master. See NOTE on 5:5. The title *epistata* is used in the Lucan Gospel elsewhere only by Jesus' own disciples. Is this use of it pre-Lucan? See H. D. Betz, "The Cleansing," 316.

have mercy on us! Or, "have pity on us." See NOTE on 16:24. The cry of the lepers formulates a prayer. It is an implicit request for help, but whether it would connote a request for alms or a miracle may be debated.

14. *and said.* Ms. D adds *tetherapeuesthe,* "be healed," and a marginal note in ms. P75 adds, *thelō katharisthēti kai eutheōs ekatharisthēsan,* "I will (it), be cleansed, and they were immediately cleansed." The note, however, is almost certainly introduced by scribal harmonization from Matt 8:3.

Go, show yourselves to the priests. Jesus sends them off unhealed, and ostensibly unaided. He alludes to the Mosaic regulation of Lev 13:49. Cf. Lev 14:2-4 (as in 5:14). The pl. "priests" does not necessarily mean the Jewish priest on duty in the Temple of Jerusalem and his Samaritan counterpart at Mount Gerizim. That would be to read more into the generic statement than may have been intended. The pl. is called for in the story because there are "ten lepers." See further NOTE on 5:14. In any case, the Lucan Jesus does not counsel against the Mosaic Law. Recall 16:17.

as they went, they happened to be made clean. Lit. "and it happened, in their going, (that) they were made clean." Luke uses *kai egeneto* with a finite vb. without *kai,* but with the dat. of the articular infin. See pp. 119-120. The cure of the lepers is not instantaneous; but the story presupposes their willingness to trust Jesus and to carry out his instructions (contrast the reaction of Naaman 2 Kgs 5:10-12). The cure that results from such obedience is effected at a distance. Recall 7:7-10; see NOTE on 7:7. The cleansing of the lepers would have meant the possibility of their incorporation again into normal Palestinian society.

15. *when he saw that he was cured.* Lit. "seeing that he was cured," with the emphasis on the ptc. *idōn,* "seeing." In the Lucan story this is an awakening; his eyes of faith were opened. The implication is that as a result of this awakening he no longer follows Jesus' injunction to show himself to the priest, but returns spontaneously. A few mss. (D, 892, 1424) and some ancient versions read *ekatharisthē,* "was cleansed," instead of *iathē,* "was cured." The sense is not, however, affected.

came back. The return of the one leper implies his conversion to Jesus. Luke uses a form of the vb. *hypostrephein,* a favorite. See p. 111.

glorifying God. Another Lucan formula. See NOTE on 5:25; cf. v. 18. Cf. also 2 Kgs 5:15; Luke 2:20; Acts 11:18.

in a loud voice. Lit. "with a great voice." See 4:33 (and NOTE there); 8:28; 19:37; 23:23,46; Acts 7:57,60; 8:7; 14:10; 16:28; 26:24.

16. *fell at the feet of Jesus.* Lit. "fell upon his face at his feet." Cf. Luke 5:12. An act of prostration symbolizes his recognition of Jesus' status. W. Grundmann *(Evangelium nach Lukas,* 337) considers the act to be the homage due to a king: "He pays homage to him as to a king." It could also be a recognition of him as an agent of God.

and thanked him. The glorification of God expresses itself in gratitude to Jesus, God's agent, through whom he had been cured of his leprosy. Only here in the NT is thanks expressed to Jesus; it is addressed elsewhere to God himself.

and he was a Samaritan. The position of this cl. at the end of the sentence expresses at once approval of the Samaritan, as in the story of the good Samaritan (10:29-37), and pathos over the "other nine" (which will be formulated in the next verse). The approval comes from one who has himself been rejected by Samaritans (9:53). The cl. carries the connotation that the Samaritan was an inferior person, like Naaman, a non-Jew, in 2 Kings 5. See NOTE on 9:52. The cl. is introduced by *kai autos,* which is usually regarded as unstressed (see p. 120); but A. Plummer *(The Gospel,* 404) takes it as emphatic. For other Samaritans reacting positively to the preached Christian word, see Acts 8:5-8.

17. *At that Jesus said.* Luke again uses *apokritheis eipen.* See p. 114.

Were not ten made clean? This is the first of three questions that the Lucan Jesus rhetorically asks. W. Grundmann *(Evangelium nach Lukas,* 337) calls attention to the chiastic arrangement of the first two.

Where are the other nine? The chiasm is better seen in a literal translation: "and the nine, where (are they)?" The interrogative adv. *pou* is placed emphatically at the end of the question. Cf. Plato, *Tim.* 17a. The contrast of nine with one further expresses the pathos, for the nine were presumably Jews, members of the house of Israel. Obedient enough to carry out Jesus' injunction to present themselves to the priests, they were cured—physically; but their failure to react responsibly (in not glorifying God and thanking Jesus) reveals that they have missed the greatest moment of their lives.

18. *Can it be that none has been found.* Lit. "have they not been found . . . ?"

give glory to God. See NOTE on v. 15.

but this stranger? Lit. "except this one of another race," i.e. not of the house of Israel, but a "foreigner." The Greek adj. *allogenēs* occurs only here in the NT; in Acts

10:28 Luke uses the classical Greek adj. *allophylos,* "of another tribe." Both occur in the LXX, the latter more frequently than the former. See further A. Plummer, *The Gospel,* 405.

19. *Get up and be on your way.* Luke combines the ptc. *anastas,* "getting up," with the impv. *poreuou;* the two vbs. were used before in 15:18. See further NOTE on 1:39 and p. 116; contrast 5:24. For the impv. *poreuou,* see 5:24; 7:50; 8:48; 10:37; Acts 9:15; 22:21; cf. Acts 8:26; 9:11; 10:20; 22:10; 24:25. The impvs. are paralleled only in Lucan writings in the NT.

Though J. Roloff *(Das Kerygma,* 157-158) has tried to maintain that v. 19 was part of the pre-Lucan tradition, this verse should rather be ascribed to Luke's compositional pen. See further R. Pesch, *Jesu ureigene Taten?* 121-122.

your faith has brought you salvation. See 7:50; 8:48; 18:42 and NOTE on 5:20. "Salvific faith presupposes the salvific activity of God operative in Jesus, but it also includes essentially the grateful praise of God and the turning of a human being to Jesus" (G. Schneider, *Evangelium nach Lukas,* 352). N. Perrin *(Rediscovering,* 137) rightly argues for the authenticity of this saying of Jesus, even though the use made of it by evangelists may at times be secondary (as in this case). In Stage I of the gospel tradition, it would not yet be an expression of Christian faith; but that might be the connotation in the Lucan use of it in Stage III. Ms. B omits the last sentence, as do some mss. of the Sahidic version. See further p. 223.

BIBLIOGRAPHY (17:11-19)

Betz, H. D. "The Cleansing of the Ten Lepers (Luke 17:11-19)," *JBL* 90 (1971) 314-328.

Bours, J. "Vom dankbaren Samariter: Eine Meditation über Lk 17,11-19," *BibLeb* 1 (1960) 193-198.

Bruners, W. *Die Reinigung der zehn Aussätzigen und die Heilung des Samariters Lk 17,11-19: Ein Beitrag zur lukanischen Interpretation der Reinigung von Aussätzigen* (Forschung zur Bibel 23; Stuttgart: Katholisches Bibelwerk, 1977).

Charpentier, E. "L'Evangile (Lc 17,11-19): L'Etranger appelé au salut," *AsSeign* os 67 (1965) 36-57; *AsSeign* ns 59 (1974) 68-79.

Conzelmann, H. *Theology,* 68-73.

Glombitza, O. "Der dankbare Samariter, Luk. xvii 11-19," *NovT* 11 (1969) 241-246.

Liese, H. "Decem leprosi mundantur: Lc. 17, 11-19," *VD* 12 (1932) 225-231.

Pesch, R. *Jesu ureigene Taten? Ein Beitrag zur Wunderfrage* (QD 52; Freiburg im B.: Herder, 1970) 114-134.

Roloff, J. *Das Kerygma,* 157-158.

115. THE COMING OF GOD'S KINGDOM
(17:20-21)

17 [20] Once Jesus was asked by the Pharisees when the kingdom of God would come, and he answered, "It is not by observation that the kingdom of God comes; [21] one will not even say, 'Look, here it is, or there!' For, in fact, the kingdom of God is among you."

COMMENT

There follows in the Lucan travel account an answer which Jesus gives to some Pharisees who ask him about the coming of the kingdom of God (17:20-21). The setting for the Pharisees' question is left unspecified, and Jesus' answer is an isolated saying which might have been uttered by him at any time during his ministry. R. Bultmann *(HST* 25) has ascribed the utterance to a Palestinian origin and recognized it as "a genuine dominical saying."

The saying is found only here in the canonical Gospels, but forms of it are to be found in the *Gospel of Thomas.* The first part is paralleled in § 113: "His disciple said to him, 'On what day will the kingdom come?' <Jesus said, > 'It comes not with expectation (of it). They will not say, "Look, here (it is)!" or "Look, there (it is)!" Rather, the kingdom of the Father is spread out over the earth, and human beings see it not!' " The latter part of it finds a parallel in both the Coptic and Greek forms of the *Gospel of Thomas.* The Coptic form of logion § 3 runs as follows: "Jesus said, 'If those who draw you on say to you, "Look, the kingdom is in heaven," then the birds of heaven will be (there) before you. If they say to you, "It is in the sea," then the fish will be (there) before you. But the kingdom is within you and outside of you. . . .' " The Greek form, preserved in OxyP § 654:9-16, is slightly different: "Je[sus] says, '[If] those who draw you on [say to you, "Look], the kingdom (is) in heav[en]," the birds of the heav[en will be (there) before you. But if they say th]at it is under the earth, the fish of the se[a will be (there) be]fore you; and the king[dom of heaven] is within you [and outside (of you)].' " (See further *ESBNT* 374-378; cf. D. Mueller, "Kingdom of Heaven.") None of these noncanonical forms, however, preserves a more primitive formulation of the canonical saying; but § 3 may be in part influenced by Deut 30:11-14. The only thing to be noted is that the first part of the saying in § 113 is addressed to disciples, whereas the Pharisees ask the question in Luke 17:20a; cf. 17:22.

(See further J.-E. Ménard, *L'Evangile selon Thomas,* 80-82, 209; W. Schrage, *Das Verhältnis,* 30-32, 199-200; cf. also *Gos. of Thom.* § 51.)

The relation of these two verses to the following Lucan episode (vv. 22-37) is a matter of debate and affects the question of the source of vv. 20-21. Indeed, some commentators (J.-D. Kaestli, *L'Eschatologie,* 28; G. Schneider, *Evangelium nach Lukas,* 354) further query whether 17:20-18:8 does not form a unit in the Lucan Gospel. Since the Son of Man appears in 18:8, one can see how the query arises with reference to 17:22-37, but the connection of vv. 20-21 to the rest is the problem. Years ago E. Klostermann *(Lukasevangelium,* 175) noted that the theme of vv. 20-21 and vv. 22-37 is similar; he ascribed the difference of addressees (Pharisees in v. 20 and disciples in v. 22) to the "redactor" (presumably, to Luke). More recently, R. Schnackenburg ("Der eschatologische Abschnitt," 214-216) has argued for vv. 20-37 as an original unit, which stood as such in "Q," and which Matthew has modified by omitting the counterpart of Luke 17:20-21. (Similarly, H. Schürmann, *Traditionsgeschichtliche Untersuchung,* 237; G. Schneider, *Evangelium nach Lukas,* 354; cf. A. Plummer, *The Gospel,* 405; J. M. Creed, *The Gospel,* 217-218.) See further B. Noack, *Das Gottesreich,* 41; H. Conzelmann, *Theology,* 123.

The treatment of vv. 20-37 as a unit or as derived wholly from "Q," however, is not entirely convincing. It reckons with a questionable understanding of the postulated source "Q" (see p. 75) and does not cope sufficiently with the otherwise noted Lucan combination of material from "L" and "Q" in this part of his Gospel. The juxtaposition of vv. 20b-21 and vv. 22-37 and their allegedly common theme do not necessarily mean that the sayings formed a unit in the pre-Lucan source. The similarity of wording in vv. 21a and 23a, which may seem to support that idea, may be precisely the catchword bonding used by Luke to join material from two different sources. Moreover, nowhere in vv. 22-37 is the kingdom mentioned; it does not reappear until 18:16. That the question in v. 20a and Jesus' answer in vv. 20b-21 are eschatological, no one will deny; that the days of the Son of Man constitute an eschatological theme is also correct. In this respect one may detect a "common theme." But the most one can say is that the two have been linked by Luke; they were not necessarily so in a pre-Lucan source. Note, moreover, the absence of any connotation of vigilance in vv. 20b-21; contrast this absence with vv. 22-37, especially with vv. 30-36. In this I agree with M.-J. Lagrange *(Luc,* 459) who saw the need to distinguish these two verses from what follows; the kingdom is something different from the days of the Son of Man, at least in this part of the Lucan Gospel (but see 21:27,31,36).

Hence vv. 20b-21 should be understood as a saying detached from its original context and used here by Luke. (So *HST* 25; W. G. Kümmel, *Promise and Fulfilment,* 32.) The saying has a certain similarity with Mark 13:21 (= Matt 24:23), but it is really superficial: What is said there about the

Messiah is referred here to the kingdom. There may have been some relation of common context in Stage I of the gospel tradition.

Luke has probably composed the introductory question (v. 20a), although *eperōtan,* "ask," is not a particularly Lucan vb. (it occurs eight times in Matthew, twenty-five times in Mark, and nineteen times in Luke-Acts). Yet, this is the view of many commentators (e.g. R. Bultmann, R. Schnackenburg, J.-D. Kaestli), whether they agree or not with the position taken above about the relation of vv. 20-21 to 22-37. Verses 20b-21, however, have probably been derived by Luke from his source "L" (see p. 84).

R. Bultmann *(HST* 25) classed the episode as a pronouncement-story, specifically of the type of scholastic dialogue, an "originally independent dominical saying . . . subsequently provided with a setting" (ibid. 54). Similarly, *FGT* 69.

Thus far in the Lucan Gospel Jesus has spoken of the coming of the kingdom in teaching his disciples the "Our Father" (11:2) and of the kingdom as something that could be seen (9:27). He has, moreover, instructed the disciples to announce that it "has drawn near" (10:9,11) and has himself proclaimed that it "has already reached" his hearers (11:20). Such remarks of the Lucan Jesus have to be understood as the background for the question now put on the lips of Pharisees: "When does it come" or "When is it going to come?" Jesus' answer to them is polemical in tone. In fact, it does not so much tell them when the kingdom will come as imply that they are misunderstanding what it is all about. It will not be attended by observable signs or omens enabling one to say, "Here it is!" or "There it is!" His answer clearly tells them that they are not to look for the *time* of its coming or the *place* of its arrival. Jesus rejects all useless speculation about the coming of the kingdom.

Rather, "the kingdom of God is among you." This affirmation repeats in effect what he had said in 11:20. The sense of the phrase *entos hymōn* has been much discussed, but one of two senses of it is likely in the Lucan Gospel: Either "among you," i.e. in the midst of you, in the presence of the person of Jesus himself and his ministry of preaching and healing; or "among you," i.e. within your grasp, reach (see NOTE on v. 21). Either of these meanings would suit not only Stage III of the gospel tradition, but also Stage I. In effect, Jesus would be putting his inquirers on the spot: Either they have not recognized what is in their presence or they have not allowed themselves to be accosted by his kingdom-preaching.

NOTES

17 20. *was asked.* Bultmann *(HST* 25) called attention to the similarity of the formula used here to that found in Greek philosophic apophthegms. See G. von Wartensleben, *Begriff der griechischen Chreia* (Heidelberg: C. Winter, 1901); or W. Gemoll, *Das Apophthegma: Literarhistorische Studien* (Vienna: Hölder-Pichler-Tempsky, 1924) 2. Cf. Aristeas, *Letter to Philocr.* § 10.

by the Pharisees. The query about the coming of the kingdom is posed by people who believe in the resurrection (see Acts 23:6-8), and this aspect of it is not to be missed. See further NOTE on 5:17. Nothing in the text suggests that they ask in contempt or by way of testing him.

would come. Lit. "when is the kingdom of God coming," or (if the pres. *erchetai* carries a fut. nuance [see C. F. D. Moule, *Idiom Book,* 7]) "when is (it) going to come?" See NOTE on 11:2; cf. 22:18; 19:11. Though the "coming" of the kingdom is not an OT idea, cp. Dan 7:14,18.

not by observation. I.e. in a way in which its appearance can be detected sensibly. The n. *paratērēsis* occurs only here in the whole Greek Bible (save for Aquila's later rendering of Exod 12:42). It is used by Hellenistic writers (such as Polybius, *Hist.* 16.22,8; Diodorus Siculus, *Bibl. hist.* 1.9,6; 1.28,1; 5.31,3) either of the watching of stars or the detection of symptoms of disease. The related vb. *paratērein,* "watch, observe," is found in the NT. See Luke 6:7; 14:1; 20:20; Acts 9:24. In Gal 4:10 it denotes the "observance" of Jewish feasts. In this Lucan context it refers neither to the (Pharisaic) "observance" of the Law nor to observance of cultic rites; it is to be understood instead in the Hellenistic sense, of watching for premonitory signs (e.g. from heaven) or of an apocalyptic allusion to "times and seasons" (e.g. Wis 8:8; 1 Thess 5:1; cf. Mark 13:32; Matt 24:36), i.e. a sort of eschatological timetable. Recall that Luke depicts the risen Jesus rejecting concern for such in Acts 1:7. See further H. J. Allen, "The Apocalyptic Discourse in S. Luke xvii," *Expos* 9/4 (1925) 59-61.

Pace A. Strobel (see BIBLIOGRAPHY, p. 1163), it is eisegetical to interpret "observation" as a Pharisaic belief in expectation of the Messiah on the night of Passover. How far back can one trace such a belief?

Jesus' words in this part of the verse reject a sign-seeking mentality such as that reflected in 11:29; 16:27. He implies that the question of the Pharisees stems from such a mentality.

21. *one will not even say.* Lit. "they will not even say"; the third pl. is used indefinitely.

here it is, or there! Lit. "behold, here or there." The same phrase is used of the Messiah in Mark 13:21, a verse omitted by Luke in his parallel treatment of the eschatological discourse in chap. 21. The best mss. (P⁷⁵, ℵ, B, L, 1241, etc.) read *idou hōde ē ekei;* but others (A, D, W, Ψ, 063, *f*¹,¹³, and the Koine text-tradition) read . . . *ē idou ekei,* "or behold, there," a minor change which does not affect the sense.

among you. The rare Greek *entos* is an adv. of place, often used as a prep. "inside, within (the limits of)." See Josephus, *J.W.* 3.7,10 § 175 *(tēs poleōs entos,* "within the city"). Elsewhere in the NT it occurs only as a n. in Matt 23:26, "the inside of the cup." The problem here is to determine what the prep. *entos* would mean with a pl. personal obj. Various meanings have been proposed:

(a) "within you," i.e. the kingdom is in your hearts as some inward, invisible power. This meaning may be supported by the use of *entos* in the LXX of Pss 39:4; 103:1; 109:22; Isa 16:11; Josephus, *Ant.* 5.1,26 § 107; Symmachus' translation of Ps 88:6. It was a common patristic understanding of the prepositional phrase (e.g. Origen, *Hom. in Luc.* 36 [GCS 49. 207]; Gregory of Nyssa, *De virg.* 12 [PL 46. 372]), was used by ancient versions (OL, Vg *[intra vos];* Peshitta; Coptic *Gos. of Thom.* § 3), and has been used by some modern commentators (e.g. J. Wellhausen, *Das Evangelium Lucae,* 95; B. H. Streeter, *Four Gospels,* 290; C. H. Dodd, *Parables,* 63 n. 2). In the present Lucan context it is inappropriate, when the answer of Jesus is addressed to Pharisees. But I. H. Marshall *(Luke* 655) tries to defend it, even in this context, by saying that "you" is actually indef. The real problem, however, is that elsewhere in Lucan writing the kingdom is never presented as an inward reality or an inner condition of human existence. E.g. the presence of the kingdom is never equated with the presence of the Spirit. See further W. G. Kümmel, *Promise and Fulfilment,* 33-34; T. W. Manson, *Sayings,* 304; J.-D. Kaestli, *L'Eschatologie,* 29. This problem would be applicable to the saying in both Stages I and III of the gospel tradition.

(b) "among(st) you, in the midst of you," i.e. the kingdom is already present to you in the person of Jesus and in the things that he does and says. This meaning may be supported by the use of *entos* in Xenophon, *Anab.* 1.10,3; *Hellen.* 2.3,19; Herodotus, *Hist.* 7.100,3 (especially when the object is pl.). Such an understanding of the phrase was used in the Sinaitic Syriac version, was adopted in the *RSV, NAB, NEB,* and has been preferred by many modern commentators, e.g. W. G. Kümmel, *Promise and Fulfilment,* 35; A. Sledd, "The Interpretation"; K. H. Rengstorf, *Evangelium nach Lukas,* 202.

A variant of it is espoused by some commentators who prefer to give the pres. tense *estin* a fut. connotation, "the kingdom of God will (suddenly) be in your midst." See C. F. D. Moule, *Idiom Book,* 7; BDF § 323. So J. Weiss; T. W. Manson, *Sayings,* 304.

The usual objection raised against it is that if Luke wanted to say "among you," he would have used the phrase he otherwise uses, *en mesō.* E.g. 2:46; 8:7; 10:3. It does not explain his use of the rare prep. *entos.*

H. Conzelmann *(Theology,* 122) has insisted on this meaning of the phrase (with the pres. *estin).* He is right in saying that for Luke "the Kingdom has appeared in Christ" (ibid. 125), but his following statement that "its presence is not now immanent in the Church," is a loaded theological affirmation devoid of any connection with the Lucan context and born of *Kontroverstheologie.*

(c) "within your reach, grasp, or possession," i.e. the kingdom is at your disposal; it can be shared in by you, if you want it—"to take it lies among your choices and within your power" (H. J. Cadbury, "The Kingdom," 172-173). This meaning seems to be supported by the use of *entos* in several papyrus texts. See G. Zereteli, *Papyri russischer und georgischer Sammlungen III* (Tiflis: Universitätslithographie, 1930) 1.3 (§ 9). Cf. C. H. Roberts, "The Kingdom"; A. Rüstow, *"Entos hymōn estin";* cf. Tertullian, *Adv. Marc.* 4.35,12 (CCLat 1. 642). However, H. Riesenfeld *("Emboleuein— Entos")* contests the meaning of *entos* in these papyrus texts, maintaining that *entos* is rather elliptical for "in one's home, at one's home." A. Wikgren *("Entos,"* 27-28) seems to support Riesenfeld's interpretation and hints that the latter meaning may be proper for Luke 17:21, but he never gives a translation of it. If the Cadbury interpretation can be substantiated, it would be preferable; if it cannot, then one is thrown back on interpretation b.

BIBLIOGRAPHY (17:20-21)

Allen, P. M. S. "Luke xvii. 21: *idou gar, hē basileia tou theou entos hymōn estin,*" *ExpTim* 49 (1937-1938) 476-477; 50 (1938-1939) 233-235.

Ballard, F. "Luke xvii. 21," *ExpTim* 38 (1926-1927) 331.

Bretscher, P. M. "Luke 17:20-21 in Recent Investigations," *CTM* 22 (1951) 895-907; 23 (1952) 149-150.

Cadbury, H. J. "The Kingdom of God and Ourselves," *Christian Century* 67 (1950) 172-173.

Conzelmann, H. *Theology,* 120-125.

Dalman, G. *Words of Jesus,* 143-147; *Die Worte Jesu,* 116-119.

Dodd, C. H. *Parables,* 62, 83, 87, 155.

Easton, B. C. "Luke 17:20-21: An Exegetical Study," *AJT* 16 (1912) 275-283.

Feuillet, A. "La venue du règne de Dieu et du Fils de l'Homme (d'après Luc, XVII,20 à XVIII,8," *RSR* 35 (1948) 544-565.

———— "La double venue du règne de Dieu et du Fils de l'homme en Luc xvii,20-xviii, 8: Recherches sur l'eschatologie des Synoptiques," *RevThom* 81 (1981) 5-33.

Glasson, T. F. "The Gospel of Thomas, Saying 3, and Deuteronomy xxx.11-14," *ExpTim* 78 (1966-1967) 151-152.

Grässer, E. *Parusieverzögerung,* 170-172.

Griffiths, J. G. *"Entos hymōn* (Luke xvii. 21)," *ExpTim* 63 (1951-1952) 30-31.

Héring, J. *Le royaume de Dieu et sa venue: Etudes sur l'espérance de Jésus et de l'apôtre Paul* (new ed.; Neuchâtel: Delachaux et Niestlé, 1959) 42-45.

Hiers, R. H. "Why Will They Not Say, 'Lo, Here!' or 'There!'?" *JAAR* 35 (1967) 379-384.

Jeremias, J. "L'Attente de la fin prochaine dans les paroles de Jésus," *L'Infallibilità* (ed. E. Castelli; Archivio di filosofia; Padua: A. Milani, 1970) 185-194.

Joüon, P. "Notes philologiques," 354-355.

Kaestli, J.-D. *L'Eschatologie,* 28-37.

Kümmel, W. G. *Promise and Fulfilment,* 32-36, 90, 103-104, 105, 151.

Müller, D. "Kingdom of Heaven or Kingdom of God?" *VChr* 27 (1973) 266-276.

Mussner, F. " 'Wann kommt das Reich Gottes?' Die Antwort Jesu nach Lk 17, 20b-21," *BZ* 6 (1962) 107-111.

Noack, B. *Das Gottesreich bei Lukas: Eine Studie zu Luk. 17,20-24* (SymBU 10; Lund: Gleerup, 1948).

Percy, E. *Die Botschaft Jesu: Eine traditionskritische und exegetische Untersuchung* (Lund: Gleerup, 1953) 216-233.

Perrin, N. *Rediscovering,* 58, 68-74, 77, 193-196.

Riesenfeld, H. *"Emboleuein—Entos,"* *Nuntius* 2 (1949) 11-12.

——— "Gudsriket—här eller där, mitt ibland människor eller inom dem? Till Luk 17:20-21," *SEA* 47 (1982) 93-101.

Roberts, C. H. "The Kingdom of Heaven (Lk. xvii. 21)," *HTR* 41 (1948) 1-8.

Rüstow, A. *"Entos hymōn estin:* Zur Deutung von Lukas 17.20-21," *ZNW* 51 (1960) 197-224.

Schnackenburg, R. "Der eschatologische Abschnitt Lk 17,20-37," *Mélanges bibliques* . . . *Béda Rigaux* (eds. A. Descamps and A. de Halleux) 213-234.

Schrey, H. H. "Zu Luk. 17,21," *TLZ* 74 (1949) 759.

Sledd, A. "The Interpretation of Luke 17,21," *ExpTim* 50 (1938-1939) 235-237.

Smith, A. G. " 'The Kingdom of God is within You,' " *ExpTim* 43 (1931-1932) 378-379.

Sneed, R. " 'The Kingdom of God is Within You' (Lk 17,21)," *CBQ* 24 (1962) 363-382.

Strobel, A. "A. Merx über Lc 17. 20f.," *ZNW* 51 (1960) 133-134.

——— "In dieser Nacht (Luk 17,34): Zu einer älteren Form der Erwartung in Luk 17,20-37," *ZTK* 58 (1961) 16-29.

——— "Die Passa-Erwartung als urchristliches Problem in Lc 17,20f.," *ZNW* 49 (1958) 157-196.

——— "Zu Lk 17,20f.," *BZ* 7 (1963) 111-113.

Wikgren, A. *"Entos,"* Nuntius 4 (1950) 27-28.

116. THE DAYS OF THE SON OF MAN
(17:22-37)

17 ²² Then he said to the disciples, "The time will be coming when you will long to see one of the days of the Son of Man, but you will not see it. ²³ Someone will say to you, 'Look, there it is; or here it is.' But do not run off in pursuit of it. ²⁴ For just as lightning flashes and lights up the sky from one end to the other, so shall the Son of Man be in his day. ²⁵ But first he must suffer many things and be repudiated by this generation.

²⁶ Just as it was in the days of Noah, so too will it be in the days of the Son of Man. ²⁷ They ate, drank, were married, and were given in marriage, until the day that *Noah went into the ark;*[a] then the flood came and destroyed them all. ²⁸ Or again, as it was in the days of Lot; they ate, drank, bought, sold, planted, and built; ²⁹ but on the day that Lot walked out of Sodom, *fire and brimstone rained down from*

[a] Gen 7:7

heaven[b] and destroyed them all. [30] It will be like that on the day when the Son of Man is revealed.

[31] On that day anyone who is on the roof and has belongings inside the house must not come down to pick them up; anyone who is out in the field must not *turn back for what is behind.*[c] [32] Just remember Lot's wife! [33] Whoever tries to save his life will lose it; and whoever loses it will keep himself alive. [34] I tell you, on that night there will be two men in one bed: One will be taken, and the other left. [35] There will be two women grinding at the same mill: One will be taken, and the other left." [36] [37] Then the disciples spoke up and asked, "Where, Lord?" And he said to them, "Where the corpse is, there the eagles will flock!"

[b] Gen 19:24   [c] Gen 19:26

COMMENT

Having answered the Pharisees' question about the coming of the kingdom, Jesus now addresses the disciples, instructing them about the day when the Son of Man is to be revealed (17:22-37). Catchword bonding is responsible for the juxtaposition of this eschatological instruction to the preceding sayings: *erchetai,* "is coming" (v. 20a) and "will be coming" (v. 22b); "Look, here it is, or there!" (v. 21a) and "Look, there it is; or here it is" (v. 23b).

Luke's compositional pen is clearly at work in v. 22a (see J. Jeremias, *Die Sprache,* 33). Whether the rest of the verse comes from Luke's redactional pen is hard to say; some commentators would ascribe it to a pre-Lucan source (e.g. C. Colpe, *"Ho huios tou anthrōpou," TDNT* 8. 450-451; H. Schürmann, *Traditionsgeschichtliche Untersuchungen,* 222: part of "Q"). In any case, it has no counterpart in Matthew and formulates a generic statement which introduces the topic proper. See *HST* 130. The enigmatic phrase, "one of the days of the Son of Man" (v. 22), sounds like a Lucanism (see pp. 121-122; cf. R. Schnackenburg, "Der eschatologische Abschnitt," 221).

Verses 23-24,26-27,33,34-35,37b have parallels in the Matthean Gospel (24:26-27,37-38; 10:39; 24:40-41,28) and are usually regarded as derived from "Q" (see p. 79). In Matthew they have been joined with material from "Mk" to compose the lengthy eschatological discourse. Matthew has not only broken up the "Q" unit, but rephrased some of the individual sayings and introduced explicit mention of the *parousia* in 24:27,37,39 as he did in 24:3 (= Mark 13:4; cf. Luke 21:7). In using the "Q" material here, in the course of the travel account, Luke has, in effect, created a doublet of his form of the eschatological discourse to be found in chap. 21 (see p. 81 and p. 1325). There is no guarantee that Jesus actually uttered these sayings about the coming of the days of the Son of Man en route to Jerusalem; though the original context of them is lost to us, there is no reason not to ascribe the substance of the "Q" material used here to him in Stage I of the gospel tradition (see R. Schnackenburg, "Der eschatologische Abschnitt," 233). See p. 1328.

Though T. W. Manson *(Sayings,* 142) maintains that v. 25 was also a part of "Q" and represents "a genuine utterance of Jesus," most commentators today are inclined to see it as a Lucan redactional corrective introduced to explain vv. 23-24 and imitating in a generic way the announcement of the passion in 9:22 and its mention of the suffering and repudiation of the Son of Man. So it should be regarded, in my opinion. I. H. Marshall *(Luke,* 662) is inclined to follow Manson.

Verses 28-32 create the biggest problem in the passage. First of all, vv. 28-29 form a parallel to vv. 26-27. But whereas the latter are clearly from "Q," the former have no counterpart in Matthew. Why would Matthew have wanted to omit them, if they were in "Q"? The linking of the examples of Noah and Lot is found elsewhere (e.g. Wis 10:4-8; 3 Macc 2:4-5; *T. Naph.* 3:4-5; Philo, *De vita Mos.* 2.10 § 52-56; 2 Pet 2:5-7; cf. D. Lührmann, *Redaktion,* 75-83). This suggests to many, along with the parallelism of phraseology in vv. 27-28, that vv. 26-29 were a unit in "Q." (See G. Schneider, *Evangelium nach Lukas,* 356; but cf. S. Schulz, *Q: Die Spruchquelle,* 277-287.) Second, v. 31 is sometimes considered as a parallel to Mark 13:15-16 and hence modeled on "Mk" (they have no real parallel in Luke 21:20-24). But the wording is quite different in this Lucan verse, and the warning in the Marcan context refers to the abomination of desolation and is addressed to the inhabitants of Palestine, not to disciples (see J. M. Creed, *The Gospel,* 221). Third, the allusion to the story of Lot's wife at the end of v. 31 and v. 32 itself ("remember Lot's wife!") forms an *inclusio* with vv. 28-29. Hence, vv. 28-32 should be regarded as a unit, probably derived from "L" (see p. 84) and joined by Luke to the mention of Noah because of the catchword bonding, "in the days of."

Verse 33 corresponds to Matt 10:39 and has been derived from "Q." It is only loosely joined here to the rest of the context, and undoubtedly stems from a different original context. It is, moreover, a doublet of Luke 9:24 (= Mark 8:35; Matt 1:25; see pp. 81, 783-788).

Verses 34-35 followed vv. 26-27 in the "Q" source (see *HST* 117); the Matthean parallel is 24:40-41. On v. 36 see NOTE. Verse 37 is a composite; the first part (37a,b) is the result of Lucan redaction; the second (37c) is a maxim derived from "Q," paralleled in Matt 24:28.

A form of v. 34 is further preserved in *Gos. of Thom.* § 61: "Jesus said, 'Two will be resting there on a bed; one will die, the other will live.' " This form of the saying is banal and set in an utterly strange context in this apocryphal Gospel; it scarcely represents a more primitive form of the saying, being rather a later interpretation of the Lucan form.

Form-critically considered, vv. 22-37 as a unit form a collection of prophetic and minatory sayings of Jesus about the coming of the day(s) of the
Son of Man. R. Bultmann *(HST* 122) regarded vv. 23-24 as an apocalyptic
prediction, a variant of that about the coming of the kingdom (vv. 20-21),
whereas vv. 26-35 were for him minatory sayings, a warning about the surprising suddenness of the parousia and its ensuing division among human
beings (ibid. 117). Neither M. Dibelius nor V. Taylor has sought to cope with
this problematic Synoptic material. I should prefer to label vv. 23-24 as an
eschatological prediction, despite its use of apocalyptic stage props (lightning
flashes), which is also minatory. The saying is not certainly a mere pre-Lucan
variant of the preceding kingdom-saying. The juxtaposition of these sayings is
Lucan, but the topic is really different. The sayings in this unit differ in
content, dealing with the revelation of the Son of Man; that is not the same as
the coming of the kingdom. Moreover, Luke has studiously avoided in it any
mention of "the Messiah" or the parousia (contrast Mark 13:21 and Matt
24:3,27,37,39). The problem that this unit creates is why Luke has made it
part of the travel account, when he is going to treat it again formally in chap.
21; but there the emphasis will shift. It seems that just as Luke included a
lament over Jerusalem within the travel account (13:34-35), so now he includes in it an eschatological instruction. All of this suits the character of the
instruction being given to those chosen to be witnesses from Galilee in the
course of this account (see p. 826). The sayings about the revelation of the
Son of Man in this unit are linked superficially to the foregoing one about
the coming of the kingdom; but it will only be in 19:11 that the latter is
formally linked with Jerusalem *(pace* H. Conzelmann, *Theology,* 121).

Bultmann has rightly noted that the saying in vv. 23-24 refers "to the
Person of Jesus in the intention of the Evangelist," i.e. for Luke Jesus is the
Son of Man who speaks of the revelation of his day. Bultmann admits that
Luke has not created this saying and denies that there is any ground for
thinking that Jesus could not have spoken it—though he would have been
referring to some other Son of Man, "not . . . his own Person" *(HST* 122).
This, however, raises the whole question of the existence of a belief in an
apocalyptic Son of Man in contemporary Palestinian Judaism (see pp. 208-
211). However one wishes to resolve that question, Luke is thinking of Jesus
as the Son of Man whose day is to be revealed. If there is any hesitation about
this, one need only refer to Acts 1:11b,c, where it is said that he will come in
the same way as he was seen going up into heaven.

Verses 26-35 contain further minatory utterances *(HST* 117), which compare the days of the Son of Man with those of Noah (vv. 26-27) and of Lot
(vv. 28-32). They not only warn about the vigilance required for the sudden
arrival of those days, but also about the discriminatory treatment of human
beings which will ensue (vv. 31-35). Finally, Jesus' answer in v. 37b is a
single-stranded maxim, which was probably uttered by Jesus in an entirely

different original context (see *FTG* 250 n. 2), but which is joined here in ominous fashion. Bultmann *(HST* 102-103, 166) may well be right in thinking that it was a secular mashal, which has been made into a dominical saying.

Thus the Lucan Jesus uses the occasion of the Pharisees' question (v. 20) to instruct his disciples, not only about the coming of the kingdom, but about the revelation of the day(s) of the Son of Man. In the main, his eschatological instruction about the latter topic proves to be an admonition, a warning which corrects any hasty conclusions about the coming of the day(s). Jesus first tells the disciples that the Son of Man will not come as soon as they wish (v. 22), instructs them about the way in which he will not come (v. 23) as well as the way in which he will (v. 24), but also tells them about what will happen first (v. 25), about the condition in which human beings will be when he does come (vv. 26-30), and about the discriminatory judgment which will be exercised on human beings "on that day" or "on that night" (vv. 31-35).

Above all, disciples are not to be misled by bogus prophets trying to declare the signs of the times or to indicate the time and place of the revelation. Jesus makes it clear that the arrival of the Son of Man will be sudden and unmistakable; it will not require other human beings to call attention to it. The image of flashing lightning does not mean merely that the arrival of his day(s) will be attended by a brilliant éclat, but rather that its suddenness will be startling. If his arrival is to be sudden and clear to all, it will also be preceded by something else that must occur "first," viz. by the suffering and repudiation of the Son of Man.

Verses 26-32, in comparing the arrival of the day(s) of the Son of Man with the days of Noah and Lot, warn against the insouciance and indifference of "this generation." As the flood destroyed all of unthinking humanity save Noah and his family and as fire and brimstone destroyed all of the indifferent populace of Sodom save Lot and his family, so too will judgment descend on humanity, male and female, on the day when the Son of Man is revealed. In the days of Noah and Lot people pursued their earthly existence with nonchalance; this is to be counteracted by vigilant expectation. Time will not be given to recover one's earthly possessions or what one has left behind. One will not be able to turn back; hence one must be prepared.

Verses 33-35 stress the discretionary or discriminatory aspect of the judgment which will occur on the day(s) of the Son of Man. Human pursuit of salvation will not guarantee it (v. 33): "Whoever tries to save his life will lose it; and whoever loses it will keep himself alive." This saying is unexplained, but in the context of vv. 27-29 it becomes clear that salvation from destruction will not be accomplished merely by eating, drinking, marrying, buying, selling, planting, or building (seven activities, the sum of human preoccupations—actually ten are mentioned [four + six], but some are repeated). It will matter little whether one is male or female, for the discriminatory judgment will affect both: No explanation is given why one is taken and not the other—

or even both! So sudden and discriminatory will be the day(s) of the Son of Man. Indeed, it will be as unmistakable in its revelation as carrion is to a bird of prey. It will need no localization, for all humanity will be subject to it.

Jesus' message is not meant for those disciples who think that they deserve a better fate than their neighbors, but for those who, in the midst of universal indifference and complacency, realize the desperateness of their situation, and ask, "What must I do to be saved?" (see further T. W. Manson, *Sayings,* 144).

This somber eschatological instruction about the day(s) of the Son of Man has undoubtedly been added by Luke because of his realization of a delay in its revelation. He has made it part of Jesus' training of his disciples as he is en route to Jerusalem so that the disciples who follow him along that way will realize the implications of it all in their own lives. See Acts 14:22. A more comprehensive form of this instruction will be given in the eschatological discourse of chap. 21, as Jesus terminates his Temple instruction and moves on to his own destiny.

NOTES

17 22. *Then he said to the disciples.* Luke again makes use of *eipen de* with *pros* + acc. See p. 116.

The time will be coming. Lit. "days will come." Luke has used this formula in 5:35 (see NOTE there) and will use it again in 21:6 (adding it to Mark 13:2). Cf. 19:43; 23:29. In the pres. tense it is frequently found in prophetic writings of the LXX. See Amos 4:2; Jer 7:32; 16:14; Zech 14:1, etc.

you will long to see. I.e. physically observe. Jesus' words indirectly allude to the first part of his answer to the Pharisees in v. 20d. Luke thus makes Jesus allude to the longing of the evangelist himself and of his contemporaries. Cf. Rev 6:10. J. Jeremias *(Die Sprache,* 250) regards the construction with *epithymein* + infin. as a pre-Lucan formulation.

one of the days of the Son of Man. This phrase is not easy to understand. Part of the problem is the fluctuation within this passage between the pl. *hēmerai,* "days," and the sg. *hēmera,* "day," and the eventual transition to *nyx,* "night" in v. 34. The "day" (sg.) seems to refer to what Acts 1:11 describes (i.e. the parousia of Jesus, even if Luke never uses that term). Then what is meant by the "days of the Son of Man"? A period? And what is "one of" them? Given the fluctuation in the passage, it seems likely that Luke has made "the day" of the Son of Man into a phrase to parallel "the days of Noah" (v. 26) and "the days of Lot" (v. 28), and that he has also introduced here his favorite expression "one of . . ." See pp. 121-122.

Other explanations, however, have been attempted for this difficult expression: (1) The cardinal "one" should be understood as the ordinal "first," as in the LXX of Gen 1:5; Num 1:1; Ezra 10:17; Mark 16:2; Luke 24:1; Acts 20:7. See A. Plummer, *The Gospel,* 407; cf. BAGD, 231-232. This would highlight the day of the revelation itself. (2) The acc. *mian* should be understood as a mistranslation for Aramaic *laḥdā'* (an adv. meaning "very much" and formed by the prep. *lĕ-* + *ḥādā',* "one," but misunderstood as the sign of the acc. *[lĕ-]* + *ḥădā').* This would mean, "you will long very much to see the days of . . ." So C. C. Torrey, *The Four Gospels: A New Translation* (New York: Harper & Bros., 1933) 312; followed by T. W. Manson, *Sayings,* 142. But that is a farfetched explanation. (3) The number should be taken to mean "even, just one." So B. Rigaux, "La petite apocalypse," 410. This is highly dubious. (4) The number should be taken as "one" but the following phrase should be regarded as an imitation of "the days of the Messiah," a rabbinic phrase which occurs in *m. Ber.* 1:5 and elsewhere (see Str-B 2.237; 4.826-829) as a designation for the messianic age. But how early is that expression? To introduce this notion into "the days of the Son of Man" in this Lucan passage is only compounding the problem. It is not at all clear that Luke is thinking in terms of a period of time, over which the Son of Man would, as it were, reign. Hence it is idle to speculate whether "one of the days" refers to the initial or the climactic day of such a period. The sense is centered on the suddenness and manifest character of the revelation, which will have its discriminatory effect on humanity. Recall 9:51, "the days when he was to be taken up." Ms. D adds the dem. pron. *toutōn,* ". . . of these days."

the Son of Man. See NOTE on 5:24 and pp. 208-211. The phrase occurs again in vv. 24,26,30. In the present context his revelation will be for judgment.

but you will not see it. I.e. not that the disciples will not live that long or that it will never come, but rather that it does not arrive "by observation" (v. 20d), or in answer to a longing. Thus Jesus' first comment includes a negative answer.

23. *Someone will say to you.* Lit. "they will say to you," i.e. people, the indef. third pl., as in 6:44. Jesus refers to the seduction to be proffered to disciples during the Period of the Church.

Look, there it is; or here it is. Lit. "behold there or behold here." This is the reading of mss. P⁷⁵ and B, but in the rest of the Greek mss. there is a great variety in the formulation of this parallel—too great to list here; none of them seriously affects the sense of the saying, save those which introduce *ho Christos,* "the Messiah" (undoubtedly under the influence of Mark 13:2). See *TCGNT* 166-167 and the *app. crit.* in N-A²⁶.

One should compare this saying with the reaction of Josephus to the oracles which circulated in Palestine prior to the destruction of Jerusalem *(J. W.* 6.5,14 § 310-315). Cf. Tacitus, *Hist.* 5.13.

do not run off in pursuit of it. Lit. "do not go off and do not pursue (it/them)." I.e. have nothing to do with such seduction; your salvation depends not on such titillating declarations about the place where the revelation is to be made. Some minuscule mss. (*f* ¹) and some Syriac versions read, "Do not believe (it/them)." Other mss. (P⁷⁵, B, *f* ¹³) and the Sahidic version read only, "Do not pursue (it/them)." Cf. 21:8.

24. *lights up.* Luke writes *lampei,* whereas Matt 24:27 has *phainetai,* "shines," which may be the more original vb. in "Q." T. W. Manson *(Sayings,* 142) has compared the differences with the Greek versions of Dan 12:3, where the LXX uses *phainein* and Theodotion has *lampein* as a translation of Hebrew *zāhar* of the shining of the "wise."

from one end to the other. This is a difficult phrase, since *ek tēs hypo ton ouranon eis tēn hyp' ouranon* is elliptical and some fem. word like *gēs* ("earth"), *meridos* ("part"), or *chōras* ("region") has to be understood with *ek tēs* (and its acc. with *eis tēn).* It should then mean something like "from the (region) under the heaven to the (region) under the heaven." The prepositional phrase *ek tēs hypo ton ouranon* is found in the LXX (Exod 17:14), where it seems to mean "from the earth." Cf. *T. Levi* 18:4. It is probably an attempt to describe the vagaries of lightning flashing from one place to another beneath the heavens. Note that Matt 24:27 simply has "as lightning goes forth from the east and shines unto the west," which probably represents a simplification of the original "Q" expression which Luke has retained.

so shall the Son of Man be. I.e. he will appear as suddenly and as manifestly as lightning bolts.

in his day. This phrase is bracketed in N-A²⁶ and *UBSGNT*³, because it is omitted in important mss. (P⁷⁵, B, D) and some ancient versions (OL, Sahidic). However, it is found in mss. ℵ, A, L, R, W, Θ, Ψ, *f* ¹,¹³, and the Koine text-tradition. Its omission may be the result of a copyist's oversight because of homoioteleuton (the copyist's eye passed from the ending *-pou* on "Man" to the ending *-tou* on the postpositive pron. *autou,* "his"). See *TCGNT* 167.

25. *But first.* The combination of *prōton de* is Lucan. See J. Jeremias, *Die Sprache,* 268; cf. Luke 9:61.

must suffer . . . repudiated. The wording echoes that of 9:22 (see NOTES there); cf. 24:26. On *dei,* "must," see p. 180. The notion of tribulation which must precede the revelation of the day of the Son of Man finds its counterpart in the life of disciples in Acts 14:22.

by this generation. See NOTES on 7:31; 9:41. In 9:22 the saying of Jesus singles out elders, chief priests, and Scribes; here the formulation is less specific and more comprehensive. On the prep. *apo,* "by/from," see NOTE on 1:26.

26. *in the days of Noah.* See 1 Pet 3:20. On this pre-patriarchal upright figure, see NOTE on 3:36. In contemporary Palestinian Judaism he was known as a paragon of righteousness ("During all my days I practiced truth," 1QapGen 6:2; see 2 Pet 2:5; cf. *WA* 162). In contrast to him, his contemporaries, not so upright, are introduced to describe "this generation" (v. 25). The following verse describes their nonchalant and complacent existence and conduct.

27. *They ate, drank, were married, and were given in marriage.* Asyndetic vbs. in the impf. tense are used to describe the conduct of Noah's contemporaries. But the activities mentioned are neutral or indifferent; yet they are meant to connote the "corruption" of the earth in God's sight mentioned in Gen 6:11. Cf. 2 Pet 2:5 (the "world of the ungodly"). The asyndetic piling up of vbs. at the beginning of a sentence (found again in v. 28b) is not characteristic of Luke, but rather a mark of pre-Lucan tradition. See J. Jeremias, *Die Sprache,* 268-269.

until the day that Noah went into the ark. The last words in this cl. allude to the LXX of Gen 7:7 ("Noah and his sons and his wife and the wives of his sons went with him into the ark"). Cf. 1 Pet 3:20.

the flood came and destroyed them all. See Gen 7:10,21 ("all flesh expired that moved upon the earth . . . , even every human being").

28. *in the days of Lot.* Lot was the son of Haran, the brother of Abraham (Gen 11:27). He was taken by Abraham as the latter left Upper Mesopotamia to go to Canaan. They encamped together at first at Shechem and then near Bethel before going down to Egypt. After their sojourn in Egypt, they returned to Bethel, but Lot

soon parted from his uncle Abraham because either the land could not support them both (Gen 13:6) or their herdsmen entered into strife (Gen 13:7). Then Lot went to dwell in the Jordan Valley (Gen 13:11), while Abraham remained in Canaan. Lot moved as far as Sodom, where "wicked men, great sinners against the Lord" dwelled (Gen 13:13). Eventually Lot and his family were induced to leave the sinful city of Sodom (Gen 19:15) and they went to Zoar (Gen 19:23) in the same valley. For a contemporary version of the story of Lot and Abraham, see 1QapGen 20:11-22:11.

they ate, drank, bought, sold, planted, and built. Again, six asyndetic vbs. in the impf. tense describe the conduct of Lot's contemporaries; none of them depict the noted sinfulness of the people of Sodom known from Genesis. But the vbs. insinuate at least the nonchalance of their existence. Several of these vbs. appear elsewhere in the Lucan story as distractions from what human existence should be about: buying (14:18,19); eating, drinking and building (12:18-19); selling (19:45). Compare Ezekiel's description of "the guilt" of Sodom (16:46-52, esp. v. 49).

29. *on the day that Lot walked out of Sodom.* In Gen 19:16-17 Lot actually lingers, and the men/angels have to seize him and induce him to leave Sodom. See NOTE on 4:35.

Sodom. One of the "cities of the valley" (Gen 13:12), through which the Jordan River flowed. Chedorlaomer and his allies made war on its king, Bera (Gen 14:1-2). Its exact location is unknown, but it is usually thought to have lain south of the Lisan (the tongue-shaped peninsula on the eastern shore of the Dead Sea). See F. G. Clapp, "The Site of Sodom and Gomorrah," *AJA* 40 (1936) 323-344; J. P. Harland, "Sodom and Gomorrah: The Location and Destruction of the Cities of the Plain," *BA* 5 (1942) 17-32; 6 (1943) 41-54; M. J. Dahood, "Eblaite and Biblical Hebrew," *CBQ* 44 (1982) 1-24, esp. 17-18.

fire and brimstone. Lit. "fire and sulphur." Allusion is made to Gen 19:24 ("Yahweh rained on Sodom . . . brimstone and fire . . . out of heaven"). The combination "fire and brimstone" occurs again, often with "smoke," in Rev 9:17-18; 14:10; 19:20; 20:10; 21:8. Cf. Philo, *De vita Mos.* 2.10 § 56. The ancient description of seismic or volcanic eruption elements became in time an apocalyptic stage prop, the means of destruction of the land or of apostates and sinners. See Deut 29:23; Job 18:15; Ps 11:6; Isa 30:33; Ezek 38:22; cf. 3 Macc 2:5. The order "fire and brimstone" is found in mss. P[75], ℵ, B, L, R, Ψ, 063, f^1, and the Koine text-tradition; but mss. A, D, K, W, Θ, f^{13} read "brimstone and fire," probably under the influence of the LXX of Gen 19:24.

30. *It will be like that.* Lit. "according to the same (things)," i.e. in the same way *(kata ta auta,* see NOTE on 6:23). Some mss. (P[75(?)], ℵ*, A, L, W, Θ, $f^{1,13}$, and the Koine text-tradition) read, however, *kai tauta,* "and these (things) will be," i.e. will occur on the day of . . . This makes the threat even more specific.

is revealed. The Matthean counterpart of this verse makes a more explicit reference to the parousia of the Son of Man (24:39, using *parousia).* The vb. that Luke uses, *apokalyptetai,* is cognate to the n. *(apokalypsin)* employed by Paul in 1 Cor 1:7, when he refers to the "revealing" of the Lord Jesus Christ. Though Luke studiously avoids the word *parousia,* the vb. used here is one of the reasons for thinking that he understands "the day(s) of the Son" as a reference to what other NT writers call the parousia.

31. *on the roof.* I.e. the flat roof of the typical Mediterranean-area house, access to which was normally gained by an exterior staircase.

must not come down to pick them up. I.e. the person must flee from the roof by the exterior staircase and leave directly, without entering the house itself to get belongings.

not turn back for what is behind. I.e. to get what is left behind. The words *mē epistrepsatō eis ta opisō* (lit. "let one not turn to what is behind") allude to the story of Lot's wife; she turned to "look at what was behind" (Gen 19:26) and thus "became a pillar of salt" and "a monument to an unbelieving soul" (Wis 10:7). In this passage another nuance has been introduced for the turning back. Josephus *(Ant.* 1.11,4 § 203) claims to have seen this pillar, which remained to his day. Local traditions still refer to various humanlike formations of crystalline rock salt in the Jebel Usdum area as "Lot's wife." See *IDB* 3.163. Cf. 9:62 for another sense of looking back.

32. *remember Lot's wife!* At first, this phrase may seem to belong to the preceding allusion to Genesis, but in the LXX one finds solely "his wife" (Gen 19:26).

33. *to save his life . . .* Lit. "seeks to preserve his soul *(psychēn)* for himself." See 9:24 and NOTES there. In this context the saying implies a need for vigilance and concern for what life is all about.

will keep himself alive. Lit. "will give life to it (i.e. the *psychē,* " viz. will preserve it alive. In "Q" this saying of Jesus followed on the reference to Noah and his family (vv. 26-27); but now it is understood of the judgment associated with the revelation of the day(s) of the Son of Man (v. 30).

34. *I tell you.* For the formula, see 7:9; it is not only asyndetically employed here, but is characteristically non-Lucan. See J. Jeremias, *Die Sprache,* 106.

two men in one bed. Lit. "two on one couch," with the cardinal number *dyo* of common gender so that one person could actually be a woman, e.g. a man and his wife, as A. Plummer *(The Gospel,* 409), G. B. Caird *(Gospel of St Luke,* 200), et al. have rightly noted. However, the immediately following *ho heis* and *ho heteros* (both masc.) suggest otherwise, not to mention the contrast in vv. 34-35 between men and women. The contrast was already present in "Q" as Matt 24:40-41 suggests: "Two (probably men) in the field, two grinders (certainly women, since the form is fem.) at the mill." *Pace* J. Ernst *(Evangelium nach Lukas,* 491), it is eisegetical to read into this expression an allusion to a Jewish belief of the arrival of the Messiah on the night of Passover ("on that night"!). How early is the attestation of that belief?

One will be taken, and the other left. It is not clear which nuance is to be given to these vbs. It could mean "taken" from destruction (or even into the kingdom) and "left" to one's own fate (or judgment); see G. Delling, *TDNT* 4. 13. It could, however, also mean "taken" for judgment and "left" for salvation. The former seems to be preferable in the light of the examples of Noah and Lot, the one taken into the ark, the other taken from the city about to be destroyed. The pass. in each case may be intended in the theological sense. See NOTE on 5:20. Divine judgment will inevitably discriminate.

35. *two women grinding at the same mill.* Lit. "there will be two grinding (fem. ptc.) together." Normally it took at least two persons to manipulate the ancient Palestinian mill, unless an animal was used. See NOTE on 17:2. For the prepositional phrase *epi to*

auto, "together," see Acts 1:15; 2:1,44,47; 4:26. Among the evangelists, only Matthew uses it, and then only once (22:34).

36. Some mss. (D, *f* ¹³, 700) and ancient versions (OL, OS) add a verse, which has traditionally been numbered: "Two will be in a field: one (masc.) will be taken, and the other (masc., except in ms. *f* ¹³) will be left." All the good Greek Lucan mss. (P⁷⁵, ℵ, A, B, L, W, Δ, Θ, Ψ, *f* ¹), however, omit the verse. Moreover, it spoils the symmetry and was undoubtedly added to some mss. by assimilation to Matt 24:40. See further *TCGNT* 168.

37. *the disciples spoke up and asked.* Lit. "and they (unspecified), answering, say to him." Luke uses the ptc. *apokritheis* (see p. 114) and the historic pres. *legousin* (see p. 107) in a redactional comment of his own pen!

Where, Lord? Thus Lucan redaction introduces the maxim to come. The question ironically asks for what Jesus warned them not to ask about in v. 23: Where is it going to happen? It marks the incomprehension of the disciples. On *kyrie,* see NOTES on 5:8,12.

Where the corpse is, there the eagles will flock! Lit. "where the body is, there the eagles will be gathered together." Jesus' use of a maxim to answer the disciples' query is expressive of his impatience; cp. 22:38b. In Matt 24:27 the maxim occurs in a different context, and Luke has undoubtedly transferred it to the present context, to achieve a climax. The maxim can have two different nuances. It can mean that the eagles will inevitably show up where the carrion is; and so the day(s) of the Son of Man will also inevitably be revealed. Or it can mean that the presence of the carrion will be detected by the overhead flight of the eagles; and so the day(s) will be detected too. The former seems to be the better.

Ever since classical Greek, the n. *sōma* was used in the sense of a corpse; likewise in Hellenistic Greek (Philo, *De Abr.* 44 § 258; Josephus, *J. W.* 6.5,1 § 276; *Ant.* 18.6,10 § 236). Cf. Luke 23:52,55; 24:3,23; Acts 9:40; but Matt 24:28 has the more current word for "corpse," *ptōma.* J. Jeremias *(Die Sprache,* 270) thinks that Luke has avoided the latter as more vulgar.

From earlier times Greek *aetos* (or *aietos*) designated the "eagle," the graceful bird of speed. Cf. Rev 4:7; 8:13; 12:14. Even though ancient natural historians knew the difference between an "eagle" and a "vulture" (cf. Aristotle, *Hist. anim.* 9.32 § 618a; Pliny, *Nat. hist.* 10.3,6-8), it was not easy to distinguish them in flight. In Job 39:30 a proverb seems to be quoted which speaks of the eagle as preying on dead bodies. This is said of Hebrew *nešer* (39:27), which is always translated in the LXX by *aetos,* the very word that Luke uses here. G. R. Driver ("Birds in the Old Testament," *PEQ* 87 [1955] 5-20, esp. 8-9) identifies the *nešer* as the griffon-vulture and distinguishes the "eagle" from the "vulture" by the carrion that it feeds on, whether alive or dead.

There may be an allusion in this reference to "eagles" to the image of an eagle carried by the Roman armies: "Next (came) the ensigns *(sēmaiai)* surrounding the eagle *(aetos),* which in the Roman army precedes every legion, because it is the king and bravest of all birds" (Josephus, *J. W.* 3.6,2 § 123).

BIBLIOGRAPHY (17:22-37)

Allen, H. J. "The Apocalyptic Discourse in S. Luke XVII," *Expos* 9/4 (1925) 59-61.

Ashby, E. "The Days of the Son of Man," *ExpTim* 67 (1955-1956) 124-125.

Borsch, F. H. *The Son of Man in Myth and History* (London: SCM; Philadelphia: Westminster, 1967) 307-308, 343, 347-357, 380-382, 399.

Bover, J. M. "Desearéis ver uno de los días del hijo del hombre (Luc. 17,22)," *Valoración sobrenatural del "cosmos": La inspiración bíblica: Otros estudios: XIV Semana bíblica española (21-26 Sept. 1953)* (Madrid: Libreria científica Medinaceli, 1954) 391-397.

Brunec, M. "Sermo eschatologicus," *VD* 30 (1952) 214-218, 265-277, 321-331; 31 (1953) 13-20, 83-94, 156-163, 211-220, 282-290, 344-351.

Colpe, C. "*Ho huios tou anthrōpou*," *TDNT* 8. 430-461.

Geiger, R. *Die lukanischen Endzeitreden: Studien zur Eschatologie des Lukas-Evangeliums* (Europäische Hochschulschriften 23/16; Bern: H. Lang; Frankfurt am M.: P. Lang, 1973).

Higgins, A. J. B. *Jesus and the Son of Man* (Philadelphia: Fortress, 1964) 82-91.

Hoffmann, P. *Studien zur Theologie der Logienquelle* (NTAbh ns 8; Münster in W.: Ashendorff, 1972) 37-42, 44, 269, 284.

Kümmel, W. G. *Promise and Fulfilment,* 29, 36-39, 43-45, 70-71, 79, 91, 154.

Leaney, R. "The Days of the Son of Man (Luke xvii. 22)," *ExpTim* 67 (1955-1956) 28-29.

Léon-Dufour, X. "Luc 17,33," *RSR* 69 (1981) 101-112.

Lührmann, D. *Redaktion,* 71-83.

——— "Noah und Lot (Lk 17:26-29)—Ein Nachtrag," *ZNW* 63 (1972) 130-132.

Marchi, J. de. " 'Ubicumque fuerit corpus, ibi congregabuntur et aquilae' (Mt. 24, 28; Lc. 17, 37)," *VD* 18 (1938) 329-333.

Meyer, D. "*Polla pathein,*" *ZNW* 55 (1964) 132.

Pesch, R. *Naherwartungen: Tradition und Redaktion in Mk 13* (Düsseldorf: Patmos, 1968) 112, 147-148.

Powell, W. "The Days of the Son of Man," *ExpTim* 67 (1955-1956) 219.

Rigaux, B. "La petite apocalypse de Luc (XVII, 22-37)," *Ecclesia a Spiritu Sancto edocta, Lumen gentium, 53: Mélanges théologiques: Hommage à Mgr Gérard Philips* (BETL 27; Gembloux: Duculot, 1970) 407-438.

Schlosser, J. "Les jours de Noé et de Lot: A propos de *Luc,* xvii, 26-30," *RB* 80 (1973) 13-36.

Schnackenburg, R. "Der eschatologische Abschnitt Lk 17, 20-37," *Mélanges bibliques . . . Béda Rigaux* (eds. A. Descamps and A. de Halleux) 213-234; reprinted, *Schriften zum Neuen Testament* (Munich: Kösel, 1971) 220-243.

Schneider, G. *Parusiegleichnisse,* 42-46.

Schulz, S. *Q: Die Spruchquelle,* 277-287, 444-446.

Tödt, H. E. *The Son of Man in the Synoptic Tradition* (London: SCM; Philadelphia: Westminster, 1965) 48-52, 104-108.

Vielhauer, P. *Aufsätze zum Neuen Testament* (Theologische Bücherei 31; Munich: Kaiser, 1965) 74-76, 108-110.

Zmijewski, J. *Die Eschatologiereden des Lukas-Evangeliums: Eine traditions- und redaktionsgeschichtliche Untersuchung zu Lk 21,5-36 und Lk 17,20-37* (BBB 40; Bonn: Hanstein, 1972) 326-540.

———— "Die Eschatologiereden Lk 21 und Lk 17: Überlegungen zum Verständnis und zur Einordnung der lukanischen Eschatologie," *BibLeb* 14 (1973) 30-40.

117. THE PARABLE OF THE DISHONEST JUDGE
(18:1-8)

18 ¹ Then Jesus proposed to them a parable about the need to pray always and never give up: ² "There was once a judge in a certain town who neither feared God nor cared about human beings. ³ In the same town there was a widow who kept coming to him, pleading, 'See that I get justice over my opponent.' ⁴ For a time the judge refused; but later he said to himself, 'Though I do not fear God and do not care about human beings, ⁵ yet, because this widow is a nuisance, I shall see that she gets justice, lest she keep coming and finally wear me out.' " ⁶ And the Lord said, "Listen to what that dishonest judge said! ⁷ Will not God then vindicate his chosen ones who cry out to him day and night? Will he delay long over them? ⁸ I tell you, he will make haste to vindicate them. But will the Son of Man find that faith on the earth when he comes?"

COMMENT

Immediately after Jesus' eschatological instruction about the day(s) of the Son of Man, Luke adds a parable to press home the point that he was making, the parable of the dishonest judge (18:1-8). The passage, however, contains more than just a parable, and relation of the other verses to it and of the whole to the preceding episode is a matter of no little debate. Indeed, some commentators have queried whether these verses are not part of the foregoing eschatological instruction in view of the mention of the Son of Man in v. 8b (see G. Schneider, *Evangelium nach Lukas,* 354 [who, however, treats vv. 1-8 separately from 17:20-37]; W. Grundmann, *Evangelium nach Lukas,* 338-348). In any case, the connection of vv. 1-8 to the foregoing instruction is tenuous, and the relation of vv. 1,7-8 to the parable proper may be looser than we realize.

Verse 1 with its introduction *elegen de parabolēn* . . . *legōn* (see 6:39; 21:29) and with its emphasis on prayer at all times (see pp. 244-247) almost certainly stems from Luke's redactional pen (see *HST* 334-335; G. Delling, "Das Gleichnis," 206-207; W. Ott, *Gebet und Heil,* 19; J. Jeremias, *Die Sprache,* 33, 124). Indeed, it seems to have been fashioned in view of v. 8b.

The parable proper includes at least vv. 2-5 and has been derived by Luke from his source "L." Verses 6-8 form various conclusions or applications of the parable, and they too seem to have been derived from "L" (see p. 84). Verse 8b, about the Son of Man finding faith when he comes, is almost universally regarded as a secondary addition made by Luke to the preceding verses. One may wonder why Luke did not use it as the conclusion to the preceding instruction after v. 35 and instead of the disciples' question and Jesus' maxim-answer in v. 37; it certainly would have been more appropriate there. In any case, the existence of it here in v. 8b is probably the reason why Luke introduces the parable with a comment stating the purpose of it as "the need to pray always and never give up." (See further *HST* 193; E. Grässer, *Parusieverzögerung,* 36-37; E. E. Ellis, *Gospel of Luke,* 212; W. Ott, *Gebet und Heil,* 32-34.)

The real problem in the passage is the relation of vv. 2-5 to vv. 6-8a; where does the parable proper end? R. Bultmann *(HST* 175), following A. Jülicher, considered vv. 6-8 to be a "certainly secondary" application of the parable (vv. 2-5). (See also E. Grässer, *Parusieverzögerung,* 36; W. Grundmann, *Evangelium nach Lukas,* 346.) But others have questioned this division, regarding vv. 6-8a as the conclusion of the parable itself. So G. Delling, "Das Gleichnis," 208-225; J. Jeremias, *Parables,* 155-157; W. G. Kümmel, *Promise and Fulfilment,* 59. Part of the problem is the way one interprets the beginning of v. 6, "And the Lord said." In this case *ho kyrios* seems to refer to Jesus himself and is different from the use in 16:8a. Part of it has to do with the meaning that one sees conveyed by the parable proper, in contrast to the applications that may be made of it.

I prefer to regard vv. 2-6 as the parable proper. From the beginning some comment seems to be called for about the attitude of the judge. If one were to regard the parable as consisting only of vv. 2-5, then the parable would not be so much one about a dishonest judge as about an importunate widow. Just as in 16:1-8a one expects some reaction to the manager's activity, so here one expects some comment on the conduct of the judge (even if *ho kyrios* refers to Jesus himself in this case—which it did not in 16:8a). With the Lucan introduction in v. 1 one can understand how the story about the helpless widow importuning the judge who neither fears God nor cares about human beings could be used to emphasize the effect of persistent prayer and the need to pray always. But those commentators who insist, as does I. H. Marshall

(Luke, 671), that two factors, the attitude of the widow and the attitude of the judge, are tightly woven into the parable are right. It is not just the picture of a persistent widow but of a judge who eventually hears her complaint and grants her request. Verse 6 calls attention to what the judge said in order to make the argument *a minori ad maius.* If a dishonest judge would yield to the persistence and prayer of a widow, how much more would the upright God and Father of all! If the helpless widow's persistent prayer accomplishes so much with a dishonest judge, how much more will the persistent prayer of Christian disciples! To this extent the parable carries the same message as that of the parable of the persistent friend (11:5-8). In a sense, then, the parable illustrates the Lucan introduction (v. 1), and in another sense it does not.

Verses 7-8a allegorize a detail in the parable itself, when they introduce the notion of "vindication." Not only is "God" introduced (so that the reader understands the judge as a symbol of God), but also his haste is stressed (so that it is made clear to the reader that God will not only hear the petitions of those who call upon him—his "elect"—but that he will not dilly-dally as did the "dishonest judge"). All of this is said apropos of God's "vindicating" his chosen ones who cry out to him day and night. This allegorization is clearly a further extension of the application of the parable proper. There is no real reason to ascribe it to Luke himself; it was undoubtedly already attached to the parable in the pre-Lucan tradition, even though it may have come from an entirely different setting in the ministry of Jesus himself.

The same has to be said for v. 8b, which still further allegorizes the parable in its present setting. In a sense, Luke has prepared for it by his introductory v. 1, for it explains that the "need to pray always" must be related to Christian faith. The mention of the Son of Man and his coming clearly relates this allegorized parable to the preceding eschatological instruction about the day(s) of the Son of Man. The Lucan Jesus' rhetorical question implies that such faith will not be found when the Son of Man's day(s) arrive, unless his disciples have learned the "need to pray always." The question echoes in its own way the exclamation of Jesus himself in 7:9, "not even in Israel have I found such faith as this." In the present context the "faith" that is meant is that which inspires persistent prayer.

In the light of the delay of the parousia, of which the evangelist is aware, Luke at this point in his travel account thus depicts Jesus recommending persistent prayer to God as a mode of Christian life (especially in the Period of the Church under stress)—not only a persistent prayer, but a faith-inspired prayer.

There is one last problem in the passage, which in a way relates this parable to that of the dishonest manager (16:1-8a). There a certain aspect of the conduct of someone who was dishonest was recommended as a model of Christian conduct. Here again, a "dishonest judge" figures in a parable and is used as a symbol of the heavenly Father—"God" is explicitly mentioned in v.

6 and the comparison is at least implied. One might be tempted, therefore, to ask what sort of an image of God this parable proposes to the reader—does the dilly-dallying of the judge really characterize God's dealings with his "chosen ones"? To concentrate on this aspect of the parable and its applications is to miss the real point of the parable. It is undoubtedly this sort of question that led to the addition of the sayings in vv. 7-8a, which serve to correct the image of God that one otherwise might be tempted to carry away from the parable.

NOTES

18 1. *Then Jesus proposed to them a parable.* This formula with the dat. *autois* (see NOTE on 5:36) is found again in 6:39 and 21:29. The more usual Lucan introductory formula employs *pros* + acc. See p. 116; cf. 5:36; 12:16,41; 14:7; 15:3; 18:9; 20:9,19.

about the need to pray always. Lit. "with reference to the need (infin. *dein)* to pray at all times." This is not to be understood of perpetual or continuous prayer (contrast 1 Thess 5:17), but of continual prayer (as the following cl. implies): of prayer that continues to mark the existence of disciples until the day of the Son of Man is revealed (17:30). The rest of the Lucan story will exemplify what is meant: Jesus on the Mount of Olives (22:41); the prayer of the Christian community during the imprisonment of Peter (Acts 12:5). See further W. Ott, *Gebet und Heil,* 68-71. Though it is not explicitly mentioned here, the object of the prayer should include that for which Jesus taught his followers to pray in 11:2, "May your kingdom come!" Note that the purpose of the parable as stated by Luke in this verse does not suit perfectly the thrust of the parable itself—which reveals that the parable's original setting is lost to us.

and never give up. Lit. "become weary" in this duty of the Christian disciple, i.e. not to lose heart, if the prayer seems not to be answered.

2. *a judge in a certain town.* Lit. "a certain judge in a certain town," with the Lucan predilection for indef. *tis* coming to the fore again. Some mss. (D, L, Ψ, 063) change the dat. *tini* to the def. art. *tē,* "in the town," undoubtedly under the influence of the expression in v. 3. Whether there was an official judicial system in each town or only prominent, capable persons who took on such tasks is immaterial to the story in the parable. See J. D. M. Derrett, "Law," for distracting trivia about Jewish courts and secular judges; the parable does not depend on such details.

neither feared God nor cared about human beings. This sort of description of figures of prominence is also found in extrabiblical writings. Cf. Josephus' description of King Jehoiakim, "neither reverent toward God nor fair toward human beings" *(Ant.* 10.5,2 § 283); Dionysius of Halicarnassus, *Rom. Ant.* 10.10,7; Livy, 22.3,4. For this reason the judge is described as "dishonest" in v. 6, as was the manager in 16:1b,8a.

3. *a widow.* As she is depicted in the story, the widow is seen as a helpless woman deprived of equity and as a plaintiff in some lawsuit. Was she one of those whose "houses" were being devoured (see 20:47)? She fits the OT picture of the widow to whom justice is often denied. See Exod 22:22-24; Deut 10:18; 24:17; Mal 3:5; Ruth 1:20-21; Lam 1:1; Isa 54:4; Ps 68:5; recall the OT implication of disgrace which was

often associated with widowhood. This makes her but another example of the "outcasts" about whom Jesus' message is concerned at this stage in the Lucan travel account. See COMMENT on 15:1-7. Note also the prominence of widows in the story of Luke-Acts (2:37; 4:25-26; 7:12; 20:47; 21:2-3; Acts 6:1; 9:39,41). Cf. Mark 12:40 (= Matt 23:14),42-43. As OT background for this parable, one may read Sir 35:12-20.

kept coming to him. The impf. expresses the continuity of her action, inspired by her desperation. Because of the position of women in the contemporary Palestinian society, she was helpless and could exert no real influence on those in power, having lost the support of the man to whom she was married. Persistence was her only weapon.

See that I get justice over my opponent. Lit. "vindicate me from my adversary," so she pleads as plaintiff in some lawsuit, seeking that the judge secure her rights as one wronged. She seeks not the punishment of her opponent, but the settling of her rights.

4. *For a time.* Or possibly, "for a long time." Ms. D adds the indef. *tina,* "for a certain time."

the judge refused. Lit. "was unwilling," but we are not told for what reason, since his inaction fits the description of him already given. Some commentators speculate; J. Jeremias *(Parables,* 153) would have us believe that the vb. used here *(ouk ethelen)* means "would not venture," i.e. he did not dare because of the influential position of the widow's opponent. But that scarcely suits the character of one who cared not about human beings. Was it out of laziness? So I. H. Marshall, *Luke,* 672. Who knows?

later. Lit. "but after these (things)," a Lucan phrase. See NOTE on 10:1.

he said to himself. Lit. "he said in himself." See 16:3. Ms. D reads rather, "he came to himself and says" (historic pres.), a reading undoubtedly influenced by 15:17. The cl. introduces soliloquy into a parable again. See NOTE on 12:17.

5. *because this widow is a nuisance.* Lit. "because this widow furnishes me with trouble." Compare the wording with 11:7-8. He realizes that the widow may keep on coming for an indefinite time. So his lack of concern for other human beings is being undermined by a helpless widow's persistence.

I shall see that she gets justice. Lit. "I shall vindicate her."

lest she keep coming and finally wear me out. Lit. "lest (by) coming, she in the end give me a black eye" or "fly in my face!" The vb. *hypōpiazein* means to "hit under the eye," an expression borrowed from boxing. See the Pauline context, where it occurs in 1 Cor 9:27 *(RSV,* "pommel"). The vb. was, however, also used in a figurative sense, "to blacken the face" (i.e. besmirch my character) or "wear out completely." See further Aristotle, *Ars rhet.* 3.11,15 § 1413a.20; Plutarch, *Mor.* 921F; Diogenes Laertius, *Vitae* 6.89. Cf. J. D. M. Derrett, "Law," 189-191; BDF § 207.3; E. Klostermann, *Lukasevangelium,* 178. Any of the figurative meanings would be possible, not to mention the physical sense itself, "lest she come and give me a black eye." He wants only peace and to be freed of the widow's continual nagging.

6. *the Lord.* The use of the absolute title reveals Lucan redaction. See NOTE on 7:13. Jesus is meant here, in contrast to 16:8a.

that dishonest judge. Lit. "the judge of dishonesty." See NOTE on the "dishonest manager" in 16:8a; cf. p. 124. As in the case of the manager, the judge is so characterized not because of his relenting and ultimate yielding to the widow's persistence (conduct that is at least indifferent), but because he was described earlier as one who "neither feared God nor cared about human beings," a characterization that implied that his conduct was not always what it should have been.

This verse implies the point of the parable as a whole: If even a dishonest judge can be prevailed upon to do justice, how much more will the upright God listen to the persistent prayer of his own.

said! This conclusion of the parable shifts the attention somewhat from the widow to the judge's conduct and way of thinking—and especially to his soliloquy. Implied: *a fortiori* God will heed the persistent petition of human beings who call upon him.

7. *Will not God then vindicate his chosen ones.* Lit. "will not God then produce the vindication of his chosen ones." Luke uses *ou mē* with the subjunc. *poiēsē* as an emphatic fut. in a rhetorical question, expecting an affirmative answer. On the Lucan eschatology involved here, see p. 234. The "chosen ones" *(eklektoi)* occurs only here in Luke-Acts. Cf. Mark 13:20,22,27; Luke 21:22. For the OT background of the expression, see Isa 42:1; 43:20; 65:9,15,23; Ps 105:6,43, where the connotation is that of election to serve Yahweh. See especially Sir 47:22, where election suggests the love of God. Here it is being used of Christian disciples.

who cry out to him day and night? Lit. "crying out (pres. ptc. of continuous action) to him day and night." On the expression "day and night," see 2:37; Acts 9:24; 20:31; 26:7. Cf. Ps 22:3. The phrase becomes a commentary on "always" of v. 1. The rhetorical question in v. 7a implies a delay in God's reaction, and may reflect the Lucan awareness of the delay of the parousia. But it does not completely eliminate all futurist eschatology.

Will he delay long over them? My translation has made this a separate sentence, whereas in the Greek it is actually a compound sentence (joined by *kai* to the foregoing). These words create a *crux intepretum,* and their sense is far from clear. Part of the problem is the shift from the emphatic fut. in the preceding rhetorical question to the pres. indic. here, *makrothymei* (the best reading in mss. ℵ, A, B, D, L, Q, R, Θ, Ψ, f^1, etc., whereas some others [W, 063, f^{13}, and the Koine text-tradition] have the pres. ptc. *makrothymōn).* Part of it is, furthermore, the very meaning of *makrothymein.* Normally, this vb. means "have patience, be long-suffering, forebearing," and some commentators have tried to use this meaning (e.g. K. H. Rengstorf, *Evangelium nach Lukas,* 205-206: "whether [understanding *kai* as *kai ei]* he is also patient with them," i.e. toward the chosen ones; J. Wellhausen, *Das Evangelium Lucae,* 98: toward the opponents). But it ill suits the rhetorical question in v. 7a (whether it be read as pres. indic. or pres. ptc.). The vb., however, is found in the LXX of Sir 35:19 (a passage which is not without possible influence on the parable as a whole), where it occurs in parallelism with the vb. *bradynein,* "be slow": *oude mē makrothymēsē ep' autois,* "nor will he (i.e. the Lord) delay over them," i.e. in executing judgment. See further H. Sahlin, *Zwei Lukas-Stellen;* H. Riesenfeld, "Zu *makrothymein* (Lk 18, 7)," *Neutestamentliche Aufsätze* (eds. J. Blinzler et al.) 214-217; A. Wifstrand, "Lukas xviii. 7"; cf. K. Beyer, *Semitische Syntax,* 268 n. 1; F. Horst, *TDNT* 4. 378, 380-381. Cf. 2 Pet 3:9.

8. *I tell you.* For this introductory formula, see NOTE on 11:8.

he will make haste to vindicate them. Lit. "he will produce their vindication in haste," an assurance that God will listen to the persistent prayers of his chosen ones and establish equity in their cause. The prepositional phrase *en tachei* is not to be

taken in the sense of "suddenly" *(pace* F. Horst, *TDNT* 4. 381; K. Bornhäuser, *Studien,* 167-168) but of "quickly" (so E. Schweizer, *Evangelium nach Lukas,* 185).
But. The strong adversative conj. *plēn* (see NOTE on 10:11) introduces a nom. absol., followed by a direct question: "But (as for) the Son of Man coming, will he find that faith on the earth?"

the Son of Man. See NOTE on 5:24; cf. pp. 208-211. In this Lucan context the phrase refers to the revelation of his day (17:30).

find that faith on the earth. I.e. the faith that inspires persistent prayer. Contrast Jesus' exclamation in 7:9; for the sense of faith, see NOTE on 5:20. Jesus' question at the end of this passage has to be related to the Lucan introduction in v. 1, for it supplies the motivation for the need to pray always. The art. in *tēn pistin* is anaphoric. See BDF § 252.

when he comes? See NOTE on 5:32. These words provide a Lucan comment on the delay of the revelation of the day(s) of the Son of Man. In effect, Luke is aware of the delay and poses to Christians of his day the *real* question whether there will still be disciples of strong faith when that revelation comes. This verse thus provides an indir. corrective and answer to the question of the Pharisees about the coming of the kingdom (17:20) and it implies a call for vigilance. Cf. Luke 12:35,40,43,46; 17:24,26-30. See further 2 Tim 4:7.

BIBLIOGRAPHY (18:1-8)

Bornhäuser, K. *Studien zum Sondergut des Lukas* (Gütersloh: Bertelsmann, 1934) 161-170.

Buzy, D. "Le juge inique," *RB* 39 (1930) 378-391.

Catchpole, D. R. "The Son of Man's Search for Faith (Luke xviii 8b)," *NovT* 19 (1977) 81-104.

Cranfield, C. E. B. "The Parable of the Unjust Judge and the Eschatology of Luke-Acts," *SJT* 16 (1963) 297-301.

Delling, G. "Das Gleichnis vom gottlosen Richter," *ZNW* 53 (1962) 1-25; reprinted, *Studien zum Neuen Testament und zum hellenistischen Judentum: Gesammelte Aufsätze 1950-1968* (ed. F. Hahn et al.; Göttingen: Vandenhoeck & Ruprecht, 1970) 203-225.

Derrett, J. D. M. "Law in the New Testament: The Parable of the Unjust Judge," *NTS* 18 (1971-1972) 178-191.

De Ru, G. "De gelijkenis van de onrechtvaardige Rechter (Lucas 18:1-8)," *NedTT* 25 (1971) 379-392.

Deschryver, R. "La parabole du juge malveillant (Luc 18, 1-8)," *RHPR* 48 (1968) 355-366.

George, A. "La parabole du juge qui fait attendre le jugement: Lc 18,1-8," *AsSeign* ns 60 (1975) 68-79.

Grässer, E. *Parusieverzögerung,* 36-38.

Harnisch, W. "Die Ironie als Stilmittel in Gleichnissen Jesu," *EvT* 32 (1972) 421-436.

Huhn, K. *Das Gleichnis von der 'bittenden Witwe': Gebetsaufruf Jesu an die Gemeinde der Endzeit* (Hamburg: Bethel, 1946).

Jeremias, J. *Parables,* 87, 93, 153-157.

Jülicher, A. *Gleichnisreden,* 2. 276-290.

Kissinger, W. S. *Parables of Jesus,* 397-398.

Leal, J. "La oración y la crisis de fe," *Manresa* 39 (1967) 213-220.

Linnemann, E. *Jesus of the Parables,* 119-124.

Ljungvik, H. "Zur Erklärung einer Lukas-Stelle (Luk. xviii. 7)," *NTS* 10 (1963-1964) 289-294.

Meecham, H. G. "The Parable of the Unjust Judge," *ExpTim* 57 (1945-1946) 306-307.

Ott, W. *Gebet und Heil,* 19, 32-72.

Perkins, P. *Hearing the Parables,* 176, 194-195.

Perrin, N. *Rediscovering,* 129-130.

Puzo, F. "¿Un texto escatológico? (Lc. 18,8b)," *EstEcl* 19 (1945) 273-334.

Robertson, G. P. "Luke xviii. 8," *ExpTim* 40 (1928-1929) 525-526.

Robertson, J. A. "The Parable of the Unjust Judge (Luke xviii. 1-8)," *ExpTim* 38 (1926-1927) 389-392.

Sabbe, M. "Het eschatologisch Gebed in Lc. 18, 1-8," *Collationes brugenses et gandavenses* 1 (1955) 361-369.

Sahlin, H. *Zwei Lukas-Stellen: Lk 6: 43-45; 18: 7* (Symbolae biblicae uppsalienses 4; Uppsala: Wretman, 1945) 9-20.

Schneider, G. *Parusiegleichnisse,* 71-78.

Spicq, C. "La parabole de la veuve obstinée et du juge inerte, aux décisions impromptues *(Lc.* xviii, 1-8)," *RB* 68 (1961) 68-90.

Stählin, G. "Das Bild der Witwe: Ein Beitrag zur Bildersprache der Bibel und zum Phänomenon der Personifikation in der Antike," *JAC* 17 (1974) 5-20.

Wifstrand, A. "Lukas xviii. 7," *NTS* 11 (1964-1965) 72-74.

Zimmermann, H. "Das Gleichnis vom Richter und der Witwe (Lk 18,1-8)," *Die Kirche des Anfangs* (eds. R. Schnackenburg et al.) 79-95.

118. THE PARABLE OF THE PHARISEE AND THE TOLL-COLLECTOR
(18:9-14)

18 9 Then Jesus addressed this parable to some who were self-confident, regarding themselves as upright and all others as worthless: 10 "Two men went up to the Temple to pray, one a Pharisee, the other a toll-collector. 11 The Pharisee took a stance and prayed thus about himself, 'I thank you, God, that I am not like the rest of mankind, robbers, evildoers, adulterers, or even like this toll-collector. 12 I fast twice a week; I pay a tithe on all that I acquire.' 13 But the toll-collector stood far off and refused even to raise his eyes to heaven; he

struck his breast and said, 'Have pity on me, O God, sinner that I am.'
14 This man, I tell you, rather than that other, is the one who went home upright in the sight of God.

For everyone who *exalts* himself will *be humbled;* and he who *humbles* himself will *be exalted.* "a

a Ezek 21:31

COMMENT

At this point in the travel account Luke adds another parable of Jesus about prayer, that of the Pharisee and the toll-collector (18:9-14). It makes a fitting finale for the specifically Lucan travel account (9:51-18:14), ending on an important Lucan theme.

Like the parable which precedes it, this one too is derived from Luke's special source "L" (see p. 84). Whether it was joined in "L" to the preceding parable because of the common topic of prayer is not clear (for reasons which may suggest the joining, see G. Schneider, *Evangelium nach Lukas,* 363; E. Schweizer, *Evangelium nach Lukas,* 186). It is hardly likely to be understood as a corrective of the preceding one (that disciples should pray for mercy rather than petition God incessantly). Luke has provided the introductory v. 9, which is written in characteristically Lucan style (see J. Jeremias, *Die Sprache,* 272; cf. *HST* 193, 335). Lighter Lucan redaction affects some of the traditional material in vv. 10-14a. Verse 14b is a doublet, echoing almost word for word 14:11; in that passage the saying has a counterpart in Matt 23:12 and a more questionable one in Matt 18:14. It may be that Luke has simply repeated 14:11 here, creating a frame (with v. 9—see H. Zimmermann, *Jesus Christus,* 105-106). But given Luke's tendency to avoid creating doublets (see p. 82), it seems more likely that he has left standing a more generic conclusion to the parable which was already present in "L"; it could have been redacted by him to bring it closer to 14:11. G. Schneider *(Evangelium nach Lukas,* 365) also regards the addition of v. 14b as Lucan redaction.

Form-critically considered, vv. 10-14a have been considered as a parable in "pure narrative" form *(HST* 178), with its point being made in v. 14a. Verse 14b would be an isolated wisdom-saying, secondarily added. M. Dibelius *(FTG* 253, 258) stresses that the purpose of the parable is parenetic, seeking to show the true attitude of human beings to God, with the hortatory conclusion of v. 14b emphasizing that. V. Taylor *(FGT* 101), however, more correctly notes that this is another of the four Lucan stories which are better understood as an "example" (in rhetoric, *exemplum;* see COMMENT on 10:29-37).

J. M. Creed *(The Gospel,* 222) linked this and the preceding episode together under the rubric "two parables on prayer," but later on sensed the inadequacy of this title for the latter of the two passages when he commented on v. 14a and said that "the doctrine of the parables of *c.* xv is reasserted" (ibid. 224-225). For in a sense this passage joins those of chap. 15 as one of the great Lucan parables of mercy—about God's mercy shown to a sinner who stands before him and acknowledges his own worthlessness.

The contrast of the two types, their stances in the Temple, and their utterances in addressing God in prayer speak eloquently. Even before the conclusion is made in v. 14a, the reader is aware of the message which the story carries. We are never told what sin the Pharisee commits or what reparation the toll-collector has made; Jesus leaves that to God's judgment (or to the listener's imagination). He declares only that one man found uprightness in God's sight and the other did not.

The Pharisee's expression of thanks to God contains a catalogue of his own virtues and is formulated as a boast, at first negatively, then positively: He is not like others (robbers, evildoers, adulterers)—the height of his *ḥuṣpā'* is reached when he expressly compares himself with "this toll-collector"; but he fasts and tithes beyond all that is required. In contrast, the toll-collector stands afar off, casts his eyes down, strikes his breast, and begs God for mercy as a "sinner." By the confession of his sinful condition, the toll-collector finds in God's sight the status of uprightness, that status for which the Pharisee himself was striving by the avoidance of thievery, adultery, and evildoing as well as by his fasting and tithing. The Pharisee's conduct and attitude turn out to be fundamentally misguided—even though he has never engaged in such a despised occupation as the collecting of tolls. In the eyes of his contemporaries he is neither a "toll-collector" nor a "sinner," but he does not succeed in being found "upright in the sight of God" because of his self-reliance.

The parable records not simply Jesus' reaction to two different kinds of piety, but gives yet another instance of his defense of his attitude toward Pharisees and toll-collectors in contemporary Palestinian society (see 5:29-32; 7:36-50).

Given the pursuit of uprightness or righteousness in God's sight which was current among many of Jesus' Palestinian contemporaries, it is not surprising that some comment of his should surface on the matter of justification, even in a Lucan form. This parable records his attitude toward such a pursuit. It shows that he recognized that righteousness in God's sight was not to be achieved by boasting or even by self-confident activity (either the avoidance of evil or the striving for good in the observance of Mosaic and Pharisaic regulations).

This saying about justification is important for it may reveal that the NT teaching about the matter is somehow rooted in Jesus' own attitude and teaching: One achieves uprightness before God not by one's own activity but by a contrite recognition of one's own sinfulness before him. Hence "the Pauline doctrine of justification has its roots in the teaching of Jesus" (J. Jeremias, *Parables,* 141), but those roots, however, are still generic. In the pre-Lucan tradition used here Jesus' teaching on justification is recorded, but it is still a far cry from justification by grace through faith; there is as yet "no reference to the saving act of the cross" (G. Schrenk, *TDNT* 2. 215). Moreover, the notion of justification does not transcend that of the OT; it is rooted in the spirit of justification which pervades such psalms as 51 or 24:3-5 or *2 Esdr.* 12:7. In other words, one should beware of reading this parable with all the connotations of Pauline justification or of thinking that it has a "Pauline ring" to it, *pace* E. E. Ellis, *Gospel of Luke,* 214.

The concluding exhortation (v. 14b) makes it clear that the parable is addressed not only to Jesus' contemporaries, but to Christian disciples at large. If the thrust of it is to insinuate that the disciple should identify himself/herself with the toll-collector rather than with the Pharisee, it should be remembered that with all the willingness thus to identify oneself there undoubtedly remains in everyone more than a little of the Pharisee.

The modern reader of the parable may think that the Pharisee was at least honest about himself, that despite his boasting before God he was trying to be upright, was trying to keep the commandments, and was even doing more, whereas the toll-collector presumably was not trying at all or at least not very hard. For this reason the modern reader might find it difficult to identify himself/herself with the toll-collector. That, however, would be to press the parable beyond its obvious intention. As we have pointed out earlier (p. 600), almost every parable of Jesus has some aspect to it that teases the reader to further reflection. But that further reflection should not obscure the main point—in which a large grain of truth lies.

NOTES

18 9. *Jesus addressed this parable to some.* See NOTES on 5:36; 18:1. Possibly one should translate *pros* + acc. in this instance as "against some." See BAGD 710 § 4 and NOTE on 20:19. The phrase "this parable" appears at the end of the verse and is omitted in ms. D; without it the verse would begin, "Then he said to some . . ."

who were self-confident, regarding themselves as upright and all others as worthless. Lit. "being convinced about themselves that *(or possibly* because) they were upright and treating the rest (of humanity) with contempt." Though Luke does not identify the "some" as Pharisees, Jesus' words in 16:14-15 would suggest such an identification. However, the reference is undoubtedly to a wider group of people. The prophet Ezekiel had already castigated his contemporaries for "trusting" in their own "righteousness" (33:13, the Greek translation of which uses terms related to those employed here by Luke). The mere fact that a Pharisee is one of the two types in the parable does not make it certain that Pharisees were the only ones to fit the description given here—much less *all* Pharisees. Jesus' own disciples were undoubtedly to be understood as among the "some." The mention of the "upright" *(dikaioi)* is preparing for the "evildoers" *(adikoi)* of v. 11; and the whole description is preparing for the Pharisee's arrogant comparison of himself with the toll-collector. All this is part of the Lucan introduction.

10. *Two men.* I.e. two types of contemporary Palestinian Jews.

went up to the Temple to pray. I.e. they went up from the city to the mount of the Temple. Cp. Ps 122:1. The vb. *anabainein* with a following infin. of purpose is found, apart from Matt 14:23, only in Luke-Acts (see 2:4-5; 9:28; Acts 10:9); the formulation here is probably of Lucan redaction. For *hieron* as "the Temple," see NOTE on 1:9. Prayer in the Temple could have occurred at any time of the day, but two periods were reserved for public prayer: at the third hour of the day or about 9 A.M. (see Acts 2:15) and at the ninth hour or about 3 P.M. (see Acts 3:1). See NOTE on 1:10; cf. *m. Tamid* 5:1 for the content of the public prayer.

a Pharisee. See NOTE on 5:17. Here one is mentioned as a type or representative of faithful Jewish observers of Mosaic regulations. See Josephus, *J.W.* 1.5,2 § 110: "a body of Jews known for surpassing the others in the observances of piety and exact interpretation of the laws."

a toll-collector. See NOTE on 3:12. A type of person often associated with "sinners." See 5:30; 7:34; 15:1; cf. 19:2-7 and COMMENT on that episode.

11. *took a stance.* I.e. he stood to pray. The circumstantial aor. pass. ptc. *statheis* is found in the NT only in Lucan writings (18:40 [contrast Mark 10:49]; 19:8; Acts 2:14; 5:20; 11:13; 17:22; 25:18; 27:21). We are not told where the Pharisee stood, but the contrast with v. 13 would imply that he moved far to the front of the Court of Israel within the Temple precincts. See *IDB* 4. 556.

prayed thus about himself. The prepositional phrase *pros heauton* follows the ptc. *statheis* in the Greek text, and some commentators (C. C. Torrey, *Our Translated Gospels,* 79; *AAGA*[3] 103) understand the phrase as the equivalent of Aramaic *leh* (an ethic dat. with the ptc.), "taking his stand." Probably to avoid the confusion which this diversity of interpretation represents, some mss. (P[75], B, ℵ, Θ, Ψ, *f*[1], etc.) have an inverted order, *tauta pros heauton,* "prayed these (things) concerning himself." Though N-A[26] prefers the first form as the more difficult reading, the latter seems preferable in view of the importance of the extrinsic witnesses, *pace TCGNT* 168. The phrase then introduces the content of the prayer which follows.

I thank you. The phrase *eucharistō soi,* addressed to God in the second sg., occurs only here in the Lucan writings. It is also found on the lips of Jesus in John 11:41. The formula is Palestinian, occurring often in the Qumran *Thanksgiving Psalms* as *'ôdĕkāh 'Ădōnāy,* "I thank you, O Lord." E.g. 1QH 2:20,31; 3:19,37; 4:5; 7:34. It is found elsewhere in Greek writings (Jdt 8:25; 2 Macc 1:11; Philo, *De spec. leg.* 2.33 § 204; Josephus, *Ant.* 1.10,5 § 193). Cf. Acts 27:35; 28:15. The Pharisee utters no prayer of petition; in his prayer of thanksgiving he undoubtedly had reason to express gratitude to God, but the reasons cited are another matter.

God. As in v. 13, the nom. with the def. art. *ho theos* is used as a voc. See NOTE on 10:21; cf. the LXX of Pss 18:48; 44:1; 54:2, etc. Luke never uses the voc. *theé.* Cf. Matt 27:46.

not like the rest of mankind. J. Jeremias *(Parables,* 142) calls attention to a similar prayer recorded in the fifth-century Babylonian Talmud *(b. Ber.* 28b), but naïvely asserts that it comes from "the first century AD." T. W. Manson *(Sayings,* 311) gives another form of it from the Palestinian Talmud *(y. Ber.* 2.7d). The latter may be about fifty years younger (from ca. A.D. 400). The Pharisee's prayer may indeed be "taken from life," but the date of that tradition is something else again. One might more plausibly appeal to Paul's boast, formulated as a Christian concerning his own Pharisaic past, in Phil 3:4-6. Cf. Gal 1:14; 2:15. As taken from life, the prayer scarcely caricatures the Pharisaic type, *pace* L. Schottroff, "Die Erzählung," 448-452. Moreover, 1QH 7:34-35 is not really parallel to the Pharisee's prayer, *pace* N. Perrin *(Rediscovering,* 122 n. 2).

robbers, evildoers, adulterers. I.e. violators of the commandments of the Decalogue (Exod 20:14-15; Deut 5:17-18). The *adikoi,* "evildoers," is generic in contrast to the other two, unless one wants to understand it more specifically of "deceivers." The n. *harpax* is used of robbers or extortioners in Josephus, *J. W.* 6.3,4 § 203. Cf. LXX Isa 10:2.

even like this toll-collector. The deprecatory dem. pron. *houtos* is used. See NOTE on 15:30. Contrast the advice attributed to Hillel in *m. Abot* 2:5: "Keep not aloof from the congregation and trust not in thyself until the day of thy death, and judge not thy fellow until thou art come to his place. . . ." Implied in this remark of the Pharisee is that, though he has committed none of the aforementioned crimes, he has not associated with "sinners" either.

12. *I fast twice a week.* On fasting, see NOTE on 5:33. Fasting was prescribed in the OT for the Day of Atonement in postexilic times (Lev 16:29,31 *[RSV:* "you shall afflict yourselves" = you shall fast]; 23:27,29,32; Num 29:7) and possibly for some other occasions (Zech 8:19; cf. 7:3,5; Esth 9:31; Neh 9:1). Fasting by individuals in OT times was an expression of mourning (2 Sam 12:21), penance (1 Kgs 21:27; Ezra 10:6), supplication (Neh 1:4; Dan 9:3). That Pharisees and disciples of John the Baptist fasted in NT times is known from elsewhere in the NT (Luke 5:33). This passage is the earliest attestation of the custom of Jews fasting twice a week. *Did.* 8:1 instructs Christians that they are not to fast "with the hypocrites" on the second and fifth days of the week, but on the fourth day and on the parasceve (= day of preparation for the Sabbath). This probably reflects a Christian tradition of about A.D. 100. The days thus mentioned for Jewish fasting, Mondays and Thursdays, are attested in *b. Ta'an.* 12a (final redaction ca. A.D. 450). There the days are explained as the day on which Moses ascended Mount Sinai (Thursday) and that on which he came down from it (Monday) after forty days; but see Str-B 2. 243 n. 2 for a more probable reason: Two days not contiguous with a Sabbath and themselves as far apart as possible, hence Monday and Thursday. From the end of the first century A.D. dates the *Mĕgillat Ta'ănît,* an Aramaic text that lists the days in each month on which it was not permitted to fast or mourn. See *MPAT* § 150. The Pharisee's mention of fasting twice a week is part of his boast about works of supererogation, as is also that about tithing.

I pay a tithe on all. See NOTE on 11:42, where there is mention of the tithing of herbs. Here the emphasis falls on "all." Deut 14:22-23 prescribes a tithe of all the produce of one's seed, grain, wine, oil, firstlings of the herd and flock—it was to be offered annually at the harvest festival. If the person lived far from the Temple, the produce could be converted to money, and that could be offered instead. See Deut 14:25-27; cf. Num 18:21-24. In other words, he ate not only "clean" food, but was also careful to eat only tithed food.

13. *stood far off.* I.e. probably just within the confines of the court of Israel.

refused even to raise his eyes to heaven. I.e. in an OT attitude of prayer; a Septuagintism is used. See p. 114. Cf. *1 Enoch* 13:5: ". . . they did raise their eyes to heaven out of shame for the sins for which they had been condemned."

struck his breast. I.e. smiting his heart as a sign of compunction, sorrow, or contrition. See Luke 23:48. The same sign occurs in Josephus, *Ant.* 7.10,5 § 252; it is apparently unknown in the OT. Cf. Arrian, *Anab.* 7.24,3.

Have pity on me, O God, sinner that I am. Lit. "O God, be merciful to me the sinner," so the toll-collector prays in the spirit of Ps 51:3, uttering a petition (for forgiveness and mercy), and not a thanksgiving. The vb. *hilaskesthai* is used only here in Luke-Acts, and in the rest of the NT only in Heb 2:17. Though in classical Greek it means "appease" the gods (Homer, *Il.* 1. 386; *Od.* 3.419; Strabo, *Geog.* 4.4,6), the dead (Herodotus, *Hist.* 5.47), or even men (ibid. 8.112), its object is never any of these in the NT. See further D. Hill, *Greek Words and Hebrew Meanings* (SNTSMS 5; Cambridge: University Press, 1967) 23-48. Here the aor. pass. impv. occurs in the sense of "be merciful, gracious" (to me). This sense is also found in the LXX (2 Kgs 5:18 [translating Hebrew *yislaḥ,* "will pardon"]; Esth 4:17h [C 10]) with the dat. of personal obj. The toll-collector's prayer resembles the spirit of the prayers found in 1QS 11:3-5,10-12; 1QH 11:15-22. He has nothing to parade before God.

14. *I tell you.* For this introductory *legō hymin,* see NOTE on 11:8.

rather than that other. The best reading is *par' ekeinon,* "beyond that one" (in mss. ℵ, B, L, Q, T, *f* ¹, Vg, etc.). It is a mode of expressing the comparative by the prep. *para,* which occurs elsewhere in Luke 13:2 (see NOTE there),4. Cf. Josephus, *Ag.Ap.* 2.32 § 234; *Barn.* 11:9. With it the ptc. *dedikaiōmenos* in the following phrase is treated like an adj. in the positive degree; together they express a comparison. J. Jeremias *(Parables,* 141-142) claims that *par' ekeinon* is an attempt to translate Aramaic *min,* but he completely misses the point. Aramaic *min* is a way of expressing comparison, and occasionally it is translated by *para* in the LXX (Ps 45:8). But that is rather the substitution of a different comparative expression, using a good Greek prep. which reflects another Aramaic way of expressing comparison (by the prep. *'al).*

Some mss. read *ē gar ekeinos* instead of *par' ekeinon* (A, W, Θ, Ψ, 063, *f* ¹³, and the Koine text-tradition); ms. D, OL, and the Peshitta have *mallon par' ekeinon ton Pharisaion,* "rather than that Pharisee." These are merely attempts to make clear the comparison. They are not to be preferred. But cf. J. B. Cortés, "The Greek Text of Luke 18:14a: A Contribution to the Method of Reasoned Eclecticism," *CBQ* 46 (1984) 255–273.

went home upright in the sight of God. Lit. "went home having been justified," with the pf. pass. ptc. *dedikaiōmenon* being used in the theological sense (see NOTE on 5:20) and expressing the condition in which the toll-collector now finds himself, despite his former sins: "justified," i.e. having been declared/made upright (by God). As T. W. Manson *(Sayings,* 312) puts it, ". . . the decisive thing is not the past record, whether good or bad, but the present attitude towards God." On the vb. *dikaioun,* as

18:9-14   IV. THE JOURNEY TO JERUSALEM   1189

used by Luke, see K. Kertelge, *EWNT* 1. 805-806; G. Schrenk, *TDNT* 2. 215. Compare the sentiment in *2 Esdr.* 12:7.

everyone who exalts himself. See NOTE on 14:11. As there, the allusion to Ezek 21:31 puts the concluding comment of the parable (v. 14a) into a larger perspective. Self-confidence and reliance on one's observance of Mosaic regulations or Pharisaic pious practices will not necessarily lead to uprightness before God. This is a warning addressed not only to contemporaries of Jesus but to Christian disciples: they are to pray as did the toll-collector and recall the sentiments of 1:45,48,52.

BIBLIOGRAPHY (18:9-14)

Bruce, F. F. " 'Justification by Faith' in the Non-Pauline Writings of the New Testament," *EvQ* 24 (1952) 66-67.

Bultmann, R. *Marburger Predigten,* 107-117.

Cerfaux, L. "Trois réhabilitations dans l'Evangile," *Recueil Lucien Cerfaux* 2. 51-59, esp. 53-55.

Charpentier, E. "Le chrétien: Un homme 'juste' ou 'justifié'?: Lc 18,9-14," *AsSeign* ns 61 (1972) 66-78.

Dreher, B. "Der Pharisäer: Biblisch-homiletische Besinnung zum Evangelium des 10. Sonntags nach Pfingsten (Lk 18,9-14)," *BibLeb* 8 (1967) 128-132.

Fernández, J. "La oración del publicano (Lc. 18, 9-14)," *CB* 5 (1948) 193-199.

Feuillet, A. "Le pharisien et le publicain (Luc 18,9-14): La manifestation de la miséricorde divine en Jésus Serviteur souffrant," *Esprit et vie* 48 (1981) 657-665.

——— "La signification christologique de Luc 18,14 et les références des évangiles au Serviteur souffrant," *Nova et vetera* 55 (1980) 188-229.

Green, L. C. "Justification in Luther's Preaching on Luke 18:9-14," *CTM* 42 (1972) 732-747.

Hengel, M. "Die ganz andere Gerechtigkeit: Bibelarbeit über Lk. 18,9-14," *Theologische Beiträge* 5 (1974) 1-13.

Hoerber, R. G. " 'God Be Merciful to Me a Sinner': A Note on Lk 18:13," *CTM* 33 (1962) 283-286.

Jeremias, J. *Parables,* 139-144.

Jülicher, A. *Gleichnisreden,* 2. 598-608.

Kissinger, W. S. *Parables of Jesus,* 347-348.

Linnemann, E. *Jesus of the Parables,* 58-64.

Merklein, H. " 'Dieser ging als Gerechter nach Hause . . .': Das Gottesbild Jesu und die Haltung der Menschen nach Lk 18,9-14," *BK* 32 (1977) 34-42.

Mottu, H. "The Pharisee and the Tax Collector: Sartrian Notions as Applied to the Reading of Scripture," *USQR* 29 (1973-1974) 195-213.

Perkins, P. *Hearing the Parables,* 38-39, 171-176.

Pesch, R. "Jesus, a Free Man," *Jesus Christ and Human Freedom* (Concilium 3/10; New York: Herder and Herder, 1974) 56-70.

Schnider, F. "Ausschliessen und ausgeschlossen werden: Beobachtungen zur Struktur des Gleichnisses vom Pharisäer und Zöllner Lk 18,10-14a," *BZ* 24 (1980) 42-56.

Schottroff, L. "Die Erzählung vom Pharisäer und Zöllner als Beispiel für die theologische Kunst des Überredens," *Neues Testament und christliche Existenz: Festschrift für Herbert Braun zum 70. Geburtstag* (eds. H. D. Betz and L. Schottroff; Tübingen: Mohr [Siebeck], 1973) 439-461.

Zimmermann, H. *Jesus Christus: Geschichte und Verkündigung* (2d ed.; Stuttgart: Katholisches Bibelwerk, 1975) 105-110.

119. JESUS BLESSES THE LITTLE CHILDREN
(18:15-17)

18 ¹⁵ People used to bring even babies to Jesus that he might hold them; but when the disciples saw it, they tried to rebuke them. ¹⁶ Then Jesus called for them and said, "Let the little children come to me, and do not try to stop them, for to such as these belongs the kingdom of God. ¹⁷ Believe me, whoever does not accept the kingdom of God as a little child shall never enter it."

COMMENT

Having finished the insertion of material from the sources "Q" and "L" into the extended travel account, Luke now resumes the use of "Mk." The present episode, which recounts Jesus' blessing of the little children (18:15-17), is not the first episode in the Marcan account of Jesus' departure for Jerusalem. That begins with Mark 10:1-12 and recounts Jesus' discussion with Pharisees about divorce. Luke omits that pericope because he has already recorded the "Q"-form of the prohibition of divorce in 16:18 (see pp. 1119-1124). (On his avoidance of doublets, see p. 82.) Instead Luke passes immediately to the second episode in the Marcan travel account (10:13-16), which forms a better sequel to the last saying in v. 14b, with which the preceding parable of the Pharisee and the toll-collector ended. The need for humility in Christian life is thus elaborated in another way. Just as the toll-collector who humbly confessed his sinfulness before God was the one who was found to be upright in his sight, so now it is one who accepts the kingdom as a little child who will find entrance into it.

Luke follows the Marcan account of Jesus' blessing of the little children fairly closely (cf. Matt 19:13-15). However, Luke eliminates the details of Jesus' anger and affection (see p. 95). Moreover, he improves at times the Greek style, using *brephē*, "babies, infants," in v. 15a, instead of the Marcan *paidia*, "children" (10:13), which he retains, however, in v. 16b. He transfers the ptc. *idontes*, "seeing" (v. 15b) to the disciples (in Mark 10:14 it appears in the sg. *idōn* of Jesus himself). Finally, he eliminates entirely the manifestation of affection in Mark 10:16, which is altered even in Matt 19:15. T. Schramm *(Markus-Stoff,* 141) calls this Lucan episode "pure Marcan material," lacking any agreements with Matthew against Mark in the Triple Tradition, any Semitisms, or Lucan peculiarities. Indeed, Luke has even retained *amēn legō hymin* (v. 17, from Mark 10:15).

Another form of the story is preserved in *Gos. of Thom.* § 22: "Jesus saw children being nursed. He said to his disciples, 'These children who are being nursed are like those who enter the kingdom.' They said to him, 'If we become children, shall we enter the kingdom?' Jesus said to them, 'When you make the two one, and when you make the inside like the outside and the outside like the inside, and the above like the below, and when you make the male and the female into a single one so that the male not be male or the female female, and when you put eyes in place of an eye, a hand in place of a hand, a foot in place of a foot, and an image in place of an image, then you will enter [the kingdom].'" This form seems to be remotely inspired by the Synoptic saying of Jesus about children and the kingdom, but it is an elaborate reworking to affirm gnostic teaching about the primordial unit. (See further J.-E. Ménard, *L'Evangile selon Thomas,* 113-115; H. C. Kee, "'Becoming a Child' in the Gospel of Thomas," *JBL* 82 [1963] 307-314.)

From a form-critical viewpoint, Bultmann *(HST* 32) has classified the episode as a pronouncement-story, of the biographical type. He is, however, reluctant to interpret the "such" of v. 16 by the further saying in v. 17. For him this verse represents "an originally independent dominical saying" which has been inserted into the present context and stems from a different context in the ministry of Jesus. This is plausible enough, but that the whole episode grew out of the saying in v. 16 in imitation of the story of Elisha and Gehazi's rejection of the Shunammite woman in 2 Kgs 4:27 "and an analogy in a Rabbinic story" is farfetched (even if the latter were told about R. Aqiba, it is drawn from the *Babylonian* Talmud, *b. Ketub.* 63a or *b. Ned.* 50a [Str-B 1.808]!). In adding the isolated prophetic saying of minatory character, Luke is simply following "Mk"; it applies to adults what the preceding material has said about little children. V. Taylor *(FGT* 72, 148) also considers the basic episode to be a pronouncement-story. (Cf. *FTG* 43, 44, 48 [among the paradigms].)

As the episode stands, it depicts Jesus preoccupied with little children who have been brought to him and with an overruling of his disciples' reaction to them. We are not told why the disciples rebuke the parents who bring the children, but it obviously stems from the disciples' lack of comprehension of Jesus and his possible relation to little children. The Lucan Jesus proceeds to call the children to himself, repeating word for word the tolerance expressed in "Mk": "Let the little children come to me . . . for to such as these belongs the kingdom of God." He does not allow his disciples to keep them away, for to these minors in human society a share in the kingdom of God is destined. The added saying in v. 17 draws still another lesson from the presence of such little ones: They are to be recognized not only as members of the kingdom, but as models for all adults who would like to accept it. Without saying so explicitly, Jesus is thus extolling the openness and sheer receptivity of these tiny human beings. Their freshness, their lack of guilt or suspicion, their loving warmth, and their lack of a claim to achievement are what is being held up to adults accosted by the message of the kingdom. The little child, whether *brephos* or *paidion,* thus becomes the symbol of the ideal entrant into the kingdom. (The modern reader may wonder about the other side of a little child's character, which is only too apparent to any parent or grandparent [cruelty to siblings, lying, shifting blame, etc.]; but once again, to reflect on that aspect of the comparison is to miss the point.) Those who are like a little child in the aspect intended are those who are "called" to Jesus himself. Coming immediately after the parable of the Pharisee and the toll-collector, this episode stresses who is really upright in the sight of God, who will enter the kingdom.

That the original *Sitz im Leben* for this episode in the life of Jesus had anything to do with the question of infant baptism is unlikely. That the episode reflects a debate about this matter in the community for which Luke was writing his Gospel is equally unlikely, *pace* O. Cullmann and J. Jeremias. The use of *brephē* instead of *paidia* by Luke stems from his redaction (see NOTE on v. 15) and scarcely reflects the practice "in the Greek church" of baptizing infants, *pace* W. Grundmann, *Evangelium nach Lukas,* 353. That this passage helped to determine later church practice in the matter of baptism is certain, but there is no way of determining how far back that practice can be traced.

NOTES

18   15. *People used to bring even babies to Jesus.* Lit. "they used to carry even babies to him." The impers. third pl. is used as a substitute for the pass. (ZBG § 1). Luke uses his favorite *brephos,* "infant" (see 1:41,44; 2:12,16; Acts 7:19); none of the other evangelists uses the word, and it occurs only twice elsewhere in the NT (2 Tim 3:15; 1 Pet 2:2). He retains the pl. *paidia* in v. 16b and the sg. *paidion* in v. 17b. It is a clear redactional change; see W. Michaelis, "Lukas," 190-191. Ms. D has *paidia,* thus harmonizing the Lucan story with Mark 10:13. The introduction of *brephos,* however, creates a bit of a problem, for it is less appropriate in that "some conscious capacity in the children seems needed to give point to the saying concerning the Kingdom of God as a little child" (J. M. Creed, *The Gospel,* 225). It would have been less of a problem if v. 17 were not already connected with the pronouncement-story which Luke takes over from Mark.

might hold them. Or "might touch them." If the latter sense were to be preferred, then it might possibly have the connotation of conveying a blessing (or a curse), as the word *haptesthai* sometimes has elsewhere (Luke 6:19; 5:13; and even in extrabiblical Greek [Antoninus Liberalis, *Metam.* 4.7; Pseudo-Apollodorus 2.1,3 § 1]). In Matt 19:13 Jesus lays his hands on the children and prays over them. The subjunc. *haptētai* follows the impf. *prosepheron*, as it may commonly do in Hellenistic Greek, where the optative mood is on the wane. See BDF § 369.1.

tried to rebuke them. I.e. in their incomprehension, the disciples probably considered attention to children a waste of Jesus' time or even an abuse of his kindness. The mss. ℵ, B, L, Q, T, *f* 1 read *epetimoun,* the conative impf. (see BDF § 326), but others (A, W, Θ, Ψ, 078, and the Koine text-tradition) have the aor. *epetimēsan.*

16. *called for them.* I.e. Jesus called for the parents to bring the children to him (as in v. 15a); his reaction to the incomprehension of the disciples is immediate. The best reading is *prosekalesato,* aor. indic. middle; mss. D and *f* 1 have the impf. *prosekaleito;* and others (mss. A, W, Θ, Ψ, 078, *f* 13, and the Koine text-tradition), along with some ancient versions (OL, Vg, Syr[h]) read the ptc. *proskalesamenos eipen.* There is little change in meaning.

do not try to stop them. Lit. "and do not hinder them." The vb. *kōlyein* has been used before by Luke (6:29; 9:49,50; 11:52) and will be used again (23:2; Acts 8:36; 10:47; 11:17; 16:6; 24:23; 27:43). In most instances it has the generic sense of "hinder, prevent, stop," but in Acts 8:36 and 10:47 it is found in questions about preventing someone from being baptized. In these two places the infin. *baptisthēnai* is explicitly added, which is not the case here in Luke 18:16. It is found later in patristic texts, with a more specific nuance; but this is clearly a development in the period beyond the NT. See BIBLIOGRAPHY that follows these NOTES.

to such as these belongs the kingdom. Jesus does not say that the kingdom belongs to "these" little ones whom he is holding, but to "such as these" *(toioutōn).* This undoubtedly gave rise to the addition of the isolated saying now found in v. 17. Recall 6:20b.

the kingdom of God. See NOTE on 4:43 and pp. 154-156.

17. *Believe me.* Lit. "amen, I say to you." See NOTE on 4:24.

accept the kingdom. This mode of speech about the kingdom is rare; but it is perfectly in line with the invitation used in 17:21. See pp. 1160-1162.

as a little child. A "little child" has been used for comparative purpose in the Lucan Gospel before. See 7:32; 9:47-48. Here the child's qualities of openness, lowliness in society, minority, helplessness, without claim of achievement, and in need of constant maternal or paternal attention are what is being alluded to. Note that the counterpart of this verse is used in a different context in Matt 18:3b, where acceptance is spelled out in terms of "turning and becoming like little children."

shall never enter it. For the kingdom as something to enter, see 18:24,25; Acts 14:22. Cf. Luke 13:24. It is also found in John 3:5. See p. 156.

BIBLIOGRAPHY (18:15-17)

Aland, K. *Did the Early Church Baptize Infants?* (Philadelphia: Westminster, 1963) 95-99.

Beasley-Murray, G. R. *Baptism in the New Testament* (London: Macmillan, 1962) 320-329.

Cullmann, O. *Baptism in the New Testament* (SBT 1; Chicago: Regnery; London: SCM, 1950) 26, 42, 76-80.

Jeremias, J. *Infant Baptism in the First Four Centuries* (London: SCM, 1960) 48-55.

―――― *The Origins of Infant Baptism: A Further Study in Reply to Kurt Aland* (SHT 1; London: SCM, 1963) 54 n. 1.

Légasse, S. *Jésus et l'enfant: "Enfants," "petits" et "simples" dans la tradition synoptique* (EBib; Paris: Gabalda, 1969) 36-43, 195-209, 326-333.

Michaelis, W. "Lukas und die Anfänge der Kindertaufe," *Apophoreta: Festschrift für Ernst Haenchen* (BZNW 30; ed. W. Eltester and F. H. Kettler; Berlin: Töpelmann, 1964) 187-193.

Percy, E. *Die Botschaft Jesu: Eine traditionskritische und exegetische Untersuchung* (Lund: Gleerup, 1953) 31-37.

Schilling, F. A. "What Means the Saying about Receiving the Kingdom of God as a Little Child *(tēn basileian tou theou hōs paidion)?* Mk x. 15; Lk xviii. 17," *ExpTim* 77 (1965-1966) 56-58.

Schramm, T. *Markus-Stoff,* 141-142.

120. THE RICH YOUNG MAN
(18:18-23)

18 [18] Once a magistrate put this question to him, "Good Teacher, what must I do to inherit eternal life?" [19] But Jesus said to him, "Why do you address me as good? No one is good except God alone. [20] You know the commandments, *'You shall not commit adultery; you shall not murder; you shall not steal; you shall not bear false witness; honor your father and mother.'* "[a] [21] And he replied, "I have observed all these since I was a youth." [22] When Jesus heard this, he said to him, "For you then one thing is still missing: Sell all that you have, dis-

[a] Deut 5:17-20

tribute it to the poor, and you shall have treasure in heaven. Then come, follow me!" [23] When he heard this, he became very sad; for he was extremely rich.

COMMENT

In this part of the travel account Luke continues to follow the order of material in Mark and now depicts Jesus confronted by a Palestinian magistrate who asks him how he is to inherit eternal life (18:18-23). Coming after the parable of the Pharisee and the toll-collector, which taught Christian disciples about the proper way to find uprightness in God's sight, and after the episode of Jesus' calling little children to himself as models of those who would enter God's kingdom, this episode continues in a loose topical way, now instructing them about how one may inherit eternal life. For uprightness in God's sight, entrance into the kingdom, and the inheritance of eternal life are clearly related; and the following episode (18:24-30) will continue the discussion of that relationship.

This episode is derived by Luke from Mark 10:17-22, and it has a parallel in Matt 19:16-22, where it forms part of the narrative episodes preparing for the last great sermon of Jesus in that Gospel. Luke drops the Marcan introduction, which refers to Jesus' making his way along the road—in this Gospel he has been on it since 9:51! Matthew has also eliminated it because of his own introduction in 19:1. Luke makes the person who poses the question to Jesus an *archōn*, "magistrate, ruler," but otherwise his question and Jesus' answer to it are taken over almost word for word from Mark. Similarly for Jesus' answer in v. 20 (with a slight inversion of the order of the commandments and the omission of one). Luke further improves the Greek of v. 21, eliminating the redundant "my" after the middle voice of the vb. *ephylax-amēn* and changing the latter to the act. (as does Matt 19:20). Luke also eliminates the mention of Jesus' emotional reaction (see Mark 10:21), as he often does elsewhere (see p. 95). He further introduces his own transitional cl. (v. 22a) and improves the Greek of the rest of that verse, adding a characteristically Lucan "all" to Jesus' demand. In v. 23 the evangelist curtails the description of the man's reaction and improves the Greek of the ending of it. Once again, T. Schramm *(Markus-Stoff,* 142) finds this passage to be "pure Marcan material," depending on no other source. The only really serious agreement of Matthew and Luke against Mark in this passage of the Triple Tradition is the common omission of "You shall not defraud" (Mark 10:19) among the commandments quoted; but in this case both Matthew and Luke have omitted it independently of each other—it is not part of the Decalogue in the OT and the rest of their quotations from it differ considerably.

Form-critically considered, this episode is a pronouncement-story (see *HST* 21-22), an apophthegm (v. 22) uttered by Jesus in answer to a question. One should note the growth in the tradition: the person in Mark is designated simply *heis,* "one"; this has become *neaniskos,* "a young man," in Matt 19:20 (whence the title commonly used for the episode); in Luke he becomes *archōn,* "magistrate, ruler" (18:18); and in the *Gospel of the Hebrews* he is *alter divitum,* "the second of the rich men" (quoted by Origen, *Comm. in Matth.* 15.14 [TU 47/2. 91]), who begins to "scratch his head" in perplexity. V. Taylor *(FGT* 66) notes how this pronouncement-story is thus on its way to becoming a Story about Jesus.

The narrative buildup in this pronouncement-story is notable. On his way to Jerusalem Jesus is accosted by a Palestinian magistrate who has obviously been listening to his teaching and has seen Jesus holding the little children (18:15-17). All of this prompts the man to address Jesus as "Good Teacher," which makes Jesus react, ascribing goodness to God alone. In effect, "Jesus reminds him that there is only one source of goodness. . . . He Himself is no exception. His goodness is the goodness of God working in Him" (A. Plummer, *The Gospel,* 422). To the question itself posed to him, "what must I do to inherit eternal life?" (v. 18c), Jesus responds with a generic answer which any teacher of the Law in his day would have given. He lines himself up with standard OT teaching: What God demands of a human being leads to eternal life. "You know the commandments" is equivalent to telling him to obey them; and Jesus proceeds to quote the second part of the Decalogue, the part of it which is concerned with a person's dealings with other human beings. The magistrate's answer, sincere though it is, is in effect a retort: "So what's new? I've been observing those since I became a youth!" To the pointed retort, Jesus addresses his specific pronouncement—in the second sg. "For you then one thing is still missing: Sell all that you have, distribute it to the poor . . . Then come, follow me." Jesus has not denied that the magistrate has actually observed the commandments; he takes the man's answer for what it is and tries to draw him on still further. Two things he asks of him: (a) to sell all that he has and distribute it to the poor; and (b) come follow him. The double injunction, though derived from the Marcan source, fits characteristically in with the demands of Christian living in the Lucan Gospel (see pp. 247-251, 241-243). Jesus' words add a further note, however, in that they promise a "treasure in heaven." When the magistrate hears this pronouncement from Jesus, he becomes very sad, because he is extremely rich. But it should be noted that in the Lucan Gospel we are not told that he "turned away" (cp. Mark 10:22; Matt 19:22). We do not know precisely the status of this magistrate: Was he a disciple or not? Does his sadness imply that he ceased being a disciple? Is the contrast one of a rich Palestinian ruler and a Christian disciple, or of one already well disposed enough to be in Jesus' entourage and seeking to go on further? His question was not posed to test

Jesus (contrast 10:25; 11:16; cf. Matt 19:3; 22:35), but was one of genuine inquiry.

The Lucan Jesus does not say to the man, as does the Matthean, "If you wish to be perfect" (19:21), which became the springboard for a certain interpretation in the Christian tradition that distinguished precepts and counsels and which found support in it for the monastic/religious vow of poverty. Obviously, the words of the Lucan Jesus imply nothing so definite. But the question remains whether he is not addressing a challenge (in the second *sg.*) to one who is already a rich, good-living person, perhaps even a disciple, to whom he tries to open a way of life beyond those duties of ordinary disciples (see M.-J. Lagrange, *Luc,* 481). It is significant that even E. Schweizer *(Evangelium nach Lukas,* 190) did not hesitate to mention the Frères de Taizé in his comment on this passage!

NOTES

18 18. *Once a magistrate put this question to him.* Lit. "and a certain (person), a magistrate, asked him, saying." See p. 122. The Greek n. *archōn,* "magistrate, ruler," has already been used in 8:41; 11:15; 12:58; 14:1 and will occur again in 23:13,35; 24:20 and often in Acts. Its specific sense in Palestinian (or other) society can only be gained by the context; it is far from clear in this case that it denotes a "religious ruler" or a "churchman," *pace* E. E. Ellis, *Gospel of Luke,* 217. Whoever the person is, he appears as a representative of pious legal observance—possibly a synagogue leader, possibly not.

Good Teacher. Luke has taken this form of address over from Mark 10:17. Matthew, however, has altered it notably: "Teacher, what good must I do that I may have eternal life" (19:16). In this Gospel Jesus has already been called *didaskale* (see NOTES on 3:12; 7:40; cf. p. 218), but a problem is created by the form used here, since it is difficult to explain why Jesus reacts to this title as he does. He seems to bristle at it. Years ago A. Plummer *(The Gospel,* 422) maintained that "there is no instance in the whole Talmud of a Rabbi being addressed as 'Good Master,' " but others have pointed out that *rab ṭāb* is indeed found in *b. Ta'an.* 24b. See Str-B 2. 24. Yet that is a fourth–fifth century A.D. usage (see I. H. Marshall, *Luke,* 684), as the use of *rab* shows. Cf. G. Dalman, *Words of Jesus,* 337. Whether or not it was a common Palestinian mode of address for a teacher in the time of Jesus, it is clear that he rejects it (in both Mark and Luke). It is not because human beings could not be called "good"; in the OT the adj. is often so used of them. See Prov 12:2; 14:4; cf. Luke 6:45. Jesus' reason for rejecting it follows in v. 19b.

In this and the following verse the Lucan text is quite uniformly transmitted and suffers none of the problems that attend the transmission of the Matthean (19:16-17). See J. W. Wenham, "Why Do You Ask Me."

to inherit eternal life? This sort of question has already been put to Jesus in 10:25. See NOTE there; cf. 18:30; Acts 13:46,48. As the background for the term, one can cite in addition Dan 12:2 *(ḥayyê 'ôlām;* Greek *zōē aiōnios); 4Q181* 1:4; cf. 1QS 4:7; CD

3:20 *(ḥayyê neṣaḥ); Pss. Sol.* 3:12; *1 Enoch* 37:4; 40:9; 58:3 (all in the Book of Parables!); *4 Macc* 15:3; 2 Macc 7:9. See further R. Bultmann, *TDNT* 2. 832-872, esp. 856-857; H. Balz, *EWNT* 1. 111-115. See also NOTES on 3:10 and p. 226.

19. *Why do you address me as good?* Many explanations have been given of this query of Jesus over the centuries; I list only the main ones: (a) The question is intended to bring the man to perceive that Jesus was divine: ". . . that he may believe in the Son of God, not as a good master, but as the Good God" (Ambrose, *De fide* 2.1 and many patristic writers; cf. M.-J. Lagrange, *L'Evangile selon Saint Marc* [4th ed.; Paris: Gabalda, 1929] 264-265). (b) Jesus rejects the epithet "good" from the questioner's point of view and seeks to correct the magistrate's flattery (so some patristic writers; see F. Spitta, "Jesus Weigerung," 19); (c) Jesus implicitly acknowledges his sinfulness. So G. Volkmar, *Die Evangelien* (Leipzig: Fues [R. Riesland], 1870) 489. (d) The adj. *agathos* should be understood in the sense of "gracious, kind" (W. Wagner). (e) Jesus is saying nothing about his own person, but directing the man's attention to God and his will as the only prescription for pleasing him (B. B. Warfield, *Christology and Criticism* [New York: Oxford University, 1929] 139). Most of these are subterfuges and one recognizes today that only the last is on the way to being the right interpretation. The contrast implied in Jesus' remark to the epithet used by the magistrate is further explained in the next sentence that Jesus utters. For a discussion of the variant form of the question in the Matthean Gospel, see J. W. Wenham, "Why Do You Ask."

No one is good except God alone. I.e. Goodness resides with God alone, who is the source of it when it is found in others through his grace. See 11:13. Hence, if the magistrate recognizes any goodness in Jesus, he is being told by him to attribute it to its rightful source: "His [Jesus'] goodness is the goodness of God working in Him" (A. Plummer, *The Gospel,* 422). Underlying Jesus' comment is the OT theme of God's goodness: Nah 1:7; 1 Chr 16:34; 2 Chr 5:13; Pss 34:9; 118:1,29. Cf. Philo, *Leg. alleg.* 1.14 § 47; *De somn.* 1.23 § 149.

20. *You know the commandments.* Compare Jesus' answer in 10:26. Now he refers to the commandments of the Mosaic Decalogue and proceeds to quote five of them from its second part. Luke has derived the list from Mark 10:19, inverting the order of the first two and omitting the Marcan fifth, "You shall not defraud." Matt 19:18-19 follows the Marcan order of the commandments, but he too omits the Marcan fifth. Whereas Luke has further preserved the form of the injunctions found in Mark (i.e. with the negative *mē* and the aor. subjunc.), Matthew has used the form found in the LXX of both Deuteronomy and Exodus (i.e. with the negative *ou* and the fut. indic.). Matt 19:19b has further added Lev 19:18b, which is found in neither Mark nor Luke (but see Luke 10:27). Whereas the Marcan and Matthean order of the first four commandments follows the order of the MT and of ms. A of the LXX (of both Deuteronomy and Exodus), the Lucan order of the first four agrees with that of Philo *(De decal.* 12 § 51); Rom 13:9; the Nash papyrus (see S. A. Cook, "A Pre-Massoretic Biblical Papyrus," *PSBA* 25 [1903] 34-56); and ms. B of the LXX of Deut 5:17-20). Cf. Jas 2:11. What is responsible for this divergence of order is not easy to say. See K. J. Thomas, "Liturgical Citations." In all three of the Synoptics the commandment to honor one's parents follows the other four.

21. *I have observed all these since I was a youth.* Lit. ". . . from youth." See Acts

26:4. The sense: since the time he reached religious and legal maturity and was obliged to fulfill all the commandments of the Mosaic Law. The term *bar miṣwāh,* "son of (the) commandment," is found in *b. B. Meṣ.* 96a; but its use to designate the occasion of the assumption of legal obligations by a Jewish boy appears only in the fifteenth century A.D. See *Encylopaedia judaica* (New York: Macmillan, 1971) 4. 243. The phrase *ek neotētos* is also found in LXX Num 22:30; 1 Macc 1:6; 16:2; Josephus, *J.W.* 4.1,5 § 33.

22. *For you then one thing is still missing.* Lit. "still one (thing) is left for you (sg.)," i.e. one thing that you still lack. Cf. Josephus, *J.W.* 4.4,3 § 257; Titus 3:13. Luke has suppressed the favorable reaction of Jesus recorded in the Marcan form of the story. Matt 19:21 adds a condition, "If you wish to be perfect . . ." a distinction that Luke does not make. Jesus' further advice is not a "commandment" (in the sense of those of the Decalogue just quoted).

Sell all that you have. Whereas Mark 10:21 reads simply *hosa echeis pōlēson,* "whatever you have, sell," Luke rhetorically adds in the emphatic first position the adj. *panta,* "all that you have" (on which see NOTES on 3:16; 4:15; 9:1 and pp. 247-248).

distribute it to the poor. In Mark 10:21d the man is told simply to "give" it to the poor; the Lucan Jesus becomes more specific. All that is mentioned in this part of the verse is clearly demanded of the magistrate as something more than mere fidelity to the commandments—that would be expected of any disciple of Jesus.

you shall have treasure in heaven. Luke derives this reward-language from Mark 10:21e; it echoes moreover the "Q" saying of Luke 12:33. This "treasure in heaven" cannot be simply equated with "eternal life" about which the magistrate initially queried. To obtain that Jesus implied that one had to keep the commandments. The "treasure in heaven" is promised for the distribution of one's wealth to the poor and the following of Jesus.

come, follow me! For the following of the Lucan Jesus, see pp. 241-243.

23. *he became very sad; for he was extremely rich.* Pace I. H. Marshall *(Luke,* 683) and G. B. Caird *(Gospel of St Luke,* 205), the magistrate is not said to have gone off, as it is recorded in Mark 10:22 and Matt 19:22. Implied only is that he could not bring himself to follow Jesus in the specific way that was proposed to him. His reaction contrasts with that of Peter, John, and James in 5:11, even though his wealth was not limited to boats and nets.

BIBLIOGRAPHY (18:18-23)

Best, E. "The Camel and the Needle's Eye (Mk 10:25)," *ExpTim* 82 (1970-1971) 83-89.

Degenhardt, H.-J. *Lukas Evangelist der Armen,* 136-159.

——— "Was muss ich tun, um das ewige Leben zu gewinnen? Zu Mk 10,17-22," *Biblische Randbemerkungen* (eds. H. Merklein and J. Lange) 159-168.

Dupont, J. *Béatitudes,* 3. 153-160.

Galot, J. "Le fondement évangélique du voeu religieux de pauvreté," *Greg* 56 (1975) 441-467.

Légasse, S. L'Appel du riche (Marc 10,17-31 et parallèles): Contribution à l'étude des fondements scripturaires de l'état religieux (Paris: Beauchesne, 1966) 184-214.

Riga, P. J. "Poverty as Counsel and as Precept," TBT 65 (1973) 1123-1128.

Schmid, J. Matthäus und Lukas, 129-131.

Schramm, T. Markus-Stoff, 142.

Spitta, F. "Jesu Weigerung, sich als 'gut' bezeichnen zu lassen," ZNW 9 (1908) 12-20.

Thomas, K. J. "Liturgical Citations in the Synoptics," NTS 22 (1975-1976) 205-214.

Tillard, J. M. R. "Le propos de pauvreté et l'exigence évangélique," NRT 100 (1978) 207-232, 359-372.

Trilling, W. Christusverkündigung, 123-145.

Wagner, W. "In welchem Sinne had Jesus das Prädikat agathos von sich abgewiesen?" ZNW 8 (1907) 143-161.

Walter, N. "Zur Analyse von Mc 10,17-31," ZNW 53 (1962) 206-218.

Ward, R. A. "Pin-Points and Panoramas: The Preacher's Use of the Aorist," ExpTim 71 (1959-1960) 267-270.

Wenham, J. W. "Why Do You Ask Me about the Good? A Study of the Relation between Text and Source Criticism," NTS 28 (1982) 116-125.

Zimmerli, W. "Die Frage des Reichen nach dem ewigen Leben," EvT 19 (1959) 90-97.

121. CONCERNING RICHES AND THE REWARDS
OF DISCIPLESHIP
(18:24-30)

18   24 When Jesus saw him becoming very sad, he said, "How hard it is for those who have money to enter the kingdom of God! 25 It is easier for a camel to pass through the eye of a needle than for a rich man to enter the kingdom of God." 26 Those who heard this statement began to say, "Well, then, who can be saved?" 27 Jesus said, "What is impossible for human beings is possible for God."

28 Then Peter said, "Look, we have left what we had and have followed you!" 29 Jesus said to them, "Believe me, no one who has left home or wife or brothers or parents or children for the sake of the kingdom of God 30 shall fail to receive many times as much in this age and, in the age to come, life eternal."

COMMENT

The Lucan Jesus, observing the magistrate's reaction to his proposal that he should sell his possessions and follow him, continues to comment on the problem that wealth can create in Christian life (18:24-30). Actually, his words deal with two topics: the problem that rich people have in entering the kingdom and the rewards of following Jesus. In this Gospel his comments are not addressed specifically to his "disciples" as in Mark 10:23; only at v. 28 does one learn that Peter is among those who "heard this statement" (v. 26).

Luke has derived the material for this episode from Mark 10:23-31; it is part of the Triple Tradition, the counterpart of it being found in Matt 19:23-30. By omitting reference to the disciples at the outset, Luke makes Jesus utter an exclamation (v. 24b), taken over word for word from Mark, "How hard it is for those who have money to enter the kingdom of God!" Luke then omits the repetitious Marcan v. 24 (feel for the same problem undoubtedly made Matthew reduce it to "Again, I say to you" [19:24]). In the saying about the camel and the needle's eye, Luke improves the Greek. He omits the amazement of the listeners at Jesus' comparison (Mark 10:26) and simplifies the statement of Jesus about what is possible to God (contrast Matt 19:26, which more closely follows Mark). Luke further modifies Peter's comment to Jesus, significantly substituting *ta idia,* "what we had," for the Marcan *panta,* "all things." Luke retains the *amēn legō hymin,* "believe me," and modifies slightly the list of things to be renounced by disciples who would follow Jesus in this way. The most significant modification here is the substitution of the motivation, "for the sake of the kingdom of God," for the Marcan form, "because of me and because of the gospel." In the promise of reward, Luke deletes the disturbing "with persecutions," which seems out of place in such a promise. Having used a form of Mark 10:30 in 13:30, Luke now omits it here (see p. 82). The upshot is that Luke has curtailed the Marcan form of this episode, but he has scarcely "greatly weakened" it, *pace* J. M. Creed, *The Gospel,* 226. Again, T. Schramm *(Markus-Stoff,* 142) rightly recognizes that this passage contains purely Marcan material; there is no evidence of the use of a source other than "Mk" here.

There are, however, two or more parts in the episode even in the Marcan Gospel. One senses that Peter's question and Jesus' answer to it in 10:28-30 are only loosely related to Jesus' preceding sayings. The latter have to do with the kingdom, whereas the promise uttered by Jesus in vv. 29-30 has to do with eternal life. Again, the query about "salvation" in 10:26 is not closely related to the sayings of Jesus in vv. 24-25. Whether they were all originally uttered as a unit is hard to say. Luke inherits them as a loose, topically arranged unit and curtails the episode slightly. The upshot is that this pericope joins the foregoing in relating eternal life, kingdom of God, salvation, and treasure in heaven.

From a form-critical point of view, Jesus' comments in this episode are to be classed as logia or isolated sayings. The first three (vv. 24b,25,27) are wisdom-sayings; that in vv. 29-30 is a prophetic saying (see *HST* 75, 81, 110-111). Notable in the episode is the form of the saying in v. 29b, "for the sake of the kingdom of God." Bultmann is inclined to think that "the logic of the saying" supports the Lucan formula as more original. The question then is whether Mark has introduced a formulation of his own, which Luke has avoided. Part of the problem is the Lucan avoidance of the word *euangelion* in his Gospel (see p. 148); part of it is the use of that word by Mark in what many regard as his own redaction. (See W. Marxsen, *Mark the Evangelist* [Nashville: Abingdon, 1969] 146; cf. G. Strecker, "Literarkritische Überlegungen zum *euangelion*-Begriff im Markusevangelium," *Neues Testament und Geschichte: Historisches Geschehen und Deutung im Neuen Testament: Oscar Cullmann zum 70. Geburtstag* [Zürich: Theologischer Verlag; Tübingen: Mohr (Siebeck), 1972] 91-104.)

Jesus' exclamation, in which he comments on the rich magistrate's reaction to his proposal, stresses the difficulty a rich person would have in entering God's kingdom. Though he was asked about inheriting eternal life, Jesus now makes it clear that such inheritance involves entry into the kingdom (see COMMENT on 18:18-23). Jesus does not say outright that it is impossible for a rich man, but his hyperbolic comparison of a camel passing through a needle's eye—Palestine's largest animal trying to get through its smallest opening—implies that it is almost so. Such is the problem of wealth (see p. 247). His exclamation and comparison then evoke from listeners an obvious question, posed in terms of salvation: Well, if rich people, who seem to be able to achieve everything else that they want, find it difficult, almost impossible, to enter the kingdom, who then can be saved? Jesus does not answer this question directly, but in a generic way gets across the all-important message: salvation of human beings depends entirely on God. God can bring even the rich to the state that they are saved. For if a person, rich or poor, is saved, it is achieved only by what is impossible for human beings, but not for God. It does not depend on wealth.

Hearing this, Peter, the spokesman, counters with an exclamation of his own: "We have left what we had and have followed you!" This is not a boast, but Peter's sincere query in the light of the foregoing comments of Jesus; recall that he, John, and James had left "everything" in 5:11. By way of reassurance, Jesus remarks that whoever gives up his possessions for the sake of the kingdom will receive in this life many times as much—but significantly leaves it unspecified—and in the age to come, life eternal. Noteworthy is the use of reward-language in this episode—and it is not exclusive to Luke. In effect, Jesus explains that "eternal life" is a form of "treasure in heaven" (v.

22). In the preceding episode Jesus made it clear that to inherit eternal life one had to keep the commandments; now he makes it clear that renunciation of possessions for the sake of the kingdom and following him is also something that can be rewarded by a "treasure in heaven" or "eternal life."

NOTES

18 24. *When Jesus saw him becoming very sad.* Even though the magistrate did not go off, his reaction to Jesus' proposal was enough to elicit from Jesus a further exclamation. Ms. B omits Jesus' name. The words "becoming very sad" are also omitted in mss. ℵ, B, L, *f* ¹, 1241, but are found in mss. A, D, R, W, Θ, Ψ, *f* ¹³, and the Koine text-tradition; they are bracketed in N-A²⁶. See *TCGNT* 168-169.

How hard it is for those who have money. I.e. to divest themselves of material possessions and all that they entail; recall "the mammon of dishonesty" of 16:9. See NOTE there. See the commentary on this verse in Hermas, *Sim.* 20.2.

to enter the kingdom of God! See NOTE on 4:43 and pp. 154-156. Contrast Luke 6:20. Luke uses the pres. indic. *eisporeuontai* instead of the Marcan fut. *eiseleusontai.* E. Klostermann *(Lukasevangelium,* 181) queries whether the present is being used in a futurist sense or whether Luke thinks of the kingdom as present. N. Perrin *(Rediscovering,* 143) thinks that both could be possible.

25. *easier for a camel to pass through the eye of a needle.* A hyperbolic comparison sums up the matter; again Jesus uses a grotesque figure. See 6:41-42; cf. Matt 23:24. The largest of Palestinian animals is compared with the tiniest of commonly known openings. Both "camel" and "eye of a needle" are to be understood literally. See O. Michel, *TDNT* 3. 592-594; S. Pedersen, *EWNT* 2. 609-611. In its own way, the comparison makes the same point as Jesus' saying about the "narrow door" (13:24).

To avoid the grotesque in the comparison, some commentators have suggested other explanations of the saying—both of them improbable: (1) Some would understand the "eye of a needle" as the name for a small entrance in a city wall through which a camel might squeeze only with the greatest difficulty. See G. Aicher, *Kamel und Nadelöhr,* 16-21, for a list of those who have proposed such an explanation. Plausible as it might seem, no one knows of the existence of such a named tiny entrance. (2) Ever since the patristic period others have suggested that *kámēlos,* which in Roman and Byzantine times would have been pronounced *káh-mee-los* (by itacism, according to which an *ēta* was pronounced as an *iōta),* should be understood as *kámilos,* which means "rope, hawser, ship's cable." Indeed, a few mss., undoubtedly affected by this interpretation, even read *kamilon* (S, *f* ¹³, 1010, etc.). This explanation was used by Origen, *Catena, frgs. in Matt.* 19.24 (GCS 41.166); Cyril of Alexandria, *Comm. in Matt.* 19.24 (PG 72.429D); Theophylact, *Enarr. in Matt.* 19 (PG 123.356D). See further J. Denk, "Camelus: 1. Kamel, 2. Schiffstau," *ZNW* 5 (1904) 256-257; "Suum cuique," *BZ* 3 (1905) 367; F. Herklotz, "Miszelle zu Mt 19,24 und Parall.," *BZ* 2 (1904) 176-177; "Nachtrag," *BZ* 3 (1905) 39. Again, plausible as it might seem, it takes something off the edge of Jesus' words. Note that the rabbinic saying about an elephant passing through the eye of a needle (Str-B 1. 828) dates from the fourth century and may well be dependent on this gospel saying.

In the best mss. (א, B, D) the "eye of a needle" is *trēmatos belonēs;* but mss. L, R, Θ read *trypēmatos,* a copyist's harmonization with the Matthean word for "eye," and mss. A, W, Ψ, *f*¹,¹³, and the Koine text-tradition have *trymalias,* a harmonization with the Marcan phrase *trymalias raphidos. Trymalia,* "perforation," is found in the LXX (Judg 6:2; 15:8,11; Jer 13:4; 16:16; 29:16 [49:16E]), used of "holes, clefts" in rocks; both Matthew and Luke avoid it. For the "needle" *(raphis,* used by both Matthew and Mark), Luke substitutes the classical Attic word *belonē.* W. K. Hobart *(Medical Language,* 60-61) tried to insist that the latter was a term for a "needle" used by doctors; but see ibid., 51-53; cf. H. J. Cadbury, "V. Luke and the Horse Doctors," *JBL* 52 (1933) 55-65, esp. 59-60.

than for a rich man to enter the kingdom. Recall 6:24.

26. *Those who heard this statement.* They are unnamed; contrast Matt 19:25, "the disciples," as in 19:23, derived from Mark 10:23. They exclaim in astonishment.

who can be saved? Recall 13:23. The *tís* refers not to "what rich person?" but simply to "what person?" Cf. Num 24:23, "Who shall live when God does this?"

27. *What is impossible for human beings is possible for God.* I.e. even the rich man can be saved by God; God can break the spell that wealth exercises over such people. Luke's simplification of the Marcan saying makes it more of an echo of the LXX of Gen 18:14. Cf. Luke 1:37. Actually, the saying is somewhat proverbial and more generic than the question posed; its emphasis is that salvation comes ultimately from God in any case.

28. *Peter.* Again he plays his role of the spokesman; note the "we." See NOTE on "Simon" (4:38) and COMMENT on 5:1-11.

we have left what we had and have followed you! The "we" is unspecified; in the Lucan Gospel it refers at least to Peter, John, and James. See 5:11 and NOTE. There Luke wrote that they left "everything" *(panta),* the very word that appears in Peter's statement in "Mk," but here Luke changes the latter to *ta idia,* lit. "(our) own things."

Recall that Peter and "the rest of the apostles and brothers of the Lord" are said in 1 Cor 9:5 to be "accompanied by a wife" *(or* by a sister as wife). What bearing that detail has on this saying of Jesus is not easy to say.

29. *Believe me.* Lit. "amen, I say to you." See NOTE on 4:24.

has left home or wife or brothers or parents or children. The first part of Jesus' answer refers to what human beings renounce for the sake of the kingdom. Luke uses only five objects of renunciation, whereas Mark 10:29, followed by Matt 19:29 (with a slightly different order), has seven: home, brothers, sisters, mother, father, children, fields. Is the fivesome related to the five commandments cited in 18:20? The Lucan form has preferred *goneis,* "parents," to the Semitic "mother and father" (see p. 110) but the sense of the saying is little affected. Ms. D adds "in this age."

for the sake of the kingdom of God. This motivation certainly suits the Lucan context better than the Marcan form, "for my sake and for the sake of the gospel." See vv. 16,17,24,25. But the phrase, "the kingdom of God," occurs five times earlier in Mark 10 too (vv. 14,15,23,24,25); this is part of the reason why some interpreters think in terms of Marcan redaction.

30. *many times as much in this age.* Ms. D and the OL version read "seven times as much" (possibly influenced by the LXX of Sir 35:10); ms. 1241 and the OS version have "a hundred times as much" (a scribal harmonization with Mark 10:30). What

this is is left unspecified. It must mean at least association with Jesus' new family. See 9:58,60,62. Note that Luke has omitted *meta diōgmōn*, "with persecutions," probably because he thought that incompatible with the reward promised.

and, in the age to come, life eternal. See NOTES on 10:25; 18:18. The Semitic distinction between "this age" and "the age to come" is found only here in the Lucan writings, and less clearly in 20:34-35. Cf. 16:8b. It reflects the Hebrew distinction between *hā-'ôlām hazzeh* and *hā-'ôlām habbā'*. Neither Philo nor Josephus makes use of this distinction of aeons, nor is it found in Qumran literature; but it occurs later in rabbinic literature. See Str-B 4/2. 815-857. In the first cl. of this comparison Luke follows Mark 10:30 in using *kairos*, not in the specific sense of determined time (see NOTE on 1:20), but as the equivalent of *aiōn*, which is found in the second cl. This second part of Jesus' answer thus promises a reward, "eternal life," which specifies the "treasure in heaven" of v. 22. Note how, with the omission of Mark 10:31, the Lucan form of this passage ends significantly with the phrase, "life eternal." See further H. Conzelmann, *Theology*, 112.

BIBLIOGRAPHY (18:24-30)

Aicher, G. *Kamel und Nadelöhr: Eine kritisch-exegetische Studie über Mt 19,24 und Parallelen* (NTAbh 1/5; Münster in W.: Aschendorff, 1908).

Celada, B. "Distribución de los bienes y seguimiento de Jésus según Lucas 18:18-30," *CB* 26 (1969) 337-340.

Galot, J. "La motivation évangélique du célibat," *Greg* 53 (1972) 731-758.

García Burillo, J. "El ciento por uno (Mc 10,29-30 par): Historia de la interpretaciones y exégesis," *EstBíb* 37 (1978) 29-55.

Klijn, A. F. J. "The Question of the Rich Young Man in a Jewish-Christian Gospel," *NovT* 8 (1966) 149-155.

Legrand, L. "Christian Celibacy and the Cross," *Scr* 14 (1962) 1-12.

Lehmann, R. "Zum Gleichnis vom Kamel und Nadelöhr und Verwandtes," *Theologische Blätter* 11 (1932) 336-338.

Minear, P. S. "The Needle's Eye: A Study in Form Criticism," *JBL* 61 (1942) 157-169.

122. THE THIRD ANNOUNCEMENT OF THE PASSION (18:31-34)

18 [31] Then Jesus took the Twelve aside and said to them, "We are now going up to Jerusalem, and there all that was written by the prophets will see fulfillment for the Son of Man. [32] He will be handed over to the Gentiles; he will be ridiculed, insulted, and spat upon.

33 They will flog him and kill him, and on the third day he will rise again." 34 But they did not comprehend any of this; this message was hidden from them, and they failed to realize what was being said to them.

COMMENT

At this point in the travel account the Lucan Jesus proceeds to instruct the Twelve in a specific way, announcing once again the destiny that awaits him in Jerusalem (18:31-34).

Luke continues to follow the Marcan order of material, inserting what corresponds to Mark 10:32-34, the third of the well-known announcements of the passion in that Gospel. In Mark it came closely on the heels of the two preceding ones (8:31; 9:31). But the Lucan expansion of the travel account with the copious material from "Q" and "L" (9:51-18:14) has brought it about that this so-called third announcement occurs almost nine chapters later than the two corresponding earlier announcements (9:22,43b-45). Moreover, Luke has included other material which has also announced in one way or another the coming opposition (see 12:50; 13:32-33; 17:25, and COMMENT on 9:22; cf. p. 91).

Whereas 9:22 was relatively close in its wording to Mark 8:31, 9:43b-45 was much more independently redacted. The same is true of this announcement in 18:31-34. Luke omits all reference to Jesus' being on the road to Jerusalem (Mark 10:32a) and the other introductory comments about the fear of the disciples (v. 32b,c). He begins with a participial cl. taken over from Mark 10:32d and adds his own typical introduction *(eipen pros autous* [see p. 116]). At first Luke follows the wording of v. 33a, but then redacts it with a typically Lucan reference to fulfillment of what was written by the prophets. Verses 32-33 cast in the pass. voice what Mark 10:33c-34 has in the act. As in 9:22, Luke again substitutes "on the third day" for the Marcan "after three days." Finally, Luke's pen composes v. 34, the evangelist's own comment on the incomprehension of the Twelve—which corresponds to nothing in Mark. It repeats the substance, but not the wording, of 9:45. In sum, then, though this episode is inspired by "Mk," it is considerably redacted by the Lucan pen. It stands in contrast to Matt 20:17-19, which is also Marcan-inspired; though it shortens the sayings, it follows the Marcan word order much more closely than Luke. T. Schramm *(Markus-Stoff,* 130-132) treated together the three announcements of the passion and was of the opinion that a "non-Marcan-type" of passion prediction had also influenced both Matthew and Luke, in addition to the Marcan. I find this opinion difficult to accept for this Lucan announcement, as I did for that in 9:43b-45 (see p. 812). The Lucan redaction of "Mk" is more likely. See also G. Schneider, *Evangelium nach Lukas,* 372; I. H. Marshall, *Luke,* 689.

From the standpoint of form criticism, this passage belongs to Sayings of Jesus. On the problem of the announcement as a *vaticinium ex eventu,* see COMMENT on 9:22.

As one draws near to the end of the Lucan travel account, one realizes the significance of this announcement by the Lucan Jesus about his coming fate. The next episode will reveal that Jesus has come to Jericho and hence is within a short distance of that city of destiny, Jerusalem. The announcement that he now makes, directed to the Twelve (in dependence on "Mk"), takes on great importance. The first two announcements occurred in the crucial chap. 9 (on which see pp. 757-758); now the third comes as the travel account, for which much in that chapter was preparing, is drawing to a close.

This announcement, however, is not a mere repetition of earlier ones. (1) Luke omits reference to the chief priests and Scribes, who—according to Mark 10:33—would condemn the Son of Man to death and deliver him to the Gentiles. In the Lucan form he is to be delivered to "the Gentiles" directly, but by whom is not said. (2) Luke does not omit the details found in Mark 10:33c-34, as he did in 9:43b-45 (cp. Mark 9:30-32), but he implies that the Gentiles will inflict the treatment so detailed. (3) Luke relates all this to the fulfillment of what was written by the prophets. (4) He adds his own comment, uttered three times over, about the incomprehension of the Twelve. In all, this announcement of the passion is preparing for the Emmaus episode, wherein the proof from prophecy will be spelled out in detail (24:27,44-45). Luke has further taken over a detail from early Christian kerygmatic preaching and joined it to the announcement of Jesus' passion and death—cp. 1 Cor 15:3-4, "according to the Scriptures." To be sure, it is now formulated in Lucan terminology.

Just as the Marcan third announcement depicted Jesus making it to "the Twelve" (10:32d), so too the Lucan. Likewise derived from Mark is the detail of "going up to Jerusalem" (v. 31a = Mark 10:33a) and what is to happen to "the Son of Man" (v. 31c = Mark 10:33b). Whereas Mark listed six things that would happen, Luke has seven, adding the detail of an insult. But Luke casts the first four in the pass., whereas the last three are retained in the act. As did Mark, so Luke says, "he will rise again." (Cp. Matt 20:19: "he will be raised.")

Luke sees the incomprehension of the disciples related to God's plan of salvation-history. Though Jesus speaks quite plainly in vv. 32-33, the import of it all is lost on them. They do not comprehend the fulfillment of what was written about by the prophets. Not until their eyes are opened will they comprehend. Thus, Luke in his own way is presenting an awareness of early Christians, which one finds expressed in the Johannine Gospel too (see 2:22; 12:16; cf. 11:51-52).

NOTES

18 31. *took the Twelve aside.* I.e. from those who were listening to him (v. 26), among whom Peter has already been identified (v. 28). Luke has used *paralambanein,* "take along with," in 9:10,28; 11:26; 17:34-35. In this instance it is derived from Mark 10:32c.

the Twelve. See NOTE on 6:13 and COMMENT on 6:12-16.

We are now going up to Jerusalem. For "going up" to the city (or the temple), see 2:42; 18:10; 19:28; Acts 3:1; 11:2; 15:2; 21:12,15; 24:11; 25:1,9; but the use is not exclusive to Luke, as Mark 10:33 reveals. Luke uses again *Ierousalēm.* See NOTES on 2:22; 10:30.

all that was written by the prophets will see fulfillment. Lit. "all that has been written by the prophets will be fulfilled," i.e. be brought to an end by God (theological pass.; see NOTE on 5:20), even though what will be done to him will be done by human beings. Thus Luke relates the coming passion of Jesus to the execution of the plan of salvation-history. See p. 180. Recall 13:32 and cf. Acts 2:23. Only Luke among the Synoptic evangelists uses the vb. *telein* in the sense of "fulfill" (12:50; 22:37; Acts 13:29), and sometimes, as here, of the fulfillment of the prophecies recorded in the OT. Cp. John 19:28,30; Rev 17:17.

For the pf. of *graphein* to express what has been "written" in Scripture, see Luke 4:17; 7:27; 10:26; 20:17; 21:22; 22:37; 24:44,46; Acts 13:29. Note, however, the substantive use of the pf. ptc. *gegrammenon* (sg. or pl.), which is distinctively Lucan.

by the prophets. Cf. Acts 2:23; 3:18; 17:3; 26:22-23.

for the Son of Man. As in the other two announcements derived from Mark, this title again appears (on its meaning see NOTES on 5:24; 9:22 and p. 210). The dat. of this title can be understood with either *gegrammenon* (i.e. written or "prescribed for Him as His course" [A. Plummer, *The Gospel,* 428]) or with the vb. *telesthēsetai* (i.e. "will be fulfilled for the Son of Man"). Many commentators prefer the former interpretation, but the latter seems preferable, since Luke never gives references to what prophets he has in mind (nor will he in chap. 24), and we have no way of telling what was prescribed in the OT as the course of the Son of Man. It is better to leave the *panta ta gegrammena* vague and understand it globally in the Lucan way: whatever was written by the prophets will see fulfillment for the Son of Man.

32. *handed over to the Gentiles.* Luke takes the pass. vb. *paradothēsetai* from Mark 10:33b and joins it with the indir. obj. of the act. form of the same vb. (which he omits) of 10:33c. Thus he eliminates reference to the chief priests and Scribes of the Jews. This detail is not found in the first announcement (Mark 8:31; cf. Luke 9:22); in the second (Mark 9:31; cf. Luke 9:43b-45) it was said that he would be "handed over into the hands of men" *(anthrōpōn).* The *anthrōpoi* become in Mark 10 at first the chief priests and Scribes, who later hand him over to "the Gentiles." In 20:20b we shall learn what is implied here (contrast Mark 12:13). In the Lucan Gospel it is not said by whom the Son of Man would be delivered. But he is to be handed over to "the Gentiles," which is noteworthy, given the tendency in the Lucan passion narrative to play down the involvement of the Romans.

H. Conzelmann *(Theology,* 201) is right when he says that "even when Luke uses the word *paradidonai* there is no trace of the idea of atonement." Apart from the misuse of the word "atonement" here, we can agree with this estimate. But it should also be noted that the double occurrence of the same vb. in Mark 10:33 is equally devoid of any soteriological significance. The same could be said of Matt 20:18-19. But why should one look for an expression of such significance in a text like this? (On the problem created by the word "atonement" in English, see my articles "The Targum of Leviticus from Qumran Cave 4," *Maarav* 1 [1978] 5-23; "Reconciliation in Pauline Theology," *No Famine in the Land* [eds. J. W. Flanagan and A. W. Robinson; Missoula, MT: Scholars, 1975] 155-177, esp. 158; reprinted, *TAG* 162-185, esp. 165-166.)

he will be ridiculed, insulted, and spat upon. The first and third of these acts are derived from Mark 10:34 (where they are used in the act.). Luke's redactional pen has added *hybristhēsetai,* "he will be insulted." Some mss. (D, L, 700, 1241, etc.) omit it (in the interest of harmonization). The shift to the pass. makes it somewhat unclear who inflicts such treatment on the Son of Man; but "the Gentiles" are presumably meant. Did Luke introduce the "insult" because of the connotation of *hybris* in the Greek world? W. Grundmann *(Evangelium nach Lukas,* 356) thinks so: "That is a Greek expression which above all had a great significance in tragedy. The tragedy of the Gentiles is played out in the passion of the Son of Man, on whom outrage is poured." Perhaps, but it seems a little farfetched.

What is predicted here will find fulfillment in the Lucan passion narrative, when Jesus is actually ridiculed (22:63; 23:11,36), in both word and deed. See further F. G. Untergassmair, *EWNT* 1. 1085-1087. "Insult" appears later too, but with a different vb., *blasphēmein.*

33. *flog him and kill him.* Lit. "flogging, they will kill him." Again, Luke derives these words from Mark 10:34; but did he understand them as an allusion to Isa 50:6, "I gave my back to those who flogged me, my cheeks to those who plucked my beard; my face I shielded not from buffets and spitting"?

on the third day. See NOTE on 9:22.

he will rise again. Luke preserves the intrans. use of *anastēsetai* from Mark 10:34 (contrast *egerthēnai* in 9:22). On the Lucan use of this vb., see p. 195. Cf. 1 Thess 4:14 and 1:10.

34. *But they.* Unstressed *kai autoi.* See p. 120.

did not comprehend any of this. The Lucan complaint echoes that said of Mary and Joseph in 2:50. It is now predicated of the Twelve, for whom God's plan of salvation is not per se evident—it needs to be properly revealed. Three times over in this verse Luke stresses this incomprehension.

this message was hidden from them. Again, Luke uses a favorite Septuagintism *(ēn kekrymmenon,* see p. 122). Cf. Luke 9:45b.

they failed to realize what was being said to them. Only in the post-resurrection experience will they comprehend. See 24:13-35. This verse amounts to Luke's excuse of the Apostles. Cf. H. Conzelmann, *Theology,* 56.

BIBLIOGRAPHY (18:31-34)
(in addition to the titles given in 9:22 and 9:43b-45)

Haenchen, E. *Der Weg Jesu,* 360-362.
Schmid, J. *Matthäus und Lukas,* 133-134.
Schneider, G. *Verleugnung,* 36-39.
Varro, R. "Annonce de la passion et guérison de l'aveugle de Jéricho selon S. Luc, 18, 31-43," *Ami du clergé* 78 (1968) 25-27.
Zimmermann, H. *Jesus Christus: Geschichte und Verkündigung* (Stuttgart: Katholisches Bibelwerk, 1973) 263-269.

123. THE HEALING OF THE BLIND MAN AT JERICHO (18:35-43)

18 35 As Jesus was drawing near to Jericho, a blind man happened to be sitting by the roadside begging. 36 Hearing a crowd passing by, he asked what was going on. 37 Someone told him, "Jesus the Nazorean is passing by." 38 Then he shouted out, "Jesus, Son of David, have mercy on me!" 39 Those in the lead rebuked him that he should be quiet; but he cried out all the more, "Son of David, have mercy on me!" 40 Jesus stopped and ordered the man to be brought to him. When he had drawn near, Jesus asked him, 41 "What do you want me to do for you?" "Sir," he answered, "I want to see again." 42 Jesus said to him, "Regain your sight! Your faith has brought you salvation!" 43 At once he was able to see again. He kept following Jesus, glorifying God; and all the people who saw it gave praise to God.

COMMENT

As the Lucan Jesus continues on his way to the city of destiny, he approaches the town of Jericho, which, as the reader has already learned (10:30), is not far from Jerusalem. Before Jesus enters Jericho, he encounters a blind man sitting by the road who hails him as Son of David and asks him for compassion. Jesus restores the man's sight, giving occasion for the glorification and praise of God (18:35-43).

This Lucan scene is clearly related to the cure of the blind man, Bartimaeus, in Mark 10:46-52, as well as to the two scenes in the First Gospel in which the Matthean Jesus cures two blind men each time (9:27-31 and 20:29-34). In Mark 10 and Matthew 20 the miracle takes place as Jesus leaves Jericho, but here it occurs before he enters the town. In Luke Jesus merely says, "Regain your sight!" whereas in Mark, "Go your way," and in Matthew Jesus *touches* the eyes in pity. Many have been the attempts across the centuries to harmonize or explain away the differences of these accounts: Three different cures of blind men; two different towns of Jericho, the Old and the New; one man, Bartimaeus, cured as Jesus entered Jericho, the other as he left. (For details, see A. Plummer, *The Gospel,* 429.) Obviously, the accounts were not composed to exercise the ingenuity of interpreters who would try to defend their historicity. The account of a cure of a blind person in the vicinity of Jericho has given rise to different literary traditions about it.

Luke has derived this episode from "Mk," but for some reason he has omitted the Marcan scene which immediately follows on the announcement of the passion and which precedes the Marcan parallel to this scene, viz. Mark 10:35-45. That Marcan scene tells of Jesus' conversation with the sons of Zebedee, who have asked him to grant them places of honor when he would come into his glory (10:35-40 [= Matt 20:20-23]). In reply, Jesus speaks of the cup that he must drink and of the baptism which he must undergo—using a saying similar to what Luke has in 12:50. But in dropping that episode, Luke also omits the sequel to it: the annoyance of the other ten disciples at the sons of Zebedee and Jesus' comment to them all about service of one another as the mark of those who would be the "great ones" among them and about his own role: "The Son of Man did not come to be served but to serve and to give his life as a ransom for many" (10:45). Why Luke was moved to omit this last verse in particular is a mystery. Because of his omission of it, he has often been said to have toned down the "soteriological significance" of "Jesus' suffering or death" (H. Conzelmann, *Theology,* 201). (See further p. 219.) Yet there is nothing in the Marcan verse which ill suits Luke's view of soteriology. He does not avoid "ransom" language, for he uses the vb. *lytrousthai,* "redeem" in 24:21 (indirectly speaking of it as a hoped-for effect of the Christ-event); he has already used the n. *lytrōsis,* "redemption," twice in the infancy narrative (1:68; 2:38). In Acts 7:35 he presents Moses as a type of Christ and calls him *lytrōtēs,* "redeemer." Whether the omission of the Marcan verse means that Luke has no theology of the cross, however, is another matter (see pp. 219-220). Here it need only be noted that Luke has not just eliminated Mark 10:45, but the whole episode (vv. 35-45). Part of the reason for the omission may be his use of the equivalent of Mark 10:38-39 in 12:50 and his use of the incident of the strife among the disciples for a comment at the Last Supper (22:24-27 [see the COMMENT there]). Whether 19:10 should be considered a Lucan variant of Mark 10:45 may be debated; it is certainly not as clear or as expressive. The omission has indeed eliminated from the Lucan Gospel the clearest expression of the soteriological value of Jesus' life in the Synoptics (by contrast it is retained in Matt 20:28). (See further F. Bovon, *Luc le théologien,* 176-177.)

In deriving the present episode of the cure of the blind man from Mark 10: 46-52, Luke modifies it somewhat. In the Marcan v. 46 Jesus has passed through Jericho and, as he leaves the town, encounters blind Bartimaeus. The Lucan Jesus, however, encounters him as he approaches the town (v. 35); this is an adjustment made by Luke in view of the next episode in which Jesus meets Zacchaeus *in* Jericho—in an episode exclusive to this Gospel, inserted into a block of Marcan material (see p. 67). In vv. 36-37 Luke's redaction better explains the situation: the blind man hears the crowd passing and inquires about it (instead of merely hearing "that it was Jesus of Nazareth"). Verse 38 corresponds closely to Mark 10:47c, and v. 39 is a slightly redacted form of 10:48. In v. 40 Luke reduces the details of the Marcan description of the blind man's coming to Jesus. Verse 41 is a Lucan redaction of Mark 10:51, making use of *kyrie* instead of the Semitic *rabbouni,* as does Matt 20:33 (because of 20:30, and also Matt 9:28). In v. 42 Luke inserts the impv. *anablepson,* "Regain your sight!" before the end of the Marcan formula. In v. 43 he adds to the end of the Marcan conclusion two characteristic formulas about "glorifying God" and people praising him, thus reducing somewhat the effect of the end of the Marcan story with its reference to the cured man "following" Jesus on the road. T. Schramm *(Markus-Stoff,* 143-145) rejects the idea that Luke has used in this episode any source other than "Mk" ("er folgt nur Mk"). The Lucan redaction of "Mk" is clear when one compares it with Matt 20:29-34 and sees what that evangelist has done with it. Schramm, however, is strikingly silent about the common omission of the details in Mark 10:49-50 by both Matthew and Luke, as well as of the name of the blind man.

Form-critically considered, the episode is a miracle-story, a healing narrative (see *HST* 213; he considers the Marcan form "a late formation," having the "secondary" characteristics of the naming of the blind man and the association of a miracle with the "Son of David"—but are these clear signs of community creation?). M. Dibelius *(FTG* 43, 51), however, considered the episode to be a paradigm "of a less pure type." But certainly the interest in the story lies more in its narrative than in Jesus' stereotyped words in Mark 10:52 (= Luke 18:42), efficacious as they may be. Elsewhere (ibid. 87) Dibelius seems to sense this.

This is the fourth and last miracle-story in the lengthy Lucan travel account, which like the others (13:10-17; 14:1-6; 17:11-19) relieves the monotony of the long list of sayings.

The Lucan Jesus is again seen in this episode making use of his power to relieve an afflicted human being of physical evil (recall 4:14,36; 5:17 [see pp. 579-580]). A blind man's sight is restored to him, and this bounty is accorded because of the faith which he has, which prompts him to cry out to Jesus, recognizing him as the Son of David (on the implications of this title see pp. 216-217). He cries to David's descendant and begs for compassion and mercy. His cry is an echo of that of the ten lepers in 17:13 and of the rich man in Hades in 16:24. Whereas Abraham could do nothing for the latter, Jesus' gracious attitude brings restoration to an outcast of humanity—one afflicted with physical evil, who had to pass his days by a roadside begging. In thus healing the man, Jesus implicitly affirms that he is the Son of David. In giving sight to the blind, he fulfills what was said of him earlier (4:18; 7:22, with allusion to Isa 61:1).

Coming immediately after the announcement of the passion, which the Twelve did not comprehend (18:31-34), this episode depicts a physically blind person coming to physical sight, but also recognizing in Jesus what others did not want him to recognize: "Those in the lead rebuked him that he should be quiet" (v. 39 [Were the Twelve among them?]). The blind man is presented as the foil to the uncomprehending Twelve. But the episode also prepares for Jesus' royal entry into Jerusalem, in foreshadowing the use of the title "Son of David" on that occasion.

NOTES

18   35. *As Jesus was drawing near.* Lit. "it happened, in his drawing near to Jericho, (that) a certain blind man was sitting . . ." Luke again uses his favorite *egeneto de* + a finite vb. without the conj. *kai* (see p. 119) in fashioning the introduction to this scene. He also employs *en* + dat. of the articular infin. as an indication of time (ibid.). On the use of *engizein,* see p. 112.

to Jericho. See NOTE on 10:30 and p. 170. Luke has taken over the name of the town because it has already been mentioned in his Gospel and thus suggests the proximity of Jesus to Jerusalem. Cf. 19:11. One may wonder how the Lucan Jesus has got to Jericho after what was said in 17:11. K. H. Rengstorf *(Evangelium nach Lukas,* 212) thinks that he may have come there via Perea. That is hardly suitable for the Lucan geographical perspective. In reality, we are not to ask; Luke has taken the locality over from Mark.

a blind man. Lit. "a certain blind person." See p. 111. Luke omits the name used in Mark, "the son of Timaeus, Bartimaeus" (probably = Aramaic *bar Ṭimai,* not found elsewhere). For speculation about the meaning of the name across the centuries, see V. Taylor, *Mark,* 448. R. Bultmann *(HST* 213) considered it possible that the name was "put into Mark at a later date, as it does not occur in Matthew or Luke." Taylor likewise considered it as possibly "a scribal gloss." The explanatory phrase, preceding the name itself in Mark, is strange. See H. Balz, *EWNT* 1. 479.

begging. The preferred reading is the ptc. *epaitōn* (from mss. ℵ, B, D, L, T, etc.), but some others (A, R, W, Θ, Ψ, *f*[1,13], and the Koine text-tradition) read *prosaitōn,* a form close to the n. *prosaitēs,* "beggar," used in Mark 10:46c. The meaning is not seriously affected. The blind man was probably sitting on the roadside near the entrance to the town.

36. *Hearing a crowd passing by.* I.e. like a group of pilgrims making their way toward Jerusalem. Cf. Luke 2:41,44. See NOTE on 3:7. So Luke clarifies what the blind man was actually hearing. Cp. Mark 10:47.

he asked what was going on. Lit. "inquired what this might be." See NOTE on 15:26. On the use of the optative in an indirect question, see p. 108.

37. *Someone told him.* Lit. "they reported to him," the indef. third pl. (see ZBG § 1), functioning like German *man* or French *on.*

Jesus the Nazorean. The name *Iēsous ho Nazōraios* is used again in Acts 2:22; 3:6; 4:10; 6:14; 22:8; 26:9. It is not, however, exclusively Lucan, being also found in Matt 2:23; 26:71; John 18:5,7; 19:19. In this Lucan passage mss. D and *f* ¹ read *Nazarēnos,* "the Nazarene," but this is probably a copyist's harmonization of the Lucan text with Mark 10:47, where that is the preferred reading, or with Luke 4:34; 24:19. Many commentators take *Nazōraios* and *Nazarēnos* as merely literary variants for "Nazarene." See H. Kuhli, *EWNT* 2. 1117-1121. Both forms have typical endings for Greek proper adjs. *(-aios,* like *Pharisaios,* "Pharisee," *Saddoukaios,* "Sadducee," *Essaios,* "Essene" [as in Philo]; *-ēnos, Gerasēnos,* "Gerasene" [8:26], *Essēnos,* "Essene" [as in Josephus]). But it is by no means certain that *Nazōraios* simply = *Nazarēnos,* and the matter has often been debated. The main interpretations are: *Nazōraios* is a Greek proper adj. formed from: (a) Greek *Nazara,* a variant of the village name *Nazaret, Nazareth* (see NOTE on 4:16), hence "a person from Nazareth, a Nazarene." Appeal to this form, however, does not explain the long *ō,* which cannot be ignored. (b) Hebrew *nāzîr,* "one consecrated by vow" (to God—see NOTE on 1:15), hence "one consecrated," a designation which would fit Jesus as one set apart for God's service. Yet it still does not explain the presence of the long *ō.* Moreover, some translations of the OT grecize the Hebrew adj./n. as *Naziraios* (just what one would expect); the asceticism associated with the Nazirite vow otherwise, is not, however, attributed to Jesus in the gospel tradition. (c) Hebrew *nēṣer,* "shoot, sprout," as in Isa 11:1, "A twig will come forth from the stump of Jesse, and a shoot *(nēṣer)* will blossom from its roots," said of a descendant expected to sit on the Davidic throne. In Aramaic targums of the Byzantine period *nēṣer* was given a clear messianic sense; and under the influence of Rev 22:16 ("I am the root and the offspring of David") patristic writers applied the Isaian term and idea to Jesus. See e.g. Justin Martyr, *Dial.* 126.1. This term may well underlie the eventual Hebrew name used for a "Christian," *noṣrî* (a name not attested in first-century Hebrew—how old is it?). Cf. Acts 11:26; 24:5. But it is still a problem to explain the long *ō;* nor can the shift from *ṣ* to *z* be accepted without further ado. (d) Aramaic *nāṣōrayyā',* allegedly "observers," a name found in later Mandean writings for a group related to John the Baptist. But there is no evidence for the use of such a name in first-century Palestine; and the use of the emphatic sibilant *ṣ* at this period of Aramaic needs further investigation. For a detailed discussion of these etymologies, along with the names of scholars who have proposed them, see R. E. Brown, *Birth,* 209-213, 223-225.

Probably the best explanation of *Nazōraios* at the moment is to regard it as a gentilic adj. meaning "a person from Nazara/Nazareth," but with the possible added nuance of either *nāzîr,* "consecrated one," or *nēṣer,* "sprout, scion" of Davidic lineage. The "scion of David" is found in Qumran literature (4QFlor 1:11; 4QPBless 1:3-4), used of a messianic figure. This title for Jesus may also represent one that comes from evangelists in Stage III of the gospel tradition, when more than *Nazarēnos* was being understood by it and more was being read back into earlier stages of the tradition.

38. *Jesus, Son of David.* The Davidic descent of Jesus has already been referred to in 1:27,32; 2:4. On its pre-Lucan and pre-Marcan use, see pp. 216-217. It will appear again in 20:41,44, where further discussion of it will be found. See NOTES there; cf. E. Lohse, *TDNT* 8. 478-488. There is no reason to think that "Son of David" on the lips of a blind man would have been heard with merely a political connotation. In the Lucan story, since the title surfaces here for the first time, it must be presupposed that the blind man has heard about Jesus' healing activity (see 4:14,37; 5:17) and that he knows what the reader of this Gospel knows of Jesus' origins.

It is, of course, another question why in Stage I of the gospel tradition he would expect a miracle, a healing, from a "Son of David." Because of this issue, Bultmann and others have regarded this episode as a creation of the early Christian community. E. Schweizer *(Evangelium nach Lukas,* 192) tries to explain this as a development of a Jewish belief in the powers of David's son Solomon over demons. See Str-B 4. 533-534. But that is a later rabbinic tradition and cannot be predicated of first-century Palestinian Judaism without further ado. Is there any awareness in pre-Christian Judaism or in that contemporary with the NT writings of an association of a messianic figure or a "Son of David" with a (miraculous) healing activity? It is often denied. See C. Burger, *Jesus als Davidssohn,* 44; F. Hahn, *Titles,* 189-190, 254. But cf. K. Berger, "Die königlichen Messiastraditionen des Neuen Testaments," *NTS* 20 (1973-1974) 1-44, esp. 3-9; D. C. Duling, "Solomon, Exorcism, and the Son of David," *HTR* 68 (1975) 235-252. Luke uses the title here because it was in "Mk," but it has no special meaning or function in this Gospel, such as it has in the Matthean Gospel.

have mercy on me! See NOTE on 16:24; cf. Matt 9:27; 20:30. So cries an afflicted outcast of human society, who expects compassion from Jesus.

39. *rebuked him.* See NOTE on 4:35.

should be quiet. The mss. B, D, L, P, T, W, Ψ read *sigēsē* (followed here), whereas mss. ℵ, A, R, Θ, 063, *f*[1,13], and the Koine text-tradition read *siopēsē,* "should keep silence." The meaning, however, is not seriously altered.

but he. Here Luke uses the literary *autos de.* See p. 120.

40. *When he had drawn near.* Luke substitutes a gen. absol. for Marcan parataxis (10:51). See p. 108.

41. *What do you want me to do for you?* The question is taken over word for word from Mark 10:51.

Sir. Luke, who usually avoids Semitic words in his sources (see p. 58), now substitutes *kyrie* for Marcan *rabbouni,* "my Master." See NOTES on 5:8,12 and p. 203.

I want to see again. Lit. "that I may see again," i.e. that is what I want!

42. *Regain your sight!* Lit. "see again," an impv. added by Luke based on the vb. in the question inherited from Mark 10:51. Cf. Acts 9:17-18.

Your faith has brought you salvation! Jesus repeats a stereotyped comment found in other miracle-stories. See NOTE on 5:20; 7:50; 8:48; 17:19.

43. *At once.* The Lucan favorite adv., added to "Mk," stresses the instantaneous cure. See NOTE on 1:64.

He kept following Jesus. As in Mark 10:52; but Luke omits "along the road." This omission is noteworthy since use of the phrase would have otherwise suited his concern about following Jesus on the road. See NOTE on 5:11; cf. pp. 241-242.

glorifying God. Recall 2:20; 5:25,26; 7:16; 13:13; 17:15; cf. 23:47.

all the people. This is a Lucan addition, since there is nothing like it in "Mk." See NOTES on 7:29; 1:10; cf. 2:10; 3:21; 8:47; 9:13; 19:48; 20:6,45; 21:38; 24:19; Acts 3:9,11; 4:10; 5:34; 10:41; 13:24; cf. H. Conzelmann, *Theology,* 164 n. 1. *Laos* is the Septuagintal word for God's people, and the frequency with which Luke uses it from now to the end of his Gospel is striking (it will appear nineteen times), and it is often used in contrast to the leaders of Jerusalem (esp. from 19:47-48 on). Mark never uses "all the people," Matthew has it only once (27:25), and John only once (8:2). The added comment shows wherein Luke's interest really lies, more in the reaction of the people than in the miracle itself.

gave praise to God. Recall 2:13,20; cf. 19:37. See NOTE on 4:15.

BIBLIOGRAPHY (18:35-43)

Burger, C. *Jesus als Davidssohn,* 42-46, 107-112.

Fisher, L. R. " 'Can This Be the Son of David?' " *Jesus and the Historian: Written in Honor of Ernest Cadman Colwell* (ed. F. T. Trotter; Philadelphia: Westminster, 1968) 82-97.

Fuchs, A. *Sprachliche Untersuchungen zu Matthäus und Lukas: Ein Beitrag zur Quellenkritik* (AnBib 49; Rome: Biblical Institute, 1971) 45-170.

Haenchen, E. *Der Weg Jesu,* 369-372.

Kertelge, K. *Die Wunder Jesu,* 179-182.

Ketter, P. "Zur Lokalizierung der Blindenheilung bei Jericho," *Bib* 15 (1934) 411-418.

Kodell, J. "Luke's Use of *Laos,* 'People,' Especially in the Jerusalem Narrative (Lk 19,28-24,53)," *CBQ* 31 (1969) 327-343.

Meynet, R. "Au coeur du texte: Analyse rhétorique de l'aveugle de Jéricho selon saint Luc," *NRT* 103 (1981) 696-710.

Pillarella, G. "Sedebat secus viam mendicans (Luc. 18,35)," *Palestra del clero* 38 (1959) 1085-1087.

Robbins, V. K. "The Healing of Blind Bartimaeus (10:46-52) in the Marcan Theology," *JBL* 92 (1973) 224-243.

Roloff, J. *Das Kerygma,* 121-126.

Schramm, T. *Markus-Stoff,* 143-145.

Trilling, W. *Christusverkündigung,* 146-164.

124. ZACCHAEUS
(19:1-10)

19 ¹ Jesus entered Jericho and was passing through it. ² There was a man there named Zacchaeus who was a chief toll-collector and quite wealthy. ³ He was eager to see who Jesus was, but because of the crowd he could not, for he was short of stature. ⁴ So he ran on ahead and climbed a sycamore tree in order to catch sight of Jesus as he would pass by. ⁵ When Jesus came to the place, he looked up and said to him, "Zacchaeus, hurry and come down, for I must stay at your house today." ⁶ He hastened to get down and was very happy to welcome him. ⁷ But all those who saw this grumbled at Jesus and said, "He has gone to lodge with a sinner." ⁸ Zacchaeus, however, just stood there and said to the Lord, "Look, Sir, I give away half of what I own to the poor. If I have extorted anything from anyone, I pay it back four times over." ⁹ Jesus said to him, "Salvation has come to this house today! For this man too is a son of Abraham! ¹⁰ For the Son of Man has come to *seek out* and to save *what was lost.*"[a]

[a] Ezek 34:16

COMMENT

As Luke comes near the end of the travel account, he inserts into the block of Marcan material (p. 67) which he has been using a story about Jesus' encounter with a chief toll-collector in the town of Jericho. He sees in this outcast of Palestinian society yet another of the "lost" whom Jesus has come to save (19:1-10). This episode thus brings to an end that part of the Lucan travel account which has been called the "Gospel of the Outcast" (see COMMENT on 15:1-7). In particular, it recalls chap. 15 as a whole.

Luke has derived this episode basically from his special source "L" (see p. 84); there are traces in it of Lucan redaction, the extent of which is, however, quite debated. It certainly includes much of his favorite vocabulary (e.g. *dierchesthai,* "pass through"; *kai idou,* "and behold"; *eipen pros* + acc. [vv. 5,8,9]; the absolute use of "the Lord" [v. 8]; unstressed *kai autos* [vv. 2,3]);

but the abundance of parataxis is undoubtedly pre-Lucan. (See further J. Jeremias, *Die Sprache,* 275-277.)

The story of Zacchaeus seems to be related to the call of Levi and his banquet in 5:27-32. J. M. Creed *(The Gospel,* 228), R. Bultmann *(HST* 34), S. M. Gilmour *(IB* 8. 320), and others have considered it to be a "later and secondary" counterpart of the call of Levi (as the healing of the ten lepers was seen by some commentators to be to that of the leper of Mark 1:40-44), i.e. the fictive elaboration of a minimal tradition into an ideal scene. However, this scarcely accounts for the concrete details of this episode, especially for the name Zacchaeus, the climbing of the tree, and the localization of the scene in Jericho (see further W. Grundmann, *Evangelium nach Lukas,* 358-359).

Bultmann *(HST* 33) may be right that the episode is "not a unitary composition," because apart from the redacted introductory v. 1, vv. 8 and 10 may have been added to the original form of the story. Verse 8 presents Zacchaeus' statement of his position; it disturbs the sequence from the murmuring of the crowd to Jesus' comment in the third pers., for v. 9 could easily follow on v. 7. Verse 8, moreover, suits a well-known Lucan theme and is marked with Lucan vocabulary *(statheis de, eipen pros* + acc., the absol. "the Lord," *ta hyparchonta).* Finally, it brings it about that *eipen pros* in v. 9 takes on a meaning that is peculiar in comparison with the usual sense of that idiom in Lucan writings. Did Luke insert that verse, or was it already part of the tradition? There is no unanimity among the interpreters. (See further J. Dupont, *Béatitudes,* 2. 250-251.) I am inclined to regard it as a Lucan insertion.

The matter of v. 10 is less clear. It is a saying appended to the story; it can rightly be compared with that in 5:32, but it has been wrongly compared with those in 7:50; 17:19, *pace* E. Schweizer, *Evangelium nach Lukas,* 192; those stereotypes are different. This may well have been an addition in "L" already, and so I prefer to regard it. See further J. Dupont, *Béatitudes,* 2. 251-253. Though the vocabulary may seem Lucan, part of it at least may be an allusion to Ezekiel which could well be pre-Lucan.

The reason for hesitation in all of this comes from the amount of traditional language in the whole passage over against the specifically Lucan. (See J. Jeremias, *Die Sprache,* 275-277.)

Form-critically considered, the episode is probably to be classed as a pronouncement-story, with its climax in v. 9, "Salvation has come to this house today! For this man too is a son of Abraham!" Bultmann *(HST* 33-34) has classed it with his biographical apophthegms. M. Dibelius, however, discussed it *(FTG* 51, 118) under both of his headings, paradigms and legends, calling it a "genuine personal-legend," full of anecdotal detail (name, place, occupation, condition, stature, activity). But V. Taylor *(FGT* 75-76) considers the Zacchaeus episode to be a Story about Jesus, because "the interest appears to lie in the incidents themselves rather than in the words of Jesus."

That is certainly truer of this episode than of many of the other pronounce-ment-stories that Taylor would reclassify. The Son of Man utterance in v. 10, which undoubtedly stems from a context in the ministry of Jesus that is lost to us and has been secondarily appended to this story, is regarded by R. Bultmann *(HST* 152) as an I-saying about Jesus' coming. If that is the correct designation for it, it then raises again the question of the surrogate meaning of the title Son of Man (see p. 209).

No matter how one analyzes the growth and development of the episode, one has to explain it in its present Lucan form, in which the statement of Zacchaeus in v. 8 creates a problem. Do the pres. tenses, *didōmi* ("I give away") and *apodidōmi* ("I give, pay back"), express a customary action of Zacchaeus, or do they express a repentant resolve or pledge? Are they "itera-tive or customary" presents or "futuristic" presents? To interpret them in the former sense seems to many commentators to understand Zacchaeus' state-ment as a bristling protest of self-righteousness. A. Plummer *(The Gospel,* 435) sums up his opposition to this mode of interpretation thus: "(1) this makes Zacchaeus a boaster; (2) *ton hyparchontōn* has to be interpreted 'in-come,' whereas its natural meaning is 'that which one has possessed all along, capital'; (3) *apodidōmi* must follow *didōmi,* and it is improbable that Zacchaeus was in the habit of making fourfold retribution for inadvertent acts of injustice. . . . Standing in Christ's presence, he solemnly makes over half his great wealth to the poor, and with the other half engages to make repara-tion to those whom he has defrauded." Plummer cites the futuristic interpre-tation of Zacchaeus' statement from patristic and modern writers. (See also J. M. Creed *[The Gospel,* 231]; J. Schmid *[Evangelium nach Lukas,* 287: "a promise for the future, the fulfillment of which only shows the genuineness of his conversion"]; I. H. Marshall *[Luke,* 697-698: "The present tense . . . is futuristic, and expresses a resolve"]; M.-J. Lagrange *[Luc,* 489: "To attribute to him that he is in the habit of giving away half of his belongings to the poor . . . would be to transform the publican into a Pharisee"]). But this vener-able understanding of Zacchaeus' statement is not without its problems.

Is it clear that Zacchaeus is really a "sinner" in the episode who repents (cp. 7:37-48; 5:20-21), despite the estimate of him attributed to "all" who were accompanying Jesus? He does not beg Jesus for mercy (cp. 17:13; 18:38) or express any sorrow (cp. 15:21; 18:13). Jesus makes no reference to Zacchaeus' faith (cp. 7:50; 8:48), repentance or conversion (cp. 15:7,10), or discipleship. Even E. Schweizer *(Evangelium nach Lukas,* 194), who speaks of Zacchaeus' "following" in the "world" and its institutions, had to admit that "Nachfolge (in the literal sense) is missing in the scene verbally and substantively" (ibid. 193). Or, as R. C. White has put it, the "form-critical analysis of the pericope reveals none of the expected characteristics of such a [salvation] story" ("Vindication for Zacchaeus?" 21). For in the episode Jesus pronounces not forgiveness but the vindication of Zacchaeus: Jesus announces salvation "to this house" because he sees that Zacchaeus is innocent, a true "son of Abraham," despite the post that he held, which branded him otherwise. *Pace* R. Bultmann *(HST* 57), he does not give "consolation to the sinner who needs it."

This problem was sensed years ago by F. Godet *(Commentaire* 2. 336-338), who admitted that one could understand *didōmi* as futuristic, "As of now I give away . . . ," but queried what sense it would make to understand *apodidōmi* similarly, "As of now I pay back . . ." whenever I extort. Would a repentant sinner foresee so clearly his new lapses? And even so reputable a grammarian of NT Greek as A. T. Robertson *(A Grammar of the Greek New Testament in the Light of Historical Research* [New York: C. H. Doran, 1914]), having listed the vbs. as futuristic (pp. 869-870), subsequently classed them under the iterative or customary present (p. 880).

Part of the problem is the modern reader's reluctance to admit that the Lucan Jesus could declare the vindication of a rich person who was concerned for the poor and even for his own customary conduct.

On his way through Jericho Jesus notices the activity of a wealthy toll-collector of the town, who because of his tiny stature takes special pains to catch a glimpse of the celebrated preacher who is passing. By way of reaction to Zacchaeus' initiative, Jesus too takes the initiative and invites himself to the toll-collector's house for lodging, probably for overnight. He goes willingly to a rich man, not to a poor man, to a toll-collector, not to an ordinary citizen, and to one regarded as a "sinner," not to one of the upright. Jesus' initiative evokes grumbling and criticism from the accompanying crowd: "He has gone to lodge with a sinner," an accusation which recalls the comments made in 5:30; 7:34. At which criticism Zacchaeus bristles; he may be a "sinner," but he gives half of his possessions to the poor and makes reparation in generous fashion for any extortion in which he may have been involved. Zacchaeus is not self-effacing, but he is not boasting either; cp. the antecedent protestation of the self-asserting Pharisee in 18:11-12 with the deferential *defense* that the toll-collector makes here. Jesus' pronouncement of salvation (v. 9) is not made to reveal his own power in forgiving sin or to imply that former sins of extortion are remitted (recall the condition in Zacchaeus' statement, "if," not "when"). His words are addressed to the grumbling crowd; they vindicate Zacchaeus and make it clear that even such a person can find salvation: He too is a "son of Abraham." This does not mean that Zacchaeus *has become* a child of Abraham in some spiritual sense (as in Pauline usage, Gal 3:7,29; Rom 4:16-17); Jesus seeks lodging from him because he is really an offspring of Abraham, a Jew, with as much claim to the salvation which Jesus brings as any other Israelite (cf. 13:16). The added saying of v. 10 sums up not only this episode (that an outcast Jewish toll-collector can be reckoned among the "lost" to whom Jesus' salvation is open), but also the soteriological message of the entire travel account—and the Lucan Gospel: As Son of

Man, Jesus has come to seek out and save the lost, alluding to the self-description of Yahweh in Ezek 34:16. There Yahweh depicted himself as a shepherd who would seek out Israel, his flock, which has been scattered, to rescue it and bring it back "from the peoples," to feed it on the mountains of Israel: "I will seek the lost, bring back the strays, bind up the crippled, give strength to the weak, and watch over the fat and the strong; I will feed them with justice."

One cannot read this passage without noting the allusions and overtones in it to ideas that have been expressed elsewhere in the Lucan Gospel: to elements in the ethical preaching of John the Baptist (3:10-14, see p. 465); to the exclusively Lucan parable of the Pharisee and the toll-collector (18:9-14); to the episode of the rich magistrate (18:18-23). In particular, Zacchaeus is seen as a foil to the last-named, who was called (in a special challenge addressed in the second sg.) to sell *all* that he had, but who could not bring himself to do so. Now wealthy Zacchaeus divests himself of half of all his possessions. He is presented in this episode as an exemplary rich person who has understood something of Jesus' ministry and message and concern for the poor and the cheated. Lastly, following on the episode of the blind man who sought compassion from Jesus that he might "see again" (18:41), this episode presents a wealthy inhabitant of Jericho taking unwonted steps "to catch sight of Jesus" as he passes. The two episodes are fitting scenes at the end of the lengthy Lucan travel account, for they prepare the reader for Jesus' approach to Jerusalem as "the Son of David" and the one who brings salvation to the "lost." For further discussion of the relation of this episode to Lucan theology as a whole, see W. P. Loewe, "Towards an Interpretation."

The soteriological thrust of the episode is evident; in its own way it makes a contribution to Lucan theology. It is, however, another question whether v. 10 is intended by Luke to express what the saying of Jesus recorded in Mark 10:45 (and omitted in Luke) actually expresses. Some commentators think it does (e.g. G. Schneider, *Evangelium nach Lukas,* 374); but v. 10 is a "variant" of that only in a very generic sense.

NOTES

19 1. *Jesus entered Jericho.* This episode presupposes the setting of the preceding one, and the formulation of the introduction here is Lucan; but that does not mean that the town was not associated with Zacchaeus in the pre-Lucan form, *pace* G. Schneider, *Evangelium nach Lukas,* 377. Cf. E. Schweizer, *Evangelium nach Lukas,* 193. If T. Schramm *(Markus-Stoff,* 143-144) were right, Luke would have transferred the introductory reference to Jericho from this episode to the preceding one. Perhaps. On Jericho, see NOTE on 10:30 and p. 170.

and was passing through it. Luke has already used *dierchesthai* in 2:15,35; 4:30; 5:15;

8:22; 9:6; 11:24; 17:11; and he will use it again twenty times in Acts. Its use vaguely continues the idea of Jesus' movement toward Jerusalem. See p. 825.

2. *There was a man there.* Lit. "and behold a man," *kai idou* is used. See p. 121.

named Zacchaeus. Lit. "by name Zacchaeus," a person who is otherwise unknown. He bears the name of the father of a famous rabbi from the end of the first century, Yoḥanan b. Zakkai. In later ecclesiastical tradition he becomes the bishop of Caesarea (Ps.-Clementine *Hom.* 3.63,1; *Recogn.* 3.66,4), appointed to the task by Peter against his will; Clement of Alexandria identified him with Matthias *(Strom.* 4.6,35).

Zakchaios is the grecized form of the Hebrew name Zakkai or Zaccai (Neh 7:14; Ezra 2:9 [which appears in the LXX as *Zakchos]),* found also in 2 Macc 10:19 as the name of an officer in the army of Judas Maccabee. Hebrew *zakkay* means "clean, innocent," a term often used in parallelism to *ṣaddîq,* "righteous, upright." *Pace* many commentators on this passage, it has nothing to do with *Zĕkaryāh,* "Zechariah," and is in no way an abbreviation of it. Zacchaeus is a Jew in the episode, and that is the point of v. 9. This has to be insisted on, despite Tertullian *(Adv. Marc.* 4.37,1), "allophylus . . . ex commercio iudaico adflatus." Cf. A. Loisy *(L'Evangile selon Luc,* 433), for whom Zacchaeus is the type of "gens sans loi." But then why give him a Jewish name?

Luke uses, as he frequently does elsewhere (e.g. 1:5; 5:27; 10:38; 16:20), the dat. of *onoma,* lit. "by name," before the proper n.; this is by no means exclusively Lucan, despite its frequency in his writings, being well attested in both classical and Hellenistic Greek and in the LXX. See BDF § 197, 160.

a chief toll-collector. The word *architelōnēs* occurs only here in all Greek literature up to this time. Did Luke coin it? Hardly. See NOTE on 3:12. Among the various places in Palestine where toll-stations were located, Jericho is often mentioned (see O. Michel, *TDNT* 8. 98); but this passage itself seems to be the only evidence for it.

and quite wealthy. Lit. "and he (was) wealthy"; cp. 18:23. The implication is that Zacchaeus' wealth came from his activity as a toll-collector. On the unstressed *kai autos,* used twice in this verse, see p. 120.

3. *eager to see who Jesus was.* Is this a mere expression of curiosity, as many commentators understand it (e.g. M.-J. Lagrange, *Luc,* 488; J. Schmid, *Evangelium nach Lukas,* 286)? Or is there something more, a vague discernment of something special about this person who was passing through and of whom he had heard (4:14,37)? There is no need to compare him with Herod (9:9), whose motivation was sign-seeking (23:8); the treatment of Zacchaeus in this episode does not suggest that.

because of the crowd he could not. Lit. "he was unable from the crowd," but the prep. *apo* is used in a causal sense (as in 21:26; 22:45b; 24:41; Acts 11:19; 12:14; 22:11). Cf. Josephus, *Ant.* 9.4,3 § 56. On *ochlos,* see NOTE on 3:7.

short of stature. I.e. Zacchaeus, not Jesus. See NOTE on 2:52. This is a mere physical description of the man; we are not to conclude from the episode that Zacchaeus "finds real 'stature' through the welcome extended him by Jesus," *pace* F. W. Danker, *Jesus and the New Age,* 191. The Greek *hēlikia* nowhere bears the connotation that the English word has in that understanding.

4. *ran on ahead.* The best reading is *prodramōn eis to emprosthen,* lit. "running ahead into the front," in mss. ℵ, A, B, K, Q, Δ, Θ, *f* 1,13, etc.; but some others read *prosdramōn,* "running to" (L, R, W, Γ, Ψ, 063, etc.). Some (D, R, W, Ψ, etc.) omit the

prepositional phrase. The problem is that the prepositional phrase is redundant. The suggestion of M. Black *(AAGA*[3] 116) that it is a mistranslation of Aramaic *lĕqadmûteh,* "to meet him," is farfetched. He appeals to Gen 29:13, where *liqrā'tô* occurs in the MT, but where the LXX has, not *emprosthen,* but *eis synantēsin autō.* What the evidence of the later Cairo Genizah targum E means in this connection is baffling. Moreover, as I. H. Marshall *(Luke,* 696) notes, "Zacchaeus' action in climbing a tree hardly supports this" interpretation.

a sycamore tree. Greek *sykamorea* occurs only here in the NT and never in the LXX. See NOTE on *sykaminos* (17:6); cf. C.-H. Hunzinger, *TDNT* 7. 758-759. J. Wellhausen *(Das Evangelium Lucae,* 103) thought that, if Jesus were really "passing through" Jericho, Zacchaeus would have climbed, not a tree, but a roof, and so argued that the scene must really have taken place elsewhere, outside of a town. R. Bultmann *(HST* 65-66) seems to agree with Wellhausen, but is aware of the objection of G. Dalman *(Orte und Wege Jesu* [3d ed.; Gütersloh: Bertelsmann, 1924] 15) that Jesus could still have been in the outskirts of Herodian Jericho. J. Finegan *(Archeology,* 85) has, however, more correctly noted that Wellhausen was obviously thinking of "a city of tight-packed houses where roofs were indeed available for the ascent of Zacchaeus, but not trees." That, he notes, might have been true of OT Jericho (Tell es-Sultan), but not of Herodian Jericho, where "the excavators draw their closest comparison with Roman cities such as Rome, Tivoli, and Pompeii. Like such cities NT Jericho undoubtedly had its parks and villas, avenues and public squares, where fine trees grew."

to catch sight of Jesus as he would pass by. Lit. "that he might see him because he was about to pass through that (way)." Cp. 18:40-41.

5. *looked up and said to him.* Luke uses *eipen pros* + acc. See p. 116. At the beginning of this verse, ms. D reads, *egeneto en tō dierchesthai eiden auton kai eipen* . . . "It happened, in his passing through, (that Jesus) saw him and said . . ."

Zacchaeus. One misses the point of the story if one asks how Jesus would have known his name or his occupation. Cf. John 1:47-48, for a Johannine way of explaining such knowledge.

I must stay at your house today. I.e. It is destined that I do this (on the connotation of impers. *dei,* "it is necessary," see p. 180). The adv. *sēmeron* will occur again in v. 9b and has special connotation in Lucan salvation-history. See p. 234. The personal pron. *sou* is put in the Greek text in emphatic position at the end of the sentence. Zacchaeus gets more than he has hoped for. A celebrity has come to a tiny man who showed initiative.

6. *and was very happy to welcome him.* Lit. "and rejoicing, welcomed him," i.e. into his house. Not a word is said of Zacchaeus' faith.

7. *all those.* Again, Lucan hyperbole. See NOTES on 3:16; 4:15; 9:11. No distinction is made between Jesus' disciples and the rest of the crowd.

grumbled at Jesus. The same vb. *(diagongyzein)* was used in 15:2 of critical Pharisees and Scribes. Cf. 5:30.

gone to lodge with a sinner. Lit. "has entered to find lodging with a sinful human being." See NOTE on 5:30. The vb. *katalyein* lit. means "loosen down," i.e. unharness pack animals (for the night), and hence "lodge, put up for the night." See NOTE on 2:7. Cf. Gen 19:2; 24:23,25.

8. *stood there.* Lit. "standing, he said . . ." Many commentators think that this

takes place inside Zacchaeus' house. E.g. E. E. Ellis *(Gospel of Luke,* 221): "at or after dinner"; M.-J. Lagrange *(Luc,* 489): "rising for a solemn toast." This is far from clear. Obviously in *such* a situation Zacchaeus' statement could sound like a boast. But Jesus' words in v. 9 are directed to the criticizing crowd. All that is meant is that Zacchaeus, having heard the grumbling of the crowd, stops and addresses Jesus deferentially.

said to the Lord. Again, *eipen pros* + acc. See p. 116. On the absol. "the Lord," see NOTE on 7:13.

Sir. See NOTE on 5:12.

I give away half of what I own to the poor. The pres. *didōmi* is to be taken as expressive of customary action. See 18:12. There is no need to understand it as futurist pres., "I am giving as of now (in pledge)." The half is to be understood of a voluntary offering (there is no indication of a regulation that he is following).

what I own. See NOTE on 8:3. As in Acts 4:32 the expression may be used more widely to mean also what one acquires.

the poor. See NOTE on 4:18.

If I have extorted anything from anyone. Lit. "if I have shaken anything down from anyone." See NOTE on 3:14; i.e. been involved in any transaction for personal gain exacted through kickbacks or blackmail. The implication is that he does not do this deliberately; but if he has discovered that he has been so involved, he takes action to repair it.

I pay it back four times over. I.e. Zacchaeus willingly restores the damage according to such regulations in the Pentateuch as Exod 21:37 (22:1E), "four sheep for a (stolen) sheep" (cf. 2 Sam 12:6); but Lev 6:5; Num 5:6-7 prescribe only an "added fifth." Compare the Palestinian restitution mentioned in Mur 19:10, a writ of divorce dated A.D. 111 (DJD 2. 105): *wmšlm lrb'yn,* "I am repaying (them [i.e. possessions destroyed or damaged in marriage]) fourfold." Cf. J. Dauvillier, "Le texte évangélique de Zachée et les obligations des publicains," *Recueil de l'Académie de Legislation* 5/1 (1952) 27-32. For later rabbinic interpretations of the OT regulations about restitution, see *m. Ketub.* 3:9; cf. Str-B 2. 250-251. Fourfold restitution is also known in Roman Law for *furtum manifestum.* See F. Raber, "Furtum," *Der kleine Pauly* 2. 647-649.

9. *to him.* Or possibly, "about him." See 20:19; cf. E. Schweizer, *Evangelium nach Lukas,* 192. The hesitation about the sense of *eipen pros* + acc. (for usual sense, see p. 116) comes from Jesus' following comment, which speaks of Zacchaeus in the third pers. His comment, however, is made for the benefit of the grumbling crowd (and thus seems to be better as a sequel to v. 7). But in the present Lucan context the comment is made to both Zacchaeus and the crowd—or better, to the crowd through him.

Salvation. The primary Lucan effect of the Christ-event surfaces on the lips of Jesus. See pp. 222-223. The restoration of even a Jew like Zacchaeus to a sound relationship with God is possible.

has come to this house today! Lit. "today *(sēmeron* in emphatic first position) salvation has occurred to this house" *(or* household, if *oikos* is to be understood as in Acts 10:2; 11:14; 16:15,31; 18:8). Some mss. (A, D) and the OS versions add the prep. *en,* "in" (this house). The saying, however, may have another connotation in that Jesus, the bringer of salvation, visits the house. The contrast of salvation coming to "this house" with the grumbling of the critical crowd is significant.

For this man too is a son of Abraham! I.e. despite his occupation as a toll-collector, he has not cut himself off from Israel; as much as any other Israelite, he is entitled to the blessings of Abraham, and especially to the form of those blessings now coming through Jesus. This is the real basis of the gift of Jesus and the salvation now available to Zacchaeus; *pace* E. Schweizer *(TDNT* 8. 365), though it might be the sole basis, the thrust of the story is such that Jesus' initiative in bringing salvation to "this house" corresponds to Zacchaeus' initiative. However, as I. H. Marshall *(Luke,* 698) points out, *kathoti,* "for, because," introduces an antecedent reason rather than a subsequent proof. Some commentators (E. E. Ellis, *Gospel of Luke,* 220-221; E. Klostermann, *Lukasevangelium,* 185), however, have tried to understand "son of Abraham" in a spiritual sense (= the Pauline usage).

10. *the Son of Man.* See NOTE on 5:24 and pp. 208-211.

has come to seek out and to save what was lost. Thus the Lucan Jesus is depicted as one sent not only to preach the kingdom (4:43), to fulfill Isaian utterances of consolation (4:18-19), but even to act as Yahweh told Ezekiel he would act toward his scattered people, as a shepherd. See pp. 154-155, 181, 188. The LXX of Ezek 34:16 reads: *to apolōlos zētēsō kai to planōmenon epistrepsō . . .* "I shall seek out what was lost and shall turn back what is going astray." Luke's Greek has recast the first three words and added "to save." An allusion to this verse of Ezekiel has been added in some mss. of Luke 9:55. See NOTE there; cf. Matt 18:11 (omitted in N-A[26]).

R. Bultmann *(HST* 155) considered this Son of Man utterance a "late formulation" because it turns the "apocalyptic title Son of Man on to the earthly Jesus"; for him it is therefore "an Hellenistic product." Similarly, F. Hahn, *Titles,* 36. But this is far from certain. See J. Jeremias, *TDNT* 6. 492; J. Dupont, *Béatitudes,* 2. 252-254. Moreover, as I. H. Marshall notes *(Luke,* 698), 1 Tim 1:15 shows what the saying would have been like in Hellenistic form. See further I. H. Marshall, "The Synoptic Son of Man Sayings in Recent Discussion," *NTS* 12 (1965-1966) 342-343. It is not impossible, however, that the title "Son of Man" has been secondarily introduced into an otherwise authentic saying of Jesus, who has indeed come to seek out and save what was lost. In *2 Clem.* 2.7 the title becomes *ho Christos,* "Christ."

BIBLIOGRAPHY (19:1-10)

Cocagnac, A.-M. "L'Evangile (Lc 19,10): Zachée, l'église et la maison des pécheurs," *AsSeign* os 91 (1964) 39-51; ns 62 (1970) 81-91.

Dupont, J. *Béatitudes,* 2. 249-254.

Ebel, B. "Das Evangelium der Kirchweihmesse (Lukas 19, 1-10), gedeutet im Geist der Väter," *Enkainia: Gesammelte Arbeiten zum 800jährigen Weihegedächtnis der Abteikirche Maria Laach am 24. August 1956* (ed. H. Edmonds; Düsseldorf: Patmos, 1956) 110-122.

Hahn, F. *Titles,* 36, 40-41.

Loewe, W. P. "Towards an Interpretation of Lk 19:1-10," *CBQ* 36 (1974) 321-331.

Löning, K. "Ein Platz für die Verlorenen: Zur Formkritik zweier neutestamentlicher Legenden (Lk 7, 36-50; 19, 1-10)," *BibLeb* 12 (1971) 198-208.

O'Hanlon, J. "The Story of Zacchaeus and the Lukan Ethic," *JSNT* 12 (1981) 2-26.

Rouillard, P. "Zachée, descends vite," *VSpir* 112 (1965) 300-306.
Salom, A. P. "Was Zacchaeus Really Reforming?" *ExpTim* 78 (1966-1967) 87.
Schneider, G. " 'Der Menschensohn' in der lukanischen Christologie," *Jesus und der Menschensohn* (eds. R. Pesch and R. Schnackenburg) 267-282, esp. 278-279.
Vogels, W. "Structural Analysis and Pastoral Work: The Story of Zacchaeus (Luke 19, 1-10)," *Lumen vitae* 33 (1978) 482-492.
Watson, N. M. "Was Zacchaeus Really Reforming?" *ExpTim* 77 (1965-1966) 282-285.
White, R. C. "A Good Word for Zacchaeus? Exegetical Comment on Luke 19:1-10," *Lexington Theological Quarterly* 14 (1979) 89-96.
——— "Vindication for Zacchaeus?" *ExpTim* 91 (1979-1980) 21.
Willcock, J. "St. Luke xix. 8," *ExpTim* 28 (1916) 236-237.

125. THE PARABLE OF THE POUNDS
(19:11-27)

19 [11] As they were listening to this, Jesus went on to add a parable, because he was now close to Jerusalem and people were thinking that the kingdom of God was going to appear immediately. [12] So he said, "There was once a man of noble birth, who journeyed to a distant land to acquire for himself the title of king, and so return. [13] But first he summoned ten of his servants and gave them ten pounds, saying to them, 'Do business with this while I am gone.' [14] His fellow-citizens, however, who disliked him, sent a delegation after him to say, 'We do not want this man to be king over us.' [15] When he returned with the title of king, he had those servants summoned to whom he had given the money, in order to find out what business they had done with it. [16] The first came and said, 'Sir, your pound has earned ten more.' [17] He said to him, 'Excellent! You are a good servant; because you have been trustworthy in a very little thing, you are to have authority over ten towns.' [18] Then the second one came and said, 'Sir, your pound has made five pounds.' [19] And to him he said, 'You too are to be over five towns.' [20] Then the other servant came and said, 'Here is your pound, Sir. I have kept it stored away in a handkerchief. [21] I was afraid of you, because you are a stern man; you carry off what you have not deposited and you reap what you have not sown!' [22] He said to him, 'You wicked servant! I shall judge you by your own words. You knew, did you, that I was a stern man, carrying off what I have not deposited and reaping what I have not sown? [23] Why, then, did you not put my

money in a bank account? I could at least have collected it with interest on my return.' 24 Then he said to his attendants, 'Take the pound
away from him and give it to the one with ten.' 25 'But, Sir,' they
exclaimed, 'he already has ten pounds!' 26 'I tell you, to everyone who
has more will be given; and from the one who has nothing even what
he has will be taken away. 27 However, as for those enemies of mine
who did not want me to be king over them, bring them here and
slaughter them before me.' "

COMMENT

The last episode in the travel account in the Lucan Gospel is a parable uttered
by Jesus about pounds entrusted to servants (19:11-27). Coming immediately
after the Zacchaeus incident (19:1-10), it makes its own comment on the
proper use of material possessions, and the two episodes together thus make
another contribution to the Lucan theme of the disciples' use of such possessions. Moreover, the Lucan form of this parable, with its reference to kingship, prepares for Jesus' own regal entry into Jerusalem in the episode that
follows upon it (19:28-40). But the parable is used in a context in which it
serves as a corrective to popular eschatological expectations, which Luke
introduces into this part of his Gospel. Even if the kingdom of God is "among
you" (17:21), there is a sense in which it is not to "appear immediately." On
Jerusalem as the terminus of the travel account, see p. 824.

The parable of the pounds has no counterpart in the Marcan Gospel, even
though Mark 13:33-37 may resemble it superficially, but it is related in some
way to the Matthean parable of the talents (see Matt 25:14-30). Yet the
differences between the two forms of the parable are such that commentators
are greatly divided over the proper interpretation of the relationship between
them.

In Matthew a man going off on a journey entrusts to three servants five,
two, and one talents. The first two do business with the talents and double
them, the third hides his in the ground. On his return the master rewards the
first two, setting them over many things and allowing them to share "the joy
of your master." But the third is condemned as "wicked and slothful," deprived of the talent entrusted to him (which is given to the one who has ten),
and further cast out into darkness where people weep and gnash their teeth
(25:30). Apart from the last verse, which is clearly a Matthean addition, and
parts of which he has used elsewhere (8:12; 13:42,50; 22:13; 24:51 [cf. Luke
13:28]), this form of the parable is fairly direct and simple. It is found in
Matthew's eschatological discourse, coming immediately after the parable of
the ten virgins, which concludes, "Be vigilant, then, because you know

neither the day nor the hour." In such a context the parable adds to vigilance for the master's return the notion of judgment about the responsible use of the goods the master has entrusted to his servants. The first two servants are not only "set over many things," but rewarded with a share in the master's joy, whereas the slothful servant is punished. The Christian disciple is thus exhorted not only to vigilance for the return of the Lord but warned to be armed with produce or income from that which was freely and graciously entrusted for the conduct of human life.

In Luke, the parable proper (roughly vv. 13-27) has much of the same thrust and buildup: A man going off on a journey entrusts to each of ten servants a pound or mina with which they are to do business in his absence. On his return, three are called to reckoning; the first two have made the pound work, tenfold and fivefold; but the third has hidden it away in a handkerchief. The first two are rewarded and set in authority over ten and five towns respectively, whereas the third "wicked" servant is deprived of his pound, which is given to the one with ten. Though the Lucan form says nothing more about the punishment of the wicked servant in exterior darkness, the main point of this much of the parable is similar to that of Matthew's. Christian disciples are again exhorted to vigilance for the return of the Lord and warned to be armed with produce or income from that which has been freely and graciously entrusted for the conduct of human life.

There is, however, more to the Lucan form of the parable, differences of considerable importance. These differences concern not merely such minor things as "talents" vs. "pounds" or the numbers (five, two, and one vs. one to each of ten—and reports on only three of the servants who make ten, five, and no pounds), or even the form of the reward (secular in Luke, both secular and spiritual in Matthew), but the significant context in which the parable is told and the additions made to it which alter the sense of the basic parable.

For in Luke the parable is uttered to offset a popular impression that the kingdom was to appear immediately (v. 11). This corrective heightens, indeed, the need for vigilance, but it also adds a dimension to the need for proper conduct of human life so that enough is made out of the pound graciously bestowed at the outset, while the master travels to "a distant land." This insinuates a delay in the appearance of the kingdom. Moreover, the man going off on a journey is not only "of noble birth," but he goes off "to acquire for himself the title of king" (v. 12). Though he is disliked by some of his fellow-citizens, who seek to thwart his obtaining the kingly authority (v. 14), he returns as king (v. 15a), not only to call the servants to an accounting, but to punish his enemy fellow-citizens (v. 27). A further minor variant is found in the added exclamation of the attendants (v. 25), "But, Sir . . . he already has ten pounds!" These additional verses in the Lucan form of the parable are only loosely connected to its main story line (which is common to Matthew and Luke). They create, however, the major problem in understanding the relationship between the two forms of the parable.

Older (mostly Roman Catholic) commentators often regarded the two forms as two distinct parables uttered by Jesus in different contexts and to different audiences. Thus, A. Feuillet, L. Fonck, N. Geldenhuys, P. Joüon, J. Knabenbauer, A. Plummer, P. Schanz, J. M. Vosté, T. Zahn, et al. Today, this solution is generally abandoned because of the obvious parallelism of the bulk of the two forms (Luke 19:13,15b-23,24b,26 = Matt 25:15,19-27,28,29), and especially because of such common (or nearly common) phrases as "Excellent . . . good servant" (19:17); "I was afraid" (19:21); "because you are a stern man" (19:21); "you reap what you have not sown!" (19:21); "wicked servant!" (19:22); "You knew, did you" (19:22); "reaping what I have not sown?" (19:22); "my money in a bank account" (19:23); "with interest on my return" (19:23); "Take the pound away from him" (19:24); "give it to the one with ten" (19:24); "from the one who has nothing even what he has will be taken away" (19:26). This parallelism seems to suggest that one parable is at the root of the two forms.

Another interpretation of the relationship of the two forms is to postulate that Luke and Matthew have derived the parable from "L" and "M" respectively. Thus, F. Hauck, A. Weiser, G. Schneider, T. W. Manson, J. Lambrecht, et al. This is certainly a more plausible solution, but it still does not explain adequately the bulk-similarity, especially in vv. 21-24a.

Many interpreters think that the bulk of the parable has been derived from "Q" by both Matthew and Luke (see p. 79; cf. S. Schulz, *Q: Die Spruchquelle,* 288-298). Is it possible, however, that the Lucan form of the parable (vv. 12-27) was in "Q" and has been reduced by Matthew? Some commentators have preferred this solution (e.g. M.-J. Lagrange, *Luc,* 490-492; J. Schmid, *Das Evangelium nach Matthäus* [RNT 1; 5th ed.; Regensburg: Pustet, 1965] 348-350). Because the reward given to the first two servants is authority over cities, this is interpreted to mean that the master was of kingly status from the outset. It is further argued that Luke would scarcely have so drastically modified a parable as to insert the additional verses (14,24a,25,27); that was not his custom. Moreover, it might seem likely that Matthew reduced the parable to make it sound like Matt 24:45-51 (parable of the faithful and prudent servant). Yet it is difficult to admit that Matthew would have so drastically reduced the parable if the Lucan form (vv. 12-27) stood in "Q"— especially since it would have suited his own context so well, viz. that of the eschatological discourse. It is difficult to explain what such a Matthean reduction would have served.

For this reason it is better to think that the bulk of the parable in Luke stood in "Q" in a form similar to Matthew, but with a few differences. It is more likely that "Q" had originally "ten servants," which Matthew has reduced to three, than that Luke would have introduced the ten only to forget about them almost immediately. Matthew has reduced and simplified the number of servants to the parabolic stereotype of three actors. But he has also changed the *mnas,* "minas, pounds" (which occur only in Luke in the NT), to *talanta* (which Matthew also uses in 18:24, but which Luke never uses). Thus Matthew obtains a more plausible amount of money with which the servants are to do business. Moreover, the reduction of a larger number to a smaller, as it exists in the Lucan form, is also found in other parables, in that of the great dinner (14:17-20, "those invited" become three who decline) and that of the dishonest manager (16:5-7, "his master's debtors" become two who change their bonds).

There is a further question about vv. 12,14,24a,27. Where did they come from, if they are not really part of the original parable? Two answers are given to this question today. Some commentators regard them as part of a separate parable (that of the throne-claimant), which has been fused with that of the pounds. Thus, W. E. Bundy, D. Buzy, G. B. Caird, E. E. Ellis, A. George, F. Hahn, A. von Harnack, E. Hirsch, J. Jeremias, G. D. Kilpatrick, P. Perkins, A. Schlatter, C. W. F. Smith, F. D. Weinert, J. Wellhausen, M. Zerwick, et al. This material would have been derived by Luke from "L," and he would have inserted it to explain the delay of the parousia because it depicts the master going to "a distant land." This solution has the advantage of tracing the additional material back to Jesus himself in some form and is supported by some traditional, non-Lucan phraseology which one detects in these verses.

Other commentators prefer to regard the additional verses as Lucan redaction, added to explain the delay in the appearance of the kingdom, which appears in v. 11 and has been composed by Luke himself. Thus, G. Bouwman, R. Bultmann, J. M. Creed, M. Didier, C. H. Dodd, E. Grässer, F. Hauck, A. Jülicher, E. Klostermann, A. Loisy, T. W. Manson, W. Michaelis, G. Schneider, S. Schulz, et al. It is not easy to judge between these two alternatives. In both cases, the solution answers the real problem about the loose connection that these verses have with the bulk of the parable itself. In favor of the latter solution, viz. Lucan redaction, is the obvious allegorizing feature which these verses give to the parable. The parable about vigilance and responsible human cooperation with God-given blessings has clearly taken on other nuances born of another time and place than Stage I of the gospel tradition.

In sum, then, v. 11 is to be ascribed to Lucan composition, as are vv. 12,14,15a,25,27. Lucan redaction is further detected in v. 13 *(eipan pros* + acc. [see p. 116]); v. 16 *(paregeneto* [p. 111]; *ho prōtos,* followed by *ho heteros);* v. 17 *(elachistō* [possibly]); v. 24a *(kai tois parestōsin eipen).* The rest (vv. 13a,15b,16b-23,24b,26) is to be ascribed to "Q." It should also be noted that Luke 19:26 is a doublet; this form is derived from "Q," whereas that in 8:18 is a redacted form of the "Mk" source (4:25; cf. p. 81).

A still further form of the parable is said to have been in the *Gospel of the Nazaraeans* § 18 (Hennecke-Schneemelcher, *NTApocrypha,* 1. 149): ". . . he [the master] had three servants: one who squandered his master's substance with harlots and flute-girls, one who multiplied the gain, and one who hid the talent; accordingly one was accepted (with joy), another merely rebuked, and another cast into prison. I wonder whether in Matthew the threat which is uttered after the word against the man who did nothing may refer not to him, but by epanalepsis to the first who had feasted and drunk with the drunken." This version is obviously a conflation of Luke's parable of the prodigal son and the Matthean form of this parable.

Form-critically, Luke 19:11-27 consists of a parable (vv. 12-24,27) with an appended dominical saying in v. 26 (the latter was already an appendage in "Q"). But vv. 12,14,15a,27 allegorize the parable proper. Together the parable and the allegorizing verses not only make their own points, but they serve as a corrective to v. 11c, the popular eschatological expectation of the appearance of the kingdom. Verse 25 is a Lucan addition.

What was the point of the parable as it was uttered by Jesus in Stage I of the gospel tradition? We may agree with C. H. Dodd *(Parables,* 118) that "the central interest lies in the scene of reckoning, and in particular in the position of the cautious servant." J. Jeremias finds the same emphasis *(Parables,* 61). But both of them find him to be the symbol of either the "pious Jew" (Dodd) or "the scribes" (Jeremias), to whom the word of God had been entrusted. Though this is not wholly impossible, it is far from certain. It seems more likely that Jesus would have been speaking to people in his own entourage to whom he had been entrusting his own message: "It has been granted to you to know the secrets of the kingdom of God" (Luke 8:10), and these disciples or "servants" of his are precisely the ones who are being admonished to do business with what has been entrusted to them in view of God's day of reckoning. (See further M. Didier, "La parabole des talents," 268; I. H. Marshall, *Luke,* 702.)

In the Lucan context, the parable takes on a further nuance in view of the corrective that the evangelist makes the parable give to the popular expectation of the appearance of the kingdom. Christian disciples are being taught that they have been entrusted with the "secrets of the kingdom," which are depicted as gracious bounties bestowed on them, and for which they may expect a reckoning depending on how responsibly they have trafficked with this God-given heritage. If the parable thus highlights the notion of rewards in human life and conduct, it also stresses the gratuity of the process which is involved. It makes clear that a Christian disciple can respond to such graciousness either with obedience (as do the first two servants) or with disobedience (as does the third). The emphasis falls on the latter by way of warning. For he has substituted for obedience to the master's command ("Do business with this") his own minimalist conception of cooperation and his own estimate of the master. He is not characterized in the Lucan form of the parable as "slothful" (as he is in Matt 25:26), but as "wicked" (pure and simple, i.e. disobedient). In the long run, he has not even done his duty and thus becomes an "unprofitable" servant (17:10) in still another sense.

The addition of the allegorizing verses make this lesson even clearer. For the man of noble birth who goes off to obtain a kingly title becomes Jesus the Son of God, who is about to begin his "ascent" to the Father from the city of destiny. In that ascent he will be recognized as king (i.e. as the glorified Messiah [see 24:26; Acts 2:32-36]) and will return in judgment (Acts 1:11; 3:20-21; 17:31). According to the allegorized parable, he will on his return do two things: (a) he himself will reckon with his servants to whom the blessings of his kingdom-preaching have been entrusted; and (b) he will take vengeance on his Palestinian compatriots who have not wanted him to be king over them (Luke 23:18; cf. Acts 3:17). For another view, see L. T. Johnson, "Lukan Kingship."

The ending of the allegorized parable in Luke is especially poignant. The pound given to the third servant becomes an added reward for the first servant (that detail has been inherited from "Q"). Despite the expostulation of the king's attendants, that the first servant already has ten, the seemingly arbitrary act of adding that extra pound to what the first has already acquired emphasizes that the retribution for human cooperation with the blessings of the kingdom, gracious as they are, will go far beyond human ability to measure either it or them. The Lord remains sovereign. He has graciously bestowed his bounty on his servants, and in the day of reckoning not only rewards them but does so far beyond all expectation or measured deserts.

This parable, in its Lucan form, has again been considered as a mark of Lucan anti-Semitism, with its frank reference to the slaughter of Jesus' enemies, "his fellow-citizens." It is perhaps more glaring here than in some of the other places where it has been allegedly found. Say what one will about it, it fits in with, on the one hand, the Lucan theme of the rejection of Jesus (which has been evident since 4:16-30); but, on the other, by the contrast of the good servants and the enemies it suits the other Lucan theme of the reconstituting of the people of God, which runs through his two volumes (see p. 191). After all, the good servants cannot be understood as Gentiles who become Christians. See further H. Conzelmann, *Theology*, 146.

NOTES

19 11. *As they were listening to this.* I.e. to Jesus' comments on Zacchaeus' defense statement and the grumbling of the bystanders (19:7-10). We are never told that Jesus actually entered Zacchaeus' house, *pace* E. Klostermann, *Lukasevangelium*, 186. Jesus and Zacchaeus are ostensibly still near the sycamore tree. Luke uses the gen. absol.

construction (see p. 108), referring to a vague audience, which would include the crowd (v. 7), disciples, and others (opponents).

went on to add a parable. Lit. "adding, he spoke a parable." Luke makes use of the aor. ptc. *prostheis* with a finite vb.; it is another Septuagintism (see p. 115 [cf. BDF § 419.4, 435b]), involving one of his favorite vbs. See p. 111. On "parable," see NOTE on 5:36.

because he was now close to Jerusalem. I.e. the goal of the travel account is noted, even though Jesus is presumably still in Jericho. Josephus *(J.W.* 4.8,3 § 474) tells us that this town was 150 *stadioi* distant from Jerusalem, i.e. about 27.75 kilometers. Whereas Jerusalem is over 2500 feet above sea level, Jericho is over 800 feet below it. The journey to the city of destiny, then, will still involve a climb, the beginning of an "ascent" which is to be undertaken in yet another sense. On the name *Ierousalēm,* see NOTES on 2:22; 10:30; cf. pp. 164-168, 824. The word order of this cl. differs in some Greek mss. (see the *app. crit.),* but the sense of it is not affected.

and people were thinking. Lit. "and they were thinking." To whom the pron. *autous* refers in this Lucan context is not clear; it has to be taken simply as indef. It is used to express a generic eschatological expectation. In the Lucan Gospel Jesus has already taught his disciples to pray that the kingdom may come (11:2), and at the beginning of Acts (1:6) they will ask the risen Christ whether he is about to restore "the kingdom" to Israel at that time. In later Jewish tradition it was thought that "the kingdom of Yahweh Sebaoth would be revealed to dwell upon Mt. Zion and . . . the might of Yahweh Sebaoth would be revealed over Jerusalem" *(Tg. Isa* 31:4-5). See H. Conzelmann, *Theology,* 74.

the kingdom of God. See NOTE on 4:43; cf. pp. 156, 232.

was going to appear. Lit. "was going to dawn or be lighted up." Cf. Josephus, *Ant.* 2.16,2 § 339; 7.13,4 § 333; *Orac. Sib.* 3.46-48; *Ass. Mos.* 10:1-7. See further S. Aalen, " 'Reign' and 'House' in the Kingdom of God in the Gospels," *NTS* 8 (1961-1962) 215-240, esp. 221. *Pace* L. T. Johnson ("Lukan Kingship," 150), *anaphainein* cannot be understood here as "was going to be declared."

immediately. On the Lucan use of this adv. *parachrēma,* see NOTE on 1:64. This time reference for the appearance of the kingdom is not put on Jesus' lips; Luke rather makes him utter a conflated parable which corrects this popular expectation. There is little connection between this expectation and Jesus' words to Zacchaeus.

12. *a man of noble birth.* The introductory phrase *anthrōpos tis,* "a certain man," has already been found in 10:30; 14:2,16; 15:11; 16:1,19; as here, it often has a modifier. For *eugenēs,* "of noble birth," see Acts 17:11; 1 Cor 1:26.

journeyed. The Lucan favorite *eporeuthē* is again used. See p. 169.

to a distant land. Cf. 15:13. This detail supplies the corrective to "immediately," at least by implication. Time is to elapse between the nobleman's departure and his return. Even though this allegorization of the parable is clearly present in the Lucan form, chronological detail is not absent in Matt 25:19, "after a long time." Cp. Mark 13:34.

to acquire for himself the title of king. Lit. "to get for himself a kingdom *(or* kingship)," i.e. to get from a Mediterranean sovereign the status of a vassal king. Though the detail may be derived from some real Palestinian historical incident, it is built into the parable only for verisimilitude.

Though the Romans had avoided the title *rex* for their own rulers for several centuries, they granted the title at times to certain ethnic rulers in the eastern provinces of the empire. Thus, in 40 B.C. Herod the Great by a *senatusconsultum* under Mark Anthony was empowered to "rule as king" *(basileuein)* and was feasted by Mark Anthony on "the first day of his reign" (Josephus, *J.W.* 1.14,4 § 284-285). But Herod had to acquire his kingdom, the former ethnarchy of Hyrcanus II, by defeating the Parthians with the aid of Roman troops. After the death of Herod the Great, Archelaus, his oldest son (by Malthace), inherited half of his father's kingdom according to a codicil in his will (i.e. Judea, Samaria, and Idumea). He too wanted the title of king and traveled to Rome in an attempt to obtain it (Josephus, *Ant.* 17.9,1-3 § 208-222; *J.W.* 2.2,2 § 18). In his case a delegation of fifty Palestinians, Jews and Samaritans, were sent by the people to oppose his kingship and to argue for autonomy (Josephus, *Ant.* 17.11,1-2 § 299-314; *J.W.* 2.6,1-2 § 80-92). Finally Augustus awarded him only the title of ethnarch. See further the instance of Herod Agrippa in Josephus, *Ant.* 18.6,11 § 238 (where *archē,* "rule," not *basileia,* "kingship," is used). For the sense of *basileia* here, see NOTE on 22:29.

13. *ten of his servants.* Lit. "his own ten servants," i.e. agents empowered to trade in his name in the then-existing finance system of Palestine.

ten pounds. Lit. "ten minas." The Greek *mna* appears only in this passage in the NT. As a monetary unit it is found widely in classical and Hellenistic Greek literature, in the papyri from Egypt (see MM 414), and in the LXX (1 Kgs 10:17; Ezra 2:69; Neh 7:71; 1 Macc 14:24). It is, however, a Semitic loanword, probably = Aramaic *mĕnā'* (related to the root *mny,* "count"). The Greek *mna* = a hundred Attic *drachmae* (roughly twenty–twenty-five dollars), and was only one sixtieth of a talent *(talanton),* the unit used in Matthew 25. The sum of one pound for each servant was, in any case, a pittance and scarcely represents abundant generosity on the part of the man of noble birth; soldiers of Mark Anthony regarded a gift of five hundred *drachmae* as stinginess (Appian, *Bell. civ.* 3.42 § 177). But to insist on that is to miss the point of the gratuitous gift made to the ten servants.

Do business. The Lucan form of the parable uses an impv., which imposes a command on the servants. Two of them obey it, the third does not. In Matt 25:15 the five, two, and one talents are given to the servants "each according to his own ability," which implies something different from the Lucan story in which they are regarded implicitly as equals.

while I am gone. The Greek vb. *erchesthai* is used in a peculiar way here, since its normal meaning is "come." Hence many commentators translate the cl., "until I come (again)." See E. Klostermann, *Lukasevangelium,* 186; BAGD 311. But this is to do violence to the prepositional phrase *en hō,* which *(pace* BDF § 383.1) is not attested elsewhere in the sense of "until." It means "while," and so *erchesthai* has to be understood in the more unusual, but attested, sense of "go." See Luke 9:23; 14:27; 15:20.

14. *a delegation.* Luke uses *presbeian,* the abstract form of the concrete *presbeis,* "envoys," actually used by Josephus in his story of Archelaus' opponents *(Ant.* 17.11,1 § 300).

15. *When he returned . . .* Lit. "and it happened, on his returning, having ob-

tained the kingship, that he ordered those servants summoned to him to whom . . ." Luke uses *kai egeneto* with the conj. *kai* and a finite vb. *(eipen)*. See p. 119.

with the title of king. Lit. "having obtained the kingship." Cf. Josephus, *Ant.* 17.13,1 § 339.

what business they had done with it. Some mss. (A, R, W, Θ, *f*[1,13], and the Koine text-tradition) read *tis tí diepragmateusato,* "what business one had done with it." But the better mss. (א, B, D, L, Ψ, etc.) have the pl., as used here.

16. *The first came.* This is followed by *ho deuteros,* "the second," in v. 18 and by *ho heteros,* "the other," in v. 20. Cf. the Lucan use of *ho prōtos,* "the first," in 14:18-20; 16:5,7.

has earned ten more. Lit. "has made ten in addition." That this is not an unlikely transaction for the Palestinian situation has been shown by J. D. M. Derrett *(ZNW* 56 [1965] 190).

17. *Excellent!* Or "well done"; the adv. *euge* is also used in the LXX (Job 31:29; 39:25; Ps 35:21).

trustworthy in a very little thing. Though *elachistos* is a favorite Lucan adj. (see p. 110), it may be derived in this case from "Q," where it would suit the small sum of one "pound" entrusted to the servant. Matt 25:21 reads rather *epi oliga,* "over a few (things)," a modification more adapted to his adjusted amounts. Cf. 16:10.

you are to have authority over ten towns. Lit. "be having authority over . . ." the impv. is periphrastic. Cf. 12:35. The "ten towns" are part of the kingdom to which the nobleman has acquired title. This secular reward is a Lucan redactional adaptation of the original to suit his allegorizing parable. It differs from the Matthean, which not only retains the secular reward (from "Q"), "I shall put you over many things," but also has a redactional addition, which has allegorized the original parable in its own way: "Enter into the joy of your Lord," i.e. have a share in the spiritual joy of the eschaton. See further J. Jeremias, *Parables,* 60 n. 42.

18. *the second one came and said.* Lit. "the second one came, saying"; so read the majority of the best Greek mss.; but ms. D reads, "The other one coming said." Cf. v. 20.

19. *You too are to be over five towns.* Lit. "you too be over five towns," expressed in this case with the simple impv. *ginou.* This saying repeats the (adjusted) reward of v. 17; the literary repetition of it is meant to heighten the contrast between the two good servants and the wicked one.

20. *the other servant.* The def. art. *ho* is omitted in a number of Greek mss. (A, W, Ψ, 063, and the Koine text-tradition), "and another came," but the best mss. (א, B, D, L, R, Θ, *f*[1,13], etc.) have the art. It was undoubtedly omitted in the first group to make the story smoother, for it initially spoke of "ten servants." The reading with the art. is the *lectio difficilior,* even though it represents the influence of the stereotyped parabolic threesome. It was probably so in "Q" already.

stored away in a handkerchief. Lit. "in a cloth for perspiration." The Greek *soudarion* is a loanword from Latin, *sudarium,* "sweat cloth," for face or neck. See Acts 19:12; John 11:44; 20:7. In Matt 25:25 the third servant went off and buried his talent in the ground; in either case the act is a sign of the servant's sloth (Matthew) or disobedience (Luke). *Pace* J. Jeremias *(Parables,* 61), the neglect of Palestinian insurance laws or customs has nothing to do with the sense of the parable.

21. *I was afraid of you.* The same note of fear is expressed in Matt 25:25. There is no need to sum up this fear as the core of the parable, constructed on an allegedly traditional saying which would reflect the postexilic sense of bitterness which Palestinian Jews experienced who thought that Yahweh had abandoned his chosen people (cf. Ps 119:120; Job 4:14; 23:13-17), whose mission it was to guard the traditions of the fathers in the time of Yahweh's absence from them. This would be to read far more into the parable than is there, *pace* L. C. McGaughy, "The Fear of Yahweh and the Mission of Judaism," 235-245. Cf. P. Perkins, *Hearing the Parables,* 149-150. It is an unnecessary allegorization of the parable. The fear is explained in the following phrases.

a stern man. The Greek adj. *austēros,* "severe, exacting, strict," is found in extrabiblical Greek texts for a governmental finance-inspector (Papyrus Tebtunis 315:19 [see MM 93]). Thus Luke uses for the master a term more appropriate than the Matthean description *sklēros,* "hard, cruel, merciless."

you carry off what you have not deposited. This cl. rings like a proverb and has been found to have counterparts in other Greek writers. See Josephus, *Ag.Ap.* 2.30 § 216; Plato, *Leges* 11.913C; Aelian, *Varia hist.* 3.46. Cf. C. Taylor, "Plato and the New Testament," *JTS* 2 (1901) 432; F. E. Brightman, "Six Notes," *JTS* 29 (1927-1928) 158-165, esp. 158. It is difficult to say whether Luke has added this saying to "Q" or whether Matthew has omitted it, since it is absent in the latter's form of the parable. The former is more likely.

you reap what you have not sown! I.e. you carry off the produce of another's farming at the harvest time. The master, who has been depicted in vv. 17,19 as richly rewarding the good servants, is now caricatured as one who exploits others.

22. *He said.* The historic pres. *legei* is retained from "Q." See p. 107.

wicked servant! In Matt 25:26 he is called a "wicked and slothful" servant, i.e. his "ability" (25:15) is there defined in terms of sloth. In the Lucan form, he is called merely "wicked" because of his disobedience. Compare the eulogy in v. 17.

I shall judge you. Or "I shall condemn you," since the vb. *krinein* sometimes carries the nuance of unfavorable judgment (= *katakrinein).* See BAGD 452 and NOTE on 20:47. In some mss. the vb. *krinō* is accented as the pres., not the fut.; others omit the acc. pron. *se.* The master does not try to defend himself, but judges the servant on his own terms and accusation. He is judged in the light of his minimalist cooperation with the master's bounty. He did not lose what the master had graciously entrusted to him at the outset; he has even returned it. But he has returned it with unproductivity.

by your own words. Lit. "out of your (own) mouth." Cf. Job 15:6.

carrying off . . . reaping. Mss. D, 892, etc. read the indic. *airō, therizō* instead of the ptcs. found in the best mss.

23. *in a bank account?* Lit. "on a (moneylender's) table." See Mark 11:15; Matt 21:12; John 2:15. Cf. Josephus, *Ant.* 12.2,3 § 28. The Greek n. *trapeza* was commonly used in this financial sense in classical and Hellenistic Greek texts. See MM 639-640.

with interest. This detail was also present in "Q." See Matt 25:27. In the light of Deut 23:20-21 (19-20E); Exod 22:24 (25E); Lev 25:36-37, the master thought that the servant could at least have lent the money to non-Jews. For an ancient expectation about money lent for trading, see the Code of Hammurabi § 99 *(ANET* 170).

on my return. Lit. "coming," the aor. ptc. is used here with a contrary-to-fact nuance (see BDF § 360.2), i.e. if I were to come.

24. *to his attendants.* Lit. "to those standing by," they are otherwise unidentified. Only by implication can one discern that the king's courtiers or gentlemen-at-arms are meant. Cf. Esth 4:2-5.

Take the pound away from him . . . One is not to ask how much an additional pound would mean to one who has already been put in charge of ten towns. That would be to miss the point. The excess of reward is the real point; the good servant comes in for an unexpected bounty, whereas the wicked one is deprived even of the bounty that was originally accorded him.

25. *he already has ten pounds!* Mss. D, W, 69, 565, and some ancient versions (OL, OS, Bohairic) omit the whole verse, but it is found in the best Greek mss. It is not only a *lectio difficilior* in a sense, but belongs here. Because it deals with "pounds" and not with "towns," it has been thought to have been originally in "Q," but it is much more likely a Lucan addition. However, it is clearly an insertion, since the master continues to speak in v. 26; he is unmoved by the attendants' exclamation. The expostulation heightens the extra unexpected bounty given to the good servant.

26. *I tell you.* Matt 25:29 has omitted this phrase from "Q." Cf. 14:24.

to everyone who has. See Luke 8:18 for the form of the doublet used there. These words of the master imply praise for human endeavor cooperating with his original bounty.

what he has. Some mss. (Θ, 69, etc.) harmonize the text with 8:18, reading *dokei echein,* "what he thinks he has." Though this is surely Lucan, it is out of place here. For the form of this saying in *Gos. of Thom.* § 41, see p. 718.

27. *However.* The strong adversative *plēn,* a Lucan favorite word (see p. 111), is used to introduce the ending of the parable. See NOTE on 10:11.

those enemies of mine. I.e. those of v. 14. Contrast the concluding verse of the Matthean parable (25:30), which allegorizes that form of the parable in a still different fashion, intensifying the punishment of the worthless servant. Here in Luke the punishment is meted out to others than the wicked servant. Luke has no reference to an eschatological punishment, as does Matthew (25:30). He may be hinting at some form of secular destruction of his enemies, possibly at the destruction of Jerusalem by the Romans and the slaughter of many of its inhabitants. So E. Grässer, *Parusieverzögerung,* 116.

slaughter them. I.e. in OT fashion, as was done by Samuel to Agag, the king of the Amalekites at Gilgal (1 Sam 15:33; cf. Luke 12:46; Plutarch, *Lysan. et Sull.* 2.4 § 476D; Caesar, *Bell. civ.* 3.28,4).

Ms. D adds a form of Matt 25:30 to the end of the Lucan parable.

BIBLIOGRAPHY (19:11-27)

Bauer, J. B. "Die Arbeit als Heilsdimension (Lk 19.26 u. 1 Tim 2,14s)," *BLit* 24 (1956-1957) 198-201.

Bouwman, G. *Das dritte Evangelium: Einübung in die formgeschichtliche Methode* (Düsseldorf: Patmos, 1968) 56-61.

Candlish, R. "The Pounds and the Talents," *ExpTim* 23 (1911-1912) 136-137.

Conzelmann, H. *Theology,* 64, 72-73, 82-83, 113, 121, 138-141, 198.

Derrett, J. D. M. "Law in the New Testament: The Parable of the Talents and Two Logia," *ZNW* 56 (1965) 184-195; reprinted, *Law,* 17-31.

Didier, M. "La parabole des talents et des mines," *De Jésus aux évangiles* (ed. I. de la Potterie) 2. 248-271.

Dodd, C. H. *Parables,* 7, 12, 100, 114-121, 127-129.

Dupont, J. "La parabole des talents (Mat. 25: 14-30) ou des mines (Luc 19: 12-27)," *RTP* 19 (1969) 376-391.

────── "La parabole des talents: Mt 25, 14-30," *AsSeign* ns 64 (1969) 18-28.

Fiedler, P. "Die übergebenen Talente: Auslegung von Mt 25,14-20," *BibLeb* 11 (1970) 259-273.

Foerster, W. "Das Gleichnis von der anvertrauten Pfunden," *Verbum Dei manet in aeternum: Eine Festschrift für Prof. D. Otto Schmitz . . .* (ed. W. Foerster; Witten: Luther-V., 1953) 37-56.

Ganne, P. "La parabole des talents," *BVC* 45 (1962) 44-53.

Grässer, E. *Parusieverzögerung,* 114-117.

Holdcroft, I. T. "The Parable of the Pounds and Origen's Doctrine of Grace," *JTS* 24 (1973) 503-504.

Jeremias, J. *Parables,* 58-63, 67, 86, 95, 99-100, 136, 166.

Johnson, L. T. "The Lukan Kingship Parable (Lk. 19:11-27)," *NovT* 24 (1982) 139-159.

Joüon, P. "La parabole des mines *(Luc,* 19, 13-27) et la parabole des talents *(Matthieu,* 25, 14-30)," *RSR* 29 (1939) 489-494.

Jülicher, A. *Gleichnisreden,* 2. 472-495.

Kaestli, J.-D. *L'Eschatologie,* 38-40.

Kamlah, E. "Kritik und Interpretation der Parabel von den anvertrauten Geldern: Mt. 25,14ff.; Lk. 19,12ff.," *KD* 14 (1968) 28-38.

Kissinger, W. S. *Parables of Jesus,* 349-351.

Lambrecht, J. *Once More,* 167-195.

Lindeskog, G. "Logia-Studien," *ST* 4 (1950) 129-189.

Lüthi, W. "Das Gleichnis vom anvertrauten Pfund: Predigt über Lk. 19,11-27," *Das Wort sie sollen lassen stahn: Festschrift für D. Albert Schädelin* (eds. H. Dürr et al.; Bern: Herbert Lang, 1950) 207-214.

McCulloch, W. "The Pounds and the Talents," *ExpTim* 23 (1911-1912) 382-383.

McGaughy, L. C. "The Fear of Yahweh and the Mission of Judaism: A Postexilic Maxim and Its Early Christian Expansion in the Parable of the Talents," *JBL* 94 (1975) 235-245.

Ollivier, M.-J. "Etudes sur la physionomie intellectuelle de N. S. J. C.: La parabole des mines (Luc, xix, 11-27)," *RB* 1 (1892) 589-601.

Pesch, W. *Der Lohngedanke in der Lehre Jesu verglichen mit der religiösen Lohnlehre des Spätjudentums* (MTS I/1; Munich: Zink, 1955) 30-39.

Resenhöfft, W. "Jesu Gleichnis von den Talenten, ergänzt durch die Lukas-Fassung," *NTS* 26 (1979-1980) 318-331.

Sanders, J. T. "The Parable of the Pounds and Lucan Anti-Semitism," *TS* 42 (1981) 660-668.

Schneider, G. *Parusiegleichnisse,* 38-42.

Schulz, S. *Q: Die Spruchquelle,* 288-298.

Simpson, J. G. "The Parable of the Pounds," *ExpTim* 37 (1925-1926) 299-302.

Spicq, C. "Le chrétien doit porter du fruit," *VSpir* 84 (1951) 605-615.

Stock, W. "The Pounds and the Talents," *ExpTim* 22 (1901-1911) 424-425.

Thiessen, H. C. "The Parable of the Nobleman and the Earthly Kingdom: Luke 19:11-27," *BSac* 91 (1934) 180-190.

Thomson, P. " 'Carry on!' (Luke xix. 13)," *ExpTim* 30 (1918-1919) 277.

Weinert, F. D. "The Parable of the Throne Claimant (Luke 19:12, 14-15a, 27) Reconsidered," *CBQ* 39 (1977) 505-514.

Weiser, A. *Die Knechtsgleichnisse der synoptischen Evangelien* (SANT 29; Munich: Kösel, 1971) 226-272.

Winterbotham, R. "Christ, or Archelaus?" *Expos* 8/4 (1912) 338-347.

Zerwick, M. "Die Parabel vom Thronanwärter," *Bib* 40 (1959) 654-674.

V. THE MINISTRY OF JESUS IN JERUSALEM

Blest Be the King,
the One Who Comes in the Name of the Lord

---

126. THE ROYAL ENTRY INTO THE JERUSALEM TEMPLE
(19:28-40)

19 ^{28} After he had said this, Jesus kept moving ahead, going up to Jerusalem. ^{29} When he drew near to Bethphage and Bethany, at the hill called the Mount of Olives, he happened to send off two of the disciples, ^{30} saying, "Go into the village opposite, and as you enter it you will find a colt tethered there on which no one has yet ridden. Untie it and lead it here. ^{31} If anyone asks you why you are untying it, simply say, 'Because the Lord has need of it.' " ^{32} Those whom he sent off went and found it just as he had told them. ^{33} As they were untying the colt, its owners asked them, "Why are you untying that colt?" ^{34} They replied, "Because the Lord has need of it." ^{35} So they led it to Jesus. They tossed their cloaks on the colt and made Jesus mount it; ^{36} and as he moved along, others kept spreading their cloaks on the road. ^{37} When he was already close to the descent of the Mount of Olives, the whole crowd of disciples began to praise God loudly in their joy over all the miracles which they had seen. ^{38} They sang out,

"*Blest be* the king,
    the one who comes in the name of the Lord![a]

Peace in heaven,
    and glory in highest heaven!"

[a] Ps 118:26

³⁹ Some of the Pharisees in the crowd said to him, "Teacher, rebuke your disciples." ⁴⁰ But he replied, "I tell you, if these grow silent, then will the stones cry out!"

COMMENT

With this episode one begins the fifth major part of the Lucan Gospel (19:28-21:38). Jesus' long journey is over, and the Lucan Gospel joins the other three in depicting his entry into Jerusalem. This part of the Lucan Gospel is mainly devoted to the ministry of Jesus in the Jerusalem Temple. The first four episodes (vv. 28-40,41-44,45-46,47-48) are really transitional because they also serve as the climax of the travel account itself which has preceded (see p. 167). At the same time they depict in a generic way Jesus' approach and initial reaction to Jerusalem, the city of his destiny, and its Temple, the house of his Father. Luke has been preparing his readers for this part of the Gospel with various references to Jerusalem which have marked the travel account that preceded (9:51,53; 10:30; 13:4,22,33,34; 17:11; 18:31; 19:11 [see p. 824]). With the first episode in this part (19:28-40) Jesus arrives at the environs of the city and prepares to make his way into it, entering it as one hailed as king (and going directly to the Temple in it, as we eventually learn). This episode is also a fulfillment of what was announced in 13:35. The entire Jerusalem-section of the Gospel, which includes also parts VI and VII, thus forms for the evangelist the geographic climax of the Gospel as a whole. (See p. 185.)

The bulk of this episode, the royal entry of Jesus into the Jerusalem Temple (19:28-40) is derived from "Mk" (= Mark 11:1-10; cf. Matt 21:1-9). Like Matthew, Luke has reworked the episode to suit his own purpose, but he thus reverts to his use of Marcan material after the two inserted preceding episodes. Verse 28 has been composed by Luke as a transitional introduction; it connects this episode with the preceding parable, the bulk of which has been derived from "Q." Verses 29-38 are a redacted form of Mark 11:1-10, with v. 37 composed by Luke himself and added. Though some interpreters (V. Taylor, *Behind the Third Gospel* [Oxford: Clarendon, 1926] 94-95; T. Schramm, *Markus-Stoff,* 144-149; H. Patsch, "Der Einzug") have tried to show that another source for vv. 29-36,38 beyond "Mk" has been used by Luke, this has never proved convincing. (See G. Schneider, *Evangelium nach Lukas,* 384-385; K. H. Rengstorf, *Evangelium nach Lukas,* 217.) Lucan redaction is clear in vv. 29 *(kai egeneto,* etc.), 30 (substitution of *agagete* for *pherete,* as in v. 35), 31 (omission of the final cl.), 33 (substitution of a gen. absol. [see p. 108]; use of *eipan pros* + acc.), 34 (substitution of the quotation of Jesus' words), 36 (gen. absol.; omission of reference to branches cut from the fields [Mark 11:8]), 38 (addition of "the king"; omission of "Hosanna," and of the reference to the kingdom of David our father; and substitution of the final accla-mation). Though in some respects the redaction may seem to resemble an element or two in the Johannine tradition, that influence—if it exists—does not argue clearly for the use of another source.

As for vv. 39-40, it is another matter. First of all, it is not certain whether these verses are to be regarded as part of this episode, since some commenta-tors relate them rather to vv. 41-44 (e.g. *SQE* 396). Second, they seem to be a form of Matt 21:15-16 (see *HST* 34, 57). Third, some interpreters would even make vv. 37-40 a unit derived from "L" (see T. W. Manson, *Sayings,* 317-319). The last view neglects too much the similarity of v. 38 and Lucan concerns which may simply account for his redaction of it from "Mk." Tak-ing vv. 39-40 as part of this episode in the Lucan Gospel, I prefer to regard these verses as derived from "L," not excluding that they may be an indepen-dent form of what Matt 21:15-16 has. (See p. 84.)

Verse 37 was added by Luke on his own in order to emphasize the locality at this crucial part of his Gospel—the geographical perspective, proximity to Jerusalem—and thus to locate the loud praise of God for the miracles that Jesus has worked in the Lucan account.

This Lucan episode might seem to have some affinity with the Johannine account of Jesus' entry into Jerusalem (John 12:12-16). There a large crowd present in Jerusalem (for Passover [12:1]) comes out to meet Jesus and his companions, having learned that he was about to enter the city. They come with palm fronds and shout, "Hosanna! Blest be the one who comes in the name of the Lord! Blest be the King of Israel!" Once a procession has begun, Jesus "finds" a young donkey *(onarion)* and sits on it, thus fulfilling the words of Zech 9:9 (in part at least, and somewhat conflated with Isa 40:9). To which the evangelist adds a comment about the failure of the disciples to understand the relation of the event to Scripture.

The affinity of the Lucan scene to the Johannine is to be noted in four things: (1) Jesus entering Jerusalem astride an animal; (2) the acclamation from Ps 118:26, "Blest be the one who comes in the name of the Lord" (also used in Mark and Matthew); (3) the additional title *ho basileus,* "the king" (which John 12:13 fills out with "of Israel" and adds to the end of the quota-tion, whereas Luke inserts it after *ho erchomenos);* and (4) the animal in Luke 19:33,35 is called *pōlos,* "colt," the word used in the Johannine quotation of Zech 9:9, after it had been called *onarion* in v. 14a.

The differences of the Lucan scene from the Johannine, however, are more significant: (1) The Lucan story knows nothing of (a) a crowd coming out of Jerusalem to meet Jesus; (b) the use of palm fronds (indeed, Luke even omit-ted reference to branches from the fields [Mark 11:8]); (c) the (possibly politi-cally oriented) addition to the regal title, "of Israel"; (d) the "finding" of the animal; (e) the use of Zech 9:9 and the fulfillment-idea [a notion not strange to Luke]; or (f) the evangelist's comment about the disciples' failure to comprehend. Moreover, (2) the Lucan story, following the Marcan, depicts Jesus (a) coming from Bethphage, Bethany, and the Mount of Olives; (b) knowing about the colt in advance; (c) sending two disciples with instructions to get it; (d) sitting on the animal covered with garments and riding on other garments strewn like a carpet along his path; (e) descending the Mount of Olives; (f) finally being greeted with "Peace in heaven and glory in highest heaven." Recall, too, that the purging of the Temple in the Johannine Gospel is not associated with this entry of Jesus into Jerusalem (see p. 1260).

The upshot is that the only significant point of contact different from "Mk" is the title *ho basileus* added to the acclamation from Ps 118:26. If that is derived by Luke from a non-Marcan source, is it certainly influenced by the developing Johannine tradition? (See p. 88; cf. R. E. Brown, *John I-XII*, 459-461.)

The bulk of the episode (vv. 28-38) is to be understood form-critically as a Story about Jesus, to which a pronouncement-story (vv. 39-40) has been attached. The relation of vv. 39-40 to the rest and the various forms in which the story of Jesus' entry into Jerusalem have come down to us raise a serious question about the amount of it that is historical. If vv. 39-40 are an independent form of what Matthew has in 21:15-16, in which children, not disciples, are criticized and Jesus' answer to his critics quotes Ps 8:3, a question is immediately raised about the original setting and form of these verses in Stage I of the gospel tradition. Moreover, the "finding" of the young donkey in the Johannine story contrasts strongly with the foreknowledge that Jesus has in the Synoptic accounts about the animal(s). Again, the use of Zech 9:9 in the differing Synoptic forms creates a problem. Luke has not the slightest reference to it, apart from the use of *pōlos* for the animal. Whereas the cl. "on which no one has yet ridden" might reflect (by implication) in Mark 11:2 the *pōlon neon*, "new (= young) animal, foal," of Zech 9:9, that cl. is simply taken over by Luke (19:30) with no interest in the reflection. However, Matt 21:4-5 explicitly quotes Zech 9:9, making it one of his famous formula-quotations. The extent to which the earliest form of the story in Mark 11 reflects Zech 9:9 is a matter of debate. In his analysis of the narrative material in the Synoptics, R. Bultmann *(HST* 261-262) considered the getting of an animal to ride on as "a manifestly legendary characteristic," and like Mark 14:12-16 "a fairy-tale motif." Moreover, he regarded the assumption that Jesus intended to fulfill the prophecy of Zech 9:9 and that the crowd recognized "the ass as the Messiah's beast of burden" as "absurd." He conceded, however, that "the historical basis" of the scene could have been Jesus' entry into Jerusalem "with a crowd of pilgrims full of joy and expectation." If one prescinds from the pejorative language of Bultmann, one has to recognize that his analysis is substantially correct. We are confronted in the differing accounts with a tradition about the arrival of Jesus at Jerusalem, probably with a group of pilgrims coming for a feast, being hailed with the usual greeting of pilgrims taken from Ps 118:26; indeed, he may even have arrived sitting on some animal and been honored at the sight of Jerusalem by his fellow-travelers. One has to remember that in the Johannine tradition Jesus went up to Jerusalem at least three times (2:13; 5:1; 12:12), whereas the Synoptics know of only one journey to Jerusalem and treat it accordingly (especially Luke). Though the Synoptic tradition relates that one journey to a Passover (Mark 14:1; Matt 26:2; Luke 22:1), it has often been thought that the trappings in the scene of Jesus' entry should be associated with the arrival of pilgrims for the feast of Dedication (Hanukkah) or Tabernacles (Succoth); see B. A. Mastin, "The Date." If there is any validity to that argument, it merely compounds the problem of the historical basis of the scene of Jesus' entry. Attempts to support the historicity of Jesus' riding on an animal by appealing to the custom of a rabbi riding and disciples following on foot are slightly idyllic.

Did Jesus' entry into Jerusalem have any messianic connotation in the minds of his companions (in Stage I of the gospel tradition)? This is difficult to answer. Certainly, the growing gospel tradition (in Stages II and III) so understood it. W. G. Kümmel argues, however,

. . . if Jesus only rode into Jerusalem on an ass amid the reverential shouts of the crowd and if this fact was remembered as something remarkable, there can be no doubt that Jesus consciously associated himself with Zech. 9.9. For the verse . . . was in early days applied by the rabbis to the Messiah and so was probably known to Jesus with this meaning. But while the messianic exegesis of Zech. 9.9 by the rabbis probably did not seriously influence the active messianic expectation, Jesus by a conscious act associates himself with the prediction and shows thereby that he wishes to be a Messiah without pomp, but yet just in this lowly action the eschatological consummation is already revealing itself (Promise and Fulfilment, 116-117).

In support of this contention, Kümmel cites only Str-B 1. 842-844 to show that "in early days" the rabbis applied Zech 9:9 to the Messiah. But P. Billerbeck clearly says that nowhere in the Pseudepigrapha is the relation of Zech 9:9 to the Messiah cited, whereas in rabbinic literature it is widely used (p. 842). The majority of Billerbeck's references, however, are to the midrash Genesis Rabbah or the Babylonian Talmud—neither of which can be used as evidence for first-century Palestinian interpretations without further ado, since they come from—at the earliest—the fourth century A.D. We are confronted in the use of Zech 9:9 (explicitly) in Matthew and John (but only possibly in Mark) with a Christian interpretation of the OT.

Working with Mark, Luke has considerably changed the nuances of the earlier account of Jesus' entry into Jerusalem. He is concerned that the arrival of Jesus in Jerusalem not be understood as an eschatological event (the arrival of the kingdom of our father David, Mark 11:10) or as a political event (the restoration of the kingdom to Israel, Acts 1:6). Jesus rather comes to Jerusalem as a pilgrim who is hailed as a king, and prepares for his destiny, his passion, his transit to the Father.

The sense of the episode in the Lucan Gospel is not difficult to discern. It can best be summed up under three headings: (a) Jesus, having made his *way* from Galilee, enters the city of destiny, the goal of all his wanderings (cf. 23:5), the place from which he will be "taken up" (cf. 9:51), and the place from which he will now make his transit to the Father (his *exodos,* cf. 9:31). (b) Jesus enters not only the city of destiny, but its Temple, and not only as a pilgrim coming for the feast of Passover, greeted with the usual pilgrim-salutation (Ps 118:26), but as "the king," and "the one who comes" (now to be understood in the full Lucan sense). This greeting recalls 13:35, where the pilgrim-salutation was already quoted at the halfway mark in the travel account. But now *ho erchomenos* not only takes on the regal nuance, expressly given to it, but echoes with the connotation of the question put in 7:19 by the messengers sent from the imprisoned John the Baptist, "Are you the 'One who is to come'?" In other words, the greeting chanted by the "whole crowd of disciples" (19:37b) is loaded with the connotation of Mal 3:1, whence the title *ho erchomenos* in the Synoptic tradition is ultimately derived (see NOTE on 7:19). Hence, Jesus enters Jerusalem as "the king," the "One who is to come," and as the fulfillment of Malachi's prophecy, "Look, I am sending forth my messenger, and he will prepare the way before me; suddenly the Lord whom you seek will come to his own temple, and the messenger of the covenant whom you look for. Look, he is coming, says the Lord Almighty" (3:1 LXX). This is why Jesus makes his way directly "into the Temple area" (19:45) in this Gospel. (c) To the objection of the Pharisees about such acclamations coming from Jesus' "disciples," Jesus, the teacher, wryly comments, "If these grow silent, then will the stones cry out!" In God's providence the acclamation will be made, even if it must come from the very stones with which Jerusalem has been so compactly built (Ps 122:3). As at the beginning of the travel account, the Samaritans rejected his entry into their villages (9:52-53), so now the Pharisees reject his entry into Jerusalem.

"The days . . . when he was to be taken up" (9:51) have, therefore, arrived in a new sense, even though "the kingdom of God" was not going "to appear immediately" (19:11). Now "all that was written by the prophets" concerning him "will see fulfillment" (18:31) in this very city. These days, moreover, will bring Jesus through his suffering to "glory" (24:26) and will open the way for salvation-history to continue on its way through the witnesses who have been accompanying him from Galilee and who have been trained by him and are yet to be commissioned (24:48). The entry into the Temple of Jerusalem is the inauguration of the period of the passion, the last phase of the Period of Jesus. Before the onset of the passion proper, however, he must exercise a ministry in Jerusalem, a ministry of teaching in the Temple. Now he arrives, as H. Conzelmann rightly notes *(Theology,* 74), in a non-eschatological, non-political sense. "He does not intend to set up 'the Kingdom' in Jerusalem." He comes as its king, and from him eventually will come the peace that is in heaven in a new way. The emphasis that appears in this entry scene on Jesus as "the king," will continue in the passion narrative itself. See further A. George, "La royauté."

Finally, one should not miss in this scene the elaborate geographical references, especially those in the added Lucan v. 37; they contribute to the geographical perspective in the Lucan writings. See pp. 165-167.

NOTES

19 28. *After he had said this.* I.e. had uttered the parable of the pounds (19:11-27), with its allegorical reference to himself as one who is to journey to a distant land to acquire for himself the title of king. Hence the "kingdom" will not arrive until he returns with that title duly bestowed. Before that return he must make his transit to the Father, his *exodos* (9:31).

Jesus kept moving ahead. The Lucan favorite vb. *poreuesthai* (see pp. 168-169) occurs in this climax scene; it is in the impf. tense, expressing continuous movement. The adv. *emprosthen*, "ahead," insinuates that Jesus leads the way, at the head of his band of companions. Cf. Mark 10:32, omitted by Luke in 18:31. He moves on from the east, from Jericho, to Jerusalem, which is roughly due west of it.

going up to Jerusalem. Cf. Mark 10:32. For a sense of the climb involved, see NOTE on 19:11. On the name used for Jerusalem here, *Hierosolyma,* see NOTES on 2:22; 10:30. Cf. pp. 164-168, 824. This "going up" foreshadows his ascent/transit to the Father.

29. *drew near to Bethphage and Bethany.* Coming up the Roman road from Jericho to Jerusalem, one would approach the villages of Bethphage and Bethany on the hill overlooking Jerusalem from the east (above the Kidron Valley). Luke follows Mark 11:1 in mentioning both and in putting Bethphage first; Matthew simplifies the reference and mentions only Bethphage (21:9).

Bethphage was a small village on the Mount of Olives, but its exact site is uncertain. Today it is often identified with Abu Dis, southeast of Bethany and lower down on the southeastern side of the Mount of Olives. From Luke's account, which follows Mark, one gets the impression that a traveler from Jericho would come first to Bethphage and then to Bethany; this may therefore account for the present-day localization of the village at Abu Dis. But little can really be deduced from the Marcan order of names about the relative location of the two villages. Since Crusader times others have located Bethphage northwest of Bethany, close to or at Kefr eṭ-Ṭur, higher up the mount. The Greek name *Bēthphagē* is usually explained as = Aramaic *bêt paggê',* "house of unripe figs" (with the name referring to a species of figs which, even when edible, never appear to be ripe). Bethphage is named only in this episode in the NT; because Matt 21:9 mentions only Bethphage, this is usually taken to be "the village opposite" in v. 30. But it is scarcely so interpreted with certainty. See further J. Finegan, *Archeology,* 88-91.

Bethany was another small village situated about 2.7 kilometers east of Jerusalem, on the eastern slope of the Mount of Olives. It is probably mentioned in Jdt 1:9 (LXX *Batanē* or *Baitanē)*, and possibly in Neh 11:32 *(RSV* Ananiah). Greek *Bēthania* probably reflects Hebrew or Aramaic *bêt 'Ănanyāh,* "House of Ananiah," or *bêt Ḥānanyāh,* "House of Hananiah." Where the explanation of it as "house of dates" (I. H. Marshall, *Luke,* 712) comes from is a mystery. Bethany will be mentioned again in 24:50. Cf. Mark 11:1,11,12; 14:3; Matt 21:17; 26:6; John 11:1,18; 12:1 (not to be confused with "Bethany beyond the Jordan" in 1:28). Today the village is called el-'Azariyeh by its Moslem inhabitants, after Lazarus, whose grave was located there by the Bordeaux Pilgrim ca. A.D. 333. See *ELS* 359-382; cf. J. Finegan, *Archeology,* 91-95. See further NOTE on 10:38.

at the hill called the Mount of Olives. The hill is part of a range of low-lying mountains overlooking Jerusalem to the east across the Kidron Valley. The range extends about two and a half miles from north to south and has three main summits, the highest of which is the northern (Mount Scopus or Ras el-Mesharif), about 2690 feet above sea level. The central summit has been traditionally regarded as the Mount of Olives; it is 2660 feet above sea level directly across the valley from the area of the Temple. Cf. Zech 14:4. On it is found Kefr eṭ-Ṭur. The southern summit rises above the village of Silwan and is often called the Mount of Corruption (see *RSV* 2 Kgs 23:13) or the Mount of Offence. See J. Finegan, *Archeology,* 88-90. On the problematic form of the Greek nom. *elaiōn* or gen. pl. *elaiōn,* see BDF § 143; I. Broer, *EWNT* 1. 1035.

send off two of the disciples. Lit. "and it happened, when he drew near . . . (that) he sent off . . ." Luke uses *kai egeneto* with a finite vb. *(apesteilen)* without the conj. *kai.* See p. 119. The temporal cl. is introduced with *hōs,* "when." Disciples were last mentioned as part of the accompanying crowd in 18:15.

30. *a colt.* Luke follows Mark 11:2 in calling the animal *pōlos;* Matt 21:2 uses *onos,* "ass," probably because of his explicit quotation of Zech 9:9 in v. 5. The meaning of *pōlos* is disputed. It means "a young animal, foal" when another is mentioned in the context; when used alone, it seems to mean either "a young horse, colt" or a "young male ass." See W. Bauer, "The 'Colt,' " 220-229; H.-W. Kuhn, "Das Reittier," 82-91; O. Michel, *TDNT* 6. 959-961; "Eine philologische Frage zur Einzugsgeschichte," *NTS* 6 (1959-1960) 81-82.

Matthew has not only changed to *onos,* but seems to depict Jesus sending for two animals, "a (she-)ass and a foal with it." The Greek of Zech 9:9 reads *epi hypozygion kai pōlon neon,* "upon a draft-animal (= an ass) and a new (= young) foal." The MT of Zech 9:9, however, reads *'al ḥāmôr wĕ'al 'ayir ben 'ătōnôt,* which should be translated, "upon an ass, even upon a colt, the foal of an ass." The LXX rendered the Hebrew conj. *wĕ-* literally by *kai.* Though the Greek *kai* could also be used adverbially (as the Hebrew *wĕ-* was intended), Matthew has understood the *kai* of the LXX as a conj. and depicted Jesus needing two animals ("them," v. 3) and eventually astride both of them ("and he sat upon them," v. 7)!

tethered there. Some commentators see in *pōlon dedemenon* an allusion to or echo of Gen 49:11, part of Jacob's blessing of Judah, "binding his foal to the vine and his ass's colt to the choice vine" *(RSV).* E.g. I. H. Marshall, *Luke,* 712, who claims that the passage in Genesis "has messianic associations." But the only word common is *pōlon,* used twice, in fact, in the LXX of Gen 49:11, whereas "binding" is an entirely different vb., *desmeuōn*. Cf., however, J. Blenkinsopp, "The Oracle of Judah." The allusion might be more evident in the Matthean form of the episode, which is more concerned with its OT allusions than Luke is.

on which no one has yet ridden. I.e. fit for "the king" who is to enter. This detail is taken over by Luke word for word from Mark 11:2. There it was possibly an allusion to Zech 9:9, *pōlon neon,* a "new foal." That nuance, however, should not be read into the Lucan passage, which otherwise has no allusion to Zechariah. Moreover, one should not wonder about Jesus riding an animal not yet broken in, and going down hill; to do so is to miss the point of the story. The description of the colt used here may be echoing the description of animals in the OT that have never borne a yoke. See Num 19:2; Deut 21:3; 1 Sam 6:7. A similar motif will recur in 23:53.

Untie it and lead it here. As did Matthew, Luke has substituted the more proper Greek vb. *agein* for the Marcan *pherein.* See J. A. Fitzmyer, "The Use of *Agein* and *Pherein* in the Synoptic Gospels," *Festschrift to Honor F. Wilbur Gingrich . . .* (eds. E. H. Barth and R. E. Cocroft; Leiden: Brill, 1972) 147-160, esp. 152. Cf. H. J. Cadbury, *Style and Literary Method of Luke,* 174.

31. *the Lord has need of it.* Luke adopts this answer from Mark 11:3, one of the two places in the Marcan Gospel where absol. *ho kyrios* is used of Jesus. See also 12:37 (David calls him "Lord"—a somewhat different use!), but note its occurrence in the Marcan appendix (16:19,20). This adoption suits the Lucan use of the phrase for the earthly Jesus. See NOTE on 7:13 and p. 203. Note, however, that the Marcan reading may not be textually certain. See G. D. Kilpatrick, " 'Kurios' in the Gospels," *L'Evangile, hier et aujourd'hui: Mélanges offerts au Professeur Franz-J. Leenhardt* (Geneva: Labor et Fides, 1968) 66-70; "Kyrios again," *Orientierung an Jesus* (eds. P. Hoffmann et al.) 214-219. The title is used in both Gospels to assert Jesus' right to send for the animal.

To some commentators the use of *kyrios* is ambiguous. It scarcely is used of Yahweh or God. In the Marcan text, one could translate, "Its master has need (of it)," but this meaning seems precluded in the Lucan text because of *hoi kyrioi* in v. 33 (changed by Luke from "those standing by"). J. D. M. Derrett ("Law," 246-247) would have us believe that even in Luke the sense is "its (real) owner," but given the Lucan frequent use of absol. *ho kyrios* (see pp. 202-203), one should use that instead. See J. A. Fitzmyer, *EWNT* 2. 818.

"We must not rationalise here. Jesus has not already ordered the colt, nor made an arrangement with its owners, but he knows beforehand what will happen, because God, who directs what is to happen is with him" (J. Wellhausen, *Evangelium Marci,* 87 [quoted in J. M. Creed, *The Gospel,* 239]). As one approaches the passion narrative in the various Synoptic Gospels, one notes the increase of reference to Jesus' superior foreknowledge. There is no need to invoke here a "prior arrangement" made by Jesus with the owners, *pace* I. H. Marshall, *Luke,* 713; G. B. Caird, *Gospel of St Luke,* 215.

The text is somewhat ambiguous here, since this comment of Jesus is actually introduced by *hoti.* My translation has understood this conj. as *hoti recitativum* (see BDF § 470.1), but other commentators have understood it as causal, "Because the Lord has need of it" (notice the difference between *UBSGNT* [3] and N-A[26] with regard to the capitalization). Similarly in v. 34.

32. *as he had told them.* Cf. 22:13.

33. *its owners.* I.e. its master and mistress, expressed merely as the pl. See A. Souter, "Interpretations of Certain New Testament Passages—Luke xix. 33," *Expos* 8/8 (1914) 94-95; cf. Acts 16:16,19; Juvenal, *Sat.* 6.4. For the Lucan change of text, see NOTE on v. 31; Matthew has none of this.

34. *has need of it.* Luke does not hesitate to repeat (dramatically) the proleptically provided answer. It enhances his picture of Jesus drawing near to his destiny.

35. *They tossed their cloaks on the colt.* I.e. the two disciples, as v. 36 makes clear.

36. *others kept spreading their cloaks on the road.* I.e. in a gesture of "red-carpet" welcome. Lucan redaction begins to depart from "Mk" considerably, probably to prepare for his form of the acclamation and the addition of vv. 37,39-40. For some reason Luke has no interest in the detail of green bows being brought from the fields. See Mark 11:8. The cloaks on the road may be an allusion to the homage paid to the newly anointed Jehu in 2 Kgs 9:13.

37. *When he was already close to the descent of the Mount of Olives.* I.e. on the western slope, going down to the Kidron Valley. Thus Luke specifies, as the other evangelists do not, the geographic spot where this earthly homage begins for Jesus "the king." The best mss. read the sg. ptc. *engizontos* here, but ms. D has the pl.

the whole crowd of disciples. Lit. "the whole multitude" *(hapan to plēthos),* again Lucan hyperbole. See NOTES on 3:16; 4:15; 9:1. Mark 11:8 simply has "many" and no indication that they were "disciples." The Lucan introduction of them contrasts with the incomprehension mentioned in 18:31-34. Some mss. (B, D) even add another "all" with "disciples." Cf. Luke 6:17.

began. The best reading is *ērxanto,* the pl. agreeing with "disciples," despite the immediately following sg. *plēthos,* "crowd"; the following ptc. *chairontes* (pl.) has to be taken with the "they" in the vb. Luke's Greek is a bit faulty here. Some mss. (D, L, R, W, etc.), however, remedy the matter by using the sg. *ērxato.*

to praise God loudly. Luke uses a favorite vb. *ainein* (see p. 112), as he does elsewhere (2:13,20; 24:53; Acts 2:47; 3:8,9 [otherwise in the NT, only in Rom 15:11; Rev 19:5]). It is probably his way of expressing the omitted "Hosanna." Recall 18:43.

all the miracles which they had seen. The past tense *eidon* is to be noted, since in the Lucan Gospel Jesus will not perform any miracles in the Jerusalem Temple—the sole exception being in 22:51 on *the Mount of Olives.* Luke again uses the pl. *dynameis,* "miracles, mighty deeds." See NOTE on 10:13. This use of it is a summary statement about all Jesus' cures, exorcisms, etc., even though only four had been witnessed by the accompanying crowds and disciples during the lengthy travel account (13:10-17; 14:1-6; 17:11-19; 18:35-43). See H. Conzelmann, *Theology,* 182-184.

Instead of *dynameōn,* some mss. (B, D, etc.) read *ginomenōn,* which is blander, "all the things which they had seen happen."

38. *They sang out.* Lit. "saying" (the ptc. *legontes).* Luke omits the grecized Aramaism *hōsanna* of Mark 11:9, which equals *hôša'-nā',* because of his usual custom of eliminating Semitic words or phrases which his intended readers would scarcely understand. See p. 58. *Hôša'-nā'* would be the Aramaic form of Hebrew *hôšîa'-nā',* used in Ps 118:25, where the LXX renders it as *sōson dē,* "save indeed." It was a supplication addressed at times to Yahweh (Ps 20:10) or to a king (2 Sam 14:4) as an entreaty for deliverance or help. Introduced into Psalm 118, it thus formed part of the Hallel

(used on the feasts of Passover or Tabernacles) to greet pilgrims coming to Jerusalem; but it had most likely lost its original connotation (of entreaty) and become something like the modern British use of "God save the king/queen!" in all sorts of contexts. See E. Lohse, *TDNT* 9. 682-684. The root *yš'*, for long unknown in Aramaic, has now turned up in 4QpsDan ar^a D2. See *MPAT* § 3D:2 (p. 6). On Luke's omission of *hōsanna*, see Jerome, *Ep.* 20.4 (CSEL 54. 108).

Blest be the king, the one who comes in the name of the Lord! In the LXX the pilgrim greeting in Ps 118:26 reads *eulogēmenos ho erchomenos en onomati kyriou*, "Blest be the one coming in the name of the Lord," a correct translation of the MT. Luke, following Mark, quotes the text exactly but inserts *ho basileus*, "the king," after the ptc. *erchomenos*. (My English translation has inverted the word order slightly.) See further NOTE on 13:35. The royal title that is thus introduced into the Lucan greeting has been foreshadowed in this Gospel in 1:32 and in 18:38,40 ("Son of David"). Cf. 23:3,37,38; Acts 17:7. See pp. 215-216; cf. H. Conzelmann, *Theology*, 198-199.

Luke omits the blessing invoked on "the coming kingdom of our father David" (Mark 11:10a), mainly because of what he has already written about the arrival of the kingdom in 19:11. He thus studiously avoids the idea that Jesus is preparing for anything other than his destiny in Jerusalem. This is why he substitutes for the Marcan secondary blessing an acclamation which recalls 2:14. See next NOTE. It is not the kingdom of David that is coming, but Jerusalem's "king" himself. Salvation through this king brings peace.

Peace in heaven, and glory in highest heaven! Lit. "in heaven peace and glory in the heights," a chiastic arrangement. At Jesus' birth the angelic host sang, "Glory to God in highest heaven; peace on earth for people whom he favors" (2:14). Whereas the heavenly choristers contrasted glory in heaven and peace on earth, the disciples near the end of Jesus' earthly career sing of peace in *heaven* and glory in its highest part. Luke thus makes this contrast without noting it explicitly. See H. Flender, *St Luke*, 8. Though Jesus instructed the disciples to bring "peace" to people (10:5,6), it is now regarded (along with glory) as a heavenly quality: "Peace in heaven" is "the gift of peace which is laid up in heaven for God's people" (J. M. Creed, *The Gospel*, 240), but which Jesus now brings in a new way; see Acts 2:33. It is not just the real *pax Augusta*, which the birth of Jesus brought to humanity, but the peace of heaven itself. See further H. Flender, *St Luke*, 61, 103-104. See pp. 224-225. A further nuance of "peace" will emerge in the next pericope, when Jesus laments over Jerusalem (vv. 41-44). Recall Bildad's speech in Job 25:2.

39. *Some of the Pharisees in the crowd.* The Pharisees (see NOTE on 5:17) emerge suddenly; but they have been in the crowd accompanying Jesus since at least 13:31. Cf. 14:1,3; 15:2; 16:14; 17:20. This is the last appearance of them in the Lucan Gospel. Cf. Acts 5:34; 15:5; 23:6-9; 26:5. They and their protest stand in contrast to the disciples and their homage.

Teacher. See NOTES on 3:12; 7:40.

rebuke your disciples. On the vb. *epitiman*, see NOTE on 4:35. Though they query Jesus' authority, the Pharisees are depicted as acknowledging his title and his following of disciples.

40. *if these grow silent.* Mss. א, A, B, L, N, R, W, Δ, etc., read the fut. indic.

siōpēsousin. This would be an unusual combination with the conj. *ean,* "if," which usually governs the subjunc. See BDF § 373.3. Some other mss. (Θ, Ψ, *f*[1,13], and the Koine text-tradition) have the aor. subjunc. *siōpēsōsin,* but that looks suspiciously like a copyist's deliberate correction. Ms. D reads the fut. indic. of another vb., *sigēsousin.* Cf. the textual problem in 18:39. *Ean* with the indic. is occasionally found elsewhere in the NT (1 Thess 3:8; 1 John 5:15), but it is surprising in a careful writer like Luke.

then will the stones cry out! This is possibly an allusion to Hab 2:11, "For a stone will cry out from a wall, and a beam from the wood-paneling will answer it," i.e. a threat uttered against a nation which plunders people and acquires gain by violence. Now in God's plan of salvation-history the arrival of Jesus in Jerusalem would make Jerusalem's stones cry out to acclaim him as the agent of it, if his disciples did not. Jesus' words are thus an indirect affirmation of the role in which he arrives at the city of destiny. In some mss. (A, R, W, Θ, Ψ, *f*[1,13], and the Koine text-tradition) *kekraxontai,* "will have cried out," is read; if it were correct, it would be the only example in the NT of a simple (non-periphrastic) fut. pf. See BDF § 65.1b. My translation follows mss. ℵ, B, L, etc. *(kraxousin,* "will cry out"). The pathos of stones crying out will be given a further nuance in v. 44b of the next episode.

BIBLIOGRAPHY (19:28-40)

Bailey, J. A. *The Traditions Common to the Gospels of Luke and John* (NovTSup 7; Leiden: Brill, 1963) 22-28.

Bauer, W. "The 'Colt' of Palm Sunday (Der Palmesel)," *JBL* 72 (1953) 220-229.

Blenkinsopp, J. "The Oracle of Judah and the Messianic Entry," *JBL* 80 (1961) 55-64.

Burger, C. *Jesus als Davidssohn: Eine traditionsgeschichtliche Untersuchung* (FRLANT 98; Göttingen: Vandenhoeck & Ruprecht, 1970) 112-114.

Conzelmann, H. *Theology,* 74-78, 110, 134, 139, 183-184, 198-199.

Davies, T. L. "Was Jesus Compelled?" *ExpTim* 42 (1930-1931) 526-527.

Derrett, J. D. M. "Law in the New Testament: The Palm Sunday Colt," *NovT* 13 (1971) 241-258.

Doeve, J. W. "Purification du temple de desséchement du figuier: Sur la structure du 21ème chapitre de Matthieu et parallèles (Marc xi.1-xii.12, Luc xix.28-xx.19)," *NTS* 1 (1954-1955) 297-308.

Flender, H. *St Luke,* 8 n., 61, 78, 92-94, 97, 103-104, 108.

Frayn, R. S. "Was Jesus Compelled?" *ExpTim* 43 (1931-1932) 381-382.

Frenz, A. "Mt xxi 5.7," *NovT* 13 (1971) 259-260.

George, A. "La royauté de Jésus selon l'évangile de Luc," *ScEccl* 14 (1962) 57-69.

——— *Etudes sur l'oeuvre de Luc* (SB; Paris: Gabalada, 1978) 274-276.

Haenchen, E. *Der Weg Jesu,* 372-379.

Hahn, F. *Titles,* 84.

Kuhn, H.-W. "Das Reittier Jesu in der Einzugsgeschichte des Markusevangeliums," *ZNW* 50 (1959) 82-91.

Mastin, B. A. "The Date of the Triumphal Entry," *NTS* 16 (1969-1970) 76-82.

Meikle, J. "Was Jesus Compelled?" *ExpTim* 43 (1931-1932) 288.

Patsch, H. "Der Einzug Jesu in Jerusalem: Ein historischer Versuch," *ZTK* 68 (1971) 1-26.

Rese, M. *Alttestamentliche Motive in der Christologie des Lukas* (SNT 1; Gütersloh: G. Mohn, 1969) 196-199.

Samuel, O. "Die Regierungsgewalt des Wortes Gottes," *EvT* 3 (1936) 1-3.

Schniewind, J. *Die Parallelperikopen bei Lukas und Johannes* (Leipzig: Hinrichs, 1914; reprinted, Darmstadt: Wissenschaftliche Buchgesellschaft, 1970) 26-28.

Schramm, T. *Markus-Stoff,* 145-149.

127. THE LAMENT OVER JERUSALEM
(19:41-44)

19 [41] As Jesus drew near to Jerusalem, he wept at the sight of the city [42] and said, "Would that you, even you, had recognized this day what would make for peace! But, as it is, that is hidden from your sight. [43] Yet the time is coming upon you when your enemies will throw up an embankment against you, encircle you, and hem you in on every side. [44] They will *dash* you and *your children*[a] within you to the ground; they will leave not a stone upon a stone within you, because you have not recognized the *time of* your *visitation.*"[b]

[a] Ps 137:9; Nah 3:10   [b] Jer 6:15; 10:15

COMMENT

The enthusiastic and shouting crowd continues to accompany Jesus as he draws closer to Jerusalem, and with fine dramatic contrast Luke now depicts Jesus himself in the midst of their tumult weeping over the city, which is unaware of its own fate (19:41-44).

The passage is exclusive to the Lucan Gospel and has been derived from "L" (see p. 84), being inserted into the block of Marcan material which the evangelist is otherwise using. The parataxis in the Greek text of this passage (six *kais* in vv. 43-44) and the unusual syntax (see NOTES on these verses) reveal that Luke is making use of an inherited piece of tradition, which he has only slightly redacted. (See further J. Jeremias, *Die Sprache,* 281-282; D. L. Tiede, "Weeping," 79-80.) The insertion of this "L" material has been prepared for by v. 37 of the preceding episode.

This passage has been classed by R. Bultmann *(HST* 36) as a biographical apophthegm, i.e. a pronouncement-story, not an "imaginary scene," even though the pronouncement itself is regarded by him as a *vaticinium ex eventu,* fitted out with an introductory setting in v. 41. More specifically, Bultmann called vv. 42-44 "apocalyptic predictions," which betray a Christian tendency *(HST* 123, 127). Others have ascribed the predictions to early Christian prophets and claimed that they were eventually attributed to Jesus in the pre-Lucan tradition. In its present Lucan form, the passage is certainly to be regarded as a pronouncement-story, not a Story about Jesus (as V. Taylor, *FGT* 76, would have it); the interest in the episode lies not in Jesus' weeping, but in the pronouncement that he utters. His utterance, though prophetic, is in reality more minatory in tone.

Is the utterance to be simply dismissed as *vaticinium ex eventu?* The question is complicated because it is involved in the dating of the Lucan Gospel (see pp. 53-57) and because vv. 43-44 are echoes of OT minatory predictions. Yet a number of commentators are reluctant to deny that the utterance goes back to Jesus himself in some form (e.g. T. W. Manson, *Sayings,* 320; E. E. Ellis, *Gospel of Luke,* 226; D. L. Tiede, "Weeping"). There is, indeed, reason to think that Jesus did actually say something similar to this prophetic pronouncement about the fate of Jerusalem or at least of its Temple. Various forms of a reminiscence surface in the gospel tradition, both Synoptic and Johannine (see John 2:19-20; Mark 13:2 [= Matt 24:2; Luke 21:6]; 14:58 [= Matt 26:61—Luke omits this]); they have been variously redacted by the evangelists. Such an utterance on the part of the historical Jesus is as plausible as the interpretation given to Hab 2:8 ("Because you yourself have plundered many nations, all the rest of the peoples shall plunder you" [not said of Jerusalem]) in the Qumran pesher on that OT book. It is interpreted of "the last priests in Jerusalem who heap up riches and wealth by plundering peoples; but at the end of days their riches, together with the fruit of their plundering will be delivered into the hands of the army of the Kittim; for it is they who are the 'rest of the peoples' " (1QpHab 9:5-7). Again, it is as plausible as the utterance pronounced by another Jesus, son of Ananias, against Jerusalem and its Temple, about whom Josephus wrote—after the fact, indeed, and with reminiscences of Jeremiah's language *(J. W.* 6.5,3 § 300-309). Four years before the first revolt of Palestinian Jews against the Romans, "when the city was especially enjoying peace and prosperity," this Jesus stood up in the Temple at the feast of Tabernacles (i.e. roughly autumn of A.D. 62) and cried out, "A voice from the east, a voice from the west, a voice from the four winds; a voice against Jerusalem and the sanctuary, a voice against the bridegroom and the bride [cf. Jer 7:34], a voice against all the people." Unheeded and opposed by some of the leading Jerusalemites, he was finally brought before the Roman governor Albinus and scourged. At each stroke he exclaimed, "Woe to Jerusalem." Considered a maniac, he continued his utterances for seven years and five months, until he died in the siege of Jerusalem itself, struck by a stone hurled from a Roman *ballista.* Are we to write off this account too as *vaticinium ex eventu?* Even if we would have to ascribe the actual formulation of the Lucan Jesus' pronouncement to "Christian prophets" at some point in Stage II of the gospel tradition (see D. Hill, "On the Evidence for the Creative Role of Christian Prophets," *NTS* 20 [1973-1974] 262-274), one has to reckon with the fact that the gospel tradition does eventually ascribe it to Jesus himself. The real question: Is it ascribed without any basis in Stage I? Did he utter something like the Lucan formulation? In less specific terms perhaps? But to ask this is to bring up another problem, or several problems.

Would not a *vaticinium ex eventu* have been more specific in its terminology? For instance, allusion to the earthworks thrown up by the Romans *(J. W.* 5.11,4 § 466 *ta chōmata),* the circumvallation of Jerusalem, a wall of thirty-nine furlongs *(stadia)* encircling the whole city *(J. W.* 5.12,2 § 508), the firing of the Temple gates *(J. W.* 6.4,1 § 228), the battering of the fortress Antonia *(J. W.* 6.1,3 § 24-28; 6.2,1 § 93). Another opinion is held by C. H. Dodd who maintains that this oracle of the Lucan Jesus is "composed *entirely* from the language of the Old Testament. . . . So far as any historical event has coloured the picture, it is not Titus's capture of Jerusalem in A.D. 70, but Nebuchadrezzar's capture in 586 B.C." ("The Fall of Jerusalem," 79). Indeed, Dodd goes so far as to insist that "there is no single trait of the forecast which cannot be documented directly out of the Old Testament" (ibid.). Although NOTES will call attention to the OT passages which the various cls. of vv. 43-44 echo, Dodd has overplayed his hand in claiming that the documentation of the single traits excludes any reference to the destruction of Jerusalem by Titus. Luke's insertion of the "L" material into the Marcan block is almost certainly inspired in part by the evangelist's knowledge that Jerusalem had fallen to the Romans. The same has to be said about L. Gaston's assertion that "the whole scene of Jesus weeping over Jerusalem could have come straight from the pages of Jeremiah" *(No Stone,* 359); he puts together a "catena of passages" to illustrate it (Jer 8:18,23 [9:1E]; 8:11 [= 6:14]; 6:6,15,8). (Gaston's discussion of the passage, however, encounters the difficulty of his distinction between the use of the catena in Proto-Luke and in Luke itself; see further D. L. Tiede, "Weeping," 68-70.) In other words, the best solution to these problems is the recognition that the Lucan oracle may well go back to Jesus in some form, but that the reformulation of it in the pre-Lucan tradition was affected both by the destruction of the city itself in A.D. 70 and by allusions to that under Nebuchadnezzar in the OT. We have to admit with D. L. Tiede that Luke has not "coolly turned the traditions against Israel" (ibid. 70). Luke does not blame the destruction of Jerusalem on the death of Jesus, as Origen would do centuries later *(Contra Celsum* 1.47; 2.8 [quoting Luke 19:44]; 4.22,32; 8.42,69; GCS 2. 97, 134, 292, 303; 3. 257, 286).

As the Lucan Jesus draws near to the city of destiny, he comes not only as God's emissary (4:43bc) and its "king," with whom heaven's peace has been associated (19:38), but also as a prophet, who comments on the sad condition of the famous city. He is not concerned with the fate that awaits *him* there, but with the fate of the city itself. The full understanding of this passage has to relate it to two other passages in the Lucan Gospel: (a) 13:34-35, the lament over Jerusalem in the midst of the travel account, and (b) 23:26-32, the road to the cross in the passion narrative. In the first scene Jesus compared himself to a mother-bird which manifests its love and concern for its fledglings; the reluctance of Jerusalem there to accept the heaven-sent bearer of God's wisdom now becomes the source of Jesus' tears over its reluctance to accept the heaven-sent bearer of heaven's peace. In the second scene, Jesus' weeping will find its counterpart in the weeping of the women of Jerusalem not only for themselves but also for their children.

In the midst of the enthusiasm and tumult that are associated with his approach to Jerusalem, Jesus weeps as he reflects on the fate of the city—because it does not realize what could make for its peace. If "peace" in v. 38 carries the full connotation of OT *šālôm*, it is used in this passage not only with the same connotation, but also more specifically with the nuance of absence of war or hostilities, as the allusions in vv. 43-44 make clear.

There is, moreover, a play on the name of Jerusalem. The old Hebrew name *Yĕrûšālayim* (Josh 10:1,3) was contracted in time to *Yĕrûšālēm*, and used in Aramaic as *Yĕrûšĕlem* (Ezra 4:8,20; Dan 5:2,3). Its original meaning is lost (see numerous attempts to explain it in *HALAT* 417). But even in OT times it came to be associated with Salem, the town from which Melchizedek came (Gen 14:18). (See Ps 76:3 ["His (God's) abode has been established in Salem, his dwelling-place in Zion (the original fortified hill of pre-Israelite Jerusalem)"].) The association is made explicit in the paraphrase of Gen 14:18 found in the *Genesis Apocryphon* of Qumran Cave 1, "Salem, that is Jerusalem" (1QapGen 22:13). Philo explained the name as meaning "the vision of peace" *(horasis eirēnēs, De somn.* 2.38 § 250), and Heb 7:2 interprets *Melchisedek basileus Salēm* (really, "M. king of Salem") as *basileus eirēnēs,* "king of peace." This popular etymology of the name of Jerusalem, identifying its last element with Hebrew *šālôm* or Aramaic *šĕlām,* thus known in pre-Christian Judaism, is undoubtedly inspired in part by Ps 122:6, "Pray for the peace of Jerusalem" (cf. Ps 147:12-14). Hence the pathos in Jesus' words, "Would that you, even you, had recognized this day what would make for peace!" (v. 42). The city, whose very name is associated with peace, fails to recognize what makes for its own peace—fails to recognize the bearer of heaven's peace, fails to recognize its "king" of peace. Its role in the peaceful existence of humanity is hidden from its eyes, for it recognizes not the time of its visitation. Thus the end of v. 44 echoes the pathos of v. 42, alluding to words of Jeremiah in the LXX of 6:15. In that passage (6:9-15) the prophet castigated Jerusalem for its obstinacy and greed and its people who cried out "Peace, peace," when there was no peace. "So they will fall among the fallen and will perish at the time of their visitation." (See also Jer 10:15.)

The OT background of vv. 42 and 44c helps to explain also the lack of peace for Jerusalem in terms of war, to which vv. 43-44ab refer. Jerusalem will be encircled and hemmed in on all sides, with an embankment thrown up against it. The terminology may be prophetic and traditional; but the implication of the horrors of war to which Jerusalem will be exposed will bring home to it another sense of its failure to achieve peace. Verse 44 continues the dire description of Jerusalem's fate, its share in the usual atrocities of ancient warfare—with allusions to Ps 137:9 (which describes the fate of Babylon) and to Nah 3:10 (the fate of Nineveh, the capital of Assyria). Not a stone will be left upon a stone.

Jesus' lament over Jerusalem in this passage contributes in its own way to the Lucan notion of the continuity of Christianity with Judaism of old. If Israel of old is to be reconstituted—not replaced by a new people of God—in the Lucan story of God's salvation-history, the Lucan Jesus can nevertheless weep over the fate of its main city, which is for him the city of destiny. It recognizes not him who comes as God's last emissary of peace. Its failure to do so, especially at this time of his visit, becomes ominous. This "visitation" will take on a new meaning. For Jerusalem, the "city that murders prophets and stones those who are sent to you" (13:34) will become the city from which goes forth "the word of the Lord" (Isa 2:3; cf. Acts 1:8). But the transformation brings tears to the eyes of this last emissary of peace, because of the city's ominous fate. Implied, but never asserted by Luke, is the glory of Jerusalem, intimately associated with Jesus' own destiny, and his transit to the Father. The Lucan Jesus weeps over Jerusalem because the evangelist takes no delight in the fate that he recognizes to have been Jerusalem's.

In its own way, the Christmas promise of 2:14 is now fulfilled.

So Luke ends his story of Jesus' approach to the city of Jerusalem with the jubilant throng; he never tells about Jesus' entry into the city proper (contrast Mark 11:15). The next episode will be concerned with the Temple.

NOTES

19 41. *As Jesus drew near to Jerusalem.* Lit. "and as he drew near." Though *engizein* is a vb. "more or less characteristic" of Luke (see p. 112), J. Jeremias *(Die Sprache,* 157 n. 15) points out the problem that one has both here and in 15:25 about its possibly traditional (pre-Lucan) usage.

he wept at the sight of the city. Lit. "seeing the city, he wept over it." This detail recalls 13:34 and accentuates the concern expressed there. The motivation for Jesus' weeping will be expressed in the following verse; it does not concern his own fate.

Jesus' weeping is to be seen as a prophetic sign, with OT parallels in such passages as 2 Kgs 8:11; Jer 9:1; 14:17. The sad condition of the city will be the reason for weeping on the part of others in 23:28. The vb. *klaiein* with the prep. *epi* is found in the LXX of Gen 50:1; Num 11:13; Judg 11:37-38. See Tacitus' description of Jerusalem *(Hist.* 5.8).

42. *Would that you, even you, had recognized.* Lit. "if you . . . had recognized," to be understood: "it would please me." There is aposiopesis here (see BDF § 482), so that the conj. *ei* with the aor. indic. *egnōs* functions as an unattainable or unfulfilled wish. See BDF § 359.1. The word order differs in some Greek mss. with an extra intensifying adv. and particle *(kai ge)* added in the Koine text-tradition; but the meaning is not radically changed. It is still an expression of deep pathos.

this day. The day of Jesus' regal approach and peaceful visit thus takes on a somber aspect. The difference in time implied here from that in v. 43a is to be noted.

what would make for peace! I.e. how you might have won a share in that "peace in heaven" now being offered and how it might have contributed to your welfare. The phrase *ta pros eirēnēn* occurred in 14:32, used with a vb. of asking and thus with a different connotation. Cf. Isa 48:18 for a similar prophetic complaint.

that is hidden from your sight. I.e. by God (theological pass., see NOTE on 5:20), because of Jerusalem's own lack of perception. Implied is the blindness of its irresponsibility. See G. Schneider, *Evangelium nach Lukas,* 388-389.

43. *the time is coming.* Lit. "days will come." Cf. 5:35; 23:29, derived from the LXX of 1 Sam 2:31; 2 Kgs 20:17—the more usual Lucan terminology. The vb. *hēxousin* is probably pre-Lucan, traditional phraseology.

upon you. This prepositional phrase is omitted in ms. D and the OS versions.

your enemies. No mention is made of the Romans, even though they are the occupiers of the country.

will throw up an embankment against you. This is the first of five descriptions of hostile activity. The reference could be to the earthworks constructed by the Roman soldiers of Titus' army. See COMMENT on p. 1255. But the vocabulary may be borrowed from the LXX of Isa 29:3, "I will encircle you [Ariel, a name for Jerusalem], throw up an embankment *[balō peri se charaka],* and set towers about you." Cf. Isa 37:33e; Jer 6:6-21; Ezek 4:1-3; Tacitus, *Hist.* 5.11.

encircle you. The second hostile activity; it could be a reference to the wall built about Jerusalem by Titus' troops. See COMMENT. See the LXX of 2 Kgs 6:14.

hem you in on every side. The third hostile activity. The vb. *synechein,* "press close," a favorite of Luke (see p. 111), denotes hard pressure being exerted. Cf. 2 Macc 9:2 (against the city of Persepolis). See Ezek 4:2; 21:22; Jer 52:5.

44. *They will dash you and your children within you to the ground.* The fourth hostile activity. The vb. *edaphizein* means to make level with the ground, but is used often in the LXX to describe the atrocity of war which resulted in a form of genocide. The detail alludes to the avenging taunt addressed to the "Daughter of Babylon" in Ps 137:9 (but only the vb. is common to the two texts). However, Hos 10:14 makes clear the hostile activity that is intended. Cf. Nah 3:10; 2 Kgs 8:12. The prepositional phrase *en soi* is omitted in ms. D, probably because it appears later in the same verse (in the following cl.). Jerusalem itself is alluded to as a mother. Cf. 23:28.

leave not a stone upon a stone. The fifth hostile activity is possibly derived from 2

Sam 17:13, "so that not even a stone will be left there" *(lithos,* "stone," as in this verse). In the Lucan context this mention of stones must be related to those in v. 40; it now specifies how the stones will cry out. See further 20:17; cf. 21:6. Thus Jesus' words become a dire verdict for Jerusalem; something like the king's verdict in the parable of 19:27. Josephus' description of the end of Jerusalem runs like this: ". . . Caesar had already commanded the entire city and the temple to be razed to the ground, leaving only the towers which projected higher than the others to stand, Phasael, Hippicus, and Mariamme, and that part of the wall which enclosed the city on the west. This was to be an encampment for the troops which would be left behind, and the towers were to reveal to posterity how great a city Jerusalem had been and what sort of fortifications Roman prowess had dominated. All the rest of the wall which encompassed the city the demolition teams levelled so that no one who would come there in the future would ever believe that the spot had been inhabited. This, then, was the end to which the frenzy of the rebels brought Jerusalem, that illustrious city of celebrated renown" *(J. W.* 7.1,1 § 1-4; cf. 7.8,7 § 375-377). Jesus' words echo a prophetic utterance of old. See Mic 3:12.

because. See NOTE on 12:3; cf. Acts 12:23.

the time of your visitation. Thus the Lucan Jesus alludes to the minatory utterance of the prophet Jeremiah against Jerusalem in the time of Josiah: Jer 6:15 (LXX) "in the time of their visitation they will perish." Cf. Jer 10:15; Isa 10:3; Wis 3:7; 1 Pet 2:12. In the LXX the n. *episkopē* frequently translates Hebrew *pĕquddāh* (or related forms of the same root, *pqd),* "commission, charge, office," but also "punishment, requital." The period of opportunity was unnoticed by Jerusalem and not exploited.

BIBLIOGRAPHY (19:41-44)

Dodd, C. H. "The Fall of Jerusalem and the 'Abomination of Desolation,' " *JRS* 37 (1947) 47-54; reprinted, *More New Testament Studies* (Grand Rapids, MI: Eerdmans, 1968) 69-83.

Dupont, J. "Il n'en sera pas laissé pierre sur pierre (Marc 13,2; Luc 19,44)," *Bib* 52 (1971) 301-320.

Galbiati, E. "Il pianto di Gesù per Gerusalemme *(Luca* 19,41-47a)," *BeO* 7 (1965) 196-204.

Gaston, L. *No Stone on Another: Studies in the Significance of the Fall of Jerusalem in the Synoptic Gospels* (NovTSup 23; Leiden: Brill, 1970).

Gnilka, J. *Die Verstockung Israels: Isaias 6,9-10 in der Theologie der Synoptiker* (SANT 3; Munich: Kösel, 1961) 137-140.

Reicke, B. "Synoptic Prophecies on the Destruction of Jerusalem," *Studies in New Testament and Early Christian Literature: Essays in Honor of Allen P. Wikgren* (ed. D. E. Aune; NovTSup 33; Leiden: Brill, 1972) 121-134.

Robinson, W. C., Jr. *Der Weg des Herrn: Studien zur Geschichte und Eschatologie im Lukas-Evangelium* (Hamburg-Bergstedt: H. Reich, 1964) 50-53, 55-56.

S. Marco, E. a, "Videns civitatem, flevit super illam (Lc. 19, 41-44)," *VD* 10 (1930) 245-248.

Schramm, T. *Markus-Stoff,* 146-147.

Tiede, D. L. "Weeping for Jerusalem," *Prophecy and History in Luke-Acts* (Philadelphia: Fortress, 1980) 65-96, 143-148.

Uhsadel, W. "Predigt zum Gedächtnistage der Zerstörung Jerusalems," *Abraham unser Vater: Juden und Christen im Gespräch über die Bibel: Festschrift für Otto Michel zum 60. Geburtstag* (eds. O. Betz et al.; Leiden: Brill, 1963) 459-466.

128. THE PURGING OF THE TEMPLE
(19:45-46)

19 ⁴⁵ Then he went into the Temple area and started to drive out those who were selling there, ⁴⁶ saying to them, "It is written in Scripture, '*My house shall be a house of prayer*';ᵃ but you have made it *a den of robbers.*" ᵇ

ᵃ Isa 56:7   ᵇ Jer 7:11

COMMENT

Jesus proceeds directly into the Jerusalem Temple and in a prophetic act purges it of those who by their mercantile traffic were profaning its character as a house of prayer (19:45-46). By this significant act, Jesus as "the king, the one who comes in the name of the Lord!" (19:38), takes possession of and transforms his "Father's house" (2:49).

Luke is in this episode inspired by the Marcan parallel of 11:11,15-19 (cf. Matt 21:12-13). In the Marcan version Jesus is portrayed explicitly entering the city of Jerusalem (11:11a), from which he goes into the Temple, where he looks around at "everything" (as if he were coming there for the first time!), and then retires to Bethany with the Twelve (11:11bc). The next morning he finds and curses the fruitless fig tree (11:12-14), then enters the Temple and purges it. Thus the Marcan parallel to the present Lucan episode is complicated by two things: (a) the spacing of Jesus' entry into the city and the Temple from the purging of the latter by the cursing of the fig tree; and (b) the close linking of the purging of the Temple to the reaction of the chief priests and the Scribes who were seeking how they might do away with Jesus (11:18). Though inspired by the Marcan version, Luke has considerably redacted the Marcan source, and yet there is no real evidence that he has used any alternate source (see T. Schramm, *Markus-Stoff,* 149; H. Conzelmann, *Theology,* 76; but cf. I. Buse, "The Cleansing," 23).

The Lucan redaction consists of the following: (a) He omits the cursing of the fig tree (Mark 11:12-14); (b) he omits the first sentence of Mark 11:15 (mention of the entry into the city); (c) he greatly curtails the description of Jesus' actions in the Temple area (11:15cd—in effect, eliminating all the violent details [see p. 98]); (d) he eliminates 11:16 completely (mention of Jesus not allowing people to carry things through the Temple); (e) he drops the reference to Jesus' teaching (11:17a), in order to use the detail more explicitly in v. 47; and (f) he omits from the quotation of Isa 56:7 the final phrase "for all the nations." The following verses (47-48), the next episode in fact, emphasize the teaching of Jesus in the Temple and make that, rather than the purging of the Temple itself, the motive for the reaction of the chief priests, the Scribes, and the leaders of the people.

Though T. Schramm (Markus-Stoff, 149) maintains that there are no agreements of Luke and Matthew against Mark in this part of the Triple Tradition, one has to note at least the common omission of Mark 11:16 (for what reason it is hard to say) and of the phrase "for all the nations" in 11:17c (see I. Buse, "The Cleansing," 23). Both Matthew and Luke were undoubtedly aware that the Temple no longer existed, and hence for them it could scarcely still be regarded as a house of prayer for all the nations, especially when both evangelists knew that "the nations" were now "finding their way into the Church, not into the Temple of the old order" (J. M. Creed, The Gospel, 242). Moreover, it may have been additionally difficult for Matthew to admit to his readers that the Jerusalem Temple was intended to be a house of prayer for all the nations, even though his Gospel was destined for a mixed Jewish/Gentile Christian community.

Though it is easy to account for what Luke has made of the Marcan material, it is another matter to assess the form-critical nature of the passage and its relation to the historical Jesus and the Johannine form of the tradition about the purging of the Temple.

From the form-critical standpoint, R. Bultmann (HST 36) considers Mark 11:15b-d,16,17 as a unit, a biographical apophthegm, but he maintains that v. 17 (with its quotation of Isaiah and Jeremiah) has actually replaced an older pronouncement of Jesus, which is still preserved in John 2:16, "Stop making my Father's house a market place." Part of the reason for this is the evangelist's introduction in Mark 11:17a ("and he taught and said to them"), which suggests that "word and action did not originally belong together." Moreover, the second part of the pronouncement ("you have made it a den of robbers") is actually addressed not to the sellers, but to "the Jews at large," which tends to make the episode into an "imaginary scene." Bultmann has clearly put his finger on the problems in the Marcan passage and its relation to the Johannine tradition. However, V. Taylor (FGT 75) prefers to regard this episode form-critically as a Story about Jesus, because he thinks that the interest lies in the dramatic incident itself rather than in the words of Jesus.

Taylor may well be right in his assessment of the tradition in Mark (and perhaps also in Matthew), but when one reflects on the curtailed form of the episode in the Lucan Gospel, one is thrust back on Bultmann's assessment of the story. It is a pronouncement-story in the Lucan form. M. Dibelius considered the Lucan form to be a chria *(FTG* 161), because he sensed the emphasis on Jesus' pronouncement.

The further problem is to explain the relation of this episode in the Synoptic tradition to that in John 2:13-17. The Johannine form of the account is actually fuller than that of Mark and complicates the issue in still another way, in that it relates the purging to the words of Jesus about the destruction and rebuilding of the Temple—words preserved elsewhere in the Marcan and Matthean Gospels, but not in Luke. Luke may well have omitted reference to these words because he knew that Jesus neither destroyed the Temple nor rebuilt it (see R. E. Brown, *John, I-XII,* 120). The differences in the four accounts of the purging of the Temple can best be seen thus:

John 2	Mark 11	Matthew 21	Luke 19
Date: Passover (13)			
Jesus in Jerusalem (13)	Jesus in Jerusalem (15)	Jesus in Jerusalem (10) as a prophet from Nazareth (11)	
Enters the Temple (14)	Enters the Temple (15)	Enters the Temple (12)	Enters the Temple (45)
Meets people selling oxen, sheep, and doves and changing money (14)			
Makes a whip (15)			
Drives out sellers of oxen and sheep (15)	Drives out sellers and buyers (15)	Drives out sellers and buyers (12)	Drives out sellers (45)
Knocks over tables of money changers (15)	Knocks over tables of money changers (15)	Knocks over tables of money changers (12)	
Tells dove-sellers to get out (16)	Knocks over seats of dove-sellers (15)	Knocks over seats of dove-sellers (12)	
Says, "Stop making my Father's house a market place" (16)	Allows no one to carry anything through the Temple (16)		
Disciples recall Scripture: "Zeal for your house will consume me" (Ps 69:9) (17)	Teaches and quotes Scripture: "House of prayer" becomes "den of robbers" (Isa 56:7; Jer 7:11) (17)	Quotes Scripture: "House of prayer" becomes "den of robbers" (Isa 56:7; Jer 7:11) (13)	Quotes Scripture: "House of prayer" becomes "den of robbers" (Isa 56:7; Jer 7:11) (46)
			Teaches daily in the Temple (47)

Whereas the Matthean and Lucan accounts are dependent on the Marcan, the relation of the Marcan and Johannine accounts raises further problems. Attempts to solve them vary from the denial of all historicity for the episode (e.g. H. Ackermann, *Jesus: Seine Botschaft und deren Aufnahme im Abendland* [Göttingen: "Musterschmidt," Wissenschaftlicher-V., 1952] 62) to the claim that Jesus actually purged the Temple twice, once at the beginning of his ministry and once at the end (e.g. A. Plummer, *The Gospel,* 453). Denial of the historicity stems mainly from the inability to explain how Jesus as a single individual could have cleaned out the great Court of the Gentiles of the sellers and money changers who did business there with the permission of Temple authorities and succeeded in it without opposition or at least the intervention of Temple police. How could he have prevented the court from being used as a thoroughfare for transporting objects (Mark 11:16)? There is, in the long run, no way of answering this question, valid though it may be; we just do not know how Jesus might have done it. The separate attestation of the incident in the Synoptic and Johannine tradition would tend to support the basic historicity of the event, even though the details may have undergone embellishment and the Scripture passages involved may have been embroidered on to the traditions. There is enough similarity in the Greek wording of the two fundamental accounts to argue for separate narratives describing the same event (see I. Buse, "The Cleansing," 22), so that one cannot be persuaded by Plummer's arguments about "the Second Cleansing." His preference for that explanation stems mainly from the "gross chronological blunder" of one tradition or the other. Whereas some commentators (e.g. C. K. Barrett ["The House," 13]) think that the Johannine account is dependent on the Marcan, the majority consider the accounts independent of each other. (See further R. E. Brown, *John, I-XII,* 116-120.) The real problem is to decide which tradition, the Johannine or the Synoptic, echoes better the original setting of the incident or its dating.

Many interpreters (e.g. M.-J. Lagrange, V. Taylor, J. A. T. Robinson) consider the Johannine dating to be more probable. In the Synoptics Jesus makes only one journey to Jerusalem, and so Mark was constrained to date the purging of the Temple to the arrival of Jesus in Jerusalem toward the end of his public ministry. The Johannine Gospel, however, which reports several journeys of Jesus to Jerusalem would seem to date it more historically toward the beginning of his career. Other interpreters (e.g. C. H. Dodd, C. K. Barrett) prefer the Synoptic dating, because such a public attack on institutions of the Jerusalem Temple would have provoked an immediate reaction from the priests and officials of the Temple. Accordingly in the Marcan tradition they put Jesus quickly on trial and sentenced him to death. Moreover, to do what he did would have been more plausible after a career of prophetic preaching, and indeed after his regal entry into Jerusalem (as in the Marcan tradition). Which seems more plausible? It is difficult to decide because of the context in which the episode is recounted in both Johannine and Marcan traditions. In the Johannine Gospel the episode is linked to words of Jesus about the destruction of the Temple and its rebuilding, whereas in the Marcan Gospel the incident becomes the reason why the authorities finally move definitively to do away with Jesus (a reason which Matthew uses, but which Luke modifies somewhat). R. E. Brown *(John, I-XII,* 118) tries to make a distinction. He would date the prophetic warning of Jesus about the destruction of the Temple to "his first journey to Jerusalem and to the Temple," a warning later recalled with vagueness in the Synoptic tradition (Mark 14:58; Matt 26:61 [omitted by Luke]), but would assign Jesus' act of purging the Temple to "the last days of his life." John would then have combined them in his own fashion, transposing the scene of the purging to the beginning of Jesus' ministry because the raising of Lazarus becomes the chief reason for Jesus' arrest in that Gospel. This is a plausible solution; but to my way of thinking the early dating of the purging of the Temple could also be related to an aspect of Jesus' ministry in the Synoptic tradition. John the Baptist depicts Jesus as one mightier than himself, and at first casts him in the role of a fiery reformer, one whose hand carries the winnowing fan and who was prepared to burn up the chaff in Israel (Luke 3:17). Even though the Jesus of the Synoptic public ministry eventually disowns that role ascribed to him (Luke 7:18-23), the one incident in the gospel tradition which associates him with violence is precisely this episode, and it would more plausibly have been associated with the beginning of the ministry. For this reason I should prefer to think of the basic episode as having a context early in Jesus' ministry in Stage I of the gospel tradition; as said above, the Synoptics would have related it to the end of ministry, because in their tradition that is the only time that Jesus arrives in Jerusalem and comes into contact with the Temple.

In this scene the Lucan Jesus climaxes his entry into Jerusalem by entering directly into its Temple and purging it of all mercantile trafficking, driving out the sellers who were installed there, and protesting like a prophet of old against the profanation of God's house which their commerce has produced. Thus Jesus, arriving as "king" (19:38), acts as a prophet (quoting the prophets of old) and takes possession of his "Father's house" (2:49). He purges the Temple to make it ready for his Jerusalem ministry, i.e. teaching in the Temple. As he did in vanquishing the devil in 4:4,8,10 (see pp. 512-513), he quotes Scripture to justify his action. The first part of his declaration is not an exact quotation, but a rephrasing of Isa 56:7, "For my house shall be called a house of prayer for all the nations" (so the MT, followed closely by the LXX, which is quoted exactly in Mark 11:17b). These words of Trito-Isaiah form part of miscellaneous post-restoration oracles (coming from after 538 B.C.) and include beatitudes pronounced over proselytes, eunuchs, and other outcasts of Israel. Verses 6-7, in particular, are directed to proselytes *(bĕnê hannēkār);* even they will find a place in that "house of prayer." That was the purpose of the Temple of Jerusalem. But what has become of it?

The second part of Jesus' declaration alludes to Jer 7:11, "Has this house, which is called by my name, become a den of robbers *(mĕ'ārat pārîṣîm,* LXX: *spēlaion lēstōn)* in your sight?" It forms part of Jeremiah's famous Temple sermon (7:1-15), directed not against the priests and officials, but the worshipers in general who desecrate it by their idolatry and lawlessness. The mercantile trafficking of the sellers in the Temple becomes in Jesus' sight a desecration tantamount to that idolatry and lawlessness of old.

In discussing the greeting shouted to Jesus as he drew near to Jerusalem, "Blest be the king, the one who comes in the name of the Lord!" (19:38), I drew attention to the connotation of *ho erchomenos* and its relation to Mal 3:1 ("the Lord whom you seek will come to his temple") and suggested that this is the reason why the Lucan Jesus makes his way directly "into the Temple" of Jerusalem (instead of first entering the city proper, as in Mark). His purpose is to purge his Father's house (2:49) of all unsuited service of mammon. Recall his words in 16:13d, "You cannot serve both God and mammon." Thus he prepares his Father's house for his own ministry of preaching. In yet another sense, his act implies the transformation of the Temple and its role in the reconstitution of Israel. Certain Jerusalem Jews are driven out of it by an authoritative act of God's last emissary, who has just uttered a dire prediction about the fate of the city in which it is. Reconstituted Israel will have no need of the Temple for its God, "who dwells not in houses made by (human) hands" (Acts 7:48); but in the meantime Jesus removes from it those who do not belong there.

Is Jesus' purging of the Temple to be understood as a messianic purification? This can be asked on two levels. Would it have been so understood in Stage I of the gospel tradition? Is it to be so understood in the Synoptic, and specifically in the Lucan, account? Many commentators consider that Jesus' act in Stage I would have been understood as "a sign that the messianic purification of the Temple was at hand" (R. E. Brown, *John, I-XII,* 121; similarly, E. E. Ellis, *Gospel of Luke,* 231; G. Schneider, *Evangelium nach Lukas,* 392; W. G. Kümmel, *Promise and Fulfilment,* 117-118). They cite Jer 7:11, Zech 14:21 (no trader in the house of Yahweh), Mal 3:1 (the Lord *[hā'ādôn]* coming to his temple, which follows on the prophet's castigation of levitical abuses in it), Isa 56:7, and other OT passages. In the light of such OT prophetic passages, Jesus' act could readily be understood as the promised purification of the Temple. Given the opposition to the Jerusalem Temple priests on the part of the Essenes of Qumran, his act would be even more plausible. But none of the OT passages nor any of the Qumran literature suggests that the purging of the Temple was expected of a *messiah.* (See further G. Schrenk, *TDNT* 3. 243-244; P. Volz, *Die Eschatologie der jüdischen Gemeinde im neutestamentlichen Zeitalter* (2d ed.; Tübingen: Mohr

[Siebeck], 1934) 217, 240. An association of the Messiah with the rebuilding of Jerusalem and its Temple does surface in the *Amidah* § 14, but is never found earlier; the question is, How early is that tradition? Nor does the concatenation of Mark 14:56-57 and 14:61 necessarily give evidence of a belief in the *messianic* rebuilding of the Temple. Would that association ever have surfaced prior to the destruction of the Second Temple itself?

As for Stage III of the gospel tradition, there is not a hint that Jesus, either in the Synoptic or Johannine tradition, purges the Temple as Messiah. The closest one could come to this is in the Marcan Gospel, where he has been hailed with the cry, "Blest be the coming kingdom of our father David" (11:10), which may imply messiahship, but then his entry into the Temple is for inspection, and only after the cursing of the fruitless fig tree does the purging take place—in a context which suggests a connotation other than messianic. As far as Luke is concerned, H. Conzelmann *(Theology,* 77) rightly notes that "it is not a question of the eschatological end of the Temple, but of its cleansing; in other words, Jesus prepares it as an area where he can stay, and from now on he occupies it as a place belonging to him," where he can teach.

NOTES

19   45. *into the Temple area.* Or "the Temple precincts," i.e. *to hieron,* which in the concrete would mean the Court of the Gentiles, not the *naos* or sanctuary proper. See NOTE on 2:27.

started to drive out those who were selling there. I.e. the sellers of animals (without blemish, Lev 1:3) for the various sacrifices in the Temple and of other forms of offerings. In John 2:14 these are listed as oxen, sheep, and pigeons (on the last mentioned, see Luke 2:24). Luke, however, omits all mention of the buyers (see Mark 11:15), the money changers (those who supplied the Tyrian silver coins, at a commission, for other coins so that the half-shekel tax levied on adult male Jews by Exod 30:11-14 could be paid in support of the Temple [see further *m. Šeqal.* 1:3; 2:1,4]), and the dove-sellers. See Mark 11:15. Some mss. of the Lucan Gospel, however, add "in it and buying" (A, C, R, W, Θ, Ψ, *f* 13, and the Koine text-tradition), thus harmonizing this verse with either Mark 11:15 or Matt 21:12. Ms. D has an even fuller harmonization, mentioning all the things omitted. Cf. Str-B 1. 850-852.

46. *saying to them.* Thus Luke makes Jesus' act of purging and his declaration simultaneous. Contrast Mark 11:17.

It is written in Scripture. Lit. "it has been written"; *gegraptai* is an abbreviated form of *kathōs gegraptai* (see NOTES on 2:23; 3:4), which Luke also used in 4:4,8,10.

My house shall be a house of prayer. This is the reading in mss. ℵ¹, B, L, R, Θ, *f* 1,13; but a few others (C², 28, 1241, 1424) read *klēthēsetai,* "shall be called," instead of *estai,* "shall be," again a copyist's harmonization with Matthew or Mark, or possibly with the LXX of Isa 56:7. For the later rabbinical understanding of this OT text, see Str-B 1. 852-853.

a den of robbers. See Jer 7:11. C. K. Barrett ("The House," 16) thinks that *lēstēs,* which elsewhere in the NT means "guerilla, nationalist rebel" (see K. H. Rengstorf, *TDNT* 4. 257-262 [who does not, however, use this meaning for Mark 11:17!]) should have this meaning here too. It would then stand in contrast with "all the nations" of Mark 11:17: I.e. God intended this place for international prayer, but you have made it a nationalist stronghold. This is ingenious, but it is scarcely of any relevance to the Lucan form of the saying, which has eliminated *pasin tois ethnesin.* Moreover, it would then deprive the second part of the saying of its allusion to Jer 7:11, which certainly does not carry that connotation.

BIBLIOGRAPHY (19:45-46)

Barrett, C. K. "The House of Prayer and the Den of Thieves," *Jesus und Paulus* (eds. E. E. Ellis and E. Grässer) 13-20.

Braun, F.-M. "L'Expulsion des vendeurs du Temple (Mt., xxi, 12-17, 23-27; Mc., xi, 15-19, 27-33; Lc., xix, 45-xx, 8; Jo., ii, 13-22)," *RB* 38 (1929) 178-200.

Buse, I. "The Cleansing of the Temple in the Synoptics and in John," *ExpTim* 70 (1958-1959) 22-24.

Derrett, J. D. M. "The Zeal of the House and the Cleansing of the Temple," *Downside Review* 95 (1977) 79-94.

Eppstein, V. "The Historicity of the Gospel Account of the Cleansing of the Temple," *ZNW* 55 (1964) 42-58.

Haenchen, E. *Der Weg Jesu,* 382-389.

Hahn, F. *Titles,* 155-157.

Hamilton, N. Q. "Temple Cleansing and Temple Bank," *JBL* 83 (1964) 365-372.

Hiers, R. H. "Purification of the Temple: Preparation for the Kingdom of God," *JBL* 90 (1971) 82-90.

Jeremias, J. "Zwei Miszellen: 1. Antik-jüdische Münzdeutungen; 2. Zur Geschicht-lichkeit der Tempelreinigung," *NTS* 23 (1976-1977) 177-180, esp. 179-180.

Manson, T. W. "The Cleansing of the Temple," *BJRL* 33 (1950-1951) 271-282.

Mendner, S. "Die Tempelreinigung," *ZNW* 47 (1956) 93-112.

Pesch, R. "Der Anspruch Jesu," *Orientierung* 35 (1971) 53-56.

Roloff, J. *Das Kerygma,* 89-110.

Roth, C. "The Cleansing of the Temple and Zechariah xiv 21," *NovT* 4 (1960) 174-181.

Schnider, F., and W. Stenger, *Johannes und die Synoptiker: Vergleich ihrer Parallelen* (Biblische Handbibliothek 9; Munich: Kösel, 1971) 26-53.

Schramm, T. *Markus-Stoff,* 149.

Trocmé, E. "L'Expulsion des marchants du Temple," *NTS* 15 (1968-1969) 1-22.

(For further bibliography, especially on the Johannine form of the story, see R. E. Brown, *John, I-XII,* 125.)

129. THE REACTION OF THE LEADERS
TO JESUS' TEACHING
(19:47-48)

19 ⁴⁷ Day after day he would teach in the Temple area, and the chief
priests and the Scribes, together with the leaders of the people, kept
looking for a way to do away with him. ⁴⁸ But they could not find a
way to do so, for the people all hung on his words.

COMMENT

Jesus' official ministry in the Jerusalem Temple now begins, and Luke sums it
up in characteristic fashion (19:47-48), just as he gave a summary of his
Galilean ministry at its outset (4:14-15).

The introductory statement, giving the summary of the ministry, is composed by Luke himself (v. 47a). After that his account is inspired by the
Marcan summary of 11:18, but he derives from it only the mention of the
attempt of the chief priests and Scribes to do away with Jesus. To the two
groups named in "Mk" Luke adds "the leaders of the people" and v. 48a
(their inability to find a way to achieve their end). Verse 48b is also inspired
by Mark 11:18c, but formulated by Luke (see p. 167).

Form-critically considered, these verses are a summary (on which see pp.
521-522; cf. *HST* 362.)

Whereas the Marcan Gospel linked closely the reaction of the Jerusalem
authorities to Jesus' act of purging the Temple, the Lucan account has interjected the daily teaching of Jesus in the Temple. This is now seen to be the
purpose for the purging of the Temple itself. But it is also part of the reason
(at least) for their attempt to do away with him. This will become still clearer
in 20:1-2, where his authority is questioned in a context of teaching and
preaching.

Jesus' ministry in Jerusalem is confined to teaching in the Temple area. (Cf.
21:37.) In 20:21 Luke will specify what Jesus has been teaching, "the way of
God." He performs, however, no miracles in Jerusalem or in its Temple (that
in 22:51 takes place on the Mount of Olives!). Indeed, the summary statement
in these verses and later references to Jesus' teaching in chaps. 20-21 would
give the impression that this ministry of Jesus was protracted, an impression

which differs from that of the other Synoptic Gospels (see H. Conzelmann, *Theology,* 77).

This summary also mentions the attempt of the Jerusalem authorities to do away with Jesus, and it thus foreshadows the passion narrative itself. Noteworthy in this regard is the distinction that Luke introduces between the chief priests, Scribes, and leaders, on the one hand, and "all the people" *(ho laos hapas),* on the other. This distinction will surface again, even though Luke will not rigorously pursue it. Thus the antagonists of the passion drama are already introduced.

NOTES

19 47. *Day after day he would teach.* Lit. "he was teaching daily." Luke uses *kai ēn* + pres. ptc. *didaskōn,* the periphrastic conjugation (see p. 122), which is expressive of the customary activity of Jesus in the Temple area. It helps to build up the impression of a protracted ministry of teaching in the Temple. Cf. 21:37; 22:53. On the prepositional phrase *kath' hēmeran,* see p. 234. On the Lucan use of *didaskein,* see p. 148.

the chief priests and the Scribes, together with the leaders of the people. This phrase, describing three groups of Jerusalem authorities, has not been met before. It may mean the same as the three groups mentioned in 9:22 (see NOTE there), chief priests, Scribes, and elders. In 20:19; 22:2; 23:10 only the first two groups will be mentioned again; in 22:4,52 we will meet with "chief priests and the Temple officers." In all of this characterization of the groups that oppose Jesus during his last days the Pharisees are conspicuously absent; they last appeared in 19:39. See NOTE there. For *prōtos* as "leader," see Mark 6:21; Acts 13:50; 17:4; 25:2; 28:7,17. Note Josephus' statement *(Ant.* 20.10,5 § 251): "After the death of these kings [Herod the Great and Archelaus] the constitution became an aristocracy, and the chief priests were entrusted with the leadership of the nation."

kept looking for a way to do away with him. Lit. "to destroy him." This is really the first indication in the Lucan Gospel of a deliberate intention on the part of Jesus' adversaries to take action against him. Preparation for such an attempt, however, was already made in 6:11; 11:53-54. Contrast Mark 3:6, where the plotting starts earlier in that Gospel. This deliberate action is part of the orchestration of the chord first struck in the infancy narrative. See p. 423.

48. *they could not find a way to do so.* Lit. "they did not find what they might do." Luke uses the acc. neut. def. art. before the indir. question. See p. 108. His comment eliminates the "fear" found in the Marcan parallel (11:18); instead Luke merely contrasts the authorities and the people.

the people all hung on his words. Lit. "for all the people, listening to him, hung (upon him)." It is impossible to say what the function of the gen. *autou* really is, whether it is the obj. of *akouōn,* "listening," or of the compound vb. *exekremato,* "hung themselves on." It is placed between the two of them. The vb. expresses a sort of intimate association and appreciation of all the people with Jesus, in contrast to the authorities. Mark 11:17 spoke of "all the crowd," but Luke uses his favorite biblical word *laos,* on which see NOTE on 18:43.

130. JESUS' AUTHORITY IS QUESTIONED
(20:1-8)

20 ¹ One day while he was teaching the people in the Temple area and was preaching, the priests and the Scribes happened to be standing by with the elders. ² So they said to him, "Tell us, what authority do you have for doing these things? Who gave you this authority?" ³ Jesus replied to them, "Let me ask you a question too. Tell me, ⁴ was John's baptism of heavenly or of human origin?" ⁵ Then they began to debate among themselves, admitting, "If we say, 'Of heavenly origin,' he will ask, 'Then why did you not believe him?' ⁶ But if we say, 'Of human origin,' then the people will all stone us, for they are convinced that John was a prophet." ⁷ So they answered that they did not know its origin. ⁸ Then Jesus said to them, "Nor shall I tell you what authority I have for doing these things."

COMMENT

During the course of Jesus' daily Temple-teaching Jerusalem authorities finally confront him explicitly and ask him what authority he has for what he has been doing. He counters with a question to them about how they judged another recent Jewish religious figure, John the Baptist, whom the people esteemed. Because these authorities feign ignorance and an inability to answer his question, he refuses to tell them what his authorization is (20:1-8). In the first of six scenes in this Lucan chapter, which the evangelist takes over from "Mk," Jesus is depicted in conflict with the Jerusalem authorities (see Mark 11:27-12:40 [except for 12:28-34, which Luke omits because of his own episode in 10:25-28]). Four of the scenes will be controversy-stories (20:1-8,20-26,27-40,41-44), one a parable to which a note of controversy is appended (20:9-19), and one a collection of isolated sayings (20:45-47).

Thus Luke continues to follow his Marcan source, substantially reproducing Mark 11:27-33, but redacting it somewhat (cf. Matt 21:23-27, which follows "Mk" still more closely). Luke substitutes for Mark 11:27a a characteristic introductory cl., which repeats the context of teaching (and preaching) in the Temple. He improves the Greek at times, substituting some of his favorite expressions; he eliminates repetitious cls. (e.g. Mark 11:29d,30b), substitutes an indirect question (v. 7; cf. Mark 11:33), and removes the note about the authorities' "fear" of the crowd (Mark 11:32). The only minor agreements of Matthew and Luke against Mark are in the mention of "teaching" (Matt 21:23; Luke 20:1), the introduction of *apokritheis* (Matt 21:24; Luke 20:3), and the use of a form of *eipein* (Matt 21:24; Luke 20:3), which, however, have to be judged as coincidental. Even T. Schramm *(Markus-Stoff,* 149-150), who is eager to maintain that Luke had known a variant source for this episode, considers it "certain" that Luke made no use of it. (See also E. Haenchen, *Der Weg Jesu,* 395; G. S. Shae, "The Question," 4.)

Form-critically considered, the episode is a pronouncement-story, with a minimum of narrative, a controversy dialogue with adversaries. In it Jesus answers them with a counter-question (v. 4), which functions as the primary pronouncement; a secondary one is found in v. 8 (his refusal to answer the authorities). In effect, the pronouncement is: He who authorized John to preach "a baptism of repentance for the forgiveness of sins" (3:3) has authorized me (Jesus) to teach and preach, to do "these things." (See *FGT* 64-65.)

R. Bultmann, who agrees with the above form-critical assessment *(HST* 20), queries the original sense of "these things" *(tauta,* v. 2), denying that it refers to Jesus' walking in the Temple (Mark 11:27) or to the preceding context of the purging of the Temple (Mark 11:15-19). He considers the original pronouncement to have been in Mark 11:30 (= "Just as the Baptist received his *exousia* from God and not from men, so also do I"). For him, however, the following verses (Mark 11:31-33) transform the original apophthegm (vv. 28-30), by introducing a Hellenistic note of belief in the Baptist and thus revealing an early Christian creation designed to disarm opponents who sought to extol the Baptist and downplay Jesus: "If you recognize the Baptist's *exousia,* you must likewise acknowledge the *exousia* of Jesus."

Bultmann's view has often been subjected to serious criticism (see J. M. Creed, *The Gospel,* 244-245; G. S. Shae, "The Question," 14-28). Whether or not the controversy dialogue conforms to rabbinical modes or not (for a detailed comparison, see G. S. Shae, "The Question," 13-14), it should be noted that none of the rabbinical parallels usually appealed to (see Str-B 1. 861-862) antedates the fourth century A.D. The dialogue-mode is very effective. Creed notes that, if Mark 11:33 (= Luke 20:8) is regarded as a secondary addition, the original apophthegm would be "an intolerably lame reply," having little force either as a saying of the historical Jesus or as a contribution to the controversy of an early Christian community (such as was imagined by Bultmann). Creed likewise calls attention to the parallel in this episode to that about the tribute due to Caesar, which Bultmann himself regards as "a genuine historical incident" (cf. *HST* 26). As others have often noted (e.g. J. Kremer, "Jesu Antwort," 129; N. Perrin, *Rediscovering,* 75), there is no reason to contest the authenticity of this account of Jesus' altercation with the

Jerusalem authorities or the substance of the dialogue. Its roots and details are to be traced to Stage I of the gospel tradition.

As for the meaning of "these things," this varies according to the present Gospel context. In Mark 11, even though the cursing of the fig tree (vv. 12-14) and its interpretation (vv. 20-25) are interposed, the episode of the challenge of the authorities made to Jesus is dated to "the next day" (11:12). Hence in Mark the *tauta* must include the purging of the Temple. The same would hold true for Matthew. But Luke, with his reference to Jesus' daily teaching in the Temple and with his distancing of the challenge from the foregoing incident ("one day while he was teaching" [v. 1]), puts the main emphasis on Jesus' teaching. It would be difficult to say that *tauta* (v. 2) does not refer to the purging of the Temple. But then one has to raise the question whether *tauta* might not also include all that Jesus has been doing in his ministry as described in the Gospel, *pace* E. Klostermann, *Markusevangelium* (HNT 3; Tübingen: Mohr [Siebeck], 1971) 119 (see J. Kremer, "Jesu Antwort," 131). Given the context of Jesus' Jerusalem teaching in this part of the Gospel, which (as already noted) is more protracted than in the other Synoptics, the main referent in *tauta* has to be understood as his authority to teach.

Having assumed possession of his "Father's house" (2:49), the Lucan Jesus teaches and preaches in the Temple and is there confronted by Jerusalem authorities, who want to know where he gets the authority *(exousia)* to do so. Instead of immediately answering them or challenging their authority, he poses a counter-question, "Was John's baptism of heavenly or of human origin?" (v. 4). The authorities sense the implication of the dilemma and immediately realize the possible reactions of Jesus and the people who are present (v. 1), if they answer. As J. M. Creed *(The Gospel,* 243) notes, the counter-question is not a mere dialectical device; having been baptized by John himself, Jesus asks his critics to "face the issue which John had already presented to them, before he consented to discuss the question of his own authority." So the Jerusalem authorities feign ignorance and say only that they do not know whence John's authority came, lest the people who consider John a prophet would react violently against them. Jesus' final reply: "Nor shall I tell you what authority I have" (v. 8). The thrust of his answer: If John's authority came from God, a fortiori mine does too, for John himself had declared Jesus to be one more powerful than himself (3:16). If John were a prophet, then Jesus would be likewise a heaven-sent spokesman of God.

Jesus' final reply (v. 8) foreshadows his answer to the Sanhedrin at his trial (22:67-68); what he will say on that occasion is actually borne out here.

This controversy dialogue has christological implications in that Jesus is indirectly portrayed as a heaven-commissioned prophet, one who speaks, teaches, and preaches in the name of God himself. It reaffirms what was implied in the episode of the purging of the Temple and will be reinforced in coming episodes, where he will be indirectly presented as a beloved "son" (20:13), the cornerstone (20:17), teacher (20:39), and David's Son and Lord (20:41-44).

The reader of the Lucan Gospel knows that Jesus' authority comes from God, for he himself revealed in 4:43 that he "was sent" to "proclaim the kingdom of God." To ask what would have happened if Jesus had given a straightforward answer to the authorities and said that he had been sent by the Father would be to miss the point of the Synoptic controversy. It would also pose a Johannine question to the Lucan Jesus.

NOTES

20 1. *One day.* Lit. "on one of the days," an obvious reference to the daily teaching mentioned in 19:47a. Compare the Lucan introduction here with 5:12,17; 8:22. For the use of *mia* with the gen., see pp. 121-122. Some mss. (A, C, R, W, Θ, *f*¹³, and the Koine text-tradition) add *ekeinōn*, "those" (days), which would make the reference to Jesus' teaching even more explicit; but it is omitted in mss. ℵ, B, D, L, Q, Ψ, *f*¹, etc.

while he was teaching the people in the Temple area and was preaching. The subordinate cl. in the *kai egeneto* construction is a gen. absol. (p. 108) which Luke substitutes for the Marcan parataxis. No real distinction is being made between Jesus' teaching and preaching (on the sense of the latter, see the explanation of *euangelizesthai* on p. 148). There is no reference to the kingdom in this episode, and it is not until v. 21 that we learn that Jesus has been teaching "the way of God."

the priests and the Scribes happened to be standing by with the elders. Lit. "and it happened on one of the days, while . . . preaching, (that) the priests were standing by with . . ." Luke uses *kai egeneto* with a finite vb. *(epestēsan)* without the intervening conj. *kai.* See p. 119. On the three groups mentioned as members of the Jerusalem Sanhedrin, see NOTE on 9:22. Cf. E. Lohse, *TDNT* 7. 860-871. Jesus is confronted not merely by the Temple police *(stratēgoi tou hierou,* 22:4,52; Acts 4:1; 5:24,26), who might have been thought to react to his purging the Temple; more is involved, and so the authorities themselves challenge him. On the vb. *ephistanai,* see NOTE on 2:19.

The word *archiereis,* "chief priests," is found in mss. ℵ, B, C, D, L, M, N, Q, R, Θ, Ψ, *f*¹,¹³, etc., but other mss. (A, E, G, H, K, W, Γ, Δ, Π, and the Koine text-tradition) read simply *hiereis,* "priests." B. M. Metzger *(The Text of the New Testament* [New York: Oxford University, 1964] 238-239) argues strongly for the latter as the correct, original reading; see also H. Greeven, "Erwägungen zur synoptischen Textkritik," *NTS* 6 (1959-1960) 281-296, esp. 295-296.

2. *So they said to him.* Lit. "speaking to him, they said"; Luke uses *legontes pros* + acc. (see p. 116), instead of the simple impf. *elegon* of Mark 11:28.

what authority do you have for doing these things? Lit. "in/with what authority do you do these (things)?" Luke has already spoken of Jesus' authority *(exousia)* in 4:32 (see NOTE there), 36; cf. 5:24. It will appear again in v. 8. See also p. 168. The Jerusalem authorities try to bring Jesus to an inquisition and demand that he declare publicly the source of his claim to teach and preach. Note the demand, "Tell us," and contrast the Johannine way of putting the question in John 2:18.

Who gave you this authority? Lit. "or who is the one giving you this authority?" The second question merely recasts more specifically the previous one in terms of the person who authorizes Jesus. The Sanhedrin realizes that Jesus is not a rabbi in the usual sense. See Str-B 2. 746-754. So they hope to catch him in some admission that would enable them to arrest him. Luke, slavishly reproducing the Marcan *Vorlage,* forgets that he has already portrayed Jesus earlier in the Gospel as one over whom the heavens opened, upon whom the holy Spirit descended in bodily form, and about whom a heavenly voice publicly declared, "You are my beloved son" (3:21-22).

3. *replied to them.* Luke substitutes his favorite *apokritheis de eipen* (see p. 114) for the simple Marcan *eipen,* "said," and *pros autous* (see p. 116) for the Marcan dat. *autois.* In his reply Jesus identifies himself neither as the Messiah nor as a prophet, but counters with a question. He does not contest the authority of the Sanhedrin to question him.

a question. Lit. "a word" *(logon),* i.e. a word of explanation about what they thought of John and his ministry of baptizing. Some mss. (A, C, D, K, Θ, Ψ, *f* 13, and the Koine text-tradition) add *hena,* "one" (word); but this is a copyist's harmonization of the Lucan text with Mark 11:29. For another counter-question in the gospel tradition, see Mark 10:3. For the Johannine Jesus' way of answering, cp. John 18:19-22.

Tell me. The counter-request of "Tell us" (v. 2).

4. *was John's baptism of heavenly or of human origin?* Lit. "was John's baptism from heaven or from human beings?" Jesus' question is more specific than that of the authorities: What did they really think of the baptism that John preached and administered? His question implies that the Baptist's *exousia* was from God and contains a "veiled claim" that his is too—not *(pace* V. Taylor, *Mark,* 470) that "Jesus Himself is the Messiah." That is too specific; there is not a hint in this passage, even in the Marcan form of it, that Jesus' messiahship is involved. See E. Haenchen, *Der Weg Jesu,* 394.

of heavenly origin or of human origin? I.e. since John was not a rabbi, but had authority that commanded the respect of people. Cf. the similar question posed by Gamaliel in Acts 5:38.

5. *began to debate among themselves.* Lit. "began to debate, saying to themselves." Put on the defensive by Jesus, the Sanhedrin resorts to debate and discussion, not about the heart of the matter, but about the consequences of their answer. Luke uses the ingressive aor. of *syllogizesthai,* "discuss, debate" (see BDF § 331), and the ptc. *legontes* with *pros* + acc., which is in this case derived from Mark 11:31. See 20:14. Cf. Matt 21:25, where the debate is inner, mental discussion, "within themselves."

Of heavenly origin. I.e. the expected natural answer in the story. "Heaven" is a circumlocution for the divine name. See NOTE on 15:18; cf. John 3:27.

Then why did you not believe him? I.e. and submit to his baptism? Cf. 7:28-30.

6. *Of human origin.* I.e. their preferred answer in the circumstances.

then the people will all stone us. Luke improves the Greek text (as does Matthew in his own way), since Mark 11:32 has an anacoluthon, "But shall we say, 'Of human origin'?—They were afraid of the people." Cf. Matt 21:26. The vb. *katalithazein,* "stone (to death)," is found only in Christian Greek writers (e.g. Epiphanius, *Pana-*

rion 26.3,5 [GCS 25.280]; Gregory of Nyssa, *Contra Eunom.* 1 [PG 45.332B]), possibly in dependence on this Lucan usage. The simple vb. *lithazein* occurs in Acts 5:26; 14:19. In the Johannine Gospel stoning is linked to the charge of blasphemy (10:31-33; cf. 8:59). This may be implied in Luke's redactional change of the text. See Lev 24:11-16.

they are convinced that John was a prophet. Again, Luke improves the Greek, using the periphrastic pf. ptc. *pepeismenos* with *estin*. See p. 122. For John as a prophet, see NOTES on 1:76; 7:26,28-30.

7. *that they did not know its origin.* Lit. "that they did not know whence (it was)." Luke substitutes indir. discourse for the Marcan direct discourse (11:33). Their reply claims ignorance, but their (feigned) ignorance is eloquent. Nothing more need be said. They may have feared stoning, but they really feared the need to admit the truth. They admit that they are incompetent to judge John; they prove thereby that they are incompetent to judge Jesus! But judge him they will.

8. *said.* Luke changes Mark's historic pres. to the aor. *eipen.* See p. 107.

Nor shall I tell you what authority I have for doing these things. Lit. "nor do I tell you in/with what authority I do these (things)." Cf. 22:67-68. In Mark 11:29d Jesus promised an answer, conditionally; in 11:33d he expresses his refusal to carry out the promise. Luke omitted the promise (even conditional); but now he repeats the refusal of an answer. Both in the counter-question and in the refusal Jesus, in effect, challenges the authorities to recognize his authority. Implied: he knows clearly what authority he has, who has commissioned him, and, in fact, who he really is.

BIBLIOGRAPHY (20:1-8)

Haenchen, E. *Der Weg Jesu,* 392-396.
Kremer, J. "Jesu Antwort auf die Frage nach seiner Vollmacht: Eine Auslegung von Mk 11,27-33," *BibLeb* 9 (1968) 128-136.
Roloff, J. *Das Kerygma,* 93-95, 101-102.
Schramm, T. *Markus-Stoff,* 149-150.
Shae, G. S. "The Question on the Authority of Jesus," *NovT* 16 (1974) 1-29.

131. THE PARABLE OF THE WICKED TENANT FARMERS
(20:9-19)

20 ⁹ Then Jesus began to propose this parable to the people. "A man planted a vineyard, leased it to farmers, and went abroad for quite some time. ¹⁰ After a while he sent a servant to the farmers that they might pay him a share of the vineyard's produce. But the farmers beat

the servant and sent him away empty-handed. [11] Again he tried, sending another servant; and they beat him too, treated him shamefully, and sent him away empty-handed. [12] Again he tried, sending a third servant; but they covered him with wounds and drove him away. [13] Then the owner of the vineyard said, 'What am I to do? Ah, I shall send my own son, one who is dear to me; perhaps they will respect him.' [14] When the farmers saw him, they discussed it among themselves: 'This is the heir; let us kill him, so that the inheritance will be ours.' [15] So they drove him out of the vineyard and murdered him. What then will the owner of the vineyard do to them? [16] He will come and destroy those farmers and lease the vineyard to others."

When they heard this, the people said, "Heaven forbid!" [17] But Jesus looked at them and said, "Then what is the meaning of this text of Scripture:

'The stone which the builders rejected
    has become the cornerstone'?[a]

[18] Everyone who trips over that stone will be broken to pieces, and anyone on whom it falls it will crush."

[19] The Scribes and the chief priests wanted to lay hands on Jesus then and there—but they feared the people—for they knew that he had directed that parable against them.

[a] Ps 118:22

COMMENT

Luke now continues his account of Jesus' teaching ministry in the Jerusalem Temple with the telling of the parable of the wicked tenant farmers (20:9-19). Though Jesus utters it in the hearing of "the people," it is really addressed to the Jerusalem authorities, for the episode ends with the significant comment of the evangelist that "The Scribes and the chief priests," some of the authorities named at the beginning of the preceding episode (20:1), realized that "he had directed that parable against them" (v. 19).

Luke has derived the parable from Mark 12:1-12, which has also preserved the added quotation of an OT passage (vv. 10-11 = Luke 20:17). Cf. Matt 21:33-46. As in "Mk," the parable is preceded by the question about Jesus' authority and followed by the episode about the tribute due to God and to Caesar. Apart from v. 18, which Luke has himself added (possibly derived from "L" [see p. 84], or possibly of Lucan composition—note its problematic presence in Matt 21:44 [bracketed]), he has otherwise abbreviated and redacted what he has derived from "Mk" (see p. 93). The elements in the Lucan form of the parable are as follows: (a) a Lucan redactional introduction (v. 9a: with the characteristic *legein pros* + acc. [see p. 116]); (b) a shortened opening of the parabolic narrative (v. 9b,c,d—with the addition of *chronous hikanous,* "for quite some time"); (c) the details about the sending of three servants and the son (vv. 10-15a, with the use of *prosetheto,* "added, did again" [vv. 11,12], the addition of the soliloquy [v. 13], and the introduction of a purpose cl. with the subjunc. [v. 14d]); (d) the conclusion of the parable (vv. 15b-16, with the reaction of the people who listened); (e) the added OT quotation (v. 17, curtailed by Luke); (f) the Lucan added saying (v. 18); and (g) the redacted comment of the evangelist about the reaction and the fear of the Scribes and chief priests (v. 19). Though the Lucan redactional modifications are numerous, they are in the long run minimal, for the bulk of the parable is clearly derived from "Mk."

Has Luke possibly used some other source instead of or in addition to "Mk"? A. T. Cadoux *(The Parables of Jesus: Their Art and Use* [London: James Clarke, 1931] 40) once tried to maintain that Luke preserved the "Q"-form of this parable; but such a position counters the basic understanding of "Q," and nothing in the differences between "Mk" and the Lucan form suggests this. T. Schramm *(Markus-Stoff,* 150-167) has argued that Luke has combined an "L" form of the parable with that of "Mk." Yet this is no more convincing than Cadoux's view. The soliloquy of v. 13 is almost certainly a Lucan creation; it is not clearly derived from "L," despite the arguments brought forth by Schramm (ibid. 162-163).

It has recently been argued by M. Lowe that "the original reference of the Parable of the Vineyard and the Wicked Husbandmen was to John the Baptist" ("From the Parable," 257). Basing himself on all sorts of questionable analyses of Synoptic relations (of R. L. Lindsey, M.-E. Boismard, E. L. Abel, and D. Flusser), he maintains that a "Baptist sequence" (consisting of the cleansing of the Temple, the question to Jesus, the parry about John, the parable of the two sons, the parable of the banquet, the parable of the vineyard, and the stone-saying) has been the basis of this and the preceding episode in the Lucan Gospel. The suggestion is ingenious, unbridled in speculation.

The real problem in the passage is the developed form of the parable which is present in the Synoptic tradition. The attempt to discern Luke's sources has to contend with the attempts to recover the parable of Stage I of the gospel tradition and with its relation to the form of it which is preserved in *Gos. of Thom.* § 65-66.

Ever since A. Jülicher's analysis of this parable, many commentators have judged the Marcan form of it to be an early Christian "allegorical presentation of the history of salvation," with the death of Jesus in retrospect: ". . . our sole source, Mark 12, is in the end to be understood as the product of early Christian theology rather than as the authentic record of a controversy-discourse of Jesus himself. . . . Early Christianity, not Jesus himself, comes to the fore in Mark 12:1-11" *(Gleichnisreden,* 2. 406). In this judgment Jülicher was followed by R. Bultmann *(HST* 177, 205: "a community product"); W. G. Kümmel *(Promise and Fulfilment,* 83; cf. "Das Gleichnis," 120-131).

Part of the reason for this assessment of the parable was the reluctance of commentators to think that Jesus could have made use of allegory; part of it was a reluctance to admit that "the murder of the 'only' *[sic]* son cannot be understood in any way as a feature of a real parable" (W. G. Kümmel, *Promise and Fulfilment,* 83); in part, it was a conviction that "Judaism did not know the messianic name 'Son of God' " [on this, see pp. 206-208, 347]; and in part, because "the transference of the promise from the Jews who reject the son to a new people of God is here described as a punishment for the *murder* of the son, whilst in other cases Jesus lets this punishment follow on the rejection of his person without mentioning his death" (ibid. 83).

However, a number of commentators (e.g. C. H. Dodd, J. Jeremias, B. T. D. Smith, V. Taylor, C. W. F. Smith, et al.) have insisted that a genuine parable uttered by Jesus himself lies at the basis of the gospel tradition (in Stage I), which has been subsequently allegorized and expanded (in Stage II). In this view, the parable told about an absentee landlord who had leased his vineyard to tenant farmers under contract to give him in due time a share of the produce. He sent his agent-servants to collect his share after the vintage, but those agents were paid off only in blows and rejection. Realizing the seriousness of the situation, the landlord eventually sent his son, thinking that he would command the respect of the tenant farmers. But the tenants murdered the son, cast his corpse out of the vineyard, and seized the property for themselves. This skeleton form of the parable was further shown to have historical verisimilitude in first-century Palestine, where economic unrest often caused landlords to live elsewhere and to lease their farms to tenant farmers (see C. H. Dodd, *Parables,* 97; J. Jeremias, *Parables,* 74-75). To this skeleton form of the parable the early tradition eventually added allusions to the OT (to Isa 5:2 at the beginning of it, and the testimony-text about the cornerstone from Ps 118:22-23) and a concluding application.

This interpretation of the parable seems to have found striking support in the form of the parable preserved in *Gos. of Thom.* § 65: "There was a good man who had a vineyard. He leased it to tenant farmers that they might cultivate it and he might get its produce from them. He sent his servant so that the tenants might give him the produce of the vineyard. They seized his servant and beat him—a little more and they would have killed him. The servant went (back) and told his master (about) it. The master said, 'Perhaps < they > did not recognize < him >.' He sent another servant; the tenants beat him too. Then the master sent his son and said, 'Perhaps they will respect my son.' Since those tenants knew that he was the heir to the vineyard, they seized him and killed him. Let the one who has ears give heed." This form of the parable is also immediately followed by an isolated saying, separately introduced (ibid. § 66): "Jesus said, 'Show me the stone which the builders have rejected; that is the cornerstone.' " Not only is the skeleton form of the parable found here (i.e. minus the additions which Dodd et al. ascribed to early tradition), but it even has the parabolic threesome (a "servant," "another servant," "his son").

Reactions to this new evidence and to its bearing on the interpretation of the Synoptic parable have been mixed. J. Jeremias, J.-E. Ménard, R. M. Wilson, J. D. Crossan regard the skeleton form of the parable as preserved in the *Gospel of Thomas* as the primitive form which Jesus would have uttered: It "vindicates the offer of the gospel to the poor" which the leaders of the people (= the tenant farmers) have opposed in their rebellion against God, who will give the vineyard to "others" (e.g. the poor and the meek [Matt 5:5]). In the subsequent (pre-Marcan) tradition the vineyard became "the house of Israel" (Isa 5:7), the rebellious tenant farmers the leaders thereof who have rejected the message of its servants the prophets (see Mark 12:5b), and the son Jesus himself who by his resurrection has become the cornerstone (Mark 12:10-11). Others, however, have tried to show that the form of the parable in the *Gospel of Thomas* is either dependent on the Synoptics, even Luke (e.g. W. Schrage, *Das Verhältnis,* 137-145; H. K. McArthur, "The Dependence of the Gospel of Thomas on the Synoptics," *ExpTim* 71 [1960] 286-287; B. Dehandschutter, "La parabole"; G. Schneider, *Evangelium nach Lukas,* 297-298), or under gnostic influence (e.g. W. R. Schoedel, "Parables").

My own reaction to this problem is the following: Even though one cannot prove that the *Gospel of Thomas* is independent of earlier tradition, it is likely that it has in this case preserved an independent tradition, a more primitive form of the parable. *Pace* M. Hengel ("Das Gleichnis," 5-6), the *Gospel of Thomas* does not display a tendency to deallegorize. It may be under gnostic influence at times, and the omission of one detail or another may be owing to gnostic exegesis (so W. R. Schoedel, "Parables"); but the allegorization of a parable in the gospel tradition is a more normal process than a change from allegory to parable. Moreover, the parabolic threesome in the *Gospel of Thomas* form (a "servant," "another servant," "his son") is scarcely a reduction from the Marcan three servants "and many others" or from the Matthean double sending of "his servants" and "other servants, more than the first," or even the Lucan "a servant," "another servant," and "a third servant," and then the son. It suits the usual threesome otherwise found in Jesus' teaching (see C. L. Mitton, "Threefoldness in the Teaching of Jesus," *ExpTim* 75 [1963-1964] 228-230). The differences in the *Gospel of Thomas* which make Schrage think that its form of the parable depends on the Synoptics, especially Luke, have all been explained by J.-E. Ménard *(L'Evangile selon Thomas,* 167). The reference to the "son" may already have had an allegorical nuance; but one cannot conclude that such a detail could not have been used by Jesus himself (see p. 600; cf. W. G. Kümmel, "Das Gleichnis," 207-217).

Form-critically, then, this episode in the Lucan Gospel is to be considered as an expanded and allegorized parable. It is, indeed, an allegorical presentation of Lucan salvation-history. Even though Luke has not retained the allusion to Isa 5:2-7 in v. 1b (cp. Mark 12:1b), the "vineyard" is still enough of a symbol for Israel in the OT that the allusion at the beginning of the Lucan form of the parable cannot be missed (see Ps 80:9-14 [8-13E]; Isa 27:2; Jer 2:21; Hos 10:1; Ezek 19:10-14, as well as Isa 5:2-7). Despite the introductory v. 9 the parable in the Lucan form is still addressed to the leaders of "the house of Israel" in Jesus' time. The produce expected of the tenant farmers who had been contracted to care for the vineyard rings a bell in the Lucan Gospel, where this parable comes shortly after the parable of the pounds (19:11-27), in which certain results were expected of servants. In that instance, the servants were to do business with the money which had been graciously put at their disposal by the master, whereas here the landlord enters into a contract with tenants who are to care for the vineyard, a contract which is not honored. Thus the Lucan theme of stewardship and responsibility is presented in another form. It may not be easy to say whom the servants sent to the tenants are meant to represent in the Lucan form of the parable (the prophets of old? [see 11:49])—if any specific group at all is intended. But the son is clearly to be understood as Jesus, the preacher of God's "way" (v. 21), whom the tenants do not respect. Note too the suggestion of God's fidelity, for "the owner in the story continues to pursue the contractual arrangements that he had with the tenants to the bitter end. Even after they have beaten three of his servants, he hopes that he can invoke the authority of the legal bond between them by sending a representative whom they should all recognize is not an impostor—his son" (P. Perkins, *Hearing the Parables,* 191). The rejection of Jesus by the leaders among his comtemporaries echoes another Lucan theme (recall 4:16-30; 7:31-35; 11:29-32,49-54; 13:34-35; Acts 4:1-3; 7:51-58). The "others" (20:16) become the rest of Jesus' contemporaries, Palestinian Jews who accepted him and Gentiles, who will together form the reconstituted Israel (see p. 191) and thus prove to be tenants worthy to care for the vineyard and bring in its produce.

In no form of the parable preserved in the canonical Gospels does it stand alone. Further allegorical additions are found: Luke 20:17, quoting Ps 118:22, functions as does that OT passage in Mark (and Matthew), even if Luke has curtailed it, in making the reader realize that Jesus' destiny does not end with his death, alluded to in v. 15a, "out of the vineyard." Why Luke eliminated v. 23 of Psalm 118, the mention of the "Lord's doing, marvelous to behold," is hard to say. But even in his form of the ending of the episode the rejected stone becomes the cornerstone, symbolizing Jesus rejected and crucified, who becomes the risen Lord. The stone that did not measure up to the expected estimate of the builders becomes instead the most important stone in the edifice; it is accorded the place of honor by the function that it plays in the whole structure. "Cornerstone" should not be misunderstood. It does not mean cornerstone as we frequently use the word in modern English (to designate the stone of a principal angle of a building, usually laid at its formal inauguration, with a date on it and often some inscription, and a hollowed-out recess for holding documents relating to the history of the structure— thus a principal stone of the building). Rather *kephalē gōnias,* lit. "(the) head of (the) corner," designated in antiquity the stone used at a building's corner to bear the weight or stress of the two walls. It would have functioned somewhat like a "keystone" or "capstone" in an arch or other architectural form. It was the stone which was essential or crucial to the whole structure. In this sense, Jesus is the "beloved son," rejected by builders (another image for the leaders of contemporary Judaism), i.e. put to death by them. By his resurrection he becomes the key figure in God's new building, the reconstituted Israel, or the chief stone of the heavenly sanctuary (to borrow a motif from Hebrews). (See further Acts 4:5-11; 1 Pet 2:4-7; cf. J. Jeremias, *TDNT* 1. 792-793; H. Krämer, *EWNT* 1. 645-648; M. Lattke, *EWNT* 2. 703.)

Luke, by adding v. 18, gives another nuance to the stone. This verse, in effect, allegorizes still further v. 17. The rejected stone becomes a stumbling block, with a probable allusion to Isa 8:14-15 (in v. 18a) and to Dan 2:34-35,44-45 (in v. 18b). The rejected stone will cause ruin and downfall, because people will trip over it (recall Simeon's words in 2:34). On the other hand, should it fall (in judgment) on someone, it will crush that person to smithereens.

The implications of the allegorized parable are not lost on the audience in the Lucan Gospel, and in particular on the Scribes and the chief priests who were among the "people" to whom Jesus proposed the parable. Though Luke has reworded the conclusion and eliminated the mention of their fear, he retains in his own way the pointed reference to the leaders found in "Mk."

NOTES

20   9. *Jesus began.* Though Luke likes to use forms of the vb. *archein* (see NOTE on 3:23), he has derived this instance of it from Mark 12:1.

to propose this parable. Instead of the Marcan phrase "to speak to them *(autois)* in parables" (pl.), Luke uses a formula employed by him elsewhere (see 5:36; 12:16; 13:6; 15:3), with *legein pros* + acc. See p. 116.

to the people. Whereas in Mark 12:1 the pron. *autois* refers to the authorities of the preceding episode, the "people" are here explicitly addressed.

A man planted a vineyard. Or "a certain man"; for the text-critical problem (some mss. read *tis),* see *TCGNT* 170-171. The *planting* of the vineyard is a detail derived from Mark 12:1; there it reflects Isa 5:2 *(ephyteusa,* "I planted"), but it scarcely has that echo in the Lucan text, because Luke has omitted the further details from Isaiah (the fence, the winepress, and the tower) retained by Mark. The *Gos. of Thom.* § 65 speaks merely of "a good man who had a vineyard," which suits the primitive form of the parable found there. However, Luke has changed the word order from "Mk," putting *anthrōpos,* "man," first. Matt 21:33 does likewise, but modifies it with *oikodespotēs,* "master of a house." This prevents the difference from Mark within the Triple Tradition from becoming a minor agreement. See pp. 72-73. Even T. Schramm *(Markus-Stoff,* 150) admits that the first place given to *anthrōpos* by Matthew and Luke is insignificant.

leased it to farmers. Lit. "gave it out to cultivators." The vb. *ekdidonai* is found in extrabiblical Greek, both classical and Hellenistic, with the meaning "let out for hire, lease." See Plato, *Leges,* 7.806E; Polybius, *Hist.* 6.17,2; MM 192; cf. the LXX of Exod 2:21. On the rare second aor. form *exedeto,* see BDF § 94.1. For details about such transactions in first-century Palestine, see M. Hengel, "Das Gleichnis"; J. D. M. Derrett, "Fresh Light"; P. Perkins, *Hearing the Parables,* 86-89. The details provide verisimilitude for the parable, but it does not depend on them for comprehension (as the parable of the dishonest manager does [16:1-8a]). See further C. E. Carlston, *The Parables,* 185.

went abroad for quite some time. Lit. "for considerable times." Cf. 23:8; 8:27; Acts 8:11; 14:3; 27:9 for other Lucan uses of *hikanos* (cf. p. 112). This temporal note helps to allegorize the Lucan form of the parable even more. Pace E. Grässer *(Parusieverzögerung,* 113), J. Schmid *(Evangelium nach Lukas,* 296), C. E. Carlston *(The Parables,* 77), et al., this note can hardly refer to the delay of the parousia, for the landlord does not symbolize Jesus. The delay depicts God's greater tolerance and patience with his people, which will in time come to an end. See further W. Grundmann, *Evangelium nach Lukas,* 372 n.

10. *After a while.* Or possibly "at a proper time." Luke uses the simple dat. of *kairos.* Cf. 12:43; see NOTE there. Reference would be to some time of vintage. Matt 21:34 has made the reference explicit, "when the time of the fruit drew near."

he sent a servant. Note the rhetorical buildup of the story: a servant, another (servant), a third servant, finally "my own son, one who is dear to me." The first three are maltreated, but not killed, but the son is eventually killed. Contrast Mark 12:4-5. The three servants may be an echo of Luke 19:16-23. In the *Gospel of Thomas* there were only two servants.

they might pay him a share of the vineyard's produce. Lit. "might give him (some) from the fruit of the vineyard." For the partitive use of the prep. *apo,* see Luke 16:21; 22:18; it may be another instance of a Septuagintism in Lucan Greek (see Exod 12:7; 17:5; Sir 26:12; 2 Macc 7:1), reflecting the Semitic use of *min* (in both Hebrew and Aramaic). The amount of the landlord's share would have been stipulated in the contract of lease.

Luke substitutes a fut. indic. *dōsousin* in the purpose cl. for the more usual Koine subjunc. *labē* (see BDF § 369.2); but some mss. (C, D, R, W, Θ, Ψ, *f* ¹, and the Koine text-tradition) have the subjunc. *dōsin.*

beat the servant. The tenants have dutifully worked the farm and have not been lazy or negligent. Indeed, they have been so successful that they grow arrogant and disregard their contract. They are ready to go to any lengths to keep for themselves what they have produced.

11. *Again he tried, sending another servant.* Lit. "and he added to send (an)other servant." Luke substitutes a Septuagintism for the simple Marcan *kai palin apesteilen,* "and he sent again." He has already used the vb. *prostithenai,* "add," in various ways (see 3:20; 12:25,31; 17:5; cf. Acts 2:41,47; 5:14; 11:24; 13:36), even once (19:11) of saying something in addition *(prostheis eipen).* But only here and in v. 12 (also in Acts 12:3) does he use this vb. with a dependent infin., in the sense of "he proceeded (in addition) to send." Cf. the LXX of Gen 8:12; Exod 9:34; 1 Sam 18:29; cf. BDF § 435a; § 392.2. See pp. 111, 115. It is impossible to say whether this second sending was at the same vintage or a later one.

12. *a third servant.* The third in Mark 12:5 is killed, but not so here.

covered him with wounds and drove him away. Lit. "having wounded him, they cast him out." On the Lucan dropping of Mark's *men . . . de* (12:5), see p. 108. Luke omits all reference to "many other" servants. See Mark 12:5c.

13. *What am I to do?* Soliloquy is thus introduced into this parable, as in other parables exclusive to Luke. See 12:17; 15:17-19; 16:3. This is clearly a Lucan redactional modification of the Marcan parable; it does not reveal that he has used another source in addition to Mark. To ask why the landlord did not go himself to the tenant farmers is to miss the thrust of the story itself.

my own son, one who is dear to me. Lit. "my beloved son," the same Greek expression is used in 3:22; 9:35 *(ho huios mou ho agapētos).* See NOTE on 3:22. The adj. is undoubtedly part of the allegorization in the pre-Marcan tradition; compare the form in the *Gospel of Thomas.* From the drift of the story the "beloved" son is not only dear to his father, but probably is his "only" son, even though this is not so expressed. Compare the use of *monogenēs* in 7:12; 8:42; 9:38. Recall the reference to son and heir in Heb 1:2. Cf. Gen 22:2 (comparing the MT and the LXX).

perhaps they will respect him. The adv. *isōs,* "perhaps," occurs only here in the NT. The Coptic equivalent *(mešak)* appears twice in *Gos. of Thom.* § 65, but it is not therefore clearly dependent on Luke. According to A. Jülicher *(Gleichnisreden,* 2. 391-392), Luke has added "perhaps" to spare God the error of not foreseeing the rejection of his son (as the words seem to imply in Mark 12:6b). However, Luke was scarcely concerned with the problems of God's foreknowledge. Luke has rather added a dramatic touch!

14. *they discussed.* This detail is peculiar to Luke. Cf. 19:47,48.

so that the inheritance will be ours. I.e. the owner will be heirless, and they as tenant farmers will have a claim to the vineyard when the owner dies. Or it might mean that they are aware that the farm has already been made over to the son as heir. See NOTES on 15:12,31.

15. *drove him out of the vineyard and murdered him.* So Luke rephrases "Mk," which says, "taking him, they murdered him and cast him (i.e. his corpse) outside the vineyard." Luke has softened the description of the indignity of not only murdering the son, but of heaping consummate disrespect on him by not even burying him properly. Here both Matthew and Luke reverse the order of actions; the son is driven

out of the vineyard and then killed. They have both undoubtedly done this in light of the passion narrative and the burial of Jesus. Cf. Heb 13:12-13; John 19:17. In doing away with the son, the Lucan tenant farmers join others in the Gospel who reject him; the chord of rejection (see p. 423) is again orchestrated.

What then will the owner . . . do to them? Luke echoes Mark 12:9, adding "then" and "to them." The query expresses the end of his long-suffering and tolerance.

16. *come and destroy those farmers.* I.e. those who refused to carry out their contract faithfully and have even become murderers of his son.

lease the vineyard to others. Lit. "give the vineyard to others." The vb. *dōsei,* "will give," derived from Mark 12:9c, may be considered as a simple form of the compound *ekdidonai* used in v. 9c. But it may also be meant more literally: Whereas the landlord had *leased* the vineyard on contract to the first tenant farmers, he now "gives" it as a gift to others. For the "others" are not clearly specified as other contract farmers. Cf. Jer 3:17.

When they heard this, the people said. Lit. "hearing this, they said." The "they" refers to the "people" of v. 9. This Lucan redactional addition thus elicits a reaction to the parable from the people and marks off the parable itself from what follows. It is also in line with the evangelist's general tendency of recording bystanders' reactions and of contrasting the reactions of the people and the authorities.

Heaven forbid! Lit. "may it not be (so)!" The people hope that such a fate for the authorities will be averted. Though the exclamation *mē genoito* occurs frequently enough in some Pauline writings (Rom 3:4,6,31; 6:2,15; 7:7,13; 9:14; 11:1,11; 1 Cor 6:15; Gal 2:17; 3:21), this is the only place where it is found in the canonical Gospels. It expresses a strong reaction or negation, used by Paul generally after a rhetorical question. The phrase is often found in the LXX as a translation of Hebrew *ḥālîlāh lî/lānû,* lit. "an abomination to me/us." E.g. Gen 44:17; Josh 22:29; 24:16; 1 Kgs 20:3 (= MT 21:3). But it is also found in extrabiblical Greek. See Lucian, *Dial. Meret.* 13.4; Demosthenes, *Orat.* 10.27; 28.21; Alciphron, *Ep. agt.* 2.5,3; Epictetus, *Disc.* 1.1,13. The positive *genoito* is used in Isa 25:1; Ps 72:19 as the translation of Hebrew *'āmēn.* On Luke's use of the optative, see p. 108 (§ 7a).

17. *Jesus looked at them.* This detail is also a Lucan addition to the story. Cf. 22:61.

what is the meaning of this text of Scripture. Lit. "what then is this (which has) been written." Luke uses his own formula to introduce a quotation from the OT, the pf. pass. ptc. of *graphein* (cf. 18:31; 21:22; 22:37; 24:44), a formula not used by either Mark or Matthew, who both employ the pf. pass. indic. *gegraptai* frequently (as does Luke; see NOTE on 19:46). Scripture is introduced to stress the divine retribution coming to the faithless tenants and the vindication of the murdered son.

The stone which the builders rejected has become the cornerstone. What Luke retains from Mark 12:10, he retains verbatim. Moreover, it corresponds exactly with the LXX of Ps 118:22 *(lithon hon apedokimasan hoi oikodomountes, houtos egenēthē eis kephalēn gōnias),* which is an accurate translation of the MT *('eben mā'ăsû habbônîm hāyĕtāh lĕrō'š pinnāh).* Psalm 118 is the last of the Hallel psalms, originally a psalm of thanksgiving for deliverance in battle. The rejection of Jesus that is implied here is another "veiled" reference to his coming death. See p. 778. The *kephalē gōnias* is an example of the Hebraic gen. See pp. 123-124.

18. *Everyone who trips over that stone will be broken to pieces.* This added Lucan

verse is proverb-like and allegorizes the stone mentioned in v. 17 by revealing how it
will function in two further ways. The cornerstone would have been firmly fixed in a
wall and people would scarcely fall over it, nor would it fall on them. Hence the
statement in this verse is clearly a Lucan additional interpretation. See T. W. Manson,
Sayings, 322. The first function assigned to the stone: It will bring disaster to those
who stumble over it, i.e. inevitable judgment. The Lucan addition probably alludes to
Isa 8:14-15: The Lord of hosts will become a "stone of offense, a rock of stumbling to
both houses of Israel, a trap and a snare to the inhabitants of Jerusalem. Many will
stumble thereon; they will fall and be broken to bits." So Yahweh warned Isaiah,
counseling him not to accept the views of Israel. The Lucan allusion thus refers to
disbelief in the risen Jesus who will cause "many in Israel" (2:34) to fall. This passage
of Isaiah is used along with 28:16 in conjunction with Ps 118:22 in 1 Pet 2:4-8. See
further my article on testimonia collections and composite quotations of the OT in the
NT, " '4QTestimonia' and the New Testament," *ESBNT* 59-89.

anyone on whom it falls it will crush. The second function of that stone: It will bring
disaster to those on whom it falls in judgment. This part of the verse may allude to
Dan 2:34-35,44-45, the stone torn loose from a mountain which smashes to pieces the
statue of fine gold, silver, bronze, iron, and clay which Nebuchadnezzar saw in his
dream. It probably is meant to refer to the risen Jesus, who becomes the judge of
human conduct. Cf. Luke 23:30. The vb. *likmēsei,* "will crush," is found in the The-
odotionic version of Dan 2:44. *Likman* properly means "to winnow." See Philo, *De
Jos.* 20 § 112; Josephus, *Ant.* 5.9,3 § 328. In Dan 2:44 the Aramaic *taddiq wĕtāsēp,*
"will break to bits and bring to an end," is translated in the LXX as *pataxei de kai
aphanisei,* "will crush and make disappear," whereas Theodotion has *leptynei kai
likmēsei,* "will comminute and crush." See LSJ 1050; MM 376. The OS and Vg
translated *likmēsei* in Luke 20:18 as "crush." See further A. Plummer, *The Gospel,*
463. For a similar proverb in later rabbinical literature, see *Midr. Esth* 3.6: "If a stone
falls on a pot, woe to the pot! If the pot falls on the stone, woe to the pot. Either way,
woe to the pot!" (Str-B 1. 877). Cf. Sir 13:2; Aesop, *Fables,* 422 (quoted by G.
Bornkamm, *TDNT* 4. 281 n. 10). These parallels show only that the saying in v. 18 is
proverb-like. For an attempt to interpret the saying as a warrior's boast ("Anyone who
attacks that stone will be crushed, anyone whom it attacks it will grind to powder"),
which takes *piptein epi* in a different sense of "fall upon" (like *epipiptein epi* [Gen
14:15; Josh 11:7]), see R. Doran, "Luke 20:18: A Warrior's Boast?" *CBQ* 45 (1983)
61-67.

19. *The Scribes and the chief priests.* I.e. those of v. 1, standing by as Jesus taught
"the people" in the Temple and addressed to them this parable. The order of the two
groups is reversed in some Greek mss.

wanted to lay hands on Jesus. Cf. 22:53. The same expression is used of disciples in
21:12. It is a Septuagintism. See Gen 22:12; Exod 7:4; 2 Sam 18:12.

then and there. Lit. "in that hour," an alleged Aramaism. See pp. 117-118. Their
"hour" has not yet come; but it will and with it "the power of darkness" (22:53). Cf.
22:1-6.

they feared the people. Luke now introduces the note of fear which he eliminated in
v. 32, thus creating again a distinction between "the people" (who expressed their
reaction in v. 16c) and the Jerusalem authorities. On *laos,* see NOTE on 18:43.

that he had directed that parable against them. Even though Luke uses a formula found elsewhere for the simple proposing of a parable to a group *(eipein/legein parabolēn pros* + acc. [see NOTE on v. 9]), the prepositional phrase *pros autous* seems here to have a more specific sense of accusation, "against them" or "with reference to them" (see BAGD 710 and NOTE on 18:9), or "meant for them" (BDF § 239.6). Cf. 11:53-54.

BIBLIOGRAPHY (20:9-19)

Bammel, E. "Das Gleichnis von den bösen Winzern (Mk. 12,1-9) und das jüdische Erbrecht," *RIDA* 3/6 (1959) 11-17.

Bartsch, H.-W. "Das Thomas-Evangelium und die synoptischen Evangelien," *NTS* 6 (1959-1960) 249-261.

Black, M. "The Christological Use of the Old Testament in the New Testament," *NTS* 18 (1971-1972) 1-14, esp. 11-14.

——— "The Parable as Allegory," *BJRL* 42 (1959-1960) 273-287.

Blank, J. "Die Sendung des Sohnes: Zur christologischen Bedeutung des Gleichnisses von den bösen Winzern Mk 12,1-12," *Neues Testament und Kirche* (ed. J. Gnilka) 11-41.

Brown, R. E. "Parable and Allegory Reconsidered," *NovT* 5 (1962) 36-45; reprinted, *New Testament Essays* (Milwaukee: Bruce, 1965) 254-264.

Bruce, F. F. "New Wine in Old Wine Skins: III. The Corner Stone," *ExpTim* 84 (1972-1973) 231-235.

Burkitt, F. C. "The Parable of the Wicked Husbandmen," *Transactions of the Third International Congress for the History of Religions* (2 vols.; eds. P. S. Allen and J. de M. Johnson; Oxford: Clarendon, 1908) 2. 321-328.

Carlston, C. E. *The Parables,* 40-45, 76-81, 178-190.

Crossan, J. D. "The Parable of the Wicked Husbandmen," *JBL* 90 (1971) 451-465.

Dehandschutter, B. "La parabole des vignerons homicides (Mc., XII, 1-12) et l'évangile selon Thomas," *L'Evangile selon Marc* (ed. M. Sabbe) 203-219.

Derrett, J. D. M. "Allegory and the Wicked Vinedressers," *JTS* 25 (1974) 426-432.

——— "Fresh Light on the Parable of the Wicked Vinedressers," *RIDA* 3/10 (1963) 11-41; reprinted (with revised title), *Law,* 286-312.

——— " 'The Stone That the Builders Rejected,' " *SE IV,* 180-186.

Dodd, C. H. *Parables,* 96-102, 127.

Dupont, J. "La parabole des ouvriers de la vigne (Matthieu, xx, 1-16)," *NRT* 79 (1957) 785-797.

Gray, A. "The Parable of the Wicked Husbandmen (Matthew xxi. 33-41; Mark xii. 1-9; Luke xx. 9-16)," *HibJ* 19 (1920-1921) 42-52.

Guillet, J. "Jésus et la politique," *RSR* 59 (1971) 531-544.

Haenchen, E. *Der Weg Jesu,* 396-405.

Hengel, M. "Das Gleichnis von den Weingärtnern Mc 12,1-12 im Lichte der Zenonpapyri und der rabbinischen Gleichnisse," *ZNW* 59 (1968) 1-39.

Higgins, A. J. B. "Non-Gnostic Sayings in the Gospel of Thomas," *NovT* 4 (1960) 292-306.

Hubaut, M. *La parabole des vignerons homicides* (Cahiers de la Revue Biblique 16; Paris: Gabalda, 1976).

Iersel, B. M. F. van. *"Der Sohn,"* 124-145.

Jeremias, J. *Parables,* 31, 41, 70-77, 86, 93, 108, 204.

Jülicher, A. *Gleichnisreden,* 2. 385-406.

Klauck, H.-J. "Das Gleichnis vom Mord im Weinberg (Mk 12,1-12; Mt 21,33-46; Lk 20,9-19)," *BibLeb* 11 (1970) 118-145.

Kümmel, W. G. "Das Gleichnis von den bösen Weingärtnern (Mark. 12. 1-9)," *Aux sources de la tradition chrétienne: Mélanges offerts à M. Maurice Goguel . . .* (Neuchâtel/Paris: Delachaux et Niestlé, 1950) 120-131; reprinted, *Heilsgeschehen und Geschichte: Gesammelte Aufsätze 1933-1964* (Marburg: Elwert, 1965) 207-217.

Léon-Dufour, X. "La parabole des vignerons homicides," *ScEccl* 17 (1965) 365-396; digested, *TD* 15 (1967) 30-36.

——— "La parabole des vignerons homicides," *Etudes d'évangiles* (Parole de Dieu; Paris: Editions du Seuil, 1965) 303-344.

Lowe, M. "From the Parable of the Vineyard to a Pre-Synoptic Source," *NTS* 28 (1982) 257-263.

MacRae, G. W. "The Gospel of Thomas—*Logia Iesou?*" *CBQ* 22 (1960) 56-71.

Merli, D. "La parabola dei vignaioli infedeli (Mc. 12,1-12)," *BeO* 15 (1973) 97-107.

Montefiore, H. "A Comparison of the Parables of the Gospel according to Thomas and of the Synoptic Gospels," *NTS* 7 (1960-1961) 220-248, esp. 236-238.

Nestle, E. "Lk 20,18," *ZNW* 8 (1907) 321-322.

Newell, J. E. and R. R. "The Parable of the Wicked Tenants," *NovT* 14 (1972) 226-237.

Orchard, B. "J. A. T. Robinson and the Synoptic Problem," *NTS* 22 (1975-1976) 346-352.

Rese, M. *Alttestamentliche Motive,* 171-173.

Robinson, J. A. T. "The Parable of the Wicked Husbandmen: A Test of Synoptic Relationships," *NTS* 21 (1974-1975) 443-461.

Schoedel, W. R. "Parables in the Gospel of Thomas: Oral Tradition or Gnostic Exegesis?" *CTM* 43 (1972) 548-560, esp. 557-560.

Schramm, T. *Markus-Stoff,* 150-167.

Snodgrass, K. R. "The Parable of the Wicked Husbandmen: Is the Gospel of Thomas Version the Original?" *NTS* 21 (1974-1975) 142-144.

Weiser, A. *Die Knechtsgleichnisse,* 49-57.

132. THE TRIBUTE DUE TO GOD AND
TO CAESAR
(20:20-26)

20 ²⁰ So they watched for their opportunity and sent spies, who pretended to be upright, in order to catch him in his speech; thus they might hand him over to the jurisdiction and authority of the prefect. ²¹ These people asked him, "Teacher, we know that what you say and teach is correct and that you show no favor to anyone; you truly teach the way of God. ²² But is it lawful for us to pay tribute to Caesar, or not?" ²³ He perceived their trickery at once and said to them, "Suppose you show me a silver coin. ²⁴ Whose image and inscription does it bear?" "Caesar's," they answered. ²⁵ So he said to them, "Well, then, pay to Caesar what is Caesar's and to God what is God's." ²⁶ And they were unable in the sight of the people to catch him in anything he said; rather they grew silent, astonished at his answer.

COMMENT

The contest between Jesus and the Jerusalem authorities continues as the latter now set out formally to entrap him, to catch him uttering something politically subversive, so that they may bring about his arrest. Those sent by the authorities attempt to catch him in a dilemma, but their attempt only elicits from him what he thinks about the payment of tribute to the Roman occupiers of Palestine and the relation of it to his preaching of God's kingdom (20:20-26).

Luke continues to follow the Marcan order of pericopes, for this episode is parallel to Mark 12:13-17 (cf. Matt 22:15-22). Luke, however, has composed his own introductory verse (v. 20), eliminating all mention of the Pharisees and Herodians (cf. Mark 12:13) and making more explicit reference to Roman political jurisdiction and the prefect's authority. Luke's reference to the pretense of the Jerusalem authorities (v. 20a) has its parallel in Mark 12:15, but Luke has recast that too. The reason for the Lucan recasting of v. 20 will appear in 23:2-5, a passage related to this one. Verses 21-25 follow the Marcan story, but with some redactional modifications. The main modifications are the following: (a) "what you say and teach is correct" (v. 21b), instead of the Marcan formulation, "we know that you are true and care about no one" (v. 14b); (b) the Septuagintism "show no favor" *(prosōpon lambanein)* is introduced (v. 21c); (c) the proper Greek term *phoros,* "tribute" (v. 22), is used to replace the Latinism *kēnsos* (v. 14); (d) the Lucan favorite *eipen pros autous* (v. 23) replaces the Marcan *eipen autois* (v. 15); (e) "trickery" is substituted for "hypocrisy" (v. 23); and (f) Luke eliminates the secondary questions, "Do we give or not give?" (vv. 14f) and "Why do you try to put me to the test?" (v. 15b). The episode closes with a statement (v. 26), clearly composed by Luke himself, but inspired by the Marcan counterpart; it records the silence to which his would-be critics are reduced in the sight of the people. Even T. Schramm *(Markus-Stoff,* 170) admits that no variant source has been used by Luke apart from "Mk"; in this he disagrees with B. Weiss *(Die Quellen des Lukasevangeliums* [Stuttgart/Berlin: J. G. Cotta, 1907] 212-214).

Forms of this story are preserved elsewhere and have to be considered. The first variant is found in a fragment of a Gospel, composed probably in the early second century A.D., the Egerton Papyrus 2, frg. 2r: "[11] [Com]ing to him in[quisitorial]ly, they tried to test him, sa[ying], 'Jesus, Teacher, we know that you have come [from God], for what you are doing bears te[stimony] beyond (that of) all th[e] prophets. [12] [Tell] us [then], Is it lawful to [pa]y kings what ap[per]tains to (their) rule? [Should we] pay [th]em or not?' [13] But Jesus, realizing [the]ir [in]tention, said [to th]em in an[ger]. 'Why do you call me with yo[ur mou]th "Master," while you list[en no]t to what I [s]ay? [14] Well indeed has Is[aiah] pro[phesi]ed [of y]ou, saying, "[Th]is [people honors] me with the[ir li]ps, [but] the[ir hea]rt sta[ys far] from me. In vai[n they reverence me]; [their] pre[cepts . . .]." ' " This variant of the story is clearly a mixture of Johannine and Synoptic sayings-material; it is dependent on the four canonical Gospels, and contains nothing that can be called more primitive than the story in the Synoptics. (See further Anon., *The New Gospel Fragments* [London: British Museum, 1951]; J. Jeremias, "An Unknown Gospel with Johannine Elements," Hennecke-Schneemelcher, *NTApocrypha* 1.94-97; A. de Santos Otero, *Los evangelios apócrifos* [BAC 148; 3d ed.; Madrid: Edica, 1979] 95-100.)

Another variant is preserved in the writings of Justin Martyr: "For about that time some people came up to him and asked him whether one ought to pay taxes to Caesar. And he answered, 'Tell me, whose image does the coin bear?' And they said, 'Caesar's.' Again he replied, 'Pay, then, to Caesar what is Caesar's and to God what is God's' " *(Apol.* 1.17,2; FP 2. 38). Jesus' first query is closer to Luke 20:24b, but his pronouncement follows Matt 22:21c. There is no independent tradition here.

Finally, a more developed form of the story is preserved in *Gos. of Thom.* § 100. It has even preserved a bit of a narrative setting—something unusual in this apocryphal Gospel. It runs: "They showed Jesus a gold (coin) and said to him, 'Caesar's agents demand of us taxes.' He said to them, 'Give Caesar the

things of Caesar; give God the things of God, and what is mine give me.' "
The silver denarius has become a gold coin, whereas the brief narrative setting is almost unintelligible (it would be so, if we did not have the fuller
canonical form on which the *Gospel of Thomas* here depends). Moreover the
saying of Jesus is expanded and acquires an added (gnostic?) climax, which
subordinates God to Jesus. (Cf. W. Schrage, *Das Verhältnis,* 189-192; J.-E.
Ménard, *L'Evangile selon Thomas,* 200-202.)

Form-critically considered, the episode is a pronouncement-story. R.
Bultmann *(HST* 26) regards its Marcan form as an "excellently constructed"
controversy dialogue (apophthegm), one which he would not consider "a
community product." It was clearly shaped in oral form (ibid. 48; cf. pp. 44,
63, 385), and the emphasis lies on the saying. Similarly, V. Taylor *(FGT* 64-
65) calls it an illustration of the pronouncement-story at its best: "Everything
leads up to the final word of Jesus, which for the early Christians must have
had the force of a pronouncement. So Jesus had spoken, and there was no
more to be said!"

The story is, however, a little more complicated than it appears at first
sight. The Lucan introduction (v. 20) makes clear the pretext which the
Jerusalem authorities are using in their attempt to involve Jesus in some
compromising political stance (such as sedition). But he succeeds in escaping
from such entrapment. Their pretense at uprightness even leads them to acknowledge in hollow tones and with fulsome praise that they know that he
speaks and teaches rightly, shows no favor to anyone, and instructs people
about God's "way." Such a pretense is intended to disarm him. But their
protestation about Jesus not showing favor to anyone cleverly prepares for
the two-pronged pronouncement with which the episode climactically ends.

Jesus turns the question the spies put to him, "But is it lawful for us to pay
tribute to Caesar or not?" back on them, by asking that *they* show him the
tribute coin. Implied in his question is this: If you "upright" Jews of Roman
Judea actually carry and use the silver denarius with the name and inscription of Caesar on it, then you acknowledge your dependence on him. He asks
them to show him the coin, because he carries none himself. His second
question, "Whose image and inscription does it bear?" (v. 24), makes them
acknowledge who is behind "the jurisdiction and authority of the prefect" (v.
20c). In answering "Caesar's," they are forced to utter the name that they
would gladly have avoided.

Jesus' pronouncement, "Well, then, pay to Caesar what is Caesar's and to
God what is God's" (v. 25), is two-pronged. At first, it seems to avoid favoritism (recall v. 21c). They are to pay Caesar his due, but a fortiori God too.
The pronouncement has nothing to do with Jesus himself; it is rather an
instruction for his disciples' conduct. Further, his answer makes no reference
to the coin or any specific tax. All of this suggests that the emphasis really
falls on the second part of the pronouncement.

Three different modes of interpreting Jesus' pronouncement have been used: *First,* the two-kingdoms interpretation, a sense given to it since patristic times. Jesus would not only be recommending the payment of the imperial tribute, but would also be inculcating a proper attitude toward political authority or the state which also affects human life. He would thus be aligning himself with older Jewish ideas (cf. Dan 2:21,37-38; Prov 8:15-16; Wis 6:1-11). The kingdom of God has been inaugurated, indeed, but it does not suppress or supplant the political kingdoms of this world. Toward the political authority Jesus himself would be manifesting a sovereign liberty, but no revolt against its legitimate claim on human subjects. The German historian L. von Ranke, who understood the words in this sense, regarded them as the most important and influential utterance that Jesus ever made. (See his *History of the Popes* [2 vols.; New York: Colonial, 1901] 1. 6-10.) This interpretation (with varying nuances) has been used by such commentators as O. Cullmann *(Dieu et César* [Paris/Neuchâtel: Delachaux et Niestlé, 1956] 37-40); E. Stauffer *(New Testament Theology* [London: SCM, 1955] 197-199); P. Bonnard *(L'Evangile selon Saint Matthieu* [CNT 1; Paris/Neuchâtel: Delachaux et Niestlé, 1963] 323); L. Goppelt ("The Freedom"); E. E. Ellis *(Gospel of Luke,* 234). This interpretation may be right in seeing a germinal appreciation of the role of the state in Jesus' thinking, but it tends to equate what is due to God with what is due to Caesar—on a more or less equal plane. (See further C. H. Giblin, " 'The Things of God,' " 512.)

Second, the ironic interpretation. To avoid the stress on the political which the first interpretation would propose, some commentators have understood the words of Jesus as irony. Jesus would not have been really interested in the tribute to Caesar; so his recommendation, "Pay to Caesar what is Caesar's," is a flash of wit, devoid of any serious import. One gives to Caesar what belongs to him, but of what importance is that vis-à-vis the kingdom of God? This interpretation (again with varying nuances) has been used by M. Dibelius ("Rom und die Christen im ersten Jahrhundert," *Botschaft und Geschichte: Gesammelte Aufsätze* [2 vols.; Tübingen: Mohr (Siebeck), 1953, 1956] 2. 178); A. Schweitzer *(Das Messianitäts- und Leidensgeheimnis: Eine Skizze des Lebens Jesu* [3d ed.; Tübingen: Mohr (Siebeck), 1956] 30-31); S. Kierkegaard *(Ecole du christianisme* [Bazoches-en-Pareds (Vendée): Berger-Levrault, 1937] 207). This interpretation pits the second part of the pronouncement against the first, whereas the conj. that separates them is *kai,* "and," and not an adversative *alla,* "but." (See further C. H. Giblin, " 'The Things of God,' " 510.)

Third, the so-called anti-Zealot interpretation. Jesus would be openly opposing the refusal to pay the Roman tribute, but his pronouncement would have no real bearing on the problem of the state. He would be telling interlocutors that they are trying to bring to the fore a question which is only secondary and that they are downplaying a real human concern. "The coin belongs to Caesar, but you to God. . . . The coin, which bears the image of Caesar, we owe to Caesar. We, however, as men who bear the image of God, owe ourselves to God" (G. Bornkamm, *Jesus of Nazareth* [New York: Harper & Row, 1975] 123). Similarly, Tertullian *(De Idol.* 15.3 [CCLat 2. 1115]); D. Cairns *(The Image of God in Man* [Fontana Library; London: Collins, 1973] 38); R. Völkl *(Christ und Welt nach dem Neuen Testament* [Würzburg: Echter-V., 1961] 113-116); R. Schnackenburg *(The Moral Teaching of the New Testament* [New York: Herder and Herder, 1965] 117-118).

The third interpretation is tending in the right direction. Jesus' saying was certainly not intended to set up two parallel but separate kingships. C. H. Giblin (" 'The Things of God,' " 520-525) tries to press the third interpretation a bit further, in stressing that the pronouncement has to be related not only to the "image" on the coin, but to the "image and inscription." When this full expression is related to "the things of God" *(ta tou theou),* it probably echoes Isa 44:5, where the prophet speaks of service of God in terms of inscribing "I belong to God" (LXX *tou Theou eimi)* on one's hand. This may be a bit subtle, and I. H. Marshall *(Luke,* 736) is probably right in calling it "a (correct) theological deduction from the saying [rather] than an inherent element in the argument, the comparison being more between Caesar and God than between coins and men."

Jesus' pronouncement presupposes a comparison of what is marked with Caesar's image and what is marked with God's image (see Gen 1:26-27). The kingdom which Jesus preaches does not call in question Caesar's rightful kingship; but that is not the all-important aspect of human life. A human being belongs to God, whose image he/she bears; God has not only a right of possession over human beings, but also a claim to a basic recognition of his lordship.

Jesus' male contemporaries had to pay a half-shekel tax to the Temple each year (see Exod 30:11-14 and NOTE on 19:45). When Pompey captured the country in 63 B.C., a tax was imposed on the Jews of Palestine for the Roman *fiscus,* which Josephus says soon came to ten thousand talents *(Ant.* 14.4,5 § 78). Julius Caesar subsequently reduced the taxes and allowed no taxes to be collected from the Jews during the sabbatical years (see Josephus, *Ant.* 14.10,5-6 § 201-202). The census of Quirinius (see pp. 399-405) was in part related to the Roman taxation of the province of Syria, and of Judea in particular (see *J. W.* 2.8,1 § 117-118; 7.8,1 § 253-258; *Ant.* 18.1,1 § 1-10; cf. Acts 5:37).

Part of the problem in first-century Palestine, which is the background for the question posed to Jesus, was how God's people (Jewish and later Christian) were to react to the pagan government of the occupying Roman forces and the imperial *fiscus.* This episode should not be read as if it were asking Jesus whether he sided with the Zealots (who allegedly resisted the payment of taxes to the Romans) or with the Pharisees (who are said to have acknowledged the obligation). Origen *(In Matth.* 17.25 [GCS 40. 655]) wrote: "It has been reported that Judas the Galilean [see Acts 5:37] . . . taught that one must not pay tribute to Caesar." (See Josephus, *J. W.* 2.8,1 § 118.) But it is far from certain that there were Zealots (i.e. a political party, with capital Z) in Jesus' time (see NOTE on 6:15). Hence, *pace* R. Eisler, *Iēsous basileus ou basileusas* (2 vols.; Heidelberg: Carl Winter, 1929, 1930) 2. 200 and S. G. F. Brandon, *Jesus and the Zealots* (New York: Scribner's, 1967) 346-349, the relation of this episode to all the political unrest in first-century Palestine is far from clear. Whatever is to be said about the historical background of this passage, Jesus' reply espouses neither the allegedly Zealot solution nor the allegedly Pharisaic solution. He shows favor to no one. He answers directly a trap question, but "his answer lifts the problem to another plane. . . . [It] transcends the question of the imperial tax as such by alluding to the universality of God's claim to dominion" (K. Weiss, *TDNT* 9. 81).

The relation of Jesus' pronouncement in this episode to Paul's instruction in Rom 13:1-7 and to that of 1 Pet 2:13-17 must not be neglected. Paul does not exhort the Roman Christians to obedience and tax payment on "the word of the Lord" (cf. 1 Thess 4:15; 1 Cor 7:10), but he does exhort them to pay tribute *(phorous teleite),* because authorities *(exousiai)* are ministers *(leitourgoi)* of God, persistently attending to these matters. Civil authority was to be obeyed and taxes were to be paid because the authority was "a servant of God for what is good" (Rom 13:4a). Whether his stance is based on a Saying of Jesus such as that recorded here (or possibly in Matt 17:27a) is hard to say. Jesus' sayings about such matters were germinal in this sense at most.

Jesus' pronouncement in this episode serves as a foil for the political accusation that will be made against him in 23:2, an accusation that is found only in this Gospel. Lucan foreshadowing is being used with subtle tones.

NOTES

20   20. *they watched for their opportunity.* Lit. "watching closely," the vb. *paratērein* is often used with a pejorative connotation, "watching maliciously, lying in wait for." See BAGD 622. For similar Lucan uses of it, see 6:7; 14:1. The subj. "they" must be understood of the Scribes and chief priests, who are mentioned at the end of the preceding episode (v. 19).

Some mss. (D, Θ, etc.) read instead the ptc. *apochōrēsantes,* "departing," i.e. leaving the Temple area, where the preceding episode took place. Similarly, ms. W reads *hypochōrēsantes* (same meaning). Both variants seem to have been occasioned by the vb. *apēlthon,* "they went off," with which the preceding episode in Mark ended (12:12), but which the best text of Luke does not follow.

sent spies, who pretended to be upright. The adj. *enkathetos* means lit. "someone hired/suborned to lie in wait (sent down into)" and is generally interpreted as a "spy."

The persons so engaged by the Jerusalem authorities put up the pretense of dedicated adherence to the Mosaic Law, since *dikaious*, "upright," must be understood of ethical conduct regulated by such legislation. E. Klostermann *(Lukasevangelium,* 195) would have us believe that these spies are Pharisees (he appeals to 18:9—but 16:15 would have been better). But the Pharisees never appear in this part of the Lucan Gospel (see NOTE on 19:39). The use of *dikaious* cannot be restricted to them. Compare Paul's sentiments in 2 Cor 11:15. On the two accs. here, see BDF § 157.2; 406.1.

to catch him in his speech. The vb. *epilambanesthai,* "catch," is used with a double gen., one objective, the other epexegetical: "him (in his) word," i.e. something he would say (BAGD 295). Cf. Xenophon, *Anab.* 4.7,12 for a parallel to the Lucan expression. The spies are concerned to see whether Jesus' position would be that of one who is "upright" vis-à-vis Roman or Mosaic law.

thus they might hand him over. Lit. "so as to hand him over," with *hōste* and an infin. *paradounai* to express the result of their planned action. See BDF § 391.3; ZBG § 352. Recall Jesus' announcement in 18:32.

to the jurisdiction and authority of the prefect. Lit. "to the rule *(archē)* and authority *(exousia)* of the (Roman) governor" (of Judea). The political overtones are thus clearly introduced by Luke; the purpose of this introduction will emerge in 23:2-5. There is nothing so overtly political in Mark 12:13 or Matt 22:15-16. On "prefect," see NOTE on 3:1.

21. *These people asked him.* Lit. "and they (the spies sent to him) asked him."

Teacher. The Greek voc. *didaskale* reappears. See NOTE on 3:12; 7:40.

what you say and teach is correct. Lit. "that you speak and teach rightly," i.e. with orthodoxy. Cf. 7:43; 10:28. In Mark 12:14b they assert that they know that Jesus is true *(or* faithful). Luke's redaction is more pointed and suited to what Jesus teaches; it prepares better for his pronouncement. Because it will be "correct" too, they will be silenced. On Jesus' role as a teacher, see pp. 148, 218.

you show no favor to anyone. Lit. "you do not lift up the face," a Septuagintism, meaning that he shows no favoritism or partiality. This too prepares for the two-pronged pronouncement to come. The Greek phrase *prosōpon lambanein* would have been unintelligible in classical or Hellenistic Greek writing, where the vb. *lambanein* means either (actively) "take, take hold of" or (receptively) "accept," and never has the sense of "raise, lift up." This meaning is found in the LXX as a translation of *nāśā' pānîm.* See p. 115. It gave rise to the n. *prosōpolēmptēs* (Acts 10:34), God is no "respecter of persons," i.e. one who, when greeted by a person bowed in prostration, lifts up the face of the person as a sign of recognition, favor, or esteem. See E. Lohse, *TDNT* 6. 779. *Pace* T. Schramm *(Markus-Stoff,* 169), this is not to be labeled a Hebraism; it is a Septuagintism and is to be clearly attributed to Luke.

truly. Lit. "in truth." See NOTE on 4:25.

the way of God. This is the height of the spies' fulsome praise; but it rings hollow. For the significance of "the way" in Lucan theology, see p. 169. In this case, however, the expression has been derived by Luke from Mark 12:14e. According to W. Michaelis *(TDNT* 5. 87), it denotes the "(divinely) commanded walk" or "the proclamation of the divine will, of the walk which God requires." On "way," see NOTE on 3:4.

22. *is it lawful for us.* I.e. for "upright" Jews, or even "upright" spies. Luke has introduced "for us," because he has omitted the second question of Mark 12:14-15. In

his context of spies who pretend to be upright, the "for us" takes on a peculiar connotation.

to pay tribute. Lit. "to give tribute." Luke substitutes the commonly used *phoros* (a generic term for the *tributum agri* and *tributum capitis)* for the Marcan Latinism *kēnsos* (= Latin *census).* See H. Balz, *EWNT* 2. 708-710. The Lucan *phoros* is the word used by Josephus when he refers to the Roman tribute (e.g. *J.W.* 1.7,7 § 154; 2.8,1 § 118) imposed by Pompey on the farmlands *(chōra)* and on Jerusalem. In this Gospel context it refers to the direct poll tax levied on inhabitants of Judea.

Caesar. I.e. the ruler of the Roman empire. At the time it was Tiberius Julius Caesar Augustus. See NOTE on 3:1. Greek *Kaisar* was the transcription of Latin *Caesar,* which was originally the cognomen of Gaius Julius Caesar. In a will dated 13 September 45 B.C. he adopted his great-nephew, C. Octavius, as his son and heir to succeed him as dictator. After Caesar's assassination by M. Brutus and C. Cassius on the Ides of March 44 B.C., C. Octavius was eventually recognized as Caesar's adopted son. Then he took the name Gaius Julius Caesar Octavianus, and succeeding "emperors" of the Julio-Claudian and later lines continued the practice of adding "Caesar" to their names so that it became a common epithet for the reigning *princeps* or dictator. Jerome *(Comm. in Matth.* 3; CCLat 77. 204) wrote: "All Roman kings from the first Gaius Caesar . . . are called Caesars." From this use of *Caesar* developed the title for the Holy Roman Emperor, *der Kaiser.*

23. *perceived their trickery.* Lit. "their craftiness," i.e. their readiness to resort to anything (even fulsome praise) to achieve their goal. See O. Bauernfeind, *TDNT* 5. 726. Luke has substituted *panourgia* for the Marcan *hypokrisis* (12:15a), "dissembling." Jesus realizes that their question does not stem from a genuine desire to learn.

show me a silver coin. Lit. "a denarius." See NOTE on 7:41.

24. *Whose image and inscription does it bear?* The silver denarius, weighing 3.8 grams, had been in use in the Roman world since 268 B.C. and continued to be used into the reign of L. Septimius Severus (A.D. 193-211). Denarii bore the head of Tiberius and the inscription *TI. CAESAR DIVI AVG. F. AVGVSTVS* (Tiberius Caesar, son of the divine Augustus, Augustus). See F. W. Madden, *Coins of the Jews* (London: Trübner; Boston: J. R. Osgood, 1881) 291-292; E. Stauffer, *Christ and the Caesars* (London: SCM, 1955) 112-113; *IDB* 1. 824. The image and inscriptions on ancient coins would have been understood as a property seal; the coins *belonged* to Caesar. Part of the background of Jesus' question, which must be understood, is that for an "upright" Jew the image of Caesar on a coin was an abomination. It was, in effect, proscribed by the current interpretation of Exod 20:4, possibly also of Exod 20:23, because it referred to Tiberius as the son of "divine Augustus." Cf. *LAE* 252.

25. *Well, then.* The particle *toinyn* precedes Jesus' injunction in mss. ℵ, B, L, whereas the classical postpositive usage is found in mss. A, C, P, W. See BDF § 451.3.

pay to Caesar what is Caesar's and to God what is God's. Luke changes the Marcan word order slightly, putting the impv. *apodote* first and prefixing to it the particle *toinyn.* See previous NOTE. Matthew also moves the vb. forward, but in a different (and independent) fashion. The expression *ta tou theou,* "the things of God," is used elsewhere in the NT: 1 Cor 2:11 (of God = his gifts graciously bestowed, contrasted with those "of man"); 2:14 (of God's Spirit = mysteries known to the Spirit); 1 Cor

7:32-34 (of the Lord, contrasted with those of "the world"); Mark 8:33 (of God, contrasted with those of human beings). In these instances *ta tou . . .* expresses concern about things due to be rendered (to the person or thing expressed in the gen.).

Some commentators try to say that *apodote* connotes an obligation to "give back, render" what is owed or due. This would be the connotation, if the second Lucan sense of the word could be pressed here. See NOTE on 10:35. It may, however, be meant in a more neutral sense. How to distinguish between them depends on the theory of interpretation which one uses. See COMMENT.

The Lucan Jesus does not forbid the use of material possessions to pay taxes to a secular ruler. See p. 247. But his instruction in this episode does not counter his utterance of 16:13d, "You cannot serve both God and mammon," because tribute to Caesar is not the same as "mammon."

26. *in the sight of the people.* This detail is important in view of the accusation to be made against Jesus by the Jerusalem authorities in 23:1-2.

to catch him in anything he said. Because Jesus did not answer the question as the spies desired, their authorities will twist his answer to their liking in 23:2c.

they grew silent, astonished at his answer. Luke's ending emphasizes the failure of the commissioned spies, "upright" though they were.

BIBLIOGRAPHY (20:20-26)

Abel, E. L. "Jesus and the Cause of Jewish National Independence," *REJ* 128 (1969) 247-252.

Barrett, C. K. "The New Testament Doctrine of Church and State," *New Testament Essays* (London: SPCK, 1972) 1-19.

Bea, A. " 'Date a Cesare quel che è di Cesare e a Dio quel che è di Dio," *CivCatt* 109/ 3 (1958) 572-583.

Bergen, P. van. "L'Impôt dû à César," *LumVieSup* 50 (1960) 12-18.

Bornkamm, G. *Jesus of Nazareth* (New York: Harper & Row, 1975) 120-124.

Cassidy, R. J. *Jesus, Politics and Society: A Study of Luke's Gospel* (Maryknoll, NY: Orbis, 1978) 55-61.

Derrett, J. D. M. " 'Render to Caesar,' " *Law,* 313-338.

Giblin, C. H. " 'The Things of God' in the Question Concerning Tribute to Caesar (Lk 20:25; Mk 12:17; Mt 22:21)," *CBQ* 33 (1971) 510-527.

Goppelt, L. "The Freedom to Pay the Imperial Tax (Mk 12,17)," *SE II,* 183-194.

——— "Die Freiheit zur Kaisersteuer (Zu Mk. 12,17 und Röm 13,1-7)," *Ecclesia und Res Publica: Festschrift für Kurt Dietrich Schmidt* (eds. G. Kretschmar and B. Lohse; Göttingen: Vandenhoeck & Ruprecht, 1961) 40-50.

Haenchen, E. *Der Weg Jesu,* 406-409.

Kennard, J. S. *Render to God: A Study of the Tribute Passage* (New York: Oxford University, 1950).

Loewe, H. M. J. *"Render unto Caesar": Religious and Political Loyalty in Palestine* (Cambridge: University Press, 1940).

Petzke, G. "Der historische Jesus in der sozialethischen Diskussion," *Jesus Christus in*

Historie und Theologie: Neutestamentliche Festschrift für Hans Conzelmann zum 60. Geburtstag (ed. G. Strecker; Tübingen: Mohr [Siebeck], 1975) 223-235.

Rist, M. "Caesar or God (Mark 12:13-17)? A Study in *Formgeschichte,*" *JR* 16 (1936) 317-331.

Schramm, T. *Markus-Stoff,* 168-170.

Sevenster, J. N. "Geeft den Keizer, wat des Keizers is, en Gode, wat Gods is," *NedTT* 17 (1962-1963) 21-31.

Stauffer, E. *Christ and the Caesars: Historical Sketches* (London: SCM, 1955) 112-137.

Stock, A. " 'Render to Caesar,' " *TBT* 62 (1972) 929-934.

133. THE QUESTION ABOUT THE RESURRECTION OF THE DEAD
(20:27-40)

20 [27] Then some of the Sadducees, who say that there is no resurrection, came up to Jesus and posed this question: [28] "Teacher, Moses wrote this for our benefit: *If a* man's *brother dies* who had married but has left no children, his *brother is to take the wife*[a] and *raise up off-spring for* his *brother.*[b] [29] Now there were seven brothers; and the first married a woman but died childless. [30] Then the second married her; [31] and then the third, and so on until all seven married her and died leaving no children. [32] Finally the woman died too. [33] Now at the resurrection whose wife will this woman be, since all seven had married her?" [34] Jesus answered, "The children of this age marry and are married; [35] but those who are considered worthy of sharing in that age and in the resurrection from the dead will neither marry nor be married, [36] for they can no longer die. They are like angels, and they are children of God, since they share in the resurrection. [37] That the dead are raised was even revealed by Moses in the story of *the burning-bush,*[c] when he speaks of the Lord as *'the God of Abraham, the God of Isaac, and the God of Jacob.'*[d] [38] Indeed, he is not a God of the dead, but of the living; for to him they are all alive."

[39] At this some of the Scribes spoke up, "Teacher, you have put it well!" [40] And they no longer ventured to put a question to him.

[a] Deut 25:5   [b] Gen 38:8   [c] Exod 3:2   [d] Exod 3:6

COMMENT

Another type of Jerusalem Jew now accosts Jesus, inquiring about his teaching. Hitherto we have not heard about the Sadducees in the Lucan Gospel (and they appear in the Marcan parallel to this episode for the first time in that Gospel). The Sadducee questioners want to know what Jesus thinks about the resurrection of the dead and pose a question to him about levirate marriage. As in the last episode, Jesus solves the casuistic problem in an unexpected way (20:27-40), so that even the Scribes commend him for his (Pharisaic) answer. In this case, the question posed concerns neither Jesus himself nor his relation to Jerusalem authorities. The problem is theoretic, possibly even a stock question customarily put by Sadducees to Pharisees.

Luke has derived this episode mainly from Mark 12:18-27, which he has at times cast into better Greek (cf. Matt 22:23-33). Lucan dependence on "Mk" is especially clear in vv. 27-34a,37,38a. The Lucan modifications in these verses consist in the following: (a) the introduction of the ptc. *proselthontes*, lit. "coming up" (v. 27) to eliminate the Marcan parataxis (12:18); (b) the use of a ptc. *echōn*, lit. "having" (v. 28), and a compound adj. *ateknos*, "childless," to avoid parataxis in the OT allusion; (c) the use of *ateknos* again in v. 29; (d) the abbreviation of v. 30 (cf. Mark 12:21), which is similar to—but not exactly—Matt 22:26; (e) the use of better Greek in vv. 31-32 *(hysteron,* "finally," instead of *eschaton* [Mark 12:22]); (f) the omission in v. 33 of the redundant *hotan anastōsin,* "when they rise" (Mark 12:23); (g) the casting of the OT quotation in v. 37 into the acc. (cf. Mark 12:26). Verses 38b-39 are clearly the Lucan conclusion to the story, composed by Luke and differing from Mark 12:27b. Verse 40 is a redacted form of Mark 12:34, which Luke moves up to this point, because he will omit the next Marcan episode. The problematic verses are 34b-36. T. Schramm *(Markus-Stoff,* 170-171) maintains that these verses, which betray a "heavy Semitizing phraseology," certainly come from a variant source in the gospel tradition and have been substituted by Luke for the first part of Jesus' answer in Mark 12:24-26a. This solution is not impossible, but unlikely. Luke eliminates Jesus' accusation of Sadducees (that they err in interpreting Scripture) and puts the answer squarely on his own lips; he teaches the Sadducees. F. Neirynck ("La matière marcienne, 176-177) more plausibly ascribes these verses to Lucan redaction, "un elargissement personnel," which, among other things, replaces the double reference to the error of the adversaries and alludes to the idea of immortality in 4 Macc 7:19. A variant tradition is unlikely. (See further G. Schneider, *Evangelium nach Lukas,* 404-405; J. Schmid, *Evangelium nach Lukas,* 298-299.)

From a form-critical viewpoint, the episode is again a pronouncement-story (see *FGT* 65) or apophthegm, another controversy dialogue *(HST* 26). Bultmann regards Mark 12:26-27 (= Luke 20:37) as an addition to the story, though not an originally independent saying: an extra argument which is "in place in a debate." He regards it as "an argument from the theological material of the Church . . . , one which betrays its origin by its thoroughgoing Rabbinic character." Yet even if one were to grant that the argument proceeds along lines well known in the Pharisaic-rabbinic tradition (with the additional OT argument [contested by D. M. Cohn-Sherbok]), one must note that there is in this part of the pericope no specific Christian element. The reference to angels and to Exod 3:6, instead of any appeal to Jesus' own resurrection, argues against the formation of this episode in a Christian matrix. Even if one admits with H. Conzelmann *(Theology,* 205-206) that the Lucan title for Jesus, "author of life" *(archēgos tēs zōēs,* Acts 3:15; cf. 5:31) is to be explained by Jesus being the "first to rise from the dead" *(prōtos ex anastaseōs nekrōn,* Acts 26:23), none of that argument is brought into the discussion here. Nor does the OT argument support a "Christian" belief in the resurrection, *pace* G. Schneider *(Evangelium nach Lukas,* 405). (See further J. Jeremias, *New Testament Theology,* 184 n. 3; I. H. Marshall, *Luke,* 738.)

In the Lucan form of the story the Sadducee questioners address Jesus as teacher and ask him how he interprets a regulation in the Mosaic Law. In a generic allusion, they conflate Deut 25:5 and Gen 38:8, giving the substance of that regulation about levirate marriages (as they came to be called later on). The custom of such marriages (a brother-in-law begetting children by intercourse with his brother's widow, to continue his brother's house) was widespread in the ancient Near East, being in vogue among the Assyrians, Hittites, and Canaanites. The custom became part of Mosaic legislation in the two pentateuchal passages cited. (See also Ruth 4:1-12 for a possibly related instance of it.) In the light of this regulation the Sadducees pose a case, wondering what sort of answer Jesus would give, one in accord with their denial of the resurrection of the dead or one in accord with the more popular (Pharisaic and possibly Essene) belief in it. The case as posed: A woman's husband has died leaving no children; his six brothers perform the levirate duty; they all die childless and finally she dies too. At the resurrection "whose wife will this woman be"? Jesus' first answer is to insist that marriage is an institution of "this age," in which men and women die; it was instituted as a way in which the human race would survive. But in "that age," when they no longer die, are "like angels," become "children of God," and "share in the resurrection," there will be no marriage. Hence the Sadducees' question involves a misunderstanding. Verses 34-36 contain Jesus' own answer, which is not an interpretation of Scripture; his pronouncement corrects the misconceived idea that the Sadducees have of the afterlife, and of Pharisaic teaching about the resurrection. The Sadducees have erroneously assumed that earthly institutions will continue in the age to come.

To support his teaching, Jesus adds an OT argument about the resurrection itself, which in the Lucan form clearly becomes an argument for immortality. He appeals to the pentateuchal passage about Yahweh's appearance to Moses at Horeb, the mountain of God, "in the flame of fire from the midst of a bush . . . the bush was burning, yet it was not consumed" (Exod 3:2). Yahweh identified himself to Moses as the God of the patriarchs who were long since dead—then they must be living in some sense, for this identification not only shows that "the dead are raised" (v. 37), but even that Yahweh is a God of the living, not of the dead, and furthermore (Luke adds) that "to him they are all alive."

In what sense are they all alive? In this regard there are two schools of thought: (a) the traditional interpretation: The patriarchs, though having died, live indeed; they are immortal. This view has been said to encounter the difficulty that it conceives of the afterlife in terms of Greek dualism, the dichotomy of body and soul, a notion uncharacteristic of OT and Palestinian Jewish teaching. But whereas this difficulty is sensed more in the Marcan form of the story, it is less so in the Lucan because the evangelist has clearly added in v. 38b an allusion to 4 Macc 7:19, which itself implies immortality. (b) E. E. Ellis ("Jesus, the Sadducees"; *Gospel of Luke,* 235) finds the former argument impossible "because it would defeat the precise point of Jesus' argument. If Abraham is now personally 'living', no resurrection would be necessary for God to be 'his God'. The premiss of the argument is the Old Testament (and Sadducean) view of death. From this premiss, the nature of the 'living' God, and God's covenant with Abraham the Lord infers the necessity of a resurrection. The question between Jesus and the Sadducees is not Plato's but Job's, not 'if a man die is he still alive' but 'if a man die shall he live again'. To this question Jesus gives a firm and positive answer: the paths of glory lead *from* the grave." But such an interpretation reduces Jesus' double answer to one, for he not only affirms that "the dead are raised," but that "they are all alive" to God (vv. 37-38). Moreover, it presupposes that there was no belief in immortality among Palestinian Jews of the first century A.D. and that the resurrection of the dead had not already developed in terms of immortality (undoubtedly under the influence of Hellenistic philosophy). But that presupposition is far from certain.

In effect, Jesus says to the Sadducees, those who quote Moses (about levirate marriage) should also listen to him (about resurrection); and the Lucan Jesus adds, even about immortality.

The background of the question is the belief among Jews about the afterlife. In NOTE on 10:15 we have already sketched briefly the general OT ideas about Sheol and Hades. Though one can see that in the bulk of the OT belief in the afterlife was very vague, almost non-existent (no praise or presence of

God in Sheol, Pss 6:6; 88:4-6; 115:17; Qoh 9:4-10; Isa 38:18-19), there does emerge in time the idea of the resurrection of the dead (Dan 12:2), along with the notion of retribution for the conduct of earthly life. (See further 2 Macc 7:9; *Jub.* 23:31 ["Their bones shall rest in the earth, and their spirits shall have much joy; they shall know that the Lord executes judgment and shows mercy to hundreds and thousands, to all that love him"]; *1 Enoch* 91:10 ["The righteous will rise from sleep, and wisdom will rise and will be given to them"]; 92:3; 103:3-4.) Some of these ideas are verging on immortality itself, which eventually surfaces also in Jewish literature (Wis 1:15; 3:4; 8:13; 15:3 [Alexandrian tradition]; 4 Macc 14:5).

Of Pharisaic belief in an afterlife, Josephus writes: They hold that "every soul is imperishable, but only the soul of the good passes into another body, whereas the souls of the wicked are punished with eternal penalties" *(J. W.* 2.8,14 § 163). He further explains the passage into another body: "Their souls remain spotless and obedient, obtain a very holy place in heaven, from which, at the turn of the ages they will again inhabit bodies" *(J. W.* 3.8,5 § 374). (Cf. *Ag.Ap.* 2.30 § 218; *Ant.* 18.1,3 § 14.) These statements have been interpreted as metempsychosis, but they are really Josephus' way of trying to describe for Greek-speaking Gentiles the Pharisaic belief in resurrection (see L. H. Feldman, LCL 9. 13 n. c).

Of Essene belief in an afterlife, Josephus says, "It is a fixed opinion of theirs that bodies are perishable and their matter non-abiding, but that souls are immortal and persist forever" *(J. W.* 2.8,11 § 154). This belief Josephus attributes to the influence of Greek thinking. (See further *Ant.* 18.1,5 § 18.)

Of Sadducee belief in an afterlife, Josephus says, "As for the persistence of the soul, penalties in death's abode, and rewards, they do away with them" *(J. W.* 2.8,14 § 165; cf. *Ant.* 18.1,4 § 16: "the souls perish along with the bodies").

Such deuterocanonical, intertestamental, and extrabiblical references seem to make it clear that at least some first-century Palestinian Jews were believing in the resurrection of the dead, and probably even in immortality. The extent to which this belief was influenced by the Greek duality of body and soul is hard to say. The Sadducees would have none of it; hence the question that they pose to Jesus.

NOTES

20   27. *some of the Sadducees.* The Greek name *Saddoukaioi* is to be related to the Hebrew proper name *Ṣādôq,* "Zadok," which appears in Greek (with a double delta) in the LXX as *Saddouk* (2 Sam 8:17; Ezek 40:46; 43:19) and in Josephus as *Saddōk* or *Saddouk* (depending on the mss., see *Ant.* 18.1,1 § 4). The descendants of Zadok *(běnê Ṣādôq)* were granted the privilege of officiating as priests in the Temple after the return

from the Babylonian Captivity. These "Zadokites" formed the nucleus of the priesthood staffing the Jerusalem Temple. 1 Chr 5:30-35 [6:4-10E] traces the lineage of Zadok back to Eleazar, elder son of Aaron. Cf. Sir 51:12 (Hebrew; lacking in the Greek and Syriac versions). The Sadducees of first-century Palestine (B.C. and A.D.) were related to this Zadokite priestly line, but they had become a tightly closed circle, no longer exclusively a priestly group. They were priestly and lay aristocrats, considerably Hellenized. Of them Josephus writes, "The Sadducees have the confidence of the well-to-do only and no following among the people" *(Ant.* 13.10,6 § 298). "This teaching [of the Sadducees] has reached but few people, yet these are men of highest esteem" *(Ant.* 18.1,4 § 17). Though they appear only here in the Lucan Gospel, they emerge again in Acts 4:1; 5:17; 23:6-8. In the Matthean Gospel they appear with more frequency (3:7; 16:1,6,11,12; 22:33,34). Like the Essenes, they practically disappear from history with the destruction of Jerusalem, though references to them do occur in the Talmud. See further J. Le Moyne, *Les Sadducéens;* J. Jeremias, *Jerusalem,* 228-232; *HJPAJC* 2. 404-414; R. Meyer, *TDNT* 7. 35-54.

who say that there is no resurrection. Lit. "those denying there is a resurrection." Cf. Acts 4:2; 23:6-8; see COMMENT on this passage. The reason for their position was undoubtedly their strict interpretation of the *written* Torah, especially its precepts on the cult and the priesthood; they would have nothing to do with oral law and the *hălākāh* of the Pharisees. Since there is no reference to the resurrection in the Torah, they found no need to believe in it. See *HJPAJC* 2. 411. In the later rabbinic tradition the question is posed: "Sectarians *[Minîm]* asked Rabban Gamaliel: When do we know that the Holy One, blessed be He, will resurrect the dead? He answered them from the Torah, the Prophets and the Hagiographa . . ." *(b. Sanh.* 90b). Appeal was made to such passages as Num 15:31; 18:28; Exod 6:4; 15:1; Deut 31:16. The rabbis also referred at times to non-pentateuchal parts of the OT: Job 19:26; Ps 16:9,11; Isa 26:19.

The word *anastasis* has already occurred in a different sense in 2:34. With reference to the dead it has been met in 14:14 and occurs again in Acts 17:32; 23:6,8; 24:15,21. Apart from this passage (vv. 27,33,35,36) it otherwise refers to Jesus' resurrection, at least indirectly (Acts 1:22; 2:31; 4:2,33; 17:18; 26:23). It is also found in the sense of resurrection of the dead in classical and Hellenistic Greek (Aeschylus, *Eumen.* 648; Ps.-Lucian, *De Salt.* 45).

Many mss. (‭א‬, B, C, D, L, N, Θ, *f*¹, 33, etc.) read simply *legontes,* "saying," but mss. A, W, *f*¹³, and the Koine text-tradition have *antilegontes,* "denying" with the negative *mē.* Nestle-Aland²⁶ reads the latter with square brackets about *anti-,* considering it the *lectio difficilior.* See *TCGNT* 171-172. The meaning is not affected. But the nom. pl. is puzzling; it apparently agrees with *tines,* "some," but in sense it must be taken with the gen. pl. *Saddoukaiōn,* because it does not mean that only some of the Sadducees did not believe in the resurrection.

came up to Jesus and posed this question. Lit. "coming up, they asked him, saying . . ."

28. *Teacher.* See NOTES on 3:12 and 7:10; also p. 218. The address may be ironic, but they may also be acknowledging his authority as an interpreter of the Mosaic Law.

Moses wrote this. Earlier references to the Mosaic law are found in 2:22; 5:14. For the introduction of OT quotations with the vb. *graphein,* "write," see my article, "The Use of Explicit Old Testament Quotations," *ESBNT* 8-10.

If a man's brother dies. These words are taken over by Luke from Mark 12:19b. The Marcan form is an abridgement of the LXX of Deut 25:5a-c, which reads, *ean de katoikōsin adelphoi epi to auto kai apothanē heis ex autōn, sperma de mē ē autō, ouk estai hē gynē tou tethnēkotos exō andri mē engizonti,* "if brothers dwell together and one of them dies, and he has no offspring, the wife of the dead man will not become (a wife) to an outsider not related." Though explicitly introduced, the words in Mark and Luke are no more than an allusion to the OT passage.

who had married but has left no children. Lit. "having a wife, and he is childless." This is Luke's paraphrase of Mark's "and leaves a wife, but leaves no child," which is again only an allusion to Deut 25:5.

his brother is to take the wife. Or possibly "the brother is to take his wife," since *autou,* "his," is ambiguously placed. Luke derives these words from Mark 12:19d, which is a paraphrase of Deut 25:5d, *ho adelphos tou andros autēs eiseleusetai pros autēn kai lēmpsetai autēn heautō gynaika kai synoikei autē,* "the brother of her husband will go into her and will take her to himself (as) a wife and will live with her." The Lucan sentence is a bit peculiar; the subjunc. *labē,* "take," is introduced by the conj. *hina,* which expresses the obj.-injunction contained in "Moses wrote" *(egrapsen);* it is a substitute for an infin. See BDF § 392.1d; ZBG § 406-408.

and raise up offspring for his brother. Luke derives these words from Mark 12:19e, which slightly rewords the LXX of Gen 38:8, *kai anastēson sperma to adelphō sou,* "and raise (impv.) up offspring for your brother."

The name for this sort of marriage is "levirate," from Latin *levir,* "husband's brother, brother-in-law" (< *laevus vir,* Nonius Marcellus *Comp. doct.* 2.20 § 557.6). A Mishnaic tractate, *Yebamot,* deals with all the details of such marriages. See also M. Burrows, "Levirate Marriage in Israel," *JBL* 59 (1940) 23-33. Cf. Str-B 1. 886-887. Such a marriage was not considered a violation of Lev 18:16; 20:21 because the brother was dead. Some commentators question whether the levirate marriage was in vogue in first-century Palestine. See J. M. Creed, *The Gospel,* 248. However, Josephus *(Ant.* 4.8,23 § 254-256) speaks of it as if it were still being practiced. If it were not, then the question of the Sadducees would have been still more theoretical. Cf. J. Jeremias, *Jerusalem,* 372.

29. *Now there were seven brothers.* Luke adds the conj. *oun.* So begins the case. It tells the story of a widow in vv. 29-32. Why "seven"? No reason emerges in the story itself; it was, however, a favorite number among the Jews and suits well a storytelling purpose. See Tob 3:8 and NOTE on 17:4. Some mss. (ℵ¹, D, q, and the Sinaitic Syriac version) read: *ēsan par' hēmin hepta adelphoi,* "there were among us seven brothers," but this is a copyist's harmonization of the Lucan text with Matt 22:25a.

A similar casuistic problem occasioned by belief in the resurrection is found in the later rabbinic tractate, *b. Nid.* 70b, whether those to be resurrected will require ritual cleansing because of contact with death and the grave.

33. *at the resurrection.* I.e. of the dead, according to popular belief, but not by the Sadducee questioners; they use it in the Pharisaic sense for the sake of argument. Implicitly they pose a dilemma for Jesus: resurrection of the dead or Mosaic Torah?

whose wife will this woman be. So runs the problem that the Sadducees envisage.

The reading *estai* (in mss. ℵ, D, L, Θ, Ψ, *f*¹, 33, etc.) is to be preferred to the pres. *ginetai*, "does she become" (of mss. A, B, R, W, *f*¹³, and the Koine text-tradition). *since all seven had married her?* Lit. "for the seven had her (as) a wife."

34. *The children of this age.* Or "of this world," since *aiōn* can mean either "world" or "age." See BAGD 27-28. A related expression is found in 16:8b (see NOTE there); here the phrase designates mortal human beings in earthly existence.

The Lucan Jesus' answer does not accuse the Sadducees of erring in their reading of Moses; instead he teaches them directly about their misconceived notions.

marry and are married. This is a succinct way of describing a primary function of mortal, earthly life. Marriage and procreation are necessary so that the human race not die out, so that the life of this age be continued. Ms. D and the OL and OS versions, along with some patristic writers, add "are born and beget," but it is far-fetched to think that this addition (or any form of it [see *AAGA*³ 227]) could "have been in the original." A "reconstructed parallelism" is no argument for originality.

35. *those who are considered worthy of sharing in that age.* Or "that world." Implied in vv. 34-35 is the Semitic contrast of the two aeons; for a slightly different way of referring to it, see 18:30 (and NOTE). The aor. pass. ptc. *kataxiōthentes*, "having been considered worthy," is to be understood as a theological pass. (see NOTE on 5:20), i.e. considered by God. Cf. Acts 13:46. On what grounds a person would be so considered is not stated; not by gnosis, but undoubtedly by God's gracious judgment. Cf. Rom 8:29-30 for a Pauline way of considering it.

and in the resurrection from the dead. I.e. those raised to "everlasting life" (Dan 12:2).

will neither marry nor be married. I.e. because then people will no longer die and the perpetuation of the race will no longer depend on such marital union. Whereas in v. 34 the Greek vbs. were *gamousin kai gamiskontai*, here the preferred reading is *gamousin kai gamizontai*, a literary variant (with the same meaning, "are given in marriage"), which copyists have sought to harmonize in mss. B, 1241, 1424, etc.

36. *for they can no longer die.* I.e. being immortal. This reason has been added by Luke; it prepares for the following descriptions of such persons. It emphasizes the mortal, transitory character of earthly marriage. Some mss. (D, W, Θ) and the OL and OS versions soften the expression, reading or implying *mellousin*, "they are not going to die."

They are like angels. I.e. disembodied spirits who do not marry. Philo *(De sacrif. Abel.* 1 § 5) speaks of Abraham, having left this mortal life, becoming "equal to the angels" *(isos angelois gegonōs)* who are "unbodied and blessed souls" *(asōmatoi kai eudaimones psychai).* Cf. *2 Apoc. Bar.* 51:10 (the risen righteous will "be made like unto the angels"). For a description of angelic life, see *1 Enoch* 15:6. The compound adj. *isangelos* occurs only here in the NT; the Marcan counterpart (12:25c) is clearly more Semitic than this Lucan phrase. If this cl. were really part of what many commentators consider heavily Semitic source material inserted into "Mk," they would have to reckon with the peculiarly Greek compound adj. In 1QSb 4:25 the priests who are blessed will be *kml'k pnym,* "like an angel of the presence," an expression applied to them in this life.

There is a certain irony in Jesus' answer to the Sadducees, seeing that they admitted neither angels nor spirits. Cf. Acts 23:8.

they are children of God. Lit. "sons of God." This description is a Lucan addition, found neither in Matthew nor Mark. In Matt 5:9 it occurs in the seventh beatitude, but in an entirely different sense. Here its eschatological connotation is evident. See J. Jeremias, *New Testament Theology,* 181. It is predicated of human beings whose life and conduct have been deemed worthy of a share in the age to come. There is, indeed, another nuance to the phrase, because "sons of God" is used in the OT as a name for angels (Gen 6:2; Job 1:6 [in the latter instance *běnê hā'ělōhîm* becomes in the LXX *hoi angeloi tou theou]).* Particularly intriguing as background to this episode and to Jesus' comparisons is the story of the "sons of God" (angels) in Gen 6:2-4 who covet "the daughters of men" and engage in marriage to beget "giants" *(gigantes* in the LXX for *něpīlîm* and *gibbōrîm* of the MT). For the Johannine sense of the phrase, see John 1:12; 1 John 3:1-2.

since they share in the resurrection. Lit. "being sons of the resurrection," i.e. born of the resurrection, they participate in the age to come. On the figurative use of *huios,* see NOTE on 10:6.

37. *That the dead are raised.* I.e. by God (again, a theological pass.; see NOTE on 5:20). This cl. is the obj. of the vb. *emēnysen,* what Moses has revealed. On the pass. of *egeirein* for raising from the dead, see NOTE on 7:14.

was even revealed by Moses. Lit. "even Moses revealed (that the dead are raised)." Thus Jesus turns the argument from Moses back on the Sadducees. Instead of *emēnysen,* mss. D, W read *edēlōsen,* "showed, made clear."

in the story of the burning-bush. Lit. "at (the passage about) the burning-bush," an allusion to Exod 3:2, *ōphthē de autō angelos kyriou en phlogi pyros ek tou batou, kai hōra hoti ho batos kaietai pyri, ho de batos ou katekaieto,* "the angel of the Lord appeared to him in a flame of fire from the bush and he saw that the bush was burning, but the bush was not burned up." Luke follows Mark 12:26b, but changes the gender of the n. *batos* from masc. (as in the LXX) to fem. *(tēs batou),* the Atticistic usage. See BDF § 49.1.

when he speaks of the Lord. I.e. Yahweh (see Exod 3:4), for whom the surrogate "angel of the Lord" is used in 3:2. See NOTE on 1:11. For *kyrios* as a title for God, see pp. 113, 201. Luke substitutes the pres. tense *(legei)* for the Marcan aor. (eipen); "speaks" = what stands written (timelessly). If the Sadducees quote what Moses had written, then they should listen to him as he "speaks." Cf. Luke 20:42; Acts 2:25,34; 7:48; 8:34.

as the God of Abraham . . . Jacob. Luke follows Mark 12:26c, but casts the titles for Yahweh in the acc., making Moses himself say that Yahweh is the God of the patriarchs. Mark has *Egō ho theos Abraam kai theos Isaak kai ho theos Iakōb.* The LXX of Exod 3:6 reads, *Egō eimi ho theos tou patros sou, theos Abraam kai theos Isaak kai theos Iakōb,* "I am the God of your father, God of Abraham and God of Isaac and God of Jacob." Cf. Exod 3:15-16; Acts 3:13; 7:32. The main point in the argument is that Yahweh identifies himself to Moses as the God of the patriarchs long after they have died.

38. *Indeed, he is not a God of the dead, but of the living.* Luke follows Mark 12:27, but puts *theos* emphatically at the head of the statement which concludes his argument from Scripture. *Theos* is, however, predicative, lacking a def. art. See ZBG § 179; BDF § 273. The argument: Only living people can have a God, and therefore

Yahweh's promise to the patriarchs that he is/will be their God requires that he maintain them in life (I. H. Marshall, *Luke*, 743).

for to him they are all alive. This last cl. is peculiarly Lucan and undoubtedly alludes to 4 Macc 7:19, *pisteuontes hoti theō ouk apothnēskousin, hōsper oude hoi patriarchai hēmōn Abraam kai Isaak kai Iakōb, alla zōsin tō theō,* "they (i.e. the martyrs who imitate Eleazar, son of Aaron, in the pursuit of piety) believe that unto God they die not, just as not even our patriarchs, Abraham, Isaac, and Jacob, but they live unto God." See also 4 Macc 16:25. This is clearly an expression of the immortality of the patriarchs. The dat. *autō*, "to him," is ethical. See BDF § 192; ZBG § 56. This Lucan addition shows how Luke has pressed the sense of the story beyond that found in "Mk." *Pace* E. E. Ellis *(Gospel of Luke,* 237), this phrase can have neither a "proleptic" sense (they live "in the prospect of a sure resurrection") nor a "spiritual" sense (referring to the "Christian's present [corporate] existence in Christ which continues in spite of his [individual] death"). The former distorts the statement of the Lucan Jesus; the latter imports a Pauline idea which is not within the Lucan perspective.

"All" refers at least to all the patriarchs, but is probably to be understood also of all those considered worthy of sharing in the resurrection and in the age to come.

39. *some of the Scribes.* Those mentioned in vv. 1,19. Thus Luke joins up this episode closely with his own story of Jesus' teaching in the Jerusalem Temple and of Jesus' altercations with Jerusalem authorities. On "Scribes," see NOTE on 5:21. Embarrassed though they may be by the unexpected answer of Jesus to his Sadducee questioners, they have to agree with him.

Teacher. See NOTE on v. 28.

you have put it well! Lit. "you have spoken well/rightly."

40. *they no longer ventured to put a question to him.* Lit. "for they no longer dared to question him about anything." Who are "they"? It could be understood of the Sadducees, since they disappear from the Lucan story. But in the immediate context, the Scribes have been mentioned. In 22:66-68 the Scribes are among those who interrogate Jesus at his trial. But that is a closed session, and the meaning here may be that the Scribes dared not *openly* question him again.

This explanatory cl., which Luke adds to finish off his story (see NOTE on 5:39), is a modified form of Mark 12:34. It is transitional to the next episode, in which Jesus continues his teaching, but he also takes the initiative in querying others (probably the Scribes [cf. Mark 12:35]).

BIBLIOGRAPHY (20:27-40)

Bartina, S. "Jesús y los saduceos: 'El Dios de Abraham, de Isaac y de Jacob' es 'El que hace existir' (Mt 22,23-33; Mc 12,18-27; Lc 20,27-40; Hebr 11,13-16)," *EstBíb* 21 (1962) 151-160.

Baumbach, G. "Der sadduzäische Konservativismus," *Literatur und Religion des Frühjudentums* (eds. J. Maier and J. Schreiner; Würzburg: Echter-V., 1973) 201-213.

Carton, G. "Comme des anges dans le ciel," *BVC* 28 (1959) 46-52.

Charpentier, E. "Tous vivent pour lui: Lc 20,27-38," *AsSeign* ns 63 (1971) 82-94.

Cohn-Sherbok, D. M. "Jesus' Defence of the Resurrection of the Dead," *JSNT* 11 (1981) 64-73.

Dreyfus, F. "L'Argument scripturaire de Jésus en faveur de la résurrection des morts (Marc, XII, 26-27)," *RB* 66 (1959) 213-224.

Ellis, E. E. "Jesus, the Sadducees and Qumran," *NTS* 10 (1963-1964) 274-279.

Gundry, R. H. *The Use of the Old Testament in St. Matthew's Gospel* (NovTSup 18; Leiden: Brill, 1967) 20-22.

Haenchen, E. *Der Weg Jesu,* 409-412.

Le Moyne, J. *Les Sadducéens* (EBib; Paris: Gabalda, 1972) 123-127, 129-135.

Meyer, R. *"Saddoukaios,"* *TDNT* 7. 35-54.

Montanti, C. "Lc. 20,34-36 e la filiazione divina degli uomini," *BeO* 13 (1971) 255-275.

Müller, K. "Jesus und die Sadduzäer," *Biblische Randbemerkungen: Schülerfestschrift für Rudolf Schnackenburg* . . . (Würzburg: Echter-V., 1974) 3-24.

Neirynck, F. "La matière marcienne dans l'évangile de Luc," *L'Evangile de Luc: Problèmes littéraires et théologiques: Mémorial Lucien Cerfaux* (BETL 32; ed. F. Neirynck; Gembloux: Duculot, 1973) 157-201.

Schramm, T. *Markus-Stoff,* 170-171.

Schubert, K. "Die Entwicklung der Auferstehungslehre von der nachexilischen bis zur frührabbinischen Zeit," *BZ* 6 (1962) 177-214.

Suhl, A. *Die Funktion der alttestamentlichen Zitate und Anspielungen im Markus-evangelium* (Gütersloh: Mohn, 1965) 67-72.

Weir, T. H. "Luke xx. 20," *ExpTim* 28 (1916-1917) 426.

Wiles, M. "Studies in Texts: Lk 20.34-36," *Theology* 60 (1957) 500-502.

134. THE QUESTION ABOUT THE SON OF DAVID
(20:41-44)

20 [41] Then he said to them, "How is it that they say that the Messiah is the son of David? [42] For David himself in the Book of Psalms has said, 'The Lord said to my lord, "Sit at my right hand [43] until I make your enemies a footstool for your feet."' 'a [44] David obviously calls him 'lord'; then how can he be David's son?"

---

a Ps 110:1

COMMENT

Jesus continues his teaching in the Temple, now posing questions himself to those listening. His questions present an exegetical problem: If Psalm 110, ascribed to David in the OT, refers to the Messiah as "lord," how can he be David's son? (20:41-44).

Luke has derived the episode about the son of David saying from Mark 12:35-37a (cf. Matt 22:41-46). He has omitted at this point from "Mk" the intervening episode (12:28-31), the commandment for eternal life (cf. Matt 22:23-33), in order to avoid a doublet (see p. 81), for he has used a different form of that episode in 10:25-28 (see COMMENT there). In taking over the son of David saying from "Mk," Luke has somewhat abridged it. He eliminates the reference to Jesus "teaching in the Temple" (Mark 12:35a) probably not only because of 19:47 but also because of the general context at this point in his Gospel. He further eliminates mention of the Scribes (Mark 12:35b), probably because he has just mentioned them in v. 39 (and they will reappear in v. 46). They are then presumed to be among those listening to him in this episode. He also changes the form of indir. discourse in v. 41 (from a *hoti* cl. to an acc. + infin.). Strangely enough, for all his emphasis on the holy Spirit in his writings (see pp. 227-231, esp. p. 228), Luke omits the detail about David speaking "in the holy Spirit" (Mark 12:36). However, along with Matt 22:45, he uses the vb. *kalei,* "calls" (v. 44), instead of the Marcan *legei,* "says" (12:37), a minor agreement in the Triple Tradition. T. Schramm *(Markus-Stoff,* 171) agrees that in this episode Luke follows only "Mk," there being no evidence of a variant source.

As for the form-critical character of the episode it is not easily classified. Is it a dominical saying or a pronouncement-story? In Mark the narrative element is at a minimum, and there is no evidence of a debate. The Lucan form even curtails the Marcan, whereas the Matthean form builds into the episode a setting, making out of it a controversy dialogue (see *HST* 51). What is essentially preserved is two questions put by Jesus to his audience (Scribes, implied in Luke; Pharisees, mentioned in Matthew). In effect, the second question that he poses (v. 44) answers implicitly the first one (v. 41). M. Dibelius *(FTG* 261), in discussing the Marcan form of the episode, regarded it as "only a saying introduced into the text . . . handed down as an example of Jesus' critique of scribal learning." V. Taylor *(FGT* 78), noting the problem that Jesus himself supplies both the question and the answer, prefers to regard it as a pronouncement-story. This it implicitly is. One can speculate, as does R. P. Gagg ("Jesus und die Davidssohnfrage,") that what has been preserved is possibly only the torso of a fuller dialogue in which others had posed the first question to Jesus ("You too teach, don't you, that the Messiah is David's son?"), which Jesus would have answered by posing a counter-question. Hence a real controversy dialogue. But that is sheer speculation (see I. H. Marshall, *Luke,* 744; my article in *ESBNT* 123-124).

Bultmann *(HST* 66, 136-137) argues that the saying or pronouncement is "secondary," being a "community product," derived either from a part of the primitive community which held that the Messiah was Son of Man rather than the son of David (perhaps to meet the objection that Jesus' Davidic descent could not be established) or from the Hellenistic church (to show that he was not only David's son but Son of God). Fresh support for the latter alternative (with some varying nuances) can be found in F. Hahn, *Titles,* 13-15.

One can agree with V. Taylor *(FGT* 78) that "in the period before the Genealogies were compiled," the passage "may well have been used by Christians in controversy with Jews who laid stress on the necessity of actual physical descent" for the Messiah. But Taylor further argues *(Mark,* 490) that the content of the story and its linguistic features suggest that it was derived from a Palestinian tradition. Moreover, "the allusive character of the saying favours the view that it is an original utterance; it half conceals and half reveals the 'Messianic Secret'. It suggests, but does not state the claim, that Jesus' . . . Sonship is no mere matter of human descent. It is difficult to think that the doctrinal beliefs of a community could be expressed in this allusive manner. . . . The one speaker to whom Mk. xii.35-37 can be credibly assigned is Jesus Himself. His words led to the free use of Psa. cx. 1 in primitive Christianity" (ibid. 493). (See further D. M. Hay, *Glory at the Right Hand,* 26, 110, 114, 158-159.) What should above all be noted is that the title "lord" is not given its full resurrection-sense and that the question in v. 44 is devoid of Christian explanation. What Luke makes of all this in Acts 2:34-36 is another question; but can that be used to claim that the episode (especially in its Marcan form) is not rooted in Stage I of the gospel tradition?

The Lucan Jesus poses a double question to those listening to him in the Jerusalem Temple. His first question, "How is it that they say that the Messiah is the son of David?" Before anyone has a chance to reply, he quotes Psalm 110:1 and asks a second question, How can David, the reputed author of the Book of Psalms, and of Psalm 110 in particular, be the father of a messianic king whom he himself calls "lord"? The implication of the second question answers the first. It is not a matter of either/or, but of both/and: Yes, the Messiah is David's son, but he is more: He is indeed David's lord.

Jesus' questions raise several problems, which must be carefully sorted out. *First,* one must recall how the messianic expectation of first-century Palestinian Judaism had developed out of an OT background (see pp. 471-472, 197-198; cf. *ESBNT* 115-121). The expectation of a Davidic Messiah (with a capital M) is traced back to the OT promise of a future David (see especially Jer 30:9; cf. 23:5). He was to be the "anointed" agent of Yahweh, sent for the restoration of Israel and the triumph of God's dominion and power. The Qumran form of this expectation (along with others) is clear in 1QS 9:11, "until the coming of a prophet and the Messiahs of Aaron and Israel." Cf. *Ps. Sol.* 17:21, "Raise up, O Lord, for them their king, the son of David, at that time that you see [fit]." In 17:32 he is referred to as "their king, the Anointed of the Lord." (Cf. P. G. R. de Villiers, *Neotestamentica* 12 [1978] 75-110.)

Second, the relation of Psalm 110 to this pre-Christian Palestinian Jewish messianic expectation is problematic. The psalm is one of the royal psalms, undoubtedly composed for the enthronement of some king in the Davidic dynasty. The king ("my lord") is addressed by Yahweh ("the Lord") and called to ascend the throne and sit at his right hand; as a result of military victory the king's enemies will be made by Yahweh a footstool for his feet. (See M. Dahood, *Psalms III: 101-150* [AB 17A; Garden City, NY: Doubleday, 1970] 112-114; H.-J. Kraus, *Psalmen* [BKAT 15/2; 3d ed.; Neukirchen-Vluyn: Neukirchener-V., 1966] 2. 755.) Though often claimed to be of Maccabean date, more recent OT scholarship tends to attribute it to the beginning of the first millennium B.C. The problem, however, is whether this psalm was understood in pre-Christian Palestinian Judaism of the enthronement of the expected Messiah. Many NT commentators confidently so interpret it, ascribing such an interpretation to "the Rabbis" of Jesus' own day (e.g. V. Taylor, *Mark,* 492; E. E. Ellis, *Gospel of Luke,* 237-238). There is not a hint, however, of such an interpretation in the LXX or in the echo of the psalm in *T. Job* 33:3 or in the Hasmonean application of it (1 Macc 14:41 [alluding to v. 4]). Allusion to Ps 110:2 is found in *T. Levi* 8:3 and possibly to Ps 110:3,6 in *T. Levi* 18:1-3,8,12 (where mention is made of a "new priest" to be raised up by the Lord—which, indeed, *sounds like* the "Messiah of Aaron" [1QS 9:11], but which says nothing explicitly of a "Messiah" or of a Davidic one). (See D. M. Hay, *Glory* 21-26; cf. E. Schweizer, *The Good News according to Mark* [London: SPCK, 1971] 255.) Moreover, Str-B (1. 525) cites only *Ps. Sol.* 17:21 for the messianic sense of "son of David" in pre-Christian times and further admits (4. 452-465) that the messianic interpretation of Psalm 110 does not appear in rabbinic literature before the second half of the third century A.D. But to argue, as some authors do, that this Synoptic passage shows that the messianic interpretation was current among Palestinian Jews in the first century and that it was avoided by Jews subsequently because of anti-Christian polemic, only to emerge still later, is a gratuitous assertion. There is simply no evidence of the Davidic messianic interpretation of Psalm 110 in pre-Christian Palestinian Judaism, *pace* T. Callan, "Psalm 110:1 and the Origin of the Expectation that Jesus Will Come Again," *CBQ* 44 (1982) 622-636. Hence, if this episode is rightly rooted in Stage I of the gospel tradition, then the messianic interpretation may have begun with Jesus—and was certainly used by early Christians after him. In *Ep. Barn.* 12.11 the psalm-verse becomes, "The Lord said to Christ my Lord."

Third, the pun in the Greek text of Jesus' quotation of Ps 110:1, *eipen Kyrios tō kyriō mou*, "The Lord said to my lord," may seem to support Bultmann's contention that the saying originated in a "Hellenistic Church." (See also F. Hahn, *Titles*, 105.) The Hebrew text of the psalm has none of this, being *ně'ūm Yhwh la'dōnî*, "oracle of Yahweh to my lord"—but then one must ask how that would have been *read* aloud in first-century Palestinian usage (see my discussion in *WA* 126-127). The NT form of Ps 110:1 corresponds to the LXX, which has *eipen ho kyrios tō kyriō mou*, with the pun. Leaving aside, however, the question whether the Old Greek translation of the psalter had already translated the tetragrammaton by *kyrios* (see P. E. Kahle, *The Cairo Geniza* [2d ed.; Oxford: Blackwell, 1959] 222; cf. my discussion of this problem in *WA* 120-123), there is the problem about what language Jesus would have been using in posing this question. Obviously, he could have quoted the Hebrew of the psalm itself (see NOTE on 4:17); but he was probably speaking Aramaic, in which language the pun would also have been perfectly possible: *'ămar māryā lěmār'î* (see further *WA* 90). (The later Targum of the Psalms is of no help, since it preserves two considerably developed paraphrases of Ps 110:1 [see *WA* 110 n. 36].)

Fourth, in what sense would Jesus have posed the double question? There are three main interpretations of it: (a) Jesus is calling in question the Davidic origin of the Messiah: "Jesus had already declared himself Messiah. But the Messiah was to be the *Son of David*, whereas Jesus was a Galilaean and the son of Joseph the carpenter! How could he be the Messiah? To evade this serious difficulty Jesus must find a passage of Scripture according to which the Messiah need not necessarily be the Son of David; and like an expert Pharisee he finds it" (J. Klausner, *Jesus of Nazareth: His Life, Times, and Teaching* [New York: Macmillan, 1926] 320; cf. C. G. Montefiore, *The Synoptic Gospels* [London: Macmillan, 1909] 1. 290-292). But the tradition about an expected Davidic Messiah was so strong by the first century A.D. that it is inconceivable that Jesus would have sought to deny it or imply that it was not correct. (Cf. John 7:41-42.) As V. Taylor *(Mark, 491)* remarks, "Such a denial on His part would have furnished a major ground for an attack against Him, but in disputes between the scribes and Himself there is no sign that on this issue any objection was taken to His teaching." The tradition about Jesus' own Davidic descent is not based solely on the Lucan and Matthean infancy narratives (see pp. 340, 344). Klausner's interpretation is sheer speculation and has found few supporters. Moreover, it stems from the period prior to the Qumran discoveries and may be dismissed on the basis of this better evidence. His further question shows that he is challenging a specific understanding of such a messianic belief.

(b) Many ancient and modern commentators have understood the question of Jesus to imply that the Messiah is to be something more than a mere son of David, one having a more exalted or transcendent origin than David, seeing that the latter calls him *kyrios.* (See V. Taylor, *Mark,* 492; A. H. McNeile, *The Gospel according to St. Matthew* [London: Macmillan, 1915] 328.) Jesus would be insinuating something about himself without claiming to be either "Messiah" or "Lord." Bultmann *(HST* 136-137) recognized this as a possible meaning of the "community product," but read into it (along with others) the title Son of God—and therefore ascribed it to a "Hellenistic Church." Cf. *Ep. Barn.* 12.10. But the title "Son of God" has nothing to do with this episode, and, even if it had, it would not necessarily stem from a Hellenistic background (on which see pp. 206-207). From the text itself in the Synoptics one can say only that the "something more" insinuates lordship (of some form).

(c) Some interpreters have pressed beyond the second interpretation to specify that Jesus would have been referring to himself as the Son of Man of Dan 7:9-13. Because Ps 110:1 and Dan 7:13 are linked in Jesus' statement to the high priest at his interrogation (Mark 14:62; Luke 22:69), that would shed light on the usage of Psalm 110 here. Jesus is indeed the son of David, but more too: He is the Son of Man (and is making a synthesis of various Palestinian Jewish beliefs). (So J. Schniewind, *Das Evangelium nach Markus* [10th ed.; NTD 1; Göttingen: Vandenhoeck & Ruprecht, 1963] 164-165; P. Bonnard, *L'Evangile selon Saint Matthieu* [CNT 1; Neuchatel: Delachaux et Niestlé, 1963] 330-331.) But the importation of the title Son of Man into this passage is as arbitrary as that of Son of God mentioned above. Simply because Ps 110:1 is linked later with Dan 7:13, that is no proof that the linkage is connoted here.

The real problem in understanding the episode is not the meaning it has in Stage III of the gospel tradition (what the evangelists imply by it), but what it would have meant in Stage I. This meaning may be wholly lost to us. There is always the danger of reading too much into it at that stage in terms of Jesus' own messianic consciousness. As in that matter in general, all that one can trace back to Stage I is an implication—Jesus implicitly hinting about himself as Messiah, without any explicit affirmation. In this episode he poses a theoretic question and insinuates a connection between the Messiah born of Davidic lineage and his lordship. This connection is undoubtedly the springboard for the early Palestinian Jewish Christian community's confession (and even proclamation) of him: "Jesus is Lord."

The Davidic descent of Jesus is heightened, of course, in the Lucan writings (recall Luke 1:32-33; 3:31). His Davidic sonship will be emphasized anew in Acts 2:25-36, where David will again be quoted (Ps 16:8-11) and called a prophet. Psalm 110:1 will be used again in proximity to a proclamation that God made Jesus "both Lord and Messiah." Thus Luke implies that the full understanding of Jesus' relation to David and of the nature of his lordship comes only with resurrection-faith (see further C. Burger, *Jesus als Davidssohn,* 116). In its own way this passage implies Jesus' Davidic sonship, but it is another matter whether from that title alone, "son of David," one is to read into its use overtones of Solomonic wisdom, or even exorcistic and therapeutic skills. The question is posed by Jesus with an entirely different perspective.

This too probably explains why Luke, who usually likes to record the reactions of bystanders, suppresses here any mention of such reaction; contrast Mark 12:37c (the reaction of the crowd).

NOTES

20   41. *Then he said to them.* The favorite Lucan introduction is used, *eipen de* with *pros* + acc. See p. 116. Neither here nor in Mark 12:35 is the audience further specified; in Matt 22:34 the Pharisees are still gathered together, and Jesus addresses them.

How is it that they say that the Messiah is the son of David? I.e. that the expected anointed agent of Yahweh to be sent for the deliverance and salvation of his people (Israel) will be born of Davidic lineage. The third pl., "they say," is indef., possibly equaling the pass., "How is it said . . . ?" In Mark 12:35b the saying is attributed to the Scribes. On the background to the saying, see COMMENT on this passage; on the title, "son of David," see pp. 216-217.

42. *David himself.* Lit. "for David himself." David, the youngest of Jesse's eight sons (according to 1 Sam 16:10-11; 17:12; but cf. 1 Chr 2:13-15, youngest of seven), was anointed king of Judah after the death of Saul, and soon thereafter became king of the northern kingdom too. He made the former Jebusite city of Jerusalem his capital and exerted his regal influence from the Euphrates to the Brook of Egypt. The legitimacy of his kingship and the continuity of his dynasty were assured to him by the oracle of Nathan (2 Sam 7:8-16). The Davidids continued to reign in Judah until the fall of Jerusalem (587 B.C.). See further NOTE on 3:31; cf. E. Lohse, *TDNT* 8. 478-482; H. Merkel, *EWNT* 1. 663-665.

We are reading here *autos gar Dauid,* as in mss. ℵ, B, L, Θ, *f*¹, 33, etc.; some other mss. (A, D, R, W, Ψ, *f*¹³, and the Koine text-tradition) have *kai autos D.,* a Lucanism. See p. 120; but cf. p. 118.

in the Book of Psalms. In 1 Sam 16:23 David is depicted playing the lyre to soothe Saul, and in 2 Sam 23:1 he is called the "sweet psalmist of Israel" *(RSV;* "singer of Israel's psalms," *NEB;* but the translation is contested). In 1 Chr 16:7 reference is made to his inauguration of Temple thanksgiving psalms. This growth in tradition accounts for seventy-three psalms being eventually attributed to him in the OT "Book of Psalms." One of them is Psalm 110. The tradition continued to grow, for in a Qumran Psalms scroll a prose insertion lists all of David's compositions (11QPsᵃ 27:2-11; DJD 4.48,91-93). It ascribes to him 3600 psalms, 364 songs for the daily holocaust ("for all the days of the year"), 52 songs for the Sabbath qorbans, 30 songs for the feasts of New Moons, solemn assemblies, and the Day of Atonement, and 4 songs for making music over the stricken. "And the total was 4050. All these he spoke in prophecy which was given to him before the Most High." (On David as a prophet, see Acts 2:30; cf. my article, "David, 'Being Therefore a Prophet . . .' (Acts 2:30)," *CBQ* 34 [1972] 332-339.) The Qumran statement makes David surpass Solomon's compositions; in 1 Kgs 5:12 (4:32E) the latter is said to have uttered 3000 proverbs and 1005 songs. But cf. the LXX of 1 Kgs 4:32.

The Lord said to my lord. The historic, enthroned king addressed by David as "my lord" is now being understood as the expected messianic king. The quotation of Ps 110:1 follows the LXX, except for the lack of a def. art. before *Kyrios* (= Yahweh). In some Lucan mss. the def. art. *ho* is read (‫א‬, A, L, R, W, Θ, Ψ, *f*[1,13], and the Koine text-tradition), but that is suspected of being a copyist's harmonization with the LXX tradition. The art. is omitted in Mark 12:36 too—from which Luke probably derives it directly. The sense is not affected. See NOTE on 1:43.

Sit at my right hand. The king is accorded a place of honor by Yahweh himself, a sign of blessing on his rule.

43. *until I make your enemies a footstool for your feet.* Luke follows the LXX more closely, using *hypopodion,* "footstool," instead of the Marcan compound prep. *hypokatō,* "until I put your enemies under your feet." For an ancient illustration of this scene, see *ANEP* § 4 (pp. 2, 249): Syrians and Negroes kneeling on the platform beneath the enthroned Amen-hotep III. M. Dahood *(Psalms III,* 114) refers to the enthroned Sennacherib in *ANEP* § 371 (pp. 129, 293), but the king's footstool there is not formed of kneeling enemy prisoners. Cf. D. J. Wiseman, *Illustrations from Biblical Archaeology* (London: Tyndale, 1958) pl. 57. Cf. *ANET* 486 (Amarna Letters 254, 270, 271).

44. *David obviously calls him 'lord.'* I.e. calls the Messiah "lord," to whom Jesus applies the Davidic utterance. Cf. Acts 2:36.

then how can he be David's son? Order in patriarchal society would demand that a son call the father lord, not vice versa. For whereas "son" would connote subordination, "lord" connotes the opposite. Implied in Jesus' second question is that the Messiah is not merely David's son, but more (i.e. "lord" in some sense, not yet defined). Luke has used *pōs,* "how," instead of Mark's *pothen,* "whence" (12:37b).

BIBLIOGRAPHY (20:41-44)

Burger, C. *Jesus als Davidssohn,* 64-70, 114-116.

Chilton, B. "Jesus *ben David:* Reflections on the *Davidssohnfrage,*" *JSNT* 14 (1982) 88-112.

Cullmann, O. *Christology,* 130-133.

Daube, D. *The New Testament and Rabbinic Judaism* (London: University of London/Athlone, 1956) 158-169.

Fitzmyer, J. A. "The Son of David Tradition and Mt 22:41-46 and Parallels," *Concilium* 20 (1967) 75-87; reprinted, *ESBNT* 113-126.

——— "The Contribution of Qumran Aramaic to the Study of the New Testament," *NTS* 20 (1973-1974) 382-407; reprinted, *WA* 85-113.

France, R. T. *Jesus and the Old Testament: His Application of Old Testament Passages to Himself and His Mission* (London: Inter-Varsity, 1971) 100-102, 163-169.

Gagg, R. P. "Jesus und die Davidssohnfrage: Zur Exegese von Markus 12,35-37," *TZ* 7 (1951) 18-30.

Hahn, F. *Titles,* 103-115, 191, 251-262.

Hay, D. M. *Glory at the Right Hand: Psalm 110 in Early Christianity* (SBLMS 18; Nashville: Abingdon, 1973) 104-121.

Iersel, B. M. F. van. *"Der Sohn,"* 171-173.

Lövestam, E. "Die Davidssohnfrage," *SEA* 27 (1962) 72-82.

Lohse, E. *"Huios Dauid,"* *TDNT* 8. 478-488.

——— "Der König aus Davids Geschlecht: Bemerkungen zur messianischen Erwartung der Synagoge," *Abraham unser Vater* (eds. O. Betz et al.) 337-345.

Michaelis, W. "Die Davidssohnschaft Jesu als historisches und kerygmatisches Problem," *Der historische Jesus und der kerygmatische Christus* (eds. H. Ristow and
K. Matthiae; 2d ed.; Berlin: Evangelische Verlagsanstalt, 1962) 317-330.

Neugebauer, F. "Die Davidssohnfrage (Mark xii. 35-7 Parr.) und der Menschensohn," *NTS* 21 (1974-1975) 81-108.

Rese, M. *Alttestamentliche Motive,* 173-174.

Schneider, G. "Die Davidssohnfrage (Mk 12, 35-37)," *Bib* 53 (1972) 65-90.

Suhl, A. "Der Davidssohn im Matthäus-Evangelium," *ZNW* 59 (1968) 57-81.

135. BEWARE OF THE SCRIBES
(20:45-47)

20 ⁴⁵ In the hearing of all the people Jesus said to his disciples,
⁴⁶ "Beware of the Scribes who like to walk about in long robes and are
fond of greetings of respect in the marketplaces, front seats in the
synagogues, and first places at dinners! ⁴⁷ They are the ones who devour the houses of widows and say long prayers for appearance' sake.
They will incur the severest condemnation."

COMMENT

Jesus continues his teaching in the Temple with a warning against the way of
life of the Scribes (20:45-47). He criticizes them for their ostentation, their
pretense, and their deceit. On them, he says, will fall God's severest condemnation.

These verses are derived by Luke from Mark 12:38-40 (cf. Matt 23:1,6
[where the Marcan material is used with some of "Q" and "M" to form the
long list of woes against the Pharisees]). Luke has substituted his own introductory v. 45, using a gen. absol. to avoid the parataxis of Mark 12:37c (see p.
108), but otherwise follows "Mk" almost word for word. He substitutes a
characteristic vb. *prosechein* (see p. 113) for the Marcan *blepein.* Verse 46 is a
doublet of 11:43, which was derived from "Q" (see pp. 81-82) and formed
part of a lengthy criticism of the Pharisees and lawyers (11:37-54).

From a form-critical viewpoint, these verses contain minatory sayings of

Jesus, warning his disciples about the conduct of Scribes (see *HST* 113-114). On the isolated character of these sayings, which may no longer be in their original context, see *FTG* 236.

Previous references to Scribes in the immediately preceding episodes were not all negative or critical of them. In v. 39 the Scribes commended Jesus for his answer to the Sadducees; in v. 41 he probably refers to a saying of theirs (so in "Mk"), which he proceeds to interpret. But now the Lucan Jesus' attention is directed against the conduct of these Jerusalem authorities. He warns his disciples against imitating their fondness for long robes, for greetings of respect from the populace in the marketplaces, for seats of honor in the synagogues, and for first places at banquets. All of this is sham and ostentation, which should not be part of a Christian disciple's way of life. The Scribes presume to pass themselves off as important, yet they are the ones who devour what little estates widows have left. They cover up such activity with the façade of religious piety, saying lengthy prayers to God. But for all this God's condemnation will eventually fall on them in the most severe fashion, because they are, in effect, leaders and teachers of the people—a position which they are abusing. Implicitly, Jesus appears in this scene as an advocate for one group that is exploited. (See pp. 191-192.)

The difficulty which the reader senses in this passage is the severe condemnation of the Scribes which allows for no exceptions or qualifications; it is a "blanket" condemnation of them. This aspect of the episode is evident not only in the Lucan form but also in the Marcan. It undoubtedly stems in part from the sharpened polemic of Stage II of the gospel tradition. G. Stählin *(TDNT* 9. 449) thinks that Jesus' prophetic warning, echoing OT descriptions of the plight of the widows (e.g. Isa 1:23; 10:2; Ezek 22:7; Job 22:9; 24:3), has been sharpened against "certain scribes." Yet the trouble is that in both Mark and Luke it is directed against *"the* Scribes," without distinction.

NOTES

20 45. *In the hearing of all the people.* Lit. "while all the people (were) listening," a gen. absol. The mention of the "people" *(laos)* and the "disciples" *(mathētai)* as the audience to which Jesus addresses his warning against the conduct of the Scribes again pits the Jerusalem authorities against the others. See NOTES on 18:43; 19:47.

his disciples. They were last mentioned in 19:39, when some Pharisees requested Jesus to rebuke them on the occasion of his royal entry into Jerusalem. The pron. *autou,* "his," is read in mss. B and D, but omitted in many others; hence the square brackets around it in N-A[26]. Note that the disciples appear also in Matt 23:1.

46. *Beware of the Scribes.* See NOTES on 12:1 and 5:21. Jesus' warning constitutes advice that the disciples should not imitate the way of life of the Scribes.

to walk about in long robes. In the LXX *stolē* is often used to translate the generic word for clothing, Hebrew *beged.* E.g. Gen 27:15; Exod 29:5,21; 31:10. But it came to be used also for priestly robes (Philo, *Leg. ad Gaium* 37 § 296; Josephus, *Ant.* 3.7,1 § 151; 11.4,2 § 80). According to Str-B (2. 31-33) *stolē* refers here to the *ṭallît,* a Hebrew word not found in the OT or in Qumran literature, but used in later rabbinic literature, for the outer cloak (= Latin *pallium)* that most people wore, but which lawyers and officers used in more ornamented or voluminous fashion, as a mark of distinction. K. H. Rengstorf ("Die *stolai,"* 402) would rather understand it of festive garments which Jews would don for the celebration of the Sabbath. The Scribes would be donning these for notoriety among the populace and to move it to imitation.

Instead of *stolais,* "long robes," the OS versions presuppose the reading *stoais,* "stoas" (i.e. roofed colonnades or porticos, as in Acts 3:11; 5:12), an interesting variant which completely changes the meaning of the verse.

fond of greetings of respect in the marketplaces. Luke adds *kai philountōn,* lit. "and loving," to smooth out the awkward Greek of "Mk." Cf. 11:43.

front seats in the synagogues. See NOTE on 11:43.

first places at dinners! See NOTE on 14:7. These were more usually assigned to elderly persons in the community.

47. *devour the houses of widows.* I.e. eat away the estates of widows; their need for judicial aid is already evident in 18:2-5. The "devouring" has been interpreted in various ways: (a) Scribes accepted payment for legal aid to widows, even though such payment was forbidden. See G. Stählin, *TDNT* 9. 445; cf. G. Schneider, *Evangelium nach Lukas,* 411. (b) Scribes cheated widows of what was rightly theirs; as lawyers, they were acting as guardians appointed by a husband's will to care for the widow's estate (J. D. M. Derrett, " 'Eating Up' "). (c) Scribes sponged on the hospitality of these women of limited means, like the gluttons and gourmands mentioned in *Ass. Mos.* 7:6 ("devourers of the goods of the < po > or, saying that they do so on the basis of their justice") (J. Jeremias, *Jerusalem,* 114). (d) Scribes mismanaged the property of widows like Anna who had dedicated themselves to the service of the Temple (T. W. Manson, *Sayings,* 306). (e) Scribes took large sums of money from credulous old women as a reward for the prolonged prayer which they professed to make on their behalf (D. E. Nineham, *The Gospel of St Mark* [Pelican Gospel Commentaries; Baltimore: Penguin, 1963] 333). (f) Scribes took the houses as pledges for debts which could not be paid (C. H. Talbert).

The trouble is that there is no explanation in the text itself. Any of the foregoing explanations might be valid; but even the meager evidence brought forth by Derrett might support the second interpretation more than others.

Luke has substituted a rel. cl. for the Marcan def. art. + pres. ptc.; this ameliorates the Greek somewhat.

and say long prayers for appearance' sake. The relation of this complaint to the preceding one is not clear. If one follows ms. D and omits the conj. *kai* and reads the ptc. *proseuchomenoi,* the cl. is joined closely to the preceding. But the best Lucan mss. read *kai* and the indic. *proseuchontai.* It is not "long prayers" which are criticized, but rather that they are done *prophasei.* However, the sense of this n. is contested. It could mean either "real, actual motive or reason, valid excuse" (so in John 15:22; Josephus, *Ant.* 13.16,5 § 427) or "pretext, ostensible reason" (as in Acts 27:30; Josephus, *J. W.* 2.16,4 § 348). Derrett prefers the former, which would mean that the real reason why the Scribes indulge in long prayers was a parade of piety to induce people to trust them—"with such an end in view." However, that is subtle and not very convincing. Moreover, most commentators prefer the latter meaning, "pretense," and understand it of the ostentatious piety by which Scribes would be pleading for the widows. Fortunately, Derrett's explanation of the "devouring" is not logically linked to his interpretation of *prophasei.*

They will incur the severest condemnation. The n. *krima* in itself means "lawsuit" or "decision, judgment, verdict" (= Greek *krisis).* But it is often used as the equivalent of *katakrima,* "negative judgment, condemnation" (as in Luke 23:40; 24:20). Cf. Rom 2:2-3; 3:8; 1 Cor 11:34; Gal 5:10; Rev 17:1. The latter is clearly the sense intended here, for it refers to the eschatological judgment of God in a negative sense against the Scribes. See NOTE on 19:22.

BIBLIOGRAPHY (20:45-47)

Derrett, J. D. M. " 'Eating Up the Houses of Widows': Jesus's Comment on Lawyers?" *NovT* 14 (1972) 1-9.

Keck, F. *Die öffentliche Abschiedsrede Jesu in Lk 20,45—21,36: Eine redaktions- und motivgeschichtliche Untersuchung* (Forschung zur Bible 25; Stuttgart: Katholisches Bibelwerk, 1976) 36-46.

Rengstorf, K. H. "Die *stolai* der Schriftgelehrten: Eine Erläuterung zu Mark. 12,38," *Abraham unser Vater* (eds. O. Betz et al.) 383-404.

136. THE WIDOW'S TINY OFFERING
(21:1-4)

21 ¹ Jesus glanced up and saw wealthy people dropping their contributions into the Temple treasury. ² Then he noticed a needy widow drop in two small coins. ³ He commented, "I can tell you truly, this poor widow has contributed more than all the rest. ⁴ For they have all given their gifts out of their abundance, but she in her need has dropped in all that she had to live on."

COMMENT

The mention of widows in the preceding episode acts as a catchword bond to join to it another episode about Jesus' comments on a poor widow who makes a tiny offering to the Temple in Jerusalem (21:1-4). These comments continue to form part of his teaching in the Temple.

Luke again derives his story from Mark 12:41-44 (Matthew omits the episode). The catchword bonding already existed in "Mk." Though Luke has fashioned his own introduction to the episode, when he comes to the crucial part, the Saying of Jesus, he follows "Mk" closely. In v. 1 he has eliminated the Marcan details of Jesus sitting down opposite the Temple treasury and the many contributions that many rich people made to the Temple. He has thus sharpened the contrast between the poor widow and the others in his version of the story. Verses 2-4 follow the Marcan form of the episode, but Luke abridges them by eliminating the Latinism *kodrantēs* (see NOTE on 12:59) and the summoning of the disciples (cf. 20:45). Luke also uses a poetic word *penichra,* "poor, needy," instead of Mark's more ordinary word *ptōchē,* "beggarly, poor," in his initial description of the widow (v. 2), only to revert to the latter in Jesus' comment itself (v. 3), as he follows his source. In v. 4 he slightly improves the Greek style. T. Schramm *(Markus-Stoff,* 171) sees no need to appeal to a variant source, apart from "Mk."

From a form-critical point of view, the episode is a pronouncement-story, a biographical apophthegm, with the saying preserved in vv. 3b-4. (See *FGT* 72; *HST* 32-33.) M. Dibelius *(FTG* 261) thought that the narrative could perhaps be traced back "to a saying of Jesus, and especially to a parable." Possibly, but that is mere speculation. H.-J. Degenhardt *(Lukas,* 93-97) thinks that the narrative setting is a secondary addition to what was only a Saying of Jesus in the earlier tradition. But Bultmann has rightly stressed the "unitary composition" of the episode, especially in its Marcan form. He further toys with the idea that the episode may depend on a similar story preserved in Buddhist tradition (see H. Haas, *'Das Scherflein der Witwe' und seine Entsprechung in Tripitaka* [Leipzig: Hinrichs, 1922]; J. B. Aufhauser, *Buddha und Jesus in ihren Paralleltexten* [KlT 157; Bonn: Marcus und Weber, 1926] 13-16). Moreover, even Bultmann sensed that the idea of small sacrifices being made by poor people as being more pleasing to the gods than the extravagant contributions of the rich is a theme common to Greek literature from at least the sixth century B.C. (see R. Herzog, *Der junge Platon* [ed. E. A. Horneffer; 2 vols.; Giessen: Töpelmann, 1922] 1. 150-157; J. Wettstein, *Novum Testamentum graecum* [2 vols.; reprinted, Graz: Akademische Druck- und Verlagsanstalt, 1962] 1. 618-619; cf. Josephus, *Ant.* 6.7,4 § 148; Euripides, *Danaë* frg. 319). See Str-B 2. 45-46 for later rabbinic parallels (esp. *Lev. Rab.* 3.107a).

What is the meaning of Jesus' comment about the widow's tiny offering? Various attempts have been made to explain it. In listing these attempts, I am following the study of A. G. Wright, "The Widow's Mites," which gives five of them: (a) The true measure of gifts is not how much is given but how much remains behind, or the percentage of one's means (the cost to the giver). (So commentators such as A. Farrer, I. H. Marshall, G. B. Caird, B. Swete, V. Taylor, et al.) (b) It is not the amount that one gives but the spirit in which the gift is given. (So E. Haenchen, F. Keck, M.-J. Lagrange, A. Plummer,

P. S. Minear, et al.) The "spirit" is, however, variously explained (e.g. self-offering, self-forgetfulness, unquestioning surrender, detachment). (c) The true gift is to give everything one has. (So D. E. Nineham.) (d) Alms and other pious gifts should correspond to one's means. (So J. Schmid.) (e) The story expresses Jesus' mind on the subject of almsgiving. (So V. Taylor *[FGT* 73], R. H. Fuller.) Wright correctly notes (p. 258) that all the explanations apart from the first have no basis in the gospel text itself. Nothing is said about the inner "spirit" of the widow. Again, the contrast in the story is between "more" and "less" not between a "true gift" and a "non-authentic gift." There is no basis in the text for giving according to one's means; the widow gives all that she has! She gives beyond her means. To reduce the point of the story to a counsel about almsgiving is to miss its main thrust; certainly almsgiving to the poor is out of question here.

In the broad context of the Marcan Gospel the episode, when it is normally understood as a comment of praise from Jesus, creates a problem. This arises from Jesus' statement about Corban in Mark 7:10-13. There he is remembered as having said that human needs take precedence over religious values, when they conflict. Compare further his words about healings on the Sabbath (e.g. 3:1-5). Given such a reaction of Jesus in other parts of the Marcan Gospel, would the Marcan Jesus become enthusiastic about and praise the widow's contribution, when it involves "all that she had to live on"? The Corban-saying seems to set limits to the interpretation of Jesus' words in this episode.

In the immediate context of both the Marcan and Lucan Gospels, moreover, Jesus has condemned the Scribes who devour the estates of widows. Now he comments: This widow has put in everything that she had, her whole livelihood or subsistence. "Her religious thinking has accomplished the very thing that the scribes were accused of doing" (A. G. Wright, "The Widow's Mites," 262). In the preceding episode Jesus was displeased with what the Scribes were doing to widows' estates; here he is no more pleased with what he sees. He heaps no praise on the widow, but rather laments the tragedy of the day: "She has been taught and encouraged by religious leaders to donate as she does, and Jesus condemns the value system that motivates her action" (ibid.). In short, Jesus' comment contains words of lament, not of praise.

NOTES

21 1. *Jesus glanced up and saw wealthy people dropping their contributions.* Thus Luke joins this episode closely to the preceding one (contrast Mark, which implies a change of scene). Moreover, in Mark 12:41 Jesus watches both "the crowd" and "many wealthy people" making their contributions. See p. 247.

into the Temple treasury. Treasure chambers in the Jerusalem Temple are mentioned in Neh 12:44; Josephus, *J.W.* 5.5,2 § 200; 6.5,2 § 282; cf. 1 Macc 14:49; 2 Macc 3:6,24,28,40. The Greek term *gazophylak(e)ion* used here has to be understood of the receptacles for collecting contributions and taxes brought to the Temple. According to *m. Šeqal.* 6:5, thirteen shofar-chests (i.e. trumpet-shaped receptacles) stood in the forecourt of the Temple for this purpose. They were inscribed with various titles: "New Shekel Dues," "Old Shekel Dues," "Bird-Offerings," "Young Birds for the Holocaust," "Wood," "Frankincense," "Gold for the Mercy-Seat," and six of them with "Freewill-Offerings."

   2. *noticed a needy widow.* Luke uses the literary adj. *penichros,* formed from the stem of *penesthai,* "toil, work," and related to the adj. *penēs.* The difference between *ptōchos* (v. 3) and *penēs* is explained by Aristophanes *(Plutus,* 553): "The life of a poor person *(ptōchos)* is to live, having nothing at all, whereas the life of a needy person *(penēs)* is to live sparingly, and dependent on toil." Luke, however, uses them in these verses synonymously. It should be noted, moreover, that nothing is said about the widow being elderly, sickly, or without dependents. It is rather implied that she has personal needs.

   drop in two small coins. Lit. "casting there two small (copper) coins," i.e. two of the smallest coins in use in Palestine of the time. See NOTE on 12:59. Ms. D adds *ho estin kodrantēs,* "which is a quadrans," a copyist's harmonization with Mark 12:42. Whether or not *kodrantēs = quadrans* and is the equivalent of *lepta dyo,* see F. Blass, "On Mark xii. 42," and W. M. Ramsay, "On Mark xii. 42.

   3. *I can tell you truly.* See NOTES on 9:27; 4:24.

   has contributed more than all the rest. So runs the sad comment of Jesus.

   4. *they have all given their gifts out of their abundance.* Lit. "for all these (people) out of what abounds to them were casting in the gifts." Some mss. (A, D, W, Θ, Ψ, *f*¹³, and the Koine text-tradition) add "of God."

   she in her need has dropped in all that she had to live on. Lit. "but she out of her need cast in all the subsistence which she had." For a similar use of *bios,* see 8:43; contrast the use of it in 15:12,30. At the end of this verse some mss. (Γ, 063, *f*¹³, 892) add, "As he said this, he called out, 'Let the one who has ears to hear take heed.' " See NOTES on 8:8 and 12:21.

BIBLIOGRAPHY (21:1-4)

Blass, F. "On Mark xii. 42 and xv. 16," *ExpTim* 10 (1898-1899) 185-187, 286-287.

Degenhardt, H.-J. *Lukas Evangelist der Armen,* 93-97.

Lee, G. M. "The Story of the Widow's Mite," *ExpTim* 82 (1971) 344.

Ramsay, W. M. "On Mark xii. 42," *ExpTim* 10 (1898-1899) 232, 336.

Simon, L. "Le sou de la veuve: Marc 12/41-44," *ETR* 44 (1969) 115-126.

Sperber, D. "Mark xii 42 and Its Metrological Background: A Study in Ancient Syriac Versions," *NovT* 9 (1967) 178-190.

Wright, A. G. "The Widow's Mites: Praise or Lament?—A Matter of Context," *CBQ* 44 (1982) 256-265.

137. THE FATE OF THE JERUSALEM TEMPLE
(21:5-7)

21 ⁵ When some of the people were talking about the Temple and about how it had been adorned with fine stones and votive offerings, Jesus said, ⁶ "As for what you are gazing at—the time is coming when not a stone of it will be left upon a stone that will not be torn down." ⁷ Then they asked him, "Teacher, when will this happen? What sign will there be when these things are to take place?"

COMMENT

As Jesus continues his teaching in the Temple, he utters a long discourse which deals with the fate of Jerusalem and its Temple and then moves on to "what is coming upon the world" (21:5-36). This part of the gospel tradition has either preserved the recollection of a lengthy discourse uttered by Jesus toward the end of his ministry about the crisis facing Jerusalem and "this generation" (not unrelated to the fate of the world) or else fashioned such a discourse out of isolated sayings that he may have uttered at various times. The latter is more likely because the different forms of this discourse in the Synoptic Gospels reveal reworkings of the material and concerns which stem even from the post-resurrection period. Moreover, the topics of the fate of Jerusalem and of the world are linked to topics which have appeared earlier in the gospel tradition, the coming of the kingdom and the day of the Son of Man. As a result, this discourse is very complicated and one of the most difficult parts of the gospel tradition to interpret. There are almost as many interpretations of it as there are heads that think about it.

It is often called Jesus' "eschatological discourse" because it deals with the *eschata*, "last things," of both Jerusalem and the world. It is also often called the Synoptic "apocalyptic discourse," because it presents those *eschata* in apocalyptic trappings. This is not the place for an elaborate distinction of "eschatological" and "apocalyptic," but for the sake of clarity about the way they will be used in the discussion of this discourse this minimum must be stressed. "Eschatology" is being understood as a content-term; a body of teaching about the *eschata* (of Jerusalem and the world [in this Gospel context—other *eschata* could be considered in other contexts]). "Apocalyptic" is an adj. that describes either a form of literature or a mode of thinking; it is a genre-term. For the details, see J. J. Collins, "Apocalypse: Towards the Morphology of a Genre," *SBL 1977 Seminar Papers* (No. 11; ed. P. J. Achtemeier; Missoula, MT: Scholars, 1977) 359-370. Whereas the whole of the discourse, especially in the Lucan form, can be called "eschatological," not every verse of it employs apocalyptic trappings or stage props. In that it seeks, as a whole, to give encouragement and exhort to vigilance, it can be regarded as a piece of apocalyptic writing.

The discourse is introduced by a question from those listening to Jesus; this question follows on a comment of Jesus about the Temple and its adornments (21:5-7). But the division of the discourse proper (vv. 8-36) is not easily made and the division may seem arbitrary at times (see COMMENT on vv. 8-11 for the outline that will be employed in this commentary). As a whole, it will be discussed in the next seven pericopes.

The Lucan eschatological discourse (21:5-36) has its parallels in Mark 13:5-37 and Matt 24:1-36, but this Lucan form echoes material already used in chap. 17 (especially vv. 23-24,26-27,33,34-35,37—derived from "Q"); this makes the form here, derived largely from "Mk," something of a doublet. Its inspiration is clearly the Marcan discourse; but it owes to that more than merely inspiration, for it occurs at the same place in the gospel tradition (after the two widow-sayings [20:45-21:4] and just before the passion narrative). It has, moreover, the same basic content (end of the world related to the end of Jerusalem) and uses much of the Marcan wording. But the further analysis of the Lucan discourse and of its relation to the Marcan material is complicated, for it is clearly not a slavish reproduction of "Mk."

The relation of the three Synoptic forms of this discourse has been well summarized by G. B. Caird *(Gospel of St Luke,* 230):

> Jesus' prediction of the destruction of the temple calls forth from the disciples a question which, in all three Synoptic Gospels, leads to a long prophetic discourse. Mark's discourse, however, is no answer to the question; it relates to the end of the present age and the signs that will foreshadow it, and one of those signs is, not the destruction, but the desecration of the temple. Matthew has removed the inconsistency by making the question fit the answer, Luke by making the answer fit the question.

Before we turn to further discussion of that relationship, four prior questions have to be considered: (1) Though the Synoptic gospel tradition preserves in this discourse the recollection of some lengthy sermon that Jesus uttered toward the end of his ministry about Jerusalem, its Temple, and the world in general, it is impossible for anyone to say today how much of that tradition is authentic, or an accurate reflection of Stage I of the tradition. One need only look at what has happened to the material in the Marcan, Matthean, and Lucan versions to realize that we have in Stage III well-explicated, overlaid forms, no one of which can be simply equated with Stage

I. As a result, there have been students of this material who have concluded, as did E. Meyer *(Ursprung und Anfänge des Christentums* [3 vols.; Berlin/ Stuttgart: Cotta, 1921, 1922, 1923] 1. 129), "It is quite clear that this whole proclamation has nothing to do with the historical Jesus. It is a creation of the first generation of the Christian community." Others like C. C. Torrey *(Documents of the Primitive Church* [New York/London: Harper, 1941] 12-22), J. Schniewind *(Evangelium nach Markus* [NTD 1; Göttingen: Vanden-hoeck & Ruprecht, 1963] 168), and M. Mahoney ("Luke 21:14-15: Editorial Rewriting or Authenticity?" *ITQ* 47 [1980] 220-238) insist that the whole discourse (at least in the Marcan form) could have been uttered by Jesus. There is, however, no way of resolving this problem.

(2) The speculation about whether the Marcan form of the discourse repre-sents a christianized version of a "Little (Jewish) Apocalypse" need not de-tain us here; if it has any validity, it is a problem for the interpreter of the Marcan Gospel. (See further W. G. Kümmel, *Promise and Fulfilment,* 95-104; R. Pesch, *Naherwartungen;* J. Lambrecht, *Die Redaktion der Markus-Apokalypse;* I. H. Marshall, *Luke,* 760.) We have given our reasons for consid-ering the Lucan Gospel as dependent in this discourse at least on "Mk."

(3) One has to note the relation of vv. 5-36 to other eschatological passages in the Lucan Gospel. In 12:35-48 the Lucan Jesus exhorts his followers to eschatological vigilance, faithfulness, and readiness. In 17:20-37 he stresses the suddenness and certainty of the coming of the day(s) of the Son of Man. Moreover, in 13:34-35 he has lamented the abandonment of the house of Jerusalem and in 19:41-44 wept over Jerusalem itself and spoken of its siege. The question then arises, why vv. 5-36 are retained and why they constitute something of a doublet. Why has Luke retained this eschatological discourse, when he elsewhere shows willingness to omit other Marcan material when it tends to create a doublet (see pp. 81-82)? The answer may be that this dis-course, inherited from "Mk" and refashioned by Luke, succeeds in bringing together all these diverse themes. For the destruction of Jerusalem and of its Temple is now seen as related to the coming of the day(s) of the Son of Man and to the proximity of the kingdom, even to the end of the world.

(4) It is to be noted that nowhere in this discourse does Luke introduce the word *parousia* or speak of the coming of the Son of Man in terms of it. In fact, it is not a Lucan word. By contrast, Matthew has introduced it into his form of the eschatological discourse (see Matt 24:3,27,37,39). Part of the reason why Luke does not use it may be the non-use of it by Mark. In any event, it should not be introduced into the discussion of the Lucan form of the discourse; Luke has his own ways of referring to the future events, and they should be respected.

We may now turn to further discussion of the relation of the Lucan escha-tological discourse to the Marcan. Three main solutions are proposed today for the problem of that relationship:

(a) Luke has used another form of the discourse beyond the "Mk"; this accounts for the differences between them. The analysis, however, is not always uniformly presented. Thus G. B. Caird *(The Gospel of St Luke,* 228) would assign vv. 5-11,16-17,21a,23a,26b-27,29-31 to "Mk," and vv. 12-15,18-20,21b-22,23b-26a,28,34-36 to "L." L. Gaston considers 21:20,21b-22,23-24,10-11,25-26a,28 to have been part of Proto-Luke, into which vv. 12-15,18-19 were later inserted, and vv. 29-36 derived from "Mk" ("Sondergut und Markus-Stoff"). T. Schramm *(Markus-Stoff,* 171-182) appeals to a non-Marcan source for 21:10-11,12-15,18-19,20,21b-22,23b-26a,28,29-31,34-36. (See further A. Salas, *Discurso escatológico* [see p. 1347]; A. Schlatter, *Evangelium des Lukas,* 412-420; V. Taylor, *Behind the Third Gospel,* 101-125; M.-E. Boismard, "Commentaire," *Synopse des quatre évangiles en français* [eds. P. Benoit and M.-E. Boismard; 3 vols.; Paris: Cerf, 1972] 2. 361; P. Winter, "The Treatment of His Sources by the Third Evangelist in Luke XXI-XXIV," *ST* 8 [1954] 138-172.) (b) Luke has simply redacted "Mk" (so J. Wellhausen, *Das Evangelium Lucae,* 116-119; E. Klostermann, *Lukasevangelium,* 197-199; J. M. Creed, *The Gospel,* 253; *HST* 122-123, 327; J. Schmid, *Evangelium nach Lukas,* 301-303, 308-310; H. Conzelmann, *Theology,* 125-126; E. Grässer, *Parusieverzögerung,* 152-170; E. Haenchen, *Der Weg Jesu,* 455; J. Zmijewski, *Die Eschatologiereden* [1972] 59-65, 311; F. Neirynck, "La matière marcienne," 177-179; G. Schneider, *Evangelium nach Lukas,* 414-415; etc.). This is the opinion of the majority of commentators on the Lucan Gospel, what I. H. Marshall *(Luke,* 755) has called "the 'orthodox' view." Whether that is the right way to put it or not is another question. (c) The Lucan form is an independent Semitic form of the tradition, echoing Ps 49:3 and Isa 50:8 and stemming from an Aramaic milieu (so M. Mahoney, "Luke 21:14-15").

It seems to me that the best solution of this problem is to admit the Lucan redaction of "Mk" in large measure and to agree that Luke has at times inserted into that redaction some material that he has derived from "L." What he has so derived is not an independent form of the whole discourse, but isolated material of the same character that could be utilized in his redaction.

Thus (1) the seventh pericope (vv. 34-36) is clearly an ending to the discourse which Luke has substituted for Mark 13:33-37 (see p. 82). Even R. Bultmann *(HST* 119) had to admit this, while insisting on the Lucan redaction of "Mk." He suggested that the terminology in these verses is so akin to Paul's that Luke has probably used a fragment of some lost epistle! Luke has made this substitution undoubtedly to avoid a doublet of 12:38-40; moreover, it suits his general concern to shift the emphasis from the *eschaton* to the *sēmeron* (see p. 234).

(2) In the first pericope about the fate of Jerusalem's Temple (vv. 5-7), Luke not only abbreviates the Marcan material, as he often does (see pp. 92-93), but he is concerned to keep Jesus in the Temple, for this discourse is the

climax of his public, daily teaching there (cp. 19:47; 20:1 with 21:37-38). Thus the Lucan Jesus does not come out of the Temple and sit down on the Mount of Olives opposite the Temple to speak only with named disciples (as in Mark 13:1,3). Moreover, in the question put to Jesus (v. 7) Luke eliminates *panta,* "all" (Mark 13:4), and changes *synteleisthai,* "be accomplished," to *ginesthai,* "happen," thus making *tauta,* "this/these things," refer solely to the destruction of the Jerusalem Temple. (Contrast Matt 24:3, which sharpens the Marcan formula in yet another way, introducing explicitly reference to the *parousia,* "your coming," and *synteleia tou aiōnos,* "the close of the age.") The slight Lucan change affects the division of the discourse (see COMMENT on vv. 8-11). Finally, a Marcan parataxis is removed by the use of a gen. absol. in v. 5 (see p. 108, a clear instance of Lucan stylistic change).

(3) In the second pericope about the signs before the end (vv. 8-11), Luke has derived most of his material from Mark 13:5-8, redacting it somewhat. Apart from the introductory cls., Luke retains thirty-seven out of the fifty-one Marcan words. Some of his redactional changes are minor stylistic alterations, but others induce a change of meaning. Thus he adds, "The time has drawn near!" (v. 8) and counsels his listeners not to run after those who make such announcements (cp. the advice of 17:23). In v. 9 Luke intensifies the time reference; Marcan *oupō,* "not yet," becomes *ouk eutheōs,* "not . . . at once." In v. 11 "plagues," "dread portents and great signs" are added and, in effect, replace the Marcan "beginning of the birth-pangs" (13:8). In eliminating the latter, Luke undoes the contrast between *to telos,* "the end," and *archē,* "beginning" (Mark 13:7,8), and thus severs "the end" from any connotation of the end of the world (like the Matthean "close of the age"). The result is that *telos* in the Lucan context still refers to the end of Jerusalem's Temple.

(4) In the third pericope about the coming persecutions (vv. 12-19), v. 18 (about the hairs of the head) is clearly a proverb added from "L," having no counterpart in "Mk" and being a doublet of Luke 12:7 (see p. 81). But an important modification of the Marcan material is made at the beginning of this pericope by the addition of *pro de toutōn pantōn,* "but before all this occurs" (v. 12). This has the effect of relegating the political and cosmic signs of vv. 10-11 to a more remote time, "the end." Again, it is not yet clear that this transcends the end of the Jerusalem Temple. In this pericope Luke recasts the Greek of Mark 13:9-13, but retains v. 13a word for word (in 21:17) and substitutes for the Marcan note of preaching the gospel (13:10) his own characteristic terminology for the role of disciples, "testifying, bearing witness" (in accord with the Lucan form of the great commission in 24:48; cf. Acts 1:8; 10:41 [see p. 243, and recall Luke's attitude toward *euangelion,* pp. 147-148]). The Lucan phrase "because of my name" is introduced into v. 12c. Verses 14-15 become a doublet of 12:11-12 (see p. 81), but whereas the Marcan Jesus promises that the holy Spirit will assist the persecuted disciples in

their trials (13:11e), the Lucan Jesus promises that he himself will supply the words and wisdom. This, then, modifies the doublet. However, it must be stressed that this is not evidence of the use of a distinct source, since it suits in general the Lucan tendency not to mention the holy Spirit in this latter part of the Gospel (see pp. 227-228). Finally, in v. 19 Luke reproduces Mark 13:13b in a more pithy form.

(5) In the fourth pericope about the desolation of Jerusalem (vv. 20-24), Luke has considerably altered Mark 13:14-20, not only redacting it, but adding material from "L" (vv. 21b,22, and 24[?]). Lucan redaction is seen in the reformulation of v. 20, which eliminates the Marcan "abomination of desolation" as too cryptic, perhaps even incomprehensible for the predominantly Gentile readers (see pp. 57-59) and which substitutes for it a reference to the Roman siege of Jerusalem. Verse 21b is substituted for Mark 13:15 because of concern not to create a doublet of 17:31 (see p. 82). As for v. 22, it seems to come from "L," but in this instance it is hard to say, since Lucan "proof from prophecy" may be at work. In v. 23 Luke clearly depends on Mark 13:17, but omits 13:18 in a very significant way—undoubtedly because he knew that Jerusalem was destroyed, not in the winter, but in late August/early September. Lucan redaction further eliminates allusion to Dan 12:1 (see Mark 13:19); again, the avoidance of *archē* eliminates the comparison with another "end," other than that of Jerusalem. Verse 24 may be derived from "L," but with its OT allusion and reference to Jerusalem "trampled upon by pagans" it could also easily be attributed to Lucan composition. (Mark 13:21-23 is omitted by Luke, to avoid a doublet of 17:23-24 [see pp. 82, 1165].)

(6) In the fifth pericope about the coming of the Son of Man (vv. 25-28), Luke has largely redacted Mark 13:24-27, eliminating above all "in those days" which thus severs the Marcan connection of the end of Jerusalem and the end that Luke now sees to be far more remote. Luke also eliminates the OT allusions in vv. 24b-25, using a formulation that imitates and resumes that of v. 11 (see E. Klostermann, *Lukasevangelium,* 197). Thus some of the apocalyptic stage props are handled differently. In v. 26a a gen. absol. reveals the Lucan hand, as it prepares for the word-for-word retention of Mark 13:26 in v. 26b. Instead of Mark 13:27 Luke substitutes v. 28, probably derived from "L" (see p. 108).

(7) In the sixth pericope, the parable of the fig tree (vv. 29-33), the Lucan redaction is clear in the introduction. Luke characteristically adds "*all* the trees" and significantly appends to the application of the parable the reference to "the kingdom of God" (v. 31). Verses 32-33 tend to allegorize the parable still further, but v. 32 is clearly Marcan in origin (even with the Amen-saying retained). Similarly, v. 33 has only slightly reworded Mark 13:31. But what is most striking is the complete omission of 13:32 by Luke; he did not want to admit that the Son was ignorant of "that day."

As F. Neirynck ("La matière marcienne," 179) rightly notes, one can scarcely conclude from a careful analysis of the Lucan and Marcan forms of this discourse that the elements peculiar to Luke in vv. 5-36 once made up a *continued sermon* which Luke would have combined with Mark 13, or even into which he would have inserted Marcan elements. The "L" material has to be limited to vv. 18,21b,22,24,28,34-36. Yet those verses scarcely argue for the existence of a separate source, containing a whole discourse.

What is evident in the Lucan recasting of the inherited eschatological discourse is (a) the clearer separation of what refers to Jerusalem and what refers to the world; (b) the clearer reference to the destruction of the city itself; after vv. 5-7 there is hardly a reference to the Temple; Jerusalem will be "surrounded by camps" (v. 20) or "trampled upon by pagans" (v. 24); one must flee from "the city" (v. 21); thus the "end" moves from the Temple to the city; (c) the clearer postponement of the *eschata* of the world, since they will not take place "in those days" (Mark 13:24, omitted by Luke [cf. 21:25]), i.e. in the days of the destruction of Jerusalem. The upshot is that Luke has retained the relation of the eschatological discourse to the destruction of Jerusalem and its Temple, but he is updating the prophetic utterance of Jesus about it in terms of the fulfillment which has already taken place. The Lucan discourse looks back at the catastrophe in Jerusalem (A.D. 70) in a microcosmic view; it sees the crisis that the earthly coming of Jesus brought into the lives of his own generation, but sees it now as a harbinger of the crisis which Jesus and his message, and above all his coming as the Son of Man, will bring to "all who dwell upon the entire face of the earth" (21:35). Both of the events are examples for Luke of God's judgment, even if their temporal connection is no longer that which Mark stressed. As Jerusalem met its fate, so will all who dwell upon the face of the earth. "The contemporary situation has made it necessary for Luke to impose an interpretation upon his source which will distinguish for his readers between fulfilled and unfulfilled prophecy" (J. M. Creed, *The Gospel,* 253).

Finally, more than the other evangelists, Luke has utilized the eschatological discourse for another exhortation to vigilance (vv. 34-36). The Christians in the Period of the Church are exhorted to perseverance, vigilance, alertness, and prayer at all times.

As for vv. 5-7 in particular, they are to be regarded as the introduction to the discourse; they set the stage for the monologue that follows. Form-critically considered, they constitute a pronouncement-story; R. Bultmann *(HST* 36) calls them a biographical apophthegm. Though V. Taylor *(FGT* 73) rejects the suggestion that they contain "a prophecy after the event" (see also R. Meyer, *Der Prophet aus Galiläa,* 16-28), the words of Jesus have been colored by the event of the destruction. Jesus' prediction about the Temple here raises the same problem as did his lament over the city in 19:41-44 (see COMMENT there).

In the midst of Jesus' public teaching in the Temple he hears some of his

audience commenting on the Herodian Temple and its magnificent adornments. His comment to them is not a warning, but a prophetic pronouncement, an ominous prediction: The time is coming when not a stone of it will
be left upon a stone—all of it will be torn down. His words are unmistakably
clear. They saw fulfillment in the burning and destruction of the Temple in
late August/early September A.D. 70. Josephus *(J. W.* 6.4,5 § 250-284) gives a
detailed description of the burning of it, but he makes it clear that the Romans were not the ones who ignited it: "The flames, however, owed their
origin and cause to God's own people" *(ek tōn oikeiōn,* § 251 [LCL 3. 449]).
Thus the fate of the Jerusalem Temple was announced to Jesus' own contemporaries.

NOTES

21   5. *When some of the people were talking.* As Jesus continues his teaching in the
Temple, "some" *(tines)* of his audience exclaim about the beauty of the Temple. They
are not the Peter, James, John, and Andrew of Mark 13:3; nor are they outside the
Temple area (e.g. on the Mount of Olives, as in Mark). The Lucan Jesus speaks only in
the Temple, not in the city itself outside the Temple (so Conzelmann, *Theology,* 79);
but his words on the Mount of Olives will be concerned with another topic. See 22:40-
53.

the Temple. After the Jews returned from the Babylonian Captivity, they reconstructed the Second Temple under Zerubbabel as a replacement of Solomon's Temple
destroyed by Nebuchadnezzar in 586 B.C. The new structure was built on the old site
and completed about 515 B.C. See Hag 1:4-15. It was less finely appointed than Solomon's structure, and Herod the Great was finally moved to refurbish it in the fifteenth
year of his reign (20-19 B.C.), "erecting new foundation-walls, enlarging the surrounding area to twice its former dimensions" (Josephus, *J. W.* 1.21,1 § 401). Work on the
reconstruction of the Temple continued for decades. The Johannine Gospel alludes to
Jesus' purging of the Temple in its forty-sixth year of building (2:20). See further Luke
4:9 (and NOTE there); Acts 3:2,10,11; 5:12; John 10:23. The reconstruction continued
until about A.D. 63, a mere seven years before it was destroyed. See further Josephus,
J. W. 5.5,1-6 § 184-227; *Ant.* 15.11,1-7 § 380-425; cf. 11QTemple 3:8-13:7; 30:?-45:7;
m. Middot; J. Finegan, *Archeology,* 117-132.

adorned with fine stones. The comment of Jesus' listeners may have been occasioned
by the work of adornment which was still going on. According to Josephus, the
Temple was built of "hard, white stones, each of which was about twenty-five cubits in
length, eight in height, and twelve in width" *(Ant.* 15.11,3 § 392; but cf. *J. W.* 5.5,1 §
189, where stones of forty cubits in length are mentioned).

The exterior of the structure lacked nothing that could astound either mind or
eye. For, being covered on all sides with massive plates of gold, the sun was no
sooner upon it than it radiated so fiery a flash that people straining to look at it were
compelled to avert their eyes, as from the rays of the sun. To approaching strangers
it appeared from afar like a snow-clad mountain; for all that was not overlaid with

gold was of purest white. From its summit protruded sharp golden spikes to prevent birds from settling upon and befouling the roof. Some of the stones in the structure were forty-five cubits in length, five in height, and six in breadth. *(J. W.* 5.5,6 § 222-224.)

votive offerings. The Greek n. *anathema* means "that which is set up" (LSJ 105) and was often used of ornaments set up in temples (Herodotus, *Hist.* 1.14,92; Sophocles, *Ant.* 286). Cf. 2 Macc 9:16; Josephus *(J. W.* 5.5,4 § 210-212; *Ant.* 15.11,3 § 395) speaks of a gate of the Temple, completely overlaid with gold, with gold vines above it, from which hung grape clusters as tall as a man, and of fine Babylonian tapestries. The luxurious trappings stand in contrast to the destruction to be mentioned. Cf. Tacitus, *Hist.* 5.8,1 who speaks of the Temple luxury: "illic immensae opulentiae templum." Cf. 2 Macc 3:2-8.

6. *As for what you are gazing at.* Lit. "(as for) those things at which you are looking," anacoluthon, a suspended acc. See BDF § 466.1; cf. Acts 7:40c. Some mss. (D, L, Ψ) omit the rel. pron. *ha,* which further complicates the analysis of the Greek here. See pp. 124-125.

the time is coming. Lit. "days will be coming." See NOTES on 5:35; 17:22; 19:43. This Lucan redactional addition sharpens the imminence of the prediction.

when not a stone of it will be left upon a stone. I.e. so utter will be the destruction of Herod's magnificent Temple. Cf. 19:44 and NOTE there. According to Josephus *(J. W.* 6.4,5 § 250), "God had long since condemned that building to the flames, and now in the turn of the years the fated day arrived, the tenth of the month of Loüs [= 29 August A.D. 70], the day on which of old it had been burned by the king of Babylon" (= tenth day of Hebrew month of Ab, Jer 52:12-13 [but cf. 2 Kgs 25:8]). For prophetic utterances in the OT against the Temple, see Jer 7:1-14; 22:5. Some mss. (א, B, L, *f* [13]) add the adv. *hōde,* "here"; but this is a scribal harmonization with Matt 24:2. Ms. D has a typical Western expansion. Cf. *TCGNT* 172.

7. *Then they asked him.* The *tines* of v. 5 are understood here (= the hearers of Jesus).

Teacher. See NOTES on 3:12; 7:40, and also p. 218. This title comes from Mark 13:1, but Luke has postponed it.

when will this happen? Here and later in the verse *tauta,* "these things," refers clearly to the destruction of the Temple. *Pace* I. H. Marshall *(Luke,* 761, 762), it does not include "the last things," since there is no reference to these in the Lucan text. Luke has changed the Marcan question, "What sign will there be when *all* these things are going *to be accomplished"* (13:4b). The Lucan formulation is directly concerned with events that do not belong to the *eschaton.* See H. Conzelmann, *Theology,* 126.

This question becomes the springboard for the eschatological discourse proper.

LUCAN ESCHATOLOGICAL DISCOURSE: GENERAL BIBLIOGRAPHY

Agua Pérez, A. del. "Derâš lucano de Mc 13 a la luz de su 'Teología del Reino': Lc 21,5-36," *EstBíb* 39 (1981) 285-313.

Bartsch, H.-W. *Wachet aber zu jeder Zeit! Entwurf einer Auslegung des Lukasevangeliums* (Hamburg-Bergstedt: H. Reich, 1963) 118-123.

Braumann, G. "Das Mittel der Zeit: Erwägungen zur Theologie des Lukasevangeliums," *ZNW* 54 (1963) 117-145, esp. 140-144.

Conzelmann, H. "Geschichte und Eschaton nach Mc 13," *ZNW* 50 (1959) 210-221.

——— *Theology*, 125-136.

Cotter, A. C. "The Eschatological Discourse," *CBQ* 1 (1939) 125-132, 204-213.

Dupont, J. *Distruzione del tempio e fine del mondo: Studi sul discorso di Marco 13* (Rome: Edizioni paoline, 1979).

——— "Les épreuves des chrétiens avant la fin du monde: Lc 21,5-19," *AsSeign* ns 64 (1969) 77-86.

Feuillet, A. "Le discours de Jésus sur la ruine du Temple d'après Marc XIII et Luc XXI, 5-36," *RB* 55 (1948) 481-502; 56 (1949) 61-92.

Flender, H. *St Luke*, 107-117.

Flückiger, F. "Die Redaktion der Zukunftsrede in Mark. 13," *TZ* 26 (1970) 395-409.

Flusser, D. "Nbw'h 'l šḥrwr Yrwšlym bbryt hḥdšh (The Liberation of Jerusalem: A Prophecy in the New Testament)," *Zalman Shazar Volume* (Eretz-Israel 10; Jerusalem: Israel Exploration Society, 1971) 226-236 (+ xvii).

Gaston, L. "Sondergut und Markus-Stoff in Luk. 21," *TZ* 16 (1960) 161-172.

——— *No Stone on Another: Studies in the Significance of the Fall of Jerusalem in the Synoptic Gospels* (NovTSup 23; Leiden: Brill, 1970) 8-64, 355-369.

Geiger, R. *Die lukanischen Endzeitsreden: Studien zur Eschatologie des Lukas-Evangeliums* (Europäische Hochschulschriften 23/16; Bern: H. Lang; Frankfurt: P. Lang, 1973) 149-258.

Grässer, E. *Parusieverzögerung*, 152-170.

Grayston, K. "The Study of Mark XIII," *BJRL* 56 (1973-1974) 371-387.

Hartman, L. *Prophecy Interpreted: The Formation of Some Jewish Apocalyptic Texts and of the Eschatological Discourse Mark 13 par.* (ConB, NT ser. 1; Lund: Gleerup, [1966]) 226-235.

Kaestli, J.-D. "Luc 21:5-36: L'Apocalypse synoptique," *L'Eschatologie*, 41-57.

Kümmel, W. G. *Promise and Fulfilment*, 95-104.

Lagrange, M.-J. "L'Avènement du Fils de l'Homme," *RB* ns 3 (1906) 382-411, 561-574.

Lambrecht, J. "Die Logia-Quellen von Markus 13," *Bib* 47 (1966) 321-360.

——— "Die 'Midrasch-Quelle' von Mk 13," *Bib* 49 (1968) 254-270.

——— "Redactio sermonis eschatologici," *VD* 43 (1965) 278-287.

——— *Die Redaktion der Markus-Apokalypse: Literarische Analyse und Strukturuntersuchung* (AnBib 28; Rome: Biblical Institute, 1967).

Lattanzi, H. "Eschatologici sermonis Domini logica interpretatio (Mt. 24,1-36; Mc. 13,1-37; Lc. 21,5-35)," *Divinitas* 11 (1967) 71-92.

Manson, T. W. *Sayings,* 323-337.

Marxsen, W. *Mark the Evangelist: Studies on the Redaction History of the Gospel* (Nashville, TN: Abingdon, 1969) 151-206, esp. 190-198.

Nicol, W. "Tradition and Redaction in Luke 21," *Neotestamentica* 7 (1973) 61-71.

Oñate, J. A. "El 'reino de Dios,' ¿tema central de discurso escatológico?" *EstBíb* 4 (1945) 15-34, 163-196, 421-446; 5 (1946) 101-110.

Parsch, P. "Un discours de Jésus," *Apprenons à lire la Bible* (Paris: Desclée de Brouwer, 1956) 166-172.

Perrot, C. "Essai sur le discours eschatologique (Mc. XIII, 1-37; Mt. XXIV, 1-36; Lc. XXI, 5-36)," *RSR* 47 (1959) 481-514.

Pesch, R. *Naherwartungen: Tradition und Redaktion in Mk 13* (Düsseldorf: Patmos, 1968).

Robinson, W. C., Jr. *Der Weg des Herrn* (Hamburg-Bergstedt: H. Reich, 1964) 47-50, 64-66.

Walter, N. "Tempelzerstörung und synoptische Apokalypse," *ZNW* 57 (1966) 38-49.

Walvoord, J. F. "Christ's Olivet Discourse on the Time of the End: Prophecies Fulfilled in the Present Age," *BSac* 128 (1971) 206-214.

Zmijewski, J. *Die Eschatologiereden des Lukas-Evangeliums: Eine traditions- und redaktionsgeschichtliche Untersuchung zu Lk 21,5-36 und Lk 17,20-37* (BBB 40; Bonn: Hanstein, 1972) 43-325, 541-572.

———— "Die Eschatologiereden Lk 21 und Lk 17: Überlegungen zum Verständnis und zur Einordnung der lukanischen Eschatologie," *BibLeb* 14 (1973) 30-40.

BIBLIOGRAPHY (21:5-7)

Meyer, R. *Der Prophet aus Galiläa: Studie zum Jesusbild der drei ersten Evangelien* (Leipzig: Hinrichs, 1940; reprinted, Darmstadt: Wissenschaftliche Buchgesellschaft, 1970) 16-18.

Vielhauer, P. *Oikodome: Aufsätze zum Neuen Testament, Band 2* (ed. G. Klein; Theologische Bücherei 65; Munich: C. Kaiser, 1979) 59-66.

138. THE SIGNS BEFORE THE END
(21:8-11)

21   ⁸ Then Jesus said, "Make sure that you are not misled. Many people will come using my name and saying, 'I am he!' and 'The time has drawn near!' But do not run after them. ⁹ When you hear of wars and rebellions, do not be terrified. For these things *must happen* first;[a]

---

[a] Dan 2:28

but the end will not follow at once." [10] He then said to them, *"Nation will rise against nation,*[b] *and kingdom against kingdom;* [11] *there will be severe earthquakes and plagues and famines in place after place; and in the sky dread portents and great signs."*

[b] 2 Chr 15:6; Isa 19:2

COMMENT

The eschatological discourse proper begins with this pericope (21:8-11). It will be a monologue, in which there are no interrupting questions, but only narrative introductions of the evangelist (vv. 10,29). In the first paragraph of the discourse Jesus mentions false prophets who will come and speak in his name, of wars and revolts, of nations rising against nations, and of natural cataclysms—"but the end will not follow at once" (v. 9c). Even though political and cosmic cataclysms are mentioned, they need not be understood as referring to anything other than the destruction of Jerusalem and its Temple. The horizon broadens, indeed, but only from the Temple (mentioned in the preceding pericope) to the city; the still broader horizon will be met in v. 26, "what is coming upon the world." The thrust of this episode is negative, warning listeners not to be misled by the startling political and cosmic events to come.

On the relation of this pericope to Mark 13:5-8, see COMMENT on vv. 5-7; cf. Matt 24:4-8.

The discourse proper falls into two main parts:

a) vv. 8-24: *What will precede the end of Jerusalem.* It is subdivided:
   (i) vv. 8-11, The Signs before the End.
   (ii) vv. 12-19, Admonitions for the Coming Persecution.
   (iii) vv. 20-24, The Desolation of Jerusalem.

b) vv. 25-36: *What will precede the end of the world.* It is subdivided:
   (i) vv. 25-28, The Coming of the Son of Man.
   (ii) vv. 29-33, The Parable of the Fig Tree.
   (iii) vv. 34-36, Concluding Exhortation to Vigilance.

Form-critically considered, vv. 8-11 are a collection of prophetic, even minatory, Sayings of Jesus, cast in apocalyptic language (esp. in vv. 9-11). R. Bultmann *(HST* 125) thinks that this is the beginning of the "Jewish Apocalypse with Christian editing." (See, however, I. H. Marshall, *Luke,* 761-762.)

In this passage the Lucan Jesus warns his listeners not to be misled by people who will come using his name and pretending to announce the dire destruction of the Temple in the near future (recall the words of Jesus, son of Ananias, quoted in COMMENT on 19:41-44). *Kairos* on the lips of such people is not to be confused with the really crucial time. (Recall Luke 9:49; Acts 8:9-24.)

Jesus uses apocalyptic language in speaking vaguely of wars and rebellions, of nations rising against nations, and of kingdoms against kingdoms. In alluding to the apocalyptic language of Dan 2:28, he stresses that such things "must happen" first; then adds emphatically that "the end" (of Jerusalem) "will not follow at once." He continues his apocalyptic description with further OT allusions, to Isa 19:2 (part of the oracle uttered against Egypt) and to 2 Chr 15:6 (the prophet Azariah's description of the distress to which God reduced Israel, which had become "without the true God"). There will be national and political catastrophes, even cosmic cataclysms (earthquakes, plagues, famines, dread portents in the sky, and great signs), all vividly expressed in apocalyptic terms. They are reminiscent of Ezek 38:19-22, the oracle against Gog of the land of Magog.

Such portents were used even by Josephus in his description (after the fact) of the burning of the Temple of Jerusalem: "Many who were already slowly dying of starvation and unable to speak, when they saw the Temple afire, gathered strength again for wailings and outcries. Perea and the surrounding mountains echoed with them, making the din still more intense" (*J. W.* 6.5,1 § 274). He tells too of six thousand refugees who perished in the flames of the Temple porticos, deluded by a "false prophet, who had on that day announced to the people in the city that God commanded them to go to the Temple to receive the signs of their salvation" (*J. W.* 6.5,2 § 285). They were deluded by charlatans and would-be messengers of God and believed not "the manifest portents which signalled the coming desolation. . . . So it was when a star, looking like a sword, stood over the city, and a comet lasted for a year" (*J. W.* 6.5,3 § 288-289). He goes on to tell of omens (lights seen in the sanctuary, a cow giving birth to a lamb) that attended the destruction.

When one considers such false prophets, portents, and ominous signs associated with the historic destruction of the Jerusalem Temple, it makes it plausible to think that "the end" (v. 9) could well be in Luke's view that of Jerusalem and its Temple. For this reason we see no need to import reference to the end of the world at this point in the Lucan eschatological discourse—which is the custom of the majority of commentators upon it.

NOTES

21 8. *Make sure that you are not misled.* Lit. "see that you are not led astray," i.e. deluded by false prophets or charlatans, as were six thousand Jerusalemites at the time of the burning of the Temple (see COMMENT). The vb. *planan,* "lead astray," occurs only here in Lucan writings; it connotes a departure from truth or fidelity. See John 7:47; 1 Cor 15:33.

Luke substitutes here for the Marcan introduction a beginning of his own. *Many people will come using my name.* Lit. "in my name." See NOTE on 9:48. Jesus refers to such people coming after his departure. Recall 5:35, where he has already spoken of his being taken away. His followers are to shun all self-styled prophets. On first-century false prophets in Palestine, see Acts 5:36-37; 21:38. Cf. Josephus, *Ant.* 18.4,1 § 85-87; 20.5,1 § 97-99; 20.8,6 § 169-172. See R. Meyer, *TDNT* 6. 826-827. Do not read into this warning specific references to false messiahs or to anti-christs; the language does not permit specific references.

I am he! I.e. a representative of Jesus, who has already insinuated his return. See Luke 12:35-48; 19:11-27. Matt 24:5 makes the declaration derived from Mark 13:5 explicit, by adding, "the Messiah" *(ho Christos).* Yet, even though in the Lucan writings it is explicitly said that "this Jesus, who has been taken up from you into heaven, will come in the same way as you saw him go" (Acts 1:11), it is not a question here of a false Messiah. Cf. John 4:25-26. See W. Manson, "The *Ego eimi* of the Messianic Presence in the New Testament," *JTS* 48 (1947) 137-145.

The time has drawn near! So will the false prophets proclaim, but they are not to be believed. This Lucan redactional addition is possibly an allusion to Dan 7:22, "the time has arrived" (LXX: *ho kairos edothē;* Theodotion: *ho kairos ephthasen).* But cf. Mark 1:15 *(peplērōtai ho kairos kai ēngiken hē basileia,* "The time has been fulfilled and the kingdom has drawn near"); Rev 1:3 *(ho gar kairos engys,* "for the time is near"; cf. Rev 22:10). Luke has added this typically apocalyptic utterance to sharpen Jesus' denial in v. 9b. Such false prophets are not to be trusted. See NOTE on 1:20.

do not run after them. I.e. do not be taken in by their rhetoric and flair.

9. *When you hear of wars and rebellions.* I.e. of signs of the Period of the Church under stress. Luke has changed the latter term, "rebellions" *(akatastasias),* from Mark's "rumors of wars" (13:7a), probably to reflect the so-called First Revolt of Palestinian Jews against the Roman occupiers (A.D. 66-70), which led to the war itself. "War" is a standard apocalyptic stage prop. Recall Dan 11:20,25,44; the Qumran *War Scroll;* Rev 6:3-4; 9:9; 12:7; 4 Ezra 13:31. The "wars and rebellions" may even refer to the rapid succession of Roman emperors between Nero and Vespasian. See *JBC* art. 75 § 161.

do not be terrified. Luke substitutes a Septuagintism *(mē ptoēthēte* [see 2 Chr 32:7; Deut 31:6; Jer 1:17; Ezek 3:9]) for the Marcan *mē throeisthe.*

these things must happen first. I.e. the appearance of impostors and national or political upheavals. Luke derives the *dei genesthai* (an allusion to Dan 2:28) from Mark 13:7c, but adds *gar tauta,* "for these things," and the adv. *prōton,* "first." In this case, *tauta* refers not to those of v. 7, but to the phenomena of vv. 8-9, which immediately precede. The *necessity* of such historical events is also an apocalyptic stage prop; it suits well the sense of Lucan salvation-history. See p. 180. The added adv. *prōton* will be explained by the Lucan redaction modification of v. 9d. On the suppression of the Marcan *archē odinōn tauta* (13:8c), which avoids the contrast with *telos,* see COMMENT on vv. 5-7.

but the end will not follow at once. In this Lucan context the "end" refers only to that of Jerusalem and its Temple, of which Jesus spoke in v. 6. To understand it of the end of the world is to import a Marcan and Matthean nuance into the Lucan context. This has to be stressed, *pace* G. Schneider, *Evangelium nach Lukas,* 418; J. Dupont,

Distruzione, 63-64; I. H. Marshall, *Luke,* 764, et al. It is not the same as Luke 17:25 or the Pauline reference in 2 Thess 2:3; 1 Cor 15:24. *Pace* E. Grässer *(Parusieverzögerung,* 158), the change from Marcan *oupō,* "not yet," to *ouk eutheōs,* "not . . . at once," has not been made to distance the revolt and the destruction of the Temple from the eschatological context of the parousia. The *prōton* and *ouk eutheōs* prepare for the next Lucan pericope in which Jesus warns his followers that even before the "end" of Jerusalem there will be persecutions which they will face. On the Lucan use of *eutheōs,* see NOTE on 17:7.

10. *He then said to them.* This Lucan redactional addition does not necessarily point to the use of a separate source. In form it resembles 6:5; 19:22; Acts 12:8. It merely separates the further cataclysms, political and cosmic, from the preceding. It does not, moreover, mark a transition to eschatological events; what follows in vv. 10bc-11 provides a context for the coming persecutions.

Nation will rise against nation. This is probably an allusion to 2 Chr 15:6, which in the LXX reads, *kai polemēsei ethnos pros ethnos kai polis pros polin,* "and nation will war against nation and city against city" (an accurate translation of the Hebrew). The contrast may also echo the MT of Isa 19:2, "I shall stir up Egyptians against Egyptians," which is changed to the third pl. in the LXX, *egerthēsontai Aigyptioi ep' Aigyptious.*

kingdom against kingdom. See 4 Ezra 13:31.

11. *severe earthquakes and plagues and famines.* Possibly this is an allusion to Ezek 38:19, *estai seismos megas epi gēs Israēl,* "there will be a great earthquake on the land of Israel," and other cataclysms are mentioned in vv. 20-22. Such apocalyptic stage props are found in the OT prophetic tradition. See Hag 2:6; the LXX of Isa 5:13-14; cf. Rev 6:12; 8:5; 11:13,19; 16:18. Luke has added the "plagues" *(loimoi),* probably under the influence of the Greek literary pair, *loimoi kai limoi.* See Hesiod, *Op.* 243; Thucydides, *Hist.* 2.54; *T. Judah* 23:3; *Sib. Or.* 8.175. In Luke's own story of the Period of the Church there is a famine in the time of Claudius (Acts 11:28) and an earthquake (Acts 16:26).

and in the sky dread portents and great signs. Lit. "and from the sky there will be dread portents and great signs." This is Luke's substitution for the Marcan phrase, "This is the beginning of the birth-pangs" (13:8), which is perhaps a more vivid apocalyptic stage prop. Luke's substitution is in line with Josephus' description of the star and comet at the burning of the Jerusalem Temple. Compare the description of the invasion of Jerusalem by Antiochus IV Epiphanes in 2 Macc 5:2-3; or *Sib. Or.* 3.796-808.

A different order of words is found in various mss., but the sense of the text is not affected thereby.

139. ADMONITIONS FOR THE COMING PERSECUTION
(21:12-19)

21   12 "But before all this occurs, people will lay their hands upon you and will persecute you; they will hand you over to synagogues and prisons, and you will be led off to kings and prefects because of my name. 13 It will lead to your having to testify. 14 So make up your minds not to rehearse your defense in advance, 15 because I myself shall supply you with lips and with a wisdom that none of your adversaries will be able to withstand or contradict. 16 You will even be handed over by parents and brothers, by relatives and friends; and they will put some of you to death. 17 You will be hated by all because of my name. 18 But not a hair of your head will be lost. 19 It is by your endurance that you will make your lives secure."

COMMENT

Jesus' discourse continues with warnings about persecutions which his followers will face before the "end" of the Jerusalem Temple (21:12-19); but the warnings quickly turn to a promise of victory.

For the relation of this pericope to Mark 13:9-13, see COMMENT on vv. 5-7; cf. Matt 24:9-14.

From a form-critical point of view, these verses contain further prophetic and hortatory Sayings of Jesus, now devoid of apocalyptic dress.

By adding "before all this occurs," Luke postpones events associated with the "end" of v. 9d (see *HST* 123). He makes it clear that the coming persecutions will precede the destruction of Jerusalem and its Temple. As background for this interpretation of the Lucan discourse, one should recall Acts 4:16-18; 8:1b-3; 12:1-5, where such persecutions are recounted in the Lucan writings themselves. (Cf. 1 Thess 2:14; Gal 1:13.) Thus this part of the discourse describes the condition of the *ecclesia pressa* (to use H. Conzelmann's terminology [see p. 182]), the Period of the Church under stress.

As Jesus describes the coming persecutions, he sees them coming from Jewish and Gentile sources, from synagogues and prisons, from kings and prefects. All of this will befall them because of "his name." Such persecution will challenge his followers to "bear witness, give testimony" that they are

"Christians" (see Acts 11:26). *Pace* G. Schneider *(Evangelium nach Lukas,* 419), they will not be called to give testimony "for the sake of the gospel," since that would be to put a Marcan interpretation on this passage in the Lucan writings which studiously avoids "gospel" (see pp. 147-148). The *martyrion* of which Jesus speaks is not yet the "martyrdom" of the later understanding of that word; but this passage undoubtedly contributed to that understanding.

In view of this persecution, Jesus exhorts his followers not to worry about or be concerned about what kind of defense they will make before Jewish or Gentile authorities, because Jesus himself—not the holy Spirit, as in Mark 13:11 (cf. Matt 24:20)—will give them words and wisdom to confound those who try them. The counsel that Jesus gives echoes that of 12:11-12. The words and wisdom that he will give will be such that their adversaries will not be able to counter them or win out over them. Implied is that victory will be theirs in such trials.

But Jesus warns that the followers will face this persecution not only from outsiders, Jewish or Gentile adversaries, but even from their own kith and kin. Members of their own families, good friends, will turn against them, because they bear his "name." Moreover, the persecution will take the form, not only of arrest and imprisonment, but of death—at least for some of them. And the reason will always be: Hatred because of "my name" (v. 17).

The Lucan Jesus exhorts his followers still further, guaranteeing them victory, in quoting for them a proverb, "not a hair of your head will be lost," an echo of Luke 12:7. For by their "endurance" (or "consistency, persistence") they will possess their lives, i.e. through their endurance they will show that they have been the seed sowed in good soil, those who have listened to the word, held on to it with noble and generous minds, and through such persistence they will yield a crop (i.e. find real lives). Cf. Luke 8:15.

This hortatory section of the eschatological discourse is the reason why the apocalytic stage props appear in other parts of it. Apocalyptic literature grew up in an OT matrix as a form of persecution-literature, intended to give hope to the persecuted. This pericope, in particular, conforms to the parenetic character of that genre of literature.

NOTES

21 12. *But before all this occurs.* This Lucan addition reiterates v. 9d, "the end will not follow at once." In adding it, Luke makes clear that much must precede the "end" of Jerusalem and its Temple.

people will lay their hands upon you. I.e. aggressively, as in 20:19. See NOTE there.

will persecute you. The vb. *diōkein,* which normally means "pursue," is used with a religious connotation, as in Luke 11:49; Acts 7:52. Social and political harassment would be involved because of religious allegiance. See O. Knoch, *EWNT* 1. 816-819.

hand you over to synagogues and prisons . . . kings and prefects. Luke adds *phylakas,* "prisons." The first two may refer to Jewish persecutions, and the second two to Gentile persecutions. See NOTES on 12:11 and 4:15. However, "prisons" could theoretically refer as well to Gentile imprisonment, just as in the next pair "kings" could refer to Jewish rulers, people like King Herod Agrippa. See Acts 12:1-11; 25:13-26:32. But "prefects" *(hēgemones)* almost certainly suggests Gentile governors, such as Felix (Acts 23:24-24:27) and Porcius Festus (Acts 24:27-26:32). In this case, the persecution of Stephen, Peter, James, and Paul in Acts would be illustrations of Christians persecuted in the Period of the Church, even before the destruction of Jerusalem.

because of my name. So Luke rewords Mark 13:9, which has simply *heneken emou,* "because of me." He is influenced by Mark 13:13, and possibly by Mark 13:6. But one should recall the Lucan emphasis on the name of Jesus in Acts. See NOTE on 9:49; cf. Acts 9:16.

13. *It will lead to your having to testify.* Lit. "it will turn out for you for bearing witness," i.e. you will be called on to act in a way which testifies (to your fidelity to me, or to what you really are). This is a redactional development of the Marcan phrase *eis martyrion autois,* "for testimony to them" (13:9d—cp. Luke 5:14, where the phrase is used with a different connotation). Having developed the cl. in accord with his own emphasis on "testimony" (see p. 243), Luke then omits Mark 13:10. See COMMENT on vv. 5-7. But he has not omitted 13:10 because of a concern to avoid any stress on the imminent expectation of the end *(pace* H.-W. Bartsch, *Wachet aber,* 121); he just avoids the mention of "gospel."

The vb. *apobainein* means "go away," but is used figuratively to express how something "turns out" (BAGD 88).

14. *not to rehearse your defense in advance.* Lit. "not to practice beforehand to be defended." Cp. Luke 12:11. The vb. *promeletan* is a technical expression for practicing or memorizing a speech in advance. See Aristophanes, *Eccles.* 117.

15. *I myself shall supply you with lips and with a wisdom.* Lit. "I shall give you a mouth and wisdom." Luke places *egō* emphatically at the head of the sentence, as he redactionally substitutes Jesus as the giver of these gifts to his persecuted followers for the Marcan "holy Spirit" (13:11f). But the "holy Spirit" is mentioned in the doublet in Luke 12:12. These followers will speak like Stephen, with eloquence and wisdom. See Acts 6:10. In Stage III of the gospel tradition Luke makes the risen Jesus say that he will supply the wisdom, just as he will dispense the Father's promise (Acts 2:33).

that none of your adversaries will be able to withstand or contradict. The triumph of the testimony is made manifest, as in v. 18. Luke is reflecting on the de facto evangelization of the eastern Mediterranean world and the idyllic success of the spread of the word in Acts, as he recasts Mark 13:11.

16. *be handed over by parents and brothers, by relatives and friends.* The first pair was used in 18:29. Luke creates the double pair by adding the opposition of "friends"; recall the double pair in v. 12. Ms. G omits "and brothers." The allusion to Mic 7:6 in Mark 13:12 is omitted by Luke, for what reason is not clear.

they will put some of you to death. As happens in the story of the Period of the Church in Acts to Stephen (7:54-60) and to James, son of Zebedee (12:1-2).

17. *will be hated by all because of my name.* This is derived word for word from Mark 13:13. The extension to "all" in this instance is not Lucan. But the contrast is intended between kin and friends and everyone outside such close circles.

18. *not a hair of your head will be lost.* I.e. because God will be protecting you in such persecution. This Lucan addition to the Marcan material, probably derived from "L," is a doublet of Luke 12:7 (= Matt 10:30). See p. 81. Its proverbial character can be seen from Acts 27:34; 1 Sam 14:45; 2 Sam 14:11; 1 Kgs 1:52. This verse, however, stands in some tension with v. 16b, which promises death for some followers. It is far from certain that this is to be understood in some spiritual sense (e.g. E. E. Ellis, *Gospel of Luke,* 244: "Although put to 'death' not a hair will 'perish.' "). It is simply another instance of Luke's lack of concern about ironing out things he puts together from various sources.

19. *by your endurance . . . you will make your lives secure.* Lit. "in your persistence win (impv.) your souls." The condition for deliverance is not *hypomonē,* simply understood as "patience," but as persistent endurance. So one will acquire, procure (real) life. For the sense of *psychē* as "life," see NOTE on 9:24. The best reading here is the aor. impv. *ktēsasthe* (in mss. ℵ, D, K, L, R, W, Ψ, 063, *f* 1, and the Koine text-tradition), but some other mss. (A, B, Θ, *f* 13, and ancient versions read the fut. indic. *ktēsesthe,* "you will acquire/procure." In English one has to use something similar, even if one follows the preferred reading. It should be noted that Luke has not followed Mark 13:13b in speaking of endurance "to the end," because he has eliminated from this part of the discourse that eschatological condition.

BIBLIOGRAPHY (21:12-19)

Fuchs, A. *Sprachliche Untersuchungen zu Matthäus und Lukas: Ein Beitrag zur Quellenkritik* (AnBib 49; Rome: Biblical Institute, 1971) 37-44, 171-191.

Giblet, J. "Les promesses de l'Esprit et la mission des apôtres dans les évangiles," *Irénikon* 30 (1957) 5-43, esp. 17-19.

Grässer, E. *Parusieverzögerung,* 158-161.

Hartman, L. *Testimonium linguae: Participial Constructions in the Synoptic Gospels: A Linguistic Examination of Luke 21,13 (ConNT* 19; Lund: Gleerup, 1963) 36-45, 57-75.

Manson, T. W. *Sayings,* 326-328.

Mahoney, M. "Luke 21:14-15: Editorial Rewriting or Authenticity?" *ITQ* 47 (1980) 220-238.

140. THE DESOLATION OF JERUSALEM
(21:20-24)

21   20 "When you see Jerusalem surrounded by camps, then you will
realize that her desolation has drawn near. 21 Then those who are in
Judea must flee to the mountains; those who are in the city itself must
get out of it; and those who are out in the open fields must not go back
into it. 22 For this is *the time of vengeance,*ᵃ when all that stands written will see fulfillment. 23 Woe to women who are pregnant or nursing
infants at that time! For great indeed will be the misery in this land
and the wrath against this people! 24 They will *fall by the edge of the
sword*ᵇ or be carried off captive *to all the nations.*ᶜ *Jerusalem* will be
*trampled upon by pagans,*ᵈ until the time of the pagans sees its fulfillment."

   ᵃ Hos 9:7   ᵇ Sir 28:18   ᶜ Deut 28:64   ᵈ Zech 12:3

COMMENT

As Jesus continues his eschatological discourse, he finally turns to the city of
Jerusalem itself and foretells its desolation and demise (21:20-24). It is not a
pleasant prospect for the city that he depicts, yet he utters it deliberately.

This is a radically reworked form of Mark 13:14-20 (see COMMENT on vv.
5-7; cf. Matt 24:15-22).

As far as the form-critical assessment is concerned, these verses contain
further prophetic Sayings of Jesus (see *HST* 123). Whether he ever uttered
them in the Lucan form is highly questionable; there is here a heavy overlay
of Lucan redaction and composition.

Jesus now returns to the "end" (21:9d) and foretells how Jerusalem will be
"surrounded by camps," which will mark unmistakably the desolation of the
holy city. There will be no escape for those who stay within it (v. 21). In v. 22
"the time of vengeance," an allusion to Hos 9:7, supplies the explanation of
the "end." This reveals why Jerusalemites will have to flee from the city, not
go back into it. Moreover, making use of apocalyptic stage props, Jesus
predicts that disaster will come upon those women of Jerusalem who are with
child or who will be nursing children at the breast. The phrase "at that time"

makes plain the historic reference of which the Lucan Jesus speaks. Even the
Marcan use of the same phrase has to be understood of the Jerusalem-catas-
trophe. "For great indeed will be the misery in this land and the wrath against
this people!" (v. 23b). The misery and wrath are, unfortunately, not further
explained; we can only speculate about their concrete manifestation. The
reader of the Lucan Gospel, however, cannot help but relate such a prediction to the words of Simeon in the infancy narrative about "the fall . . . of
many in Israel" (2:34) or to the reaction of Jesus' own townspeople (4:29) or
even to the words of Jesus himself about Jerusalem, which murders those who
are sent to it (13:34). Making use of OT allusions (Sir 28:18; Deut 28:64),
Jesus foretells that the inhabitants of Jerusalem will be put to the sword or
carried off as captives to foreign countries. Moreover, Jerusalem itself will be
trampled upon by pagans until they have their fill of carnage and their domination is complete.

In reading this Lucan version of Jesus' words about the desolation of Jerusalem, one notes how Luke has suppressed all mention of the "abomination of
desolation." He retains from it only the mention of Jerusalem's "desolation."
In substituting for it the picture of Jerusalem "surrounded by camps" and in
introducing the mention of its inhabitants falling by the sword and being
carried off into captivity, and finally in depicting Jerusalem as "trampled
upon by pagans," Luke has obviously been influenced by the historic events
associated with the destruction of Jerusalem in A.D. 70. Luke never read
Josephus' account of the destruction, and his formulations of Jesus' prophetic
utterances are colored by OT phraseology; but the details of Josephus' account can be used to illustrate the Lucan description.

The surrounding of Jerusalem by Titus' army and camps is described by
Josephus in *J. W.* 5.2,1-5 § 47-97; 6.2,1 § 93; 6.2,7 § 149-156. Indeed, he uses
the very word *stratopedon,* "camp," that Luke uses (21:20). Josephus numbers the Jews of Jerusalem and Judea put to the sword by the Romans as
1,100,000 (see *J. W.* 6.5,1 § 271-273; 6.9,3 § 420). Jewish captives are described as part of Titus' triumphal procession at Rome and numbered as
97,000 (see *J. W.* 7.5,3 § 118; 7.5,5 § 138; 7.5,6 § 154; 6.9,3 § 420). To illustrate the woe uttered by Jesus over women with children, one can point to the
story recorded by Josephus about Mary, a woman from Perea, who was
among the Jews starving in Jerusalem and who seized her child, an infant at
her breast, slew it, and roasted it for food for herself *(J. W.* 6.3,4 § 201-211).
(Cf. 2 Kgs 6:24-31.) For desolated Jerusalem, visited later by Titus, who
walked among its ruins, see *J. W.* 7.5,2 § 112-115. (See also Tacitus, *Hist.* 5.8-
13.)

In discussing Luke 19:41-44, Jesus' lament over Jerusalem, we referred to
C. H. Dodd's contention that that passage and this one depend far more on
the description of the destruction of Jerusalem under Nebuchadnezzar in the
sixth century B.C. than on Titus' capture of it in A.D. 70 (see COMMENT on p.

1255; cf. F. Flückiger, "Luk. 21,20-24"). That may be, as far as the terminology is concerned, for Luke likes to make his accounts echo similar OT stories. But the question remains, Why has he substituted these covert references to the destruction of Jerusalem under the Romans for the Danielic "abomination of desolation"? Luke never names the Romans any more than Mark names either Antiochus IV Epiphanes or the Romans—saying only, "Let the reader understand." Though Luke does not follow Mark in using such indirection, he knows that, since he writes after the event, he will be understood. (For J. A. T. Robinson's use of this passage, see *Redating the New Testament* [Philadelphia: Westminster, 1976] 13-30, 86-117; cf. pp. 54-56 above.) Cf. G. Schneider, *Die Apostelgeschichte I. Teil* (HTKNT 5; Freiburg: Herder, 1980) 119.

No one will contest that Luke has overlaid his form of Jesus' utterances about Jerusalem's coming desolation with various OT allusions, some of them more explicit than others (e.g. Hos 9:7 in v. 22; Sir 28:18 and Deut 28:64 in v. 24ab; and Zech 12:3 in v. 24c). The effect of this is to present the destruction of Jerusalem as an event in Lucan salvation-history. The "end" of v. 9 is now seen as "the time of vengeance," when "all that stands written will see fulfillment" (v. 22). "All that stands written" refers at least to the four allusions to OT writings mentioned above, which, though they are not all prophetic in themselves, are regarded by Luke (as is his wont, see p. 180), not only as prophetic, but even as predictive.

Moreover, Jesus' words against Jerusalem not only have to be understood in terms of prophetic utterances of the OT against Jerusalem (e.g. Mic 3:12; Jer 7:1-14; 22:5), but also have to be related to his utterances against the Galilean towns of Bethsaida and Chorazin (10:13-15), where eschatological judgment was also pronounced.

However, what Jesus says here about the coming desolation of Jerusalem forms a springboard for a wider development, for this pericope brings to an end the first part of the eschatological discourse, and now Jesus will move on to speak of what is coming upon the world.

NOTES

21 20. *Jerusalem surrounded by camps.* Or possibly by "armies." The word *stratopedon* properly means "camp," and is so used by Josephus, *J. W.* 5.2,1 § 47; 5.2,2 § 65; 5.2,3 § 68, etc., but it is also often used as the equivalent of *stratia,* "army" (Polybius, *Hist.* 1.16,1; 2.1,6). The ptc. *kykloumenēn* is pres., hence "being surrounded." Luke uses the form *Ierousalēm.* See NOTES on 2:22; 10:30. Cf. Tacitus, *Hist.* 5.11.

her desolation has drawn near. "Desolation" *(erēmōsis)* is derived by Luke from Mark 13:14, where *bdelygma tēs erēmōseōs,* "abomination of desolation," is used, drawn by that evangelist from the LXX of Dan 12:11. Cf. 9:27; 11:31. That Greek phrase is an attempt to translate Hebrew *šiqqûṣ šōmēm* (12:11) or *šiqqûṣîm mĕšōmēm* (9:27) or *haššiqûṣ mĕšōmēm* (11:31), "desolating abomination(s)," i.e. the detestable thing causing the desolation of the Temple, the Danielic way of describing the desecration of the Temple caused by the statue of Zeus Olympius erected by Antiochus IV Epiphanes in 167 B.C. (2 Macc 6:2; but cf. 1 Macc 1:54). The new desolation will be seen in encircling camps (see Luke 19:43), and the "end" (v. 9) will soon follow. Thus the Lucan Jesus corrects the claim of the false prophets that "the time has drawn near," in now saying that Jerusalem's desolation has indeed "drawn near." Recall his words about its "abandoned house" in 13:35.

21. *those who are in Judea must flee to the mountains.* Lit. "let them flee," expressed by the third pl. impv. *(pheugetōsan),* as again in the two following cls. Luke derives this part of Jesus' utterance from Mark 13:14d. The "mountains" would be those mostly to the east, north, and south of Jerusalem.

Does this detail echo any historic flight of people from Jerusalem? It is often so interpreted, and in the Lucan form of the discourse it would be more plausibly so interpreted than in the Marcan. For Eusebius *(H.E.* 3.5,3) records that "people of the church in Jerusalem were commanded by a certain oracle before the war to those in the city who were worthy of it to depart and dwell in one of the cities of Perea called Pella." There is, however, no way of knowing whether Luke was aware of this.

Judea. The name is used in the specific sense. See NOTE on 1:5.

must get out of it. Lit. "let them withdraw." Strangely enough, ms. D, which usually smooths out difficulties in the Lucan text, reads rather the vb. *ekchōreitōsan* with the negative *mē* before it, "let them not withdraw."

must not go back into it. Lit. "let them not enter it."

22. *this is the time of vengeance.* Lit. "these are the days of vengeance," an allusion to Hos 9:7, which in the LXX reads, *hēkasin hai hēmerai tēs ekdikēseōs,* "the days of vengeance have come," an accurate translation of Hebrew, *bā'û yĕmê happĕqûdāh.* The phrase forms part of Hosea's complaint against Israel, which has rejected Yahweh and paid no heed to his prophet; it must then face the punishment/visitation which will ensue. Luke has introduced this detail into the Marcan form of the discourse, probably from "L." But note that Luke does not explain in what sense the desolation of Jerusalem is "vengeance." Vengeance for what? Recall, however, Luke 18:7. Cf. Deut 32:35; Jer 46:10 [LXX, 26:10] for similar OT expressions of God's vengeance.

when all that stands written will see fulfillment. Lit. "for all that is written to be fulfilled," the gen. of the articular infin. to express purpose. See BDF § 400. For *gegrammena* in the sense of OT Scripture, see NOTES on 18:31; 20:17. The "all" that stands written cannot be restricted to the three passages to which allusion is made in v. 24. We meet here again the Lucan rhetorical use of *panta.* See NOTES on 3:16; 4:15; 9:1. Other oracles against Jerusalem can be found in Mic 3:12; Jer 6:1-8; 26:1-9; Zech 8:1-8. The destruction of Jerusalem will mean its "end" in God's salvation-history. It will have been the city of destiny in Jesus' career, the place where salvation is accomplished, and the city from which the word of God spreads to the end of the earth. See pp. 166-168. But all of that will see its "end." For the theme of "fulfillment" in Lucan writings, see pp. 179-180, and NOTE on 9:51.

23. *Woe.* See NOTE on 6:24.

women who are pregnant. Lit. "to those (fem.) having in the belly," a common Septuagintism for women bearing children. See the LXX of Gen 16:4,5,11; 38:24,25; Judg 13:3,5,7; 2 Sam 11:5, etc.

nursing infants. Lit. "to those (fem.) giving suck," another Septuagintism. See the LXX of Gen 21:7. In this verse Luke has been following Mark 13:17, but he omits 13:18, with its reference to Jerusalem's possible destruction in the winter. As G. Schneider *(Evangelium nach Lukas,* 423-424) notes, "In the deletion of Mark v. 18 ("Pray that your flight be not in the winter!") is seen the Lucan 'adaptation' of the promise to the events of the year 70; for the siege of the city lasted from April to late August. In view of this one cannot assert (with Flückiger *[TZ* 28 (1972)] 389f.) that Luke makes no 'historical allusions' to the events of the past (about which he would not have known), but rather interprets Mark 13,14-18 only on the basis of OT prophetic sayings."

at that time! Lit. "in those days." See NOTES on 1:39; 4:2; here the dem. adj. *ekeinais* is used. The phrase refers to the "time of vengeance" of v. 22.

great indeed will be the misery in this land. Lit. "there will be great need upon the/ this land." The def. art. *tēs* probably has dem. force in view of the dem. adj. *toutō* used in the following phrase coordinated with this one. Hence *epi tēs gēs* is not to be understood merely as "on the earth," for the reference is to the destruction of Jerusalem and *gē* would be referring to Judea (see v. 21). Cf. J. M. Creed, *The Gospel,* 257. This part of v. 23 is a Lucan substitution for Mark 13:19, with its allusion to Dan 12:1; Luke has probably composed this himself.

and the wrath against this people! Lit. "and wrath for this people." See NOTE on 3:7.

24. *fall by the edge of the sword.* This is an allusion to Sir 28:18, which in the LXX reads, *polloi epesan en stomati machairas,* "many fell by the edge (lit. "mouth") of the sword" (the Hebrew for this verse is not preserved). The phrase comes from a sapiential part of Sirach which has to do with the evils of slander in human conduct. Thus the allusion made to such a text is a sheer accommodation of the OT text. See also p. 115.

carried off captive to all the nations. This is an allusion to Deut 28:64, which in the LXX reads *kai diasperei se kyrios ho theos sou eis panta ta ethnē,* "and the Lord your God will scatter you among all the nations," which is an accurate rendering of the Hebrew, *wehĕpîṣĕkā Yhwh bĕkol hā'ammîm.* In Deuteronomy the cl. forms part of Moses' final (second) address to the Hebrews, in which he blesses them and explains the curses (vv. 20-46,47-68) of the preceding chap. 27. In the Lucan context the captivity would refer to that of the Romans. Luke has introduced this verse (possibly from "L") to stress the fate of Jerusalem Jews. Cf. Ezek 30:3; 32:9; Jer 21:7; Ezra 9:7.

Jerusalem will be trampled upon by pagans. This is an allusion to Zech 12:3, which in the LXX runs, *kai estai en tē hēmera ekeinē thēsomai tēn Ierousalēm lithon katapatoumenon pasin tois ethnesin,* "and it will come to pass on that day (that) I shall make Jerusalem a stone trampled upon by all the nations," which is something of a paraphrase of the Hebrew, *wĕhāyāh bayyôm hahû' 'āśîm 'et-Yĕrûśālayim 'eben ma'āmāsāh lĕkol hā-'ammîm,* "and it will come to pass on that day (that) I shall make Jerusalem a heavy lifting-stone for all the nations." The sentence forms part of Zechariah's oracle against Jerusalem, which needs to be cleansed of sin and infidelity, a heavy burden for any nation to bear. Luke follows the Greek text of the LXX. Cf. Dan 8:13; Rev 11:2. For *ethnē* in the sense of "pagans," see Luke 12:30.

until the time of the pagans sees its fulfillment. I.e. until the triumph of the Romans over Jerusalem is complete. When the "end" of Jerusalem comes, the pagans take over. It is the *kairoi ethnōn,* the "appointed/determined times of the pagans." See NOTE on 1:20. Cf. Tob 14:5; Rom 11:25. *Pace* W. Marxsen *(Mark the Evangelist* [see p. 173], 190), this cl. cannot refer to the "epoch of the Gentile mission [which] precedes the end." The fulfillment of the time of the pagans can only mean the period after A.D. 70, when the city of Jerusalem and Judea are again dominated by the Romans (the pagans) after the unsuccessful revolt of the Jews. It is a wrong-headed reading of the phrase to think that "this is Luke's own time" (ibid.).

Luke does not agree with Mark's remark about God's shortening the days "for the sake of the chosen" (13:20), for he emphasizes rather the duration of "the time of vengeance." But even the time of the pagans will give way to the coming of the Son of Man. Cp. Dan 2:44-45; 7:18,21-27. See G. Schneider, *Evangelium nach Lukas,* 424. See NOTE on 9:31.

BIBLIOGRAPHY (21:20-24)

Braumann, G. "Die lukanische Interpretation der Zerstörung Jerusalems," *NovT* 6 [Rengstorf Festschrift] (1963) 120-127.

Conzelmann, H. *Theology,* 125-132.

Dodd, C. H. "The Fall of Jerusalem" (see p. 1259).

Flückiger, F. "Luk. 21.20-24 und die Zerstörung Jerusalems," *TZ* 28 (1972) 385-390.

Holst, R. "God's Truth in a Kaleidoscope: Using a Synopsis," *CurrTM* 3 (1976) 347-354.

Pedersen, S. "Zum Problem der vaticinia ex eventu (Eine Analyse von Mt. 21,33-46 par.; 22,1-10 par.)," *ST* 19 (1965) 167-188.

Reicke, B. "Synoptic Prophecies on the Destruction of Jerusalem," *Studies in the New Testament and Early Christian Literature: Essays in Honor of Allen P. Wikgren* (NovTSup 33; Leiden: Brill, 1972) 121-134.

Salas, A. *Discurso escatológico prelucano: Estudio de Lc. XXI, 20-36* (El Escorial: Ciudad de Dios, 1967). Cf. J. Schmid, *BZ* 14 (1970) 290-292.

Taylor, V. "A Cry from the Siege: A Suggestion Regarding a Non-Marcan Oracle Embedded in Lk. xxi 20-36," *JTS* 26 (1924-1925) 136-144.

Wainwright, A. W. "Luke and the Restoration of the Kingdom to Israel," *ExpTim* 89 (1977-1978) 76-79.

141. THE COMING OF THE SON OF MAN
(21:25-28)

21 25 "Then there will be signs in the sun, the moon, and the stars; and on the earth distress among nations in their perplexity at the roaring and surging of the sea. 26 People will stop breathing out of fear and foreboding of what is coming upon the world. For *the forces of heaven*a will be shaken loose. 27 People will then see *the Son of Man coming on a cloud* b with power and great glory. 28 When all this begins to take place, stand erect and hold your heads high, because your deliverance is near."

a Isa 34:4   b Dan 7:13

COMMENT

As the Lucan Jesus continues his eschatological discourse, his words take on another dimension. He has just foretold the "end" of Jerusalem, which is to be desolated and "trampled upon by pagans" (v. 24), but now he moves on to another "end," to "what is coming upon the world" (v. 26). The first part of the discourse was a prophetic utterance, formulated with hindsight by the evangelist about the end of Jerusalem; it had the overtones of prophecy fulfilled. Now Jesus utters prophetic utterances about the future, with overtones of prophecy yet to be fulfilled. Thus he begins here the second part of the discourse (vv. 25-36) and returns to the topic of the coming of the Son of Man (21:25-28), a topic already touched upon in 17:22-37.

For the relation of this passage to Mark 13:24-27, see COMMENT on vv. 5-7; see p. 1328. (Cf. Matt 24:29-31.)

From a form-critical point of view, these verses contain prophetic Sayings of Jesus, most of them making use of clear OT apocalyptic stage props.

By his redactional omission of *en ekeinais tais hemerais,* "in those days" (Mark 13:24), Luke clearly distinguishes what Mark had linked together, the "end" of Jerusalem and the "end" of the world. What is still to come will not happen "in those days," i.e. right after the destruction of Jerusalem. As R. Bultmann *(HST* 123) notes, Luke wants to postdate the coming of the Son of Man and "separate it from vv. 12-14 by a long interval."

Jesus now counsels his followers about "what is coming upon the world," admitting that cosmic signs will attend it, signs in the sun, moon, stars, and in the roaring and surging sea. They will cause distress among people of all nations. Fear and foreboding will snatch the breath away from people, as the forces of the heavens are shaken loose. All of this will be a sign of the coming of the Son of Man on a cloud with power and great glory. He will bring deliverance to Christian disciples who will have to learn to "shape up" and hold their heads high in joyful expectation. For the judgment passed on Jerusalem merely presages a judgment of greater dimension and import. As Jerusalem was faced with a crisis when Jesus appeared to teach there, so will the world be faced when he comes as the Son of Man. In contrast to the judgment to be passed on the world, Christian disciples will then realize that their deliverance is near. In the context of the Lucan discourse that deliverance would include release from persecutions such as those of vv. 12-19.

NOTES

21 25. *signs in the sun, the moon, and the stars.* Jesus' positive answer to the question of his listeners in v. 7c now makes mention of "signs," of cosmic signs. The things predicted in vv. 10-11 were not to be misunderstood, even though they too had to happen first. Jesus speaks of similar things but in a different sense. Jesus' words are an abbreviation of Mark 13:24-25, but they are cast in the form of vv. 10-11 above. They make use of apocalyptic stage props similar to those of Joel 3:3-4 (2:30-31E), "I shall set portents in the heavens and on the earth, blood and fire and columns of smoke; the sun will be turned to darkness and the moon to blood." Such portents are common in OT prophetic utterances. See Isa 13:10 (used in Mark 13:24b-25a); 34:4; Hag 2:6,21; Ezek 32:7.

on the earth distress among nations in their perplexity. I.e. to the cosmic signs correspond terrestrial catastrophes. This is possibly an allusion to Isa 24:19, which in the LXX reads, *tarachē tarachthēsetai hē gē kai aporia aporēthēsetai hē gē,* "with distress will the earth be distressed, and with perplexity will it be perplexed," a slightly nuanced version of the Hebrew. Cf. Ps 65:8.

at the roaring and surging of the sea. Possibly an allusion to Ps 46:4, which in the LXX runs *ēchēsan kai etarachthēsan ta hydata autōn, etarachthēsan ta orē en tē krataiotēti autou,* "their waters echoed and were disturbed, the mountains were shaken by its forceful tumult," said with reference to the sea(s). Cf. Ps 89:10. The force of the earth's elements becomes an apocalyptic stage prop.

26. *People will stop breathing out of fear and foreboding.* Lit. "as human beings stop breathing from . . ." a gen. absol. added by Luke. See p. 108. The expression could refer to either fainting or death. See 4 Macc 15:18; Josephus, *Ant.* 19.1,5 § 114. "Fear and foreboding" are normal human reactions, but they stand in contrast in this passage to the stance of Christians expressed in v. 28.

of what is coming upon the world. Lit. "of the things coming upon the inhabited earth" *(oikoumenē,* on which see NOTE on 4:5). Cf. Acts 11:28. This phrase has been added by Luke; it has no counterpart in the Marcan or Matthean discourse, and it clearly sets off this part of the Lucan discourse from the first, which had to do with Jerusalem. Thus the judgment of the world is distinct from that of Jerusalem, although the latter is a microcosmic view of the former. On the vb. *eperchesthai,* "come upon," see NOTE on 1:35.

the forces of heaven will be shaken loose. This is usually considered an allusion to Isa 34:4, "all their host shall fade away" (LXX: *kai panta ta astra pesetai,* "and all the stars will fall"). A variant, however, in mss. B, L of the LXX reads, *takēsontai pasai hai dynameis tōn ouranōn,* "all the powers of heaven will be dissolved," i.e. the heavenly bodies conceived of as armies. Luke has derived the saying from Mark 13:25 and slightly modified it. In Isaiah the words form part of an oracle about the terrifying end of God's enemies, who are symbolically depicted as the hosts of heaven. Implied is the reversal of the created order and the return to chaos. Cf. Acts 17:26.

27. *People will then see.* Recall the words addressed by the two men in white robes to the disciples at Jesus' ascension in Acts 1:11, "This Jesus, who was taken up from you into heaven, will come in the same way as you *saw* him go into heaven."

the Son of Man coming on a cloud. Luke has derived this verse directly from Mark 13:26, changing only the pl. *nephelais,* "clouds," to the sg. *nephelē.* It is an allusion to Dan 7:13, which in the LXX reads, *epi tōn nephelōn tou ouranou hōs huios anthrōpou ercheto,* "upon the clouds of heaven (one) like a son of man (= a human being) was coming." In this Lucan eschatological discourse the saying refers to the glorious appearance of the risen Christ as the Son of Man coming in judgment (see 12:8-9) to deliver his own. On "Son of Man," see NOTE on 5:24 and pp. 208-211, 233-234. The function of the Son of Man in Mark 13:26-27 is double, judgment (v. 26) and gathering in of the chosen (v. 27). In Luke the former task is retained, but *deliverance* of Christian disciples is envisaged (v. 28).

with power and great glory. See Mark 13:26 and pp. 196, 789.

28. *stand erect and hold your heads up high.* I.e. Jesus' followers are not to share the fear and foreboding mentioned in v. 26; in contrast, their attitude will be one of rising and upright, joyful expectation. They will stand to welcome their deliverance.

because your deliverance is near. I.e. your "redemption" *(apolytrōsis).* This compound form appears only here in Lucan writings; the simple form *lytrōsis* occurs in 1:68. See NOTE there. As A. Plummer *(The Gospel,* 485) notes, *apolytrōsis* is used in the sense of "release, deliverance," without any connotation of "ransom" *(lytron).* Jesus' advice now stands in contrast to that of v. 21, about flight from Jerusalem. But "deliverance/redemption" is not associated with Christ's death or resurrection, but with his coming again. Cf. Acts 3:19-21; Rom 8:23; Eph 4:30. See pp. 181, 222. Cf. *I Enoch* 51:2-3.

The following parable will illustrate the proximity of such deliverance.

BIBLIOGRAPHY (21:25-28)

Gardiner, J. A. "Studies in Texts: Luke 21.28," *Theology* 59 (1956) 460-462.

George, A. "La venue du Fils de l'Homme: Lc 21,25-28. 34-36," *AsSeign* ns 5 (1969) 71-78.

Lauras, A. "Le commentaire patristique de Lc. 21,25-33," *Studia patristica* 7 (TU 92; Berlin: Akademie, 1966) 503-515.

Salas, A. "Los signos cósmicos de Lc. XXI, 25-28, a la luz del concepto bíblico 'día de Yahvé,' " *Ciudad de Dios* 180 (1967) 43-85.

—— " 'Vuestra liberación está cerca' (Lc 21,28): Dimensión histórico-salvífica de la teología de la liberación," *CB* 31 (1974) 157-163.

—— " 'Vuestra liberación está cerca' (Lc 21,28): Dimensión liberacionista del acto redentor," *Ciudad de Dios* 189 (1976) 3-22.

Varro, R. "Le Christ est notre avenir (Luc, 21, 25-33)," *AmiCl* 78 (1968) 659-662.

——, G. Becquet, and R. Beauvery. "Le Christ est notre avenir," *Esprit et vie* 90 (1970) 605-608.

Vico Gargano, C. a. "Secundus Christi adventus," *VD* 19 (1939) 338-346.

142. THE PARABLE OF THE FIG TREE
(21:29-33)

21 [29] Then Jesus proposed to them a parable: "Look at the fig tree, and all the trees. [30] Once they have put forth their leaves, you can see and tell for yourselves that summer is near. [31] So it is with you; when you see all this happen, realize that the kingdom of God is near. [32] Believe me, it will all happen before this generation passes away. [33] The sky and the earth will pass away, but my words will not."

COMMENT

To stress the need of a proper reaction to his words about "what is coming upon the world" (v. 26) and about the proximity of deliverance, Jesus now adds a parable about a fig tree (21:29-33), and draws several lessons from it.

For the relation of this passage to Mark 13:28-32, see COMMENT on vv. 5-7. (Cf. Matt 24:32-36.)

Form-critically considered, these verses contain a parable (vv. 29-30) and an application (v. 31), to which are appended two minatory Sayings of Jesus, probably derived from isolated, independent original contexts. R. Bultmann *(HST* 123) admits the originality of this parable as part of the eschatological discourse, but cannot say whether it was uttered by Jesus or derived from Jewish or Christian tradition (ibid. 125). However, N. Perrin *(Rediscovering,* 202) argues that Mark 13:28 may well be authentic, but v. 29 has been added to adapt the parable itself to the service of "early Christian apocalyptic," such as is found in 1 Thess 4:16; 1 Cor 16:22 *(marana tha).* There is no real reason to deny the authenticity of the Marcan form of the parable itself; whether it originally formed part of the eschatological discourse is another matter (cf. Matt 16:2-3[?]).

In the Lucan form Jesus draws a lesson from the fig tree and all other trees: Once they have put forth their leaves, a person knows that summer is near, for blossoms and leaves are the sign of summer fruit. Then he concludes: Learn to read these other signs too; when you see them, realize that the kingdom of God is near. So runs the Lucan parable and its conclusion.

To bolster up his contention, Jesus utters two further sayings, one to stress the imminence of the coming kingdom (and by implication the coming of the Son of Man), and the other to emphasize the seriousness of what he says. In the first saying Luke retains a bit of futurist eschatology, despite the distinction made earlier in the discourse between what must happen first and the "end." How imminent the coming of the kingdom is meant to be no one can say. In any case, it is a warning to "this generation" (cp. 7:31; 9:41; 11:29-32,50-51; 16:8; 17:25; Acts 2:40).

What is preserved here is undoubtedly an utterance of Jesus about something that "this generation" would live to see; but what that was is mostly lost to us. Similar forms of the saying are preserved in Matt 10:23 and Mark 9:1. The fact that such an utterance is used in different gospel-contexts reveals that the early Christians had already applied (and probably redacted) it to suit diverse purposes of their own. Here it is made to suit the early Christian expectation of an imminent coming of the kingdom. The early Christians may well have inherited from Jesus himself an expectation of something important, but the precise nature of it is another matter.

NOTES

21   29. *Then Jesus proposed to them a parable.* See Luke 6:39; 18:1. On "parable," see NOTE on 5:36.

Look at the fig tree. Recall the parable of the barren fig tree (13:6-9). In Mark 13:28 (Matt 24:32) the common Palestinian fig tree is the sole tree used to draw the lesson, but Luke adds, "and all the trees," spoiling the parabolic style, according to R. Bultmann *(HST* 123). The reason for the Lucan addition is not only his fondness for the rhetorical "all" (see NOTES on 3:16; 4:15; 9:1), but also his recognition that the lesson to be drawn is not exclusive to the fig tree. It is not that Luke lacked any idea about the sprouting of the Palestinian fig tree or that he was writing the parable for those who did not know what a fig tree was. It is a rhetorical extension. In Joel 2:22-23 the fig tree and the vine are signs of God's blessing on Israel; this OT motif, however, does not enter into the meaning of the parable.

30. *Once they have put forth their leaves.* Lit. "when they put forth," with no obj. expressed; it is understood. They are the young leaves, which announce the season of summer and its fruit. See Josephus, *Ant.* 4.8,19 § 226.

you can see and tell for yourselves. Luke's Greek is cumbersome here; lit. it reads, "seeing, you know from yourselves." He had redacted the simpler Marcan formula, by adding *blepontes ap' heautōn,* in order to stress that no other instruction or teaching will be necessary (E. Klostermann, *Lukasevangelium,* 204).

that summer is near. This is the point of the parable: the leaves are the sign of summer's proximity.

31. *So it is with you.* I.e. with those who hear my words and ponder them. The same expression is found in 17:10.

when you see all this happen. Jesus draws his conclusion, applying the lesson of the parable to the "signs" that have been mentioned in vv. 11,25.

the kingdom of God is near. So Luke allegorizes the parable, adding the reference to the kingdom, which is not present in Mark 13:29. The kingdom is as near as summer is; it will come as surely as summer comes after the leaves sprout. Recall Jesus' words about the proximity of the kingdom in 10:9,11; 19:11. What v. 28 said of deliverance, this verse now affirms of the kingdom. Jesus' affirmation about the nearness of the kingdom stands in contrast with that of the *kairos* proclaimed by the false prophets of 21:8; its nearness is like the proximity of Jerusalem's desolation (21:20). Thus the appearance of the kingdom is brought into relation to the coming of the day of the Son of Man (vv. 25-28). On the "kingdom," see pp. 154-156.

32. *Believe me.* Lit. "Amen, I tell you," on which see NOTE on 4:24. Luke has retained this asseveration, which he often omits, from Mark 13:30.

it will all happen. Lit. "this generation will not pass away until all happens." Luke derives the affirmation from Mark 13:30, deleting only *tauta,* "these things." The verse echoes the sentiment of 9:27. See NOTE there. This solemnly introduced affirmation does not refer solely to Jerusalem, but to the end of the world as well. The destruction of Jerusalem is the *type* for the end of the world, the coming of the kingdom and of the day of the Son of Man. "All" is not part of Lucan rhetoric here, because he has derived it from Mark; but it does not refer to the apocalyptic stage props as much as to the "end" of Jerusalem or of the world, in whatever way that comes.

To what does "this generation" refer? This is a difficult question to answer, and in the long run the most difficult phrase to interpret in this complicated eschatological discourse. Different answers have been proposed: (a) Jesus' own contemporary generation: So A. Plummer, W. G. Kümmel, et al.; (b) the Jewish people: So W. Grundmann, W. Marxsen, et al.; (c) human beings in general or all humanity: So A. R. C. Leaney, J. Zmijewski, et al.; (d) the generation of the end-signs: So H. Conzelmann, G. Schneider, et al. If one insists on answer *a,* it would have to be understood of Stage I of the gospel tradition, and it may be correct for that stage; but there is no certainty of the application of this saying in that stage. See COMMENT on these verses. Answer *b* is irrelevant; and only answers *c* or *d* merit attention for the Lucan Gospel. In that Luke is writing after the destruction of Jerusalem, the best answer for Stage III would seem to be *d,* since "all humanity" is scarcely envisaged. See further NOTES on 7:31; 9:41.

33. *The sky and the earth will pass away.* See NOTE on 16:17.

but my words will not. Jesus identifies the permanence of his prophetic utterance with the constancy of Yahweh's word found in the OT (see Isa 40:8; 55:10-11; Ps

119:89), for his words are more solid than the heavens and the earth. No matter how long the interval may seem to be, assurance is given for the reality of the "end." Recall the risen Christ's words about the authority reserved to the Father in Acts 1:7.

On the omitted Marcan verse about the ignorance of the Son (13:32), see R. Pesch, *Naherwartungen,* 195.

BIBLIOGRAPHY (21:29-33)

Berger, K. *Die Amen-Worte Jesu* (BZNW 39; Berlin: de Gruyter, 1970) 68-69.
Dupont, J. "La parabole du figuier qui bourgeonne *(Mc,* XIII, 28-29 et par.)," *RB* 75 (1968) 526-548.
Jeremias, J. *Parables,* 119-120.
Jülicher, A. *Gleichnisreden,* 2. 3-11.
Lövestam, E. "En problematisk eskatologisk utsaga: Mark. 13:30 par.," *SEA* 28-29 (1963-1964) 64-80.
Manson, T. W. *Sayings,* 332-333.
Schneider, G. *Parusiegleichnisse,* 55-61, 62-66.

143. CONCLUDING EXHORTATION TO VIGILANCE
(21:34-36)

21 34 "Be on your guard, then, that your minds be not dulled by carousing, drunkenness, and worldly cares, or that day will come upon you by surprise, 35 like *a trap.* For so will it come upon all who *dwell upon* the entire face of *the earth.*a 36 Be on the alert and pray at all times for the strength to come safely through all that is going to happen and so to stand before the Son of Man."

a Isa 24:17

COMMENT

Jesus concludes his eschatological discourse with an exhortation to vigilance and prayer (21:34-36); it is intended as a preparation for the coming of the day of the Son of Man.

This conclusion is peculiar to Luke; part of it may depend on material from his source "L" (see p. 84), but Lucan composition cannot be wholly excluded, as J. M. Creed *(The Gospel,* 254) notes. For its relation to Mark 13:33-37, see

COMMENT on vv. 5-7. Matthew has a longer form of the eschatological discourse, because he appends to "Mk" materials from "Q" (parallel to Luke 17:26-27,34-35; 12:39-46; 19:12-27) and from "M" (Matt 25:1-13,31-46).

Form-critically considered, vv. 34-36 contain hortatory and monitory Sayings of Jesus, with an OT allusion in v. 35. R. Bultmann *(HST* 119, 166) finds the Lucan formulation in this conclusion to be "quite late" and "Hellenistic," even akin to Pauline terminology. How it can be akin to Paul and late, however, is not explained.

Jesus now enjoins his listeners and followers to beware that their way of life be not burdened or dulled by dissipation, intoxication, or excessive solicitude for material things. These are scarcely the ways one should prepare for the coming day of the Son of Man. His reason for the injunction: The Day of the Son of Man's appearance will come of a sudden, and it may catch human beings like a snare or a trap. For it will come upon all who dwell on earth, not just on Palestinians, but on the whole *oikoumenē* (v. 26). Therefore, Jesus counsels, "Be on the alert and pray at all times for the strength" (v. 36) to come through the ordeal and be able to stand upright before the Son of Man, who comes in judgment.

Especially to be noted in this conclusion is the idea of the universality of judgment which will "come upon all who dwell upon the entire face of the earth" (v. 35). This may echo OT themes, but it is particularly significant as a solemn injunction coming from Jesus, who is now about to face his own passion and death, his transit to the Father.

His followers are urged to "Be on the alert and pray at all times" to be ready for the appearance of the coming Son of Man. So Luke emphasizes once again his theme of prayer in Christian life (see pp. 244-247) and uses the tradition of Jesus' eschatological discourse to exhort Christians of "this generation" to readiness—thus he shifts the emphasis from the *eschaton* to the *sēmeron* (see p. 234).

NOTES

21 34. *Be on your guard.* See NOTE on 12:1.

that your minds be not dulled. Lit. "that your hearts be not weighed down," i.e. lose their sensitivity. Luke uses an OT expression. See Exod 7:14; 8:11[LXX]; 9:7. But "to be heavy with wine" was an expression well known in Greek literature too (from Homer on: see *Od.* 3.139; 19.122). Cf. G. Schwarz, *"Mēpote barēthōsin hymōn hai kardiai,"* BN 10 (1979) 40.

carousing, drunkenness, and worldly cares. I.e. by distracting, degrading, mundane pursuits. Recall Jesus' words in 12:22-31,45. Cf. Mark 4:19, but also the Pauline exhortations of 1 Thess 5:7; Rom 13:13; cp. Eph 5:18. Cf. Isa 5:11-12.

that day will come upon you by surprise. Lit. "of a sudden." Cf. 1 Thess 5:2. As is evident from v. 36, it is the day of the Son of Man (cf. 17:22,24,26,30). For "that day," see 10:12; 17:31. On the vb. *ephistanai,* "come upon," see NOTE on 2:9.

35. *like a trap.* I.e. one set for an unsuspecting animal. This is probably an allusion to Isa 24:17, which reads in the LXX, *phobos kai bothynos kai pagis eph' hymas tous enoikountas epi tēs gēs,* "fear and pit and trap upon you, O inhabitants of the earth," which renders the Hebrew original accurately, save for the alliteration of the first three words *(paḥad wāpaḥat wāpaḥ)* and the pl. for the sg. It forms part of Isaiah's oracle about universal judgment. Cf. Jer 48:43; 25:29. The Greek phrase *hōs pagis* forms the end of a sentence, but the beginning of a verse; on the problem, see *TCGNT* 173.

all. Again Lucan rhetoric for the universality of judgment. See 17:37; 21:26.

36. *Be on the alert.* Lit. "keep yourselves awake." This counsel is the Lucan substitute for the last, emphatic word in the Marcan form of the discourse, *grēgoreite,* "be awake" (13:37). Cf. 1 Thess 5:6; Matt 26:41; 1 Pet 4:7; 1 Esdr 8:58.

pray at all times. Lit. "praying at every season." Whether *kairos* here carries the nuance of "appointed/determined time" (see NOTE on 1:20) may be debated. See 4:13 (and NOTE there). Cf. 18:1,7-8; Rom 12:12. The phrase *en panti kairō* is exclusive to Luke.

for the strength to come safely through all that is going to happen. Lit. "that you may be strong (enough) to flee from all these things being about to happen." Some mss. (A, C, D, R, Θ, *f*[13], and the Koine text-tradition) read *kataxiōthēte,* "that you may be judged worthy"; but the better reading is *katischysēte,* "you may be strong" (mss. ℵ, B, L, W, Ψ, *f*[1], 33, etc.).

and so to stand before the Son of Man. I.e. to face his judgment and come through with flying colors. Ms. D, the OL and Syriac versions read *stēsesthe,* "and you will stand." On "Son of Man," see NOTE on v. 27.

BIBLIOGRAPHY (21:34-36)

Joüon, P. "Notes philologiques," esp. 355.

Lövestam, E. *Spiritual Wakefulness in the New Testament,* 122-132.

Manson, T. W. *Sayings,* 334-337.

Ott, W. *Gebet und Heil,* 73-90.

Schneider, G. " 'Der Menschensohn' in der lukanischen Christologie," *Jesus und der Menschensohn* (eds. R. Pesch and R. Schnackenburg) 267-282, esp. 268-271.

Stout, J. C. "*Agrypnein*—Luke 21:36," *Biblical Review* 3 (1918) 621-623.

Tödt, H. E. *The Son of Man,* 94-112.

144. THE MINISTRY OF JESUS IN JERUSALEM
(21:37-38)

21 ³⁷ Jesus used to spend the days teaching in the Temple area, but then he would go and spend the nights on the hill called the Mount of Olives. ³⁸ And in the morning all the people would rise early to come and listen to him in the Temple.

COMMENT

Having concluded Jesus' eschatological discourse in the Jerusalem Temple, Luke appends two verses which sum up his story of the Temple ministry (21:37-38).

These verses could be derived from "L" (see p. 84 and cp. Mark 14:26), but they are even more probably to be ascribed to Lucan composition.

They are a summary of Jesus' Temple activity and have to be compared with other Lucan summaries or editorial statements (see COMMENT on 4:14-15; cf. *HST* 362). Note the difference between this conclusion to Jesus' Jerusalem ministry and that in Mark 13:37, which concludes with Jesus' last words, "What I say to you, I say to all, 'Be awake.' " That existential challenge is replaced by Luke's bland summary of the Jerusalem Temple ministry.

During the day Jesus taught in the Temple area, but he would spend the night on the Mount of Olives opposite the town. Each morning, however, people came at an early hour to listen to him. The main emphasis in the summary is thus not on Jesus' nightly bivouac, but on his daily teaching in the Temple; the secondary emphasis is on the eagerness of the people to listen to him. Implied is the opposition of the Jerusalem authorities (see 19:47; 20:1-2); and that will surface again soon enough (22:2-4).

This notice of Jesus' activity has to be joined to that in 19:47-48 and 20:1. Together they depict Jesus engaged in a "third epoch" of his ministry (H. Conzelmann, *Theology,* 77), one equal in importance to the Galilean ministry and to that during the journey to Jerusalem, even if not as protracted as either of them. (Cf. 22:53.) Jesus purged the Temple that he might teach in it, but he has performed no miracle there, not because of the psychological reason assigned to him by Conzelmann (ibid. 76 n. 3), but because there were no miracles in "Mk," and Luke saw no reason to introduce any at this point in the Gospel.

NOTES

21 37. *Jesus used to spend the days teaching in the Temple area.* Lit. "(during) the
days he was teaching in the Temple." Luke uses the periphrastic conjugation
(*ēn* + pres. ptc.) to emphasize Jesus' customary procedure. See pp. 122-123. The
phrase *tas hēmeras* is an acc. of duration of time. See BDF § 161.2. Cp. 19:47-48; on
Jesus' teaching in general, see p. 148.

   then he would go and spend the nights. Lit. "and going out, he used to find lodging
(during) the nights." The vb. *aulizesthai* does not necessarily mean "spend the night in
the open." See Matt 21:17; *Did.* 11:6; Ps 30:6 (LXX).

   on the hill called the Mount of Olives. See NOTES on 19:29; 6:12. Luke uses the prep.
eis instead of *en.* See BDF § 205. This notice prepares for 22:39,47.

   38. *all the people would rise early to come and listen to him.* Lit. "all the people used
to get up very early in the morning (to come) to him in the Temple (and) hear him."
The Hellenistic vb. *orthrizein,* "get up early in the morning," is also used in the LXX
(Exod 24:4; 32:6; 34:4; 2 Kgs 6:15). The infin. *akouein,* "to listen," expresses purpose
(BDF § 390).

   After this verse mss. *f*¹³ (i.e. mss. 13,69,124,346,543,788,826,983) add the story of
the woman taken in adultery (= John 7:53-8:11). Compare the setting of John 8:1-2
with this Lucan summary to see the reason for the association of that passage with this
part of the Lucan Gospel. See further R. E. Brown, *John, I-XII,* 332-338; U. Becker,
*Jesus und die Ehebrecherin: Untersuchungen zur Text- und Überlieferungsgeschichte
von Joh. 7,53-8,11* (BZNW 28; Berlin: Töpelmann, 1963) 8-14; H. J. Cadbury, "A
Possible Case of Lukan Authorship (John 7:53-8:11)," *HTR* 10 (1917) 237-244.

VI. THE PASSION NARRATIVE

*Please, Father, take this cup away from me. Yet not
my will, but yours be done!*

A. The Preliminary Events

145. THE CONSPIRACY OF THE LEADERS
(22:1-2)

22 ¹ Now the feast of Unleavened Bread, called the Passover, was
close at hand. ² The chief priests and the Scribes were seeking for some
way to do away with Jesus, for they were afraid of the people.

COMMENT

Having depicted Jesus' ministry in the Jerusalem Temple (19:28-21:38), Luke
now begins another important part of his Gospel. In it Jesus will come to the
climax of his "departure" *(exodos,* 9:31), as he begins his "ascent" to the
Father. This is the point at which Luke joins the other three evangelists in
incorporating into his narrative account *(diēgēsis,* see pp. 172-174) his own
form of the passion narrative (22:1-23:56a). It constitutes the sixth major part
of his Gospel (after the prologue). The "ascent" which is now begun will be
completed in the final (seventh) part of the Gospel, the resurrection narrative
(23:56b-24:53). Whereas up till now Luke has pictured Jesus exercising a
ministry of teaching exclusively in the Temple, what ensues in chaps. 22-23
will run its course in the city of Jerusalem itself and in its environs. Before
taking up the details of the various pericopes that make up the passion narrative, we must devote a few paragraphs to the general character of a passion
narrative in the gospel tradition and to the Lucan passion narrative as a
whole.

I. *A Passion Narrative.* Like the infancy narrative and the resurrection narrative, the passion narrative is a subform in the literary genre of gospel. Since the days of M. Kähler (1896), K. L. Schmidt (1919), and M. Dibelius (1919), it has been customary to regard the passion narrative as the first part of the gospel tradition to attain the form of a continuous or connected narrative *(FTG* 180). Kähler labeled the Gospels as "passion narratives with extended introductions" *(So-Called Historical Jesus,* 80 n. 11). With varying nuances this view of the genesis of the gospel tradition has been held by R. Bultmann, W. Bussmann, V. Taylor, J. Jeremias, et al. Leaving aside for the moment the question of whether this part of tradition was already consigned to writing in a pre-Marcan stage, we may consider the following points, which argue for the formation of such a connected narrative, at least in an oral form:

1) Paul is aware of "the story of the cross" *(ho logos ho tou staurou,* 1 Cor 1:18 [written ca. A.D. 56]). Even though *logos* can scarcely be restricted in meaning in this passage to a "narrative," it is for Paul a summary way of referring to the known and oft-repeated string of events of Jesus' crucifixion and death (recall the sense of *logos* in Acts 1:1).

2) Though he manifests but little interest in Jesus' sayings (e.g. 1 Thess 4:15; 1 Cor 7:10-11; 11:23-25), Paul makes countless allusions or references to Jesus' passion, death, and burial: his Last Supper (1 Cor 11:23-25), his betrayal (ibid.), his "sufferings" (Phil 3:10), his "cross" (Phil 2:8), his "crucifixion" (Gal 2:20; 3:1; 1 Cor 1:23; 2 Cor 13:4), his being "hung on a tree" (Gal 3:13), his "death" (1 Thess 5:10; 1 Cor 11:26; 15:3; Rom 4:25; 5:8-10; 6:3), his "burial" (1 Cor 15:3; Rom 6:4); even to "the Jews who killed the Lord Jesus" (1 Thess 2:14-15) or to his being "crucified" by the "rulers of this age" (1 Cor 2:8). (The possibly Deutero-Pauline Col 2:14 speaks of his being "nailed" to the cross.) Even though these allusions are isolated in Paul's writings and often made in a context more theological than historical, they reveal that Paul was aware of a "story of the cross" in the sense of a connected narrative.

3) All four canonical Gospels, Synoptic as well as Johannine, have a passion narrative with a certain striking similarity (betrayal of Jesus by Judas, Last Supper with the disciples, arrest in an outdoor area outside the city, Peter's denials, an interrogation before a high priest, an appearance before P. Pilate, being led off to death, crucifixion, title on the cross, death, burial)—a similarity which is scarcely manifest elsewhere in the Jesus-story and one which "has the nature of a connected historical account more than any other part of the tradition"; it "suggests that the Evangelists had access to a relatively fixed complex of stories" *(FGT* 44-45).

4) This primitive nucleus of connected stories seems to have been the first expansion of such a proclamation as the kerygmatic fragment preserved in 1 Cor 15:3-4: Christ died for our sins . . . was buried . . . was raised on the third day. (Those who would accept C. H. Dodd's analysis of the early speeches in Acts as containing fragments of a Jerusalem kerygma would find

further support for such an expansion. (See his *Apostolic Preaching and Its Developments,* 46-47; cf. further pp. 159-161 above, especially the literature cited on p. 160.)

5) The need for such a continuous or connected account undoubtedly arose from the experience of early Christian preachers or missionaries confronted with the objection, "Well, if he were God's Messiah, then why did he end up crucified? If he were God's agent for human salvation, why did God allow him to die a criminal's death on a cross?" As such, he quickly became "a stumbling block to Jews, and to Gentiles foolishness" (1 Cor 1:23). As M. Dibelius *(FTG* 22-23) once phrased it:

> If what was preached was a witness of salvation, then, among all the materials which were related, only this one, the Passion, was of real significance in the message. For what it dealt with was the first act of the end of the world as then believed and hoped. Here salvation was visible not only in the person and the word of the Lord, but also in the succession of a number of events. To set these matters in their connection corresponded to a need, and all the more as only a description of the consequences of the Passion and of Easter resolved the paradox of the Cross, only the organic connection of the events satisfied the need of explanation, and only the binding together of the individual happenings could settle the question of responsibility *(Schuldfrage).*

To that question Peter's words made an answer, "This Jesus whom you crucified God has made both Lord and Messiah" (Acts 2:36).

Did, however, a continuous story exist as a primitive passion narrative in written form in the pre-Marcan stage? This is a very difficult question to answer. Some scholars like J. Finegan and K.-H. Schelkle tended to identify the Marcan passion narrative with the primitive form inherited. But the divergences which exist among the Marcan, Lucan, and Johannine forms suggest that a briefer narrative than the Marcan account was what that evangelist inherited. Scholars such as J. Jeremias *(Eucharistic Words,* 89-96) and X. Léon-Dufour ("Passion," 1425) have argued for a briefer form which began with the arrest of Jesus. They note that the Johannine passion narrative agrees with the Marcan only generically from the entry into Jerusalem up to the arrest, but more closely thereafter; that the second and third announcements of the passion in the Synoptic tradition (Mark 9:31; 10:33 and parallels) begin with the handing over of Jesus to his adversaries (cf. 1 Cor 11:23); and that Mark 14:43 introduces Judas on his arrival at Gethsemane as "one of the Twelve," as if he had not already been so identified in 14:10 (the repetition is taken as a sign of a separate "source").

Such scholars postulate a development of the tradition similar to this: (a) a kerygmatic proclamation, such as 1 Cor 15:3b-5; (b) a *short* passion narrative, beginning with the arrest of Jesus; (c) a *long* passion narrative, beginning with Jesus' entry into Jerusalem and including the purging of the Temple, the questioning of Jesus' authority, the announcement of Judas' betrayal, the Last Supper, and Gethsemane prayer; (d) the Marcan passion narrative. (For a convenient presentation of V. Taylor's study of the Marcan passion narrative and its two sources, see R. E. Brown, *John, XIII-XXI,* 788; cf. S. Temple, "Two Traditions.")

It has, however, been shown in more recent times by detailed redaction-critical studies of various episodes in the Marcan passion narrative that they are made up of traditional material *and Marcan redaction* in almost every instance. The details of this analysis do not concern us here; it will suffice to cite the conclusion of one author alone who has made a comprehensive study of the Marcan passion narrative:

> All redaction-critical work on the Gospel of Mark which has been done so far has set out from the presupposition that a connected passion narrative already lay before Mark. This presupposition, as we have been able to show, is not evident. The redaction-critical investigation of Mark's Gospel has to begin once again and has to face the fact that the evangelist has built the passion narrative out of individual traditions as he has the rest of the Gospel. (E. Linnemann, *Studien,* 174-175)

(See further J. R. Donahue, *Are You the Christ?;* D. Dormeyer, *Die Passion Jesu;* E. Lohse, *History;* L. Schenke, *Der gekreuzigte Christus;* G. Schille, "Das Leiden"; E. Schweizer, *Good News according to Mark,* 226-363.)

II. *Motifs at Work in the Passion Narrative.* To anyone who reads carefully the passion narratives of the canonical Gospels it soon becomes evident that they have not been composed solely as accounts of factual details. The differences alone among the Marcan, Matthean, Lucan, and Johannine narratives are of such a nature as to preclude such a conclusion. More is at stake in these narratives, and the *Schuldfrage* already alluded to explains why other factors or motifs have been worked into the accounts. We must try to set forth briefly some of these features before looking further at the Lucan passion narrative. The additional features are mainly of two sorts, theological and apologetic.

A. Among the *theological* motifs or factors we may mention the following: (1) *The dominance of faith in the risen Christ.* This echo of the primitive kerygma (recall 1 Cor 15:3-5; Rom 4:25; Acts 2:36; 4:10) brings it about that, though the story of the cross is recounted, it inevitably finds its climax in the *praeconium paschale* ("the Easter proclamation"), "He is not here, but has been raised!" (Luke 24:6; cf. Mark 16:6; Matt 28:6). The details of the arrest, interrogation, trial before Pilate, and crucifixion are not recounted merely as a setback to Jesus' ministry, but are all ordered toward the proclamation of his victory over those events through the power of God. The patristic and medieval theme of *Christus victor mortis* merely spells out what is an implicit thrust of the passion narrative itself. (2) *The accomplishment of God's will.* This is seen above all in the allusion to or quotation of pertinent OT passages: Luke 22:37 (quoting the Servant Song of Isa 53:12); 23:34b-35 (alluding to the psalm of the righteous individual, Ps 22:8,19); 23:36 (alluding to Ps 69:22); 23:46 (alluding to Ps 31:6). (See further Mark 14:61; Matt 26:67; 27:12, etc.) (3) *The tendency to hint at a more-than-human condition of Jesus.* The vague foreknowledge and announcement of his betrayal (Mark 14:18-21; Luke 22:21-23) become explicit, with Judas' name mentioned (Matt 26:25; John 13:21-26). Or the hint at his power: Compare the simple arrest in Mark 14:46 (= Matt 26:50) with the reference to his Father's "twelve legions of angels" (Matt 26:53) and his majestic "I am he" (John 18:6), which fells his would-be captors. Or the significant rewording of Jesus' last cry on the cross: In Mark 15:34 it is "My God, my God, why have you forsaken me?" (Ps 22:1; cf. Matt 27:46). This cry is omitted by Luke, perhaps because he felt it inappropriate on the lips of the Son of God; instead one finds, "Father, into your hands I entrust my spirit" (23:46; cp. Ps 31:6). In John (19:30) the cry becomes, "It is finished." (Cp. *Gos. Peter* 5.19, "My power, O power, you have forsaken me!" [Hebrew *'ēlî* is now understood as a common n., not a proper name].)

B. Among the *apologetic* motifs or factors we may mention: (1) *The emergence of declarations of Jesus' innocence.* A verdict against him occurs in Mark 14:64c; Matt 26:66b; it disappears in Luke (see 22:71), where a triple declaration of his innocence emerges instead (23:4,14-15,22; cp. John 18:38; 19:4,6; Acts 3:13). (2) *The tendency to exculpate the Roman prefect Pontius Pilate and to inculpate the Jewish leaders.* This tendency is not detected in any one passion narrative, but when the four are compared. In Mark 14:1,43,53,55; 15:1,11 the Jewish leaders are mentioned, and in 15:15 Pilate too is implicated, "wishing to satisfy the crowd." The Matthean passion narrative differs little from the Marcan in the parallel passages (26:3,47,57,59; 27:1,20). But peculiarly Matthean additions modify the depiction of Pilate's role: (a) His wife warns him to have nothing to do "with that innocent man" (27:19); (b) Pilate washes his hands and openly declares his non-involvement, "I am innocent of the blood of this man; see to it yourselves." And all the people replied, "His blood be upon us and upon our children" (27:24-25). (c) The chief priests and Pharisees demand of Pilate a guard at the tomb (27:62). The Lucan passion narrative, which also depends on the Marcan but is independent of the Matthean, continues the tendency differently. Luke often distinguishes "the people" or "the crowd" (22:2; 23:27,35a,48) from "the leaders" or the "elders, chief priests, and Scribes" (22:2,52,54; 23:1,4,13,35b,51). He eliminates all reference to false witnesses or to accusations about destroying the Temple and instead presents Jesus accused by the leaders solely of political agitation (23:2,5,18-19). Pilate declares Jesus innocent three times over (23:4,14-15,22). When Pilate finally yields, Luke makes it clear that "their voices prevailed" and that Pilate handed Jesus "over to their will" (23:23-25); and "they led Jesus away" (to crucifixion, v. 26). In these verses the "they/their" can refer only to the "chief priests, the leaders, and the people" (v. 13). Only at v. 36 do (Roman) soldiers appear! Ironically, a Roman centurion declares, "This man was really innocent" (v. 47). Finally, in the Johannine passion narrative what was emerging in the Lucan comes to fuller expression. Caiaphas declares the expediency of Jesus' death (11:47-53, esp. v. 50). Soldiers and officers from the chief priests and Pharisees deal with Judas (18:3,12-14 [the Johannine tradition may be ambiguous here; see R. E. Brown, *John, XIII-XXI,* 807-813]). When Jesus is brought before Pilate, he is again declared innocent three times over (18:38; 19:4,6), and Pilate seeks to release him (18:31; 19:12). When Pilate finally does yield (19:16), he hands Jesus over "to them" (the chief priests of v. 15), and *"they* took Jesus; and he went out, bearing his own cross" (19:17). The tendency thus detected in the canonical Gospels reaches yet another climax in the *Gospel of Peter,* where Pilate, seeing that none of the Jews, "neither Herod nor any of his judges would agree to wash their hands," as he had done symbolically, walks out on them. "Then Herod the king commanded that the Lord should be marched off" (§ 1-2; see Hennecke-Schneemelcher, *NTApocrypha* 1. 183). See further M. Kiddle, "The Passion Narrative." (3) *The tendency to excuse the desertion of the disciples.* In Mark 14:50 "they all forsook him," and the extreme form of that desertion is symbolically depicted by the flight of the young man naked, leaving his "linen cloth" *(sindōn)* behind (14:51-52). Luke has no parallel to Mark 14:50, but includes among those standing by at the crucifixion not only the women who had come with Jesus from Galilee, but also "all his acquaintances" *(pantes hoi gnōstoi* [masc.!], 23:49). In John 18:8c Jesus gives them permission to go! Whereas the prediction of desertion concerns all of the disciples in Mark 14:27 and Matt 26:31, only Peter will fall victim to Satan in Luke 22:31-34 (and he will be converted!).

These motifs and factors color the passion narratives, then, and reveal features in them which transcend the concern of factual reporting. There is a hortatory character to the passion narratives as well, for the passion of Jesus quickly became the pattern for the suffering and persecution of his followers. Stephen's martyrdom in Acts 7:54-8:1 is recounted in imitation of Jesus' death. Certain motifs (vigilance, prayer, Jesus' resignation) were worked into the narrative almost certainly for this reason.

It is also clear that some of the differences among the canonical passion narratives are owing to the selection of materials. The motifs and tendencies detected may account for some of this selection or for the ordering of them. But it should be obvious that no one evangelist has told the whole story as it actually happened. If the gospel tradition at this point has retained the best contact with the historical facts, it has also colored them with these motifs and tendencies. It should also be clear that the part that this section of the gospel tradition played in the life of the early church was not merely that of telling what actually happened. It was far more important that what was being preached dealt with what Jesus of Nazareth had accomplished for mankind. We are faced in this part of the tradition not only with some sort of a factual account of what happened in the last days of Jesus, but (much more) with an early privileged—because inspired—interpretation of it. This interpretation is echoed in various ways in the rest of the NT writings.

III. *The Lucan Passion Narrative.* The Marcan passion narrative is the shortest of the four canonical accounts and is devoid of any peculiar traditions of its own, save that of the flight of the naked young disciple (14:51-52). If one counts that story of flight separately from the account of Jesus' arrest (14:43-50), the Marcan narrative consists of eighteen episodes. The twenty episodes of the Lucan passion narrative, as I have subdivided it (see pp. 141-142), correspond to fourteen of the Marcan episodes *in almost the same order.* The continuous thread of his account is based on Mark. The significant correspondence argues strongly for Lucan dependence on the Marcan narrative in this part of his Gospel. The difference between Luke and Mark in this respect is mainly one of minor omissions and additions. Luke has omitted four episodes: the anointing in Bethany (Mark 14:3-9, because of Luke 7:36-50 [see pp. 685-686]); Jesus' prediction of the desertion of the disciples (Mark 14:27-28, because the disciples do not desert Jesus in this Gospel); the flight of the naked young disciple (along with the preceding v. 50, Mark 14:51-52); and the mocking of the soldiers (Mark 15:16-20abc). But Luke has added a four-part discourse at the end of the account of the Last Supper (22:21-23,24-30,31-34,35-38), and two narratives (Jesus sent to Herod, 23:6-12; and Pilate's judgment, 23:13-16). For differences (omissions) of lesser scope, see COMMENTS on respective passages.

The material within the episodes in the Lucan passion narrative is, however, sometimes quite diverse from that in the Marcan parallels. As elsewhere in this Gospel, Luke has been inspired by the passion narrative in "Mk," especially its order, but he has either incorporated into what he has derived from it other material (from "L") or redacted the Marcan material—perhaps more heavily than elsewhere—or even freely composed some of the verses. Evidence of "Q" in the Lucan passion narative is limited only to 22:28-30.

In this century the question has been posed whether Luke has used another, independent connected account of the passion in addition to "Mk." The question has been answered affirmatively by such commentators as E. Bammel, P. Benoit, M. Black, R. E. Brown, F. C. Burkitt, B. S. Easton, A. George, J. Hawkins, J. Jeremias, A. M. Perry, F. Rehkopf, F. Spitta, B. H. Streeter, V. Taylor, B. Weiss, P. Winter, et al. Three main reasons have been proposed in support of it: (a) the large amount of "L" material used with what comes from "Mk" at this point in the Gospel (see p. 84); (b) the remarkable number of instances where the Johannine and Lucan passion narratives share common, precise details absent from the Marcan or Matthean narratives; and (c) when Luke retains Marcan vocabulary or phrases in this section of the Gospel, it is far less in percentage than in earlier parts of the Gospel (27 percent here vs. 50 percent earlier). Those who espouse the Proto-Luke hypothesis (see pp. 89-91) would simply agree (in general) with this proposal.

However, there is an almost equally long litany of modern scholars who have insisted that Luke has only modified the passion narrative in "Mk" by adding separate stories or sayings from "L" (or in one instance from "Q"), by redacting "Mk," and by freely composing some material. Thus, J. Blinzler, R. Bultmann, J. M. Creed, M. Dibelius, J. Finegan, H. J. Holtzmann, G. Iber, H. C. Kee, H. Lietzmann, R. H. Lightfoot, A. Loisy, G. Schneider, et al. This seems to me to be the better solution. The heavy use of "L" material in the passion narrative does not argue immediately for a *connected written source* independent of "Mk" (even though some have at times so concluded; see pp. 83-85).

Moreover, the impressive list of contacts between the Lucan and Johannine passion narratives, which such scholars as E. Osty, J. A. Bailey, and F. L. Cribbs have pointed out (see pp. 88-89), establishes only that "Luke knew an early form of the developing Johannine tradition" (R. E. Brown, *John, XIII-XXI*, 791) or, as I should prefer to put it, "early forms" of that tradition. The common, precise details will be pointed out in the NOTES on pertinent passages, but they are at most a part of "L" as mentioned above.

Finally, the smaller percentage of Marcan vocabulary means only that Luke has more heavily modified "Mk" at this point in the Gospel. My main hesitations about the claim for the Lucan use of a connected written account independent of "Mk" are two: (i) the three main reasons mentioned above do not conclude absolutely enough; and (ii) the order of the fourteen Lucan pericopes similar to the Marcan would have to postulate an independent source in almost the same order as "Mk"—which is difficult to admit (Occam's razor: *Entia non sunt multiplicanda sine necessitate!*).

The Lucan passion narrative resembles the Marcan in including (a) preliminary events (22:1-38) and (b) the passion, death, and burial of Jesus (22:39-56a). In this it differs from the Johannine narrative, at least as it is sometimes understood by some commentators (e.g. R. E. Brown, who begins the Johannine passion narrative only after the story of the Last Supper *[John XIII-XXI, 787-962]*). In the Synoptics the preliminary events have to be considered part of the passion narrative.

The Lucan passion narrative is concerned to present the destiny of Jesus in a very specific way. The following elements characterize the Lucan form:

a) The setting of the drama is no longer the Temple. The Temple, "my Father's house" (2:49), has been purged in order to become the scene of Jesus' Jerusalem teaching ministry. There Jesus pronounced judgment on Jerusalem itself (21:20) and its leaders (20:19). Now the city Jerusalem and its leaders will pronounce judgment on Jesus. This part of the Gospel opens with the conspiracy of the leaders and will climax in Jesus' trial.

b) Jesus' victory over evil is depicted in the role of Satan, the personification of evil. Having departed from Jesus "for a while" in Luke's story (4:13 [see NOTE there]), he now returns, "entering into Judas" (22:3), seeking to "sift" all the disciples "like wheat" (22:31), and succeeding in making Peter deny Jesus, because it is now his "hour," and his is "the power of darkness" (22:53). (As for whether the intervening Period of Jesus was wholly Satan-free, as H. Conzelmann would have it, or not, see pp. 186-187; cf. S. Brown, *Apostasy and Perseverance,* 6-12.) Satan's involvement in the passion narrative is unique to Luke in the Synoptic tradition; but it is an element that he shares with John (13:2,27—indeed, with specific, precise wording). Hence, it is not primarily the Romans who govern Jesus' fate, but a Satan-possessed disciple, a Palestinian Jewish follower, one "numbered among the Twelve" (22:3). Jesus' victory over Satanic evil, however, is implied in his prayer for Peter (22:31) and in his words to the penitent criminal on the cross (23:43).

c) The Lucan passion narrative shares with the other Synoptic accounts the picture of Jesus serenely facing his death with a realization that it is the Father's will for him (22:39-46). But a specific Lucan expression is given to it in 22:37 at the Last Supper (cf. 24:7,26). This caps all the special Lucan emphasis on Jesus' mercy, forgiveness, healing power, prayer, and compassion. The Lucan Jesus faces death, moreover, not deserted, lonely, and isolated, as in Mark, but attended by lamenting "Daughters of Jerusalem" (23:28), "women who had come with him from Galilee," and "all" his "acquaintances" (23:49). Indeed, the consummate expression of his compassion is made to the penitent criminal as he hangs dying, "Today you shall be with me in Paradise" (23:43). As for the significance of this for the soteriological meaning of Jesus' death, see p. 23.

d) The Lucan passion narrative is a continuation of the travel account in that it is now above all the "way" that Jesus begins to travel in his transit to the Father (recall 9:51; 17:25; cf. 24:7,26). He goes along it in a special sense as precursor, pioneer, and pathfinder—indeed, as one driven by compulsion to face his destiny (see 13:33; 17:25; 22:37). Yet he faces this destiny in Jerusalem as the upright one (23:41,47), and above all willingly (22:42,51).

e) Jesus' victory over Satanic evil also gives to the Lucan passion narrative a hortatory aspect that the other Gospels do not have. According to M. Dibelius *(FTG* 201):

> The suffering Saviour is the Man of God who is attacked by evil powers and who, with His patience and forgiveness, is a model of innocent suffering. Luke regards these events in the place where he consequently puts them not as the completion of salvation, but as the story of a saintly man closely united with God. The literary consequence of this view is that Luke presents the Passion as a martyrdom.

What is mainly affirmed here is correct, the Lucan Jesus does die as "a model of innocent suffering," but he also accomplishes salvation for humanity, even if his death is a form of martyrdom. X. Léon-Dufour has better characterized the Lucan passion narrative as a drama in which the reader is invited to participate, to engage himself like Simon of Cyrene, carrying his own cross behind Jesus:

> The reader is invited, no longer to make a simple act of faith in God who fulfills the Scriptures and in Jesus the Son of God made manifest in his death. Unlike Mark, Luke explains, as does Matthew, the mystery which he unfolds. The reader is no longer specially invited to adore the person of Jesus who presents himself as the Son of God, the all-powerful Lord (Matthew), but to recognize his own weakness with Peter and his malice with all those who have condemned Jesus, to adore the infinite mercy of Jesus . . . and to participate especially in his patience. . . . Jesus is not simply a model; he is the type of the persecuted upright one, resuming in his person the persecution of all times and revealing by his triumph the victory of his own followers. ("Passion," 1476)

(See further pp. 241-243; cf. Acts 14:22.)

IV. *Comment on 22:1-2.* The first episode in the Lucan passion narrative is the notice about the conspiracy of the Jerusalem leaders against Jesus (22:1-2). It is closely followed by the plot of Judas and these leaders (22:3-6 [see COMMENT there]). These initial verses sound an ominous note and serve to mark off this part of the Gospel as the beginning of a new section in it.

The Lucan notice is a redacted form of Mark 14:1-2 and should be compared with the expanded form of the redacted introduction to the Matthean passion narrative (26:1-5). Even those commentators who believe that Luke used an independent connected non-Marcan account in addition to "Mk" usually ascribe these verses (as well as vv. 3-6) to "Mk" (see J. Jeremias, *Die Sprache,* 285; V. Taylor, *Passion Narrative,* 42; T. Schramm, *Markus-Stoff,* 182-184): wholly dependent on Mark. Luke's redaction can be seen in the use of his favorite vb. *engizein,* "be close at hand, draw near" (v. 1) instead of the mere vb. "to be" (Mark 14:1 [see p. 112]). He has also introduced the indirect question (v. 2) with the acc. neut. def. art. *to* (see p. 108). He further eliminates the Marcan detail about "not on the feast day," probably because he realizes that his account (following Mark) will depict the arrest of Jesus happening precisely on that day. He has also omitted the mention of "stealth" *(dolos).*

The usual categories of form criticism have not normally been applied to episodes in the passion narrative, mainly because it was considered a primitive and connected piece of narrative material which the pioneers of form-critical study did not further analyze. But in more recent times it is seen that these parts of the gospel tradition can be analyzed similarly, even though the majority of the episodes will still be part of the narrative tradition (i.e. Stories about Jesus). But some of the Lucan additions will fall into other categories. The conspiracy of the leaders and the plot of Judas, which introduce the passion narrative, do "contain historical narrative," *pace* R. Bultmann *(HST*

262). If there were ever a part of the gospel tradition which must be so characterized, this is it. Even Bultmann had to reject the suggestion of J. M. Robertson (*Jesus and Judas* [London: Watts & Co., 1927]) that the betrayer Judas was an invention of Gentile Christians concocted to discredit Jewish Christians. Moreover, it is far from clear that Mark "invented" the introductory verses which Luke has inherited from him (with redaction), *pace* L. Schenke (*Studien,* 64-66).

The purpose of these initial verses in the Lucan passion narrative is to situate the coming drama of Jesus' last days in Jerusalem in time—in a relationship with a celebration of the solemn national Jewish feast, the yearly Passover. They present once again, in a formal way, the striving of the Jerusalem authorities, the chief priests and the Scribes, to do away with Jesus (recall 11:53-54 [see COMMENT there]; 19:47; 20:1,19). These verses also note the awareness of the authorities about the difference of their reaction to Jesus from that of the ordinary populace. That difference was already noted in 19:48; now it is repeated in terms of "fear," as it was in 20:19.

The occasion of the passion to which Jesus will now be subjected is the Passover (Greek *pascha,* Hebrew *pesaḥ* [see NOTE on 2:41, for its relation to the feast of Unleavened Bread). Because *pascha* is mentioned at the beginning of the passion narrative, it did not take long for a Christian popular etymology of that name to develop. A connection was soon seen between *pascha* and the vb. *paschein,* "suffer" (see Melito of Sardis, *Homily on Pasch.* 46; cf. Irenaeus, *Adv. haer.* 4.10,1; PG 7. 1000). Thus "Passover" and "passion" were related. Eventually, one pressed even further—at the time of the Quartodeciman controversy, when some held that the day of the resurrection (Easter) was to be celebrated on the day of Passover (see Eusebius, *Pasch.* 8; PG 24. 704A). So "paschal" became a designation of something far wider than the day in the Jewish calendar on which the evangelists have located the beginning of their passion narratives.

NOTES

22 1. *the feast of Unleavened Bread, called the Passover.* So Luke identifies the two feasts. Cf. Mark 14:1. See NOTE on 2:41. The pilgrim character of this annual feast would explain the presence of added crowds in Jerusalem. See 22:6,47; 23:4,48. The connection of the events to occur with the Passover finds an echo in the extrabiblical reference to Jesus *(Yēshu)* preserved in the Babylonian Talmud, in a baraita (an "outside" addition to the Mishnaic tradition) found in *b. Sanh.* 43a (third century A.D. at the earliest), which speaks of him as having practiced magic and led Israel into apostasy, as having disciples, and as having been "hanged on the eve of Passover."

was close at hand. Lit. "was drawing close." Mark 14:1 states specifically that it was still two days off. Luke has changed the Marcan specific dating to a more generic reference, speaking only of its "approach," because of his wider interest in the historicization of the Jesus-story. See *FTG* 199-200.

2. *The chief priests and the Scribes.* This phrase, which implicates the Jerusalem authorities, is derived from Mark 14:1. The pair has already been mentioned in 19:47-48. See NOTE there; 20:1,19. Again, it stands in contrast to the people *(ton laon)* of v. 2c. Cf. v. 6.

to do away with Jesus. Thus Luke tones down the starker Marcan description of their concern, "how to arrest him by stealth and kill him." On the vb. *anairein,* "do away with," which occurs here for the first time, see p. 112.

for they were afraid of the people. As in 20:19.

PASSION NARRATIVE: GENERAL BIBLIOGRAPHY

Bammel, E., ed. *The Trial of Jesus.*

Benoit, P. *The Passion and Resurrection of Jesus.*

Bertram, G. *Die Leidensgeschichte Jesu und der Christuskult: Eine formgeschichtliche Untersuchung* (FRLANT ns 15; Göttingen: Vandenhoeck & Ruprecht, 1922).

Bornhäuser, K. *The Death and Resurrection of Christ* (London: [Independent Press], 1958).

Bruce, F. F. "The Book of Zechariah and the Passion Narrative," *BJRL* 43 (1960-1961) 336-353.

Conzelmann, H. "Historie und Theologie in den synoptischen Passionsberichten," *Zur Bedeutung des Todes Jesu: Exegetische Beiträge* (eds. H. Conzelmann et al.; 3d ed.; Gütersloh: G. Mohn, 1968) 35-53.

Delling, G. *Der Kreuztod Jesu in der urchristlichen Verkündigung* (Berlin: Evangelische Verlagsanstalt, 1971).

Dibelius, M. "La signification religieuse des récits évangeliques de la passion," *RHPR* 13 (1933) 30-45.

Donahue, J. R. *Are You the Christ? The Trial Narrative in the Gospel of Mark* (SBLDS 10; Missoula: Scholars, 1973).

Dormeyer, D. *Die Passion Jesu als Verhaltensmodell* (NTAbh ns 11; Münster in W.: Aschendorff, 1974).

Finegan, J. *Die Überlieferung der Leidens- und Auferstehungsgeschichte Jesu* (BZNW 15; Giessen: Töpelmann, 1934).

Gollwitzer, H. *The Dying and Living Lord* (London: SCM, 1960).

Hillmann, W. *Aufbau und Deutung der synoptischen Leidensberichte* (Freiburg im B.: Herder, 1941).

Innitzer, T. *Kommentar zur Leidens- und Verklärungsgeschichte Jesu Christi* (4th ed.; Vienna: Herder, 1948).

Jeremias, J. *Eucharistic Words,* 89-96.

Kähler, M. *The So-Called Historical Jesus and the Historic Biblical Christ* (Philadelphia: Fortress, 1964).

Karavidopoulos, I. *To pathos tou Christou kata ta synoptika euangelia* (Saloniki: St. Theodora, 1974).

Lehmann, M. *Synoptische Quellenanalyse und die Frage nach dem historischen Jesus.*

Léon-Dufour, X. "Autour des récits de la Passion," *RSR* 48 (1960) 489-507.

———— "Passion (Récits de la)," *DBS* 6 (1960) 1419-1492.

Linnemann, E. *Studien.*

Lohse, E. *History.*

Ramsey, M. *The Narratives of the Passion* (Contemporary Studies in Theology 1; London: Mowbray, 1962).

Richardson, P. "The Israel-Idea in the Passion Narratives, *The Trial of Jesus* (ed. E. Bammel) 1-10.

Riedl, J. "Die evangelische Leidensgeschichte und ihre theologische Aussage," *BLit* 41 (1968) 70-111.

Schelkle, K. H. *Die Passion Jesu in der Verkündigung des Neuen Testaments: Ein Beitrag zur Formgeschichte und zur Theologie des Neuen Testaments* (Heidelberg: Kerle, 1949).

Schenke, L. *Der gekreuzigte Christus* (SBS 69; Stuttgart: Katholisches Bibelwerk, 1974).

———— *Studien.*

Schille, G. "Das Leiden des Herrn," *ZTK* 52 (1955) 161-205.

Schmid, J. "Die Darstellung der Passion Jesu in den Evangelien," *Geist und Leben* 27 (1954) 6-15.

Schmidt, K. L. *Der Rahmen der Geschichte Jesu: Literarkritische Untersuchungen zur ältesten Jesusüberlieferung* (Berlin: Trowitzsch & Sohn, 1919; reprinted, Darmstadt: Wissenschaftliche Buchgesellschaft, 1964).

Schneider, G. "Gab es eine vorsynoptische Szene 'Jesus vor dem Synedrium'?" *NovT* 12 (1970) 22-39.

———— *Die Passion Jesu nach den drei älteren Evangelien* (Biblische Handbibliothek 4; Munich: Kösel, 1973).

Schreiber, J. *Die Markuspassion: Wege zur Erforschung der Leidensgeschichte Jesu* (Hamburg: Furche-V., 1969).

Scroggs, R., et al. "Reflections on the Question: Was There a Pre-Markan Passion Narrative? (Report Prepared by the Markan Task Force for the 1971 Meeting of the Society of Biblical Literature)," *Seminar Papers* (2 vols.; Missoula, MT: Scholars, 1971) 2. 503-566.

Sloyan, G. S. *Jesus on Trial: The Development of the Passion Narratives and Their Historical and Ecumenical Implications* (Philadelphia: Fortress, 1973).

Taylor, V. *FGT* 13, 44-62.

———— "The Origin of the Markan Passion-Sayings," *NTS* 1 (1954-1955) 159-167.

Temple, S. "The Two Traditions of the Last Supper, Betrayal, and Arrest," *NTS* 7 (1960-1961) 77-85.

Trilling, W. "Die Passion Jesu in der Darstellung der synoptischen Evangelien," *Lebendiges Zeugnis* 1 (1966) 28-46.

Vanhoye, A. *Structure and Theology of the Accounts of the Passion in the Synoptic Gospels* (Collegeville, MN: Liturgical Press, 1967).

LUCAN PASSION NARRATIVE: GENERAL BIBLIOGRAPHY

Blevins, J. L. "The Passion Narrative: *Luke* 19:28-24:53," *RevExp* 64 (1967) 513-522.
Blinzler, J. "Passionsgeschehn und Passionsbericht des Lukasevangeliums," *BK* 24 (1969) 1-4.
Borgen, P. "John and the Synoptics in the Passion Narrative," *NTS* 5 (1958-1959) 246-259.
Buse, S. I. "St John and the Passion Narratives of St Matthew and St Luke," *NTS* 7 (1960-1961) 65-76.
Creed, J. M. "The Supposed 'Proto-Luke' Narrative of the Trial before Pilate: A Rejoinder," *ExpTim* 46 (1934-1935) 378-379.
Cribbs, F. L. "A Study of the Contacts That Exist between St. Luke and St. John," *SBL 1973 Seminar Papers* (2 vols.; ed. G. W. MacRae; Cambridge, MA: Society of Biblical Literature, 1973) 2. 1-93.
Fransen, I. "Le baptême de sang (Luc 22,1-23,56)," *BVC* 25 (1959) 20-28.
Galizzi, M. "La passione secondo Luca," *Parole di vita* 6 (1971) 444-460.
Kiddle, M. "The Passion Narrative in St Luke's Gospel," *JTS* 36 (1935) 267-280.
Klein, H. "Die lukanisch-johanneische Passionstradition," *ZNW* 67 (1976) 155-186.
Osty, E. "Les points de contact entre le récit de la Passion dans saint Luc et dans saint Jean," *Mélanges Jules Lebreton I* (= *RSR* 39 [1951]) 146-154.
Perry, A. M. "Luke's Disputed Passion-Source," *ExpTim* 46 (1934-1935) 256-260.
––––––– *The Sources of Luke's Passion Narrative* (Chicago: University of Chicago, 1920).
Schneider, G. *Verleugnung,* 11-72, 174-220.
Schramm, T. *Markus-Stoff,* 182-184.
Stöger, A. "Eigenart und Botschaft der lukanischen Passionsgeschichte," *BK* 24 (1969) 4-8.
Taylor, V. *Passion Narrative.*
Vööbus, A. *The Prelude to the Lukan Passion Narrative: Tradition-, Redaction-, Cult-, Motif-Historical and Source-Critical Studies* (Stockholm: ETSE, 1968).
Winter, P. "Sources of the Lucan Passion Narrative," *ExpTim* 68 (1956-1957) 95.
––––––– "The Treatment of His Sources by the Third Evangelist in Luke xxi-xxiv," *ST* 8 (1954) 138-172.

BIBLIOGRAPHY (22:1-2)

Dugmore, C. W. "A Note on the Quartodecimans," *Studia patristica IV* (TU 79; Berlin: Akademie, 1961) 410-421.
Schenke, L. *Studien,* 12-66.
Segal, J. B. *The Hebrew Passover: From the Earliest Times to A.D. 70* (London Oriental Series 12; London/New York: Oxford University, 1963).
Turner, H. E. W. "The Chronological Framework of the Ministry," *Historicity and*

Chronology in the New Testament (eds. D. E. Nineham et al.; Theological Collections 6; London: SPCK, 1965) 59-74, esp. 68-74.

Wambacq, B. N. *"Pesaḥ—Maṣṣôt,"* Bib 62 (1981) 499-518.

Zerafa, P. "Passover and Unleavened Bread," *Ang* 41 (1964) 235-250.

146. THE BETRAYAL OF JESUS BY JUDAS
(22:3-6)

22 ³ Then Satan entered into Judas, who was called Iscariot and was numbered among the Twelve. ⁴ He went off and conferred with the chief priests and the Temple officers about how he might hand Jesus over to them. ⁵ They were very glad and consented to give him a sum of money. ⁶ He agreed and kept seeking for an opportunity to hand him over to them apart from a crowd.

COMMENT

The sequel to the notice about the conspiracy of the chief priests and Scribes to do away with Jesus is the account of his betrayal by Judas Iscariot (22:3-6). In the COMMENT on the preceding episode we have noted how closely related these two episodes are in the Lucan Gospel because of Luke's omission of the anointing of Jesus in Bethany (Mark 14:3-9). He has omitted this episode, probably because of the very similar story in 7:36-50 (see pp. 82, 684-686), possibly also because of its reference to the preaching of "the gospel" (see p. 148), and possibly because in his story the body of Jesus is to be anointed after death (see 23:56-24:1; see further J. Schmid, *The Gospel according to Mark* [Staten Island, NY: Alba House, 1968] 246). Luke has undoubtedly restored the original connection of vv. 1-2 to vv. 3-6 of the more primitive passion narrative (of the pre-Marcan form). See *FTG* 178; G. Schneider, *Evangelium nach Lukas,* 440.

This episode has been derived by Luke from Mark 14:10-11, save for the introductory note of v. 3a about Satan entering Judas (derived probably from "L," since it has a precise echo in the Johannine tradition, 13:27 [cf. 13:2]). Even for V. Taylor, "Mark is Luke's source" *(Passion Narrative,* 44; cf. J. Jeremias, *Die Sprache,* 285). Lucan redaction can be seen in the addition of "the Temple officers" (v. 4), the use of the acc. neut. def. art. *to* before the indir. question (v. 4 [see p. 108]), and the additional phrase at the end "apart from a crowd" (v. 6—only Luke uses the prep. *ater* in the NT [see 22:35]). As does Mark, so Luke recounts the negotiations with Judas in indir. discourse, whereas Matthew (26:14-16) casts it in dir. discourse and embellishes the text with an OT allusion ("thirty pieces of silver" [Zech 11:12]).

Form-critically considered, the episode is another piece of the narrative tradition, a Story about Jesus (see *HST* 262).

The Lucan form of this episode ascribes to Satanic influence the reason why one of Jesus' own disciples, Judas Iscariot, turns against him. The story of opposition to Jesus in this Gospel thus comes to a dramatic climax. He has been rejected not only by the people of his own town (4:28-29), by leaders of his own nation (11:53-54; 19:47-48; 20:1,19), but now even by one of his own disciples—one of those whom he "called" and "chose," one of "the Twelve" (6:12-16). The frequency with which that description of Judas—or something similar to it—appears in the NT, whenever his name is mentioned, stands as a testimony to the horror which early Christians associated with his name (see Luke 6:13,16; Mark 14:10,20,43; John 6:70-71; 12:4). Luke never describes Judas, as does John (12:6), as a "thief" and one who "used to take what was put into" the common purse. Instead, he invokes Satanic influence and lets the bare account of the story of Judas' machinations with the chief priests and Temple officers make its impact on the reader: "He went off," "conferred," "agreed" to take money, and "kept seeking for an opportunity" to hand Jesus over. Baffled as to how he should explain the sinister betrayal of Jesus by one of his own, Luke is the only Synoptic evangelist who makes evil "enter" Judas as "Satan."

Between the plot of Judas to deliver Jesus to the chief priests and the Temple officers (22:3-6) and the arrest itself (22:47-53) stands the scene of Jesus' last intimate meal with his own, the Twelve.

NOTES

22   3. *Satan entered into Judas.* Though Satan has been mentioned in Luke 10:18 (see NOTE there); 11:18; and 13:16, Luke introduces him now in an allusion to 4:13, where he was called "the devil" *(ho diabolos),* who having put Jesus to the test "departed from him for a while." Now he returns explicitly as an explanation of the defection of one of the Twelve and as the cause of the sinister influence that dominates the passion narrative. See 22:31,53. The identical expression, *eisēlthen ho satanas,* occurs in John 13:27. Cf. 13:2; cf. T. Schramm, *Markus-Stoff,* 182. For the protological belief about demons or spirits "entering" people or animals, see Mark 5:12-13; Luke 8:30-32. Cf. *Mart. Isa.* 3:11 ("Beliar dwelt in the heart of Manasseh and in the heart of the princes of Judah and Benjamin and of the eunuchs and councillors of the king" *[APOT* 2. 162]). Cf. 1 Cor 2:8.

Judas, who was called Iscariot. See NOTE on 6:16. Whereas the more Semitic form *Iskariōth* (without a Greek ending) is found in 6:16, the grecized form *Iskariōtēs* is used here.

numbered among the Twelve. Lit. "being of the number of the Twelve." See pp. 253-255. Cf. Acts 4:4; 5:36; 6:7; 11:21; 16:5.

4. *conferred*. I.e. entered into a pact with the chief priests and Temple officers to deliver Jesus to them.

the chief priests and the Temple officers. On "chief priests," see NOTE on 9:22. Instead of "Scribes" (see v. 2) we now read about *stratēgoi*, who appear again in 22:52, where their association with "the Temple" is made clear. In Acts 4:1; 5:24,26 Luke speaks of *stratēgos* (in the sg.), who is probably to be understood as the same as the *stratēgos* of whom Josephus writes, the leader of the Temple guards *(phylakes, J.W.* 6.5,3 § 294; *Ant.* 20.6,2 § 131). This figure was probably the same as the *sāgān* or the *sĕgan hakkôhānîm,* "the captain of the priests," known from later rabbinic tradition *(m. Abot* 3:2; *m. Yoma* 2:1,9). The pl. *stratēgoi* to whom Luke refers (vv. 4,52) are more likely to be understood of the Temple proctors (at least seven of whom were known to function in a regulatory capacity). They may well be the *'ămarkĕlîn* of later tradition, "accountants," related to the Temple treasury (the term *'ămarkĕlîn* is a dissimilated form of *hamarkarayyā',* known from fifth-century B.C. Aramaic papyri *[AP* 26:4,23; *AD* 8:1; 9:1; 10:1,3], a Persian loanword, *hamarakara;* see J. C. Greenfield, "*Hamarakara > 'Amarkal," *W. B. Henning Memorial Volume* [Asia Major Library; London: L. Humphries, 1970] 180-186). If so, it is interesting to see that Luke introduces mention of them in a negotiation in which Judas is to be given money. See further J. Jeremias, *Jerusalem,* 165; G. Schrenk, *TDNT* 3. 270-271; *HJPAJC* 2. 282-283.

hand Jesus over to them. The vb. *paradidonai,* "hand over, deliver," has also appeared in 9:44; 18:32; 21:12,16. See further 22:6,21,22,48; 23:5; 24:7,20.

5. *They were very glad.* Lit. "they rejoiced," as in Mark 14:11.

to give him a sum of money. Lit. "to give him silver." Only Matt 26:15 specifies the amount; Luke follows Mark 14:11. Given the Lucan reaction to money, mammon, and material possessions (see p. 247), this detail takes on a significantly ominous nuance. It specifies the Satanic element in the evil that Judas does.

6. *kept seeking for.* The vb. *ezētei* is in the impf. tense and expresses iterative effort (see BDF § 325) in contrast with the aor. *exōmologēsen,* "he agreed" (punctiliar action). The contrast lies between the pact made and the efforts to execute the details of it.

an opportunity. I.e. since Judas does not yet know of the room in which the Passover meal will be celebrated.

apart from a crowd. Recall 19:48; 20:26. The prep. *ater* occurs only here and in 22:35 in the NT.

BIBLIOGRAPHY (22:3-6)

Brown, S. *Apostasy and Perseverance,* 82-97.

Hein, K. "Judas Iscariot: Key to the Last-Supper Narratives?" *NTS* 17 (1970-1971) 227-232.

Jonge, M. de. "Judas Iskarioth, de verrader," *Homiletica en biblica* 18 (1959) 149-156, 178-181.

——— "Judas Iskarioth, de verrader II: Problemen rondom de Nieuw-Testamen-tische verhalen," ibid. 19 (1960) 38-45.
——— "III. De mens Judas," ibid. 69-80.
Preisker, H. "Der Verrat des Judas und das Abendmahl," *ZNW* 41 (1942) 151-155.
Schenke, L. *Studien,* 119-150.

147. PREPARATION FOR THE PASSOVER MEAL
(22:7-14)

22 ⁷ The day of Unleavened Bread arrived, when the Passover lamb was to be slaughtered, ⁸ and Jesus sent Peter and John with these instructions, "Go and make preparations for us to eat the Passover supper." ⁹ They asked him, "Where do you want us to make the preparations?" ¹⁰ He said, "As soon as you have entered the city, a man carrying a jug of water will meet you. Follow him to the house where he is going, ¹¹ and say to the master of the house, 'The Teacher asks of you, "Where is the guest room where I can eat the Passover supper with my disciples?" ' ¹² He will show you a large room upstairs already furnished; there you will prepare." ¹³ So they went off and found it just as he had told them; and there they made preparations for the Passover supper. ¹⁴ When the hour came, Jesus reclined at table, and the apostles with him.

COMMENT

Luke's passion narrative continues with the story of the preparations for the eating of the Passover meal by Jesus and his apostles (22:7-14). It is a matter of debate whether v. 14 should be included with vv. 7-13 or treated as the opening of the following episode (see *SQE* 430-431). It is, in reality, a minor issue, since it is clearly a transitional verse.

As a whole the episode (vv. 7-14) is a redacted form of Mark 14:12-17; its Matthean counterpart is found in 26:17-20. "Lk. xxii. 7-13 is derived from Mark with no more than editorial and stylistic changes" (V. Taylor, *Passion Narrative,* 46); similarly, H. Schürmann, who has engaged in a minute analysis of the entire passage *(Der Paschamahlbericht,* 76-104). Apart from minor details (for which see H. Schürmann, ibid.), the Lucan redaction consists mainly in making Jesus take the initiative in sending the two disciples and in identifying them as Peter and John (v. 8 is wholly of Lucan composition;

contrast Mark 14:12b-13, where unnamed disciples pose the question to Jesus and two of them are sent off). Schürmann (ibid. 107-110) regards v. 14 likewise as a redacted form of Mark 14:17 (cf. H. J. Cadbury, *Style and Literary Method of Luke,* 105), whereas F. Rehkopf *(Sonderquelle,* 91-106), V. Taylor *(Passion Narrative,* 48-49), and others would ascribe it to the non-Marcan continuous source. This diversity of opinion about one verse merely highlights the subjectivity involved in such analysis. There is, however, enough Lucan vocabulary in the verse to justify the view that it is a redactional form of "Mk." The only striking element in it is the use of *hōra,* "hour," which rings with a Johannine tone (see John 13:1).

From a form-critical viewpoint the episode is again part of the narrative gospel tradition, a Story about Jesus. R. Bultmann *(HST* 264) considers the passage as a not independent unit of tradition, "a secondary composition" which presupposes "a story of the Passover meal" and which has been written to fit it. (Cf. L. Schenke, *Studien,* 181-194.) Bultmann further compares Jesus' foreknowledge in it with that of Samuel sending off Saul in 1 Sam 10:2-13. There may be some similarity between Jesus' and Samuel's foretelling, but in the latter case telling Saul what he would encounter was to be *a sign* for him that Yahweh had anointed Saul to be a prince over his people—a detail without any meaning in this episode (Jesus' foreknowledge is without sign value). Indeed, one may wonder who sees the connection between Jesus and Samuel, Bultmann or the evangelist? In this Gospel Luke is merely using a detail that he inherits from the Marcan account.

The Lucan episode is in itself simple in purpose and intent: it is introductory to the following episode, the account of the Last Supper. The Lucan emphasis is on Jesus taking the initiative on the parasceve (the day of preparation), solicitous to celebrate the yearly feast of Passover with his chosen apostles according to OT prescriptions: "at the place the Lord God chooses, to make his name dwell in it. . . . There you shall offer the Passover sacrifice, in the evening at the going down of the sun, at the time you came out of Egypt" (Deut 16:6). At least since the days of King Josiah it was to be eaten in the court of the Jerusalem Temple (2 Chr 35:16-19; cf. *Jub.* 49:15-16); but in time because of the number of pilgrims, that injunction was interpreted to mean the city of Jerusalem, after the lambs had been slaughtered in the forecourt of the Temple. Luke has inherited the detail of Jesus' prophetic foreknowledge about the man with the jug of water and the master of the house from "Mk." There is no way of telling whether or not either evangelist intends the reader to think that Jesus had made a prior arrangement with the master; such an interpretation cannot be ruled out.

The reason for Jesus' desire to eat the Passover meal with his apostles will emerge in the next episode. The directions given to Peter and John may seem vague, but in the course of the story it is evident that they are so formulated as to prevent Judas from learning the place where Jesus will be "apart from a crowd" (v. 6).

The reader will detect a certain similarity in this episode to that of the story of Jesus' regal entry into the Jerusalem Temple, especially in the sending of two disciples (in that case, unnamed) to find the colt (19:29). The similarity means no more than that the tradition stems from a commonly authored source; indeed, the sending of emissaries (human or divine) in pairs is of ancient custom.

Lastly, the emphasis on Jesus' foreknowledge in the episode is merely an example of the control over elements in the passion that is ascribed to Jesus, one of the motifs in the passion narratives (see p. 1363).

Though the episode in itself is without complication, it raises three classic problems when it is considered with other elements in the passion narrative: (1) Was the so-called Last Supper a Passover meal? (2) How is it related to the Johannine tradition about the Last Supper? (3) According to what calendar is "the day of Unleavened Bread" to be reckoned? Some brief comments on each of these questions have to be made.

1) The term "Last Supper" is never found in the NT itself. It has been developed from the reference to Jesus' "dining" with his disciples "on the night on which he was betrayed" (1 Cor 11:23-25; cf. John 13:1-2). Paul is clearly aware of a rite being celebrated among early Christians ca. A.D. 56 (1 Cor 10:16-21), which he eventually calls "the Lord's Supper" (11:20) and relates to his own account of the actions and words of Jesus on the night of his betrayal. This account he had inherited from earlier tradition. Though in those passages of 1 Corinthians 10-11 no mention is made of the Last Supper as a Passover meal, Paul seems to be aware already of a Passover-interpretation of that Last Supper when he speaks of "Christ, our Passover lamb" (RSV, to pascha hēmōn . . . Christos, 5:7) in a context dealing with "leaven" and further mentions "the cup of blessing" (10:16), probably alluding to the cup of wine over which a thanksgiving was uttered at the end of the Passover meal (see Str-B 3. 419; 4. 628, 630).

The Synoptic evangelists present that Last Supper as a Passover meal (Mark 14:1-2,12-17; Luke 22:1,7-14; Matt 26:2,5,17-20), and Luke more pronouncedly than the others. The disciples clearly prepare for a meal to be eaten at sundown, at the end of the fourteenth day of the first month, Nisan (= March-April), as the Passover itself (15 Nisan) is beginning. Moreover, according to the Synoptic Gospels Jesus is arrested that same night (Mark 14:26,43-46,53; Luke 22:39,47-54; Matt 26:30,47-50,57) and put to death in the course of the following day, still 15 Nisan (Mark 15:1,15,37; Luke 22:66-23:1,25,46; Matt 27:1,26,50). Further, that day is said explicitly to have been "the day of preparation, the day before the Sabbath" (Mark 15:42; Luke 23:54-56; cf. Matt 27:62). In other words, that year Passover (15 Nisan) coincided with the parasceve of a Sabbath (what we would call a Friday). All of this suggests that the Last Supper that Jesus ate with his disciples was a Passover meal.

2) The date of the Last Supper in the Johannine tradition is, however, differently reckoned. John 13:1 speaks of Jesus with "his own" eating a supper "before the feast of Passover" (13:1-2). That notice is vague enough, but after the supper Jesus is taken captive (18:2-3,12-13) and on the next day he is led to Pilate's praetorium, which his captors refuse to enter lest they defile themselves and not be able to eat the Passover meal at the coming sundown (18:28). Jesus is crucified and dies "on the day of preparation of the Passover" (19:14). In 19:31 it is further explained as the day before a "Sabbath," indeed even annotated as "a solemn feast day" *(megalē hē hēmera),* i.e. a doubly holy feast, being both a Sabbath and a Passover (see R. E. Brown, *John, XIII-XXI,* 934). This Johannine tradition suggests, therefore, that Jesus ate the Last Supper at sundown on 13 Nisan, as the parasceve of Passover and of a Sabbath (14 Nisan) was beginning, i.e. a day before the date in the Synoptic tradition. Though both traditions, Synoptic and Johannine, date the death of Jesus to the eve of a Sabbath, the Johannine tradition implies that the Last Supper was not a meal eaten at the start of a Passover. This discrepancy between the Synoptic and Johannine traditions has given rise to the classic debate about whether the last meal which the historical Jesus ate with his disciples "on the night on which he was betrayed" was a Passover meal or not.

The liturgical tradition has followed the Johannine, celebrating the feast of the Lord's Supper on a Thursday and the day of his death on a Friday—in the latter case it follows the Synoptic tradition as well. The difference between the Synoptic and Johannine traditions, the eating of the Last Supper at the beginning of Passover or the evening before, has often been given a *theological* interpretation: The Synoptics date the Last Supper to sundown at the beginning of 15 Nisan because they wanted to enhance that meal with Passover connotations, whereas the Johannine tradition, which had earlier identified Jesus as "the Lamb of God" (1:29,36), sought to depict him going to his death about the hour when the Passover lambs would have been slaughtered —before the sundown at which Passover (15 Nisan) would begin (recall further John 19:31-37, esp. v. 36b, with its quotation of the OT prescription of not breaking a bone of the Passover lamb, Exod 12:46c). Whichever interpretation may be valid, a problem still remains about the date of this historical Last Supper and its Passover-character. (See further J. Jeremias, *Eucharistic Words,* 220-225.)

3) In recent times another solution to the difference in the traditions has been proposed, viz. a calendaric explanation. The Jewish priests (John 18:13-14,28) would have been following an official calendar, whereas Jesus and his followers would have been using a different calendar. For some scholars the former would have been the Sadducee calendar, whereas the latter would

have been the Pharisaic calendar (e.g. G. Ricciotti, *The Life of Christ* [Milwaukee, WI: Bruce, 1947] 567-568; Str-B 2. 847-853). For others, the former would have been a Judean calendar, whereas the latter would have been a Galilean calendar (e.g. M.-J. Lagrange, *The Gospel of Jesus Christ* [2 vols.; New York: Benziger, 1939] 2. 195). But these explanations are hypothetical and speculative; there is no evidence that these postulated calendars existed in first-century Palestine.

More recently, however, it has been discovered that some Jews of first-century Palestine (Essenes) were indeed using an older solar calendar of 364 days, which differed from an "official" calendar, which was lunar or luni-solar. The solar calendar has been traced to passages in the OT which speak merely of (for example) "the first month, the fourteenth day" (Lev 23:5). Traces of it may be found in intertestamental writings such as *1 Enoch* and *Jubilees* (see the writings of A. Jaubert and E. Ruckstuhl in the BIBLIOGRAPHY on p. 1385; but cf. R. T. Beckwith, "The Earliest Enoch Literature and Its Calendar: Marks of Their Origin, Date and Motivation," *RevQ* 10 [1980-1981] 365-403; J. C. VanderKam, "The Origin, Character and Early History of the 364-Day Calendar," *CBQ* 41 [1979] 390-411; "2 Macc 6:7a and Calendrical Change in Jerusalem," *JSJ* 12 [1981] 1-23; P. R. Davies, "Calendrical Change and Qumran Origins," *CBQ* 45 [1983] 80-89). The clearest reference to its existence is found in 11QPs[a] 27:6-7 ("David's Compositions"): He wrote "songs to sing before the altar over the whole-burnt *tamid* offering every day, for all the days of the year, 364" (DJD 4. 48, 92). That this calendar was in conflict with another has been deduced from 1QpHab 11:4-8, which tells of the "Wicked Priest," some enemy of the Essene community of Qumran, who not only persecuted their Teacher of Righteousness but even appeared on "the feast of rest of the Day of Atonement" in their "place of exile." The text raises the question how a priest (of Jerusalem?) could travel to Qumran on a solemn feast, if another calendar were not being followed. A strong case has been made for the existence of a calendar being employed by some Palestinian Jews that differed from the one normally used.

Utilizing such evidence, A. Jaubert has proposed that the Synoptics would be depicting Jesus preparing for the Passover meal and eating it according to the Essene calendar, whereas he would have been put to death (as in the Johannine story) on the eve of Passover according to the "official" calendar. She would reconstruct the details of the week thus:

Solar Calendar		*Luni-solar (official) Calendar*
Tues.—Before sundown	14 Nisan: Preparation for the Passover (Mark 14:12-16)	
About sundown	15 Nisan: Last Supper (Passover meal, Mark 14:17-25)	12 Nisan

Night	Arrest; Interrogation before Annas (Mark 14:53a; John 18:13); Peter's Denials Led to Caiaphas (John 18:24)	
Wed.—Before sundown	15 Nisan: First Appearance before the Sanhedrin (Mark 14:55)	12 Nisan
At sundown	16 Nisan	13 Nisan
Thurs.—Before sundown	16 Nisan: Second Appearance before the Sanhedrin (Mark 15:1a) Jesus is led to Pilate (Mark 15:1b) Jesus is sent to Herod (Luke 23:6-12) People are stirred up to demand Barabbas' release (Mark 15:11)	13 Nisan
At sundown	17 Nisan	14 Nisan
Night	Dream of Pilate's Wife (Matt 27:19)	
Fri.—Before sundown	17 Nisan: Jesus is led to Pilate again (Luke 23:13) Barabbas released (Mark 15:15) Jesus delivered to be crucified; death on the cross (Mark 15:15-37)	14 Nisan: Preparation for the Passover (John 18:28)
At sundown	18 Nisan: Sabbath Jesus in the tomb (Mark 15:42-46)	15 Nisan: Sabbath and Passover (John 19:31)
Sat.—Before sundown	18 Nisan: Sabbath Jesus in the tomb	15 Nisan: Sabbath

According to this solution, Jesus would have eaten the Last Supper according to the solar (Essene) calendar (about sundown on 15 Nisan, Tuesday evening) and been crucified according to the luni-solar calendar (on 14 Nisan, the preparation day of both the Passover and the Sabbath).

Initial reactions to the Jaubert proposal were favorable; but they came mainly from OT scholars and conservative NT interpreters. It was eventually recognized that there are many problems with it, among which the two main ones are these: (a) There is no indication elsewhere in the gospel tradition that Jesus was following a solar calendar in opposition to the luni-solar (official) calendar. Indeed, the only way that anything might be established in this regard comes solely from the Johannine Gospel, where he seems to have celebrated three Passovers. (b) The harmonization of the Synoptic and Johannine material in the proposal rides roughshod over the long-accepted analyses of so many of the passages involved according to form-critical methods that it cannot be taken seriously. Moreover, in this regard it manifests an unmistakably fundamentalist concern. For further difficulties with the proposal, see the articles of P. Benoit, J. Blinzler, H. Braun, R. E. Brown, and J. Delorme in the BIBLIOGRAPHY on p. 1385. The upshot is that we cannot answer the question when the historical Jesus ate the Last Supper or whether he ate it as a Passover meal. But that is a problem of Stage I of the gospel tradition. There is no doubt, however, that in the Lucan Gospel the Last Supper is understood as a Passover meal, and so it must be interpreted in this form of Stage III of that tradition. No attempt should be made to harmonize the Synoptic and Johannine traditions.

NOTES

22 7. *The day of Unleavened Bread arrived.* For the relation of the feast of Unleavened Bread to Passover, see NOTES on 22:1 and 2:41. The notice stands in contrast to v. 1, which spoke only of its approach. Luke's redaction of Mark 14:12 has eliminated somewhat the difficulty sensed in the Marcan text, which mentions the "first day of Unleavened Bread, when they used to slaughter the Passover lamb." The words of G. Dalman *(Jesus—Jeshua,* 105) have often been quoted apropos of that Marcan verse: "No instructed Jew could have called the eve of the Feast 'the first day of the Feast'; only a Gentile could possibly have thought of the day of the offering of the Passover lamb and the night of the Passover meal as the first day of the Feast." The Lucan formulation removes some of the problem, but then it has been said that it gives the impression that the feast of Unleavened Bread lasted for only one day. That is probably the reason for the changes in some mss.; Codex Bezae and the OL and OS versions have "of Passover" instead of "of Unleavened Bread." But what is probably operative in both the Marcan and Lucan formulations is popular (inexact) usage. Cp. Josephus, *J.W.* 5.3,1 § 99; *Mekilta* 3:24-27 (on Exod 12:15).

when the Passover lamb was to be slaughtered. Lit. "when it was necessary for the Passover lamb to be slaughtered." Luke follows Mark 14:12 in using *to pascha* in the sense of "Passover lamb." See the LXX of Exod 12:21; Deut 16:2,6; Ezra 6:20. For the "necessity" stemming from the pentateuchal prescription, see Exod 12:6, the MT of which reads, "and the whole assembly of Israel shall kill it between the two evenings," which came to mean "at twilight," and then roughly from 2:30-5:30 P.M. In the first century this was to be done in the court of the priests, by the *paterfamilias* or his representative. As I. H. Marshall *(Luke,* 791) notes, the vb. *thyein* "carries a sacrificial sense in this context." Cf. the LXX of Exod 16:6, where *thyein* renders Hebrew *zbḥ,* used of the Passover.

8. *Peter and John.* The "two of his disciples" (Mark 14:13) who are sent off by Jesus become in the Lucan redaction of the story Peter and John. John the son of Zebedee is meant. See NOTES on 6:14. They are two of the trio often mentioned in the Lucan story. See 8:51; 9:28; cf. Acts 3:1,3,4,11; 4:13,19; 8:14. They are the two most important disciples of Jesus in that story, and those who will become the "leaders" are now made to "serve." See 22:26; cf. H. Schürmann ("Der Dienst"), who concedes that these names are not to be ascribed to a non-Marcan source. Luke has added them in

his redaction. (One wonders why Mark would have omitted them, if he were abbreviating Luke according to the Griesbach hypothesis.)

to eat the Passover supper. Or "to eat the Passover lamb," as in v. 7. Lit. "going, prepare for us the Passover supper/lamb that we may eat (it)." H. Chadwick ("The Shorter Text of Luke XXII. 15-20," *HTR* 50 [1957] 257) thought that "to eat the *pascha*" was an "odd" expression, because in the LXX "the *pascha* is either 'sacrificed' or 'done.'" But C. K. Barrett ("Luke XXII. 15: To Eat the Passover," *JTS* 9 [1958] 305-307) has shown that "to eat" the *pascha* is also a good ancient expression. See Exod 12:11 (MT, LXX, *Tg. Onq.);* 12:43-46; Num 9:11; Deut 16:7; 2 Chr 30:18; Ezra 6:21; cf. *Jub.* 49:1-2,6,9,12-13,16-17,20; Philo, *Quis rer. div. heres* 51 § 255.

9. *Where do you want us to make the preparations?* The "traditional request" (M.-J. Lagrange, *Luc,* 541) is picked up by Luke from the Marcan source.

10. *As soon as you have entered.* Luke eliminates the parataxis of Mark 14:13b, substituting for it *idou* ("behold") and a gen. absol. See p. 108. However, the "absolute" character of the cl. is not preserved, for Luke follows it up with the dat. pron. *hymin,* "you" (obj. of "meet").

a man carrying a jug of water. Lit. "a human being *(anthrōpos)* . . .";* but to use the latter meaning would deprive the saying of its intent, since the meeting of a person with a jug of water would not necessarily be as out of the ordinary as the saying seems to imply, a "man" carrying a jug of water. That may well have been a task for a woman in first-century Palestine. See Gen 24:11; John 4:7. Jesus' foreknowledge is evident, in the detail that Luke has preserved from Mark. But cf. Matt 26:18: "Go into the city to so-and-so," which clearly implies prearrangement on the part of Jesus.

where he is going. Lit. "into which he enters." Some mss. (D, W, Θ, 063, *f*[1.13], and the Koine text-tradition) actually read *hou,* "where." The better reading, however, is *eis hēn* (mss. ℵ, B, C, L, Ψ, etc.).

11. *the master of the house.* Lit. "the house-master of the house." It is a mystery why Luke, who is usually careful with his language, has added *tēs oikias,* which is not in the Marcan source. It introduces an unneeded pleonasm. See BDF § 484. The master is to be understood as someone different from the man who was carrying the jug of water.

The Teacher asks of you. Lit. "the Teacher says to you." Such an identification is sufficient, either because of a previous arrangement of Jesus' or because the master is to be understood as a disciple. Recall the similar directive of 19:31. On "Teacher," see p. 218; cf. F. Hahn, *Titles,* 80.

the guest room. The n. *katalyma* has been used in Luke 2:7 in the sense of "lodge." See NOTE there. The reader of the Greek text would catch it as an echo.

eat the Passover supper. See NOTE on v. 8.

12. *a large room upstairs.* Lit. "a big room-under/on-the-roof," depending on the shape of the Palestinian house. Ms. D reads *oikon,* "a house," and ms. Θ has *oikon mega,* "a great house"(?).

already furnished. The detail is derived from Mark 14:15. In LXX Ezek 23:41 *klinē estrōmenē,* "a spread couch," suggests the cushions needed for reclining at table.

13. *and found it just as he had told them.* The Lucan redaction strips down the description of what Peter and John found.

made preparations. I.e. they bought the lamb, had it slaughtered and roasted; they would have had to prepare the other victuals too, as well as arrange the room for the thirteen.

14. *When the hour came.* I.e. sundown of 14 Nisan, when the feast of Passover (15 Nisan) was beginning. The term *hōra* does not mean merely "evening" (see Mark 14:17), but carries a salvation-history connotation. Cf. 22:53b. At a critical moment in that history Jesus celebrates the Last Supper with his apostles—a supper to which the Christian Eucharist is related.

reclined at table. The practice of standing at the Passover meal, ready for a hasty departure (see Exod 12:11), had long since been given up. The reclining at table at the Passover meal was taken as "a ritual duty," "a symbol of freedom . . . for the poorest man in Israel" *(m. Pesah.* 10:1). See J. Jeremias, *Eucharistic Words,* 48-49. Luke used the vb. *anapiptein* for "reclining" at a meal in 11:37; 14:10; 17:7.

and the apostles with him. I.e. "reclined with him"; no vb. is expressed in the elliptical cl. For Luke the "apostles" are the Twelve whom he called and so named in 6:13-16. This is part of Luke's redaction of Mark 14:17, which speaks rather of "with the Twelve." *Hoi apostoloi* is the reading of mss. P⁷⁵, ℵ*, B, D, and of the OL and OS versions. However, the corrector of ms. ℵ and mss. L, 1241 read instead *dōdeka,* "the Twelve," harmonizing the text with Mark and Matthew. A second corrector of ms. ℵ added *dōdeka* to *hoi apostoloi,* creating "the Twelve apostles," a conflate reading which is found in many mss. of the Koine text-tradition besides C, A, W, Θ, and f¹·¹³. See NOTE on 6:13 and pp. 253-255.

BIBLIOGRAPHY (22:7-14)

Black, M. "The Arrest and Trial of Jesus and the Date of the Last Supper," *New Testament Essays: Studies in Memory of Thomas Walter Manson 1893-1958* (ed. A. J. B. Higgins; Manchester: Manchester University, 1959) 19-33.

Dalman, G. *Jesus—Jeshua: Studies in the Gospels* (London: SPCK 1929; reprinted, New York: Ktav, 1971) 86-184.

Edanad, A. "Institution of the Eucharist according to the Synoptic Gospels," *Bible Bhashyam* 4 (1978) 322-332.

Foster, J. " 'Go and Make Ready' (Luke xxii.8, John xiv.2)," *ExpTim* 63 (1951-1952) 193.

MacMillan, H. "The Man Bearing a Pitcher of Water: Luke xxii. 10," *ExpTim* 3 (1891-1892) 58-60.

Schenke, L. *Studien,* 152-198.

Schürmann, H. "Der Abendmahlsbericht Lk 22,7-38 als Gottesdienstordnung, Gemeindeordnung, Lebensordnung," *Ursprung und Gestalt,* 108-150; *Le récit de la dernière cène, Luc 22,7-38: Une règle de célébration eucharistique, une règle communautaire, une règle de vie* (Le Puy: X. Mappus, 1966).

—— "Der Dienst des Petrus und Johannes," *TTZ* 60 (1951) 99-101; reprinted, *Ursprung und Gestalt,* 274-276.

—— *Der Paschamahlbericht Lk 22, (7-14.) 15-18.*

Winter, P. "Luke 22, 7-18," *Vox theologica* 26 (1955-1956) 88-91.

Zerwick, M. "Praehistoria textus sacri—cui bona?" *VD* 36 (1958) 154-160.

BIBLIOGRAPHY ON THE DATE OF THE LAST SUPPER

Benoit, P. "La date de la cène," *Exégèse et théologie,* 1. 255-261.

Blinzler, J. "Qumran-Kalender und Passionschronologie," *ZNW* 49 (1958) 238-251.

Braun, H. *Qumran und das Neue Testament* (2 vols.; Tübingen: Mohr [Siebeck], 1966) 2. 43-54.

Brown, R. E. "The Problem of Historicity in John," *New Testament Essays* (Milwaukee, WI: Bruce, 1965) 143-167, esp. 160-167.

Delorme, J. "Jésus a-t-il pris la dernière cène le mardi soir?" *Ami du clergé* 67 (1957) 218-223, 229-234.

Jaubert, A. "Le calendrier des Jubilés et de la secte de Qumrân: Ses origines bibliques," *VT* 3 (1953) 250-264.

———— "Le calendrier des Jubilés et les jours liturgiques de la semaine," *VT* 7 (1957) 35-61.

———— "La date de la dernière Cène," *RHR* 146 (1954) 140-173.

———— *The Date of the Last Supper* (Staten Island, NY: Alba House, 1965).

Ruckstuhl, E. *Chronology of the Last Days of Jesus: A Critical Study* (New York: Desclée, 1965).

(For further bibliography, both on the Essene calendar itself and on its relation to the NT accounts of the Last Supper, see my book *The Dead Sea Scrolls: Major Publications and Tools for Study* [SBLSBS 8; Missoula, MT: Scholars, 1977] 131-132, 136-137.)

148. THE LAST SUPPER
(22:15-20)

22 ¹⁵ Jesus said to them, "How *intensely have I desired*[a] to eat this Passover supper with you before I suffer! ¹⁶ For I tell you, never again shall I eat it until it has found its fulfillment in the kingdom of God." ¹⁷ Then he took a cup, and after giving thanks said, "Take this and divide it among yourselves; ¹⁸ for I tell you, from now on I shall not drink of the fruit of the vine until the kingdom of God comes." ¹⁹ Then he took up some bread, and after giving thanks, broke it, and gave it to them, saying, "This is my body, which is given for you. Do

[a] Gen 31:30

this in remembrance of me." [20] And he did the same with the cup after the meal, saying, "This cup is the new covenant with my blood, which is poured out for you."

COMMENT

The Lucan Passion narrative continues with the account of Jesus' Last Supper (22:15-20). In it Jesus celebrates the Passover meal and reinterprets it, sharing bread and wine with his apostles, giving these elements a new meaning, and instructing them to repeat such a meal in memory of him in future times. Though it seems to be a straightforward account, "the Lucan account of the Last Supper is a scholar's paradise and a beginner's nightmare" (G. B. Caird, *Gospel of St Luke,* 237).

Notoriously different is this account of the Last Supper from that preserved in the Johannine Gospel, where five long chapters are devoted to it (13-17). There it records a meal that Jesus took with "his own," during which he performs a symbolic act (washing the feet of those present as "an example" [13:15] of the service that sums up his own life), announces his betrayal by one of those intimate with him (13:2-3,18-19,27-30), and delivers a lengthy, composite farewell discourse (13:31-17:26). The Johannine account clearly enshrines the way the Last Supper was recalled in the community of the Beloved Disciple and differs considerably from the Synoptic accounts, which have in general little to do with it. Where there are scattered contacts, they significantly appear more with the Lucan than with the Marcan or Matthean accounts.

The Lucan account has its counterpart in Mark 14:22-25 (and Matt 26:26-29), being almost twice as long as either of the other Synoptic accounts. Though inspired by the Marcan account, Luke has done two main things in this passage: (1) He has transposed the mention of Judas' betrayal (Mark 14:18-21), slightly changing the Marcan order (see p. 71) to create a better "discourse" after the meal itself. He thus relates Jesus' words about Judas to three other sayings, casting them all in a form of a farewell discourse. (2) He has substituted for the Marcan account of the Last Supper proper a form derived from "L" (certainly for vv. 15-17 and 19cd,20, and probably also for v. 18 [one may hesitate about the latter because of its similarity to Mark 14:25]). It is impossible that vv. 15-18 are a mere reworking of Mark 14:25, *pace* G. Schneider *(Evangelium nach Lukas,* 444), or that vv. 19-20 are dependent on 1 Cor 11:24-25. In the first case, the work of H. Schürmann *(Der Paschamahlbericht,* 1-74) is telling (cf. V. Taylor, *Passion Narrative,* 49-50; J. Jeremias, *Die Sprache,* 286-288)—one does not have to conclude that vv. 15-18 once formed part of a *continuous* passion narrative derived from a non-Marcan source. In the latter case, Luke does not depend on the Pauline parallel—which would imply that Luke had read the Pauline letter (see pp. 28, 51). The Pauline parallel gives evidence only of a pre-Lucan source used by Luke. Verse 19ab, however, is a clear reworking of Mark 14:22; apart from that partial verse, the rest of vv. 19-20 is to be ascribed to "L." (Cf. H. Schürmann, *Der Einsetzungsbericht,* 17-81.)

Lucan redaction can be seen in the use of *eipen* with *pros* + acc. (v. 15a); possibly in the Septuagintism *epithymiā epethymēsa* (v. 15b), though H. Schürmann *(Der Paschamahlbericht,* 5-7) prefers to consider it pre-Lucan; in the use of the prep. *pro* + gen. of the articular infin. (see J. Jeremias, *Die Sprache,* 286); and in the absolute use of *pathein* in the sense of "suffer" (death—cf. 24:46; Acts 1:3; 3:18; 17:3). This redaction is minimal. (Cf. G. Schneider, *Evangelium nach Lukas,* 437.)

Form-critically considered, this episode is again a piece of the narrative tradition, a Story about Jesus. That the account, in Mark as well as in Luke, has been influenced by a liturgical tradition is to be admitted, without necessarily borrowing the pejorative connotation of R. Bultmann's "cult legend" (used of Mark 14:22-25, *HST* 265). Bultmann may, however, be right in calling the Lucan account an "older tradition . . . preserved in a more complete form" and having "the original connection with the preparation of the [Passover] meal (Lk. 22⁷⁻¹³)" *(HST* 265-266). Because Bultmann considers vv. 19-20 "an interpolation in its entirety" *(HST* 266 n. 1), his view is now antiquated and vitiates the rest of his analysis of the Lucan passage and its alleged "parallelism." We do not know why the Johannine Gospel lacks any real counterpart to this section of the Synoptic tradition. The scene in John 13 is, indeed, "not thought of as a Passover"; but that may be due to the chronological problem discussed above (see p. 1379). There is certainly no evidence that the Johannine Gospel preserves "a more primitive account of the Last Supper"; the emphasis lies on something else (see p. 1379). That there is an "aetiological" aspect to the Synoptic accounts of the Last Supper, especially to the Lucan, may well be admitted, in that the evangelist(s) sought to anchor the celebration of the Lord's Supper or the Eucharist in these accounts—but there is a sense in which that is true of the entire Lucan Gospel (see p. 9).

Before we continue with further analysis of the Lucan account of the Last Supper, we must remark on the text-critical problem involved in this episode, since it is probably the most notorious one in the entire Gospel. It mainly concerns vv. 19b-20 (or, more accurately, 19cd-20): " '. . . which is given for you. Do this in remembrance of me.' And he did the same with the cup after the meal, saying, 'This cup is the new covenant with my blood, which is poured out for you.' "

The textual evidence for these verses is complicated and, in some cases, involves vv. 17-18 as well. Six forms of the text-tradition are known:

a) The so-called long text (vv. 17-20, as given in my translation), read in mss. P[75], ℵ, A, B, C, K, L, T, W, X, Δ, Θ, Π, Ψ, 063, *f*[1,13], many minuscules, and ancient versions (Vg, Syr[Pal], Coptic, Armenian, and Georgian).

b) The so-called short text (vv. 17,18,19ab, in my translation, down to and including "This is my body"), read in ms. D and in mss. underlying some of those of the OL version (a, d, ff[2], i, l).

These variants (a and b) are the two main contenders; the rest of the variants are abridged and/or conflate forms of a and b.

c) Verses 19ab,17,18 of my translation, read in mss. b,e of the OL version (sometimes with a difference of a word or two).

d) Verses 19,17,18 of my translation (with "given" omitted and some words in a different order), read in the Curetonian OS version.

e) Verses 19,20a ("and after the meal"),17,20b ("This is my blood, the new covenant" [no cup mentioned]),18, read in the Sinaitic OS version.

f) Verses 19-20 (vv. 17-18 being omitted), read in the Syriac Peshitta and some copies of the Bohairic version.

When B. F. Westcott and F. J. A. Hort published a critical text of the Greek NT in 1881, they preferred the short text, considering vv. 19cd-20 to be one of the "Western Non-Interpolations" and therefore bracketing them (see pp. 130-131). Given the lengthy list of external witnesses to the long text, one wonders today why Westcott and Hort were able to exert such influence, for their decision was followed by other critical texts (e.g. Nestle [up to the 25th ed.], British and Foreign Bible Societies, 2d ed.), versions (e.g. *RSV* [up to 1972], *NEB),* and numerous scholars (e.g. F. C. Burkitt, H. Chadwick, J. M. Creed, G. D. Kilpatrick, E. Klostermann, M. Rese, C. H. Talbert, A. Vööbus). At length, some text-critics and commentators began to question the Westcott and Hort decision (e.g. P. Benoit, J. C. Cooper, A. R. Eagar, E. E. Ellis, J. Ernst, F. Hahn, J. Jeremias [having once preferred the short text], F. G. Kenyon, W. G. Kümmel, P. Parker, K. T. Schaefer, H. Schürmann, B. H. Throckmorton, Jr.). Verses 19cd-20 are restored to full status by K. Aland in N-A[26] and by H. Greeven in his new edition of Huck's *Synopse der drei ersten Evangelien* (Tübingen: Mohr [Siebeck], 1981) 248, as well as in the last edition of the NT in the *RSV, NAB,* and *NIV.* In favor of the long text is not only the overwhelming number of Greek mss. which support it, but the principle of *lectio difficilior,* which restores the two cups to the Lucan account. The real objection against it is the difficulty of explaining the genesis of the other, shorter or conflate, readings, if the long text were the original. But even though the evidence in the OL and OS versions might seem to argue for an early date for this tradition, it is still suspect *(pace* A. Vööbus, *The Prelude,* 86-87), because it does not explain the widespread use of the long text. The rating of "C" given in *UBSGNT*[3] 302 is decidedly too low; it should be a "B" at least (see p. 131). See further *TCGNT* 173-177.

Once one recognizes that vv. 19cd-20 are really part of the Lucan account of the Last Supper, one can better reckon with this Lucan unit (vv. 15-20). It contains in reality two parts: (a) vv. 15-18, Jesus' celebration of the Passover Supper; and (b) vv. 19-20, Jesus' reinterpretation of that meal, or his institution of the Lord's Supper. The first part, vv. 15-18, is clearly marked by a parallelism, vv. 15-16 and vv. 17-18 (in each case the second verse supplies a reason [introduced by "For I tell you"] and relates what is being done to the kingdom of God, understood eschatologically). A different parallelism can be seen in vv. 19 and 20 (words over the bread and words over the cup after the meal). Part *a* (vv. 15-18) also contains clearer traces of the elements of a Passover meal than do the parallel accounts in the other Synoptics. Above (pp. 1379-1382) we discussed the calendaric problem about the dating of the Last Supper that the historical Jesus would have eaten; its Passover character is often denied, however, for other reasons than the mere dating problem (see, among other things, NOTE on *to pascha* at 22:7). References to the Passover in Mark 14:22-25 are vague, if existent at all, whereas in this Lucan passage there is explicit mention of *to pascha* (v. 15). If, then, this piece of gospel tradition happens to be "older" than the Marcan, its Passover character has to be recognized.

Other proposals for the character of the Last Supper which the historical Jesus would have eaten have been made in this century, and they have been scrutinized at length by J. Jeremias *(Eucharistic Words,* 26-36). There is no need to summarize his criticism here; it will suffice to mention the proposals: The Last Supper has been understood: (1) as a *Qiddûš* meal (a meal with a special blessing to "sanctify" it, taken at the beginning of a Sabbath); (2) as a *ḥăbûrāh* meal (one participated in by a "company" [of friends] or a "fraternity" of religious Jews); or (3) as an Essene meal (one celebrated in common by members of the ascetic community of Essenes, known to us from Josephus, *J.W.* 2.8,5 § 129-131 and from 1QS 6:4-6; 1QSa 2:17-22). None of these proposals has carried full conviction, and the strongest case has been made (by Jeremias himself) for the historical Last Supper having been eaten as a Passover meal, for the fragments of evidence in the Gospels reveal that (a) Jesus sent two of his own disciples to make preparations for such a meal (Mark 14:12-13,17; cf. John 13:1); (b) he celebrated it with his disciples *in Jerusalem;* (c) he celebrated it there *at night* (Mark 14:17; 1 Cor 11:23; John 13:30); (d) he *reclined* at table (see NOTE on 22:14); (e) he broke bread during the course of the meal (Mark 14:22,23), in the Lucan story even after drinking wine (22:19); and (f) the meal ended with the singing of a hymn (Mark 14:26). A few further details (see J. Jeremias, *Eucharistic Words,* 41-84) are debatable; but in the long run this is still the best explanation of the Last Supper in Stage I of the gospel tradition. As for the Lucan form in Stage III, the Passover character also furnishes the best explanation of that.

To understand better the thrust of the Lucan account, one should recall briefly what is known of a first-century Passover meal in Palestine. According to J. Jeremias (ibid. 84-88), it consisted of four parts:

1) Preliminary Course: A blessing *(qiddûš)* to sanctify the feast day, cup I of wine, and the preliminary dish of herbs (green herbs, bitter herbs, and the *ḥărôset* [fruit purée with spices and vinegar]). The meal was served, but not yet eaten; cup II of wine was poured.

2) Passover Liturgy: Recited by the *paterfamilias* in Aramaic in response to a question asked by the youngest boy, "Why is this night different?" *(m. Pesaḥ.* 10:4). It was followed by the singing in Hebrew of the Hallel, part I (Psalm 113 [according to the school of Shammai]; Psalms 113-114 [according to the school of Hillel]), and the drinking of cup II (the *haggādāh* cup).

3) The Meal Proper: A blessing was pronounced over the *maṣṣôt,* "unleavened bread"; the Passover lamb was eaten with the *maṣṣôt* and bitter herbs (Exod 12:8); cup III, "the cup after the meal" (the "cup of blessing," 1 Cor 10:16—*kôs šel běrākāh),* was blessed.

4) Conclusion: Part II of the Hallel (Psalms 114-118 [school of Shammai]; Psalms 115-118 [school of Hillel]) was sung. (It is disputed whether a fourth cup of wine concluded the meal in first-century Palestine.) See further G. J. Bahr, "The Seder of Passover," 187-188.

Among first-century Palestinian Jews the Passover meal was celebrated annually in Jerusalem as a re-presentation and a reliving of the experience of their ancestors described in Exod 12:3-14; Num 9:1-14; Deut 16:1-8, emphasizing above all their deliverance from Egyptian bondage. It was a "memorial" *(anamnēsis)* in a pregnant sense. (See *m. Pesaḥ.* 10:5 for a graphic presentation of this meaning of the feast.) But also associated with this reliving of their historic liberation was an anticipation of an eschatological, even messianic, deliverance. In this sense the second part of the Hallel was sung, especially Ps 118:26, "Blest be the one who comes in the name of the Lord."

This double dimension of the Passover meal can still be seen in the Lucan account of the Last Supper. It is clearly referred to as a Passover meal (v. 15; cf. vv. 1,7-8,13). *To pascha* may refer to the lamb itself; the bread and the two cups hint at the courses of the Passover meal: The first Lucan cup (v. 17) would refer to either cup I *(qiddûš* cup) or cup II *(haggādāh* cup), whereas the second Lucan cup, described as "the cup after the meal" (v. 20a), would refer to cup III, the "cup of blessing." The eschatological dimension is also present in the double reference to the kingdom of God. The Passover meal, which Jesus shall never again eat, will find fulfillment in God's kingdom— another reference to the so-called messianic banquet (even though the messianic aspect is completely missing here—see NOTE on 13:29).

In the second part of the account Jesus reinterprets elements of the Passover meal in terms of himself. His words over the bread and "the cup after the meal" are to be understood as a reinterpretation of the declaration of the *paterfamilias* over the bread taken with the meal proper, "This is 'the bread of affliction' (Exod 16:3), which our fathers had to eat as they came out of Egypt" (see J. Jeremias, *Eucharistic Words*, 54; G. Dalman, *Jesus—Jeshua*, 139). Instead of identifying the unleavened *maṣṣôt* as "the bread of affliction," Jesus identifies the bread with his "body," i.e. with himself.

The Lucan Jesus goes further, adding about the bread/body, "which is given for you" (v. 19). This adds a vicarious dimension of meaning to his "body," and probably also a sacrificial nuance (see NOTE on *didonai* on v. 19). Thus a soteriological nuance of the reinterpreted bread is presented by Jesus at this supper. When this is set in the context of v. 15, it implies a soteriological value to Jesus' own "suffering." Jesus' words refer to his coming death. No matter what one would say about the character of the meal that the historical Jesus took with his disciples in Stage I, whether a mere fellowship meal (like those of Acts 2:42,46 with an eschatological connotation) or a memorial of his death (like that referred to by Paul in 1 Cor 11:23-26)—a problem that does not concern us here—the reference to Jesus' death and the connection with it of this reinterpreted Passover in the Lucan account is unmistakable, even though implicit.

The vicarious and soteriological character of Jesus' reinterpretation come out still more clearly in his words over the "cup after the meal": "This cup is the new covenant with my blood, which is poured out for you" (v. 20). The Lucan form of the reinterpretative words is no less "sacrificial" than the Marcan, *pace* J. M. Creed, *The Gospel*, 265. The last cl. of v. 20 is as vicarious and soteriological in its thrust as is v. 19c. Indeed, "poured out" is even more connotative of death than "given." But even though we do not have "my blood-of-the-covenant," as in Mark 14:24, which is a clear allusion to Exod 24:8, yet the identification of the cup of wine with "the new covenant with my blood" is scarcely any less of an allusion to the covenantal sacrifice of Exod 24:3-8 than the Marcan formula, even though it may be overlaid now with an allusion to Jer 31:31, the "new covenant." The allusion to the Sinai pact, when Moses sprinkled the blood of twelve sacrificed oxen, half of it on the altar representative of Yahweh and half of it on the people of the twelve tribes, as a conclusion of the covenant, is still clear in the Lucan formula. Because it is now a "new covenant," the pact is concluded not with the blood of sacrificed oxen, but "with my blood," which will be poured out. (For the fut. sense of the pres. ptcs. in vv. 19c,20 see NOTES there. See the articles of K. W. Goetz and E. Lohmeyer in the BIBLIOGRAPHY on p. 1404 for further aspects of this "sacrificial" debate.)

Moreover, the Lucan Jesus instructs the apostles that they are to "Do this in remembrance of me" (v. 19). Just as the Passover meal was for Palestinian Jews a yearly *anamnēsis*, so too Jesus now gives a directive to repeat such a meal with bread and wine as a mode of re-presenting to themselves their experience of him (especially at this Last Supper). The backward thrust of the

Passover meal would take on a new referent in this reinterpretation. Thus Jesus gives himself, his "body" and his "blood," as a new mode of celebrating Israel's feast of deliverance. His own body and blood will replace the Passover lamb as the sign of the way God's kingdom will be realized from now on, even though its fullness will not be achieved until the eschaton.

Within the Lucan Gospel this supper scene is the "last" in another sense, for the evangelist has been preparing for this climax by the foreshadowing in six other banquet/dinner scenes: 5:29-32; 7:36-50; 9:12-17; 10:38-42; 11:37-44; 14:1-24. An echo of it will be heard in 24:28-32, and possibly in 24:41-43 (though there only Jesus eats!).

The words of Jesus in this scene at table with his apostles have to be understood in the context of the actions that he has performed as he utters them. They are not merely "a double simile" occasioned by the twin terms "body" and "blood," as J. Jeremias *(Eucharistic Words,* 224) would have it: ". . . the broken bread a simile of the fate of his body, the blood of the grapes a simile of his outpoured blood," in the manner of OT prophets announcing parabolically future events (Ezek 4:1-17; 5:1-17; Jer 19:1-5). Jesus is not merely saying, "I go to death as the true Passover sacrifice," i.e. the meaning of Jesus' last parable (ibid.). Rather, the words are what X. Léon-Dufour has called "performative": "[Jesus] addresses the disciples, not in order to propose to them a definition of the bread which he has just broken and distributed, but to invite them to recognize in the bread shared his own body and to constitute in this way a community" among them; he thus "inaugurates a new mode of presence among his disciples, not through some prolonged form of the incarnation, but as the risen One who will thus sustain the life" of his own ("Prenez!" 239 [slightly modified]). This meaning will become clearer in the scene in which the risen Christ appears to the disciples at Emmaus and they recognize him in the "breaking of the bread." See COMMENT on p. 1559.

Two further comments are called for in this discussion of the Lucan Last Supper. First, one should note the diverse forms of the words of institution in the Synoptic Gospels and Paul. Jesus' words pronounced over the bread are given thus:

- a) 1 Cor 11:24: *Touto mou estin to sōma to hyper hymōn* (note order of Greek words!)
  "This is my body which is for you" *(RSV).*
- b) Mark 14:22: *Labete, touto estin to sōma mou*
  "Take; this is my body" *(RSV).*
- c) Matt 26:26: *Labete, phagete, touto estin to sōma mou*
  "Take, eat; this is my body" *(RSV).*
- d) Luke 22:19: *Touto estin to sōma mou to hyper hymōn didomenon*
  "This is my body, which is given for you" *(RSV).*

To complete the picture, we add a bit of the Johannine tradition which may be an attempt to reflect Jesus' own words at the Last Supper:

e) John 6:51:   *Egō eimi ho artos ho zōn ho ek tou ouranou katabas.*
ean tis phagē ek toutou tou artou, zēsei eis ton aiōna. kai
ho artos de hon egō dōsō hē sarx mou estin hyper tēs tou
kosmou zōēs
"I am the living bread which came down from heaven; if any one eats of this bread, he will live forever; and the bread which I shall give for the life of the world is my flesh" *(RSV).*

Jesus' words over the cup of wine are recorded thus:

f) 1 Cor 11:25:   *Touto to potērion hē kainē diathēkē estin en tō emō*
haimati
"This cup is the new covenant in my blood" *(RSV).*

g) Mark 14:24:   *Touto estin to haima mou tēs diathēkēs to ekchyn-*
nomenon hyper pollōn
"This is my blood of the covenant, which is poured out for many" *(RSV).*

h) Matt 26:27-28: *Piete ex autou pantes, touto gar estin to haima mou tēs*
diathēkēs to peri pollōn ekchynnomenon eis aphesin
hamartiōn
"Drink of it, all of you; for this is my blood of the covenant, which is poured out for many for the forgiveness of sins" *(RSV).*

i) Luke 22:20:   *Touto to potērion hē kainē diathēkē estin en tō haimati*
mou to hyper hymōn ekchynnomenon
"This cup which is poured out for you is the new covenant in my blood" *(RSV).*

Though one might like to believe that of all the sayings attributed to Jesus in the NT we come closest to his very words in the institution of the Lord's Supper, such a diversity reveals an immediate problem. The words of the first part of the saying over the bread have a certain similarity in the Pauline and Synoptic traditions ("This is my body," despite the difference in word order), but the saying over the cup of wine varies considerably. The Lucan formula over the bread and the wine is closer to the Pauline and is often judged today as an echo of an Antiochene liturgy, which both would reflect independently. The Marcan formula may reflect a Jerusalem liturgy, which Matthew has redacted on his own.

The Marcan form is said to be the more Semitic and closer to the original formula (see J. Jeremias, *Eucharistic Words,* 189-191); but almost the same claim has been made for the Lucan (see H. Schürmann, *Einsetzungsbericht,* 83-132). The twentieth-century reader should realize that we have no way of ascertaining the exact form of the words that Jesus pronounced over the bread and the wine at the Last Supper. The whole matter is compounded when one recalls that what has been preserved in the Christian writings of the NT about that event is in Greek, whereas Jesus most probably made use of a Semitic language on that occasion.

This brings us to the second comment. Though a strong case can be made out for Aramaic as the usual language that Jesus of Nazareth would have spoken, G. Dalman, M. Black, and J. Jeremias have tried to reckon with the possibility that Jesus used Hebrew at this part of the Last Supper. This is indeed a *possibility*, but one so remote that it is not worth pursuing. The real question is which form of the words of institution reflect—or reflect better— an Aramaic substratum, the Marcan or the Lucan/Pauline? Both can be retrojected into contemporary Aramaic—with almost equal ease and problems.

Luke 22:19b-20	Mark 14:22-23
dēn[1] *biśrî*[2] *(hû')*[3]	*dēn biśrî (hû').*
This my flesh (is)	This my flesh (is).
dî yĕhîb[4] *'ălêkōn.*	
which (is) given for you.	
'ăbîdû dā'[5] *lĕdukrānî.*[6]	
Do this in my memory.	
kāsā'[7] *dēn (hû') qĕyāmā'*[8] *ḥădatĕtā' bidmî*	*dēn dĕmî dî qĕyāmā'*[10] *(hû')*
This cup (is) the new covenant with my blood	This (is) my blood of the covenant
dî šĕpîk[9] *'ălêkōn.*	*dî šĕpîk 'al saggî'în.*[11]
which (is) poured out for you.	which (is) poured out for many.

Notes on the Aramaic Retroversion

[1] Or the fuller form *dĕnāh*. For the pronominal use of *dēn/dĕnāh*, see 11QtgJob 5:5 (= Hebrew 21:25); 1QapGen 22:34. It would also have been possible to substitute the deictic particle *hā'*, "behold," for the dem. pron. (see 11QtgJob 28:3).

[2] A suffixal form of *biśrā'* is found in 11QtgJob 36:8 (= Hebrew 41:15). (Cf. *MPAT* 7:4.1.)

[3] The copulative use of the personal pron. *hû'* can be found in 11QtgJob 28:3 *(hā' 'elāhā' rab hû'*, "Behold, God is great" [= Hebrew 36:26]); cf. 1QapGen 19:7. (See further NOTE on 22:19 [about the copula].)

[4] For *dî* with a ptc., see 11QtgJob 15:8 (= Hebrew 30:4 [article + ptc.]). (Cf. 1QapGen 20:8; 21:9; 22:10.)

[5] For the pronominal use of the dem. *dā'*, see 11QtgJob 29:5 (= Hebrew 37:14). (Cf. 1QapGen 19:19.)

[6] A similar use of *dukrānî* can be found in *Tg. Onq.* of Exod 3:15. (Cf. *MPAT* 9:1.)

[7] For *kāsā'*, see *AP* 61:4,14; *BMAP* 7:14.

[8] For *qĕyāmā'*, "covenant," see 11QtgJob 35:7 (= Hebrew 40:28 [41:4E]).

[9] For the vb. *špk*, see 4QEn[a] 1 iv 7 *(dm sgy šp[yk]*, "much blood poured out"); 4QEn[b] 1 iii 8.

[10] *Tg. Onq.* of Exod 24:8 reads: *hā' dēn dam qĕyāmā'*, "Behold, this (is) the blood of the

covenant." For the phrase "of the covenant" following a suffixal form of *dam,* "blood," see the parallel construction in Hebrew: Ps 71:7 *(mahăsî 'ōz,* "my strong refuge"); Hab 3:8 *(markĕbōtêkā yĕšû'āh,* "your chariots of deliverance"); Qoh 4:1 *('ōšĕqêhem kōah,* "their powerful oppressors"); Ps 35:19 *('ōyĕbay šeqer,* "my enemies of deceit"); Ps 38:20 *(šōnĕ'ay šāqer,* "my enemies of deceit"). (Cf. GKC § 131r; J.-E. David, *"To haima mou tēs diathēkēs* Mt 26,28: Un faux problème," *Bib* 48 (1967) 291-292.) For similar constructions in later Aramaic/Syriac texts, see J. A. Emerton, "The Aramaic Underlying *to haima mou tēs diathēkēs* in Mk. xiv. 24," *JTS* ns 6 (1955) 238-240; 12 (1962) 111-117; 15 (1964) 58-59.

[11] For the absolute use of *saggî'în,* see 11QtgJob 26:4 (= Hebrew 35:9 *[rabbîm]*).

The Lucan account of the Last Supper, like those of Mark and Matthew, is clearly seeking to root the Christian celebration of the "Lord's Supper" (even though none of them uses that term) in the words and deeds of Jesus at that meal. Paul in 1 Corinthians refers to such a rite being celebrated among early Christians (10:14-22), even before he comes to mention the "Lord's Supper" (11:20) or gives his form of the words of institution (11:23-25). What steps intervened in the development between the Last Supper and the Lord's Supper is a matter of speculation and deduction; it is scarcely possible to reconstruct that development with accuracy today. For attempts to do so, see R. H. Fuller, "The Double Origin"; J. Reumann, "The Last and the Lord's Supper," 22-31; W. Marxsen, *The Beginnings of Christology,* 87-122.

Finally, the reference that the Lucan Jesus makes at the Last Supper to his suffering (v. 15) relates this account to the theology that one finds in both the Epistle to the Hebrews and 1 Peter, where the death of Jesus on the cross is likewise presented in terms of *paschein* (Heb 9:26; 13:12; 1 Pet 2:21-23; 3:18; cf. W. Michaelis, *TDNT* 5. 913). It is in the long run part of the Lucan theme of the necessity of Jesus' death (on which see further COMMENT on 23:44-49).

NOTES

22 15. *Jesus said to them.* Lit. "and he said to them" *(eipen pros +* acc.). See p. 116.

How intensely have I desired. Lit. "with a desire have I desired"; the dat. of the abstract cognate n. *(epithymia)* is used to intensify the vb. *(epithymein).* This is a Septuagintism (found verbatim in Gen 31:30). See p. 114; cf. BDF § 198.6; ZBG § 60. It could also translate a construction now attested in Palestinian Aramaic (1QapGen 20:10-11), "and I Abram wept with a grievous weeping"; see *WA* 99.

The expression has been variously interpreted:

a) According to F. C. Burkitt and A. E. Brooke ("St Luke xxii 15,16"), Jesus had desired to eat the coming Passover meal but knew that he would die first, before it came. This interpretation is based on the view that Jesus did not eat the Last Supper as a Passover meal. Apart from the historical question, it seeks to interpret the Lucan text according to the Johannine dating of the Last Supper, which is unacceptable (see

p. 1379). Moreover, it demands that the aor. *epethymēsa* be understood as a pluperfect, which, in a main cl., is difficult to accept.

b) According to J. Jeremias *(Eucharistic Words,* 208), the aor. *epethymēsa* expresses an unfulfilled or unrealizable wish, "I would very gladly have eaten this passover lamb with you before my death," and the reason is given in vv. 16 and 18. Jesus would have given the cup to the apostles, but would not have drunk of it himself. Comparison is made with Luke 15:16, where one finds a similar use of the impf. *epethymei.* See BDF § 359.2. Moreover, vv. 16 and 18 are to be understood as an avowal of abstinence; Jesus will drink of the cup only in the kingdom. While not impossible as an interpretation, it is suspect because it tends to read too much into the text.

c) According to J. M. Creed *(The Gospel,* 265), "the meaning is that Jesus had earnestly desired to eat this passover, and that his desire is fulfilled." This is the *prima facie* understanding of the text: an ardent, real, attainable wish, now being accomplished or realized. It is the more common interpretation and is to be preferred. See further E. Schweizer, *Evangelium nach Lukas,* 223.

to eat this Passover supper. Or "this Passover lamb," i.e. that which lies before him (the dem. *touto* being emphatic); it is not a merely generic reference to the celebration of Passover that year. See NOTE on v. 7. It thus becomes the farewell feast to which Jesus has ardently looked forward.

with you. His apostles are to share in this act in which Jesus brings the old Passover to new fruition. The apostles are present as the new people with whom the "new covenant" (v. 20) is to be established. To them he gives his body as food, and for them his blood will be poured out.

before I suffer! The vb. *paschein* is being used absolutely in the sense of suffering death, as elsewhere in the Lucan writings (see 24:46; Acts 1:3; 3:18; 17:3) and in other NT books (1 Pet 2:21,23; Heb 2:18; 9:26; 13:12). See W. Michaelis, *TDNT* 5. 913, but cf. J. Kremer, *EWNT* 3. 123. The Lucan Jesus relates the eating of the Passover meal (or lamb) to his own suffering. In this form of Stage III of the gospel tradition, there is not only a hint of the death of Jesus, but also of its significance. It is thus the first announcement at the supper of the imminent passion; see its parallel in v. 18.

16. *For I tell you.* Note the parallel emphasis in v. 18. J. Jeremias *(Die Sprache,* 110, 286) regards *legō gar hymin* as a pre-Lucan formula.

never again shall I eat it. I.e. after this occasion. The statement in this verse concerns "eating," whereas its parallel in v. 18 will concern "drinking." It is an emphatic statement of fact about the future, not the declaration of a resolve to abstain even from partaking of this (last) Passover.

The best reading is the simple emphatic negative (with the subjunc.), *hoti ou mē phagō* (as found in mss. P⁷⁵, ℵ, A, B, L, Θ). To bring out the emphasis I have added "never" for the sake of translation; but this reading lit. would be: "Eat it I shall not." The same need has brought some other mss. to read simply *ouketi,* "no longer" (ms. D has *ouketi mē phagomai),* or even to add it to *ou mē* (mss. C*, X, K, P, W, Δ, Π, Ψ).

until. Luke uses *hēos hotou,* as in 12:50; 13:8. The second word *hotou* is an unusual form of the gen. sg. neut. of *hostis,* but is often used with preps. See BAGD 335, 587. It occurs as a variant also in 15:8; 22:18.

it has found its fulfillment in the kingdom of God. Lit. "until it is (ful)filled . . ."

the vb. *plēroun* being used as in 4:21; 9:31; 24:44; Acts 1:16; 3:18. Jesus thus gives a new eschatological dimension to the Passover meal being taken with his apostles. The Passover meal was not merely a commemoration of the deliverance of the Hebrews from Egyptian bondage, but one which also looked for deliverance of a new sort (in messianic expectation). The connection that is now made by Jesus between the newly interpreted Passover and the kingdom of God introduces a different eschatological dimension; it will be further explained in v. 18 (where the kingdom is again mentioned) and in v. 19d (where he gives a directive). The prep. *en* is being understood in a temporal sense, "in the kingdom," but it is not impossible that it is to be understood in an instrumental sense, "through/by the kingdom." See ZBG § 119. On dining in the kingdom, see 13:29 (and NOTE there); 14:15.

M. Black ("The 'Fulfilment' in the Kingdom of God") sought to give the pass. vb. *plērōthē* an impersonal meaning so that the "fulfillment" would refer to the kingdom itself, "until *there is a consummation* in the kingdom of God" (his italics). But that seems to violate the grammar of the verse, in which something other than the kingdom is the subj.; that something finds fulfillment in (the time of) or by the kingdom, i.e. the Passover meal or lamb, which is now being understood as a type of prefigurement.

On the kingdom, see NOTE on 4:43 and pp. 154-156; on the theological pass., see NOTE on 5:20.

A different eschatological nuance is associated with the Lord's Supper in 1 Cor 11:26, where the meal is regarded as a proclamation of Jesus' death "until he comes." There the eschatology concerns not the kingdom, but the parousia.

17. *he took a cup.* Lit. "having received a cup," i.e. handed to him by one of the table companions. Whereas participants in the Passover meal usually drank from their own cups, Jesus introduces a different element. His first action concerns one of the earlier cups of the Passover meal (cup I or cup II?). The formulation of his actions in this verse (with four verbal forms) is probably traditional.

Many commentators who favor the short text of this account (vv. 15-19b) argue that *Did.* 9:1-3 can be invoked in support of a Lucan account of the Last Supper which had only the cup-bread sequence, such as vv. 15-19b would have without the additional material in vv. 19cd-20. The passage in the *Didache* runs as follows: [1] "Now concerning the Eucharist, give thanks in this way. [2] First, about the cup (say), 'We thank you, our Father, for the holy vine of David your child (servant?), which you made known to us through Jesus your child (servant?); to you be glory forever.' [3] And about the broken bread (say), 'We thank you, our Father, for the life and knowledge which you have made known to us through Jesus your child (servant?). To you (be) glory forever!' " (There follows a further prayer relating the broken bread to the church.) It should be noted, however, that there is in the *Didache* no reference to the Last Supper. What appears there is an interpretation of the Eucharist. Moreover, it would have to be shown that what is said in this paragraph reflects liturgical practice rather than the author's interpretation of the Eucharist. Again, even if it did reflect liturgical practice, one would still have to show that such a practice was equally as primitive as that recorded in the Lucan account and that it was meant as the order in which the words were uttered at the Last Supper. Lastly, the translation of the passage in the LCL is slightly tendentious, since *eucharistēsate,* which I have translated above simply as "give thanks in this way," appears as "hold Eucharist thus"; this clearly has a different connotation, suggesting a difference of order.

after giving thanks. I.e. to God. The absol. aor. ptc. *eucharistēsas* will appear again in v. 19. Cf. 17:16; 18:11. Most frequently this vb. is used in the NT of "giving thanks" to God in a religious sense (as in the later books of the LXX [Jdt 8:25; 2 Macc 1:11; 10:7], in Philo *[De spec. leg.* 2.33 § 204; 3.1 § 6], and in Josephus *[Ant.* 1.10,5 § 193]). From the use of this vb. in these verses, in Mark 14:23, and in Matt 26:27 and 1 Cor 11:24 comes the common name "Eucharist" for the Christian rite which carries out Jesus' directive in v. 19d. The "thanksgiving" connotes God's blessing on what is given. Whereas it is often considered to be a term derived from Hellenistic Judaism, one should recall that it probably has a Palestinian background in the attitude expressed by many of the Qumran *Thanksgiving Psalms.* Cf. J. M. Robinson, "Die Hodajot-Formel," 194-235; J.-P. Audet, "Esquisse historique du genre littéraire de la 'bénédiction' juive et de l' 'eucharistie' chrétienne," *RB* 65 (1958) 371-399. See further H. Patsch, *EWNT* 2. 219-221; J. Jeremias, *Die Sprache,* 287. The connotation of "thanksgiving" is well expressed in 1 Tim 4:4-5: "Every creature of God is good, and nothing is to be rejected, when it is received with thanksgiving; for (then) it is sanctified through the word of God and prayer."

Take this and divide it among yourselves. It is impossible to say whether the evangelist means that Jesus himself tasted of it first (see A. Plummer, *The Gospel,* 495); if it is to be so understood, then the further comment would have the same connotation as v. 16. The Lucan Jesus' directive invites the apostles to a communal sharing in this new meal. Recall the more abstract, theological explanation provided by Paul in 1 Cor 10:16-21. It is a "participation" in the "table of the Lord."

18. *for I tell you.* See NOTE on v. 16.

from now on. The phrase *apo tou nyn* is characteristically Lucan. See p. 110. On the lips of the Lucan Jesus it refers to the imminence of his suffering, as a result of which he will no longer be present at a Passover meal with the apostles. Some mss. (A, C, Θ, Ψ, *f*[13], and the Koine text-tradition) and Latin versions omit this prepositional phrase; but it is to be retained with mss. P[75], ℵ, B, K, L, W, 892, 1241, etc.

I shall not drink of the fruit of the vine. I.e. as an element of the Passover meal. These words are neither an avowal of abstention nor a vow taken by Jesus against the drinking of wine. The drinking of the wine is parallel to the eating of the Passover meal/lamb of v. 16. For *to genēma tēs ampelou,* "the product of the vine," as an expression for grapes (or wine made therefrom), see LXX Deut 22:9; Isa 32:12 (where it translates Hebrew *gepen pōriyyāh,* "a fruitful vine"). In *m. Ber.* 6:1 *pěrî haggepen,* "fruit of the vine," is used in a blessing over wine. The combination of the vb. *pinein,* "drink," with the prep. *apo/ek* (Mark 14:25) is likewise found in the LXX (Gen 9:21; Sir 26:12); it probably represents the partitive use of Hebrew or Aramaic *min.* The more common Greek and Semitic expression is "to drink wine/water from a cup/river." See Exod 7:18,21; 1 Kgs 17:4,6. Cf. John 4:13,14; Rev 14:10; 18:3.

until the kingdom of God comes. This is another way of expressing the eschatological fulfillment of the Passover meal in the kingdom. See v. 16. On the "coming" of the kingdom, see NOTES on 11:2; 17:20.

19. *took up some bread.* Or "a loaf of bread." This refers to the bread eaten at the beginning of the main meal. See J. Jeremias, *Eucharistic Words,* 87. Luke derives from Mark 14:22 the participial phrase *labōn arton,* "having taken bread," the first of four formulaic vbs. Though J. Wellhausen *("Arton eklasen* Mc 14, 22," *ZNW* 7 [1906] 182) once argued that *artos* had to refer to "leavened bread" and concluded that, therefore, the Last Supper could not have been a Passover meal (see also J. M. Creed, *The Gospel,* 264-265), that interpretation was questioned by G. Beer *(Die Mischna II/3: Pesachim* [Giessen: Töpelmann, 1912] 96) and others. That *artos* can mean "unleavened bread" is seen from the LXX of Exod 29:2 (= Hebrew *leḥem maṣṣôt);* Lev 2:4; 8:26; Num 6:19. Cf. Philo, *De spec. leg.* 2.28 § 158; Josephus, *Ant.* 3.6,6 § 142. See further H. Balz, *EWNT* 1. 383-386; J. Jeremias, *Eucharistic Words,* 62-65.

after giving thanks. If Luke is following Mark 14:22 here, he has changed the ptc. *eulogēsas,* "having given praise" or "having blessed" (God or the bread), to parallel the phrase in v. 17. However, *eucharistēsas* also occurs in 1 Cor 11:24, and so it may have been in "L" as well. (In the LXX the vb. *eulogein* regularly translates the Hebrew *brk,* and only rarely the hiphil of *ydy* [e.g. Isa 12:1 (mss. B,5); 38:19], which would mean "thank"; this at least shows the kinship of *eulogēsas* and *eucharistēsas.)* On the connotation of "giving thanks," see NOTE on v. 17.

broke it, and gave it to them. I.e. the one loaf is divided in order to be shared. These vbs. are derived from Mark 14:22; note that Paul in 1 Cor 11:24 has "broke and said." Again they are part of a traditional (probably liturgical) formula with four vbs. From the form used here Luke will develop his formula, "the breaking of the bread" (24:35; Acts 2:42; 20:7,11). The vb. *klan,* "break," is used in the NT only in the context of breaking bread at a meal. See Luke 24:30; Acts 2:46; 20:7,11; 27:35; cf. 1 Cor 10:16; 11:24; Mark 8:6,19; 14:22; Matt 14:19; 15:36; 26:26. The *paterfamilias* shares the bread with others present, showing his relation to them.

This is my body. The sentence *touto estin to sōma mou* is derived from Mark 14:22b verbatim (as it is also in Matt 26:26c); cp. 1 Cor 11:24, where the word order differs. As the *paterfamilias* at the Passover meal interpreted the unleavened bread with a reference to Deut 16:3 *(leḥem 'ŏnî,* "bread of affliction"), so Jesus interprets the bread of this new Passover meal, as he identifies it with himself. He gives his companions not only bread to eat, but his own self. Greek *sōma* probably has to be understood not merely in the sense of "body," but even of "self"—a sense found elsewhere in the NT (see 1 Cor 9:27; 13:3; Rom 12:1; Phil 1:20), and also in classical and Hellenistic Greek. See Aeschines, *Orat.* 2.58; Xenophon, *Anab.* 1.9,12; Appian, *Rom. Hist.* 11.7,41; cf. MM 621). R. Bultmann caught the nuance well when he wrote, ". . . man does not have a *soma;* he is *soma"* (*Theology,* 1. 194).

In the Greek of the LXX *sōma* translates a variety of Hebrew words, but most frequently it is *bāśār,* "flesh." The word which becomes in rabbinic, medieval, and modern Hebrew "body" is *gûp* or *gûpāh* (fem.); in biblical Hebrew this word is found only in 1 Chr 10:12, and then in the sense of "corpse." Though G. Dalman *(Jesus— Jeshua,* 142) tried to suggest that this word was used by Jesus, it is unlikely. See I. H. Marshall, *Luke,* 802. The influence of Greek philosophical thinking may well have aided the development of *gûp* from "corpse" to "body" (even in a living sense); but we have no evidence that that development took place in the time of Jesus. In the OT

Hebrew *bāśār*, "flesh," carried the connotation not only of "body" (see Ezek 11:19; 36:26; Ps 63:2; Job 4:15), but even of "person" or "self" (Num 16:22; 27:16; Isa 40:5-6; Ps 145:21). See Luke 3:6, where *pasa sarx*, lit. "all flesh," i.e. "all human beings," translates *kol bāśār* of Isa 40:5. In the late pre-Christian period of Palestinian Judaism "flesh and blood" is used to designate the human unit or person (Sir 14:18; 17:31; *1 Enoch* 15:4; cf. Philo, *Quis rer. div. heres* 11 § 57; Gal 1:16; Matt 16:17; 1 Cor 15:50; Heb 2:14—perhaps also Ezek 39:17). Is this usage in the background of the distinction of bread = body and wine = blood, as used by Jesus in vv. 19 and 20? See further J. Jeremias, *Eucharistic Words,* 198-201; J. Bonsirven, "Hoc est corpus meum: Recherches sur l'original araméen," 205-219; X. Léon-Dufour, "Prenez!" 225-227.

From a philological viewpoint, it is impossible to tell whether the vb. *estin* is to be understood to mean "is really, is identical with," which seems to be the sense in Luke 3:22; 4:34; 6:5; Matt 3:17; 10:2; 13:55; 14:2, or "is symbolically/spiritually," "it means," which seems to be the sense in John 10:7-11; 11:25; 15:1; 1 Cor 10:4; Gal 4:24. The Pauline interpretive passage in 1 Cor 11:26-29 became the basis for an early Christian understanding of the vb. in the realistic sense—a sense that was not questioned until the Middle Ages (Berengar of Tours, eleventh century), but eventually was reaffirmed in church tradition at the Council of Trent (DS 1636, 1651). If the historical Jesus were using Aramaic, or even Hebrew, at the Last Supper, no vb. would have been used, since the juxtaposition of the subj. and predicate suffices to express the pres. tense of the vb. to be: *dēn biśrî.* However, one could also add the third pers. pron. as the copula, which would not change the sense: *dēn biśrî hû'* (lit. "This is my flesh").

which is given for you. Lit. "that being given for you" or "that to be given for you," since the pres. ptc. here and in v. 20 is to be understood as denoting "a relatively fut. action," i.e. "which is to be given." See BDF § 339.2b; ZBG § 282-283. This participial phrase is not found in either the Marcan or Matthean parallels, but 1 Cor 11:24 has a simpler form, "which is for you" *(to hyper hymōn).* The Lucan form adds the ptc. *didomenon.* (Some mss. of 1 Corinthians [$\aleph^2$, C^3, D^2, F, G, Ψ, and the Koine text-tradition] add the ptc. *klōmenon,* "which is broken for you," an addition, which, though different from the Lucan ptc., supports the latter.) It is difficult to say whether the Lucan or the Pauline form is the more primitive.

The first problem that this phrase creates is to determine the antecedent to which the art. and ptc. are to be referred. Is it *touto* (the dem. pron. "this," i.e. this piece of bread)? Or is it *to sōma mou,* "my body"? That it could refer to a forward-looking dem. is certainly possible. See R. Kühner and B. Gerth, *Ausführliche Grammatik der griechischen Sprache: Satzlehre* (4th ed.; Hannover: Hahn, 1955) 1. 658-659. But the more obvious referent is "my body," because the dem. pron. *touto* is already used in the neut. to agree with the predicate *sōma* and not with the masc. *artos* (see BDF § 132.1), and the art. + ptc. are being used as the equivalent of a rel. cl. (BDF § 412).

The second problem is the sense of the vb. *didonai,* "give." Elsewhere it is sometimes found with the connotation of giving in offering, in sacrifice, and even in death. See Luke 2:24; cf. Mark 10:45; Gal 1:4; 2 Cor 8:5; John 6:51; 1 Tim 2:6; Titus 2:14; 1 Macc 2:50; 6:44; Thucydides, *Hist.* 2.43,2 (with *sōmata!); Ignatius, *Smyr.* 4.2

—see further BAGD 193; W. Popke, *EWNT* 1. 774-775. This is the sense that should be understood here too.

No matter how one resolves the first two problems, the "for others" aspect of this added phrase is unmistakable. The vicarious gift of himself is the Lucan Jesus' intention in reinterpreting the Passover offering of old; it implies the soteriological aspect of his life and death. For the vicarious sense of the prep. *hyper,* see Josephus, *Ant.* 13.1,1 § 6 *(apothnēskein hyper autōn,* "to die for them"); *J.W.* 2.10,5 § 201 *(hyper tosoutōn hetoimōs epidōsō tēn emautou psychēn,* "for the sake of so many I shall readily give my own life"). Cf. Sir 29:15; Rom 5:6; 8:32; 2 Macc 7:9; 8:21; 4 Macc 1:9,10; John 11:50; 1 Cor 15:3,29; 2 Cor 5:14; 1 Pet 2:21. See further E. H. Blakeney, *"Hyper* with the Genitive in N.T.," *ExpTim* 55 (1943-1944) 306; X. Léon-Dufour, "Prenez!" 227-230. This vicarious aspect of Jesus' life and death is affirmed here without any connection with the Servant motif, which will appear in v. 37 but in a different sense. As for the relation of this phrase to the death of Jesus in Lucan writings, see COMMENT on 23:44-49 (p. 1516).

Do this in remembrance of me. I.e. perform this action in memory of me. This memento-directive is not found in either the Marcan or Matthean parallels, but occurs in 1 Cor 11:24c (and there it is repeated after the cup). Both Paul and Luke inherit the word *anamnēsis* from an earlier tradition. *Touto poieite* is a reinterpretation of the *anamnēsis* which the Passover meal itself was intended to be: "that you may remember the day of your departure from the land of Egypt all the days of your life" (Deut 16:3d). As Jesus has substituted himself for the Passover lamb, so the memento of him is to replace the *anamnēsis* of the Passover itself. This memento is further explained in the Pauline reference to the celebration of the Lord's Supper in 1 Cor 11:20,26. It is not a mere recollection of Jesus, but a re-presenting of him and his act at the Last Supper to the awareness of the apostles: "Continually do this in order to bring me to mind" (A. Plummer, *The Gospel,* 498). The attempt to understand the vb. *poiein* in a sacrificial sense is eisegetical (ibid. 497).

The directive is undoubtedly both pre-Lucan and pre-Pauline, even though it stems immediately from a liturgical tradition different from that in the Marcan and Matthean accounts. It may well have *not* been part of the liturgical tradition at first, when the celebration was actually carrying out the rubric-like direction. In time, the rubric became part of the formula to be recited, and so it was inherited independently by both Paul and Luke. See further P. Benoit, "Le récit," 386.

The directive carries the nuance of a farewell commission. Paul understands it as a memorial of "the Lord's death" (1 Cor 11:26); for Hellenistic parallels, see H. Lietzmann, *An die Korinther I-II* (HNT 9; 5th ed.; Tübingen: Mohr [Siebeck], 1969) 58, 186. These parallels provide a good background for the understanding of the directive, but one does not have to draw all the questionable analogies and conclusions that Lietzmann once did from them. J. Jeremias *(Eucharistic Words,* 244-246) rightly points to Palestinian memorial formulas as well, but goes too far in trying to establish the meaning of the directive as ". . . that God may remember me," i.e. the Messiah (ibid. 252). The absence of the directive in the Marcan and Matthean accounts led A. Schweitzer to an eschatological interpretation of the Last Supper and the Lord's

Supper. See J. Reumann, "The Last," 23; cf. Exod 3:15e and the targumic renderings of it.

(Later Christian tradition understood the directive in still another way, in terms of the Sacrament of Orders [see Thomas Aquinas, *Summa theologica*, Supp. 37, 5 ad 2; the Council of Trent, sess. XXII (DS 1740, 1752)].)

20. *the cup after the meal.* I.e. "the cup of blessing" (1 Cor 10:16), cup III, the cup over which a blessing is pronounced. 1 Cor 11:25 has the same words in a slightly different order. See L. Goppelt, *TDNT* 6. 154-156; I. H. Marshall, *Luke,* 805. For a triadic blessing over a meal, see *Jub.* 22:6-9.

This cup is the new covenant with my blood. The Lucan formula identifies the cup with the new covenant, whereas Mark 14:28 more directly identifies it with the blood itself: "This (the cup or its contents) is my blood of the covenant." Though the Marcan formulation is closer to Exod 24:8, the Lucan has scarcely dropped "the sacrificial language" of Mark, *pace* J. M. Creed, *The Gospel,* 265, and G. B. Caird, *Gospel of St Luke,* 238. The Lucan formulation is less direct in its identification, but is almost the same as that in 1 Cor 11:25b.

The "new covenant" is an allusion to Jer 31:31, the promise made by Yahweh of a pact that he would make with "the house of Israel and the house of Judah"—a phrase taken over also by the Essenes of Qumran to describe their community (CD 6:19; 1QpHab 2:4-6). This new "covenant" reflects the "old covenant" (see 2 Cor 3:14), made by Yahweh and the people of Israel on the mountain, when Moses took the blood of twelve sacrificed oxen and sprinkled it, half on the people and half on the altar in token of the pact: "See, the blood of the covenant which the Lord has made" (Exod 24:8). In this new form the covenant is established "with my blood": Jesus' own blood is now involved in the *thysia sōtēriou,* "sacrifice of salvation" (Exod 24:5 LXX). Cf. B. Cooke, "Synoptic Presentation of the Eucharist as Covenant Sacrifice," *TS* 21 (1960) 1-44. For a figurative use of "cup," recall Ps 116:13 *(kôs yĕšû'ôt,* "cup of salvation").

Still another connotation of "blood" in the OT has to be considered, since Jesus' words over the cup imply, as did those over the bread, that his "life" is involved. According to Lev 17:14, "the life *(nepeš)* of all flesh is its blood," and "I have put it for you on the altar to make expiation for your lives" (17:11). Thus the cultic overtones of Jesus' words are unmistakable. See O. Böcher, *EWNT* 1. 88-93; V. Taylor, *Mark,* 545. Cf. A. Metzinger, "Die Substitutionstheorie und das alttestamentliche Opfer mit besonderer Berücksichtigung von Lev 17:11," *Bib* 21 (1940) 159-187, 247-272, 353-377.

which is poured out for you. Lit. "that being poured out for you" or "that to be poured out for you." See NOTE on the participial phrase in v. 19. Mark 14:24 reads, "which is poured out for many," and Matt 26:27, "which is poured out for many for the remission of sins." No such participial phrase occurs at 1 Cor 11:25. The Marcan seems to be the more original, whereas the Matthean is clearly a secondary (liturgical) development. See J. Schmid, *Das Evangelium nach Matthäus* (RNT 1; Regensburg: Pustet, 1965) 361. Luke (or his source) has restricted the scope of the vicarious offering in the change from "for many" to "for you" (this agrees with the ending of the earlier participial phrase in v. 19).

Again, one can ask about the antecedent of this participial phrase; is it *touto to potērion,* "this cup," or *tō haimati mou* (in the dat.), "with my blood"? K. Goetz ("Das vorausweisende Demonstrativum in Lc 22.19,20 und I Cor 11.24," *ZNW* 38 [1939] 189) insisted that it must go with the former, and "so is scarcely to be understood in any other way than as a sort of offering or libation according to ancient custom, as it has often been understood by ancient Greek and Latin Church Fathers." Yet that connotation may be present, even if the articular ptc. (in the nom.) is taken to agree, in sense, but not in case, with *tō haimati mou.*

In the OT *haima ekchein,* "pour out blood," is a way of expressing death. E.g. Gen 9:6; Ezek 18:10; Isa 59:7 (cf. Rom 3:15); cf. Luke 11:50. Many commentators think that the joining of this expression with "for you/for many" is an allusion to Isa 53:12, the Servant Song ("he poured out his life *[napšô]* in death and was counted among transgressors, yet he bore the sin of many").

BIBLIOGRAPHY (22:15-20)

Bacon, B. W. "The Lukan Tradition of the Lord's Supper," *HTR* 5 (1912) 322-348.

Bahr, G. J. "The Seder of Passover and the Eucharistic Words," *NovT* 12 (1970) 181-202.

Beck, N. A. "The Last Supper as an Efficacious Symbolic Act," *JBL* 89 (1970) 192-198.

Benoit, P. "The Accounts of the Institution and What They Imply," *The Eucharist in the New Testament* (ed. J. Delorme) 71-101.

Black, M. "The 'Fulfilment' in the Kingdom of God," *ExpTim* 57 (1945-1946) 25-26.

Blakiston, H. E. D. "The Lucan Account of the Institution of the Lord's Supper," *JTS* 4 (1902-1903) 548-555.

Bonsirven, J. "Hoc est corpus meum: Recherches sur l'original araméen," *Bib* 29 (1948) 205-219.

Bornkamm, G. *Jesus of Nazareth* (New York: Harper & Row, 1960) 160-162.

Box, G. H. "The Jewish Antecedents of the Eucharist," *JTS* 3 (1901-1902) 357-369.

——— "St Luke xxii 15,16," *JTS* 10 (1908-1909) 106-107.

Burkitt, F. C., and A. E. Brooke. "St Luke xxii 15,16: What Is the General Meaning?" *JTS* 9 (1907-1908) 569-572.

Christie, W. M. "Did Christ Eat the Passover with His Disciples? or, The Synoptics *versus* John's Gospel," *ExpTim* 43 (1931-1932) 515-519.

Cohn-Sherbok, D. "A Jewish Note on *to potērion tēs eulogias,*" *NTS* 27 (1980-1981) 704-709.

Cullmann, O. "La signification de la Sainte-Cène dans le christianisme primitif," *RHPR* 16 (1936) 1-22.

——— and F. J. Leenhardt. *Essays on the Last Supper* (Ecumenical Studies in Worship 1; London: Lutterworth, 1958).

Feneberg, R. *Christliche Passafeier und Abendmahl: Eine biblisch-hermeneutische Untersuchung der neutestamentlichen Einsetzungsberichte* (SANT 27; Munich: Kösel, 1971).

Flusser, D. "The Last Supper and the Essenes," *Immanuel* 2 (1973) 23-27.

Fuller, R. H. "The Double Origin of the Eucharist," *BR* 8 (1963) 60-72.

Goetz, K. W. "Zur Lösung der Abendmahlsfrage," *TSK* 108 (1937) 81-107.

Hahn, F. "Die alttestamentlichen Motive in der urchristlichen Abendmahlsüberlieferung," *EvT* 27 (1967) 337-374.

——— "Zum Stand der Erforschung des urchristlichen Herrenmahls," *EvT* 35 (1975) 553-563.

Higgins, A. J. B. "The Origins of the Eucharist," *NTS* 1 (1954-1955) 200-209.

Holtzmann, O. "Zu Lukas 22,20," *ZNW* 3 (1902) 359.

Jeremias, J. *Eucharistic Words.*

——— *New Testament Theology,* 288-292.

——— "This Is My Body . . . ," *ExpTim* 83 (1972) 196-203.

——— "Zur Exegese der Abendmahlsworte Jesu," *EvT* 7 (1947-1948) 60-63.

Kaestli, J.-D. *L'Eschatologie,* 58-59.

Kertelge, K. "Die soteriologischen Aussagen in der urchristlichen Abendmahlsüberlieferung und ihre Beziehung zum geschichtlichen Jesus," *TTZ* 81 (1972) 193-202.

Kilmartin, E. J. *The Eucharist in the Primitive Church* (Englewood Cliffs, NJ: Prentice-Hall, 1965).

Kosmala, H. "Das tut zu meinem Gedächtnis," *NovT* 4 (1960-1961) 81-94.

Kuhn, K.-G. "The Lord's Supper and the Communal Meal at Qumran," *The Scrolls and the New Testament* (ed. K. Stendahl; New York: Harper & Row, 1957) 65-93.

Lambert, J. C. "The Passover and the Lord's Supper," *JTS* 4 (1902-1903) 184-193.

Léon-Dufour, X. " 'Faites ceci en mémoire de moi': Luc 22,19—I Corinthiens 11,25," *Christus* 24 (1977) 200-208.

——— "Jésus devant sa mort à la lumière des textes de l'institution eucharistique et des discours d'adieu," *Jésus aux origines* (ed. J. Dupont) 141-168.

——— "Das letzte Mahl Jesu und die testamentarische Tradition nach Lk 22," *ZKT* 103 (1981) 33-55.

——— *Le partage du pain eucharistique selon le Nouveau Testament* (Parole de Dieu; Paris: Editions du Seuil, 1982) 266-284.

——— " 'Prenez! Ceci est mon corps pour vous,' " *NRT* 104 (1982) 223-240.

Lohmeyer, E. "Vom urchristlichen Abendmahl," *TRu* ns 9 (1937) 168-227; 10 (1938) 81-99.

Marxsen, W. *The Beginnings of Christology: Together with the Lord's Supper* (Philadelphia: Fortress, 1979) 87-122.

Merklein, H. "Erwägungen zur Überlieferungsgeschichte der neutestamentlichen Abendmahlstraditionen," *BZ* 21 (1977) 88-101, 235-244.

Monks, G. G. "The Lucan Account of the Last Supper," *JBL* 44 (1925) 228-260.

Nestle, E. "Zu Lukas 22,20," *ZNW* 3 (1902) 252.

——— "Zu Lc 22,20," *ZNW* 7 (1906) 256-257.

Pesch, R. "The Last Supper and Jesus' Understanding of His Death," *Bible Bhashyam* 3 (1977) 58-75.

——— *Wie Jesus das Abendmahl hielt: Der Grund der Eucharistie* (Freiburg im B.: Herder, 1977).

Porporato, F. X. "Hoc facite in meam commemorationem: Lc. 22, 19; 1 Cor. 11, 24.25," *VD* 13 (1933) 264-270.

Reumann, J. "The Last and the Lord's Supper," *Lutheran Theological Seminary Bulletin* 62 (1982) 17-39.

Richardson, R. D. "The Place of Luke in the Eucharistic Tradition," *SE I* (TU 73; Berlin: Akademie, 1959) 663-675.

Roloff, J. "Anfänge der soteriologischen Deutung des Todes Jesus (Mk. x. 45 und Lk. xxi. 27)," *NTS* 19 (1972-1973) 38-64.

Schenke, L. *Studien,* 286-347.

Schürmann, H. "Abendmahl, letztes A. Jesu," *LTK* 1 (1957) 26-31.

——— "Der Abendmahlsbericht Lk 22,7-38" (see p. 1384).

——— *Der Einsetzungsbericht Lk 22,19-20* (NTAbh 20/4; Münster in W.: Aschendorff, 1955).

——— "Die Gestalt der urchristlichen Eucharistiefeier," *MTZ* 6 (1955) 107-131; reprinted, *Ursprung und Gestalt,* 77-99.

——— "Die Semitismen im Einsetzungsbericht bei Markus und bei Lukas," *ZKT* 73 72-77.

Schweitzer, A. *The Problem of the Lord's Supper according to the Scholarly Research of the Nineteenth Century and the Historical Accounts, Volume 1: The Lord's Supper in Relationship to the Life of Jesus and the History of the Early Church* (ed. J. Reumann; Macon, GA: Mercer University, 1982).

Schweizer, E. "Abendmahl," *RGG* 1. 10-21: translated, *The Lord's Supper according to the New Testament* (FBBS 18; Philadelphia: Fortress, 1967).

——— "Das Herrenmahl im Neuen Testament," *TLZ* 79 (1954) 577-592.

——— Reviews of H. Schürmann, *TLZ* 80 (1955) 156-157; 81 (1956) 217-219.

Smith, M. A. "The Lukan Last Supper Narrative," *SE VI* (TU 112; Berlin: Akademie, 1973) 502-509.

Sparks, H. F. D. "St. Luke's Transpositions," *NTS* 3 (1956-1957) 219-223.

Sykes, M. H. "The Eucharist as 'Anamnesis,'" *ExpTim* 71 (1959-1960) 115-118.

Vööbus, A. *The Prelude to the Lukan Passion Narrative* (Papers of the Estonian Theological Society in Exile 17; Stockholm: ETSE, 1968).

Wanke, J. *Beobachtungen zum Eucharistieverständnis des Lukas auf Grund der lukanischen Mahlberichte* (Erfurter theologische Schriften 8; Leipzig: St. Benno, 1973).

Ziesler, J. A. "The Vow of Abstinence: A Note on Mark 15:25 and Parallels," *Colloquium* 5 (1972) 12-14.

——— "The Vow of Abstinence Again," *Colloquium* 6 (1973) 49-50.

BIBLIOGRAPHY ON THE TEXT-CRITICAL PROBLEM OF LUKE 22:19CD-20

Aland, K. "Die Bedeutung des P75 für den Text des Neuen Testaments: Ein Beitrag zur Frage der 'Western Non-Interpolations,'" *Studien zur Überlieferung des Neuen Testaments und seines Textes* (AzNTT 2; Berlin: de Gruyter, 1967) 155-172, esp. 160, 164-165.

Bate, H. N. "The 'Shorter Text' of St Luke xxii 15-20," *JTS* 28 (1927) 362-368.

Benoit, P. "Luc xxii, 19b-20," *JTS* 49 (1948) 145-147.

——— "Le récit de la cène dans Lc xxii, 15-20: Etude de critique textuelle et littéraire," *RB* 48 (1939) 357-393; reprinted, *Exégèse et théologie,* 1. 163-209.

Burkitt, F. C. "On Luke xxii 17-20," *JTS* 28 (1926-1927) 178-181.

Cooper, J. C. "The Problem of the Text in Luke 22:19-20," *LQ* 14 (1962) 39-48.

Eagar, A. R. "St. Luke's Account of the Last Supper: A Critical Note on the Second Sacrament," *Expositor* 7/5 (1908) 252-262, 343-361.

Fitzmyer, J. A. "Papyrus Bodmer XIV: Some Features of Our Oldest Text of Luke," *CBQ* 24 (1962) 170-179, esp. 177.

Geerlings, J. *Family 13—The Ferrar Group: The Text according to Luke* (Studies and Documents 20; Salt Lake City, UT: University of Utah, 1961).

Hahn, F. "Die alttestamentlichen Motive," 342.

Jeremias, J. *Eucharistic Words,* 139-159.

Kenyon, F. G., and S. C. E. Legg. "The Textual Data," *The Ministry and the Sacraments* (ed. R. Dunkerley: London: Student Christian Movement, 1937) 271-286, esp. 285-286.

Kilpatrick, G. D. "Luke xxii. 19b-20," *JTS* 47 (1946) 49-56.

Metzger, B. M. *TCGNT* 173-177.

Parker, P. "Three Variant Readings in Luke-Acts," *JBL* 83 (1964) 165-170, esp. 165-167.

Porporato, F. X. "De lucana pericopa 22,19b-20," *VD* 13 (1933) 114-122.

Rese, M. "Zur Problematik von Kurz- und Langtext in Luk. xxii. 17ff.," *NTS* 22 (1975-1976) 15-31.

Schäfer, K. T. "Zur Textgeschichte von Lk 22,19b.20," *Bib* 33 (1952) 237-239.

Schürmann, H. "Lk 22,19ᵇ-20 als ursprüngliche Textüberlieferung," *Bib* 32 (1951) 364-392, 522-541; reprinted, *Traditionsgeschichtliche Untersuchungen,* 159-192.

——— "Lk 22,42a das älteste Zeugnis für Lk 22,20," *MTZ* 3 (1952) 185-188; reprinted, *Traditionsgeschichtliche Untersuchungen,* 193-197.

Snodgrass, K. " 'Western Non-Interpolations,' " *JBL* 91 (1972) 369-379.

Throckmorton, B. H., Jr. "The Longer Reading of Luke 22:19b-20," *ATR* 30 (1948) 55-56.

Vööbus, A. "A New Approach to the Problem of the Shorter and Longer Text in Luke," *NTS* 15 (1968-1969) 457-463.

Westcott, B. F., and F. J. A. Hort. *The New Testament in the Original Greek,* 2. 63-64 (Appendix).

149. JESUS FORETELLS HIS BETRAYAL
(22:21-23)

22 ²¹ "Yet look! The hand of the one who is handing me over is with me at this table. ²² For the Son of Man goes his way, as it has been determined. Yet woe to that man by whom he is handed over!" ²³ Then they began to ask one another which of them it could be who would do that.

COMMENT

The Lucan story of the Last Supper continues with Jesus addressing his apostles after they have eaten. Unlike the Marcan account, in which they end the meal with the singing of a hymn and then go forth to the Mount of Olives, Luke depicts Jesus delivering a discourse to his table companions (22:21-38). In this detail the Lucan story is unique among the Synoptics. It agrees, however, with the Johannine tradition, wherein Jesus gives a long, final discourse to his disciples (chaps. 14-17). The repetitious character of the Johannine discourse has given rise to speculation about its nature as a collection of various independent traditions about what Jesus said on that last occasion, which have been conflated (see further R. E. Brown, *John, XIII-XXI,* 582-597). What we have in the Lucan account of the Last Supper is undoubtedly related to independent traditions in the early community about such a discourse at the Last Supper. But the details of the Lucan and Johannine discourses differ so greatly that there can be nothing more than a superficial similarity between them. Only in the first part of the Lucan discourse (vv. 21-23) is there anything similar to a detail in the Johannine passion narrative; but that is found in John 13:26, prior to the Johannine discourse itself. Moreover, whereas the Johannine final discourse is a good example of the genre of a farewell speech attributed to famous men before death, the Lucan form has little of this character (see the detailed analysis of the genre and its use in the Johannine Gospel by R. E. Brown, *John, XIII-XXI,* 598-601).

The Lucan discourse is made up of four parts, which are not well connected: (1) the foretelling of the betrayal of Jesus (vv. 21-23); (2) Jesus' remarks about the disciples and their place in the kingdom (vv. 24-30); (3) the foretelling of Peter's denial of Jesus (vv. 31-34); and (4) the saying about two swords (vv. 35-38). The topics are only loosely joined and reflect the composite nature of the Lucan discourse. The coherence of the parts is the greatest problem. In fact, some commentators (e.g. G. Schneider, *Evangelium nach Lukas,* 444) do not consider vv. 21-23 to be part of the discourse at all, because v. 24, being narrative in character, seems to introduce the discourse. But then one has to reckon with the character of those verses, which parallel Mark 14:18-21, and with the reason for the Lucan transposition of them. To this point we shall return below.

The conflated character of this part of the passion narrative can be seen from the following: Verses 21-23 are either a redactional reworking of Mark 14:18-21 or a parallel to it, derived from elsewhere. Verses 24-30 are composite; v. 24 stems from Luke's compositional pen; vv. 25-26 are a reworking of Mark 10:42-45; v. 27 seems to come from "L"; and part of vv. 28-30 from "Q." Again, vv. 31-34 are composite; vv. 31-32 are from "L," and vv. 33-34 a redactional reworking of Mark 14:29-30. Finally, vv. 35-38 are probably derived from "L." For details, see pp. 1412, 1421, 1429.

Though H. Schürmann *(Abschiedsrede,* 139-142) argues for a pre-Lucan conflation of this material, it seems much more likely that Luke himself has been responsible for the conflation of the Marcan material (from chap. 14) with material from either other parts of Mark or "L" and "Q." One sees here the use of material that other Synoptic evangelists preserve in different parts of the ministry of Jesus; Luke introduces it into the discourse of the Last Supper. "Luke's editing" is at work (see *HST* 280).

As for the Lucan story of the prediction of Jesus' betrayal by one of his own disciples (22:21-23), different solutions have been proposed for its Synoptic relationship. F. Rehkopf *(Sonderquelle,* 7-30) argues for the use by Luke of a form of the story from "L," and V. Taylor *(Passion Narrative,* 59-61) concludes that "the narrative is non-Markan and that probably verse 22 is a Markan insertion." Taylor goes so far as to think that the account antedates the narratives of Mark, Matthew, and John. But surely the view of J. M. Creed *(The Gospel,* 266-267) is better, for he sees vv. 21-23 to be merely "a briefer version" of Mark 14:17-21. The differences that one notes between Mark 14:22 and Luke 22:21-22 are owing to Lucan redaction (see NOTES on these verses). Verse 23 could be of Lucan composition, but then it has a certain (distant) relationship with John 13:22-24. (See further H. Schürmann, *Abschiedsrede,* 3-21; J. Finegan, *Überlieferung,* 9-13.)

If we are right in regarding this material as basically a reworking of Mark 14:18-21, then one has to reckon with it as a transposition of Marcan material (see p. 71). In the Marcan Gospel the foretelling of Judas' betrayal preceded the institution of the Lord's Supper (cf. the expanded form of Mark in Matt 26:21-25). Luke's use of an older tradition to introduce the institution (see pp. 1386-1387) is in part responsible for the transposition; but undoubtedly a more important reason is his decision to include something of the tradition about a final discourse of Jesus at the supper. This then is the reason for looking at the Lucan discourse as composed of four parts, even if a few narrative verses are interjected (v. 23 and v. 24). Note that if one regards the Johannine discourse as beginning at 13:31, it too has narrative interruptions (13:36; 14:8; 16:29; 17:1).

By making the foretelling of the betrayal of Jesus part of the last discourse, Luke has intensified the nature of the offense. Though he does not mention Judas (among the Synoptics only Matthew does that, 26:25), he implies that Judas has shared in the Last Supper with Jesus and has partaken of the interpreted bread and wine along with the other apostles. The usual horror of the early Christian community over his deed surfaces in the query among the others about who would do such a thing.

The meaning of these verses is not hard to discern. Jesus' declaration not only reveals his awareness that he would be betrayed by one of his own, a betrayal that will lead to death, but it emphasizes that it will come from one from whom he had expected the utmost loyalty. The Lucan transposition thus heightens the contrast between Judas' share in the Last Supper and the action that he is about to perform. It is not easy to say to what extent the lament of Ps 41:9 is operative in the account of the betrayal: "Even my bosom friend in whom I trusted, who ate of my bread, has lifted his heel against me." The reader of the Lucan account cannot help but perceive the anguish experienced by the Lucan Jesus as he admits that his being handed over will come about by "the hand" of one who "is with me at this table." Yet Jesus knows that such infidelity is foreseen in the Father's plan; he reckons with "betrayal" as part of the destiny of the Son of Man. The first part of the Lucan discourse is thus notably parenetic: Participation in the Lord's Supper is no guarantee that a disciple will not betray his Lord.

From the viewpoint of form criticism, these verses preserve Sayings of Jesus, prophetic pronouncements about his own fate, which is related to what has been determined in God's will for him.

NOTES

22 21. *Yet look!* Luke continues his story of the Last Supper with the emphatic adversative conj. *plēn,* followed by the exclamation *idou* (lit. "behold"). J. Jeremias (*Die Sprache,* 288) claims that the use of *plēn* is non-Lucan, but that is scarcely correct. See p. 111, and NOTE on 10:11. In any case, it marks the sharp contrast between this episode and the preceding.

The hand of the one who is handing me over. This is the Lucan abridgement of Mark 14:18. The evangelist introduces synecdoche in speaking of the "hand" of the traitor being on the table. Cf. 1 Sam 24:13-15. The early material in Mark 14:18 is unnecessary in the Lucan account, because Jesus and the apostles have already been depicted as having eaten.

with me. This prepositional phrase is missing in some mss. (D, 063). See Mark 14:18c.

at this table. Lit. "at/on the table," but the def. art. probably carries a demonstrative force in this context. The phrase will appear again in v. 30 with a different connotation. It is part of the Lucan redaction.

22. *the Son of Man.* See NOTE on 5:24. The phrase is used in the surrogate sense, and is derived from Mark 14:21.

goes his way. Instead of the Marcan vb. *hypagei* (14:21), Luke makes use of his favorite *poreuetai* (see pp. 166-169), because he presents Jesus speaking of his own progress to his destiny. See NOTE on 4:30.

as it has been determined. The Marcan parallel speaks of the Son of Man "going as it has been written of him." The words used in Mark, *kathōs gegraptai,* are found elsewhere in Lucan writings (2:23; Acts 7:42; 15:15), but here Luke introduces a different notion, probably because no OT passage was actually cited in the "Mk" source. Luke writes *kata to hōrismenon,* lit. "according to that (which has been) determined," i.e. by God (theological pass.; see NOTE on 5:20). For the Lucan use of *horizein,* see Acts 2:23; 10:42; 11:29; 17:26,31. In four of these passages the reference is to God's will. With this phrase Luke has related the betrayal of Jesus by Judas to the Father's plan of salvation-history. This plan provides the background for the necessity of Jesus' suffering and death. Recall 13:33. See K. L. Schmidt, *TDNT* 5. 452-453; G. Schneider, *EWNT* 2. 1300-1301.

Yet woe to that man. Instead of the Marcan introduction *ouai de,* Luke uses again his emphatic adversative *plēn ouai,* as he introduced his woes in 6:24; 17:1. See p. 108. Why J. Jeremias *(Die Sprache,* 288) ascribes this expression to tradition, rather than redaction, is baffling. In ms. D and the OL versions "man" *(anthrōpō)* is omitted, but the better mss. read it, and it is probably used for a play on "Son of Man" above.

Luke suppresses the judgment recorded in Mark 14:21c: "It would have been better for that man had he not been born." See p. 96.

23. *Then they began to ask one another.* The verse is introduced by the unstressed *kai autoi.* See p. 120. This is really the Lucan reworking of Mark 14:19; there the question is posed to Jesus, but Luke poses the question among the apostles.

which of them it could be who would do that. Lit. "which of them it would be, the one about to do this." The sentence is a bit heavy, but has clearly Lucan traits: the introduction of the indir. question with the acc. neut. def. art. (see p. 108) and the use of the optative in it (ibid.). The question echoes the horror of the early Christian community over the betrayal of Jesus by one of his own. According to the Lucan story, Judas must be assumed to be present among them, since the reader has heard nothing about his departure. Contrast Matt 26:25; John 13:26-30. The Lucan form of this verse has definite hortatory overtones. See COMMENT.

BIBLIOGRAPHY (22:21-23)

Christensen, J. "Le fils de l'homme s'en va, ainsi qu'il est écrit de lui," *ST* 10 (1956-1957) 28-39.
LaVerdiere, E. A. "A Discourse at the Last Supper," *TBT* 71 (1974) 1540-1548.
Rehkopf, F. *Sonderquelle,* 7-30.
Schenke, L. *Studien,* 199-285.
Schürmann, H. *Abschiedsrede,* 3-21.
Taylor, V. *Passion Narrative,* 59-61.

150. JESUS' REMARKS ON THE DISCIPLES AND THEIR PLACES IN THE KINGDOM (22:24-30)

22 [24] Then an invidious dispute developed among them: Which one of them would seem to be the greatest? [25] But Jesus said to them, "The kings of the pagans lord it over them; and those in authority call themselves 'Benefactors.' [26] But this must not be the way with you. No, the greatest among you must become like the youngest; the one who leads like the one who serves. [27] For who is the greater, the one reclining at table or the one waiting on him? Surely it is the one who reclines. Yet I am here among you as the one who serves. [28] You are indeed the ones who have stood by me in my trials. [29] And I confer on you a kingship such as my Father has conferred on me, [30] that you may eat and drink at my table in my kingdom and sit upon thrones as the judges of the twelve tribes of Israel."

COMMENT

The second part of the discourse at the Last Supper in the Lucan Gospel records comments of Jesus about a strife among his apostles, who were at table with him and who were concerned about who was the greatest among them, and further remarks about the rewards that awaited them (22:24-30). This episode has no parallel in other Synoptic accounts of the Last Supper— but then they have no discourse at it. Parts of the verses (25-26) have a parallel earlier in the Marcan Gospel (10:42-45 [cf. Matt 20:25-28]), and parts of vv. 28,30 have an echo in Matt 19:28. The result is that this Lucan episode is composite. It manifests some of Luke's concern to have a discourse at the Last Supper; and the collocation of the material at this point in it may be explained by the relation of the strife and Jesus' comments on it to the immediately preceding announcement of the betrayal of Jesus by one of his own. If that is the nadir to which a chosen and called disciple can sink, then who is the greatest? This seems to be the logic in the Lucan collocation of the parts of the discourse. Jesus' complete answer will steer the concern of the apostles away from such a question. His remarks about the strife, however, make the same point in an abstract way that his example gives in the Last Supper scene of the Johannine Gospel: "Yet I am here among you as the one who serves"—that is given concrete illustration in John 13:3-16.

Concerning these verses the first question is whether or not they form a unit. Verses 25-27 preserve Sayings of Jesus occasioned by a narrative comment of the evangelist about a dispute that arose among the apostles (v. 24). Jesus' comments are partly censorious, partly hortatory. Then in vv. 28-30 the apostles are told of a reward that awaits them, a reward for their fidelity to Jesus in his trials. As a result, commentators are divided about the treatment of these verses; some take the episode as two passages, vv. 24-27, vv. 28-30 (thus M.-J. Lagrange, J. M. Creed, E. Lohmeyer, I. H. Marshall, et al.). Others keep the two passages together as a unit (thus A. Plummer, V. Taylor, J. Schmid, J. Ernst, E. Schweizer, et al.). The joining of the materials used in vv. 24-30 is clearly secondary (see next paragraph), and the thrust of the exhortation is directed primarily at leaders of the Christian community in Luke's day: Those directed to repeat the rite of the Lord's Supper are now exhorted not to lord it over the community, but to serve it. The question, however, still remains about the unitary conception of the Lucan paragraph. In favor of it is the link provided in vv. 27c and 28, where the "you" refers to the apostles who are at table with Jesus, the "you" of vv. 16,18,19,20,26. But this first question is of minor importance.

Of greater importance is the Lucan redaction or composition that is involved. The narrative v. 24, with which the episode opens, is of Lucan composition, even though Luke has been aware of a tradition about strife among Jesus' followers. It begins with his favorite *egeneto de* and contains an indir. question introduced with the acc. neut. def. art. (see p. 108; cf. J. Jeremias, *Die Sprache,* 290). Verse 25 has a traditional (non-Lucan) introduction, *pace* H. Schürmann, *Abschiedsrede,* 70, and the rest of it is a Lucan redaction of Mark 10:42bc. Verse 26 is also a redacted and abridged form of Mark 10:43-44; the verbless first cl. is an abridgment of "Mk" (cp. 1:5c). Instead of Mark 10:45—*the* Marcan Jesus' soteriological pronouncement—Luke has introduced v. 27, an entirely different Saying of Jesus, and probably derived from "L" (see J. Jeremias, *Die Sprache,* 290); it echoes Jesus' servant-action in John 13:15-16. In v. 28 the phrase "the ones who have stood by me" are a parallel to Matt 19:28c, "the ones who have followed me," and the latter part of v. 30 is a Lucan parallel to the last part of Matt 19:28, in effect, something derived from "Q"—indeed, both E. Bammel ("Das Ende") and S. Schulz regard this as the original end of the "Q" document. It is a matter of debate, however, which evangelist has preserved the more original form of "Q" in this instance. Luke has certainly dropped the introductory *amēn legō hymin* (see NOTES on 9:27; 4:24), whereas the mention of the Son of Man and of "regeneration" *(palingenesia)* have to be ascribed to Matthean redaction. The upshot is that the latter part of v. 30 undoubtedly preserves a more original form of "Q" than does its Matthean counterpart (see H. Schürmann, *Abschiedsrede,* 37-54), *pace HST* 159; E. Klostermann, *Lukasevangelium,* 209. Luke has not only put this Saying of Jesus in the Last Supper context, but has further adapted it by the addition of vv. 29,30a; these may represent Lucan composition, or possibly have been derived by him from "L," as J. Schmid *(Evangelium nach Lukas,* 330) prefers. It is possible to admit that the instruction concerns early church leaders, as noted above; but it is far from clear that the sayings are "unquestionably" those of "the risen Lord" (so R. Bultmann, *HST* 158, who even goes further to maintain that "we are dealing with a formulation deriving from the early Church, for it was there that the Twelve were first held to be the judges of Israel in the time of the end" [see pp. 614-620]).

This analysis of the episode is, however, not without its problems. Other analysts differ. J. M. Creed *(The Gospel,* 267), who is otherwise skeptical of the theory about a continuous non-Marcan independent passion narrative being available to Luke, thinks that in this case "the differences both in wording and thought make it probable that Lk. is dependent on a non-Marcan source." Similarly, V. Taylor *(Passion Narrative,* 61-64) ascribes vv. 24-30 to "L". (See also T. W. Manson, *Sayings,* 337; B. H. Streeter, *The Four Gospels,* 288.) Verse 27 clearly comes from a non-Marcan source ("L"), but it is far from certain that the differences in vv. 25-26 are to be explained only by use of such a source (see J. Finegan, *Überlieferung,* 13-14). Rightly has I. H. Marshall *(Luke,* 811) noted the parallelism in structure between the Marcan and Lucan forms of the sayings; that suggests a link between them. Moreover, that Matt 19:28 (which parallels parts of Luke 22:28,30) is "affected by its Markan context" and reflects "the imagery of Matt. xxv.31" can also be admitted (V. Taylor, *Passion Narrative,* 64); "the hand of Matthew" redacting "Q" is clear. But that does not amount to sufficient evidence that all of vv. 28,30 are from "L" (see N. Perrin, *Rediscovering,* 17).

The striking element in Luke's redaction of Mark 10:42-44 is the omission of anything equivalent to v. 45, the soteriological Saying of Jesus about his "giving his life as a ransom for many" *(dounai tēn psychēn lytron anti pollōn),* which would have suited the Lucan context so well here. In addition to what has been said about this problem in COMMENT on 18:35-43 (p. 1212), one may note that the Marcan ending of that saying may be omitted by Luke because of what has been said by Jesus at the end of v. 20. This presupposes, of course, the originality of the long text in the Lucan Last Supper scene. Those who insist on the short text have greater difficulty in justifying the Lucan omission of Mark 10:45. But that may well involve circular reasoning.

The omission of anything like Mark 10:45 by Luke, even in this pericope, raises, however, further problems. Those who like to castigate Luke for doing so should recall what R. Bultmann has written apropos of that Marcan verse *(HST* 93): "A well-known dogmatic transformation can be seen in Mk. 10⁴⁵, the original form of which may well be found in Lk. 22²⁷. . . ." Bultmann even went so far as to claim that the addition (about Jesus' life being a ransom for man) is an "alteration which Mk. 10⁴⁵ . . . has taken from his source (Lk. 22²⁷)"! "Indeed, at the end Lk. 22²⁷ is doubtless original over against Mk. 10⁴⁵, which has formed its conception of Jesus from the redemption theories of Hellenistic Christianity" (ibid. 144). Bultmann's judgment has been echoed by others. E. Schweizer *(Good News according to Mark,* 219) even argues from the absence of anything like Mark 10:45 in the Lucan Last Supper discourse "that v. 45 is an explanation which has been added by the church." (See further E. Haenchen, *Der Weg Jesu,* 369.) If all this were true, why would the Lucan Gospel be at fault in its omission of such a soteriological detail? But I am inclined to agree with C. E. B. Cranfield *(Mark,* 342-343) that 10:45 is an authentic part of the Marcan Gospel tradition. (See further R. Pesch, *Das Markusevangelium II. Teil* [HTKNT 2/ 2; 2d ed.; Freiburg im B.: Herder, 1980] 164-165; V. Taylor, *Mark,* 445-446; S. H. T. Page, "The Authenticity of the Ransom Logion," *Gospel Perspectives* [eds. R. T. France and D. Wenham] 1. 137-161.)

From a form-critical viewpoint, vv. 25-27 and 28-30 preserve Sayings of Jesus. With the introductory v. 24 in the Lucan setting, they take on the character of a multiple pronouncement; and so perhaps it would be better to regard the whole Lucan form as a pronouncement-story. In vv. 25-27, as we have already noted, the sayings are mainly hortatory. In v. 27c a Synoptic I-saying of Jesus is present *(HST* 151). However, T. W. Manson *(Sayings,* 337) also rightly notes that v. 27 is a "saying in parabolic form" and vv. 28-30 have the character of a "farewell-saying." One notes in it a certain similarity to the rewards and duties of disciples which are found in the Lucan parable of the pounds (19:11-27). There is no reason why the hortatory sayings in vv. 25-27 should not be traced back in some form to the historical Jesus (i.e. without the Lucan redaction and the Lucan use of them at the Last Supper).

A dispute among the apostles reclining with Jesus at table about who would seem to be the most important among them is occasioned by Jesus' revelation that one of them could even betray him. From betrayal Jesus turns to another problem in discipleship, that chosen and called disciples, even apostles, could dispute about their importance. Betrayal by one of them implies differences could exist among them; if so, who then is the best, the greatest, the most important? The first two parts of Jesus' table-discourse thus unmask two all-too-human characteristics of those who may be chosen: infidelity or betrayal and struggle for position or esteem. Apropos of the latter, Jesus recalls the mentality of pagan lords; because they are in power, they let their power be felt. The domineering spirit of pagan kings and overweening self-aggrandizement of all authority figures are well known. Jesus flatly states: "This must not be the way with *you*" (v. 26). The "greatest," an echo of the dispute of v. 24, "must become like the youngest" (v. 26), i.e. the newest arrival in their structured group, the least important in their apostolic college. "The one who leads like the one who serves" (v. 26). Thus for the Christian disciple the roles are reversed; they *may not* conduct themselves as do pagan kings and lords. The Lucan Jesus presents himself as an example to them: "I am here among you as the one who serves" (v. 27). What John 13:3-16 presents in symbolic narrative and comment, Luke states in a simple abstract contrast: Jesus has not come to be served by disciples (as the one reclining at table by a waiter), but rather as one who serves and ministers to the needs of others. These words of his at the Last Supper are a commentary on the counsel that he gave in 12:37: He is the master who puts on an apron and serves the faithful servant.

This note of fidelity in the service of apostles surfaces in Jesus' further words in v. 28. He recognizes that the apostles have persevered with him, standing by him in the trials that faced him in his ministry. He gladly acknowledges that fidelity and promises them a reward for it, a share in the regal status that his heavenly Father is about to confer on him. That share is expressed, first, in terms of a right to dine with him at his kingdom banquet (see vv. 16,18; cf. 13:28-29; 14:24); and second, to act as regal judges of his own people, reconstituted anew. The twelve tribes of Israel will be subject to his kingly status in a new way, and his apostles will become like the "judges" of Israel of old, not merely charismatic leaders, but regal figures. This is the greatness and authority which the apostles will have, not the sham power of mere human lordship, the dominance of pagan kings and princes. Their share, however, in such authority and rule will have to be like his own: "I am here among you as the one who serves" (v. 27). Real apostolic leadership must be service of others!

There is yet another aspect of the Sayings of Jesus in this passage: He instructs his apostles to look for community with him *in glory* rather than distinction in earthly rank. Community in that sphere will depend not on who is greatest among them in mortal esteem, but on their perseverance with him in his trials. His words, in effect, foreshadow the coming passion, and more so the words that he will address to the disciples on the road to Emmaus, "Was not the Messiah bound to suffer all this before entering into his glory?" (24:26).

The question always arises whether this final verse with its reference to the twelve tribes of Israel has a bearing on the tradition in the Gospels about the choosing of the Twelve by Jesus. (See p. 617.) I have already set forth (see pp. 253-254) the reasons for attributing to Jesus himself the origin of the Twelve. That he may have adopted that number in imitation of the twelve tribes of Israel is quite possible. The connection between the Twelve and the twelve tribes is certainly pre-Lucan (see Matt 19:28), no matter how important it becomes in Acts 1:15-26 (by implication). Theoretically, the Twelve could have been derived by Jesus as a number for the inner circle of disciples from the use of twelve as a round number among the Jews (see Mark 5:25; Acts 24:11; 19:7). Apart from the Twelve, allusion is made to the twelve tribes in Acts 26:7 (cf. Acts 7:8; Jas 1:1). That the Twelve could also be considered apart from the twelve tribes seems clear in the pre-Pauline kerygmatic tradition of 1 Cor 15:5; cf. Acts 6:1. (See further T. Holtz, *EWNT* 1. 878.)

NOTES

22   24. *Then an invidious dispute developed among them.* I.e. among the apostles. The Lucan introduction is generic and vague; it makes no mention of the ambition of the sons of Zebedee (cp. Mark 10:35-37) or the indignation of the others that it caused (10:41). Luke had no need to introduce such details into the context in which he now uses Jesus' sayings about apostolic ministry. The Greek n. *philoneikia* occurs only here in the NT (the adj. *philoneikos,* "contentious," is found in 1 Cor 11:16); it is a good Hellenistic term to describe the situation, "love of strife."

would seem to be the greatest? I.e. the most important. Lit. "seems to be greater," but the comparative *meizōn* is used for the superlative, as normally in Hellenistic Greek, where the superlative begins to disappear from the language. See BDF § 244; ZBG § 148-150. The need to translate the comparative as the superlative in English obscures the play on *meizōn* in vv. 26,27. The dispute or strife is expressed in terms of appearances *(dokei,* "seems to be . . ."), i.e. how they will be seen in the eyes of others.

25. *The kings of the pagans lord it over them.* Or "the kings of the nations." Jesus' comment on the dispute appeals first to the normal pagan experience. Among them *kyrioi* act as *kyrioi* and make their political power felt. *Ethnē* is used in the sense of "pagans" or "heathens" in 12:30; 18:25. Jesus' answer or comment does not solve the dispute; we never learn who the greatest or most important was. He concentrates instead on how the greatest or most important should conduct himself/herself. Luke's story has already singled out Peter and John (v. 8); the prominence given to them in the sequel (Acts 3-5) makes them prime examples of followers to whom Jesus' words could refer.

those in authority call themselves "Benefactors." The vb. *kalountai* is middle pass. in form and is often taken as pass. (so *RSV, NAB, NEB),* but the middle voice suits the context better. So *NIV, BJ* (se font appeler). It could also mean "let themselves be called" (see BDF § 317). Cf. A. Plummer, *The Gospel,* 501 (he compares the claim of the apostles themselves).

Euergetēs, "benefactor," was a title often given in the Hellenistic world to gods, princes, and Caesars. Caesar Augustus was implicitly so hailed in the Priene inscription, celebrating his birthday and giving thanks for his *euergēmata,* "benefactions" *(OGIS* 2. § 458.I,17) as well as in the Decree of the Hellenes in Asia (ibid. § 458.II,46), recalling his *euergesia,* "benefaction" (abstract). Nero was given the title *euergetēs* (along with *sōtēr,* "savior") in an inscription from the Fayyum in Egypt (ibid. 2. § 668,4). See further A. D. Nock, *"Soter and Euergetes," The Joy of Study: Papers on New Testament and Related Subjects to Honor Frederick Clifton Grant* (ed. S. L. Johnson; New York: Macmillan, 1951) 127-148; reprinted, *Essays on Religion and the Ancient World* (2 vols.; ed. Z. Stewart; Cambridge, MA: Harvard University, 1972) 2. 720-735; F. W. Danker, *Benefactor,* 323-324; G. Schneider, *EWNT* 2. 191-193.

26. *this must not be the way with you.* Lit. "but you not thus." Jesus' injunction must be rightly understood; he does not eliminate distinction or rank in Christian life. He insists only that greatness must serve lowliness. His words are not to be understood in an egalitarian sense, which would be an unrealistic interpretation of them.

No. Lit. "but," a stronger conj. *(alla)* than the *de* which introduced v. 26.

the greatest among you must become like the youngest. I.e. in terms of conduct and way of living. Note how Luke has redacted "Mk": Marcan (and Matthean) *megas,* "great," has become the comparative *meizōn,* to agree with the Lucan compositional introduction (v. 24); Luke has already explained who is *megas* (9:48a). Marcan *diakonos,* "servant," has become *ho neōteros,* "the youngest" (lit. "newer, younger" [cf. Gen 42:20]), a term used elsewhere by Luke (15:12,13; Acts 5:6). Marcan *prōtos,* "first," becomes *hēgoumenos,* "leader" (lit. "leading one"), because the Marcan contrast of *prōtos* and *doulos* is not apt. Finally, Marcan *doulos,* "slave, servant," becomes *ho diakonōn,* "(one) serving, ministering." This last choice of vocabulary may represent the service *(diakonein)* of the church in Luke's day. See Acts 6:2. Recall, too, the play on *meizōn* throughout. See NOTE on v. 24. Note the difference in emphasis in the Lucan form of the saying: it takes for granted that one or other is the greatest. But in Mark 10:43 Jesus says, "Whoever wants to become great among you . . ." In all, the "greatest" must act like the last one to arrive on the scene, the youngest, the least significant. It is sometimes queried whether *neōteroi* refers to a special group within organized early Christian communities. See Acts 5:6; 1 Tim 5:1; Tit 2:6; 1 Pet 5:5; see G. Schneider, *EWNT* 2. 1138; H. Schürmann, *Abschiedsrede,* 76-77. It is, however, eisegetical to introduce into the discussion of these verses the distinction between *presbyteros* and *diakonos* or *episkopos, pace* I. H. Marshall, *Luke,* 813.

the one who leads like the one who serves. The vb. *hēgeisthai* is never used by Mark, occurs only once in Matthew (2:6, where it is part of an OT quotation from Mic 5:1, found only in ms. A of the LXX), but is found five times in Lucan writings (Acts 7:10; 14:12; 15:22; 26:2 besides this occurrence).

27. *who is the greater, the one reclining at table or the one waiting on him?* I.e. according to normal ways of judging or estimating roles in human society. Recall 22:8,

where two prominent members of the Twelve, Peter and John, were sent by Jesus to prepare the supper.

Surely it is the one who reclines. Lit. "is it not the one reclining?" Jesus answers his first rhetorical question with another one, again summarizing the normal mode of estimation—a mode which his next comment will correct.

Yet I am here among you as the one who serves. So the Lucan Jesus sums up his own life and ministry. Possibly his words mean that he is actually serving the Passover meal. Though in a real sense he is actually *ho meizōn,* he is among them as *ho diakonōn,* "the one serving." As in 12:37, the image is derived from table-serving, not from the Servant motif of Deutero-Isaiah. Jesus' life (and his coming passion and death) are thus interpreted as service, and it is all to be taken as the norm of apostolic ministry. No matter what rank the disciple or apostle may achieve in human eyes and by human estimate, their role as Christians is to serve in a lowly, humble way. The soteriological implication of the saying is not to be missed. See R. Tannehill, "A Study"; J. Roloff, "Anfänge."

28. *You are indeed.* Emphasis is on the "you," the same "apostles" (v. 14), who have just been exhorted to lowly service; they now become the subj. of a further comment. Luke has suppressed the *amēn legō hymin* of Matt 19:28 ("Q"). In ms. D one reads the beginning of this verse so: *kai hymeis ēuxēthēte en tē diakonia mou hōs ho diakonōn,* "and you have grown/increased in my service as one who serves," which supplies more of a connection with the preceding, but is suspect because it seems to give a different motive for the reward.

the ones who have stood by me in my trials. I.e. the apostles have persevered with Jesus in the *peirasmoi* that have come to Jesus during his entire ministry from all the rejection and opposition that were his. H. Conzelmann *(Theology,* 80-81) tried to claim that *peirasmoi* refers not to "Jesus' whole life as a temptation, for this would be false. It is now [i.e. in the passion—my addition] that the *peirasmoi* hold sway. Previously they were far away." The period from 4:13 to 22:3 has been interpreted by Conzelmann as Satan-free, and this is the basis for his view of the *peirasmoi.* But now "temptation by Satan" returns. See 22:31-34,39-46. However, as S. Brown *(Apostasy and Perseverance,* 8-9) argues, the limitation of Jesus' *peirasmoi* in this verse to "the passion" would be "grammatically indefensible," since the ptc. *diamemenēkotes* is pf., not pres., and "denotes the *continuance* of completed action." This ptc. is the Lucan equivalent of Matthean aor. *akolouthēsantes,* "having followed" (19:28c), now expressed in terms of Lucan perseverance. Recall 8:15. In the Lucan story the apostles *remain* with Jesus in his passion (see Brown, *Apostasy and Perseverance,* 62-74), and that is "the continuation of their fidelity to him during the public ministry." In Luke's story, the disciples do not always comprehend, but they do not desert him (see 23:49), save for Peter (and he will be converted). Cp. W. Grundmann, *Evangelium nach Lukas,* 403-404. See NOTE on 4:13.

It is well to recall that in the Marcan story (8:33) Peter is called Satan by Jesus himself, because what Peter said showed that he was not on the side of God, but of men. Though Luke drops that detail in his story, it is an example of the *peirasmoi* that came to Jesus during his ministry.

29. *I confer on you a kingship such as my Father has conferred on me.* This is the reward that the Lucan Jesus promises to his apostles for their perseverance with him

in his trials: they will share his regal glory. We learn here for the first time in the Lucan Gospel of Jesus' own kingship *(basileian)*. Cf. 23:42. It is, however, the climax of a number of earlier references that have implied it (1:32-33; 19:11-27,28-40; cf. 22:69 [by indirection]). See further A. George, "La royauté de Jésus selon l'évangile de Luc," 57-69. See pp. 154-157.

Basileia is to be understood as "kingship," as in 1 Kgs 1:46 (MT, *'al kissē' hammĕlûkāh;* LXX, *epi thronon tēs basileias;* cf. P. Joüon, "Notes philologiques," 355). When so understood, it removes the problem that J. M. Creed *(The Gospel,* 269) had with the word in vv. 29,30, since "kingship" can well imply "kingdom."

This verse (whether composed by Luke or derived from "L" [see COMMENT on p. 1413]) echoes a theme about the relation of Jesus to the Father and to his followers, which one finds in the Johannine Gospel. See John 15:9; 17:18,21,22; 20:21. See further J. Guillet, "Luc 22,29." Recall also Luke 12:32.

Some mss. read the beginning of this verse thus: *kagō diatithemai hymin diathēkēn,* which may mean "I make a covenant with you," or more likely "I leave to you a testament/last will" (so mss. A, Θ, 1579, etc.). The addition of *diathēkē* would give to Jesus' words either a covenantal or farewell-speech nuance. Yet even without the addition of *diathēkē,* either sense is already connoted in the vb. *diatithemai.* The "idea of a will or testament" is scarcely excluded, because God is the subject, *pace* I. H. Marshall *(Luke,* 816): it is used figuratively, "I bequeath to you." Cf. Josephus, *Ant.* 13.16,1 § 407.

30. *that you may eat and drink at my table in my kingdom.* I.e. at the banquet of the kingdom of God, to be inherited by Jesus. See 13:29 and NOTE there; 14:15. Note the repetition of the possessive pron. *mou,* "my."

sit upon thrones as the judges of the twelve tribes of Israel. "Twelve thrones" are found in Matt 19:28, probably the original form of "Q." Luke has omitted "twelve" because of Judas' defection, not because of a "broader understanding of apostolic leadership" in his day, *pace* E. E. Ellis, *Gospel of Luke,* 256. The omission reflects the difficulty the early church had in assigning a throne to the betrayer.

The imagery of the saying may reflect Ps 122:4-5, "Jerusalem . . . , to which the tribes go up, the tribes of the Lord, . . . There thrones for judgment were set, the thrones of the house of David." The reference to thrones does not restrict the role of the apostles to "judgment." They are in the Lucan context kingly thrones, and "judging" has to be taken in the OT sense of "ruling." See 1 Sam 8:20 *[ûšĕpāṭānû];* Dan 9:12, which both the LXX and Theodotion translate by *krinein;* Judg 3:10. The apostles will thus become the rulers of reconstituted Israel, the reconstituted people of God. The sense is not that they will sit on thrones in judgment of the Jews who had persecuted them and been involved in the death of Jesus. See further G. Lohfink, *Sammlung,* 79-83. Cf. p. 188 for the relation of this passage to the choosing of Matthias in Acts 1:15-26.

BIBLIOGRAPHY (22:24-30)

Bammel, E. "Das Ende von Q," *Verborum veritas* (eds. O. Böcher and K. Haacker) 39-50.

Brown, S. *Apostasy and Perseverance,* 62-63.

Danker, F. W. *Benefactor: Epigraphic Study of a Graeco-Roman and New Testament Semantic Field* (St. Louis, MO: Clayton, 1982).

Dupont, J. "Le logion des douze trônes (Mt 19,28; Lc 22,28-30)," *Bib* 45 (1964) 355-392.

Feuillet, A. "Le logion sur la rançon," *RSPT* 51 (1967) 365-402.

George, A. "La royauté de Jésus selon l'évangile de Luc," *ScEccl* 14 (1962) 57-69.

Guillet, J. "Luc 22,29: Une formule johannique dans l'évangile de Luc?" *RSR* 69 (1981) 113-122.

Joüon, P. "Notes philologiques [see p. 433]," 345-359, esp. 355.

Lohfink, G. *Die Sammlung Israels,* 79-84.

Moulder, W. J. "The Old Testament Background and the Interpretation of Mark x. 45," *NTS* 24 (1977-1978) 120-127.

Rickards, R. R. "Luke 22:25—They Are Called 'Friends of the People,'" *BT* 28 (1977) 445-446.

Roloff, J. "Anfänge der soteriologischen Deutung des Todes Jesu (Mk. x. 45 und Lk. xxii. 27)," *NTS* 19 (1972-1973) 38-64.

Schlosser, J. "La genèse de *Luc,* XXII, 25-27," *RB* 89 (1982) 52-70.

Schulz, S. *Q: Die Spruchquelle,* 330-336.

Tannehill, R. "A Study in the Theology of Luke-Acts," *ATR* 43 (1961) 195-203.

151. PETER'S DENIAL FORETOLD
(22:31-34)

22 ³¹ "Simon, Simon, beware! Satan has sought you all out to sift you like wheat. ³² But I have prayed for you that your faith might not give out. Indeed, you yourself will turn back; then reinforce your brothers." ³³ "But Lord," he replied, "I am ready to go with you to prison and to death." ³⁴ Jesus answered, "I tell you, Peter, a cock will not crow today before you will have denied three times over that you know me."

COMMENT

The third part of the discourse at the Last Supper in the Lucan Gospel records a Saying of Jesus about the coming trial of the apostles and a dialogue between him and Simon Peter, in which he foretells the trial that Peter is to face and how he will deny that he knows Jesus (22:31-34). Two Sayings of Jesus are thus preserved in it: one about the satanic trial which will test all the apostles, Jesus' own prayer for Peter, and Peter's eventual reaction to it; the other announcing the nadir to which Peter himself will sink in that trial.

The episode is again composite, as the shift in names (Simon in v. 31, Peter in v. 34) immediately suggests. Verses 31-32 are, in fact, exclusive to the Lucan Gospel and have been derived from "L" in general. H. Schürmann (Abschiedsrede, 99-116) regards it as basically a "pre-Lucan piece of tradition" with some traces of Lucan redaction. The latter may be the exclamation idou, the name Satan, the infin. introduced by tou ("to sift you"), and the last words of v. 32 (epistrephein, stērizein, adelphous). (See also HST 267; G. Klein, "Die Verleugnung des Petrus"; E. Linnemann, Studien, 72; V. Taylor, Passion Narrative, 65-66; but cf. F. Rehkopf, Sonderquelle, 91-99.) These verses compensate for the omission of Mark 14:26-28,31 (the Marcan Jesus' prediction of "all" being scandalized over him); they prepare too for what Luke will adopt from Mark about Peter's denial. Verses 33-34 are often regarded as a Lucan redaction of Mark 14:29-30 (thus J. Finegan, Überlieferung, 14-15; H. Schürmann, Abschiedsrede, 21-35). There can be little doubt about v. 34, where "half its words (8/15) are common to Luke and Mark" (V. Taylor, Passion Narrative, 65). But the problematic verse is 33, which not only differs considerably from Mark 14:29, but has a certain resonance with John 13:37, so that one ought to consider it as derived from a non-Marcan source. (See further T. W. Manson, Sayings, 339-340.) There are, however, some commentators (A. Plummer, The Gospel, 503; K. Rengstorf, Evangelium nach Lukas, 248) who hesitate to think of v. 34 as a mere reworking of Mark 14:30. Luke seems to be following a tradition, known also from the Johannine Gospel, according to which the foretelling of Peter's denial takes place in the room where the Last Supper was eaten and not on the way to the Mount of Olives, as in the Marcan and Matthean tradition.

Form-critically considered, the episode contains, first, a prophetic utterance of Jesus (vv. 31-32), which attributes to the disciples a sifting of them by Satan. Pace M. Dibelius (FTG 200), it is far from clear that Luke has "invented the speeches at table during the last Supper" or that "the word to Simon" is the clearest example of such invention. Though Luke is generally reluctant to depict the apostles as having deserted Jesus (he has no parallel to

Mark 14:27-28 or 14:50 and hints instead at their presence at the crucifixion in 23:49 [see NOTE there]), he does preserve here a Saying of Jesus foretelling how they will react to the satanic plot about to unfold. Luke could have suppressed v. 31 entirely as not suited to his general portrait of the disciples at Jesus' passion; but he has not done so. Moreover, the shift from the pl. *hymas,* "you" (v. 31), to the sg. *sou/sy,* "you" (four times in v. 32, referring to Peter), suggests that Luke is using a source with which he has tampered little. Second, in vv. 33-34 Jesus' further statement, likewise prophetic, is occasioned by the narrative record of Peter's protest of his own fidelity; in effect, Jesus' utterance here becomes a pronouncement. Even though one may have to reckon with Marcan redaction in his account of the prediction, as well as with Lucan redaction in certain parts of this episode, what is recorded in both traditions (Marcan and Lucan) is something that is derived from a pre-Marcan and pre-Lucan tradition, as the Johannine evidence makes clear (see R. E. Brown, *John, XIII-XXI,* 614-616).

Having spoken of one of the Twelve who would betray him and commented on the dispute that arose among the apostles about the "greatest" among them, a dispute probably occasioned by the realization of differences existing among them, Jesus passes on to another form of infidelity that will surface among his close followers. Having just spoken of the reward that awaited those who had persevered with him in the trials of his ministry, he makes it clear to them that that fidelity is to be further tested. The coming satanic plot that will engulf him will affect them too, even his chosen apostles. Like the house of Israel of old, they will be sifted like wheat (Amos 9:9). Jesus has, however, prayed for Simon Peter that his "faith" will not fail (permanently); he implies that that prayer has been efficacious. As a result of it, Peter will be converted from what he will become during that satanic experience and is told by Jesus that his task will be to reinforce and strengthen the rest in their fidelity to him. These words of the Lucan Jesus serve to soften the following prediction of Peter's denial of Jesus. Having protested against the implication of Jesus' words about the fidelity of the apostles (himself included), Peter emphatically asserts, "I am ready to go with you to prison and to death" (v. 33). In the Lucan story this protestation is made only once in contrast to the double form of it in Mark 14:29,31. Jesus' comment to Peter is that, even so, that very day before a cock crows he will quickly deny that he knows him.

Simon Peter is clearly being singled out by the Lucan Jesus; though he is part of the apostolic group that will be tested by the coming satanic plot and though he will sink lower than the rest of them, Jesus has prayed for him. He will have the task of strengthening their dedication to Jesus, once he has come back himself, but not by virtue of any trait of character, but simply because he will be assisted by the effective prayer of Jesus. The "brothers" whom he will reinforce or strengthen will be immediately the rest of the apostles, but in view of the fact that they are never depicted as stumbling in the Lucan story or as sheep being scattered (contrast Mark 14:27) and that the term *adelphoi* is used in Acts in a wider sense of Christians (1:15; 15:23,32), Jesus' words to Peter are preparing for the missionary role that he will play in the rest of the Lucan story. He will strengthen them by his primary witness to the resurrection (24:34), by his initiative to reconstitute the Twelve (Acts 1:15-26), by his leadership at Pentecost (Acts 2:14-41) and in Jerusalem (Acts 1-5), by his visits to converts in Samaria, Lydda, and Joppa (Acts 8-9), by his involvement in the conversion of the Roman centurion Cornelius (Acts 10-11), and by his decisive voice at the Jerusalem "council" (Acts 15:7-11).

Though Peter protests his fidelity to Jesus, Jesus foretells his denial, "I tell you, Peter, a cock will not crow today before you will have denied three times over that you know me" (v. 34). In Mark and Matthew the denial of Peter concerns the person of Jesus himself; in Luke the stress is on his knowledge of Jesus. This may point to a different way of thinking about the *pistis,* "faith," of Peter which is involved.

Luke has no equivalent of Matt 16:16b-19 (see p. 771). O. Cullmann *(Peter: Disciple, Apostle, Martyr* [2d ed.; Philadelphia: Westminster, 1962] 191) once raised the question whether those additional Matthean verses might not have had their original context in the Last Supper, i.e. whether they might not be an equivalent of Luke 22:31-32. In both passages Peter's faith is something that stems not from himself alone; in Luke, it depends on Jesus' prayer; in Matthew, on a revelation from the Father. In both Peter is singled out for a community role. The Matthean verses, however, have been more plausibly explained as a retrojection of sayings addressed by the risen Christ to Peter and as the equivalent of the Johannine sayings (John 21:15-17). Moreover, the difference in further details between the Matthean and Lucan episodes makes the Cullmann suggestion rather improbable. (See further R. E. Brown et al. [eds.], *Peter,* 85, 124-125; cf. NOTE on 24:34.)

As we noted at the beginning of this comment, Jesus' remarks on the trial about to face both the apostles as a group and Peter as an individual have to be seen in the context of his comments on the betrayal of himself by one of his own and on the apostles' query about who the "greatest" among them might be. For a test of fidelity can come even to one who will prove to be the "greatest" among them, the one most ready to protest of his readiness to go with Jesus to prison or to death. The Lucan Jesus is making it clear to the reader of the Gospel that no disciple, not even the one for whom Jesus has prayed, will be safe from a test to his/her loyalty and fidelity.

NOTES

22 31. *Simon, Simon.* This name first surfaced in 4:38 (see NOTE there); on the connotation of the repetition of it, see NOTE on 10:41. The Lucan repetition stands in contrast to the single use of *Petre* in v. 34. The latter, Simon's other—significant—name, surfaced in 6:14. In this pre-Lucan tradition, Jesus makes use of Peter's original name as part of the ominous mention of the satanic plot that is about to unfold. A certain similarity in form between this saying and that in 13:34-35 can be detected.

The saying to Simon is introduced abruptly; but some mss. (‌‌‌א, A, D, W, Θ, Ψ, *f* 1,13, and the Koine text-tradition) have an introductory cl., *eipen de ho kyrios,* "but the Lord said." This cl., however, is omitted in mss. P75, B, L, T, 1241, and in some ancient versions (Sinaitic Syriac, Coptic). The transition here is really no more abrupt than that at the beginning of the Lucan discourse (22:21). *Lectio brevior potior.* The abruptness is also owing in part to Luke's making this saying part of the discourse, whereas in the Marcan context there is a narrative introduction (14:26) and a more generic comment of Jesus directed to the group (14:27-28), after which Peter's protestation emerges. Here Jesus takes the initiative.

beware! Lit. "behold" *(idou).*

Satan. See NOTES on 10:18; 22:3. The evil that will affect Jesus will spread to others in different ways. Apart from John 13:27 ("Then Satan entered into him"), Satan occurs in the passion narrative only in the Lucan Gospel; hence Luke may be responsible for the introduction of his name here, creating a link immediately with 22:3 and more remotely with 4:13. It also foreshadows 22:53.

has sought you all out. I.e. "you" pl. *(hymas),* all the apostles, including Simon Peter, and not just Judas and Peter, *pace* E. E. Ellis, *Gospel of Luke,* 256. Satan's seeking out may be an allusion to his roaming to and fro upon the earth in Job 1:7; 2:2. H. Stählin *(TDNT* 1. 194) presses the image still further and thinks that the vb. *exaitein* means "to demand the surrender of" the disciples. See Josephus, *Ant.* 5.2,9 § 152. For an attempt to understand the pron. *hymas* as referring to Simon alone, see A. W. Argyle, "Luke xxii. 31f.," and F. J. Botha, "*'Umâs* in Luke xxii. 31." Cf. *T. Benj.* 3:3. See pp. 509-510.

to sift you like wheat. I.e. to separate the chaff from the wheat. The satanic plot that will bring about the passion of Jesus will test the fidelity of the apostles; it will be their hour of trial too. The phrase is introduced by the gen. of the def. art. (with the infin.). See p. 108 § 9. The phrase may contain an allusion to Amos 9:9: "And I shall shake the house of Israel among all the nations, as one shakes with a sieve." Though the thought content is similar, the formulation in the LXX is different: *kai likmiō en pasi tois ethnesin ton oikon Israēl, hon tropon likmatai en tō likmō,* "and I shall winnow the house of Israel among all the nations, the way one winnows with a winnowing fan/ basket." No little part of the problem is the rare vb. *siniazein,* "sift," which Luke uses; it is not classical (see MM 575). Attempts to specify the image further are not successful. See I. H. Marshall, *Luke,* 820-821. Enough of the sense of the expression comes through without further specification.

32. *But I have prayed for you.* I.e. for Simon Peter, since *sou* is sg., as are the following second-pers. vbs. and prons. The contrast of Satan and Jesus is noteworthy: Jesus stands at Simon's side as an advocate, pleading against the *śāṭān,* the "accuser." The vb. form, *edeēthē,* may come from Luke's pen; *deisthai* is never used by Mark or John, occurs only once in Matthew (9:38), but is found fifteen times in Luke-Acts. See H. Schürmann, *Abschiedsrede,* 105-106; but cf. J. Jeremias, *Die Sprache,* 291. Jesus makes it clear that his influence in Peter's experience will be felt. His prayer actually foreshadows his glance in 22:61. Recall that in the Johannine Last Supper discourse Jesus prayed for "the men given to him from the world" by the Father (17:6,20). *Pace* E. E. Ellis *(Gospel of Luke,* 256), there is not the slightest hint that Jesus' prayer is to be understood in terms of "priestly intercession." Instead, he plays the advocate's role.

that your faith might not give out. I.e. might not prove permanently wanting. Even though R. Bultmann *(HST* 267 n. 2) denies that this is the sense of Jesus' words, they have to be so understood in this Lucan context. Jesus' prayer has been uttered for Peter and it will be efficacious, but it is announced prior to the denial that will be subsequently foretold. This means that the *pistis* of Peter will meet with a test and will be found wanting—but in the long run, not wholly wanting—not because it is *Peter's* faith, but because of Jesus' prayer for him. Though Peter is not said in the Lucan Gospel to have been a "man of little faith" (see Matt 14:31), the theme finds Lucan expression here. Peter's *pistis* is to be understood in this context as "fidelity, loyalty." Recall v. 28. One should not try to understand it in terms of the later distinction between *fides quae* and *fides qua.* In this context it would include both of those. See further p. 236.

Indeed, you yourself will turn back. Lit. "and as for you (emphatic), turning (back), strengthen . . ." The aor. ptc. *epistrepsas* modifies the following impv. *stērison.* But the exact meaning of the ptc. has been a matter of no little debate. Theoretically, it could be taken in a trans. sense, as in Luke 1:16,17 (cf. Sir 48:10), and mean "turn (i.e. convert) your brothers and strengthen (them)." So R. E. Lee, "Luke xxii. 32." The vb. *epistrephein,* however, is used quite frequently in the Lucan writings in an intrans. sense, either neutrally or geographically, "return, turn back/to" (Luke 2:39; 8:55; 17:31; Acts 9:40; 15:36; 16:18), or in a moral, religious sense, "return, turn back, be converted" (Luke 17:4; Acts 3:19; 9:35; 11:21; 14:15; 15:19; 26:18,20). This is the more common interpretation of the ptc. in this verse (thus P. Thomson, *"Epistrephō";* BAGD 301; S. Légasse, *EWNT* 2. 101-102). It is to be preferred and would mean: When Simon has repented of his denial of Jesus, or when he has turned back from his (period of) infidelity. The attempt to understand *epistrepsas* as a Semitism, equaling Hebrew *śûb,* "do again," hence "strengthen again . . ." is misguided. True, the ptc. is found in such a translation in the LXX of 1 Kgs 19:6; but it would imply that Peter had already, even during Jesus' earthly ministry, exercised such a supporting role, which would be difficult to show. See further J. Jeremias, *Die Sprache,* 291.

Whether or not the saying of Jesus echoes 2 Sam 15:20 may be debated. There is a superficial resemblance in the LXX: *epistrepsou kai epistrepson tous adelphous sou.* This was apparently first noticed by W. K. Lowther Clarke, "The Use of the Septuagint in Acts," *Beginnings of Christianity* (eds. F. J. Foakes Jackson and K. Lake; see p. 280 above) 2. 104. However, both Hebrew *śûb* and Greek *epistrephein* are used there in the neutral, geographical sense, not in a moral or religious sense, even though "the verbal echoes" may seem to be "possibly not accidental" (J. M. Creed, *The Gospel*, 269).

A more serious problem is whether the ptc. *epistrepsas* has been added to a pre-Lucan tradition that knew nothing of Peter's denial—that Jesus prayed for Peter so that his faith would not fail. So G. Klein, "Die Verleugnung." Supposedly, Luke would have added the ptc. to link this inherited tradition with the Marcan tradition about Peter's denial in vv. 33-34. See also *HST* 267. All of that, however, is highly speculative; it seems to be more aimed at the denial to Peter of any leadership role.

reinforce your brothers. Lit. "make your brothers firm," i.e. in their fidelity to me. Among the evangelists only Luke uses *stērizein* (9:51; 16:26; Acts 18:23). It is, moreover, far from certain that this vb. belongs to pre-Lucan vocabulary *in the gospel tradition, pace* F. Rehkopf, *Sonderquelle,* 97. On "brothers," see COMMENT on p. 1422; cf. H. Schürmann, *Abschiedsrede,* 110-112. Recall that in Acts 15:41; 16:5; 18:23 others beside Peter (Paul, Barnabas, Judas, Silas) are depicted in a strengthening role. Cp. Matt 16:19 with Matt 18:18.

33. *Lord.* On the voc. *kyrie,* see NOTE on 5:12.

I am ready to go with you to prison and to death. Peter's emphatic reply states his allegiance to his "Lord." Compare the form of the protestation in John 13:37c, "I will lay down my life for you." Both in Luke and John, Peter is less confident than in Mark (14:29,31) or Matthew (26:33,35). The reference to Peter's imprisonment has made commentators query whether the Lucan formulation is colored by the later experience of Peter in Acts 5:18; 12:3.

34. *I tell you.* Luke omits the Marcan asseverative *amēn* (14:30). See NOTE on 4:24.

Peter. The voc. *Petre* is again found in Acts 10:13; 11:7, used by a voice from heaven. Here it is part of the Lucan redaction of v. 34, being lacking in Mark 14:30. Some commentators see in the change of name from "Simon" (v. 31) to "Peter" an ironic reference to the meaning of the latter name; but his rocklike strengthening will come, however, not from his character, but from Jesus' prayer. See further I. H. Marshall, *Luke,* 823.

a cock will not crow today before you will have denied three times over that you know me. Despite Peter's enthusiastic stress on going to prison or death "with" Jesus, the latter now counters with a frank avowal of Peter's coming cowardly defection. Luke has modified Mark 14:30, which reads, "Today, this very night, before a cock crows twice you will deny me thrice," i.e. your triple denial will come so quickly that a cock will not even be able to crow twice. If the Marcan Jesus' prediction is understood thus, it eliminates the query often posed, How could Peter have gone on to further denials of Jesus after the first crowing of the cock? Would he not have recalled the words the first time the crowing was heard? The emphasis is clearly on the rapidity with which the association of Peter with Jesus will elicit the denials. There is no need to invoke reference to the third division of the Roman night, called *gallicinium* or (in Greek) *alektorophōnia,* "cockcrow." That is a subterfuge. If Luke has been moved to excise from his Gospel the rebuke of Peter in chap. 9, he has retained the prediction of Peter's denial from Mark, softening it a bit—as did other parts of the gospel tradition (Matt 26:34; John 13:38).

Finally, note that whereas in Mark 14:30 Peter will deny Jesus *himself* (also in Matt 26:35), the denial in the Lucan Gospel refers to Peter's *knowledge* of Jesus.

Is the cock known in the OT? According to the Vg, "gallus" appears in Isa 22:17; Job 38:36; and Prov 30:31. In Isa 22:17 it is the translation of *geber*, which most modern versions render as "man." In Job 38:36 it renders *śekwî*, the meaning of which is quite disputed *(RSV:* "mists"; *NIV, NJV:* "mind"; *NAB:* "cock" [this meaning is defended by E. Dhorme, "Notice bibliographique," *RHR* 120 (1939) 209]). In Prov 33:31 it renders *zarzîr*, the meaning of which is again disputed *(RSV, NAB:* "cock"; *NIV:* "rooster"). The LXX has in these places (respectively) *andra, poikiltikēn,* and *alektōr.* Moreover, the Vg of Tob 8:11 has *circa pullorum cantum,* lit. "about the crowing of chickens," a part of the night, "cockcrow." But nothing corresponds to this in the LXX, and this part of Tobit is not preserved in Aramaic in the Qumran fragments of Qumran Cave 4 (see J. T. Milik, "La patrie de Tobie," *RB* 73 [1966] 522-530, esp. 522 n. 3). The meaning of all these passages has recently been called in question by G. Brunet ("Et aussitôt le coq chanta," *CCER* 108 [1979] 9-12), who also points out that according to *m. Bab. Qam.* 7:7 it was forbidden to "raise chickens in Jerusalem because of the holy things," and priests were forbidden to raise them anywhere in the land of Israel. See further *b. Bab. Qam.* 79b. Brunet's contentions for Isa 22:17 and Prov 30:31 have to be regarded as serious; that concerning Job 38:36 is highly questionable. About Tob 8:11 no one can say anything. But in 3 Macc 5:23 another word for "rooster, cock," *alektryōn,* does appear: "As soon as the cock had crowed in the morning." (3 Maccabees comes from the end of the first century B.C., but probably of Alexandrian provenience.) Though the Mishnaic regulation is not certainly valid for pre-70 Jerusalem, the prohibition may have been in force then. Where does that leave the historical cockcrow?

BIBLIOGRAPHY (22:31-34)

Argyle, A. W. "Luke xxii. 31f.," *ExpTim* 64 (1952-1953) 222.

Botha, F. J. "'*Umâs* in Luke xxii. 31," *ExpTim* 64 (1952-1953) 125.

Brown, R. E., et al., eds. *Peter,* 119-125.

Dietrich, W. *Das Petrusbild der lukanischen Schriften* (BWANT 94; Stuttgart: Kohlhammer, 1972) 116-139.

Foerster, W. "Lukas 22, 31f.," *ZNW* 46 (1955) 129-133.

Fridrichsen, A. "Scholia in Novum Testamentum, 1. Luk. 22:31," *Professor Johannes Lindbom* (= *SEA* 12 [1947]) 124-131.

Gundry, R. H. "The Narrative Framework of Mt 16,17-19: A Critique of Cullmann's Hypothesis," *NovT* 7 (1964-1965) 1-9.

Klein, G. "Die Berufung des Petrus," *ZNW* 58 (1967) 1-44, esp. 39-44; reprinted, *Rekonstruktion und Interpretation: Gesammelte Aufsätze zum Neuen Testament* (BEvT 50; Munich: Kaiser, 1969) 11-48.

——— "Die Verleugnung des Petrus: Eine traditionsgeschichtliche Untersuchung," *ZTK* 58 (1961) 285-328; reprinted, *Rekonstruktion und Interpretation,* 49-98.

Lattey, C. "A Note on Cockcrow," *Scr* 6 (1953) 53-55.

Lee, R. E. "Luke xxii. 32," *ExpTim* 38 (1926-1927) 233-234.

Lehmann, M. *Synoptische Quellenanalyse,* 103-106.

Linnemann, E. *Studien,* 70-108.

—— "Die Verleugnung des Petrus," *ZTK* 63 (1966) 1-32.

O'Callaghan, R. T. " 'Et tu aliquando conversus,' St. Luke 22,32," *CBQ* 15 (1953) 305-314.

Ott, W. *Gebet und Heil,* 75-81.

Pickar, C. H. "The Prayer of Christ for Saint Peter," *CBQ* 4 (1942) 133-140.

Prete, B. "Confirma fratres tuos," *Sacra doctrina* 15 (1970) 181-218.

—— *Il primato e la missione di Pietro: Studio esegetico-critico del testo di Lc. 22,31-32* (RivBSup 3; Brescia: Paideia, 1969).

—— "Il senso di *epistrepsas* in Luca 22,32," *San Pietro: Atti della xix settimana biblica* (Brescia: Paideia, 1967) 113-135.

Refoulé, F. "Primauté de Pierre dans les évangiles," *RevScRel* 38 (1964) 1-41.

Schneider, G. " 'Stärke deine Brüder!' (Lc 22,32): Die Aufgabe des Petrus nach Lukas," *Catholica* 30 (1976) 200-206.

Schürmann, H. *Abschiedsrede,* 21-35, 116-139.

Sutcliffe, E. F. " 'Et tu aliquando conversus,' St. Luke 22,32," *CBQ* 15 (1953) 305-310.

Thomson, P. "*Epistrephō* (Luke xxii. 32)," *ExpTim* 38 (1926-1927) 468.

Tobin, W. J. "The Petrine Primacy: Evidence of the Gospels," *Lumen vitae* 23 (1968) 27-70.

152. THE TWO SWORDS
(22:35-38)

22 [35] Then Jesus said to them, "When I sent you out without a purse, knapsack, or sandals, was there anything that you lacked?" "Not a thing!" they replied. [36] "But now the one who has a purse had better carry it; and his knapsack too. If one does not have them, he must sell his cloak and buy a sword. [37] For I tell you, what has been written in Scripture must find its final sense in me: *He was classed even with outlaws.*[a] In fact, all that concerns me comes now to its end." [38] And they said, "Look, Lord, here are two swords." But he merely replied, "Enough of that!"

[a] Isa 53:12

COMMENT

The final part of the discourse at the Last Supper in the Lucan Gospel records a dialogue of Jesus with his apostles in which he comments on advice that he once gave to them and now modifies in view of a crisis impending on him and eventually on all of them—a crisis that they still fail to comprehend (22:35-38). Jesus' words in this episode allude to the instructions that he gave to the Twelve when during his ministry he sent them out to proclaim the kingdom and to cure diseases. But now there is need in view of the crisis that looms ahead to make preparations in a different way. This episode has often been called traditionally "the Two Swords," but it is not really appropriate for the subject matter in it; T. W. Manson and V. Taylor have used "Then and Now," but that does not help much, since it is so vague. The topic treated in this episode accentuates the disparate character of the Last Supper discourse in this Gospel (see pp. 1407–1408).

This part of the discourse has no counterpart in any of the other Gospels. If there is tradition behind it, it must be ascribed to "L" (see p. 84). Though A. Loisy *(L'Evangile selon Luc,* 521) and J. Finegan *(Überlieferung,* 16) have been inclined to attribute the passage to Lucan composition (e.g. as a preparation for the use of the sword in 22:49-50), most commentators regard the verses as derived from a pre-Lucan source, although there has been some light Lucan redaction in them. The fact that Jesus, in speaking (v. 35) to the "apostles" who are still with him at table, alludes not to 9:3 (part of the instructions given at the sending-out of "the Twelve"), but to 10:4 (the instructions given at the sending-out of the seventy[-two] others) is an obvious pointer to the use of source material. However, the verses have not come to Luke as a preformed unit; it is Luke who has derived bits of "L" material and put them together in the present form. (See further F. Hahn, *Titles,* 154-155; cf. H. Schürmann, *Abschiedsrede,* 116-139; V. Taylor, *Passion Narrative,* 66-68; J. Jeremias, *Die Sprache,* 292-293.) Moreover, there is "a notable absence of words and phrases characteristic of Luke" in the episode (V. Taylor, *Passion Narrative,* 67). The Lucan redaction has been found in the following elements: the prep. *ater,* "without" (v. 35); the substantived neut. pf. ptc. *to gegrammenon* = "Scripture" (see NOTE on v. 37); the impers. *dei,* lit. "it is necessary" (v. 37; see pp. 179-180); *telesthai en emoi,* "find its final sense in me" (v. 37; see NOTE there); and *to peri emou,* "what concerns me" (v. 37).

From a form-critical point of view, these verses are not easily characterized. The setting is that of a dialogue between Jesus and his apostles. Verses 36-37 could be understood as a pronouncement, but that characterization suits much better the final words of Jesus in v. 38d—yet these hardly constitute the point of the episode. Hence it is probably best to regard these verses as isolated Sayings of Jesus from a pre-Lucan tradition, which Luke has strung together. The saying in v. 36 is partly hortatory, partly minatory; that in v. 37 is prophetic; and that in v. 38 is an ironic comment cutting off further discussion.

Jesus' question in v. 35 is supposed to be a reference to the instructions that he gave to the apostles when the Twelve were sent out (9:1-6; recall 6:13cd). But the items without which they were to go forth, "purse, knapsack, or

sandals," are found in the instructions for the "seventy(-two) others" (10:1-
12; cp. 9:3 and 10:4). How this situation has come about has already been
explained in the COMMENT on 10:1-12 (see p. 843). Luke now makes no effort
to resolve the inconsistency. No matter whether the allusion be to the
sending-out of the apostles or of the seventy(-two), the time has come when
the Lucan Jesus must correct the instructions. The "but now" with which v.
36 begins is emphatic; it alludes to a coming crisis for which the apostles must
now begin to prepare. The opposition to Jesus, which has been mounting in
the Lucan story (recall 6:11; 11:53-54; 19:47; 20:19; 22:2), provides the
background for his admonition to the apostles. They must be on their guard
and must provide for themselves, for they are to be part of crisis. Jesus
mentions three of the things that he instructed disciples earlier not to carry
along with them; now he refers to the same threesome (purse, knapsack, or
sandals) but instructs them solemnly and symbolically that they are to take
them up. Even though the apostles' task eventually will be to continue the
proclamation of the kingdom, what is to ensue shortly will draw them into
the opposition that has faced Jesus in his ministry. The reason for his new
instruction is his awareness that what has been written in Scripture about him
must find its fulfillment. The opposition will come to the point that he will be
reckoned as a transgressor, as lawless. The Lucan Jesus casts himself in the
role of the Servant of Yahweh, about whom the prophet of old had written:
". . . because he poured out his life unto death and was numbered among
the transgressors; yet he bore the sin of many and made intercession for the
transgressors" (Isa 53:12). But the Lucan Jesus singles out only one cl. of that
prophecy and intimates by the use of it that he will be classed with the
outlaws. What Deutero-Isaiah said of the Servant of old finds new meaning
now in the crisis that faces Jesus. The OT prophetic utterance is used, in
typically Lucan fashion, as a prediction that is to find realization in the
passion and death of Jesus.

For a number of commentators the crisis that is in the offing is to be
restricted to "the passion of Jesus" (thus P. S. Minear, "A Note"). Obviously,
that is part of the immediate reference of "but now." However, in the total
complex of the Lucan writings it cannot be limited to that alone. What
happens to the kingdom-preacher in the ensuing episodes of the Lucan story
is but a symbol of the experience that the witnesses to the word are going to
have in Luke's second volume.

The episode ends with a note of the incomprehension of the apostles.
Because Jesus introduces in v. 36 a new item with which the apostles have to
equip themselves, viz. a sword, they take his word literally, and comment,
"Look, Lord, here are *two* swords" (v. 38). With no little irony the Lucan
Jesus exclaims, "Enough of that!" His disillusionment is complete. As T. W.
Manson *(Sayings,* 341) once put it, "This short dialogue throws a brilliant

light on the tragedy of the Ministry. It goes with the Q lamentation over Jerusalem (Lk. 13³⁴ᵇ ‖ Mt. 23³⁷⁻³⁹); and, like that elegy, it is full of bitter disappointment. The grim irony of v. 36 is the utterance of a broken heart."

NOTES

22 35. *Then Jesus said to them.* So Luke introduces the new topic.

without a purse, knapsack, or sandals. See NOTE on 10:4. The last of this threesome, *hypodēmata,* is omitted in ms. Γ and a few others; but even without "sandals," the allusion to 9:3 (the sending of the Twelve) does not become clear. On *ater,* "without," see 22:6.

was there anything that you lacked? Lit. "you did not lack anything, did you?" Jesus' question expects a negative answer. Implied is the ready hospitality that they met from people among whom they proclaimed the kingdom and cured diseases.

Not a thing! Luke uses the Hellenistic form *outhenos* instead of the classical *oudenos.* Apart from 1 Cor 13:2; 2 Cor 11:9, the Hellenistic form otherwise occurs only in Lucan writings in the NT (23:14; Acts 15:9; 19:27; 20:33; 26:26). The apostles' answer echoes the reaction of the disciples on their return in 10:17.

36. *But now.* I.e. in view not only of the passion of Jesus soon to begin but also of the new period of salvation-history to be inaugurated on the heels of that passion. Though emphatic, *alla nyn* does not merely refer to that very moment in which it is spoken. Before Jesus' passion begins, he will prepare himself by prayer on the Mount of Olives. A fortiori, the phrase does not demarcate the end of Period II (of Jesus) and the beginning of Period III (of the church). It looks forward, however, to both. See pp. 182-186. I. H. Marshall *(Luke,* 824) thinks that the contrast lies only between the peaceful ministry up to this point and the crisis of the passion about to ensue. Such a contrast is present, but it is not restricted to that, since the Lucan Jesus' words are also addressed to the readers of Luke's Gospel. H. Conzelmann *(Theology,* 103 n. 1) insists on the different character of the period that comes after *nyn;* indeed, it will be different since Jesus will no longer be physically and visibly present to his disciples, and his presence will be felt through his Spirit.

the one who has a purse had better carry it; and his knapsack too. Lit. "let the one having a purse carry (it), and likewise a knapsack." Another possible, but less likely, translation would be, "let the one having carry a purse, and likewise a knapsack." The first translation would almost spontaneously be adopted were it not for the parallel *ho mē echōn,* "the one not having," with an obj. implied in v. 36d. The relation between these parts of v. 36 is quite complicated.

If one does not have them, he must sell his cloak and buy a sword. Lit. "let the one not having (an obj. understood) sell his cloak and buy a sword." The relation between the parts of this elliptical verse have given rise to four different interpretations: (1) *ho echōn* and *ho mē echōn* have the same objs., *ballantion,* "purse," and *pēran,* "knapsack." So I have understood the relation in my translation. Similarly, A. Plummer *(The Gospel,* 505) and J. Finegan *(Überlieferung,* 16). The sense: The one who has purse and knapsack had better take them along; the one who does not have (them) must sell what clothing he has to get a sword. (2) *ho echōn* has the objs.

ballantion and *pēran*, but *ho mē echōn* has as obj. *machairan,* "a sword," understood from the end of the sentence. This is probably the most common interpretation, being used by the RSV, NAB, NEB, NIV. The sense: One needs purse, knapsack, *and sword.* (3) *ho echōn* has the objs. *ballantion* and *pēran,* but *ho mē echōn* is used absolutely: The sense: Let the one having a purse carry it, and a knapsack too; the one having no(thing) must sell his cloak and buy a sword. So G. Schneider *(Evangelium nach Lukas,* 454-455). (4) *ho echōn* and *ho mē echōn* are both used absolutely: The sense: The one who has (one) had better carry his purse, and his knapsack too; the one who has not must sell his cloak and buy a sword. The contrast is between the affluent and the destitute. So E. Klostermann *(Lukasevangelium,* 214).

It is difficult to be sure which sense is preferable; something can be said in favor of each possibility. No matter which is preferred, instead of the threesome, purse, knapsack, and sandals, a different threesome appears, purse, knapsack, *and sword.* The introduction of the "sword" signals the difference in the periods; the Period of the Church will be marked with persecution, as the later Lucan story makes clear. See Acts 8:1b-3; 9:1-2; 12:1-5. But whoever sets out in Jesus' name must be fully equipped —not with material armor, but with armor in his sense.

This verse has no zealot tendency (see F. Hahn, *Titles,* 153); nor does it reflect any awareness of the flight of Jewish-Christians from Jerusalem to Pella, *pace* H.-W. Bartsch, "Jesu Schwertwort." Moreover, it cannot be used to support the purchase of physical weapons in modern society; for the connection between the recommendation here and vv. 49-50 of this same chapter has yet to be shown.

Jesus' words about equipping oneself with purse, knapsack, and sword have to be taken in a symbolic sense, even if one may not read into it the sense of spiritual armor of Eph 6:11-17. The symbolic sense of his counsel is derived from the reaction that he gives to the literal interpretation of his words in v. 38.

37. *For I tell you.* See NOTE on 22:16.

what has been written in Scripture. Lit. "that having been written," a dem. pron. + the substantived pf. pass. ptc. *to gegrammenon* is used to = "Scripture." See 20:17 (sg. as here); 18:31 (see NOTE there); cf. J. Jeremias, *Die Sprache,* 292-293. The specific OT passage will be quoted in the subsequent part of the verse.

must find its final sense in me. Lit. "must be brought to an end in me." On the vb. *telein,* see NOTE on 18:31; again, as there, used as the theological pass.

He was classed even with outlaws. An explicit quotation of the Servant Song of Isa 53:12, the only place in the gospel tradition where it is so quoted. The LXX reads, *kai en tois anomois elogisthē,* "and he was classed among the outlaws," whereas the MT reads *wĕ'et pōšĕ'îm nimnāh* (1QIsaᵃ 44:21-22: *w't pwš'ym nmn'),* "and with transgressors was he counted." D. L. Jones ("The Title Pais") rightly stresses that Luke uses the Servant motif as part of a " 'humiliation-exaltation' theme" in the Lucan writings, without any reference to it in a vicarious sense. Luke develops the latter independently.

Luke's quotation is a closer reflection of the Hebrew than of the LXX. A. Plummer *(The Gospel,* 506) objects to the translation of *kai* as "even," maintaining that it is the conj. "and." So it is in the Hebrew and in the LXX; but in the Lucan context that sense of *kai* is difficult; hence the translation proposed. In Deutero-Isaiah the Servant is regarded as part of sinful humanity, the object of both God's judgment and mercy.

As used here, the cl. refers to the human judgment to be passed on Jesus, as a result of which God's judgment will bring him to victory: "This Jesus whom you crucified God has made both Lord and Messiah" (Acts 2:36). But the real meaning of introducing the quotation from Isaiah is to make clear that if Jesus is to be so treated, so will his followers. Hostility toward the apostles is grounded in the hostility to Jesus himself *(qualis rex, talis grex)*.

Jesus' association with two *kakourgoi* will take place in the crucifixion scene (23:32-33); but all the political implications of his ministry (see 23:2-5) as well as of the early Christian community, which grows out of his preaching, in Acts fill out the implication of his being classed with outlaws in the sense of Deutero-Isaiah.

To interpret the *anomoi,* "outlaws," of the Deutero-Isaiah passage as a reference to "the disciples," as do P. S. Minear ("A Note") and F. W. Danker *(Jesus and the New Age,* 225), can only be described as strange; not even the episode of 22:49-50 calls for that.

all that concerns me comes now to its end. Lit. "that which (is) about me has an end." The meaning of this sentence and its relation to the preceding are a matter of dispute. The expression *echein telos,* lit. "have an end," can be understood in several ways: (1) "is at an end," which with *to peri emou* referring to Jesus' earthly life would mean: "my life's work is at an end," i.e. comes to cessation in a temporal sense. So T. W. Manson, *Sayings,* 342; E. Klostermann, *Lukasevangelium,* 214. Cf. Josephus, *Life* 31 § 154: *ta men peri ekeinous tout' esche to telos,* "and so ended their affairs"; Diodorus Siculus, 20.95; Plutarch, *Mor.* 615E. This would add another reason beyond that from the OT. (2) "has its fulfillment," i.e. all that has been foreseen in God's plan comes to realization, fulfillment. Since the vb. *telein* has been used in the preceding sentence in the sense of "fulfill," *telos,* the cognate n., is given the same sense here. This would then reiterate the OT reason. See Luke 24:27 (and possibly 24:19). So J. M. Creed, *The Gospel,* 271; BAGD 811. (3) "(now) reaches its goal," understanding *telos* as that toward which all Jesus' life and ministry have been aimed. See Plato, *Symp.* 211b, 210e; *Clit.* 410e; *Resp.* 613c; Aristotle, *Nic. Eth.* 1094a 18. This would add a telic nuance to the reason based on the OT. The second sense seems least apt, since it is repetitious of what has just been said. For *ta peri* + gen., see 24:19,27: Acts 1:3; 8:12; 18:25; 19:8; 23:11,15; 24:10; 28:7,15,23,31.

38. *Look, Lord, here are two swords.* I.e. not just one, as in v. 36. So literally the apostles take Jesus' words in v. 36; if he is for fighting, they are with him. See T. W. Manson, *Sayings,* 341. They miss the point of what he was talking about, and one of them will still be armed in vv. 49-50.

Since the time of John Chrysostom *(Hom. in Matt.* 84; PG 58. 752) attempts have been made (see F. Field, *Notes,* 76-77) to translate *machaira* other than "sword," e.g. of the daggerlike butcher knife used for the slaughter of the Passover lamb. In its earliest use in the Greek language (Homer, *Il.* 11.844; 18.597) it was so understood; but from Herodotus on *(Hist.* 6.75; 7.225) it came to designate "sword" generically and is used in the LXX of various types of swords. See W. Michaelis, *TDNT* 4. 524-527; E. Plümacher, *EWNT* 2. 978-980.

G. Schwarz *("Kyrie")* has recently tried to explain the misunderstanding of Jesus' words about a sword by the apostles, appealing to Jesus' mother tongue, Aramaic, in which *sêpā'* means either "end" (= Greek *telos)* or "sword." However, he cites only dictionaries of rabbinic and targumic Aramaic (J. Levy, G. Dalman) and never asks himself about the problems that his suggestion raises. The usual word in Aramaic of the contemporary period would be *saypā'*, which could be contracted to *sêpā'*, the form he uses. The usual form of the word for "end" is *sĕyāpā'*, which could never be contracted to *sêpā'*. Where this last form occurs is also problematic. Moreover, Schwarz never tells us how a misunderstanding could arise between *to peri mou telos echei*, which might be in Aramaic *lĕkol dî 'alay sĕyāp* (or even *sêp*) and *māryā', hā' trê saypîn tĕnāh* (= *Kyrie, idou machairai hōde dyo*). Serious consideration of the Aramaic substratum of Jesus' words must pass beyond such naïve comparison of mere dictionary forms of (often alleged) homonyms.

For later, medieval interpretations of the "two swords," see J. Lecler ("L'Argument") and Pope Boniface VIII, *Unam Sanctam* (DS 870-875, esp. 873).

On the voc. *kyrie,* see NOTE on 5:12.

Enough of that! I.e. the apostles have so misunderstood the import of my words. He will refuse to explain further, for he realizes that he faces his destiny alone. He has said what he considered necessary to warn them about the crisis that is to begin.

These last words have often been understood otherwise. Either literally, as if Jesus meant that two real swords would suffice for the encounter to come (so A. Loisy, *L'Evangile selon Luc,* 524), or even ironically, "That's more than enough" *(satis superque;* so since Cyril of Alexandria *[Comm. in Luc.* 22.38; PG 72. 917]).* But the irony concerns not the number of the swords, but the whole mentality of the apostles. Jesus will have nothing to do with swords, even for defense. Whether the ironic sense of *hikanon estin* is a Semitism, related somehow to the Hebrew *(rab-lāk)* of Deut 3:26 (cf. the LXX *[hikanousthō soi]),* is problematic; there is no need to appeal to that since the irony is in the context.

BIBLIOGRAPHY (22:35-38)

Bartsch, H.-W. "Jesu Schwertwort, Lukas xxii. 35-38: Überlieferungsgeschichtliche Studie," *NTS* 20 (1973-1974) 190-203.

Bischinger, M. *Die Zwei-Schwerter-Theorie: Exegesegeschichtliche Untersuchung über die Interpretation von Lk 22,35-38* (Vienna: Dissertation, 1971).

Cullmann, O. *Jesus and the Revolutionaries* (New York: Harper & Row, 1970) 47-50.

Finlayson, S. K. " 'The Enigma of the Swords,' " *ExpTim* 50 (1938-1939) 563.

Hahn, F. *Titles,* 153-155.

Hall, S. G. "Swords of Offence," *SE I* (TU 73) 499-502.

Hobhouse, S. " 'And He that Hath No Sword, Let Him . . . Buy One' (Luke xxii. 35-38)," *ExpTim* 30 (1918-1919) 278-280.

Jones, D. L. "The Title *Pais* in Luke-Acts," *SBLSP 1982,* 217-226.

Larkin, W. J. "Luke's Use of the Old Testament as Key to His Soteriology," *JETS* 20 (1977) 325-335.

Lecler, J. "L'Argument des deux glaives (Luc xxii,38) dans les controverses politiques au moyen âge," *RSR* 21 (1931) 299-339; 22 (1932) 151-177, 280-303.

Lehmann, M. *Synoptische Quellenanalyse,* 148-152.

McDowell, E. A. "Exegetical Notes," *RevExp* 38 (1941) 44-48.

Maurer, C. "Knecht Gottes und Sohn Gottes im Passionsbericht," *ZTK* 50 (1953) 1-38.

Minear, P. S. "A Note on Luke xxii 36," *NovT* 7 (1964-1965) 128-134.

Napier, T. M. "The Enigma of the Swords," *ExpTim* 49 (1937-1938) 467-470.

────── " 'The Enigma of the Two Swords' (Luke xxii. 35-38)," *ExpTim* 51 (1939-1940) 204.

Reinach, S. "Les deux épées," *Revue archéologique* 4/19 (1912) 435.

────── "Encore les deux épées," ibid. 5/10 (1919) 370-371.

Schlatter, A. *Die beiden Schwerter: Lukas 22,35-38. Ein Stück aus der besonderen Quelle des Lukas* (BFCT 20/6; Gütersloh: Bertelsmann, 1916).

Schürmann, H. *Abschiedsrede,* 116-139.

Schwarz, G. *"Kyrie, idou machairai hōde dyo,"* *BN* 8 (1979) 22.

Western, W. " 'The Enigma of the Swords,' " *ExpTim* 50 (1938-1939) 377.

────── "The Enigma of the Swords, St. Luke xxii, 38," *ExpTim* 52 (1940-1941) 357.

Wright, R. F. "Studies in Texts," *Theology* 44 (1942) 296-300.

B. The Passion, Death, and Burial of Jesus

153. THE PRAYER ON THE MOUNT OF OLIVES
(22:39-46)

22 [39] Then Jesus went out and made his way as usual to the Mount of Olives, and his disciples too followed him. [40] When he had reached the spot, he said to them, "Pray that you enter not into temptation." [41] Then he withdrew from them about a stone's throw, knelt down, and prayed, [42] "Please, Father, take this cup away from me. Yet not my will, but yours be done!" [43-44][a] [45] When he rose from his prayer, he came to the disciples and found them sleeping, because of grief. [46] He said to them, "Why do you sleep? Get up and pray that you enter not into temptation."

[a] Verses 43-44 are omitted in many mss. See NOTE at the end of the pericope.

COMMENT

The passion narrative now moves into another phase which presents the Lucan account of Jesus' passion, death, and burial (22:39-23:56a). In its first episode Jesus retreats after the Last Supper to the Mount of Olives and prays to his Father, expressing his readiness to face what awaits him (22:39-46). In each of the Synoptic accounts this scene deals with Jesus' inner reaction to his coming passion and with his basic orientation to his Father's will and the heavenly plan of salvation, which is about to unfold in its climactic moment.

Not only do the Synoptic parallels (Mark 14:26,32-42; Matt 26:30,36-46) record Jesus' withdrawal with his disciples after the Last Supper to a spot (east of the Kidron), but also John's Gospel has a bit of the same tradition (18:1,11; see p. 88). In the latter Jesus goes with the disciples to "a garden" (kēpos, possibly an allusion to 2 Sam 15:23?), whereas in the Synoptics he goes to a spot on "the Mount of Olives." The Marcan Gospel, however, has more echoes in the Johannine (see R. E. Brown, *New Testament Essays*, 192-198) than the Lucan. Again, both Mark (14:32) and Matthew (26:36) name the spot, Gethsemane (Gethsēmani, probably a grecized form of Hebrew/

Aramaic *gat-šĕmānî,* "oil-press"). This Semitic place name is omitted by Luke, who contents himself with the generic locality (v. 39), as in Mark 14:26.

The Lucan account is clearly inspired by the Marcan. Because Luke has put the foretelling of Peter's denial into his Last Supper discourse, he brings Jesus directly to the Mount of Olives without mention of anything that happened en route. It is, however, a matter of no little debate whether Luke presents here a redacted form of "Mk" or has made use of an independent non-Marcan source. For the Lucan account is considerably shorter than the Marcan, and it may contain some details that are wholly absent from the latter.

When one compares the Lucan and Marcan accounts, one notes:

1) In Luke Jesus proceeds to the Mount of Olives (generically named), followed by unnamed disciples, whereas in Mark he goes to Gethsemane, on the Mount of Olives.

2) In Luke Jesus exhorts the disciples to pray, whereas in Mark he tells them to sit there, while he goes to pray; he further singles out Peter, James, and John and tells them of his distress and anxiety—none of which is noted in Luke.

3) In Luke Jesus withdraws from (all) the disciples "about a stone's throw" (v. 41) and prays, whereas in Mark he withdraws "a little further" from Peter, James, and John.

4) In Mark part of Jesus' prayer is recounted in indir. discourse, but in Luke the content of his prayer is given entirely in dir. discourse.

5) Though the substance of what he utters to the Father is the same in Mark and Luke, the latter eliminates the Aramaic address *'abbā'* and its Greek literal translation, *ho patēr,* using the more correct voc. *páter.*

6) In Mark Jesus prays three times and returns to Peter, James, and John after each prayer, whereas in Luke he prays only once and then returns to (all) the disciples.

7) In Mark Jesus finds Peter, James, and John asleep, whereas in Luke he finds all the disciples asleep—and because of grief.

8) Jesus' counsel to pray lest they enter into temptation is common to Mark and Luke, but in the latter it forms an *inclusio* which frames his own prayer.

9) If vv. 43-44 in the Lucan account are authentic, Jesus receives heavenly reassurance and strength in his traumatic experience, a detail that is wholly lacking in Mark.

From this comparison it is clear that Luke has either radically abridged the Marcan form or has made use of another shorter account (which may even have had details different from the Marcan). The Marcan form of the story is the subject of much analysis and debate itself (see K. G. Kuhn, T. Lescow, E. Linnemann, L. Schenke), a problem that does not concern us here.

Many commentators maintain that, since the Lucan account is so different from the Marcan in details, it must have been derived from an independent non-Marcan source. (So A. Schlatter, *Evangelium des Lukas,* 432-433; A. Loisy, *L'Evangile selon Luc,* 525; M.-J. Lagrange, *Luc,* 558; W. Grundmann, *Evangelium nach Lukas,* 411; K. G. Kuhn, "Jesus in Gethsemane," 271; V. Taylor, *Passion Narrative,* 69-72; F. Rehkopf, *Sonderquelle,* 84; T. Lescow, "Jesus in Gethsemane bei Lukas und im Hebräerbrief"; E. Haenchen, *Der Weg Jesu,* 495; et al.) Yet such a solution may be all too simple, for, if one prescinds from the text-critical problem of vv. 43-44 for the moment, the rest of the Lucan verses can be explained as either a Lucan redaction of some Marcan verses or Lucan omission and composition. A number of commentators have judged similarly: J. Finegan, *Überlieferung,* 18; J. M. Creed, *The Gospel,* 272; J. Schmid, *Evangelium nach Lukas,* 335; E. Linnemann, *Studien,* 34-40 (her discussion is the best); E. Klostermann, *Lukasevangelium,* 215; G. Schneider, *Evangelium nach Lukas,* 457; et al.

Verse 39 is clearly dependent on Mark 14:26, even if Luke has used some of his own formulation: aor. *eporeuthe* instead of the Marcan *exēlthon; kata to ethos,* "according to custom." In v. 40b Jesus' counsel to the disciples to pray is influenced by the advice given to the disciples later on in Mark 14:38; Luke thus creates an *inclusio* (see v. 46b) to frame the prayer of Jesus. Verse 40a has been composed by Luke himself (for details, see NOTES). In v. 41 one finds the unstressed *kai autos* (see p. 120), the Lucan use of *hōsei* (see NOTE on v. 43), and the Lucan expression for "knelt down"—all of which suggests a Lucan redaction of Mark 14:35. In v. 42 Luke omits the Marcan reference to the "hour" (probably because it is saying almost the same thing as the "cup") and the Aramaic address *abba,* but keeps the substance of Mark 14:36, casting the mention of the Father's will only in the abstract. Yet he retains the Marcan "take this cup away from me." Verse 45 begins with two Lucan ptcs. *anastas* and *elthōn,* lit. "rising" and "coming," and a typically Lucan shift of the Marcan historical pres. *heuriskei* to second aor. *heuren* (see p. 107). Lucan redaction excuses the sleeping disciples, "because of grief" (v. 45). In v. 46 Luke's esteem for Peter makes him address Jesus' complaining query to (all) the disciples, "Why do you (pl.) sleep?" Again, he substitutes his favorite ptc. *anastantes* (see p. 110) for the Marcan impv. *grēgoreite,* "wake up" (14:38). He models the rest of v. 46 on 14:38b, but drops completely vv. 38c-42.

The result is a stark abridgment of the Marcan account, one that centers on Jesus' relation to his Father much more than on his concern about the nonchalance of the uncomprehending disciples. As one might expect in this Gospel, the Lucan Jesus emphasizes the need for prayer in the lives of the disciples who are "following" him into the ordeal that is about to unfold. His double exhortation to them to pray forms a frame for his own prayer. The centrality which is thus given to it highlights Jesus' filial submission to his Father's will.

It is also clear that the disciples come off better in the Lucan story than they do in the Marcan—and this is undoubtedly responsible for the omission of the three comings from and goings to prayer. For this reason too he excuses the disciples who sleep "because of grief" (v. 45).

Form-critically considered, the episode is another Story about Jesus, part of the narrative gospel tradition. R. Bultmann *(HST* 267-268) considered the Marcan form to be "an individual story of a thorough-going legendary character, which has not survived intact in Mark." He reckons with secondary additions, which attached themselves to a core, as the scene was read for Christian edification. The problem is how to account for the origin of the scene and especially the prayer of Jesus. Having withdrawn from the disciples, and even from Peter, James, and John (see 14:32b,33a,35a) to commune with the Father, who would have heard him utter the words ascribed to him? This difficulty is compounded when one recalls the sleep of the disciples. (The Lucan account would exaggerate the distance, changing "a little further" to "a stone's throw.") We are, in fact, confronted with the type of episode met in 4:1-13 (see p. 509). Though many commentators follow Bultmann in maintaining the legendary character of the episode, many others point to the echoes of the tradition in John 12:27; 18:11 and even more so in Heb 5:7, which in a more developed form records, "Who in the days of his flesh offered prayers and supplications, with mighty cries and tears, to him who was capable of saving him from death; and he was heard because of his piety." Although these echoes scarcely *establish* the connection with an event and a prayer in the life of the historical Jesus, they do argue in favor of a presumption that the story is not a fabrication out of whole cloth. V. Taylor *(Mark,* 551) not only cites the view of A. E. J. Rawlinson (that the basis of the story is "certainly historical and beyond the reach of invention") but also mentions a "consensus of opinion shared by radical and conservative critics alike" that the tradition goes back to a historical nucleus. (See further R. S. Barbour, "Gethsemane in the Tradition of the Passion.") No one will deny that the different accounts have been overlaid with nuances that reveal the later, often hortatory or apologetic, use of the episode.

Having reinterpreted the Passover meal for his disciples and having given them his last instructions, Jesus withdraws, according to custom, to the Mount of Olives (recall 21:37), to a spot well known to Judas, to devote himself to prayer (see pp. 244-245). The Lucan Jesus reveals none of the emotional reactions to the coming ordeal that the Marcan Jesus does. With sober brevity he exhorts his disciples to prayer, then withdraws from them, kneels, and makes his supplication: "Please, Father, take this cup away from me" (v. 42), using an OT figure for the cup of destiny that he soon must drink (see NOTE there). Though he does not see clearly the shape that that ordeal is going to take, he adds, "Yet not my will, but yours be done!" (v. 42). As Son, he submits to what his filial dedication to his Father demands of him; he expresses his readiness to see the climactic moment of the Father's plan of salvation reached. His dedication thus faces its ultimate challenge, because it involves his human existence itself. When the Lucan Jesus began his ministry, he announced, "I must proclaim the kingdom of God . . . for that is what I was sent for" (4:43). And "As the days were drawing near when he was to be taken up to heaven," he resolutely set his face "toward Jerusalem" (9:51). En route to that city of destiny, he further declared, "Today, tomorrow, and the next day, I must keep on my way, because it is impossible that a prophet will perish outside of Jerusalem" (13:33). Now comes the climax in the drama which has been running its course. And yet he remains in control; he faces the ordeal, whatever it is going to be, with equanimity, not with fear and trembling; and the "baptism" of 12:50 has to be read in this light.

In stark contrast to his filial submission and dedication stand his own followers' insouciance and lack of comprehension. They sleep. They pay no attention to his counsel to pray. At the end he exhorts them again, "Get up and pray that you enter not into temptation" (v. 46). In the other Synoptics the trial that they face results in their defection and abandonment of Jesus (Mark 14:50—and the utter dereliction is symbolized by the flight of the young man naked, leaving behind even the sheet that had covered him—a detail omitted in Matt 26:56b). Luke delicately omits all that, but one cannot help but detect even in his account the lack of comprehension on their part of what it was all about. (See further D. M. Stanley, *Jesus in Gethsemane.*)

Later tradition used this episode from the Synoptic Gospels in various ways: to emphasize the humanity of Jesus in face of Docetic denials (see Irenaeus, *Adv. haer.* 3.22,2 [PG 7. 956-957]); to invalidate the claims to his divinity (thus Celsus, Julian the Apostate, the Arians); to emphasize the conflict between Jesus' liberty and his obedience. Countless orators and homilists bent on psychoanalyzing him and his "agony" have sought to determine what caused it: the amount of human sin in the world, the number of those damned, having rejected the salvation that his passion offered. His foresight of all this would have caused the distress and the agony. Yet there is not a word in the NT texts about any of this.

NOTES

22   39. *Then Jesus went out and made his way.* Lit. "and going out, he made his way," i.e. in the moonlit night of Passover. Luke omits the detail about their singing (see Mark 14:26), i.e. the last part of the Hallel. On the Lucan vb. *poreuesthai,* see NOTE on 4:30 and p. 169.

as usual. Lit. "according to custom." See 1:9; 2:42, where the same phrase has already been used. It recalls 21:37, Jesus' wont to spend the nights on the Mount of Olives. The addition of this detail further implies the freedom of Jesus' choice to go to a spot well known to Judas the betrayer. Cf. Origen, *Contra Cels.* 2.10 (GCS 2. 137-138).

the Mount of Olives. See NOTES on 19:29; 21:37. For the Lucan motif of Jesus' prayer on a mountain, see NOTES on 6:12; 9:28. Cf. H. Ott, *Gebet und Heil,* 84.

and his disciples too. Whereas those who were with Jesus at the Last Supper were called *apostoloi* (22:14), Luke, now influenced by Mark 14:32, refers to them as *mathētai,* "disciples," a term that usually denotes a group more numerous than the Twelve, but which here has to be understood of the Eleven, since Judas is not among them, yet will appear shortly (v. 47). Some mss. (B*, 69, etc.) omit the intensive adv. *kai,* "too."

followed him. On the use of the vb. *akolouthein,* see NOTE on 5:11 and p. 242. This detail in the Lucan story implies the eventual identification of the disciples with Jesus in his trial and destiny. It thus has a hortatory aspect for the readers of the Lucan Gospel; they too are being invited to follow.

40. *When he had reached the spot.* Lit. "being at the place," i.e. arriving at it. For this use of the vb. *ginesthai* with the prep. *epi,* see Luke 3:2; 24:22; Acts 21:35—exclusively Lucan in the Synoptics. The spot is unnamed. Cf. Mark 14:32. The use of *topos,* "place, spot," in John 18:2 (Judas' knowledge of the spot) is scarcely an indication that Luke has drawn on a source close to the Johannine tradition, *pace* V. Taylor, *Passion Narrative,* 69.

Pray that you enter not into temptation. Whereas the Marcan Jesus says at first that he is going to pray (14:32b), the Lucan Jesus instructs those accompanying him to pray. He will repeat the counsel again in v. 46, where it has a parallel in Mark 14:38. Luke has thus introduced the counsel earlier, creating an *inclusio.* In teaching his followers the "Our Father," Jesus instructed them to say, "Bring us not into temptation" (11:4c [see NOTE there]). Now he implies that the ordeal that faces him will become a test of their fidelity and perseverance too—indeed, the test par excellence. But communing with God is suggested by him as a way of preventing the apostasy. What Jesus faces is not a renewed temptation for him (see S. Brown, *Apostasy and Perseverance,* 9-10, 15-16), but it will prove to be a testing of his followers. See NOTE on 4:13. To "enter into" temptation means to succumb to its evil power.

41. *he withdrew from them about a stone's throw.* Lit. "he was pulled away from them"; the vb. *apospan* is used again in Acts 21:1, where Paul tears himself away from his friends, the elders of Ephesus summoned to Miletus, as he departs for Jerusalem. Cf. 4 Macc 13:18. In the Lucan account the distance of Jesus' withdrawal is measured by a colloquial expression, found already in classical Greek (see Thucydides, *Hist.* 5.65,2: *mechri men lithou kai akontiou bolēs echōrēsan,* "and they withdrew as far as a stone's or javelin's throw"). Similar, but not exact, expressions can be found in Gen 21:16; Homer, *Il.* 3.12. Implied in the distance mentioned is that Jesus was not completely out of sight, but was out of earshot.

knelt down. Lit. "placing (his) knees," i.e. on the ground. Though the expression *tithenai gonata* is found once in Mark 15:19 (at the mocking of Jesus), it occurs four other times in Lucan writings (Acts 7:60; 9:40; 20:36; 21:5); cf. *Herm. Vis.* 1.1,3; 2.1,2;

3.1,5. By contrast, Mark 14:35 says that Jesus fell to the ground *(epipten epi tēs gēs)*. The expression is often said to be a Latinism (= *genua ponere,* see BDF § 5.3). Yet it occurs in Euripides, *Troad.* 1307 *(gony tithēmi gaia).* Jesus has adopted a pose of supplication.

prayed. See p. 245. The substance of his prayer is the same as in Mark 14:36 and Matt 26:39.

42. *Please, Father.* Lit. "Father, if you wish." So Luke reformulates the Marcan introductory phrase, "Abba, Father, all things are possible for you." The Lucan Jesus uses the voc. *páter,* as in 11:2 (see NOTE there); the Aramaic *'abbā'* and its translation as *ho patēr* are omitted.

take this cup away from me. Lit. "carry off . . ." Luke follows the wording of Mark 14:36c, changing only the position of the dem. *touto.* "Cup" *(potērion)* carries the OT sense of the cup of destiny. See Isa 51:17,22; Jer 25:15; 49:12; Lam 4:21; Pss 11:6; 75:9; cf. C. E. B. Cranfield, "The Cup Metaphor in Mark xiv. 36 and Parallels," *ExpTim* 59 (1947-1948) 137-138; M. Black, "The Cup Metaphor in Mk. xiv. 36," ibid. 195; cf. *AAGA*[3] 298; L. Goppelt, *TDNT* 6. 148-158, esp. 152-153. The idea of a cup of destiny may be reflected in the phrase "cup of death" found in the late *Tg. Yer. II* at Gen 40:23 *(ks' dmwt').* Note the Matthean formulation ("let this cup pass from me," 26:39) and the Johannine, "As for the cup which the Father has given to me, shall I not drink it?" (18:11). With these words the Lucan Jesus expresses a natural revulsion for the fate that waits for him. Nowhere else in the gospel tradition is the humanity of Jesus so evident as here. His reaction refers not only to the physical suffering and psychic anguish that are coming, but probably includes as well inner distress and doubt about the meaning of it all.

Yet not my will, but yours be done! So Luke formulates abstractly what Mark 14:36 states more concretely, "Not what I want, but what you want." The n. *thelēma* refers not to a capricious whim of the Father who subjects his son to death in satisfaction for human sins and offenses against divine majesty, but rather to the Father's plan of salvation for humanity, as the n. is used in Acts 21:14; 22:14. See p. 179. Though the saying echoes a wish of the "Our Father," that is not part of the Lucan form of it. Cf. Matt 6:10. This part of the Lucan Jesus' prayer expresses his basic filial orientation and submission.

43-44. See pp. 1443-1445.

45. *he came to the disciples.* I.e. all of them, not just Peter, James, and John. Contrast Mark 14:37, where he addresses Peter.

and found them sleeping. Recall 9:32.

because of grief. Lit. "from grief." Just as Luke explained Peter's uncomprehending remark in 9:33e (cp. Mark 9:6), so now he explains away the disciples' sleep. Usually grief has the opposite effect, insomnia. In the Lucan story there is no explanation given why the disciples should be grieving, nor even why Jesus withdrew to pray, whereas in the Marcan story Jesus has revealed to Peter, James, and John at least that his soul was *perilypos,* "very sad," a detail that Luke has chosen to omit. For an interpretation of *lypē* as a cardinal passion, related to sin and guilt, and for reasons why Luke has excised all mention of Jesus' emotions and depicted only the disciples under such sway, see J. H. Neyrey, "The Absence."

46. *Why do you sleep?* Or possibly, "What! Do you sleep?" The vb. *katheudete* is second pl.

Get up and pray that you enter not into temptation. See NOTES on 1:39; 22:40. Jesus advises the disciples to rise above such human reactions as sleep and grief. Recall his counsel in 18:1. These are the last words that he addresses to them before the curtain rises on the drama of the passion. The whole episode has served as the overture to it.

[43-44]. These verses read: 43 Now a heavenly angel appeared to him to strengthen him, 44 and in his anxiety he prayed still more earnestly. His sweat became like drops of blood that fall to the ground.

The following Greek mss. and ancient versions omit these verses: P69(apparently), P75, ℵ(first corrector), A, B, N, R, T, W, 579, 0171*, *f*13, syrsin, sah, boh(in part); they are also omitted by Marcion, Clement of Alexandria, Origen, Athanasius, Ambrose, Cyril, and John Damascene.

The following Greek mss. and ancient versions include these verses: ℵ*, D, K, L, X, Γ, Δ, Θ, Ψ, 0171(corrector), *f*1, 565, 700, lat, syrcur, pesh, boh(in part); they are read by Justin Martyr, Irenaeus, Hippolytus, Eusebius, Didymus, and Jerome. The minuscule family *f*13 inserts them after Matt 26:39, where some lectionaries put vv. 43-45a.

The decision to admit them into the text or to omit them from it is not easy; the matter is hotly debated among textual critics today. See further *TCGNT* 177; J. A. Fitzmyer, "Papyrus Bodmer XIV," 177-179; J. Duplacy, "La préhistoire"; B. D. Ehrman and M. A. Plunkett, "The Angel."

The external witnesses to the text are almost equally divided, with what are usually considered the better Greek mss. on the side of omitting the verses. Whether they are part of the problem of the so-called Western Non-Interpolations (see pp. 130-131) is also debated. Nor is it easy to decide whether the omission or the reading of these verses is the *lectio difficilior.* L. Brun ("Engel und Blutschweiss") argued for the inclusion of the verses, because, even though the Lucan story has a consistency without them, the evangelist usually compensates for his abridgment of Marcan material in the passion narrative by the addition of new material of his own, drawn from elsewhere.

There is no doubt that a tradition about Jesus' agony in the garden as found in these verses is ancient. See Justin Martyr, *Dial.* 103.8; a fourteenth–fifteenth-century writing, *Historia passionis Domini* (f. 32r), claims that it was read in the *Gospel of the Nazarenes* (often called the *Gospel according to the Hebrews).* Yet none of these ancient testimonies shows that the verses actually *belonged to the original text of the Lucan Gospel.* Epiphanius *(Ancoratus* 31.4-5 [GCS 25.40] ca. A.D. 374) knew that the verses were found in some "uncorrected copies" of the Lucan Gospel and that some orthodox theologians of his day were perplexed at the apparent incompatibility of the strong human emotion depicted in these verses with Jesus' divinity. J. Duplacy ("La préhistoire") notes the part that they played in the controversies about monothelism and monergism; but his discussion attests only to what he calls the "prehistory" of the text, and he has been unable to show that any *early* ancient testimonies attributed the verses to *Luke.* This would clearly not be the first instance where later theological concerns affected the textual history of the Greek NT.

In the first edition of the *UBSGNT* the editorial committee labeled the omission of vv. 43-44 as C (i.e. with a considerable degree of doubt whether the text or the apparatus contains the superior reading). In the third edition they labeled the insertion of them into the text (in double square brackets) as C. Though the verses are bracketed in *UBSGNT*[3], N-A[26], J. M. Creed, and the *RSV* (1972), they have been retained by A. Merk, J. M. Bover, British and Foreign Bible Societies text, *BJ* (one volume, 1973), A. Huck and H. Greeven, *Synopse,* and the *NEB* (which omits 22:19cd-20!). For a fuller list of commentators who omit or admit the verses in the Lucan text, see L. Brun, "Engel and Blutschweiss," 265; I. H. Marshall, *Luke,* 831-832.

They have been omitted in my translation, because (1) *lectio brevior potior;* (2) they have no counterpart in the parallel Synoptic accounts; (3) they militate against the thrust of the Lucan passage in that they add emotional details to what is otherwise a sober abridgment of the Marcan text; (4) they are absent from the oldest ms. of Luke (P[75]); and (5) they betray later parenetic or hortatory concerns. One cannot, however, be apodictic about the matter.

(For Roman Catholics they are, however, generally considered to be canonical verses; see *Enchiridion biblicum* § 392; cf. D. M. Stanley, *Jesus in Gethsemane,* 206-207.)

The appearance of the strengthening angel would be the Father's answer to Jesus' prayer—an example of prayer heard, assuring Christians that that is so even in the moments of darkest anxiety and trouble. In imitation, they too should pray in such moments all the "more earnestly."

43. *a heavenly angel.* Lit. "an angel from heaven." Cf. 17:29; 21:11.

appeared to him. Lit. "was seen to (= by) him." On the aor. pass. *ōphthē,* which occurs in Mark only in 9:4 and in Matthew only in 17:3, see NOTE on 1:11. Luke often uses it.

to strengthen him. Lit. "strengthening him." The Greek text has the pres. ptc. *enischyōn,* but gives no hint as to the kind of support, whether to body or spirit. Cf. Acts 9:19.

44. *in his anxiety.* Lit. "being in an agony." The Greek n. *agōnia* is found only here in the NT; neither Mark nor Matthew uses it to depict Jesus' experience in the garden. *Agōnia* can denote a struggle for victory, a contest. But it is also well attested for a state of mind associated with fear or anguish because of some impending, uncertain experience or phenomenon. See W. R. Paton, *"Agōnia* (Agony)." It has nothing to do in this context with a final or death spasm.

he prayed still more earnestly. The adv. *ektenōs* is also used of prayer in Acts 12:5.

His sweat became like drops of blood that fall to the ground. Both *idrōs,* "sweat," and *thrombos,* "drop," are *hapax legomena* in the NT. The comparison is made between profuse perspiration and copious drops of blood splashing to the ground; the text does not hint at a comparison of color. Cf. W. Grundmann, *Evangelium nach Lukas,* 412. The text is often misunderstood as if it referred to a "bloody sweat," i.e. that Jesus sweated blood. Ancient and modern interpreters have often restricted the meaning to the comparison of quantity (thus Theophylact, Euthymius Zigabenus, T. Zahn, J. Jeremias). A. Feuillet ("Le récit lucanien") has tried to undermine this interpretation by appealing to the Lucan use of *hōs* or *hōsei* in the sense of real identity (15:19; 16:1; Acts 2:3), a highly dubious interpretation. Apart from the text-critical problem involved, it is stretching matters to invoke alleged instances of *haematidrōsis.*

For the approximative sense of *hōsei,* see Luke 3:23; 9:14,28; 22:41,59; 23:44; 24:11; Acts 1:15; 2:3,41; 10:3; 19:7,34.

The ptc. *katabainontes* refers to the "drops," but a few mss. (𝖭*,², lat) read *katabainontos,* which would refer to the "blood" that falls to the ground.

BIBLIOGRAPHY (22:39-46)

Ambruster, C. J. "The Messianic Significance of the Agony in the Garden," *Scr* 16 (1964) 111-119.

Aschermann, H. "Zum Agoniegebet Jesu, Lc. XXII, 43sq.," *Theologia viatorum* 5 (1953-1954) 143-149.

Barbour, R. S. "Gethsemane in the Tradition of the Passion," *NTS* 16 (1969-1970) 231-251.

Bate, H. N. "Luke xxii 40," *JTS* 36 (1935) 76-77.

Benoit, P. *Passion and Resurrection,* 1-23.

Bishop, E. F. F. "A Stone's Throw," *ExpTim* 53 (1941-1942) 270-271.

Boman, T. "Der Gebetskampf Jesu," *NTS* 10 (1963-1964) 261-273.

Brun, L. "Engel und Blutschweiss Lc 22,43-44," *ZNW* 32 (1933) 265-276.

Carle, P.-L. "L'Agonie de Gethsémani: Enquête exégétique et théologique du Père Feuillet," *Divinitas* 21 (1977) 429-432.

Colunga, A. "La agonía de Jesús en Getsemani," *CB* 16 (1959) 13-17.

Cullmann, O. *Immortality of the Soul or Resurrection of the Dead? The Witness of the New Testament* (London: Epworth, 1958) 21-27.

Daube, D. "A Prayer Pattern in Judaism," *SE I* (TU 73) 539-545.

Dibelius, M. "Gethsemane," *Crozer Quarterly* 12 (1935) 254-265; reprinted, *Botschaft und Geschichte,* 1. 258-271.

Duplacy, J. "La préhistoire du texte en Luc 22:43-44," *New Testament Textual Criticism* (eds. E. J. Epp and G. D. Fee) 77-86.

Eltester, W. " 'Freund, wozu du gekommen bist' (Mt. xxvi 50)," *Neotestamentica et patristica* (ed. W. C. van Unnik) 70-91.

Feuillet, A. *L'Agonie de Gethsémani: Enquête exégétique et théologique suivie d'une étude du 'Mystère de Jésus' de Pascal* (Paris: Gabalda, 1977) 13-141.

——— "Le récit lucanien de l'agonie de Gethsémani (Lc xxii. 39-46)," *NTS* 22 (1975-1976) 397-417.

Fillion, L.-C. "L'Ange et la sueur de sang à Gethsémani," *Essais d'exégèse* (Lyon/Paris: Briday, 1884) 101-127.

Fitzmyer, J. A. "Papyrus Bodmer XIV: Some Features of Our Oldest Text of Luke," *CBQ* 24 (1962) 170-179, esp. 177-179.

Galizzi, M. *Gesù nel Getsemani (Mc 14,32-42; Mt 26,36-46; Lc 22,39-46)* (Biblioteca di scienze religiose 4; Zürich: Pas-V., 1972).

Gamba, G. G. "Agonia di Gesù," *RivB* 16 (1968) 159-166.

Héring, J. "Simples remarques sur la prière à Gethsémané: Matthieu 26.36-46; Marc 14.32-42; Luc 22.40-46," *RHPR* 39 (1959) 97-102.

——— "Zwei exegetische Probleme in der Perikope von Jesus in Gethsemane

(Markus XIV 32-42; Matthäus XXVI 36-46; Lukas XXII 40-46)," *Neotestamentica et patristica* (ed. W. C. van Unnik) 64-69.

Holleran, J. W. *The Synoptic Gethsemane: A Critical Study* (AnGreg 191; Rome: Gregorian University, 1973).

Holzmeister, U. "Exempla sudoris sanguinei (Lc. 22,44)," *VD* 18 (1938) 73-81.

Kelber, W. H. "Mark 14,32-42: Gethsemane: Passion Christology and Discipleship Failure," *ZNW* 63 (1972) 166-187.

Kuhn, K. G. "Jesus in Gethsemane," *EvT* 12 (1952-1953) 260-285.

Larkin, W. J. "The Old Testament Background of Luke xxii. 43-44," *NTS* 25 (1978-1979) 250-254.

Lescow, T. "Jesus in Gethsemane," *EvT* 26 (1966) 141-159.

―――― "Jesus in Gethsemane bei Lukas und im Hebräerbrief," *ZNW* 58 (1967) 215-239.

Linnemann, E. *Studien,* 34-40, 178-179.

Moffatt, J. "Exegetica: Luke xxii. 44," *Expos* 8/7 (1914) 90-92.

Mohn, W. "Gethsemane (Mk 14,32-42)," *ZNW* 64 (1973) 194-208.

Neyrey, J. H. "The Absence of Jesus' Emotions—The Lucan Redaction of Lk 22,39-46," *Bib* 61 (1980) 153-171.

Ott, W. *Gebet und Heil,* 82-90.

Paton, W. R. *"Agōnia* (Agony)," *CRev* 27 (1913) 194.

Radl, W. *Paulus und Jesus im lukanischen Doppelwerk: Untersuchungen zu Parallelmotiven im Lukasevangelium und in der Apostelgeschichte* (Europäische Hochschulschriften 23/49; Bern/Frankfurt: Lang, 1975) 159-168.

Schenke, L. *Studien,* 461-560.

Schneider, G. "Engel und Blutschweiss (Lk 22, 43-44): 'Redaktionsgeschichte' im Dienste der Textkritik," *BZ* 20 (1976) 112-116.

Schürmann, H. "Lk 22,42a das älteste Zeugnis für Lk 22,20?" *MTZ* 3 (1952) 185-188; reprinted, *Traditionsgeschichtliche Untersuchungen,* 193-197.

Skard, E. "Kleine Beiträge zum Corpus hellenisticum NT," *Symbolae osloenses* 30 (1953) 100-103.

Smith, H. "Acts xx. 8 and Luke xxii. 43," *ExpTim* 16 (1904-1905) 478.

Stanley, D. M. *Jesus in Gethsemane* (Ramsey, NJ: Paulist, 1980).

Trémel, Y.-B. "L'Agonie de Jésus," *Lumière et vie* 13 (1964) 79-103.

154. THE ARREST OF JESUS
(22:47-53)

22 [47] While Jesus was still speaking, a crowd suddenly appeared with one of the Twelve, the one named Judas, at their head. He drew near to Jesus to kiss him. [48] But Jesus said to him, "Is it with a kiss, Judas, that you hand over the Son of Man?" [49] Those who were about Jesus, realizing what was going to happen, said, "Lord, shall we strike with a

sword?" ⁵⁰ Then one of them struck the high priest's servant and cut off his right ear. ⁵¹ But Jesus spoke up, "Let them be, even this far!" And he touched the ear and healed it. ⁵² Then Jesus addressed the chief priests, the Temple officers, and the elders who had come to him, "Did you come out, as it were against a robber, with swords and clubs? ⁵³ Day after day, when I was with you in the Temple area, you did not lay a hand on me. But now this is your hour, and the power of darkness."

COMMENT

The first real episode of Jesus' passion is the story of his arrest on the Mount of Olives (22:47-53). What has been predicted in vv. 21-23 now comes to fulfillment, the betrayal of Jesus by Judas Iscariot. The episode has its parallels not only in the Synoptic Gospels (Mark 14:43-52; Matt 26:47-56), but also in the Johannine Gospel (18:2-11).

When compared with the Marcan account, the Lucan story of the arrest depicts Jesus himself dominating the scene. Yet it is shorter than the Marcan form, and significantly omits details that one would consider necessary for comprehension. At the least, the Lucan account is more intelligible, if one has read the Marcan. Thus Luke does not reveal why Judas comes to Jesus to kiss him (see Mark 14:44-45); yet that is presupposed by v. 48. Again, the attack on the servant of the high priest, which in Mark 14:47 is narrated as an attempt to free Jesus, who has already been seized, appears in the Lucan account as an act of defense, prepared for by only a vague premonition of what was about to happen (22:49-50). Though the Lucan account is shorter, it alone recounts the healing of the ear by Jesus (v. 51b). Moreover, the flight of the disciples (Mark 14:50) is completely omitted, in order not to denigrate the disciples, who in this Gospel never leave the Jerusalem area and will be numbered among his "acquaintances (masc.)" standing not far from the cross at the crucifixion (23:49). Moreover, the dialogue that Jesus carries on with Judas and with the disciple who wields the sword gives a more dramatic touch to the episode.

This difference in the Lucan and Marcan accounts of Jesus' arrest raises the question about the source of the episode in the Lucan Gospel. W. Grundmann (*Evangelium nach Lukas,* 413), V. Taylor (*Passion Narrative,* 72-76), K. H. Rengstorf (*Evangelium nach Lukas,* 254), F. Rehkopf (*Sonderquelle,* 31-85 [most elaborate treatment]), I. H. Marshall (*Luke,* 834), et al., would have us believe that Luke has combined "Mk" with material from an independent non-Marcan source (e.g. vv. 52b-53a would be derived from "Mk" and inserted into the non-Marcan source material). But

Rehkopf's discussion reveals, in particular, how questionable that position is. Hence it is better to say with J. Finegan *(Überlieferung,* 20-21), J. M. Creed *(The Gospel,* 272), J. Schmid *(Evangelium nach Lukas,* 337), G. Schneider *(Evangelium nach Lukas,* 460-461), et al., that the Lucan account results from a redaction of "Mk" along with Lucan omission and composition. (Whether the Marcan account itself is composite or not need not detain us here; for details see E. Linnemann, *Studien,* 41-69; G. Schneider, "Die Verhaftung Jesu.")

In general, the sequence of the Lucan narrative follows that of "Mk." Verse 47 is clearly a redacted form of Mark 14:43ab,45, with the omission of the intervening material. Verse 48 stems from Luke's pen; J. Jeremias *(Die Sprache,* 295) can find no traditional matter in it. V. Taylor *(Passion Narrative,* 74) maintains that no "linguistic details" in it show that Luke is redacting, and so he concludes that Luke "is using a source." Yet why could not Luke be freely composing? Verse 49 is freely composed. The phrase *hoi peri auton* is Lucan; see its parallel in Acts 21:8 *(hoi peri ton Paulon),* a construction never found in Mark or Matthew. The dir. question introduced by *ei* is often used by Luke (13:23; 22:67; Acts 1:6; 7:1; 19:2; 21:37; 22:25; 26:23[bis]—see J. Jeremias, *Die Sprache,* 231, 295). Verse 50 is a redacted form of Mark 14:47, retaining *heis tis,* "one," and substituting *ex autōn,* "of them," for *tōn parestēkotōn,* "of the bystanders" (because Luke has just mentioned "those who were about Jesus" [v. 49a]). The rest of the verse is dependent on Mark 14:47, but Luke makes it the "right" ear (see NOTE on v. 50). Verse 51 begins with a typically Lucan introduction, the use of a Septuagintism *apokritheis eipen* (see p. 114). The difficult sentence *eate heōs toutou* is like *hikanon estin* of v. 38, a peremptory comment of the Lucan Jesus. That the Lucan Jesus heals the ear of the servant is not surprising; it is exactly what one would expect Luke to introduce (see pp. 257-258 [§ 9]). Verse 52 begins with another typically Lucan introduction (see p. 116, *pros +* acc.; and p. 111 *paraginesthai);* but it continues with a redacted form of Mark 14:43b and 48. Similarly for v. 53a (= Mark 14:49a); v. 53b is freely composed, introducing again a reference to "the hour" (see 22:14) to replace the Marcan vague reference to Scripture. Though it is not clear why Luke has so abridged the story of the arrest, there is no detail in the Lucan account that cannot be explained on the basis of the Marcan, save for the "right" ear and its cure.

Form-critically considered, this episode is a Story about Jesus, another piece of the narrative gospel tradition. R. Bultmann *(HST* 268) was of the opinion that the narrative was "coloured by legend in the motif of the betrayal by a kiss" and in Jesus' comment in vv. 52b-53a (= "Church apologetics and dogmatics"). No one will deny that the story has grown under Luke's pen (the "crowd" from the chief priests, Scribes, and elders in "Mk" becoming the chief priests, Temple officers, and elders; the "right" ear;

Jesus' dominance of the scene). Yet, even though one is hard put to establish the historicity of Judas' kiss, the substance of the episode of the arrest has to be reckoned as historical; even Paul (1 Cor 11:23) knows of the betrayal of Jesus at night (and, by implication, of his arrest) after the Last Supper.

The sense of the episode is not difficult to grasp. The Jerusalem authorities, led by Judas—who is again branded as "one of the Twelve"—come out to the spot on the Mount of Olives to which Jesus has retired for the night, intending to take him captive, "apart from a crowd" (22:6). The scene contains three elements: (a) Jesus' reaction to the arrival of his captors and the betrayer; as Judas approaches to greet him with a kiss, Jesus queries, "Is it with a kiss, Judas, that you hand over the Son of Man?" (v. 48). The mark of supreme affection, respect, and love becomes the sign of betrayal. Judas uses it to offend his Lord; the nadir of infidelity is reached. (b) Jesus' reaction to the impulsive action of one of his followers who would defend him and ward off arrest, striking one of the opposite party with a sword. Jesus' comment is, in effect, "No more of this!" And in the moment of his betrayal and arrest, he manifests again compassion; he heals the wounded servant's ear. He performs a miracle—on the Mount of Olives, but not in the city of Jerusalem (see p. 1269). (Cf. 4:23; 5:17.) Jesus thus uses the moment of his arrest as the occasion for manifesting his healing power even toward one of those who is among his enemies. It betokens the symbolic value of his passion; through his arrest and death will come forgiveness. As God's agent he reverses the evil done by human beings. Finally, (c) Jesus serenely interprets the whole event, relating the evil that is about to be worked against him to his Father's salvific plan. With irony he queries the Jerusalem authorities whether they have come out to seize him as if he were a robber or an insurrectionist; he asks this, who shortly before in the Lucan story had predicted that he was to be classed with outlaws (22:37). He sees it all as a manifestation of the hour of evil, the climactic moment in the Father's plan when it encroaches on his own very human existence. The power that these Jerusalem authorities have over him is that of "darkness," for they sit in darkness, and the light that he was to bring (see 1:79) has not shone upon them. That darkness will in time spread over the whole earth (23:44). They come in the physical dark of the night to cover up the moral darkness of their deeds.

NOTES

22 47. *While Jesus was still speaking.* I.e. to the disciples whom he was rousing from sleep. Luke has taken over the gen. absol. from Mark 14:43, omitting, however, the characteristic Marcan introduction *kai euthys,* "and immediately."

a crowd suddenly appeared. Lit. "behold a crowd." See p. 121. Luke brings forward in his sentence the mention of this group; it is not further identified here, but see NOTE on v. 52. The Synoptics know nothing of the presence of Roman troops with Judas (contrast John 18:3,12). Ms. D and the OS versions add the adj. *polys,* "a great crowd."

with one of the Twelve, one named Judas, at their head. Lit. "and the one named Judas, one of the Twelve, was preceding them." See NOTES on 6:16; 22:3 and p. 253. Luke has intensified the role of Judas by placing him at the head of the group (see Acts 1:16); in Mark 14:43 the crowd was simply "with him." Mss. D and a few others read *ho kaloumenos Iskariōth,* "the one called Iscariot." Again, mss. D and *f*[1] read *proēgen,* "was walking ahead of" instead of the more common *proērcheto.*

The identification of Judas as one of the Twelve is the echo of the horror that the early church associated with his deed—he was one of that chosen few! It does not point with any certainty to the beginning of a shorter passion narrative, as some have at times argued. See E. Schweizer, *Evangelium nach Lukas,* 229.

He drew near to Jesus to kiss him. In Mark 14:45 Judas actually kisses Jesus; in the Lucan text we never learn whether he succeeded in kissing Jesus or not. It can be interpreted either way. This is perhaps the reason why some mss. (P[69], D) and ancient versions have a different reading, *engisas ephilēsen ton Iēsoun,* "drawing near, he kissed Jesus." And at the end of the sentence, some mss. (D, E, H, Θ, *f*[13], 700, etc.) add an explanation, *touto gar sēmeion dedōkei autois· hon an philēso autos estin,* "he had given them this sign, 'Whomever I kiss, that is he.'" This is, however, a form of Mark 14:44 and reads suspiciously like a copyist's harmonization. Luke omitted the Marcan preliminary verse undoubtedly because he considered Jesus sufficiently well known to the crowd and the authorities that he would not need such identification, even at night.

The vb. *philein* really means "to love," but it was also used in a concrete sense for the mark of love. Mark 14:44-45 uses both the simple form *philein* and the compound *kataphilein.*

48. *Is it with a kiss, Judas, that you hand over the Son of Man?* This query, exclusive to the Lucan Jesus, begins emphatically with *philēma,* "a kiss," at the head of the sentence. There is no counterpart to this query in Mark, where Jesus does not speak to Judas at all; but cp. Matt 26:50, *hetaire, eph' ho parei,* a difficult cl., possibly meaning, "Colleague, why are you here?" For the stereotyped expression, "hand over the Son of Man," recall 9:44; 18:31-32; 22:22; cf. 24:7. The surrogate use of the Son of Man occurs here. See NOTE on 5:24 and pp. 208-211.

49. *Those who were about Jesus.* I.e. his disciples, who display a positive role in this Lucan account, a willingness to intervene. They will not be said to have fled, as in Mark 14:50.

realizing what was going to happen. Lit. "seeing the coming-to-be"; Luke uses the fut. ptc. *esomenon* in a substantival form. Cf. Sir 48:25. Mss. D, 0171, and some ancient Latin and Syriac versions read *genomenon,* "what was happening." In the Marcan parallel Jesus has already been seized; and so the attempt of the disciples is to free him and not to ward off the seizure as here.

Lord. See NOTE on 5:12.

shall we strike with a sword? This question is asked by one of the two who carried the swords mentioned in 22:38 (there too Jesus is addressed as *Kyrie*). In John 18:10

Simon Peter is named as the one who wields the sword. The dir. question, introduced by *ei* (lit. "if"), is a Septuagintism. See Gen 17:17; 44:19; Amos 3:3-6; 6:12. F. Rehkopf *(Sonderquelle,* 59) says this construction is found elsewhere in Lucan writings only in 13:23 and Acts 1:6; see COMMENT on p. 1448, however, for the many other instances of it. Cf. BAGD 219b; ZBG § 401: BDF § 440.3.

50. *struck the high priest's servant.* Or possibly "the servant of a chief priest," if one is inclined not to press the def. art. before *archiereōs* (sg.).

cut off his right ear. The Johannine account records too that it was the right ear; this has been taken as a sign that Luke has used a source. But the question is, In which direction did the influence go? Here one must recall Luke 6:6, "right hand" (see NOTE there), in contrast to Mark 3:1. If the Lucan form of the story has grown here, so has the Johannine—even more, for the servant there acquires a name, "Malchus" (18:10). Cf. M. Rostovtzeff, *"Ous dexion apotemnein,"* *ZNW* 33 (1934) 196-199.

51. *Let them be, even this far!* So the Lucan Jesus addresses the unnamed disciple who has resorted to violence to defend him. He will have none of it. In John 18:11 Jesus tells Peter to put his sword back into its scabbard. The meaning of Jesus' words, *eatō heōs toutou,* is not easy to determine; literally, they mean, "Let him/it (be) as far as *(or* up to) this." In the context it may mean something like "Stop! No more of this!" (so BAGD 212) or "Stop! That's enough." For J. M. Creed *(The Gospel,* 274) the pron. *toutou* "this," might refer to the assault ("Suffer your resistance to go thus far— but not further") or better to the arrest ("Let events take their course—even to my arrest"). See LXX 2 Sam 7:18; Aristotle, *Hist. anim.* 9.46.

he touched the ear and healed it. Lit. "touching the earlet, he healed him." Whereas Luke has used the word *ous,* "ear," in v. 50, he now uses a form, which is really diminutive, *ōtion,* but which in Hellenistic Greek had lost its force and has become a common name for the (outer) ear, of humans or animals. See BDF § 111.3. Matt 26:51 uses the same word, whereas the best mss. of Mark 14:47 have still another word, *ōtarion,* which is also found in John 18:10. See D. C. Swanson, "Diminutives in the Greek New Testament," *JBL* 77 (1958) 134-151. Cf. P. Joüon, "Luc 22,50-51: *to ous, tou ōtiou,"* *RSR* 24 (1934) 473-474.

52. *the chief priests, the Temple officers, and the elders.* So Luke finally identifies the crowd of v. 47. In Mark 14:43 the threesome was "chief priests, Scribes, and elders," which appears in Luke 9:22. See NOTE there. Luke now substitutes "Temple officers" *(stratēgous tou hierou)* for the Scribes, persons whom he had associated with the chief priests in 22:4. See NOTE there.

as it were against a robber. Or possibly "an insurrectionist"; on the n. *lēstēs,* see NOTE on 10:30. For *lēstēs* as "revolutionary," see Josephus, *J.W.* 2.13,2-3 § 253-254. Luke omits the Marcan detail, *syllabein me,* "to take hold of me," because he depicts Jesus tolerating his arrest; he is in charge and permits it.

53. *Day after day.* For the prepositional phrase *kath' hēmeran,* see NOTE on 11:3. In this case, Luke has derived it from Mark 14:49.

when I was with you in the Temple area. Luke substitutes a gen. absol. for the Marcan parataxis (see p. 108 § 2) and strangely omits the ptc. *didaskōn,* "teaching." Cf. 19:47. See further John 18:20.

you did not lay a hand on me. Lit. "you did not stretch forth your hands against me." This verse finds an interesting parallel in John 7:30.

now this is your hour. I.e. the climactic moment when the force of evil in such human beings is to be marshaled against him, the moment in history when salvation for humanity is to be achieved (despite them). This sentence replaces the Marcan allusion to the fulfillment of Scripture (14:49b); it is replaced by Luke probably because of its vagueness, even though he too will quote Scripture similarly. See 24:27,44-46.

and the power of darkness. I.e. when darkness and all that it symbolizes will hold sway and even stifle the good. The utterance resembles those of the Johannine Jesus (see John 13:30; 19:11); the contrast of light and darkness is not so prominent in Lucan writings, but it is not wholly absent. See 11:35; Acts 26:18. The Lucan Jesus plays upon the physical darkness of night, when the Jerusalem authorities arrive to take him "apart from a crowd" (22:6), and the moral darkness that they represent. The irony is that they themselves now constitute a "crowd" (see vv. 47,52a), in a sense quite different from the crowd whom they feared (22:2).

BIBLIOGRAPHY (22:47-53)

Benoit, P. *Passion and Resurrection,* 25-48.

Black, M. "The Arrest and Trial of Jesus" (see p. 1384) 19-33.

Brandon, S. G. F. *The Trial of Jesus of Nazareth* (New York: Stein and Day, 1968).

Dibelius, M. "Judas und der Judaskuss," *Botschaft und Geschichte,* 1. 272-277.

Doeve, J. W. "Die Gefangennahme Jesu in Gethsemane: Eine traditionsgeschichtliche Untersuchung," *SE I* (TU 73, 1959) 458-480.

Hall, S. G. "Swords of Offence," ibid. 499-502.

Linnemann, E. *Studien,* 41-69.

Rehkopf, F. *Sonderquelle,* 31-82.

Rice, G. E. "The Role of the Populace in the Passion Narrative of Luke in Codex Bezae," *AUSS* 19 (1981) 147-153.

Schneider, G. *Passion Jesu,* 43-55.

——— "Die Verhaftung Jesu: Traditionsgeschichte von Mk 14,43-52," *ZNW* 63 (1972) 188-209.

155. PETER'S DENIALS; JESUS BEFORE THE COUNCIL
(22:54-71)

22 ⁵⁴ They arrested Jesus and led him away, bringing him to the house of the high priest; and Peter followed at a distance. ⁵⁵ He sat down in the midst of those who had kindled a fire in the courtyard and were sitting around it. ⁵⁶ When a servant-girl saw him sitting there at

the fire, she stared at him and said, "This fellow too was with him." [57] But Peter denied it, "Woman, I do not know him." [58] A little later someone else noticed him and remarked, "You too are one of them." But Peter said, "No, Sir, I am not." [59] About an hour later someone else insisted, "I assure you, this fellow too was with him; he is even a Galilean!" [60] And Peter said, "Sir, I do not know what you are talking about!" At once, as he was still speaking, a cock crowed. [61] The Lord turned and looked at Peter. Then Peter remembered the Lord's saying, how he said to him, "Before a cock crows today, you will have denied me three times over." [62] And he went outside and wept bitterly.

[63] The men who were holding Jesus in custody began to ridicule him and beat him. [64] They blindfolded him and kept taunting, "Now prophesy! Who is it that hits you?" [65] And they kept leveling many other insults at him.

[66] When it was day, the elders of the people, both chief priests and Scribes, assembled, and Jesus was brought before their Council. [67] "Tell us," they said to him, "are you the Messiah?" He answered, "If I tell you, you will not believe me. [68] If I ask you a question, you will not answer. [69] But from now on *the Son of Man* [a] will be *seated at the right hand* [b] of the power of God." [70] At that they all said, "You are, then, the Son of God?" And he answered them, "It is you who say I am." [71] So they said, "What further need have we of testimony? We have heard it ourselves from his own lips."

[a] Dan 7:13   [b] Ps 110:1

COMMENT

Having been taken captive on the Mount of Olives by the Jerusalem authorities, Jesus is led to the house of the high priest, where he is denied three times by Peter, mistreated, and interrogated at daybreak by the Sanhedrin (22:54-71). We are again dealing with a part of the tradition that is preserved not only in the Synoptic Gospels (see also Mark 14:53-15:1a; Matt 26:57-27:1), but also in the Johannine (John 18:13-27). This and the following episodes, in which Jesus is brought to trial before Pilate (23:1-5,13-16), are the most crucial in the passion narrative and have given rise to many problems of interpretation.

The Lucan account of Jesus' appearance before the council of Jewish authorities is composite, being made up of three incidents (the denial by Peter, vv. 54-62; the mistreatment of Jesus, vv. 63-65; and the interrogation of him regarding his messiahship and divine sonship, vv. 66-71), all neatly set off one from the other. It differs considerably from the Marcan story, where the interrogation begins immediately on Jesus' arrival at the high priest's house— at night (14:55-64), with a verdict being given. It is then followed by the mistreatment of Jesus (14:65) and by Peter's denials (14:66-72). But there also follows a further consultation of the Jewish council at daybreak (15:1a). In other words, the Marcan story tells of two sessions of the council. In this sequence Mark is followed by Matthew (26:59-66,67-68,69-75; 27:1—with the only difference being the naming of the high priest, 26:57). This transposition of Marcan material (see p. 71) and the difference between the Marcan/ Matthean and Lucan stories of the interrogation of Jesus about his messiahship and of the verdict have given rise to the classic problem about the historicity of this event.

The problem is compounded by the sequence of events in the Johannine Gospel, where Jesus is led "first . . . to Annas," the father-in-law of Caiaphas, "who was the high priest of that year" (18:13). At Annas' house Peter denies Jesus for the first time (18:15-18). Then "the high priest interrogates Jesus about his disciples and his teaching" (but not about his messiahship or divine sonship, vv. 19-21). Jesus is mistreated (18:22). Then Annas sends Jesus "bound to Caiaphas the high priest" (18:24), after which we learn of Peter's further denials (18:25-27), but nothing is recorded of an interrogation before Caiaphas. Finally, Jesus is led from Caiaphas' house to the pretorium (18:28). To appreciate the discrepancies that are present in the Gospel accounts of this part of the passion narrative, it is good to see the details schematically set forth. One should note in particular that not "all the synoptic Gospels presuppose that Jesus had two hearings before the Jewish authorities," pace E. E. Ellis, Gospel of Luke, 259.

Jesus before the Jewish Authorities

Mark 14-15*	Luke 22-23	John 18
14:53 They lead Jesus "to the high priest," with council assembled (Matt 26:57: "to Caiaphas, the high priest")	22:54 "Bringing him to the house of the high priest"	18:13 "First they led him to Annas"
54 Peter in "the courtyard of the high priest," sitting at the fire	55 Peter sits with those who had kindled a fire in the courtyard	15-17 Peter admitted to the house; his first denial of Jesus at the gate
		18 Peter sits at the fire

* Matthew follows Mark very closely, except for the identification of the high priest in 26:57 (added by Matthew).

Mark 14-15	Luke22-23	John 18
55-63 Chief priest and council interrogate Jesus about messiahship; witnesses	56-62 Peter denies Jesus three times	19-21 "The high priest interrogates Jesus about his disciples and his teaching"
64 Verdict: blasphemy, deserving death		
65 Jesus is mistreated by members and assistants	63-65 Jesus is mistreated by those who hold him	22 Jesus is mistreated by one of the assistants ("of the Jews" [v. 12])
66-72 Peter denies Jesus three times		
15:1a As soon as it is morning, the council holds a consultation and decides to put Jesus to death	66-71 When it is day, the council interrogates Jesus about messiahship and divine sonship (no record of witnesses or verdict)	24 "Annas sent him bound to Caiaphas the high priest" (no record of interrogation or verdict)
		25-27 Peter denies Jesus a second and third time
1b They bind Jesus, lead him away, and hand him over to Pilate	23:1 "the whole assembly of them rose and led Jesus to Pilate"	28 "They led Jesus from the house of Caiaphas to the pretorium"

The discrepancies in these details raise a further question about who was responsible for the death of Jesus. Actually one has to consider the following episodes about the trial before Pilate as well. But the problem begins here. For though the handling of Peter's denials, whether *before* the interrogation of Jesus (Luke) or *after* it (Mark/Matthew) or whether in *one* place (the Synoptics) or possibly in *two* (John: at Annas' house, 18:15-18; at Caiaphas' house, 18:25-27), is really a minor issue (for details see the comparative chart in R. E. Brown, *John, XIII-XXI,* 838-839), it is nevertheless part of the larger problem of the session(s) of the Sanhedrin and what happened at them (a verdict or not). The way one resolves the relation of the Synoptic and Johannine stories of interrogation of Jesus by Jewish authorities bears on the answer of responsibility for Jesus' death in the long run.

The historical reconstruction of the interrogation of Jesus before the Jewish authorities and of his trial before Pilate has been attempted many times. The main problem that modern readers of the Gospels have, both Christian and Jewish, is the tendency to treat both these Gospel accounts and the record of regulations for the conduct of criminal cases in the Mishnah as if these writings were actually case records or *acta* of the "trial" of Jesus itself. Both the Gospels and the Mishnah *(Sanh.* 4:1) were written for purposes quite different. The historical reconstruction of the scene does not concern us, especially in a commentary on the Lucan Gospel. R. E. Brown *(John, XIII-XXI,* 791-802) has presented all the major points that have to be considered and has described the "four views" usually advocated in modern times. There is no need to repeat all that here. I personally class myself with those who hold the second view (ibid. 792-793), that, though Jewish authorities were deeply involved in the "trial," all the main legal formalities were carried out by the Roman governor. (See further the books in the BIBLIOGRAPHY on pp. 1468-1471 by J. Blinzler, D. R. Catchpole, H. Cohn, R. W. Husband, G. Sloyan, P. Winter, and S. Zeitlin for a variety of views; also the controversy started by H. Lietzmann ["Der Prozess Jesu"] and the reactions of F. Büchsel, M. Dibelius, M. Goguel, and G. D. Kilpatrick, also listed there.)

A further remark needs to be made about the background of the different Gospel accounts of the interrogation of Jesus by Jewish authorities. The Marcan and Johannine accounts suggest (in different ways) a double appearance of Jesus before those authorities; such a double appearance was possibly historical. However, it is more likely that Luke has preserved a better recollection of the time when the interrogation about Jesus' messiahship took place—in the morning, not at night. We know nothing of what happened at the house of Caiaphas to which Jesus was led (John 18:24), apart—*possibly*—from Peter's second and third denials, if they are to be located there (see vv. 25-27). It would mean, then, that Mark has moved up the interrogation about Jesus' messiahship to the night session (14:55-64), being aware of a tradition about *an* interrogation before *a* high priest (called Annas in John 18:19-21), but not of *the substance* of that interrogation (much less that reported by John). In Mark 14:53 Jesus is led simply "to the high priest"; similarly in Luke 22:54, "to the house of the high priest." Whereas in John 18:13 he was led "first . . . to Annas," whose relation to Caiaphas is explained, Matthew has identified the person to whom Jesus was at first led as "Caiaphas the high priest" (26:57). At the time of Matthew's writing (A.D. 80-85), when Caiaphas has long since been deposed (see NOTE on 3:22), the evangelist simply recalls that Caiaphas was the high priest of that year and inserts his name into his Marcan source. (Cf. P. Benoit, *Passion and Resurrection,* 79-80, 99.)

In considering the Synoptic relationship of this Lucan episode, we note again its composite character. We shall take each part in turn. As for the denial of Peter (vv. 54-62), these verses are mainly a redacted form of Mark 15:53-54,66-72. However, K. H. Rengstorf *(Evangelium nach Lukas,* 257), W. Grundmann *(Evangelium nach Lukas,* 416), G. Klein ("Die Verleugnung," 290-294), D. R. Catchpole *(The Trial,* 160-174), I. H. Marshall *(Luke,* 839-840), et al. prefer to regard this form of the story as derived from Luke's special source. But others, such as J. Finegan *(Überlieferung,* 23-24), V. Taylor *(Passion Narrative,* 77-78), G. Schneider *(Verleugnung,* 73-96; *Evangelium nach Lukas,* 464), E. Linnemann *(Studien,* 97-101), M. Lehmann *(Synoptische Quellenanalyse,* 106-112), et al., more rightly have seen that the episode is marked with no little Lucan redaction and that the rest can be explained from "Mk." V. Taylor, who normally argues for a non-Marcan source, admits in this instance that "Mk" is "perhaps his only written source," which was likewise the source of the prediction in v. 34. This seems to be true for 22:54-60,61b. In v. 54a Luke introduces the technical word for arrest, *syllabontes*, from Mark 14:48 and adds his favorite *eisēgagon*, "led away" (see 2:27; 14:21; Acts 7:45; 9:8; 21:28,29,37; 22:24); he omits mention of the threesome that make up the Sanhedrin, having just mentioned a threesome in v. 52. In v. 54b Luke redacts Mark 14:54a slightly. In v. 55 the Lucan redactional hand can be seen in the phrase *en mesō* + gen., "in the midst of" (used in Luke-Acts ten times, against two in "Mk"), and in the compound vb. *synkathizein*, "sit with" (see J. Jeremias, *Die Sprache*, 86-87). Again, in v. 56 the Lucan redaction is seen in the addition of indef. *tis*, in the use of the ptc. *atenisasa*, lit., "staring at" (see p. 112; cf. J. Jeremias, ibid. 122), and in the prep. *syn*, "with," instead of the Marcan *meta*. In v. 57 Luke has redactionally simplified the Marcan formula, as he often does. In v. 58 he has substituted a male servant for the servant girl at the second accusation. Note also the sequence, *tis* (v. 56), *heteros* (v. 58), *allos tis* (v. 59). (Cf. 9:57,59,61; see J. Jeremias, ibid. 110-111.) The temporal use of *brachy*, "a little later," is exclusively Lucan, as is also the voc. of *anthrōpos* (Luke 5:20; 12:14; 22:58,60— *pace* J. Jeremias, ibid. 215). The Lucan hand is further evident in the ptc. *diastasēs* in v. 59 (see 24:51; Acts 27:28; cf. Acts 5:7) in a gen. absol. (see p. 108) and in conjunction with *hōsei* with a number, "about an hour later"; it is also evident in the phrase *ep' alētheias*, "I assure you" (4:25; 20:21; Acts 4:27; 10:34), instead of the Marcan *alēthōs*, "truly." In v. 60a Luke again uses the voc. *anthrōpe* and simplifies the rest; in v. 60b he substitutes his favorite *parachrēma*, "at once, instantly" (see NOTE on 1:64) for Marcan *kai euthys* and uses a gen. absol. (p. 108)—the rest is Marcan save for the omitted *ek deuterou*, "a second time." Verse 61b is a slightly redacted form of Mark 14:72b.

Only vv. 61a and 62 create a problem. The former tells of Jesus' turning and looking at Peter after the denials. This is exclusive to Luke and probably stems from his compositional pen—the type of detail that Luke would like to include (see *FTG* 116; G. Schneider, *Verleugnung*, 91-93). Verse 62 is problematic because it is identical to Matt 26:75, and not found in Mark at all. Under other circumstances one would expect such a verse to come from "Q," but that is scarcely the case here, since the verse is narrative. It is, however, absent in the Lucan ms. 0171 and an OL version, and some commentators (P. Benoit, *Passion and Resurrection*, 67; G. Schneider, *Verleugnung*, 95-96) prefer to regard it as a copyist's addition, harmonizing the Lucan text with Matthew. Certainly, the Lucan story could have ended with the notice of the cockcrow; but the verse is otherwise well attested in the Lucan Gospel text-tradition, and that solution is too easy. It may be that we should have to ascribe it to "L," which is going to be the source of the following verses.

As for the scene of the mistreatment of Jesus (vv. 63-65), it draws its inspiration from "Mk," but there it does not occur in the same sequence; Luke has transposed it. In this instance there is a majority agreement among commentators that Luke is making use of an independent, non-Marcan source ("L"). (So A. Plummer, *The Gospel*, 517; W. Grundmann, *Evangelium nach Lukas*, 417-418; V. Taylor, *Passion Narrative*, 79-80 [Luke's "own re-writing of material from his special source"]; B. H. Streeter, *The Four Gospels*, 222; D. R. Catchpole, *The Trial*, 174-183; J. Ernst, *Evangelium nach Lukas*, 616; I. H. Marshall, *Luke*, 845; et al.) For hesitancy about such a source, see J. M. Creed, *The Gospel*, 277-278; J. Finegan, *Überlieferung*, 24. (Cf. G. Schneider, *Verleugnung*, 96-104.)

Luke has only six out of twenty-seven words in common with Mark, the most prominent of which is the impv. *prophēteuson*, "prophesy!" The note-worthy item in the scene, however, is again the word-for-word agreement of "Who is it that hits you?" (v. 64c) with Matt 26:68, which is absent in "Mk." This is simply a strong reason for ascribing this passage to "L." (See *HST* 271.)

Finally, as for the interrogation scene proper, the source of the verses is quite contested. The first part (vv. 66-68) is almost certainly to be attributed to "L," although some Lucan rewording may be detected in it. Similarly for v. 70, the second question put to Jesus, and his half-answer. If v. 69 comes from the same source, then it has been assimilated to Mark 14:62, either by Luke or by the source before him. Again, v. 71 has some resemblance to Mark 14:63b, but is devoid of the charge of blasphemy and the verdict (14:64); so the chances are that it too stems from "L." Ascription of vv. 66-71 to "L" seems to be a better solution than a mere redaction of the Marcan parallel, though one cannot be apodictic about it.

Even V. Taylor *(Passion Narrative,* 84) had to admit that in this case "the character of the narrative is very difficult to determine. It is difficult to believe that it is based solely on Mark or that it is entirely independent of Mark." Those who prefer to regard the episode as a revision of "Mk" are: M.-J. Lagrange *(Luc,* 571-574); J. M. Creed *(The Gospel,* 276: "The dependence upon Mark is . . . unmistakable in the account of the Trial"); J. Schmid *(Evangelium nach Lukas,* 340-341); J. Finegan *(Überlieferung,* 24); H. Conzelmann *(Theology,* 84 n. 3). Those who prefer to regard the episode as basically derived from a non-Marcan source are: W. Grundmann *(Evangelium nach Lukas,* 418-419 [except for v. 69]); K. H. Rengstorf *(Evangelium nach Lukas,* 257); D. R. Catchpole *(The Trial,* 183-203); G. Schneider *(Evangelium nach Lukas,* 468: for vv. 66-68, whereas vv. 69-71 are from "Mk"); J. Ernst *(Evangelium nach Lukas,* 617-618); et al. J. Jeremias *(Die Sprache,* 299-300) seems to consider v. 70 as composed by Luke himself.

From a form-critical point of view, the three-part episode belongs to Stories about Jesus, further portions of the narrative gospel tradition. Though R. Bultmann *(HST* 269) was willing to admit that Luke had made use of an "older tradition" than Mark for the denial scene and that the appearance of the servants in vv. 58,59 and Peter's not leaving the courtyard are from Luke's editorial pen, he still concludes that "the story of Peter is itself legendary and literary." We have already admitted the Lucan redaction of "Mk," which does change the character of the story, making it perhaps more "literary" and softening the depiction of Peter (in Luke he does not curse or swear [Mark 14:71]), and eliminates the problem that the double crowing of the cock causes for plausibility (see p. 1426). Yet that does not enable one to conclude that the episode is "legendary." If there is one piece of historical truth in the passion narrative that comes through as such, it is the denial of Jesus by Peter three times over. Why would there be such unanimity about it otherwise? Though Luke sought to soften the flow of the story, by giving it a more forensic cast (see W. Dietrich, *Das Petrusbild,* 145-157), he passes on to us the essence of the story. (See further I. H. Marshall, *Luke,* 840.)

As for the mistreatment scene, R. Bultmann *(HST* 271) argues for the plausibility of the Lucan position of it, after the arrest and before the interrogation.

In the episode of the interrogation, I shall prescind from the nature of the Marcan scene and its historical character (on which see now J. R. Donahue, *Are You the Christ?* cf. D. Juel, *Messiah and Temple).* Even if one prescinds from the differences between the Marcan and Lucan forms of the interrogation, the fact of the interrogation about messiahship by a threefold group of Jewish authorities is clear. Whether Luke deliberately chose to eliminate the charge of blasphemy and the verdict or merely preferred to follow "L," which lacked these elements, we shall never know. To conclude one way or the other about the historicity of these elements of the interrogation scene is impossible. One must merely note that the Lucan story agrees with the Johannine in the omission of them, against the tradition preserved in Mark and Matthew.

The suggestion of P. Winter *(On the Trial of Jesus,* 27-43) that the interrogation scene was a later addition to the passion narrative is sheer speculation and does not merit serious consideration.

In the Lucan story of the sequel to Jesus' arrest Peter at first occupies the center of attention. It is the story of his *peirasmos,* "temptation, testing," and it takes place at night. Peter has not yet abandoned Jesus (Mark 14:50 puts it even more strongly—they *all* fled; Luke is rather silent about the whereabouts of the others), but he has "followed," if even at a distance. Having entered the courtyard of the high priest's house, Peter takes a seat with unnamed persons, probably servants, who have kindled a fire and have been sitting about it, warming themselves against the chill of a spring night. The scene involving Peter develops in three stages: (a) A servant girl, catching sight of him, stares at him (the Lucan stress on the mode of recognition), and immediately associates him with the captive just brought in: "This fellow too was with him" (v. 56). Guilt by association! This implied accusation evokes from Peter his first denial, "Woman, I do not know him" (v. 57), as he rejects the accusation of the witness against him, who happens to be a woman. Peter's denial does not stem from fear, *pace* E. E. Ellis, *Gospel of Luke,* 260. Unlike Mark 14:68, where Peter then retires to a forecourt and a cock crows, the Lucan Peter continues to sit at the fire in the courtyard. (b) A little while later someone else, a servant boy *(heteros,* masc.; contrast Mark 14:69, where the same servant girl continues her accusation), apparently unaware of the girl's remark, makes another implied accusation, "You too are one of them" (v. 58). The accusation begins with emphatic *kai sy* (cf. John 18:25). Again Peter denies that he is. The first accusation involved association with Jesus; the second, association with his disciples—Peter denies his discipleship! Moreover, Luke introduces it with *anthrōpe,* "Man," in contrast to the *gynai,* "Woman," of v. 57. About an hour later yet another servant boy *(allos tis,* masc.) repeats the allegation with asseveration, insisting, "I assure you, this fellow too was with him," and adds a reason, "He is even a Galilean!" (v. 59). How the servant recognized Peter as a Galilean we are not told (see Matt 26:73 for a Matthean explanation: Peter's manner of speech gives him away). Then for a third time Peter makes a denial, "Sir, I do not know what you are talking about!" (v. 60). Two denials are uttered against male accusers. (c) At that instant, before Peter's words are at an end, a cock is heard crowing. And the Lucan Jesus, now called "the Lord," turns—apparently from a spot in the courtyard—and looks at Peter, who recalls at once the prediction of v. 34; he goes out and weeps bitterly. The servant girl and the two servant boys have played the role of Satan in Peter's *peirasmos*—associating Peter with the "guilty" Jesus, soon to be accused. Peter has thus faced the sifting process and been shown to be mere chaff in the sieve of discernment. Unlike Judas, he has not handed Jesus over for money (22:5) nor made a travesty of his intimacy with him by seeking to greet him with a kiss (22:47); but it is a callous defection, a denial three times over, stemming from Peter's failing faith (22:32). The Lucan form of the story has made the accusation of Peter even more official than the Marcan, by showing Peter challenged not only by a servant-girl, whose testimony might be questioned, but even by two servant boys, two male witnesses (recall Deut 19:15; cf. Josephus, *Ant.* 4.8,15 § 219; *m. Roš. Haš.* 1:8; cf. E. Schweizer, *Evangelium nach Lukas,* 234). Thus Peter alone in the Lucan passion narrative becomes a deserter of Jesus; but Jesus has prayed for him, not that he would not defect, but having done so and been converted would then become a support for his brethren. Jesus' glance in this form of the denial story starts the process of remorse; it is the prevenient grace given to him who had been ready to go with Jesus "to prison and to death" (v. 33). In this scene he has been tried and found wanting. Once again, Peter finds himself in Jesus' presence as "a sinner" (recall his protestation at the catch of fish, 5:8). As Jesus there promised Peter that he would henceforth "be catching human beings" (5:10), so now his glance at Peter recalls not only his prediction of Peter's denials, but also his prayer for the role destined for Peter (22:31-32). (See further W. Dietrich, *Das Petrusbild*, 154-157.

After Peter's exit and departure, the men holding Jesus in the courtyard of the high priest's house begin to ridicule or mock him; they blindfold and buffet him, taunting him with jibes, Play the prophet for us! Who is it that hits you? Whereas the Marcan/Matthean Jesus is eventually to be accused of blasphemy, the only place the vb. *blasphēmein* is used in the Lucan episode is of the "insults" leveled at *him* by these jesters. Whereas in the Marcan account the actors in this part of the episode were *tines*, "some" (14:65a), which in the context could refer only to the *pantes*, "all," of v. 64, i.e. "the chief priests and the whole Sanhedrin" (14:55), and also "assistants" *(hypēretai,* 14:65d), in the Lucan account the actors are unnamed. "The men who were holding Jesus" (22:63) are not simply to be identified with the Jewish authorities; they are rather underlings. (No intimation is given that any Roman soldiers are involved; even in John 18:22 it is one of the *hypēretai,* who in v. 12 have been identified as attendants "of the Jews.") In all the mistreatment the Lucan Jesus utters not a word (contrast John 18:23). Once again he gives the impression of one who is in control of the scene; he tolerates what is happening to him, because he is aware that this forms part of the consequences of the Father's will. He has already announced ridicule as part of the coming passion (18:32; see further Luke 23:11,36). It is part of the way that a prophet meets his fate in Jerusalem (13:33). The blindman's buff played on him heightens his humiliation and lonely dereliction. Disowned by Peter, he is now ridiculed by those who hold power over him (recall "the power of darkness," 22:53). From this status of ridicule and humiliation he will move to the interrogation by the authorities of his own people. (For similar acts of degradation and humiliation inflicted on a prophet, see 1 Kgs 22:24-28; Jer 28:10-16, as D. N. Freedman recalls to me.)

In the interrogation scene itself, before the assembled elders, chief priests, and Scribes (= the Jerusalem Sanhedrin), where no witnesses are introduced (contrast Mark 14:55-59) and no reference is made to Jesus having spoken of the destruction of the Temple (contrast Mark 14:58), the entire questioning is addressed to Jesus himself. (What he said in 19:44 or 21:6 does not become a pretext for accusation.) The questioning concerns his messiahship and his divine sonship alone. The answers that he gives to the questions, half-affirmative at best, are interpreted as "testimony" coming "from his own lips" (v. 71). And this, strangely enough, becomes the basis for leading him off to Pilate (23:1). For all the Lucan concern to exculpate the Roman authorities and inculpate the Jewish leaders (see p. 1363), it is surprising that Luke has retained nothing of the charge of "blasphemy" in this scene, or of any verdict passed against Jesus (contrast Mark 14:64, which Luke must have read).

The emphasis in the Lucan interrogation scene is christological. Luke uses the occasion to affirm once again who Jesus is: "Are you the Messiah?" (v. 67). "You are, then, the Son of God?" (v. 70). These questions, posed by the supreme Jewish authorities, echo the double angelic announcement in the infancy narrative about the child to be born: One who would sit upon "the throne of his father David" and would "be called Son of God" (1:32,35). Thus the child "marked for the fall and the rise of many in Israel" and destined "to be a symbol that will be rejected" (2:34) becomes the Jesus who is interrogated by authorities of his own people about his messiahship and divine sonship. What was foreshadowed in the infancy narrative, where the chords were first struck (1:32,35; 2:11,26), reaches with crescendo its climax in this scene, having been orchestrated in various ways in the Gospel up to this point (recall 3:15; 9:20; 20:41—3:22; 4:3,9,41; 8:28; 9:35). Faint echoes of it will again be heard in the Gospel's coda (23:2,35,39; 24:26)—and often in the Lucan second volume, where Jesus himself will become the preached one: not merely Messiah, and Son of God, but even the Son of Man standing at God's right hand (Acts 2:32-33,36; 7:55).

Jesus' answers to the Council in this Gospel are not explicit or direct. To the first one about his messiahship he retorts, "If I tell you, you will not believe me" (v. 67). He does not challenge the authority of his questioners, but he implies the uselessness of it all. Strikingly, he does not formulate his answer as an unreal (contrary-to-fact) condition, but as a future-more-vivid, with an emphatic fut. apodosis *(ou mē* + subjunc. *pisteusēte),* as if to predict the de facto negative reaction of the Sanhedrin members. But he does not stop with such a retort; he goes on to affirm something about himself: "From now on the Son of Man will be seated at the right hand of the power of God" (v. 69). In an allusion to Dan 7:13 and Ps 110:1 Jesus insinuates his coming heavenly destiny. In their original contexts these OT passages speak of something else: In the former, the seer beheld in a vision of the night "one like a son of man" coming to "the Ancient of Days" and being presented before him, who had taken his seat on the (heavenly) throne(s). From that Danielic passage comes (in part at least) the title "Son of Man" so often used of Jesus throughout the Lucan Gospel (see pp. 208-211). Here it bears a surrogate sense (= me), and implies a heavenly status for Jesus. In the second allusion Jesus' words refer to the royal Psalm 110, "Sit at my right hand till I make your enemies your footstool." This was addressed by Yahweh to some king about to be crowned and seated on the historic dynastic throne of David (recall Jesus' query about its meaning in 20:41-44 [pp. 1308-1316]). Now, confronted by interrogating Jewish authorities, who adopt an adversary position toward him, Jesus uses the words of that psalm again in his answer about his messiahship (i.e. Davidic kingship), not to make a direct, affirmative answer (as in Mark 14:62, "I am"), but indirectly to assert his victory over his adversaries—for he will be invested with the "power of God." The Lucan formulation (v. 69), if modeled on Mark 14:62bc, has divested the answer of some of its apocalyptic stage props (the coming with the clouds of heaven) and eliminated the personification of "Power" (an OT substitute for God himself; see Ps 54:3; Jer 16:21; Exod 9:16). Luke, however, has added *apo tou nyn,* "from now on," referring to the transit to the Father that is about to begin in the passion and death confronting Jesus.

From Jesus' first answer the Sanhedrin concludes, "You are, then, the Son of God?" (v. 70). The title *huios tou theou* is not to be understood as a mere equivalent of *christos,* i.e. being understood in a mere messianic sense (see pp. 206, 339); more is implied. And they have drawn this conclusion from the complete answer that Jesus gave them.

Jesus' second answer is a half-affirmative answer. He does not deny their conclusion, but merely comments, "It is you who say I am" (v. 70). The reason for this formulation is the legal situation in which he finds himself; he is being interrogated and refuses to play into the interrogators' hands. Luke (or his source) may well have known the Marcan tradition of 14:62a, *egō eimi,* "I am." That sort of answer is avoided. Jesus, in effect, throws the implied accusation back on his interrogators. He stresses that they are actually saying it, even if they do not believe it.

The Sanhedrin's conclusion: No need for witnesses to accuse Jesus; what he has said is enough to convict him out of his own mouth and it justifies their coming action of turning him over to the Roman governor. Thus, though the Sanhedrin may not be wholly responsible for what eventually happens to Jesus, it is not without some involvement in it. In this involvement a political reason has not yet emerged in the Lucan Gospel; all has hinged only on what Jesus' relation to God himself is. One cannot miss once again the mastery of Jesus in the interrogation scene; he may have been confronted by adversaries, but he has insinuated his ultimate victory over them.

NOTES

22   54. *They arrested Jesus.* Luke has no equivalent of Mark 14:46, but derives the vb. *syllabein* from 14:48 (where he had omitted it) and makes a ptc. of it, *syllabontes,* "arresting (him)." Cf. Acts 1:16; 12:3; 23:27. The subj. of the sentence must be the threesome mentioned in v. 52. They arrest Jesus because he tolerates it; he is in control of the situation. See G. Schneider, *Verleugnung,* 63, 73-74; recall v. 53.

bringing him to the house of the high priest. Lit. "and they led him (in)to . . ." The high priest goes unnamed, as in Mark 14:53. Cf. Matt 26:57, Caiaphas. See NOTE on 9:22 and p. 177. Some mss. (D, Γ, Θ, ƒ¹) and some ancient versions (Latin, Syriac) omit the vb. *eisēgagon,* "they led (in)to," because it follows *ēgagon,* "led away" and seems redundant. But it is read in the best mss. and is retained as the *lectio difficilior;* it may have been omitted by parablepsis (homoeoteleuton).

Peter followed. The presupposition is that the other ten disciples have gone off, but Luke never says that; Peter alone follows (out of curiosity? desire to manifest loyalty?). An ancient interpretation is that he follows out of love, but at a distance out of fear (see A. Plummer, *The Gospel,* 515); but is that really apparent in the Lucan text? He is called Peter, as in vv. 55,58,60,61, not Simon. See NOTE on 4:38.

at a distance. Luke eliminates the redundant prep. *apo* (see Mark 14:54), which Mark always uses with the adv. *makrothen* ("from a distance") and which Luke himself has in 16:23; 23:49.

55. *He sat down.* Lit. "when they had kindled a fire in the middle of the courtyard and were sitting together, Peter seated himself in the midst of them." The "they" is not easily determined; it is scarcely the same as the subj. of v. 54; more likely it is to be understood of those to be named in v. 63, "the men who were holding Jesus," the underlings of the threesome named in v. 52. Two gen. absols. begin the sentence, only to have their absol. character spoiled by the phrase at the end, *mesos autōn.* The first ptc., *periapsantōn,* is problematic, because it should mean lit. "kindling all around"; its sense, however, is pregnant, for it means that having kindled a fire they were sitting around it. But the problem is further compounded by the second ptc., *synkathisantōn,* which should mean "sitting together." This compound difficulty is the cause of the variant readings in mss. Instead of *periapsantōn,* mss. A, D, W, Γ, Δ, Θ, Ψ, 063, 0135, *f* [1,13], and the Koine text-tradition read the simple form *hapsantōn,* "kindling"; and instead of *synkathisantōn,* a few mss. (D, G, *f* [1]) have *perikathisantōn,* "sitting about." The sequence *periapsantōn . . . synkathisantōn* is found in mss. P[75], ℵ, B, L, T, 0124, etc. See further P. Joüon, "Notes philologiques," 356.

in the courtyard. Lit. "in the middle of the courtyard." In the Lucan account the three denials of Peter take place here.

56. *saw him sitting there at the fire.* Lit. "in/at the light."

stared. See NOTE on 4:20.

This fellow too was with him. The girl's statement is, in effect, an accusation. See W. Dietrich, *Das Petrusbild,* 144-145. The derogatory dem. pron. *houtos* is used, lit. "this one." Cf. Acts 4:13.

57. *Woman, I do not know him.* Peter uses *ouk oida,* "I do not know," usually used to express knowledge of facts. See v. 34. See NOTE on 9:26. He adds to his denial the voc. *gynai,* "Woman!" This detail is not found in the other Synoptics; it is preparing for the use of voc. *anthrōpe,* "Sir" (lit. "Man"), which in this case must be understood of a male human being because of the contrast. Recall 13:18,21.

58. *someone else.* The Greek text has the masc. pron. *heteros.* See COMMENT on p. 1457. In Mark 14:69 the second accusation comes from the same servant girl.

You too are one of them. I.e. one of those who were on the Mount of Olives with Jesus. The position of *kai sy* at the head of the sentence is emphatic.

No, Sir, I am not. Lit. "Man, I am not." See NOTE on 5:20. Peter has thus distanced himself not only from Jesus but also from the rest of the disciples.

59. *About an hour later.* Lit. "when about one hour had passed *(or* had distanced itself)," a gen. absol. For the approximative use of *hōsei,* see NOTE on 22:44.

someone else. Luke uses *allos tis,* implying someone different from either the servant girl or the second accuser. In Mark 14:70 the third accusation stems from "bystanders." In John 18:26 the third accusation comes from a servant of the high priest, a relative of Malchus.

insisted. The vb. *diischyrizesthai* occurs only here and in Acts 12:15, meaning, "maintain firmly, insist" (BAGD 195).

I assure you. See NOTE on 4:25; cf. 20:21.

this fellow too. See NOTE on v. 56.

even a Galilean! This identification will be used of Jesus himself in 23:6. See NOTE on 17:11. The reason for the identification given in Matt 26:73 (Peter's manner of speech) is exclusive to that Gospel; compare the reason in John 18:26 (recognition by one who had seen him in the garden).

60. *I do not know what you are talking about!* Though dependent here on "Mk," Luke has significantly omitted Peter's cursing and swearing, for he has too high an esteem for Peter to include that. See p. 564.

At once. See NOTE on 1:64.

a cock crowed. I.e. for the first and only time in the Lucan story; there is no awareness of a double crowing.

61. *The Lord turned and looked at Peter.* The evangelist's narrative style again uses the title *ho kyrios.* See NOTE on 7:13 and pp. 202-203. Peter is still presumably sitting in the middle of the courtyard (v. 55); Luke never explains where Jesus has been during the denials; the reader has to presume that he has been somewhere in the courtyard.

the Lord's saying. I.e. the foretelling of the denial in v. 34, which is not exactly quoted. The evangelist uses *tou rhēmatos tou Kyriou,* a phrase that will recur in Acts 11:16. Some mss., however, read *logou* instead (thus A, D, W, Θ, Ψ, 063, 0135, *f*¹, and the Koine text-tradition), which does not change the meaning.

62. *he went outside and wept bitterly.* This verse is omitted by ms. 0171 and various mss. of the OL version (a, b, e, ff², i, l*, r); but this is scarcely sufficient external testimony to exclude the verse from the Lucan text. See *TCGNT* 178. The problem that the verse creates is that it agrees verbatim with Matt 26:75c. Since it is scarcely owing to a copyist's harmonizing tendency, it has to be reckoned as one of the minor agreements of Matthew and Luke against Mark in the Triple Tradition. See pp. 72-73. Save for *pikrōs,* "bitterly," every word in the cl. is otherwise well attested in Lucan vocabulary. It could be of Lucan composition; but more likely it is derived by him from "L." In any case, in the Lucan story the sentence poignantly depicts Peter abandoning Jesus—with remorse.

63. *The men who were holding Jesus in custody.* Lit. "him" *(auton),* which must refer to Jesus, despite the immediate context. The vb. *synechein* is a Lucan favorite. See p. 111.

began to ridicule him and beat him. The vb. *enepaizon* is a sort of conative impf. See BDF § 326. For OT background of the mistreatment of prisoners or adversaries, see Isa 50:5-6; 53:3-5 (esp. LXX); 2 Macc 7:1-2,7,12; 4 Macc 6:3-30; 8:12-14:10. Recall the ridicule predicted in 18:32.

64. *blindfolded.* Lit. "covered/concealed all around."

Now prophesy! Who is it that hits you? The impv. *prophēteuson* is common to Mark 14:65 and Matt 26:67, whereas the rest of the taunt is not found in Mark, but is in

Matthew. It is another minor agreement of Matthew and Luke against Mark, but in this case it almost certainly comes from "L," as does the rest of this part of the episode. *Pace* R. Bultmann *(HST* 271), it is scarcely a "wholly secondary conformation [of Luke] to Matthew"!

65. *they kept leveling many other insults at him.* Lit. "reviling (him in) many other ways," the adjs. *polla hetera* act as an adverbial acc. to the ptc. *blasphēmountes.* This additional notice has no counterpart in either Mark or Matthew. Recall the insults of 18:32 (where the vb. differs).

66. *When it was day.* I.e. daybreak of 15 Nisan or Passover, which began with sunset on the previous evening. This timing agrees with Mark 15:1, but there it is the time for the second consultation of the Sanhedrin in the Marcan account, during which no interrogation of Jesus about messiahship (or sonship) occurs. According to J. M. Creed *(The Gospel,* 278), Luke "interpolates here an account of the interrogation of Jesus based on the narrative of Mk. xiv. 55f." But is it so based? The time indication is one of the major differences in the Lucan and Marcan/Matthean accounts. Fixing the interrogation about messiahship and divine sonship to a morning meeting of the Sanhedrin may actually be a more historical recollection. E. Linnemann *(Studien,* 109 n. 1) rightly notes that the Marcan account of the interrogation about messiahship is actually devoid of any time reference. For later rabbinic regulations about the holding of capital cases at night, see *m. Sanh.* 4:1.

the elders of the people, both chief priests and Scribes, assembled. Lit. "there assembled the elders-council of the people, both chief priests and Scribes." In this Lucan formulation the phrase "both chief priests and Scribes" seems to be an appositive to *presbytērion tou laou,* "the elders-council of the people." See BDF § 444.4. To make his formulation refer clearly to the three groups often mentioned as the components of the Sanhedrin, Luke should have used another *te* (with the first n.). Codex Bezae solves the problem by using *pr. kai archiereis kai grammateis.* Though the Lucan text adds *tou laou,* "of the people," it does not necessarily implicate the whole people along with the authorities. Luke normally distinguishes them. See NOTE on 18:43.

Jesus was brought before. Lit. "they (indef.) led him away," or the third pl. may refer to "the men who were holding Jesus in custody" (v. 63).

their Council. Or possibly, "their Council hall." See P. Winter, *On the Trial of Jesus,* 27-43. Luke uses the n. *synedrion,* as does Mark 14:55 and Matt 26:46, which in itself means "a (general) council" (lit. "a sitting together"). It is found on Greek inscriptions to designate a "council of elders" in the eastern Mediterranean world. E.g. at Philadelphia, *CIG* 3417; see MM 604. Josephus uses it to designate the high council of Palestinian Jews. See *Ant.* 14.9,3 § 167; 14.9,4 § 168; 20.9,1 § 200, 202; in *Ant.* 12.3,3 § 142 he speaks of its three components as *hē gerousia kai hoi hiereis kai hoi grammateis.* From this Greek word comes the Hebrew form *Sanhedrîn* used in the Mishnaic tractate of the same name, whence the commonly used English title. See further E. Lohse, *TDNT* 7. 862-866; *HJPAJC* 2. 199-216.

67. *are you the Messiah?* This first of two questions put to Jesus is not idle; the interrogators are dead serious. Were Jesus to answer yes, the political nuances of the title could be exploited. He is challenged by Jewish authorities to admit whether he considers himself to be such. On the meaning of *christos,* see NOTES on 2:11, 3:15 and pp. 197-200. In Stage I of the gospel tradition the question would have been asked in

the political sense. But in Stage III Luke obviously intends the question to carry a deeper christological nuance as well. The political aspect will emerge in 23:1-5. There is undoubtedly an echo of this sort of interrogation in the Johannine tradition within the ministry itself. See John 10:24-26.

If I tell you, you will not believe me. Cf. Luke 20:8. Jesus does not contest the Sanhedrin's authority, but merely calls attention to the pointlessness of an answer from him. Cp. Jer 45:15 (LXX; MT 38:15). What Jesus implies about his interrogators is actually verified in v. 71.

68. *If I ask you a question, you will not answer.* Some mss. (Θ, *f*¹) add *moi*, "me"; ms. D and the Koine text-tradition add *moi ē apolysēte,* ". . . answer me or release (me)." Jesus' reply spells out a little more explicitly a possible sense of this peculiar statement in the Lucan form of the interrogation. It is a parallel to the preceding statement of Jesus, but it is peculiar on the lips of the one being interrogated. It is the type of variant that is characteristic, however, of ms. D in that it removes unclarity in the text. It heightens the dramatic irony of the scene as a whole. See further J. Duplacy, "Une variante méconnue du texte reçu." Cf. Luke 20:3.

69. *But from now on.* For *apo tou nyn* in Lucan writings, see NOTES on 1:48; 5:10. Nothing corresponds to this phrase in "Mk," but note the coincidental agreement, in sense but not in wording, in Matt 26:64 *(ap' arti).* Cf. Luke 22:18 and Matt 26:29. The "now" refers to the time of the *exodos* (recall 9:31), after which the Period of the Church begins. See further H. Conzelmann, *Theology,* 84 n. 3.

the Son of Man will be seated at the right hand of the power of God. Jesus' declaration combines a phrase from Dan 7:13 (LXX and Theodotion: *hōs huios anthrōpou)* and from Ps 110:1 (LXX: *kathou ek dexiōn mou).* In Mark 14:62 and Matt 26:64 a form of this conflated declaration is also found. But the Lucan form differs in not mentioning a vision ("you will see"—for Luke only a believer will behold it; see Acts 7:55-56) or the apocalyptic stage props ("the clouds of heaven"). Jesus' declaration asserts the exaltation of himself as the Son of Man and his investiture with power. See Luke 21:27; cf. O. Linton, "The Trial." If the title "Son of Man" is intended to have a judicial connotation (so C. Colpe, *TDNT* 8. 435), as it seems to have in 11:30, then Jesus declares that as such he will turn out to be the judge of those who interrogate him now. Cf. 12:8-9. Whereas *dynamis* was used in Mark 14:62 in a personified sense for God himself, it is in the Lucan form "power of God," something with which the Son of Man will be invested. For the OT background of this phrase, see Josh 4:24; 1 Chr 12:23(LXX), Wis 7:25; 2 Macc 3:24,38; 9:8; cf. 1QM 1:11,14; 4:4,12; 6:2,6; 10:5. Cf. G. Friedrich, *EWNT* 1. 860-867. Cf. Eph 1:20; 1 Pet 3:22. For a different, Pauline sense of *dynamis theou,* see 1 Cor 1:18-25; Rom 1:16.

70. *they all said.* The Lucan predilection for "all" is probably a redactional addition to "L" here. See NOTES on 3:16; 4:15; 9:1. It implicates the whole Sanhedrin.

You are, then, the Son of God? On the title, see pp. 205-208. The separate question about his divine sonship heightens the drama of the Lucan interrogation. It is a question that does not disclose the belief, but only sinister implications. The separation of the questions about messiahship and sonship parallels the declarations of the angel in 1:32-33,35. Whereas H. Conzelmann *(Theology,* 84) was inclined to regard the two titles (Messiah and Son of God) as fundamentally identical, that is exactly what they are not; their basis in the OT itself is distinct, and the connotations of each have to be respected. See further J. M. Creed *(The Gospel,* 278): "To Luke and his readers Son of God is the supreme title of Jesus, which was capable of expressing his universal significance, whereas the use of 'Christ' as a title naturally tended to become subordinate." Similarly, E. Schweizer, *Evangelium nach Lukas,* 233.

The conj. *oun* does not merely repeat the former question, but draws a conclusion from Jesus' answer to the first question; the matter is debated, however. See J. Schmid, *Evangelium nach Lukas,* 341.

It is you who say I am. Lit. "you (emphatic) say that I (emphatic) am!" In effect, this is a half-yes answer (BDF § 441.3), which does not refuse a reply; it implies an affirmation, yet stresses that it is their way of putting it. Note the contrast in *sy oun* (v. 70b) and *hymeis* (v. 70d). The irony, of course, is that they may say it, but in reality deny it. This is not a mere accepted formula of assent, *pace* I. Abrahams, *Studies in Pharisaism and the Gospels* (2 vols.; Cambridge: University Press, 1917, 1924) 2. 1-2, as J. M. Creed *(The Gospel,* 279) long ago pointed out. Cf. Euripides, *Hipp.* 352.

71. *What further need have we of testimony?* In the Lucan scene of the interrogation there has been no testimony thus far (cp. Mark 14:55-59; Matt 26:59-61). But a different reason will be given in the following cl.

We have heard it ourselves from his own lips. Lit. "from his mouth." What the Sanhedrin has heard is not made explicit; but it is clear that "from his own lips" these leaders have heard that he is the Son of God. The admission made here on the part of all the members of the Sanhedrin leads to the next step in the narrative; the intention expressed in 20:20 will now find political expression in 23:2. Verse 71 shows that Luke has at least read Mark 14:53-61.

BIBLIOGRAPHY (22:54-71)

Benoit, P. *Passion and Resurrection,* 49-72, 73-92, 93-114.

——— "Les outrages à Jésus prophète (Mc xiv 65 par.)," *Neotestamentica et patristica* (ed. W. C. van Unnik) 92-110.

Birdsall, J. N. *"To rhēma hōs eipen autō ho Iēsous:* Mark xiv. 72," *NovT* 2 (1957) 272-275.

Blinzler, J. "Geschichtlichkeit und Legalität des jüdischen Prozesses gegen Jesus," *Stimmen der Zeit* 147 (1950-1951) 345-357.

——— "Das Synedrium von Jerusalem und die Strafprozessordnung der Mischna," *ZNW* 52 (1961) 54-65.

——— *The Trial of Jesus: The Jewish and Roman Proceedings against Jesus Christ Described and Assessed from the Oldest Accounts* (Westminster: Newman, 1959); *Der Prozess Jesu* (3d ed.; Regensburg: Pustet, 1960).

Boyd, W. J. P. "Peter's Denials—Mark xiv.68; Luke xxii.57," *ExpTim* 67 (1955-1956) 341.

Büchsel, F. "Die Blutgerichtsbarkeit des Synedrions," *ZNW* 30 (1931) 202-210.

——— "Noch einmal: Zur Blutgerichtsbarkeit des Synedrions," *ZNW* 33 (1934) 84-87.

Burkill, T. A. "The Trial of Jesus," *VC* 12 (1958) 1-18.

Cantinat, J. "Jésus devant le Sanhédrin," *NRT* 75 (1953) 300-308.

Catchpole, D. R. "The Problem of the Historicity of the Sanhedrin Trial," *The Trial of Jesus* (ed. E. Bammel) 47-65.

―――― *The Trial of Jesus* (SPB 18; Leiden: Brill, 1971) 153-220.

Cohn, H. *The Trial and Death of Jesus* (New York: Harper & Row, 1967).

Danby, H. "The Bearing of the Rabbinical Criminal Code on the Jewish Trial Narratives in the Gospels," *JTS* 21 (1919-1920) 51-76.

Delorme, J. "Le procès de Jésus ou la parole risquée (Lc 22,54-23,25)," *RSR* 69 (1981) 123-146.

Derrett, J. D. M. "Midrash in the New Testament: The Origin of Luke XXII 67-68," *ST* 29 (1975) 147-156.

Dibelius, M. "Das historische Problem der Leidensgeschichte," *ZNW* 30 (1931) 193-201.

Dietrich, W. *Das Petrusbild,* 139-157.

Donahue, J. R. *Are You the Christ? The Trial Narrative in the Gospel of Mark* (SBLDS 10; Missoula, MT: Scholars, 1973).

Duplacy, J. "Une variante méconnue du texte reçu: '. . . ē apolysēte' (Lc 22, 68)," *Neutestamentliche Aufsätze* (eds. J. Blinzler et al.) 42-52.

Evans, C. A. " 'Peter Warming Himself': The Problem of an Editorial 'Seam,' " *JBL* 101 (1982) 245-249.

Feuillet, A. "Le triomphe du fils de l'homme d'après la déclaration du Christ aux Sanhédrites (Mc., xiv, 62; Mt., xxvi, 64; Lc., xxii, 69)," *La venue du Messie* (RechBib 6; Bruges: Desclée de Brouwer, 1962) 149-171.

Flender, H. *St Luke,* 44-50.

Gnilka, J. "Die Verhandlungen vor dem Synhedrion und vor Pilatus nach Markus 14,53-15,5," *EKK Vorarbeiten* 2 (1970) 5-21.

Goguel, M. "A propos du procès de Jésus," *ZNW* 31 (1932) 289-301.

Grant, F. C. *"On the Trial of Jesus:* A Review Article," *JR* 44 (1964) 230-237.

Herranz, M. "El proceso ante el Sanhedrín y el ministerio público de Jesús," *EstBíb* 34 (1975) 83-111.

Husband, R. W. *The Prosecution of Jesus: Its Date, History and Legality* (Princeton: Princeton University, 1916).

Jaubert, A. "Les séances du Sanhédrin et les récits de la passion," *RHR* 166 (1964) 143-169; 167 (1965) 1-33.

Jeremias, J. "Zur Geschichtlichkeit des Verhörs Jesu vor dem Hohen Rat," *ZNW* 43 (1950-1951) 145-150.

Juel, D. *Messiah and Temple: The Trial of Jesus in the Gospel of Mark* (SBLDS 31; Missoula, MT: Scholars, 1977).

Kempthorne, R. "The Marcan Text of Jesus' Answer to the High Priest (Mark xiv 62)," *NovT* 19 (1977) 197-208.

Kilpatrick, G. D. *The Trial of Jesus* (London: Oxford University, 1953).

Klein, G. "Die Verleugnung" (see p. 1427) 285-328.

Lamarche, P. "La déclaration de Jésus devant le Sanhédrin," *Christ vivant: Essai sur la christologie du Nouveau Testament* (LD 43; Paris: Cerf, 1966) 147-163.

Lampe, G. W. H. "St. Peter's Denial," *BJRL* 55 (1972-1973) 346-368.

Légasse, S. "Jésus devant le Sanhédrin: Recherche sur les traditions évangéliques," *RTL* 5 (1974) 170-197.

Lehmann, M. *Synoptische Quellenanalyse*, 106-112.

Lietzmann, H. "Bemerkungen zum Prozess Jesu," *ZNW* 30 (1931) 211-215.

———— "Der Prozess Jesu," *SPAW* phil.-hist. Kl., Heft 14 (1931) 313-322; reprinted, *Kleine Schriften 2: Studien zum Neuen Testament* (ed. K. Aland; TU 68; Berlin: Akademie-V., 1958) 251-263.

Linnemann, E. "Die Verleugnung des Petrus," *ZTK* 63 (1966) 1-32.

———— *Studien*, 70-135.

Linton, O. "The Trial of Jesus and the Interpretation of Psalm cx," *NTS* 7 (1960-1961) 258-262.

Lührmann, D. "Markus 14.55-64: Christologie und Zerstörung des Tempels im Markusevangelium," *NTS* 27 (1980-1981) 457-474.

Masson, C. "Le reniement de Pierre: Quelques aspects de la formation d'une tradition," *RHPR* 37 (1957) 24-35.

Meyer, F. E. "Einige Bemerkungen zur Bedeutungen des Terminus 'Synhedrion' in den Schriften des Neuen Testaments," *NTS* 14 (1967-1968) 545-551.

Miller, D. L. "*Empaizein:* Playing the Mock Game (Luke 22:63-64)," *JBL* 90 (1971) 309-313.

Pesch, R. "Die Verleugnung des Petrus: Eine Studie zu Mk 14,54.66-72 (und Mk 14,26-31)," *Neues Testament und Kirche* (ed. J. Gnilka) 42-62.

Rese, M. *Alttestamentliche Motive*, 199-200.

Rosenblatt, S. "The Crucifixion of Jesus from the Standpoint of the Pharisaic Law," *JBL* 75 (1956) 315-321.

Rudberg, G. "Die Verhöhnung Jesu vor dem Hohenpriester," *ZNW* 24 (1925) 307-309.

Schneider, G. "Gab es eine vorsynoptische Szene 'Jesus vor dem Synedrium'?" *NovT* 12 (1970) 22-39.

———— "Jesus vor dem Synedrium," *BibLeb* 11 (1970) 1-15.

———— *Verleugnung*, 73-104, 105-134, 211-220.

Schubert, K. "Die Juden und die Römer," *BLit* 36 (1962-1963) 235-242.

———— "Das Verhör Jesu vor dem Hohen Rat," *Bibel und zeitgemässer Glaube II* (ed. J. Sint; Klosterneuburg: Buch- und Kunstverlag, 1967) 97-130.

Sloyan, G. *Jesus on Trial* (Philadelphia: Fortress, 1973).

Tyson, J. B. "The Lukan Version of the Trial of Jesus," *NovT* 3 (1959) 249-258.

Unnik, W. C. van. "Jesu Verhöhnung vor dem Synedrium (Mc 14.65 par.)," *ZNW* 29 (1930) 310-311; reprinted, *Sparsa collecta* I (NovTSup 29; Leiden: Brill, 1973) 3-5.

Valentin, P. "Les comparutions de Jésus devant le Sanhédrin," *RSR* 59 (1971) 230-236.

Walaskay, P. W. "The Trial and Death of Jesus in the Gospel of Luke," *JBL* 94 (1975) 81-93.

Winter, P. "Luke XXII 66b-71," *ST* 9 (1955) 112-115.

———— "Marginal Notes on the Trial of Jesus," *ZNW* 50 (1959) 14-33, 221-251.

———— *On the Trial of Jesus* (2d ed.; rev. T. A. Burkill and G. Vermes; Studia judaica 1; Berlin/New York: de Gruyter, 1974).

———— "The Trial of Jesus," *Commentary* 38/3 (1964) 35-41.

———— "The Trial of Jesus and the Competence of the Sanhedrin," *NTS* 10 (1963-1964) 494-499.

Zeitlin, S. *Who Crucified Jesus?* (New York: Harper & Row, 1942).

156. JESUS IS DELIVERED TO PILATE; THE TRIAL
(23:1-5)

23 ¹ Then the whole assembly of them arose and led Jesus to Pilate. ² They proceeded to accuse him, "This man we have found subverting our nation, obstructing the payment of taxes to Caesar, and even claiming to be an anointed king." ³ Then Pilate questioned Jesus, "Are you the king of the Jews?" He answered him, "It is you who say this!" ⁴ Then Pilate said to the chief priests and the crowds, "I find nothing in this man that calls for his death." ⁵ But they kept insisting, "He has been stirring up our people all throughout Judea with his teaching, beginning from Galilee even to this place."

COMMENT

Having been interrogated by the Jerusalem Sanhedrin about his messiahship and divine sonship and having been judged to have furnished with "his own lips" (v. 71) what its members were looking for, Jesus is brought by them before the supreme authority of the Roman occupying power, the prefect Pontius Pilate, who questions him further (23:1-5). The accusations that are now made against Jesus by the Sanhedrin have nothing to do with the interrogation of him concluded in the preceding episode, save his messiahship.

This episode is inspired by Mark 15:1b-5 (cf. Matt 27:2,11-14, where the story of the death of Judas is inserted, vv. 3-10). Verse 3 is clearly derived from Mark 15:2, being almost word-for-word identical (apart from a few obvious Lucanisms, simple *erōtan* and pleonastic *legōn*). But vv. 1-2,4-5 create a problem. Apart from v. 4b they are so heavily Lucan in formulation that they raise many questions. Verse 4b resembles John 18:38c in a striking way:

Luke: *ouden heuriskō aition en tō anthrōpō toutō,* "I find nothing guilty in this man."

John: *egō oudemian heuriskō en autō aitian,* "I find no guilty cause in him."

Because of this one would be tempted to say that the rest of vv. 1-2,4-5 is from "L"; but it is not so simple. Luke may well have derived from "L" the tradition of Pilate's triple declaration of Jesus' innocence (see vv. 14-15,22), a tradition found also in John 18:38; 19:4,6 (see p. 88). A number of commentators (e.g. W. Grundmann, *Evangelium nach Lukas,* 421; K. H. Rengstorf, *Evangelium nach Lukas,* 261; V. Taylor, *Passion Narrative,* 86-87; I. H. Marshall, *Luke,* 852; J. Ernst, *Evangelium nach Lukas,* 621; et al.) maintain that Luke has used here an independent non-Marcan source. But, if he has, then he has heavily reworked it. For the amount of Lucan formulation in vv. 1-2,4-5 is remarkable. For this reason another group of commentators refuses to see anything more than a Lucan redaction of "Mk" along with Lucan composition—with at most a recognition of "L" behind v. 4b (so, with varying nuances, J. M. Creed, *The Gospel,* 279; J. Schmid, *Evangelium nach Lukas,* 342; G. Schneider, *Evangelium nach Lukas,* 471; E. Klostermann, *Lukasevangelium,* 221; et al.). The latter view is preferable. For in v. 1 the ptc. *anastan,* "arising," is the typically Lucan pleonastic form (see pp. 110, 114); similarly the expression "the whole assembly of them" (see NOTE). Though v. 2 has no counterpart in any of the other Gospel trial scenes, it clearly spells out the *polla,* "many things," of Mark 15:3, putting the accusations before Pilate's question in order to provide a psychological background for the question (recall the Lucan psychological background to the call of Peter, p. 560). In Mark 15:3 Pilate's question comes like a bolt from the blue; the Lucan preparation makes it more understandable. Moreover, v. 2 is filled with Lucan vocabulary (see J. Jeremias, *Die Sprache,* 300), which V. Taylor *(Passion Narrative,* 86-87) has overly reduced to a mere four words. There is really no evidence that a "non-Markan narrative" (ibid.) lies behind v. 2; it is the result of Lucan composition. Verse 4a is introduced with a clear Lucanism *(eipen pros* + acc., p. 116); on *archiereis kai ochlous,* "the chief priests and the crowds," see NOTE. Finally, v. 5 is clearly a piece of Lucan composition. It presents again the political motivation (stirring up the people), alludes to the geographical perspective of Lucan theology (see pp. 164-171, esp. 168), and uses phrases that will reappear in Acts 10:38 ("all throughout Judea, beginning from Galilee"). Though J. Jeremias *(Die Sprache,* 301) would have us believe that *heōs hōde,* "even up to this place," is pre-Lucan, the evangelist has used both *heōs* and *hōde* so frequently in the Gospel that the argument is questionable.

From the viewpoint of form criticism, the episode is another Story about Jesus, part of the narrative gospel tradition. In form it is similar to Mark 15:1b-5, with accusations of the Sanhedrin, a question of Pilate, and an answer of Jesus. Luke has eliminated the refusal of Jesus to answer Pilate further and the latter's surprise. Pilate's question has been introduced here because of the title that will eventually be put on the cross. R. Bultmann *(HST* 282) labels it an "apologetic motive." That is not impossible.

When the Marcan and Lucan accounts of Jesus' appearance before Pilate are compared, questions about historicity arise. A real political charge against Jesus was part of the pre-Lucan and pre-Marcan tradition; that aspect surfaces in the Johannine tradition as well, and the fourfold testimony to the *titulus* on the cross supports the conclusion that a political charge was part of the early tradition. But in the present accounts of Jesus' appearance before Pilate, only Luke gives details of real political character. Jesus is accused of subverting the nation; this is specified in two ways: by obstructing the payment of taxes to Caesar, and by the claim to be an anointed king. Even in the lengthy account of the Johannine scene of Jesus' appearance before Pilate (18:29-38) he is accused only of being an "evildoer" (v. 30), and when Pilate poses there the same question as in v. 4b here, the dialogue plays on Jesus' kingship, but in an entirely different sense. Where Luke derives the two specific accusations brought against Jesus is unclear; it is far from clear that they have come to him from an independent, non-Marcan source. More likely they have been introduced by Luke himself to provide psychological preparation for Pilate's question. Having read 20:20-25, the reader knows immediately that the first accusation is false; and the second has its own qualifications in the course of the Lucan Gospel.

As far as the development of the Lucan passion narrative is concerned, this scene begins the major act in it: Jesus is accused by Jewish authorities before the supreme authority of the Roman occupying secular power, the prefect. This is the beginning of the real repudiation of the Son of Man by "the elders, chief priests, and Scribes" (9:22), as he is "handed over into the hands of men" (9:44), "handed over to the Gentiles" (18:32). Jesus may indeed have subverted the nation in warning the crowds against the "leaven of the Pharisees" (12:1), i.e. subverted it in a religious sense. But such action in a political sense has not been evident thus far in the Gospel. The first specific accusation, which is about obstructing the payment of taxes to Caesar, distorts his pronouncement in 20:25 (about giving Caesar his due). Similarly, the accusation about his claim to be an anointed king makes the reader recall not only Peter's confession (9:20), but also Jesus' strict orders to the disciples that they were not to repeat what Peter had said (9:21). In the preceding episode Jesus may have indirectly admitted that he was a Messiah, but he qualified it by referring to himself as the exalted Son of Man and Son of God (22:67-70). Such details in the Gospel dull the edge of the implied political accusation.

Lurking in the background of the accusation, however, is the welcome tendered Jesus when he approached Jerusalem, "Blest be the king . . ." (19:38). This provides the psychological background in the Lucan story for Pilate's question, "Are you the king of the Jews?" (v. 3), to which Jesus replies, "It is you who say this!" One has to accept the Lucan story here at face value. It is clearly a telescoped version of an interrogation of Jesus by Pilate. The prefect may have feared someone who, he somehow learned, was hailed as a king and who has now been brought before him, the supreme political authority, on a political charge. But the Lucan story says nothing of an investigation of such a charge by Pilate. It tells only of a question put to Jesus by Pilate, which Jesus in effect refuses to answer. From such a summary questioning, indeed, Pilate turns to the chief priests and the crowds with, "I find nothing in this man that calls for his death" (v. 4)—his first declaration of Jesus' innocence (see vv. 14-15,22; recall the similar declaration by Roman officials about Paul's innocence in Acts 23:29; 25:25; 26:30-32; 28:21). The evangelist is interested only in the conclusion reached by Pilate.

The upshot is that Jesus is now being reckoned with outlaws (see 22:37), haled into court on political charges; yet Pilate's answer to Jesus' accusers makes it clear that he is the wronged, suffering, upright one. The accusation, however, persists: Jesus is a rabble-rouser, one who stirs up the people with his preaching, from Galilee, throughout all Judea, and even in Jerusalem. What comes across clearly in 23:1-5 is that the Lucan Jesus is guilty of no crime in Roman eyes; he is guiltless even when the charge of sedition is leveled against him.

NOTES

23 1. *the whole assembly of them.* I.e. of the members of the Sanhedrin, mentioned in 22:66. Whereas *plēthos,* "assembly," is used only once by Mark and never by Matthew, it occurs twenty-four times in Luke-Acts. Moreover, the expression *(ha)pan to plēthos* (usually with a dependent gen.) is uniquely Lucan. See 1:10; 8:37; 19:37; Acts 15:12; 25:24. The Lucan hyperbolic use of *pas/hapas* is again in evidence (see NOTES on 3:16; 4:15; 9:1); note the correction that Luke will make in 23:51.

arose. Lit. "arising," the pleonastic use of *anastan.* See NOTE on 1:39.

led Jesus to Pilate. Luke omits all mention of the binding of Jesus. See Mark 15:1b. The reader of the Lucan Gospel has to conclude at this point that Jesus was judged guilty in the Sanhedrin session of something that merited his being brought before the Roman prefect, who "had received from Caesar authority even in capital cases" *(mechri tou kteinein labōn para Kaisaros,* lit. "even up to death," Josephus, *J. W.* 2.8,1 § 117). Recall Tacitus (A.D. 56[?]-116[?]), *Annales* 15.44,3: *auctor nominis eius* [i.e. Christiani] *Christus Tiberio imperitante per procuratorem Pontium Pilatum supplicio adfectus erat,* "Christ, the source of that name [Christian] was executed by the procurator, Pontius Pilate, while Tiberius was reigning." (On the anachronism of "procurator," see NOTE on 3:1 about Pilate.) On the Lucan use of the vb. *agein,* see p. 112; cp. John 18:28.

2. *They proceeded to accuse him.* Lit. "they began . . ." The "they" refers to "of them" (v. 1). The first accusation is generic, as W. Grundmann *(Evangelium nach Lukas,* 422) rightly saw; it is not a question of three accusations. The cl. has an echo in Josephus, *Ant.* 1.19,1 § 314 *(ērxato katēgorein autou,* of Laban accusing Jacob).

This man we have found. Lit. "this one we have found," again the derogatory use of the dem. pron. *houtos,* emphatically placed at the head of the sentence. Cf. 22:56,59.

subverting our nation. I.e. misleading people with his teaching, even subverting them. This generic accusation is repeated in v. 5. The vb. *diastrephein* means "make crooked," often having the figurative sense of "pervert" (as here, cf. 9:41; Acts 13:8,10; 20:30). Cf. U. Busse, *EWNT* 1. 751-752; in the OT, Exod 5:4; 1 Kgs 18:17,18. This accusation is really based on the attempts made by the Jewish authorities to trap Jesus earlier (19:48; 20:6,19,26; 22:2—instances all found in the Marcan source of these passages).

Marcion and OL mss. add a further accusation at this point: *kai katalyonta ton nomon kai tous prophētas,* "and doing away with the law and the prophets," i.e. adding a religious accusation to the preceding political one. This reading, however, is so poorly attested, so obviously dependent in wording on Matt 5:17, and so glaringly in accord with Marcion's views that it cannot be taken seriously.

obstructing the payment of taxes to Caesar. No evidence of this is offered. Cf. to the contrary Luke 20:20-25. For *Kaisar* as a title of the reigning Roman emperor, see NOTE on 20:22; cf. 2:1; 3:1. The taxes were the capitation fees imposed by Rome on the populace in all the provinces (police tax, guard tax, baths tax, etc.) and the poll tax *(laographia).* The *fiscus iudaicus* came into being only when Vespasian ordered the Jews, who had been paying a half-shekel or didrachm each year for the Jerusalem Temple, to pay it for the temple of Jupiter Capitolinus. See V. A. Tcherikover and A. Fuks, *Corpus papyrorum judaicarum* (Cambridge, MA: Harvard University, 1960) 2. 110-113.

Marcion and OL mss. add here, *kai apostrephonta tas gynaikas kai ta tekna,* "and misleading women and children." See *TCGNT* 178; cf. Epiphanius, *Pan.* 42.11,6 (GCS 31. 116).

even claiming to be an anointed king. Or "to be a messiah, a king," or perhaps even, "to be Christ, a king." The emphasis falls on the last word, "king," a political author- ity, a rival of Rome itself. It would make little difference to Pilate that Jesus was "anointed" (a feature rooted in Jewish tradition, see 1 Sam 9:16). On *christos,* see NOTE on 3:15 and pp. 197-200. Though Rome allowed certain eastern allied rulers to be called "kings" (e.g. Herod the Great [see NOTE on 1:5]), Romans were by tradition very distrustful of kings because of the tyrannous reign of such rulers in early Roman history. This well-known tradition is being exploited in the accusation of the Sanhe- drin against Jesus as he stands before the Roman prefect. See further p. 215.

3. *Are you the king of the Jews?* This question is found not only in Mark 15:2; Matt 27:11c, but also in John 18:23. *Ho basileus tōn Ioudaiōn* will appear again in the *titulus* on the cross (Luke 23:38; Mark 15:26; Matt 27:37; John 19:19). In the Lucan context Pilate ignores the first accusation and draws an implication from the second one. Josephus *(Ant.* 15.10,5 § 373) reports that an Essene, named Manaēmos, once hailed Herod, while still a boy, as *basilea Ioudaiōn,* "king of the Jews," which shows that the title had some Palestinian currency.

It is you who say this! Lit. *"you* say (it)," with emphatic *sy* preceding *legeis.* The answer is the same in all four Gospels, but developed in John 18:37. It is the same sort of half-yes answer as in 22:67c-68,70. Though Westcott-Hort wondered whether this sentence was to be understood as a question (in margin, *ad loc.),* it is scarcely that. See further E. Schweizer, *Evangelium nach Lukas,* 233.

4. *the chief priests and the crowds.* The "chief priests" must be understood in the

context as a shortened way of referring to the Sanhedrin. See v. 1a. For the first time we learn that more than the Sanhedrin were present. Though Luke normally distinguishes the Jewish authorities from the "crowds" or "the people" (see 19:47-48; 20:1,6,9,19,26,45; 22:2,6; 23:5), the "crowds" are here associated with the authorities. But note that it is in a sentence in which the evangelist reports Pilate addressing them; it does not necessarily mean that the crowds side with all the Sanhedrin's accusations. Similarly v. 13. Verse 18 is problemˀtic. See NOTE there. On "crowds," see NOTE on 3:7.

I find nothing in this man that calls for his death. Lit. "I find nothing guilty in this man," i.e. deserving capital punishment. Pilate concludes (from what it is not clear) that Jesus is "a harmless enthusiast" (A. Plummer, *The Gospel,* 521). The reader of the Lucan Gospel recognizes the truth of Pilate's conclusion: Jesus and his disciples constitute no threat to Roman authority.

5. *they kept insisting.* Who is "they"? It refers at least to the "chief priests" of v. 4; it is questionable whether one is to include the "crowds" as well. Note the contrast with "people" in the following accusation.

He has been stirring up our people . . . with his teaching. Lit. "he has been stirring up the people, teaching . . ." This repeats the generic accusation of v. 2b. H. Conzelmann *(Theology,* 86) sees this verse as a summary showing that from the beginning "all Judea" has been thought of as the sphere of Jesus' ministry along with Galilee. This verse would primarily bring to the fore "the political element." It would establish that Jesus has already appeared in the territory of Pilate as well as of Herod. Because of this, the mention of Samaria would be superfluous. But though this view has some plausibility, it is scarcely "a pre-Lucan summary" (ibid. n. 1), for it is so clearly expressed in Lucan terminology, and makes use of the Lucan motif of moving Jesus from Galilee to the city of destiny. The repeated accusation, interestingly enough, centers not on Jesus' kingship or on his obstruction of the payment of taxes, but on his stirring up people by his teaching. See pp. 148, 168, 182-183.

all throughout Judea. Lit. "throughout the whole of Judea." It is not easy to say whether the word *Ioudaia* is to be understood in the specific sense (as in 1:65; 2:4; 21:21) or in the generic sense (= the land of the Jews). See NOTE on 1:5. The mention of Galilee and "this place" might suggest the former meaning; but then Samaria is omitted, and because it is, *Ioudaia* could have the generic sense. Moreover, the way Galilee and "this place" are used, they could be meant as subdivisions of "Judea" in the broad sense. Cf. Acts 9:31; 10:37.

beginning from Galilee. For "Galilee," see NOTE on 17:11; on *arxamenos,* see NOTES on 1:2 and 3:23. Cf. 24:47; Acts 1:8,22; 10:37.

even to this place. I.e. Jerusalem. Lit. "up to here."

After *hōde,* "here," some mss. of the OL version add: *et filios nostros et uxores avertit a nobis, non enim baptizantur/baptizatur* (c) *sicut (et* [e]) *nos,* "and he turns our children and our wives away from us, for they/he are/is not baptized, as we (too) are." These strange words are obviously a Christian gloss on the original Lucan text; they are probably related to the Marcionite Greek additions mentioned above. See further *TCGNT* 178-179.

BIBLIOGRAPHY (23:1-5)
(in addition to the titles given in 22:54-71)

Allen, J. E. "Why Pilate?" *The Trial of Jesus* (ed. E. Bammel) 78-83.

Bailey, J. A. *The Traditions Common,* 64-77.

Benoit, P. *Passion and Resurrection,* 115-151.

Besnier, R. "Le procès du Christ," *Revue de l'histoire du droit* 18 (1950) 191-209.

Bickermann, E. "Utilitas crucis; Observations sur les recits du procès de Jésus dans les évangiles canoniques," *RHR* 112 (1935) 169-241.

Blinzler, J. *Trial of Jesus,* 164-193; *Der Prozess Jesu* (3d ed., 1960) 175-204.

Braumann, G. "Markus 15,2-5 und Markus 14,55-64," *ZNW* 52 (1961) 273-278.

Burkill, T. A. "The Condemnation of Jesus: A Critique of Sherwin-White's Thesis," *NovT* 12 (1970) 321-342.

Catchpole, D. R. *The Trial of Jesus* (see p. 1469) 221-260.

Colin, J. "Sur le procès de Jésus devant Pilate et le peuple," *Revue des études anciennes* (Bordeaux) 67 (1965) 159-164.

Conzelmann, H. *Theology,* 86-88.

Creed, J. M. "The Supposed 'Proto-Lucan' Narrative of the Trial before Pilate: A Rejoinder," *ExpTim* 46 (1934-1935) 378-379.

Doeve, J. W. "Jodendom en koningschap bij het begin van onze jaartelling," *Vox theologica* 32 (1961) 69-83.

Doyle, A. D. "Pilate's Career and the Date of the Crucifixion," *JTS* 42 (1941) 190-193.

Finegan, J. *Die Überlieferung,* 25-27.

Horvath, T. "Why Was Jesus Brought to Pilate?" *NovT* 11 (1969) 174-184.

Juster, J. *Les juifs dans l'empire romain: Leur condition juridique, économique et sociale* (2 vols.; Paris: Geuthner, 1914) 2. 94, 127-149.

Kastner, K. *Jesus vor Pilatus: Ein Beitrag zur Leidensgeschichte des Herrn* (NTAbh 4/2-3; Münster in W.: Aschendorff, 1912) 64-78.

Lietzmann, H. "Der Prozess Jesu" (see p. 1470) 313-322.

Maier, P. L. "Sejanus, Pilate, and the Date of the Crucifixion," *Church History* 37 (1968) 3-13.

Robinson, W. C., Jr. *Der Weg des Herrn* (see p. 261) 30-36.

Schneider, G. *Passion Jesu,* 83-94.

Sherwin-White, A. N. "The Trial of Christ in the Synoptic Gospels," *Roman Society and Roman Law in the New Testament* (Sarum Lectures, 1960-1961; Oxford: Clarendon, 1963) 24-47.

Strobel, A. *Die Stunde der Wahrheit: Untersuchungen zum Strafverfahren gegen Jesus* (WUNT 21; Tübingen: Mohr [Siebeck], 1980).

Winter, P. *On the Trial of Jesus* (see p. 1470) 70-89.

———— "The Trial of Jesus," *Jewish Quarterly* (London) 16 (1968) 31-37.

157. JESUS IS SENT TO HEROD
(23:6-12)

23 ⁶When Pilate heard this, he asked whether the man were a Galilean. ⁷Learning that he was from Herod's jurisdiction, he sent Jesus off to Herod, who was also in Jerusalem during those days.

⁸Now at the sight of Jesus Herod was very pleased, since he had been desirous of seeing him for some time, because he had been hearing about him. He even hoped to watch some miracle performed by Jesus. ⁹Herod tried to question him at length, but he would not answer him at all. ¹⁰Meanwhile the chief priests and the Scribes stood by, vigorously accusing him. ¹¹So Herod and his soldiers treated Jesus with contempt and ridicule; putting a gorgeous robe on him, he sent him back to Pilate. ¹²That very day Herod and Pilate became friends, whereas previously they had been at odds with one another.

COMMENT

The Lucan passion narrative is unique in breaking up the trial of Jesus before Pilate with the insertion of his appearance before Herod Antipas (23:6-12). It is occasioned by Pilate's hearing about the Galilean matrix of Jesus' teaching. Jesus is therefore sent to the Galilean authority, who questions him but gets no answer; accordingly, he treats Jesus with contempt and sends him back to Pilate. And Herod and Pilate become friends after a long period of enmity.

The episode has often been regarded as a Lucan creation (so M. Dibelius, "Herodes und Pilatus"; *HST* 273: "a legend that has developed out of Ps. 2¹ᶠ·, "in which Herod and Pilate represent the *basileis* and *archontes* who in the psalm plot against the Lord's anointed; A. Loisy, *L'Evangile selon Luc,* 544-545: comparing this episode with Acts 26:2-32, he regards them as "deux fictions . . . parallèles et de la même main"; J. M. Creed, *The Gospel,* 280; J. Finegan, *Überlieferung,* 27-29; et al.). Reasons proposed for this view: (1) Acts 4:27-28 speaks of Herod and Pilate gathered in Jerusalem against God's holy servant, alluding to Ps 2:1-2; this is the tradition that Luke has spun into a yarn. (2) If the scene were historical, how could Mark have failed to come across it? (3) Is it likely that Pilate would have sent a political prisoner to be tried before Herod within *his own* jurisdiction? (4) The chief priests and

Scribes seem to accompany Jesus to Herod (23:10); but v. 15 implies that they have remained with Pilate ("back to us"). (5) Ridicule of Jesus by Herod and his soldiers (23:11) is introduced here to compensate for Mark 15:16-17, which Luke omits. Yet none of these reasons is without a countering consideration. (1) Why is Acts 4:27-28 not merely a reflection of Luke 25:6-12, the normal expectation in the second volume of any author's work? That there may be an allusion to Ps 2:1-2 is acceptable; but does that allusion certainly explain the genesis of the story? Its details? The allusion is at best vague. (2) Apart from Herod's involvement in the execution of John the Baptist (Mark 6:14-22), how much interest does Mark display in Herod? He could have omitted the scene, just as John did. (3) Pilate may have sent Jesus to Herod to get a problem off his hands (see pp. 1473-1474). (4) Verse 15 does not tell whether the chief priests and Scribes had accompanied Jesus when he returned to Pilate. Pilate's use of "us" could also refer to himself and his entourage, apart from the priests and Scribes. (5) The reason for the Lucan omission is obvious in the course of his passion narrative, where Roman soldiers do not appear until 23:36. The upshot is that, though one cannot be apodictic about the matter, the evidence does not all point toward Lucan fabrication. The appearance of Jesus before Herod could be just as historical as the Lucan depiction of the morning session of the Sanhedrin interrogation. (See further A. W. Verrall, "Christ before Herod"; J. Blinzler, *Der Prozess Jesu*, 205-219; H. W. Hoehner, *Herod Antipas* [see p. 457] 224-250.)

Other commentators prefer to ascribe the passage to "L," while admitting some Lucan reworking of the material. (Thus P. Benoit, *Passion and Resurrection*, 144-146; A. N. Sherwin-White, *Roman Society*, 28-32; G. Schneider, *Evangelium nach Lukas*, 474; I. H. Marshall, *Luke*, 854-855; J. Ernst, *Evangelium nach Lukas*, 343.) Whence would have come the "L" tradition? One can only speculate (Joanna, the wife of Chuza, 8:3; Manaen, Acts 13:1?).

Lucan redaction in the episode can be detected in the following points: (1) the use of *anapempein*, "send off/back" (vv. 7,11; cf. v. 15; Acts 25:21)— apart from Phlm 12, it occurs only in Lucan writings in the NT; (2) "during those days," a common Lucan phrase; (3) the periphrastic use of *ēn* + ptc. *thelōn* (see pp. 122-123); (4) the use of the adj. *hikanos*, "some, many" (vv. 8,9; see p. 112); (5) the use of the articular infin. *(to akouein*, v. 8) with a prep. *dia;* (6) the literary use of *autos de* (see p. 120); (7) the prep. *syn;* (8) v. 12 (the sort of inconsequential explicative note that Luke likes to add; (9) "that very day," see pp. 117-118. (See further the comparative chart of the mockery scenes in R. E. Brown, *John, XIII-XXI,* 887.)

Form-critically considered, the episode is another Story about Jesus. The relation of it to Ps 2:1-2 is tenuous indeed, and this psalm can scarcely be considered as the origin of the episode, since the question is, Who is seeing the connections, Luke or the modern reader? Once the reader has read Acts 4:27-28, a connection may seem clearer; but it is scarcely patent here.

Why does Pilate send Jesus to Herod? The question is not easily answered. In view of the sequence of verses, one would say that Pilate, hoping to get rid of a problem, seizes upon the mention of Galilee (v. 5) to send off this unwanted political prisoner, whom he regards as a "harmless enthusiast," to the one who exercises authority in the district to which Jesus belongs, to the tetrarch of Galilee (3:1), who also happens to be in Jerusalem for the festival of Passover. Yet it is a gesture that ends in the reconciliation of the two authorities (see v. 12). Hence commentators have at times wondered whether such a reason adequately explains Pilate's conduct in the scene. Did he not perhaps do it to honor Herod? Or maybe he did it out of fear of Herod? Such motives have been suggested, but there is no way of being certain about them.

Herod, who has been anxious to see Jesus (9:9), now gets his opportunity. Curiosity to watch this Galilean thaumaturge at work excites him. Though he questions Jesus at length, he gets no answer—and Jesus proves by his silence that he is once again in command of the scene. Though the chief priests and Scribes who have accompanied him to Herod seek to accuse him still further (no specifics are mentioned), they do not succeed in getting Herod to pass any judgment on him. Finally, Herod's curiosity yields to contempt. He and his minions act like sulking children; they treat Jesus with ridicule, decking him out in elegance (in reality a "sign" of his guiltlessness), and send him back to Pilate. The supreme irony of the scene is expressed in the final explicative comment of the evangelist: "That very day Herod and Pilate became friends, whereas previously they had been at odds with one another" (v. 12). In the moment of his humiliation Jesus brings about the reconciliation of enemies. Though Jesus is really incomprehensible to these rulers, he makes them become "friends." In other words, despite the power that they wield as prefect and tetrarch they cannot free this person who stands before them guiltless. In such weakness they find camaraderie, similarity of reaction, and friendship. So as Luke sees it, Jesus, who is humiliated by such powerful figures, brings about their reconciliation. It is another Lucan way of insinuating an effect of the Christ-event.

In the Lucan passion narrative this scene is actually a minor one. It has no significance for the understanding of Jesus' person or fate. Its importance lies wholly in the testimony that Herod brings to the story; he finds nothing worthy of punishment in Jesus and sends him back to Pilate. The scene enhances Jesus' innocence, because it discloses that *two* Palestinian authorities bear witness by their actions to his innocence (recall Deut 19:15; see further W. Grundmann, *Evangelium nach Lukas,* 424).

To consider this episode as a Lucan effort to parallel Daniel's appearance before Darius and Cyrus or as a penetration of the Daniel-haggadah into the passion narrative is sheer eisegesis, *pace* J. D. M. Derrett ("Daniel and Salvation-History," *Downside Review* 100 [1982] 62-68).

NOTES

23 6. *whether the man were a Galilean.* See NOTE on 13:1. Though born in Bethlehem (2:4-7), Jesus would have been regarded as a Galilean because of his parents. See 1:26; 2:4. Moreover, Nazareth in Galilee has been called his *patris* (4:24). Recall 22:59; cf. John 7:41,52.

7. *from Herod's jurisdiction.* The n. *exousia* denotes "authority," but here carries the connotation of the "domain" in which that authority is exercised. See 4:6, Acts 23:34. On Herod Antipas, see NOTE on 3:1; cf. 3:19; 8:3; 9:7,9; 13:31. See further *HJPAJC* 1. 340-353.

he sent Jesus off. The vb. *anapempein* has the technical sense of remanding a person or a prisoner to another (or higher) authority, as in Acts 25:21. Cf. Josephus, *J.W.* 2.20,5 § 571; MM 37; J. Jeremias, *Die Sprache,* 301.

who was also in Jerusalem. One normally supposes that the reason that Herod Antipas was in Jerusalem was for the feast of Passover. But his father Herod the Great, was "a commoner and an Idumean, i.e. a half-Jew" (Josephus, *Ant.* 14.15,2 § 403), and one wonders about his Jewish allegiance. Be that as it may, Herod Antipas probably lodged in the family's Hasmonean palace in Jerusalem. See P. Benoit, *Passion and Resurrection,* 144; cf. Josephus, *J.W.* 2.16,3 § 344. Cf. Acts 12:3-4. On the form *Hierosolyma,* see NOTE on 2:22.

during those days. Luke again uses *en tautais tais hēmerais,* as in 1:39; 6:12; 24:18; Acts 1:15; 11:27; for the same expression but with *ekeinais,* see 2:1; 4:2; 5:35; 9:36; 21:23; Acts 2:18; 7:41; 9:37. See NOTE on 1:39.

8. *desirous of seeing him.* See Luke 9:9c, where the foreshadowing of this meeting occurs.

for some time. Lit. "from many times" *(ex hikanōn chronōn).* See NOTE on 20:9.

because he had been hearing about him. Lit. "on account of the hearing about him." Luke uses the prep. *dia* + the acc. of the articular infin. See 2:4; 6:48; 8:6; 9:7; 11:8; 18:5; 19:11; Acts 4:2; 8:11; 12:20; 18:2,3; 27:4,9; 28:18.

some miracle. Lit. "some sign" *(sēmeion).* Herod is thus depicted as one of the sign-seekers of Jesus' generation. See 11:16,29. Cf. John 12:21.

9. *tried to question him at length.* Lit. "kept questioning him with many words/sayings" *(en logois hikanois).*

he would not answer him at all. Jesus' reaction to Herod's questions is quite different from that manifested to the high priest (22:67,70) and to Pilate (23:3). His serene assurance before his tormentor only heightens the mockery that is to follow. Luke begins this cl. with the literary *autos de.* See p. 120.

10. *the chief priests and the Scribes.* See NOTE on 9:22; cf. 22:66.

vigorously accusing him. Luke never spells out the accusations. In the Sinaitic Syriac version vv. 10-12 are omitted, and this version has been followed by some modern commentators (e.g. J. Wellhausen, *Das Evangelium Lucae,* 129-130). It has been thought that the omission is owing to an apparent contradiction between v. 10 (chief priests and Scribes accompanying Jesus to Herod) and v. 15 (the chief priests and

Scribes staying with Pilate, to whom Jesus is sent back). But the verses are in the best Greek mss.

11. *Herod and his soldiers.* Lit. "Herod with his soldiers," i.e. probably bodyguards or retinue. The prep. *syn* has the Lucan sense of "and." See 20:1; Acts 14:5; 15:22; 16:32. The real difficulty in this phrase is the presence of *kai* before Herod's name in good mss. (P⁷⁵, ℵ, L, T, X, 1079, etc.). Its presence is hard to explain. If original, it would mean, "Then even/also Herod and his soldiers treated Jesus with contempt." Since, however, *kai* is absent in mss. B, A, D, Γ, Δ, Θ, 063, and the Koine text-tradition, it has been bracketed in *UBSGNT*³ and N-A²⁶. See further *TCGNT* 179.

with contempt and ridicule. Lit. "despising, ridiculing, and tossing (a garment) about (him)." Three aor. ptcs. express the supreme contempt and mistreatment of Jesus.

a gorgeous robe. Lit. "a bright shining garment." See P. Joüon, "Luc 23,11: *esthēta lampran,*" *RSR* 26 (1936) 80-85. The adj. *lampran* does not necessarily mean "white." There is no suggestion in this Lucan episode that the gorgeous robe has anything to do with Jesus' alleged kingship. That is to read a Marcan nuance into it. It is chosen to mock his guiltlessness. Contrast Mark 15:16-17.

he sent him back. See NOTE on v. 7. Pilate was presumably staying at the Fortress Antonia.

12. *That very day.* See pp. 117-118.

Herod and Pilate became friends. The relationship is carried further in the *Gospel of Peter,* where in 2:5 Herod addresses the Roman prefect as "Brother Pilate." See Hennecke-Schneemelcher, *NTApocrypha* 1. 183.

previously they had been at odds with one another. Lit. "for they existed before, being in hostility toward themselves." Luke uses the vb. *pro-hyp-archein,* with a ptc. *ontes.* Cf. Acts 8:9; Josephus, *Ant.* 4.6,5 § 125; BDF § 414.1. The enmity of the two is otherwise unknown. It is understandable that a tetrarch would be ill at ease with an overlord, especially one that represented an occupying power. Sometimes commentators speculate whether Pilate's conduct described in 13:1 might have alienated Herod. See J. Blinzler, "Die Niedermetzelung von Galiläern durch Pilatus," *NovT* 2 (1958) 24-49; cf. H. W. Hoehner, *Herod Antipas,* 175-176; Philo, *Leg. ad Gaium* 38 § 299-305.

This is one more of Luke's inconsequential explicative notes, which he likes to add to his story. Cf. 1:66; 2:50; 3:15; 8:29; 9:14; 12:1; 16:14; 20:20; Acts 1:15; 17:21; 23:8. Cf. J. Jeremias, *Die Sprache,* 72, 302.

BIBLIOGRAPHY (23:6-12)

Blinzler, J. "Herodes und der Tod Jesu," *Klerusblatt* 37 (1957) 118-121.

———— *Der Prozess Jesu* (3d ed.) 205-219.

Bornhäuser, K. "Die Beteiligung des Herodes am Prozesse Jesu," *NKZ* 40 (1929) 714-718.

Buck, E. "The Function of the Pericope 'Jesus before Herod' in the Passion Narrative of Luke," *Wort in der Zeit* (eds. W. Haubeck and M. Bachmann) 165-178.

Corbin, M. "Jésus devant Hérode: Lecture de *Luc* 23, 6-12," *Christus* 25 (1978) 190-197.

Dibelius, M. "Herodes und Pilatus," *ZNW* 16 (1915) 113-126.

Harlow, V. E. *The Destroyer of Jesus: The Story of Herod Antipas, Tetrarch of Galilee* (2d ed.; Oklahoma City: Modern Publishers, 1954).

Hoehner, H. W. *Herod Antipas* (see p. 457) 175-176, 224-250.

——— "Why Did Pilate Hand Jesus over to Antipas?" *Trial of Jesus* (ed. E. Bammel) 84-90.

Jervell, J. "Herodes Antipas og hans plass i evangelieoverleveringen," *NorTT* 61 (1960) 28-40.

O'Neill, J. C. "The Silence of Jesus," *NTS* 15 (1968-1969) 153-167.

Verrall, A. W. "Christ before Herod (Luke xxiii 1-16)," *JTS* 10 (1908-1909) 321-353.

158. PILATE'S JUDGMENT
(23:13-16)

23 [13] Pilate then summoned the chief priests, the leaders, and the people [14] and said to them, "You have brought before me this man as one who has been subverting the people. Now then, I have examined him in your presence and have found in this man no basis for any charge that you bring against him. [15] Neither has Herod, for he sent him back to us. Obviously, he has done nothing that calls for his death. [16] Therefore, I will discipline him and release him." [17][a]

[a] Verse 17 is omitted in many mss.; see NOTE there.

COMMENT

Having been ridiculed by Herod and his retinue, Jesus is returned to the Roman prefect, Pilate, who repeats his declaration about Jesus' innocence and appeals to Herod's reaction. So Pilate decides to discipline Jesus and release him (23:13-16).

The Synoptic relationship of these verses is tied up with that of the foregoing vv. 6-12, since the episode is exclusive to Luke. Here too the source is probably "L" (see p. 84). But the episode is composite: v. 15 alone refers to Herod, whereas v. 14 presents Pilate's second declaration about Jesus' innocence. What we have here is probably the Lucan conflation of disparate elements of tradition which have come to him from "L." The Lucan redaction of what has been inherited can be seen in the use of *eipen pros* + acc. (v. 14, see p. 116), the double use of *kai idou* (vv. 14,15, see p. 121), and in the prep. *enōpion,* "before" (p. 114).

The episode is another Story about Jesus in form-critical terminology. It is a logical sequel to vv. 6-12 and difficult to separate from them.

Pilate again appears before the Jewish authorities and the people, whom he has summoned. The opinion that he expressed in v. 4b he now reiterates with greater solemnity: Jesus has not been subverting the people. Moreover, he draws the logical conclusion from Herod's action: even the Galilean authority did not take legal action against this supposed rabble-rouser. But the logic in the following v. 16 is peculiar; Pilate pronounces publicly, "Therefore I will discipline him and release him." This is the only reference in the Lucan Gospel to the so-called scourging of Jesus—a mere suggestion that he will subject Jesus to it (one never learns in this Gospel whether it takes place). It is part of the Lucan attempt to tone down the crude aspects of the passion narrative (see pp. 94-95). But the logic in the "therefore" is what puzzles. Pilate uses a euphemism for the terrible Roman *flagellatio,* probably to salve his own conscience. It would serve to warn Jesus about future run-ins with authority, once he is released. But how even that is justified, if Pilate really considered Jesus innocent of the charges brought against him, is puzzling. He makes the statement, about Jesus' innocence, undoubtedly because he has summed up Herod's reaction as nothing deserving death.

NOTES

23 13. *summoned.* Luke uses the vb. *synkalein,* on which see NOTE on 9:1.

the chief priests. See NOTE on 9:22.

the leaders. On *archontes,* see NOTE on 14:1. Here it must refer to the elders, chief priests, and Scribes of 22:66.

the people. See NOTE on v. 4. Pilate may be depicted summoning the "people" as well as the rulers because of the hope of finding support among the populace for Jesus in opposition to the leaders. "The people" will occur again in v. 14b. For an attempt to read rather *tou laou,* "of the people," see G. Rau, "Das Volk"; but that has no support in the mss. That this notice has anything to do with the tradition in John 18:38-39; 19:1 is highly dubious, *pace* E. Schweizer, *Evangelium nach Lukas,* 234. Cf. 3 Macc 5:24: "The crowds in the city assembled for the piteous spectacle."

14. *You have brought before me this man.* Pilate begins with a factual statement, alluding to 23:1.

as one who has been subverting the people. So Pilate sums up the main charge of 23:2b, repeated in v. 5 and explained in v. 23cd. Luke uses *apostrephein* (cf. Acts 3:26) instead of the *diastrephein* of v. 2; the sense is the same.

Now then. Lit. "and behold." See p. 121.

examined him in your presence. This is an allusion to v. 3. The vb. *anakrinein* often had in the Hellenistic world of the time a technical sense denoting strict legal procedure; whether that is intended here is hard to say. Luke uses it again in Acts 4:9; 12:19; 24:8; 28:18.

have found in this man no basis for any charge that you bring against him. Lit. "nothing have I found guilty in this man as to what you accuse him." Pilate's second declaration of Jesus' innocence is thus more solemnly put; it will be repeated in v. 15c.

15. *Neither has Herod.* Lit. "but not even Herod."

sent him back to us. This is the reading of mss. P75, ℵ, B, K, L, T, Θ, etc., but other mss. (A, D, W, Γ, Δ, 063, *f*¹, and the Koine text-tradition) read *anepempsa gar hymas pros auton,* "for I sent you to him" (which B. M. Metzger calls "utterly banal" [*TCGNT* 179]). Still others (*f*¹³) and some old versions (Vg, Syr) have *anepempsa gar auton pros hymas,* "for I sent him [i.e. Herod] to you" (which Metzger, ibid., calls "totally nonsensical"). The text-tradition seems to be hopelessly confused, if one does not stay with the reading in the best Greek texts.

Obviously, he has done nothing that calls for his death. Lit. "and behold, nothing deserving death has been done by him." The last word is the dat. of the pers. pron. *autō,* which is widely taken as a dat. of agency, even though this is almost unique in the NT. See BDF § 191; ZBG § 59. This is probably the reason why some mss. (D, N, Γ, *f*¹³) read the prep. *en* before it. Conceivably, however, it could be the dat. of indir. obj.: "has been done to him," i.e. by Herod; in other words, Herod did nothing to Jesus that would make us conclude that he deserved to be put to death. This statement reiterates, as a conclusion from Herod's conduct, the declaration that Pilate made in v. 14d.

16. *Therefore, I will discipline him and release him.* Lit. "having disciplined him, I will release (him)." The vb. *paideuein* means "instruct, educate," but also carries the nuance "discipline, chasten," i.e. to teach someone a lesson, occurring in this sense in the LXX of 1 Kgs 12:11,14; 2 Chr 10:11,14 (along with *en mastinxin,* "with whips"). See further G. Bertram, *TDNT* 5. 621; G. Schneider, *EWNT* 3.8.

On the treatment of the scourging of Jesus in this Gospel, see pp. 94-95.

[17]. In some mss. (ℵ, D, W, Θ, Ψ, 063, *f*¹,¹³, and the Koine text-tradition) and various ancient versions (Latin, Syriac, and Bohairic) one reads an addition to v. 16: "He had to release someone to them on (the) feast" *(anankēn de eichen apolyein autois kata heortēn hena,* lit. "he had a need to . . ."). This verse is, however, omitted in mss. P75, A, B, K, L, T, 0124, 1241, etc., and some other ancient versions (OL, Sahidic). The evidence may seem at first sight more or less balanced. But in ms. D it appears after v. 19, and in a word order agreeing with that of mss. Θ and Ψ. Moreover, it looks suspiciously like a gloss introduced into the Lucan text from Mark 15:6; Matt 27:15, even if the wording differs slightly. Though Merk⁹ reads it, most critical texts today omit it (thus N-A²⁵, N-A²⁶, *UBSGNT*³, *SQE*¹⁰, and A. Huck and H. Greeven, *Synopse).* See further *TCGNT* 179-180; cf. G. D. Kilpatrick, "The Greek New Testament Text of Today and the *Textus Receptus,"* The New Testament in Historical and Contemporary Perspective: Essays in Memory of G. H. C. Macgregor (eds. H. Anderson and W. Barclay; Oxford: Blackwell, 1965) 189-208, esp. 195. The similarity of the beginning of vv. 17 and 18 is not sufficient to explain the omission of v. 17!

Part of the problem is that the "custom" (John 18:39) to which the verse refers, the so-called *privilegium paschale,* "the Passover privilege," is unknown outside the gospel tradition. The promise mentioned in *m. Pesah.* 8:6 has nothing to do with this Gospel incident. See further P. Winter, *On the Trial of Jesus,* 131-143; C. B. Chavel, "The Releasing"; H. A. Rigg, "Barabbas"; H. Cohen, *The Trial,* 162-169; Str-B 1. 1031. If, however, v. 17 is omitted, then the mention of Barabbas in v. 18 may seem to be abrupt and unprepared for. Yet this clearly makes the omission of the verse the *lectio difficilior.* The choice to be made between Barabbas and Jesus in the following scene may be part of a genuine historical tradition, but the text-tradition in Luke is garbled and it raises the question about whether it was ever part of the original Lucan Gospel. Moreover, it should be noted that the Lucan text is really intelligible without any reference to the *privilegium paschale;* commentators who claim that the mention of Barabbas in v. 18 is abrupt are too much influenced by the Marcan form of the story, which Luke for some reason has decided to abandon. That privilege plays little part in this Gospel.

BIBLIOGRAPHY (23:13-16)

Blinzler, J. *Der Prozess Jesu* (3d ed.) 249-262.
Brandon, S. G. F. *The Trial of Jesus of Nazareth* (New York: Stein and Day, 1968) 107-139.
Chavel, C. B. "The Releasing of a Prisoner on the Eve of Passover in Ancient Jerusalem," *JBL* 60 (1941) 273-278.
Cohen, H. *The Trial and Death of Jesus* (New York: Harper & Row, 1967).
Juster, J. *Les juifs dans l'empire romain: Leur condition juridique, économique et sociale* (2 vols.; Paris: Geuthner, 1914).
Rau, G. "Das Volk in der lukanischen Passionsgeschichte, eine Konjektur zu Lc 23:13," *ZNW* 56 (1965) 41-51.
Rigg, H. A. "Barabbas," *JBL* 64 (1945) 417-456.
Trilling, W. *Fragen zur Geschichtlichkeit Jesu* (Düsseldorf: Patmos, 1966) 130-141; *Jésus devant l'histoire* (Paris: Cerf, 1968) 175-188.

159. JESUS IS HANDED OVER TO BE CRUCIFIED
(23:18-25)

23 18 Then all together they kept shouting back, "Away with this man! Release to us Barabbas!" 19 (The latter had been imprisoned for murder and for some riot that had broken out in the city.) 20 Pilate, wishing rather to release Jesus, addressed them again, 21 but they kept shouting at him, "Crucify, crucify him!" 22 Yet a third time he spoke to them, "What wrong has this man done? I have found nothing in him that calls for his death. Therefore, I will discipline him and release

him." ²³ Then with loud outcries they persisted in demanding that Jesus be crucified; and their voices prevailed.

²⁴ Pilate decided that their demand should be met. ²⁵ So he released the man they asked for, the one who had been imprisoned for rioting and murder; but Jesus he handed over to their will.

COMMENT

The trial of Jesus before Pilate comes to an end in this scene, in which the Roman prefect yields to the cries and demands of all those whom he had summoned—before whom he had hoped once again to declare Jesus innocent and to release him. But instead he finally decides that their cries of "Crucify him!" should be heeded and so he hands Jesus "over to their will" (23:18-25).

The scene is inspired by Mark 15:6-15, as Luke returns to the Marcan material and order of the trial after the insert about Herod. As in the Marcan scene, it contains the cry for the release of Barabbas instead of Jesus (v. 18; cf. Mark 15:11), an identification of Barabbas (v. 19; cf. Mark 15:7), the shout "Crucify him!" (v. 21; cf. Mark 15:13), the persistence of the demands (v. 23; cf. Mark 15:14c), a decision to yield to their demands (v. 24; cf. Mark 15:15a), to release Barabbas (v. 25a; cf. Mark 15:15b), and to hand Jesus over (v. 25c; cf. Mark 15:15c). In typical fashion Luke has again abridged a Marcan scene, eliminating all reference to the so-called *privilegium paschale,* the inciting of the people by the chief priests, and the taunting references to "the king of the Jews." He substitutes instead v. 20, a formulation probably inspired by Mark 15:12, but which makes explicit Pilate's attempt to release Jesus, v. 22, which in part echoes Mark 15:14b ("What wrong has he done?"), but which introduces (probably from "L") the third declaration of innocence, and v. 25c, "to their will," Luke's way of removing some responsibility from Pilate, and putting some of it on the Jews who clamored for Jesus' death.

Apart from the third declaration of innocence, everything that is in this episode can be found in Mark 15:6-15, even though it has been differently formulated. Since Lucan style and phraseology are evident in the episode, it is best ascribed to a Lucan redactional working of "Mk." See J. Jeremias, *Die Sprache,* 303-304, where almost everything is ascribed to redaction. V. Taylor *(Passion Narrative,* 88-89) struggles valiantly, but in vain, to save vv. 18-25 for his independent source: "The origin of 18-25 is more speculative. It *appears* to be derived from a non-Marcan source" (my emphasis). His discussion includes v. 17—failing to acknowledge the *lectio difficilior* aspect of its omission. That *aire,* "away with" (v. 18), has anything to do with John 19:15 is not obvious. It could be coincidental in this case, given the difference of context; it is a word often used by all the evangelists. Taylor himself acknowledges that the best parallels are in Acts 21:36; 22:22. Moreover, he has to acknowledge Luke's dependence on "Mk" for the description of Barabbas, and for the question, "What wrong has this man done?" (v. 22). Taylor's rhetorical question wonders whether Luke returns to "his special source" in vv. 23-24, without querying whether Lucan redaction would not also explain these verses (aside from saying that the "agreements" with Mark are negligible). Thus, the Taylor suggestion is not convincing.

Lucan redaction in vv. 18-25 is detected in the following points: (1) the pleonastic ptc. *legontes* (vv. 18,21; see J. Jeremias, *Die Sprache*, 67-70); (2) emphatic *touton*, "this man" (used eight times in Luke and ten in Acts; see J. Jeremias, ibid. 212); (3) *hostis* instead of the simple rel. pron. *hos* (thirteen times in Luke, eighteen in Acts; ibid. 43-44); (4) *prosphōnein*, "address" (see p. 111); (5) *epiphōnein*, "shout at" (used by Luke alone in the NT: Acts 12:22; 21:34; 22:24); (6) *eipen pros* + acc. (see p. 116); (7) the third declaration of innocence, echoing those of vv. 4,14-15; (8) *paideusas*, "having disciplined," an echo of v. 16; (9) *epikrinein*, "decided" (v. 24), exclusive to Luke in the NT; (10) description of Barabbas (v. 25), an echo of that in v. 19. (See further the comparative chart in R. E. Brown, *John, XIII-XXI*, 870-871.)

Form-critically considered, the episode is again a Story about Jesus. R. Bultmann *(HST* 282), following H. Lietzmann, rightly recognizes the "apologetic motive," which surfaces above all in this Lucan form of the story—the tendency to exculpate the Roman prefect and to inculpate the Jewish authorities (this being done through the emphatic declaration of Jesus' innocence [vv. 4,14-15,22] and the evangelist's own statement about Pilate's attempt to release Jesus [v. 20]). This clearly colors one's estimate of the historicity of the *mode* in which the final verdict was given. The Lucan form calls explicit attention to the *three* declarations of innocence, and that finds an echo in John 18:38; 19:4,6. Yet it is a tendentious aspect of the scene and may be covering up greater complicity of Pilate in the verdict than one realizes (for what reason, see pp. 10, 178-179).

So far in the appearance of Jesus before Pilate, the latter has made it clear that he sees no basis in the charges of the Jewish authorities, who have brought Jesus before him, for any action on his part. He has also appealed to Herod's reaction to Jesus, having concluded from it that Herod did not fundamentally disagree with his estimate of the situation. Thus testimony has been given by "two witnesses" (Deut 19:15), by two authorities, one Roman and one Palestinian. There is not sufficient evidence for execution in a capital criminal case. Pilate has decided instead to discipline Jesus and release him.

But Pilate has spoken the neuralgic word, "release." That sparks a reaction, and the prefect is now confronted with a shouting mob. Luke's predilection for rhetorical hyperbole, using forms of the word *pas*, "all," appears again, as "all together they kept shouting back." The "they" must now refer to all those assembled there, including "the people" (v. 13) or "the crowds"

(v. 4), as well as "the whole assembly of them" (v.1, *hapan to plēthos autōn*, "all the assembly of them," i.e. the Sanhedrin). The "people" have been caught up in mob psychology (even though Luke does not say that the chief priests incited them, as does Mark 15:11), and they shout, "Away with this man! *Release* to us Barabbas!" A substitute criminal is demanded in place of a criminal! The irony of the scene is apparent. Moreover, they scream for the release of one called Barabbas, "son of the father," and reject him who is really the Father's son (recall 2:49; 10:21-22; 11:2; 22:29,42).

Yet another attempt of the prefect to release Jesus brings only more specific cries for Jesus' death, "Crucify, crucify him!" Those present demand that Pilate execute Jesus as he would other criminals (see v. 32). In the minds of those assembled before Pilate, Jesus has been "classed even with outlaws" (22:37; cf. Isa 53:12). The demand for this form of death surfaces now for the first time in the Lucan passion narrative—on the lips of the Jerusalem crowd, assembled with their religious leaders before the Roman prefect.

Despite Pilate's *third* attempt to declare Jesus' innocence and his question, "What wrong has this man done?" he not only repeats his former conclusion to go against his conscience, in disciplining "this man," but even to yield to their outcries that he be crucified. Pilate finally yields, releases Barabbas, the known criminal, and hands Jesus, whom he has publicly declared three times to be innocent, over "to their will." Thus Pontius Pilate, the prefect of Judea, becomes the coward of history. Luke makes sure that his readers understand who was weak and who was strong. "The power of darkness" (22:53) has prevailed over all of the crowd assembled. It is not "the kings of the earth" or "the rulers" who have taken counsel together against God and his anointed one (recall Ps 2:2), but the people who still "walk in darkness," who have refused to see the "great light" (Isa 9:1), which has shone among them. So Luke would have Pilate's verdict understood. In the end, it is Pilate's verdict that sends Jesus to the cross.

NOTES

23 18. *all together they kept shouting back.* In reaction to Pilate's use of the vb. "release," they shout instead for the release of someone else. Luke uses the adv. *pamplēthei,* a compound of *pas,* "all," and *plēthos,* "number, crowd, assembly," meaning something like "in full number." In the immediate context it must refer to the chief priests, leaders, and people of v. 13, unless one would try to argue that it is merely another way of saying *hapan to plēthos autōn,* "the whole assembly of them" (23:1), which meant the Sanhedrin. Though Luke does not say that the chief priests incited the people (as does Mark 15:11), it would be naïve to think that he refers merely to the leaders.

Away with this man! Lit. "carry this one off" *(aire touton),* in the sense of doing away with him (from life). See Acts 8:33 (= Isa 53:8); 21:36; 22:22. A different form of the same vb. *(aron,* second aor. impv.) is used in John 19:15.

Release to us. The shouters pick up the word "release" that Pilate used. The best commentary on this shout is found in Acts 3:13-15. See H. Conzelmann, *Theology,* 87.

Barabbas! Nothing is known of this person beyond the description given in the next verse (and its parallels in the other Gospels). Luke has derived the name from Mark 15:7,11,15. Cf. Matt 27:16-17,20-21,26; John 18:40. The name is a grecized form of Aramaic *Bar-'Abbā',* "Son of Abba" (or, more lit. "son of the father"). The Aramaic name is attested in sixth–fifth-century texts: *[N]ḥsy br 'b'* (from Neirab; *Revue assyriologique* 25 [1928] 60); *'ytn br 'bh* (from Elephantine, *AP* 6:16). In form, it is like *Barsabbas* (Acts 1:23; 15:22), a grecized form of Aramaic *bar-Sabbā',* "Son of Sabba" (or, more lit. "son of the old man"); the latter is attested extrabiblically too (from Palestine: *Bar-Śabbā',* Mur 25:1.4 [DJD 2. 135]; *Bar-Sabbā',* Talpioth Ossuary 1 *[MPAT* § 44:1.4; § 118]). *Pace* A. Plummer *(The Gospel,* 525), evidence is not wanting that Abba was a personal name; the form *'abbāh* is found as a clear name on a first-century (B.C. or A.D.) funerary inscription from Givʿat Ha-Mivṭar near Jerusalem. See E. S. Rosenthal, "The Givʿat ha-Mivtar Inscription," *IEJ* 23 (1973) 72-81; cf. *MPAT* § 68. If this man had a son, he would have been called "X bar Abba," or in Greek *Barabbas.* One of the third–fourth-century Babylonian Amoraic rabbis was named *Ḥiyya bar 'Abba';* he is quoted in *Lev. Rab.* 3.1 (Soncino ed., 35). The use of a patronymic alone is also well attested. E.g. the eighth-century Bar-Rākib inscription; Mur 25:1.4 (DJD 2. 135).

Origen (Scholia fragments of a *Comm. in Matt.* 60 [PL 17.308]) interpreted the name to mean "Son of the Teacher"; Jerome *(Lib. interp. hebr. nom.* 60 [PL 23.883]) gives the meaning as "filium magistri nostri," "Son of our Teacher." Cf. CCLat 72.135, where some mss. read "filium magistri eorum," "Son of their Teacher"; see also *Comm. in Matt.* 4.27,16 (CCLat 77.265). This implies that the name was read in Greek as *barrabbas* (with two r's) and understood as = Aramaic *bar-Rabban,* "Son of our Teacher," or *bar-Rabbam,* "Son of their Teacher." See E. Nestle, *Introduction to the Textual Criticism of the Greek New Testament* (London: Williams and Norgate, 1901) 259. This seems to be the result of a confusion of titles for teachers in the rabbinic period, which became known to patristic writers.

In some mss. of Matt 27:16-17 (Θ, *f*[1], 700*) and a few ancient versions (some Syriac, Armenian, Georgian) the name is even given as *Iēsoun Barabban/Iēsoun ton Barabban,* "Jesus Barabbas." This form, bracketed, has been used in *UBSGNT*[3] and N-A[26] and labeled as a C reading (with "a considerable degree of doubt whether the text or the apparatus contains the superior reading"). How the committee behind the *UBSGNT* ever came to that decision, given the weak external attestation of the reading in Matthean mss., is baffling. If the reading is to be retained (even with square brackets), it should be labeled D (with "a very high degree of doubt concerning the reading selected for the text). Fortunately, this does not affect the Lucan text; but the matter is brought up simply to warn the reader of the Lucan Gospel not to import that reading into this episode.

For idle speculation whether the historical Jesus' full name was Jesus Barabbas, see H. A. Rigg, Jr., "Barabbas"; H. Z. Maccoby, "Jesus"; and S. L. Davies, "Who Is Called Bar Abbas."

19. *imprisoned for murder and for some riot.* Nothing more about these incidents is known than what is stated here and in the Gospel parallels. Whereas Matt 27:16 identifies Barabbas as a "notorious prisoner" *(desmion epismon)* and John 18:40 calls him a "robber" *(lsts),* Luke uses almost the same description as Mark 15:7, rewording it slightly.

20. *wishing rather to release Jesus.* So Luke depicts the Roman prefect in a statement of his own.

21. *Crucify, crucify him!* Whereas both Mark (15:13) and Matthew (27:22) formulate the cry only once, Luke has doubled it, and John has it both ways, doubled in 19:6 (but without the obj.), and single in 19:15. For this reason it is hard to say that the double cry comes to Luke from "L." Luke likes to double vocs. (see 10:41; 13:34; 22:31), and that may have carried over here. Luke uses the pres. middle impv. of *stauroun,* viz. *staurou,* whereas Mark 15:13 and John 19:6,15 have the second aor. act. impv. *staurson* and Matt 27:22 the aor. pass. third pers. impv. *stauroth,* "let him be crucified."

The vb. *stauroun* is denominative, i.e. formed from the n. *stauros,* "stake." Being a factitive formation in -*o,* it basically means "fix a stake, fit with stakes" (e.g. to build a palisade or stockade [Thucydides, *Hist.* 7.25,7]) or "fix on a stake" (e.g. when a severed head is so impaled [Herodotus, *Hist.* 4.103,2; 7.238,1]; it can also be used of a living person fixed to a stake [Herodotus, *Hist.* 7.194,1], who is later taken down and described as "having been hung up" *[anakremasthentos],* and even a corpse [Herodotus, *Hist.* 3.125,3]). The historian Polybius uses the vb. of crucifixion *(Hist.* 1.86,4 [see W. R. Paton, LCL, 1. 232-233]). This sense is also admitted for the word in H. Frisk, *Griechisches etymologisches Wörterbuch* (Indogermanische Bibliothek; Heidelberg: C. Winter) Lief. 18 (1967) 778.

In the NT *stauroun* is used exclusively of crucifixion. See J. Schneider, *TDNT* 7. 572-584. In the same period, when Josephus, a Jewish historian who writes in Greek, tells of the execution of eight hundred Jewish enemies of the Hasmonean king Alexander Janneus, he uses a compound of this vb., which is almost always interpreted of crucifixion *(anastaursai, Ant.* 13.14,2 § 380; cf. *J. W.* 1.4,5-6 § 93-98; for an attempt to interpret these Josephus references as "impalement," see P.-E. Guillet, "Les 800 'crucifiés' d'Alexandre Jannée," *CCER* 100 [1977] 11-16). The incident to which Josephus refers is also alluded to in 4QpNah 3-4 i 7-8, where it is spoken of as a "hanging alive" on a tree (DJD 5.37-42), an obvious euphemism for the reality. Whether or not the Jews under the Roman occupation could have executed anyone by crucifixion, this mode of execution, in the same figurative language, is recommended for two crimes in some of their literature (treason, i.e. the passing on of information to an enemy of Israel; and evasion of due process of law in a case of capital punishment). As to the question whether historically the Jews of Roman Palestine had the authority to execute anyone for a capital crime, see R. E. Brown, *John, XIII-XXI,* 849-850. There is no need to rehash all that in a commentary on the Lucan Gospel. As for the Jewish use of crucifixion, see my article, "Crucifixion in Ancient Palestine, Qumran Literature, and the New Testament," *CBQ* 40 (1978) 493-513; slightly revised in *TAG* 112-146, esp. 125-146.

22. *Yet a third time.* This is Lucan counting; he misses no chance to repeat Pilate's declaration of Jesus' innocence.

What wrong has this man done? Pilate has seen no validity in any of the charges leveled against Jesus (23:4). Luke has derived these words from Mark 15:14.

nothing . . . that calls for his death. An echo of 23:15.

I will discipline him and release him. An echo of 23:16.

23. *with loud outcries they persisted in demanding.* Lit. "they kept pressing on (him), demanding with great voices." The terminology is Lucan. For *epikeisthai,* see 5:1; Acts 27:20. Though the phrase *phōnē megalē* is pre-Lucan (see Mark 1:26; 5:7; 15:34,37 [cf. Luke 4:33, moved up; 8:28; 23:46]), it is used more by Luke than any other NT writer. See further 17:15; 19:37; Acts 7:57,60; 8:7; 16:28. See NOTE on 17:15. For the middle of *aitein* with a dependent infin., see Acts 3:14; 7:46; 13:28.

that Jesus be crucified. Lit. "that he be crucified."

their voices prevailed. Lit. "the voices of them" *(autōn),* to which some mss. (A, D, W, Θ, Ψ, 063, 0250, *f* 1,13, and the Koine text-tradition) add *kai tōn archiereōn,* "and of the chief priests." The latter phrase is thought to be omitted in other mss. (P75, ℵ, B, L, 0124, 1241, etc.) and some versions (Latin, Coptic) because of homoeoteleuton. The question is whether the longer form is original and later shortened or whether it is the result of a copyist's desire to make sure that the priests' voices were mentioned.

24. *decided.* Luke uses *epikrinein,* which could have the technical nuance of issuing an official sentence. See 2 Macc 4:47; 3 Macc 4:2.

that their demand should be met. Lit. "should be done" or "should take place."

25. *imprisoned for rioting and murder.* The identification of Barabbas is repeated from v. 19.

he handed over to their will. So Luke concludes the sentencing of Jesus, making sure that the account ends with *to thelēmati autōn,* "their will." Mark 15:15b has "and having scourged Jesus, he handed him over to be crucified" (followed by Matt 27:26b) —which puts more of the blame on Pilate. Luke has made it clear that Pilate has capitulated to the "loud outcries" of the mob before him. Recall John 19:17-42, which insinuates the same. Cf. p. 88. Luke has, however, not completely exonerated Pilate; he is involved. To appreciate this, one has only to look at the *Gos. Peter* 1:1-2: "But of the Jews none washed their hands [as Pilate had done, Matt 27:24], neither Herod nor any one of his judges. And as they would not wash, Pilate arose. And then Herod the king commanded that the Lord should be marched off, saying to them, 'What I have commanded you to do to him, do ye' " (Hennecke-Schneemelcher, *NTApocrypha* 1. 183). The Lucan story involves Pilate, as does the (partly interpolated?) account in Josephus, *Ant.* 18.3,3 § 64. Cf. Tacitus, *Annales* 15.44,3.

The Lucan account omits all reference to the scourging of Jesus. See Mark 15:15b.

BIBLIOGRAPHY (23:18-25)

Bajsić, A. "Pilatus, Jesus und Barabbas," *Bib* 48 (1967) 7-28.

Bartsch, H.-W. "Wer verurteilte Jesu zum Tode?" *NovT* 7 (1964-1965) 210-216.

Blinzler, J. "Der Entscheid des Pilatus: Exekutionsbefehl oder Todesurteil," *MTZ* 5 (1954) 171-184.

——— *Der Prozess Jesu* (3d ed.) 220-235.

Brandon, S. G. F. *Jesus and the Zealots* (New York: Scribner's, 1967) 4-5.

Cohn H. H. *The Trial and Death of Jesus* (New York: Harper & Row, 1968) 166.

Colin, J. *Les villes libres de l'orient gréco-romain et l'envoi au supplice par acclamations populaires* (Collection Latomus 82; Brussels-Berchem: Latomus, 1965).

Davies, S. L. "Who Is Called Bar Abbas," *NTS* 27 (1980-1981) 260-262.

Finegan, J. *Die Überlieferung,* 29-30.

Herranz Marco, M. "Un problema de crítica histórica en el relato de la pasión: La liberación de Barrabás," *EstBib* 30 (1971) 137-160.

Lohfink, G. *Sammlung,* 42-43.

Maccoby, H. Z. "Jesus and Barabbas," *NTS* 16 (1969-1970) 55-60.

Rigg, H. A., Jr. "Barabbas," *JBL* 64 (1945) 417-456.

Schulte, F. W. C. "Bar-Abbas een bijnaam," *Nieuwe theologische studiën* 3 (1920) 114-118.

Sloyan, G. *Jesus on Trial* (Philadelphia: Fortress, 1973) 68.

Winter, P. *On the Trial of Jesus* (see p. 1470) 94.

160. THE ROAD TO THE CROSS
(23:26-32)

23 ²⁶ As they led Jesus away, they seized upon Simon, a certain Cyrenian, who was just coming in from a field, and they put on him a cross to carry behind Jesus. ²⁷ A large crowd of people was following him, many of them women who were beating their breasts and wailing at his fate. ²⁸ At one point Jesus turned to them and said, "Daughters of Jerusalem, do not weep for me. Weep rather for yourselves and for your children. ²⁹ The time is coming indeed when it will be said, 'Blessed are the childless, the wombs that have never given birth and the breasts that have never given suck!' ³⁰ Then people will begin to *say to the mountains, 'Fall upon us,' and to the hills, 'Cover us up!'*ᵃ ³¹ For if this is what is done with green wood, what will happen to the dry?"

³² Two others were also led off with him, criminals who were to be put to death.

ᵃ Hos 10:8

COMMENT

Luke continues his passion narrative, not with the scourging and mistreatment of Jesus, which follows in the Marcan Gospel (15:16-20a), but with an extended account of Jesus being led to the place of execution. In it the cross on which he is to be hung is carried by Simon of Cyrene, and people of Jerusalem, especially mourning women, line the road. Jesus addresses words of warning to them, and the episode ends with his wry prophetic comment and the notice that two others, criminals who were to be put to death, were being led off at the same time (23:26-32).

Verse 26 is a Lucan redaction of Mark 15:20b-21, having ten Marcan words out of nineteen (cf. Matt 27:31b-32). Luke has abridged what he takes from "Mk," retaining only the mention of Jesus' being led away and the pressing of Simon a Cyrenian, "coming in from a field" (v. 26) into service to carry Jesus' cross. The Lucan touch is evident in the addition of "behind Jesus." He eliminates the unneeded mention of Simon's sons, as does Matt 27:32.

The rest of the episode (vv. 27-32) is exclusive to Luke, probably derived from "L" (see pp. 67, 84). V. Taylor *(Passion Narrative,* 90) concluded: ". . . verse 26 is a Markan addition prefixed to a non-Markan narrative." Though J. Finegan *(Überlieferung,* 30-31) was inclined to regard vv. 27-32 as a Lucan composition based on 21:23 and Hos 10:8, that is scarcely convincing. The amount of Lucan composition or redaction in this episode is minimal (see J. Jeremias, *Die Sprache,* 304-305). It can be seen in *plēthos tou laou,* "a crowd of people" (v. 27, exclusive to Luke in the NT: 1:10; 6:17; Acts 21:36); *eipen pros* + acc. (v. 28; see p. 116); and the use of the strong adversative conj. *plēn* (v. 28; see NOTE on 10:11). Though Mark 15:27 would presuppose that the two criminals had also been led off, the Marcan account does not mention this detail, which Luke alone has (and the three words in v. 32 that are common to Mark 15:27 are coincidental and no proof that they were not in "L"). Cf. B. Rinaldi, "Beate le sterili"; W. Käser, "Exegetische," for attempts to show the composite form of this episode.

A shortened form of the beatitude of v. 29 is found in *Gos. of Thom.* § 79: "Blessed is the womb that has not conceived and the breasts that have not given milk." There it is joined to that of 11:27-28. However, conception is substituted for parturition, and the sg. "womb" for the Lucan pl. "wombs." In Luke the beatitude is uttered over barrenness or simple childlessness; but in the *Gospel of Thomas* it is over voluntary abandonment of conception (see J.-E. Ménard, *L'Evangile selon Thomas,* 180-181).

Form-critically considered, the episode may seem at first to be another Story about Jesus, but R. Bultmann *(HST* 37) has more rightly classed it as a pronouncement-story (among his biographical apophthegms). He considers the apophthegm (vv. 28bc-30) to be "a Christian prophecy [placed] in the mouth of Jesus on his way to the cross," not a genuine Saying of Jesus, but one "constructed from material supplied by primitive Christian apologetic," though from an old, possibly even Aramaic tradition (cf. *HST* 127). Bultmann tends to regard the episode as a motif found in other ancient literature which recounts the story of famous persons faced with death. Such a suspicion cannot be completely excluded, as the difficulty in interpreting v. 31 reveals. V. Taylor *(FGT* 56) also classes the episode as a pronouncement-story, even as a "Lukan addition" to the passion narrative. M. Dibelius *(FTG* 202-203) saw in the passage the characteristics of a story of martyrdom, in which the martyr informs mourners "that all this affects themselves and that their own fate is to be deplored." However, W. Käser ("Exegetische") has maintained that vv. 27-28 were the original unit, and that Luke has added vv. 29-30 to make the pronouncement of Jesus refer to the destruction of Jerusalem, just as 19:39-44 and 21:5-36 did; underlying vv. 29-30 is an allusion to Isa 54:1-10. All of this is highly speculative, but Käser may be right in regarding the unit of vv. 29-30 as not original. How much any of this can really be traced to Jesus himself is a question; but perhaps v. 28 was uttered in a different context, and perhaps it has been used by Luke in this context with the hindsight of the destruction of Jerusalem. The whole episode acts as another minatory utterance of Jesus against Jerusalem (see the end of COMMENT on 11:37-54).

Unlike the Johannine account, where Jesus carries his own cross to the place of execution (19:17), the Lucan Jesus is led off unscourged with the cross carried behind him by Simon of Cyrene—who carries it as a disciple would be expected to do (9:23; 14:27; cf. pp. 241-243). The Lucan theme of the "way" (part of the geographical perspective, see pp. 164-171) is hinted at again.

The distinctive elements in the Lucan expansion of the account of Jesus' being led off are the following of a great crowd of people and of the "daughters of Jerusalem," whom Jesus addresses. The latter come out in the character of professional mourners to bewail in anticipation the fate of this Jesus, upon whose words the people of Jerusalem all hung (19:48). Hailed and greeted on his approach to Jerusalem as "the king, the one who comes in the name of the Lord" (19:38), Jesus is now led out of that city to be crucified as the King of the Jews, accompanied by its inhabitants who lament and bewail his destiny. "They raise the death-wail over Him in anticipation. He in His turn raises, as it were, the death-wail over Jerusalem in anticipation" (T. W. Manson, *Sayings,* 343).

Luke depicts Jesus addressing these women, drawing a lesson from his own fate to warn them. For they cannot be sure that the forces of evil that have brought him to this hour of darkness are not going to have an effect in their own lives. Facing his destiny, the Lucan Jesus counsels these mourners not to

weep for him but for themselves, and their children. What the present generation of Jerusalemites is doing will affect even its offspring. The coming fate of
Jerusalem will be so terrible that people will consider childless women
"blessed," and the horrors of it so great that people will seek for catastrophic
relief from it. Underlying the beatitude that Jesus refers to is the Jewish belief
that a childless woman was cursed; instead, in this case, she will be blessed.
Just as did apostate Israel of old, which cried out because of the trouble that
had come upon it as a consequence of its rebellion against God, begging that
mountains fall upon its people and hills cover them up (an allusion to Hos
10:8), those of this generation of Jerusalem with children will cry out in like
fashion.

Finally, Jesus makes an ironic comment, using a proverb. He compares his
situation in this confrontation with evil to green wood, difficult to kindle, and
that of Jerusalem, when faced with similar forces of evil, to dry wood, easy to
kindle and susceptible to destruction by consuming fire. The meaning of the
proverb, however, is quite disputed; see NOTE.

Finally, he is associated in the march to the cross with two others, criminals who were to be put to death. Thus, the foretelling of 22:37 finds its
realization: he is classed with outlaws.

NOTES

23   26. *As they led Jesus away.* Who is "they"? It cannot refer to Pilate, and though
some commentators are inclined to think that the Romans are the subject (M.-J.
Lagrange, *Luc,* 584; J. Schmid, *Evangelium nach Lukas,* 346; G. B. Caird, *Gospel of St
Luke,* 249; I. H. Marshall, *Luke,* 863), this is to miss an important aspect of the Lucan
passion narrative. The "they" has to refer to those who "asked for" the release of
Barabbas and to whom Pilate handed over Jesus according to "their will" (v. 25). This
must include "the chief priests, the leaders, and the people" of v. 13 (cf. vv. 4,18,23).
Cf. John 19:16, where *autois,* "to them," refers to the "chief priests" of v. 15. In the
Lucan story the (Roman) soldiers will appear eventually (vv. 36,47), but to read them
into this vague assertion is to miss the point of the way Luke is handling the passion
narrative.

On *hōs,* "as." See 12:58; 24:32.

seized upon. Lit. "took hold of." Luke uses *epilambanesthai* instead of the foreign
word *angareuein,* "press into service," of Mark 15:21.

Simon, a certain Cyrenian. Otherwise unknown; Luke omits the identification of
him as the father of Alexander and Rufus, both known to the Marcan audience
(15:21). Presumably he was a Jew, but it is uncertain that he was already a disciple of
Jesus, *pace* E. E. Ellis, *Gospel of Luke,* 266.

In Cyrene on the coast of northern Africa (modern Libya) a Jewish colony had been
founded by Ptolemy I Soter, son of Lagus (Josephus, *Ag.Ap.* 2.4 § 44). Josephus,
quoting Strabo, says that four groups made up the population of Cyrene: *politai,*

"citizens," *geōrgoi,* "farmers," *metoikoi,* "resident aliens," and *Ioudaioi,* "Jews." See further Josephus, *Ant.* 16.6,1-5 § 160-170; 1 Macc 15:23; 2 Macc 2:23; Acts 2:10; 11:20. The description of Simon in the following phrase would imply that he was not just visiting Jerusalem for the feast of Passover. One can only speculate that he may have been a member of the synagogue mentioned in Acts 6:9.

The best mss. (P75, ℵ, B, L, 0124, *f* 13, 33, etc.) read Simon's name and description in the acc. *Simōna . . . ;* but some (A, W, Θ, Ψ, 063, *f* 1, and the Koine text-tradition) have it in the gen. *Simōnos tinos Kyrēnaiou erchomenou . . .* the more common construction with the compound vb. The sense is not affected.

coming in from a field. This detail is derived from Mark 15:21, with the same wording. One may wonder what a Jew would be doing in a field on the feast of Passover. Cf. Luke 15:25. But see J. Jeremias, *Eucharistic Words,* 77.

they put on him a cross. Lit. "the stake." See NOTE on 9:23. According to Plutarch *(De sera num. vind.* 9 554B), "each of the criminals carries forth his own cross" *(hekastos tōn kakourgōn ekpherei ton heautou stauron).* Luke gives no hint why or how Simon was pressed into service for such a job. "It must therefore be presumed that Jesus was breaking down under the weight, so that the soldiers found it necessary to force Simon to aid him" (I. H. Marshall, *Luke,* 863). That may be a valid presumption for Stage I of the gospel tradition, in which Jesus was presumably scourged; but we know nothing of that in the Lucan story, and there has not yet been any mention of "soldiers." On the basis of Matt 5:41, G. B. Caird *(Gospel of St Luke,* 249) concludes that "the Roman army had the power to requisition assistance from civilians"!

to carry behind Jesus. Without saying that Simon was a disciple, Luke thus depicts him in the attitude of a Christian disciple. See 9:23; 14:27; and especially COMMENT on 9:23-27.

27. *A large crowd of people.* I.e. inhabitants of Jerusalem and, presumably, visitors for the festival. They will reappear in vv. 35,48 as witnesses of the crucifixion. So Luke begins to separate them again from "the leaders." See v. 35.

following him. The vb. *akolouthein* is used in a physical sense. See p. 242. For what purpose were they following, sympathy or curiosity? E. Klostermann *(Lukasevangelium,* 227) quotes Lucian, *De morte Peregr.* 34, in support of the latter: ". . . he [Peregrinus] was being escorted by crowds and getting his fill of glory as he gazed at the number of his admirers, not knowing, poor wretch, that men on their way to the cross or in the grip of the executioner have many more at their heels."

women who were beating their breasts and wailing at his fate. Lit. "who were beating themselves and bewailing him." The two vbs. *koptesthai* and *thrēnoun* are used by Josephus *(Ant.* 6.14,8 § 377) to describe the mourning for King Saul at Jabesh-gilead (1 Sam 31:11-13). This may be a literary motif adopted from Zech 12:10-14. The women who come out are not necessarily disciples; but, devout and sympathetic, they have come to bewail the execution of a human being. Whether this was customary or not is unknown, but they should not be confused with those who are to appear later in vv. 49,55-56. See NOTE on 8:52. J. Schmid *(Evangelium nach Lukas,* 346) maintains that lamentation for criminals to be executed was not permitted in public and that the women really came out to protest the condemnation of Jesus and to make known that he was really the king of their people. But that is to read a great deal into the Lucan text, and no evidence of the prohibition is offered.

28. *Daughters of Jerusalem.* The mourning female inhabitants of Jerusalem are addressed by Jesus with a term often used in the OT. See Cant 2:7; 5:16; 8:4 in the pl.; Isa 37:22; Zeph 3:14; Zech 9:9 in the sg. But the connotation differs here. The address carries the note of Jesus' sadness about the daughters of the city where he meets his own destiny. Cf. Jer 9:19 (9:20E).

do not weep for me. See 7:13. This mild prohibition stands in chiastic arrangement with the following: "Do not weep for me, but for yourselves weep—and for your children." Cp. Luke 10:20 for the form. The sense: If you only knew what was coming, you would better weep for yourselves.

29. *The time is coming.* Lit. "behold, days are coming." See NOTE on 5:35; cf. 19:43. The expression comes from the LXX (Jer 7:32; 16:14; 38:31 [= MT 31:31]).

Blessed are the childless. Lit. "blessed are the barren ones (fem.)." Cp. 21:23; this is an echo of Isa 54:1, cast in the form of a beatitude or macarism. See NOTE on 6:20. See, in fact, the entire episode Isa 54:1-10. The blessing falls not on women with children, usually considered blessed for having them (recall 11:27), but on those without them, who will have none to offer as booty to death. They will be spared the added torture of seeing them put to death. This notion is found in much of classical literature: Euripides, *Androm.* 395; *Alces.* 882; Tacitus, *Annales* 2.75; Elder Seneca, *Controv.* 2.5,2; Apuleius, *Apol.* 85 § 571.

30. *say to the mountains . . . us up!* Jesus' words allude to Hos 10:8 but invert the impvs.: "They shall say to the mountains, Cover us up, and to the hills, Fall upon us." The words of Hosea describe Israel's cry for relief from the punishment of its own apostasy from Yahweh. This Hosean cry is heard again in the mourning of the daughters of Jerusalem and Jesus' comment on it, which thus relates the city's reaction to him to the apostasy of Israel of old. Cf. Rev 6:16.

31. *if this is what is done with green wood.* Lit. "if they (indef.) do this with the damp wood." Jesus uses a proverbial formulation to argue *a minore ad maius.* A similar contrast between a "green tree" *(xylon chlōron)* and a "dry tree" *(xylon xēron)* is found in Ezek 17:24, but with another sense. Jesus compares himself to damp, soggy wood, difficult to kindle, and some aspect of the "daughters of Jerusalem" to dry wood, easily combustible. But in what sense? Commentators differ: (1) If the Romans so treat me, whom they admit to be innocent, how will they treat those who revolt against them? *But* this is to introduce the Romans into a text in which they have not yet been mentioned; moreover, it seems to neglect the implied comparison of Jesus with the daughters of Jerusalem. (2) If Jews so treat me who have come to save them, how will they be treated for destroying me? (3) If human beings so behave before their cup of wickedness is full, what will they do when it overflows? (4) If "God has not spared Jesus, . . . how much more will Judaism, if impenitent, learn the seriousness of divine judgment" (J. Schneider, *TDNT* 5. 38). With slightly different wording, this view is held by J. M. Creed, *The Gospel,* 286; T. W. Manson, *Sayings,* 343; ZBG § 2; G. Schneider, *Evangelium nach Lukas,* 481 (specifying the contrast as between the execution of Jesus and the destruction of Jerusalem). The first three senses are reported by A. Plummer, *The Gospel,* 529. Some form of the fourth seems to be best: If God allows the innocent Jesus *(en tō hygrō xylō,* "damp wood") to suffer such a fate as Jerusalem prepares for him, what will be the fate of Jerusalem *(en tō xerō,* "dry wood")? The contrast is further between the wood on which Jesus is crucified (not

consumed by flames) and the wood of Jerusalem (consumed by flames) in its destruction. Cf. Isa 10:16-19; Ezek 20:47; Prov 11:31; 1 Pet 4:17-18.

what will happen. The vb. *genētai* is subjunc., used as a substitute for an emphatic fut. in a deliberative question (see BDF § 366.1), "what will really happen?" Some mss. (D, K, etc.), however, read the fut. indic. *genēsetai.*

32. *Two others were also led off with him.* Lit. "and there were led off others, two criminals, with him." Because the word order *heteroi kakourgoi dyo,* the reading in mss. P[75], א, B, could suggest that Jesus was also a criminal, many mss. invert the word order to *heteroi dyo kakourgoi* (so A, C, D, L, W, Θ, Ψ, 0117, 0124, 0250, *f*[1,13], and the Koine text-tradition). One ms. (l) of the OL even supplies the names of the two criminals, *Ioathas* and *Maggatras.*

criminals. Recall 22:37. Verse 32 thus prepares for vv. 33,39-43. In this account of the road to the cross there is nothing of later legendary traditions about the falls of Jesus, the meeting with his mother or with Veronica. See P. Benoit, *Passion and Resurrection,* 166.

BIBLIOGRAPHY (23:26-32)

Bailey, J. A. *The Traditions Common,* 78-84.
Benoit, P. *Passion and Resurrection,* 153-180.
Finegan, J. *Die Überlieferung,* 30-31.
Käser, W. "Exegetische und theologische Erwägungen zur Seligpreisung der Kinderlosen Lc 23,29b," *ZNW* 54 (1963) 240-254.
Neyrey, J. H. "Jesus' Address to the Women of Jerusalem (Lk. 23. 27-31)—A Prophetic Judgment Oracle," *NTS* 29 (1983) 74-86.
Rinaldi, B. "Beate le sterili (Lc. 23,29b)," *BeO* 15 (1973) 61-64.
Schreiber, J. *Theologie des Vertrauens: Eine redaktionsgeschichtliche Untersuchung des Markusevangeliums* (Hamburg: Furche, 1967) 22-82.

161. THE CRUCIFIXION
(23:33-38)

23   33 When they had reached the place called The Skull, they crucified Jesus there together with the criminals, one on his right, the other on his left. [34a][a] 34b *Dividing up* his *garments, they cast lots*[b] for them, 35 as the people stood by and *looked on.*[c] The leaders too *kept sneering,*[c] saying, "He saved others; let him save himself, if he is really

---

[a] Verse 34a is omitted in many mss.; see NOTE there.   [b] Ps 22:19
[c] Ps 22:8-9

God's Messiah, his Chosen One." [36] Even the soldiers ridiculed him; they would come up, offer their *sour wine*,[d] [37] and say, "If you are really the King of the Jews, save yourself!"

[38] There was an inscription above him, "This is the King of the Jews."

[d] Ps 69:22

COMMENT

In this scene of the Lucan passion narrative Jesus of Nazareth meets his fate. He is crucified at the place called The Skull between two criminals, insulted by leaders and Roman soldiers, and officially identified as "the King of the Jews" (23:33-38).

Of the ninety-eight Greek words in this passage, twelve occur in a partial verse (34a), which may not have belonged to the original text of the Lucan Gospel. Of the remaining eighty-six Greek words thirty-six have counterparts in Mark 15:22-32a (cf. Matt 27:33-43). Luke has abridged and reordered the Marcan material, making no use of the Aramaic name Golgotha, the wine mixed with myrrh offered to Jesus, his refusal to drink of it, the third hour of the day, the wagging of the heads of passersby, the taunt referring to the destruction of the Temple, or the title "King of Israel."

The peculiarly Lucan details in this episode are: the name "criminals" (*kakourgoi*, see v. 32) for those crucified with him (Mark and Matthew call them *lēstai*, "robbers"; John 19:18 has merely "two others"); Jesus' prayer for forgiveness, if v. 34a were authentic to the text; the addition of "This (is) . . ." to the inscription on the cross (v. 38); the extra title, "his Chosen One" (v. 35); and the distinguishing of the people standing by from "the leaders" (v. 35).

Luke, though using "Mk," writes his own form of the story in this scene, mingling with the Marcan material other information derived from "L." The question in this case is, Has Luke introduced Marcan material into an account from "L," or has he inserted the "L" material into "Mk"? Who can say for sure? I think it is the latter, since he is basically following the Marcan order of episodes. Hence vv. 33,34b,35bcd,38 would be redacted forms of Mark 15:22-24,26-27,31, whereas vv. 35a,36-37 (and also v. 34a, if original) would be derived from "L."

The more specific Lucan redaction can be seen in the following points: (1) the elimination of the Aramaic name Golgotha (Mark 15:22) and the use of the ptc. *kaloumenon*, "called" (v. 33, see J. Jeremias, *Die Sprache*, 53); (2) the mention of the crucifixion of the criminals at his right and left (with *aristeron*

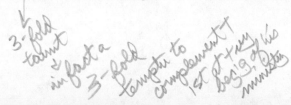

for "left"), moved up (cf. Mark 15:27); (3) the elimination of the time of the day (probably because the early morning session of the Sanhedrin and the appearance of Jesus before Herod would make the "third hour" [Mark 15:25] implausible); (4) in v. 35cd he has simplified and redacted Mark 15:31b, using pleonastic *legontes* (see J. Jeremias, ibid. 67-70) and adding *tou theou*, "God's" (see NOTE on 9:20). Even V. Taylor *(Passion Narrative,* 99) had to agree that vv. 34b and 38 are Marcan, but his attempt to relate vv. 33,35bcd to a non-Marcan source is not convincing; they could just as easily be Lucan redaction and simplification of Mark 15. (See G. Schneider, *Evangelium nach Lukas,* 482-483; cf. J. Jeremias, "Perikopen-Umstellungen bei Lukas?" *NTS* 4 [1957-1958] 115-119; W. Grundmann, *Evangelium nach Lukas,* 431.)

From a form-critical point of view the episode is another Story about Jesus, part of the narrative gospel tradition. R. Bultmann *(HST* 272-273) called the Marcan form of this scene (15:22-26) "a legendary editing of what is manifestly an ancient historical narrative," preserved in vv. 20b-24. The legendary accretion would include v. 26 (the casting of lots for Jesus' garments), developed out of Ps 22:8-9,19 (= Luke 23:34b-35) and other OT allusions. Further, the mocking of the crucified Jesus (15:29-32) is "a legendary formulation" based on Ps 22:8 (or Lam 2:15). One cannot deny that the account of this event has been embellished with OT references—whether by Mark himself or the pre-Marcan tradition does not concern us here. The question is whether such embellishment necessarily makes "legendary" the details that the scene would recount: the crucifixion of Jesus between two criminals, the mocking of Jesus, the inscription on the cross, and even the disposition of Jesus' garments. Three of these four details are recounted in the Johannine tradition (crucifixion, 19:17-18; the title, 19:19-23; the disposition of the garments, 19:23-24 [even with the reference to Ps 22:19]), though in an expanded and even more embellished form. Only the mocking of the crucified Jesus is missing, and even part of that, the offering of wine to him by soldiers (see Luke 23:36), has a counterpart in John 19:29. Literary embellishment is obvious, whereas "legendary editing" is too pejorative.

The peculiar thrust of the Lucan crucifixion scene has been well caught by V. Taylor *(Passion Narrative,* 96), when he contrasts the figure of Jesus and all the other actors in the episode. For Luke distinguishes the silent crowd which stands by and observes from the other persons who utter the taunts: "the leaders" (v. 35), "the soldiers" (v. 36), and—in the next scene—one of the "criminals" (v. 39). Thus the *threefold* taunt forms the nucleus of the extended Lucan crucifixion scene. All three of them make use of the vb. *sōzein,* "save." The first and second taunts have counterparts in Mark 15:30,31; but the added Lucan taunt (v. 39), making a threesome, highlights the salvific significance of Jesus' crucifixion in the Lucan Gospel: He is crucified precisely as "savior," a major theme in Lucan theology (see pp. 204-205, 222-223). (See further D. Flusser, "The Crucified One.")

Jesus has been led to the place called The Skull and is there crucified between two criminals. The climax of his suffering has been reached; his *exodos* (9:31) from this life has moved to its definitive stage. The "power of darkness" (22:53) has closed in against him.

Jesus is not merely crucified, but he is also deprived of his last earthly claims, his garments (for which others cast lots) and his human dignity (of which the sneering leaders seek to deprive him even in his humiliation). The allusion to Ps 22:8-9,19 in vv. 34b-35 identifies him with the suffering upright one of old for whom the psalmist composed his lament. Misery aggravated by mockery and despoilment comes to him from the "leaders" of his own people: "He saved others" (which recalls 7:50; 8:48,50; 17:19; 18:42 in this Gospel); "let him save himself if he is really God's Messiah" (v. 35). Let him manifest himself with éclat so that we may believe in him. (Recall 4:9-12.) Only Luke gives the crucified Jesus the added title, "Chosen One" (v. 35), echoing the heavenly identification of Jesus in 9:35. So the peak of opposition to Jesus in the Lucan Gospel is finally formulated. The crucified Messiah is exposed to the sight of all "the people"; he who was earlier called "Messiah" (9:20; 22:67) has now become in the Lucan Gospel the suffering Messiah (see pp. 200-201), a description or a title that will soon be given him (24:26,46; Acts 3:18; 17:3; 26:23).

Three titles are used of him in this episode, "God's Messiah," his "Chosen One," and "King of the Jews," the last appearing not only in the soldiers' taunt (possibly echoing Pilate's question, 23:3), but also in the inscription on the cross.

The inscription on the cross is the only thing we know of which was *written about* Jesus during his lifetime. Anything else that might have been written about him has disappeared. Yet, as Luke says later on in his story, "this was not done in a corner" (Acts 26:26). Even so, only the inscription on the cross has come down to us from Jesus' lifetime—but in four different forms (see p. 215):

Mark 15:26   *ho basileus tōn Ioudaiōn,* "The King of the Jews."

Luke 23:38   *ho basileus tōn Ioudaiōn houtos,* "This (is) the King of the Jews."

Matt 27:37   *houtos estin Iēsous ho basileus tōn Ioudaiōn,* "This is Jesus, the King of the Jews."

John 19:19   *Iēsous ho Nazōraios ho basileus tōn Ioudaiōn,* "Jesus the Nazorean, the King of the Jews" (written *hebraïsti, rhōmaïsti, hellēnisti,* "in Hebrew, Latin, Greek" [19:20]).

Despite the variants the substance of the title is present in each case.

If v. 34a were originally part of the Lucan Gospel, it would add still another dimension to this scene: Jesus crucified praying for his executioners, begging his Father for mercy toward them, and excusing their deed because of their ignorance. In the spirit of his own teaching, Jesus at this supreme moment communes with the Father and asks for pardon for what is done to him. (See pp. 244-245.)

NOTES

23 33. *the place called The Skull.* Luke retains from Mark 15:22 "the place" *(epi ton topon)* but omits the foreign word (see p. 58) *Golgotha,* a grecized form of Aramaic *gulgultā',* "skull" (which has undergone a Greek dissimilation [so BDF § 39.6]); compare the omission of *Gethsēmani* in 22:39. The place was probably so called because of the physical shape of a hill, not because it was a place of skulls. For the likely location, see L. H. Vincent and F. M. Abel, *Jerusalem nouvelle* (Paris: Gabalda, 1914) 92-93; J. Jeremias, *Golgotha* (Angelos 1; Leipzig: E. Pfeiffer, 1926); A. Parrot, *Golgotha and the Church of the Holy Sepulchre* (SBA 6; London: SCM, 1957); C. Coüasnon, *The Church of the Holy Sepulchre in Jerusalem* (Schweich Lectures 1972; London: British Academy, 1974) 12-13. For the legend about Golgotha being the burial place of Adam, see Jerome, *Comm. in Matt.* 4 (CCLat 77.270).

they crucified Jesus there. The vb. is *estaurōsan* (see NOTE on 23:21), an aor. that Luke substitutes for Mark's historic pres. See p. 107. In the crucifixion accounts of the Synoptic Gospels no mention is made of nails; but cf. John 20:25; Col 2:14 (see my article, *TAG* 125-129). For reactions of ancient writers to the kind of death crucifixion was, see Josephus, *J.W.* 7.6,4 § 203 ("the most pitiable of deaths"); Cicero, *Act. in C. Verr.* 5.66,169-170 ("the worst extreme of tortures inflicted on slaves"). Cf. E. Bammel, "Crucifixion"; M. Hengel, *Crucifixion,* 84-90.

the criminals, one on his right, the other on his left. From the very beginning of the scene the Lucan Jesus is depicted crucified between two criminals. Cf. John 19:18. Luke does this to make clear what "the people" observed. Possibly there is an echo of 22:37 and its allusion to Isa 53:12. To mark the positions of the criminals, Luke uses *men . . . de.* See p. 108.

[34a]. *Jesus said, "Father, forgive them; they do not realize what they are doing."* Though found in some mss. (א*, C, Dᶜ, L, Γ, Δ, 0117, *f*¹·¹³, and the Koine text-tradition) and some ancient versions (Vg, Curetonian Syriac, Peshitta), these words are omitted in very early and important mss. from diverse geographical areas (P⁷⁵, B, אᶜ, D*, W, Θ, 0124, 579, 1241) and some ancient versions (Sinaitic Syriac, Coptic). Because of this the question is raised whether they really formed part of the original text of Luke. They interrupt the flow of the story of the crucifixion and sound like the prayer of Stephen in Acts 7:60b (cf. also the story of the stoning of James the Just in Eusebius, *Hist. eccl.* 2.23,16). Moreover, they introduce a motif of ignorance, which is otherwise found in Acts (3:17; 13:27; 17:30). See E. J. Epp, "The 'Ignorance Motif' in Acts and the Antijudaic Tendencies in Codex Bezae," *HTR* 55 (1962) 51-62. In defense of the reading of v. 34a, see A. von Harnack, "Probleme im Texte der Leidensgeschichte Jesu," *SPAW* 11 (1901) 251-266, esp. 255-261; similarly B. H. Streeter, *The Four Gospels,* 138-139; *TCGNT* 180; G. Schneider, *Evangelium nach Lukas,* 483.

If the words are considered original, to whom do they refer? Scarcely to the Roman soldiers. Apart from the fact that the soldiers have not yet been mentioned (see v. 36), the "ignorance motif" of Acts would have to be invoked to explain the sense of "them," i.e. the Jewish "leaders" of the context, those who were crucifying and mocking him. Cf. 1 Pet 2:21; Acts 2:36. See H. Conzelmann, *Theology*, 89.

On "Father," see NOTES on 11:2 and 10:21. The suffering upright one obtains forgiveness from his Father for those who make him suffer both physically and mentally.

34b. *Dividing up his garments*. Luke follows "Mk" in alluding to Ps 22:19, "They divide (LXX: divided) my garments among them, and for my raiment they cast (LXX: have cast) lots." The allusion to the psalm is reduced in Luke. For the use of this psalm in the Lucan passion narrative, see H. Gese, "Psalm 22 und das Neue Testament," *ZTK* 65 (1968) 1-22, esp. 16-17; J. R. Scheifler, "El salmo 22."

35. *the people stood by and looked on*. Once again the "people" are contrasted with the "leaders." The mention of the people looking on is another allusion to Ps 22:8-9, but with a correction, "All who look upon me have sneered at me," since the contrast of the people and leaders is made clear. Luke has omitted the wagging of the heads (Mark 15:29) and attributes the sneering to the leaders. The contrast prepares for the reaction of the people in v. 48.

The leaders too. The reading *kai hoi archontes* is found in mss. P[75], ℵ, B, C, L, Q, Ψ, 0124, 33, 892, 1241, etc. The *kai* seems to be adverbial, since it follows *de;* but then one asks, "Who besides the leaders were sneering?" This accounts for a variety of attempts on the part of copyists to remedy the text. Ms. D reads instead of the three words simply *auton*, "him," meaning that the people kept sneering at him. Other mss. (*f*[1,13], 1424) and some ancient versions read *auton hoi archontes syn autois*, "and the leaders kept sneering at him with them" (presumably the people). Others have a variant of the latter, *kai hoi archontes syn autois*, "and the leaders with them kept sneering." The text in the lemma is the *lectio difficilior* and for that reason is retained. Possibly the *kai* carries here the nuance of contrast (see BDF § 442.1), "and yet the leaders . . ."

kept sneering. Luke has already used the vb. *ekmyktērizein* in 16:14. Now he substitutes it for the Marcan *empaizein* (15:31), which he himself had used in 22:63 and 23:11 and will use again in v. 36 for the soldiers.

let him save himself. The remark drips with sarcasm; only so can he fill the leaders' idea of messiahship! Mark 15:31c formulates the taunt in a question, "Is he not able to save himself?"

if he is really God's Messiah. So Luke reformulates Mark 15:32, which reads, "Now let the Messiah, the king of Israel, come down from the cross that we may see and believe." In changing the taunt as he has, Luke has eliminated the mention of "Israel" and substituted the form of the title he had used in 9:20. See NOTE there and pp. 197-200. Codex Bezae (ms. D) has cast the whole taunt in the second sg., "You saved others; save yourself if you are the Son of God, if you are the Messiah." The second sg. may be derived from 23:39.

his Chosen One. Lit. "the chosen one." This may be an additional title, joined as an appositive to the preceding; so I prefer to take it because of 9:35. See NOTE there. In itself it is not a messianic title, but is used here of the Messiah. However, one should note the fluctuation in various mss. that have tried to join this title more closely to the preceding or make it a mere modifier of the foregoing one. Thus mss. A, Γ, Δ, Θ,

0135, etc., have "the Messiah, the Chosen One of God"; mss. P[75], 0124, *f* [13], etc., have "the Messiah, the chosen Son of God."

The "Chosen One" is used in Enochic literature as a title *(1 Enoch* 45:3; 49:2; 50:5; 51:3,5; 52:6,9; 53:6; 55:4; 61:5,8,10), but there is no Aramaic part of Enochic literature that corresponds to this from Qumran. See *ESBNT* 127-160.

36. *Even the soldiers ridiculed him.* This is the first time that we learn in the Lucan account that soldiers, presumably Roman soldiers or Roman and other mercenaries in Pilate's service, are present at the crucifixion of Jesus. It reflects a historical detail, even though Luke has sought to play down their involvement and presence.

sour wine. The word *oxos* was used in the ancient eastern Mediterranean area to designate a dry wine, distinguished from the sweet wine usually called *oinos.* It was called *oxos* (from *oxys,* "sharp") because it was sharper or more piquant; it was the ordinary wine used by soldiers stationed at Hermopolis in Egypt and elsewhere and is frequently mentioned in papyri. See MM 452-453. Part of the reason why it is mentioned here is its occurrence in the LXX of Ps 69:22; the allusion is more obvious in Mark 15:36, but it is not clear there who offers the wine to Jesus on a sponge (one of the bystanders); cf. H. Conzelmann, *Theology,* 88 n. 2. What the motivation of the offering is is not clear, since Luke has omitted the anesthetic wine and myrrh of Mark 15:23. There is no mention of Elijah, because Luke has eliminated the cry of Jesus on the cross (Mark 15:34), not for the avoidance of an Elijah motif, but because he normally eliminates Aramaic phrases. See p. 58.

37. *If you are really the King of the Jews.* An allusion to Pilate's question (23:3) as well as to the inscription on the cross itself (23:38), which follows.

38. *an inscription.* Following Mark 15:26, Luke writes *epigraphē,* whereas John 19:19 has the Latinism *titlos* (= Latin *titulus),* the technical Roman name for the plaque bearing (usually) the name and the charge. See p. 773. For another example of the *titulus,* see Eusebius, *Hist. eccl.* 5.1,44 ("This is Attalus, the Christian," written *rhōmaïsti,* "in Latin"); Suetonius, *Calig.* 32.2.

above him. Some mss. (א*, A, C³, D, R, W, Θ, Ψ, 0117, 0135, 0250, *f* [1.13], and the Koine text-tradition) read *(epi)gegrammenē ep' autō grammasin hellēnikois kai rhōmaïkois kai hebraïkois* (not all with the same word order or with all the *kai*'s), "written over him in Greek, Latin, and Hebrew letters." This reading, though widespread, is almost certainly a gloss taken over from John 19:20. It is absent from "several of the earliest and best witnesses" *(TCGNT* 181), viz. P[75], B, C*, and from many ancient versions (Sinaitic and Curetonian Syriac, Coptic, and some of the OL mss.).

This is the King of the Jews. Luke has simply redacted the Marcan formula, "The King of the Jews." By putting it at the end of this scene, Luke makes it more climactic than it is in "Mk." Matthew and John have added the name of Jesus to the inscription. Attempts have often been made to identify the original form among the four that have come down to us (see G. M. Lee, "The Inscription on the Cross"; P.-F. Regard, "Le titre de la croix"), one as more Latin or another as more Hebrew; but the differences in the suggestions belie the fantasy which belongs to them. Only John's Gospel attributes the inscription to Pilate himself. It is to be understood as a taunt against Jesus, and not as a taunt against the Jews (see J. Schmid, *Evangelium nach Lukas,* 349). For the role which the inscription undoubtedly played in the development of the title

Christos for the risen Jesus, see pp. 198-99. —Note the form that the inscription takes in *Gos. Peter* 4:11: "This is the King of Israel" (Hennecke-Schneemelcher, *NTApocrypha* 1. 184). See W. Trilling, "Le Christ."

BIBLIOGRAPHY (23:33-38)

Bammel, E. "Crucifixion as a Punishment in Palestine," *The Trial of Jesus* (ed. E. Bammel) 162-165.

Cantinat, J. "Le crucifiement de Jésus," *VSpir* 84 (1951) 142-153.

Conzelmann, H. *Theology*, 88-93.

Dammers, A. H. "Studies in Texts: Luke xxiii, 34a," *Theology* 52 (1949) 138-139.

Daube, D. " 'For They Know Not What They Do': Luke 23,34," *Studia patristica* 4 (TU 79; Berlin: Akademie, 1961) 58-70.

Démann, P. " 'Père pardonnez-leur' (Lc 23,34)," *Cahiers sioniens* 5 (1951) 321-336.

Feuillet, A. "Souffrance et confiance en Dieu: Commentaire du psaume xxii," *NRT* 70 (1948) 137-149.

Finegan, J. *Die Überlieferung*, 31-32.

Fitzmyer, J. A. "Crucifixion in Ancient Palestine, Qumran Literature, and the New Testament," *CBQ* 40 (1978) 493-513; reprinted, *TAG* 125-146.

Flusser, D. "The Crucified One and the Jews," *Immanuel* 7 (1977) 25-37.

Hengel, M. *Crucifixion in the Ancient World and the Folly of the Message of the Cross* (Philadelphia: Fortress, 1977).

Henry, D. M. " 'Father, Forgive Them; for They Know Not What They Do' (Luke xxiii. 34)," *ExpTim* 30 (1918-1919) 87.

Karavidopoulos I. D. *"To pathos tou doulou tou theou epi tou staurou kata tēn diēgēsin tou euangelistou Louka* (23,33-49)," *Deltion* 1 (1972) 189-211.

Lee, G. M. "The Inscription on the Cross," *PEQ* 100 (1968) 144.

Lindars, B. *New Testament Apologetic: The Doctrinal Significance of Old Testament Quotations* (Philadelphia: Westminster, 1961) 88-93.

Linnemann, E. *Studien*, 136-170.

Moffatt, J. "Exegetica: Luke xxiii. 34," *Expos* 8/7 (1914) 92-93.

Regard, P.-F. "Le titre de la croix d'après les évangiles," *RevArch* 28 (1928) 95-105.

Reid, J. "The Words from the Cross, I: 'Father, Forgive Them' (Lk. xxiii.34)," *ExpTim* 41 (1929-1930) 103-107.

Scheifler, J. R. "El salmo 22 y la crucifixión del Señor," *EstBíb* 24 (1965) 5-83.

Taylor, V. "The Narrative of the Crucifixion," *NTS* 8 (1961-1962) 333-334.

——— *Passion Narrative*, 91-99.

Trilling, W. "Le Christ, roi crucifié; Lc 23,35-43," *AsSeign* 65 (1973) 56-65.

Westermann, C. *Gewendete Klage: Eine Auslegung des 22. Psalms* (BibS[N] 8; 2d ed.; Neukirchen: Neukirchener-V., 1957).

Wilkinson, J. "The Seven Words from the Cross," *SJT* 17 (1964) 69-82.

162. THE TWO CRIMINALS ON CROSSES
(23:39-43)

23 [39] One of the criminals who hung there kept insulting him, "Are you really the Messiah? Then save yourself, and us too!" [40] But the other answered him with a rebuke, "Don't you even fear God? After all, you are under the same sentence yourself. [41] For us it represents justice; we are only getting what our deeds deserve. But this man has done nothing improper." [42] Then he said, "Jesus, remember me when you come into your kingdom!" [43] Jesus replied to him, "Believe me, today you shall be with me *in Paradise.*"[a]

[a] *Ps. Sol.* 14:3

COMMENT

The Lucan passion narrative is unique in having a scene in which one of the criminals crucified with Jesus joins in the mocking of Jesus explicitly. He is in time corrected by the other criminal, who acknowledges Jesus' innocence and begs to be remembered when Jesus comes into his kingly heritage. Jesus answers with the promise that he will be with him in Paradise that very day (23:39-43).

The episode is inspired by Mark 15:32c, which reads simply, "And those crucified with him kept taunting him." This brief notice is expanded by Luke into an incident that corrects it, probably derived from "L." Lucan redaction in this episode is at a minimum (see J. Jeremias, *Die Sprache,* 306-307): *kakourgoi,* "criminals" (see vv. 32,33); *kremasthentōn,* "hung" (see Acts 5:30; 10:39; 28:4); *apokritheis . . . ephē* (see p. 114); *hēmeis men . . . houtos de* (see p. 108); the attracted rel. pron., "what our deeds deserve" (see J. Jeremias, ibid. 88). The list that V. Taylor gives *(Passion Narrative,* 95) needs checking, even if one agrees that "Luke is editing a pre-Lukan source."

Form-critically considered, this episode is another pronouncement-story in the Lucan passion narrative. However, V. Taylor *(FGT* 56) would rather regard it as another Story about Jesus, which could even "be told apart from the Passion Narrative as a whole"(?). Certainly, the emphasis is on the Saying of Jesus to the second criminal. M. Dibelius *(FTG* 203) saw the episode as an example of a classic promise of special reward made to a martyr: the penitent criminal who acknowledges Jesus is promised a share in his own blessed lot. R. Bultmann *(HST* 309-310) cites the episode as an example of the growth in the narrative tradition as it differentiates and individualizes: the account of those crucified with Jesus and taunting him (Mark 15:32c) becomes a story in which one sides with him and the other against. This may be. E. Lohse *(History,* 97) calls the scene a "legendary elaboration that one of the two criminals repented." Being unique to the Lucan Gospel, the episode is subject to this sort of suspicion; but who can say for sure that it did not take place?

In a sense this episode becomes the peak of the Lucan scene of crucifixion, for it not only presents the third taunt against Jesus, yet another (implicit) declaration of his innocence, but a manifestation of his salvific mercy to one of the dregs of humanity. As did the leaders and the soldiers in the preceding episode, so now one of the criminals adds his taunt about Jesus' kingship and salvific activity. But this third taunt becomes a foil for a rebuke from the fellow criminal, who reminds the first that he too is about to die, being "under the same sentence" (v. 40, condemnation to crucifixion). Indeed, he too will soon face God. This crucifixion of himself and of the other criminal is viewed by the second criminal as justice rightly taking its course: "We are only getting what our deeds deserve" (v. 41). Thus implicitly, Jesus' innocence is formulated again, this time not by the Roman prefect, but unofficially by a Palestinian criminal sentenced to the same punishment. He recognizes that justice has been denied Jesus, that the latter has not been judged *dikaiōs,* "rightly, justly," and that he has not even done anything improper, much less criminal. To ask how the man knew all this about Jesus is to miss the point of the story.

Addressing Jesus, this criminal, having thus admitted his own guilt, acknowledges Jesus' kingly status, "Remember me when you come into your kingdom!" (v. 42). He begs for remembrance in the unknown future that awaits them all. He calls him not "Lord," but "Jesus," using his given name, and asks for a share in the mercy that only a king can dispense.

The crucified Jesus, the one soon to die on the gibbet of infamy, replies to this criminal, "Believe me, today you shall be with me in Paradise" (v. 43). As Ambrose put it centuries ago, "More abundant is the favor shown than the request made" *(Expos. ev. sec. Luc.* 10.121 [CCLat 14.379]). Whatever the final prepositional phrase in Jesus' answer means (see NOTE on p. 1510), he promises the criminal a share in Christian destiny. In Lucan fashion, it echoes what Paul promises the living and the dead in 1 Thess 4:17: to be "always with the Lord." (See further Paul's debate with himself in Phil 1:22-23; cf. 1 Thess 5:10; 2 Cor 5:8; Rom 6:8.) It is an acquittal uttered by him who is "the one ordained by God to be the judge of the living and the dead" (Acts 10:42).

This episode, then, is Luke's way of presenting the salvific aspect of Jesus' death: the regal status that he will achieve, once he has entered "his glory" (24:26) and been exalted (Acts 2:32-36), will not be without saving effect on *right but whether is to be?*

suffering human beings, even crucified criminals. This sums up the Lucan
theologia crucis (see p. 23). Recall the threefold use of *sōzein,* "save," in vv.
35,36,39, which clearly hints at the salvific character of Jesus' crucifixion and
death—in a Lucan way, to be sure.

Thus, among the evangelists, only Luke makes clear that the destiny of the
Christian is something that transcends this life and the death with which it
ends. That destiny is freely granted by the Savior-King to one who is repentant (who has experienced *metanoia)* and turns to the source of salvation (in
epistrophē). Even though these themes of Lucan theology are not made explicit in the scene, they are implied and are not to be missed (see pp. 237-239).

Luke makes use of this third scene of mockery to let it become a manifestation of mercy; he could not let the mockery end on a negative note. Instead it
becomes an implicit affirmation of the victory over death that Jesus himself
will experience, for the penitent criminal, who will be with him "in Paradise,"
will thus be sharing in that victory. What that victory will be is not yet
apparent, but in the next scene Jesus will consign himself to his Father's
hands.

NOTES

23 39. *One of the criminals.* Luke again calls them *kakourgoi,* as in vv. 32,33. We are
not told whether they are Jews or pagans. That either of them was "a person of Zealot
outlook" (I. H. Marshall, *Luke,* 871, following K. H. Rengstorf, *Evangelium nach
Lukas,* 262) is sheer speculation. It has nothing to do with the Lucan story.

kept insulting him. Lit. "kept blaspheming him." See 22:65.

Are you really the Messiah? This is an echo of the taunt of the "leaders" (v. 35; see
NOTE there).

save yourself. The third reference to Jesus' salvific power; it is uttered with sarcasm,
and the addition "and us too" brings out its selfish aspect. It becomes the foil to the
rebuke of the other criminal, who will appeal for salvation in his own way.

40. *the other.* Traditionally called Dismas or Dysmas, which name first appears in
the apocryphal *Acts of Pilate* 10:2 (sometimes called the *Gospel of Nicodemus,* see
Hennecke-Schneemelcher, *NTApocrypha* 1. 459). See further J. Blinzler, LTK² 3. 419.
For a summary of the ways in which patristic writers explained the "conversion" of
this criminal, see A. Plummer, *The Gospel,* 533-534.

with a rebuke. Lit. "rebuking (him)." See NOTE on 4:35.

Don't you even fear God? I.e. when you are on the threshold of death itself. The
oude, "not even," modifies the vb. *phobē,* not the pron. *sy,* "you," *pace* I. H. Marshall,
Luke, 871-872; see A. Plummer, *The Gospel,* 534.

41. *For us it represents justice.* Lit. "even we suffer justly." Thus the second criminal
recognizes his guilt, and implicitly expresses his *metanoia* before God.

But this man has done nothing improper. Lit. "nothing out of place" *(a-topon;* see
Acts 25:5; 28:6), i.e. not to mention anything criminal. This becomes yet another
declaration of Jesus' innocence, from an unofficial source, and from one suffering

under the same condemnation *(krima,* lit. "judgment"). Instead of *atopon,* ms. D reads *ponēron,* "evil."

42. *Then he said.* Some mss. (A, C³, W, Γ, Δ, Θ, 0124, 0135) and some ancient versions (Syriac, Coptic) read *elegen tō Iēsou, mnēsthēti mou, kyrie,* "he said to Jesus, 'Lord, remember me . . .' " which seems to be an effort to avoid having Jesus addressed by his name. Ms. D has *strapheis pros ton kyrion eipen autō,* "turning to the Lord, he said to him," which sounds peculiar when predicated of a crucified person.

remember me when you come into your kingdom! This is the reading in mss. P⁷⁵, B, L, and the Latin versions. Many others, however, (mss. א, A, C², R, W, Ψ, 0124, 0135, *f*¹,¹³, and the Koine text-tradition) have *en tē basileia sou,* "in/with your kingdom," and the latter is defended by a number of modern commentators. E.g. M.-J. Lagrange, *Luc,* 591; A. Plummer, *The Gospel,* 535; G. Schneider, *Evangelium nach Lukas,* 485; A. Huck and H. Greeven, *Synopse,* 268. *UBSGNT*³ rightly prefers the text in the lemma and labels it with a C (with "a considerable degree of doubt whether the text or the apparatus contains the superior reading"). It is "more consonant with Lukan theology (compare 24.26)" *(TCGNT* 181), for death and exaltation will initiate Jesus' own kingly rule (cf. 1:33; 22:30). The alternate reading might rather be understood of Jesus' parousiac coming, a less likely sense for this Lucan passage. Ms. D reads *en tē hēmera tēs eleuseōs,* "in the day of your coming," which is even less likely. For an attempt to justify this last reading as original, see F. Altheim and R. Stiehl, "Aramäische Herrenworte."

The request for remembrance may echo OT passages such as Gen 40:14 or Ps 106:4. These requests are found at times in Jewish funerary inscriptions. See *IEJ* 5 (1955) 234; cf. *TDNT* 5. 770. The criminal begs of Jesus remembrance, apparently judging that Jesus' fate may be different from his own. His request plays on the title given to Jesus in the inscription on the cross. His plea is for gracious remembrance, for he can do nothing to merit it now.

43. *Jesus replied to him.* Lit. "he said to him." Many mss. insert the name *ho Iēsous.*

Believe me. Lit. "Amen I say to you." See NOTE on 4:24. This is the only place in the six instances of *amēn* in the Lucan Gospel, where the pron. "you" is sg.; as in 4:24, it is used in a passage that has no counterpart in Mark and may stem from "L" itself.

today you shall be with me. The criminal phrased his request vaguely, "when you come . . . ," but Jesus' answer replies specifically, not *when,* but *"today,"* with the adv. *sēmeron* placed emphatically immediately after the asseverative cl. "Today" refers not to "the calendar day of the crucifixion" (E. E. Ellis, "Present and Future," 37), but to the day of "messianic salvation inaugurated by" the death of Jesus. The criminal will share the kingly condition of Jesus that very day. "For life is to be with Christ, because where Christ is, there is the kingdom" (Ambrose, *Expos. ev. sec. Luc.* 10:121 [CCLat 14.379]). See G. W. MacRae, "With Me"; P. Grelot, " 'Aujourd'hui.' "

in Paradise. The n. *paradeisos* occurs further in the NT in 2 Cor 12:4 and Rev 2:7 and has often been thought to be the biblical word for heaven. Its background, however, is something else again. It came into the Greek language from Old Persian *(pairidaêza,* "enclosed space, precinct"). It is attested in Greek from the time of Xenophon *(Anab.* 1.2,7; 2.4,14; *Cyrop.* 1.3,14) in the sense of an "enclosed park, garden." It turns up likewise in Hebrew as *pardēs* (Cant 4:13; Qoh 2:5; Neh 2:8), meaning "a treed park." Greek *paradeisos* is used in the LXX to translate *gan,* "garden" (Gen 2:8, "a garden in Eden"; Gen 13:10, "the garden of God"). Cf. Philo, *De opif. mund.* 153-155, etc.; Josephus, *Ant.* 1.1,3 § 37, etc. From the Genesis use it developed in time an eschatological nuance, a place of expected bliss (e.g. Ezek 31:8), and even more specifically as the mythical place or abode of the righteous after death *(T. Levi* 18:10-11; *Ps. Sol.* 14:3; *1 Enoch* 17-19; 60:8; 61:12). The last sense could be what is intended in this Lucan passage. See further P. Grelot, " 'Aujourd'hui.' "

The joining of "today" and "in Paradise" in this verse creates a problem when one tries to relate it to the credal "descent into Hell," and even with 1 Pet 3:19-20. That, however, is a question about which Luke never dreamed.

BIBLIOGRAPHY (23:39-43)

Altheim, F., and R. Stiehl. "Aramäische Herrenworte," *Die Araber in der alten Welt* (5 vols.; Berlin: de Gruyter) 5/2 (1969) 361-367.

Berger, K. *Die Amen-Worte Jesu* (see p. 536), 87.

Boulogne, C.-D. "La gratitude et la justice depuis Jésus-Christ," *VSpir* 96 (1957) 142-156.

Calle, F. de la. " 'Hoy estarás conmigo en el Paraíso'; Visión inmediate de Dios o purificación en el 'más allá'?" *Biblia y fe* 3 (1977) 276-289.

Ellis, E. E. "Present and Future Eschatology in Luke," *NTS* 12 (1965-1966) 27-41.

George, A. "La royauté de Jésus selon l'évangile de Luc," *ScEccl* 14 (1962) 57-69.

Grelot, P. " 'Aujourd'hui tu seras avec moi dans le Paradis' (Luc, XXIII, 43)," *RB* 74 (1967) 194-214.

Hope, L. P. "The King's Garden," *ExpTim* 48 (1936-1937) 471-473.

Leloir, L. "Hodie, mecum eris in paradiso (Lc., XXIII, 43)," *Revue diocésaine de Namur* 13 (1959) 471-483; *VD* 28 (1950) 372-380 (slightly different Latin form).

Lewis, A. S. "A New Reading of Luke xxiii.39," *ExpTim* 18 (1906-1907) 94-95.

Macgregor, W. M. "The Words from the Cross, II: The Penitent Thief (Lk. xxiii. 39-43)," *ExpTim* 41 (1929-1930) 151-154.

MacRae, G. W. "With Me in Paradise," *Worship* 35 (1961) 235-240.

Martin, G. C. "A New Reading of Luke xxiii. 39," *ExpTim* 18 (1906-1907) 334-335.

Nestle, E. "Luke xxiii. 43," *ExpTim* 11 (1899-1900) 429.

Schneider, G. *Parusiegleichnisse,* 81-84.

Smith, R. H. "Paradise Today: Luke's Passion Narrative," *CurrTM* 3 (1976) 323-336.

Trilling, W. "L'Evangile (Lc 23,33-43): La promesse de Jésus au bon larron," *AsSeign* os 96 (1967) 31-39.

Weisengoff, J. P. "Paradise and St. Luke 23:43," *AER* 103 (1940) 163-168.

Wulf, W. "Jesus, gedenke meiner, wenn du in dein Königtum kommst (Lk 23,42)," *Geist und Leben* 37 (1964) 1-3.

163. THE DEATH OF JESUS
(23:44-49)

23 ⁴⁴ It was already about noon, and darkness began to hang over the whole land until three in the afternoon, ⁴⁵ for the sunlight had failed and the curtain in front of the sanctuary was torn in two. ⁴⁶ Then Jesus uttered a loud cry and said, "Father, *into your hands I entrust my spirit.*"ᵃ Saying this, he breathed his last. ⁴⁷ The centurion who saw this happen glorified God: "Indeed, this man was innocent."

⁴⁸ The crowds too that had gathered for this spectacle, when they gazed at what happened, all returned home beating their breasts. ⁴⁹ All Jesus' acquaintances and the women who had come with him from Galilee stood at a distance, looking on.

ᵃ Ps 31:6

COMMENT

The Lucan passion narrative continues with its climactic episode, which recounts the death of Jesus (23:44-49), depicting Jesus serene in his final torment and utterly dedicated to his Father. His death is attended by darkness over the whole land and the rending of the Temple veil. Once again, he is declared innocent, this time by a subordinate Roman official. His death is witnessed—by crowds, who withdraw shaken by the incident, and by acquaintances and Galilean women who had known him.

The episode is inspired by Mark 15:33-40a (cf. Matt 27:45-55a), following its order and using some of its wording. But Luke has greatly abridged and redacted the Marcan parallel: (1) he has supplied an explanation for the darkness, the failure of sunlight (v. 45a); (2) he has moved up the notice about the rending of the Temple veil to join it to the cataclysmic darkness (in Mark it occurs *after* Jesus has breathed his last [15:38]), thus creating a more dramatic backdrop for the event; (3) he has eliminated Jesus' Aramaic cry of dereliction and the subsequent association of it with Elijah (Mark 15:34-36); (4) he makes use of a different OT psalm to explain the "loud cry" of Mark 15:37, as Jesus breathes his last (v. 46); (5) he has changed the comment of the centurion who stood by; and (6) he has created his own ending of the episode (vv. 48-49), slightly modifying what he retains of Mark 15:40a.

The passage is filled with Lucan terminology and stylistic expressions (see J. Jeremias, *Die Sprache,* 307-309; V. Taylor, *Passion Narrative,* 95-96). The main redactional or compositional traits are: *hōsei,* "about" (v. 44a; see NOTE on 22:44); the adverbial use of *mesos,* lit. "in the middle" (v. 45; cf. Acts 1:18); "uttered a loud cry" (v. 46; see NOTE on 23:23); the use of *hekatontarchēs* for the "centurion," avoiding the Latinism of Mark 15:39 (v. 47); "glorified God" (v. 47; see NOTE on 5:25); "this happen," "what happened" (vv. 47,48; see 8:34,35,56; 9:7; 24:12; Acts 4:21; 5:7; 13:12); hyperbolic "all" (vv. 48,49; see NOTES on 3:16; 4:15; 9:1).

Does Luke make any use of "L" in this passage? This is much debated. What might seem to stem from "L" is the omission of the cry of dereliction, since John 19:28-30 knows nothing of it either (only Mark and Matthew record it). Again, the centurion's comment may actually be a bit of authentic historical tradition, which has come to Luke from "L." V. Taylor *(Passion Narrative,* 96), after conceding a great number of " 'Lukan' words" in the passage, concludes to a "Lukan re-setting of an earlier source supplemented by Markan additions in vv. . . . 44f. and 49." But other commentators insist that the episode is the result solely of Lucan redaction or editing of "Mk." (See G. Schneider, *Evangelium nach Lukas,* 486; even I. H. Marshall, *Luke,* 874, has to admit that "the case for a separate passion narrative used by him [Luke] is at its weakest here." I agree.

Form-critically considered, the episode is another Story about Jesus, a piece of the narrative gospel tradition. R. Bultmann *(HST* 274) thought that "Luke was offended by the cry of dereliction" and so eliminated the use of Ps 22:2. That may be, but then perhaps there was another tradition in the early church that he preferred to follow.

Luke follows "Mk" in dating the event of Jesus' death to sometime after noon on the day of Passover. He creates a symbolic backdrop for the death by the reference to two cataclysmic events that accompanied it: darkness over the whole land (of Palestine) and the rending of the Temple veil (in Jerusalem). Several things have to be noted about this dramatic setting that Luke has provided. *First of all,* as G. B. Caird *(The Language and Imagery of the Bible* [Philadelphia: Westminster, 1980] 213-214) has pointed out, Mark's arrangement of the references to these cataclysms shows that he intended them to be taken figuratively. In Mark 15:37-39 Jesus utters a loud cry and breathes his last; the veil is rent in two; the centurion who stands by sees that Jesus has expired and makes his comment. Verses 37 and 39 take place on Golgotha; the evangelist's comment (v. 38) refers to an event not on Golgotha, something which the centurion could not have seen; it is not the cause of his remark. If so, the comment can only be taken logically in a figurative sense. Matthew (27:51-53) expands "Mk" and relates the rending of the Temple veil to other cataclysmic events (earthquake, etc.), and Luke (23:44-45) does so too, but not in the same way. "It would appear that what began as a figurative statement has ended as a literal one: interpretation has been taken as actuality" (ibid. 214; see also pp. 185-186). So it may seem at least. *Second,* even in the Lucan account, where the two cataclysmic events are recorded at the beginning, they are obviously intended by the evangelist as a setting for the death of Jesus. Referring to the rending of the Temple veil, P. Benoit *(Passion and Resurrection,* 201) rightly stresses, "This event is not to be taken too literally either. . . . We must go straight for the symbolism and decide what the gospels mean by the event, since they are not interested in anecdote for its own sake." Given the Lucan presentation of Jesus in this Gospel, almost from the very beginning, as "a light to give revelation to the Gentiles and glory to your people Israel" (2:32), and given the various ways Jesus experienced rejection, fulfilling Simeon's comment about him, "This child is marked for the fall and the rise of many in Israel, to be a symbol that will be rejected" (2:34), the darkness over the whole land and the rending of the Temple veil take on a clear symbolic connotation. The death of Jesus, attended by such cataclysmic events, is to have an ominous effect on the "whole land" (v. 44) and on the Temple in Jerusalem (recall 21:5-7). *Third,* there may be even more intended, since the Temple veil served to separate the presence of Yahweh in his Temple from those outside. That connotation of the veil is also known in the Lucan Gospel from the first episode (after the prologue), in which Zechariah the priest entered "the sanctuary of the Lord" *(ton naon tou kyriou)* to burn incense (1:9). Here it is *to katapetasma tou naou* (v. 45), which is rent. Luke may well be suggesting in his own way what the Epistle to the Hebrews does more explicitly (9:6-28), that by the death of Jesus access to the intimate presence of God has been made possible for human beings, even those not serving in the priestly courses of old. Similarly, it may be Luke's way of expressing what the Epistle to the Ephesians calls "the dividing wall of hostility" between Jew and Greek (2:14-16), broken down "through the cross." The dramatic setting in vv. 44-45 should be understood as the Lucan symbolic backdrop for the death of Jesus on the cross.

Though the Lucan Jesus does not cry out in the words of Ps 22:2, he does consign himself to his Father's care. Making use of Ps 31:6, he once again prays to his Father, saying, "Into your hands I entrust my spirit" (v. 46). He who several times over in this Gospel has been depicted as one to be handed over "into the hands of men" *(eis cheiras anthrōpōn,* 9:44; cf. 18:32; 20:19; 22:53; 24:7) now entrusts himself (his "spirit") into the hands of the Father. He has fulfilled his role: the preaching of the kingdom of God, for which he was sent (4:43), has led to this. The *exodos* that he was destined to complete in Jerusalem (9:31), the transit to the Father, is now summed up in these words. Having quoted Ps 31:6, he breathes his last. Jesus of Nazareth, the one destined to sit on "the throne of his father David," to "be king over the house of Jacob forever," and of whose "kingship there will be no end" (1:32-33), now dies classed "with outlaws" (22:37). In suffering all this, he enters "into his glory" (24:26); he becomes in the Lucan Gospel alone the suffering Messiah (see p. 200). He who in this Gospel was the bringer of peace (see pp. 224-225) now dies in peace, entrusting himself to the Father.

The significance of this death is not lost on those who stand by. The evangelist's narrative comment about the pagan Roman centurion practically makes a Christian (or at least a Jew) out of him: he "glorified God," as he acknowledged, "Indeed, this man was innocent" (v. 47). Luke avoids the Marcan formulation (either because he prefers an older tradition ["L"] or thinks that "son of God" on the lips of a pagan might be misunderstood by his own readers). But the centurion's declaration of Jesus' innocence constitutes his glorifying God, for he recognizes the meaning of the innocent death in God's plan. So Luke, writing from Stage III of the gospel tradition, would have us understand it. Indeed, in that stage of the tradition Jesus may even be God's upright one (see NOTE on v. 47).

The centurion, however, is not the only witness to the death of Jesus. The role of witness is important in Lucan theology (see p. 243), and in a sense it begins here in a special way. Chapter 24 will make much of it. But those who stand by and look on are both "crowds" who gaze at all that happens as if it were a spectacle, and Jesus' "acquaintances" (male) and the women of Galilee. Luke does not name the latter (contrast Mark 15:40b), since the reader knows from 8:2-3 who they are: Mary called Magdalene, out of whom seven demons had come, Joanna, the wife of Chuza, Herod's steward, Susanna, and many others. (Like Mark, he knows nothing of the presence of the mother of Jesus at the cross; cf. John 19:25-27.) Only in this Gospel are we told that the people regretted what had happened—"beating their breasts" (v. 48).

So dies Jesus of Nazareth in the Lucan Gospel, peaceful and forgiving, attended by cataclysms and witnessed by sympathizers. He is not depicted as having given his life "as a ransom for many" (Mark 10:45) or as "put to death for our trespasses" (Rom 4:25; cf. 1 Cor 15:3). Yet he has been clearly portrayed dying as a savior, implicitly so acknowledged by the taunts of "the leaders" (23:35), the "soldiers" (23:36-37), and even one of the "criminals" (23:39). That his salvific activity has helped "others" has likewise been acknowledged (23:35); and shortly before he breathes his last, the crucified Jesus assures the penitent criminal that that very day he shall be with him in bliss (23:43). So Luke, the storyteller, dramatizes an effect of the Christ-event: What Jesus of Nazareth by his death has achieved for humanity is salvation (see pp. 222-223).

Still another aspect of Jesus' death becomes clearer when one relates what has been synthesized in the foregoing paragraph to what Jesus has been portrayed as saying at the Last Supper. Now the real meaning of his words emerges: what he meant by "suffering" (22:15), by his "body, which is given for you" (22:19), and by "the new covenant with my blood, which is poured out for you" (22:20). With these elements of an earlier part of the passion narrative in mind, the reader of the Lucan Gospel can understand the implication that Jesus' death has been a sacrifice. Luke does not yet express the meaning of Jesus' death as clearly as the Epistle to the Ephesians does, "Christ loved us and gave himself up for us, a fragrant offering and a sacrifice to God" (5:2), or as explicitly as does the Epistle to the Hebrews, "(he has) put away sin by the sacrifice of himself" (9:26), or even as clearly as 1 Pet 2:24, "He himself carried our sins in his body up onto the tree, that we might die to sin and live to uprightness," but Luke does insinuate the vicarious and salvific aspects of the death of Jesus. Recall too the motif of the forgiveness of sins, which runs through the whole Gospel (see pp. 223-224) and is to be understood as a Lucan expression of an effect of the Christ-event. Again, once crucified (and raised by God), he is proclaimed as the one through whose name forgiveness of sins is achieved (Acts 10:39-43; cf. 13:38-39).

All of this further explains why the Lucan Jesus describes to his apostles at the Last Supper his presence among them as service (22:27c). Luke may have changed the Marcan "for many" (14:24) to "for you" (22:19-20), but that change has scarcely eliminated or even reduced the notion of service or the vicarious character of the giving up of his life. Again, Luke has summed up Jesus' life (and death) in the explicit reference to the Isaian Servant passage of Isa 53:7-8 in Acts 8:30-35. One may wonder why Luke has not made more of the expiation of sins (in OT fashion) when speaking of Jesus' death; but he may have avoided that *hilaskesthai* terminology precisely because of the persons for whom he was writing and the wrong impression it might have caused in a predominantly Gentile Christian community (see F. Büchsel, *TDNT* 3. 310-312). However, the idea of a death vicariously purifying a nation of its sins was not foreign to Hellenistic Judaism (see 4 Macc 6:28-29; 17:20-22).

But the real question is whether or not Luke depicts the crucifixion and death of Jesus solely as a deed done in ignorance because of a misunderstanding of OT prophecies, a deed which God himself then corrected by raising Jesus from the dead (see Acts 2:36-3:17; 13:27; cf. H. Conzelmann, *Theology,* 89-90). Or to put it another way, in Lucan theology "the forgiveness of sins is tied to the messiahship of Jesus which is based on the resurrection (vs. 37 [i.e. Acts 2:37]), and also 'nothing is said in this connection about the particular significance of his death.' " (So P. Vielhauer, "On the 'Paulinism' " [see p. 61], 41-42.) True, Luke does in certain places of Acts so present the death of Jesus, without reference to the salvific significance of it. That he has not stressed the latter as Paul has would also have to be admitted (see pp. 27-29). Yet part of the explanation for such a view of Luke is the polemical character of certain passages in Acts; the ignorance motif in Acts cannot be denied. Whether it emerges in the passion narrative is another matter, related to the questionable v. 34a of this chapter. But it is certainly an exaggeration to present such an understanding of Jesus' death as the sole way in which Luke understands it. (See further J.-D. Kaestli, *L'Eschatologie,* 86-91; I. H. Marshall, *Luke: Historian,* 170-175; A. George, "Le sens," 185-212; cf. pp. 219-221.)

Finally, it should be noted that the Lucan account of Jesus' death is no less soteriological in its description than is that of Mark or Matthew. Whatever there is of this aspect in the Matthean Gospel, it has to be found in the added verses (27:51bc,52,53); but one may really ask whether that is the intent of such additions as the mention of the earthquake, the opening of tombs, etc. These phenomena are intended to be symbolic, but there is much debate about the symbolism involved. The question is whether it is soteriological.

NOTES

23 44. *It was already about noon.* Lit. "about (the) sixth hour," i.e. of the day, which would mean halfway through the twelve-hour period of daylight. The time indication is derived from Mark 15:33a (cf. John 19:14), but Luke makes use of parataxis, against his normal practice (see p. 108), eliminating a Marcan gen. absol. (obviously because he will use one later in the sentence). He has also added *hōsei,* "about."

darkness began to hang over the whole land. Lit. "and darkness began to be over the whole land," i.e. Palestine, a detail derived from Mark 15:33. Cf. *Gos. Peter* 5:15, "Now it was midday and a darkness covered all Judea" (Hennecke-Schneemelcher, *NTApocrypha* 1. 184). The darkness should be understood as one of the cosmic phenomena often associated with the Day of Yahweh in the OT (Zeph 1:15; Joel 2:10; 3:3-4 [2:20-31E]; cf. M. Rese, *Alttestamentliche Motive,* 54). This and the following detail are scarcely to be understood as "photographic snapshots or on-the-spot reporting" (P. Benoit, *Passion and Resurrection,* 199). The n. *gē* is taken here as in 4:25; 21:23; Acts 7:3,33. For the expression *ginesthai epi,* see 1:65; 3:2; 4:25,36; 22:40; 24:22; Acts 5:5,11; 8:1; 10:10.

until three in the afternoon. Lit. "until (the) ninth hour," a detail derived from Mark 15:33, but which Luke has changed. Mark dates the cry of dereliction to the ninth hour, and shortly thereafter Jesus' last cry and death. But here in Luke (as in John 19) we do not learn at what hour Jesus dies; the span from noon to 3 P.M. tells of the darkness over the land. According to H. Conzelmann *(Theology,* 88), Jesus died "soon after the crucifixion."

45. *for the sunlight had failed.* Luke's added explanation of the darkness. Instead of the gen. absol. *(tou hēliou eklipontos),* many mss. (C³, A, D, R, W, Γ, Θ, Ψ, 0117, *f* 1,13, and the Koine text-tradition) read *kai eskotisthē ho hēlios,* "and the sun was darkened," but the gen. absol. is found in the best mss. (P⁷⁵, B, ℵ, C*, etc.) with *eklipontos* (aor.), or in some cases with *ekleipontos* (pres.), "for the sunlight was failing."

Some commentators (e.g. W. Manson, *Gospel of Luke,* 261) have tried to translate *eklipontos* as "was in eclipse." The vb. *ekleipein,* when used with the sun, can sometimes have that meaning. But it is usually considered an impossible meaning here, because it would imply an eclipse at Passover (full-moon time); so M.-J. Lagrange, *Luc,* 592. J. M. Creed *(The Gospel,* 288) thinks that Luke simply did not realize "the impossibility of a solar eclipse at the time of the Paschal full moon." It is this difficulty that probably led to the variant reading mentioned above, preferred by Origen *(Comm. in Matt.* ser. 134 [GCS 11.274]). However, it should be noted that Thucydides *(Hist.* 2.28) speaks of an eclipse of the sun at *noumēnia,* "new moon." The darkening of the sun is otherwise known in the Mediterranean area, as an effect of the *ḥamsîn* or searing sirocco. See G. R. Driver, "Two Problems in the New Testament," 331-335.

The darkness and the failure of the sun's light are intended as an ominous background to the death of Jesus. Their symbolism can be seen in a comment made in a letter of Mark Antony to Hyrcanus, the high priest and ethnarch of the Jews (42 B.C.), in which he tells how the battle waged by him to regain Asia was conducted against those "who were guilty both of lawless deeds against men and of unlawful acts against the gods, from which we believe the very sun turned away, as if it too were loath to look upon the foul deed against Caesar" (Josephus, *Ant.* 14.12,3 § 309).

the curtain in front of the sanctuary was torn in two. Lit. "the curtain of the sanctuary was torn (in the) middle." Jesus' death had a bearing not only on the whole land but particularly on Jerusalem's Temple. Luke transposes a verse from a later point in the Marcan scene (15:38) and modifies the wording; cp. the Matthean expansion (27:51-53); John's Gospel knows nothing of any of this. Indeed, the curtain is rent prior to the death of Jesus in Luke's story. In Luke 1:9,21,22 *naos* clearly means a sanctuary of the Jerusalem Temple, specifically, the "holy place" *(hagia,* cf. Heb 9:2). Luke has taken over the word *naos* from Mark, who used it in 14:58; 15:29 for the whole Temple.

Which veil is meant? In the Temple there hung thirteen veils or curtains *(pārōkôt).* The two main ones were the one at the entrance of the "holy place" (see Josephus, *J.W.* 5.5,4 § 212: "a veil . . . of Babylonian tapestry, with embroidery of blue and fine linen, of scarlet also and purple, wrought with marvellous skill. . . . It typified the universe" [cf. LXX Exod 26:36]) and one at the entrance of the "holy of holies" (ibid. 5.5,5 § 219: "screened in like manner from the outer portion by a veil" [cf. Heb 6:19; 9:3; 10:20]). Str-B 1. 1043-1045 thinks that it is impossible to say which of these two is meant. Older commentators in general merely assumed that the veil before the "holy of holies" was intended. So Thomas Aquinas *(Summa theologica* 1-2. 102, 4 ad 4); A. Plummer *(The Gospel,* 537); J. Schmid *(Mark,* 296); BAGD 416; E. E. Ellis *(Gospel of Luke,* 269). But others insist on the veil at the entrance to the "holy place": A. Pelletier ("Le 'voile' du temple de Jérusalem est-il devenu la portière du temple d'Olympie?" *Syria* 32 [1955] 289-307; 35 [1958] 218-226; "La tradition synoptique du 'voile déchiré' à la lumière des réalités archéologiques," *RSR* 46 [1958] 161-180); L.-H. Vincent *(Jérusalem de l'Ancien Testament* [Paris: Gabalda, 1956] 2. 468); P. Benoit *(Passion and Resurrection,* 201); G. R. Driver ("Two Problems," 335-336). This seems to be more likely. The rending of the Temple veil is mentioned also in *T. Benj.* 9:4 and *T. Levi* 10:3, but these are generally suspected of being Christian interpolations. See Str-B 1. 1044-1045; M. de Jonge, *Studies on the Testaments of the Twelve Patriarchs: Text and Interpretation* [SVTP 3; Leiden: Brill, 1975] 233-237).

H. Conzelmann *(TDNT* 7. 439) thinks that such details have been added to the account of Jesus' death "to stress the saving significance" of that death "by ref. to its eschatological and cosmic dimension." There might be some truth in this view, if it is applied to the Matthean account, but it is difficult to see any "saving significance" in the Lucan form. The darkness and the rending of the Temple veil may have an apocalyptic and cosmic dimension; but they should rather be related to the Lucan idea of evil's "hour" and "the power of darkness" (22:53), which reign as Jesus dies; they are signs of this domination.

46. *uttered a loud cry.* Lit. "having voiced with a great voice," see Acts 16:28; Rev 14:18. Having given the substance of Jesus' Aramaic cry of dereliction in 15:34, Mark omits the content of the final cry (v. 37); Luke, having omitted the former, now supplies the content of the latter.

Father. In this Gospel Jesus has already addressed God so (10:21 [see NOTE there]; 11:2; 22:42 [23:34a ?]); now the climax of that mode of filial prayer is reached.

into your hands I entrust my spirit. So the dying Jesus expresses his supreme human dedication. See p. 193. These words are a quotation of Ps 31:6 (31:5E), agreeing with the LXX form save for the pres. tense *paratithemai* instead of the fut. *parathēsomai,* which by scribal harmonization also enters the textual tradition of this verse (see mss. L, Δ, 0117, and the Koine text-tradition). The psalmist prays for deliverance from enemies, expressing his confidence in God. Stephen in Acts 7:59 will utter a similar act of resignation, addressed then to Jesus. By "spirit" would be meant the whole of the living person (so E. Schweizer, *Evangelium nach Lukas,* 240), as the parallel in Acts shows.

In the later rabbinical tradition Ps 31:6 was used as part of the evening prayer that a disciple should utter before going to sleep. See *b. Berak.* 5a; cf. Str-B 2. 269.

That Luke has taken over a prayer of early Christian liturgy and substituted it for the Aramaic cry of dereliction is a possible explanation; but it has not been clearly shown that Ps 31:6 was in pre-Lucan liturgical usage. For an attempt to show that Jesus' cry was really *'ēlî 'attāh,* "You are my God" (Ps 118:28), see T. Boman, "Das letzte Wort Jesu."

he breathed his last. Lit. "he expired," the vb. *exepneusen* is derived from Mark 15:37. The vb. *ekpnein* was used in both classical and Hellenistic Greek to mean "die." See Sophocles, *Ajax* 1026; cf. Josephus, *Ant.* 12.9,1 § 357. Matt 27:50 has *aphēken to pneuma,* "he gave up the spirit," whereas John 19:30 reads, "bowing his head he handed over the spirit *(or* the Spirit)," with typical Johannine ambiguity. See R. E. Brown, *John, XIII-XXI,* 931. None of the evangelists says simply that he "died" or "fell asleep"; from this detail Augustine argued for the *voluntary* character of Jesus' death (see *Tr. in Joh.* 19:30 [CCLat 36. 660])!

47. *The centurion.* Luke avoids the Latinism of Mark 15:39, *kentyriōn* (= "centurio"), using instead *hekatontarchēs* ("commander of a hundred"), which he had used in 7:2,6. The Gentile centurion represents the occupying power of Rome at the execution; but he is a mere subordinate, for Pilate is in the pretorium. Later legend *(Acts of Pilate* 11:2 [recens. B]) gives him the name "Longinus" (i.e. the soldier with the "spear" *[lonchē,* John 19:34]). See J. R. Michaels, "Centurion's Confession."

who saw this happen. Lit. "seeing what was going on," the phrase *to genomenon* may refer to the darkness (the Temple veil would scarcely be visible from the place called The Skull), but more likely in the Lucan story it refers to Jesus' words to the penitent criminal and then his prayer to the Father (vv. 43,46). In the Marcan parallel the centurion's comment follows on his noticing that Jesus "had breathed his last" (15:39), whereas in Matt 27:54 he sees "the earthquake and the things happening."

glorified God. I.e. as a good Jew or Christian would. Cf. 2:20; 5:25 (and NOTE there),26; 13:13; 17:15; 18:43; Acts 4:21; 11:18; 21:20.

Indeed, this man was innocent. The comment of the centurion in the Lucan story stands in striking contrast to that in Mark 15:39, "Truly this man was the Son of God." Luke has chosen not to follow Mark, but rather a tradition from "L." On the lips of the historical centurion, *dikaios* would have meant "innocent." This meaning is found in the LXX, where it translates Hebrew *nāqî*, "clean, guiltless" (Prov 6:17; Joel 4:19; Jonah 1:14). Cf. Matt 23:35; 27:19. See further E. J. Goodspeed, *Problems of New Testament Translation* (Chicago: University of Chicago, 1945) 90-91; G. D. Kilpatrick, "A Theme of the Lucan Passion Story"; but cf. R. P. C. Hanson, "Does *dikaios* in Luke xxiii.47 Explode the Proto-Luke Hypothesis?" *Hermathena* 60 (1942) 74-78. That suits the problem of Stage I of the gospel tradition, but at Stage III one can ask whether Luke may not have meant more, since Jesus is at times called the "Righteous One" in Lucan writings (Acts 3:14; 7:52; 22:14; cf. M.-J. Lagrange, *Luc,* 593). The centurion's reaction to Jesus joins those of Pilate (23:4,14-15,22), Herod (23:11), and the criminal (23:41).

48. *The crowds.* We are not told who made up these "crowds." See NOTE on 3:7. A curious parallel is found in 3 Macc 5:24: "The crowds in the city assembled for the piteous spectacle," as soon as the cock had crowed.

spectacle. Luke uses the n. *theōrian,* which also occurs in 3 Macc 5:24. Recall the description of the "people" in 23:35.

gazed at what happened. Lit. "contemplating the goings on," *ta genomena,* the pl. of the phrase used for the centurion in v. 47. See 24:12,18; Acts 13:12.

all returned home. Lit. "they returned," the vb. *hypostrephein* is being used absolutely, as in 2:20,43; 8:37,40; Acts 8:28.

At the end of v. 48 there are many variant readings in the ancient versions that heighten the poignancy of the Lucan summary; in general they depict Jerusalemites expressing woes on themselves and relating the destruction of Jerusalem to Jesus' death. See further *TCGNT* 182.

beating their breasts. In Luke 18:13 the gesture is a clear sign of guilt and contrition, as in Arrian, *Anab.* 7.24,3; cf. Josephus, *Ant.* 7.10,5 § 252, used of David's mourning for the death of Absalom. It could obviously be taken in the latter sense here, mourning for the death of Jesus. If it were meant in the former sense, then it would connote responsibility for what had happened.

49. *All Jesus' acquaintances.* Lit. "all those known to him" *(autō,* but some mss. [Ψ, C, D, R, W, Γ, Θ, Ψ, and the Koine text-tradition] read *autou,* "all his acquaintances"). See Luke 2:44 for a similar use of *gnōstoi.* In the Lucan Gospel the onlookers are not merely women, as in Mark 15:40-41, but male acquaintances too, not more specifically identified (either as "relatives" [cf. *syngeneis,* 14:12; 21:16], "brethren" *[adelphoi,* Acts 1:15], or "disciples" *[mathētai,* 6:13]). Since Luke has never recounted the flight of the disciples (contrast Mark 14:50; Matt 26:56), some of them at least must be presumed to be included in the "acquaintances."

the women who had come with him from Galilee. Lit. "who were following along with him." Instead of the pres. ptc. *synakolouthousai* some mss. (A, D, R, W, Θ, Ψ, 0177, and the Koine text-tradition) read the aor. ptc. *synakolouthēsasai,* probably with the nuance of "who had followed along with him." They are the women mentioned in

8:2-3: Mary called Magdalene, Joanna, wife of Chuza (Herod's steward), Susanna, and many others; in the light of 24:10 one would be inclined to include among the latter "Mary, the mother of James."

Galilee. See Notes on 4:14; 17:11. The women from Galilee are clearly distinguished from the "daughters of Jerusalem" (23:28).

stood at a distance, looking on. Actually the last role is played in the Greek text by the women alone, for the ptc. is fem., *horōsai,* "seeing." They are witnesses of Jesus' death; their function is not that of the idle crowds, "gazing at" *(theōrēsantes)* the spectacle (v. 48). The two vbs., *horan* and *theōrein,* are also used together in John 16:19.

It is sometimes queried whether there is an allusion in these words to Ps 38:12 ("my kinsmen stood at a distance") or to Ps 88:9 ("you have made my acquaintances distance themselves from me"). There may, indeed, be such allusion here, even though Luke derives part of his description from Mark 15:40a. Both psalms are prayers of personal lament and could suit the situation.

BIBLIOGRAPHY (23:44-49)

Abramowski, L., and A. E. Goodman. "Luke xxiii. 46 *Paratithemai* in a Rare Syriac Rendering," *NTS* 13 (1966-1967) 290-291.

Benoit, P. *Passion and Resurrection,* 181-204.

Bligh, J. "Christ's Death Cry," *HeyJ* 1 (1960) 142-146.

Boman, T. "Das letzte Wort Jesu," *ST* 17 (1963) 103-119.

Bratcher, R. G. "A Note on *huios theou* (Mark xv. 39)," *ExpTim* 68 (1956) 27-28.

Celada, B. "El velo del Templo," *CB* 15 (1958) 109-112.

Chronis, H. L. "The Torn Veil: Cultus and Christology in Mark 15:37-39," *JBL* 101 (1982) 97-114.

Conzelmann, H. "Historie und Theologie in den synoptischen Passionsberichten," in H. Conzelmann (ed.), *Zur Bedeutung,* 35-53.

Driver, G. R. "Two Problems in the New Testament," *JTS* 16 (1965) 327-337.

Harris, R. "The Origin of a Famous Lucan Gloss," *ExpTim* 35 (1923-1924) 7-10.

Jonge, M. de. "De berichten over het scheuren van het voorhangsel bij Jezus' dood in de synoptische evangeliën," *NedTT* 21 (1966-1967) 90-114.

——— "Het motief van het gescheurde voorhangsel van de tempel in een aantal vroegchristlijke geschriften," *NedTT* 21 (1966-1967) 257-276.

Kilpatrick, G. D. "A Theme of the Lucan Passion Story and Luke xxiii. 47," *JTS* 43 (1942) 34-36.

Lange, J. "Zur Ausgestaltung der Szene vom Sterben Jesu in den synoptischen Evangelien," *Biblische Randbemerkungen: Schülerfestschrift für Rudolf Schnackenburg zum 60. Geburtstag* (eds. H. Merklein and J. Lange; Würzburg: Echter-V., 1974) 40-55.

Légasse, S. "Les voiles du Temple de Jérusalem: Essai de parcours historique," *RB* 87 (1980) 560-589.

Léon-Dufour, X. "Le dernier cri de Jésus," *Études* 348 (1978) 667-682.

Lindeskog, G. "The Veil of the Temple," *In honorem A. Fridrichsen sexagenarii* *(ConNT* 11; Lund: Gleerup, 1947) 132-137.

Lindijer, C. H. "De tekenen bij Jezus' dood," *Homiletica en biblica* 25 (1966) 55-59.

Lowther Clarke, W. K. "St Luke and the Pseudepigrapha: Two Parallels," *JTS* 15 (1913-1914) 597-599.

Michaels, J. R. "The Centurion's Confession and the Spear Thrust," *CBQ* 29 (1967) 102-109.

Pobee, J. "The Cry of the Centurion—A Cry of Defeat," *The Trial of Jesus* (ed. E. Bammel) 91-102.

Rese, M. *Alttestamentliche Motive,* 200-202.

Sawyer, J. F. A. "Why Is a Solar Eclipse Mentioned in the Passion Narrative (Luke xxiii. 44-45)?" *JTS* 23 (1972) 124-128.

Taylor, V. "The Narrative of the Crucifixion," *NTS* 8 (1961-1962) 333-334.

Trilling, W. *Christusverkündigung,* 191-211.

Yates, T. "The Words from the Cross, VII: 'And When Jesus Had Cried with a Loud Voice, He said, Father into Thy Hands I Commend My Spirit (Luke xxiii. 46),' " *ExpTim* 41 (1929-1930) 427-429.

Bibliography on the Death of Jesus in the Lucan Gospel

Büchele, A. *Der Tod Jesu im Lukasevangelium: Eine redaktionsgeschichtliche Untersuchung zu Lk 23* (Frankfurter theologische Studien 26; Frankfurt am M.: Knecht, 1978).

Conzelmann, H., ed. *Zur Bedeutung des Todes Jesu: Exegetische Beiträge* (Gütersloh: G. Mohn, 1967).

Delling, G. *Der Kreuzestod Jesu in der urchristlichen Verkündigung* (Berlin: Evangelische Verlagsantalt, 1971) 75-97.

Dupont, J. *Le discours de Milet: Testament pastoral de Saint Paul (Actes 20, 18-36)* (LD 32; Paris: Cerf, 1962) 182-198.

Friedrich, G. *Die Verkündigung des Todes Jesu im Neuen Testament* (Biblisch-theologische Studien 6; Neukirchen-Vluyn: Neukirchener-V., 1982).

George, A. "Le sens de la mort de Jésus pour Luc," *RB* 80 (1973) 186-217; reprinted, *Etudes sur l'oeuvre de Luc* (SB; Paris: Gabalda, 1978) 185-212.

Hengel, M. *The Atonement: The Origins of the Doctrine in the New Testament* (Philadelphia: Fortress, 1981) 65-75.

Lohse, E. *Märtyrer und Gottesknecht: Untersuchungen zur christlichen Verkündigung vom Sühntod Jesu Christi* (Göttingen: Vandenhoeck & Ruprecht, 1955) 113-146.

Roloff, J. "Anfänge der soteriologischen Deutung des Todes Jesu (Mk. x. 45 und Lk. xxii. 27)," *NTS* 19 (1972-1973) 38-64.

Schneider, G. *Verleugnung,* 169-210.

Schürmann, H. *Jesu ureigener Tod* (Freiburg im B.: Herder, 1975) 56-63, 66-96.

Schütz, F. *Der leidende Christus: Die angefochtene Gemeinde und das Christuskerygma der lukanischen Schriften* (BWANT 89; Stuttgart: Kohlhammer, 1969).

Untergassmair, F. G. "Thesen zur Sinndeutung des Todes Jesu in der lukanischen Passionsgeschichte," *TGl* 70 (1980) 180-193.

Voss, G. *Die Christologie*, 99-130.

Zehnle, R. "The Salvific Character of Jesus' Death in Lucan Soteriology," *TS* 30 (1969) 420-444.

164. THE BURIAL OF JESUS
(23:50-56a)

23   50 Now there was a man named Joseph, a member of the Council, a good and upright man, 51 for he had not consented to their decision or their action. He was from the Jewish town of Arimathea and lived in expectation of the kingdom of God. 52 This man approached Pilate and asked him for the body of Jesus. 53 He took it down, wrapped it in a linen cloth, and laid it in a rock-cut tomb, where no one had yet been laid.

54 It was the day of Preparation, and the Sabbath was drawing near. 55 The women who had come with Jesus from Galilee followed along and noted the tomb and saw how his body had been placed. 56a Then they went back home and prepared spices and ointments.

COMMENT

The Lucan passion narrative ends with the episode of the burial of Jesus by Joseph of Arimathea (23:50-56a). Having requested permission from the Roman prefect, Pontius Pilate, Joseph takes Jesus' body down from the cross, wraps it in linen, and lays it in a newly cut tomb. Galilean women, who had followed him, took note of how Jesus had been buried, and went home to prepare burial spices and ointments for a return to the tomb after the Sabbath.

The episode is mainly a Lucan redaction of Mark 15:42-47 (cf. Matt 27:57-61). The earlier, possibly pre-Marcan forms of the account of Jesus' burial do not concern us here (see I. Broer, *Die Urgemeinde und das Grab Jesu;* R. Pesch, "Der Schluss"). Only vv. 53c,56a of the Lucan account may have to be traced to the source "L" (see p. 84). Otherwise, Luke has abridged the Marcan account, omitting such details as Joseph's courage (Mark 15:43), Pilate's checking on Jesus' death (15:44-45—as does Matt 27:58), Joseph's buying the linen cloth (15:46a), the closing of the tomb (15:46d), and the naming of the women (15:47—for which Luke substitutes a mere reference to the women "from Galilee," v. 55). Finally, Luke uses the Marcan detail about the day of Preparation and the coming Sabbath (15:42) later in the episode to situate not Joseph's actions, but those of the women (v. 54). Luke knows nothing of the posting of a guard at the tomb (cf. Matt 27:62-66).

Even V. Taylor *(Passion Narrative,* 99-103) agrees that in the Lucan account of the burial of Jesus (vv. 50-54) the "source is Mark, without any clear sign of a second source except a knowledge of Johannine tradition" (the latter being confined to v. 53c, "where no one had yet been laid"; see John 19:41). But Taylor would ascribe vv. 55-56a to a "non-Markan" source—never considering the possibility of Lucan composition for v. 55, which seems clear. W. Grundmann *(Evangelium nach Lukas,* 436) would attribute vv. 50,51a, 53b,54-56 to Luke's special source. That is certainly too much, since Lucan redaction of "Mk" accounts adequately for most of that.

Lucan redaction can be found in the following points: (1) *kai idou anēr,* "Now there was a man" (see p. 121; also 5:12,18; 9:30,38; 19:2; 24:4; Acts 1:10; 8:27; 10:17,19,30); (2) *onomati,* "by name" (see 10:38; 16:20; Acts 8:9; 9:33; 10:1; 16:1; cf. J. Jeremias, *Die Sprache,* 15); (3) the ptc. *hyparchōn,* "being," a favorite Lucan substitute for the vb. to be (ibid. 163); (4) *mnēmeion,* "tomb" (v. 55, in contrast to the Marcan word *mnēma* [disputed reading!] used in v. 53; see Luke 11:44,47; 24:2,9,12,22,24; cf. ibid. 207).

From a form-critical point of view, the episode is another Story about Jesus. Of Mark 15:42-47 R. Bultmann *(HST* 274) wrote: "This is an historical account which creates no impression of being a legend apart from the women who appear again as witnesses in v. 47, and vv. 44-45 [Pilate's checking on Jesus' death] which Matthew and Luke in all probability did not have in their Mark." (Bultmann thus reckons with Urmarkus as the "Mk.") Bultmann is also skeptical about the description of Joseph of Arimathea in both Matt 27:57 ("a rich man") and Luke 23:50-51 ("a good and upright man," not a party to the Sanhedrin's resolution). Yet both of these are redactional additions of the evangelists to the simple Marcan description.

In this Lucan scene the crucified and dead Jesus of Nazareth is accorded an honorable and reverent burial. Though associated with criminals in vv. 32,39, he is not given the treatment of executed criminals, who were often laid in a common grave. His body is not allowed to hang beyond sundown (cf. Deut 21:22-23, applied in the time of the Roman occupation of Palestine to crucified persons [see my article "Crucifixion," *TAG* 125-146, esp. 134-139]). Cf. Josephus, *Ag.Ap.* 2.29 § 211; Tob 1:17-18. Jesus is cared for not by his relatives or disciples but by devout Jewish people of Palestine, Joseph of Arimathea and women from Galilee. Joseph was identified in the Marcan story as a member of the Sanhedrin and *euschēmōn,* "prominent, highly respected," and Luke makes him a "good and upright man," one who "had not consented to their decision or their action" (v. 51), thus stressing not so much his social standing as his moral character. Like the pious Jerusalemites of the infancy narrative, he is depicted as one who "lived in expectation of the kingdom of God" (v. 51), a description that Luke derives from Mark 15:43. Such an upright Jew goes to the Roman prefect and requests permission to take Jesus' body down from the cross. Wrapping it in a linen cloth, Joseph lays Jesus' body in a previously unused rock-cut tomb. In this manner Jesus of Nazareth joins his human forebears in death, "gathered to his people" (see Gen 25:8; Ezek 32:22-27)—or so it seems.

Since it is already late on the day before the Sabbath (see p. 1379), the women from Galilee who had followed Joseph take note of how Jesus has been buried; they return home, planning to come with burial spices and ointments to give Jesus a more proper burial according to the usual customs of the Jews of the time—but after the Sabbath is over.

The "burial" of Jesus, which is recorded here in the Lucan Gospel (in dependence on "Mk"), was already part of the pre-Lucan and pre-Pauline primitive kerygma (see 1 Cor 15:4; cf. Acts 13:29). Luke will make much of it in the speech of Peter on Pentecost, the first feast of the Jews to occur after the Passover, which is now ending (Acts 2:29-31). To claim, as had been done in modern times, that Jesus' body was either left lying on the ground or thrown into a common grave for criminals is a preference for speculation that goes against the multiple attestation of NT witnesses about the burial (Synoptics, John, Paul). The posting of the guard at the tomb in Matt 27:62-66 is obviously apologetic, and the allusion to the burial of Christ made by Paul in Rom 6:3-4 is clearly theological, but those uses do not cast suspicion over the other testimonies.

The striking detail in the Lucan account is the notice in v. 53c, "where no one had yet been laid." This detail is known also to John (19:41); see pp. 87-89. It is a detail that sets off the burial of Jesus from that of common criminals; it is a grave that has been found worthy of Jesus, "the King of the Jews." It is provided by one who comes from (lit.) a town of the Jews (v. 51b). And the women from Galilee, who earlier were portrayed as "providing" for him (8:3) will now become those who serve him in another way, providing for his proper burial. Judea and Galilee surface as two parts of Jesus' homeland that have not entirely ignored or forgotten him. A certain irony runs through the Lucan account with its contrast of the town of the Jews and "the women . . . from Galilee"; it plays on the geographical perspective in the Lucan Gospel in its own way.

NOTES

23 50. *a man named Joseph.* Joseph of Arimathea is otherwise unknown; but in all four Gospels he is linked to the burial of Jesus, clearly a historical reminiscence being used. Who would invent him? It is sheer coincidence that "a man named Joseph" appears in the Lucan story of Jesus' birth (1:27) and his burial.

a member of the Council. Luke derives this description from Mark 15:43; these are the only places in the NT where this designation is used. In the Marcan and Lucan contexts, however, it cannot be understood as anything else but a reference to the Council (22:66: *synedrion).* Whether he was a chief priest, a Scribe, or an elder is impossible to say.

a good and upright man. This and the following phrase are Lucan additions to the description of Joseph, derived from Mark. Unlike Matt 27:57, Luke does not make a disciple of Joseph. The Lucan description makes him an upright and law-observing Jew. See J. Schreiber, "Die Bestattung Jesu." In *Gos. Peter* 2:3 (Hennecke-Schneemelcher, *NTApocrypha* 1. 183) he is described further as a "friend of Pilate and of the Lord." So the legend grows. He even asks for permission to bury Jesus *before* Jesus is crucified; and Pilate has to send to Herod and beg for the body, i.e. beg for it from him who earlier "commanded that the Lord should be marched off."

51. *had not consented to their decision or their action.* The "decision" may refer either to the plot of the chief priests and Temple officers with Judas (22:4-5) or to the sentence implied in the Council's assertion that no further testimony was needed (22:71). The "action" is the handing of Jesus over to Pilate (23:1). Luke adds this to explain how a member of the Council could now act as Joseph does, being solicitous for Jesus' burial. The vb. *synkatatithenai,* "agree with, consent," is also found in Exod 23:32.

from the Jewish town of Arimathea. Lit. "from Arimathea, a town of the Jews." The latter phrase is undoubtedly intended to identify the town as Judean, and not as one of the Decapolis, or of the Samaritans, or even of Galilee. That Joseph is so described may mean that he is now resident in Jerusalem, having once come from Arimathea. For the type of appositive used here, see 4:31 (perhaps also 8:26). The identification of the town echoes the title of Jesus as "the King of the Jews" (23:38).

Arimathea. The town *Arimathaia* has been identified with Ramathaim-zophim (1 Sam 1:1), Rathamin (1 Macc 11:34), and Ramathain (Josephus, *Ant.* 13.4,9 § 127), all considered as variants of the same place-name. It has been identified by Eusebius *(Onomas.* [GCS 144:28]) as Remphis or Remfthis, a place about ten miles northeast of Lydda (Lod) or ten miles southeast of Antipatris. For attempts to identify it with Ramallah, see W. F. Albright, "Excavations and Results at Tell el-Ful (Gibeah of Saul)," AASOR 4 (1922-1923) 112-115; or Beit Rimeh, see H. M. Wiener, "The Ramah of Samuel," *JPOS* 7 (1927) 109-111. See also F.-M. Abel, *Géographie de la Palestine* (2 vols.; EBib; 2d ed.; Paris: Gabalda, 1938) 2. 428-429; cf. M. du Buit, *Géographie de la Terre Sainte* (2 vols.; Paris: Cerf, 1958) 1. 220.

lived in expectation of the kingdom of God. Though the description of Joseph is pre-Lucan, being derived from Mark 15:43, it links Joseph in this Gospel with the pious eschatologically-minded Jews of Jerusalem in the infancy narrative, Simeon (2:25) and Anna (2:38). For an expectation of a manifestation of God's kingship among Jews of Palestine, see 1QM 6:6 ("Kingship shall belong to the God of Israel, and he shall display his power through the holy ones of his people" [probably an allusion to Obad 21]).

52. *approached Pilate.* The ptc. *proselthōn* implies that Joseph went to Pilate in the pretorium. According to the Lucan story, he goes *after* the death of Jesus.

the body of Jesus. Luke, in agreement with Mark 15:43 and Matt 27:58, uses *sōma* for "body"; contrast Mark 15:45, *ptōma*, "corpse." Cf. John 19:38,40. See NOTE on v. 50, about the request in the *Gospel of Peter.*

53. *He took it down.* Cf. Acts 13:29. No mention is made of the washing of the body; but that is included in the *Gos. Pet.* 6:21-24: "Then the Jews drew the nails from the hands of the Lord and laid him on the earth. And the whole earth shook, and there came a great fear. Then the sun shone <again>, and it was found to be the ninth hour. The Jews rejoiced and gave his body to Joseph that he might bury it, since he had seen all the good that he [Jesus] had done. He took the Lord, washed him, wrapped him in linen, and brought him into his own sepulchre, called Joseph's Garden" (Hennecke-Schneemelcher, *NTApocrypha* 1. 185).

wrapped it in a linen cloth. The Greek *sindōn* means "fine cloth," and was regularly used of fine linen cloth. In Mark 14:51-52 it designates the cloth/garment left behind by the young disciple of Jesus who fled naked from Gethsemane. Cf. the LXX of Judg 14:12-13; Prov 31:24. Here it is to be understood of a burial shroud, as in Mark 15:46 and Matt 27:60. Cf. B. P. Grenfell and A. S. Hunt, *New Classical Fragments, and Other Greek and Latin Papyri* (Oxford: Clarendon, 1897) 2. 77,27, where it has the same sense. Unfortunately, nothing is said of the shape of this linen burial cloth. See J. Blinzler, "Sindon in evangeliis," *VD* 34 (1956) 112-113.

Only the Synoptic tradition speaks of a *sindōn* as the wrapping of Jesus' body: "a linen cloth" (Mark, Luke), "a clean linen cloth" (Matthew). No mention is made here of a *soudarion,* "kerchief" (see NOTE on 19:20), or of the pl. *othonia,* "linen wrappings," which are the cloths mentioned in the Johannine tradition (19:40; 20:5-7 [see R. E. Brown, *John, XIII-XXI,* 942, 986]), much less of *keiriai,* "bandages," in which Lazarus is said to have been bound (John 11:44). In the episode of the women at the empty tomb, the first part of the Synoptic resurrection narrative, *othonia* are mentioned, but only in Luke 24:12, a verse with difficulties of its own. See p. 131 and NOTE on 24:12.

Moreover, only the Johannine tradition speaks of Jesus' body having been actually treated with "myrrh and aloes" or with "spices" (19:39-40), *before* the burial, as was customary in Jewish burials. In the Synoptics, however, the bringing of such materials to the tomb after the Sabbath is given as the reason why the women visit it (Mark 16:1; Luke 23:56-24:1). Again, only in the Johannine tradition is Jesus' side pierced with a lance so that "blood and water" flow forth from it (19:34). Since these Johannine details are not mentioned in the Synoptic tradition, which alone speaks of the *sindōn,* one should be wary of harmonizing such disparate data. The NT itself does not suggest that any trace of the spices, lance wound, or blood and water was associated with the *sindōn.* This has to be stressed in view of the following modern problem.

Santa Sindone di Torino is said to be the burial cloth of which the Synoptic tradition speaks. This linen cloth, roughly fourteen feet three and a half inches by three feet seven inches, was folded up for decades of its existence, with only the face on it visible; but it is now rolled on a staff and has been stored in a multilayered cask in the Duomo San Giovanni in Turin, since at least 1694. The cloth bears the frontal and dorsal images of a man who died a violent death, seemingly by crucifixion. It is sepia in color, with the "stains of blood" a deep burgundy or garnet. The wrists and feet seem to bear "nail marks," the left side of the chest a "lance wound," the head encircling "specks of blood," and the back and legs "wounds of a lashing." The eyes of the person seem to have been covered with coins.

The Shroud of Turin remains, however, of unproven antiquity. It first surfaced in history in A.D. 1357, when it was publicly displayed in the collegiate church of Lirey, France. From fourteenth-century bishops, who inveighed against the exposition and veneration of the shroud—"cunningly painted . . . by a clever sleight-of-hand" (Pierre d'Arcis, Bishop of Troyes, A.D. 1389), to twentieth-century scholars, historians, and scientists (Ulysse Chevalier, Herbert Thurston, Walter C. McCrone), it has been denounced as a fabrication (medieval or otherwise). Nonetheless, "scientific" investigators of varied backgrounds in this century (P. Barbet, P. Vignon, Y. Delage, The Shroud of Turin Research Project, Inc. [STURP], of Los Alamos, NM), clerical proponents (W. Bulst, P. M. Rinaldi, A. J. Otterbein, F. L. Filas), and pious associations (the American Holy Shroud Guild, the British Society for the Shroud of Turin) have argued for its antiquity—even for its authenticity. "Shreds of evidence" have been amassed by X-ray fluorescence analysis, infrared thermography, microphotography, computer-aided image enhancement, microanalysis of particles lifted from the cloth by sticky tape, pollen samples, tonal distortions in image photography, or by the discovery of the "negative image," of the three-dimensional character of the image, of the wrist (not palm) wounds, of the impressions of *lituus* coins minted by Pilate in A.D. 29. But such shreds of evidence remain just that, *shreds,* never enough, even cumulatively, to enable one to come to a positive conclusion.

The crucial test, dating by Carbon-14, has not yet been made! This is remarkable, since such a dating technique has been so developed and refined in recent years that a very small piece of the cloth (scarcely two inches square) would suffice to run the test —and there is plenty of it under the patches sewn on the burns that the image would not be damaged.

Even if that test were to be run and if the antiquity of the cloth were to be established, who could show that it wrapped the dead body of Jesus of Nazareth—and not that of some other crucified person of first-century Palestine?

Church authorities, from the Avignon Pope Clement VII, to whom Bishop d'Arcis first reported the "discovery" of the shroud, to Pope Paul VI ("L'ostensione televisiva della sacra sindone," *Insegnamenti di Paolo VI* 11 [1973] 1138-1140), have consistently hedged in encouraging belief in its authenticity. As a recent writer put it, ". . . the matter of the shroud's authenticity is one of those superficially trivial issues on which whole systems of belief converge. Some partisans have invested so much of themselves in the debate that, one suspects, were the decision to go against them, their entire world view would collapse . . ." (C. Murphy, "Shreds," 45). Belief in the authenticity of the Shroud of Turin is at best a tenet of *fringe Christianity.* It is hardly of the essence of Christian faith or even a norm of Christian dedication; it serves only to distract Christians, especially "fearful fundamentalists" (to use J. A. T. Robinson's term, *Can We Trust the New Testament?* [Grand Rapids, MI: Eerdmans, 1977] 16.), from what is essential. As Horace put it centuries ago, "Let . . . Apella believe it; I don't" *(Credat Iudaeus Apella, non ego, Serm.* 1.5,100). See further P. Benoit, *Passion and Resurrection,* 253-255.

laid it. Reading *auto,* "it," with mss. P⁷⁵, A, L, W, Γ, Δ, Θ, and the Koine text-tradition, instead of *auton,* "him," found in many other mss. (ℵ, B, C, D) and preferred by N-A²⁶ and *UBSGNT* ³.

in a rock-cut tomb. The adj. *laxeutos* is a hapax legomenon in the NT, but is found in the LXX of Deut 4:49. Tombs hewn out of rock, dating from the first century, are found in abundance in the area around Jerusalem. See J. Finegan, *Archeology,* 191-196; "Tombs," *Jerusalem Revealed: Archaeology in the Holy City 1968-1974* (ed. Y. Yadin; New Haven: Yale University, 1976) 63-74.

where no one had yet been laid. Luke adds to the Synoptic tradition a detail found in the Johannine (19:41). Only Matthew (and the *Gospel of Peter,* probably in dependence on Matthew) makes it explicit that the tomb was "new" *(kainon)* and Joseph's "own" *(autou).* According to the custom of the time, the body was so buried until the flesh decomposed. Later a "second burial" took place, when the bones were gathered and deposited in an ossuary.

Since the fourth century the tomb has been traditionally associated with a spot located at present within the Church of the Holy Sepulchre. See *ELS* 619-705; C. Coüasnon, *The Church* (p. 1503); K. M. Kenyon, *Jerusalem,* 146-154. On "Gordon's Tomb" or the so-called Garden Tomb, see L.-H. Vincent, "Garden Tomb," 401-431; J. Simons, *Jerusalem in the Old Testament,* 282-343, esp. 287-290. Cf. L. E. Cox Evans, "The Holy Sepulchre," *PEQ* 100 (1968) 112-136.

54. *the day of Preparation.* This phrase could mean either the day before the Sabbath or the day before the Passover; given the following cl., Luke means it in the former sense. See further v. 56b. Mark 15:42 had explicitly identified *paraskeuē* as *prosabbaton.* This is more of a problem in the Johannine story. See p. 1379.

the Sabbath was drawing near. Lit. "was beginning to dawn *(or* break forth)." The vb. *epiphōskein* cannot refer to the real "dawn" of the Sabbath day, but refers to the beginning of the Sabbath at sundown. E. Lohse *(TDNT* 7. 20 n. 159) refers the expression to the shining of the first star as the Sabbath comes. Others have referred it to the light of Venus or to the light of the Sabbath candles! See P. Benoit, *Passion and Resurrection,* 217. Note the reference to the beginning of the Sabbath in CD 10:14-17: "Let no one do work on the sixth day from the time when the orb of the sun is distant from the gate by its own fullness, for that is what it means, 'Guard the day of Sabbath to keep it holy.' "

55. *The women . . . from Galilee.* See NOTE on 23:49.

followed along. The vb. *katakolouthein* would mean lit. "follow down," but it is not to be pressed, as if it meant into some subterranean sepulcher. It should be understood merely as "followed after" Joseph (and his assistants). See Acts 16:17.

noted the tomb. Whereas in v. 53 Luke may use the Marcan word *mnēma,* he now uses his own term *mnēmeion* (see COMMENT on v. 55). This detail is found in all three Synoptics, and prepares for the story of the empty tomb.

saw how his body had been placed. In Mark 15:47 the stress is on "where" he had been laid, but in Luke it is on the "how," i.e. the insufficient washing and anointing. This prepares for v. 56.

56a. *prepared spices and ointments.* Or "aromatic oils/salves" and "perfumes" *(myra).* When the women could have done this, after what has been said in v. 54b, is a mystery; it may reveal something about Luke's understanding of Jewish practices. In Mark 16:1 the women go to buy the spices after the Sabbath. The details of such "preparation" are absent from Mark and Matthew and may have come to Luke from "L." Note the later Mishnaic regulation: "They may make ready [on the Sabbath] all that is needful for the dead, and anoint it and wash it . . ." *(m. Šabb.* 23:5). Would that have been permitted in pre-70 A.D. Jerusalem?

BIBLIOGRAPHY (23:50-56a)

Benoit, P. *Passion and Resurrection,* 205-230.

Blinzler, J. "Die Grablegung Christi in historischer Sicht," *Resurrexit* (ed. E. Dhanis) 56-107.

——— *Der Prozess Jesu* (3d ed.) 282-308.

Braun, F.-M. "La sépulture de Jésus," *RB* 45 (1936) 34-52, 184-200, 346-363.

Broer, I. *Die Urgemeinde und das Grab Jesu: Eine Analyse der Grablegungsgeschichte im Neuen Testament* (SANT 31; Munich: Kösel, 1972) 138-200.

Finegan, J. *Die Überlieferung,* 34-35.

Goulder, M. D. "Mark xvi. 1-8 and Parallels," *NTS* 24 (1977-1978) 235-240.

Heeren, A. van der. "In narrationem evangelicam de sepultura Christi," *Collationes brugenses* 19 (1914) 435-439.

Kenyon, K. M. *Jerusalem: Excavating 3000 Years of History* (London: Thames and Hudson; New York: McGraw-Hill, 1967) 146-154.

Mercurio, R. "A Baptismal Motif in the Gospel Narratives of the Burial," *CBQ* 21 (1959) 39-54.

Pesch, R. "Der Schluss der vormarkinischen Passionsgeschichte und des Markus-evangeliums: Mk 15,42—16,8," *L'Evangile selon Marc: Tradition et rédaction* (BETL 34; ed. M. Sabbe; Gembloux: Duculot, 1974) 365-409.

Schreiber, J. "Die Bestattung Jesu: Redaktionsgeschichtliche Beobachtungen zu Mk 15,42-47 par," *ZNW* 72 (1981) 141-177.

Simons, J. *Jerusalem in the Old Testament: Researches and Theories* (Leiden: Brill, 1952) 282-343.

Vincent, L.-H. "Garden Tomb: Histoire d'un mythe," *RB* 34 (1925) 401-431.

Winter, P. "Lucan Sources," *ExpTim* 68 (1957) 285.

Bibliography on the Shroud of Turin

Abbott, W. "Shroud, Holy," *Catholic Encyclopedia Suppl.* II, sect. 7 (vol. 18 [1957] unpaginated).

Barbet, P. *A Doctor at Calvary: The Passion of Our Lord Jesus Christ as Described by a Surgeon* (New York: Kenedy, 1953).

Baumgarten, P. M. "Das 'Grabtuch Christi' von Turin: Ein Bericht," *Historisches Jahrbuch* 24 (1903) 319-343.

Beecher, P. A. *The Holy Shroud: Reply to the Rev. Herbert Thurston, S.J.* (Dublin: Gill, 1928).

Bortin, V. "Science and the Shroud of Turin," *BA* 43 (1980) 109-117.

Bulst, W. *The Shroud of Turin* (Milwaukee: Bruce, 1957).

Chevalier, U. *Etude critique sur l'origine du saint suaire de Lirey-Chambéry-Turin* (Paris: A. Picard, 1900).

—— *Le S' Suaire de Lirey-Chambéry-Turin et les défenseurs de son authenticité* (Bibliothèque liturgique 5/3; Paris: A. Picard, 1902).

Cohn-Sherbok, D. "The Jewish Shroud of Turin? *ExpTim* 92 (1980) 13-16.

Culliton, B. J. "The Mystery of the Shroud of Turin Challenges 20th-Century Science," *Science* 201 (1978) 235-239.

Fossati, L. *Breve saggio critico di bibliografia e di informazione sulla sacra sindone: Dal primo congresso nazionale di studi (1939) al secondo congresso internazionale (1978)* (Turin: Bottega d'Erasmo, 1978).

Ghiberti, G. "Sepolchro, sepoltura e panni sepolcrali di Gesù: Reconsiderando i dati biblici relativi alla Sindone di Torino," *RivB* 27 (1979) 123-158.

Habermas, G. R. "The Shroud of Turin and Its Significance for Biblical Studies," *JETS* 24 (1981) 47-54.

Murphy, C. "Shreds of Evidence," *Harper's Magazine* 263 (November 1981) 42-65.

Pellicori, S., and M. S. Evans. "The Shroud of Turin through the Microscope," *Archaeology* 34/1 (1981) 34-43.

Robinson, J. A. T. "Re-investigating the Shroud of Turin," *Theology* 80 (1977) 193-197.

—— "The Holy Shroud in Scripture," *Tablet* (London) 232 (1978) 817-820.

Sox, H. D. "The Authenticity of the Turin Shroud," *Clergy Review* 63 (1978) 250-256.

Stevenson, K., ed. *Proceedings of the 1977 United States Conference of Research on The Shroud of Turin* (Bronx, NY: Holy Shroud Guild, 1977, reprinted, 1979; available from E. J. Jumper, The Shroud of Turin Research Project, Inc., 1700 Radcliffe Rd., Dayton, OH 45406).

Thurston, H. "The Holy Shroud and the Verdict of History," *The Month* 101 (1903) 17-29 [Engl. tr. of letter of Bishop d'Arcis to Pope Clement VII].

—— "The Holy Shroud as a Scientific Problem," *The Month* 101 (1903) 162-178.

—— "Shroud, The Holy," *Catholic Encyclopedia* 13 (1912) 762-763.

Vignon, P. *The Shroud of Christ* (Westminster [London]: Constable, 1902).

Walsh, J. *The Shroud* (New York: Random House, 1963).

Weaver, K. F. "Science Seeks to Solve . . . the Mystery of the Shroud," *National Geographic* 157 (1980) 730-752.

Wilcox, R. K. *Shroud* (New York: Macmillan, 1977).

Wild, R. A. "The Shroud of Turin," *Biblical Archaeology Review* 10 (1984) 30-46.

Wilson, I. *The Shroud of Turin: The Burial Cloth of Jesus Christ?* (Garden City, NY: Doubleday, 1978).

—— "Tomb to Turin: The Burial Shroud of Christ Jesus?" *Ampleforth Journal* 83 (1978) 9-23.

Wood, F. H. "Again the Turin Shroud," *ExpTim* 92 (1980-1981) 315-316.

VII. THE RESURRECTION
NARRATIVE

Why Do You Look for the Living among the Dead?
He Is Not Here, but Has Been Raised!

---

165. THE WOMEN AT THE EMPTY TOMB
(23:56b–24:12)

23 56b The women rested on the Sabbath in obedience to the commandment. 24 1 But on the first day of the week at the crack of dawn they came to the tomb, bringing the spices they had prepared. 2 They found the stone rolled back from the tomb, 3 and going inside they failed to find the body of the Lord Jesus. 4 While they were perplexed at this, suddenly two men in gleaming robes happened to stand by them. 5 The women were startled and bowed down to the ground. But the men addressed them: "Why do you look for the living among the dead? 6 He is not here, but has been raised! Remember what he told you while he was still in Galilee: 7 'The Son of Man must be handed over into the hands of sinful men and be crucified; and he must rise again on the third day!' " 8 Then they recalled his words. 9 They returned from the tomb and reported all this to the Eleven and all the others.

10 The women were Mary Magdalene, Joanna, and Mary, the mother of James; they and the others kept repeating these things to the apostles. 11 But their stories seemed to them to be so much nonsense, and they would not believe the women. 12 But Peter got up and ran to the tomb. He peered in and saw only the linen wrappings, and he went home, wondering about what had happened.

COMMENT

The seventh and final part of the Lucan Gospel is the resurrection narrative, the part in which Jesus' "departure" *(exodos,* 9:31) is completed, as he is "raised" (24:6), enters "his glory" (24:26), and is finally "parted from" his disciples and "carried up into heaven" (24:51). It is the climax of the Lucan Gospel as a whole and forms a transition to the Lucan second volume, the Acts of the Apostles. The centrality of Jerusalem appears, for it is the city in which Jesus' destiny is reached—from it he enters "his glory." It acts, more-over, as a focal point in the Lucan geographical perspective (see pp. 164-171), as it will become the place from which the word about him "must be preached to all the nations—beginning from Jerusalem" (24:47; cf. Acts 1:8). Furthermore, the resurrection narrative is the story of one day alone; all that is recounted here happens on this "first day of the week," slightly extended (v. 1; cf. vv. 13,33,36,44,50-51), resurrection, appearances, ascension.

This part of the Lucan Gospel coincides with the other three Gospels in beginning its account with the story of the women who visit the tomb and find it empty (23:56b-24:12; cf. Mark 16:1-8; Matt 28:1-8; John 20:1-13). But after that each Gospel goes its own way. This situation calls for some generic comments on the nature of a resurrection narrative, on the resurrection itself, and on the Lucan resurrection narrative as a whole prior to further consider-ation of this episode.

I. *A Resurrection Narrative.* Like the infancy narrative and the passion narrative, the resurrection narrative is a subform of the literary genre of gospel. It has not always been treated separately from the passion narrative (e.g. W. Bussman, *Synoptische Studien* [3 vols.; Halle an der S.: Waisenhaus, 1925-1931] 3. 180-192; and V. Taylor, *Passion Narrative,* 103-115, 130-132 treat it as a part or an appendage of the passion narrative). Yet, given the diversity of the gospel tradition found here, it deserves separate treatment. Moreover, one may ask whether this part of the gospel tradition is as primi-tive or as old as that of the passion narrative. Some fragments of the primitive pre-Pauline kerygma ("of Jerusalem origin," H. Conzelmann *[RGG* 1. 699]) embedded in NT writings include not only the mention of Jesus' resurrection (e.g. 1 Thess 1:10; 1 Cor 15:4; Rom 4:24-25; 10:8-9), but also appearances of the risen Christ (e.g. 1 Cor 15:5-7) so that the *basic content* of the resurrection narrative must have been part of that early proclamation ("Christ died . . . was buried . . . has been raised . . . and appeared . . ."); it also has *a character just as primitive* as the basic content of the passion narrative. This must be stressed, even if one realizes that the formulation of the individual accounts in the resurrection narrative comes possibly from a later time in the tradition.

Moreover, there is also a pre-Pauline tradition that refers to the *exaltation* of Jesus to heavenly status as a sequel to his death on the cross, but without any mention of the resurrection (see Phil 2:8-11). Compare too the ambiguous expressions about Jesus being "lifted up" in the Johannine tradition, where one wonders whether it refers to his being lifted up on the cross or to heavenly glory or to both (John 3:14; 8:28; 12:32,34 [see R. E. Brown, *John, I-XII,* 145-146]). Similarly, the transit from the sacrifice of the cross to the heavenly sanctuary in Heb 9:12,24-26. Such passages do not deny the resurrection, much less contradict it; but they may reflect an earlier mode of speaking about Christ's exaltation without reference to the resurrection.

None of the four Gospels tries to recount the resurrection itself, as the *Gospel of Peter* (§ 35-42) does, or as Luke does for the ascension (Acts 1:9-11), yet both the Synoptics and the Johannine Gospels have an account of the finding of the empty tomb, which in the Synoptic tradition also enshrines the fundamental *praeconium paschale,* "Easter proclamation." It is impossible to say when or how this tradition about the empty tomb emerged. Certain accretions to it in the Matthean Gospel, affecting not only the end of the passion narrative (the posting of the guard, 27:62-66), but the resurrection narrative as well (the fright of the guards, 28:4; the bribing of them by the chief priests and elders, 28:11-15), are clearly of later origin, apologetic in character, and designed to answer the charge that the tomb was empty because disciples came by night and stole Jesus' body. Such a development within the gospel tradition cannot be used to label the basic tradition about the empty tomb and its related *praeconium paschale* as apologetic. It is, moreover, sometimes argued that the empty tomb formed no part of the primitive kerygma and is actually passed over in 1 Cor 15:3-5: Yet the parallelism of that bit of early kerygmatic preaching alerts us to its stylized formulation; the fourfold use of *hoti* to introduce the vbs., *"that* Christ died . . . *that* he was buried . . . *that* he has been raised . . . *that* he appeared to Cephas . . ." emphasizes the parallelism of the traditional formula (even if one agrees with J. Murphy-O'Connor ["Tradition and Redaction in 1 Cor 15:3-7," *CBQ* 43 (1981) 582-589] that the last three instances of *kai hoti* were added by Paul to sharpen the formulation, the parallelism is still there). And to that stylized parallelism the mention of the empty tomb may have been sacrificed. Note too the parallel with the formulation in Acts 13:28-31 (death, burial, resurrection, appearances). The formulaic character of the proclamation was clearly of greater importance than the inclusion of all the details. Even if the formulation of the *narrative account* of the discovery of the empty tomb came about later than the kerygmatic tradition, does such later formulation exclude factuality? (See further R. H. Stein, "Was the Tomb Really Empty?" *JETS* 20 [1977] 23-29.)

Apart from the story of the empty tomb (and its *praeconium paschale* in the Synoptic tradition), however, the lack of concord in the resurrection narratives of the Gospels is noteworthy. Indeed, it is strikingly in contrast with the agreement of the foregoing passion narratives. That agreement was explained (see p. 1361) as having emerged from a need for a continuous or connected account of how and why Jesus' life ended as it did (the *Schuldfrage*). The need for a *continuous story* of the appearances of the risen Christ neither emerged nor could have been seen as crucial. As V. Taylor *(FGT* 59-60) once put it:

> Here the immediate need was assurance about a new and astounding fact. Was it true that Jesus had risen and had appeared to His own? To satisfy this clamant need single stories were enough; there was no demand for a continuous Story such as the modern man desires. Testimony, witness-bearing to the fact of the Appearances, was the first essential for preachers and hearers alike. We can understand therefore that different cycles of stories would become current at various centres of Palestinian and Syrian Christianity, but that there would be no continuous account which traced the succession of events from the Tomb to the final parting of Jesus from His disciples.

This explains further why one cannot put the stories of the appearances of the risen Christ in parallel columns in a synopsis. (In this regard there is a certain similarity between these isolated scenes and the scenes in the infancy narratives of the Lucan and Matthean Gospels—clearly with different reasons to explain this similarity.)

The diversity of this part of the gospel tradition is clear when one reckons with the six forms which it takes (or with six resurrection narratives):

1) *Mark 16:1-8*, the conclusion of the Marcan Gospel in the best Greek mss. of that Gospel (א, B, 304) and some ancient versions. Verses 1-8 report the discovery of the empty tomb at sunrise on the first day of the week by women (Mary Magdalene; Mary, the mother of James; and Salome), who came to anoint Jesus' body with aromatic spices; the *praeconium paschale* is made to them by a young man sitting at the right of the tomb, and he charges them to go and tell the disciples and Peter that Jesus goes before them to Galilee, where they will see him; the women flee and say nothing to anyone "for they were afraid." (There is no description of the resurrection, and no appearances of the risen Christ.)

2) *Matt 28:1-20*, the conclusion of the Matthean Gospel. Verses 1-8 report the discovery of the empty tomb by the women (Mary Magdalene and the other Mary) at dawn on the first day of the week; the *praeconium paschale* is made to them by the angel of the Lord who had descended from heaven to roll back the stone; he further charges the women to go and tell the disciples that Jesus has been raised and goes before them to Galilee. With fear and great joy they run to break the news, but in vv. 9-10 Jesus appears to them en route to repeat the angel's charge. Verses 11-15 report the bribery of the guard, and vv. 16-20 the appearance of the risen Christ to the Eleven in Galilee, as he commissions them to make other disciples, to teach, and to

baptize. (Again, no description of the resurrection; appearances of Christ in Jerusalem and in Galilee; no withdrawal of the risen Christ [e.g. by ascension].)

3) *Luke 23:56b-24:53,* the conclusion of the Lucan Gospel, with five episodes: (a) The finding of the empty tomb by the women (Mary Magdalene; Mary, the mother of James; Joanna, and others) at the crack of dawn on the first day of the week (23:56b-24:12); the *praeconium paschale* is announced to them by two men in gleaming robes suddenly standing by them. These persons charge the women to recall the words that Jesus had addressed to them while he was still in Galilee; the women leave and report it all to the Eleven, who regard their stories as so much nonsense. Peter alone goes off to see for himself (and to him Christ appears first, as one learns in v. 34). (b) The risen Christ appears to disciples walking to Emmaus; they return to make known what they had experienced (vv. 13-35). (c) Christ appears to the Eleven and their companions in Jerusalem (vv. 36-43). (d) These he commissions to be "witnesses of this" and to preach in his name (vv. 44-49); and finally (e) he leads them out to Bethany, where he is parted from them and carried off to heaven on Easter Sunday night (vv. 50-53). (Again, no description of the resurrection; appearances only in Jerusalem and its vicinity; his parting from them by ascension.)

4) *John 20:1-29,* the real conclusion of the Johannine Gospel. Verses 1-10 give an elaborate account of the finding of the empty tomb by Mary Magdalene, who tells Simon Peter and the Beloved Disciple; the appearance of the risen Christ to Mary, to whom he speaks of ascending (vv. 11-18); his appearance to disciples in Jerusalem on Easter Sunday evening, with Thomas absent (vv. 19-23); and his appearance a week later, with Thomas present (vv. 24-29). (Again, no description of the resurrection; three appearances of the risen Christ, all in Jerusalem; no mention of his withdrawal.)

5) *John 21:1-23,* the appendix to the Johannine Gospel (added by redactors?). The risen Christ appears to seven disciples who have gone fishing at the Sea of Tiberias (vv. 1-14), after which Simon Peter is commissioned to feed Christ's sheep, and the contrasting roles of Peter and the Beloved Disciple are set forth (vv. 15-23). (No reference to the resurrection or empty tomb; one protracted appearance of Christ in Galilee.)

6) *Mark 16:9-20,* the Marcan appendix, added—to the original ending of Mark (16:1-8)? or to a form of the Marcan Gospel with its ending lost? It is found only in some mss. of Mark (A, C, D, L, W, Γ, Δ, Θ, Ψ, $f^{1,13}$, and the Koine text-tradition), with an expanded form of v. 8 (in mss. L, Ψ, 099, 0112) or with the so-called Freer Logion, added to v. 14 (in ms. W). Verses 9-20 are not of Marcan authorship (but considered as part of canonical Mark by Roman Catholics). They make up for the lack of appearances of the risen Christ in Mark 16:1-8; three appearances in the Jerusalem area on the first day of the week: the first to Mary Magdalene (vv. 9-11); the second to two

disciples walking into the country, who go back and report it to disbelieving disciples (vv. 12-13); and then to the Eleven, whom he upbraids for disbelief and finally commissions to preach the gospel to all creation (vv. 14-18). Finally, after Christ has finished speaking, he is taken up into heaven and seated on the right hand of God and the disciples go forth to preach (vv. 19-20). (No reference to the resurrection or empty tomb; three appearances in the Jerusalem area; ascension on the night following the first day of the week.) (See further the chart of the variant Gospel narratives of the post-resurrectional appearances in R. E. Brown, *John, XIII-XXI,* 968.)

Apart from the empty tomb (and the *praeconium paschale* in the Synoptics), the only parallels to be noted are these: (a) the appearance of Christ to disciples on the road to Emmaus (Luke 24:13-25) and vv. 12-13 of the Marcan appendix; and (b) the ascension of Christ (Luke 24:50-51) and v. 19 of the Marcan appendix. Though undoubtedly of independent origin, they both reflect a later development in the tradition of the resurrection narrative.

The *praeconium paschale,* the essential Easter proclamation in the Synoptics, takes, moreover, three different forms, even though the substance is found in each:

a) Mark 16:6:   *Mē ekthambeisthe. Iēsoun zēteite ton Nazarēnon ton estaurōmenon. ēgerthē. ouk estin hōde.*

           Do not be alarmed. You are looking for Jesus the Nazarene, the one crucified. He has been raised! He is not here!

b) Matt 28:5:   *Mē phobeisthe hymeis, oida gar hoti Iēsoun ton estaurōmenon zēteite. ouk estin hōde, ēgerthē gar kathōs eipen.*

           Do not fear, for I know that you are looking for Jesus, the one crucified. He is not here; for he has been raised, as he said!

c) Luke 24:5-6:   *Tí zēteite ton zōnta meta tōn nekrōn; ouk estin hōde, alla ēgerthē.*

           Why do you look for the living among the dead? He is not here, but has been raised!

II. *The Resurrection.* Before proceeding to the detailed discussion of the Lucan resurrection narrative, I have to add a few lines about the way the NT itself speaks of the resurrection of Jesus. This topic has been touched upon briefly on pp. 193-194; but further detail is now called for. In Acts 1:22, in the episode in which Matthias is selected to take Judas' place among the Twelve, one of the criteria for membership is given as one who has been "a witness to the resurrection." Yet from what we have just seen, neither Luke nor any of the other evangelists has depicted anyone *witnessing the resurrection,* i.e. visibly perceiving God's act of raising the dead Jesus. For no one witnessed it, and that is not implied even in Matt 28:2b, where the angel of the Lord descends from heaven and rolls back the stone from before the tomb's entrance, a detail unique to the Matthean Gospel. In Acts Luke's meaning is clear: someone must take Judas' place that the Twelve be reconstituted, but someone who has been a "witness" *to the risen Christ.* However, he states the matter abstractly because he is listing criteria for membership. (See further Acts 4:33, *to martyrion . . . tēs anastaseōs tou kyriou Iēsou,* apostles giving "testimony about the resurrection of the Lord Jesus".)

What the writers of the NT have not recounted apropos of the resurrection, the apocryphal gospel tradition will supply. See *Gos. Pet.* § 35-42:

> 35 Now in the night in which the Lord's day dawned, when the soldiers were keeping guard, two by two in every watch, there rang out a loud voice in heaven. 36 They saw the heavens opened, and two men came down from there in great brightness and drew near to the sepulchre. 37 That stone which had been laid against the entrance to the sepulchre started to roll of itself and gave way to the side, and the sepulchre was opened, and both the young men entered in. 38 When then these soldiers saw this, they woke up the centurion and the elders—for they also were there to assist at the watch. 39 And while they were relating what they had seen, they again saw three men come out of the sepulchre, and two of them sustaining the other, and a cross following them. 40 They saw the heads of the two reaching to heaven, but that of him who was led by them by the hand surpassing the heavens. 41 Then they heard a voice crying out of the heavens, "Hast thou preached to them that sleep?" 42 And from the cross there was heard the answer, "Yes." (Cf. Hennecke-Schneemelcher, *NTApocrypha* 1. 185-186.)

This description of the resurrection clearly represents an effort to answer later queries about how it happened, *pace* H. Koester, "Apocryphal and Canonical Gospels," *HTR* 73 (1980) 105-130. It is a development beyond the Matthean additions to the story of the empty tomb, but undoubtedly of the same generic character.

Though Luke eventually puts an interval between Jesus' resurrection (on Easter Sunday morning) and his ascension (some forty days later, Acts 1:3— but cf. Acts 13:31, simply "for many days" *[hēmeras pleious]),* he never portrays the risen Christ as inhabiting the earth or appearing like someone who was ensconced behind an arras. Though Luke depicts Christ walking along the road with the disciples going to Emmaus (24:15), he tells us that when Christ is finally recognized, he vanishes from their sight. Indeed, Luke strives explicitly (24:37-39) to dispel the idea that Christ was like a spook or a ghost, insisting on the reality of his risen person, portraying him eating broiled fish, and stressing that his body experienced no decay (Acts 2:27; 13:35,37).

No NT writer, moreover, ever depicts the resurrection of Jesus as if it were a mere resuscitation or a return to a former mode of natural, terrestrial existence (like the resuscitated son of the widow of Nain [Luke 7:15] or Jairus' daughter [8:54-55], or even like Lazarus [John 11:43-44; 12:1-2]). Luke, in particular, insists that the risen Christ, who walks with the disciples to Emmaus, has already entered "his glory" (24:26: "Was not the Messiah bound to suffer all this before entering into his glory?"), said by the one who, when finally recognized by the disciples at Emmaus, *vanished from their sight!* Whither? Clearly, to "his glory"! In other words, it is from "glory," i.e. from his Father's presence, that the risen Christ appears to his disciples, not only in the interval before his "ascension" but in that appearance too, the "ascension" itself, which is nothing more than the appearance from glory in which he takes his final (visible) leave from his assembled followers.

The primitive kerygma, which affirmed Jesus' resurrection from the dead, was formulated in Palestine and in a culture which would have scarcely been able to conceive of it as anything but a "bodily" resurrection. It thus emerged in a milieu that was not yet fully dominated by the Greek philosophical dichotomy of body and soul or the doctrine of the immortality of the soul. (Recall what was said about *sōma* in NOTE on 22:19.) The latter idea is known in the Book of Wisdom (3:4; 4:1, etc.), but that is of Alexandrian Jewish provenience. The matrix of the kerygma was one that reckoned with "resurrection" (see Dan 12:2; recall that Luke will depict Paul exploiting that belief in Acts 23:6-8). Yet even such a belief had to reckon with a difference between the earthly body and the risen body, even as several indications in the NT itself reveal apropos of the risen Christ himself. Luke 24:16 portrays the disciples en route to Emmaus failing to recognize Christ initially. If that is related to Mark 16:12, we learn why they failed: "He was made manifest in another form *(en hetera morphē)* to two of them." Similarly, Mary Magdalene had trouble recognizing the risen Christ at first (John 20:14-16). However this is to be explained, one has to recall the admission that Paul makes in 1 Cor 15:42-44 about the difference between a "physical body" *(sōma psychikon),* which is sown as perishable, with dishonor, and with weakness, and a "spiritual body" *(sōma pneumatikon),* which is raised as imperishable, with glory, and with power. When Paul brings himself to say something about the risen body, he indulges in oxymoron and identifies the one and the same "body" with all that is not body, viz. with spirit. Though he may know as little as anyone else about the constitution of the risen body, Paul is struggling, perhaps not too successfully, to preserve the reality of it. As H. Conzelmann has put it, "A differentiation according to body and soul is far removed" from the NT thinking on the subject *(RGG* 1. 699).

The early Christian kerygma, which finds a dramatic formulation in the first episode of each of the four canonical resurrection narratives, was scarcely content to affirm merely that Jesus was alive (the Lucan form says that [v. 5], but it goes on!) or that he had become only a living influence in the lives or minds of his disciples and followers. It included indeed the affirmation that he had been "raised" to the state of glory in the presence of the Father, and it meant thereby "in bodily form" (without explaining it further). (See further W. L. Craig, "The Bodily Resurrection of Jesus," *Gospel Perspectives* [eds. R. T. France and D. Wenham] 1. 47-74.)

The "resurrection" of Christ is called in question in modern times because of attempts to square it with the dichotomy of body and soul inherited from Greek philosophy and common to all modern Western thought. Or it is called in question because of other philosophical difficulties that people have with the idea, born of scientific objections or of modern sophisticated (post-Enlightenment) ways of regarding human existence. But it should be recalled that the NT writers who formulated the resurrection narratives and incorporated the primitive kerygma about the resurrection were scarcely trying to cope with this sort of thinking. Denials of the "resurrection" were current already in Paul's time (as 1 Corinthians 15 attests), but not even he was trying to cope with the modern problems; and it is somewhat anachronistic to expect theologians to answer such problems on the basis of the first-century texts themselves. Luke too sought to cope with the manifestation of doubt about the resurrection, but he does it in a less philosophical way than Paul (see 24:41-43; Acts 1:3a; 10:41).

III. *The Lucan Resurrection Narrative.* The episodes that comprise the Lucan resurrection narrative have been set forth above (see pp. 1535-1537). One needs to note now that it includes no account of any appearance of Christ in Galilee. The only reference to that area is found in v. 6, where the two men in gleaming robes tell the women, not that Jesus goes before them and the disciples to Galilee, as in Mark 16:7, but that they should recall what he had told them when he was with them in Galilee. Thus the mention of Galilee is preserved, but it serves a different function. Having come from Galilee to Jerusalem, Jesus does not return there in the Lucan story, for the geographical perspective takes over. Jerusalem will become the focal point for the rest of the chapter and then function in an important way at the beginning of Acts (especially in its programmatic verse, 1:8). Luke undoubtedly knew of the appearances of Christ in other areas; but he has chosen to eliminate them in the interest of his overarching literary perspective.

The Lucan resurrection narrative will end with the mention of the disciples spending their time in the Temple of Jerusalem, "constantly praising God" (24:53), thus bringing the Gospel to a close in the area in which it began. For the first episode dealt with Zechariah's service in the Jerusalem Temple (1:5-24), during which the birth of John the Baptist was announced.

One should also note in this chapter how the Lucan resurrection narrative is marked by the motif of the fulfillment of OT prophecy and of Jewish hopes. Note in particular vv. 19b-21,25-27,44-46. Proof from prophecy will serve to emphasize the continuity of Christianity with Judaism of old, for in this way Israel will be reconstituted.

Finally, one should attend to the contrast that runs through the chapter: the *praeconium paschale* or the proofs of the resurrection of Jesus are confronted throughout by human incredulity and lack of perception. Luke has not depicted the disciples of Jesus fleeing and deserting him at his passion; but he has not played down their obtuseness at his resurrection.

Comment on 23:56b-24:12. In the first episode of the resurrection narrative, the story of the visit of the women to the empty tomb, Luke not only follows the Marcan order, but presents a redacted form of Mark 16:1-8 in vv. 1-9. Verse 56b, about the women resting on the Sabbath, may come to Luke from "L," as does 24:12; but this last verse has been worked by Luke into what F. Neirynck ("The Uncorrected Historic Present in Lk. xxiv. 12," 549, following J. Muddiman) has called a "parenthetic unit," composed by Luke on the basis of Mark 16:1a and some earlier tradition. Mark 16:7 had singled out Peter alongside of "his disciples," and Luke 24:34 ("he has appeared to Simon" [cf. 1 Cor 15:5]) shows that he was aware of an old tradition that told of the visit not only of women to the empty tomb, but also of Peter (and perhaps some other disciple[s]—see 24:24 *[tines,* "some of our own number"]). This unit ends with v. 12, which has striking affinity to John 20: 3,4,5,6,10, and which has been derived from a source common to Luke and John.

This seems to be the view of the majority of present-day interpreters of this passage: thus, with some variations, R. Bultmann, *HST* 287; J. Finegan, *Überlieferung,* 86-87; P. Schubert, "The Structure," 167; H. Grass, *Ostergeschehen und Osterberichte,* 32-35; G. Schneider, *Evangelium nach Lukas,* 490-492; R. J. Dillon, *From Eye-Witnesses,* 1 (esp. n. 1). However, a small group of interpreters prefer to think that Luke uses here an independent narrative derived from a non-Marcan source, which would have been similar to Mark 16:1-8 and into which some Marcan details have been inserted: so, with variations, V. Taylor, *Passion Narrative,* 103-109; W. Grundmann, *Evangelium nach Lukas,* 439; I. H. Marshall, *Luke,* 882-883. *Pace* M. D. Goulder, "Mark xvi. 1-8 and Parallels," *NTS* 24 (1977-1978) 235-240, Luke did not use Matthew.

The main differences in the Lucan account are the resting of the women on the Sabbath (presupposed but not mentioned in "Mk"), the lack of concern about who will roll the stone back, the explicit notice that the women did not find the body of Jesus, the mention of "two men" instead of a young man, the reformulation of the message addressed to the women, the delayed mention of the names of the women, and Peter's verification of the empty tomb.

Some of the minutiae of Lucan redaction can be seen in the following points: (1) "at the crack of dawn" (24:1; see 24:22; 21:38; Acts 5:21); (2) the mention of the "prepared" *arōmata* (24:1b; see 23:56a); (3) "failed to find" (24:3; see J. Jeremias, *Die Sprache,* 82 and n. 10); (4) the *kai egeneto* construction (24:4; see p. 119 [with *kai idou,* p. 121]); (5) the gen. absol. with a form of *genomenos* (24:5; see J. Jeremias, ibid. 311); (6) *eipen/elegon pros* + acc. (24:5,10; see p. 116); (7) reference to Jesus' words in Galilee (24:6-8; see 9:22,44); (8) the rhetorical hyperbole involving "all" (24:9 bis); (9) the mention of "the Eleven" (see 24:33; Acts 1:26; 2:14 [otherwise only in Matt 28:16]); (10) "got up" *(anastas,* 24:12 [see p. 114]); (11) *thaumazōn* + acc., "wondering at" (24:12; see p. 110); (12) "what had happened" *(to gegonos,* 24:12; see 8:34,35,36; Acts 4:21; 5:7; 13:12). (See further the comparative chart in R. E. Brown, *John, XIII-XXI,* 974.)

Verse 12 creates a special problem in this episode. Since it is absent in ms. D and some mss. of the OL version (for the details, see F. Neirynck, "Lc. xxiv 12"), it was judged by Westcott and Hort to be a "Western Non-Interpolation" (see pp. 130-131), and their influence affected a large number of modern scholars until recently (e.g. the *NEB;* J. M. Creed, *The Gospel,* 294; R. E. Brown, *John, XIII-XXI,* 969, 1000 [added to the Lucan text by a redactor!]). Moreover, since it has such verbal similarities with John 20, this seems to compound the problem. Thus, in v. 12 *ho Petros,* "Peter," is used (but in v. 34 "Simon")—cf. John 20:3; *to mnēmeion,* "the tomb"—cf. John 20:3; "ran"— cf. John 20:4; *parapkypsas blepei,* "peered in and saw" (in the same historic pres.)—cf. John 20:5; *ta othonia,* "linen wrappings" (but *sindōn* is used in 23:53)—cf. John 20:5; *apēlthen pros,* "he went home"—cf. John 20:10. (See K. P. G. Curtis, "Linguistic Support.") These phrases in v. 12 have been labeled "Johannisms." But, in reality, they argue for nothing more than dependence on a common source for both Luke and John, as many writers have more recently recognized. Along with vv. 3b,6a, v. 12 has to be regarded as part of the original text of the Lucan Gospel. Luke has thus combined with what he had redacted from Mark 16:1-8 a bit of another tradition about others visiting the empty tomb besides the women.

Form-critically considered, the episode would have to be regarded as another Story about Jesus, even if he appears in it only by implication; it is part of the narrative gospel tradition. R. Bultmann *(HST* 284-285) rightly sensed that Mark 16:1-8 originally did not follow on Mark 15, for the women (already named in 15:40,47) would not have been named again at the beginning of it. Moreover, their intention to anoint the body of Jesus ill accords with 15:46, which scarcely hints that those present considered the burial to be "incomplete or provisional." Luke, however, in reworking "Mk," has eliminated some of that inconsistency by identifying the women only later (v. 10, which becomes a combination of Mark 16:1 and his own reference to the women in 8:2).

The heart of the scene is the *praeconium paschale* in v. 6a: "He is not here, but has been raised!" At the beginning of the episode Luke depicts the Galilean women, having prepared the spices and ointments, resting on the Sabbath "in obedience to the commandment" (v. 56b). Thus the proclamation is made first to pious, observant Jewish women, who happen to be followers of Jesus. They now come dutifully to the tomb to do for Jesus' body what Joseph of Arimathea had not had time for (recall 23:55d, *"how* his body had been placed"). They find the tomb, but fail to find his body there. Then they are charged by two men in gleaming robes who proclaim Jesus' resurrection: "Remember what he told you while he was still in Galilee." Only in the

Lucan resurrection narrative is reference thus made to the predictions of Jesus' death and resurrection. Having recalled his words, the women carry the report back to the Eleven and others, who fail to give it credence.

The testimony about the resurrection—which will become an important issue in the rest of the chapter and in Acts—is thus first made to women of Galilee. Yet their testimony does not engender faith; it does not give "assurance" *(asphaleia)*. The Lucan story even singles out the "apostles" as the ones who discredit the report. Their faith will have to depend on their own seeing (see Acts 1:22). Peter alone of them is aroused, but only to curiosity; he goes off to see for himself, and comes home "wondering about what had happened" (v. 12), not yet believing. That will take an appearance of the risen Christ, about which we learn in v. 34.

This story will be summarized in 24:22-24 (by Luke himself?) in preparation for the news about Simon Peter.

The purpose of this episode, which centers on the *praeconium paschale,* is to present Jesus as the victor over death. Through his "suffering" he has become the risen Christ and Lord (see Acts 2:36); he has passed from the status of earthly teacher and healer to the exalted Son, who will pour forth the "promise of my Father" (Acts 1:4; cf. 2:33) on all those who will know him in the breaking of the bread. Death no longer holds him in its grip. In this episode we witness how difficult it was for even dedicated followers to comprehend his victory over death. This difficulty will become even more evident in the following episodes, when the risen Christ manifests himself to such persons and only gradually comes to be recognized by them for what he is. The words addressed to the repentant criminal now take on meaning: "Today you shall be with me in Paradise" (23:43). As the victor over death, Jesus has indeed come into his kingdom. A share in it awaits the faithful disciple who recognizes him now as the risen Lord.

NOTES

23 56b. *The women.* I.e. those from Galilee who had prepared the spices and ointments. See NOTES on 23:49,56a. In the Greek text note the use of *men . . . de* (see p. 108); it shows that 23:56b really belongs with 24:1.

rested on the Sabbath. I.e. from the sundown at the end of the day of Passover or the day of Preparation for the Sabbath (23:54) until the sundown ending the Sabbath itself. The following verse will make it clear that the women did not go to the tomb immediately at the end of the Sabbath—in the dark.

in obedience to the commandment. Lit. "according to the commandment." See Exod 20:10; Deut 5:12-15; cf. Exod 16:22-30. For the formula used, see CD 10:14: *ʾl hš[b]t lšmrh kmšptḥ,* "concerning the Sa[bb]ath, to observe it according to its regulation." Cf. Josephus, *J.W.* 4.19,12 § 582.

24 1. *on the first day of the week.* Lit. "on the (day) one of the week." Luke follows

Mark 16:2, which uses the cardinal instead of the ordinal in dating. Cf. Matt 28:1; John 20:1; see BDF § 247.1; Josephus, *Ant.* 1.1,1 § 29. The expression is found in the title to Psalm 24 in the LXX *(tēs mias sabbatōn)*. Cf. Psalm 48. See further E. C. Maloney, *Semitic Interference in Marcan Syntax* (SBLDS 51; Chico, CA: Scholars, 1981) 144-150.

at the crack of dawn. Lit. "at deep dawn," a gen. of time when. See BDF § 186.2. Cf. 23:38; 24:22; Acts 26:13 for related uses of the root *orthro-*. This is the Lucan substitute for the Marcan *lian prōi . . . anateilantos tou hēliou,* "very early . . . when the sun had risen." See F. Neirynck, "Le récit," 432.

they came to the tomb. Notice of it was taken explicitly in 23:55. One should read here *mnēmeion* with mss. P⁷⁵, ℵ, C*, Δ, X, etc. See J. Jeremias, *Die Sprache,* 310. *UBSGNT* ³ and N-A²⁶ read *mnēma,* following mss. A, W, Γ, *f* ¹·¹³, and the Koine text-tradition.

Ms. D omits *arōmata,* understanding the verse, "bringing what they had prepared." But then it also adds, "and they were pondering within them, 'Who will roll away the stone?' And when they had come, they found . . ." But Luke has not told us about a stone having been rolled before the entrance of the tomb (contrast Mark 15:46d and Luke 23:53c). So he omits this detail about their query. Ms. D has thus harmonized the account with Mark 16:3. But just as in Mark 16, Luke gives no hint as to *how* the stone was rolled back. Cf. Matt 28:2, where it is opened by the angel of the Lord who has descended from heaven, an embellishment of the story of the sort that continues in the apocryphal *Gospel of Peter.* See R. J. Dillon, *From Eye-Witnesses,* 7.

2. *found the stone rolled back.* Tombs in the neighborhood of Jerusalem from the first century A.D. have been found fitted with huge circular stone discs that were set in a transverse channel hollowed out of stone, along which the discs would be rolled in front of a rectangular doorway opening on to the tomb proper. As one faced the doorway from the outside, the stone would be rolled from left to right (or vice versa) to open or close the tomb. One such disc is found before the so-called Herodian Family tomb (see F.-M. Abel, "Deux tombeaux à meule à Abou Ghoch," *RB* 34 [1925] 275-279; cf. Josephus, *J.W.* 5.12,2 § 507; 5.3,2 § 108) and before the tomb of Queen Helena of Adiabene. See L.-H. Vincent, *Jérusalem de l'Ancien Testament* (Paris: Gabalda, 1954) 1/1. 349; cf. J. Finegan, *Archeology,* 198, 202.

3. *they failed to find the body of the Lord Jesus.* The last phrase "of the Lord Jesus" is omitted in ms. D and in several mss. (a, b, d, e, ff², l, r) of the OL version. The omission is influenced by v. 23. However, it is read in the important mss. P⁷⁵, ℵ, A, B, C, W, Θ, *f* ¹·¹³, etc. This so-called Western Non-Interpolation is to be regarded as part of the original text of the Lucan Gospel. See pp. 130-131. The phrase is otherwise Lucan. See Acts 1:21; 4:33; 8:16. Here once again *kyrios* is used in a statement of the evangelist. See NOTE on 7:13 and p. 203.

4. *While they were perplexed at this.* Lit. "and it happened, in their being perplexed about this, that behold two men stood by them . . ." This is another instance of the Lucan use of *kai egeneto* with the conj. *kai* + finite vb. See p. 119 and NOTE on 2:9. The temporal expression uses *en* + the articular infin. See p. 119.

two men in gleaming robes. This phrase is introduced by *kai idou.* See p. 121. Whereas Mark 16:5 speaks merely of "a young man" *(neaniskos)* sitting on the right and dressed in a white robe, Luke has two men. The "gleaming robes" are apparently intended to suggest their otherworldly nature, but neither Mark nor Luke goes so far as to call them angels (as does Matt 28:2,4). However, in the Lucan summary of this episode in v. 23, the "two men" will become "angels." Cf. Acts 1:10; 10:30.

5. *The women were startled.* Though ms. D. uses finite vbs. here, the best textual tradition has the gen. absol., the Lucan way to avoid parataxis. See p. 108.

bowed down to the ground. Lit. "inclined their faces to the ground," a detail added by Luke.

addressed them. Lit. "spoke to them" *(eipan pros* + acc.; see p. 116).

Why do you look for the living among the dead? This query is exclusive to Luke; it replaces the assurance given to the women in the other Synoptics, the negative impv. "Do not be alarmed," Mark 16:6; Matt 28:5. The Lucan summary in v. 23 will again refer to Jesus as "alive." See further Acts 1:3, "he showed himself alive"; cf. R. J. Dillon, *From Eye-Witnesses,* 28). "Life" is one of the effects of the Christ-event in Lucan theology (see p. 226); this is a fitting way to depict the risen Christ. Cf. Rom 14:9.

6. *He is not here, but has been raised!* I.e. by God. These words have been omitted in ms. D and in several mss. of the OL version. See NOTE on 3b. They are found, however, in P⁷⁵, ℵ, A, B, C, W (this last ms. reads the intrans. *anestē,* "he is risen"). It can no longer be regarded as a Western Non-Interpolation. See pp. 130-131.

Most of the mss. read the aor. pass. indic. *ēgerthē,* used here of someone who has died, as in 7:22; 9:7,22; 20:37; 24:34. See NOTE on 7:14. Because the same aor. pass. is used in 11:8; 13:25 with an intrans. meaning, "has got up" or "has risen," attempts have often been made to translate it so here (thus the *RSV, NIV;* J. A. Lacy, *"Ēgerthē* —He Has Risen," *TBT* 36 [1968] 2532-2535; and others [see *TAG* 214]). Yet elsewhere Luke clearly ascribes the resurrection of Jesus to "God" (using the act. of *egeirein* in Acts 3:15; 4:10; 5:30; 10:40; 13:30,37) rather than to Jesus' self-activity, as do other writers in the NT (e.g. Paul in 1 Thess 1:10; Rom 4:24; 8:11; 10:9; 1 Cor 6:14); it is better, therefore, to understand the form as a real pass., "he has been raised." Compare the analogous use of *anelēmphthē,* "he has been taken up" (Acts 1:11,22) and of *anaphereto,* "he was carried up" (Luke 24:51). It is a use of the theological pass. (ZBG § 236). Cf. J. Kremer, "Auferstanden—auferweckt," *BZ* 23 (1979) 97-98. Cf. Ignatius, *Smyrn.* 2.1; 7.1.

while he was still in Galilee. Instead of instructions to go and tell Peter and the others that the risen Christ will precede them to Galilee *(or* lead them forth to Galilee), Luke rephrases the messengers' words to make of them a recollection of what was said by Jesus in Galilee. This rephrasing preserves an association of the risen Christ with "Galilee," but only by way of recollection. It enables Luke to omit any reference to appearances of Christ outside of the Jerusalem vicinity. As H. Conzelmann *(Theology,* 93) noted, this verse "shows that Luke is deliberately giving a different picture from Mark." On "Galilee," see NOTE on 17:11.

7. *The Son of Man must be handed over . . .* Lit. "saying (of) the Son of Man that he must be . . ."; for the proleptic position of *ton huion tou anthrōpou,* see 9:31 *(exodon);* Acts 13:32-33; this is simply a Lucan usage, and there is no need to invoke an underlying Aramaic expression, *pace AAGA³,* 53, 75-76. The words of Jesus allude to 9:22, where there is mention of the "Son of Man," *dei,* "must," and of resurrection on "the third day." The latter is expressed there by the aor. pass. infin. of *egeirein,*

whereas here Luke uses the intr. *anastēnai,* "rise." Cf. 9:44. See further p. 195. On "Son of Man," see NOTE on 5:24 and COMMENT on 9:22 and p. 210. On the use of *dei,* see p. 180. See further N. Perrin, "The Use of *(para)didonai.*"

into the hands of sinful men. I.e. sinful human beings *(anthrōpōn).* Though *hamartōlos,* "sinful," is used elsewhere by Luke (e.g. 5:8,30,32), it is never found in any of the announcements of the passion (9:22,43b-45; 18:31-34).

be crucified. This specific mode of death appears in none of the announcements of the passion; its earliest occurrence in this Gospel is in 23:21,23,33. In 9:22 Jesus is said to "suffer much" and "be repudiated." Even though those announcements have been formulated with some hindsight, this specific mode of death was not introduced into them.

rise again. Luke will use *anastēnai* again in 24:46. Though it may correspond to a mode of speech more common in Luke's own day, it was already found in the earliest of NT writings (1 Thess 4:14). See NOTE on v. 6. Cf. Ignatius, *Smyrn.* 2.1 ("he raised himself").

on the third day! See NOTE on 9:22 and 2:46.

8. *they recalled his words.* I.e. the gist of what he had said in Galilee. This is the sense of the recollection, since the messengers' charge does not repeat 9:22 (or 9:44) verbatim. Not even Luke has been so consistent as to quote the words of the Lucan Jesus exactly.

9. *from the tomb.* This phrase is again omitted in ms. D and mss. of the OL version.

reported all this to the Eleven. I.e. the Twelve without Judas Iscariot. This detail is exclusively Lucan and intended to prepare for the rest of this resurrection narrative, which from this point on will go its own way. The Eleven will appear again in v. 33; Acts 1:26; 2:14; cf. Matt 28:16; Mark 16:14. See further J. Plevnik, " 'The Eleven.' "

all the others. Though no hint is given as to who these might be, this is a Lucan addition to prepare for the Emmaus incident (24:13, *ex autōn).* See next note.

10. *The women were.* Lit. "but they were." Both the textual transmission and the syntax of this verse are difficult. It sounds as though it is an attempt to explain who "all the others" (of the end of the last verse) were. This would be an explanation of masc. *pasin tois loipois* by a list of women. I have inserted "women" into the translation as subj. of *ēsan de,* "but they were," with which the verse begins. Mss. A, D, W, Γ, 1010, 1241, and some OS versions omit *ēsan de;* if these words are omitted, then one would translate, "Mary . . . and the others with them kept repeating . . ." Other mss. (ℵ², K, Θ, Ψ, 063, etc.) read the fem. rel. pron. *hai* before the vb. *elegon,* "The women were Mary . . . and the others with them, who kept repeating . . ." One could also punctuate the text differently: "Now the women were Mary . . . James; and the others with them kept repeating . . ." or possibly, "Now the women were Mary . . . James, and the others with them; they kept repeating . . ." No one knows for sure how the verse should be taken. See further I. H. Marshall, *Luke,* 887.

Mary Magdalene. See NOTE on 8:2.

Joanna. The wife of Chuza, Herod's steward. See NOTE on 8:3.

Mary, the mother of James. Lit. "Mary, the one of James," which could theoretically mean "the daughter of James," "the wife of James," or "the mother of James." The latter is usually preferred because Luke has taken over the name from Mark 16:1, where the same phrase occurs, but which refers to 15:40 where she is said to be the "mother of James and Joses." See Mark 6:3. Luke has not previously mentioned this "Mary," but she must be presumed to have been among the women from Galilee who stood at some distance from the cross (23:49).

they and the others. Lit. "and the other (women) with them." Those mentioned in 23:49,55.

kept repeating. Lit. "kept saying to . . ." *elegon pros* + acc. See p. 116.

the apostles. This title now emerges for the Eleven. Recall 6:13 and NOTE there.

11. *so much nonsense.* The Lucan phrase stresses the apostles' unbelief, i.e. their refusal to accept the testimony of the women. Though they have not as a group defected and were among his "acquaintances" on Calvary, they treat the report of the women *hōsei lēros,* "as if (it were) humbug."

H. Conzelmann *(Theology,* 93 n. 2) comments on v. 11:

> The significance of xxiv, 11 is that it expresses the truth that the Resurrection cannot be deduced from an idea (of Messiahship) or from the historical life of Jesus, but that it is announced as something new. It is only in retrospect that it casts light on Jesus' life, and it is not until now that the disciples understand what they should have understood long ago. Now, after the event, their misunderstanding really becomes inconceivable. That this motif cannot be explained psychologically . . . springs from the fact that the Lucan misunderstanding expresses the fundamental conviction that faith cannot be deduced, in other words, that faith is something that is possible only by faith itself. The Emmaus story shows a remarkable awareness of this problem.

Conzelmann's comment is correct, if he means by "the Lucan misunderstanding" the Lucan motif of the *disciples' misunderstanding.* It would be otherwise, if Conzelmann meant that Luke has some sort of misunderstanding of the resurrection or of faith.

12. *But Peter got up and ran to the tomb.* This verse is found in the best mss. (P[75], ℵ, A, B, K, L, W, X, Δ, Θ, Ψ, etc.); its inclusion in the original text of the Lucan Gospel merits more than a D in the *UBSGNT*[3] rating. See p. 131. The use of the name Peter may relate it to a source similar to that used in John 20:3; but that source is different from the one to which v. 34 belongs ("Simon").

He peered in and saw. The phrase is *parakypsas blepei,* identical with that in John 20:5, where it is used of the "other disciple," not of Peter. Despite the etymology of *kyptein,* "bend forward," the sense of the compound *parakyptein* is not, as has been pointed out many times (M.-J. Lagrange, *Luc,* 602, in dependence on F. Field, *Notes,* 80; MM 486), "stoop down" (so I. H. Marshall, *Luke,* 889; *NAB; JB; KJV; RSV;* BAGD 619), but "peer in," i.e. stretching forward to get a good look (whether it be up or down—*para* means "along"). See Gen 26:8; Prov 7:6; Sir 21:23. For a full discussion of the meaning of this word, see F. Neirynck, *"Parakypsas blepei."* See also the discussion of this phrase by K. P. G. Curtis, "Linguistic Support" refuted by J. Muddiman, "A Note." The translation of the phrase by R. E. Brown *(John, XIII-XXI,* 979), "He bent down to peer in and saw," would have the best of both worlds; but it is scarcely accurate.

only the linen wrappings. Luke has undoubtedly added *mona,* "alone," to the *ta othonia* of his source. See John 20:6, where that evangelist had added *keimena,* "the linen wrappings lying there." The n. *othonion* is a diminutive form of *othonē,* "linen sheet/cloth." See Acts 10:11; 11:5. But it need not have the diminutive connotation at this stage in the Greek language. See BDF § 111.3-111.4. *Othonion* is used in the LXX (Judg 14:13 [ms. B, *othonia* parallel to *sindonas];* Hos 2:7,11) of "linen garments," a meaning that it often has in Greek texts from Egypt (Rosetta Stone; *OGIS* § 90.18). It was also used specifically for burial wrappings. See W. Brunet de Presle and E. Egger, *Les papyrus grecs du Musée du Louvre* . . . (Paris: Imprimerie impériale, 1866) 53.8,42; O. Eger et al., *Griechische Papyri* . . . *zu Giessen* (2 vols.; Leipzig/Berlin: Teubner, 1910-1912) 1.68,11: *othonia euōna,* "fine linen wrappings" for a mummy. The word, however, says nothing of the shape of the cloth. Bands such as those used on Egyptian mummies are unknown for corpses in Palestine; hence that sense is out of question here. The pl. *othonia* is used also in John 19:40; 20:5-7 for the burial of Jesus. This suggests that Luke has derived this term from a source common to John and himself; but he has not taken the pains to change it so that it would agree with *sindōn* of 23:53. See NOTE there. One cannot facilely conclude that *othonia* (pl.) is just another name for *sindōn* or that *othonia* (pl.) are parts of *sindōn* (sg.), or even that "wrappings" were used along with the *sindōn.* The words simply come from different gospel traditions and mean nothing more than the "cloth(s)" in which Jesus was wrapped. That *sindōn* is a specific form of generic *othonia* is far from clear, *pace* R. E. Brown, *John, XIII-XXI,* 942. One should beware of harmonizing these accounts. For further discussion, see A. Vaccari, *"Edēsan auto othoniois* (Ioh. 19,40): Lessicografia ed esegesi," *Miscellanea biblica B. Ubach* (Scripta et documenta 1; ed. R. M. Díaz; Montserrat: [Benedictine Abbey], 1953) 375-386; J. Blinzler, "Othonia," *Philologus* 99 (1955) 158-166.

In some mss. (A, Γ, Δ, Θ, 079, *f*[1,13], and the Koine text-tradition, the ptc. *keimena* is found, whereas it is omitted in others (mss. P[75], ℵ, B, etc.). It is undoubtedly a copyist's gloss derived from the Johannine parallel (20:5 or 6). However, the adj. *mona* is to be retained (as in mss. P[75], ℵ[c], B, W).

he went home. Though the phrase *pros heauton* appears between the vb. *apēlthen,* lit. "he went off," and the ptc. *thaumazōn* and therefore creates a question about what it modifies, the best explanation is to take it with the preceding vb. Ever since the Vg *(abiit secum mirans,* "he went off wondering to himself"), attempts have been made to use it with the following ptc. See T. Zahn, *Evangelium des Lucas,* 714 n. 46. But see John 20:10; Num 24:25 (parallel to *eis ton topon autou);* Ezek 17:12; Josephus, *Ant.* 8.4,6 § 124; also the evidence amassed by F. Neirynck, *"Apēlthen pros heauton,"* 110-114.

wondering about what had happened. This is a Lucan addition to the traditional material, revealing Luke's inclination to use *thaumazein* (see p. 110), in this case with a dir. obj. *(to gegonos,* cf. 2:15; 8:34,35,56; Acts 4:21; 13:12). Peter's seeing leads only to "wonder," not belief; but the obj. of the seeing is only the empty tomb, not the risen Christ.

THE RESURRECTION AND THE RESURRECTION NARRATIVES: GENERAL BIBLIOGRAPHY

Albertz, M. "Zur Formgeschichte der Auferstehungsberichte," *ZNW* 21 (1922) 259-269.

Benoit, P. *Passion and Resurrection,* 231-342.

Brown, R. E. *The Virginal Conception and Bodily Resurrection of Jesus* (New York: Paulist, 1973) 69-129.

Clark, N. *Interpreting the Resurrection* (London: SCM, 1967).

Clark, W. R. "Jesus, Lazarus, and Others: Resuscitation or Resurrection?" *Religion in Life* 49 (1980) 230-241.

Conzelmann, H. "Auferstehung Christi," *RGG* 1. 698-700.

Daalen, D. H. van. *The Real Resurrection* (London: Collins, 1972).

Delling, G. "The Significance of the Resurrection of Jesus for Faith in Jesus Christ," *The Significance of the Message of the Resurrection for Faith in Jesus Christ* (SBT 2/8; ed. C. F. D. Moule; Naperville, IL: Allenson, 1968) 77-104.

Descamps, A. "La structure des récits évangéliques de la Résurrection," *Bib* 40 (1959) 726-741.

Dhanis, E., ed. *Resurrexit: Actes du symposium international sur la résurrection de Jésus (Rome 1970)* (Vatican City: Libreria Vaticana, 1974).

Dodd, C. H. "The Appearances of the Risen Christ: An Essay in Form-Criticism of the Gospels," *Studies in the Gospels: Essays in Memory of R. H. Lightfoot* (ed. D. E. Nineham; Oxford: Blackwell, 1957) 9-35; reprinted, *More New Testament Studies* (Grand Rapids, MI: Eerdmans, 1968) 102-133.

Dupont, J. "Ressuscité 'le troisième jour,'" *Bib* 40 (1959) 742-761.

Fuller, R. H. *The Formation of the Resurrection Narratives* (New York: Macmillan, 1971).

——— "The Resurrection of Jesus Christ," *BR* 4 (1960) 8-24.

Gander, G. "La notion chrétienne primitive de la résurrection," *VCaro* 8 (1954) 33-51.

Geyer, H.-G. "The Resurrection of Jesus Christ: A Survey of the Debate in Present Day Theology," *The Significance of the Message* (ed. C. F. D. Moule) (see above) 105-135.

Goguel, M. *"La foi à la résurrection de Jésus dans le christianisme primitif* (Bibliothèque de l'Ecole des Hautes Etudes, sc. rel. 57; Paris: Leroux, 1933).

Grass, H. *Ostergeschehen und Osterberichte* (2d ed.; Göttingen: Vandenhoeck & Ruprecht, 1962) 15-93.

Gutbrod, K. *Die Auferstehung Jesu im Neuen Testament* (Stuttgart: Calwer, 1969).

Hodges, Z. C. "Form-Criticism and the Resurrection Accounts," *BSac* 124 (1967) 339-348.

Hooke, S. H. *The Resurrection of Christ as History and Experience* (London: Darton, Longman & Todd, 1967).

Kegel, G. *Auferstehung Jesu—Auferstehung der Toten* (Gütersloh: Mohn, 1970).

Kremer, J. *Die Osterevangelien—Geschichten um Geschichte* (Stuttgart: Katholisches Bibelwerk, 1977).

Lampe, G. W. H., and D. M. MacKinnon. *The Resurrection: A Dialogue* (ed. W. Purcell; Philadelphia: Westminster, 1966).

Leipoldt, J. "Zu den Auferstehungsgeschichten," *TLZ* 73 (1948) 737-742.

Léon-Dufour, X. *Resurrection and the Message of Easter* (New York: Holt, Rinehart and Winston, 1971) 80-194.

Lohfink, G. "Die Auferstehung Jesu und die historische Kritik," *BibLeb* 9 (1968) 37-53.

Lorenzen, T. "Ist der Auferstandene in Galiläa erschienen?" *ZNW* 64 (1973) 209-221.

Marxsen, W. "The Resurrection of Jesus as a Historical and Theological Problem," *The Significance of the Message* (ed. C. F. D. Moule) (see above) 15-50.

—— *The Resurrection of Jesus of Nazareth* (Philadelphia: Fortress, 1970).

Michaelis, W. *Die Erscheinungen des Auferstandenen* (Basel: Majer, 1944).

Moule, C. F. D. "The Post-Resurrection Appearances in the Light of Festival Pilgrimages," *NTS* 4 (1957-1958) 58-61.

Mussner, F. *Die Auferstehung Jesu* (Biblische Handbibliothek 7; Munich: Kösel, 1969).

O'Collins, G. *What Are They Saying about the Resurrection?* (New York: Paulist, 1978).

Perrin, N. *The Resurrection according to Matthew, Mark and Luke* (Philadelphia: Fortress, 1977).

Ponthot, J. "Gospel Traditions about Christ's Resurrection: Theological Perspectives and Problems of Historicity," *Lumen vitae* 21 (1966) 66-90.

Ramsey, A. M. *The Resurrection of Christ: An Essay in Biblical Theology* (rev. ed.; London: G. Bles, 1956).

Rengstorf, K. H. *Die Auferstehung Jesu: Form, Art und Sinn der urchristlichen Osterbotschaft* (4th ed.; Witten/Ruhr: Luther-V., 1960).

Rigaux, B. *Dieu l'a ressuscité: Exégèse et théologie biblique* (Gembloux: Duculot, 1973) 171-307.

Robinson, J. A. T. "Resurrection in the New Testament," *IDB* 4. 43-53.

Robinson, W. C. "The Bodily Resurrection of Christ," *TZ* 13 (1957) 81-101.

Russel, R. "Modern Exegesis and the Fact of the Resurrection," *Downside Review* 76 (1958) 251-264, 329-343.

Schlier, H. *Über die Auferstehung Jesu Christi* (Kriterien 10; Einsiedeln: Johnnes-V., 1968).

Schmitt, J. "Auferstehung Christi," *LTK* 1. 1028-1035.

—— "Résurrection de Jésus dans le kérygme, la tradition, la catéchèse," *DBS* 10. 487-582.

Schnider, F., and W. Stegner. *Die Ostergeschichten der Evangelien* (Schriften zur Katechetik 13; Munich: Kösel, 1970).

Seidensticker, P. *Die Auferstehung Jesu in der Botschaft der Evangelisten: Ein traditionsgeschichtlicher Versuch zum Problem der Sicherung der Osterbotschaft in der apostolischen Zeit* (SBS 26; Stuttgart: Katholisches Bibelwerk, 1967).

Surgy, P. de, ed. *La résurrection du Christ et l'exégèse moderne* (LD 50; Paris: Cerf, 1969).

Turner, H. E. W. "The Resurrection," *ExpTim* 68 (1956-1957) 369-371.

Vögtle, A., and R. Pesch. *Wie kam es zum Osterglauben?* (Düsseldorf: Patmos, 1975) 85-98.

Wilckens, U. *Auferstehung: Das biblische Auferstehungszeugnis historisch untersucht und erklärt* (Themen der Theologie 4; Stuttgart/Berlin: Kreuz-V., 1970).

——— "The Tradition-History of the Resurrection of Jesus," *The Significance of the Message* (ed. C. F. D. Moule) (see above) 51-76.

LUCAN RESURRECTION NARRATIVE: GENERAL BIBLIOGRAPHY

Bailey, J. A. *The Traditions Common,* 85-102.

Bouwmann, G. "Die Erhöhung Jesu in der lukanischen Theologie," *BZ* 14 (1970) 257-263.

Brändle, M. "Auferstehung Jesu nach Lukas," *Orientierung* 24 (1960) 84-89.

Dillon, R. J. *From Eye-Witnesses.*

Dupont, J. "Les discours de Pierre dans les Actes et le chapitre XXIV de l'évangile de Luc," *L'Evangile de Luc* (ed. F. Neirynck) 329-374.

Guillaume, J.-M. *Luc interprète des anciennes traditions sur la résurrection de Jésus* (EBib; Paris: Gabalda, 1979).

Hebbelthwaite, P. "Theological Themes in the Lucan Post-Resurrection Narratives," *Clergy Review* 50 (1965) 360-369.

Leaney, A. R. C. "The Resurrection Narratives in Luke (xxiv. 12-53)," *NTS* 2 (1955-1956) 110-114.

Lohse, E. *Die Auferstehung Jesu Christi im Zeugnis des Lukasevangeliums* (BibS[N] 31; Neukirchen: Neukirchener-V., 1961).

Marshall, I. H. "The Resurrection in the Acts of the Apostles," *Apostolic History and the Gospel: Biblical and Historical Essays Presented to F. F. Bruce on His 60th Birthday* (eds. W. W. Gasque and R. P. Martin; Exeter: Paternoster; Grand Rapids, MI: Eerdmans, 1970) 92-107.

O'Toole, R. F. "Activity of the Risen Jesus in Luke-Acts," *Bib* 62 (1981) 471-498.

Plevnik, J. "The Origin of Easter Faith according to Luke," *Bib* 61 (1980) 492-508.

Schmitt, J. "Le récit de la résurrection dans l'évangile de Luc: Etude de critique littéraire," *RevScRel* 25 (1951) 119-137, 219-242.

Schubert, P. "The Structure and Significance of Luke 24," *Neutestamentliche Studien* (ed. W. Eltester) 165-186.

BIBLIOGRAPHY (23:56b-24:12)

Baldensperger, G. "Le tombeau vide," *RHPR* 12 (1932) 413-443; 13 (1933) 105-144; 14 (1934) 97-125.

Benoit, P. *Passion and Resurrection,* 231-261.

Bickermann, E. "Das leere Grab," *ZNW* 23 (1924) 281-292.

Bode, E. L. *The First Easter Morning: The Gospel Accounts of the Women's Visit to the Tomb of Jesus* (AnBib 45; Rome: Biblical Institute, 1970) 59-71, 105-126.

————— "A Liturgical Sitz-im-Leben for the Gospel Tradition of the Women's Easter Visit to the Tomb of Jesus?" *CBQ* 32 (1970) 237-242.

Campenhausen, H. von. "Der Ablauf der Osterereignisse und das leere Grab," *Sitzungsberichte der heidelberger Akademie der Wissenschaften,* Heft 2 (2d ed.; Heidelberg, 1958).

Craig, W. L. "The Empty Tomb of Jesus," *Gospel Perspectives* (eds. R. T. France and D. Wenham) 2. 173-200.

Cronin, H. S. " 'They Rested the Sabbath Day according to the Commandment: Luke xxiii. 56," *ExpTim* 16 (1904-1905) 115-118.

Curtis, K. P. G. "Linguistic Support for Three Western Readings in Luke 24," *ExpTim* 83 (1971-1972) 344-345.

————— "Luke xxiv. 12 and John xx. 3-10," *JTS* 22 (1971) 512-515.

Dillon, R. J. *From Eye-Witnesses,* 1-68.

Ellicott, C. J. "The Testimony of the Tomb," *ExpTim* 14 (1902-1903) 508-511.

Feuillet, A. "La découverte du tombeau vide en Jean 20,3-10 et la foi au Christ ressuscité," *Esprit et vie* 87 (1977) 257-266, 273-284.

Grayston, K. "The Empty Tomb," *ExpTim* 92 (1980-1981) 263-287.

Guillaume, J.-M. *Luc interprète,* 15-66.

Hodges, Z. C. "The Women and the Empty Tomb," *BSac* 123 (1966) 301-309.

Kremer, J. "Zur Diskussion über 'das leere Grab,' " *Resurrexit* (ed. E. Dhanis) 137-168.

Mangatt, G. "At the Tomb of Jesus," *Bible Bhashyam* 3 (1977) 91-96.

Muddiman, J. "A Note on Reading Luke xxiv.12," *ETL* 48 (1972) 542-548.

Nauck, W. "Die Bedeutung des leeren Grabes für den Glauben an den Auferstandenen," *ZNW* 47 (1956) 243-267.

Neirynck, F. "*Apēlthen pros heauton:* Lc 24,12 et Jn 20,10," *ETL* 54 (1978) 104-118; reprinted, *ALBO* 5/30 (1978).

————— "Lc. xxiv 12: Les témoins du texte occidental," *Miscellanea neotestamentica: Studia ad Novum Testamentum praesertim pertinentia . . .* (2 vols.; eds. T. Baarda et al.; NovTSup 47-48; Leiden: Brill, 1978) 1. 45-60.

————— "*Parakypsas blepei:* Lc 24, 12 et Jn 20, 5," *ETL* 53 (1977) 113-152.

————— "Le récit du tombeau vide dans l'évangile de Luc (24,1-12)," *Miscellanea in honorem Josephi Vergote* (Orientalia lovaniensia periodica 6/7; eds. P. Naster et al.; Louvain: Departement oriëntalistiek, 1975-1976) 427-441.

————— "The Uncorrected Historic Present in Lk. xxiv. 12," *ETL* 48 (1972) 548-553.

Odenkirchen, P. C. " 'Praecedam vos in Galilaeam' (Mt 26,32 cf. 28,7.10; Mc 14,28; 16,7 cf. Lc 24,6)," *VD* 46 (1968) 193-223.

Perrin, N. "The Use of *(para)didonai* in Connection with the Passion of Jesus in the New Testament," *Der Ruf Jesu* (eds. E. Lohse et al.) 204-212.

Plevnik, J. " 'The Eleven and Those with Them' according to Luke," *CBQ* 40 (1978) 205-211.

Prete, B. "L'annunzio dell'evento pasquale nella formulazione di *Luca* 24,5-7," *Sacra doctrina* 16 (1971) 485-523.

Schenke, L. *Auferstehungsverkündigung und leeres Grab: Eine traditionsgeschichtliche Untersuchung von Mk 16,1-8* (SBS 33; Stuttgart: Katholisches Bibelwerk, 1968; 2d ed., 1969).

Stauffer, E. "Der Auferstehungsglaube und das leere Grab," *ZRGG* 6 (1954) 146-148.

166. JESUS APPEARS ON THE ROAD TO EMMAUS
(24:13-35)

24   [13] Now that same day two of them were making their way to a village called Emmaus, about seven miles distant from Jerusalem. [14] They were talking together about all that had occurred. [15] As they were talking and discussing, Jesus himself happened to draw near and began to walk with them. [16] But their eyes were held from recognizing him.

[17] He said to them, "What is all this talk that you exchange with one another as you walk along?" They stopped momentarily, full of gloom, [18] and one of them named Cleopas said to him, "Are you the only stranger in Jerusalem who has not learned what happened there these last few days?" [19] "What is that?" he asked them. They said to him, "All that happened to Jesus of Nazareth who was a prophet mighty in deed and word in the eyes of God and all the people; [20] how our chief priests and leaders handed him over to be sentenced to death and had him crucified. [21] We were hoping that he would be the one to deliver Israel. And besides all that, it is three days since this happened. [22] Some women from our group have really astounded us; they went to the tomb early this morning [23] and, failing to find his body, came back with the report that they had even seen a vision of angels who told them that he was alive. [24] Then some of our own number also went to the tomb and found it to be just as the women had said; but him they did not see." [25] Jesus said to them, "How foolish you are and slow of wit to believe in all that the prophets have said! [26] Was not the Messiah bound to suffer all this before entering into his glory?" [27] Then he began with Moses and all the prophets and interpreted for them what pertained to himself in every part of Scripture.

[28] They had drawn near to the village to which they were going, and Jesus pretended to be going on farther. [29] But they urged him strongly, "Stay with us because it is almost evening, and the day is already far

spent." So he went into the village to stay with them. [30] Now when he had reclined at table with them, he happened to take bread and utter a blessing; he broke it and offered it to them. [31] Then their eyes were opened, and they recognized him; but he vanished from their sight. [32] And they admitted to each other, "Were not our hearts on fire within us, as he was speaking to us on the road and opened to us the sense of the Scriptures!"

[33] Even at that late hour they rose up and returned to Jerusalem. They found that the Eleven and their companions had gathered together [34] and were saying, "It is really true! The Lord has been raised and he has appeared to Simon." [35] Then they explained what had happened on the road and how he became known to them in the breaking of the bread.

COMMENT

After the episode of the visit of the women and Peter to the empty tomb, Luke adds in his resurrection narrative accounts of the appearance of the risen Christ. In the remaining four episodes three appearances of Christ are mentioned: one is reported at third hand, not narrated (the appearance to Simon, v. 34); the other two are narrated, one at some length in a dramatic story (Christ's appearance to the two disciples on their way to Emmaus, vv. 13-35), and the other at less length (his appearance to the Eleven and others gathered in Jerusalem, vv. 36-53: Christ appears to them [vv. 36-43], commissions them to be witnesses of him [vv. 44-49], and then leads them out to Bethany for his final leave-taking, his ascension [vv. 50-53]). Thus the second narrated appearance, when finally completed, becomes almost as long as the first narrative story (vv. 13-35), with which we begin.

We have already noted that after the story of the visit to the empty tomb, each evangelist goes his own way in the resurrection narrative. The use of "Mk" by Luke has come to an end. If there is any tradition behind the Lucan appearance stories, it comes to the evangelist from "L." That there is some tradition behind the first episode, Christ's appearance to the disciples going to Emmaus, may be seen in the following ways: (a) There is the brief notice of a similar appearance of the risen Christ in two verses of the Marcan appendix (16:12-13): "Afterwards he made himself manifest in another form to two of them walking along, making their way into the country. Then they went back and reported it to the others; but they did not believe them." *Pace* I. H. Marshall *(Luke,* 889), it is far from certain that Mark 16:12-13 is "based on Lk." It is the kind of snippet of pre-Lucan tradition that enables this evangelist to build it into his dramatic story. (b) The destination of the two disciples, Emmaus, is also to be reckoned as part of the pre-Lucan tradition (even if one cannot settle the text-critical problem of its distance from Jerusalem). (c) The same has to be said for the name of one of the disciples, Cleopas; if Luke had invented that name, he would undoubtedly have done the same for the other disciple as well. (d) Verse 34, "It is really true! The Lord has been raised and he has appeared to Simon." Not only does it echo the kerygma of 1 Cor 15:4-5 (the same vbs.: pass. forms of *egeirein,* and *ōphthē),* but if it were from Luke's pen, he would almost certainly have used *Petrō* (as in v. 12) instead of *Simōni* (cf. 22:31; recall 6:14; Acts 10:5,18,32; 11:13). (e) Verses 22-24 may be an independent summary of the foregoing episode, derived from a non-Marcan source. It has often been regarded as a mere Lucan summary of vv. 1-12 (for J. Wellhausen, *Das Evangelium Lucae,* 139, they are an interpolation into the Lucan story); but J. Jeremias *(Die Sprache,* 316) argues that they are not the product of Lucan redaction, but of tradition. Note that the "two men in gleaming robes" (24:4) now become "angels" (24:23). Finally (f) traditional formulation is present in the four vbs. of v. 30 ("take," "utter a blessing," "broke," and "offered"), which could, however, simply echo Lucan formulation elsewhere (e.g. 9:16). These elements in the story suggest that Luke, who has otherwise heavily redacted (or even composed) parts of the story, has derived other parts of it from a tradition ("L") before him. V. Taylor *(Passion Narrative,* 109-112) has analyzed the episode in detail, noting the characteristic Lucan vocabulary and constructions, and concluded that "Luke has embellished an existing tradition with unusual freedom." That freedom, however, includes the insertion of many typically Lucan theological motifs. For other detailed analyses of the Lucan redaction, see J. Wanke, *Die Emmauserzählung,* 23-126; R. J. Dillon, *From Eye-Witnesses,* 69-155; J.-M. Guillaume, *Luc interprète,* 67-159; cf. I. H. Marshall, "The Resurrection of Jesus in Luke," *Tyndale Bulletin* 24 (1973) 55-98, esp. 75-78. Cf. W. R. Farmer, *The Last Twelve Verses of Mark* (SNTSMS 25; Cambridge: University Press, 1974).

The Lucan redaction/composition is manifest in the following points: (1) *kai idou,* lit. "and behold" (v. 13; see p. 121); (2) *en autē tē hōra/hēmera,* lit. "that same hour/day" (vv. 13,33; see pp. 117-118); (3) the periphrastic ptc. with the vb. to be, *ēsan poreuomenoi,* lit. "were making their way"; *kaiomenē ēn,* lit. "was burning" (vv. 13,32; see p. 121 [especially with the vb. *poreuesthai]);* (4) *Ierousalēm* (vv. 13,18,33; see NOTE on 2:22); (5) *hē onoma Emmaus,* "called Emmaus," a Septuagintism (dat. + *onoma* + name), used only by Luke (v. 13; see NOTE on 1:26; cf. J. Jeremias, *Die Sprache,* 313); (6) unstressed *kai autoi/autos* (vv. 14,25,28,31,35; see p. 120); (7) *pros* + acc. with vb. of speaking (vv. 14,17bis,18,25,32; see p. 116); (8) *kai egeneto* construction (vv. 15,30; see p. 119); (9) the articular infin. (vv. 16,25,29; see pp. 108-109; cf. J. Jeremias, ibid. 314); (10) *apokritheis eipen,* "answering, he said" (v. 18; see p. 114); (11) *onomati,* "by name" (v. 18; see p. 111); (12) "these last few days" (v. 18; see NOTE on 23:7); (13) *ta peri,* "the things concerning" (vv. 19,27; see NOTE on 23:37); (14) *anēr prophētēs,* "a prophet" (v. 19; see 5:8; 11:32; Acts 1:11,16; 2:14,22,29,37; 3:12,14; 5:35, etc.); (15) *dynatos en,* "mighty in" (v. 19; see Acts 7:22; 18:24); (16) hyperbolic use of *pas,* "all" (vv. 19,21,25; see NOTES on 3:16; 4:15; 9:1); (17) *archontes,* "leaders" (v. 20; see NOTE on 14:1); (18) *tines,* "some" (v. 22; see p. 111); (19) *orthrinai,* "early" (v. 22; see NOTE on 24:1); (20) *arxamenos,* "began" (v. 27; see NOTES on 1:2; 3:23; 23:5); (21) pleonastic ptc. *anastantes,* "rose up" (v. 33; see p. 114); (22) absolute use of *hypostrephein,* "returned" (v. 33; see p. 111); (23) *tous hendeka,* "the Eleven" (v. 33; see NOTE on 24:9); (24) *tē klasei tou artou,* "breaking of the bread" (v. 35; uniquely Lucan).

For R. Bultmann *(HST* 286 [in dependence on H. Gunkel]) this episode "has the character of a true legend"—Christ appears as the unknown traveler, as God of old (see Gen 16:7-14; 18:1-22) liked to walk among men, in simple human form (motifs known in Greek and Chinese literature). H. D. Betz ("The Origin") seeks to rescue the characterization of the episode by presenting it as a "cult legend" in the form of a narrative so that the reader will appreciate the principal teaching, that Christian faith must be understood as faith in the resurrected Jesus of Nazareth. That there is a resemblance in the episode to legends of this sort is undeniable; but whether that is all there is is another matter. A reader in the twentieth century may well ask whether there is a basis in fact for such an episode: ". . . there seems to be no good reason why the story should not be founded on fact" (J. M. Creed, *The Gospel,* 290).

As C. H. Dodd showed years ago ("The Appearances," p. 1549), one cannot really classify the post-resurrection appearance-stories according to the categories used for the rest of the gospel tradition. Instead, he suggested the distinction of three kinds of appearance-stories, which made use of early traditions: (1) *Concise Narratives,* which tell nothing but what is absolutely essential to a bare report of what happened and which have an easily recognizable common pattern, resulting from being often repeated and hence rubbed down and polished by repetition—a self-contained unit without reference to other stories. Their common pattern: (a) Situation—Christ's followers bereft and distraught; (b) Appearance—Christ is suddenly among them; (c) Greeting; (d) Recognition; (e) Word of Command. According to Dodd, the following episodes are concise narratives: Matt 28:8-10 (appearance of Christ to the women on the road); 28:16-20 (appearance to the Eleven in Galilee); John 20:19-23 (appearance to the disciples in Jerusalem, without Thomas). (2) *Circumstantial Narratives* (also called "tales" by Dodd, a term that like Bultmann's "legends" has an excessively pejorative tone), which manifest the art and craft of the storyteller, his concern for dramatic development, vivid and arresting details, traits of character, conversation, etc. The two prime examples of this kind of narrative are Luke 24:13-35 (Christ's appearance to the disciples on the way to Emmaus), and John 21:1-14 (his appearance to seven disciples fishing at the Sea of Tiberias). (3) *Mixed Narratives*, which are concise stories developing into circumstantial narratives. Thus Mark 16:14-15 (Christ's appearance to the Eleven at table and his commission to them); John 20:11-17 (his appearance to Mary Magdalene); John 20:26-29 (his appearance to the disciples in Jerusalem, with Thomas present); and Luke 24:36-49.

One can also follow Dodd in his view of the genesis and development of such appearance-stories, adapting it slightly thus: (1) In the beginning there was a mere *list of witnesses*, something like 1 Cor 15:5-7: he appeared to Cephas (cf. Luke 24:34; Matt 16:16b-19 [see R. E. Brown et al., eds., *Peter*, 83-101]); to the Twelve (cf. Luke 24:36-53); to more than five hundred (unnoted elsewhere); to James (even to one of the unbelieving "brothers," John 7:5 [recorded in the *Gospel of the Hebrews* according to Jerome, *De vir. ill.* 2 (TU 14.8); see Hennecke-Schneemelcher, *NTApocrypha* 1. 165]); to all the apostles (not restricted to the Lucan sense of *apostolos;* unnoted elsewhere). (2) From the bare list developed *statements* or reports that disciples or apostles had been witnesses to the risen Christ (Luke 24:34; Acts 1:3-4; 10:39-40; 13:28-31; Mark 16:9,12-13). (3) *Concise* Narratives developed in time, as details were learned, reflecting corporate oral tradition; see preceding paragraph. (4) *Mixed* Narratives, corporate tradition being embellished; and (5) *Circumstantial* Narratives, reflecting the literary style and interest of the individual evangelist.

The appearance-stories cannot be harmonized, being too different from one another in character and detail. Yet it is important to realize that in general they are devoid of apocalyptic stage props (the only preternatural element associated with one of them is Christ's appearance to the disciples in Jerusalem with the doors locked [John 20:26]—which is no problem if it is recalled that he is appearing from "glory" [see p. 1539]). Compare, however, the appearance of the risen Christ to the seer John in Rev 1:12-20, where apocalyptic trappings enhance the vision. In the gospel tradition there is none of this; though the gospel christophanies can be compared with the theophanies of the OT, in none of the latter does anyone appear who has been raised from the dead.

The appearance of the risen Christ to the two disciples on the road to Emmaus is, then, a circumstantial narrative, an appearance-story, yet one devoid of apologetic concerns: Once he is recognized, Christ vanishes. We do not even learn whether he ate anything at table in Emmaus; contrast 24:41-43 (where the apologetic concern emerges).

The episode, however, is filled with Lucan theological motifs. These are: 1) *Geographical*, but these as elsewhere are clearly subordinated to Lucan theology. The disciples are en route to Emmaus, "making their way" *(poreuomenoi,* v. 13) and Christ comes to "walk with them" *(syneporeueto autois,* v. 15). Note the double use of *en tē hodō,* "on the road" (vv. 32,35). It is precisely the geographical setting in which Christ instructs them about the sense of the Scriptures. Thus at the end of the Lucan Gospel the appearance-story *par excellence* takes place, not only in the vicinity of the city of destiny, toward which Jesus' entire movement in the Gospel has been directed, but his final and supreme instruction about the relation of his destiny to that which Moses and the prophets of old had announced is given "on the road." The subtle, yet highly deliberate, use of this Lucan motif is not to be missed (see further pp. 164-171).

2) *Revelatory,* for the risen Christ is only gradually made manifest in his new status to these journeying disciples. At first "their eyes were held from recognizing him" (v. 16); this is not an accurate recollection, but a literary device to advance the story. Satan is not involved, but mere human incredulity reigns. Before the veil is removed from their sight, they have to be instructed. The dramatic suspense enhances the revelation of him. One wonders how the disciples could fail to recognize him "on the road" if his explanation of Moses and the prophets were actually firing their hearts. Thus Luke subtly builds the suspense. Finally, they come to recognize him, not by seeing (looking at him), but with the eyes of faith, in the breaking of the bread. So he is finally made manifest to them—and he vanishes.

3) *Christological as fulfilling OT prophecy:* Though the disciples regarded Jesus as "a prophet mighty in deed and word" (v. 19), one who, they thought, was to deliver Israel, the risen Christ corrects their impression of him, insisting on *"all* that the prophets have said!" (v. 25). He is now manifested to them not only as a prophet but as the suffering Messiah, of whom Moses and all the prophets had written. It is the Lucan proof-from-prophecy theology (P. Schubert, "Structure," 165-186) that is at work. The Lucan Christ catechizes the disciples, setting their hearts afire with his interpretation of OT Scriptures. He gives no specific references to the *Tôrāh* or to the *Nĕbî'îm,* and the modern reader will look in vain for the passages in the OT to which the Lucan Christ refers when he speaks of "what pertained to himself in every part of Scripture" (v. 27), especially to himself as "the Messiah" who was "bound to suffer" (v. 26). This is the Lucan way of casting the OT data; it is his global christological use of the OT (see p. 200). Luke has his own way of reading the OT and here puts it on the lips of Christ himself; a (Christian) interpretation of the OT thus surfaces in this episode and will be continued in Acts. Such a reading of the OT explains what Luke meant when in the prologue of the Gospel he spoke of "the events that have come to fulfillment among us" (1:1). What has happened, and what Luke has reported in his whole Gospel, is not merely "the things which have been accomplished among us" *(RSV,* 1:1). He has recounted the suffering of Jesus of Nazareth, now recognized as "Lord and Messiah" (Acts 2:36), and of the one who has

entered "his glory" (Luke 24:26). All this is seen as the fulfillment of what Moses and the prophets were writing about. This motif will appear again in vv. 44-46.

4) *Eucharistic*, a Lucan motif that begins here, but which will be picked up in Luke's second volume. For this scene with Christ reclining at table with the disciples of Emmaus, taking bread, uttering a blessing, breaking the bread, and offering it to them (v. 30), not only recalls the Last Supper (22:19ab), but becomes the classic Lucan way of referring to the Eucharist. The lesson in the story is that henceforth the risen Christ will be present to his assembled disciples, not visibly (after the ascension), but in the breaking of the bread. So they will know him and recognize him, because *so* he will be truly present among them. (This presence will be modified later, when one learns that it will not be its only mode, since he will also be present to them in "what my Father has promised" [24:49]—not yet identified; but see Acts 1:4-5.)

"In this story Luke's artistic powers are seen at their height" (J. M. Creed, *The Gospel,* 290). Every reader senses the suspense and the excitement of the account, which develops in four parts: (1) *The meeting* (vv. 13-16). Two dejected disciples set out from Jerusalem to return to their home village three days after the crucifixion; they are met by Christ, who joins them, but whom they fail to recognize. (2) *The conversation en route* (vv. 17-27). When Christ inquires about the topic of their conversation, Cleopas exclaims, "Are you the only stranger in Jerusalem who has not learned what happened there these last few days?" When pressed further, Cleopas and his companion tell of Jesus of Nazareth, a prophet who they had hoped would deliver Israel, but who was put to death by Jewish authorities. In their gloom they would not give credence to the reports of women who had gone to the tomb and found it empty and who told of angels who declared that he was alive. For some of their group had gone to the tomb, found it empty, but "him they did not see." Then the risen Christ catechizes the disciples, teaching them the import of the Scriptures: that the Messiah was destined to suffer all this before he entered into his glory. So he sought to turn their dejection and gloom into faith and hope. (3) *The Emmaus meal* (vv. 28-32). Coming to Emmaus, they realize that their companion would go on further, but they prevail upon him to stay with them. When Christ reclines at table with them, he takes bread, utters a blessing, breaks it, and offers it to them—and their eyes are finally opened. They recognize him in the breaking of the bread. Then upon reflection they recall how their hearts were afire on the road as he opened to them the sense of the Scriptures. (4) *The return to Jerusalem* (vv. 33-35). Even late in the evening, they set out to return to Jerusalem. There they find that the Eleven and others have gathered and are already aware that "the Lord has been raised and he has appeared to Simon" (v. 34). Then they explain what happened "on the road" and how he became known to them in the breaking of the bread. A similar sequence, though less obvious, will appear in the next (composite) episode: an appearance that is not comprehended, a revelation through exposition of Scripture and a meal, and the departure of the risen Christ.

The story inevitably raises a question: Did Christ celebrate the Eucharist before them? We have already pointed out the Eucharistic motif which gives rise to the question. The question is asked, however, anachronistically. What is meant is, Did the risen Christ in Stage I of the gospel tradition break bread in the sense of celebrating the Eucharist? No one can answer that question. Moreover, it must be recalled that these two disciples were not among the "apostles" (22:14) with whom Jesus celebrated the Last Supper. The recognition of Christ which the episode recounts would have to be based on a scene like 9:10-17, where Jesus is depicted taking five loaves (and two fish), looking up to heaven, blessing them, breaking them, and giving them to the disciples. . . . Such a background would suffice to explain the recognition in Stage I of the tradition. But it is another question whether in Stage III of the tradition Luke intended a Eucharistic connotation. We have already implied an affirmative answer to that in discussing the Lucan motifs in the episode, especially in light of the way the expression "the breaking of the bread" is used in Acts.

A further question has often been asked, whether the thrust of the account is reminiscent of early Christian liturgical celebrations. One points to the use of OT Scriptures (liturgy of the word), the proclamation of resurrection faith (v. 34), the meal setting with the breaking of the bread. Such elements are there and they suggest clearly a relation to the Eucharist, but whether they also reflect the *mode* of a primitive eucharistic celebration is another matter. This may be more eisegetical than exegetical. We know very little about liturgical celebrations in the first century. (See further J. Wanke, *Die Emmauserzählung,* 120-122.)

Similarly, parallelism between this episode and that of the conversion of the Ethiopian eunuch in Acts 8:26-40 has also been noted (see J. Dupont, "The Meal at Emmaus," 119-120). One cannot deny the similarity of structure in the stories, but there is also enough dissimilarity to caution one from overinterpreting the former.

NOTES

24 13. *Now that same day.* Lit. "and behold two of them on that day," i.e. the first day of the week (24:1). This phrase explicitly links the appearance of the risen Christ chronologically with the day of the discovery of the empty tomb, or with the day of the resurrection itself. Other indications will be given below (see v. 33 in this episode) to ensure that the reader understands that all the events in this last chapter occur within twenty-four hours. Because each of the episodes makes a reference to this new day, after the Sabbath (vv. 1,13,33), E. E. Ellis *(Gospel of Luke,* 276) thinks this is

symbolic and "identifies Jesus' resurrection as the beginning of a new creation." But that is to read a Pauline motif into the Lucan story; it is scarcely Lucan.

two of them. This refers to v. 9, "and all the others," since Cleopas, named as one of them in v. 18, is not among "the apostles" (24:10), as this term is understood by Luke (see 6:13)—a fortiori, not among the Eleven. However, one cannot exclude the possibility that the unnamed disciple is one of the Eleven.

were making their way. See NOTE on 4:30 and p. 169. Implied is their return home after the celebration of Passover in Jerusalem.

to a village called Emmaus, about seven miles distant from Jerusalem. Lit. "to a village 60 stadia distant from Jerusalem, the name of which (was) Emmaus." Three different questions have to be discussed in the interpretation of this difficult verse: (a) the text-critical problem of the distance from Jerusalem; (b) the identification of the village; and (c) why is Emmaus mentioned at all?

a) *Stadious hexēkonta,* "60 stadia," is the reading in mss. P[75], A, B, D, K[2], L, W, X, Δ, Ψ, 063, 0124, *f*[1,13] and many others, as well as in most of the ancient versions. However, mss. ℵ, K*, Θ, Π, 079, 1079*, and some patristic writers (Eusebius, Jerome, Sozomen) read *stadious hekaton hexēkonta,* "160 stadia." The better reading is clearly "60 stadia." See A. Vaccari, "L'Emmaus di S. Luca: Punti sugli i," *Antonianum* 25 (1950) 493-500; M.-J. Lagrange, *Luc,* 617-619.

As a measure of distance, Greek *stadion* equaled 600 Greek feet, 625 Roman feet, 607 English feet, or 185 meters (BAGD 764). Hence "60 stadia" would equal roughly 6.8 miles, and "160 stadia" roughly 18.4 miles.

b) What is known of a village called *Emmaous?* All the Greek mss. and ancient versions read *Emmaus,* save ms. D, which strangely enough has *onomati Oulammaous* (which is well-nigh inexplicable, unless it is a corruption of the ancient name of Bethel *[Oulamlous]* in LXX Gen 28:19). In the main, three places vie for the identification:

1) *Ammaous (RSV,* "Emmaus"), known from Maccabean times. It is mentioned in 1 Macc 3:40,57; 4:3 as the place "in the plain" where Judas Maccabee attacked the forces from Syria and Philistia; it was later fortified by Bacchides (1 Macc 9:50; see Josephus, *Ant.* 13.1,3 § 15). Josephus also speaks of this *Ammaous (J.W.* 2.4,3 § 63; 2.5,1 § 71) or *Emmaous (Ant.* 17.10,7 § 282; 17.10,9 § 291) as a village later burned to the ground at the order of Quintilius Varus (legate of Syria, 6-4 B.C.) in revenge for the slaying of Romans. This village was apparently rebuilt, because it appears later as the chief town in a list of Roman toparchies in A.D. 66 *(J.W.* 3.3,5 § 55 *[Ammaous]).* This place was located some twenty miles west northwest of Jerusalem. In A.D. 223 its name was changed to Nicopolis *(Chronicon paschale* [PG 92. 657]). Eusebius *(Onomasticon* [GCS 3/1. 90]) identified it as the town from which Cleopas came, "the present Nicopolis, a famous town of Palestine." He was followed by Jerome (ibid. 91), and in the fifth century by Sozomen, *Hist. eccl.* 5.21 (GCS 50. 228). None of these writers mentions the distance of Nicopolis from Jerusalem, nor do we know what reading they preferred in 24:13. The modern name of this village is '*Amwas* (the Arabic form of Greek *Emmaous),* near Latrun. Its distance from Jerusalem creates a real difficulty in identifying it with the place intended by Luke. How could the two disciples have traveled that distance by foot and returned the same day? The reading

of "160 stadia" was undoubtedly introduced into the text-tradition (by Origen? by Julius Africanus?) to identify Emmaus as Nicopolis.

This identification is used by G. Dalman (*Sacred Sites and Ways* [London: SPCK, 1935] 226-231); F.-M. Abel ("La distance de Jérusalem à Emmaüs," *RB* 34 [1925] 347-367); L.-H. Vincent and F.-M. Abel (*Emmaüs: Sa basilique et son histoire* [Paris: Leroux, 1932]). See further BIBLIOGRAPHY on pp. 1571-1572.

2) Another *Ammaous* is known to Josephus (*J.W.* 7.6,6 § 217) as a place, "30 stadia" distant from Jerusalem, where Vespasian settled eight hundred veterans discharged from the Roman army. It lay roughly 3.5 miles northwest of Jerusalem in the direction of Joppa and was called in modern times *Kuloniyeh* (= Latin *colonia*, a term often used for such Roman installations), until it was destroyed in the fighting of 1948. It lay on the site of ancient Mozah (Josh 18:26), and was known in the Mishnah *(m. Sukk.* 4:5) as the place from which willow branches were brought to Jerusalem for the feast of Tabernacles. Such a place lay clearly within walking distance for the disciples, both to and fro on the same day. Do Luke's "60 stadia" represent the figure of the round trip?

This identification has been used by J. M. Creed, *The Gospel,* 295; *HJPAJC* 1. 512-513 n. 142; P. Benoit, *Passion and Resurrection,* 271-274; J. Wellhausen, *Das Evangelium Lucae,* 138. If one had to choose, this would be preferable.

3) Since the time of the Crusaders the village of el-Qubeibeh, about 63 stadia from Jerusalem on the road to Lydda, has been identified as the Lucan Emmaus. Some modern Arabs refer to this village as 'Amwas (but this custom does not antedate the beginning of this century). It would be within walking distance of Jerusalem and would be close to the Lucan "60 stadia." But this site is unknown in the first century A.D.

This identification is used by P.-M. Viaud, *Qoubeibeh Emmaus évangélique: Etude archéologique de son église et de la maison qu'elle enclave* (Jerusalem: Saint-Sauveur, 1930); cf. L.-H. Vincent, *RB* 40 (1931) 57-91; A. de Guglielmo, "Emmaus," *CBQ* 3 (1941) 293-301.

c) Why is Emmaus mentioned at all? Even though there is no possibility in modern times of being certain about the location of the village to which the two disciples were walking (given the textual problem and the possibilities of identification), and also given the problem that one has in general about Luke's knowledge of Palestinian geography (see p. 164), the reason why Luke has mentioned this place is merely to keep it within the vicinity of Jerusalem. If Luke were pressed, he would have to admit that Christ did not appear to these disciples in "Jerusalem," but his overarching geographical perspective should not be so pressed. After all, he allowed Jesus during his Galilean ministry to go to "the region of the Gerasenes" (8:26), but he was careful to note that it was "opposite Galilee," lest the reader be distracted from the Galilean setting of such a ministry. So too here. Emmaus is in the vicinity of Jerusalem, and that is all that matters.

14. *They were talking together.* Lit. "and they were conversing with one another." *about all that had occurred.* Lit. "about all those things which had come about/together." For the substantive use of the pf. ptc. *ta symbebēkota,* see 1 Macc 4:26; Josephus, *J.W.* 4.1,6 § 43; *Ant.* 13.6,3 § 194. Note the difference between this neutral expression and *peplērophorēmena* in Luke 1:1. See NOTE there.

15. *As they were talking and discussing.* Lit. "and it happened, in their conversing and discussing, that Jesus himself, drawing near, began to walk with them." Luke uses *kai egeneto* with the conj. *kai* and a finite vb. *(syneporeueto).* See p. 119. The accompanying temporal expression makes use of two articular infins., introduced by *en tō.* See p. 119.

Jesus himself. The *kai autos* is here intensive. See p. 120. Instead of this phrase, ms. B* reads *autous,* "them," as subj. of the infin. *syzētein,* unnecessarily. Ms. D has simply *kai ho* before the proper n. *Iēsous.* Mark 16:12 says that he "appeared in another form" *(en hetera morphē).*

happened to draw near. Christ overtakes them from the rear; he is regarded then as another pilgrim to Jerusalem, returning home from the celebration of Passover. For the risen Christ walking the earth, see p. 193.

16. *their eyes were held.* Lit. "were held back, restrained." Though they saw Christ physically, they failed to recognize who he was. Cf. John 20:14-15, where Mary Magdalene mistakes the risen Christ for a gardener. This comment of the evangelist matches those found in 9:45; 18:34; here it is part of the dramatic concealment used by Luke to build up suspense. Probably the pass. is to be understood as theological. See ZBG § 236.

from recognizing him. Luke uses the gen. of the articular infin. (see p. 108) to express the obj. of restraint.

17. *What is all this talk.* Lit. "what are these words" So Luke makes the risen Christ stage the dramatic story that begins to unfold; he asks about the subj. of their discussion.

that you exchange with one another. For the use of *antiballein,* see 2 Macc 11:13.

18. *Cleopas.* This name is a shortened form of the Greek name *Kleopatros,* the masc. form of Cleopatra (cp. *Antipas* and *Antipatros);* the shortened form is found on Greek ostraca from Egypt. See BDF § 125.2. Though commentators have often associated it with *Klōpas,* the name of the husband or father of a Mary who stands at the cross of Jesus in John 19:25, it really has nothing to do with it, since the latter is a grecized form of a Semitic name, either *qlwp'* (known from Palmyrene texts) or *qlwpw* (an Aramaic name used in Mur 33:5 [DJD 2. 151]).

Since the time of Origen *(Contra Cels.* 2.62,68 [GCS 2. 184, 190]) attempts have been made to identify the companion of Cleopas as Peter. See R. D. Sawyer, "Was Peter the Companion of Cleopas on Easter Afternoon," *ExpTim* 61 (1949-1950) 191-193; J. H. Crehan, "St Peter's Journey to Emmaus," *CBQ* 15 (1953) 418-426; R. Annand, " 'He Was Seen of Cephas', A Suggestion about the First Resurrection Appearance to Peter," *SJT* 11 (1958) 180-187). But this is unlikely in view of v. 34. Other attempts to identify the companion make her Cleopas' wife (because of confusion with John 19:25?). See J. E. Adams, "The Emmaus Story, Lk. xxiv. 13-25: A Suggestion," *ExpTim* 17 (1905-1906) 333-335; C. E. Charlesworth, "The Unnamed Companion of Cleopas," *ExpTim* 34 (1922-1923) 233-234. In yet another late tradition the companion is even named *Emmaous.* See A. Souter, " 'Emmaus' Mistaken for a Person," *ExpTim* 13 (1901-1902) 429-430; E. Nestle, " 'Emmaus' Mistaken for a Person," ibid. 477; A. Bonus, "Emmaus Mistaken for a Person," ibid. 561-562. A tenth-century tradition identifies him with Nathanael.

For Luke the companion is unnamed; and this raises the question why he names

Cleopas at all. There is no need for it; and so the best explanation is that it was already part of the pre-Lucan tradition.

Are you the only stranger in Jerusalem. Lit. "are you sojourning alone in Jerusalem and have not learned . . . ?" The vb. *paroikein* often means to inhabit a place without citizenship, dwell as a resident alien; it can also be used of temporary visitors (which would suit the sojourn of a Passover pilgrim). See the LXX of Gen 17:8; Exod 6:4. Parallels to this sort of rhetorical question have been found in Cicero, *Pro Milone* 12.33; *Pro Rabir. perduell.* 10.28.

what happened there. This is another instance of the Lucan attempt to anchor the Christ-event in human history; so he calls the reader's attention to the far-reaching consequences of what has happened to Jesus. See p. 172. On *genomena,* see NOTE on 23:48.

19. *What is that?* Lit. "what sort of things" *(poia?).* It is a leading question, and they take the bait.

All that happened to. Lit. "the things concerning," *ta peri.* See NOTE on 22:37.

Jesus of Nazareth. Lit. "the Nazarene," *Nazarēnou* being the reading in mss. P[75], ℵ, B, L, 079, 0124, etc. (see 4:34), whereas a number of other mss. (A, D, K, P, W, X, Θ, Ψ, 063, *f*[1,13], and the Koine text-tradition) read *Nazōraiou,* "the Nazorean," the form used in 18:37. See NOTE there.

a prophet mighty in deed and word. For the identification of Jesus as a "prophet," see Luke 7:16,39; 9:8,19. Cf. p. 213. See also F. Hahn, *Titles,* 379-388. For the phrase "mighty in deed and word," see Acts 7:22. For the combination "deed and word" or "word and deed," see Rom 15:18; Col 3:17; 2 Thess 2:17.

in the eyes of God. Lit. "before God." The prep. *enantion* is exclusively Lucan in the NT. See 1:6; 20:26; Acts 7:10; 8:32 (= Isa 53:7).

all the people. See NOTE on 18:43.

20. *our chief priests and leaders.* The same collocation of "chief priests" and (other) "leaders" is found in 23:13. Thus at the end of the Gospel Luke makes one of the subordinate characters point his finger again directly at the Jewish authorities as responsible for the death of Jesus, without any mention of Pilate or the Romans.

The conj. *hopōs,* in the sense of *pōs,* "how," is strange; it introduces an indir. question (see BDF § 300.1), which is unusual, and is probably the reason why ms. D has rather *hōs touton paredōkan,* "that . . . handed him over."

handed him over to be sentenced to death and had him crucified. Lit. "handed him over to a death sentence and crucified him." These words allude to 22:71 and 23:24-33. For the form *paredōkan,* see NOTE on 1:2.

21. *We were hoping.* So the disciples express their disappointment. Their words echo Jer 14:8, where Yahweh himself is called "the hope of Israel, its savior in time of trouble."

the one to deliver Israel. I.e. delivering Israel from Roman occupation (see 1:68 [and NOTE there]; 2:38), a hope alive among Palestinian Jews of the time, rooted in such OT passages as Isa 41:14; 43:14; 44:22-24; 1 Macc 4:11, and echoed in *Ps. Sol.* 9:1. The expression *lg'wlt yśr'l,* "for the redemption of Israel," is found in the date of a deed from the Second Revolt (Mur 22:1; see also 25:1 [DJD 2. 118, 135]). Cf. Acts 1:6.

it is three days since this happened. The translation of the Greek words *tritēn tautēn hēmeran agei aph' hou tauta egeneto* is problematic. The vb. *agein* in a temporal sense is found in extrabiblical Greek, used transitively, in the meaning "to spend" (time), "to celebrate" (a feast). But it usually does not occur impersonally, as it seems to do here; and so some commentators have suggested that "Jesus" should be understood as the subj. of *agei:* "(Jesus) is spending this, the third day, since this happened." See BAGD 14; BDF § 129; *EWNT* 1. 58. But others insist on the impersonal, intrans. sense. See J. M. Creed, *The Gospel,* 296; A. Plummer, *The Gospel,* 554. Cf. W. Arndt, *"Agei,* Luke 24:21," *CTM* 14 (1943) 61. On "the third day," see NOTES on 2:46; 9:22.

22. *Some women from our group.* The ms. D omits the prepositional phrase *ex hymōn.*

really astounded us. See NOTE on 2:47. The report of the women, who first noted the empty tomb, brings not credence, but astonishment, incredulous astonishment.

they went to the tomb early this morning. Lit. "being early at the tomb." This and the two following verses are a summary of 23:56b-24:9, and seemingly they have come to Luke independently of Mark 16:1-8.

23. *came back with the report.* Lit. "came, saying."

a vision of angels. See NOTE on 24:4.

that he was alive. See NOTE on 24:5c.

24. *some of our own number.* Lit. "some of those with us." But according to v. 12 only "Peter" went to the tomb to verify the women's report. This suggests that Luke is using a summary of the visit, which he did not simply create on the basis of vv. 1-12. It shows, as does the Johannine tradition, that not only women went to the empty tomb.

but him they did not see. The obj. "him" *(auton)* is placed emphatically at the head of the sentence. In spite of the empty tomb and the reports of the women, the disciples remain skeptical and are resigned about it all; no one saw *him!*

25. *Jesus said to them.* Lit. "and he said to them," unstressed *kai autos* and *eipen pros* + acc. are used. See pp. 116, 120.

to believe in all that the prophets have said! In this generic statement Luke introduces a major point in his theology. Again he indulges in the hyperbolic "all" *(pasin),* yet refrains from specifying the passages in OT prophetic writings that he has in mind. He thus becomes the model for much of later Christian global reading of the OT as *praeparatio evangelica.* Cf. 18:31. Luke uses the articular infin. (see p. 108) to explain the preceding adjs., "foolish" and "slow of wit" (lit. "slow of heart"). For the combination of *pisteuein* and the prep. *epi,* see BAGD 287.

26. *Was not the Messiah bound to suffer all this.* Recall 17:25. With a rhetorical question Christ goes to the heart of the matter. This is the first occurrence of the specifically Lucan christologoumenon that the Messiah must suffer; see v. 46; Acts 3:18; 17:3; 26:23 (using instead the verbal adj. *pathētos,* "suffering" [Messiah]). The notion of a suffering Messiah is not found in the OT or in any texts of pre-Christian Judaism. Str-B (2. 273-299) says that the "old Synagogue" knew of "a suffering Messiah, for whom no death was determined, i.e. the Messiah ben David" and "a dying Messiah, of whom no suffering was mentioned," i.e. the Messiah ben Joseph (ibid. 273-274). Yet when it cites the passages from rabbinic literature (ibid. 282-291) that speak of the suffering Messiah ben David, they are all drawn from late texts, which scarcely show that the expectation of such a figure existed among *Palestinian* Jews in or prior to the time of Jesus. The same has to be said of the texts about the dying

Messiah ben Joseph (ibid. 292-299). Str-B rightly rejects the implication found at times in Christian commentators that Mark 8:31; 9:31; Matt 16:21 refer to a "suffering Messiah," since, if any title is used in these passages, it is a suffering "Son of Man," and the latter is not a "messianic" title without further ado. Where in pre-Christian Judaism does one find a "Son of Man" as an agent of Yahweh anointed for the salvation, deliverance of his people? True, in *Tg. Jonathan* the "servant" of Isa 52:13 is identified as "the Messiah": "See, my servant, the Messiah, shall prosper; he will be exalted, great, very mighty"; and 53:10c is made to read, "They will look upon the kingdom of their Messiah, many sons and daughters will be theirs." Yet no use of "Messiah" is made in the crucial verse, 53:12. It is not surprising that the "Servant" of Isaiah 52-53 was eventually identified with a messiah in the Jewish tradition; but it still remains to be shown that this identification existed in pre-Christian Judaism or in Judaism contemporary with the NT. Compare S. H. Levey, *The Messiah: An Aramaic Interpretation: The Messianic Exegesis of the Targum* (New York: Hebrew Union College—Jewish Institute of Religion, 1974) 63-67 (to be used with great caution); see D. J. Harrington, *CBQ* 37 (1975) 388-389; J. A. Fitzmyer, *JBL* 94 (1975) 473-477; cf. *HJPAJC* 2. 547-549, which agrees in general with the comments made above; but one has to scrutinize the dates and sources of the (usually *Babylonian)* "sundry rabbinic passages" quoted on p. 549. *(Tg. Jonathan* of the prophets is to be dated sometime between A.D. 200 and 500, and probably comes from Babylonia, as far as its final redaction is concerned. That it uses earlier [even Palestinian] traditions may be admitted; but how does one sort out such traditions from the final redaction without Palestinian controls? Moreover, as Str-B notes [p. 284], this targum, though it understands Isa 52:13-53:12 in a messianic sense, has "ingeniously interpreted away everything that could have referred to the suffering and death of a Messiah," for "the sufferings of the Messiah are turned into those of the people of Israel [52:14; 53:3,4,8,10] or into those of the nations and their rulers [53:3,7,8].") Note, however, that in Justin Martyr, *Dial. cum Tryph.* (68 [PG 6. 635]) the Messiah is *pathētos*—a term probably derived from Acts 26:23!

In using the vb. *edei,* "it was necessary," Luke relates the suffering Messiah motif to his idea of salvation history. See pp. 179-180.

Note how the comment in J. M. Creed *(The Gospel,* 296-297) about "the Pauline ideas of the Cross and redemption" distorts the Lucan view of Jesus' suffering and death. See further pp. 27-29.

before entering into his glory? Lit. "and (so) to enter . . ." Luke 9:26 (see NOTE there) makes it clear that "glory" is the condition of Jesus as "Messiah" or "Son of Man." I.e. that he already enjoys the company of his heavenly Father. See pp. 194, 794. "Glory" *(doxa)* is the splendor associated with the presence of Yahweh in the OT (Exod 14:4,17-18; 16:7,10; 24:16; 40:34-35; Pss 26:8; 72:19), and even in an eschatological sense (Isa 43:7; 58:8; 60:1-2). Cf. Luke 21:27; Acts 7:2,55. Here "glory" represents the term of Jesus' transit to the Father; his destiny has been reached. Even while he converses on the road to Emmaus, he tells the disciples that he has *already entered* upon that status—he is in "glory," and from there he appears to them.

Just as Christ had to suffer all this in order to enter his "glory," so "must" the Christian disciple suffer tribulations to enter the kingdom of God (Acts 14:22).

27. *he began with Moses and all the prophets.* Two parts of the Hebrew OT are

singled out, as in Luke 16:31; Acts 26:22; 28:23. Though Matt 11:13 speaks of "all the prophets and the law" and John 1:45 has a similar phrase, this coupling of the *Tôrah* and the *Nĕbî'îm* is really Lucan in the NT. But Luke is using a mode of expression known from Palestinian Judaism. See 1QS 1:3; 4QDibHam 3:12; cf. 1QS 8:15-16; CD 5:21-6:1; 6QD 3:4.

interpreted for them what pertained to himself in every part of Scripture. Lit. "in all the Scriptures." See Acts 8:35. This would seem to suggest that "all the Scriptures" were included in "Moses and all the prophets." The latter should be understood in the usual Jewish sense of the "former prophets" (Joshua, Judges, 1-2 Samuel, 1-2 Kings) and the "latter prophets" (Isaiah, Jeremiah, Ezekiel, and the Twelve Minor Prophets). Yet note that in v. 44 the "Psalms" (part of the *Kĕtûbîm*, the third part of the Hebrew Bible) are added. Again, Luke supplies no specific references to what "pertained to him" in these Scriptures. On *ta peri*, see NOTE on 22:37.

The sense of Christ's words to the two disciples is that from one end of the Hebrew Scriptures to the other they bear testimony about him and his fate, for "Christ is the goal and the centre of all the Scriptures" (E. Lohse, *Die Auferstehung* [see p. 1551] 29). One can agree with A. Loisy *(L'Evangile selon Luc,* 579) that "the evangelist envisages all the passages of the OT wherein primitive Christianity thought it recognized messianic prophecies, chiefly the texts cited by himself in this book and in Acts." But it is another matter to become so specific as does A. Plummer *(The Gospel,* 555), "Such prophecies as Gen. iii. 15, xxii. 18; Num. xxiv. 17; Deut. xviii. 15, and such types as the scape-goat, the manna, the brazen serpent, and the sacrifices, are specially meant." Plummer is not alone in this sort of endeavor. See J. Ernst, *Evangelium nach Lukas,* 662; N. Geldenhuys, *Commentary,* 634; K. H. Rengstorf, *Evangelium nach Lukas,* 284. It might be tolerable to specify those OT passages to which Luke himself makes reference, but to cite such a passage as Gen 3:15 is highly questionable.

28. *to which they were going.* The double use of *poreuesthai* in this and the following cl. calls attention once again to the geographical perspective of Luke. See NOTE on 4:30. The goal of their walk is reached, but it is also the climax of the story.

pretended to be going on farther. The pretense is a literary foil for the disciples to urge him to stay with them; they so react out of a motive of hospitality for a stranger.

29. *they urged him strongly.* Lit. "prevailed upon him." See Acts 16:15, and the use of the simple vb. in Luke 16:16. See NOTE there.

it is almost evening, and the day is already far spent. Lit. "it is toward evening, and (the day) has declined." In Jewish calendaric reckoning this would mean that "the first day of the week" (24:1) has come to an end; but Luke disregards that, considering the hours after sundown as part of the same day. The first phrase *pros hesperan* is a Septuagintism (see Gen 8:11; Exod 12:6; Num 9:11), and the LXX of Jer 6:4 shows that *hē hēmera* is to be understood with the vb. *kekliken,* which can also be used impersonally of the waning of the day. Cf. 9:12 and NOTE there. So Christian disciples beg their risen Lord to be with them.

to stay with them. I.e. in the house that belonged to one of them. The risen Christ deigns to accept the invitation of such disciples. The articular infin. (see p. 108) is used to express purpose.

30. *Now when he had reclined.* Lit. "and it happened, in his reclining (at table) with

them, (that) he, having taken bread, blessed (it? God?), and having broken (it) offered (it) to them." Luke again uses *kai egeneto* with a finite vb. but without the conj. *kai* (see p. 119); the temporal cl. is expressed by *en* + dat. of the articular infin. See p. 119.

to take bread and utter a blessing; he broke it and offered it to them. Though he is the guest, he assumes the role of the host or *paterfamilias*. Two of the words echo the vbs. of 22:19, the ptcs. *labōn* and *klasas,* "taking" and "breaking." Cf. 9:16. Luke depicts the risen Christ performing the same basic actions that he had performed at the multiplication of the loaves and at the Last Supper. No words of interpretation, however, are pronounced over the bread.

31. *their eyes were opened.* I.e. by God (theological pass.), so that they might see with the eyes of faith. Luke makes use of a Septuagintal expression. See 2 Kgs 6:17.

they recognized him. I.e. as the risen Christ. The same vb. *epiginōskein* is used as in v. 16.

he vanished from their sight. Lit. "and he became (someone) disappearing from them," i.e. without physical locomotion. The goal of the story has been reached. The prepositional phrase *ap' autōn* is a bit peculiar; but it imitates a phrase often used with the pass. of the cognate vb. *aphanizein* ("to be made invisible, disappear") in the LXX (Judg 21:16; Job 2:9b). Cf. 2 Macc 3:34. In classical Greek the adj. is used of disappearing gods. See Euripides, *Hel.* 606.

32. *on fire within us, as he was speaking to us.* A rhetorical exclamation sums up the reaction of the disciples, when they realize the full import of his catechesis and his actions. The words, "within us, as he was speaking to us," are omitted in whole or in part in various ways in different mss. Thus mss. P75, B, D, et al., omit "as he was speaking to us"; others omit "within us." It is best to keep them all; the omission of any of them scarcely changes the sense of the verse in a substantial way. See further *TCGNT* 186. However, some Latin versions change "on fire" (the ptc. *kaiomenē,* "burning") to "blinded" *(excaecatum,* ms. c) or "obtuse" *(optusum,* ms. l); this is obviously a different matter, but it is confined to the Latin versions.

on the road. The prepositional phrase *en tē hodō* again strikes the chord of the geographical motif. See p. 169.

opened to us the sense of the Scriptures! Lit. "opened up for us the Scriptures." Cf. Acts 17:2-3.

33. *Even at that late hour.* Lit. "at that hour," a Septuagintism (see pp. 117-118), i.e. after having dissuaded Christ from going farther because it was evening, and the day was already far spent, they themselves decide to go back to Jerusalem. "The first day of the week" in Jewish reckoning is over; but this is of little concern to Luke.

rose up. For the pleonastic use of the ptc. *anastantes,* see p. 114.

returned to Jerusalem. I.e. whence they had set out earlier in the day, in order to tell the others of their experience.

the Eleven and their companions. See NOTE on 24:9. This would certainly include Thomas; beware of restricting this phrase to those mentioned in John 20:19-23, even though the Lucan tradition here coincides with the Johannine about an appearance of the risen Christ to disciples in Jerusalem on the evening following the discovery of the empty tomb.

gathered together. I.e. as the nucleus community in Jerusalem. See p. 251.

34. *and were saying.* All the mss. read the acc. of the ptc. *legontas* (i.e. the gathered Eleven and others were saying), except for ms. D, which reads instead the nom. pl. *legontes,* which would mean that the two disciples are reporting that the Lord has been truly raised. This much of it would make sense. But how would they have known about the appearance to Simon?

The Lord has been raised. Luke makes use here of a kerygmatic formula, possibly inserting himself *ho Kyrios,* though that may have been part of it originally (see pp. 201-204), for it is not at all impossible that the title formed part of the original kerygma. See pp. 201-204. See NOTES on 7:13-14. The formula used by Luke employs the same vb. *egeirein* as in 1 Cor 15:4; but whereas there it appears in the pf. pass. *egēgertai,* it is used here in the aor. pass. *ēgerthē.*

and he has appeared to Simon. Lit. "and there was seen to Simon," a stereotyped formula for appearances. See NOTE on 1:11; see p. 117. Simon is to be understood as Simon Peter. See NOTE on 4:38. This appearance to Simon makes him the first official witness of the resurrection. Cf. 1 Cor 15:4; Matt 16:16b-19. See p. 1536. The appearance is not narrated, but merely reported; and so one must suppose that it took place after Peter's visit to the empty tomb (v. 12). Nothing is said either by Luke or in Paul's use of the kerygmatic fragment about where the appearance took place. But the Lucan tradition would suggest a locale in Jerusalem, which would not be the same as John 21:1-23. See further H. Conzelmann, *RGG* 1. 699; cf. R. H. Fuller, *McCormick Quarterly* 20 (1967) 309-315. This appearance to Simon Peter is the basis on which he will reinforce his brothers (see Luke 22:32); it is the grace given by the risen Christ to the one who will play the leading role in the Christian community depicted in Luke's second volume. See COMMENT on 22:31-34. See further W. Dietrich, *Das Petrusbild,* 158-163.

35. *what had happened on the road.* Lit. "the things on the road" *(ta en tē hodō);* cp. the end of v. 27 and the prepositional phrase in v. 32.

how he became known to them. Lit. "how he was known to them," the aor. pass. of *ginōskō* is used in the sense of *gnōrizein,* "make known." See BAGD 163.

in the breaking of the bread. This Lucan abstraction, *hē klasis tou artou,* first appears here; it occurs again in Acts 2:42. The concrete verbal form is found further in Acts 2:46; 20:7,11; 27:35. E. Haenchen *(Acts,* 584) understands Acts 20:7,11 to refer to a celebration of the Lord's Supper, but the other passages (2:46; 27:35) to ordinary (perhaps sumptuous) meals. Yet it is difficult to see a reason for the distinction. True, it is not always said that the bread was distributed, but we are clearly confronted here with an abstract way of referring to the Eucharist, which was current in Luke's time. He has read it back into these instances (even into this one) at Stage III of the gospel tradition (say what one might about Stage I). This is the way that Luke wants it to be understood.

What is above all important is that the disciples report that they knew him "in the breaking of the bread" (v. 35) and not by seeing him.

BIBLIOGRAPHY (24:13-35)

Benoit, P. *Passion and Resurrection,* 263-287.

Betz, H. D. "The Origin and Nature of Christian Faith according to the Emmaus Legend (Luke 24:13-32)," *Int* 23 (1969) 32-46.

Bowen, C. R. "The Emmaus Disciples and the Purposes of Luke," *BW* 35 (1910) 234-245.

Brunot, A. "Emmaüs, cité pascale de la fraction du pain," *BTS* 36 (1961) 4-11.

Buzy, D. "Emmaüs dans l'évangile et la tradition," *BTS* 36 (1961) 4-5.

Certeau, M. de. "Les pèlerins d'Emmaüs," *Christus* 13 (1957) 56-63.

D'Arc, J. "Catechesis on the Road to Emmaus," *Lumen vitae* 32 (1977) 143-156.

———— "Un grand jeu d'inclusions dans 'les pèlerins d'Emmaüs,' " *NRT* 99 (1977) 62-76.

Desremaux, J. "Les disciples d'Emmaüs: Luc 24,13-32," *BVC* 56 (1964) 45-46.

Dillon, R. J. *From Eye-Witnesses,* 69-155.

Dupont, J. "Les pèlerins d'Emmaüs (Luc xxiv, 13-35)," *Miscellanea biblica B. Ubach* (Scripta et documenta 1; ed. R. M. Díaz; Montserrat: [Benedictine Abbey], 1953) 349-374.

———— "The Meal at Emmaus," *The Eucharist* (ed. J. Delorme) 105-121.

Ehrhardt, A. "The Disciples of Emmaus," *NTS* 10 (1963-1964) 182-201.

———— "Emmaus, Romulus and Apollonius," *Mullus: Festschrift Theodor Klauser* (JAC Ergänzungsband 1; Münster in W.: Aschendorff, 1964) 93-99.

Feuillet, A. "L'Apparition du Christ à Marie Madeleine *Jean 20,11-18:* Comparaison avec l'apparition aux disciples d'Emmaus *Luc 24,13-35,* " *Esprit et vie* 88 (1978) 193-204, 209-223.

———— "Les pèlerins d'Emmaüs (Lc 24, 13-35)," *Nova et vetera* (Genoa) 47 (1972) 89-98.

———— "La recherche du Christ dans la Nouvelle Alliance d'après la christophanie de Jo. 20,11-18: Comparaison avec Cant. 3,1-4 et l'épisode des pèlerins d'Emmaüs," *L'Homme devant Dieu: Mélanges H. de Lubac* (Théologie 56; Paris: Aubier, 1963) 1. 93-112.

Fichtner, J. A. "Christ Humiliated and Exalted," *Worship* 36 (1961-1962) 308-313.

Gaide, G. "Les apparitions du Christ ressuscité d'après S. Luc, Luc 24,13-48," *As-Seign* ns 24 (1969) 38-56.

Gils, F. "Pierre et la foi au Christ ressuscité," *ETL* 38 (1962) 5-43.

Guillaume, J.-M. *Luc interprète,* 67-159.

Hahn, F. *Titles,* 376-382.

Huffman, N. "Emmaus among the Resurrection Narratives," *JBL* 64 (1945) 205-226.

Iersel, B. van. "Terug van Emmaüs: Bijdragen tot een structurele tekstanalyse van Lc. 24, 13-35," *TvT* 18 (1978) 294-323.

Kremer, J. " 'Der Herr ist wahrhaft auferstanden': Zur Überlieferung und Form von Lk 24,34," *Liturgie und Mönchtum* 42 (1968) 33-41.

Lee, G. M. "The Walk to Emmaus," *ExpTim* 77 (1965-1966) 380-381.

Liefeld, W. L. "Exegetical Notes: Luke 24:13-35," *Trinity Journal* 2 (1981) 223-229.

Losada, D. A. "El episodio de Emaús: Lc 24,13-35," *RevistB* 35 (1973) 3-13.
Meissner, S. R. de. "The Journey to Emmaus," *BSac* 84 (1927) 158-166.
Menoud, P.-H. "Les Actes des Apôtres et l'eucharistie," *RHPR* 33 (1953) 21-36.
Meynet, R. "Comment établir un chiasme: A propos des 'pèlerins d'Emmaüs,' " *NRT* 100 (1978) 233-249.
Michael, J. H. "The Text of Luke xxiv. 34," *ExpTim* 60 (1948-1949) 292.
Orlett, R. "The Influence of the Early Liturgy upon the Emmaus Account," *CBQ* 21 (1959) 212-219.
Perella, C. M., and A. Vaccari. "De vi critices textus et archaeologiae circa Lc. 24,13-38," *VD* 17 (1937) 186-191.
Perella, G. M. " 'Cognoverunt eum in fractione panis' (Lc xxiv 35)," *Divus Thomas* 3 (1936) 349-357.
Riedl, J. " 'Wirklich, der Herr ist auferweckt worden und dem Simon erschienen' (Lk 24,34): Entstehung und Inhalt des neutestamentlichen Osterglaubens," *BLit* 40 (1967) 81-110.
Schnider, F., and W. Stenger. "Beobachtungen zur Struktur der Emmausperikope (Lk 24,13-35)," *BZ* 16 (1972) 94-114.
Stöger, A. "L'Esprit synodal," *Christus* 18 (1971) 406-419; "Weggefährten *(synodoi)* der Auferstandenen," *BLit* 44 (1971) 155-164.
Stravinskas, P. M. J. "The Emmaus Pericope: Its Sources, Theology and Meaning for Today," *Bible Bhashyam* 3 (1977) 97-115.
Suasso, P. H. "Een moderne evangelie-exegese: De Emmausgangers," *Bijdragen* 16 (1955) 204-207.
Thévenot, X. "Emmaüs, une nouvelle Genèse? Une lecture psychanalytique de Genèse 2-3 et Luc 24, 13-35," *MScRel* 37 (1980) 3-18.
Veloso, M. "Una lectura viviente de la Biblia según san Lucas," *RevistB* 39 (1977) 197-209.
Walker, W. O., Jr. "Postcrucifixion Appearances and Christian Origins," *JBL* 88 (1969) 157-165.
Wanke, J. *Die Emmauserzählung: Eine redaktionsgeschichtliche Untersuchung zu Lk 24,13-25* (Erfurter theologische Studien 31; Leipzig: St. Benno, 1973).
——— " '. . . wie sie ihn beim Brotbrechen erkannten': Zur Auslegung der Emmauserzählung Lk 24, 13-35," *BZ* 18 (1974) 180-192.
Wulf, F. "Sie erkannten ihn beim Brechen des Brotes (Lk 24,35)," *Geist und Leben* 37 (1964) 81-83.

Bibliography on the Site of Emmaus

Arce, P. A. "Emaús y algunos textos desconocidos," *EstBíb* 13 (1954) 53-90.
Bataini, G. "L'Emmaus del vangelo (Luc. 24,13-35)," *Divus Thomas* 3/21-23 (1944-1946) 96-123.
——— "L'Emmaus di S. Luca, punti sugli," *Palestra del clero* 24 (1955) 241-249.
Bishop, E. F. F. "Where Was Emmaus? Why Not 'Imwas?'" *ExpTim* 55 (1943-1944) 152-153.

Crowfoot, J. W. *Early Churches in Palestine* (Schweich Lectures 1937; London: British Academy, 1941) 71.

Duvignau, P. *Emmaüs: Le site—le mystère* (Paris: Leroux, 1937).

Mackowski, R. M. "Where is Biblical Emmaus?" *ScEsp* 32 (1980) 93-103.

Sandoli, S. de. *Emmaus—El Qubeibeh* (2d ed.; Jerusalem: Franciscan Press, 1980).

Spadafora, F. "Emmaus: Critica testuale e archeologia," *RivB* 1 (1953) 255-268.

Vincent, L.-H. "L'Année archéologique 1924-1925 en Palestine: I.-1. Fouilles de l'Ecole à la basilique d'"Amwas," *RB* 35 (1926) 117-121.

——— "La chronologie du groupe monumentale d'"Amwas," *RB* 55 (1948) 348-375.

167. JESUS APPEARS TO THE DISCIPLES IN JERUSALEM
(24:36-43)

24 [36] While they were still talking about this, Jesus himself stood in their midst and said to them, "Peace be with you!" [37] Terrified and startled, they thought that they were seeing a ghost. [38] He said to them, "Why are you alarmed? Why do doubts arise in your minds? [39] Look at my hands and my feet and see that it is really I. Touch me and see; no ghost has flesh and bones such as you see I have." [40] As he said this, he showed them his hands and his feet. [41] Because they were still incredulous, overjoyed yet wondering, Jesus said to them, "Do you have anything here to eat?" [42] And they offered him a piece of fish that they had broiled; [43] he took it and ate it in front of them.

COMMENT

The third appearance of the risen Christ in the Lucan resurrection narrative takes place in Jerusalem itself on the same evening following the discovery of the empty tomb, immediately after the return of the two disciples from Emmaus with their report. Christ appears to the nucleus Christian community, the house-church of his followers, gathered together in bewilderment, astonishment, and incredulity (24:36-43).

In reality, this episode is but the threshold to the coming scene (vv. 44-49), in which the risen Christ instructs the Eleven and those with them from Scripture and commissions them to be his witnesses, and then in the last scene (vv. 50-53) takes his final departure from them by ascension. Verses 36-53 are really a literary unit, for they recount but one appearance of the risen

Christ. Indeed, though there is an inkling of recognition in the "joy" that attends the incredulity (v. 41), the real recognition of Christ does not come until v. 52, where, having been instructed by him from Scripture, they finally worship him. Moreover, the parallelism, which we noted above, between this composite scene and the Emmaus incident has to be noted. There is again an appearance that is not comprehended; an instruction based on Scripture, which leads to proper revelation; a meal (taken by Jesus himself), and finally his departure (not by vanishing, but by ascension). The only element that is added, which was not present in the Emmaus episode, is the commission that Christ gives to his disciples. If we divide this unit into three smaller scenes, it is not to deny its basic unity, but merely to facilitate the interpretation of it, because the Lucan unit has been made up of various elements from the gospel tradition.

In these scenes we encounter once again several verses that have been regarded as Western Non-Interpolations: vv. 36bc,40,51b,52a. For the reasons why they are no longer to be so regarded and why they are here considered as genuine parts of the original text of the Lucan Gospel, see pp. 130-131. On this point we insist, *pace* J. Schmid, *Evangelium nach Lukas,* 359-363; J. Ernst, *Evangelium nach Lukas,* 666; A. Huck and H. Greeven, *Synopse,* 280-281.

In the first scene of this unit (vv. 36-43) the evangelist makes use of some earlier tradition, for what one meets here is a developed form of the snippet of tradition preserved in 1 Cor 15:5 ("he appeared . . . then to the Twelve") and of material that John 20:19-21 has also employed. Moreover, another form of the tradition is undoubtedly to be found in the Marcan appendix (16:14-15), which tells of an appearance of Christ to the Eleven as they sat at table on Easter Sunday night; he upbraids them for their incredulity and finally commissions them to preach the gospel. The language and style in the Marcan appendix are so different that there can be no dependence on the Lucan Gospel; and so it is an independent testimony (from "L") to the same appearance. But the similarity of the tradition used in common by Luke and John is another matter: Some details can be seen in the following points: (1) "stood in their midst" (v. 36b, *estē en mesō autōn;* John 20:19c, *estē eis to meson);* (2) "and said to them, 'Peace be with you!' " (v. 36c, *kai legei autois, eirēnē hymin* [with historic pres.]; John 20:19d); (3) "As he said this, he showed them his hands and his feet" (v. 40); "As he said this, he showed them his hands and his side" (John 20:20a—clearly a Johannine redactional change in view of 19:34, where alone in the gospel tradition the "side" of Jesus is pierced); (4) the mention of "joy" (v. 41—out of place in this context; John 20:20b). The main difference in the Lucan and Johannine scenes is the treatment of the reactions of the disciples: in John, they rejoice at seeing the Lord (who commissions them and breathes the Spirit upon them); in Luke, they are terrified, astounded, and incredulous. There are, moreover, two other minor elements in this Lucan scene that have counterparts in other Johannine verses: (a) The challenge of the Lucan Christ, "Touch me and see" (v. 39b), is similar to the challenge extended to Thomas in John 20:27; and (b) the "fish" that is offered to the risen Christ in v. 42 recalls the fish that he would offer to the seven disciples in John 21:9 (though the terminology differs).

Lucan stylistic redaction in the episode is at a minimum: (1) The gen. absol. in v. 36a (see Acts 4:1); (2) the doubled participial phrases in v. 37a, "terrified and startled" (see Luke 21:9; 24:5); (3) the vb. "offered" in v. 42 *(epididonai,* see p. 110); and (4) the prep. *enōpion,* "in front of them," in v. 43 (see p. 110). (See further J.-M. Guillaume, *Luc interprète,* 171-201 [but beware of his conclusion that this episode stems from "tradition johannique"].)

This scene constitutes the beginning of a *mixed* appearance-story (see COMMENT on 24:13-35). Some of the elements of Dodd's concise pattern are present in it: (a) Situation: The disciples still talking about the report of the two who had returned from Emmaus (v. 36a); (b) Appearance (v. 36b); (c) Greeting (v. 36c); (d) Recognition: only an inkling of it in v. 41, "overjoyed yet wondering"; the full recognition is held until v. 52; (e) Word of command: to come in vv. 47-49. But these elements are dressed with Lucan embellishment, which takes on three forms: (a) the multiple description of the reaction of the disciples confronted with the risen Christ: they are terrified, startled, full of doubt, incredulous, overjoyed yet wondering; (b) an apologetic motif: Christ challenges them to touch him, look at his hands and feet, flesh and bones; and he asks them for something to eat, which he consumes in their sight; and (c) the instruction of them through an explanation of Scripture. The unit lacks the dramatic suspense of the Emmaus story, mainly because of the first two forms of Lucan embellishment.

In this first scene of the unit the risen Christ again appears from "glory" and shows himself alive to the Eleven and those with them, who have just learned from the two who have come back from Emmaus about how they recognized him in the breaking of the bread. Christ thus appears to his nucleus Christian community with the message of "Peace" (one of the effects of the Christ-event in Lucan theology [see pp. 224-225]). That the members of this household are incredulous or mistake him for a ghost is at first understandable. But their rapt silence in the episode is striking; Christ is the only one who speaks. He tries to dispel their doubts "with many proofs" (Acts 1:3).

Finally, he asks for something to eat and is given a piece of broiled fish; we are not told that they were at table, but that is the gist of the story, for later in Acts we learn that the risen Christ did "eat with" his apostles (Acts 1:4, *synalizomenos* [of disputed meaning, see BAGD 783-784]; Acts 10:41, "we ate and drank with him"). (Cf. R. J. Dillon, *From Eye-Witnesses,* 197-203.)

Though the motif of the meal is there and helps fill out the parallelism of this unit with the Emmaus incident, one cannot help but realize that the scene is intended also to stress the identity and the physical reality of the risen Christ who has appeared to his disciples. Thus Luke develops his own form of a tradition of early Christianity; it is but another way that he builds up the assurance *(asphaleia)* for the reader Theophilus (1:3-4). Though there is a certain parallelism with John 20:19-21, the whole piece has become far more realistic. The Johannine tradition too was coping with that problem, but it does it in a different way by introducing the Thomas episode (John 20:24-29 —recall that Thomas was not mentioned in the verses that parallel this Lucan episode; it is an afterthought).

Further comments on this appearance-story will follow in the next two scenes.

NOTES

24   36. *While they were still talking about this.* This transitional cl., of Lucan redaction, ensures the dating of this appearance of the risen Christ to "the first day of the week." See 24:1,13,33. *Pace* J. Ernst *(Evangelium nach Lukas,* 666), the connection is not "loose"; it is rather "clear," as G. Schneider *(Evangelium nach Lukas,* 501) notes.

Jesus himself. Lit. "he himself," according to the reading of the best mss. (P[75], ℵ, B, D, L, 1241) and many ancient versions. But something more is needed for the sake of the sense, and *Iēsous* has been added in mss. A, W, Θ, Ψ, *f*[1.13], and the Koine text-tradition. Though we recognize the better reading, we have added "Jesus" for the sake of the English translation.

stood in their midst. See John 20:19, which may preserve the original formulation, since *en mesō autōn* is used elsewhere by Luke (2:46; 8:7; 10:3; 22:27,55; Acts 4:7; 27:21).

and said to them, "Peace be with you!" Though these words are omitted in ms. D and the OL version, they are included in all the best Greek mss. (P[75], ℵ, A, B, K, L, X, Δ, Θ, Π, Ψ, *f*[1.13], and many others). Just because they are word-for-word identical with John 20:19, they are not to be regarded as a gloss introduced from the Johannine Gospel. Nor do they show that Luke is dependent necessarily on the Johannine tradition; the most one can say is that both Luke and the Johannine tradition have used common material.

Some minor mss. (P, W, 579) and some ancient versions (Vg, Syriac) add, "It is I; do not be afraid." But this addition cannot be put in the same class with the foregoing words. The greeting that the risen Christ uses makes one recall 10:5, part of the mission-charge, when Jesus sent the seventy(-two) out to preach; for the implications of its use in this scene, see R. J. Dillon, *From Eye-Witnesses,* 187.

37. *Terrified and startled.* Lit. "terrified and being fearful." For the latter phrase *(emphoboi genomenoi),* see 24:5.

they were seeing a ghost. Lit. "seemed to gaze at a spirit." Instead of *pneuma,* "spirit," read by most of the Greek mss., ms. D has *phantasma,* "apparition, ghost," a term probably derived from Matt 14:26. This sense of *pneuma,* as the bodiless independent being of a person after death is not used elsewhere by Luke, but it does occur in 1 Pet 3:19; Heb 12:23.

38. *Why do doubts arise in your minds?* Lit. "Because of what do thoughts mount in your heart/hearts" (depending on the reading *kardia* [sg.] or *kardiais* [pl.]). Mss. P⁷⁵, B, D have the sg. *kardia;* the majority of the rest of the Greek mss. have the pl. *kardiais.* The sg. would have to be understood collectively. On *dialogismoi,* "thoughts, doubts," see NOTE on 2:35. The risen Christ perceives the problem facing the disciples who behold him.

39. *Look at my hands and my feet.* I.e. the hands and feet pierced in the act of crucifixion. His challenge to the disciples to look and to touch is aimed at establishing his identity; but his challenge reveals the incredulity that still besets them. Luke presupposes here details of the crucifixion that he did not recount, e.g. the use of nails.

see that it is really I. Lit. "that I myself exist." This cl. is explanatory or epexegetical to the impv. "Look at . . ."

Touch me and see. A second challenge is offered to the disciples. Luke never tells us whether any of the disciples took up the challenge and touched the risen Christ, just as John never tells whether Thomas touched him (20:27). Ignatius of Antioch *(Smyrn.* 3.1) supplies what all readers suppose: "And they immediately touched him and believed, being mingled both with his flesh and spirit."

no ghost has flesh and bones such as you see I have. This cl. begins with an ambiguous conj. *hoti,* which could mean ". . . and see that no ghost . . ."; or ". . . and see, because no ghost . . ."; or it could be taken as *hoti recitativum,* introducing dir. discourse, as I have taken it. Either the second or third possibility is preferable.

Luke is not concerned with the type of question that Paul discusses in 1 Cor 15:44; and his explanation of a *sōma pneumatikon* should not be invoked to explain this Lucan verse. By way of contrast, see Lucian's description of the existence of "heroes," *Vera historia* 2.12. Cf. Homer, *Od.* 11. 218-219.

40. *As he said this, he showed them his hands and his feet.* These words are omitted in ms. D and in the OL and OS versions, and by Marcion; yet they are found in all the best Greek mss. (P⁷⁵, ℵ, A, B, K, L, W, X, Δ, Θ, Π, Ψ, *f* ¹,¹³, and many others). Just because they are almost word-for-word identical with John 20:20, they are not to be regarded as a gloss introduced from the Johannine Gospel. Nor do they show that Luke is dependent necessarily on the Johannine tradition; the most one can say is that both Luke and the Johannine tradition have used common material. Here Luke has probably preserved the more original formulation, "his hands and his feet." See COMMENT. Another problem is often seen in this case (not true of v. 36bc) in that v. 40 is redundant after v. 39. Yet that may be precisely the reason why ms. D and the OL and OS versions have removed it.

41. *incredulous, overjoyed yet wondering.* Lit. "being still disbelieving from joy and wondering," a gen. absol. to introduce the sentence. See p. 108. Though the detail of "joy" is probably retained by Luke from his source "L," he makes it the excuse for the disciples' disbelief (see v. 11), just as he earlier explained away their sleep in 22:45, "because of grief." For *apo,* expressing cause, see 21:26; 22:45; Acts 12:14. "Joy" is mentioned in John 20:20.

Do you have anything here to eat? Lit. "anything edible," i.e. left over from their evening meal. The adv. *enthade,* "here," occurs only in Lucan writings in the NT, apart from John 4:15-16. See Acts 10:18; 16:28; 17:6; 25:17,24.

42. *they offered.* On the vb. *epedōkan,* see NOTE on 1:2.

a piece of fish that they had broiled. Lit. "part of a broiled fish *(ichthyos optou),*" actually the adj. *optos* could mean "broiled," "roasted," or "baked." The food offered makes the reader think of John 21:9: Jesus on the shore of the Sea of Tiberias with fish *(opsarion)* on coals and bread ready for the disciples' breakfast.

A few mss. (Θ, Ψ, *f*[1.13], and the Koine text-tradition) and some versions (Latin, Syriac) add: "and some honeycomb." But they are not significant enough to be considered seriously. See further E. Nestle, "The Honeycomb in Luke xxiv," *ExpTim* 22 (1910-1911) 567-568.

More of a problem is the objection raised about this request of Jesus and what is offered to him, fish (in Jerusalem). Is this possibly an indication that Luke is using a tradition about an appearance of Christ in Galilee and centering it in Jerusalem? Who can say? See further I. H. Marshall, *Luke,* 903; M.-J. Lagrange, *Luc,* 613. This is the kind of question that should not be asked of the Lucan Gospel. It does not make any difference to Luke what was offered to Jesus (in Stage I of the tradition); the important thing is that he ate it in front of them (Stage III of the tradition).

43. *he took it and ate it in front of them.* Only Luke among the evangelists indulges in this sort of realism about the existence of the risen Christ; and for this he is castigated, by twentieth-century readers! In 20:27-29 John as an evangelist has his own way of stressing the reality, yet he is rarely castigated in the same way. See further M.-E. Boismard, "Le réalisme." For eating on the part of "angels" and others like them, see Gen 18:8; 19:3; Tob 6:5.

A few mss. (K, Π, *f*[13], etc.) add, "and taking the rest, he gave it to them." This addition would nicely support the contention that this is really a meal-scene; but that is never said in the main texts.

BIBLIOGRAPHY (24:36-43)

Bishop, E. F. F. "With Saint Luke in Jerusalem from Easter Day till Pentecost," *ExpTim* 56 (1944-1945) 192-194, 220-223.

Boismard, M.-E. "Le réalisme des récits évangéliques," *Lumière et vie* 107 (1972) 31-41.

Dillon, R. J. *From Eye-Witnesses,* 157-203.

George, A. "Les récits d'apparitions aux Onze à partir de Luc 24, 36-53," *La résurrection du Christ et l'exégèse moderne* (LD 50; eds. P. de Surgy et al.; Paris: Cerf, 1969) 75-104.

Guillaume, J.-H. *Luc interprète,* 163-201.

Martini, C. M. "L'apparizione agli Apostoli in Lc,36-43 nel complesso dell'opera lucana," *Resurrexit* (ed. E. Dhanis), 230-245.

168. JESUS' FINAL COMMISSION
(24:44-49)

24 44 Then Jesus said to them, "Now this is what my words meant which I addressed to you while I was still with you: All that was written about me in the Law of Moses, in the Prophets, and in the Psalms must see fulfillment." 45 Then he opened their minds to an understanding of the Scriptures. 46 "This," he said, "is what stands written: The Messiah shall suffer and rise from the dead on the third day. 47 In his name repentance for the forgiveness of sins shall be preached to all the nations—beginning from Jerusalem! 48 You are witnesses of this! 49 Now take note: I am sending upon you what my Father has promised. You are to remain here in the city until you are invested with power from on high."

COMMENT

The sequel to the threshold scene of the appearance of Christ to the disciples in Jerusalem on Easter Sunday evening tells of his instruction of them on the basis of the Scriptures and his commissioning of them to be his witnesses, announcing repentance for the forgiveness of sins in his name to all the nations. But they are to wait in Jerusalem until they have been invested with "what my Father has promised" (24:44-49).

This episode really belongs to the Lucan literary unit of vv. 36-53 (see COMMENT on 24:36-43). It also has parallels with other parts of the gospel tradition, which have now to be considered.

This passage is remotely related to the finale of the Matthean Gospel (29:19-20a) and to the Marcan appendix (16:15-16) in that like them it preserves an early tradition about an appearance of the risen Christ in which he commissioned disciples to carry out a future mission in his name. This commission is couched specifically in vv. 47-49 of this episode. However, strikingly enough, the commission in each case is made *in its formulation* to suit a major theme in the theology of each Gospel. In the Marcan appendix—not composed by Mark himself, but echoing in part some Marcan themes—the commission is worded thus:

16:15-16:   *poreuthentes eis ton kosmon hapanta, kēryxate to euangelion pasē*
            tē ktisei. Ho pisteusas kai baptistheis sōthēsetai, ho de apistēsas
            katakrithēsetai.
            "Go into the whole universe and preach the gospel to every crea-
            ture. The one who believes (it) and is baptized will be saved; the
            one who does not believe will be damned."

In this "Marcan" commission the disciples are to "preach the gospel" (see
Mark 1:1,14,15; 8:35; 10:29; 13:10; 14:9), a theme that Luke has studiously
avoided in his Gospel (see pp. 172-174).

Matthew does not express the final commission in terms of "gospel" either,
but phrases it to express his own concerns thus:

28:19-20a: *poreuthentes oun mathēteusate panta ta ethnē, baptizontes autous*
            eis to onoma tou patros kai tou huiou kai tou hagiou pneumatos,
            didaskontes autous tērein panta hosa eneteilamēn hymin.
            "Go, therefore, and make disciples of all the nations, baptizing
            them in the name of the Father, and of the Son, and of the holy
            Spirit, teaching them to observe all that I have commanded
            you."

In this Matthean commission the disciples are to baptize, as in Mark 16:16,
but the distinctive element is the charge to "make disciples of all the nations"
and to *teach* "them to observe all that I have commanded you." The latter in
particular is so well suited to the Gospel in which the evangelist has grouped
Jesus' "teaching" in five great discourses and has made an important issue of
discipleship *(mathētēs,* used seventy-three times in Matthew, forty-six times
in Mark, and thirty-seven times in Luke; only Matthew uses *mathēteuein*
[three times]).

In contrast to the two foregoing commissions, the Lucan formulation of the
charge stands out; it is also the beginning of a theme that will be important in
the rest of the Lucan writings. It runs thus:

24:47-49:   . . . *kērychthēnai epi tō onomati autou metanoian eis aphesin*
            hamartiōn eis panta ta ethnē, arxamenoi apo Ierousalēm. hymeis
            martyres toutōn, kai idou egō apostellō tēn epangelian tou patros
            mou eph' hymas. hymeis de kathisate en tē polei heōs hou en-
            dysēsthe ex hypsous dynamin.
            "In his name repentance for the forgiveness of sins shall be
            preached to all the nations—beginning from Jerusalem! You are
            witnesses of this! Now take note: I am sending upon you what my
            Father has promised. You are to remain here in the city until you
            are invested with power from on high."

One is not surprised to see *metanoia,* "repentance," or *aphesis hamartiōn,*
"forgiveness of sins," surface here (see pp. 237-238, 223-224); but the theme
of "testimony" now begins, and it will be picked up in the programmatic
verse of Acts (1:8) and used often thereafter (see p. 243). What is striking,
however, is the way the Lucan Christ relates this function of the disciples to

the OT Scriptures. They tell not only about the suffering Messiah who is to rise, but they become the basis for the testimony that the disciples are to bear and the preaching that they are to carry out in his name. Eyewitnesses are to become testifiers, and indeed "ministers of the word" (1:2). Though this becomes one of the criteria for the member who will replace Judas in the Twelve (Acts 1:21-22), it is not limited to such a member, as this episode makes clear, in that the commission is addressed to "the Eleven and all the others" (24:9,33). They are the ones who are to carry to the end of the earth "the word" *(ton logon,* Acts 4:4,29; 8:4; 10:36,44; 11:19,22; 14:25; 16:6; 17:11; 18:5; 19:20); "the word of God/the Lord" *(ho logos tou theou/kyriou,* Acts 4:31; 6:2,7; 8:14,25; 11:1; 12:24; 13:5,7,44,46,48,49; 15:36; 16:32; 17:13; 18:11; 19:10); "the word of salvation" (Acts 13:26); "the word of the gospel" (Acts 15:7). (See further R. J. Dillon, *From Eye-Witnesses,* 203-225.)

All of this is, in effect, part of the Father's plan of salvation-history (see pp. 179-187). This is the reason why the disciples have to wait in Jerusalem itself to be invested "with power from on high." It is the place from which the word is destined to go forth (cp. v. 47b and Acts 1:8). The disciples are not to proceed on their own; Christ's commission to them clearly involves a grace, but it is also an authorized commission, one invested with *dynamis,* which they will need to carry it out. The word *dynamin* comes emphatically at the end of the verse, and it rings a bell for the careful reader of the Lucan Gospel. For it was "with the power of the Spirit" that Jesus himself withdrew to Galilee after his encounter in the desert with the devil (4:14). Moreover, it was with "the power of the Lord" *(Kyriou* = Yahweh, 5:17) that he healed people. And the power that "went forth from him" (6:19) is precisely the "power" with which his disciples are now to be invested (see Acts 2:32-33). Though it is not yet made clear what "my Father has promised" (24:49) is, that will be clarified in Acts 1:4b,5b; 2:2-4,32-33.

Luke has inherited from "L" a tradition about a final commission of the disciples by the risen Christ (see p. 84), a tradition known to Matthew and the author of the Marcan appendix as well. This tradition told about a sending-out of the disciples (Matthew and Mark: *poreuthentes* [dir. impv.]; Luke: *apostellō* [dir. statement]); to preach/teach (Mark: *kēryxate;* Luke: *kērychthēnai;* Matthew: *didaskontes);* what they are to preach/teach (Mark: *euangelion;* Matthew: "all that I have commanded you"; Luke: "repentance for the forgiveness of sins"); and above all to whom (Mark: "to every creature"; Matthew and Luke: "all the nations").

Specifically Lucan redaction in this scene can be seen in the following elements: (1) *eipen/elalēsa pros* + acc., "said to" (v. 44ab; see p. 116); (2) "while I was still with you" (v. 44c; see p. 111 *[syn]);* (3) "all that was written" (v. 44d; see 18:31; 21:22; Acts 13:29; 24:14 [also hyperbolic "all"]); (4) "the Law of Moses," (v. 44d; see 2:22; Acts 13:38; 15:5); (5) "opened" (v. 45; see p. 110 *[dianoigein]);* (6) articular infin. with *tou* (v. 45b; see p. 108); (7)

"the Messiah shall suffer" (v. 46; see NOTE on 24:26); (8) "in his name repentance for the forgiveness of sins" (v. 47); (9) "beginning from" (v. 47c; see NOTE on 23:5); (10) "witnesses" (v. 48); (11) "what my Father has promised" (v. 49; see Acts 1:4b). (For further analysis, see J.-M. Guillaume, *Luc interprète,* 181-187; J. Jeremias, *Die Sprache,* 321-322.)

The scene is thus largely a Lucan embellishment of the element in C. H. Dodd's concise pattern called the Word of Command ("The Appearances," p. 1556). The "word" itself would be those details that this Lucan scene shares in common with the Marcan appendix and the Matthean finale in their commissions; the Lucan embellishment makes the scene part of the mixed appearance-story. For the commissioning form, see B. J. Hubbard, "Commissioning Stories in Luke-Acts."

The risen Christ in this scene recalls to the disciples in the light of his resurrection the meaning of the "words" that he had so often addressed to them during his ministry. Those words would have included not only his teaching and parables, but above all the announcements of his passion and death (recall 9:22,44; 17:25; 18:31-33; 22:37 [see COMMENT on 9:22]). Now come his last words to them, his testament. This time, they are directed to his nucleus community, gathered in their silence as they intently listen to his exposition of what pertained to him in the Law of Moses, the Prophets, and the Psalms—in the *Tôrāh,* the *Něbî'îm,* and at least part of the *Kětûbîm.* In the salvific plan of his Father all had to be fulfilled, and indeed has now been fulfilled. Only in the light of his resurrection can the Scriptures of old be understood. Once again, the Lucan Christ cites no specific passages from the OT, and the Lucan global interpretation of the Hebrew Scriptures takes over. "This . . . is what stands written: The Messiah shall suffer and rise from the dead on the third day" (v. 46). But it is impossible to find any of these elements precisely in the OT, either that the Messiah shall suffer, or that he is to rise, or that it will happen on the third day. This is Lucan use of the OT in the service of his christology.

However, the risen Christ does not stop there, for he even traces to Scripture the preaching in his name of repentance for the forgiveness of sins to all the nations. Thus Luke adumbrates already the sequel to the suffering, death, and resurrection of the Christ, a sequel that he will develop and present in his second volume.

Jerusalem, which had been the goal of Jesus' missionary wanderings (23:5), is now explicitly named as the focal point; from *goal* it becomes the *starting point,* whence the "word" will spread to the end of the earth (Acts 1:8).

In the Matthean finale (28:20), the eleven disciples who have been commissioned to make other disciples, to baptize, and to teach all the nations are assured by Christ, "Look, I am with you during all the days until the close of the age." The Lucan Christ assures his followers too, but in a different way: His heavenly Father has promised to invest them with power from on high.

This will be the basis of the boldness with which Peter and the others will speak (Acts 2:29; 4:13,29,31; 28:31). But they are not yet told what form that *dynamis,* "power," will assume. That is to be revealed in Acts 1-2 as "the holy Spirit," who will assist their "testimony" as they carry the "word" to the "end of the earth" (Acts 1:8; see 2:33,38; 5:32; 13:4,9; 16:6; 20:23). Thus, in and through the Spirit, who is "what my Father has promised," Christ will be present to his commissioned followers in their testimony. (See further R. F. O'Toole, "Activity" [p. 1551].) For parallels between this passage and the commission given to Paul in Acts 26:16-23, see J. Dupont, "La mission de Paul."

This commissioning of the Eleven had been foreshadowed in the Lucan Gospel by the mission of the Twelve (9:1-6) and the mission of the seventy(-two) (10:1-12). Now, when the commissioning of "the Eleven and all the others" (vv. 9,33) takes place with the charge of the risen Christ, one sees a further meaning in the double mission of the disciples in the ministry of Jesus. This will be further exploited in Acts 6, when the Twelve decide to appoint seven others to assist them. (See COMMENT on 9:1-6.)

Lastly, it is to be recalled that these instructions and the commission are given by Christ in this Gospel on the night following the discovery of the empty tomb. *Pace* A. Plummer *(The Gospel,* 561), they are not to be understood as "a condensation of what was said by Christ to the Apostles between the Resurrection and the Ascension, partly on Easter Day and partly on other occasions." Such an interpretation is based on the negative view that Plummer adopts toward v. 51b, as if it were not clear in this Gospel that Christ was "carried up" into heaven on the evening of the day of the resurrection itself.

NOTES

24   44. *Then Jesus said to them.* Lit. "then he said to them," words that might seem to mark a break, but they stem from Luke's own pen and are redactional.

what my words meant. Lit. "These (were) my words which I addressed to you." It is not so much the words themselves that Christ recalls for them as their meaning, which the following statements (vv. 44b,45,46) make clear.

while I was still with you. I.e. during the pre-crucifixion earthly ministry. The words as such are to be found nowhere else in the Lucan account; the closest are the announcements of his passion in 9:22,44; 17:25; 18:31-33; 22:37. Certainly, his remarks do not refer to what is found in 24:26.

All that was written about me. This is an echo of v. 25c. See Acts 13:29; cf. John 5:39; 20:9 for the Johannine way of putting the same idea. However, John 12:16 more accurately reflects what was happening in the early Christian community, from which this mode of reading the OT springs: "His disciples did not understand this at first;

but when Jesus was glorified, then they remembered that this had been written of him and had been done to him."

in the Law of Moses. See 2:22; 24:27; Acts 24:14; cf. John 5:39,46. Peter's speech in Acts 3:22 will refer to Moses, who promises "a prophet" to be raised up "like me" (Deut 18:15-18), and will identify Christ with him; indeed, it will even refer to him as the suffering Messiah (3:18). Yet, if one looks in the Pentateuch for a *māšîaḥ,* one will find this title used only of the "anointed" high priest of old (Lev 4:3,5,16; 6:15), never of an expected Davidic king, much less one that is expected to suffer.

in the Prophets. See 1:70; 16:16,29; 18:31; 24:25,27; Acts 3:18a,21b,24 (where "Samuel and those who came afterward" are called prophets); 10:43; 24:14. The *Gos. of Thom.* § 52 puts it this way: "His disciples said to him, 'Twenty-four prophets have spoken in Israel, and all of them spoke concerning you.' But he said to them, 'You have forsaken the Living One who is before you and have spoken about the dead.' " The title *māšîaḥ* is found in the writings of the prophets, but only of a historical king on David's throne. Thus, in the "former prophets," see 1 Sam 24:7 bis,11; 26:9,11,16,23; 2 Sam 1:14,16; see also 1 Sam 2:10,38; 12:3,5; 16:6 (of Saul or some king in a generic sense); cf. 2 Sam 19:22; 23:1; 22:51 (of David himself). In the "latter prophets," it is found only in Isa 45:1 (of Cyrus!) and Hab 3:13 (of whom?). If one were to include Daniel among the "prophets" (in the Hebrew Scriptures the Book of Daniel is part of the *Kĕtûbîm,* "Writings"), then (for the first time in the OT) the title is used of an expected figure, "an anointed one, a prince" *(māšîaḥ nāgîd,* 9:25).

in the Psalms. Does the tripartite division of the Hebrew Scriptures found in this verse reflect an awareness of a "canon" of Scripture? This has often been suggested, but the psalms scarcely stand for all the *Kĕtûbîm.* Cf. the prologue of Sirach ("the law itself, the prophecies, and the rest of the books"). In the psalms the title *māšîaḥ* is found in Pss 2:2; 18:51; 20:7; 28:8; 84:10; 89:39,52; 132:10,17 (of David or a Davidic king); in Ps 105:15 (of prophets? patriarchs?).

must see fulfillment. See NOTES on 1:1,20 and p. 180.

45. *he opened their minds to an understanding of the Scriptures.* I.e. the evangelist describes the risen Christ himself interpreting the OT Scriptures in a new way, referring them to himself and to his career in God's salvation-history. See further Luke 24:27. For the idea of "opening" minds or eyes, see 24:31; Acts 16:14; 26:17-18; cf. John 12:16. Nothing is said about how this "opening" takes place; *pace* A. Plummer *(The Gospel,* 562), it is not yet done through the Spirit, because that is not yet given in the Lucan story. If anything, the scene seems to suggest that it is faith in the risen Christ himself that is the key. See further J. Ernst, "Schriftauslegung." Contrast the situation described in 9:45; 18:34.

46. *This . . . is what stands written.* Lit. "so it has been written," and the following *hoti* is *recitativum.* See BDF § 397.5; § 470.1. Some mss. (A, C², W, Θ, Ψ, 063, *f*¹,¹³, and the Koine text-tradition) and some ancient versions (Vg, Syriac) add *kai houtōs edei,* "and so it was necessary (that)"; but this reading is usually judged influenced by v. 26. Mss. P⁷⁵, ℵ, B, C, D, L, etc., lack the words.

The Messiah shall suffer. Lit. "the Messiah suffers." See NOTE on v. 26.

and rise from the dead. See NOTE on 9:8 and pp. 195, 221. Once again, there is no known passage in pre-Christian Jewish literature where one can find mention of a messiah who shall rise from the dead. This is a Lucan christologoumenon. Luke is reading the OT in the light of the Christian kerygma. See 1 Cor 15:4 ("has been raised on the third day according to the Scriptures"). Ms. D and the Sahidic version omit "from the dead."

on the third day. See NOTES on 2:46; 9:22; cf. 18:33; 24:7,21; Acts 10:40. It is derived by Luke from the kerygmatic proclamation. See preceding NOTE.

47. *In his name.* See NOTE on 9:48, for the OT sense of this expression. The story in Acts will depict the disciples constantly so baptizing and preaching: 2:38; 3:6; 4:10,17-18; 5:28,40; 8:12,16; 9:27-28; 10:48, etc. Jesus' status as the risen Messiah will be the basis for all that is preached about him.

repentance for the forgiveness of sins. See NOTE on 3:3 and pp. 237-239; cf. Acts 5:31. The preferred reading here is *metanoian eis aphesin hamartiōn* (in mss. P⁷⁵, ℵ, B); the variant *kai* instead of *eis* would mean "repentance *and* forgiveness of sins" (in mss. A, C, D, L, W, Θ, Ψ, 063, *f*¹·¹³, and the Koine text-tradition and in many ancient versions) and is an obvious copyist's correction to avoid two preps. *eis* in proximity. But both formulae are attested in Lucan writings elsewhere: *metanoian eis* (3:3) and *metanoian kai* (Acts 5:31).

shall be preached. This word too is dependent on "what stands written" (v. 46). See pp. 147, 175.

to all the nations. See Luke 12:30; Acts 14:16; 15:17 (= Amos 9:12). The same phrase occurs in Matt 28:19. In this Gospel it serves the universalism of Lucan theology. See pp. 187-192.

beginning from Jerusalem! See NOTES on 1:2; 3:23; 23:5; cf. Acts 1:8,22; 10:37. This phrase forms the transition to the second volume of the Lucan writings; the programmatic verse of Acts (1:8) will echo it.

The phrase is, however, variously attested in the manuscripts. The best reading *(arxamenoi,* mss. ℵ, B, C*, L, N, 33, etc.) is a dangling ptc., masc. nom. pl. It can also be related to the beginning of v. 48; it would then mean, "Beginning from Jerusalem, you are (to be) witnesses of this!" Three other variants are attested: (a) *arxamenon,* a dangling neut. nom. (or acc.) sg. ptc. (in mss. P⁷⁵, A, C³, K, W, 063, *f*¹·¹³, and the Koine text-tradition); it would refer to all that precedes in v. 47; (b) *arxamenōn,* a gen. pl. ptc. with "you" understood, "with you beginning from J." (in mss. D, Δ² and some Latin versions); (c) *arxamenos,* a masc. nom. sg. ptc. (in mss. Θ, Ψ, 565), which would have to be related to the distant subj. in "he said" (v. 46), which makes little sense. Though the phrase is important in Lucan theology, the sense of it is not compromised by these textual difficulties.

48. *witnesses.* Luke introduces here for the first time the important role that Christ's disciples are to play in the third phase of salvation-history, in the Period of the Church. See further Acts 1:8,22; 2:32; 3:15; 5:32; 10:39,41; 13:31; 22:15; 26:16; cf. 4:33; 22:20. Thus eyewitnesses are to become testifiers. See further p. 243.

of this! Lit. "of these things," i.e. of the ministry of Jesus. See Acts 1:21-22 as well as of his resurrection, all that pertains to him.

49. *Now take note.* Lit. "and behold." See p. 121. Ms. ℵ reads *kagō,* "and I" (cf. mss. P⁷⁵, D *kai egō*). But most mss. (A, B, C, Θ, Ψ, 063, *f*¹·¹³, and the Koine text-tradition) have *kai idou egō,* which is preferable. N-A²⁶ and *UBSGNT*³ put *idou* in square brackets. It makes little difference as to the sense.

I am sending upon you. I.e. to authorize your preaching, for they are not to go forth to spread abroad mere personal opinions, but his own authentic message. Related to the vb. *apostellō* is the use of *apostolous* in Acts 1:2. See Luke 6:13.

what my Father has promised. Lit. "the promise of my Father," i.e. the holy Spirit, as Acts 1:4b,5b makes clear. The Spirit will be the source of the "power" in the following sentence. See further pp. 227-231.

You are to remain here in the city. Lit. "You remain here!" The independent personal pron. emphatically precedes the impv. See Acts 1:4.

invested with power from on high. The n. *dynamis* is put emphatically at the end of the sentence in the Greek text. "Power" in Jesus' ministry was noted in 4:14; 5:17; 9:1. For the OT background to the idea, see Isa 32:15 ("until the Spirit is poured upon us from on high"); Wis 9:17.

BIBLIOGRAPHY (24:44-49)

Asensio, F. "Trasfondo profético-evangélico del *pasa exousia* de la 'Gran Misión,' " *EstBíb* 27 (1968) 27-48.

Benoit, P. *Passion and Resurrection,* 313-342.

Bockel, P. "Luc 24,45: 'Il leur ouvrit l'esprit à l'intelligence des écritures,' " *BTS* 36 (1961) 2-3.

Dillon, R. J. "Easter Revelation and Mission Program in Luke 24:46-48," *Sin, Salvation, and the Spirit: Commemorating the Fiftieth Year of the Liturgical Press* (ed. D. Durken; Collegeville, MN: Liturgical Press, 1979) 240-270.

——— *From Eye-Witnesses,* 203-220.

Duesberg, H. "He Opened Their Minds to Understand the Scriptures," *Concilium* 30 (1968) 111-121.

Dupont, J. "La mission de Paul d'après Actes 26.16-23 et la mission des apôtres d'après Luc 24.44-49 et Actes 1.8," in *Paul and Paulinism: Essays in Honour of C. K. Barrett* (eds. M. D. Hooker and S. G. Wilson; London: SPCK, 1982) 290-301.

——— "La portée christologique de l'évangélisation des nations d'après Luc 24,47," *Neues Testament und Kirche* (ed. J. Gnilka) 125-143.

Ernst, J. "Schriftauslegung und Auferstehungsglaube bei Lukas," *TGl* 60 (1970) 360-374; reprinted, *Schriftauslegung* (ed. J. Ernst; Munich: Schöningh, 1972) 177-192.

George, A. "L'Intelligence des écritures (Luc 24,44-53)," *BVC* 18 (1957) 65-71.

Hubbard, B. J. "Commissioning Stories in Luke-Acts; A Study of Their Antecedents, Form and Content," *Semeia* 8 (1977) 103-126.

Kümmel, W. G. *Promise and Fulfilment,* 105.

169. THE ASCENSION
(24:50-53)

24   ⁵⁰ Then Jesus led them out as far as Bethany and, lifting up his hands, he began to bless them. ⁵¹ While he was blessing them, he happened to be parted from them and was carried up into heaven. ⁵² But they worshiped him and returned with great joy to Jerusalem, ⁵³ and they spent their time in the Temple, constantly praising God.

COMMENT

The conclusion to the Lucan Gospel consists of the end of the appearance of the risen Christ to the disciples in Jerusalem. He leads them out of the city to Bethany, where, as he blesses them, he is parted from them and carried up to heaven. Having finally recognized him and worshiped him, the disciples return to Jerusalem, where they spend the ensuing days in the Temple praising God (24:50-53). This scene is the climax of the appearance-story that began in v. 36 (see COMMENT on 24:36-43).

Nothing corresponds in the Matthean or Johannine Gospels to this scene in which Christ departs at the end of his appearance. Only the Marcan appendix has something of a parallel; there Christ, having appeared to the Eleven at table in Jerusalem, is carried up similarly to heaven (16:19): "Then after the Lord Jesus had spoken to them, he was taken up to heaven and took his seat at the right hand of God." One may wonder whether this account depends on the Lucan; but except for the prepositional phrase *eis ton ouranon* ("into heaven"), which is common to both, the rest of the wording differs so much from the Lucan that one is inclined to regard it as a separate tradition. The main difference from the Lucan is that the ascension takes place from indoors, and in Jerusalem itself. Despite the misgivings which M.-J. Lagrange had about Jesus' departure from his disciples "at night," as the Lucan context suggests *(Luc,* 616), the Marcan appendix seems to suggest the same. Whereas the Lucan account uses the vb. *anephereto,* "was carried up," the Marcan appendix has *anelēmpthē,* "was taken up," the same form that is used in Acts 1:2 (cf. 1:11), but not in Acts 1:9, which has *epērthē,* "was lifted up." However, the Johannine Gospel depicts Christ appearing to Mary Magdalene at the tomb and saying to her on Easter Sunday morning, "Do not cling to me, for I have not yet ascended *(oupō anabebēka)* to my Father and your Father . . ." (20:17).

The early tradition which Luke makes use of is otherwise expressed in terms of Jesus' exaltation (see the pre-Pauline formulation of it in Phil 2:9); even Luke himself has something of that in Acts 2:33, where he speaks of the pouring out of the promise of the holy Spirit from the Father by the "exalted" Jesus (cf. Acts 5:31). Again, in the early hymn embedded in 1 Tim 3:16 the exaltation is expressed in terms of being "taken up" *(anelēmphthē)*. If Luke is the only NT writer who has depicted the ascension of Jesus as a visibly perceptible event, he has hardly "invented the Ascension as a physical event," *pace* A. R. C. Leaney ("Why There Were Forty Days between the Resurrection and the Ascension in Acts 1,3," *SE IV* 417). One would have to insist on that, even if one admits the Lucan formulation and terminology (G. Lohfink, *Die Himmelfahrt Jesu,* 212).

This episode not only forms the end of the Lucan Gospel, but it is the climax of the whole latter part of it—from the crucial chap. 9 on. In 9:31 the transfigured Jesus converses with Moses and Elijah about his "departure" *(exodos),* which he is to complete in Jerusalem. Again, in 9:51 the reader learns about the days that were drawing near "when he was to be taken up to heaven." That *exodos,* which has been explained as "his entire transit to the Father" through death and resurrection "ending in the ascension" (p. 800), has now been achieved. The goal and destiny toward which the Lucan Jesus has been resolutely moving have now been reached. It is the status to which he referred in his answer to the Sanhedrin in 22:69, "From now on the Son of Man will be seated at the right hand of the power of God." Indeed, from that "glory" (v. 26) he has appeared to Simon (v. 34), to the two disciples at Emmaus (vv. 15-31), and finally to the Eleven and all the others in this literary unit (vv. 36-53).

It is well known that Luke, having ended his Gospel with this scene in which Christ is "carried up into heaven" (v. 51b), begins the second volume of his writing with a description of the ascension itself:

> "Having said this, while they were looking on, Jesus was lifted up, and a cloud took him up out of their sight. As they were staring into the sky, as he moved away, two men in white garments suddenly stood by them and said to them, 'Galileans, why do you stand here looking into the sky? This Jesus, who has been taken up from you into heaven, will come in the same way in which you have seen him moving into heaven.'" (Acts 1:9-11)

This Lucan description of the ascension has been decked out with apocalyptic stage props: a rapture with motion upward through the heavens, a cloud as the elevator, and angel interpreters (for a study of the form involved, see G. Lohfink, *Die Himmelfahrt Jesu,* 32-79). OT and Jewish background for similar raptures (ascensions or assumptions) can be found in the stories about

Enoch (Gen 5:24; Sir 44:16; Heb 11:5), Elijah (2 Kgs 2:11; Sir 48:9; 1 Macc 2:58), Ezra *(2 Esdr.* 14:9), and Moses *(Ass. Mos.* 10.12[?]; cf. Origen, *De princip.* 3.2,1 [GCS 22. 244]; *Hom. in Jos.* 2.1 [GCS 30. 397]). According to Philostratus, the life of Apollonius of Tyana ended with his assumption *(Vita Apol.* 8.30).

In itself the Lucan description of the ascension of Jesus in Acts says little more than what is found in v. 51b. But the problem is that whereas that statement about the ascension in Luke 24 dates it to Easter Sunday night (as does the reference in Acts 1:2), the description in Acts 1:9-11 refers to an event which took place some "forty days" later (see Acts 1:3; cf. 13:31, *epi hēmeras pleious,* "for many days" *[RSV]).* Why Luke has dated the ascension of Jesus in these two different ways no one will ever know. There is no reason to think that Luke considers them two different events. P. Benoit ("The Ascension," 242; *Exégèse et théologie,* 1. 399) considered it possible that Luke came upon the precise information about the interval between resurrection and ascension only after he had finished the Gospel and before he began to write Acts. That would mean that the beginning of Acts is a deliberate correction of the end of the Gospel. The double reference to the ascension, at the end of the Gospel and at the beginning of Acts, makes it clear that one has to reckon with it as the crucial marker not only in the phases of Christ's existence, but in the phases of salvation-history itself. It demarcates the Period of the Church from the Period of Jesus. This is why one must reckon with a three-phased division of salvation-history (see p. 181), *pace* W. S. Kurz *(CBQ* 44 [1982] 674). What will be recounted in Acts 2, in dependence on Joel 3:1-2, may be a sign of the eschatological period; but that is already alluded to in v. 49, "what my Father has promised." Is it not significant that that promise is mentioned again in the context of the ascension in Acts 1:4-5? After all, the story in the Book of Acts is not the story of the "final days," but the story of the church, the narrative of the Period of the Church.

What is much more important, however, is to get an accurate impression of what the "ascension" is in Lucan and other NT writings. For of itself "ascension" means motion upward, i.e. through the "heavens" (Eph 4:10) or the celestial spheres (cf. Aristotle, *Metaph.* 12.8 § 1073a). These are clearly time-conditioned modes of expression. The essential NT affirmation about the ascended Christ is that he is with his heavenly Father in "glory" (v. 26) when he sends the holy Spirit on his followers, investing them with "power from on high" (v. 49; see pp. 194-195). Here one need only emphasize that the crucified Jesus, raised from the dead, entered his "glory," and from there has manifested himself to Peter, to Cleopas and his companion, and now to the Eleven and all the others. Hence the "ascension" is nothing more than this appearance of the risen Christ to his assembled disciples, in which for the last time he is visibly perceptible, as he takes his leave from them, gathered as the nucleus community. No longer will they behold him in this manner; hereafter he will be present to them not in visibly perceptible form, but in "the breaking of the bread" (v. 35) and through "what my Father has promised" (v. 49; Acts 1:4-5; 2:31). This, moreover, explains why the Johannine Jesus could say to Mary Magdalene that, though he was appearing to her from "glory," he had "not yet ascended to my Father" (John 20:17), i.e. had not yet taken his final leave of his assembled followers. This explains too why, even after the ascension, it is narrated that he appeared to Saul on the road to Damascus (Acts 9:4-6; 22:6-11; 26:14-17). That was a special appearance to an *individual* after the final leave-taking from the group, for the purpose of designating "a chosen instrument" (Acts 9:15), "a witness" in a special sense (Acts 22:15), and one to stand in the line of Moses and the prophets of old (Acts 26:22). (For Paul's own way of referring to that experience, see Gal 1:15; 1 Cor 9:1.)

Early Christian tradition continued to speak of the ascension of Christ on Easter Sunday itself. E.g. see *Barn.* 15:9: "Therefore we also celebrate with joy the eighth day, on which Jesus rose from the dead and having been made manifest ascended into heaven" *(anebē eis ouranous)*. Similarly, the *Gospel of Peter*, after referring (§ 50) to "early in the morning of the Lord's day," tells how Mary Magdalene and the women came to the tomb and saw a young man sitting in it, who announced to them (§ 55-56): "He is risen and gone. But if you do not believe (it), stoop and look at the place where he lay, for he is not here. He is risen and is gone there whence he was sent" (Hennecke-Schneemelcher, *NTApocrypha* 1. 187). (See further the Christian interpolation in *T. Benj.* 9:5 ["Ascending from Hades, he shall pass from the earth up into heaven"(?)]; Tertullian, *Adv. Iud.* 13.23 [CCLat 2. 1389]; Eusebius, *De eccl. theol.* 3.5 [PG 24. 1009].)

NOTES

24 50. led them out. Luke uses the vb. *exagein,* the word used in the LXX for Yahweh leading his people out of Egyptian bondage in the exodus. See Exod 3:10; 6:6-8; Lev 19:36; see further G. Lohfink, *Die Himmelfahrt Jesu,* 163-164. The transmission of the text is a bit disturbed here, for after the compound vb. N-A[26] reads *[exō] heōs pros,* lit. "outside unto toward," which is redundant. This is why some mss. (P[75], ℵ, B, C*, L, 1, 33, etc.) omit the *exō,* and probably rightly so. Mss. A, C[3], W, Θ, Ψ, 063, *f* [13], and the Koine text-tradition read all three words. But some of them change the last prep. *pros* to *eis,* "into" (mss. A, C[3], W[c], Θ, Ψ, 063, *f* [13]). For the use of the prep. *heōs* with a place, see Acts 17:14 *(heōs epi);* 21:5 *(heōs exō);* 26:11 *(heōs kai eis),* a usage derived from the LXX (Gen 38:1, *heōs pros;* Ezek 48:1). Cf. Josephus, *Ant.* 16.3,3 § 90.

as far as Bethany. For the location of Bethany, see NOTE on 19:29. That "the setting of the Ascension in Bethany in v. 50 . . . flatly contradicts the geographical reference in Acts i,12 [the Mount of Olives]" (H. Conzelmann, *Theology,* 94) is highly questionable. Since Bethany was on that mount, both modes of speech would be tolerable. Moreover, Conzelmann's conclusion that vv. 50-53 were not "an original part of the gospel" is matched only by his equally questionable attitude toward the Lucan infancy narrative. See p. 310.

lifting up his hands. I.e. in a hieratic or priestly blessing, as did Aaron in Lev 9:22, or the high priest, Simon II, son of Onias, in Sir 50:20-21 ("Then Simon came down and lifted up his hands over the whole congregation of the children of Israel to pronounce the blessing [probably an allusion to Num 6:23-26] of the Lord with his lips and to glory in his name"). See further P. A. van Stempvoort, "The Interpretation." What Zechariah (1:21-22) could not do, that Jesus does to his silent followers. Cf. 1 Tim 2:8.

he began to bless them. As the first part of v. 51 makes clear, the aor. *eulogēsen* is to be understood as inceptive. See BDF § 331. The ascending Christ calls down God's favor upon them as a token of his leave-taking. See Acts 3:25-26. See further NOTES on 2:34; 9:16. Though Luke depicts Christ performing a hieratic act, his theology is not concerned with Jesus as priest (this is the sole reference to it and it is implicit, rather than explicit).

51. *While he was blessing them.* Lit. "and it happened, in his blessing them, (that) he was parted from them and . . ." Luke uses again *kai egeneto* with a finite vb. *(diestē)* without the conj. *kai* (see p. 119); also *en tō* with an infin. in a temporal cl. (p. 119). Instead of the vb. *diestē*, "was parted," ms. D reads *apestē*, with no difference of meaning.

and was carried up into heaven. The words *kai anephereto eis ton ouranon* are read in mss. P75, ℵc, A, B, C, K, L, W, X, Δ, Θ, Π, Ψ, *f*1,13, and the Koine text-tradition; they are omitted only in ℵ*, D, and the OL and Sinaitic Syriac versions. See E. J. Epp, "The Ascension," 135-136 for fuller discussion. There is no longer any real reason to regard these words as a Western Non-Interpolation (see pp. 130-131); they should be regarded as part of the original text of the Lucan Gospel. They may have been omitted in an effort to remove the conflict with Acts 1:3,9-11 concerning the date of the ascension; or they may have been simply omitted by a copyist's parablepsis, for vv. 51b and 52a both begin with KAIA . . . KAIA. See J. Jeremias, *Eucharistic Words,* 151; K. Aland, "Neue neutestamentliche Papyri II," *NTS* 12 [1965-1966] 193-210, esp. 208-209).

The passive of the vb. *anephereto* should be noted, as well as the vbs. of Acts 1:9,11,22; cp. John 20:17 *(oupō anabebēka);* Eph 4:9 *(anebē)*—which both probably reflect a later stage of early Christian awareness about Christ. See NOTE on *ēgerthē,* "he was raised," v. 6.

52. *But they worshiped him.* Lit. "and worshiping him, they . . ." This is the real recognition of Christ by the disciples; silently they bow down in adoration, as did the Jews before the high priest Simon (Sir 50:22) to receive his blessing. Cf. Lev 9:24d. Again, these words are found in all the Greek mss. except ms. D and the OL and Sinaitic Syriac versions; they are to be judged as those in v. 51b.

returned with great joy. It is difficult to explain this "great joy" if the recognition implied in vv. 51b,52a is omitted, because *diestē,* "was parted," would then stand unexplained and it would mean no more than that he "vanished" from them, as in v.

31c. So internal reasons support the external evidence for the originality of vv. 51b,52a in the Lucan text.

to Jerusalem. Thus the Lucan Gospel ends where it began. See 1:5: Zechariah in the Temple of Jerusalem; cf. p. 165.

53. *they spent their time in the Temple.* Lit. "they were constantly in the Temple, praising God." Thus Luke begins the description of the community-life of the nucleus church. See Acts 2:46; 3:1; 5:42. The importance of the Temple in the Lucan story emerges again. See F. D. Weinert, "The Meaning." See p. 251.

praising God. See Luke 1:64; 2:28. So ends the Lucan Gospel on the note that the evangelist would elicit from all his readers. Contrast the endings of the other Gospels (Mark 16:8, "for they were afraid"; Matt 28:20, "even to the close of the age"; John 21:24-25, those strange apologetic verses, pleading for credibility; the Marcan appendix, 16:20c, with an apologetic notice of confirmatory "signs"). Only Luke has the courage to depict his Christian community engaged in what it should be doing.

As at the end of all the other gospels, *amēn* has been added in many mss. (A, B, C², Θ, Ψ, 063, *f* 13, and the Koine text-tradition; but the liturgical ending has been omitted in mss. P⁷⁵, ℵ, C*, D, L, W, 1, 33.

THE ASCENSION: GENERAL BIBLIOGRAPHY

Alsup, J. E. *The Post-Resurrection Appearance Stories of the Gospel Tradition: A History of Tradition Analysis with Text-Synopsis* (Calwer theologische Monographien 5; Stuttgart: Calwer, 1975) 145.

Argyle, A. W. "The Ascension," *ExpTim* 66 (1954-1955) 240-242.

Belser, J. E. *History of the Passion, Death, and Glorification of Our Saviour, Jesus Christ* (adapted by F. A. Merks; St. Louis, MO: B. Herder, 1929) 644-658.

Benoit, P. "The Ascension," *Jesus and the Gospel: Volume 1* (New York: Herder and Herder, 1973) 209-253; originally, *RB* 56 (1949) 161-203; see *Exégèse et théologie*, 1. 363-411.

Bertram, G. "Die Himmelfahrt Jesu vom Kreuz aus und der Glaube an seine Auferstehung," *Festgabe für Adolf Deissmann zum 60. Geburtstag 7. November 1926* (Tübingen: Mohr [Siebeck], 1927) 187-217.

Bouwman, G. "Die Erhöhung Jesu in der lukanischen Theologie," *BZ* 14 (1970) 257-263.

Davies, J. G. *He Ascended into Heaven: A Study in the History of Doctrine* (London: Lutterworth; New York: Association, 1958).

Devor, R. C. "The Ascension of Christ and the Dissension of the Church," *Encounter* 33 (1972) 340-358.

Flicoteaux, E. "La glorieuse ascension," *VSpir* 76 (1947) 664-675.

Haroutunian, J. "The Doctrine of the Ascension: A Study of the New Testament Teaching," *Int* 10 (1956) 270-281.

Jansen, J. F. "The Ascension, the Church, and Theology," *TTod* 16 (1959) 17-29.

Kern, W. "Das Fortgehen Jesu und das Kommen des Geistes *oder* Christi Himmelfahrt," *Geist und Leben* 41 (1968) 85-90.

Lake, K. "Note III. The Ascension," *Beginnings* (see p. 280) 5. 16-22.

Larrañaga, V. "De ascensione Domini in Act. I,3-13," *VD* 17 (1937) 129-139.

—— *L'Ascension de Notre-Seigneur dans le Nouveau Testament* (Scripta pontificii instituti biblici; Rome: Biblical Institute, 1938).

—— "Historia de la crítica en torno al misterio de la Ascensión del Señor," *EstEcl* 15 (1936) 145-167.

Léon-Dufour, X. *Resurrection and the Message of Easter* (New York: Holt, Rinehart & Winston, 1974) 80-94.

Lohfink, G. "Der historische Ansatz der Himmelfahrt Christi," *Catholica* 17 (1963) 44-84.

Mann, C. S. "The New Testament and the Lord's Ascension," *CQR* 158 (1957) 452-465.

Metzger, B. M. "The Ascension of Jesus Christ," *Historical and Literary Studies: Pagan, Jewish, and Christian* (NTTS 8; Grand Rapids, MI: Eerdmans, 1968) 77-87.

—— "The Meaning of Christ's Ascension," *Search the Scriptures: New Testament Studies in Honor of Raymond T. Stamm* (Gettysburg Theological Studies 3; eds. J. M. Meyers et al.; Leiden: Brill, 1969) 118-128.

Milligan, W. *The Ascension and Heavenly Priesthood of Our Lord* (London: Macmillan, 1901) 1-60.

Miquel, P. "Le mystère de l'Ascension," *Questions liturgiques et paroissiales* 40 (1959) 105-126.

Ramsey, A. M. "What Was the Ascension?" *Historicity and Chronology in the New Testament* (ed. D. E. Nineham; London: SPCK, 1965) 135-144.

Schillebeeckx, E. "Ascension and Pentecost," *Worship* 35 (1960-1961) 336-363.

Schmitt, A. *Entrückung—Aufnahme—Himmelfahrt: Untersuchungen zu einem Vorstellungsbereich im Alten Testament* (Forschung zur Bible 10; Stuttgart: Katholisches Bibelwerk, 1974).

Seidensticker, P. *Zeitgenössische Texte zur Osterbotschaft der Evangelien* (SBS 27; Stuttgart: Katholisches Bibelwerk, 1967) 65-68.

Selwyn, E. G. "Our Lord's Ascension," *Theology* 12 (1926) 241-244.

Vögtle, A. " 'Erhöht zur Rechten Gottes': Braucht der Osterglaube die Krücken des antiken Weltbildes?" *Orientierung* 45 (1981) 78-80.

Wilson, S. G. "The Ascension: A Critique and an Interpretation," *ZNW* 59 (1968) 269-281.

Bibliography (24:50-53)

Bacon, B. W. "The Ascension in Luke and Acts," *Expos* 7/7 (1909) 254-261.

Davies, J. G. "The Prefigurement of the Ascension in the Third Gospel," *JTS* 6 (1955) 229-233.

Dillon, R. J. *From Eye-Witnesses,* 220-225.

Doeve, J. W. "De hemelvaart in het Evangelie naar Lucas," *Homiletica en biblica* 20 (1961) 75-79.

Enslin, M. S. "The Ascension Story," *JBL* 47 (1928) 60-73.

Epp, E. J. "The Ascension in the Textual Tradition of Luke-Acts," *New Testament Textual Criticism* (eds. E. J. Epp and G. D. Fee) 131-145.

Fitzmyer, J. A. "The Ascension of Christ and Pentecost," *TS* 45 (1984) 409-440.

Fridrichsen, A. "Die Himmelfahrt bei Lukas," *TBl* 6 (1927) 337-341.

Guillaume, J.-M. *Luc interprète,* 203-274.

Lohfink, G. *Die Himmelfahrt Jesu: Untersuchungen zu den Himmelfahrts- und Erhöhungstexten bei Lukas* (SANT 26; Munich: Kösel, 1971) 147-176.

——— " 'Was steht ihr da und schauet' (Apg 1,11): Die 'Himmelfahrt Jesu' im lukanischen Geschichtswerk," *BK* 20 (1965) 43-48.

Lowther Clarke, W. K. "St Luke and the Pseudepigrapha: Two Parallels," *JTS* 15 (1914) 597-599.

Menoud, P.-H. "Remarques sur les textes de l'ascension dans Luc-Actes," *Neutestamentliche Studien für Rudolf Bultmann zu seinem siebzigsten Geburtstag am 20. August* (BZNW 21; ed. W. Eltester; Berlin: Töpelmann, 1954) 148-156.

Michaelis, W. *Die Erscheinungen des Auferstandenen* (Basel: Majer, 1944) 89-91.

——— "Zur Überlieferung der Himmelfahrtsgeschichte," *TBl* 4 (1925) 101-109.

Odasso, G. "L'ascensione nell'evangelo di Luca," *BeO* 13 (1971) 107-118.

Plooij, D. *The Ascension in the 'Western' Textual Tradition* (Mededelingen der koninklijke Akademie van Wetenschappen, Afd. Letterkunde, Deel 67, ser. A/2; Amsterdam: Noord-Hollandsche Uitg., 1929) 39-60.

Schille, G. "Die Himmelfahrt," *ZNW* 57 (1966) 183-199.

Schlier, H. *Essais sur le Nouveau Testament* (LD 46; Paris: Cerf, 1968) 263-278.

Stempvoort, P. A. van. "The Interpretation of the Ascension in Luke and Acts," *NTS* 5 (1958-1959) 30-42.

Weinert, F. D. "The Meaning of the Temple in Luke-Acts," *BTB* 11 (1981) 85-89.

Woolsey, T. D. "The End of Luke's Gospel and the Beginning of the Acts: Two Studies," *BSac* 39 (1882) 593-619.

Wulf, F. " 'Und sie kehrten mit grosser Freude nach Jerusalem zurück' (Lk 24,52)," *Geist und Leben* 27 (1954) 81-83.

ADDENDA BIBLIOGRAPHICA FOR VOLUME 28
(Italicized page numbers preceding the items relate them to
existing bibliographies of volume 28)

Pp. 29-34

Agua Pérez, A. del. "Boletín de literatura lucana," *EstBíb* 38 (1979-1980) 166-174.

Cambe, M. "Bulletin de Nouveau Testament: Etudes lucaniennes," *ETR* 56 (1981) 159-167.

Giles, K. "Is Luke an Exponent of 'Early Protestantism?': Church Order in the Lukan Writings (Part I)," *EvQ* 54 (1982) 193-205.

Guillet, J. "Bulletin d'exégèse lucanienne," *RSR* 69 (1981) 425-442.

Rasco, E. "Estudios lucanos," *Bib* 63 (1982) 266-280.

Rese, M. "Neuere Lukas-Arbeiten: Bemerkungen zur gegenwärtigen Forschungslage," *TLZ* 106 (1981) 225-237.

Taeger, J.-W. "Paulus und Lukas über den Menschen," *ZNW* 71 (1980) 96-108.

Pp. 103-104

Dehandschutter, B. "The Gospel of Thomas and the Synoptics: The Status Quaestionis," *SE VII* (TU 126 [1982]) 157-160.

Pp. 105-106

Ades, J. I. "Literary Aspects of Luke," *Papers on Language & Literature* 15 (1979) 193-199.

Pp. 126-127

Delebecque, E. "L'Hellénisme de la 'relative complexe' dans le Nouveau Testament et principalement chez saint Luc," *Bib* 62 (1981) 229-238.

P. 133

Quecke, H. "Eine koptische Bibelhandschrift des 5. Jahrhunderts II (PPalau Rib. Inv.-Nr. 181)," *SPap* 16 (1977) 7-11.

Pp. 259-260

Bovon, F. "Le Dieu de Luc," *RSR* 69 (1981) 279-300.

Fabris, R. "La ricerca di Dio nell'opera di Luca," *Quaerere Deum* (Settimana biblica 25; eds. A. Bonora et al.; Brescia: Paideia, 1980) 235-260.

Karris, R. J. "Missionary Communities: A New Paradigm for the Study of Luke-Acts," *CBQ* 41 (1979) 80-97.

McDowell, E. A. "The Gospel of Luke," *Southwestern Journal of Theology* 10 (1967-1968) 7-24.

P. 261

Bachmann, M. *Jerusalem und der Tempel: Die geographisch-theologischen Elemente in der lukanischen Sicht des jüdischen Kultzentrums* (BWANT 109; Stuttgart: Kohlhammer, 1980).

P. 262

Villiers, P. G. R. de. "Lukas als heilshistoriese Evangelis," *Nederuits gereformeerde teologiese Tydskrif* 19 (1978) 249-259.

Pp. 262-263

Flanagan, N. M. "The Position of Women in the Writings of St. Luke," *Marianum* 40 (1978) 288-304.

P. 263

Bouttier, M. "L'Humanité de Jésus selon saint Luc," *RSR* 69 (1981) 33-43.

Kingsbury, J. D. *Jesus Christ in Matthew, Mark, and Luke* (Philadelphia: Fortress, 1981).

Pp. 265-266

Donahue, J. R. "The Good News of Peace," *The Way* 22 (1982) 88-99.

Pp. 266-267

Chevallier, M.-A. "Luc et l'Esprit saint: A la mémoire du P. Augustin George (1915-1977)," *RevScRel* 56 (1982) 1-16.

George, A. "L'Esprit-Saint dans l'oeuvre de Luc," *RB* 85 (1978) 500-542.

Turner, M. M. B. "Jesus and the Spirit in Lucan Perspective," *Tyndale Bulletin* 32 (1981) 3-42.

——— "The Significance of Receiving the Spirit in Luke-Acts: A Survey of Modern Scholarship," *Trinity Journal* 2 (1981) 131-158.

——— "Spirit Endowment in Luke/Acts: Some Linguistic Considerations," *Vox evangelica* (London) 12 (1981) 45-63.

P. 267

Gaventa, B. R. "The Eschatology of Luke-Acts Revisited," *Encounter* 43 (1982) 27-42.

Mattill, A. J., Jr. *Luke and the Last Things: A Perspective for the Understanding of Lukan Thought* (Dillsboro, NC: Western North Carolina, 1979).

Pp. 268-269

Dupont, J. "La prière et son efficacité dans l'évangile de Luc," *RSR* 69 (1981) 45-55.

Martini, C. M. *Itinerario di preghiera con l'evangelista Luca* (Sul monte della presenza 7; Rome: Paolina, 1981).

Medivilla, R. "La oración de Jesús en el tercer evangelio," *Mayéutica* 4 (1978) 5-34, 163-183.

Scaria, K. J. "Christian Prayer," *Bible Bhashyam* 7 (1981) 201-224.

——— "Jesus' Prayer and Christian Prayer," ibid. 160-185.

P. 269

Nickelsburg, G. W. E. "Riches, the Rich, and God's Judgment in 1 Enoch 92-105 and the Gospel according to Luke," *NTS* 25 (1978-1979) 324-344.

Pp. 269-270

Giles, K. N. "The Church in the Gospel of Luke," *SJT* 34 (1981) 121-146.

Prete, B. " 'Il popolo che Dio si è scelto' negli scritti di Luca," *Sacra doctrina* 26 (1981) 173-204.

Rodriguez Carmona, A. "La comunidad cristiana a la luz de los escritos de Lucas," *Communio* 14 (1981) 311-334.

P. 270

Bovon, F. "Luc: Portrait et project," *LumVie* 30 (1981) 9-18.

Pp. 271-276
Beck, B. E. "Commentaries on Luke's Gospel," *Epworth Review* 6 (1979) 81-85.
Marshall, I. H. *The Gospel of Luke: A Commentary on the Greek Text* (The New International Greek Testament Commentary; Grand Rapids, MI: Eerdmans, 1978).
Schweizer, E. *Das Evangelium nach Lukas übersetzt und erklärt* (NTD 3; 18th ed.; Göttingen: Vandenhoeck & Ruprecht, 1982).
Talbert, C. H. *Reading Luke: A Literary and Theological Commentary on the Third Gospel* (New York: Crossroad, 1982).

Pp. 279-281
Edwards, O. C., Jr. *Luke's Story of Jesus* (Philadelphia: Fortress, 1981).
Schweizer, E. *Luke: A Challenge to Present Theology* (Atlanta, GA: John Knox, 1982).
Talbert, C. H. *The Certainty of the Gospel: The Perspective of Luke-Acts* (Deland, FL: Stetson University, 1980).
Wilson, S. G. *Luke and the Pastoral Epistles* (London: SPCK, 1979).

(The following items are listed according to the chaps. and vv. to which they refer)

1-2	Farris, S. C. "On Discerning Semitic Sources in Luke 1-2," *Gospel Perspectives* (eds. R. T. France and D. Wenham) 2. 201-237.
1:1-4	Omanson, R. L. "A Note on Luke 1.1-4," *BT* 30 (1979) 446-447.
	Radaelli, A. "I racconti dell'infanzia nel contesto del prologo all'evangelo," *Ricerche bibliche e religiose* 15 (1980) 7-26, 199-227; 16 (1981) 292-330.
1:1-4:22a	Brodie, L. T. "A New Temple and a New Law: The Unity and Chronicler-based Nature of Luke 1:1—4:22a," *JSNT* 5 (1979) 21-45.
1:5-38	O'Fearghail, F. "The Literary Forms of Lk 1,5-25 and 1,26-38," *Marianum* 43 (1981) 321-444.
1:5-56	Peretto, E. "Zaccaria Elisabetta Giovanni visti dal primo lettore di Luca (Cap. I)," *Marianum* 40 (1978) 350-370.
1:26-38	Stock, K. "Die Berufung Marias (Lk 1,26-38)," *Bib* 61 (1980) 457-491.
	Tourón del Pie, E. "María en la escatología de Lucas," *Ephemerides mariologicae* 31 (1981) 241-466.
1:34	Orsatti, M. "Verso la decodificazione di una insolita espressione: Analisi filologica di *andra ou ginōskō (Lc.* 1,34)," *RivB* 29 (1981) 343-357.
	Prete, B. "Il significato di Luca 1,34 nella struttura del racconto dell'annunziazione," *Marianum* 40 (1978) 248-276.
1:38,49	McGovern, J. J. "María, 'Sierva de Yahveh' en Lc 1. 38,49," *Estudios teológicos* 7 (1980) 3-15.
1:46-55	Dupont, J. "Le Magnificat comme discours sur Dieu," *NRT* 102 (1980) 321-343.
	Hamel, E. "Le Magnificat et le renversement des situations: Reflexion théologico-biblique," *Greg* 60 (1979) 55-84.

Mínguez, D. "Poética generativa del Magnificat," *Bib* 61 (1980) 55-77.

1:49   Serra, A. M. " 'Fecit mihi magna' (Lc 1,49a): Una formula comunitária?" *Marianum* 40 (1978) 305-343.

Trèves, M. "Le Magnificat et le Benedictus," *CCER* 27 (1979) 105-110.

1:68   Bonnard, P.-E. "Le psaume 72: Ses relectures, ses traces dans l'oeuvre de Luc?" *RSR* 69 (1981) 259-278.

Globe, A. "Some Doctrinal Variants in Matthew 1 and Luke 2, and the Authority of the Neutral Text," *CBQ* 42 (1980) 52-72.

2:1-21   Kaufmann, L. "Geburt des Messias: Text und Kontext einer guten Nachricht," *Orientierung* 44 (1980) 250-253.

Schrage, W. "Was fällt dem Exegeten zu Weihnachten ein?" *Der evangelische Erzieher* 31 (1979) 338-344.

Thorley, J. "When Was Jesus Born?" *GR* 28 (1981) 81-89.

———— "The Nativity Census: What Does Luke Actually Say?" *GR* 26 (1979) 81-84.

Tremel, B. "Le signe du nouveau-né dans la mangeoire: A propos de Lc 2,1-20," *Mélanges Dominique Barthélemy* (eds. P. Casetti et al.) 593-612.

2:14   Soderlund, S. K. "Christmas as the *Shalōm* of God," *Crux* 16 (1980) 2-4.

2:19   Serra, A. *Sapienza e contemplazione di Maria secondo Luca 2,19.51b* (Scripta pontificiae facultatis theologicae 'Marianum' ns 8; Rome: Marianum, 1982).

2:22   Potterie, I. de la. "Les deux noms de Jérusalem dans l'évangile de Luc," *RSR* 69 (1981) 57-70.

2:41-50   Manns, F. "Luc 2, 41-50 témoin de la bar mitswa de Jésus," *Marianum* 40 (1978) 344-349.

2:52   Couroyer, B. "A propos de Luc, II, 52," *RB* 86 (1979) 92-101.

3:17   Schwarz, G. *"To de achyron katakausei,"* *ZNW* 72 (1981) 264-271.

3:21-22   Dennison, C. G. "How Is Jesus the Son of God? Luke's Baptism Narrative and Christology," *CTJ* 17 (1982) 6-25.

Uprichard, R. E. H. "The Baptism of Jesus," *Irish Biblical Studies* 3 (1981) 187-202.

3:23-38   Lerle, E. "Die Ahnenverzeichnisse Jesu: Versuch einer christologischen Interpretation," *ZNW* 72 (1981) 112-117.

Overstreet, R. L. "Difficulties of New Testament Genealogies," *Grace Theological Journal* 2 (1981) 303-326.

Ride, G. E. "Luke 3:22-38 in Codex Bezae: The Messianic King," *AUSS* 17 (1979) 203-208.

4:14-44   Agua Pérez, A. del. "El cumplimiento del reino de Dio en la misión de Jesús: Programma del evangelio de Lucas (Lc. 4, 14-44)," *EstBíb* 38 (1979-1980) 269-293.

4:16-21   Chilton, B. "Announcement in Nazara: An Analysis of Luke 4:16-21," *Gospel Perspectives* (eds. R. T. France and D. Wenham) 2. 147-172.

4:16-30   Menezes, F. "The Mission of Jesus according to Lk 4:16-30," *Bible Bhashyam* 6 (1980) 249-264.

Rodgers, M. "Luke 4:16-30—A Call for a Jubilee Year?" *RTR* 40 (1980) 72-82.

Sanders, J. A. "Isaiah in Luke," *Int* 36 (1982) 144-155.

Seccombe, D. "Luke and Isaiah," *NTS* 27 (1981) 252-259.

Sloan, R. B., Jr. *The Favorable Year of the Lord: A Study of Jubilary Theology in the Gospel of Luke* (Austin, TX: Schola, 1977).

4:22   Nolland, J. "Impressed Unbelievers as Witnesses to Christ (Luke 4:22a)," *JBL* 98 (1979) 219-229.

4:23   Nolland, J. "Classical and Rabbinic Parallels to 'Physician, Heal Yourself' (Lk. iv 23)," *NovT* 21 (1979) 193-209.

4:25   Thiering, B. E. "The Three and a Half Years of Elijah," *NovT* 23 (1981) 41-55.

5:1   Kilpatrick, G. D. "Three Problems of New Testament Text," *NovT* 21 (1979) 289-292, esp. 290.

5:1-11   Rice, G. E. "Luke's Thematic Use of the Call to Discipleship," *AUSS* 19 (1981) 51-58.

5:12   Hulse, E. V. "The Nature of Biblical 'Leprosy' and the Use of Alternative Medical Terms in Modern Translations of the Bible," *PEQ* 107 (1975) 87-105.

5:12-16   Boismard, M.-E. "La guérison du lépreux (Mc 1,40-45 et par.)," *Salmanticensis* 28 (1981) 283-291.

5:17   Ziesler, J. A. "Luke and the Pharisees," *NTS* 25 (1978-1979) 146-157.

5:17-26   Klauck, H.-J. "Die Frage der Sündenvergebung in der Perkope von der Heilung des Gelähmten (Mk 2,1-12 parr)," *BZ* 25 (1981) 223-248.

5:36   Diamond, G. "Reflections upon Recent Developments in the Study of Parables in Luke," *ABR* 29 (1981) 1-9.

6:1   Isaac, E. "Another Note on Luke 6:1," *JBL* 100 (1981) 96-97.

6:1-5   Lindemann, A. " 'Der Sabbat ist um des Menschen willen geworden . . .': Historische und theologische Erwägungen zur Traditionsgeschichte der Sabbatperikope Mk 2,23-28 parr." *Wort und Dienst* 15 (1979) 79-105.

6:4   Morgan, C. S. " 'When Abiathar Was High Priest' (Mark 2:26)," *JBL* 98 (1979) 409-410.

6:16   Arbeitman, Y. "The Suffix of Iscariot," *JBL* 99 (1980) 122-124.

6:24-26   Klein, P. "Die lukanischen Weherufe Lk 6:24-26," *ZNW* 71 (1980) 150-159.

6:20-49   Topel, L. J. "The Lukan Version of the Lord's Sermon," *BTB* 11 (1981) 48-53.

6:35   Schwarz, G. *"Mēden apelpizontes,"* *ZNW* 71 (1980) 133-135.

6:43-49   Duplacy, J. "Le véritable disciple: Un essai d'analyse sémantique de Luc 6,43-49," *RSR* 69 (1981) 71-86.

6:47-49   Abou-Chaar, K. "The Two Builders: A Study of the Parable in Luke 6:47-49," *Near East School of Theology Theological Review* 5 (1982) 44-58.

7:14   Hachlili, R. "The Goliath Family in Jericho: Funerary Inscriptions from a First Century A.D. Jewish Monumental Tomb," *BASOR* 235 (1979) 31-65, esp. 33 (on *soros).*

7:18-23   Lambrecht, J. " 'Are You the One Who Is to Come, or Shall We Look for Another?' The Gospel Message of Jesus Today," *Louvain Studies* 8 (1980) 115-128.

7:36-50   Dupont, J. "Le pharisien et la pécheresse (Lc 7, 36-50)," *Communautés et liturgies* 4 (1980) 260-268.

8:5-8   Horman, J. "The Source of the Version of the Parable of the Sower in the Gospel of Thomas," *NovT* 21 (1979) 326-343.

           Houston, T. "Preaching to the People of Luke's Time Today," *Christianity Today* 25 (1981) 731-734.

9:3-4   Legrand, L. "Bare-Foot Apostles? The Shoes of St. Mark (Mk. 6:6-9 and Parallels)," *Indian Theological Studies* 16 (1979) 201-219.

9:10-17   Bagatti, B. "Dove avvenne la moltiplicazione dei pani?" *Salmanticensis* 28 (1981) 293-298.

9:28-36   Best, F. "The Transfiguration: A Select Bibliography," *JETS* 24 (1981) 157-161.

           Pamment, M. "Moses and Elijah in the Story of the Transfiguration," *ExpTim* 92 (1980-1981) 338-339.

9:46-50   Wenham, D. "A Note on Mark 9:33-42/Matt. 18:1-6/Luke 9:46-50," *JSNT* 14 (1982) 113-118.

9:51-18:14 Enslin, M. S. "The Samaritan Ministry and Mission," *HUCA* 51 (1980) 29-38.

           Wenham, J. W. "Synoptic Independence and the Origin of Luke's Travel Narrative," *NTS* 27 (1980-1981) 507-515.

9:51   Evans, C. A. " 'He Set His Face': A Note on Luke 9,51," *Bib* 63 (1982) 545-548.

9:60   Schwarz, G. *"Aphes tous nekrous thapsai tous heautōn nekrous,"* *ZNW* 72 (1981) 272-276.

Miscellany

Downing, F. G. "Common Ground with Paganism in Luke and in Josephus," *NTS* 28 (1982) 546-559.

CORRIGENDA IN VOLUME 28
(beyond the corrections already made in its second edition, first printing)

Page	Line* (* = from bottom)	Delete	Substitute (or *Add*)
4	16*	1953	1954
29	6	Anderson	Andersen
	6	Zeugnisse,"	Zeugnisse!"

Page	Line* (* = from bottom)	Delete	Substitute (or *Add*)
84	12*	22:63-71(?)	22:62-71
	5*	23:46,47b-49 Death of Jesus	
	2*	24:44-49 Jesus' final commission	
84			(Add line omitted at bottom of page:) the Third Gospel to an oral source alone. Luke's dependence on eyewit-
110			(add to col. 2:) *eutheōs* (at once, 6)
			(add to col. 2:) *hikanos* (temporal sense, 11)
111			(add to col. 1:) *poreuesthai* (make one's way, 50)
205	22	high priest's	Sanhedrin's
207	22	high priest	Sanhedrin
268	9	*TBT*	*BTB*
293	8*		(add:) See NOTE on 24:14.
330	6	J.-M.	J.-P.
363	22	Horten	Horton
370	1*	Balague M.	Balagué, M.
417	2*	Wobbe. J.	Wobbe, J.
457	16*	become	became
536	6*	ger,	ger
583	14	22:58	22:58,60
586	1	17:15	17:16
835	4	9:55	9:56

INDEXES

INDEX OF MODERN AUTHORS

(Vol. 28: i–xxvi, 1–837; vol. 28A: i–xxxvi, 839–1600. Umlauts have been disregarded in the alphabetizing of the names.)

Aalen, S. 156, 260, 972, 1055, 1058, 1234
Abbott, E. A. 99
Abbott, L. 271
Abbott, W. 1530
Abel, E. L. 504, 1278, 1297
Abel, F.-M. 535, 736, 1503, 1526, 1544, 1562
Abou-Chaar, K. 1598
Abrahams, I. 1140, 1468
Abramowski, L. 1521
Accame, S. 415
Achtemeier, P. J. 659–60, 733, 743
Ackermann, H. 1264
Acton, J. (Lord) 16
Adam, A. 1078
Adams, J. E. 1563
Ades, J. I. 1594
Aerts, T. 569
Agnew, F. 570
Agouridès, S. 632, 645
Agua Pérez, A. del 1332, 1594, 1597
Ahern, B. M. 754
Aicher, G. 1204, 1206
Aland, K. xxiii, xxiv, 37, 128, 130–33, 532, 573, 592, 628, 824, xxiv, xxvii, xxviii, 845, 979, 1195, 1388, 1405, 1590
Albertz, M. 52, 54, 586, 1549
Albright, W. F. 42, 44–45, 920, 1526
Aldama, J. A. de 352
Alexandre, M. 1135
Allard, M. 352
Allegro, J. M. 339, 411, 666
Allen, H. J. 1160, 1174
Allen, J. E. 1477
Allen, P. M. S. 1162
Allen, W. C. 101
Allgeier, A. 352
Allis, O. T. 1019
Alon, A. 28A: xxx, 863, 979, 1017
Alonso Díaz, J. 1092
Alsup, J. E. 1591
Altheim, F. 1510–11
Ambruster, C. J. 1445
Andersen, W. 29, 268
Anderson, F. C. 1111
Anderson, H. 528, 534, 539

Anderson, J. G. C. 403
Annen, F. 741
Antoniadis, S. 125
Arbeitman, Y. 620, 1598
Arce, P. A. 369, 1571
Argyle, A. W. 35, 59, 73, 100–1, 447, 643, 1424, 1427, 1591
Arndt, W. F. xvii, 271, 810, xx, 1565
Arvedsen, T. 865, 871–72, 875
Aschermann, H. 1445
Asensio, F. 1585
Ashby, E. 1174
Ashton, J. 907
Asting, R. K. 260
Audet, J.-P. 330, 335, 349, 352, 607, 1398
Auffret, P. 390
Aufhauser, J. B. 1320
Augsten, M. 895
Avanzo, M. 980
Avi-Yonah, M. 343, 352
Aytoun, R. A. 370

Baarda, T. 353, 970
Bachmann, M. 1594
Bacon, B. W. 59, 99, 297, 301, 797, 937, 1403, 1592
Badham, F. P. S. 97, 333
Baer, H. von 19, 29, 181, 266
Bagatti, B. 1131, 1599
Bahr, G. J. 1403
Bailey, J. A. 88, 104, 313, xxx, 1252, 1366, 1477, 1499, 1551
Bailey, K. E. 912, 1102
Baily, M. 414
Baird, W. 260, 271
Bajsić, A. 1492
Baker, A. 895, 908
Baker, J. 59, 1058
Balagué, M. 370–71
Baldensperger, G. 1551
Baldi, D. xix, 343, 517, 538, 769, 798, xxi, 886
Balducelli, R. 294
Ballard, F. 1162
Ballard, P. H. 1056, 1058
Balmforth, H. 271

Swidler, L. 928
Sybel, L. von 694
Sykes, M. H. 1405
Syme, R. 403–5, 416
Synge, F. C. 603

Taeger, J.-W. 1594
Talbert, C. H. 5, 11, 33, 96–98, 106, 164, 260, 281, 363, 541, 547, 1318, 1388, 1596
Talmon, S. 536
Tannehill, R. 33, 265, 371, 527, 537, 540, 1418, 1420
Tarelli, C. C. 970
Tarn, W. W. 405
Tatum, W. B. 227, 267, 310, 332
Taylor, A. B. 511, 519
Taylor, C. 1237
Taylor, L. R. 417
Taylor, R. O. P. 294
Taylor, T. M. 460, 462
Taylor, V. xix, 89, 102–5, 166, 266, 305, 312, 336, 436, 461, 527, 555, 573, 588, 649–50, 656, 663, 684, 686, 706–7, 716, 727, 757–58, 762–63, 785, 795–96, 799, 806, 816, 819, 827, 833, xxii, xxxv, 891–92, 965, 1010, 1028, 1039, 1183, 1192, 1197, 1214, 1242, 1254, 1261, 1264, 1275, 1279, 1291, 1310–13, 1320–21, 1326, 1329, 1347, 1360, 1362, 1365, 1368, 1371–73, 1376–77, 1386, 1402, 1408, 1411–14, 1421, 1429, 1438–39, 1447–48, 1456–58, 1472, 1487–88, 1494–95, 1501, 1506–7, 1513, 1522, 1524, 1533, 1535, 1541, 1555
Tcherikover, V. A. 1475
Temple, P. J. 444, 448
Temple, S. 1371
Tenney, M. C. 25, 276, 759
Ter-Minassiantz, E. 371
Ternant, P. 661, 1009
Testa, E. 755
Thackeray, H. St. J. 1066–77
Thévenot, X. 1571
Thibaut, R. 445, 448, 938
Thiering, B. E. 1119, 1598
Thiessen, H. C. 1240
Thomas, J. 460
Thomas, K. J. 880–81, 1199, 1201
Thompson, G. H. P. 276, 520
Thompson, P. J. 332, 505
Thompson, W. G. 269
Thomson, P. 880, 1240, 1425, 1428
Thorley, J. 1597
Thrall, M. E. 28A: xxxvi, 848, 928
Throckmorton, B. H. 266, 505, 628, 1388, 1406
Thurston, H. 1528, 1531
Thüsing, W. 857–58
Thyen, H. 266, 462

Thysman, R. 268
Tiede, D. L. 1254–55, 1260
Tilborg, S. van 908
Tillmann, F. 1097
Tinsley, E. J. 276
Tobin, W. J. 1428
Tödt, H. E. 782, xxxvi, 938, 958, 961, 991, 1174, 1356
Tolbert, M. O. 260, 276, 1094
Topel, J. 1079, 1104, 1598
Torrance, T. F. 462
Torrey, C. C. 363, 370, 620, xxxvi, 941, 1169, 1325
Tosato, A. 1124
Tourón del Pie, E. 1596
Trantham, H. 343
Trémel, Y.-B. 1446, 1597
Trèves, M. 1597
Trevijano Etcheverría, R. 1124
Trilling, W. 475, 621, xxxvi, 1059, 1079, 1139, 1217, 1371, 1486, 1506, 1511, 1522
Troadec, H. 612
Trocmé, E. 51, 293, 297, 302, 1268
Troeltsch, E. 23
Trompf, G. W. 832
Trudinger, L. P. 890
Turner, C. H. 486
Turner, H. E. W. 103, 1050, 1061, 1372, 1550
Turner, M. M. B. 1595
Turner, N. 101, 108, 123–25, 283, 332, 355, 361, 401, 738
Tuya, M. de 276
Tyson, J. B. 99, 1028, 1030, 1033, 1470

Ubach, B. M. 1102
Uhsadel, W. 1260
Ulrich, E. C. 1026
Unnik, W. C. van 3, 4, 8, 11, 33, 106, 266, 413, 415, 646, xxxvi, 1470
Untergassmair, F. G. 1210, 1523
Uprichard, R. E. H. 1597
Urrutia, J. L. de 694
Usener, H. 332

Vaccari, A. 415, 837, 1548, 1561, 1571
Vaganay, L. 73, 75, 811, 818
Valensin, A. 276
Valentin, P. 1470
Van Bruggen, J. 908
VanderKam, J. C. 1380
Vanhoye, A. 390, 1371
Vardaman, E. J. 343
Varela, A. T. 433
Vargas-Machuca, A. 1124
Varro, R. 1211, 1351
Vassiliadis, P. 102
Vattioni, F. 1109

INDEX OF SUBJECTS